Basic Standard Deduction Amounts

Filing Status	Standard Deduction Amount 1993	1992
Single	$3,700	$3,600
Married, filing jointly	6,200	6,000
Surviving spouse	6,200	6,000
Head of household	5,450	5,250
Married, filing separately	3,100	3,000

Amount of Each Additional Standard Deduction

Filing Status	1993	1992
Single	$900	$900
Married, filing jointly	700	700
Surviving spouse	700	700
Head of household	900	900
Married, filing separately	700	700

Income Tax Rates—Corporations

Taxable Income	Tax Rate
$50,000 or less	15%
Over $50,000 but not over $75,000	25%
Over $75,000	34%
$100,000–$335.000	5%

*Additional tax, "phases out" the lower marginal brackets.

1994 ANNUAL EDITION

WEST'S FEDERAL TAXATION:

COMPREHENSIVE VOLUME

1994 Annual Edition

West's Federal Taxation:

Comprehensive Volume

General Editors

Eugene Willis, Ph.D., C.P.A. **William H. Hoffman, Jr.,** J.D., Ph.D., C.P.A.

David M. Maloney, Ph.D., C.P.A. **William A. Raabe,** Ph.D., C.P.A.

Contributing Authors

James H. Boyd,
Ph.D., C.P.A.
Arizona State University

D. Larry Crumbley,
Ph.D., C.P.A.
Texas A & M University

Steven C. Dilley,
J.D., Ph.D., C.P.A.
Michigan State University

Patrica C. Elliott,
D.B.A., C.P.A.
University of New Mexico

Mary Sue Gately,
Ph.D., C.P.A.
Texas Tech University

Jerome S. Horvitz
J.D., LL.M. in Taxation
Suffolk University

William H. Hoffman, Jr.,
J.D., Ph.D., C.P.A.
University of Houston

David M. Maloney,
Ph.D., C.P.A.
University of Virginia

Marilyn Phelan,
J.D., Ph.D., C.P.A.
Texas Tech University

William A. Raabe,
Ph.D., C.P.A.
University of Wisconsin-Milwaukee

Boyd C. Randall,
J.D., Ph.D.
Brigham Young University

W. Eugene Seago,
J.D., Ph.D., C.P.A.
Virginia Polytechnic Institute and State University

James E. Smith,
Ph.D., C.P.A.
College of William and Mary

Eugene Willis,
Ph.D., C.P.A.
University of Illinois at Urbana

West Publishing Company

Minneapolis/St. Paul New York Los Angeles San Francisco

Copyediting: Patricia A. Lewis
Index: Catalyst Communication Arts
Composition: Carlisle Communications, Ltd.
Cover and
Interior Design: John Rokusek

West's Commitment to the Environment

In 1906, West Publishing Company began recycling materials left over from the production of books. This began a tradition of efficient and responsible use of resources. Today, up to 95 percent of our legal books and 70 percent of our college and school texts are printed on recycled, acid-free stock. West also recycles nearly 22 million pounds of scrap paper annually—the equivalent of 181,717 trees. Since the 1960s, West has devised ways to capture and recycle waste inks, solvents, oils, and vapors created in the printing process. We also recycle plastics of all kinds, wood, glass, corrugated cardboard, and batteries, and have eliminated the use of styrofoam book packaging. We at West are proud of the longevity and the scope of our commitment to the environment.

Production, Prepress, Printing and Binding by West Publishing Company.

Printed in the United States of America
00 99 98 97 96 95 94 93 8 7 6 5 4 3 2 1

Library of Congress
Cataloging in Publication Data

Main entry under title:
West's Federal Taxation.
Includes index.
1. Income tax—United States—Law
I. Hoffman, William H. III. Willis, Eugene

ISBN 0–314–02240–6, 0–314–02532–4
KF6335.H63 343'.73'04 76–54355

ISSN 0270–5265
1994 ANNUAL EDITION

PREFACE

West's Federal Taxation: Comprehensive Volume is an abridged version of *West's Federal Taxation: Individual Income Taxes* and *West's Federal Taxation: Corporations, Partnerships, Estates, and Trusts.* In condensing all of this material to a manageable form, it was necessary to utilize our editorial license to pick and choose. Thus, a great deal of useful, but not essential, information had to be pruned in order to arrive at the final product. What to cover or not to cover in any abridgement process is, understandably, a judgment call. We can only hope that we acted correctly in making our decisions.

The *Comprehensive Volume* is designed to provide flexibility for those who offer only one course in Federal taxation or for a two-course sequence. In cases where the *Comprehensive Volume* is used for only one course, a broad scope of coverage could be the ultimate objective. Although the income taxation of individuals may be stressed, it is conceivable that some may wish to devote significant classroom time to other areas of Federal taxation. For example, the allocation of course coverage might be structured as follows: 60 percent to the individual income tax (Chapters 1–15) and 40 percent to the tax treatment of corporations, partnerships, etc. (Chapters 16–28).

For those who encounter time constraints and/or want to emphasize some areas and not others, the last segment of the text (Chapters 16–28) possesses potential for selectivity. For example, an instructor who wants to cover corporations (Chapters 16–21) and tax practice (Chapter 25), but not the other subjects (Chapters 22–24 and 26–28), can proceed accordingly without disrupting the flow of the material. In this regard, the last segment of the text offers the flexibility for partial coverage through a number of different combinations (e.g., for a "light" coverage of corporations, select Chapters 16 through 18, but for a "heavy" concentration, assign Chapters 16–21).

Special Features

A variety of pedagogical devices is used to assist the student in the learning process. Each chapter begins with a statement of the learning objectives for the chapter. The learning objectives are followed by a topical outline of the material in the chapter. Page references appear in the outline to provide easy access to each topic. The following features enhance the readability of the material in the text.

- Including three levels of headings that aid in organization and presentation.
- Italicizing key words to emphasize their importance.

- Avoiding legal terminology except where it is beneficial.
- Using Concept Summaries to synthesize important concepts in chart or tabular form.
- Organizing material in lists with bullets rather than presenting it in lengthy sentences.
- Using examples frequently to help the student understand the tax concept being discussed.

If the *Comprehensive Volume* is to be used in whole (or in part) for a one-course tax offering, the pace of coverage of the subject matter may have to be accelerated. In recognition of this fact, we have followed certain guidelines.

- In an accelerated setting, a decided constraint is placed on the amount of problem solving that can be expected from the reader. We have, therefore, limited the quantity of the problem materials. In this connection, we have strived to maintain the integrity of the quality of the materials.
- Although not eliminated entirely, the research orientation has been kept to a minimum. Restricting judicial analysis and controlling the number of footnotes spare the reader some measure of distraction. The result is a quicker coverage of the textual material.
- For those users who feel the need for some material on research methodology, the last chapter in the text, "Working with the Tax Law," is available. Along with the usual problem materials, this chapter also includes numerous research problems, arranged by chapter, dealing with the subject matter treated in the text. Instructors who emphasize research can assign Chapter 28 early in the course and then select from these problems as other chapters are covered.
- Once knowledge of the tax law has been acquired, it needs to be used. The tax minimization process normally requires careful planning. Because we recognize the importance of planning procedures, most chapters include a separate section (called *Tax Planning Considerations*) illustrating the applications of such procedures to specific areas.
- The appendixes to the text contain a great deal of useful material. In addition to the usual Subject Index, the following items are included: Tax Rates and Tables (Appendix A); Tax Forms (Appendix B); Glossary of Tax Terms (Appendix C); Table of Code Sections Cited (Appendix D); and Comprehensive Tax Return Problems for 1992 (Appendix E).

The coverage on ethics is expanded in the 1994 edition. Also, in recognition of the increasing emphasis on communication in accounting and tax education, some of the cumulative problems and tax research problems have been modified to include a communication component. These problems ask the student to prepare a tax client letter and a memorandum for the files. The discussion of the tax research process in Chapter 28 includes an illustration of both of these items.

Supplements

Other products in our 1994 instructional package include the following:

- The 1994 *Instructor's Guide with Lecture Notes* contains lecture notes that can be used as lecture outlines, as well as teaching aids and information not contained in the text. It also includes solutions to the research problems (Chapter 28 in the text) and the comprehensive tax return problems

(Appendix E in the text). For the 1994 edition, we have added synopses of many interesting and unusual court cases that can be used to illustrate technical points in the tax law. The lecture notes are also available on disk in ASCII files.

- A *Solutions Manual* that has been carefully checked to ensure accuracy. A matrix is included indicating topic coverage for each problem, as well as which problems are new, modified, or unchanged in the new edition. The solutions are referenced to pages in the text.
- A *Test Bank* with a comprehensive set of examination questions and solutions. The answers to these are referenced to pages in the text. The questions are arranged in accordance with the sequence of the material in the chapter. To assist the professor in selecting questions for an examination, all questions are labeled by topical coverage in a matrix that also indicates which questions are new, modified, or unchanged in the new edition. Approximately 20 percent of the questions in the 1994 edition are new or modified.
- *Westest,* a microcomputer test generation program for IBM PCs and compatibles and the Macintosh family of computers.
- *West's CD-ROM Federal Tax Library* (Compact Disk with Read-Only Memory) provides a complete tax research library on a desktop. The *Federal Tax Library* is a set of compact disks with a software package that reads the disks through a PC. Each disk has a remarkable storage capacity—roughly 1,000 times more than a single-sided floppy disk. A brief list of the library contents includes the complete IRS Code and Regulations, the 1986 Tax Reform Act with Amendments and legislative History, Federal Court cases on tax, Tax Court cases, Revenue Rulings, and Revenue Procedures. The CD-ROM library is available to qualified adopters.
- Limited free use to qualified adopters of WESTLAW, a computer-assisted tax and legal research service that provides access to hundreds of valuable information sources.
- A *Student Study Guide* prepared by David M. Maloney, University of Virginia, and William A. Raabe, University of Wisconsin (Milwaukee). This *Study Guide* includes a chapter review of key concepts and self-evaluation tests with solutions that are referenced to the text.
- *Transparency Masters* for selected complex and cumulative problems, with a larger typeface for greater readability.
- *Transparency Acetates* containing charts and tables that can be used to enhance classroom presentations.
- *Instructor's Resource Notebook*—this three-ring binder can be used to house all or portions of the supplements and text. The 1994 edition is offered in looseleaf form so the instructor can reorganize the book and incorporate supplemental materials to fit course lectures.
- *WFT Individual Practice Sets* and *WFT Corporation, S Corporation, and Partnership Practice Sets* 1993–94 edition, prepared by John B. Barrack, University of Georgia. They are designed to cover most of the common forms that would be used by a tax practitioner for the average client.
- *West's Internal Revenue Code of 1986 and Treasury Regulations: Annotated and Selected: 1994 Edition* by James E. Smith, College of William and Mary. This provides the opportunity for the student to be exposed to the Code and the Regulations in a single-volume book, which also contains useful annotations.
- *West's Federal Taxation Newsletter* is mailed to adopters twice a year. It focuses on new tax legislation and updated information.

Software

The trend toward increased use of the computer as an essential tool in tax practice has accelerated. To ensure that the West's Federal Taxation instructional package continues to set the pace in this important area, the following products are available to be used with the 1994 edition:

- *TurboTax* © Personal/1040 by Chipsoft, Inc., is a commercial tax preparation package. It enables students to prepare over 80 forms, schedules, and worksheets and automatically performs all mathematical calculations and data transfers. *TurboTax* also assists students with tax planning and helps them prepare "anticipated" tax returns. The *TurboTax* package, available for student purchase includes disks bound with a 200-page workbook containing exercises and problems. The software runs on IBM PCs and compatibles with 512K memory. Both DOS and Windows versions of *TurboTax* are available. Also available is *MacInTax,* the best-selling tax preparation software for the Macintosh.
- *Corporation and Partnership Tax Return Preparation with TurboTax* Pro Series 1120/1120S/1065 is a commercial tax preparation package which includes disks bound with a workbook containing exercises and problems.
- *West's Federal Taxation: Tax Planning with Electronic Spreadsheets,* prepared by Sam A. Hicks, Jr., Virginia Polytechnic Institute and State University, contains Lotus-based tax computation and planning templates for individual taxpayers and is available free to adopters.

These software products are powerful, easy to learn, and easy to use. We believe that tax education can be raised to a higher level through the use of computers and well-designed software. These software packages take the drudgery out of performing the complex computations involved in solving difficult tax problems. This allows students to concentrate on applying concepts and interpreting results.

To enable students to take advantage of these software products, the text contains numerous tax return and tax planning problems. The tax planning problems allow students to evaluate alternative tax planning strategies and calculate the effects of various alternatives on the taxpayer's liability. Problems that lend themselves to solutions using the software packages described above are identified by a computer symbol to the left of the problem number. The instructions for each of these problems indicate which software packages are appropriate for solving the problems.

Tax Forms Coverage

- Although it is not our purpose to approach the presentation and discussion of taxation from the standpoint of preparation of tax returns, some orientation to forms is necessary. Because 1993 forms will not be available until later in the year, most tax return problems in this edition are written for tax year 1992. The 1992 problems may be solved manually, or many may be solved using the tax return preparation software (*MacInTax®* or *TurboTax*) that may be purchased by students who use this text.
- Appendix E contains comprehensive tax return problems written for tax year 1992. Each of these problems lends itself for use as a term project because of the sophistication required for satisfactory completion. Solutions to the problems in Appendix E are contained in the *Instructor's Guide with Lecture Notes.*

- For the reader's convenience, Appendix B contains a full reproduction of most of the 1992 tax forms frequently encountered in actual practice. Most tax textbooks are published in the spring, long before tax forms for the year of publication are available from the government. We believe that students should be exposed to the most current tax forms. As a result, we write several new forms problems and provide adopters with reproducible copies of these problems, along with blank tax forms and solutions on the new forms. Shortly after the beginning of 1994, adopters will receive selected tax return problems, updated and solved on 1993 forms.

Tax Law Updates

Since the original edition was issued in 1983, we have followed a policy of annually revising the text material to reflect statutory, judicial, and administrative changes in the Federal tax law and to correct any errors or other shortcomings.

In the event of *significant* tax law changes, a supplement will be written for the three texts in the West series. Our aim is to provide a timely, complete, and easy-to-use supplement.

Acknowledgments

As is the case with any literary undertaking, we welcome user comments. Please rest assured that any such comments will not be taken lightly and, we hope, will lead to improvements in later editions of *West's Federal Taxation: Comprehensive Volume*.

We are most appreciative of the many suggestions that we have received for revising the text, many of which have been incorporated in past editions and in the 1994 edition. In particular, we would like to thank all those users who have called or written with suggestions for improving the book, and those who did detailed reviews for this edition. They include Cindy Lou Beale, Pace University; Lee Daniel, Troy State University; Sue N. Hinrichs, University of the Pacific; John E. Karayan, California State Polytechnic University, Pomona; Margaret McCrory, Marist College; and James P. Trebby, Marquette University. We would also like to thank those people who have painstakingly worked through all the problems and test questions and generally acted as problem checkers to ensure the accuracy of the book and ancillary package. They are Tracey A. Anderson, Indiana University at South Bend; Caroline K. Craig, Illinois State University; Frank Linton, Illinois State University; Mark B. Persellin, St. Mary's University; Debra L. Sanders, Washington State University; Randall K. Serrett, University of Alaska at Fairbanks; Thomas Sternburg, Arizona State University; and Raymond F. Wacker, Southern Illinois University at Carbondale.

Finally, this 1994 Edition would not have been possible without the technical assistance of and the manuscript review by Bonnie Hoffman, CPA, and Freda Mulhall, CPA. We are indebted to them for their efforts.

Eugene Willis
William H. Hoffman, Jr.
David M. Maloney
William A. Raabe

April 1993

Contents in Brief

Table of Contents

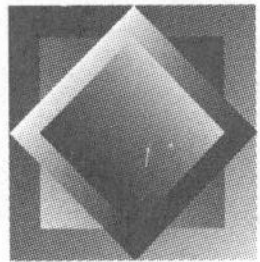

1994 Annual Edition

West's Federal Taxation:

Comprehensive Volume

CHAPTER

AN INTRODUCTION TO TAXATION AND UNDERSTANDING THE FEDERAL TAX LAW

OBJECTIVES

Provide a brief history, including trends, of the Federal income tax.

Describe some of the criteria for selecting a tax structure.

Explain the different types of taxes imposed in the United States at the Federal, state, and local levels.

Introduce the Federal income tax on individuals and corporations.

Describe the major employment taxes such as the Federal Insurance Contributions Act (FICA) and the Federal Unemployment Tax Act (FUTA).

Briefly review the role of the audit process in tax administration.

Explain the economic, social, equity, and political considerations that justify various aspects of the tax law.

Review the role played by the IRS and the courts in the evolution of the Federal tax system.

OUTLINE

The primary objective of this chapter is to provide an overview of the Federal tax system. Among the topics discussed are the following:

- A brief history of the Federal income tax.
- The different types of taxes imposed at the Federal, state, and local levels.
- Some highlights illustrating how the tax laws are administered.
- Tax concepts that help explain the reasons for various tax provisions.
- The influence that the Internal Revenue Service (IRS) and the courts have had in the evolution of current tax law.

HISTORY OF U.S. TAXATION

Early Periods

The concept of an income tax can hardly be regarded as a newcomer to the Western Hemisphere. An income tax was first enacted in 1634 by the English colonists in the Massachusetts Bay Colony, but the Federal government did not adopt this form of taxation until 1861. In fact, both the Federal Union and the Confederate States of America used the income tax to raise funds to finance the Civil War. Although modest in its reach and characterized by broad exemptions and low rates, the income tax generated $376 million of revenue for the Federal government during the Civil War.

When the Civil War ended, the need for additional revenue disappeared and the income tax was repealed. As was true before the war, the Federal government was able to finance its operations almost exclusively from customs duties (tariffs). It is interesting to note that the courts held the Civil War income tax was not contrary to the Constitution.

When a new Federal income tax on individuals was enacted in 1894, its opponents were prepared to and did again challenge its constitutionality. The U.S. Constitution provided that ". . . No Capitation, or other direct, Tax shall be laid, unless in Proportion to the Census or Enumeration herein before directed to be taken." In *Pollock v. Farmers' Loan and Trust Co.*,[1] the U.S. Supreme Court found that the income tax was a direct tax that was unconstitutional because it was not apportioned among the states in proportion to their populations.

A Federal corporate income tax, enacted by Congress in 1909, fared better in the judicial system. The U.S. Supreme Court found this tax to be constitutional because it was treated as an excise tax.[2] In essence, it was a tax on the right to do business in the corporate form. As such, it was likened to a form of the franchise tax. Note that the corporate form of doing business was developed in the late nineteenth century and was an unfamiliar concept to the framers of the U.S. Constitution. Since a corporation is an entity created under law, jurisdictions possess the right to tax its creation and operation. Using this rationale, many states still impose franchise taxes on corporations.

The ratification of the Sixteenth Amendment to the U.S. Constitution in 1913 sanctioned both the Federal individual and corporate income taxes and, as a consequence, neutralized the continuing effect of the *Pollock* decision.

---

1. 3 AFTR 2602, 15 S.Ct. 912 (USSC, 1895). See Chapter 28 for an explanation of how judicial decisions are cited.

2. *Flint v. Stone Tracy Co.*, 3 AFTR 2834, 31 S.Ct. 342 (USSC, 1911).

Revenue Acts

Following ratification of the Sixteenth Amendment, Congress enacted the Revenue Act of 1913. Under this Act, a flat 1 percent tax was levied upon the income of corporations. Individuals paid a normal tax rate of 1 percent on taxable income after deducting a personal exemption of $3,000 for a single individual and $4,000 for a married taxpayer. Surtax rates of 1 to 6 percent were applied to high-income taxpayers.

Various revenue acts were passed during the period from 1913 to 1939. In 1939, all of these revenue laws were codified into the Internal Revenue Code of 1939. In 1954, a similar codification of the revenue law took place. The current law is the Internal Revenue Code of 1986, which largely carries over the provisions of the 1954 Code. The Code has been amended several times since 1986. This matter is discussed further in Chapter 28 under Origin of the Internal Revenue Code.

Historical Trends

The income tax has proved to be a major source of revenue for the Federal government. As Figure 1–1 shows, estimated income tax collections from individuals and corporations amount to 41 percent of the total receipts.[3]

The need for revenues to finance the war effort during World War II converted the income tax into a *mass tax*. For example, in 1939, less than 6 percent of the U.S. population was subject to the Federal income tax. In 1945, over 74 percent of the population was subject to the Federal income tax.[4]

Certain changes in the income tax law are of particular significance in understanding the Federal income tax. In 1943, Congress passed the Current Tax Payment Act, which provided for the first pay-as-you-go tax system. A pay-as-you-go income tax system requires employers to withhold for taxes a specified portion of an employee's wages. Persons with income from other than wages must make periodic (e.g., quarterly) payments to the taxing authority (the Internal Revenue Service) for estimated taxes due for the year.

One trend that has caused considerable concern has been the increased complexity of the Federal income tax laws. Often, under the name of tax reform, Congress has added to this complexity by making frequent changes in the tax laws. Increasingly, this has forced many taxpayers to seek the assistance of tax professionals. At this time, therefore, substantial support exists for tax law simplification.

FIGURE 1–1
Federal Budget Receipts—1993

Individual income taxes	34%
Corporation income taxes	7
Social insurance taxes and contributions	29
Excise taxes	3
Borrowing	23
Other	4
	100%

3. *Budget of the United States Government for Fiscal Year 1993*, Office of Management and Budget (Washington, D.C.: U.S. Government Printing Office, 1992).

4. Richard Goode, *The Individual Income Tax* (Washington, D.C.: The Brookings Institution, 1964), pp. 2–4.

Criteria Used in the Selection of a Tax Structure

In the eighteenth century, Adam Smith identified the following *canons of taxation,* which are still considered when evaluating a particular tax structure:[5]

- *Equality.* Each taxpayer enjoys fair or equitable treatment by paying taxes in proportion to his or her income level. Ability to pay a tax is the measure of how equitably a tax is distributed among taxpayers.
- *Convenience.* Administrative simplicity has long been valued in formulating tax policy. If a tax is easily assessed and collected and its administrative costs are low, it should be favored. An advantage of the withholding (pay-as-you-go) system is its convenience for taxpayers.
- *Certainty.* A tax structure is *good* if the taxpayer can readily predict when, where, and how a tax will be levied. Individuals and businesses need to know the likely tax consequences of a particular type of transaction.
- *Economy.* A *good* tax system involves only nominal collection costs by the government and minimal compliance costs on the part of the taxpayer. Although the government's cost of collecting Federal taxes amounts to less than one-half of 1 percent of the revenue collected, the complexity of our current tax structure imposes substantial taxpayer compliance costs.

By these canons, the Federal income tax is a contentious product. *Equality* is present as long as one accepts ability to pay as an ingredient of this component. *Convenience* exists due to a heavy reliance on pay-as-you-go procedures. *Certainty* probably generates the greatest controversy. Certainty is present in the sense that a mass of administrative and judicial guidelines are available to aid in interpreting the tax law. In another sense, however, certainty does not exist since many questions remain unanswered, and frequent changes in the tax law by Congress lessen stability. *Economy* is present if one considers only the collection efforts of the IRS. Economy is not present, however, if taxpayer compliance efforts are the central focus.

The Tax Structure

Tax Base

A tax base is the amount to which the tax rate is applied. In the case of the Federal income tax, the tax base is *taxable income.* As noted later in the chapter (Figure 1–2), taxable income is gross income reduced by certain deductions (both business and personal).

Tax Rates

Tax rates are applied to the tax base to determine a taxpayer's liability. The tax rates may be proportional or progressive. A tax is *proportional* if the rate of tax remains constant for any given income level.

5. *The Wealth of Nations,* Book V, Chapter II, Part II (New York: Dutton, 1910).

EXAMPLE 1

Bill has $10,000 of taxable income and pays a tax of $3,000, or 30%. Bob's taxable income is $50,000, and the tax on this amount is $15,000, or 30%. If this constant rate is applied to all levels of income, the tax is proportional. ◆

A tax is *progressive* if a higher rate of tax applies as the tax base increases. The Federal income tax, Federal gift and estate taxes, and most state income tax rate structures are progressive.

EXAMPLE 2

If Cora, a married individual filing jointly, has taxable income of $10,000, her tax for 1993 is $1,500 for an average tax rate of 15%. If, however, Cora's taxable income is $50,000, her tax will be $9,203 for an average tax rate of 18.41%. The tax is progressive since higher rates are applied to greater amounts of taxable income. ◆

Incidence of Taxation

The degree to which the total tax burden is shared by various segments of society is difficult to assess. Assumptions must be made concerning who absorbs the burden for payment of the tax. For example, since dividend payments to shareholders are not deductible by a corporation and are generally taxable to shareholders, a form of double taxation on the same income is being levied. Concern over double taxation is valid to the extent that corporations are *not* able to shift the corporate tax to the consumer through higher product prices. Many research studies have shown a high degree of shifting of the corporate income tax. When the corporate tax can be shifted, it becomes merely a consumption tax that is borne by the ultimate purchasers of goods.

The U.S. Federal income tax rate structure for individuals is becoming less progressive. For example, for 1986 there were 15 rates, ranging from 0 to 50 percent. Subsequently, these rates have been reduced to 15 percent, 28 percent, and 31 percent. Because many deductions and other tax savings procedures have been eliminated, Congress expects the lower rates to reach a larger base of taxable income.

MAJOR TYPES OF TAXES

Property Taxes

Normally referred to as *ad valorem* taxes because they are based on value, property taxes are a tax on wealth, or capital. In this regard, they have much in common with death taxes and gift taxes, discussed later in the chapter. Although property taxes do not tax income, the income actually derived (or the potential for any income) may be relevant insofar as it affects the value of the property being taxed.

Property taxes fall into two categories: those imposed on realty and those imposed on personalty. Both have added importance since they usually generate a deduction for Federal income tax purposes (see Chapter 10).

Ad Valorem Taxes on Realty. Property taxes on realty are exclusively within the province of the states and their local political subdivisions (e.g., cities, counties, school districts). They represent a major source of revenue for local governments, but their importance at the state level has waned over the past few years.

This is especially true in jurisdictions that do not impose ad valorem taxes on personalty. How realty is defined can have an important bearing on which assets are subject to tax. Primarily a question of state property law, *realty* generally includes real estate and any capital improvements that are classified as fixtures. Simply stated, a fixture is something so permanently attached to the real estate that its removal will cause irreparable damage. A built-in bookcase might well be a fixture, whereas a movable bookcase would not be a fixture. Certain items such as electrical wiring and plumbing cease to be personalty when installed in a building and become realty.

The following are some of the characteristics of ad valorem taxes on realty:

- Property owned by the Federal government is exempt from tax. Similar immunity usually is extended to property owned by state and local governments and by certain charitable organizations.
- Some states provide for lower valuations on property dedicated to agricultural use or other special uses (e.g., wildlife sanctuaries).
- Some states partially exempt the homestead portion of property from taxation. Modern homestead laws normally protect some or all of a personal residence (including a farm or ranch) from the actions of creditors pursuing claims against the owner.
- Lower taxes may apply to a residence owned by an elderly taxpayer (e.g., age 65 and older).
- When non-income-producing property (e.g., a personal residence) is converted to income-producing property (e.g., a rental house), typically the appraised value increases.
- Some jurisdictions extend immunity from tax for a specified period of time (a *tax holiday*) to new or relocated businesses.

Unlike the ad valorem tax on personalty (see the next section), the tax on realty is difficult to avoid. Since real estate is impossible to hide, a high degree of taxpayer compliance is not surprising. The only avoidance possibility that is generally available is associated with the assessed value of the property. For this reason, the assessed value of the property and, particularly, a value that is reassessed upward may be subject to controversy and litigation.

Four methods are currently used for assessing the value of real estate:

1. Actual purchase or construction price.
2. Contemporaneous sales prices or construction costs of comparable properties.
3. Cost of reproducing a building, less allowance for depreciation and obsolescence from the time of actual construction.
4. Capitalization of income from rental property.

Because all of these methods suffer faults and lead to inequities, a combination of two or more is not uncommon. For example, when real estate values and construction costs are rising, the use of actual purchase or construction price (method 1) places the purchaser of a new home at a definite disadvantage compared with an owner who acquired similar property years before. As another illustration, if the capitalization of income (method 4) is used for property subject to rent controls, the property may be undervalued.

Ad Valorem Taxes on Personalty. *Personalty* can be defined as all assets that are not realty. It may be helpful to distinguish between the *classification* of an asset (realty or personalty) and the *use* to which it is placed. Both realty and personalty can be either business use or personal use property. Examples include a residence (realty that is personal use), an office building (realty that is business use), surgical instruments (personalty that is business use), and regular wearing apparel (personalty that is personal use). The distinction, important for ad valorem and for Federal income tax purposes, often becomes confused when personalty is referred to as *personal* property to distinguish it from *real* property. This designation does not give a complete picture of what is involved. The description *personal residence* is clearer since one can identify a residence as being realty. What is meant, in this case, is realty that is personal use property.

Personalty can also be classified as tangible property or intangible property. For ad valorem tax purposes, intangible personalty includes stocks, bonds, and various other securities (e.g., bank shares).

Some generalizations can be made about ad valorem taxes on personalty:

- Particularly with personalty devoted to personal use (e.g., jewelry, household furnishings), taxpayer compliance ranges from poor to nonexistent. Some jurisdictions do not even attempt to enforce the tax on these items. For automobiles devoted to personal use, many jurisdictions have converted from value as the tax base to arbitrary license fees based on the weight of the vehicle. Some jurisdictions consider the vehicle's age (e.g., automobiles six years or older are not subject to the ad valorem tax because they are presumed to have little, if any, value).
- For personalty devoted to business use (e.g., inventories, trucks, machinery, equipment), taxpayer compliance and enforcement procedures are measurably better.
- Which jurisdiction possesses the authority to tax movable personalty (e.g., railroad rolling stock) always has been and continues to be a troublesome issue.
- Some jurisdictions impose an ad valorem tax on intangibles.

Transaction Taxes

Transaction taxes, which characteristically are imposed at the manufacturer's, wholesaler's, or retailer's level, cover a wide range of transfers. Like many other types of taxes (e.g., income taxes, death taxes, and gift taxes), transaction taxes usually are not within the exclusive province of any level of taxing authority (Federal, state, or local). As the description implies, these levies place a tax on transfers of property and normally are determined by multiplying the value involved by a percentage rate.

Federal Excise Taxes. Long one of the mainstays of the Federal tax system, Federal excise taxes had declined in relative importance until recently. In late 1982 and in 1990, Congress substantially increased the Federal excise taxes on such items as tobacco products, fuel and gasoline sales, telephone usage, and air travel passenger tickets. Other Federal excise taxes include the following:

- Manufacturers' excise taxes on trucks, trailers, tires, firearms, sporting equipment, coal, and the gas guzzler tax on automobiles.
- Alcohol taxes.
- Certain luxury items. These include passenger cars (on sales price in excess of $30,000); boats (on sales price in excess of $100,00); aircraft (on sales price in excess of $250,000); jewelry (on sales price in excess of $10,000); and furs (on sales price in excess of $10,000).
- Miscellaneous taxes (e.g., the tax on wagering).

The list of transactions covered has diminished over the years. At one time, for example, there was a Federal excise tax on admission to amusement facilities (e.g., theaters) and on the sale of such items as leather goods and cosmetics.

When reviewing the list of both Federal and state excise taxes, one should recognize the possibility that the tax laws may be trying to influence social behavior. For example, the gas guzzler tax is intended to encourage the automobile companies to build fuel-efficient cars. It is imposed on the manufacturers of automobiles and increases as the mileage ratings per gallon of gas decrease.

Since many consider alcohol and tobacco to be harmful to a person's health, why not increase their cost by imposing excise taxes and thereby discourage their use? Unfortunately, the evidence on the correlation between imposition of an excise tax and consumer behavior is mixed.

State Excise Taxes. Many state and local excise taxes parallel the Federal version. Thus, all states tax the sale of gasoline, liquor, and tobacco products; however, the rates vary significantly. For example, compare the 26 cents per gallon of gasoline imposed by the state of Rhode Island with the 9 cents per gallon levied by the state of Wyoming. For tobacco, contrast the 2.5 cents per pack of cigarettes in effect in Virginia with the 51 cents per pack applicable in Massachusetts. Is it surprising that the smuggling of cigarettes from low-tax jurisdictions for resale elsewhere is so widespread?

Other excise taxes found at some state and local levels include those on admission to amusement facilities; hotel occupancy and the rental of various other facilities; and the sale of playing cards, oleomargarine products, and prepared foods. Most states impose a transaction tax on the transfer of property that requires the recording of documents (e.g., real estate sales). Some extend the tax to the transfer of stocks and other securities.

General Sales Taxes. The distinction between an excise tax and a general sales tax is easy to make. One is restricted to a particular transaction (e.g., the 14.1 cents per gallon Federal excise tax on the sale of gasoline), while the other covers a multitude of transactions (e.g., a 5 percent tax on *all* retail sales). In actual practice, however, the distinction is not always that clear. Some state statutes exempt certain transactions from the general sales taxes (e.g., sales of food to be consumed off the premises, sales of certain medicines and drugs). Also, it is not uncommon to find that rates vary depending on the commodity involved. Many states, for example, allow preferential rates for the sale of agricultural equipment or apply different rates (either higher or lower than the general rate) to the sale of automobiles. With many of these special exceptions and various rates, a general sales tax can take on the appearance of a collection of individual excise taxes.

A *use tax* is an ad valorem tax, usually at the same rate as the sales tax, on the use, consumption, or storage of tangible property. The purpose of a use tax is to prevent the avoidance of a sales tax. Every state that imposes a general sales tax levied on the consumer also has a use tax. Alaska, Delaware, Montana, New Hampshire, and Oregon have neither tax.

EXAMPLE 3

Susan resides in a jurisdiction that imposes a 5% general sales tax but lives near a state that has no sales or use tax. She purchases an automobile for $10,000 from a dealer located in the neighboring state. Has Susan saved $500 in sales taxes? The state use tax is designed to pick up the difference between the tax paid in another jurisdiction and what would have been paid in the state in which Susan resides. ◆

The use tax is difficult to enforce for many purchases and is therefore often avoided. In some cases, for example, it may be worthwhile to make purchases through an out-of-state mail-order business. In spite of shipping costs, products such as computer components may be cheaper due to the avoidance of the local sales tax. Some states are taking steps to curtail this loss of revenue. For items such as automobiles (refer to Example 3), the use tax probably will be collected when the purchaser registers the item in his or her home state.

Local general sales taxes, over and above those levied by the state, are common. It is not unusual to find taxpayers living in the same state who pay different general sales taxes due to the location of their residence.

Severance Taxes. Severance taxes are an important source of revenue for many states. These transaction taxes are based on the notion that the state has an interest in its natural resources (e.g., oil, gas, iron ore, coal). Therefore, a tax is imposed when they are extracted.

Death Taxes

A *death tax* is a tax on the right to transfer property or to receive property upon the death of the owner. Consequently, a death tax falls into the category of an excise tax. If the death tax is imposed on the right to pass property at death, it is classified as an *estate tax*. If it taxes the right to receive property from a decedent, it is termed an *inheritance tax*. As is typical of other types of excise taxes, the value of the property transferred provides the base for determining the amount of the death tax.

The Federal government imposes only an estate tax. State governments, however, levy inheritance taxes, estate taxes, or both.

EXAMPLE 4

At the time of her death, Wilma lived in a state that imposes an inheritance tax but not an estate tax. Mary, one of Wilma's heirs, lives in the same state. Wilma's estate is subject to the Federal estate tax, and Mary is subject to the state inheritance tax. ◆

The Federal Estate Tax. The Revenue Act of 1916 incorporated the estate tax into the tax law. Never designed to generate a large amount of revenue, its original purpose was to prevent large concentrations of wealth from being kept within a family for many generations. Whether this objective has been accomplished is debatable. Like the income tax, estate taxes can be reduced through various planning procedures.

The gross estate includes property the decedent owned at the time of death. It also includes life insurance proceeds when paid to the estate or when paid to a beneficiary other than the estate if the deceased-insured had any ownership rights in the policy. Quite simply, the gross estate represents property interests subject to Federal estate taxation. All property included in the gross estate is valued as of the date of death or, if the alternate valuation date is elected, six months later.

Deductions from the gross estate in arriving at the taxable estate include funeral and administration expenses, certain taxes, debts of the decedent, casualty losses incurred during the administration of the estate, contributions to charitable organizations, and, in some cases, the marital deduction. The marital deduction is available for amounts actually passing to a surviving spouse (a widow or widower).

Once the taxable estate has been determined and certain taxable gifts have been added to it, the estate tax can be computed. From the amount derived from the appropriate tax rate schedules, various credits are subtracted to arrive at the tax, if any, that is due. Although many credits are available, probably the most significant is the unified transfer tax credit. The main reason for this credit is to eliminate or reduce the estate tax liability for modest estates. For deaths after 1986, the credit is $192,800. Based on the estate tax rates, the credit covers a tax base of $600,000.

EXAMPLE 5

Ned made no taxable gifts before his death in 1993. If his taxable estate amounts to $600,000 or less, no Federal estate tax is due because of the application of the unified transfer tax credit of $192,800. Under the tax law, the estate tax on a taxable estate of $600,000 is $192,800. ◆

State Death Taxes. As noted earlier, states usually levy an inheritance tax, an estate tax, or both. The two forms of death taxes differ according to whether the tax is imposed on the heir or on the estate.

Characteristically, an inheritance tax divides the heirs into classes based on their relationship to the decedent. The more closely related the heir, the lower the rates imposed and the greater the exemption allowed. Some states completely exempt amounts passing to a surviving spouse from taxation.

Gift Taxes

Like a death tax, a *gift tax* is an excise tax levied on the right to transfer property. In this case, however, the tax is imposed on transfers made during the owner's life and not at death. Also, a gift tax applies only to transfers that are not supported by full and adequate consideration.

EXAMPLE 6

Carl sells property worth $20,000 to his daughter for $1,000. Although property worth $20,000 has been transferred, only $19,000 is a gift since this is the portion not supported by full and adequate consideration. ◆

The Federal Gift Tax. First enacted in 1932, the Federal gift tax was intended to complement the estate tax. In the absence of a tax applicable to lifetime transfers by gift, it would be possible to avoid the estate tax and escape taxation entirely.

Only taxable gifts are subject to the gift tax. For this purpose, a taxable gift is measured by the fair market value of the property on the date of transfer less the annual exclusion of $10,000 per donee and, in some cases, less the marital deduction, which allows tax-free transfers between spouses. Each donor is allowed an annual exclusion of $10,000 for each donee. The purpose of the annual exclusion is to avoid the need to report and pay a tax on "modest" gifts. Without the exclusion, the IRS could face a real problem of taxpayer noncompliance.

EXAMPLE 7

On December 31, 1992, Vera (a widow) gives $10,000 to each of her four married children, their spouses, and her eight grandchildren. On January 3, 1993, she repeats the same procedure. Although D transferred $160,000 [$10,000 × 16 (number of donees)] in 1992 and $160,000 [$10,000 × 16 (number of donees)] in 1993 for a total of $320,000 ($160,000 + $160,000), she has not made a taxable gift as a result of the annual exclusion. ◆

A special election applicable to married persons allows one-half of the gift made by the donor-spouse to be treated as being made by the nondonor-spouse. This election to split gifts of property made to third persons has the effect of increasing the number of annual exclusions available. Also, it allows the use of the nondonor-spouse's unified transfer tax credit and may lower the tax brackets that will apply.

For taxable gifts made after 1976, the gift tax rate schedule is the same as that applicable to the estate tax. The schedule is commonly referred to as the *unified transfer tax schedule*. See Appendix A.

The Federal gift tax is *cumulative* in effect. What this means is that the tax base for current taxable gifts includes past taxable gifts. Although a credit is allowed for prior gift taxes, the result of adding past taxable gifts to current taxable gifts is to push the donor into a higher tax bracket. Like the Federal estate tax rates, the Federal gift tax rates are progressive.

The unified transfer tax credit is available for all taxable gifts made after 1976. As with the Federal estate tax, this credit is $192,800. There is, however, only one unified transfer tax credit, and it applies both to taxable gifts and to the Federal estate tax. In a manner of speaking, therefore, once the unified transfer tax credit has been exhausted for Federal gift tax purposes, it is no longer available to insulate a decedent from the Federal estate tax. For further information on the Federal gift tax, see Chapter 26.

In summary, transfers by gift and transfers by death made after 1976 are subject to the unified transfer tax. The same rates and credits apply. Further, taxable gifts made after 1976 are added to the taxable estate in arriving at the tax base for applying the unified transfer tax at death.

State Gift Taxes. Connecticut, Delaware, Louisiana, New York, North Carolina, and Tennessee currently impose a state gift tax. Most of the laws provide for limited lifetime exemptions and annual exclusions. Like the Federal gift tax, the state taxes are cumulative in effect. But unlike the Federal version, the amount of tax depends on the relationship between the donor and the donee. Like state inheritance taxes, larger exemptions and lower rates apply when the donor and donee are closely related to each other.

Income Taxes

Income taxes are levied by the Federal government, most states, and some local governments. The trend in recent years has been to rely more heavily on this method of taxation. This trend is not consistent with what is happening in other countries, and in this sense, the U.S. system of taxation is somewhat different.

Income taxes generally are imposed on individuals, corporations, and certain fiduciaries (estates and trusts). Most jurisdictions attempt to assure the collection of income taxes by requiring certain pay-as-you-go procedures (e.g., withholding requirements for employees and estimated tax prepayments for other taxpayers).

Federal Income Taxes. Chapters 2 through 15 deal primarily with the application of the Federal income tax to individuals. The procedure for determining the Federal income tax applicable to individuals is summarized in Figure 1–2.

The application of the Federal corporate income tax does not require the computation of adjusted gross income (AGI) and does not provide for the standard deduction and personal and dependency exemptions. All allowable deductions of a corporation fall into the business-expense category. In effect, therefore, the taxable income of a corporation is the difference between gross income (net of exclusions) and deductions.

Chapter 16 summarizes the rules relating to the tax formula for corporations.

State Income Taxes. All but the following states impose an income tax on individuals: Alaska, Florida, Nevada, South Dakota, Texas, Washington, and

Wyoming. New Hampshire and Tennessee have an income tax, but it applies only to dividend and interest income.

Nearly all states have an income tax applicable to corporations. It is difficult to determine those that do not because a state franchise tax sometimes is based in part on the income earned by the corporation.

Local Income Taxes. Cities imposing an income tax include, but are not limited to, Baltimore, Cincinnati, Cleveland, Detroit, Kansas City (Mo.), New York, Philadelphia, and St. Louis.

Employment Taxes

Classification as an employee usually leads to the imposition of employment taxes and to the requirement that the employer withhold specified amounts for income taxes. This discussion concentrates on the two major employment taxes: FICA (Federal Insurance Contributions Act—commonly referred to as the Social Security tax) and FUTA (Federal Unemployment Tax Act). Both taxes can be justified by social and public welfare considerations: FICA offers some measure of retirement security, and FUTA provides a modest source of income in the event of loss of employment.

FICA Taxes. The FICA tax is comprised of Social Security tax (old age, survivors, and disability insurance) *and* Medicare tax (hospital insurance). The tax rates and wage base under FICA are not constant, and as Figure 1–3 indicates, the increases over the years have been quite substantial. There appears to be every reason to predict that the rate and base amount will continue to rise in the future. Until 1991, the maximum wage that was subject to the Medicare portion of FICA was the same as that applicable to the Social Security portion. Since 1991, however, the ceiling amounts differ ($135,000 for the Medicare portion in 1993 and $57,600 for the Social Security portion). Also note that Figure 1–3 represents the employee's share of the tax.

A spouse employed by another spouse is subject to FICA. However, children under the age of 18 who are employed in a parent's trade or business are exempted.

FIGURE 1–2
Formula for Federal Income Tax on Individuals

Income (broadly conceived)	$xx,xxx
Less: Exclusions (income that is not subject to tax)	(x,xxx)
Gross income (income that is subject to tax)	$xx,xxx
Less: Certain business deductions (usually referred to as deductions *for* adjusted gross income)	(x,xxx)
Adjusted gross income	$xx,xxx
Less: The greater of certain personal and employee deductions (usually referred to as *itemized deductions,* *or* The standard deduction (including any *additional* standard deduction) *and*	(x,xxx)
Less: Personal and dependency exemptions	(x,xxx)
Taxable income	$xx,xxx
Tax on taxable income (see Tax Table and Rate Schedules in Appendix A)	$ x,xxx
Less: Tax credits (including Federal income tax withheld and other prepayments of Federal income taxes)	(xxx)
Tax due (or refund)	$ xxx

FUTA Taxes. The purpose of FUTA is to provide funds that the states can use to provide unemployment benefits. This leads to the somewhat unusual situation of one tax being handled by both Federal and state governments. The end result of this joint administration is that the employer must observe a double set of rules. Thus, state and Federal returns must be filed and payments made to both governmental units.

FUTA applies at a rate of 6.2 percent in 1993 on the first $7,000 of covered wages paid during the year to each employee. The Federal government allows a credit for FUTA paid (or allowed under a merit rating system) to the state. The credit cannot exceed 5.4 percent of the covered wages. Thus, the amount required to be paid to the IRS could be as low as 0.8 percent (6.2% – 5.4%).

States follow a policy of reducing the unemployment tax on employers who experience stable employment. Thus, an employer with little or no employee turnover might find that the state rate drops as low as 0.1 percent or, in some states, even to zero. The reason for the merit rating credit is that the state has lower unemployment benefits to pay when employment is steady.

FUTA differs from FICA in that the incidence of taxation falls entirely upon the employer. A few states, however, levy a special tax on employees either to provide disability benefits or supplemental unemployment compensation, or both.

Other U.S. Taxes

To complete the overview of the U.S. tax system, some missing links need to be covered that do not fit into the classifications discussed elsewhere in this chapter.

Federal Customs Duties. One tax that has not yet been mentioned is the tariff on certain imported goods. Generally referred to as a customs duty or levy, this tax, together with selective excise taxes, provided most of the revenues needed

FIGURE 1–3
FICA Rates and Base

	Social Security Portion				Medicare Portion				
	Percent	×	Base Amount	+	Percent	×	Base Amount	=	Maximum Tax
1978	5.05%	×	$17,700	+	1.00%	×	$ 17,700	=	$1,070.85
1979	5.08%	×	22,900	+	1.05%	×	22,900	=	1,403.77
1980	5.08%	×	25,900	+	1.05%	×	25,900	=	1,587.67
1981	5.35%	×	29,700	+	1.30%	×	29,700	=	1,975.05
1982	5.40%	×	32,400	+	1.30%	×	32,400	=	2,170.80
1983	5.40%	×	35,700	+	1.30%	×	35,700	=	2,391.90
1984	5.40%	×	37,800	+	1.30%	×	37,800	=	2,532.60
1985	5.70%	×	39,600	+	1.35%	×	39,600	=	2,791.80
1986	5.70%	×	42,000	+	1.45%	×	42,000	=	3,003.00
1987	5.70%	×	43,800	+	1.45%	×	43,800	=	3,131.70
1988	6.06%	×	45,000	+	1.45%	×	45,000	=	3,379.50
1989	6.06%	×	48,000	+	1.45%	×	48,000	=	3,604.80
1990	6.20%	×	51,300	+	1.45%	×	51,300	=	3,924.45
1991	6.20%	×	53,400	+	1.45%	×	125,000	=	5,123.30
1992	6.20%	×	55,500	+	1.45%	×	130,200	=	5,328.90
1993	6.20%	×	57,600	+	1.45%	×	135,000	=	5,528.70
1994	*		*		*		*		**

*Not yet determined by Congress.
**Cannot be computed until the wage base is set by Congress.

by the Federal government during the nineteenth century. In view of present times, it is remarkable to note that tariffs and excise taxes alone paid off the national debt in 1835 and enabled the U.S. Treasury to pay a surplus of $28 million to the states.

In recent years, tariffs have served the nation more as an instrument for carrying out protectionist policies than as a means of generating revenue. Thus, a particular U.S. industry might be saved from economic disaster, so the argument goes, by placing customs duties on the importation of foreign goods that can be sold at lower prices. Protectionists contend that the tariff neutralizes the competitive edge held by the producer of the foreign goods.

Protectionist policies seem more appropriate for less-developed countries whose industrial capacity has not yet matured. In a world where a developed country should have everything to gain by encouraging international free trade, such policies may be of dubious value. History shows that tariffs often lead to retaliatory action on the part of the nation or nations affected.

Miscellaneous State and Local Taxes. Most states impose a franchise tax on corporations. Basically, a *franchise tax* is levied on the right to do business in the state. The base used for the determination of the tax varies from state to state. Although corporate income considerations may come into play, this tax most often is based on the capitalization of the corporation (either with or without certain long-term indebtedness).

Closely akin to the franchise tax are *occupational taxes* applicable to various trades or businesses, such as a liquor store license, a taxicab permit, or a fee to practice a profession such as law, medicine, or accounting. Most of these are not significant revenue producers and fall more into the category of licenses than taxes. The revenue derived is used to defray the cost incurred by the jurisdiction in regulating the business or profession in the interest of the public good.

Value Added Taxes

At least in the Common Market countries of Western Europe, the *value added tax* (VAT) has gained acceptance as a major source of revenue. Although variously classified, a VAT resembles a national sales tax since it taxes the increment in value as goods move through production and manufacturing stages to the marketplace. A VAT has its proponents in the United States as a partial solution to high Federal budget deficits and increases in employment taxes. Its incorporation as part of our tax system in the near future is problematical, however.

TAX ADMINISTRATION

Internal Revenue Service

The responsibility for administering the Federal tax laws rests with the Treasury Department. Administratively, the IRS is part of the Department of the Treasury and is responsible for enforcing the tax laws.

The Commissioner of Internal Revenue, who is appointed by the President, is responsible for establishing policy and supervising the activities of the entire IRS organization. The National Office organization of the IRS includes a Senior Deputy Commissioner and several Deputy Commissioners and Assistant Commissioners who have supervisory responsibility over field operations.

The Audit Process

Selection of Returns for Audit. Due to budgetary limitations, only a small minority of returns are audited. For calendar year 1992, for example, only 0.94 percent of *all* individual income tax returns were examined.

The IRS utilizes mathematical formulas and statistical sampling techniques to select tax returns that are most likely to contain errors and to yield substantial amounts of additional tax revenues upon audit. Though the IRS does not openly disclose all of its audit selection techniques, the following observations may be made concerning the probability of selection for audit:

- Certain groups of taxpayers are subject to audit much more frequently than others. These groups include individuals with gross income in excess of $50,000, self-employed individuals with substantial business income and deductions, and taxpayers with prior tax deficiencies. Also vulnerable are cash businesses (e.g., cafes and small service businesses) where the potential for tax avoidance is high.

Example 8

Jack owns and operates a liquor store on a cash-and-carry basis. Since all of his sales are for cash, Jack might well be a prime candidate for an audit by the IRS. Cash transactions are easier to conceal than credit transactions. ◆

- If information returns (e.g., Form 1099, Form W–2) are not in substantial agreement with reported income, an audit can be anticipated.
- If an individual's itemized deductions are in excess of norms established for various income levels, the probability of an audit is increased.
- Filing of a refund claim by the taxpayer may prompt an audit of the return.
- Certain returns are selected on a random sampling basis under the Taxpayer Compliance Measurement Program (TCMP). TCMP is used to develop, update, and improve the mathematical formulas and statistical sampling techniques used by the IRS.
- Information obtained from other sources (e.g., informants, news items). The tax law permits the IRS to pay rewards to persons who provide information that leads to the detection and punishment of those who violate the tax laws. The rewards may not exceed 10 percent of the taxes, fines, and penalties recovered as a result of the information.

Example 9

After 15 years of service, Rita is discharged by her employer, Dr. Smith. Shortly thereafter, the IRS receives an anonymous letter informing it that Dr. Smith keeps two separate sets of books, one of which substantially understates his cash receipts. ◆

Example 10

During a divorce proceeding, it is revealed that Leo, a public official, kept large amounts of cash in a shoe box at home. The information is widely disseminated by the news media and comes to the attention of the IRS. Needless to say, the IRS would be interested in knowing whether the cash originated from a taxable source and, if so, whether it was reported on Leo's income tax returns. ◆

Tax Practice

The area of tax practice is largely unregulated. Virtually anyone can aid another in complying with the various tax laws. If a practitioner is a member of a profession, such as law or public accounting, he or she must abide by certain ethical standards. Furthermore, the Internal Revenue Code imposes penalties upon the preparers of Federal tax returns who violate proscribed acts and procedures.

Ethical Guidelines. The American Institute of CPAs has issued numerous guides for CPAs engaged in tax practice. Called "Statements on Responsibilities in Tax Practice," some of these are summarized below.

- Do not take questionable positions on a client's tax return in the hope that the return will not be selected for audit by the IRS. Any positions taken should be supported by a good-faith belief that they have a realistic chance of being sustained if challenged.
- A practitioner can use a client's estimates if they are reasonable under the circumstances. If the tax law requires verification (e.g., receipts), the client should be so advised.
- Every effort should be made to answer questions appearing on tax returns.
- Upon learning of an error on a past tax return, advise the client to correct it. Do not, however, inform the IRS of the error. If the error is material and the client refuses to correct it, consider withdrawing from the engagement. This will be necessary if the error has a carryover effect and prevents the current year's tax liability from being determined correctly.

Statutory Penalties Imposed on Tax Return Preparers. In addition to ethical constraints, a tax return preparer may be subject to certain statutorily sanctioned penalties, including the following:

- Various penalties involving procedural matters. Examples include failing to furnish the taxpayer with a copy of the return; endorsing a taxpayer's refund check; failing to sign the return as a preparer; failing to furnish one's identification number; and failing to keep copies of returns or maintain a client list.
- Understatement of a tax liability based on a position that lacks any realistic possibility of being sustained. If the position is not frivolous, the penalty can be avoided by disclosing it on the return.
- Any willful attempt to understate taxes. This usually results when a preparer disregards or makes no effort to obtain pertinent information from a client.

UNDERSTANDING THE FEDERAL TAX LAW

The Federal tax law is a mosaic of statutory provisions, administrative pronouncements, and court decisions. Anyone who has attempted to work with this body of knowledge would have to admit to its complexity. For the person who has to trudge through a mass of rules to find the solution to a tax problem, it may be of some consolation to know that the law's complexity can generally be explained. Whether sound or not, there is a reason for the formulation of every rule. Knowing these reasons, therefore, is a considerable step toward understanding the Federal tax law.

The Federal tax law has as its *major objective* the raising of revenue. But although the fiscal needs of the government are important, other considerations explain certain portions of the law. Economic, social, equity, and political factors also play a significant role. Added to these factors is the marked impact the IRS and the courts have had and will continue to have on the evolution of Federal tax law. The remainder of the chapter examines these matters, referring wherever appropriate to subjects covered later in the text.

Revenue Needs

The foundation of any tax system has to be the raising of revenue to cover the cost of government operations. Ideally, annual outlays should not exceed anticipated revenues, thereby leading to a balanced budget with no deficit. Many states have achieved this objective by passing laws or constitutional amendments precluding deficit spending. Unfortunately, the Federal government has no such conclusive prohibition, and mounting annual deficits have become an increasing concern for many.

When finalizing the Tax Reform Act (TRA) of 1986, a deficit-conscious Congress was guided by the concept of *revenue neutrality*. The concept means that the changes made in the tax law will neither increase nor decrease the net result reached under the prior rules. Revenue neutrality does not mean that any one taxpayer's tax liability will remain the same, as this will depend upon the circumstances involved. Thus, one taxpayer's increased tax liability could be another's tax savings. Although revenue-neutral tax reform does not reduce deficits, at least it does not aggravate the problem.

One can expect budget deficit considerations to play an ever-increasing role in shaping future tax policy. The Revenue Reconciliation Act of 1990 is intended to generate considerable revenue. Although it contains certain revenue loss provisions, these are more than made up by new taxes and increases in tax rates.

Economic Considerations

The use of the tax system in an effort to accomplish economic objectives has become increasingly popular in recent years. Generally, proponents of this goal amend the Internal Revenue Code through tax legislation designed to help control the economy or encourage certain activities and businesses.

Control of the Economy. Congress has used depreciation write-offs as a means of controlling the economy. Theoretically, shorter asset lives and accelerated methods should encourage additional investment in depreciable property acquired for business use. Conversely, longer asset lives and the required use of the straight-line method of depreciation dampen the tax incentive for capital outlays.

Compared with past law, TRA of 1986 generally cut back on faster write-offs for property acquired after 1986. Particularly hard hit was most depreciable real estate, where class lives were extended from 19 years to as long as 31½ years and the straight-line method was made mandatory. These changes were made in the interest of revenue neutrality and in the belief that the economy was stable.

A change in the tax rate structure has a more immediate impact on the economy. With lower tax rates, taxpayers are able to retain additional spendable funds. Although TRA of 1986 lowered tax rates for most taxpayers, it also reduced or eliminated many deductions and credits. Consequently, lower rates may not lead to lower tax liabilities.

Encouragement of Certain Activities. Without passing judgment on the wisdom of any such choices, it is quite clear that the tax law does encourage certain types of economic activity or segments of the economy. For example, the favorable treatment allowed research and development expenditures can be explained by the desire to foster technological progress. Under the tax law, such expenditures can be either deducted in the year incurred or capitalized and amortized over a period of 60 months or more. In terms of timing the tax savings, these options usually are preferable to capitalizing the cost with a write-off over the estimated useful life of the asset created. If the asset developed has an indefinite useful life, no write-off would be available without the two options allowed by the tax law.

Is it desirable to encourage the conservation of energy resources? Considering the world energy situation and our own reliance on foreign oil, the answer to this question has to be yes. The concern over energy usage was a prime consideration in the enactment of legislation to make various tax savings for energy conservation expenditures available to taxpayers.

Is preserving the environment a desirable objective? Ecological considerations explain why the tax law permits a 60-month amortization period for costs incurred in the installation of pollution control facilities.

Is saving desirable for the economy? Saving leads to capital formation and thereby makes funds available to finance home construction and industrial expansion. The tax law encourages saving by granting preferential treatment to private retirement plans. Not only are contributions to Keogh (H.R. 10) plans and certain Individual Retirement Accounts (IRAs) deductible, but income from the contributions accumulates free of tax. As noted below, the encouragement of private-sector pension plans can also be justified under social considerations.

Encouragement of Certain Industries. No one can question the proposition that a sound agricultural base is necessary for a well-balanced national economy. Undoubtedly, this can explain why farmers are accorded special treatment under the Federal tax system. Among the benefits are the election to expense rather than capitalize certain soil and water conservation expenditures and fertilizers and the election to defer the recognition of gain on the receipt of crop insurance proceeds.

Encouragement of Small Business. At least in the United States, a consensus exists that what is good for small business is good for the economy as a whole. Whether valid or not, this assumption has led to a definite bias in the tax law favoring small business.

In the corporate tax area, several provisions can be explained by the desire to benefit small business. One provision permits the shareholders of a small business corporation to make a special election that generally will avoid the imposition of the corporate income tax. Furthermore, the election enables the corporation to pass through to its shareholders any of its operating losses. Known as the S election, it is discussed in Chapter 21.

Social Considerations

Some provisions of the Federal tax law, particularly those dealing with the income tax of individuals, can be explained by social considerations. The following are some notable examples with their rationales:

- Certain benefits provided to employees through accident and health plans financed by employers are nontaxable to employees. Encouraging such plans is considered socially desirable, since they provide medical benefits in the event of an employee's illness or injury.

- Most premiums paid by an employer for group term insurance covering the life of the employee are nontaxable to the employee. These arrangements can be justified on social grounds in that they provide funds for the family unit to help it adjust to the loss of wages caused by the employee's death.
- A contribution made by an employer to a qualified pension or profit sharing plan for an employee receives special treatment. The contribution and any income it generates will not be taxed to the employee until the funds are distributed. Such an arrangement also benefits the employer by allowing a tax deduction when the contribution is made to the qualified plan. Private retirement plans are encouraged to supplement the subsistence income level the employee otherwise would have under the Social Security system.
- A deduction is allowed for contributions to qualified charitable organizations. The deduction attempts to shift some of the financial and administrative burden of socially desirable programs from the public (the government) to the private (the citizens) sector.
- A tax credit is allowed for amounts spent to furnish care for certain minor or disabled dependents to enable the taxpayer to seek or maintain gainful employment (see Chapter 11). Who could deny the social desirability of encouraging taxpayers to provide care for their children while they work?
- A tax deduction is not allowed for certain expenditures deemed to be contrary to public policy. This disallowance extends to such items as fines, penalties, illegal kickbacks, bribes to government officials, and gambling losses in excess of gains. Social considerations dictate that the tax law should not encourage these activities by permitting the deduction.

Many other examples could be included, but the conclusion would be unchanged. Social considerations do explain a significant part of the Federal tax law.

Equity Considerations

The concept of equity is relative. Reasonable persons can, and often do, disagree about what is fair or unfair. In the tax area, moreover, equity is most often tied to a particular taxpayer's personal situation. To illustrate, compare the tax positions of those who rent their personal residences with those who own their homes. Renters receive no Federal income tax benefit from the rent they pay. For homeowners, however, a large portion of the house payments they make may qualify for the Federal interest and property tax deductions. Although renters may have difficulty understanding this difference in tax treatment, the encouragement of home ownership can be justified on both economic and social grounds.

In the same vein, compare the tax treatment of a corporation with that of a partnership. Although the two businesses may be of equal size, similarly situated, and competitors in the production of goods or services, they are not treated comparably under the tax law. The corporation is subject to a separate Federal income tax; the partnership is not. Whether the differences in tax treatment can be justified logically in terms of equity is beside the point. The point is that the tax law can and does make a distinction between these business forms.

Equity, then, is not what appears fair or unfair to any one taxpayer or group of taxpayers. It is, instead, what the tax law recognizes. Some recognition of equity does exist, however, and explains part of the law. The concept of equity appears in tax provisions that alleviate the effect of multiple taxation and postpone the recognition of gain when the taxpayer lacks the ability or wherewithal to pay the tax. Equity considerations also mitigate the effect of the application of the annual accounting period concept and cope with the eroding results of inflation.

Alleviating the Effect of Multiple Taxation. The income earned by a taxpayer may be subject to taxes imposed by different taxing authorities. If, for example, the taxpayer is a resident of New York City, income might generate Federal, state of New York, and city of New York income taxes. To compensate for this apparent inequity, the Federal tax law allows a taxpayer to claim a deduction for state and local income taxes. The deduction does not, however, neutralize the effect of multiple taxation since the benefit derived depends on the taxpayer's Federal income tax rate. Only a tax credit, rather than a deduction, would eliminate the effects of multiple taxation on the same income.

Equity considerations can explain the Federal tax treatment of certain income from foreign sources. Since double taxation results when the same income is subject to both foreign and U.S. income taxes, the tax law permits the taxpayer to choose between a credit and a deduction for the foreign taxes paid.

The Wherewithal to Pay Concept. The *wherewithal to pay* concept recognizes the inequity of taxing a transaction when the taxpayer lacks the means to pay the tax. It is particularly suited to situations in which the taxpayer's economic position has not changed significantly as a result of the transaction.

An illustration of the wherewithal to pay concept is the provision of the tax law dealing with the treatment of gain resulting from the sale of a personal residence. If the proceeds are rolled over (reinvested) in another personal residence within a specified time period, the gain will not be taxed (see Chapter 12).

EXAMPLE 11

Ron sells his personal residence (cost of $60,000) for $100,000 and moves to another city. Shortly thereafter, he purchases a new personal residence for $100,000. ◆

In Example 11, Ron has a realized gain of $40,000 [$100,000 (selling price) − $60,000 (cost of residence)]. It would be inequitable to force him to pay a tax on this gain for two reasons. First, without disposing of the property acquired (the new residence), Ron would be hard-pressed to pay the tax. Second, his economic position has not changed significantly.

Mitigating the Effect of the Annual Accounting Period Concept. For purposes of effective administration of the tax law, all taxpayers must report to and settle with the Federal government at periodic intervals. Otherwise, taxpayers would remain uncertain as to their tax liabilities, and the government would have difficulty judging revenues and budgeting expenditures. The period selected for final settlement of most tax liabilities, in any event an arbitrary determination, is one year. At the close of each year, therefore, a taxpayer's position becomes complete for that particular year. Referred to as the annual accounting period concept, its effect is to divide each taxpayer's life, for tax purposes, into equal annual intervals.

The finality of the annual accounting period concept could lead to dissimilar tax treatment for taxpayers who are, from a long-range standpoint, in the same economic position.

EXAMPLE 12

José and Alicia, both sole proprietors, have experienced the following results during the past four years:

Year	Profit (or Loss) José	Alicia
1990	$50,000	$150,000
1991	60,000	60,000
1992	70,000	70,000
1993	50,000	(50,000)

Although José and Alicia have the same profit of $230,000 over the period from 1990 to 1993, the finality of the annual accounting period concept places Alicia at a definite disadvantage for tax purposes. The net operating loss procedure offers Alicia some relief by allowing her to apply some or all of her 1993 loss to the earliest profitable years (in this case, 1990). Thus, with a net operating loss carryback, Alicia is in a position to obtain a refund for some of the taxes she paid on the $150,000 profit reported for 1990. ◆

The same reasoning used to support the deduction of net operating losses can explain the special treatment the tax law accords to excess capital losses and excess charitable contributions. Carryback and carryover procedures help mitigate the effect of limiting a loss or a deduction to the accounting period in which it was realized. With such procedures, a taxpayer may be able to salvage a loss or a deduction that might otherwise be wasted.

Coping with Inflation. Because of the progressive nature of the income tax, a wage adjustment to compensate for inflation can increase the income tax bracket of the recipient. Known as *bracket creep*, its overall impact is an erosion of purchasing power. Congress recognized this problem and began to adjust various income tax components, such as tax brackets, standard deduction amounts, and personal and dependency exemptions through an indexation procedure. Indexation is based upon the rise in the consumer price index over the prior year.

Political Considerations

A large segment of the Federal tax law is made up of statutory provisions. Since these statutes are enacted by Congress, is it any surprise that political considerations influence tax law? For purposes of discussion, the effect of political considerations on the tax law is divided into the following topics: special interest legislation, political expediency situations, and state and local government influences.

Special Interest Legislation. There is no doubt that certain provisions of the tax law can largely be explained by the political influence some pressure groups have had on Congress. Is there any other realistic reason, for example, that prepaid subscription and dues income are not taxed until earned while prepaid rents are taxed to the landlord in the year received?

Special interest legislation is not necessarily to be condemned if it can be justified on economic, social, or some other utilitarian grounds. At any rate, it is an inevitable product of our political system.

A recent example of special interest legislation was a last-minute amendment to the TRA of 1986 made by former Senator Long (Louisiana) and Representative Pickle (Austin, Texas). Under the amendment, a charitable deduction was allowed for donations to certain institutions of higher education that enabled the donor to receive choice seating at athletic events. The definition of institutions of higher education was so limited, however, that only Louisiana State University and the University of Texas were qualified recipients. It was not until two years later that Congress modified the tax law to neutralize this apparent preferential treatment (see Chapter 10).

Political Expediency Situations. Various tax reform proposals rise and fall in favor with the shifting moods of the American public. That Congress is sensitive to popular feeling is an accepted fact. Therefore, certain provisions of the tax law can be explained by the political climate at the time they were enacted.

Measures that deter more affluent taxpayers from obtaining so-called preferential tax treatment have always had popular appeal and, consequently, the support of Congress. Provisions such as the alternative minimum tax, the imputed interest rules, and the limitation on the deductibility of interest on investment indebtedness can be explained on this basis (see Chapters 10 and 11).

Other changes explained at least partially by political expediency include the lowering of individual income tax rates, the increase in the personal and dependency exemptions, and the increase in the amount of the earned income credit.

State and Local Government Influences. Political considerations have played a major role in the nontaxability of interest received on state and local obligations. In view of the furor that has been raised by state and local political figures every time any modification of this tax provision has been proposed, one might well regard it as next to sacred.

Somewhat less apparent has been the influence state law has had in shaping our present Federal tax law. Of prime import in this regard has been the effect of the community property system employed in some states.[6] At one time, the tax position of the residents of these states was so advantageous that many common law states actually adopted community property systems. Needless to say, the political pressure placed on Congress to correct the disparity in tax treatment was considerable. To a large extent this was accomplished in the Revenue Act of 1948, which extended many of the community property tax advantages to residents of common law jurisdictions.

The major advantage extended was the provision allowing married taxpayers to file joint returns and compute the tax liability as if the income had been earned one-half by each spouse. This result is automatic in a community property state since half of the income earned by one spouse belongs to the other spouse. The income-splitting benefits of a joint return are now incorporated as part of the tax rates applicable to married taxpayers. See Chapter 2.

6. The nine states with community property systems are Louisiana, Texas, New Mexico, Arizona, California, Washington, Idaho, Nevada, and Wisconsin. The rest of the states are classified as common law jurisdictions. The difference between common law and community property systems centers around the property rights possessed by married persons. In a common law system, each spouse owns whatever he or she earns. Under a community property system, one-half of the earnings of each spouse is considered owned by the other spouse. Assume, for example, Henry and Wanda are husband and wife and their only income is the $40,000 annual salary Henry receives. If they live in New York (a common law state), the $40,000 salary is attributed to Henry. If, however, they live in Texas (a community property state), the $40,000 salary is divided equally, in terms of ownership, between Henry and Wanda.

Influence of the Internal Revenue Service

The influence of the IRS is apparent in many areas beyond its role in issuing the administrative pronouncements that make up a considerable portion of our tax law. In its capacity as the protector of the national revenue, the IRS has been instrumental in securing the passage of much legislation designed to curtail the most flagrant tax avoidance practices (to close tax loopholes). In its capacity as the administrator of the tax law, the IRS has sought and obtained legislation to make its job easier (to attain administrative feasibility).

The IRS as Protector of the Revenue. Innumerable examples can be given of provisions in the tax law that stem from the direct influence of the IRS. Usually, such provisions are intended to prevent a loophole from being used to avoid the tax consequences intended by Congress. Working within the letter of existing law, ingenious taxpayers and their advisers devise techniques that accomplish indirectly what cannot be accomplished directly. As a consequence, legislation is enacted to close the loopholes that taxpayers have located and exploited. Some tax law can be explained in this fashion and is discussed in the chapters to follow.

In addition, the IRS has secured from Congress legislation of a more general nature that enables it to make adjustments based on the substance, rather than the formal construction, of what a taxpayer has done. One such provision permits the IRS to make adjustments to a taxpayer's method of accounting when the method used by the taxpayer does not clearly reflect income (see Chapter 15).

Example 13

Tina, an individual cash basis taxpayer, owns and operates a pharmacy. All drugs and other items acquired for resale (e.g., cosmetics) are charged to the purchases account and written off (expensed) for tax purposes in the year of acquisition. As this procedure does not clearly reflect income, it would be appropriate for the IRS to require that Tina establish and maintain an ending inventory account. ◆

Administrative Feasibility. Some of the tax law is justified on the grounds that it simplifies the task of the IRS in collecting the revenue and administering the law. With regard to collecting the revenue, the IRS long ago realized the importance of placing taxpayers on a pay-as-you-go basis. Elaborate withholding procedures apply to wages, while the tax on other types of income must be paid at periodic intervals throughout the year. The IRS has been instrumental in convincing the courts that accrual basis taxpayers should pay taxes on prepaid income in the year received and not when earned. The approach may be contrary to generally accepted accounting principles, but it is consistent with the wherewithal to pay concept.

Of considerable aid to the IRS in collecting revenue are the numerous provisions that impose interest and penalties on taxpayers for noncompliance with the tax law. Provisions such as the penalties for failure to pay a tax or to file a return that is due, the negligence penalty for intentional disregard of rules and regulations, and various penalties for civil and criminal fraud serve as deterrents to taxpayer noncompliance.

One of the keys to an effective administration of our tax system is the audit process conducted by the IRS. To carry out this function, the IRS is aided by provisions that reduce the chance of taxpayer error or manipulation and therefore simplify the audit effort that is necessary. An increase in the amount of the standard deduction, for example, reduces the number of individual taxpayers who will choose the alternative of itemizing their personal deductions. With fewer deductions to check, the audit function is simplified.

Influence of the Courts

In addition to interpreting statutory provisions and the administrative pronouncements issued by the IRS, the Federal courts have influenced tax law in two other respects. First, the courts have formulated certain judicial concepts that serve as guides in the application of various tax provisions. Second, certain key decisions have led to changes in the Internal Revenue Code.

Judicial Concepts Relating to Tax. A leading tax concept developed by the courts deals with the interpretation of statutory tax provisions that operate to benefit taxpayers. The courts have established the rule that these relief provisions are to be narrowly construed against taxpayers if there is any doubt about their application.

EXAMPLE 14

When a taxpayer has a gain on the sale of a personal residence, the gain is not subject to Federal income tax if the proceeds from the sale are reinvested in another principal residence. The tax law specifies a period of time within which the reinvestment must take place. The courts have held that the nontaxability of gain is a relief provision to be narrowly construed. Thus, failure to meet the replacement period requirements, even if beyond the control of the taxpayer, will cause the gain to be taxed. ◆

Important in this area is the *arm's length* concept. Particularly in dealings between related parties, transactions may be tested by looking to whether the taxpayers acted in an arm's length manner. The question to be asked is: Would unrelated parties have handled the transaction in the same way?

EXAMPLE 15

Rex, the sole shareholder of Silver Corporation, leases property to the corporation for a yearly rental of $6,000. To test whether the corporation should be allowed a rent deduction for this amount, the IRS and the courts will apply the arm's length concept. Would Silver Corporation have paid $6,000 a year in rent if the same property had been leased from an unrelated party (rather than from the sole shareholder)? Suppose it is determined that an unrelated third party would have paid an annual rental for the property of only $5,000. Under these circumstances, Silver will be allowed a deduction of only $5,000. The other $1,000 it paid for the use of the property represents a nondeductible dividend. Accordingly, Rex will be treated as having received rent income of $5,000 and dividend income of $1,000. ◆

Judicial Influence on Statutory Provisions. Some court decisions have been of such consequence that Congress has incorporated them into statutory tax law. For example, many years ago the courts held that stock dividends distributed to the shareholders of a corporation were not taxable as income. This result was largely accepted by Congress, and a provision in the tax statutes now covers the issue.

On occasion, however, Congress has reacted negatively to judicial interpretations of the tax law.

EXAMPLE 16

Nora leases unimproved real estate to Wade for 40 years. At a cost of $200,000, Wade erects a building on the land. The building is worth $100,000 when the lease terminates and Nora takes possession of the property. Does Nora have any income either when the improvements are made or when the lease terminates? In a landmark decision, a court held that Nora must recognize income of $100,000 upon the termination of the lease. ◆

Congress felt that the result reached in Example 16 was inequitable in that it was not consistent with the wherewithal to pay concept. Consequently, the tax law was amended to provide that a landlord does not recognize any income either when the improvements are made (unless made in lieu of rent) or when the lease terminates.

Summary

In addition to its necessary revenue-raising objective, the Federal tax law has developed in response to several other factors:

- *Economic considerations*. The emphasis here is on tax provisions that help regulate the economy and encourage certain activities and types of businesses.
- *Social considerations.* Some tax provisions are designed to encourage (or discourage) certain socially desirable (or undesirable) practices.
- *Equity considerations.* Of principal concern in this area are tax provisions that alleviate the effect of multiple taxation, recognize the wherewithal to pay concept, mitigate the effect of the annual accounting period concept, and recognize the eroding effect of inflation.
- *Political considerations.* Of significance in this regard are tax provisions that represent special interest legislation, reflect political expediency, and exhibit the effect of state and local law.
- *Influence of the IRS.* Many tax provisions are intended to aid the IRS in the collection of revenue and the administration of the tax law.
- *Influence of the courts.* Court decisions have established a body of judicial concepts relating to tax law and have, on occasion, led Congress to enact statutory provisions to either clarify or negate their effect.

These factors explain various tax provisions and thereby help in understanding why the tax law developed to its present state.

PROBLEM MATERIALS

DISCUSSION QUESTIONS

1. Irene, a middle management employee, is offered a pay increase by her employer. As a condition of the offer, she must move to another state. What tax considerations should Irene weigh before making a decision on whether to accept the offer?
2. A tax protester refuses to pay the Federal income tax on the grounds that the tax is unconstitutional. Any comment?
3. Before the ratification of the Sixteenth Amendment to the U.S. Constitution, the Federal income tax on corporations was held to be constitutional, whereas the Federal income tax on individuals was not. Why?
4. A tax law that was enacted in 1953 would be part of which Internal Revenue Code (i.e., 1939, 1954, or 1986)? Explain.
5. How does the pay-as-you-go procedure apply to wage earners? To persons who have income from other than wages?
6. Analyze the Federal income tax in light of Adam Smith's canons of taxation.
7. Is FICA a proportional or progressive tax? Explain.

8. What difference does it make whether a capital improvement to real estate is classified as a *fixture*?
9. Matt buys a new home for $150,000, its cost of construction plus the usual profit margin for the builder. The new home is located in a neighborhood largely developed 10 years ago when the homes sold for approximately $50,000 each. Assuming the homes of his neighbors are worth (in current values) in the vicinity of $150,000, could Matt be at a disadvantage with regard to the ad valorem tax on realty?
10. Freda's personal residence is appraised at the same amount as is her next-door neighbor's residence. The neighbor is retired. Freda is somewhat surprised to learn that her neighbor pays less real estate property tax to the city than she does. Could there be a logical explanation for the apparent inequity?
11. While out of town on business, Paul stays at a motel with an advertised room rate of $30 per night. When checking out, he is charged $33. What would be a plausible reason for the extra $3 Paul had to pay?
12. On a recent trip to a nearby supermarket, Nancy spent $42.00, of which $2.00 was for general sales tax. If Nancy lives in a jurisdiction that imposes a 6% general sales tax on foodstuffs, why was the bill not $42.40?
13. Earl, a resident of Wyoming (which imposes a general sales tax), goes to Montana (which does not impose a general sales tax) to purchase his automobile. Will Earl successfully avoid the Wyoming sales tax? Explain.
14. Why might a person who purchases a product from an establishment located in jurisdiction X wish to take delivery in jurisdiction Y? Would it matter whether or not the person resided in jurisdiction X? Explain.
15. When Alaska became a major oil producer, the state repealed its state income tax. Is there any correlation between these two events? Explain.
16. A death tax has been characterized as an excise tax. Do you agree? Why or why not?
17. Explain the difference between an inheritance tax and an estate tax.
18. What was the original objective of the Federal estate tax?
19. A decedent who leaves all of his property to his surviving spouse and to qualified charitable organizations will not be subject to a Federal estate tax. Explain.
20. How much property can Ida, a widow, give to her three married children, their spouses, and five grandchildren over a period of 12 years without making a taxable gift?
21. When married persons elect to split a gift, what tax advantages do they enjoy?
22. Contrast the Federal income tax scheme applicable to individuals with that applicable to corporations, pointing out the major differences.
23. When a state uses a "piggyback" approach for its state income tax, what is the state doing?
24. Chee lives in a state that imposes an income tax. His Federal income tax return for 1991 is audited in 1993, and, as a result of several adjustments made by the IRS, Chee has to pay additional Federal income tax. Several months later, Chee is notified that his 1991 state income tax return is to be audited. Are these two incidents coincidence or does a reasonable explanation exist?
25. At a social function you attended in early July of 1993, you overheard a guest, the CEO of a corporation, remark, "Thank goodness this is the end of FICA for a while!" Interpret this remark.
26. Keith, a sole proprietor, owns and operates a grocery store. His wife and his 17-year-old son work in the business and are paid wages. Will the wife and son be subjected to FICA? Explain.
27. Dan, the owner and operator of a construction company that builds outdoor swimming pools, releases most of his construction personnel during the winter months. Should this hurt Dan's FUTA situation? Why or why not?

28. Compare FICA and FUTA in connection with each of the following:

   a. Incidence of taxation.
   b. Justification for taxation.
   c. Reporting and filing requirements.
   d. Rates and base involved.

29. What is a value added tax (VAT) and how does it operate?
30. Norm, the owner and operator of a cash-and-carry military surplus retail outlet, has been audited many times by the IRS. When Norm mentions this fact to his next-door neighbor, an employee with Ford Motor Company, he is somewhat surprised to learn that the neighbor has never been audited by the IRS. Is there any explanation for this apparent disparity in treatment?
31. While Dr. Jones and her family are out of town on vacation, their home is burglarized. Among the items stolen and reported to the police are $35,000 in cash and gold coins worth $80,000. Shortly after the incident, Dr. Jones is audited by the IRS. Could there be any causal connection between the burglary and the audit? Explain.
32. What is meant by revenue-neutral tax reform?
33. Discuss the probable justification for the following provisions of the tax law:

   a. The election permitted certain corporations to avoid the corporate income tax.
   b. A provision that excludes from income certain benefits furnished to employees through accident and health plans financed by employers.
   c. Nontaxable treatment for an employee for premiums paid by an employer for group term insurance covering the life of the employee.

34. What purpose is served by allowing a deduction for home mortgage interest and property taxes?
35. The tax law encourages the creation and operation of private retirement plans. How is this done? What purpose(s) are served by this special tax treatment?
36. The tax law encourages private retirement plans and contributions to charitable organizations. In terms of nonrevenue objectives, what is the common justification for this special tax treatment?
37. Forcing accrual basis taxpayers to recognize prepaid income when received (as opposed to when earned) accomplishes what objective?

CHAPTER

TAX DETERMINATION; PERSONAL AND DEPENDENCY EXEMPTIONS; AN OVERVIEW OF PROPERTY TRANSACTIONS

OBJECTIVES

Explain how an individual's Federal income tax liability is determined.

Develop greater understanding of the components of the tax formula for individuals, including gross income, exclusions, the standard deduction, itemized deductions, and exemptions.

Apply the rules for determining dependency exemptions and filing status.

Introduce the basic concepts of property transactions and their effect on taxable income.

Discuss several basic tax planning ideas for individual taxpayers.

OUTLINE

Individuals are subject to Federal income tax based on taxable income. This chapter explains how taxable income and the income tax of an individual taxpayer are determined.

To compute taxable income, it is necessary to understand the tax formula in Figure 2–1. Although the tax formula is rather simple, determining an individual's taxable income can be quite complex. The complexity stems from the numerous provisions that govern the determination of gross income and allowable deductions.

After computing taxable income, the appropriate rates must be applied. This requires a determination of the individual's filing status, since different rates apply for single taxpayers, married taxpayers, and heads of household. The basic tax rate structure is progressive, with rates of 15 percent, 28 percent, and 31 percent.[1]

Once the individual's tax has been computed, prepayments and credits are subtracted to determine whether the taxpayer owes additional tax or is entitled to a refund.

When property is sold or otherwise disposed of, a gain or loss may result, which could affect the determination of taxable income. Although property transactions are covered in detail in Chapters 12 and 13, an understanding of certain basic concepts is helpful in working with some of the materials to follow. The concluding portion of this chapter furnishes an overview of property transactions, including the distinction between realized and recognized gain or loss, the classification of such gain or loss (ordinary or capital), and treatment for income tax purposes.

TAX FORMULA

Most individuals compute taxable income using the tax formula shown in Figure 2–1. Special provisions govern the computation of taxable income and the tax liability for certain minor children who have unearned income in excess of specified amounts. These provisions are discussed under Tax Determination—Unearned Income of Children under Age 14 Taxed at Parents' Rate later in the chapter.

FIGURE 2–1
Tax Formula

Income (broadly conceived)	$xx,xxx
Less: Exclusions	(x,xxx)
Gross income	$xx,xxx
Less: Deductions *for* adjusted gross income	(x,xxx)
Adjusted gross income	$xx,xxx
Less: The greater of—	
Total itemized deductions *or* the standard deduction	(x,xxx)
Personal and dependency exemptions	(x,xxx)
Taxable income	$xx,xxx

1. The 1993 Tax Table was not available from the IRS at the date of publication of this text. The Tax Table for 1992 and the Tax Rate Schedules for 1992 and 1993 are reproduced in Appendix A. For quick reference, the 1992 and 1993 Tax Rate Schedules are also reproduced inside the front cover of this text.

Before illustrating the application of the tax formula, a brief discussion of the components of the formula is necessary.

Components of the Tax Formula

Income (Broadly Conceived). This includes all the taxpayer's income, both taxable and nontaxable. Although it is essentially equivalent to gross receipts, it does not include a return of capital or receipt of borrowed funds.

EXAMPLE 1

Dave needed money to purchase a house. He sold 5,000 shares of stock for $100,000. He had paid $40,000 for the stock. In addition, he borrowed $75,000 from a bank. Dave has taxable income of $60,000 from the sale of the stock ($100,000 selling price – $40,000 return of capital). He has no income from the $75,000 he borrowed from the bank because he has an obligation to repay that amount. ◆

Exclusions. For various reasons, Congress has chosen to exclude certain types of income from the income tax base. The principal income exclusions are discussed in Chapter 4. A partial list of these exclusions is shown in Figure 2–2 on the following page.

Gross Income. The Internal Revenue Code defines gross income broadly as "all income from whatever source derived."[2] It includes, but is not limited to, the items in the partial list in Figure 2–3 on the following page. It does not include unrealized gains. Gross income is discussed in Chapters 3 and 4.

EXAMPLE 2

Beth received the following amounts during the year:

Salary	$30,000
Interest on savings account	900
Gift from her aunt	10,000
Prize won in state lottery	1,000
Alimony from ex-husband	12,000
Child support from ex-husband	6,000
Damages for injury in auto accident	25,000
Increase in the value of stock held for investment	5,000

FIGURE 2–2
Partial List of Exclusions from Gross Income

- Accident insurance proceeds
- Annuities (to a limited extent)
- Bequests
- Child support payments
- Cost-of-living allowance (for military)
- Damages for personal injury or sickness
- Death benefits (up to $5,000)
- Gifts received
- Group term life insurance, premium paid by employer (for coverage up to $50,000)
- Inheritances
- Life insurance paid on death
- Meals and lodging (if furnished for employer's convenience)
- Military allowances
- Minister's dwelling rental value allowance
- Railroad retirement benefits (to a limited extent)
- Scholarship grants (to a limited extent)
- Social Security benefits (to a limited extent)
- Veterans' benefits
- Welfare payments
- Workers' compensation benefits

2. § 61(a).

Review Figures 2–2 and 2–3 to determine the amount Beth must include in the computation of taxable income and the amount she may exclude. Then check your answer in footnote 3.[3] ◆

Deductions for Adjusted Gross Income. Individual taxpayers have two categories of deductions: (1) deductions *for* adjusted gross income (deductions to arrive at adjusted gross income) and (2) deductions *from* adjusted gross income.

Deductions *for* adjusted gross income (AGI) include ordinary and necessary expenses incurred in a trade or business, one-half of self-employment tax paid, alimony paid, certain payments to an Individual Retirement Account, forfeited interest penalty for premature withdrawal of time deposits, the capital loss deduction, and others.[4] The principal deductions *for* AGI are discussed in Chapters 5 through 9.

Adjusted Gross Income (AGI). AGI is an important subtotal that serves as the basis for computing percentage limitations on certain itemized deductions, such

FIGURE 2–3
Partial List of Gross Income Items

- Alimony
- Annuities
- Awards
- Back pay
- Bargain purchase from employer
- Bonuses
- Breach of contract damages
- Business income
- Clergy fees
- Commissions
- Compensation for services
- Death benefits in excess of $5,000
- Debts forgiven
- Director's fees
- Dividends
- Embezzled funds
- Employee awards (in certain cases)
- Employee benefits (except certain fringe benefits)
- Employee bonuses
- Estate and trust income
- Farm income
- Fees
- Gains from illegal activities
- Gains from sale of property
- Gambling winnings
- Group term life insurance, premium paid by employer (for coverage over $50,000)
- Hobby income
- Interest
- Jury duty fees
- Living quarters, meals (unless furnished for employer's convenience)
- Mileage allowance
- Military pay (unless combat pay)
- Notary fees
- Partnership income
- Pensions
- Prizes
- Professional fees
- Punitive damages (in certain cases)
- Reimbursement for moving expenses
- Rents
- Rewards
- Royalties
- Salaries
- Severance pay
- Strike and lockout benefits
- Supplemental unemployment benefits
- Tips and gratuities
- Travel allowance (in certain cases)
- Wages

3. Beth must include $43,900 in computing taxable income ($30,000 salary + $900 interest + $1,000 lottery prize + $12,000 alimony). She can exclude $41,000 ($10,000 gift from aunt + $6,000 child support + $25,000 damages). The unrealized gain on the stock held for investment is not included in gross income. Such gain will be included in gross income only when it is realized upon disposition of the stock.

4. § 62.

as medical expenses and charitable contributions. For example, medical expenses are deductible only to the extent they exceed 7.5 percent of AGI, and charitable contribution deductions may not exceed 50 percent of AGI. These limitations might be described as a 7.5 percent *floor* under the medical expense deduction and a 50 percent *ceiling* on the charitable contribution deduction.

EXAMPLE 3

Keith earned a salary of $23,000 in the current tax year. He contributed $2,000 to his Individual Retirement Account (IRA) and sustained a $1,000 capital loss on the sale of Wren Corporation stock. His AGI is computed as follows:

Gross income		
Salary		$23,000
Less: Deductions *for* AGI		
IRA contribution	$2,000	
Capital loss	1,000	3,000
AGI		$20,000

◆

EXAMPLE 4

Assume the same facts as in Example 3, and that Keith also had medical expenses of $1,800. Medical expenses may be included in itemized deductions to the extent they exceed 7.5% of AGI. In computing his itemized deductions, Keith may include medical expenses of $300 [$1,800 medical expenses – $1,500 (7.5% × $20,000 AGI)]. ◆

Itemized Deductions. As a general rule, personal expenditures are disallowed as deductions in arriving at taxable income. However, Congress has chosen to allow specified personal expenses as itemized deductions. Such expenditures include medical expenses, certain taxes and interest, and charitable contributions.

In addition to these personal expenses, taxpayers are allowed itemized deductions for expenses related to (1) the production or collection of income and (2) the management of property held for the production of income.[5] These expenses, sometimes referred to as *nonbusiness expenses,* differ from trade or business expenses (discussed previously). Trade or business expenses, which are deductions *for* AGI, must be incurred in connection with a trade or business. Nonbusiness expenses, on the other hand, are expenses incurred in connection with an income-producing activity that does not qualify as a trade or business. Such expenses are itemized deductions.

EXAMPLE 5

Leo is the owner and operator of a video game arcade. All allowable expenses he incurs in connection with the arcade business are deductions *for* AGI. In addition, Leo has an extensive portfolio of stocks and bonds. Leo's investment activity is not treated as a trade or business. All allowable expenses that Leo incurs in connection with these investments are itemized deductions. ◆

Itemized deductions include, but are not limited to, the expenses listed in Figure 2–4. See Chapter 10 for a detailed discussion of itemized deductions.

Standard Deduction. The standard deduction is a specified amount set by Congress, and the amount depends on the filing status of the taxpayer. The effect

5. § 212.

of the standard deduction is to exempt a taxpayer's income, up to the specified amount, from Federal income tax liability. In the past, Congress has attempted to set the tax-free amount represented by the standard deduction approximately equal to an estimated poverty level,[6] but it has not always been consistent in doing so.

The standard deduction is the sum of two components: the *basic* standard deduction and the *additional* standard deduction.[7] Figure 2–5 lists the basic standard deduction allowed for taxpayers in each filing status. All taxpayers allowed a *full* standard deduction are entitled to the applicable amount listed in Figure 2–5. The standard deduction amounts are subject to adjustment for inflation each year.

Certain taxpayers are not allowed to claim *any* standard deduction, and the standard deduction is *limited* for others. These provisions are discussed later in the chapter.

A taxpayer who is age 65 or over *or* blind qualifies for an *additional standard deduction* of $700 or $900, depending on filing status (see amounts in Figure 2–6). Two additional standard deductions are allowed for a taxpayer who is age 65 or over *and* blind. The additional standard deduction provisions also apply for a qualifying spouse who is age 65 or over or blind, but a taxpayer may not claim an additional standard deduction for a dependent who is 65 or over or blind.

FIGURE 2–4
Partial List of Itemized Deductions

- Medical expenses in excess of 7.5% of AGI
- State and local income taxes
- Real estate taxes
- Personal property taxes
- Interest on home mortgage
- Investment interest (to a limited extent)
- Charitable contributions
- Casualty and theft losses in excess of 10% of AGI
- Moving expenses
- Miscellaneous expenses (to the extent such expenses exceed 2% of AGI)
  - Union dues
  - Professional dues and subscriptions
  - Certain educational expenses
  - Tax return preparation fee
  - Investment counsel fees
  - Unreimbursed employee business expenses (after 20% reduction for meals and entertainment)

FIGURE 2–5
Basic Standard Deduction Amounts

Filing Status	Standard Deduction Amount 1992	Standard Deduction Amount 1993
Single	$3,600	$3,700
Married, filing jointly	6,000	6,200
Surviving spouse	6,000	6,200
Head of household	5,250	5,450
Married, filing separately	3,000	3,100

6. S.Rep. No. 92–437, 92nd Cong., 1st Sess., 1971, p. 54. Another purpose of the standard deduction was discussed in Chapter 1 under Influence of the Internal Revenue Service—Administrative Feasibility. The size of the standard deduction has a direct bearing on the number of taxpayers who are in a position to itemize deductions. Reducing the number of taxpayers who itemize also reduces the audit effort required from the IRS.

7. § 63(c)(1).

To determine whether to itemize, the taxpayer compares the *total* standard deduction (the sum of the basic standard deduction and any additional standard deductions) to total itemized deductions. Taxpayers are allowed to deduct the greater of itemized deductions or the standard deduction. Taxpayers whose itemized deductions are less than the standard deduction compute their taxable income using the standard deduction rather than itemizing.

EXAMPLE 6

Sara, who is single, is 66 years old. She had total itemized deductions of $4,500 during 1993. Her total standard deduction is $4,600 ($3,700 basic standard deduction plus $900 additional standard deduction). Sara will compute her taxable income for 1993 using the standard deduction ($4,600), since it exceeds her itemized deductions ($4,500). ◆

Exemptions. Exemptions are allowed for the taxpayer, the taxpayer's spouse, and for each dependent of the taxpayer. The exemption amount is $2,300 in 1992 and $2,350 in 1993.

Application of the Tax Formula

The tax formula shown in Figure 2–1 is illustrated in Example 7.

EXAMPLE 7

Grace, age 25, is single and has no dependents. She is a high school teacher and earned a $20,000 salary in 1993. Her other income consisted of a $1,000 prize won in a sweepstakes contest and $500 interest on municipal bonds received as a graduation gift in 1989. During 1993, she sustained a deductible capital loss of $1,000. Her itemized deductions were $3,800. Grace's taxable income for the year is computed as follows:

Income (broadly conceived)		
Salary		$20,000
Prize		1,000
Interest on municipal bonds		500
		$21,500
Less: Exclusion—		
Interest on municipal bonds		(500)
Gross income		$21,000
Less: Deduction *for* adjusted gross income—		
Capital loss		(1,000)
Adjusted gross income		$20,000
Less: The greater of—		
Total itemized deductions	$3,800	
or the standard deduction	$3,700	(3,800)
Personal and dependency exemptions		
(1 × $2,350)		(2,350)
Taxable income		$13,850

◆

FIGURE 2–6
Amount of Each Additional Standard Deduction

Filing Status	1992	1993
Single	$900	$900
Married, filing jointly	700	700
Surviving spouse	700	700
Head of household	900	900
Married, filing separately	700	700

The structure of the individual income tax return (Form 1040, 1040A, or 1040EZ) differs somewhat from the tax formula in Figure 2–1. On the tax return, gross income generally is the starting point in computing taxable income. With few exceptions, exclusions are not reported on the tax return.

Individuals Not Eligible for the Standard Deduction

The following individual taxpayers are ineligible to use the standard deduction and must therefore itemize:[8]

- A married individual filing a separate return where either spouse itemizes deductions.
- A nonresident alien.
- An individual filing a return for a period of less than 12 months because of a change in annual accounting period.

Special Limitations for Individuals Who Can Be Claimed as Dependents

Special rules apply to the standard deduction and personal exemption of an individual who can be claimed as a dependent on another person's tax return.

When filing his or her own tax return, a *dependent's* basic standard deduction is limited to the greater of $600 or the individual's earned income for the year.[9] However, if the individual's earned income exceeds the normal standard deduction, the standard deduction is limited to the appropriate standard deduction amount shown in Figure 2–5. These limitations apply only to the basic standard deduction. A dependent who is 65 or over or blind or both is also allowed the additional standard deduction amount on his or her own return (refer to Figure 2–6). These provisions are illustrated in Examples 8 through 11.

EXAMPLE 8

Susan, who is 17 years old and single, is claimed as a dependent on her parents' tax return. During 1993, she received $1,000 interest (unearned income) on a savings account. She also earned $400 from a part-time job. When Susan files her own tax return, her standard deduction is $600 (the greater of $600 or earned income of $400). ◆

EXAMPLE 9

Assume the same facts as in Example 8, except that Susan is 67 years old and is claimed as a dependent on her son's tax return. In this case when Susan files her own tax return, her standard deduction is $1,500 [$600 (the greater of $600 or earned income of $400) + $900 (the additional standard deduction allowed because Susan is 65 or over)]. ◆

EXAMPLE 10

Peggy, who is 16 years old and single, earned $1,000 from a summer job and had no unearned income during 1993. She is claimed as a dependent on her parents' tax return. Her standard deduction for 1993 is $1,000 (the greater of $600 or earned income). ◆

8. § 63(c)(6).

9. § 63(c)(5). The $600 amount is subject to adjustment for inflation each year. The amount was also $600 for 1992.

Example 11

Jack, who is a 20-year-old, single, full-time college student, is claimed as a dependent on his parents' tax return. He worked as a musician during the summer of 1993, earning $3,800. Jack's standard deduction is $3,700 (the greater of $600 or $3,800 earned income, but limited to the $3,700 standard deduction for a single taxpayer). ◆

The taxpayer who claims an individual as a dependent is allowed to claim an exemption for the dependent. The dependent cannot claim a personal exemption on his or her own return.

Personal and Dependency Exemptions

The use of exemptions in the tax system is based in part on the idea that a taxpayer with a small amount of income should be exempt from income taxation. An exemption frees a specified amount of income from tax ($2,300 in 1992 and $2,350 in 1993). The exemption amount is indexed (adjusted) annually for inflation. An individual who is not claimed as a dependent by another taxpayer is allowed to claim his or her own personal exemption. In addition, a taxpayer may claim an exemption for each dependent.

Example 12

Bonnie, who is single, supports her mother and father, who have no income of their own, and claims them as dependents on her tax return. Bonnie may claim a personal exemption for herself plus an exemption for each dependent. On her 1993 tax return, Bonnie may deduct $7,050 for exemptions ($2,350 per exemption × 3 exemptions). ◆

Personal Exemptions

The Code provides a personal exemption for the taxpayer and an exemption for the spouse if a joint return is filed. However, when separate returns are filed, a married taxpayer cannot claim an exemption for his or her spouse unless the spouse has no gross income and is not claimed as the dependent of another taxpayer.

The determination of marital status generally is made at the end of the taxable year, except when a spouse dies during the year. Spouses who enter into a legal separation under a decree of divorce or separate maintenance before the end of the year are considered to be unmarried at the end of the taxable year. The following table illustrates the effect of death or divorce upon marital status:

	Marital Status for 1993
1. Walt is the widower of Helen who died on January 3, 1993.	Walt and Helen are considered to be married for purposes of filing the 1993 return.
2. Bill and Jane entered into a divorce decree that is effective on December 31, 1993.	Bill and Jane are considered to be unmarried for purposes of filing the 1993 return.

Dependency Exemptions

As indicated in Example 12, the Code allows a taxpayer to claim a dependency exemption for each eligible individual. A dependency exemption may be claimed for each individual for whom the following five tests are met:

- Support.
- Relationship or member of the household.
- Gross income.
- Joint return.
- Citizenship or residency.

Support Test. Over one-half of the support of the individual must be furnished by the taxpayer. Support includes food, shelter, clothing, medical and dental care, education, etc. However, a scholarship received by a student is not included for purposes of computing whether the taxpayer furnished more than one-half of the child's support.[10]

EXAMPLE 13

Hal contributed $2,500 (consisting of food, clothing, and medical care) toward the support of his son, Sam, who earned $1,500 from a part-time job and received a $2,000 scholarship to attend a local university. Assuming that the other dependency tests are met, Hal may claim Sam as a dependent since he has contributed more than one-half of Sam's support. The $2,000 scholarship is not included as support for purposes of this test. ◆

If the individual does not spend funds that have been received from any source, the unexpended amounts are not counted for purposes of the support test.

EXAMPLE 14

Emily contributed $3,000 to her father's support during the year. In addition, her father received $2,400 in Social Security benefits, $200 of interest, and wages of $600. Her father deposited the Social Security benefits, interest, and wages in his own savings account and did not use any of the funds for his support. Thus, the Social Security benefits, interest, and wages are not considered as support provided by Emily's father. Emily may claim her father as a dependent if the other tests are met. ◆

Capital expenditures for items such as furniture, appliances, and automobiles are included in total support if the item does, in fact, constitute support.[11]

EXAMPLE 15

Norm purchased a television set costing $150 and gave it to his minor daughter. The television set was placed in the child's bedroom and was used exclusively by her. Norm should include the cost of the television set in determining the support of his daughter. ◆

EXAMPLE 16

Mark paid $6,000 for an automobile that was titled and registered in his name. Mark's minor son is permitted to use the automobile equally with Mark. Since Mark did not

10. Reg. § 1.152–1(c).
11. Rev.Rul. 57–344, 1957–2 C.B. 112; Rev.Rul. 58–419, 1958–2 C.B. 57.

give the automobile to his son, the $6,000 cost is not includible as a support item. However, out-of-pocket operating expenses incurred by Mark for the benefit of his son are includible as support. ◆

One exception to the support test involves a *multiple support agreement.* A multiple support agreement permits one of a group of taxpayers who furnish more than half of the support of an individual to claim a dependency exemption for that individual even if no one person provides more than 50 percent of the support.[12] Any person who contributed more than 10 percent of the support is entitled to claim the exemption if each person in the group who contributed more than 10 percent files a written consent. This provision frequently enables one of the children of aged dependent parents to claim an exemption when none of the children meets the 50 percent support test. Each person who is a party to the multiple support agreement must meet all other requirements (except the support requirement) for claiming the exemption. A person who does not meet the relationship or member-of-household requirement, for instance, cannot claim the dependency exemption under a multiple support agreement. It does not matter if he or she contributes more than 10 percent of the individual's support.

EXAMPLE 17

Wanda, who resides with her son, Adam, received $6,000 from various sources during 1993. This constituted her entire support for the year. She received support from the following:

	Amount	Percentage of Total
Adam, a son	$2,880	48
Bob, a son	600	10
Carol, a daughter	1,800	30
Diane, a friend	720	12
	$6,000	100

If Adam and Carol file a multiple support agreement, either may claim the dependency exemption for Wanda. Bob may not claim Wanda because he did not contribute more than 10% of her support. Bob's consent is not required in order for Adam and Carol to file a multiple support agreement. Diane does not meet the relationship or member-of-household test and cannot be a party to the agreement. The decision as to who claims Wanda rests with Adam and Carol. It is possible for Carol to claim Wanda, even though Adam furnished more of Wanda's support. ◆

A second exception to the 50 percent support requirement can occur for a child of parents who are divorced or separated under a decree of separate maintenance. Under decrees executed after 1984, the custodial parent is allowed to claim the exemption unless that parent agrees in writing not to claim a dependency exemption for the child.[13] Thus, claiming the exemption is dependent on whether or not a written agreement exists, *not* on meeting the support test.

EXAMPLE 18

Ira and Rita obtain a divorce decree in 1989. In 1993, their two children are in Rita's custody. Ira contributed over half of the support for each child. In the absence of a written agreement on the dependency exemptions, Rita (the custodial parent) is

12. § 152(c).

13. § 152(e).

entitled to the exemptions in 1993. However, Ira may claim the exemptions if Rita agrees in writing. ◆

For the noncustodial parent to claim the exemption, the custodial parent must complete Form 8332 (Release of Claim to Exemption for Child of Divorced or Separated Parents). The release can apply to a single year, a number of specified years, or all future years. The noncustodial parent must attach a copy of Form 8332 to his or her return. Form 8332 is not required if there is a pre-1985 agreement that allows the noncustodial parent to claim the exemption and the noncustodial parent provides at least $600 of support for each child.

Relationship or Member-of-the-Household Test. To be claimed as a dependent, an individual must be either a relative of the taxpayer or a member of the taxpayer's household. The Code contains a detailed listing of the various blood and marriage relationships that qualify. Note, however, that the relationship test is met if the individual is a relative of either spouse. Once a relationship is established by marriage, it continues regardless of subsequent changes in marital status.

The following individuals may be claimed as dependents of the taxpayer if the other tests for dependency are met:[14]

Cousins are not included

- A son or daughter of the taxpayer, or a descendant of either (grandchild).
- A stepson or stepdaughter of the taxpayer.
- A brother, sister, stepbrother, or stepsister of the taxpayer.
- The father or mother of the taxpayer, or an ancestor of either (grandparent).
- A stepfather or stepmother of the taxpayer.
- A son or daughter of a brother or sister (nephew or niece) of the taxpayer.
- A brother or sister of the father or mother (uncle or aunt) of the taxpayer.
- A son-in-law, daughter-in-law, father-in-law, mother-in-law, brother-in-law, or sister-in-law of the taxpayer.
- An individual who, for the entire taxable year of the taxpayer, has as his or her principal place of abode the home of the taxpayer and is a member of the taxpayer's household. This does not include an individual who, at any time during the taxable year, was the spouse of the taxpayer.

The following rules are also prescribed in the Code:[15]

- A legally adopted child is treated as a natural child.
- A foster child qualifies if the child's principal place of abode is the taxpayer's household.

Gross Income Test. The dependent's gross income must be less than the exemption amount ($2,350 in 1993) unless the dependent is a child of the taxpayer and is under 19 or a full-time student under the age of 24.[16] A parent may claim a dependency exemption for his or her child, even when the child's gross income exceeds $2,350, if the parent provided over half of the child's support and the child, at year-end, is under 19 or is a full-time student under 24.

14. § 152(a). However, under § 152(b)(5), a taxpayer may not claim someone who is a member of his or her household as a dependent if their relationship is in violation of local law. For example, the dependency exemption was denied because the taxpayer's relationship to the person claimed as a dependent constituted *cohabitation*, a crime under applicable state law. *Cassius L. Peacock, III*, 37 TCM 177, T.C.Memo. 1978–30.

15. § 152(b)(2).

16. § 151(c)(1).

However, if the parent claims a dependency exemption, the dependent child may not claim a personal exemption on his or her own income tax return.

A child is defined as a son, stepson, daughter, stepdaughter, adopted son, or adopted daughter and may include a foster child.[17] For the child to qualify as a student for purposes of the dependency exemption, he or she must be a full-time student at an educational institution during some part of five calendar months of the year.[18] This exception to the gross income test for dependent children who are under 19 or full-time students under 24 permits a child or college student to earn money from part-time or summer jobs without penalizing the parent with the loss of the dependency exemption.

Joint Return Test. If a dependent is married, the supporting taxpayer (e.g., the parent of a married child) generally is not permitted a dependency exemption if the married individual files a joint return with his or her spouse.[19] However, if neither the dependent nor the dependent's spouse is *required* to file a return but they file a joint return solely to claim a refund of all tax withheld and no tax liability exists for either spouse on separate returns, the joint return rule does not apply. See Figure 2–8 later in the chapter and the related discussion concerning income level requirements for filing a return.

Example 19

Paul provides over half of the support of his son Quinn. He also provides over half of the support of Vera, who is Quinn's wife. In 1993, Quinn had wages of $1,500, and Vera earned $1,800. Quinn and Vera file a joint return for the year. Neither Quinn nor Vera was required to file a return because each had income below the $2,350 level required for married taxpayers filing separate returns. Paul is allowed to claim both as dependents. ◆

Citizenship or Residency Test. To be a dependent, the individual must be either a U.S. citizen, resident, or national or a resident of Canada or Mexico for some part of the calendar year in which the tax year of the taxpayer claiming the exemption begins.

Phase-out of Exemptions. For tax years beginning after December 31, 1990, and before January 1, 1996, personal exemptions and exemptions for dependents are phased out as AGI exceeds specified threshold amounts. For 1993, phase-out begins at the following threshold amounts:

Joint returns/Surviving spouse	$162,700
Head of household	135,600
Single	108,450
Married, filing separately	81,350

These threshold amounts will be indexed for inflation in future years.

Exemptions are phased out by 2 percent for each $2,500 (or fraction thereof) by which the taxpayer's AGI exceeds the threshold amounts. For a married taxpayer filing separately, the phase-out is 2 percent for each $1,250 or fraction thereof.

The allowable exemption amount can be determined with the following steps:

17. Reg. § 1.151–3(a).

18. Reg. §§ 1.151–3(b) and (c).

19. § 151(c)(2).

1. AGI – threshold amount = excess amount
2. Excess amount ÷ $2,500 = reduction factor [rounded up to the next whole increment (e.g., 18.1 = 19)] × 2 = phase-out percentage
3. Phase-out percentage (from step 2) × exemption amount = amount of exemptions phased out
4. Exemption amounts – phase-out amount = allowable exemption deduction

EXAMPLE 20

Rex is a single taxpayer with AGI of $194,450. He has only one exemption.

1. $194,450 – $108,450 = $86,000 excess amount
2. $86,000 ÷ $2,500 = 34.4 (rounded to 35) × 2 = 70% (phase-out percentage)
3. 70% × $2,350 = $1,645 amount of exemption phased out
4. $2,350 – $1,645 = $705 allowable exemption deduction ◆

EXAMPLE 21

Fred and Wilma file a joint return claiming two personal exemptions and one dependency exemption for their child. Their AGI is $272,700.

1. $272,700 – $162,700 = $110,000 excess amount
2. $110,000 ÷ $2,500 = 44 × 2 = 88% (phase-out percentage)
3. 88% × $7,050 (3 × $2,350) = $6,204 amount of exemptions phased out
4. $7,050 – $6,204 = $846 allowable exemption deduction ◆

EXAMPLE 22

Frederico is married but files a separate return. His AGI is $101,350. He is entitled to one personal exemption.

1. $101,350 – $81,350 = $20,000 excess amount
2. [($20,000 ÷ $1,250) × 2] = 32% (phase-out percentage)
3. 32% × $2,350 = $752 amount of exemption phased out
4. $2,350 – $752 = $1,598 allowable exemption deduction ◆

Note that the exemption amount is completely phased out when the taxpayer's AGI exceeds the threshold amount by more than $122,500 ($61,250 for a married taxpayer filing a separate return), calculated as follows:

$122,501 ÷ $2,500 = 49.0001, rounded to 50 and multiplying by 2 = 100% (phase-out percentage).

EXAMPLE 23

Bill and Isabella file a joint return claiming two personal exemptions and one dependency exemption for their child. Their AGI equals $286,700.

$286,700 – $162,700 = $124,000 excess amount

Since the excess amount exceeds $122,500, the exemptions are completely phased out. ◆

TAX DETERMINATION

Tax Table Method

Most taxpayers compute their tax using the Tax Table. Taxpayers who are eligible to use the Tax Table compute taxable income (as shown in Figure 2–1) and determine their tax by reference to the Tax Table. The following taxpayers, however, may not use the Tax Table method:

- An individual who files a short period return (see Chapter 15).
- Individuals whose taxable income exceeds the maximum (ceiling) amount in the Tax Table. The 1992 Tax Table applies to taxable income below $100,000 for Form 1040.
- An estate or trust.

The 1993 Tax Table was not available at the date of publication of this text. Therefore, the 1992 Tax Table will be used to illustrate the tax computation using the Tax Table method.

Example 24

Pedro, a single taxpayer, is eligible to use the Tax Table. For 1992, he had taxable income of $25,025. To determine Pedro's tax using the Tax Table (see Appendix A), find the $25,000 to $25,050 income line. The first column to the right of the taxable income column is for single taxpayers. Pedro's tax for 1992 is $4,219. ◆

Tax Rate Schedule Method

The Tax Rate Schedules contain rates of 15, 28, and 31 percent. Separate schedules are provided for the following filing statuses: single, married filing jointly, married filing separately, and head of household. The rate schedules for 1992 and 1993 are reproduced inside the front cover of this text and also in Appendix A.

The rate schedules are adjusted for inflation each year. Comparison of the 1991 and 1992 schedules shows that the rates were 15, 28, and 31 percent in both years, but the amount of taxable income to which each rate applies changed in 1992.

The 1993 rate schedule for single taxpayers is reproduced in Figure 2–7. This schedule is used to illustrate the tax computations in Examples 25, 26, and 27.

Example 25

Pat had $20,000 of taxable income in 1993. His tax is $3,000 ($20,000 × 15%). ◆

Several terms are used to describe tax rates. The rates in the Tax Rate Schedules are often referred to as *statutory* (or nominal) rates. The *marginal* rate is the highest rate that is applied in the tax computation for a particular taxpayer. In Example 25, the statutory rate and the marginal rate are both 15 percent.

Example 26

Chris, who is single, had taxable income of $41,450 in 1993. Her tax is $8,733 [$3,315 + 28%($41,450 – $22,100)]. ◆

If Taxable Income Is			
Over	But Not Over	The Tax Is:	Of the Amount Over
$ -0-	$22,100	15%	$ -0-
22,100	$53,500	$ 3,315 + 28%	22,100
53,500		$12,107 + 31%	53,500

Figure 2–7
1993 Tax Rate Schedule for Single Taxpayers

The *average* rate is equal to the tax liability divided by taxable income. In Example 26, Chris had statutory rates of 15 percent and 28 percent, and a marginal rate of 28 percent. Chris's average rate was 21.1 percent ($8,733 tax liability ÷ $41,450 taxable income).

Note that $3,315, which is the starting point in the tax computation in Example 26, is 15 percent of the $22,100 taxable income in the first bracket. Income in excess of $22,100 is taxed at a 28 percent rate. This reflects the *progressive* (or graduated) rate structure on which the United States income tax system is based. A tax is progressive if a higher rate of tax applies as the tax base increases.

EXAMPLE 27

Carl had taxable income of $81,900 in 1993. His tax is $20,911 [$12,107 + 31% ($81,900 – $53,500)]. Note that the effect of this computation is to tax part of Carl's income at 15%, part at 28%, and part at 31%. An alternative computational method provides a clearer illustration of the progressive rate structure:

Tax on $22,100 at 15%	$ 3,315
Tax on $53,500 – $22,100 at 28%	8,792
Tax on $81,900 – $53,500 at 31%	8,804
Total	$20,911

◆

A special computation limits the tax rate on long-term capital gain to 28 percent of the gain. The alternative tax on long-term capital gain is discussed in detail in Chapter 13.

Computation of Net Taxes Payable or Refund Due

The pay-as-you-go feature of the Federal income tax system requires payment of all or part of the taxpayer's income tax liability during the year. These payments take the form of Federal income tax withheld by employers or estimated tax paid by the taxpayer or both.[20] These payments are applied against the tax from the Tax Table or Tax Rate Schedules to determine whether the taxpayer will get a refund or pay additional tax.

Employers are required to withhold income tax on compensation paid to their employees and to pay this tax over to the government. The employer notifies the employee of the amount of income tax withheld on Form W–2 (Wage and Tax Statement). The employee should receive this form by January 31 after the year in which the income tax is withheld.

Taxpayers who receive income that is not subject to withholding, or income from which not enough tax is withheld, must pay estimated tax. These individuals must file Form 1040–ES (Estimated Tax for Individuals) and pay in quarterly installments the income tax and self-employment tax estimated to be due.

The income tax from the Tax Table or the Tax Rate Schedules is reduced first by the individual's tax credits. There is an important distinction between tax credits and tax deductions. Tax credits reduce the tax liability dollar-for-dollar. Tax deductions reduce taxable income on which the tax liability is based.

EXAMPLE 28

Gail is a taxpayer in the 28% tax bracket. As a result of incurring $1,000 in child care expenses (see Chapter 11 for details), she is entitled to a $200 child care credit ($1,000 child care expenses × 20% credit rate). She also contributed $1,000 to the American

20. § 3402 for withholding; § 6202 for estimated payments.

Cancer Society and included this amount in her itemized deductions. The child care credit results in a $200 reduction of Gail's tax liability for the year. The contribution to the American Cancer Society reduces taxable income by $1,000 and results in a $280 reduction in Gail's tax liability ($1,000 reduction in taxable income × 28% tax rate). ◆

Tax credits are discussed in Chapter 11. The following are several of the more common credits:

- Earned income credit.
- Credit for child and dependent care expenses.
- Credit for the elderly.
- Foreign tax credit.

Computation of an individual's net tax payable or refund due is illustrated in Example 29.

EXAMPLE 29

Kelly, age 30, is a head of household with two dependents. During 1993, Kelly had the following: taxable income, $30,000; income tax withheld, $3,950; estimated tax payments, $600; and credit for child care expenses, $200. Kelly's net tax payable is computed as follows:

Income tax (from 1993 Tax Rate Schedule, Appendix A)		$ 4,552
Less: Tax credits and prepayments—		
Credit for child care expenses	$ 200	
Income tax withheld	3,950	
Estimated tax payments	600	(4,750)
Net taxes payable or (refund due if negative)		$ (198)

◆

Unearned Income of Children under Age 14 Taxed at Parents' Rate

Before the Tax Reform Act (TRA) of 1986, a dependent child could claim an exemption on his or her own return even if claimed as a dependent by the parents. This enabled a parent to shift investment income (such as interest and dividends) to a child by transferring ownership of the assets producing the income. The child would pay no tax on the income to the extent that it was sheltered by the child's exemption.

For pre-1987 years, an additional tax motivation existed for shifting income from parents to children. Although a child's unearned income in excess of the exemption amount was subject to tax, it was taxed at the child's rate, rather than the parents' rate.

To reduce the tax savings that result from shifting income from parents to children, the net unearned income (commonly called investment income) of certain minor children is now taxed as if it were the parents' income.[21] Unearned income includes such income as taxable interest, dividends, capital gains, rents, royalties, pension and annuity income, and income (other than earned income) received as the beneficiary of a trust. This provision, commonly referred to as the *kiddie tax*, applies to any child for any taxable year if the child has not reached age 14 by the close of the taxable year, has at least one living parent, and has

21. § 1(i).

unearned income of more than $1,200. The *kiddie tax* provision does not apply to a child 14 or older. However, the limitation on the use of the standard deduction and the unavailability of the personal exemption do apply to such a child as long as he or she is eligible to be claimed as a dependent by a parent.

The term *parent* is defined in the Senate Finance Committee Report as a parent or stepparent of the child. No statutory definition exists for the term.

Net Unearned Income. Net unearned income of a dependent child is computed as follows:

Unearned income
Less: $600
Less: The greater of
- $600 of the standard deduction *or*
- The amount of allowable itemized deductions directly connected with the production of the unearned income

Equals: Net unearned income

If net unearned income is zero (or negative), the child's tax is computed without using the parent's rate. If the amount of net unearned income (regardless of source) is positive, the net unearned income will be taxed at the parent's rate. The $600 amounts in the preceding formula are subject to adjustment for inflation each year (refer to footnote 9).

Tax Determination. If a child under age 14 has net unearned income, there are two options for computing the tax on the income. A separate return may be filed for the child, or the parents may elect to report the child's income on their own return. If a separate return is filed for the child, the tax on net unearned income (referred to as the *allocable parental tax*) is computed as though the income had been included on the parents' return. Form 8615 (reproduced in Appendix B) is used to compute the tax. The steps required in this computation are illustrated below.

EXAMPLE 30

Olaf and Olga have a child, Hans (age 10). In 1993, Hans received $2,600 of interest and dividend income and paid investment-related fees of $200. Olaf and Olga had $69,450 of taxable income, not including their child's investment income. Olaf and Olga do not make the parental election.

1. **Determine Hans's net unearned income.**

Gross income	$ 2,600
Less: $600	(600)
Less: The greater of	
■ $600 or	
■ Investment expense	(600)
Equals: Net unearned income	$ 1,400

2. **Determine allocable parental tax.**

Parents' taxable income	$69,450
Plus: Hans's net unearned income	1,400
Equals: Revised taxable income	$70,850

Tax on revised taxable income (rounded)	$ 15,041
Less: Tax on parents' taxable income	(14,649)
Allocable parental tax	$ 392

3. **Determine Hans's nonparental source tax.**

Hans's AGI	$ 2,600
Less: Standard deduction	(600)
Less: Personal exemption	(–0–)
Equals: Taxable income	$ 2,000
Less: Net unearned income	(1,400)
Nonparental source taxable income	$ 600
Equals: Tax ($600 × 15% rate)	$ 90

4. **Determine Hans's total tax liability.**

Nonparental source tax (step 3)	$ 90
Allocable parental tax (step 2)	392
Total tax	$ 482

◆

Election to Claim Certain Unearned Income on Parent's Return. If a child under 14 meets all of the following requirements, the parent may elect to report the child's unearned income on the parent's own tax return:

- Gross income is from interest and dividends only.
- Gross income is more than $600 and less than $5,000.
- No estimated tax has been paid in the name and Social Security number of the child, and the child is not subject to backup withholding.

The child, then, is treated as having no gross income and is not required to file a tax return.

The parent(s) must also pay an additional tax equal to the smaller of $90 or 15 percent of the child's gross income over $600. If the child has any interest from certain private activity bonds, that amount is a tax preference to the parents for purposes of the parents' alternative minimum tax (see Chapter 14). Parents who have substantial itemized deductions based on AGI (see Chapter 10) may find that making the parental election increases total taxes for the family unit. Taxes should be calculated both with and without the parental election to determine the appropriate choice.

Other Provisions. If parents have more than one child subject to the tax on net unearned income, the tax for the children is computed as shown in Example 30 and then allocated to the children based on their relative amounts of income. For children of divorced parents, the taxable income of the custodial parent is used to determine the allocable parental tax. This parent is the one who may elect to report the child's unearned income. For married individuals filing separate returns, the individual with the greater taxable income is the applicable parent.

FILING CONSIDERATIONS

Under the category of filing considerations, the following questions need to be resolved:

- Is the taxpayer required to file an income tax return?
- If so, which form should be used?
- When and how should the return be filed?
- In computing the tax liability, which column of the Tax Table or which Tax Rate Schedule should be used?

The first three of these questions are discussed under Filing Requirements, and the last is treated under Filing Status.

Filing Requirements

General Rules. An individual must file a tax return if certain minimum amounts of gross income have been received. The general rule is that a tax return is required for every individual who has gross income that equals or exceeds the sum of the exemption amount plus the applicable standard deduction.[22] For example, a single taxpayer under age 65 must file a tax return in 1993 if gross income equals or exceeds $6,050 ($2,350 exemption plus $3,700 standard deduction). Figure 2–8 lists the income levels[23] that require tax returns under the general rule, and also lists amounts that require tax returns under certain special rules.

The additional standard deduction for being 65 or older is considered in determining the gross income filing requirements. For example, note in Figure 2–8 that the 1993 filing requirement for a single taxpayer 65 or older is $6,950 ($3,700 basic standard deduction + $900 additional standard deduction + $2,350

FIGURE 2–8
Filing Levels

Filing Status	1992 Gross Income	1993 Gross Income
Single		
Under 65 and not blind	$ 5,900	$ 6,050
Under 65 and blind	5,900	6,050
65 or older	6,800	6,950
Married, filing joint return		
Both spouses under 65 and neither blind	$10,600	$10,900
Both spouses under 65 and one or both spouses blind	10,600	10,900
One spouse 65 or older	11,300	11,600
Both spouses 65 or older	12,000	12,300
Married, filing separate return		
All—whether 65 or older or blind	$ 2,300	$ 2,350
Head of household		
Under 65 and not blind	$ 7,550	$ 7,800
Under 65 and blind	7,550	7,800
65 or older	8,450	8,700
Qualifying widow(er)		
Under 65 and not blind	$ 8,300	$ 8,550
Under 65 and blind	8,300	8,550
65 or older	9,000	9,250

22. The gross income amounts for determining whether a tax return must be filed are adjusted for inflation each year.

23. § 6012(a)(1).

exemption). However, the additional standard deduction for blindness is not taken into account. The 1993 filing requirement for a single taxpayer under 65 and blind is $6,050 ($3,700 basic standard deduction + $2,350 exemption).

Filing Requirements for Dependents. Computation of the gross income filing requirement for an individual who can be claimed as a dependent on another person's tax return is subject to more complex rules. Such an individual must file a return if he or she has either of the following:

- Earned income only and gross income that is more than the total standard deduction (including any additional standard deduction) that the individual is allowed for the year.
- Unearned income only and gross income of more than $600 plus any additional standard deduction that the individual is allowed for the year.
- Both earned and unearned income and gross income of more than the larger of earned income (but limited to the applicable basic standard deduction) or $600, plus any additional standard deduction that the individual is allowed for the year.

Thus, the filing requirement for a dependent who has no unearned income is the total of the *basic* standard deduction plus any *additional* standard deduction, which includes the additional deduction for blindness. For example, the 1993 filing requirement for a single dependent who is under 65 and not blind is $3,700, the amount of the basic standard deduction for 1993. The filing requirement for a single dependent under 65 and blind is $4,600 ($3,700 basic standard deduction + $900 additional standard deduction).

A self-employed individual with net earnings of $400 or more from a business or profession must file a tax return regardless of the amount of gross income.

Even though an individual has gross income below the filing level amounts and does not owe any tax, he or she must file a return to obtain a tax refund of amounts withheld. A return is also necessary to obtain the benefits of the earned income credit allowed to taxpayers with little or no tax liability. Chapter 11 discusses the earned income credit.

Selecting the Proper Form. The 1993 tax forms had not been released at the date of publication of this text. The following comments apply to 1992 forms. It is possible that some provisions will change for the 1993 forms.

Individual taxpayers file a return on either Form 1040 (the long form), Form 1040A (the short form), or Form 1040EZ (see Appendix B). Taxpayers who cannot use either Form 1040EZ or Form 1040A must use Form 1040. These forms are reproduced in Appendix B. Examine the forms and the instructions to the forms to determine which form is appropriate for a particular taxpayer.

When and Where to File. Tax returns of individuals are due on or before the fifteenth day of the fourth month following the close of the tax year. For the calendar year taxpayer, the usual filing date is on or before April 15 of the following year.[24] When the due date falls on a Saturday, Sunday, or legal holiday, the last day for filing falls on the next business day. If the return is mailed to the proper address with sufficient postage and is postmarked on or before the due date, it is deemed timely filed.

---

24. § 6072(a).

If a taxpayer is unable to file his or her return by the specified due date, a four-month extension of time can be obtained by filing Form 4868 (Application for Automatic Extension of Time to File U.S. Individual Income Tax Return).[25] Further extensions may be granted by the IRS upon a showing of good cause by the taxpayer. For this purpose, Form 2688 (Application for Extension of Time to File U.S. Individual Income Tax Return) should be used. An extension of more than six months will not be granted if the taxpayer is in the United States.

Although obtaining an extension excuses a taxpayer from a penalty for failure to file, it does not insulate against the penalty for failure to pay.[26] If more tax is owed, the filing of Form 4868 should be accompanied by an additional remittance to cover the balance due.

The return should be sent or delivered to the Regional Service Center of the IRS for the area where the taxpayer lives.[27]

If an individual needs to file an amended return (e.g., because of a failure to report income or to claim a deduction or tax credit), Form 1040X is filed. The form generally must be filed within three years of the filing date of the original return or within two years from the time the tax was paid, whichever is later.

Filing Status

The amount of tax will vary considerably depending on which Tax Rate Schedule is used. This is illustrated in the following example.

EXAMPLE 31

The following amounts of tax are computed using the 1993 Tax Rate Schedules for a taxpayer (or taxpayers in the case of a joint return) with $40,000 of taxable income (see Appendix A).

Filing Status	Amount of Tax (rounded)
Single	$8,327
Married, filing joint return	6,403
Married, filing separate return	8,802
Head of household	7,352

◆

Rates for Single Taxpayers. A taxpayer who is unmarried or separated from his or her spouse by a decree of divorce or separate maintenance and does not qualify for another filing status must use the rates for single taxpayers. Marital status is determined as of the last day of the tax year, except when a spouse dies during the year. In that case, marital status is determined as of the date of death. State law governs whether a taxpayer is considered married, divorced, or legally separated.

Under a special relief provision, however, married persons who live apart may be able to qualify as single. Married taxpayers who are considered single under the *abandoned spouse rules* are allowed to use the head-of-household rates. See the discussion of this filing status under Abandoned Spouse Rules later in the chapter.

Rates for Married Individuals. The joint return [Tax Rate Schedule Y, Code § 1(a)] was originally enacted in 1948 to establish equity between married

25. Reg. § 1.6081–4.

26. For an explanation of these penalties, refer to Chapter 1.

27. The Regional Service Centers and the geographical area each covers can be found on the back cover of *Your Federal Income Tax,* IRS Publication 17 for 1992.

taxpayers in common law states and those in community property states. Before the joint return rates were enacted, taxpayers in community property states were in an advantageous position relative to taxpayers in common law states because they could split their income. For instance, if one spouse earned $100,000 and the other spouse was not employed, each spouse could report $50,000 of income. Splitting the income in this manner caused the total income to be subject to lower marginal tax rates because each spouse would start at the bottom of the rate structure.

Taxpayers in common law states did not have this income-splitting option, so their taxable income was subject to higher marginal rates. This inconsistency in treatment was remedied by the joint return provisions. The progressive rates in the joint return Tax Rate Schedule are constructed based on the assumption that income is earned equally by the two spouses.

If married individuals elect to file separate returns, each reports only his or her own income, exemptions, deductions, and credits, and each must use the Tax Rate Schedule applicable to married taxpayers filing separately. It is generally advantageous for married individuals to file a joint return, since the combined amount of tax is lower. However, special circumstances (e.g., significant medical expenses incurred by one spouse subject to the 7.5 percent limitation) may warrant the election to file separate returns. It may be necessary to compute the tax under both assumptions to determine the most advantageous filing status.

The Code places some limitations on deductions, credits, etc., when married individuals file separately. If either spouse itemizes deductions, the other spouse must also itemize. Married taxpayers who file separately cannot take either of the following:

- The credit for child and dependent care expenses (in most instances).
- The earned income credit.

The joint return rates also apply for two years following the death of one spouse, if the surviving spouse maintains a household for a dependent child.[28] This is referred to as surviving spouse status.

EXAMPLE 32

Fred dies in 1992 leaving Ethel with a dependent child. For the year of Fred's death (1992), Ethel files a joint return with Fred (presuming the consent of Fred's executor is obtained). For the next two years (1993 and 1994), Ethel, as a surviving spouse, may use the joint return rates. In subsequent years, Ethel may use the head-of-household rates if she continues to maintain a household as her home that is the domicile of the child. ◆

Rates for Heads of Household. Unmarried individuals who maintain a household for a dependent (or dependents) are entitled to use the head-of-household rates.[29] The tax liability using the head-of-household rates falls between the liability using the joint return Tax Rate Schedule and the liability using the Tax Rate Schedule for single taxpayers.

Single parent family

To qualify for head-of-household rates, a taxpayer must pay more than half the cost of maintaining a household as his or her home. The household must also be the principal home of a dependent relative as defined in § 152(a).[30] As a general rule, the dependent must live in the taxpayer's household for over half the year.

---

28. § 2(a).

29. § 2(b).

30. § 2(b)(1)(A)(i).

The general rule has two exceptions. One exception is that an unmarried child (child also means grandchild, stepchild, or adopted child) need not be a dependent in order for the taxpayer to qualify as a head of household. This exception also applies to a married child if the child is claimed by the noncustodial parent as a result of a written agreement between the custodial parent and the noncustodial parent (refer to Example 18).

EXAMPLE 33

Nancy maintains a household where she and Dan, her nondependent unmarried son, reside. Since Dan is not married, Nancy qualifies for the head-of-household rates. ◆

Another exception to the general rule is that head-of-household status may be claimed if the taxpayer maintains a separate home for his or her parent or parents if at least one parent qualifies as a dependent of the taxpayer.[31]

EXAMPLE 34

Rick, an unmarried individual, lives in New York City and maintains a household in Detroit for his dependent parents. Rick may use the head-of-household rates even though his parents do not reside in his New York home. ◆

Abandoned Spouse Rules. When married persons file separate returns, several unfavorable tax consequences result. For example, the taxpayer must use the Tax Rate Schedule for married taxpayers filing separately. To mitigate such harsh treatment, Congress enacted provisions commonly referred to as the abandoned spouse rules. These rules allow a married taxpayer to file as a head of household if all of the following conditions are satisfied:

- The taxpayer does not file a joint return.
- The taxpayer paid more than one-half the cost of maintaining his or her home for the tax year.
- The taxpayer's spouse did not live in the home during the last six months of the tax year.
- The home was the principal residence of the taxpayer's child, stepchild, or adopted child for more than half the year.
- The taxpayer could claim the child, stepchild, or adopted child as a dependent.[32]

GAINS AND LOSSES FROM PROPERTY TRANSACTIONS—IN GENERAL

Gains and losses from property transactions are discussed in detail in Chapters 12 and 13. Because of their importance in the tax system, however, they are introduced briefly at this point.

When property is sold or otherwise disposed of, gain or loss may result. Such gain or loss has an effect on the income tax position of the party making the sale or other disposition when the *realized* gain or loss is *recognized* for tax purposes.

31. § 2(b)(1)(B).

32. The dependency requirement does not apply, however, if the taxpayer could have claimed a dependency exemption except for the fact that the exemption was claimed by the noncustodial parent under a written agreement. Refer to Example 18 and the related discussion.

Without realized gain or loss, generally, there can be no recognized gain or loss. The concept of realized gain or loss can be expressed as follows:

$$\text{Amount realized from the sale} - \text{Adjusted basis of the property} = \text{Realized gain (or loss)}$$

The amount realized is the selling price of the property less any costs of disposition (e.g., brokerage commissions) incurred by the seller. Simply stated, adjusted basis of the property is determined as follows:

Cost (or other original basis) at date of acquisition[33]	
Add:	Capital additions
Subtract:	Depreciation (if appropriate) and other capital recoveries (see Chapter 9)
Equals:	Adjusted basis at date of sale or other disposition

All realized gains are recognizable (taxable) unless some specific part of the tax law provides otherwise (see Chapter 12 dealing with certain nontaxable exchanges). Realized losses may or may not be recognizable (deductible) for tax purposes, depending on the circumstances involved. Generally, losses realized from the disposition of personal use property (property neither held for investment nor used in a trade or business) are not recognizable.

EXAMPLE 35

During the current year, Ted sells his sailboat (adjusted basis of $4,000) for $5,500. Ted also sells one of his personal automobiles (adjusted basis of $8,000) for $5,000. Ted's realized gain of $1,500 from the sale of the sailboat is recognizable. On the other hand, the $3,000 realized loss on the sale of the automobile is not recognized and will not provide Ted with any deductible tax benefit. ◆

Once it has been determined that the disposition of property results in a recognizable gain or loss, the next step is to classify the gain or loss as capital or ordinary. Although ordinary gain is fully taxable and ordinary loss is fully deductible, the same may not hold true for capital losses.

GAINS AND LOSSES FROM PROPERTY TRANSACTIONS—CAPITAL GAINS AND LOSSES

For tax years beginning after 1990, preferential tax treatment may apply to gains on capital assets that have been held for more than a year. The maximum rate on *net capital gain* (see Chapter 13 for details) is 28 percent. This provision could save 3 percent for taxpayers in the 31 percent bracket. Because of the potential tax savings on long-term capital gains, property transactions are important factors in effective tax planning.

Definition of a Capital Asset

Capital assets are defined in the Code as any property held by the taxpayer *other than* property listed in § 1221. The list in § 1221 includes inventory, accounts

33. Cost usually means purchase price plus expenses related to the acquisition of the property and incurred by the purchaser (e.g., brokerage commissions). For the basis of property acquired by gift or inheritance and other basis rules, see Chapter 12.

receivable, and depreciable property or real estate used in a business. Thus, the sale or exchange of assets in these categories usually results in ordinary income or loss treatment (see Chapter 13).

EXAMPLE 36

Kelly owns a pizza parlor. During the current year, he sells two automobiles. The first automobile, which had been used as a pizza delivery car for three years, was sold at a loss of $1,000. Because this automobile is an asset used in his business, Kelly has an ordinary loss deduction of $1,000, rather than a capital loss deduction. The second automobile, which Kelly had owned for two years, was his personal car. It was sold for a gain of $800. The personal car is a capital asset. Therefore, Kelly has a capital gain of $800. ◆

The principal capital assets held by an individual taxpayer include assets held for personal (rather than business) use, such as a personal residence or an automobile, and assets held for investment purposes (e.g., corporate securities and land).

Computation of Net Capital Gains and Losses

Capital gains and losses must be classified as short term (those on assets held for one year or less) and long term (those on assets held for more than one year). Short-term capital losses (STCL) are offset against short-term capital gains (STCG). The result is either net short-term capital gain (NSTCG) or net short-term capital loss (NSTCL).

Long-term capital losses (LTCL) are offset against long-term capital gains (LTCG), and the result is either net long-term capital gain (NLTCG) or net long-term capital loss (NLTCL).

Several combinations are possible after this first round of offsetting. For example, if the taxpayer has NSTCL and NLTCG, these amounts are offset. Likewise, if the taxpayer has NLTCL and NSTCG, a similar offsetting is required. In general, the offsetting continues as long as there is gain in any category and loss in any other category.

EXAMPLE 37

In the current year, Polly has the following capital gains and losses: STCL of $4,000, STCG of $3,000, LTCG of $6,000, and LTCL of $2,000. This results in NSTCL of $1,000 ($4,000 STCL – $3,000 STCG) and NLTCG of $4,000 ($6,000 LTCG – $2,000 LTCL). The $1,000 NSTCL is used to offset the $4,000 NLTCG, resulting in an excess of NLTCG over NSTCL of $3,000. ◆

Capital Loss Limitation

Capital losses are first offset against capital gains (as illustrated in Example 37). If, after this offsetting, an individual taxpayer has net capital losses, such losses are deductible as a deduction *for* AGI to a maximum of $3,000 per year. Any unused amounts are carried over for an indefinite period.

EXAMPLE 38

During the year, Tina has $1,000 of NLTCL and $2,000 of NSTCL. Tina's other income is $100,000. Her capital loss deduction for the year is $3,000, which consists of $2,000 NSTCL and $1,000 NLTCL. ◆

When a taxpayer has both short-term and long-term capital losses, and the losses together exceed $3,000, the short-term losses must be used first in applying the $3,000 limitation.

Example 39

Matt has NSTCL of $2,500 and NLTCL of $5,000 for the year. His other income is $50,000. Matt uses the losses as follows:

NSTCL	$2,500
NLTCL	500
Maximum capital loss deduction	$3,000

The remaining NLTCL of $4,500 ($5,000 NLTCL – $500 used) may be carried forward for an indefinite period until used. See Chapter 13 for a detailed discussion of capital loss carryovers. ◆

Corporate Capital Losses. Corporate taxpayers may offset capital losses only against capital gains. Capital losses in excess of capital gains may not be used to reduce ordinary income of a corporation. A corporation's unused capital losses are subject to a carryback and carryover. Capital losses are initially carried back three years and then carried forward five years to offset capital gains that arise in those years. See Chapter 13 for a discussion of capital losses of corporate taxpayers.

Taking Advantage of Tax Rate Differentials

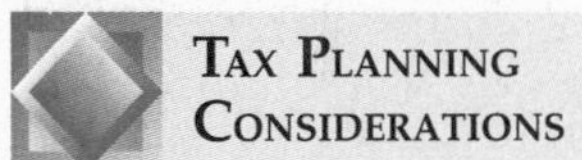
Tax Planning Considerations

It is natural for taxpayers to be concerned about the tax rates they are paying. How does a tax practitioner communicate information about rates to clients? There are several possibilities.

The marginal rate (refer to Examples 25 through 27) provides information that can help a taxpayer evaluate a particular course of action or structure a transaction in the most advantageous manner.

Example 40

Ron, who is in the 28% marginal tax bracket for 1993, is considering the sale of corporate stock he has held as an investment for a $10,000 gain in December. If he sells the stock, his income tax increases by $2,800 ($10,000 gain × 28% marginal rate), and he has $7,200 of after-tax income ($10,000 – $2,800). ◆

Example 41

Assume the same facts as in Example 40 and that Ron plans to retire early in 1994. Upon retirement, Ron's only source of income will be nontaxable Social Security benefits and municipal bond interest. If Ron waits until 1994 to sell the stock, his tax on the gain is $1,500, and his after-tax income is $8,500 ($10,000 gain – $1,500 tax). By being aware of the effect of marginal tax rates, Ron can save $1,300 in tax. ◆

The marginal rate analysis illustrated in Examples 40 and 41 for an income item can also help a taxpayer obtain the greatest tax benefit from a deductible expense. For example, a taxpayer who is in the 15 percent bracket this year and expects to be in the 31 percent bracket next year should, if possible, defer payment of deductible expenses until next year to maximize the tax benefit of the deduction.

A note of caution is in order with respect to shifting income and expenses between years. Congress has recognized the tax planning possibilities of such shifting and has enacted many provisions to limit a taxpayer's ability to do so. Some of these limitations on the shifting of income are discussed in Chapters 3, 4, and 15. Limitations that affect a taxpayer's ability to shift deductions are discussed in Chapters 5 through 10 and in Chapter 15.

A taxpayer's *effective rate* can be an informative measure of the effectiveness of tax planning. The effective rate is computed by dividing the taxpayer's tax liability by the total amount of income. A low effective rate can be considered an indication of effective tax planning.

One way of lowering the effective rate is to exclude income from the tax base. For example, a taxpayer might consider investing in tax-free municipal bonds rather than taxable corporate bonds. Although pre-tax income from corporate bonds is usually higher, after-tax income may be higher if the taxpayer invests in tax-free municipals.

Another way of lowering the effective rate is to make sure that the taxpayer's expenses and losses are deductible. For example, losses on investments in passive activities may not be deductible (see Chapter 6). Therefore, a taxpayer who plans to invest in an activity that will produce a loss in its early years should take steps to ensure that the business is treated as active rather than passive. Active losses are deductible while passive losses are not.

Income of Minor Children

Taxpayers can use several strategies to avoid or minimize the effect of the rules that tax the unearned income of certain minor children at the parents' rate. The kiddie tax rules do not apply once a child reaches age 14. Parents should consider giving a younger child assets that defer taxable income until the child reaches age 14. For example, U.S. government Series EE savings bonds can be used to defer income until the bonds are cashed in (see Chapter 3).

Growth stocks typically pay little in the way of dividends. However, the profit on an astute investment may more than offset the lack of dividends. The child can hold the stock until he or she reaches age 14. If the stock is sold then at a profit, the profit is taxed at the child's low rates.

Taxpayers in a position to do so can employ their children in their business and pay them a reasonable wage for the work they actually perform (e.g., light office help, such as filing). The child's earned income is sheltered by the standard deduction, and the parents' business is allowed a deduction for the wages. The kiddie tax rules have no effect on earned income, even if it is earned from the parents' business.

Alternating between Itemized Deductions and the Standard Deduction

When total itemized deductions are approximately equal to the standard deduction from year to year, it is possible for cash basis taxpayers to save taxes by proper timing of payments. To obtain a deduction for itemized deductions in one year and make use of the standard deduction in the next year, taxpayers should shift deductions from one year to the other. This results in a larger benefit over the two-year period than otherwise would be available.

EXAMPLE 42

Terry, who is single, is a cash basis, calendar year taxpayer. For tax years 1992 and 1993, Terry's itemized deductions are as follows:

	1992	1993
Charitable contribution	$1,800	$1,800
Other itemized deductions (e.g., interest, taxes)	1,300	1,300
Total itemized deductions	$3,100	$3,100

As presently structured, in neither year is Terry able to benefit from these itemized deductions, since they do not exceed the standard deduction applicable to a taxpayer claiming single status ($3,600 in 1992 and $3,700 in 1993). Thus, Terry's benefit for both years totals $7,300 ($3,600 + $3,700), all based on the standard deduction. ◆

EXAMPLE 43

Assume the same facts as in Example 42, except that in late 1992 Terry prepays the charitable contribution for 1993. With this change, Terry's position for both years becomes:

	1992	1993
Charitable contribution	$3,600	$ -0-
Other itemized deductions	1,300	1,300
Total itemized deductions	$4,900	$1,300

Under these circumstances, Terry claims itemized deductions of $4,900 for 1992 and the standard deduction of $3,700 for 1993. A comparison of the total benefit of $8,600 ($4,900 + $3,700) with the result reached in Example 42 of $7,300 ($3,600 + $3,700) clearly shows the advantage of this type of planning. ◆

Dependency Exemptions

The Joint Return Test. A married person can be claimed as a dependent only if that individual does not file a joint return with his or her spouse. If a joint return has been filed, the damage may be undone if separate returns are substituted on a timely basis (on or before the due date of the return).

EXAMPLE 44

While preparing a client's 1992 income tax return on April 10, 1993, the tax practitioner discovered that the client's daughter filed a joint return with her husband in late January of 1993. Presuming the daughter otherwise qualifies as the client's dependent, the exemption is not lost if she and her husband file separate returns on or before April 15, 1993. ◆

An initial election to file a joint return must be considered carefully in any situation in which the taxpayers might later decide to amend their return and file separately. As indicated above, separate returns may be substituted for a joint return only if the amended returns are filed on or before the normal due date of the return. If the taxpayers in Example 44 attempt to file separate returns after April 15, 1993, the returns will not be accepted, and the joint return election will be binding.[34]

Keep in mind that the filing of a joint return will not be fatal to the dependency exemption if the parties are filing solely to recover all income tax withholdings, neither is required to file a return, and no tax liability would exist on separate returns. The filing requirement for married persons filing separate returns applies. The application of these rules can be interesting when contrasting common law and community property jurisdictions.

EXAMPLE 45

In 1993, Abdel furnished 80% of the support of his son (Rashad) and daughter-in-law (Veneia). During the year, Veneia earned $2,400 from a part-time job. As a result, Veneia

34. Reg. § 1.6013–1(a)(1).

and Rashad filed a joint return to obtain a refund of all the income tax withheld. All parties reside in New York (a common law state). Presuming the joint return stands (refer to Example 44), Abdel cannot claim either Rashad or Veneia as his dependent. Although Veneia and Rashad filed a joint return to recover Veneia's withholdings, Veneia was required to file (she had gross income of $2,350 or more). ◆

EXAMPLE 46

Assume the same facts as in Example 45, except that all parties reside in Arizona (a community property state). Under these circumstances, Abdel may claim both Rashad and Veneia as dependents. Not only have they filed a joint return to recover all of Veneia's withholdings, but neither was required to file. Recall that in a community property state (unless otherwise altered by agreement between spouses, if permitted by state law), half of the wages of a spouse are attributable to the other spouse. Thus, Rashad and Veneia will be treated as each having earned $1,200, which is less than the filing requirement for married persons filing separate returns. ◆

The Gross Income Test. The exception to the gross income test for a person under the age of 19 or a full-time student under the age of 24 applies only to a child of the taxpayer. The term *child* is limited to a son, stepson, daughter, stepdaughter, adopted son, or adopted daughter and may include a foster child.

EXAMPLE 47

Assume the same facts as in Example 45, except that Rashad and Veneia (the son and daughter-in-law) do not file a joint return. Further assume that Veneia (the person who had gross income of $2,400) is a full-time student under age 24. Even though Abdel may claim Rashad as a dependent, Veneia does not qualify since she has gross income of $2,350 or more. The student exception to the gross income test does not apply because Veneia is not a *child* of Abdel. ◆

As was true with Example 46, the residence of the parties in a common law or a community property state can produce different results.

EXAMPLE 48

In 1993, Abdel furnishes 60% of the support of his son (Rashad) and daughter-in-law (Veneia), both over the age of 19. During the year, Veneia earns $4,800 from a part-time job, while Rashad is unemployed and not a full-time student. All parties reside in New Jersey (a common law state). Abdel may claim Rashad as a dependent, but Veneia does not qualify because of the gross income test. ◆

EXAMPLE 49

Assume the same facts as in Example 48, except that all parties reside in Washington (a community property state). Abdel may not claim either Rashad or Veneia as dependents because of the application of the gross income test. Each spouse is treated as having gross income of $2,400 (one-half of $4,800), which is not below the $2,350 filing level. ◆

The Support Test. Adequate records of expenditures for support should be maintained in the event a dependency exemption is questioned on audit by the IRS. The maintenance of adequate records is particularly important for exemptions arising from multiple support agreements.

Relationship to the Deduction for Medical Expenses. Generally, medical expenses are deductible only if they are paid on behalf of the taxpayer, his or her spouse, and their dependents. Since deductibility may rest on dependency status, planning is important in arranging multiple support agreements.

Example 50

During the year, Zelda will be supported by her two sons (Vern and Vito) and her daughter (Maria). Each will furnish approximately one-third of the required support. If the parties decide that the dependency exemption should be claimed by the daughter under a multiple support agreement, any medical expenses incurred by Zelda should be paid by Maria. ◆

In planning a multiple support agreement, take into account which of the parties is most likely to exceed the 7.5 percent limitation (see Chapter 10). In Example 50, for instance, Maria might be a poor choice if she and her family do not expect to incur many medical and drug expenses of their own.

One exception permits the deduction of medical expenses paid on behalf of someone who is not a spouse or a dependent. If the person could be claimed as a dependent *except* for the gross income or joint return test, the medical expenses are, nevertheless, deductible.

Example 51

During the year, Tara pays for all of the medical expenses of her uncle (Ed) and her married son (Gary). Ed otherwise qualifies as Tara's dependent, except that he had gross income of $2,500. Also, Gary otherwise qualifies as a dependent, except that he filed a joint return with his wife. Even though Tara may not claim dependency exemptions for Ed and Gary, she can claim the medical and drug expenses she paid on behalf of each. ◆

Problem Materials

Discussion Questions

1. Rearrange the following components to show the formula for arriving at the amount of Federal taxable income:

   a. Deductions *for* AGI.
   b. The greater of the standard deduction or itemized deductions.
   c. Income (broadly conceived).
   d. Adjusted gross income.
   e. Exclusions.
   f. Personal and dependency exemptions.
   g. Gross income.

2. Jane earned a salary of $40,000 in the current year. To obtain money for a down payment on a house, she sold 100 shares of Falcon Corporation stock for $25,000. She had paid $18,000 for the stock five years ago. What is Jane's gross income?
3. Ivan purchased 100 shares of Dove Corporation common stock in June 1993 for $100 per share. On December 15, he sold 50 shares for $120 per share. The remaining shares are worth $125 each on December 31, 1993. How much income must Ivan report with respect to the stock in 1993?
4. Adam earned a salary of $63,000 and incurred a $3,500 capital loss in the current year. He incurred medical expenses of $5,500. He had other itemized deductions of $6,100. Compute Adam's total itemized deductions.
5. Contrast the treatment of expenses incurred in a trade or business with the treatment of expenses incurred in connection with the management of property held for the production of income.

6. Discuss the special limitations that apply to the personal exemption and standard deduction of an individual who can be claimed as a dependent of another taxpayer.
7. Carlos is a student at Lakeland Community College. He earned $6,500 during 1993. Under what circumstances will Carlos's parents be allowed to claim him as a dependent?
8. If an individual who may qualify as a dependent does not spend funds that he or she has received (e.g., wages or Social Security benefits), are these unexpended amounts considered in applying the support test? Are they included in applying the gross income test?.
9. Earl contributed $2,100 toward the support of his son, Wade, who is 18 years old and a full-time college student. Wade earned $1,100 interest on a savings account and $900 working at a supermarket during the summer. Wade used all his earnings for his support. He also received a $1,000 scholarship from the college he attended. Can Earl claim Wade as a dependent? Explain.
10. Lana's only income was $2,200 in Social Security benefits she received during the year. She spent $1,700 of this amount toward her own support. Lana lives with her daughter Eve, who contributed $1,500 toward Lana's support. Can Eve claim Lana as a dependent? Explain.
11. Freda purchased a stereo system for her son Wes, age 16. The stereo was placed in Wes's room and used exclusively by him. Freda also purchased a new sports car, titled and registered in her own name, that was used 90% of the time by Wes. Should the cost of these items be considered as support in determining whether Freda may claim Wes as a dependent?
12. Seth, who is a dependent of his parents, is a full-time student at Central City College. During the current year, Seth, age 20, earned $1,500 from a part-time job. Because he is claimed as a dependent by his parents, Seth will not be allowed to claim an exemption for himself when filing his own tax return. True or false? Explain.
13. Carol provided 75% of the support of Debra, her niece. Debra was a full-time student during the year and earned $3,800 from a part-time job. Can Carol claim Debra as a dependent?
14. Otis, age 20 and a full-time student at Midwestern State University, is claimed as a dependent on his parents' tax return. During the summer of 1993, Otis earned $3,500 from a part-time job. Otis's only other income consisted of $1,500 in interest on a savings account. Compute Otis's taxable income for 1993.
15. Cora's support is provided by her daughter (40%), her son (30%), and an unrelated friend (30%). Can Cora be claimed as a dependent by any of the individuals who contributed to her support? Explain.
16. Lynn, who is married, must use either (a) the rates for married taxpayers filing jointly or (b) the rates for married taxpayers filing separately. True or false? Explain.
17. Jan is married to Bill, who left her and their six minor children in May of the current year. Jan does not know where Bill is and has not seen him since he left. She works two jobs to maintain a home for her children. What is the most advantageous filing status available to Jan?
18. A single individual age 65 or over and blind is required to file a Federal income tax return in 1993 if he or she has gross income of $6,950 or more (refer to Figure 2–8).
    a. Explain how the $6,950 filing requirement was computed.
    b. In general, explain the effect of the additional standard deduction on the determination of gross income requirements for filing.
19. Jim and Jane are engaged to be married. Each has gross income of $40,000 for 1993. Assume that they plan to make use of the standard deduction and have no dependency exemptions or tax credits. If they marry before the end of 1993, what is the overall effect on the total Federal income taxes that they will pay?
20. Kim, age 67 and blind, earned $4,600 of interest and received Social Security benefits of $7,200 in 1993. Is Kim required to file a tax return?

21. Ali, age 67, is married to Leila, who is age 62 and blind. Ali and Leila file a joint return. How much gross income can they earn before they are required to file an income tax return for 1993?
22. Alicia, a high school student, earned $1,000 from a summer job during the current year. Alicia is aware that this amount is below the income level that will require her to file a return and therefore does not plan to file. Do you have any advice for Alicia?
23. Karen has been ill and will not be able to complete her Federal income tax return by April 15. Based on preliminary calculations, she estimates that she will owe $600 when she files her return. What procedure should Karen follow?
24. During the current year, Andre had a $5,000 long-term capital loss on the sale of common stock he had held as an investment. In addition, he had a $3,000 loss on the sale of his personal automobile, which he had owned for a year. How do these transactions affect Andre's taxable income?
25. Ten years ago, Ann purchased a personal residence for $140,000. In the current year, she sells the residence for $105,000. Ann's friend tells her she has a recognizable loss of $35,000 from the sale. Do you agree with the friend's comment? Elaborate.
26. List some assets that are not capital assets and some that are capital assets. Why is it important to determine whether an asset is an ordinary asset or a capital asset?
27. During the current year, Kate earned a salary of $40,000. She sold 20 shares of Robin Corporation common stock at a loss of $2,500 and sold her personal automobile at a gain of $1,500. Compute Kate's AGI.
28. If Cole has a salary of $41,000, net short-term capital gain of $1,000, and net long-term capital losses of $4,500, what is his AGI?
29. If a corporation has net short-term capital losses of $12,000 and net long-term capital gains of $8,500, what amounts are deductible by the corporation? How are any unused losses treated?

PROBLEMS

30. Compute the taxpayer's taxable income for 1993 in each of the following cases:

    a. Jack is married and files a joint return with his wife Jill. Jack and Jill have two dependent children. They have AGI of $50,000 and $8,300 of itemized deductions.
    b. Pete is an unmarried head of household with two dependents. He has AGI of $45,000 and itemized deductions of $5,200.
    c. Iris, age 22, is a full-time college student who is claimed as a dependent by her parents. She earned $3,800 from a part-time job and had interest income of $1,500.
    d. Matt, age 20, is a full-time college student who is claimed as a dependent by his parents. He earned $2,500 from a part-time job and had interest income of $4,100. His itemized deductions related to the investment income were $700.

31. Determine the standard deduction and exemption amount for 1993 for the following taxpayers:

    a. Ned, age 65, is a single taxpayer with no dependents.
    b. Nina, age 36, is a single taxpayer with no dependents.
    c. Nora is a full-time college student, age 22, who is claimed as a dependent on her parents' Federal income tax return in 1993. She earned interest of $900.
    d. Assume the same facts as in (c), except that Nora also earned $4,000 from a summer job.

Note: Problems 32 through 34 can be solved by referring to Figures 2–1 through 2–6 and the discussion under Deductions for Adjusted Gross Income in this chapter.

32. Compute taxable income for Ned on the basis of the following information:

Filing Status	Head of Household
Salary	$45,000
Inheritance	20,000
Capital loss	2,500
Deductible contribution to IRA	2,000
Charitable contributions	7,000
Medical expenses	5,000
State and local income taxes	2,800
Interest on home mortgage	5,000
Number of dependents	2
Age	51

33. Compute taxable income for Lori on the basis of the following information:

Filing Status	Single
Salary	$57,000
Alimony received	10,000
Child support payments received	9,000
Gain from illegal activities	8,000
Deductible contribution to IRA	2,000
Moving expenses	6,500
Theft loss (deductible portion)	5,100
State and local income taxes	900
Interest on home mortgage	3,900
Number of dependents	2
Age	34

34. Compute taxable income for Kevin and Helen on the basis of the following information:

Filing Status	Married, Joint
Kevin's salary	$47,000
Bonus from Kevin's employer	8,000
Gift from Helen's uncle	9,000
Deductible contribution to IRA	2,000
Helen's lottery winnings	10,000
Charitable contributions	400
State and local income taxes	3,100
Interest on home mortgage	1,800
Number of dependents	2
Kevin's age	66
Helen's age	64

35. Sungho, age 37, was divorced from his wife in 1992. He has provided the following information and asked you to compute his taxable income for 1992:

Income:	
Salary and commissions	$62,000
Interest and dividends received	2,100
Money won in door prize drawing	1,000
Long-term capital gain from sale of stock	3,000
Expenditures and losses:	
Alimony paid to former wife	24,000
Child support paid to former wife	12,000
Short-term capital loss on sale of bonds	7,000
Deductible contribution to IRA	2,000
Cash contributed to charity	1,200
Interest on home mortgage	3,800
State income tax	1,400

Sungho lives alone and has no dependents. What amount should he report as taxable income for 1992?

36. Tim, who is single, earned $70,000 in 1993. He incurred a short-term capital loss of $2,000 and had total itemized deductions of $9,700. Compute Tim's taxable income for 1993.

37. Gus, age 65, is single and has no dependents. His salary for 1993 was $64,000. He received interest of $9,100 from First National Bank and dividends of $250 from Acme Computer Corporation. Gus incurred a capital loss of $3,500 on the sale of Greene Corporation common stock and had a capital gain of $1,850 on the sale of his personal automobile. He deposited $2,000 in his IRA, for which he is allowed a deduction. He incurred medical expenses of $2,200, mortgage interest of $3,200 and real estate taxes on his home of $1,700. Gus contributed $2,400 to the United Fund. Compute Gus's taxable income for the year.

38. Rosa, age 32, is single and has no dependents. She has custody of her 9-year-old son, who lives with her for 10 months during the year, but he is claimed as a dependent by his father. Rosa's salary for 1993 was $71,000, and she earned interest of $1,900 on Robin Corporation bonds. She received alimony of $8,400 and child support of $6,000 from her former husband. Her itemized deductions were $6,500. Compute Rosa's tax liability for the year.

39. Fred and Ethel are married and file a joint return. Fred is 66 years of age, and Ethel is 65. Fred's salary for 1993 was $33,000, and Ethel earned $41,000. Ethel won $10,000 in the state lottery and inherited $25,000 from her aunt. Fred incurred a $2,500 capital loss on stock he sold in December. Fred and Ethel provided 90% of the support for Cora, their 23-year-old daughter, who is a full-time student. Fred and Ethel also provided over half of the support of Jim, who is Cora's husband. Jim joined the army in March and earned $2,100. Cora and Jim filed a joint return. Fred and Ethel also provide over half of the support of Ethel's mother, Abby, who lives in a nursing home. Abby earned interest of $2,200 on a savings account and received Social Security benefits of $6,400. Fred and Ethel had total itemized deductions of $7,800.

    a. Compute taxable income for Fred and Ethel for 1993.
    b. Assume the same facts, except that Jim earned $6,100 in 1993. Compute taxable income for Fred and Ethel for 1993.

40. Bob, age 13, is a full-time student supported by his parents who claim him on their tax return for 1993. Bob's parents present you with the following information and ask that you prepare Bob's 1993 Federal income tax return:

Wages from summer job	$2,100
Interest on savings account at First National Bank	950
Interest on City of Chicago bonds Bob received as a gift from his grandfather two years ago	750
Dividend from Owl Corporation	200

a. What is Bob's taxable income for 1993?
b. Bob's parents file a joint return for 1993 on which they report taxable income of $66,000. Compute Bob's 1993 tax liability.

41. Don is a wealthy executive who had taxable income of $200,000 in 1993. He is considering transferring title in a duplex he owns to his son Sam, age 16. Sam has no other income and is claimed as a dependent by Don. Net rent income from the duplex is $10,000 a year, which Sam will be encouraged to place in a savings account. Will the family save income taxes in 1993 if Don transfers title in the duplex to Sam? Explain.

42. José and Marta, both 40 years of age, are married and have no children. They file separate returns for 1993. José claims itemized deductions of $6,600, and Marta's itemized deductions total $1,700. Because her itemized deductions are less than the standard deduction, Marta intends to use the standard deduction for computing her taxable income. What is the amount of the standard deduction Marta may claim? Explain.

43. Dena, age 22, is single and lives with her parents, who provide 70% of her support. Dena, a part-time student at Parkland Community College, earned a salary of $11,200 in 1993 and had itemized deductions of $2,600. What is Dena's taxable income for the year?

44. Compute the 1993 tax liability for each of the following taxpayers:

a. Norm and Nancy, both age 46, are married, have two dependent children, and file a joint return. Their combined salaries totaled $75,000. They had deductions *for* AGI of $6,000 and total itemized deductions of $8,100.
b. Juan, age 45, is single and has no dependents. He had a salary of $62,000, deductions *for* AGI of $3,000, and total itemized deductions of $7,100.
c. Yoon and Ling, both age 65, are married, have no dependents, and file a joint return. Their combined salaries were $92,000. They had deductions *for* AGI of $2,000 and itemized deductions of $17,000.

45. Compute the 1993 tax liability for each of the following taxpayers:

a. Ed, age 65, is single and has no dependents. He earned $94,260, had deductions *for* AGI of $4,000, and had itemized deductions of $3,700.
b. Ahmed, who is single and has no dependents, has taxable income of $85,000.
c. Preeti, who is single and has no dependents, has taxable income of $95,000.
d. Gus and Grace, both age 34, have one dependent child, Gail, age 10. Gus and Grace have taxable income of $96,000. Gail receives interest income of $3,000 during the year. Compute Gail's tax liability.

46. Pablo, age 12, is claimed as a dependent on his parents' 1993 Federal income tax return, on which they reported taxable income of $95,000. During the summer, Pablo earned $2,500 from a job as a model. His only other income consisted of $1,700 in interest on a savings account. Compute Pablo's taxable income and tax liability.

47. Carmen, who is 12 years old, is claimed as a dependent on her parents' tax return. During 1993, she received $12,200 in dividends and interest and incurred itemized deductions of $800 related to the management of her portfolio assets. She also earned $2,000 wages from a part-time job. Compute the amount of income that is taxed at her parents' rate.

48. Hun, who is 14 years old, is claimed as a dependent on his parents' tax return. During 1993, he received $9,000 in dividends and interest and incurred itemized deductions of $800 related to the management of his portfolio assets. He also earned $1,700 wages from a part-time job. Compute the amount of income that is taxed at Hun's own rate.

49. Paul, age 67 and single, is claimed as a dependent by his daughter. He earned $900 interest and $1,050 wages from a part-time job. Compute Paul's taxable income for 1993.

50. Mary, who earned a salary of $43,000, sold her personal car for $4,500. The car had an adjusted basis of $6,000. She also sold Whyte Corporation common stock for $1,200. Her adjusted basis for the stock was $3,300. Compute Mary's AGI.

51. Ted and Sara are married and have no dependents. Ted has AGI of $92,300, and Sara has AGI of $67,000 in 1993.

a. Compute the exemption deduction for Ted and Sara if they file a joint return.
b. Compute the exemption deductions for Ted and Sara if they file separate returns.
c. Explain why your answers to parts (a) and (b) differ.

52. Determine the correct number of personal and dependency exemptions in each of the following independent situations:

a. Rick, age 66 and disabled, is a widower who maintains a home for his unmarried daughter who is 24 years old. The daughter earned $3,000 and attends college on a part-time basis. Rick provides more than 50% of her support.
b. Wes, a bachelor age 45, provides more than 50% of the support of his father, age 70. Wes's father had gross income of $3,500 from a part-time job.
c. Dan, age 45, is married and has two dependent foster children who live with him and are totally supported by Dan. One of the foster children, age 14, had $2,200 of gross income. Dan and his spouse file a joint return.
d. Leo, age 67, is married and has a married daughter, age 22. His daughter attended college on a full-time basis and was supported by Leo. The daughter filed a joint return with her spouse. Leo filed a joint return with his spouse, age 62.

53. Carlos and Alicia, who are married and file a joint return, have four dependent children. They have AGI of $193,700. What is their allowable exemption deduction for 1992?

54. Compute the number of personal and dependency exemptions in the following independent situations:

a. Mark, a single individual, provides 60% of the support of his mother, age 69. Mark's mother received dividend income of $1,000 and $1,500 in Social Security benefits.
b. Adam, a married individual filing a joint return, provides 100% of the support of his son, age 21, who is a part-time student. Adam's son earned $2,500 during the year from part-time employment.
c. Vern is divorced and provides $2,000 of child support for his child who is living with her mother, who provides support of $2,500. An agreement executed in 1986 between Vern and his former wife provides that the noncustodial parent is to receive the dependency exemption. Vern's former wife provides him with a completed Form 8332.

55. Carl, who is single, is a branch manager for Second National Bank. He earned a salary of $85,000 in 1993. He also received cash dividends of $3,100 and interest income of $2,200, and won a $10,000 prize in the state lottery.

Carl provided 60% of the support of Abe, his father, who lived in a nursing home during the entire year. Carl also paid medical expenses of $3,000 for Abe, who did not have enough income to pay the expenses he incurred.

Carl pays Ellen, his former wife, $8,000 alimony and $5,000 child support for Amy, his daughter. Ellen, who has custody of Amy, contributed $4,200 toward her support. Carl paid $3,200 of state income tax and incurred a $5,000 loss on the sale of Whyte Corporation stock that he had owned for 10 months.

What is Carl's taxable income for 1993?

56. Has Ned provided more than 50% support in the following situations?

a. Ned paid $6,000 for an automobile that was titled in his name. His 19-year-old son, Bill, uses the automobile approximately 50% of the time while attending a local college on a full-time basis. Bill earned $4,000 from a part-time job that was used to pay his college and living expenses. The value of Bill's room and board provided by Ned amounted to $1,200.

b. Ned contributed $4,000 to his mother's support during the year. His mother received $5,000 in Social Security benefits that she placed in her savings account for future use.
c. Assume the same facts as in (b), except that Ned's mother used the funds for her support during the year.

57. Kevin contributed the following items toward the support of his son, Pete:

Food, clothing, shelter	$2,300
Television set given to Pete as a Christmas present	300
Books for college	250

Pete, age 23, is a full-time student at the University of Georgia College of Law. In June, he married Peggy, who is supported by her parents. Pete earned $3,500 during the summer and contributed the following items toward his own support:

Clothing	$ 600
Used car purchased for transportation to college	1,000
Insurance, maintenance, and operating expenses for car	800
Entertainment	420

Pete received a $2,000 scholarship from the University of Georgia. Which of the following statements is correct?

a. Kevin provided over half of Pete's support but cannot claim Pete as a dependent because Pete's gross income exceeds the maximum amount allowable for a dependent.
b. Pete's income will not prevent Kevin from claiming Pete as a dependent. However, Kevin cannot claim Pete as a dependent because he provided less than half of Pete's support.
c. Kevin cannot claim Pete as a dependent for two reasons: Kevin did not provide over half of Pete's support, and Pete's income exceeds the maximum amount allowable for a dependent.
d. Based on the facts given, nothing would prevent Kevin from claiming Pete as a dependent. However, if Pete and Peggy file a joint return, Kevin will not be allowed to claim Pete as a dependent.
e. None of the above.

58. Eli, Moshe, and Vairam contribute to the support of their mother, Zina, age 67. Zina lives with each of the children for approximately four months during the year. Her total living costs amounted to $6,000 and were paid as follows:

From Zina's Social Security benefits	$1,700
By Eli	500
By Moshe	1,300
By Vairam	1,300
By Sarojini, Zina's unrelated friend	1,200
	$6,000

a. Which, if any, of these individuals may claim Zina as a dependent (assume no multiple support agreement is filed)?
b. If a multiple support agreement is filed, who must be a party to it, and who may claim the exemption for Zina under the agreement?

59. Calculate the allowable exemption amount for the following taxpayers for 1993:

a. Vairam is single and has no dependents for 1993. His AGI for 1993 is $125,000.
b. Don and Dena are married and file a joint return for 1993. They have two qualifying dependents for the year. Their AGI for 1993 is $180,000.
c. Olaf files as head of household during 1993. He is entitled to claim one dependent. His AGI for 1993 is $160,000.

d. Sandra is married filing a separate return in 1993. She is entitled to claim two dependents for 1993. Her AGI for the year is $90,000.

60. Which of the following individuals are required to file a tax return for 1993? Should any of these individuals file a return even if filing is not required? Why?

 a. Diego is married and files a joint return with his spouse, Juanita. Both Diego and Juanita are 47 years old. Their combined gross income was $9,000.
 b. Sid is a dependent child under age 19 who received $1,000 in wages from a part-time job and $1,900 of dividend income.
 c. Ray is single and is 67 years old. His gross income from wages was $5,800.
 d. Ann is a self-employed single individual with gross income of $4,400 from an unincorporated business. Business expenses amounted to $3,900.

61. Which of the following taxpayers must file a Federal income tax return for 1993?

 a. Bob, age 19, is a full-time college student. He is claimed as a dependent by his parents. He earned $3,900 wages during the year.
 b. Anita, age 12, is claimed as a dependent by her parents. She earned interest of $900 during the year.
 c. Earl, age 16, is claimed as a dependent by his parents. He earned wages of $2,700 and interest of $1,100 during the year.
 d. Karen, age 16 and blind, is claimed as a dependent by her parents. She earned wages of $2,600 and interest of $1,200 during the year.
 e. Pat, age 17, is claimed as a dependent by her parents. She earned interest of $300 during the year. In addition, she earned $550 during the summer operating her own business at the beach, where she painted caricatures of her customers.

62. Can the taxpayer use Tax Rate Schedule Z (head of household) in 1993?

 a. Ron's wife died in 1992. Ron maintained a household for his two dependent children during 1993 and provided over one-half of the cost of the household.
 b. Jack is unmarried and lives in an apartment. He supported his aged parents, who live in a separate home. He provides over one-half of the funds used to maintain his parents' home. Jack also claimed his parents as dependents since he provided more than one-half of their support during the year.
 c. Phil is unmarried and maintains a household (over one-half of the cost) for his 18-year-old married daughter and her husband. His daughter filed a joint return with her husband solely for the purpose of obtaining a refund of income taxes that were withheld. Neither Phil's daughter nor her husband was required to file a return.

63. Indicate in each of the following situations which of the Tax Rate Schedules the taxpayer should use for calendar year 1993:

 a. Vicki, the mother and sole support of her three minor children, was abandoned by her husband in late 1992.
 b. Wilma is a widow whose husband died in 1992. She furnishes all of the support of her household, which includes two dependent children.
 c. Edna furnishes all of the support of her parents, who live in their own home in a different city. Edna's parents qualify as her dependents. She is not married.
 d. Rachel's household includes an unmarried stepchild, age 18, who has gross income of $6,000 during the year. Rachel furnishes all of the cost of maintaining the household. She is not married.

64. Henry died on January 1, 1991. He was survived by his wife, Sue, and their 19-year-old son, Mike, who was a college sophomore. Mike was a full-time student in 1992 and earned $3,000 for the year. In 1993, Mike reduced his school load and became a part-time student. He earned $5,200 in 1993. Mike continues to live with his mother, who provides over half of his support. What is Sue's filing status in 1991, 1992, and 1993?

65. Jim is a struggling songwriter, and Ann is a business executive. Jim earned royalties of $3,900 during 1993, and Ann earned a salary of $110,000. Jim and Ann have the following people as members of their household:

- Sam and Sue, Ann's two children from a former marriage. Sam is 19 years old and is a part-time student at Oakland Community College. He earned $4,500 during the year. Sue, 23 years of age, is a full-time student at Indiana University. She earned $7,000 during the year. Their father paid child support of $4,000 for each of them during the year and claims that he provided more than half of their support.
- Ann's mother, Ruth, who moved from Israel on June 12 to live with Jim and Ann. Ruth is still considered a citizen of Israel. She had no income of her own during the year. Jim and Ann provided all of her support from January 1 until she moved in with them.
- Jim's brother, Ted, was released from prison and moved in with them on July 3. Ted became ill in September, and Jim and Ann paid his medical expenses. As a result of the high medical bills, Jim and Ann can prove that they provided over half of Ted's support for the year.

Jim paid his former wife, Sarah, $2,000 child support for Ron and Don, two sons from his previous marriage. Sarah has custody of the children, who spend June, July, and August with Jim and Ann each year.

a. Assume Jim and Ann are unmarried. How many personal and dependency exemptions can Ann claim on her 1992 Federal income tax return, and what is her filing status?

b. Assume Jim and Ann are married and file separate returns. How many personal and dependency exemptions can Ann claim on her 1992 Federal income tax return?

c. Assume Jim and Ann are married and file a joint return. How many personal and dependency exemptions can they claim on their 1992 Federal income tax return?

66. Tracy, age 66, is a widow. Her husband died in 1991. Tracy maintains a home in which she and her 28-year-old son reside. Her son Koji is a piano player at a local nightclub, where he earned $12,000 during 1993. Koji contributed $3,000 of his income toward household expenses and put the remainder in a savings account that he used to return to college full-time to pursue a master's degree in music starting in August 1993. Tracy contributed $12,000 toward household expenses. What is the most favorable filing status available to Tracy for 1993, and how many exemptions may she claim?

67. In the current year, Jill earned a salary of $50,000 and had a long-term loss of $6,000 on the sale of stock. She also had a $2,500 short-term gain on the sale of land held as an investment and a $2,000 gain on the sale of her personal automobile. She had owned the automobile for two years. Compute Jill's AGI.

68. Hazel, age 39, is single. She maintains a household that is the residence of her two children, Fran, age 8, and Sam, age 11. The children are claimed as dependents by their father, who provides $2,000 child support for each of them. During 1993, Hazel earned a salary of $100,000. Other items that affected her taxable income are as follows:

Total itemized deductions	$ 6,500
Capital gains	
Short-term	1,200
Long-term	3,500
Capital losses	
Short-term	(900)
Long-term	(7,600)
Interest income	2,100

Hazel provides all the support for her mother, Mabel, who lives in a nursing home. Mabel qualifies as Hazel's dependent.

a. Compute Hazel's AGI and taxable income for 1993.
b. What is Hazel's filing status for 1993?

69. Tina, age 61, earned a salary of $63,000 in 1993. She sold common stock that she had owned for 10 months at a loss of $1,500, and sold a fishing boat that she had bought in 1988 at a loss of $4,000. Tina also sold an antique desk for a gain of $10,000. She had acquired the desk in 1953. Compute Tina's AGI for 1993.

70. Lee is a single, cash basis, calendar year taxpayer. For the years 1992 and 1993, he expects AGI of $20,000 and the following itemized deductions:

Church pledge	$2,300
Interest on home mortgage	1,200
Property taxes	500

Discuss the tax consequences of the following alternatives:

a. In 1992, Lee pays his church pledge for 1992 and 1993 ($2,300 for each year).
b. Lee does nothing different.

71. Gina, a cash basis taxpayer, is single and has no dependents. She provides you with the following estimates for 1992 and 1993:

	1992	1993
Adjusted gross income	$56,000	$60,000
Charitable contributions	2,200	2,400
Interest on home mortgage	1,000	1,200
Property taxes	700	900

a. Can Gina decrease taxable income over the two-year period by prepaying her 1993 charitable contributions in 1992?
b. Advise Gina on when she should pay her charitable contributions. Compute the amount of Federal income tax she can save if she follows your recommendation.

72. Ivan and Olga, who are married and file a joint return, have no dependents. They have gross income of $85,000 for the year. Their itemized deductions total $5,800 for the year.

a. Compute Ivan and Olga's taxable income assuming the year is 1992.
b. Compute Ivan and Olga's taxable income assuming the year is 1993, and explain what causes the difference from (a).
c. Why is the tax liability higher in 1992 than in 1993?

73. Ahmad and Yolanda are married and have no dependents. Ahmad has AGI of $40,000, medical expenses of $5,400, and other itemized deductions of $2,800. Yolanda has AGI of $50,000, medical expenses of $1,400, and other itemized deductions of $2,800. Should Ahmad and Yolanda file a joint return or separate returns for 1993? Support your answer by computing tax liabilities.

74. Diego and Felicia are married and have no dependents. For 1993, Diego has AGI of $49,300 and itemized deductions of $2,800. Felicia has AGI of $51,900 and itemized deductions of $7,800.

a. Compute the tax liability for Diego and Felicia if they file a joint return.
b. Compute the lowest combined tax liability for Diego and Felicia if they file separate returns.

CUMULATIVE PROBLEMS

75. John and Karen Sanders, both age 25, are married and file a joint return for 1992. They have one child, Linda, who was born on June 30, 1992. John's Social Security number is 266–77–2345, and Karen's is 467–33–1289. They live at 105 Bradley, Columbus, OH 43211.

John, a computer programmer, earned $53,000, and his employer withheld $8,800. Karen, a medical student at Ohio State University, received $20,000 of income from a trust her father had established to pay for her education. This amount must be included in computing taxable income. In addition, Karen was awarded a $10,000 nontaxable scholarship by the medical school in 1992.

In examining their records, you find that John and Karen are entitled to the following itemized deductions:

State and local income taxes	$1,800
Real estate taxes	1,900
Home mortgage interest	2,800
Charitable contributions	1,500

John and Karen made estimated Federal tax payments of $1,900 in 1992.

Part 1—Tax Computation

Compute (a) adjusted gross income, (b) taxable income, and (c) net tax payable or refund due for John and Karen. Suggested software (if available): *TurboTax* or *MacInTax* for tax return solutions or WFT tax planning software.

Part 2—Tax Planning

Assume that all amounts from 1992 will be approximately the same in 1993 except for the following:

a. John's salary will increase by 10%.
b. John's employer will withhold $9,100 of Federal income tax.

How much estimated tax should the Sanders pay in 1993 so they will neither owe any tax nor receive any refund for 1993? Suggested software (if available): *TurboTax* or *MacInTax* for tax return or WFT tax planning software.

76. Henry and Wanda Black, 4030 Beachside Drive, Longboat Key, FL 33548, file a joint Federal income tax return for 1992. Henry, age 66, is a restaurant manager for Gourmet Tacos. His Social Security number is 344–99–7642. Wanda, who is 54, is a manager at Timothy's Beauty Salon. Her Social Security number is 654–33–7890.

The Blacks come to you in early December 1992 seeking tax advice. They have received or will receive the following amounts during 1992:

a. Henry's salary, $40,000.
b. Wanda's salary, $54,000.
c. Interest on bonds issued by the City of Sarasota, $900.
d. Life insurance proceeds received on the death of Henry's mother, $75,000.
e. Value of property inherited from Henry's mother, $130,000.

In examining the Blacks' records, you find the following items of possible tax consequence (all applicable to 1992):

f. The Blacks had other itemized deductions as follows:

- Real estate taxes, $4,400.
- Home mortgage interest, $4,300.
- Charitable contributions (cash), $3,900.

g. Henry's employer withheld $6,400 of Federal income tax, and Wanda's employer withheld $7,800. In addition, they made estimated tax payments of $2,700.

Henry and Wanda's son Steven lived with the Blacks during 1992 except for nine months during which he was away at college. Steven, age 23, is a law student and plans to graduate in 1994. During the summer, Steven earned $2,500 and used the money he earned to pay for his college expenses. His parents contributed $3,000 toward his support.

Part 1—Tax Computation

Compute the following amounts for the Blacks if they file a joint return for 1992: gross income, adjusted gross income, taxable income, and net tax payable or refund due. Suggested software (if available): *TurboTax* or *MacInTax* for tax return solutions or WFT tax planning software.

Part 2—Tax Planning

The Blacks are contemplating a divorce and would prefer not to file jointly. They have asked you to compute their tax liabilities if they file separately rather than jointly. If they file separately, they will split itemized deductions and estimated tax payments equally. Each spouse will report one-half of the bond interest since they owned the City of Sarasota bonds jointly (refer to item c). Wanda will claim an exemption for Steven (assume he qualifies as her dependent). Will the Blacks have to pay more tax if they file separately? Explain. Suggested software (if available): *TurboTax* or *MacInTax* for tax return solutions or WFT tax planning software.

CHAPTER

GROSS INCOME: CONCEPTS AND INCLUSIONS

OBJECTIVES

Explain the all-inclusive concept of gross income and the underlying realization requirement.

Distinguish between the economic, accounting, and tax concepts of income.

Describe the cash and accrual methods of accounting for gross income.

Explain the principles applied to determine who is subject to tax on a particular item of income.

Analyze the sections of the Internal Revenue Code that describe the determination of gross income from the following specific sources: alimony, below-market interest rate loans, annuities, prizes and awards, group term life insurance, unemployment compensation, and Social Security benefits.

Identify tax planning strategies for minimizing gross income.

OUTLINE

Gross income is defined in § 61(a) as all income from whatever source derived. This definition is seemingly broad enough to include all amounts, cash or noncash, that the taxpayer receives. In reality, the law produces a much different result.

EXAMPLE 1

Bob is an accountant employed by Greene Corporation. His salary for the year was $80,000. He owns stock in Whyte Corporation on which he received dividends of $3,000 during the year. He won $10,000 in the state lottery. Bob also embezzled $5,000 from his church, where he serves as treasurer. All of these items are included in gross income, so Bob must report $98,000 income on his Federal income tax return.

Betty, who is independently wealthy, earned interest of $80,000 on municipal bonds. She received $3,000 in child support from her former husband. Betty sued the *Times-Gazette* over an unflattering newspaper story and received $10,000 damages for libel. She was the beneficiary under a life insurance policy and received $5,000 on the death of her aunt. Betty is not required to report any of the $98,000 as income on her Federal income tax return. ◆

In addition to the broad definition in § 61(a), the Code provides special rules for determining and reporting certain types of income, such as alimony, prizes, and Social Security benefits. These provisions are discussed in this chapter.

It is clear from Example 1 that some types of income are *excluded* from gross income. Exclusions, such as interest on municipal bonds, damages, and life insurance proceeds, are discussed in Chapter 4.

GROSS INCOME—WHAT IS IT?

Definition

Section 61(a) of the Internal Revenue Code defines *gross income* as follows:

> Except as otherwise provided in this subtitle, gross income means all income from whatever source derived.

This definition is derived from the language of the Sixteenth Amendment to the Constitution.

Supreme Court decisions have made it clear that all sources of income are subject to tax unless Congress specifically excludes the type of income received:

> The starting point in all cases dealing with the question of the scope of what is included in "gross income" begins with the basic premise that the purpose of Congress was to use the full measure of its taxing power.[1]

Although at this point we know that *income* is to be broadly construed, we still do not have a satisfactory definition of the term *income.* Congress left it to the judicial and administrative branches to thrash out the meaning of income. Early in the development of the income tax law, a choice was made between two competing models: economic income and accounting income.

1. *James v. U.S.*, 61–1 USTC ¶9449, 7 AFTR2d 1361, 81 S.Ct. 1052 (USSC, 1961).

Economic and Accounting Concepts

The term *income* is used in the Code but is not separately defined. Thus, early in the history of our tax laws, the courts were required to interpret "the commonly understood meaning of the term which must have been in the minds of the people when they adopted the Sixteenth Amendment to the Constitution."[2] In determining the definition of income, the Supreme Court rejected the economic concept of income.

Economists measure economic income by first determining the fair market value of the individual's net assets at the beginning and end of the year (change in net worth). After the change in net worth is determined, economic income is calculated as the individual's change in net worth plus the value of goods and services actually consumed during the period. Economic income also includes imputed values for such items as the rental value of an owner-occupied home and the value of food grown for personal consumption.

EXAMPLE 2

Helen's economic income is calculated as follows:

Fair market value of Helen's assets on December 31, 1993	$220,000	
Less liabilities on December 31, 1993	(40,000)	
Net worth on December 31, 1993		$180,000
Fair market value of Helen's assets on January 1, 1993	$200,000	
Less liabilities on January 1, 1993	(80,000)	
Net worth on January 1, 1993		120,000
Increase in net worth		$ 60,000
Consumption		
Food, clothing, and other personal expenditures		25,000
Imputed rental value of Helen's home she owns and occupies		12,000
Economic income		$ 97,000

◆

The need to value assets annually would make compliance with a tax law based on the economic concept of income burdensome and would cause numerous controversies between the taxpayer and the IRS over valuation. In addition, using market values to determine income for tax purposes could result in liquidity problems. That is, the taxpayer's assets may increase in value even though they are not readily convertible into the cash needed to pay the tax (e.g., commercial real estate).

In contrast, the *accounting concept of income* is founded on the realization principle. According to this principle, income is not recognized until it is realized. For realization to occur, (1) an exchange of goods or services must take place between the accounting entity and some independent, external group, and (2) the accounting entity must receive assets in the exchange that are capable of being objectively valued. Thus, the mere appreciation in the market value of assets before a sale or other disposition is not sufficient to warrant income recognition. In addition, the imputed savings that arise when an individual creates assets for his or her own use (e.g., feed grown for a farmer's own livestock) are not income because no exchange has occurred.

---

2. *Merchants Loan and Trust Co. v. Smietanka*, 1 USTC ¶42, 3 AFTR 3102, 41 S.Ct. 386 (USSC, 1921).

The Supreme Court expressed support for the accounting concept of income when it adopted the realization requirement in *Eisner v. Macomber*:[3]

> Income may be defined as the gain derived from capital, from labor, or from both combined, provided it is understood to include profit gained through a sale or conversion of capital assets.... Here we have the essential matter: not a gain accruing to capital; not a *growth* or *increment* of value *in* investment; but a gain, a profit, something of exchangeable value, *proceeding from* the property, *severed from* the capital however invested or employed, and *coming in*, being "*derived*"—that is, *received* or *drawn by* the recipient for his separate use, benefit and disposal—that is, income derived from the property.

Comparison of the Accounting and Tax Concepts of Income

Although income tax rules frequently parallel financial accounting measurement concepts, differences do exist. Of major significance, for example, is the fact that unearned (prepaid) income received by an accrual basis taxpayer often is taxed in the year of receipt. For financial accounting purposes, such prepayments are not treated as income until earned. Because of this and other differences, many corporations report financial accounting income that is substantially different from the amounts reported for tax purposes (see Chapter 16, Reconciliation of Taxable Income and Accounting Income).

The Supreme Court provided an explanation for some of the variations between accounting and taxable income in a decision involving inventory and bad debt adjustments.[4] The relevant portion of the opinion follows:

> The primary goal of financial accounting is to provide useful information to management, shareholders, creditors, and others properly interested; the major responsibility of the accountant is to protect these parties from being misled. The primary goal of the income tax system, in contrast, is the equitable collection of revenue.... Consistently with its goals and responsibilities, financial accounting has as its foundation the principle of conservatism, with its corollary that 'possible errors in measurement [should] be in the direction of understatement rather than overstatement of net income and net assets.' In view of the Treasury's markedly different goals and responsibilities, understatement of income is not destined to be its guiding light.
>
> ... Financial accounting, in short, is hospitable to estimates, probabilities, and reasonable certainties; the tax law, with its mandate to preserve the revenue, can give no quarter to uncertainty.

In some instances, the tax law specifically permits rapid write-offs (e.g., immediate expensing under § 179 versus normal depreciation) and deferrals of income that are not available in financial accounting.

Form of Receipt

Gross income is not limited to cash received. "It includes income realized in any form, whether in money, property, or services. Income may be realized [and recognized], therefore, in the form of services, meals, accommodations, stock or other property, as well as in cash."[5]

3. 1 USTC ¶32, 3 AFTR 3020, 40 S.Ct. 189 (USSC, 1920).

4. *Thor Power Tool Co. v. Comm.*, 79–1 USTC ¶9139, 43 AFTR2d 79–362, 99 S.Ct. 773 (USSC, 1979).

5. Reg. § 1.61–1(a).

EXAMPLE 3

ABC Corporation allows Bill, an employee, to use a company car for his vacation. Bill realizes income equal to the rental value of the car for the time and mileage. ◆

EXAMPLE 4

Rashad, an XYZ Corporation shareholder, buys real estate from the company for $10,000 when the property is worth $15,000. Rashad realizes income (a constructive dividend) of $5,000, the difference between the fair market value of the property and the price he paid. ◆

EXAMPLE 5

Terry owes $10,000 on a mortgage. The creditor accepts $8,000 in full satisfaction of the debt. Terry realizes income of $2,000 from retiring the debt. ◆

Recovery of Capital Doctrine

The Constitution grants Congress the power to tax income but does not define the term. Because the Constitution does not define income, it would seem that Congress could simply tax gross receipts. Although certain deductions are allowed, none are constitutionally required. However, the Supreme Court has held that there can be no income subject to tax until the taxpayer has recovered the capital invested.[6] This concept is known as the *recovery of capital doctrine.*

In its simplest application, this doctrine means that a seller can reduce the gross receipts (selling price) by the adjusted basis of the property sold. This net amount, in the language of the Code, is gross income.

EXAMPLE 6

Dave sold common stock for $15,000. He had purchased the stock for $12,000. Dave's gross receipts are $15,000. This amount consists of a $12,000 recovery of capital and $3,000 of gross income. ◆

YEAR OF INCLUSION

Taxable Year

The annual accounting period or taxable year is a basic component of our tax system. Generally, an entity must use the *calendar year* to report its income. However, a *fiscal year* (a period of 12 months ending on the last day of any month other than December) can be elected if the taxpayer maintains adequate books and records. This fiscal year option generally is not available to partnerships, S corporations, and personal service corporations, as discussed in Chapter 15.

Determining the year in which the income will be taxed is important for determining when the tax must be paid. But the year each item of income is subject to tax can also affect the total tax liability over the entity's lifetime. This is true for the following reasons:

- With a progressive rate system, a taxpayer's marginal tax rate can change from year to year.

6. *Doyle v. Mitchell Bros. Co.*, 1 USTC ¶17, 3 AFTR 2979, 38 S.Ct. 467 (USSC, 1916).

- Congress may change the tax rates.
- The relevant rates may change because of a change in the entity's status (e.g., a person may marry or a business may be incorporated).
- Several provisions in the Code are dependent on the taxpayer's gross income for the year (e.g., whether the person can be claimed as a dependent, as discussed in Chapter 2).

Accounting Methods

The year an item of income is subject to tax often depends upon which acceptable accounting method the taxpayer regularly employs. The three primary methods of accounting are (1) the cash receipts and disbursements method, (2) the accrual method, and (3) the hybrid method. Most individuals use the cash receipts and disbursements method of accounting, whereas most corporations use the accrual method. The Regulations require the accrual method for determining purchases and sales when inventory is an income-producing factor.[7] Some businesses employ a hybrid method that is a combination of the cash and accrual methods of accounting.

In addition to these *overall accounting methods,* a taxpayer may choose to spread the gain from the sale of property over the collection periods by using the *installment method* of income recognition. Contractors may either spread profits from contracts over the periods in which the work is done (the *percentage of completion method*) or defer all profit until the year in which the project is completed (the *completed contract method,* which can be used only in limited circumstances).

The Commissioner has the power to prescribe the accounting method to be used by the taxpayer. Section 446(b) grants the IRS broad powers to determine if the accounting method used *clearly reflects income:*

> Exceptions—If no method of accounting has been regularly used by the taxpayer, or *if the method used does not clearly reflect income, the computation of taxable income shall be made under such method as, in the opinion of the Secretary does clearly reflect income.*

A change in the method of accounting requires the consent of the IRS.

Cash Receipts Method. Under the *cash receipts method,* property or services received are included in the taxpayer's gross income in the year of *actual* or *constructive* receipt by the taxpayer or agent, regardless of whether the income was earned in that year. The income received need not be reduced to cash in the same year. All that is necessary for income recognition is that property or services received have a fair market value—a cash equivalent. Thus, if a cash basis taxpayer receives a note in payment for services, he or she has income in the year of receipt equal to the fair market value of the note. However, a creditor's mere promise to pay (e.g., an account receivable), with no supporting note, usually is not considered to have a fair market value. Thus, the cash basis taxpayer defers income recognition until the account receivable is collected.

EXAMPLE 7

Dana, an accountant, reports her income by the cash method. In 1993, she performed an audit for Orange Corporation and billed the client for $5,000, which was collected in 1994. In 1993, Dana also performed an audit for Blue Corporation. Because of Blue's

7. Reg. § 1.446–1(c)(2)(i). See the Glossary of Tax Terms in Appendix C for a discussion of the terms "accrual method," "accounting method," and "accounting period." Other circumstances in which the accrual method must be used are presented in Chapter 15.

precarious financial position, Dana required Blue to issue an $8,000 secured negotiable note in payment of the fee. The note had a fair market value of $6,000. Dana collected $8,000 on the note in 1994. Dana's gross income for the two years is as follows:

	1993	1994
Fair market value of note received from Blue	$6,000	
Cash received		
From Orange on account receivable		$ 5,000
From Blue on note receivable		8,000
Less: Recovery of capital		(6,000)
Total gross income	$6,000	$ 7,000

◆

Generally, a check received is considered a cash equivalent. Thus, a cash basis taxpayer must recognize the income when the check is received. This is true even if the taxpayer receives the check after banking hours.[8]

Accrual Method. Under *accrual accounting,* an item is generally included in the gross income of the year in which it is earned, regardless of when the income is collected. The income is earned when (1) all the events have occurred that fix the right to receive the income and (2) the amount to be received can be determined with reasonable accuracy.

Generally, the taxpayer's rights to the income accrue when title to property passes to the buyer or the services are performed for the customer or client. If the rights to the income have accrued but are subject to a potential refund claim (e.g., under a product warranty), the income is reported in the year of sale, and a deduction is allowed in subsequent years when actual claims accrue.

Where the taxpayer's rights to the income are being contested (e.g., when a contractor fails to meet specifications), the year in which the income is subject to tax depends upon whether payment has been received. If payment has not been received, no income is recognized until the claim is settled. Only then is the right to the income established. However, if the payment is received before the dispute is settled, the court-made *claim of right doctrine* requires the taxpayer to recognize the income in the year of receipt.[9]

EXAMPLE 8

A contractor completed a building in 1993 and presented a bill to the customer. The customer refused to pay the bill and claimed that the contractor had not met specifications. A settlement with the customer was not reached until 1994. No income accrues to the contractor until 1994. If the customer paid for the work and then filed suit for damages, the contractor could not defer the income (the income would be taxable in 1993). ◆

The measure of accrual basis income is generally the amount the taxpayer has a right to receive. Unlike the cash basis, the fair market value of the customer's obligation is irrelevant in measuring accrual basis income. 

EXAMPLE 9

Assume the same facts as in Example 7, except Dana is an accrual basis taxpayer. Dana must recognize $13,000 ($8,000 + $5,000) income in 1993, the year her rights to the income accrued. ◆

8. *Charles F. Kahler,* 18 T.C. 31 (1952).

9. *North American Oil Consolidated Co. v. Burnet,* 3 USTC ¶943, 11 AFTR 16, 52 S.Ct. 613 (USSC, 1932). See the Glossary of Tax Terms in Appendix C for a discussion of the term "claim of right doctrine."

Hybrid Method. The hybrid method is a combination of the accrual method and the cash method. Generally, when the hybrid method is used, inventory is an income-producing factor. Therefore, the Regulations require that the accrual method be used for determining sales and cost of goods sold. In this circumstance, to simplify record keeping, the taxpayer accounts for inventory using the accrual method and uses the cash method for all other income and expense items (e.g., dividend and interest income). The hybrid method is primarily used by small businesses.

Exceptions Applicable to Cash Basis Taxpayers

Constructive Receipt. Income that has not actually been received by the taxpayer is taxed as though it had been received—the income is *constructively received*—under the following conditions:

- The amount is made readily available to the taxpayer.
- The taxpayer's actual receipt is not subject to substantial limitations or restrictions.

The rationale for the constructive receipt doctrine is that if the income is available, the taxpayer should not be allowed to postpone the income recognition. For instance, a taxpayer is not permitted to defer income for December services by refusing to accept payment until January. However, determining whether the income is *readily available* and whether *substantial limitations or restrictions exist* necessitates a factual inquiry that sometimes leads to a judgment call. The following are examples of the application of the constructive receipt doctrine.

EXAMPLE 10

Ted is a member of a barter club. In 1993, Ted performed services for other club members and earned 1,000 points. Each point entitles him to $1 in goods and services sold by other members of the club; the points can be used at any time. In 1994, Ted exchanged his points for a new color TV. Ted must recognize $1,000 income in 1993 when the 1,000 points were credited to his account. ◆

EXAMPLE 11

On December 31, an employer issued a bonus check to an employee but asked her to hold it for a few days until the company could make deposits to cover the check. The income was not constructively received on December 31 since the issuer did not have sufficient funds in its account to pay the debt. ◆

EXAMPLE 12

Rick owns interest coupons that mature on December 31. The coupons can be converted to cash at any bank at maturity. Thus, the income is *constructively received* on December 31. ◆

EXAMPLE 13

GM Company mails dividend checks on December 31, 1993. The shareholders do not receive the checks until January and do not realize income until 1994. ◆

The constructive receipt doctrine does not reach income that the taxpayer is not yet entitled to receive, even though he or she could have contracted to receive the income at an earlier date.

EXAMPLE 14

Sara offers to pay Ivan $100,000 for land in December 1993. Ivan refuses but offers to sell the land to Sara on January 1, 1994, when he will be in a lower tax bracket. If Sara accepts Ivan's offer, the gain will be taxed to Ivan in 1994 when the sale is completed. ◆

Original Issue Discount. Lenders frequently make loans that require a payment at maturity of more than the amount of the original loan. The difference between the amount due at maturity and the amount of the original loan is actually interest but is referred to as *original issue discount.* Under the general rules of tax accounting, the cash basis lender would not report the original issue discount as interest income until the year the amount is collected, although an accrual basis borrower deducts the interest as it accrues. However, the Code puts the lender and borrower on parity by requiring that the original issue discount be reported by the lender when it is earned, regardless of the taxpayer's accounting method.[10]

EXAMPLE 15

On July 1, 1993, Chee, a cash basis taxpayer, paid $82,645 for a 24-month certificate of deposit with a maturity value of $100,000. The effective interest rate on the certificate was 10%. Chee must report $4,132 interest income for 1993:

$$(.10 \times \$82,645)(\tfrac{1}{2} \text{ year}) = \underline{\underline{\$4,132}}$$

◆

The original issue discount rules do not apply to U.S. savings bonds (discussed in the following paragraphs) or to obligations with a maturity date of one year or less from the date of issue.

Series E and Series EE Bonds. Certain U.S. government savings bonds (Series E before 1980 and Series EE after 1979) are issued at a discount and are redeemable for fixed amounts that increase at stated intervals. No interest payments are actually made. The difference between the purchase price and the amount received on redemption is the bondholder's interest income from the investment.

The income from these savings bonds is generally deferred until the bonds are redeemed or mature. Furthermore, Series E bonds can be exchanged within one year of their maturity date for Series HH bonds, and the interest on the Series E bonds can be further deferred until maturity of the Series HH bonds. Thus, U.S. savings bonds have attractive income deferral features not available with corporate bonds and certificates of deposit issued by financial institutions.

Of course, the deferral feature of government bonds issued at a discount is not an advantage if the investor has insufficient income to be subject to tax as the income accrues. In fact, the deferral may work to the investor's disadvantage if he or she has other income in the year the bonds mature or the bunching of the bond interest into one tax year creates a tax liability. Fortunately, U.S. government bonds have a provision for these investors. A cash basis taxpayer can elect to include in gross income the annual increment in redemption value.

EXAMPLE 16

Kate purchases Series EE U.S. Savings bonds for $500 on January 2 of the current year. If the bonds are redeemed during the first six months, no interest is paid. At December 31, the redemption value is $519.60.

---

10. §§ 1272(a)(3) and 1273(a).

If Kate elects to report the interest income annually, she must report interest income of $19.60 for the current year. If she does not make the election, she will report no interest income for the current year. ◆

When a taxpayer elects to report the income from the bonds on an annual basis, the election applies to all such bonds the taxpayer owns at the time of the election and to all such securities acquired subsequent to the election. A change in the method of reporting the income from the bonds requires permission from the IRS.

Amounts Received under an Obligation to Repay. The receipt of funds with an obligation to repay that amount in the future is the essence of borrowing. Because the taxpayer's assets and liabilities increase by the same amount, no income is realized when the borrowed funds are received. Because amounts paid to the taxpayer by mistake and customer deposits are often classified as borrowed funds, receipt of the funds is not a taxable event.

EXAMPLE 17

A landlord receives a damage deposit from a tenant. The landlord does not recognize income before the deposit is forfeited because he is obliged to repay the deposit if no damage occurs. However, if the deposit is in fact a prepayment of rent, it is taxed in the year of receipt. ◆

Exceptions Applicable to Accrual Basis Taxpayers

Prepaid Income. For financial reporting purposes, advance payments received from customers are reflected as prepaid income and as a liability of the seller. However, for tax purposes, the prepaid income often is taxed in the year of receipt.

EXAMPLE 18

In December 1993, a tenant pays his January 1994 rent of $1,000. The accrual basis landlord must include the $1,000 in his 1993 income for tax purposes, although the unearned rent income is reported as a liability on the landlord's December 31, 1993, balance sheet. ◆

Taxpayers have repeatedly argued that deferral of income until it is actually earned properly matches revenues and expenses. Moreover, a proper matching of income with the expenses of earning the income is necessary to clearly reflect income, as required by the Code. The IRS responds that § 446(b) grants it broad powers to determine whether an accounting method clearly reflects income. The IRS further argues that generally accepted financial accounting principles should not dictate tax accounting for prepaid income because of the practical problems of collecting Federal revenues. Collection of the tax is simplest in the year the taxpayer receives the cash from the customer or client.

Over 40 years of litigation, the IRS has been only partially successful in the courts. In cases involving prepaid income from services to be performed at the demand of customers (e.g., dance lessons to be taken at any time in a 24-month period), the IRS's position has been upheld.[11] In such cases, the taxpayer's argument that deferral of the income was necessary to match the income with

11. *Automobile Club of Michigan v. U.S.*, 57–1 USTC ¶9593, 50 AFTR 1967, 77 S.Ct. 707 (USSC, 1957); *American Automobile Association v. U.S.*, 61–2 USTC ¶9517, 7 AFTR2d 1618, 81 S.Ct. 1727 (USSC, 1961); *Schlude v. Comm.*, 63–1 USTC ¶9284, 11 AFTR2d 751, 83 S.Ct. 601 (USSC, 1963).

expenses was not persuasive because the taxpayer did not know precisely when each customer would demand services and, thus, when the expenses would be incurred. However, taxpayers have had some success in the courts when the services were performed on a fixed schedule (e.g., a baseball team's season-ticket sales).[12]

Against this background of mixed results in the courts, congressional intervention, and taxpayers' strong resentment of the IRS's position, in 1971 the IRS modified its prepaid income rules, as explained in the following paragraphs.

Deferral of Advance Payments for Goods. Generally, a taxpayer can elect to defer recognition of income from *advance payments for goods* if the taxpayer's method of accounting for the sale is the same for tax and financial reporting purposes.[13]

Example 19

Brown Company will ship goods only after payment for the goods has been received. In December 1993, Brown received $10,000 for goods that were not shipped until January 1994. Brown can elect to report the income for tax purposes in 1994, assuming the company reports the income in 1994 for financial reporting purposes. ◆

Deferral of Advance Payments for Services. Revenue Procedure 71–21[14] permits an accrual basis taxpayer to defer recognition of income for *advance payments for services* to be performed by the end of the tax year following the year of receipt. No deferral is allowed if the taxpayer might be required to perform any services, under the agreement, after the tax year following the year of receipt of the advance payment. Revenue Procedure 71–21 does not apply to prepaid rent or prepaid interest.

Example 20

Yellow Corporation, an accrual basis taxpayer, sells its services under 12-month, 18-month, and 24-month contracts. The corporation provides services to each customer every month. In 1993, Yellow Corporation sold the following customer contracts with service periods beginning April 1:

Length of Contract	Total Proceeds
12 months	$6,000
18 months	3,600
24 months	2,400

Fifteen hundred dollars of the $6,000 may be deferred (3/12 × $6,000), and $1,800 of the $3,600 may be deferred (9/18 × $3,600) because those amounts will not be earned until 1994. However, the entire $2,400 received on the 24-month contracts is taxable in the year of receipt (1993), since a part of the income will still be unearned by the end of the tax year following the year of receipt. ◆

Amounts received under guarantee or warranty contracts are not eligible for deferral unless the goods are also sold without such contracts. The reason these amounts cannot be deferred is to prevent the seller of goods from simply carving a service charge out of the selling price for the goods and attempting to defer the income from a service charge that may in reality be part of the price of the goods.

---

12. *Artnell Company v. Comm.*, 68–2 USTC ¶9593, 22 AFTR2d 5590, 400 F.2d 981 (CA–7, 1968). See also *Boise Cascade Corp. v. U.S.*, 76–1 USTC ¶9203, 37 AFTR2d 76–696, 530 F.2d 1367 (Ct. Cls., 1976).

13. Reg. § 1.451–5(b). See Reg. § 1.451–5(c) for exceptions to this deferral opportunity. The financial accounting conformity requirement does not apply to contractors who use the completed contract method.

14. 1971–2 C.B. 549.

INCOME SOURCES

Personal Services

It is a well-established principle of taxation that income from personal services must be included in the gross income of the person who performs the services. This principle was first established in a Supreme Court decision, *Lucas v. Earl.*[15] Mr. Earl entered into a binding agreement with his wife under which Mrs. Earl was to receive one-half of Mr. Earl's salary. Justice Holmes used the celebrated *fruit* and *tree* metaphor to explain that the fruit (income) must be attributed to the tree from which it came (Mr. Earl's services). A mere *assignment of income* does not shift the liability for the tax.

However, services performed by an employee for the employer's customers are considered performed by the employer. Thus, the employer is taxed on the income from the services provided to the customer, and the employee is taxed on any compensation received from the employer.[16]

EXAMPLE 21

Dr. Shontelle incorporated her medical practice and entered into a contract to work for the corporation for a salary. All patients contracted to receive their services from the corporation, and those services were provided through the corporation's employee, Dr. Shontelle. The corporation must include the fees charged the patients in its gross income. Dr. Shontelle must include her salary in her gross income. The corporation will be allowed a deduction for the reasonable salary paid to Dr. Shontelle (see the discussion of unreasonable compensation in Chapter 5). ◆

In the case of a child, the Code specifically provides that amounts earned from personal services must be included in the child's gross income. This result applies even if the income is paid to other persons (e.g., the parents).

Income from Property

Income from property (interest, dividends, rent) must be included in the gross income of the *owner* of the property. If a parent clips interest coupons from bonds shortly before the interest payment date and gives the coupons to a child, the interest will still be taxed to the parent. A parent who assigns rents from rental property to a child will be taxed on the rent since the parent retains ownership of the property.

Often income-producing property is transferred after income from the property has accrued but before the income is recognized under the transferor's method of accounting. For interest income and dividend income, the IRS and the courts have developed rules to allocate the income between the transferor and the transferee.

Interest. According to the IRS, interest accrues daily. Therefore, the interest for the period that includes the date of the transfer is allocated between the transferor and transferee based on the number of days during the period that each owned the property.

15. 2 USTC ¶496, 8 AFTR 10287, 50 S.Ct. 241 (USSC, 1930).

16. *Sargent v. Comm.*, 91–1 USTC ¶50,168, 67 AFTR2d 91–718, 929 F.2d 1252 (CA–8, 1991).

Example 22

Floyd, a cash basis taxpayer, gave his son, Seth, bonds with a face amount of $10,000 and an 8% stated annual interest rate. The gift was made on January 31, 1993, and the interest was paid on December 31, 1993. Floyd must recognize $68 in interest income (8% × $10,000 × 31/365). Seth will recognize $732 in interest income ($800 – $68). ◆

When the transferor must recognize the income from the property depends upon the method of accounting and the manner in which the property was transferred. In the case of a gift of income-producing property, the donor must recognize his or her share of the accrued income at the time it would have been recognized had the donor continued to own the property.[17]

Example 23

Assume the same facts as in Example 22, except the interest that was payable as of December 31 was not actually or constructively received by the bondholders until January 3, 1994. As a cash basis taxpayer, Floyd generally does not recognize interest income until it is received. If Floyd had continued to own the bond, the interest would have been included in his gross income in 1994, the year it would have been received. Therefore, Floyd must include the $68 accrued income in his gross income as of January 3, 1994.

Further assume that Floyd sold identical bonds on the date of the gift. The bonds sold for $9,900, including accrued interest. On January 31, 1993, Floyd must recognize $68, the accrued interest on the bonds sold. Thus, the selling price of the bonds is $9,832 ($9,900 – $68). ◆

Dividends. Unlike interest, dividends do not accrue on a daily basis because the declaration of a dividend is at the discretion of the corporation's board of directors. Generally, dividends are taxed to the person who is entitled to receive them—the shareholder of record as of the corporation's record date. Thus, if a taxpayer sells stock after a dividend has been declared but before the record date, the dividend generally will be taxed to the purchaser.

If a donor makes a gift of stock to someone (e.g., a family member) after the declaration date but before the record date, the Tax Court has held that the donor does not shift the dividend income to the donee. The *fruit* has sufficiently ripened as of the declaration date to tax the dividend income to the donor of the stock.[18]

Example 24

On June 20, the board of directors of Black Corporation declares a $10 per share dividend. The dividend is payable on June 30, to shareholders of record on June 25. As of June 20, Maria owned 200 shares of Black Corporation's stock. On June 21, she sold 100 of the shares to Norm for their fair market value and gave 100 of the shares to Sam (her son). Assume both Norm and Sam are shareholders of record as of June 25. Norm (the purchaser) will be taxed on $1,000, since he is entitled to receive the dividend. However, Maria (the donor) will be taxed on the $1,000 received by Sam (the donee) because the gift was made after the declaration date of the dividend. ◆

Income Received by an Agent

Income received by the taxpayer's agent is considered to be received by the taxpayer. A cash basis principal must recognize the income at the time it is received by the agent.[19]

---

17. Rev.Rul. 72–312, 1972–1 C.B. 22.

18. *M. G. Anton*, 34 T.C. 842 (1960).

19. Rev.Rul. 79–379, 1979–2 C.B. 204.

EXAMPLE 25

Jack, a cash basis taxpayer, delivered cattle to the auction barn in late December. The auctioneer, acting as Jack's agent, sold the cattle and collected the proceeds in December. The auctioneer did not pay him until the following January. Jack must include the sales proceeds in his gross income in the year the auctioneer received the funds. ◆

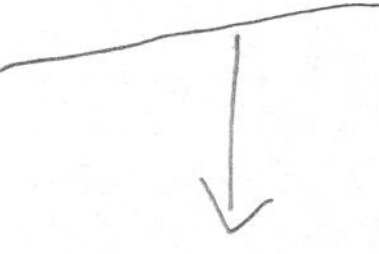

Income from Partnerships, S Corporations, Trusts, and Estates

A *partnership* is not a separate taxable entity. Rather, the partnership merely files an information return (Form 1065), which provides the data necessary for determining the character and amount of each partner's distributive share of the partnership's income and deductions. Each partner must then report his or her distributive share of the partnership's income and deductions for the partnership's tax year ending within or with his or her own tax year. Each partner must report the income in the year it is earned, even if it is not actually distributed to the partners. Because a partner pays tax on income as the partnership earns it, a distribution by the partnership to the partner is treated under the recovery of capital rules.

EXAMPLE 26

Tara owned a one-half interest in the capital and profits of T & S Company (a calendar year partnership). For tax year 1993, the partnership earned revenue of $150,000 and had operating expenses of $80,000. During the year, Tara withdrew from her capital account $2,500 per month (for a total of $30,000). For 1993, Tara must report $35,000 as her share of the partnership's profits [½ × ($150,000 – $80,000)] even though she withdrew only $30,000. ◆

A *small business corporation* may elect to be taxed similarly to a partnership. Thus, the shareholders, rather than the corporation, pay the tax on the corporation's income. The electing corporation is referred to as an *S corporation* (because it is subject to the rules of Subchapter S of the Code). Generally, the shareholder reports his or her proportionate share of the corporation's income and deductions for the year, whether or not the corporation actually makes any distributions to the shareholder.

The *beneficiaries of estates and trusts* generally are taxed on the income earned by the estates or trusts that is actually distributed or required to be distributed to them. Any income not taxed to the beneficiaries is taxable to the estate or trust.

Income in Community Property States

General Rules. State law in Louisiana, Texas, New Mexico, Arizona, California, Washington, Idaho, Nevada, and Wisconsin is based upon a community property system. All other states have a common law property system. The basic difference between common law and community property systems involves the property rights of married persons. Questions about community property income most frequently arise when the husband and wife file separate returns.

Under a *community property* system, all property is deemed either to be separately owned by the spouse or to belong to the marital community. Property may be held separately by a spouse if it was acquired before marriage or received by gift or inheritance following marriage. Otherwise, any property is deemed to be community property. For Federal tax purposes, each spouse is taxed on one-half of the income from property belonging to the community.

The laws of Texas, Louisiana, and Idaho distinguish between separate property and the income it produces. In these states, the income from separate property belongs to the community. Accordingly, for Federal income tax purposes, each spouse is taxed on one-half of the income. In the remaining community property states, separate property produces separate income that the owner-spouse must report on his or her Federal income tax return.

What appears to be income, however, may really be a recovery of capital. A recovery of capital and gain realized on separate property retains its identity as separate property. Items such as nontaxable stock dividends, royalties from mineral interests, and gains and losses from the sale of property take on the same community property or separate property classification as the assets to which they relate.

In all community property states, income from personal services (e.g., salaries, wages, income from a professional partnership) is generally treated as if one-half is earned by each spouse.

Items Specifically Included in Gross Income

The general principles of gross income determination (discussed in the previous sections) as applied by the IRS and the courts have on occasion yielded results Congress found unacceptable. Consequently, Congress has provided more specific rules for determining the gross income from certain sources. Some of these special rules appear in §§ 71–90 of the Code.

Alimony and Separate Maintenance Payments

When a married couple divorce or become legally separated, state law generally requires a division of the property accumulated during the marriage. In addition, one spouse may have a legal obligation to support the other spouse. The Code distinguishes between the support payments (alimony or separate maintenance) and the property division in terms of the tax consequences.

Alimony and separate maintenance payments are *deductible* by the party making the payments and are *includible* in the gross income of the party receiving the payments. Thus, income is shifted from the income earner to the income beneficiary, who is required to pay the tax on the amount received.

Example 27

Pete and Tina were divorced, and Pete was required to pay Tina $15,000 of alimony each year. Pete earns $61,000 a year. The tax law presumes that because Tina received the $15,000, she is more able than Pete to pay the tax on that amount. Therefore, Tina must include the $15,000 in her gross income, and Pete is allowed to deduct $15,000 from his gross income. ◆

A transfer of property other than cash to a former spouse under a divorce decree or agreement is not a taxable event. The transferor is not entitled to a deduction and does not recognize gain or loss on the transfer. The transferee does not recognize income and has a basis equal to the transferor's basis.

Example 28

Paul transfers stock to Rosa as part of a 1993 divorce settlement. The basis of the stock to Paul is $12,000, and the stock's value at the time of the transfer is $15,000. Rosa later sells the stock for $16,000. Paul is not required to recognize gain from the transfer of the stock to Rosa, and Rosa has a realized and recognized gain of $4,000 ($16,000 – $12,000) when she sells the stock. ◆

In the case of cash payments, however, it is often difficult to distinguish payments under a support obligation (alimony) and payments for the other spouse's property (property settlement). In 1984, Congress developed objective rules to classify the payments.

Post-1984 Agreements and Decrees. Payments made under post-1984 agreements and decrees are *classified as alimony* only if the following conditions are satisfied:

1. The payments are in cash.
2. The agreement or decree does not specify that the cash payments are not alimony.
3. The payer and payee are not members of the same household at the time the payments are made.
4. There is no liability to make the payments for any period after the death of the payee.

Requirement 1 simplifies the law by clearly distinguishing alimony from a property division; that is, if the payment is not in cash, it is treated as a property division.

Requirement 2 allows the parties to determine by agreement whether or not the payments will be alimony. The prohibition on cohabitation— requirement 3—is aimed at assuring the alimony payments are associated with duplicative living expenses (maintaining two households). Requirement 4 is an attempt to prevent alimony treatment from being applied to what is, in fact, a payment for property rather than a support obligation. That is, a seller's estate generally will receive payments for property due after the seller's death. Such payments after the death of the payee could not be for the payee's support.

Front-Loading. As a further safeguard against a property settlement being disguised as alimony, special rules apply to post-1986 agreements if payments in the first or second year exceed $15,000. If the change in the amount of the payments exceeds statutory limits, *alimony recapture* results to the extent of the excess alimony payments. In the *third* year, the payor must include the excess alimony payments for the first and second years in gross income, and the payee is allowed a deduction for these excess alimony payments.

The recapture computation provides an objective technique for determining alimony recapture. Thus, at the time of divorce, the taxpayers can ascertain the

CONCEPT SUMMARY 3–1 TAX TREATMENT OF PAYMENTS AND TRANSFERS PURSUANT TO POST-1984 DIVORCE AGREEMENTS AND DECREES

	Payer	Recipient
Alimony	Deduction *for* AGI.	Included in gross income.
Alimony recapture	Included in gross income of the third year.	Deducted from gross income of the third year.
Child support	Not deductible.	Not includible in income.
Property settlement	No income or deduction.	No income or deduction; basis for the property received is the same as the transferor's basis.

tax consequences of the alimony arrangement. The general concept is that if the alimony payments decrease by over $15,000 between years, there will be alimony recapture with respect to the *decrease* in excess of $15,000 each year.

EXAMPLE 29

Henry and Wanda enter into a post-1986 divorce agreement under which Wanda is to receive alimony payments of $30,000 in Year 1, $20,000 in Year 2, and $15,000 in Year 3. There is no alimony recapture because payments did not decrease by more than $15,000 per year. ◆

Alimony recapture is required if payments decrease by more than $15,000 between years. Step 1 in the alimony recapture computation is to determine the decrease from Year 2 to Year 3. Year 2 alimony is recaptured to the extent this decrease exceeds $15,000. Step 2 requires that the *average* payments for Years 2 and 3 be compared with the Year 1 payment. For this computation, *revised* alimony for Year 2 is used. Revised alimony is equal to the amount of alimony deducted by the payer in Year 2 minus the amount of Year 2 alimony that is recaptured in step 1. The excess of Year 1 alimony over average alimony for Years 2 and 3 is recaptured to the extent that it exceeds $15,000.

EXAMPLE 30

Wes and Rita enter into a post-1986 divorce decree under which Rita is to receive alimony payments of $60,000 in Year 1, $40,000 in Year 2, and $20,000 in Year 3.

Step 1: Year 2 alimony recapture:	
Year 2 alimony	$40,000
Minus: Year 3 alimony	20,000
Decrease	$20,000
Minus: Allowable decrease	15,000
Year 2 alimony recapture	$ 5,000
Step 2: Year 1 alimony recapture:	
Year 1 alimony	$60,000
Minus: Average of revised Year 2 alimony and Year 3 alimony*	27,500
Decrease	$32,500
Minus: Allowable decrease	15,000
Year 1 alimony recapture	$17,500

*[($40,000 Year 2 alimony – $5,000 recaptured) + $20,000 Year 3 alimony] divided by 2.

The total amount of alimony recaptured is $22,500 ($5,000 of Year 2 payments + $17,500 of Year 1 payments). ◆

Post-1984 agreements are not subject to alimony recapture if the decrease in payments is due to the death of either spouse or the remarriage of the payee because these events typically terminate alimony under state law. In addition, the recapture rules do not apply to payments that are contingent in amount (e.g., a percentage of income from certain property or a percentage of the payer spouse's compensation), are to be made over a period of three years or longer (unless death, remarriage, or other contingency occurs), and involve contingencies beyond the payer's control.

EXAMPLE 31

Under a 1992 divorce agreement, Emilio was to receive an amount equal to one-half of Sharon's income from certain rental properties for 1992–1995. Payments were to cease upon the death of Emilio or Sharon or upon the remarriage of Emilio. Emilio received $50,000 in 1992 and $50,000 in 1993; however in 1994, the property was vacant, and Emilio received nothing. Sharon, who deducted alimony in 1992 and 1993, is not required to recapture any alimony in 1994 because the payments were contingent. ◆

Pre-1985 Agreements and Decrees. Alimony payments were subject to a different set of rules before 1985. Because payments will continue to be made under pre-1985 agreements for many years, these provisions continue to apply to certain taxpayers. In these situations, it will be necessary to review pre-1985 law.

Child Support. A taxpayer does not realize income from the receipt of child support payments made by his or her former spouse. This result occurs because the money is received subject to the duty to use the money for the child's benefit. The payer is not allowed to deduct the child support payments because the payments are made to satisfy the payer's legal obligation to support the child.

In many cases, it is difficult to determine whether an amount received is alimony or child support. Under post-1984 law, if the amount of payments to the former spouse is reduced upon the happening of a contingency related to a child (e.g., the child attains the age of 21 or dies), the amount of the future reduction in the payment will be deemed child support, rather than alimony.

EXAMPLE 32

Matt is required to make alimony payments of $500 per month to Grace. However, when Matt and Grace's child reaches age 21, marries, or dies (whichever occurs first), the payments will be reduced to $300 per month. Grace has custody of the child. Under post-1984 rules, $200 per month is treated as child support, and $300 is treated as alimony. ◆

Imputed Interest on Below-Market Loans

As discussed earlier in the chapter, generally no income is recognized unless it is realized. Realization generally occurs when the taxpayer performs services or sells goods and thus becomes entitled to a payment from the other party. It follows that no income is realized if the goods or services are provided at no charge. Under this interpretation of the realization requirement, before 1984, interest-free loans were used to shift income between taxpayers.

EXAMPLE 33

Veneia (daughter) is in the 20% tax bracket and has no investment income. Kareem (father) is in the 50% tax bracket and has $200,000 in a money market account earning 10% interest. Kareem would like Veneia to receive and pay tax on the income earned on the $200,000. Because Kareem would also like to have access to the $200,000 should he need the money, he does not want to make an outright gift of the money, nor does he want to commit the money to a trust.

Before 1984, Kareem could achieve his goals as follows. He could transfer the money market account to Veneia in exchange for her $200,000 non-interest-bearing note, payable on Kareem's demand. As a result, Veneia would receive the income, and the family's taxes would be decreased by $6,000.

Decrease in Kareem's tax—	
(.10 × $200,000).50 =	($10,000)
Increase in Veneia's tax—	
(.10 × $200,000).20 =	4,000
Decrease in the family's taxes	($ 6,000)

◆

Under the 1984 amendments to the Code, Kareem in Example 33 is required to recognize imputed interest income. Also, Veneia is deemed to have incurred interest expense equal to Kareem's imputed interest income. Veneia's interest may be deductible on her return as investment interest if she itemizes deductions (see Chapter 10). To complete the fictitious series of transactions, Kareem is then deemed to have given Veneia the amount of the imputed interest she did not pay. The gift received by Veneia is not subject to income tax (see Chapter 4), although Kareem may be subject to the unified transfer tax on the amount deemed to be a gift to Veneia (see Chapter 26).

Imputed interest is calculated using the rate the Federal government pays on new borrowings and is compounded semiannually. This Federal rate is adjusted monthly and is published by the IRS. Actually, there are three Federal rates: short-term (not over three years and including demand loans), mid-term (over three years but not over nine years), and long-term (over nine years).

Example 34

Assume the Federal rate applicable to the loan in Example 33 is 7% through June 30 and 8% from July 1 through December 31. Kareem made the loan on January 1, and the loan is still outstanding on December 31. Kareem must recognize interest income of $15,280, and Veneia has interest expense of $15,280. Kareem is deemed to have made a gift of $15,280 to Veneia.

Interest calculations	
January 1–June 30—	
.07 ($200,000) (½ year)	$ 7,000
July 1–December 31—	
.08 ($200,000 + $7,000)(½ year)	8,280
	$15,280

◆

If interest is charged on the loan but is less than the Federal rate, the imputed interest is the difference between the amount that would have been charged at the Federal rate and the amount actually charged.

Example 35

Assume the same facts as in Example 33, except that Kareem charged 6% interest, compounded annually.

Interest at the Federal rate	$ 15,280
Less interest charged (.06 × $200,000)	(12,000)
Imputed interest	$ 3,280

◆

The imputed interest rules apply to the following *types* of below-market loans:

1. Gift loans (made out of love, affection, or generosity, as in Example 33).
2. Compensation-related loans (employer loans to employees).
3. Corporation-shareholder loans (a corporation's loans to its shareholders).

The effects of these types of loans on the borrower and lender are summarized in Concept Summary 3–2.

Exceptions and Limitations. No interest is imputed on total outstanding *gift loans* of $10,000 or less between individuals, unless the loan proceeds are used to purchase income-producing property. This exemption eliminates from these complex provisions immaterial amounts that do not result in apparent shifts of income. However, if the proceeds of such a loan are used to purchase income-producing property, the limitations discussed in the following paragraphs apply.

On loans of $100,000 or less between individuals, the imputed interest cannot exceed the borrower's net investment income for the year (gross income from *all* investments less the related expenses). As discussed above, one of the purposes of the imputed interest rules is to prevent high-bracket taxpayers from shifting income to relatives in a lower marginal bracket. This shifting of investment income is considered to occcur only to the extent the borrower has investment income. Thus, the income imputed to the lender is limited to the borrower's net investment income. As a further limitation, or exemption, if the borrower's net investment income for the year does not exceed $1,000, no interest is imputed on loans of $100,000 or less.

EXAMPLE 36

Vicki made interest-free gift loans as follows:

Borrower	Amount	Borrower's Net Investment Income	Purpose
Susan	$ 8,000	$ –0–	Education
Dan	9,000	500	Purchase of stock
Bonnie	25,000	–0–	Purchase of a business
Megan	90,000	15,000	Purchase of a residence
Olaf	120,000	–0–	Purchase of a residence

Assume that tax avoidance is not a principal purpose of any of the loans. The loan to Susan is not subject to the imputed interest rules because the $10,000 exception applies. The $10,000 exception does not apply to the loan to Dan because the proceeds were used to purchase income-producing assets. However, under the $100,000 exception, the imputed interest is limited to Dan's investment income ($500). Since the $1,000 exception also applies to this loan, no interest will be imputed.

No interest is imputed on the loan to Bonnie because the $100,000 exception applies. Interest will be imputed on the loan to Megan based on the lesser of (1) the borrower's $15,000 net investment income or (2) the interest as calculated by applying the Federal rate to the outstanding loan. None of the exceptions apply to the loan to Olaf because the loan was for more than $100,000.

CONCEPT SUMMARY 3–2
EFFECT OF CERTAIN BELOW-MARKET LOANS ON THE LENDER AND BORROWER

Type of Loan		Lender	Borrower
Gift	Step 1	Interest income	Interest expense
	Step 2	Gift made	Gift received
Compensation-related	Step 1	Interest income	Interest expense
	Step 2	Compensation expense	Compensation income
Corporation to shareholder	Step 1	Interest income	Interest expense
	Step 2	Dividend paid	Dividend income

Assume the relevant Federal rate is 10% and the loans were outstanding for the entire year. Vicki would recognize interest income, compounded semiannually, as follows:

Loan to Megan:	
First 6 months (.10)($90,000)(6/12)	$ 4,500
Second 6 months (.10)($90,000 + $4,500)(6/12)	4,725
	$ 9,225
Loan to Olaf:	
First 6 months (.10)($120,000)(6/12)	$ 6,000
Second 6 months (.10)($120,000 + $6,000)(6/12)	6,300
	$12,300
Total imputed interest ($9,225 + $12,300)	$21,525

◆

As with gift loans, there is a $10,000 exemption for *compensation-related* loans and *corporation-shareholder* loans. However, the $10,000 exception does not apply if tax avoidance is one of the principal purposes of a loan. This vague tax avoidance standard makes practically all compensation-related and corporation-shareholder loans suspect. Nevertheless, the $10,000 exception should apply when an employee's borrowing is necessitated by personal needs (e.g., to meet unexpected expenses) rather than tax considerations.

Tax Avoidance and Other Below-Market Loans. In addition to the three specific types of loans that are subject to the imputed interest rules, the Code provides a catchall provision for *tax avoidance loans* and other arrangements that have a significant effect on the tax liability of the borrower or lender. The Conference Report provides an example of an arrangement that might be subject to the imputed interest rules.[20]

CONCEPT SUMMARY 3–3
EXCEPTIONS TO THE IMPUTED INTEREST RULES FOR BELOW-MARKET LOANS

Exception	Eligible Loans	Ineligible Loans and Limitations
De minimis—aggregate loans of $10,000 or less	Gift loans	Proceeds used to purchase income-producing assets.
	Employer-employee	Principal purpose is tax avoidance.
	Corporation-shareholder	Principal purpose is tax avoidance.
Aggregate loans of $100,000 or less	Between individuals	Principal purpose is tax avoidance. For all other loans, interest is imputed to the extent of the borrower's net investment income (NII), if the borrower's NII exceeds $1,000.

20. H. Rep. No. 98–861, 98th Cong., 2d Sess., 1984, p. 1023.

EXAMPLE 37

Annual dues for the Goode Health Club are $400. In lieu of paying dues, a member can make a $4,000 deposit, refundable at the end of one year. The club can earn $400 interest on the deposit.

If interest were not imputed, an individual with $4,000 could, in effect, earn tax-exempt income on the deposit. That is, rather than invest the $4,000, earn $400 in interest, pay tax on the interest, and then pay $400 in dues, the individual could avoid tax on the interest by making the deposit. Thus, income and expenses are imputed as follows: interest income and nondeductible health club fees for the club member; income from fees and interest expense for the club. ◆

Many commercially motivated transactions could be swept into this below-market loans category. However, the temporary Regulations have carved out a frequently encountered exception for customer prepayments. If the prepayments are included in the recipient's income under the recipient's method of accounting, the payments are not considered loans and, thus, are not subject to the imputed interest rules.[21]

EXAMPLE 38

Landlord, a cash basis taxpayer, charges tenants a damage deposit equal to one month's rent on residential apartments. When the tenant enters into the lease, the landlord also collects rent for the last month of the lease.

The prepaid rent for the last month of the lease is taxed in the year received and thus is not considered a loan. The security deposit is not taxed when received and is therefore a candidate for imputed interest. However, neither the landlord nor the tenant derives an apparent tax benefit, and thus the security deposit should not be subject to the imputed interest provisions. But if making the deposit would reduce the rent paid by the tenant, the tenant could derive a tax benefit, much the same as the club member in Example 37. ◆

Limitations for loans of $100,000 or less do not apply if a principal purpose of a loan is tax avoidance. If a principal purpose of a loan is to shift income to a taxpayer in a lower tax bracket (as illustrated in Example 33), the purpose is a proscribed one. Therefore, in such a case, interest is imputed, and the imputed interest is not limited to the borrower's net investment income.

Income from Annuities

Annuity contracts generally require the purchaser (the annuitant) to pay a fixed amount for the right to receive a future stream of payments. Typically, the issuer of the contract is an insurance company and will pay the annuitant a cash value if the annuitant cancels the contract. The insurance company invests the amounts received from the annuitant, and the income earned increases the cash value of the policy. No income is recognized at the time the cash value of the annuity increases because the taxpayer has not actually received any income.

The tax accounting problem associated with receiving payments under an annuity contract involves apportioning the amounts received between recovery of capital and income. The rules differ depending on whether collections start on or after the annuity starting date or before the annuity starting date.

Collections on and after the Annuity Starting Date. The annuitant can exclude from income (as a recovery of capital) the proportion of each payment that the

21. Temp. Reg. § 1.7872–2(b)(l)(i).

investment in the contract bears to the expected return under the contract. The *exclusion amount* is calculated as follows:

$$\frac{\text{Investment}}{\text{Expected return}} \times \text{Annuity payment} = \text{Exclusion amount}$$

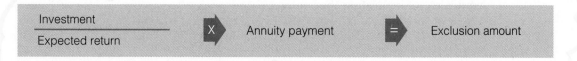

The *expected return* is the annual amount to be paid to the annuitant multiplied by the number of years the payments will be received. The payment period may be fixed (a *term certain*) or for the life of one or more individuals. When payments are for life, the taxpayer must use the annuity table published by the IRS to determine the expected return (see Figure 3–1). This is an actuarial table that contains life expectancies.[22] The expected return is calculated by multiplying the appropriate multiple (life expectancy) by the annual payment.

EXAMPLE 39

Carl, age 54, purchases an annuity from an insurance company for $90,000. He is to receive $500 per month for life. His life expectancy (from Figure 3–1) is 29.5 years from the annuity starting date. Thus, his expected return is $500 × 12 × 29.5 = $177,000, and the exclusion amount is $3,051 [($90,000 investment/$177,000 expected return) × $6,000 annual payment]. The $3,051 is a nontaxable return of capital, and $2,949 is included in gross income. ◆

The exclusion ratio (investment ÷ expected return) applies until the annuitant has recovered his or her investment in the contract. Once the investment is recovered, the entire amount of subsequent payments is taxable.

Collections before the Annuity Starting Date. Generally, an annuity contract specifies a date on which monthly or annual payments will begin—the annuity starting date. Often the contract will also allow the annuitant to collect a limited amount before the starting date. The amount collected may be characterized as either an actual withdrawal of the increase in cash value or a loan on the policy. In 1982, Congress changed the rules applicable to these withdrawals and loans.

Collections (including loans) equal to or less than the post–August 13, 1982, increases in cash value must be included in gross income. Amounts received in excess of post–August 13, 1982, increases in cash value are treated as a recovery of capital until the taxpayer's cost has been entirely recovered. Additional amounts are included in gross income. The taxpayer may also be subject to a penalty on early distributions of 10 percent of the income recognized. The penalty generally applies if the amount is received before the taxpayer reaches age 59 ½ or is disabled.

EXAMPLE 40

Juan, age 50, purchased an annuity policy for $30,000 in 1992. In 1994, when the cash value of the policy has increased to $33,000, he withdraws $4,000. Juan must recognize $3,000 of income ($33,000 cash value – $30,000 cost) and must pay a penalty of $300 ($3,000 × 10%). The remaining $1,000 is a recovery of capital and reduces his basis in the annuity policy. ◆

22. The life expectancies in Figure 3–1 apply for annuity investments made on or after July 1, 1986. See *Pension and Annuity Income,* IRS Publication 575 (Rev. Nov. 87), pp. 22–24 for the IRS table to use for investments made before July 1, 1986.

The 1982 rules were enacted because Congress perceived that the recovery of capital rule was being abused. Previously, individuals could purchase annuity contracts that guaranteed an annual increase in cash value and withdraw the equivalent of interest on the contract but recognize no income. This is no longer possible. In addition, the individual must recognize income from borrowing on the contract (e.g., pledging the contract as security for a loan) as well as from an actual distribution.

Prizes and Awards

Before 1954, the taxability of prizes and awards was not always clear. Taxpayers often sought to treat prizes and awards as nontaxable gifts. In many situations, it

FIGURE 3–1
Ordinary Life Annuities: One Life–Expected Return Multiples

Age	Multiple	Age	Multiple	Age	Multiple
5	76.6	42	40.6	79	10.0
6	75.6	43	39.6	80	9.5
7	74.7	44	38.7	81	8.9
8	73.7	45	37.7	82	8.4
9	72.7	46	36.8	83	7.9
10	71.7	47	35.9	84	7.4
11	70.7	48	34.9	85	6.9
12	69.7	49	34.0	86	6.5
13	68.8	50	33.1	87	6.1
14	67.8	51	32.2	88	5.7
15	66.8	52	31.3	89	5.3
16	65.8	53	30.4	90	5.0
17	64.8	54	29.5	91	4.7
18	63.9	55	28.6	92	4.4
19	62.9	56	27.7	93	4.1
20	61.9	57	26.8	94	3.9
21	60.9	58	25.9	95	3.7
22	59.9	59	25.0	96	3.4
23	59.0	60	24.2	97	3.2
24	58.0	61	23.3	98	3.0
25	57.0	62	22.5	99	2.8
26	56.0	63	21.6	100	2.7
27	55.1	64	20.8	101	2.5
28	54.1	65	20.0	102	2.3
29	53.1	66	19.2	103	2.1
30	52.2	67	18.4	104	1.9
31	51.2	68	17.6	105	1.8
32	50.2	69	16.8	106	1.6
33	49.3	70	16.0	107	1.4
34	48.3	71	15.3	108	1.3
35	47.3	72	14.6	109	1.1
36	46.4	73	13.9	110	1.0
37	45.4	74	13.2	111	.9
38	44.4	75	12.5	112	.8
39	43.5	76	11.9	113	.7
40	42.5	77	11.2	114	.6
41	41.5	78	10.6	115	.5

was difficult to determine whether the prize or award was in the nature of a gift. In 1954, Congress added § 74 to eliminate this uncertainty.

The fair market value of prizes and awards must be included in income. Therefore, TV giveaway prizes, door prizes, and awards from an employer to an employee in recognition of performance are fully taxable to the recipient.

An exception permits a prize or award to be excluded from gross income if all of the following requirements are satisfied:

- The prize or award is received in recognition of religious, charitable, scientific, educational, artistic, literary, or civic achievement.
- The organization that gives the prize or award pays it directly to a qualified governmental unit or nonprofit organization.
- The recipient was selected without any action on his or her part to enter the contest or proceeding.
- The recipient is not required to render substantial future services as a condition for receiving the prize or award.

Because the transfer of the property to a qualified governmental unit or nonprofit organization ordinarily would be a charitable contribution (an itemized deduction as discussed in Chapter 10), the exclusion produces beneficial tax consequences in the following situations:

- The taxpayer does not itemize deductions and thus would receive no tax benefit from the charitable contribution.
- The taxpayer's charitable contributions exceed the annual statutory ceiling on the deduction.
- Including the prize or award in gross income would reduce the amount of deductions the taxpayer otherwise would qualify for because of gross income limitations (e.g., the adjusted gross income floor in calculating the medical expense deduction).

Certain employee achievement awards in the form of tangible personal property (e.g., a gold watch) may be excluded from gross income. The awards must be made in recognition of length of service or safety achievement. Generally, the ceiling on the excludible amount is $400. However, if the award is a qualified plan award, the ceiling on the exclusion is $1,600.

Group Term Life Insurance

Before 1964, the IRS did not attempt to tax the value of life insurance protection provided to an employee by the employer. Some companies took undue advantage of the exclusion by providing large amounts of insurance protection for executives. Therefore, Congress enacted § 79, which created a limited exclusion. Current law allows an exclusion for premiums on the first $50,000 of group term life insurance protection.

The benefits of this exclusion are available only to employees. Proprietors and partners are not considered employees. Moreover, the Regulations generally require broad-scale coverage of employees to satisfy the *group* requirement (e.g., shareholder-employees would not constitute a qualified group). The exclusion applies only to term insurance (protection for a period of time but with no cash surrender value) and not to ordinary life insurance (lifetime protection plus a cash surrender value that can be drawn upon before death).

As mentioned, the exclusion applies to the first $50,000 of group term life insurance protection. For each $1,000 coverage in excess of $50,000, the employee must include the amounts shown in Figure 3–2 in gross income.

EXAMPLE 41

XYZ Corporation has a group term life insurance policy with coverage equal to the employee's annual salary. Anna, age 52, is president of the corporation and receives an annual salary of $75,000. Anna must include $144 in gross income from the insurance protection for the year.

$$\left(\frac{\$75{,}000 - \$50{,}000}{\$1{,}000}\right) \times .48 \times 12 \text{ months} = \$144$$

◆

If a group term insurance plan discriminates in favor of certain key employees (e.g., officers), the key employees are not eligible for the exclusion. In that case, the key employees must include in gross income the greater of actual premiums paid by the employer or the amount calculated from the Uniform Premiums table. The other employees are still eligible for the $50,000 exclusion and continue to use the Uniform Premiums table to compute the income from excess insurance protection.

Unemployment Compensation

Many employers are required to make FUTA contributions (refer to Chapter 1) to provide for unemployment compensation for their employees. Such unemployment compensation is included in gross income by the recipient.

Social Security Benefits

If a taxpayer's income exceeds a specified base amount, as much as one-half of Social Security retirement benefits must be included in gross income. The taxable amount of Social Security benefits is the *lesser* of the following:

- .50(Social Security benefits)
- .50[modified adjusted gross income + .50(Social Security benefits) – base amount]

Modified adjusted gross income is, generally, the taxpayer's adjusted gross income from all sources (other than Social Security), plus the foreign earned

FIGURE 3–2
Uniform Premiums for $1,000 of Group Term Life Insurance Protection

Attained Age Last Day of the Employee's Tax Year	Cost per $1,000 of Protection for One-Month Period
Under 30	8 cents
30–34	9 cents
35–39	11 cents
40–44	17 cents
45–49	29 cents
50–54	48 cents
55–59	75 cents
60–64	$1.17
65–69	$2.10
70 and over	$3.76

income exclusion and any tax-exempt interest received. The *base amount* is as follows:

- $32,000 for married taxpayers who file a joint return.
- $0 for married taxpayers who do not live apart for the entire year but file separate returns.
- $25,000 for all other taxpayers.

Example 42

A married couple filing jointly with adjusted gross income of $40,000, no tax-exempt interest, and $11,000 of Social Security benefits must include one-half of the benefits in gross income. This works out as the lesser of the following:

1. .50($11,000) = $5,500
2. .50[$40,000 + .50($11,000) – $32,000] = .50($13,500) = $6,750

If the couple's adjusted gross income were $15,000 and their Social Security benefits totaled $5,000, none of the benefits would be taxable since .50[$15,000 + .50($5,000) – $32,000] is not a positive number. ◆

Tax Planning Considerations

The materials in this chapter have focused on the following questions:

- What is income?
- When is the income recognized?
- Who is the taxpayer?

Planning strategies suggested by these materials include the following:

- Maximize economic benefits that are not included in gross income.
- Defer the recognition of income.
- Shift income to taxpayers who are in a lower marginal tax bracket.

Some specific techniques for accomplishing these strategies are discussed in the following paragraphs.

Nontaxable Economic Benefits

Home ownership is the prime example of economic income from capital that is not subject to tax. If a taxpayer uses capital to purchase investments, but pays rent on a personal residence, he or she will pay the rent from after-tax income. However, if the taxpayer purchases a personal residence instead of the investments, he or she will give up gross income from the forgone investments in exchange for the rent savings. The rent saved as a result of owning the home is not subject to tax. Thus, the homeowner will have substituted nontaxable for taxable income.

Tax Deferral

General. Since deferred taxes are tantamount to interest-free loans from the government, the deferral of taxes is a worthy goal of the tax planner. However, the tax planner must also consider the tax rates for the years the income is shifted from and to. For example, a one-year deferral of income from a year in which the taxpayer's tax rate was 15 percent to a year in which the tax rate will be 28 percent would not be advisable if the taxpayer expects to earn less than a 13 percent after-tax return on the deferred tax dollars.

The taxpayer can often defer the recognition of income from appreciated property by postponing the event triggering realization (the final closing on a sale or exchange of property). If the taxpayer needs cash, obtaining a loan by using the appreciated property as collateral may be the least costly alternative. When the taxpayer anticipates reinvesting the proceeds, a sale may be inadvisable.

EXAMPLE 43

Ira owns 100 shares of Brown Company common stock with a cost of $20,000 and a fair market value of $50,000. Although the stock's value has increased substantially in the past three years, Ira thinks the growth days are over. If he sells the Brown stock, Ira will invest the proceeds from the sale in other common stock. Assuming Ira is in the 28% marginal tax bracket, he will have only $41,600 [$50,000 – .28($50,000 – $20,000)] to reinvest. The alternative investment must substantially outperform Brown stock in the future in order for the sale to be beneficial. ◆

Selection of Investments. Because no tax is due until a gain has been recognized, the law favors investments that yield appreciation rather than annual income.

EXAMPLE 44

Vera can buy a corporate bond or an acre of land for $10,000. The bond pays $1,000 of interest (10%) each year, and Vera expects the land to increase in value 10% each year for the next 10 years. She is in the 40% (combined Federal and state) tax bracket. Assuming the bond will mature or the land will be sold in 10 years and Vera will reinvest the interest at a 10% before-tax return, she would accumulate the following amount at the end of 10 years.

		Bonds	Land
Original investment		$10,000	$10,000
Annual income	$1,000		
Less tax	(400)		
	$ 600		
Compound amount reinvested for 10 years at 6% after-tax	×13.18	7,908	
		$17,908	
Compound amount, 10 years at 10%			×2.59
			$25,900
Less tax on sale: 40%($25,900–$10,000)			(6,360)
			$19,540

Therefore, the value of the deferral that results from investing in the land rather than in the bond is $1,632 ($19,540 – $17,908). ◆

Series EE bonds can also be purchased for long-term deferrals of income. As discussed in the chapter, Series E bonds can be exchanged for new Series HH bonds to further postpone the tax. In situations where the taxpayer's goal is merely to shift income one year into the future, bank certificates of deposit are useful tools. If the maturity period is one year or less, all interest is reported in the year of maturity. Time certificates are especially useful for a taxpayer who realizes an unusually large gain from the sale of property in one year (and thus is in a high tax bracket) but expects his or her income to be less the following year.

Cash Basis. The timing of income from services can often be controlled through the use of the cash method of accounting. Although taxpayers are somewhat constrained by the constructive receipt doctrine (they cannot turn their backs on income), seldom will customers and clients offer to pay before they are asked. The usual lag between billings and collections (e.g., December's billings collected in January) will result in a continuous deferring of some income until the last year of operations. A salaried individual approaching retirement may contract with his or her employer before the services are rendered to receive a portion of the compensation in the lower tax bracket retirement years.

Prepaid Income. For the accrual basis taxpayer who receives advance payments from customers, the transactions should be structured to avoid payment of tax on income before the time the income is actually earned. Revenue Procedure 71–21 provides the guidelines for deferring the tax on prepayments for services, and Reg. § 1.451–5 provides the guidelines for deferrals on sales of goods. In addition, both the cash and accrual basis taxpayer can sometimes defer income by stipulating that the payments are deposits rather than prepaid income. For example, a landlord should require an equivalent damage deposit rather than prepayment of the last month's rent under the lease.

Shifting Income to Relatives

The tax liability of a family can be minimized by shifting income from higher-bracket to lower-bracket family members. This can be accomplished through gifts of income-producing property. Furthermore, in many cases, the shifting of income can be accomplished with no negative effect on the family's investment plans.

Example 45

Adam, who is in the 28% tax bracket, would like to save for his children's education. All of the children are under 14 years of age. Adam could transfer income-producing properties to the children, and the children could each receive income of up to $600 each year (refer to Chapter 2) with no tax liability. The next $600 would be taxed at the child's tax rate. After a child has more than $1,200 income, there is no tax advantage to shifting more income to the child (because the income will be taxed at the parents' rate) until the child is 14 years old (when all income will be taxed at the child's tax rate). ◆

The Uniform Gifts to Minors Act, a model law adopted by all states (but with some variations among the states), facilitates income shifting. Under the Act, a gift of intangibles (e.g., bank accounts, stocks, bonds, life insurance contracts) can be made to a minor but with an adult serving as custodian. Usually, a parent who makes the gift is also named as custodian. The state laws allow the custodian to sell or redeem and reinvest the principal and to accumulate or distribute the income, practically at the custodian's discretion provided there is no commingling of the child's income with the parent's property. Thus, the parent can give appreciated securities to the child, and the donor custodian can then sell the securities and reinvest the proceeds, thereby shifting both the gain and annual income to the child. Such planning is limited by the tax liability calculation provision for a child under the age of 14 (refer to Chapter 2).

A parent can purchase U.S. government bonds (Series EE) for his or her children. When this is done, the children generally should file a return and elect to report the income on the accrual basis.

EXAMPLE 46

Abby pays $7,500 for Series EE bonds in 1993 and immediately gives them to Wade (her son), who will enter college the year of original maturity of the bonds. The bonds have a maturity value of $10,000. Wade elects to report the annual increment in redemption value as income for each year the bonds are held. The first year the increase is $250, and Wade includes that amount in his gross income. If Wade has no other income, no tax will be due on the $250 bond interest since such an amount will be more than offset by his available standard deduction. The following year, the increment is $260, and Wade includes this amount in income. Thus, over the life of the bonds, Wade will include $2,500 in income ($10,000 – $7,500), none of which will result in a tax liability, assuming he has no other income. However, if the election had not been made, Wade would be required to include $2,500 in income on the bonds in the year of original maturity, if they were redeemed as planned. This amount of income might result in a tax liability. ◆

In some cases, it may be advantageous for the child not to make the accrual election. For example, a child under age 14 with investment income of more than $1,200 each year and parents in the 28 percent tax bracket would probably benefit from deferring the tax on the savings bond interest. The child would also benefit from the use of the usually lower tax rate (rather than subjecting the income to his or her parents' tax rate) if the bonds mature after the child is age 14 or older.

Alimony

The person making alimony payments favors a divorce settlement that includes a provision for deductible alimony payments. On the other hand, the recipient prefers that the payments do not qualify as alimony. If the payer is in a higher tax bracket than the recipient, both parties may benefit by increasing the payments and structuring them so that they qualify as alimony.

EXAMPLE 47

Carl and Polly are negotiating a divorce settlement. Carl has offered to pay Polly $10,000 each year for 10 years, but payments would cease upon Polly's death. Polly is willing to accept the offer, if the agreement will specify that the cash payments are not alimony. Carl is in the 31% tax bracket, and Polly's marginal rate is 15%.

If Carl and Polly agree that Carl will pay her $12,000 of alimony each year, Polly as well as Carl will have improved after-tax cash flows.

	Annual Cash Flows	
	Carl	**Polly**
Nonalimony payments	$(10,000)	$10,000
Alimony payments	$(12,000)	$12,000
Tax effects		
.31($12,000)	3,720	
.15($12,000)		(1,800)
After-tax cash flows	$ (8,280)	$10,200
Benefit of alimony option	$ 1,720	$ 200

Both parties benefit at the government's expense if the $12,000 alimony option is used. ◆

PROBLEM MATERIALS

DISCUSSION QUESTIONS

1. Which of the following would be considered "income" for the current year by an economist but would not be gross income for tax purposes? Explain.
   a. Securities acquired two years ago for $10,000 had a value at the beginning of the current year of $12,000 and a value at the end of the year of $13,000.
   b. An individual lives in the home he owns.
   c. A corporation obtained a loan from a bank.
   d. A shareholder paid a corporation $3,000 for property worth $5,000.
   e. An individual owned property that was stolen. The cost of the property three years ago was $2,000, and an insurance company paid the owner $6,000 (the value of the property on the date of theft).
   f. An individual found a box of seventeenth-century Spanish coins while diving off the Virginia coast.
   g. An individual received a $200 rebate from the manufacturer upon the purchase of a new car.
2. According to economists, because our tax system does not impute income to homeowners for the rental value of their homes, the nonhomeowner who invests in securities (rather than a home) is taxed more heavily than the homeowner. This leads to overinvesting in homes. Why do you suppose the laws are not changed to tax homeowners on the rental value of their homes?
3. Evaluate the following alternative proposals for taxing the income from property:
   a. All assets would be valued at the end of the year, any increase in value that occurred during the year would be included in gross income, and any decrease in value would be deductible from gross income.
   b. No gain or loss would be recognized until the taxpayer sold or exchanged the property.
   c. Increases or decreases in the value of property traded on a national exchange (e.g., the New York Stock Exchange) would be reflected in gross income for the years the changes in value occurred. For all other assets, no gain or loss would be recognized until the property was sold or exchanged.
4. Able Utility Corporation's common stock pays $1 per share in dividends. However, the stock is highly unlikely to increase in value because Able is regulated by a public utility commission that will not allow the company to increase its charges to customers. In addition, market interest rates are not expected to decrease. Baker Technology Corporation does not pay any dividends, but the prospects for increases in the value of the stock are excellent because of the company's new products. How might the realization requirement of the income tax law affect an investor's decision between Able and Baker stock?
5. Leif had owned a tract of land for several years when the local government decided to build an airport near the property. The cost of the property to Leif was $50,000. The local government paid Leif $10,000 for invasion of his airspace. What is Leif's gross income from the receipt of the $10,000?
6. A corporation pays all of its monthly salaried employees on the last Friday in each month. What would be the tax consequences to the employees if the date of payment were changed to the first Monday of the following month?
7. LMN, Inc., receives all of its income from repairing computers. The company reports its income by the cash method. On December 31, an employee went to a customer's office and repaired a computer. The customer gave LMN's employee a check for $300, but the employee did not remit the check to LMN until January of the following year. When is LMN required to recognize the income?

8. Marta is a cash basis surgeon who is usually paid through claims filed with insurance companies. Normally, it takes 60 days from the date of an operation until the charge is collected. What would be the consequences if Marta were required to change to the accrual method of accounting?
9. Is a cash basis taxpayer ever taxed on income before cash or its equivalent is actually or constructively received?
10. Pat, an accrual basis taxpayer, performed services for a customer in 1993. Pat's total charge was $500, and the customer paid $200 when the work was begun. When Pat completed the services, the customer refused to pay the balance due of $300. In addition, at the end of 1993, the customer filed a lawsuit against Pat for the return of the $200 because the customer claimed Pat's work did not meet contract specifications. The suit was settled in 1994 when the customer paid an additional $100. What is Pat's 1993 income from the contract?
11. In 1993, Nora, an accrual basis taxpayer, rendered services for a customer with a poor credit rating. Nora's charge for the service was $1,000. Nora sent a bill to the customer for $1,000 but reported only $500 of income. She justified reporting only $500 as follows: "I'm being generous reporting $500. I'll be lucky if I collect anything." How much should Nora include as gross income from the contract in 1993?
12. In January 1993, Carol, a cash basis taxpayer, purchased for $2,000 a five-year Series EE U.S. government bond with a maturity value of $3,000. She also purchased for $2,000 a three-year bank certificate of deposit with a maturity value of $2,500. Is Carol required to recognize any interest income in 1993?
13. Quinn (father) paid $200 for an automobile that needed repairs. He worked nights and weekends to restore the car. Several individuals offered to purchase the car for $2,800. Quinn gave the car and a list of potential buyers to Ron (son), whose college tuition was due in a few days. Ron sold the car for $2,800 and paid his tuition. Does Quinn have any taxable income from the transaction?
14. Olga, a cash basis taxpayer, sold a bond with accrued interest of $750, for $10,250. Her basis in the bond was $9,000. Compute Olga's income from this transaction.
15. Father gave Son 100 shares of PDQ Corporation stock on June 20. PDQ Corporation had declared a $1 per share dividend on the stock on June 15, payable on June 30 to holders of record as of June 25. Who must report the dividend income, Father or Son?
16. Isabella transferred rental properties to a corporation that she owned. Isabella's objective was to minimize her liability for injuries that may occur on the property. The tenants continued to pay rents to Isabella. Who must include the rents in gross income?
17. Who pays the tax on (a) the income of an S corporation and (b) the undistributed income of an estate?
18. What is the purpose of the front-loading rules related to alimony?
19. A post-1984 divorce agreement between Earl and Cora provides that Earl is to pay Cora $500 per month for 13 years. Earl and Cora have a child who is 8 years old. Termination of the monthly payments will coincide with the child's attaining age 21. Can the monthly payments qualify as alimony?
20. Hal and Nancy were divorced. They jointly owned a home in the mountains with a basis of $50,000 and a fair market value of $80,000. According to the terms of the divorce, Nancy gave Hal $40,000 for his one-half interest in the mountain home. Nancy later sold the house for $85,000. What is Nancy's gain from the sale?
21. In the case of a below-market loan between relatives, why is the lender required to recognize income although it is the borrower who appears to receive the economic benefit?
22. Mother loaned $80,000 to Son who used the money to buy a personal residence. Mother did not charge interest on the loan, although the market rate of interest was 8%. Son had investment income of $2,000. Do the imputed interest rules apply?
23. Tim is an employee and the sole shareholder of RST Corporation. The corporation loaned Tim $50,000 and did not charge him interest. The IRS agent imputed interest on the loan, which the agent characterizes as a corporation-shareholder loan. Tim insists that the loan is an employer-employee loan. What difference does it make?

24. Suppose the annuity tables used by the IRS were outdated and that people lived longer than the tables indicated. How would this affect Federal revenues?

25. Discuss the difference in tax treatment, if any, between a taxpayer who wins the Nobel Prize and a taxpayer who is crowned Miss America.

26. Gail is a full-time employee of Purple Corporation. One of the fringe benefits the company offers its employees is group term life insurance protection equal to twice the employee's annual salary. Gail is 32 years old, and her annual salary is $45,000. What is Gail's gross income from the life insurance protection for the year?

27. When a taxpayer is receiving Social Security benefits, could a $1,000 increase in income from services cause the taxpayer's adjusted gross income to increase by more than $1,000?

28. What is the rationale for excluding at least one-half of an individual's Social Security benefits from income?

PROBLEMS

29. Determine the effects of the following on Anne's gross income for the year:

    a. Anne bought a used sofa for $25. After she took the sofa home, she discovered $15,000 in a secret compartment. She was unable to determine who placed the money in the sofa. Therefore, Anne put the money in her bank account.
    b. Anne also discovered oil on her property during the year, and the value of the land increased from $10,000 to $3,000,000.
    c. One year later, Anne found a diamond in the sofa she had purchased. Apparently, the diamond was in the sofa when she purchased it. The value of the diamond was $6,000, and Anne could not determine the former owner.
    d. Anne's bank charges a $3 per month service charge. However, the fee is waived if the customer maintains an average balance for the month of at least $1,000. Anne's account exceeded the minimum deposit requirement, and as a result she was not required to pay any service charges for the year.

30. Compute the taxpayer's (1) economic income and (2) gross income for tax purposes from the following events:

    a. The taxpayer sold securities for $10,000. The securities cost $6,000 in 1989. The fair market value of the securities at the beginning of the year was $12,000.
    b. The taxpayer sold his business and received $15,000 under a covenant not to compete with the new owner.
    c. The taxpayer used her controlled corporation's automobile for her vacation. The rental value of the automobile for the vacation period was $800.
    d. The taxpayer raised vegetables in her garden. The fair market value of the vegetables was $900, and the cost of raising them was $100. She ate some of the vegetables and gave the remainder to neighbors.
    e. The local government changed the zoning ordinances so that some of the taxpayer's residential property was reclassified as commercial. Because of the change, the fair market value of the taxpayer's property increased by $10,000.
    f. During the year, the taxpayer borrowed $50,000 for two years at 9% interest. By the end of the year, interest rates had increased to 12%, and the lender accepted $49,000 in full satisfaction of the debt.

31. Kevin, a cash basis taxpayer, received the following from his employer during 1993:

    - Salary of $70,000.
    - Bonus of $10,000. In 1994, the company determined that the bonus had been incorrectly computed and required Kevin to repay $2,000.
    - Use of a company car for his vacation. Rental value for the period would have been $800. Kevin paid for the gas.
    - $4,000 advance for travel expenses. Kevin had spent only $2,500 at the end of the year.

    Determine the effects of these items on Kevin's gross income.

32. Determine the taxpayer's income for tax purposes in each of the following cases:

   a. In the current year, JKL Corporation purchased $1,000,000 par value of its own bonds and paid the bondholders $980,000 plus $50,000 of accrued interest. The bonds had been issued 10 years ago at par and were to mature 25 years from the date of issue. Does the corporation recognize income from the purchase of the bonds?
   b. A shareholder of a corporation sold property to the corporation for $60,000 (the shareholder's cost). The value of the property on the date of sale was $50,000. Does the taxpayer have any gross income from the sale?
   c. Rex was a football coach at a state university. Because of his disappointing record, he was asked to resign and accept one-half of his pay for the remaining three years of his contract. Rex resigned, accepting $75,000.

33. Which of the following investments will yield the greater after-tax value assuming the taxpayer is in the 40% tax bracket (combined Federal and state) in all years and the investments will be liquidated at the end of five years?

   a. Land that will increase in value by 10% each year.
   b. A taxable bond yielding 10% before tax, and the interest can be reinvested at 10% before tax.
   c. Common stock that will increase in value at the rate of 5% (compounded) each year and pays dividends equal to 5% of the year-end value of the stock. The dividends can be reinvested at 10% before tax.
   d. A tax-exempt state government bond yielding 8%. The interest can be reinvested at a before-tax rate of 10%, and the bond matures in 10 years.

   Given: Compound amount of $1 at the end of five years:

Interest Rate	Factor
6%	1.33
8%	1.47
10%	1.61

   Compound value of annuity payments at the end of five years:

Interest Rate	Factor
6%	5.64
8%	5.87
10%	6.11

34. Determine the taxpayer's income for tax purposes in each of the following cases:

   a. Zelda borrowed $30,000 from the First National Bank. She was required to deliver to the bank stocks with a value of $30,000 and a cost of $10,000. The stocks were to serve as collateral for the loan.
   b. Zelda owned a lot on Sycamore Street that measured 100 feet by 100 feet. The cost of the lot to Zelda is $10,000. The city condemned a 10-foot strip of the land so that it could widen the street. Zelda received a $2,000 condemnation award.
   c. Zelda owned land zoned for residential use only. The land cost $5,000 and had a market value of $7,000. Zelda spent $500 and several hundred hours petitioning the county supervisors to change the zoning to A–1 commercial. The value of the property immediately increased to $20,000 when the county approved the zoning change.

35. Ali is an attorney who conducts his practice as a sole proprietor. During the year, he received cash of $85,000 for legal services rendered. At the beginning of the year, he had fees receivable of $50,000. At the end of the year, he had fees receivable of $40,000. Compute Ali's gross income from his law practice:

   a. Using the cash basis of accounting.
   b. Using the accrual basis of accounting.

36. The taxpayer began operating a grocery store during the year. Her only books and records are based on cash receipts and disbursements, but she has asked you to compute her gross profit from the business for tax purposes.

Sales of merchandise	$260,000
Purchases of merchandise	190,000

You determine that as of the end of the year the taxpayer has accounts payable for merchandise of $9,000 and accounts receivable from customers totaling $1,500. The cost of merchandise on hand at the end of the year was $4,000. Compute the grocery store's accrual method gross profit for the year.

37. Dance, Inc., is a dance studio that sells dance lessons for cash, on open account, and for notes receivable. The company also collects interest on bonds held as an investment. The company's cash receipts for 1993 totaled $219,000:

Cash sales	$ 70,000
Collections on accounts receivable	120,000
Collections on notes receivable	20,000
Interest on bonds	9,000
Total cash receipts	$219,000

The balances in accounts receivable, notes receivable, and accrued interest on bonds at the beginning and end of the year were as follows:

	1-1-93	12-31-93
Accounts receivable	$17,000	$20,000
Notes receivable	9,000	13,000
Accrued interest on bonds	2,500	4,000
	$28,500	$37,000

The fair market value of the notes is equal to 75% of their face amount. There were no bad debts for the year, and all notes were for services performed during the year. Compute the corporation's gross income:

a. Using the cash basis of accounting.
b. Using the accrual basis of accounting.
c. Using a hybrid method—accrual basis for lessons and cash basis for interest income.

38. Determine the effect of the following on the taxpayer's gross income for 1993:

a. Received his paycheck for $3,000 from his employer on December 31, 1993. He deposited the paycheck on January 2, 1994.
b. Received a bonus of $5,000 from his employer on January 10, 1994. The bonus was for the outstanding performance of his division during 1993.
c. Received a dividend check from IBM on November 28, 1993. He mailed the check back to IBM in December requesting that additional IBM stock be issued to him under IBM's dividend reinvestment plan.

39. Mohammed owns a life insurance policy. The cash surrender value of the policy increased $1,500 during the year. He purchased a certificate of deposit on June 30 of the current year for $41,322. The certificate matures in two years when its value will be $50,000 (interest rate of 10%). However, if Mohammed redeems the certificate before the end of the first year, he receives no interest. Mohammed also purchased a Series EE U.S. government savings bond for $6,000. The maturity value of the bond is $10,000 in six years (yield of 9%), and the redemption price of the bond increased by $400 during the year. Mohammed has owned no other savings bonds. What is Mohammed's current year gross income from the above items?

40. ACK, Inc., an accrual basis taxpayer, sells and installs consumer appliances. Determine the effects of each of the following transactions on the company's 1993 gross income:

a. In December 1993, the company received a $1,200 advance payment from a customer. The payment was for an appliance that ACK specially ordered from the manufacturer. The appliance had not arrived at the end of 1993.

b. At the end of 1993, the company installed an appliance and collected the full price of $750 for the item. However, the customer claimed the appliance was defective and asked the company for a refund. The company conceded that the appliance was defective, but claimed that the customer should collect from the manufacturer. The dispute had not been settled by the end of 1993. In early 1994, it was determined that ACK did not install the appliance properly and the company was required to refund the full sales price.

c. At the end of 1993, a customer refused to pay for merchandise delivered in 1992. The customer claimed that the merchandise was defective. In 1993, the company replaced the merchandise at no charge to the customer.

d. The company sold an appliance for $1,200 (plus a market rate of interest) and received the customer's note for that amount. However, because of the customer's poor credit rating, the value of the note was only $700.

41. Freda is a cash basis taxpayer. Determine her 1993 gross income from the following transactions:

a. In 1991, Freda negotiated her 1992 salary. The employer offered to pay her $200,000 in 1992. Freda countered that she wanted $10,000 each month in 1992 and the remaining $80,000 in January 1993. Freda wanted the $80,000 income shifted to 1993 because she expected her 1993 tax rates to be lower. The employer agreed to Freda's terms.

b. In 1992, Freda was running short of cash and needed money for Christmas. Her employer loaned her $20,000 in November 1992. Freda signed a note for $20,000 plus 10% interest, the applicable Federal rate. In January 1993, the employer subtracted the $20,000 and $333 interest from the $80,000 due Freda and paid Freda $59,667.

c. On December 31, 1993, Zina offered to buy land from Freda for $30,000 (Freda's basis was $8,000). Freda refused to sell in 1993, but at that time, she contracted to sell the land to Zina in 1994 for $30,000.

42. The ZZZ Apartments requires its new tenants to pay the rent for the first and last months of the annual lease and a $400 damage deposit, all at the time the lease is signed. In December 1993, a tenant paid $600 for January 1994 rent, $800 for December 1994 rent, and $400 for the damage deposit. In January 1995, ZZZ refunded the tenant's damage deposit. What are the effects of these payments on ZZZ's taxable income for 1993, 1994, and 1995?

a. Assume ZZZ is a cash basis taxpayer.

b. Assume ZZZ is an accrual basis taxpayer.

43. Leo has asked you to review portions of his tax return. He provides you with the following information:

Gain on redemption of a 2-year 7% certificate of deposit		
Proceeds received, June 30, 1993	$10,000	
Purchase price, July 1, 1991	(8,735)	
Gain		$1,265
Gain on redemption of a 6-month 6% certificate of deposit		
Proceeds received, March 31, 1993	$ 5,000	
Purchase price, October 1, 1992	(4,855)	
Gain		$ 145
Gain from 8% Series E savings bond		
Proceeds received, September 30, 1993	$ 2,500	
Purchase price, June 30, 1980	(780)	
Gain		$1,720
Distributions from a family partnership		$1,500

Leo's share of the partnership's earnings were $1,400. Determine Leo's 1993 gross income from the preceding items.

44. a. An automobile dealer has several new cars in inventory but often does not have the right combination of body style, color, and accessories. In some cases, the dealer makes an offer to sell a car at a certain price, accepts a deposit, and then orders the car from the manufacturer. When the car is received from the manufacturer, the sale is closed, and the dealer receives the balance of the sales price. At the end of the current year, the dealer has deposits totaling $8,200 for cars that have not been received from the manufacturer. When is the $8,200 subject to tax?

b. Gray Corporation, an exterminating company, is a calendar year taxpayer. It contracts to provide service to homeowners once a month under a one-year or a two-year contract. On April 1 of the current year, the company sold a customer a one-year contract for $60. How much of the $60 is taxable in the current year if Gray is an accrual basis taxpayer? If the $60 is payment on a two-year contract, how much is taxed in the year the contract is sold?

c. Vera, an accrual basis taxpayer, owns an amusement park whose fiscal year ends September 30. To increase business during the fall and winter months, Vera sells passes that allow the holder to ride free from October through March. During September, Vera collected $6,000 from the sale of passes for the upcoming fall and winter. When will the $6,000 be taxable to Vera?

d. The taxpayer is in the office equipment rental business and uses the accrual basis of accounting. In December, he collected $5,000 in rents for the following January. When is the $5,000 taxable?

45. a. Gus is a cash basis taxpayer. On December 1, 1993, Gus gave a corporate bond to his son, Hans. The bond had a face amount of $10,000 and paid $900 of interest each January 31. Also on December 1, 1993, Gus gave common stocks to his daughter, Dena. Dividends totaling $720 had been declared on the stocks on November 30, 1993, and were payable on January 15, 1994. Dena became the shareholder of record in time to collect the dividends. What is Gus's 1994 gross income from the bond and stocks?

b. In 1993, Gus's mother was unable to pay her bills as they came due. Gus, his employer, and his mother's creditors entered into an arrangement whereby Gus's employer would withhold $500 per month from his salary and would pay the $500 to the creditors. In 1993, $3,000 was withheld from Gus's salary and paid to the creditors. Is Gus required to pay tax on the $3,000?

c. Gus is considering purchasing a zero coupon (no interest is paid until maturity) corporate bond for himself and for his minor son, Hans (age 4). The bonds have an issue price of $300 and pay $1,000 at the end of 10 years. Gus is in the 28% tax bracket, and Hans has no other taxable income. Would the zero coupon bond be an equally suitable investment for Gus and Hans?

46. Tracy, a cash basis taxpayer, is employed by AGA Corporation, also a cash basis taxpayer. Tracy is a full-time employee of the corportion and receives a salary of $60,000 per year. He also receives a bonus equal to 10% of all collections from clients he serviced during the year. Determine the tax consequences of the following events to the corporation and to Tracy:

a. On December 31, 1993, Tracy was visiting a customer. The customer gave Tracy a $3,000 check payable to the corporation for appraisal services Tracy performed during 1993. Tracy did not deliver the check to the corporation until January 1994.

b. The facts are the same as in (a), except that the corporation is an accrual basis taxpayer and Tracy deposited the check on December 31, but the bank did not add the deposit to the corporation's account until January 1994.

c. The facts are the same as in (a), except the customer told Tracy to hold the check until January when the customer could make a bank deposit that would cover the check.

47. Eve, Fran, and Gary each have a one-third interest in the capital and profits of the EFG Partnership. At the beginning of the year, each partner had a $50,000 balance in his or her capital account. The partnership's gross income for the year was $280,000, and its total expenses were $96,000. During the year, Eve contributed an additional $10,000 to the partnership and did not have any withdrawals from her capital account. Fran withdrew $30,000, and Gary withdrew $9,000. Compute each partner's taxable income from the partnership for the year.

48. Nell and Kirby are in the process of negotiating their divorce agreement. What would be the tax consequences to Nell and Kirby if the following, considered individually, become part of the agreement?

 a. Nell is to receive $1,000 per month until she dies or remarries. She also is to receive $500 per month for 12 years for her one-half interest in their personal residence. She paid for her one-half interest in the house out of her earnings.
 b. Nell is to receive a principal sum of $100,000. Of this amount, $50,000 is to be paid in the year of the divorce and $5,000 per year will be paid to her in each of the following 10 years or until her death.
 c. Nell is to receive the family residence (value of $120,000 and basis of $75,000). The home was jointly owned by Nell and Kirby. In exchange for the residence, Nell relinquished all of her rights to property accumulated during the marriage. She also is to receive $1,000 per month until her death or remarriage but for a period of not longer than 10 years.

49. Under the terms of a post-1986 divorce agreement, Al is to receive payments from Karen as follows: $50,000 in Year 1, $40,000 in Year 2, and $20,000 each year for Years 3 through 10. Al is also to receive custody of their minor son. The payments will decrease by $5,000 per year if the son dies or when he attains age 21 and will cease upon Al's death.

 a. What will be Al's taxable alimony in Year 1?
 b. What will be the effect of the Years 2 and 3 payments on Al's taxable income?

50. Under the terms of their divorce agreement, Barry is to transfer common stock (cost of $25,000, market value of $60,000) to Sandra. Barry and Sandra have a 14-year-old child. Sandra will have custody of the child, and Barry is to pay $300 per month as child support. In addition, Sandra is to receive $1,000 per year for 10 years. However, the payments will be reduced to $750 per month when their child reaches age 21. In the first year under the agreement, Sandra receives the common stock and the correct cash payments for six months. How will the terms of the agreement affect Sandra's gross income?

51. a. Marge (mother) is in the 28% tax bracket, and Louis (son) is in the 15% tax bracket. Marge loans Louis $50,000, and he invests the money in a bond that yields an 8% return. If Marge had not made the loan, she would have purchased the bond. The relevant Federal rate is 9%. There are no other loans between the family members. What is the effect of the preceding transactions on Marge's and Louis's combined tax for the year?
 b. Rocky, an individual, had outstanding interest-free loans receivable as follows:

Borrower	Amount of Loan	Use of the Loan Proceeds
Mike, Rocky's son	$ 15,000	Medical school tuition
Sue, Rocky's daughter	25,000	Start of an unincorporated business
Janet, Rocky's employee	2,000	Payment of medical bills
Walt, Rocky's brother	110,000	Payment of attorney fees

Mike had $1,500 net investment income for the year. Sue's income was $5,000 earned by the business and $1,500 of dividends. Janet's only income was her $12,000 salary. Walt is in prison serving 145 years to life and has no income.

All loans were outstanding for the entire year, and the Federal rate is 9% compounded semiannually (9.21% effective annual rate).

Compute Rocky's imputed interest income.

52. On June 30, 1993, Ridge borrowed $52,000 from his employer. On July 1, 1993, Ridge used the money as follows:

Interest-free loan to Ridge's controlled corporation (operated by Ridge on a part-time basis)	$21,000
Interest-free loan to Tab (Ridge's son)	11,000
National Bank of Grundy 9% certificate of deposit ($15,260 due at maturity, June 30, 1994)	14,000
National Bank of Grundy 10% certificate of deposit ($7,260 due at maturity, June 30, 1995)	6,000
	$52,000

Ridge's employer did not charge him interest. The applicable Federal rate was 12% throughout the relevant period. Tab had investment income of $800 for the year, and he used the loan proceeds to pay medical school tuition. There were no other outstanding loans between Ridge and Tab. What are the effects of the preceding transactions on Ridge's taxable income for 1993?

53. Vito is the sole shareholder of Vito, Inc. He is also employed by the corporation. On June 30, 1993, Vito borrowed $8,000 from Vito, Inc., and on July 1, 1994, he borrowed an additional $3,000. Both loans were due on demand. No interest was charged on the loans, and the Federal rate was 10% for all relevant dates. Vito used the money to purchase stock, and he had no investment income. Determine the tax consequences to Vito and Vito, Inc., in each of the following situations.

   a. The loans are considered employer-employee loans.
   b. The loans are considered corporation-shareholder loans.

54. Otis purchased an annuity from an insurance company for $12,000 on January 1, 1993. The annuity was to pay him $1,500 per year for life. At the time he purchased the contract, his life expectancy was 10 years.

   a. Determine Otis's gross income from the annuity in the first year.
   b. Assume Otis lives 20 years after purchasing the contract. What would be his gross income in the nineteenth year?

55. In 1993, Ahmad purchased an annuity for $50,000. He was 59 at the time he purchased the contract. Payments were to begin when Ahmad attained age 62. In 1993, when the cash surrender value had increased to $51,000, Ahmad exercised a right to receive $1,500 and accept reduced payments after age 62. In 1995, when he had a life expectancy of 22.5 years, Ahmad received his first annual $3,000 payment under the contract.

   a. What is Ahmad's income from the contract in 1993?
   b. Compute Ahmad's taxable collections under the annuity contract in 1995.

56. Determine the amount that should be included in gross income for each of the following:

   a. Joe was selected as the most valuable player in the Super Bowl. In recognition of this, he was awarded a sports car worth $60,000 and $50,000 in cash.
   b. Wanda won the Mrs. America beauty contest. She received various prizes valued at $75,000.
   c. George was awarded the Nobel Peace Prize. He instructed the Nobel committee to pay the $345,000 check directly to State University, his alma mater.

57. The LMN Partnership has a group term life insurance plan. Each partner has $100,000 protection, and each employee has protection equal to twice his or her annual salary. Employee Alice (age 44) had $90,000 insurance under the plan, and partner Kay (age 46) had $100,000 coverage. The cost of Alice's coverage for the year was $180, and the cost of Kay's protection was $380.

   a. Assuming the plan is nondiscriminatory, how much must Alice and Kay include in gross income from the insurance?

b. Assuming the plan is discriminatory, how much must Kay include in her gross income from the insurance?

58. Hubert was employed during the first nine months of the year. For this period, he earned $60,000. He was unemployed during the last three months of the year and received unemployment compensation of $2,400. Hubert was actively seeking employment during this period, but was unable to find another job because of the depressed nature of the industry in which he had been employed. He earned $1,000 of interest income on his savings account and withdrew $800 of the interest earned. Calculate Hubert's gross income for the year.

59. Linda and Don are married and file a joint return. In 1993, they received $9,000 in Social Security benefits and $28,000 taxable pension benefits, interest, and dividends.

a. Compute the couple's adjusted gross income on a joint return.
b. If Linda works part-time and earns $6,000, how much would Linda and Don's adjusted gross income increase?
c. Assume Don cashed certificates of deposit that had paid $8,000 in interest each year and purchases State of Virginia bonds that pay $6,000 in interest each year. How much would Linda and Don's adjusted gross income decrease? (Assume Don had no gain or loss from cashing the certificates.)

60. Melissa and James are married and file a joint return. They receive $8,000 a year in Social Security benefits, $25,000 pension benefits (all taxable), and $10,000 a year in taxable interest and dividends. Melissa is considering doing some consulting and would earn a fee of $5,000. Assuming that Melissa and James have $12,000 in itemized deductions and personal and dependency exemptions, how much will their taxable income increase if Melissa receives the $5,000 fee?

61. Donna does not think she has an income tax problem but would like to discuss her situation with you just to make sure she will not get hit with an unexpected tax liability. Base your suggestions on the following relevant financial information:

a. Donna's share of the SAT Partnership income is $40,000, but none of the income can be distributed because the partnership needs the cash for operations.
b. Donna's Social Security benefits totaled $8,400, but Donna loaned the cash received to her nephew.
c. Donna assigned to a creditor the right to collect $1,200 interest on some bonds she owned.
d. Donna and her husband lived together in California until September, when they separated. Donna has heard rumors that her husband had substantial gambling winnings since they separated.

CUMULATIVE PROBLEMS

62. Thomas R. Rucker, age 42, is single and is employed as a plumber for Ajax Plumbing Company. Tom's Social Security number is 262–06–3814. Tom lives at 252 Mason Place, Grand View, WV 22801. His salary was $45,000, and his employer withheld Federal income tax of $6,100.

Tom's mother, Sue Rucker, age 68, lives in a small house Tom bought for her in Florida. She has no income of her own and is totally dependent on Tom for her support. To provide his mother with some spending money, Tom assigned to her the income from some XYZ Corporation bonds he owns. The interest received by Tom's mother was $2,100. Tom retained ownership of the bonds but surrendered all rights to the interest on the bonds.

Over the years, Tom and his physician, Joe Zorn, have become good friends. During 1993, Tom incurred doctor bills of $350. Instead of paying Zorn in cash, Tom did the plumbing work for a new bar Zorn had installed in his basement in September 1993. Tom and Zorn agreed that the value of Tom's services was equal to the $350 in medical bills.

On September 5, 1993, Tom sold 100 shares of ABC Corporation stock for $1,800. He had acquired the stock on May 2, 1982, for $5,100.

Tom's itemized deductions for 1993 were as follows:

State income tax withheld	$1,910
Real estate taxes paid	750
Home mortgage interest (paid to Grand View Savings and Loan)	3,500
Cash contributions to First Church	900

Part 1—Tax Computation

Compute Tom's 1993 Federal income tax payable (or refund due). Suggested software (if available): *TurboTax* or *MacInTax* for tax return or WFT tax planning software.

Part 2—Tax Planning

For 1994, assume that all items of income and expense will be approximately the same as in 1993, except for the following:

- Tom expects a 10% increase in salary and in state and Federal income taxes withheld beginning January 1, 1994.
- He does not expect to incur any medical expenses.
- His real estate taxes will increase to $800.
- He expects to contribute $1,200 to First Church.
- He does not expect to have any capital gains or losses in 1994.

Tom plans to marry in June 1994. His fiancée, Sarah, intends to quit her job in Pittsburgh and move to Grand View to be with Tom. She does not plan to seek employment after the move. Sarah will earn $18,000 through May 1994. Her employer will withhold Federal income tax of $3,600, and state income tax of $900.

Compute the estimated total tax liability for the Ruckers for 1994. Should Tom ask his employer to withhold more or less than the amount withheld last year? How much? Suggested software (if available): WFT tax planning software.

63. Dan and Freida Butler, husband and wife, file a joint return. The Butlers live at 625 Oak Street, Corbin, KY 27521. Dan's Social Security number is 482–61–1231, and Freida's is 162–79–1245.

During 1993, Dan and Freida furnished over half of the total support of each of the following individuals:

a. Gina, their daughter, age 22, who was married on December 21, 1992, has no income of her own, and for 1993 files a joint return with her husband, who earned $8,500 during 1993.

b. Sam, their son, age 17, who had gross income of $2,500 and dropped out of high school in February 1993.

c. Ben Brow, Freida's brother, age 21, who is a full-time college student with gross income of $2,500.

Dan, a radio announcer for WJJJ, earned a salary of $36,000 in 1993. Freida was employed part-time as a real estate salesperson by Corbin Realty and was paid commissions of $18,000 in 1993. Freida sold a house on December 30, 1993, and will be paid a commission of $1,500 (not included in the $18,000) on the January 10, 1994, closing date.

Dan and Freida collected $15,000 on a certificate of deposit that matured on September 30, 1993. The certificate was purchased on October 1, 1991, for $12,397, and the yield to maturity was 10%.

Dan and Freida had itemized deductions as follows:

State income tax withheld	$1,900
Real estate taxes paid	900
Interest on home mortgage (paid to Corbin Savings and Loan)	5,600
Cash contributions to the Boy Scouts	420

Their employers withheld Federal income tax of $7,400 (Dan $4,400, Freida $3,000), and the Butlers paid estimated tax of $800.

Part 1—Tax Computation

Compute Dan and Freida's 1993 Federal income tax payable (or refund due). Suggested software (if available): *TurboTax* or *MacInTax* for tax return or WFT tax planning software.

Part 2—Tax Planning

Dan plans to reduce his work schedule and work only halftime for WJJJ in 1994. He has been writing songs for several years and wants to devote more time to developing a career as a songwriter. Because of the uncertainty in the music business, however, he would like you to make all computations assuming he will have no income from songwriting in 1994. To make up for the loss of income, Freida plans to increase the amount of time she spends selling real estate. She estimates she will be able to earn $33,000 in 1994. Assume all other income and expense items will be approximately the same as they were in 1993. Will the Butlers have more or less disposable income (after Federal income tax) in 1994? Write a letter to the Butlers that contains your advice and prepare a memo for the tax files. Suggested software (if available): WFT tax planning software.

CHAPTER

GROSS INCOME: EXCLUSIONS

OBJECTIVES

Explain that statutory authority is required for exclusions from income.

Analyze the Sections of the Internal Revenue Code that permit the following exclusions:

- Gifts and inheritances
- Life insurance proceeds
- Employee death benefits
- Scholarships
- Compensation for injuries and sickness
- Employer-sponsored accident and health plan coverage and benefits
- Meals and lodging
- Employee fringe benefits
- Foreign earned income
- Interest on government obligations
- Dividends
- Educational savings bonds interest

Discuss the extent to which receipts can be excluded under the tax benefit rule.

Describe the circumstances under which income must be reported from the discharge of indebtedness.

Suggest tax planning strategies for obtaining the maximum benefits from allowable exclusions.

OUTLINE

Items Specifically Excluded from Gross Income

Chapter 3 discussed the concepts and judicial doctrines that affect the determination of gross income. If an income item is within the all-inclusive definition of gross income, the item can be excluded only if the taxpayer can locate specific authority for doing so. Chapter 4 focuses on the exclusions Congress has authorized.

Statutory Authority

Sections 101 through 150 provide the authority for excluding specific items from gross income. In addition, other exclusions are scattered throughout the Code. For each exclusion, there is a legislative history and reason for enactment. Certain exclusions are intended as a form of indirect welfare payments. Other exclusions prevent double taxation of income or provide incentives for socially desirable activities (e.g., nontaxable interest on certain U.S. government bonds where the owner uses the funds for educational expenses).

In some cases, Congress has enacted exclusions to rectify the effects of judicially imposed decisions. For example, the Supreme Court held that the fair market value of improvements (not made in lieu of rent) made by a tenant to the landlord's property should be included in the landlord's gross income upon termination of the lease.[1] The landlord was required to include the value of the improvements in gross income even though he or she had not sold or otherwise disposed of the property. Congress reacted to this decision by enacting § 109, which defers taxing the value of the improvements until the property is sold.

Gifts and Inheritances

Beginning with the Income Tax Act of 1913 and continuing to the present, Congress has allowed the recipient of a gift to exclude the value of the property from gross income. The exclusion applies to gifts made during the life of the donor (*inter vivos* gifts) and transfers that take effect upon the death of the donor (bequests and inheritances). However, as discussed in Chapter 3, the recipient of a gift of income-producing property is subject to tax on the income subsequently earned from the property. Also, as discussed in Chapter 1, the donor or the decedent's estate may be subject to gift or estate taxes on the transfer.

In numerous cases, gifts are made in a business setting. For example, a salesperson gives a purchasing agent free samples; an employer gives cash to a retiring employee; a corporation makes payments to employees who were victims of a natural disaster; a corporation makes a cash payment to a deceased employee's spouse. In these and similar instances, it is frequently unclear whether the payment was a gift or whether it represents compensation for past, present, or future services.

1. *Helvering v. Bruun,* 40–1 USTC ¶9337, 24 AFTR 652, 60 S.Ct. 631 (USSC, 1940).

The courts have defined a *gift* as "a voluntary transfer of property by one to another without adequate [valuable] consideration or compensation therefrom."[2] If the payment is intended to be for services rendered, it is not a gift, even though the payment is made without legal or moral obligation and the payer receives no economic benefit from the transfer. To qualify as a gift, the payment must be

CONCEPT SUMMARY 4–1
SUMMARY OF PRINCIPAL EXCLUSIONS FROM GROSS INCOME

1. Donative items
   - Gifts, bequests, inheritances, and employee death benefits [§§ 102 and 101(b)]
   - Life insurance proceeds paid by reason of death (§ 101)
   - Scholarships (§ 117)
2. Personal and welfare items
   - Injury or sickness payments (§ 104)
   - Public assistance payments (Rev. Rul. 71–425, 1971–2 C.B. 76)
   - Amounts received under insurance contracts for certain living expenses (§ 123)
   - Reimbursement for the costs of caring for a foster child (§ 131)
3. Wage and salary supplements
   - a. Fringe benefits
     - Accident and health benefits (§§ 105 and 106)
     - Lodging and meals furnished for the convenience of the employer (§ 119)
     - Rental value of parsonages (§ 107)
     - Employee achievement awards [§ 74(c)]
     - Employer contributions to employee group term life insurance (§ 79)
     - Group legal service plan benefits (§ 120)*
     - Cafeteria plans (§ 125)
     - Educational assistance payments (§ 127)*
     - Child or dependent care (§ 129)
     - Services provided to employees at no additional cost to the employer (§ 132)
     - Employee discounts (§ 132)
     - Working condition and *de minimis* fringes (§ 132)
     - Athletic facilities provided to employees (§ 132)
     - Qualified transportation fringe (§ 132)
     - Tuition reductions granted to employees of educational institutions (§ 117)
   - b. Military benefits
     - Combat pay (§ 112)
     - Mustering-out pay (§ 113)
     - Housing, uniforms, and other benefits (§ 134)
   - c. Foreign earned income (§ 911)
4. Investor items
   - Interest on state and local government obligations (§ 103)
   - Improvements by lessee to lessor's property (§ 109)
5. Benefits for the elderly
   - Social Security benefits, except in the case of certain higher-income taxpayers (§ 86)
   - Gain from the sale of personal residence by elderly taxpayers (§ 121)
6. Other benefits
   - Income from discharge of indebtedness (§ 108)
   - Recovery of a prior year's deduction that yielded no tax benefit (§ 111)
   - Educational savings bonds (§ 135)

*Exclusion treatment applies for tax years beginning before July 1, 1992, for amounts paid before July 1, 1992.

2. *Estate of D. R. Daly*, 3 B.T.A. 1042 (1926).

made "out of affection, respect, admiration, charity or like impulses."[3] Thus, the cases on this issue have been decided on the basis of the donor's intent.

In a landmark case, *Comm. v. Duberstein*,[4] the taxpayer (Duberstein) received a Cadillac from a business acquaintance. Duberstein had supplied the businessman with the names of potential customers with no expectation of compensation. The Supreme Court concluded:

> . . . despite the characterization of the transfer of the Cadillac by the parties [as a gift] and the absence of any obligation, even of a moral nature, to make it, it was at the bottom a recompense for Duberstein's past service, or an inducement for him to be of further service in the future.

Duberstein was therefore required to include the fair market value of the automobile in gross income.

In the case of cash or other property received by an employee from his or her employer, Congress has eliminated any ambiguity. Transfers from an employer to an employee cannot be excluded as a gift. It is possible, however, that a transfer will fit into one of the other statutory exclusion provisions.

Life Insurance Proceeds

Insurance proceeds paid to the beneficiary by reason of the death of the insured are exempt from income tax.

Example 1

Mark purchased an insurance policy on his life and named his wife Linda as the beneficiary. Mark paid $24,000 in premiums. When he died, Linda collected the insurance proceeds of $50,000. The $50,000 is exempt from Federal income tax. ◆

Congress chose to exempt life insurance proceeds for the following reasons:

- For family members, life insurance proceeds serve much the same purpose as a nontaxable inheritance.
- In a business context (as well as in a family situation), life insurance proceeds replace an economic loss suffered by the beneficiary.

Example 2

Gold Corporation purchased a $100,000 life insurance policy on its key employee. The employee dies, and the corporation receives $100,000 from the insurance company. If the proceeds were taxable, the corporation would require more insurance coverage to pay the tax as well as to cover the economic loss of the employee. ◆

Exceptions to Exclusion Treatment

The income tax exclusion applies only when the insurance proceeds are received by reason of the death of the insured. If the owner cancels the policy and receives the cash surrender value, he or she must recognize gain to the extent of the excess of the amount received over the cost of the policy (but a loss is not deductible).

3. *Robertson v. U.S.*, 52–1 USTC ¶9343, 41 AFTR 1053, 72 S.Ct. 994 (USSC, 1952).

4. 60–2 USTC ¶9515, 5 AFTR2d 1626, 80 S.Ct. 1190 (USSC, 1960).

Another exception to exclusion treatment applies if the policy is transferred after it is issued by the insurance company. If the policy is *transferred for valuable consideration,* the insurance proceeds are includible in the gross income of the transferee to the extent the proceeds received exceed the amount paid for the policy by the transferee plus any subsequent premiums paid.

EXAMPLE 3

Adam pays premiums of $500 for an insurance policy in the face amount of $1,000 upon the life of Beth and subsequently transfers the policy to Carol for $600. Carol receives the proceeds of $1,000 on Beth's death. The amount that Carol can exclude from gross income is limited to $600 plus any premiums she paid subsequent to the transfer. ◆

The Code, however, provides exceptions to the rule illustrated in the preceding example. The four exceptions that permit exclusion treatment include transfers to the following:

1. A partner of the insured.
2. A partnership in which the insured is a partner.
3. A corporation in which the insured is an officer or shareholder.
4. A transferee whose basis in the policy is determined by reference to the transferor's basis.

The first three exceptions facilitate the use of insurance contracts to fund buy-sell agreements in business situations.

EXAMPLE 4

Rick and Sam are equal partners who have an agreement that allows either partner to purchase the interest of a deceased partner for $50,000. Neither partner has sufficient cash to actually buy the other partner's interest, but each has a life insurance policy on his own life in the amount of $50,000. Rick and Sam could exchange their policies (usually at little or no taxable gain), and upon the death of either partner, the surviving partner could collect tax-free insurance proceeds. The proceeds could then be used to purchase the decedent's interest in the partnership. ◆

The fourth exception applies to policies that were transferred pursuant to a tax-free exchange or were received by gift.

Interest on Life Insurance Proceeds

Investment earnings arising from the reinvestment of life insurance proceeds are generally subject to income tax. Often the beneficiary elects to collect the insurance proceeds in installments. In this case, each installment received by the beneficiary is comprised of a pro rata portion of the principal (face amount) of the policy plus interest on the proceeds left with the insurance company. The annuity rules (discussed in Chapter 3) are used to apportion the installment payment between the principal element (excludible) and the interest element (includible).

EXAMPLE 5

Harry is the beneficiary of a $100,000 life insurance policy on his wife. Under the terms of the policy, Harry elects to collect the proceeds as an annuity of $15,000 each year. His life expectancy is 10 years. Thus, Harry's investment in the contract is $100,000, his expected return is $150,000 (10 × $15,000), and his exclusion ratio is 100/150. Each payment Harry receives during the initial 10-year period is a recovery of capital of $10,000 [$15,000 × (100/150)] and $5,000 of interest income. ◆

EMPLOYEE DEATH BENEFITS

Gift versus Compensation

Frequently, an employer makes payments to a deceased employee's surviving spouse, children, or other beneficiaries. If the decedent had a nonforfeitable right to the payments (e.g., the decedent's accrued salaries), the amounts are generally taxable to the recipient just the same as if the employee had lived and collected the payments. But where the employer makes voluntary payments, the gift issue arises. Generally, the IRS considers such payments to be compensation for prior services rendered by the deceased employee.[5] However, some courts have held that payments to an employee's surviving spouse or other beneficiaries are gifts if the following are true:[6]

- The payments were made to the surviving spouse and children rather than to the employee's estate.
- The employer derived no benefit from the payments.
- The surviving spouse and children performed no services for the employer.
- The decedent had been fully compensated for services rendered.
- Payments were made pursuant to a board of directors' resolution that followed a general company policy of providing such payments for families of deceased employees (but not exclusively for families of shareholder-employees).

When all of the above conditions are true, the payment is presumed to have been made *as an act of affection or charity.* When one or more of these conditions is not true, the surviving spouse and children may still be deemed the recipients of a gift if the payment is made in light of the survivors' financial needs.

Section 101(b) attempts to eliminate or reduce controversy in this area by providing an *automatic exclusion* for the first $5,000 paid by the employer to the employee's beneficiaries by reason of the death of the employee. The $5,000 exclusion must be apportioned among the beneficiaries on the basis of each beneficiary's percentage of the total death benefits received.

EXAMPLE 6

When Antonio died, his employer paid his accrued salary of $3,000 to Josefina, Antonio's widow. The employer's board of directors also authorized payments to Josefina ($4,000), Antonio's daughter ($2,000), and his son ($2,000) "in recognition of Antonio's many years of service to the company."

The $3,000 accrued salary is compensation for past services and was owed to Antonio at the time of his death. Therefore, the $3,000 is includible in gross income. The additional payments to the widow and children were not owed to Antonio. Because the payments were made in recognition of Antonio's past service, under the *Duberstein* decision, the payments are not gifts. However, the employee death benefit exclusion enables the widow and children to exclude the following amounts:

5. Rev.Rul. 62–102, 1962–2 C.B. 37.

6. *Estate of Sydney J. Carter v. Comm.*, 72–1 USTC ¶9129, 29 AFTR2d 332, 453 F.2d 61 (CA–2, 1972), and cases cited there.

Josefina	$\frac{\$4,000}{\$8,000} \times \$5,000 =$	$2,500
Daughter	$\frac{\$2,000}{\$8,000} \times \$5,000 =$	1,250
Son	$\frac{\$2,000}{\$8,000} \times \$5,000 =$	1,250
		$5,000

◆

When the employer's payments exceed $5,000, the beneficiaries may still be able to exclude the entire amount received as a gift if they are able to show gratuitous intent on the part of the employer.

SCHOLARSHIPS

General Information

Payments or benefits received by a student at an educational institution may be (1) compensation for services, (2) a gift, or (3) a scholarship. If the payments or benefits are received as compensation for services (past or present), the fact that the recipient is a student generally does not render the amounts received nontaxable.

EXAMPLE 7

State University waives tuition for *all* graduate teaching assistants. The tuition waived is *intended* as compensation for services and is therefore included in the graduate assistant's gross income. Tuition waivers are also awarded to some graduate students who are not teaching assistants. These waivers, which are based on merit, are treated as nontaxable scholarships. ◆

The scholarship rules are intended to provide exclusion treatment for education-related benefits that cannot qualify as gifts but are not compensation for services. According to the Regulations, "a scholarship is an amount paid or allowed to, or for the benefit of, an individual to aid such individual in the pursuit of study or research."[7] The recipient must be a candidate for either a graduate or an undergraduate degree at an educational institution.

EXAMPLE 8

Terry enters a contest sponsored by a local newspaper. Each contestant is required to submit an essay on local environmental issues. The prize is one year's tuition at State University. Terry wins the contest. The newspaper has a legal obligation to Terry (as contest winner). Thus, the benefits are not a gift. However, since the tuition payment aids Terry in pursuing her studies, the payment is a scholarship. ◆

A scholarship recipient may exclude from gross income the amount used for tuition and related expenses (fees, books, supplies, and equipment required for courses), provided the conditions of the grant do not require that the funds be used for other purposes. Amounts received for room and board are *not* excludible and are treated as *earned income* for purposes of calculating the standard deduction for a taxpayer who is a dependent of another taxpayer.

7. Prop.Reg. § 1.117–6(a)(3)(i).

EXAMPLE 9

Kelly received a scholarship of $9,500 from State University to be used to pursue a bachelor's degree. She spent $4,000 on tuition, $3,000 on books and supplies, and $2,500 for room and board. Kelly may exclude $7,000 ($4,000 + $3,000) from gross income. The $2,500 spent for room and board is includible in her gross income.

The scholarship was Kelly's only source of income. Her parents provided more than 50% of her support and claimed her as a dependent. Kelly's standard deduction will equal her $2,500 gross income. Thus, she has no taxable income. ◆

Timing Issues

Frequently, the scholarship recipient is a cash basis taxpayer who receives the money in one tax year but pays the educational expenses in a subsequent year. The amount eligible for exclusion may not be known at the time the money is received. In that case, the transaction is held *open* until the educational expenses are paid.

EXAMPLE 10

In August 1993, Sanjay received $10,000 as a scholarship for the academic year 1993–1994. His expenditures for tuition, books, and supplies were as follows:

August–December 1993	$3,000
January–May 1994	4,500
	$7,500

Sanjay's gross income for 1994 includes $2,500 ($10,000 – $7,500) that is not excludible as a scholarship. ◆

Disguised Compensation

Some employers make scholarships available solely to the children of key employees. The tax objective of these plans is to provide a nontaxable fringe benefit to the executives by making the payment to the child in the form of an excludible scholarship. However, the IRS has ruled that the payments are generally includible in the gross income of the parent-employee.[8]

Qualified Tuition Reduction Plans

Employees (including retired and disabled former employees) of nonprofit educational institutions are allowed to exclude a tuition waiver from gross income, if the waiver is pursuant to a *qualified tuition reduction plan*.[9] The plan may not discriminate in favor of highly compensated employees. The exclusion applies to tuition waivers for the employee, the employee's spouse, and the employee's dependent children. The exclusion also extends to undergraduate tuition reductions granted by any nonprofit educational institution to employees of any other nonprofit educational institution (under reciprocal agreements).

EXAMPLE 11

Central University allows the dependent children of Midwest University employees to attend Central University with no tuition charge. Midwest University grants reciprocal

8. Rev.Rul. 75–448, 1975–2 C.B. 55. *Richard T. Armantrout*, 67 T.C. 996 (1977).

9. § 117(d).

benefits to the children of Central University employees. The dependent children can also attend tuition-free the university where their parents are employed. Employees who take advantage of these benefits are not required to recognize gross income. ◆

Generally, the exclusion is limited to undergraduate tuition waivers. However, in the case of teaching or research assistants, graduate tuition waivers may also qualify for exclusion treatment. According to proposed Regulations, the exclusion is limited to the value of the benefit in excess of the employee's reasonable compensation.[10] Thus, a tuition reduction that is a substitute for cash compensation cannot be excluded.

EXAMPLE 12

Susan is a graduate research assistant. She receives a $5,000 salary for 500 hours of service over a nine-month period. This pay, $10 per hour, is considered reasonable compensation for Susan's services. In addition, Susan receives a tuition waiver of $6,000, which is not intended as compensation. Susan may exclude the tuition waiver from gross income. ◆

COMPENSATION FOR INJURIES AND SICKNESS

Damages

A person who suffers harm caused by another is often entitled to compensatory damages. The tax consequences of the receipt of damages depend on the type of harm the taxpayer has experienced. The taxpayer may seek recovery for a loss of income, expenses incurred, property destroyed, or personal injury.

Generally, reimbursement for a loss of income is taxed the same as the income replaced. The recovery of an expense is not income, unless the expense was deducted. Damages that are a recovery of the taxpayer's previously deducted expenses are generally taxable under the tax benefit rule, discussed later in this chapter.

EXAMPLE 13

Hun's business automobile was damaged in 1993 when a mechanic left a bolt in the oil pan. Hun had to rent an automobile for the remainder of 1993. He deducted the rent as a business expense on his 1993 tax return. In 1994, the mechanic admits liability and reimburses Hun for the rent. Hun must include the recovery of the prior deduction in his 1994 gross income. ◆

A payment for damaged or destroyed property is treated as an amount received in a sale or exchange of the property. Thus, the taxpayer has a realized gain if the damage payments received exceed the property's basis.

Personal Injury. The legal theory of personal injury damages is that the amount received is intended "to make the plaintiff [the injured party] whole as before the injury or to compensate the taxpayer for damages sustained."[11] It follows that if the *compensatory* damage payments received were subject to tax, the after-tax amount received would be less than the actual damages incurred and the injured party would not be "whole as before the injury."

10. Prop.Reg. § 1.117–6(d).

11. *C. A. Hawkins*, 6 B.T.A. 1023 (1928).

Congress has specifically excluded from gross income the amount of any damage payments received (whether by suit or agreement) on account of personal injuries or sickness. The courts have applied the exclusion to any personal wrong committed against the taxpayer (e.g., breach of promise to marry, invasion of privacy, libel, slander, assault, battery). The exclusion also applies to compensation for loss of income (ordinarily taxable, as previously discussed) and recovery of expenses (except medical expenses deducted by the taxpayer) resulting from the personal injury. According to the Supreme Court, however, the damages are taxable if under the Federal or state law establishing the taxpayer's right of recovery, the recovery is limited to the loss of income.[12]

In libel and slander cases, a single event can cause both a personal injury and damage to a business reputation. Damage to a business reputation is measured on the basis of estimated loss of income. Taxpayers argue that the amount received for loss of income in these cases is no different from the payments in other personal injury cases and thus should be excluded. According to the IRS, however, the business reputation damages are separate from the personal injury and are taxable.[13]

EXAMPLE 14

Tom, a television announcer, was dissatisfied with the manner in which Ron, an attorney, was defending the television station in a libel case. Tom stated on the air that Ron was botching the case. Ron sued Tom for slander, claiming damages for loss of income from clients and potential clients who heard Tom's statement. Ron's claim is for damages to his business reputation, and the amounts received are taxable.

Ron collected on the suit against Tom and was on his way to a party to celebrate his victory when a negligent driver, Norm, drove his truck into Ron's automobile, injuring him. Ron filed suit for the personal injuries and claimed as damages the loss of income for the period he was unable to work as a result of the injury. All amounts Ron received from Norm, including the reimbursement for lost income, are nontaxable because the claims are based on a personal injury. ◆

CONCEPT SUMMARY 4–2
TAXATION OF DAMAGES

Type of Claim	Taxation of Award or Settlement
Contract (generally loss of income)	Taxable.
Property damages	Recovery of cost, gain to the extent of the excess over basis, or loss to the extent of basis over the amount realized.
Personal injury	
Physical	All amounts (compensatory and punitive) are excluded unless previously deducted (e.g., medical expenses).
Nonphysical, general	Compensatory damages are excluded (unless previously deducted), and punitve damages are taxable.
Nonphysical, only compensation is loss of income	Taxable.

12. *U.S. v. Burke*, 69 AFTR2d 92–1293 (USSC, 1992).

13. Rev.Rul. 85–143, 1985–2 C.B. 55, in which the IRS announced it would not follow the Ninth Court of Appeals decision in *Roemer v. Comm.*, 83–2 USTC ¶9600, 52 AFTR2d 83–5954, 716 F.2d 693 (CA–9, 1983). See also *Wade E. Church*, 80 T.C. 1104 (1983).

Punitive Damages. In addition to seeking *compensatory* damages, the injured party may seek *punitive* damages, which are often awarded to punish the defendant for gross negligence or the intentional infliction of harm. Punitive damages are includible in gross income *unless* the claim arises out of physical injury or physical sickness. Thus, punitive damages received for loss of personal reputation are taxable, although the compensatory damages are excludible. Punitive damages arising out of a *physical* injury claim are excludible.

Workers' Compensation

State workers' compensation laws require employers to pay fixed amounts for specific job-related injuries. The state laws were enacted so that the employee will not have to go through the ordeal of a lawsuit to recover the damages (and possibly not collect damages because of some defense available to the employer). Although the payments are intended, in part, to compensate for a loss of income, Congress has specifically exempted workers' compensation benefits from inclusion in gross income.

Accident and Health Insurance Benefits

The income tax treatment of accident and health insurance benefits depends on whether the policy providing the benefits was purchased by the taxpayer or the taxpayer's employer. Benefits collected under an accident and health insurance policy *purchased by the taxpayer* are excludible. In this case, benefits collected under the taxpayer's insurance policy are excluded even though the payments are a substitute for income.

Example 15

Bonnie purchased a medical and disability insurance policy. The insurance company paid Bonnie $200 per week to replace wages she lost while in the hospital. Although the payments serve as a substitute for income, the amounts received are tax-exempt benefits collected under Bonnie's insurance policy. ◆

Example 16

Joe sustains an injury that results in partial paralysis of his left foot. As a result of the injury, he receives $5,000 from his accident insurance company, under a policy he had purchased. The $5,000 accident insurance proceeds are tax-exempt. ◆

A different set of rules applies if the accident and health insurance protection was *purchased by the individual's employer,* as discussed in the following section.

Employer-Sponsored Accident and Health Plans

Congress encourages employers to provide employees, retired former employees, and their dependents with accident and health and disability insurance plans. The *premiums* are deductible by the employer and excluded from the employee's income. Although § 105(a) provides the general rule that the employee has includible income when he or she collects the insurance *benefits,* two important exceptions are provided.

Section 105(b) generally excludes payments received for medical care of the employee, spouse, and dependents. However, if the payments are for expenses that do not meet the Code's definition of medical care, the amount received must be included in gross income. In addition, the taxpayer must include in gross income the amounts received for medical expenses that were deducted by the taxpayer on a prior return.

EXAMPLE 17

In 1994, Tab's employer-sponsored health insurance plan paid $4,000 for hair transplants that did not meet the Code's definition of medical care. Tab must include the $4,000 in his gross income for 1994.

Also in 1994, Tab was reimbursed for medical expenses he had paid in 1993. He was reimbursed $3,000, which was the amount of his actual expenses. The expenses met the definition of medical care, and Tab had claimed the $3,000 as an itemized deduction on his 1993 return. His adjusted gross income for 1993 was $30,000, and he had no other medical expenses. Because only medical expenses in excess of 7.5% of adjusted gross income (refer to Chapter 10) may be claimed as a deduction, the expenses reduced taxable income by only $750 [$3,000 – .075($30,000)] on Tab's 1993 return. As a result of the reimbursement, Tab is required to include in gross income for 1994 only $750, the amount by which 1993 taxable income was reduced. ◆

Section 105(c) excludes payments for the permanent loss or the loss of the use of a member or function of the body or the permanent disfigurement of the employee, spouse, or a dependent. Payments that are a substitute for salary (e.g., related to the period of time absent) are includible.

EXAMPLE 18

Jill lost an eye in an automobile accident unrelated to her work. As a result of the accident, Jill incurred $2,000 of medical expenses, which she deducted on her return. She collected $10,000 from an accident insurance policy carried by her employer. The benefits were paid according to a schedule of amounts that varied with the part of the body injured (e.g., $10,000 for loss of an eye, $20,000 for loss of a hand). Because the payment was for loss of a *member or function of the body,* § 105(c) applies and the $10,000 is excluded from income. Jill was absent from work for a week as a result of the accident. Her employer provided her with insurance for the loss of income due to illness or injury. Jill collected $500, which is includible in gross income. ◆

Medical Reimbursement Plans

In lieu of providing employees with insurance coverage for hospital and medical expenses, an employer may agree to reimburse the employee for these expenses. Employees may exclude amounts received through insurance coverage (insured plan benefits) under § 105 (as previously discussed). However, due to cost considerations, the insurance companies that issue this type of policy usually require a broad coverage of employees. An alternative is to have a plan that is not funded with insurance (a self-insured arrangement). Employees can exclude benefits received under a self-insured plan if the plan does not discriminate in favor of highly compensated employees.

MEALS AND LODGING

Furnished for the Convenience of the Employer

As discussed in Chapter 3, income can take any form, including meals and lodging. However, § 119 excludes from income the value of meals and lodging provided to an employee and the employee's spouse and dependents under the following conditions:

- The meals and/or lodging are *furnished* by the employer, on the employer's *business premises,* for the *convenience of the employer.*
- In addition to the above requirements, in the case of lodging, the employee is *required* to accept the lodging as a condition of employment.

The courts have construed both of these requirements strictly.

At least two questions have been raised with regard to the *furnished by the employer* requirement:

- Who is considered an *employee?*
- What is meant by *furnished?*

The IRS and some courts have reasoned that because a partner is not an employee, the exclusion does not apply to a partner. However, the Tax Court and the Fifth Court of Appeals have ruled in favor of the taxpayer on this issue.[14]

The Supreme Court held that a cash meal allowance was ineligible for the exclusion because the employer did not actually furnish the meals.[15] Similarly, one court denied the exclusion where the employer paid for the food and supplied the cooking facilities but the employee prepared the meal.[16]

The *on the employer's business premises* requirement, applicable to both meals and lodging, has resulted in much litigation. The Regulations define business premises as simply "the place of employment of the employee,"[17] but there is not universal agreement as to what this means. The Sixth Court of Appeals held that a residence, owned by the employer and occupied by an employee, two blocks from the motel that the employee managed was not part of the business premises.[18] However, the Tax Court considered an employer-owned house across the street from the hotel that was managed by the taxpayer to be on the business premises of the employer.[19] Perhaps these two cases can be reconciled by comparing the distance from the lodging facilities to the place where the employer's business was conducted. The closer the lodging to the business operations, the more likely the convenience of the employer is served.

The *convenience of the employer* test is intended to focus on the employer's motivation for furnishing the meals and lodging rather than on the benefits received by the employee. If the employer furnishes the meals and lodging primarily to enable the employee to perform his or her duties properly, it does not matter that the employee considers these benefits to be a part of his or her compensation.

The Regulations give the following examples in which the tests for excluding meals are satisfied:[20]

---

14. Rev.Rul. 80, 1953–1 C.B. 62; *Comm. v. Doak,* 56–2 USTC ¶9708, 49 AFTR 1491, 234 F.2d 704 (CA–4, 1956); *Comm. v. Moran,* 56–2 USTC ¶9789, 50 AFTR 64, 236 F.2d 595 (CA–8, 1956); *Robinson v. U.S.,* 60–1 USTC ¶9152, 5 AFTR2d 315, 273 F.2d 503 (CA–3, 1959); *Briggs v. U.S.,* 56–2 USTC ¶10020, 50 AFTR 667, 238 F.2d 53 (CA–10, 1956), but see *G. A. Papineau,* 16 T.C. 130 (1951); *Armstrong v. Phinney,* 68–1 USTC ¶9355, 21 AFTR2d 1260, 394 F.2d 661 (CA–5, 1968).

15. *Comm. v. Kowalski,* 77–2 USTC ¶9748, 40 AFTR2d 6128, 98 S.Ct. 315 (USSC, 1977).

16. *Tougher v. Comm.,* 71–1 USTC ¶9398, 27 AFTR2d 1301, 441 F.2d 1148 (CA–9, 1971).

17. Reg. § 1.119–1(c)(1).

18. *Comm. v. Anderson,* 67–1 USTC ¶9136, 19 AFTR2d 318, 371 F.2d 59 (CA–6, 1966).

19. *J. B. Lindeman,* 60 T.C. 609 (1973).

20. Reg. § 1.119–1(f).

- A waitress is required to eat her meals on the premises during the busy lunch and breakfast hours.
- A bank furnishes a teller meals on the premises to limit the time the employee is away from his booth during the busy hours.
- A worker is employed at a construction site in a remote part of Alaska. The employer must furnish meals and lodging due to the inaccessibility of other facilities.

The *employee required* test applies only to lodging. If the employee's use of the housing would serve the convenience of the employer, but the employee is not *required* to use the housing, the exclusion is not available.

EXAMPLE 19

VEP, a utilities company, has all of its service personnel on 24-hour call for emergencies. The company encourages its employees to live near the plant so that the employees can respond quickly to emergency calls. Company-owned housing is available rent-free. Only 10 of the employees live in the company housing because it is not suitable for families.

Although the company-provided housing serves the convenience of the employer, it is not required. Therefore, the employees who live in the company housing cannot exclude its value from gross income. ◆

In addition, if the employee has the *option* of cash or lodging, the *required* test is not satisfied.

EXAMPLE 20

Khalid is the manager of a large apartment complex. The employer gives Khalid the option of rent-free housing (value of $6,000 per year) or an additional $5,000 per year. Khalid selects the housing option. Therefore, he must include $6,000 in gross income. ◆

Other Housing Exclusions

Employees of Educational Institutions. An employee of an educational institution may be able to exclude the value of campus housing provided by the employer. Generally, the employee does not recognize income if he or she pays annual rents equal to or greater than 5 percent of the appraised value of the facility. If the rent payments are less than 5 percent of the value of the facility, the deficiency must be included in gross income.

EXAMPLE 21

Southcentral University provides on-campus housing for its full-time faculty during the first three years of employment. The housing is not provided for the convenience of the employer. Professor Smith pays $3,000 annual rent for the use of a residence with an appraised value of $100,000 and an annual rental value of $12,000. Professor Smith must recognize $2,000 gross income [.05($100,000) – $3,000 = $2,000] for the value of the housing provided. ◆

Ministers of the Gospel. Ministers of the gospel can exclude (1) the rental value of a home furnished as compensation or (2) a rental allowance paid to them as compensation, to the extent the allowance is used to rent or provide a home. The housing or housing allowance must be provided as compensation for the conduct of religious worship, the administration and maintenance of religious organizations, or the performance of teaching and administrative duties at theological seminaries.

Example 22

Pastor Brown is allowed to live rent-free in a house owned by the congregation. The annual rental value of the house is $6,000 and is provided as part of the pastor's compensation for ministerial services. Assistant Pastor Clark is paid a $4,500 cash housing allowance. He uses the $4,500 to pay rent and utilities on a home he and his family occupy. Neither Pastor Brown nor Assistant Pastor Clark is required to recognize gross income associated with the housing or housing allowance. ◆

Military Personnel. Military personnel are allowed housing exclusions under various circumstances. Authority for these exclusions generally is found in Federal laws that are not part of the Internal Revenue Code.

Other Employee Fringe Benefits

Specific Benefits

In recent years, Congress has enacted exclusions to encourage employers to (1) finance and make available child care facilities, (2) provide the means for employees to obtain legal services, (3) provide athletic facilities for employees, and (4) finance certain employees' basic education. These provisions are summarized as follows:

- The employee does not have to include in gross income the value of child and dependent care services paid for by the employer and incurred to enable the employee to work. The exclusion cannot exceed $5,000 per year ($2,500 if married and filing separately). For a married couple, the annual exclusion cannot exceed the earned income of the spouse who has the lesser amount of earned income. For an unmarried taxpayer, the exclusion cannot exceed the taxpayer's earned income.
- Any benefit received by employees from coverage under qualified group legal service plans provided by the employer is excluded. The exclusion is limited to an annual premium value of $70 per employee.
- The value of the use of a gymnasium or other athletic facilities by employees, their spouses, and their dependent children may be excluded from an employee's gross income. The facilities must be on the employer's premises, and substantially all of the use of the facilities must be by employees and their family members.
- Qualified employer-provided educational assistance (tuition, fees, books, and supplies) at the undergraduate and graduate levels is excludible from gross income. The exclusion is subject to an annual employee statutory ceiling of $5,250.

Cafeteria Plans

Generally, if an employee is offered a choice between cash and some other form of compensation, the employee is deemed to have constructively received the cash even when the noncash option is elected. Thus, the employee has gross income regardless of the option chosen.

The cafeteria plan rules provide an exception to this constructive receipt treatment. Under such a plan, the employee is permitted to choose between cash and nontaxable benefits (e.g., group term life insurance, health and accident protection, and child care). If the employee chooses the otherwise nontaxable benefits, the cafeteria plan rules enable the benefits to remain nontaxable.

Cafeteria plans provide *flexibility* in tailoring the employee-pay package to fit individual needs. Some employees (usually the younger group) prefer cash, while others (usually the older group) will opt for the fringe benefit program.

EXAMPLE 23

Orange Corporation offers its employees (on a nondiscriminatory basis) a choice of any one or all of the following benefits:

	Cost
Group term life insurance	$ 200
Hospitalization insurance for family members	2,400
Child care payments	1,800
	$4,400

If a benefit is not selected, the employee receives cash equal to the cost of the benefit. Tina, an employee, has a spouse who works for another employer that provides hospitalization insurance but no child care payments. Tina elects to receive the group term life insurance, the child care payments, and $2,400 of cash. Only the $2,400 must be included in Tina's gross income. ◆

General Classes of Excluded Benefits

An employer can confer numerous forms and types of economic benefits on employees. Under the all-inclusive concept of income, the benefits are taxable unless one of the provisions previously discussed specifically excludes the item from gross income. The amount of the income is the fair market value of the benefit. This reasoning can lead to results that Congress considers unacceptable, as illustrated in the following example.

EXAMPLE 24

Vern is employed in New York as a ticket clerk for Trans National Airlines. His mother in Miami, Florida, is ill, but Vern has no money for plane tickets. Trans National has daily flights from New York to Miami that often leave with empty seats. The cost of a ticket is $400, and Vern is in the 28% tax bracket. If Trans National allows Vern to fly without charge to Miami, under the general gross income rules, he has income equal to the value of a ticket. Therefore, Vern must pay $112 tax (.28 × $400) on a trip to Miami. Because Vern does not have $112, he cannot visit his mother, and the airplane flies with another empty seat. ◆

If Trans National in Example 24 will allow employees to use resources that would otherwise be wasted, why should the tax laws interfere with the employee's decision to take advantage of the available benefit? Thus, to avoid the undesirable results that occur in Example 24 and in similar situations as well as to create uniform rules for fringe benefits, Congress established five broad classes of nontaxable employee benefits:[21]

- No-additional-cost services.
- Qualified employee discounts.
- Working condition fringes.

21. See, generally, § 132.

- *De minimis* fringes.
- Qualified transportation fringe.

No-Additional-Cost Services. Example 24 illustrates the *no-additional-cost* type of fringe benefit. The services will be nontaxable if all of the following conditions are satisfied:

- The employee receives services, as opposed to property.
- The employer does not incur substantial additional cost, including forgone revenue, in providing the services to the employee.
- The services are offered to customers in the ordinary course of the business in which the employee works.

EXAMPLE 25

Assume that Vern in Example 24 can fly without charge only if the airline cannot fill the seats with paying customers. That is, Vern must fly on standby. Although the airplane may burn slightly more fuel because Vern is on the airplane and he may receive the same meal as paying customers, the additional costs are not substantial. Thus, the trip qualifies as a no-additional-cost service.

On the other hand, assume that Vern is given a reserved seat on a flight that is frequently full. The employer would be forgoing revenue to allow Vern to fly. This forgone revenue is a substantial additional cost, and thus the benefit is taxable. ◆

Note that if Vern were employed in a hotel owned by Trans National, the receipt of the airline ticket would be taxable because he did not work in that line of business. However, the Code allows the exclusion for reciprocal benefits offered by employers in the same line of business.

EXAMPLE 26

Grace is employed as a desk clerk for Plush Hotels, Inc. The company and Chain Hotels, Inc., have an agreement that allows any of their employees to stay without charge in either company's resort hotels during the off-season. Grace is not required to recognize income from taking advantage of the plan by staying in a Chain Hotel. ◆

The no-additional-cost exclusion extends to the employee's spouse and dependent children and to retired and disabled former employees. In the Regulations, the IRS has conceded that partners who perform services for the partnership are employees for purposes of the exclusion.[22] However, the exclusion is not allowed to highly compensated employees unless the benefit is available on a nondiscriminatory basis.

Qualified Employee Discounts. When the employer sells goods or services (other than no-additional-cost benefits just discussed) to the employee for a price that is less than the price charged regular customers, the employee realizes income equal to the discount. However, the discount can be excluded from the gross income of the employee, subject to the following conditions and limitations:

- The exclusion is not available for real property (e.g., a house) or for personal property of the type commonly held for investment (e.g., common stocks).
- The property or services must be from the same line of business in which the employee works.

---

22. Reg. § 1.132–1(b).

- In the case of *property*, the exclusion is limited to the *gross profit component* of the price to customers.
- In the case of *services*, the exclusion is limited to 20 percent of the customer price.

EXAMPLE 27

Silver Corporation, which operates a department store, sells a television set to a store employee for $300. The regular customer price is $500, and the gross profit rate is 25%. The corporation also sells the employee a service contract for $120. The regular customer price on the contract is $150. The employee must recognize $75 income.

Customer price for property	$ 500
Less: Gross profit (25%)	(125)
	$ 375
Employee price	300
Income	$ 75
Customer price for service	$ 150
Less: 20%	(30)
	$ 120
Employee price	120
Income	$–0–

◆

As in the case of no-additional-cost benefits, the exclusion applies to employees (including service partners), employees' spouses and dependent children, and retired and disabled former employees. However, the exclusion does not apply to highly compensated individuals unless the discount is available on a nondiscriminatory basis.

Working Condition Fringes. Generally, an employee is not required to include in gross income the cost of property or services provided by the employer if the employee could deduct the cost of those items if he or she had actually paid for them.

EXAMPLE 28

Mitch is a certified public accountant employed by an accounting firm. The employer pays Mitch's annual dues to professional organizations. Mitch is not required to include the payment of the dues in gross income because if he had paid the dues, he would have been allowed to deduct the amount as an employee business expense (as discussed in Chapter 9). ◆

In many cases, this exclusion merely avoids reporting income and an offsetting deduction. However, in two specific situations, the working condition fringe benefit rules allow an exclusion where the expense would not be deductible if paid by the employee:

- Automobile salespeople are allowed to exclude the value of certain personal use of company demonstrators (e.g., commuting to and from work).
- The employee business expense would be eliminated by the 2 percent floor on miscellaneous deductions under § 67 (see Chapter 10).

Unlike the other fringe benefits discussed previously, working condition fringes can be made available on a discriminatory basis and still qualify for the exclusion.

De Minimis **Fringes.** As the term suggests, *de minimis* fringe benefits are so small that accounting for them is impractical. The House Report contains the following examples of *de minimis* fringes:

- The typing of a personal letter by a company secretary, occasional personal use of a company copying machine, occasional company cocktail parties or picnics for employees, occasional supper money or taxi fare for employees because of overtime work, and certain holiday gifts of property with a low fair market value are excluded.
- Subsidized eating facilities (e.g., an employees' cafeteria) operated by the employer are excluded if located on or near the employer's business premises, if revenue equals or exceeds direct operating costs, and if nondiscrimination requirements are met.

When taxpayers venture beyond the specific examples contained in the House Report and the Regulations, there is obviously much room for disagreement as to what is *de minimis.* However, note that except in the case of subsidized eating facilities, the *de minimis* fringe benefits can be granted in a manner that favors highly compensated employees.

Example 29

Tann Corporation's officers are allowed to have personal letters typed by company secretaries. On the average, a secretary will spend one hour each month on the letters. The benefit is *de minimis,* which means accounting for the cost is impractical in view of the small amount of money involved. If the costs are too small to be of concern, whether the benefits are discriminatory is also immaterial. ◆

Qualified Transportation Fringe. The Energy Policy Act of 1992 created a new category of nontaxable employee benefits called the qualified transportation fringe. The intent of the legislation with respect to this provision is to encourage the use of mass transit associated with commuting to and from work. The term *qualified transportation fringe* encompasses the following transportation benefits provided by the employer to the employee:

1. Transportation in a commuter highway vehicle between the employee's residence and the place of employment.
2. A transit pass.
3. Qualified parking.

Statutory dollar limits on the amount of the exclusion are provided. Categories (1) and (2) above are combined for purposes of applying the limit. In this case, the limit on the exclusion is $60 per month. Category (3) has a separate limit of $155 per month. Both of these dollar limits are to be indexed annually for inflation.

A *commuter highway vehicle* is any highway vehicle for which the seating capacity (excluding the driver) is at least 6 adults. In addition, at least 80 percent of the use of the vehicle must be for transporting employees between their residences and place of employment.

Qualified parking includes the following:

- Parking provided to an employee on or near the employer's business premises.
- Parking provided to an employee on or near a location from which the employee commutes to work via mass transit, in a commuter highway vehicle, or in a carpool.

Qualified transportation fringes may be provided directly by the employer or may be in the form of cash reimbursements.

EXAMPLE 30

Gray Corporation's offices are located in the center of a large city. The company pays for parking spaces to be used by the company officers. Steve, a vice president, receives $250 of such benefits each month. The parking space rental is a qualified transportation fringe. Of the $250 benefit received each month by Steve, $155 is excludible from gross income. The balance of $95 is included in his gross income. The same result would occur if Steve paid for the parking and was reimbursed by his employer. ◆

Nondiscrimination Provisions. For no-additional-cost services and qualified employee discounts, if the plan is discriminatory in favor of highly compensated employees, these key employees are denied exclusion treatment. However, the non-highly compensated employees who receive benefits from the plan can still enjoy exclusion treatment for the no-additional-cost services and qualified employee discounts.

EXAMPLE 31

Black Company's officers are allowed to purchase goods from the company at a 25% discount. Other employees are allowed only a 15% discount. The company's gross profit margin on these goods is 30%.

Peggy, an officer in the company, purchases goods from the company for $750 when the price charged to customers is $1,000. Peggy must include $250 in gross income because the plan is discriminatory.

Leo, an employee of the company who is not an officer, purchases goods for $850 when the customer price is $1,000. Leo is not required to recognize income because he received a qualified employee discount. ◆

De minimis and working condition fringe benefits can be provided on a discriminatory basis. The *de minimis* benefits are not subject to tax because the accounting problems that would be created are out of proportion to the amount of additional tax that would result. A nondiscrimination test would simply add to the compliance problems. In the case of working condition fringes, the types of services required vary with the job. Therefore, a nondiscrimination test probably could not be satisfied, although usually there is no deliberate plan to benefit a chosen few.

Taxable Fringe Benefits

If the fringe benefits cannot qualify for any of the specific exclusions or do not fit into any of the general classes of excluded benefits, the taxpayer must recognize gross income equal to the fair market value of the benefits. Obviously, determining the value frequently leads to problems. The IRS has issued extensive Regulations addressing the valuation of personal use of an employer's automobiles and meals provided at an employer-operated eating facility.[23]

If a fringe benefit plan discriminates in favor of highly compensated employees, generally, the highly compensated employees are not allowed to exclude the benefits they receive that other employees do not enjoy. However, the highly compensated employees, as well as the other employees, are generally allowed to exclude the nondiscriminatory benefits.

23. Reg. § 1.61–2 T(j). Generally, the income from the personal use of the employer's automobile is based on the lease value of the automobile (what it would have cost the employee to lease the automobile). Meals are valued at 150% of the employer's direct costs (e.g., food and labor) of preparing the meals.

EXAMPLE 32

Greene Company has a medical reimbursement plan that reimburses officers for 100% of their medical expenses, but reimburses all other employees for only 80% of their medical expenses. Mr. Greene, the president of the company, was reimbursed $1,000 during the year for medical expenses. He must include $200 in gross income [(1 – .80) × $1,000 = $200]. Mike, an employee who is not an officer, received $800 (80% of his actual medical expenses) under the medical reimbursement plan. None of the $800 is includible in his gross income. ◆

FOREIGN EARNED INCOME

A U.S. citizen is generally subject to U.S. tax on his or her income regardless of the income's geographic origin. The income may also be subject to tax in the

CONCEPT SUMMARY 4–3
GENERAL CLASSES OF EXCLUDED BENEFITS

Benefit	Description and Examples	Coverage Allowed	Effect of Discrimination
1. No-additional-cost services	The employee takes advantage of the employer's excess capacity (e.g., free passes for airline employees).	Current, retired, and disabled employees; their spouses and dependent children; spouses of deceased employees. Partners are treated as employees.	No exclusion for highly compensated employees.
2. Qualified discounts on goods	The employee is allowed to purchase the employer's merchandise at a price that is not less than the employer's cost.		No exclusion for highly compensated employees.
3. Qualified discounts on services	The employee is allowed a discount on services the employer offers to customers. A maximum discount of 20% is excludible.		No exclusion for highly compensated employees.
4. Working condition fringes	Expenses paid by the employer that would be deductible if paid by the employee (e.g., a mechanic's tools). Also, includes parking and auto salesperson's use of a car held for sale.	Current employees, partners, directors, and independent contractors.	No effect.
5. *De minimis* items	Expenses so immaterial that accounting for them is not warranted (e.g., occasional supper money, personal use of the copy machine).	*Any recipient* of a fringe benefit.	No effect.
6. Qualified transportation fringe	Transportation benefits provided by the employer to employees, including commuting in a commuter highway vehicle, a transit pass, and qualified parking.	Current employees.	No effect.

foreign country, and thus the taxpayer carries a double tax burden. Out of a sense of fairness and to encourage U.S. citizens to work abroad (so that exports might be increased), Congress has provided alternative forms of relief from taxes on foreign earned income. The taxpayer can elect *either* (1) to include the foreign income in his or her taxable income and then claim a credit for foreign taxes paid or (2) to exclude the foreign earnings from his or her U.S. gross income. The foreign tax credit option is discussed in Chapter 11, but as is apparent from the following discussion, most taxpayers will choose the exclusion.

Foreign earned income consists of the earnings from the individual's personal services rendered in a foreign country (other than as an employee of the U.S. government). To qualify for the exclusion, the taxpayer must be either

- a bona fide resident of the foreign country (or countries), or
- present in a foreign country (or countries) for at least 330 days during any 12 consecutive months.

EXAMPLE 33

Sandra took the following trips to and from a foreign country in connection with her work:

Arrived in Foreign Country	Arrived in United States
March 10, 1992	February 1, 1993
March 7, 1993	June 1, 1993

During the 12 consecutive months ending on March 10, 1993, Sandra was present in the foreign country for at least 330 days (365 days less 28 days in February and 7 days in March 1993). Therefore, all income earned in the foreign country through March 10, 1993, is eligible for the exclusion. The income earned from March 11, 1993, through May 31, 1993, is also eligible for the exclusion because Sandra was present in the foreign country for 330 days during the 12 consecutive months ending on May 31, 1993. ◆

The exclusion is *limited* to $70,000 per year. For married persons, both of whom have foreign earned income, the exclusion is computed separately for each spouse. Community property rules do not apply (the community property spouse is not deemed to have earned one-half of the other spouse's foreign earned income). A taxpayer who is present in the country for less than the entire year must compute the maximum exclusion on a daily basis ($70,000 divided by the number of days in the entire year and multiplied by the number of days present in the foreign country during the year).

EXAMPLE 34

Keith qualifies for the foreign earned income exclusion. He was present in France for all of 1993 except for 7 days in December. During this period, he was in the United States. Keith's salary for 1993 is $90,000. If Keith had been in France for all of the 365 days in 1993, he would have been able to exclude $70,000. However, since he was not present in the foreign country for 7 days, his exclusion is limited to $68,658 as follows:

$$\$70{,}000 \times \frac{358 \text{ days in foreign country}}{365 \text{ days in the year}} = \$68{,}658$$

◆

In addition to the exclusion for foreign earnings, the *reasonable housing costs* incurred by the taxpayer and the taxpayer's family in a foreign country in excess of a base amount may be excluded from gross income. The base amount is 16 percent of the U.S. government pay scale for a GS-14 (Step 1) employee, which varies from year to year.

As previously mentioned, the taxpayer may elect to include the foreign earned income in Federal adjusted gross income and claim a credit (an offset against U.S. tax) for the foreign tax paid. The credit alternative may be advantageous if the individual's foreign earned income far exceeds the excludible amount so that the foreign taxes paid exceed the U.S. tax on the amount excluded. However, once an election is made, it applies to all subsequent years, unless affirmatively revoked. A revocation is effective for the year of the change and the four subsequent years.

INTEREST ON CERTAIN STATE AND LOCAL GOVERNMENT OBLIGATIONS

At the time the Sixteenth Amendment was ratified by the states, there was some question as to whether the Federal government possessed the constitutional authority to tax interest on state and local government obligations. Taxing the interest on these obligations was thought to violate the doctrine of intergovernmental immunity in that the tax would impair the ability of state and local governments to finance their operations.[24] Thus, interest on state and local government obligations was specifically exempted from Federal income taxation. However, the Supreme Court recently concluded that there is no constitutional prohibition against levying a nondiscriminatory Federal income tax on state and local government obligations. Nevertheless, currently the statutory exclusion still exists.

Obviously, the exclusion of the interest reduces the cost of borrowing for state and local governments. A taxpayer in the 31 percent tax bracket requires only a 5.52 percent yield on a tax-exempt bond to obtain the same after-tax income as a taxable bond paying 8 percent interest [5.52% ÷ (1 – .31) = 8%].

The lower cost for the state and local governments is more than offset by the revenue loss of the Federal government. Also, tax-exempt interest is considered to be a substantial loophole for the very wealthy. For these reasons, bills have been proposed to Congress calling for Federal government subsidies to state and local governments that voluntarily choose to issue taxable bonds. The proposals would not eliminate the tax-exempt status of existing bonds.

DIVIDENDS

General Information

A *dividend* is a payment to a shareholder with respect to his or her stock. Dividends to shareholders are taxable only to the extent the payments are made from *either* the corporation's *current earnings and profits* (in many cases the same as net income per books) or its *accumulated earnings and profits* (somewhat similar

24. *Pollock v. Farmer's Loan & Trust Co.*, 3 AFTR 2602, 15 S.Ct. 912 (USSC, 1895).

to retained earnings per books). Distributions that exceed earnings and profits are treated as a nontaxable recovery of capital and reduce the shareholder's basis in the stock. Once the shareholder's basis is reduced to zero, any subsequent distributions are taxed as capital gains (see Chapter 13).

Some payments that are referred to as dividends are not considered dividends for tax purposes:

- Dividends received on deposits with savings and loan associations, credit unions, and banks are actually interest (a contractual rate paid for the use of money).
- Patronage dividends paid by cooperatives (e.g., for farmers) are rebates made to the users and are considered reductions in the cost of items purchased from the association. The rebates are usually made after year-end (after the cooperative has determined whether it has met its expenses) and are apportioned among members on the basis of their purchases.
- Mutual insurance companies pay dividends on unmatured life insurance policies that are considered rebates of premiums.
- Shareholders in a mutual investment fund are allowed to report as capital gains their proportionate share of the fund's gains realized and distributed. The capital gain and ordinary income portions are reported on the Form 1099 that the fund supplies its shareholders each year.

Stock Dividends

When a corporation issues a simple stock dividend (e.g., common stock issued to common shareholders), the shareholder has merely received additional shares that represent the same total investment. Thus, the shareholder does not realize income.[25] However, if the shareholder has the *option* of receiving either cash or stock in the corporation, he or she realizes gross income whether stock or cash is received. A taxpayer who elects to receive the stock could be deemed to be in constructive receipt of the cash he or she has rejected. However, the amount of the income in this case is the value of the stock received, rather than the cash the shareholder rejected. See Chapter 13 for a detailed discussion of stock dividends.

EDUCATIONAL SAVINGS BONDS

The cost of a college education has risen dramatically during the past 10 years, increasing at a rate almost twice the change in the general price level. The U.S. Department of Education estimates that by the year 2007, the cost of attending a publicly supported university for four years will exceed $60,000. For a private university, the cost is expected to exceed $200,000.[26] Congress has attempted to assist low- to middle-income parents in saving for the college education of their children.

The assistance is in the form of an interest income exclusion.[27] The interest on Series EE U.S. government savings bonds may be excluded from gross income if the bond proceeds are used to pay qualified higher education expenses. The exclusion applies only if both of the following requirements are satisfied:

25. *Eisner v. Macomber*, 1 USTC ¶32, 3 AFTR 3020, 40 S.Ct. 189 (USSC, 1920); § 305(a).

26. See generally, Knight and Knight, "New Ways to Manage Soaring Tuition Costs," *Journal of Accountancy* (March 1989), p. 207.

27. § 135.

- The savings bonds are issued after December 31, 1989.
- The savings bonds are issued to an individual who is at least 24 years old at the time of issuance.

The exclusion is not available for a married couple who file separate returns.

The redemption proceeds must be used to pay qualified higher education expenses. *Qualified higher education expenses* consist of tuition and fees paid to an eligible education institution for the taxpayer, spouse, or dependents. In calculating qualified higher education expenses, the tuition and fees paid are reduced by excludible scholarships and veterans' benefits received. If the redemption proceeds (both principal and interest) exceed the qualified higher education expenses, only a pro rata portion of the interest will qualify for exclusion treatment.

EXAMPLE 35

Tracy's redemption proceeds from qualified savings bonds during the taxable year were $6,000 (principal of $4,000 and interest of $2,000). Tracy's qualified higher education expenses were $5,000. Since the redemption proceeds exceed the qualified higher education expenses, only $1,667 ($5,000/$6,000 × $2,000) of the interest is excludible. ◆

The exclusion is limited by the application of the wherewithal to pay concept. That is, once the modified adjusted gross income exceeds a threshold amount, the phase-out of the exclusion begins. *Modified adjusted gross income* is adjusted gross income prior to the § 911 foreign earned income exclusion and the educational savings bond exclusion. The threshold amounts are adjusted for inflation each year. For 1993, the phase-out begins at $45,500 ($68,250 on a joint return). The phase-out is completed when modified adjusted gross income exceeds the threshold amount by more than $15,000 ($30,000 on a joint return). The otherwise excludible interest is reduced by the amount calculated as follows:

$$\frac{\text{Modified AGI} - \$45{,}500}{\$15{,}000} \times \begin{array}{c}\text{Excludible interest}\\ \text{before phase-out}\end{array} = \begin{array}{c}\text{Reduction in}\\ \text{excludible interest}\end{array}$$

On a joint return, $68,250 is substituted for $45,500 (in 1993), and $30,000 is substituted for $15,000.

EXAMPLE 36

Assume the same facts as in Example 35, except that Tracy's modified adjusted gross income for 1993 is $50,000. The phase-out will result in Tracy's interest exclusion being reduced by $500 [($50,000 – $45,500)/$15,000 × $1,667]. Therefore, Tracy's exclusion is $1,167 ($1,667 – $500). ◆

TAX BENEFIT RULE

Generally, if a taxpayer obtains a deduction for an item in one year and in a later year recovers all or a portion of the prior deduction, the recovery is included in gross income in the year received.

EXAMPLE 37

A taxpayer deducted as a loss a $1,000 receivable from a customer when it appeared the amount would never be collected. The following year, the customer paid $800 on the receivable. The taxpayer must report the $800 as income in the year it is received. ◆

However, § 111 provides that no income is recognized upon the recovery of a deduction, or the portion of a deduction, that did not yield a tax benefit in the year it was taken.

INCOME FROM DISCHARGE OF INDEBTEDNESS

A transfer of appreciated property in satisfaction of a debt is an event that triggers the realization of income. The transaction is treated as a sale of the appreciated property followed by payment of the debt. Foreclosure by a creditor is also treated as a sale or exchange of the property.

EXAMPLE 38

Juan owed the State Bank $100,000 on an unsecured note. He satisfied the note by transferring to the bank common stock with a basis of $60,000 and a fair market value of $100,000. Juan must recognize $40,000 gain on the transfer. Juan also owed the bank $50,000 on a note secured by land. When his basis in the land was $20,000 and the land's fair market value was $50,000, the bank foreclosed on the loan and took title to the land. Juan must recognize a $30,000 gain on the foreclosure. ◆

In some cases, a creditor will not exercise his or her right of foreclosure and will even forgive a portion of the debt to assure the vitality of the debtor. In such cases, the debtor realizes income from discharge of indebtedness.

EXAMPLE 39

Brown Corporation is unable to meet the mortgage payments on its factory building. Both the corporation and the mortgage holder are aware of the depressed market for industrial property in the area. Foreclosure would only result in the creditor's obtaining unsalable property. To improve Brown's financial position and thus improve the corporation's chances of obtaining the additional credit from other lenders necessary for survival, the creditor agrees to forgive all amounts past due and to reduce the principal amount of the mortgage. ◆

Generally, the income realized by the debtor from the forgiveness of a debt is taxable.[28] A similar debt discharge (produced by a different creditor motivation) associated with personal use property is illustrated in Example 40.

EXAMPLE 40

In 1988, Joyce borrowed $60,000 from National Bank to purchase her personal residence. Joyce agreed to make monthly principal and interest payments for 15 years. The interest rate on the note was 8%. In 1993, when the balance on the note had been reduced to $48,000 through monthly payments, the bank offered to accept $45,000 in full settlement of the note. The bank made the offer because interest rates had increased to 12%. Joyce accepted the bank's offer. As a result, she must recognize $3,000 ($48,000 – $45,000) income. ◆

The following discharge of indebtedness situations are subject to special treatment:[29]

1. Creditors' gifts.
2. Discharges under Federal bankruptcy law.
3. Discharges that occur when the debtor is insolvent.

28. *U.S. v. Kirby Lumber Co.*, 2 USTC ¶814, 10 AFTR 458, 52 S.Ct. 4 (USSC, 1931), codified in § 61(a)(12).

29. §§ 108 and 1017.

4. Discharge of the farm debt of a solvent taxpayer.
5. A seller's cancellation of the buyer's indebtedness.
6. A shareholder's cancellation of the corporation's indebtedness.
7. Forgiveness of loans to students.

If the creditor reduces the debt as an act of *love, affection or generosity,* the debtor has simply received a nontaxable gift (situation 1). Rarely will a gift be found to have occurred in a business context. A businessperson may settle a debt for less than the amount due, but as a matter of business expediency (e.g., high collection costs or disputes as to contract terms) rather than generosity.

In situations 2, 3, and 4, the Code allows the debtor to reduce his or her basis in the assets by the realized gain from the discharge.[30] Thus, the realized gain is merely deferred until the assets are sold (or depreciated). Similarly, in situation 5 (a price reduction), the debtor reduces the basis in the specific assets financed by the seller.

A shareholder's cancellation of the corporation's indebtedness to him or her (situation 6) usually is considered a contribution of capital to the corporation. Thus, the corporation's paid-in capital is increased, and its liabilities are decreased by the same amount.

Many states make loans to students on the condition that the loan will be forgiven if the student practices a profession in the state upon completing his or her studies. The amount of the loan that is forgiven (situation 7) is excluded from gross income.

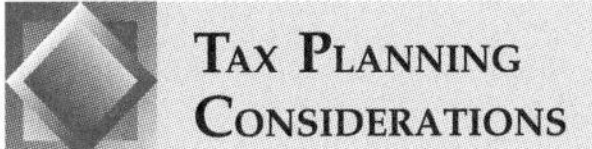

Tax Planning Considerations

The present law excludes certain types of economic gains from taxation. Therefore, taxpayers may find tax planning techniques helpful in obtaining the maximum benefits from the exclusion of such gains. Following are some of the tax planning opportunities made available by the exclusions described in this chapter.

Life Insurance

Life insurance offers several favorable tax attributes. As discussed in Chapter 3, the annual increase in the cash surrender value of the policy is not taxable (because no income has been actually or constructively received). By borrowing on the policy's cash surrender value, the owner can actually receive the policy's increase in value in cash without recognizing income.

Employee Benefits

Generally, employees view accident and health insurance, as well as life insurance, as necessities. Employees can obtain group coverage at much lower rates than individuals would have to pay for the same protection. Premiums paid by the employer can be excluded from the employees' gross income. Because of the exclusion, employees will have a greater after-tax and after-insurance income if the employer pays a lower salary but also pays the insurance premiums.

Example 41

Pat receives a salary of $30,000. The company has group insurance benefits, but Pat is required to pay his own premiums as follows:

30. §§ 108(a), (e), and (g). Note that § 108(b) provides that other tax attributes (e.g., net operating loss) will be reduced by the realized gain from the debt discharge prior to the basis adjustment unless the taxpayer elects to apply the basis adjustment first.

Hospitalization and medical insurance	$1,400
Term life insurance ($30,000 coverage)	200
Disability insurance	400
	$2,000

To simplify the analysis, assume Pat's tax rate on income is 28%. After paying taxes of $8,400 (.28 × $30,000) and $2,000 for insurance, Pat has $19,600 ($30,000 – $8,400 – $2,000) for his other living needs.

If Pat's employer reduced his salary by $2,000 (to $28,000) but paid his insurance premiums, Pat's tax liability would be only $7,840 ($28,000 × .28). Thus, Pat would have $20,160 ($28,000 – $7,840) to meet his other living needs. The change in the compensation plan would save $560 ($20,160 – $19,600). ◆

Similarly, employees must often incur expenses for child care and parking. The employee can have more income for other uses if the employer pays these costs for the employee but reduces the employee's salary by the cost of the benefits.

The employees' discount provision is especially important for manufacturers and wholesalers. Employees of manufacturers can avoid tax on the manufacturer's, wholesaler's, and retailer's markups. The wholesaler's employees can avoid tax on an amount equal to the wholesale and retail markups.

It should be recognized that the exclusion of benefits is generally available only to employees. Proprietors and partners must pay tax on the same benefits their employees receive tax-free. By incorporating and becoming an employee of the corporation, the former proprietor or partner can also receive these tax-exempt benefits. Thus, the availability of employee benefits is a consideration in the decision to incorporate.

Investment Income

Tax-exempt state and local government bonds are almost irresistible investments for many high-income taxpayers. To realize the maximum benefit from the exemption, the investor can purchase zero coupon bonds. These investments pay interest only at maturity, just as a Series EE U.S. government savings bond does. The advantage of the zero coupon feature is that the investor can earn tax-exempt interest on the accumulated principal and interest. If the investor purchases a bond that pays the interest each year, the interest received may be such a small amount that an additional tax-exempt investment cannot be made. In addition, reinvesting the interest may entail transaction costs (broker's fees). The zero coupon feature avoids these problems.

Series EE U.S. government savings bonds can earn tax-exempt interest if the bond proceeds are used for "qualified higher education expenses." Many taxpayers can foresee these expenditures being made for their children's educations. However, in deciding whether to invest in the bonds, the investor must take into account the income limitations for excluding the interest from gross income.

PROBLEM MATERIALS

DISCUSSION QUESTIONS

1. Tim owned land that was leased to a corporation under a 20-year lease with no renewal options. In 1979, when 15 years were remaining on the lease, the tenant constructed a building on the property. The value of the building was $100,000, and its estimated useful life was 35 years. In 1993, the lease expired, the tenant moved,

and Tim began using the building. The building's value when the lease expired was $75,000. Does Tim realize income from these events?

2. Bob gave DEF Company common stock to his son, Earl, before any dividends had been declared. Bob gave his mother the right to collect dividends on 100 shares of DEF Company common stock, but otherwise retained all incidents of ownership of the stock. Later in the year of the gifts, DEF Company paid $1 per share dividends. What are the tax consequences of these transactions to Bob, Earl, and Bob's mother?
3. Violet Company gave $500 to each household in the community that had suffered a flood loss. The purpose of the payments was to help the flood victims. If some of the recipients are employees of Violet Company, can the employees exclude the payments from gross income?
4. Matt's truck was stalled on the side of the road. Abby stopped to help and called Al, who agreed to repair the truck, for $75. Matt paid Al $75 and Abby $25. The payment to Al was made because of a contractual obligation and therefore is not a gift. The payment to Abby was not made because of a contractual obligation. Does this mean that the payment Abby received is a gift?
5. What are the two principal tax benefits of buying life insurance that has a cash surrender value?
6. Black Corporation purchased a $1,000,000 insurance policy on the life of the company's president. The company paid $100,000 of premiums, the president died, and the company collected the face amount of the policy. How much must Black Corporation include in gross income?
7. Grace died while employed by RST Company. The company paid Grace's husband $2,000 in sales commissions that Grace had earned and $3,000 under the company's policy of making payments to the spouses of deceased employees. Is any of the $5,000 that Grace's husband received subject to income tax?
8. Yellow Company provides its employees with $10,000 group term life insurance. Red Company does not provide insurance but generally gives the family of a deceased employee $10,000. Compare the tax consequences of the insured and uninsured plans.
9. James received an academic scholarship to State University. Under the scholarship agreement, he received tuition ($1,500), books ($400), and room and board ($5,000). What is James's gross income from the scholarship?
10. José is a graduate assistant at State University. He receives $7,000 a year in salary. In addition, tuition of $4,000 is waived. The tuition waiver is available to all full- and part-time employees. The fair market value of José's services is $11,000. How much is José required to include in his gross income?
11. Ted and Olaf were traveling together in a defectively manufactured automobile. As a result of the defects, the automobile ran off the road and crashed into a tree. Ted and Olaf each broke an arm in the accident. Ted was a baseball pitcher and was unable to pitch for one year as a result of the accident. He received a $400,000 damage award in a suit against the automobile manufacturer. Olaf was a 65-year-old retiree and received $25,000 as an award for damages. The difference in the damage awards was largely due to Ted's greater loss of earnings. Is Ted taxed on any of the $400,000 received?
12. Sara was injured in an automobile accident by a person who was intoxicated at the time of the accident. She settled with the defendant's insurance company and received $15,000 for the medical expenses associated with a whiplash, $6,000 for lost wages, and $5,000 of punitive damages. How much of the settlement is Sara required to include in gross income?
13. Wes purchases an accident and health insurance plan that was advertised in the Sunday newspaper. The annual premiums are $400. During the year, Wes received payments of $1,200 under the plan.

    a. How much of the $1,200 must Wes include in his gross income?
    b. Would the tax consequences differ if the $1,200 represented amounts paid by the insurance company to replace lost wages while Wes was hospitalized?

14. What nontaxable fringe benefits are available to employees that are not available to partners and proprietors?
15. How does one determine if meals and lodging supplied by an employer are to serve a valid business purpose? Is the tax treatment of meals and lodging affected if the employer advertises that the meals and lodging provided are one of the employees' fringe benefits?
16. Paula is employed by a telemarketing firm that pays a fixed amount for unlimited long-distance telephone calls. Employees are allowed to use the toll-free line for 5 minutes each month, at no charge to the employee. The normal charge for the calls Paula made during the year was $75. How much is Paula required to include in gross income?
17. JKL Life Insurance Company pays its employees $.25 per mile for driving their personal automobiles to and from work. For employees who ride the bus, the company reimburses the employee $45 a month for the cost of a pass. Tom collected $60 for his automobile mileage and Ted received $45 as reimbursement for the cost of a bus pass.
    - **a.** What are the effects of the above on Tom and Ted's gross incomes?
    - **b.** Assume that Tom and Ted are in the 28% marginal tax bracket, and the actual before-tax cost for Tom to drive to and from work is $.25 per mile. What are Tom and Ted's after-tax costs of commuting to and from work?
18. Jane works at a bakery and is allowed to take home bread that could not be sold during the day. The bakery gives the day-old bread to the employees because it has no other use for the goods. Is Jane required to recognize income as a result of receiving the bread?
19. Gary is employed by MVP, Inc., an automobile manufacturing company. MVP sold Gary a new automobile at company cost of $12,000. The price charged a dealer would have been $14,000, and the retail price of the automobile was $17,000. What is Gary's gross income from the purchase of the automobile?
20. EFG Company provides officers with a 30% discount on merchandise, but provides other employees with only a 10% discount. The company's gross profit rate on the goods is 40%. If Zack, an officer in the company, is allowed to buy goods for $70 when the regular price is $100, how much is he required to include in gross income?
21. Rashad, a U.S. citizen, worked in a foreign country for the period July 1, 1993, through May 31, 1994. Is Rashad entitled to any foreign earned income exclusion for 1993?
22. FGH Corporation is opening a branch in Kazonbi, an African country that does not levy an income tax on citizens of foreign countries. Carl, a U.S. citizen, is considering two offers from his employer, FGH Corporation. He can work for 6 months in Kazonbi and 6 months in the United States and receive a salary of $4,000 per month, or he can work in Kazonbi for 12 months at the same monthly salary. Carl would like to spend as much time in the United States as possible and prefers the first alternative. However, he asks your advice as to how income taxes might affect his decision.
23. Ivan received a $100,000 condemnation award when the state took his real estate for a new school. Ivan used the money to purchase State of Virginia bonds, which paid him $7,500 interest in 1993. The state condemned other property owned by Ivan. However, he contested the amount the state was willing to pay for this second piece of property. At the end of 1993, the court awarded him $100,000 for the land and $7,500 interest on the condemnation award. How much of the interest is Ivan required to include in gross income?
24. Donna and George are married, file a joint return, and are in the 31% marginal tax bracket. They would like to save for their child's education. What would be the advantage of buying State of Virginia bonds as compared to buying Series EE U.S. government bonds?
25. Chee owns 100 shares of stock in XYZ Corporation. The corporation declares a dividend that gives Chee the option of receiving 10 additional shares of XYZ stock or

$200 cash. Chee elects to receive 10 additional shares of stock. What are the tax consequences to Chee?

26. In 1993, Mary received a $2,000 sales commission. However, in 1994, her employer discovered that Mary should have received only a $1,500 commission in 1993. Therefore, the employer withheld $500 from Mary's 1994 commission. Mary's standard deduction and personal exemption for 1993 exceeded her gross income. What effect would the tax benefit rule have on Mary's gross income for 1994?

27. In 1993, Helen received a $400 factory rebate on supplies purchased and deducted as a business expense in 1992. In 1993, Rosa received a $400 factory rebate on a personal use automobile purchased in December 1992. Both Helen and Rosa had over $10,000 of taxable income in 1992 and 1993. Is the receipt of $400 taxable to Helen or Rosa?

28. How does the tax treatment of a corporation's income generated by the retirement of bonds for less than book value (issue price plus amortized discount or less amortized premium) differ from the income derived from a shareholder's forgiveness of the corporation's indebtedness?

29. In 1983, Moustafa purchased real estate for $50,000. By 1991, the property had appreciated to $150,000. In 1991, Moustafa borrowed $120,000 and gave a mortgage on the property as security for the debt. In 1993, when the value of the property equaled the balance on the mortgage ($120,000), Moustafa transferred the property to the mortgagee in satisfaction of the debt. Did Moustafa realize income from discharge of indebtedness?

30. While attending medical school, Gail received loans totaling $40,000 under a State of Virginia student loan program. The loan program provides that the loan will be forgiven if Gail practices medicine for three years in specified rural areas in the western part of the state. If the loan is forgiven, what amount should Gail include in her gross income?

PROBLEMS

31. Determine whether the following may be excluded from gross income as gifts, bequests, scholarships, prizes, or life insurance proceeds:

    a. Uncle told Nephew, "Come live with me and take care of me in my old age and you can have all my property after my death." Nephew complied with Uncle's request. Uncle's will made Nephew sole beneficiary of the estate.

    b. Uncle told Nephew, "If you study hard and make the dean's list this year, I will pay your tuition for the following year." Nephew made the dean's list, and Uncle paid the tuition.

    c. Uncle told Nephew, "If you make the dean's list this year, I will pay you $500." Nephew made the dean's list, and Uncle paid the $500.

    d. Diane cashed in her life insurance contract and collected $10,000. She had paid premiums totaling $7,000.

    e. Fred received $500 from his employer to pay his child's medical expenses. The payment was not part of a medical reimbursement plan, and the employer made the payment out of compassion.

32. Determine the taxable life insurance proceeds in the following cases:

    a. Manuel purchased a sports franchise and player contracts from Steve. As part of the transaction, Manuel purchased a life insurance contract on a key player from Steve for $50,000. One month later, the player was killed in an automobile accident, and Manuel collected $500,000 on the life insurance contract.

    b. Kareem and Vito formed a partnership and agreed that upon the death of either partner, the surviving partner would purchase the decedent's partnership interest. Kareem purchased a life insurance policy on Vito's life and paid $5,000 in premiums. Upon Vito's death, Kareem collected $100,000 on the life insurance policy and used the proceeds to purchase Vito's interest in the partnership.

    c. Same as (b), except the partnership was incorporated and Kareem and Vito owned all the stock. Upon incorporation, Kareem and Vito transferred their life insurance policies to the corporation in exchange for stock. When Vito died, the corporation redeemed (purchased) his stock, using the $100,000 life insurance proceeds.

33. Determine whether the taxpayer has gross income in each of the following situations:

a. Jim is a waiter in a restaurant. The rule of thumb is that a customer should leave the waiter a tip equal to 15% of the customer's bill for food and beverages. Jim collected $6,000 in tips during the year.
b. Tara works at a grocery store, bagging groceries and carrying them to the customers' automobiles. Her employer posts a sign saying that the employees are paid by the hour and the customer is not expected to tip them. Tara received $1,800 in tips from customers.
c. Sheila worked at a hotel. Her home was damaged by a fire. Sheila's employer allowed her to stay at the hotel for no charge until she could return to her home. The normal charge for the room Sheila occupied during this period was $500, and the hotel had several vacant rooms.

34. Donald died at age 35. He was married and had four minor children. His employer, XYZ Painting Company, made payments to Donald's wife as follows:

Donald's accrued salary at date of death	$4,000
Family death benefits under long-standing company policy ($2,000 is paid to the spouse and $1,500 is paid to each child of a deceased employee)	2,000
A payment authorized by the board of directors to help his wife pay debts accumulated by Donald	7,000

In addition, Donald's wife was the beneficiary of her husband's life insurance policy of $50,000. XYZ Painting Company had paid for the policy. Donald had excluded all of the premiums paid by the employer from gross income as group term life insurance. His wife left the insurance proceeds with the insurance company and elected to receive an annuity of $4,000 each year for life. Her life expectancy is 40 years. She collected one $4,000 payment at the end of the current year. A joint return was filed in the year of Donald's death. Which of the above amounts must be included in gross income?

35. Alejandro was awarded an academic scholarship to State University. He received $5,000 in August and $6,000 in December 1993. Alejandro had enough personal savings to pay all expenses as they came due. His expenditures for the relevant period were as follows:

Tuition, August 1993	$2,900
Tuition, December 1993	3,200
Room and board	
August–December 1993	3,000
January–May 1994	2,400
Books and educational supplies	
August–December 1993	800
January–May 1994	950

Determine the effect on Alejandro's gross income for 1993 and 1994.

36. Walt made the all-state football team during his junior and senior years in high school. He accepted an athletic scholarship from State University. The scholarship provided the following:

Tuition and fees	$4,000
Room and board	2,500
Books and supplies	500

Determine the effect of the scholarship on Walt's gross income.

37. Determine the taxpayer's taxable damages in each of the following cases:

 a. Orange Corporation collected $500,000 for damages to its business reputation.
 b. Don collected $100,000 in lost wages caused by age discrimination by his employer. Under the relevant law, a successful plaintiff can recover only lost wages.
 c. Kirby was injured in an automobile accident and collected $10,000 for loss of the use of his left arm, $15,000 for pain and suffering, $9,000 in lost wages, $5,000 for medical expenses, and $10,000 of punitive damages. None of the medical expenses had been deducted because Kirby's insurance policy paid the hospital and doctor.
 d. Nell received $10,000 of damages for invasion of her privacy by a photographer and $5,000 of punitive damages.

38. Cole was injured in an accident that was not related to his employment. He incurred $12,000 in medical expenses and collected $4,000 on a medical insurance policy he purchased. He also collected $9,000 in medical benefits under his employer's group plan. Originally, the doctor diagnosed Cole's injury as requiring no more than 3 months of disability. Because of subsequent complications, Cole was unable to return to work until 14 months after the accident. While away from the job, Cole collected $200 per week on his employer's wage continuation plan. Cole also owned an insurance policy that paid him $100 per week while he was disabled. What are the tax consequences to Cole of the receipt of the following?

 a. $10,000 medical benefits.
 b. $300 per week to replace Cole's wages.

39. Rex, age 45, is an officer of Blue Company, which provided him with the following nondiscriminatory fringe benefits in 1993:

 a. Hospitalization insurance for Rex and his dependents. The cost of coverage for Rex was $450, and the additional cost for his dependents was $400.
 b. Reimbursement of $700 from an uninsured medical reimbursement plan available to all employees.
 c. Group term life insurance protection of $120,000. (Each employee received coverage equal to twice his or her annual salary.)
 d. Salary continuation payments of $2,600 while Rex was hospitalized for an illness.

 While Rex was ill, he collected $1,600 on a salary continuation insurance policy he had purchased. Determine the amounts Rex must include in gross income.

40. Ramon served as the manager of an orphanage in 1993. In this connection, he had the following transactions:

 a. He received no salary from his job but was given room and board (valued at $9,600) on the premises. No other person was employed by the orphanage, which is a tax-exempt organization.
 b. The orphanage paid $500 in tuition for a night course Ramon took at a local university. The course was in the field of philosophy and dealt with the meaning of life. The payment was authorized by the orphanage's trustees in a written resolution.
 c. The orphanage paid $900 of the premiums on Ramon's life insurance policy and all of his medical expenses of $1,800. Again, the payment was made pursuant to a resolution approved by the trustees.

 Determine the effect of these transactions on Ramon's gross income.

41. The UVW Union and HON Corporation are negotiating contract terms. What would be the tax consequences of the following options? (Assume the union members are in the 28% marginal tax bracket and all benefits would be provided on a nondiscriminatory basis.)

 a. The company would eliminate the $100 deductible on health insurance benefits, and the employees would take a $100 reduction in pay. Most employees incur more than $100 in medical expenses each year.

b. The employees would get an additional paid holiday with the same annual income (the same pay but less work) or an increase in pay equal to the holiday pay but no additional paid holiday (more pay and the same work).
c. An employee who did not need health insurance (because the employee's spouse works and receives family coverage) would be allowed to receive the cash value of the coverage.

42. Determine the taxpayer's gross income for each of the following:

a. Alice is the manager of a plant. The company owns a house one mile from the plant (rental value of $6,000) that Alice is allowed to occupy.
b. Pam works for an insurance company that allows employees to eat in the cafeteria for 50¢ a meal. Generally, the cost to the insurance company of producing a meal is $5, and a comparable meal could be purchased for $4. Pam ate 150 meals in the cafeteria during the year.
c. Wade is a Methodist minister and receives a housing allowance of $600 per month from his church. Wade is buying his home and uses the $600 to make house payments ($450) and to pay utilities ($150).
d. Floyd is a college professor and lives in campus housing. He is not charged rent. The value of the house is $100,000, and the annual rental value is $7,200.

43. Does the taxpayer recognize gross income in the following situations?

a. Ann is a registered nurse working in a community hospital. She is not required to have her lunch on the hospital premises, but she can eat in the cafeteria at no charge. The hospital adopted this policy to encourage employees to stay on the premises and be available in case of emergencies. During the year, Ann ate most of her meals on the premises. The total value of those meals was $750.
b. Ira is the manager of a hotel. His employer will allow him to live in one of the rooms rent-free or to receive a $600 per month cash allowance for rent. Ira elected to live in the hotel.
c. Seth is a forest ranger and lives in his employer's cabin in the forest. He is required to live there, and because there are no restaurants nearby, the employer supplies Seth with groceries that he cooks and eats on the premises.
d. Rocky is a partner in the ABC Ranch (a partnership). He is the full-time manager of the ranch. ABC has a business purpose for Rocky's living on the ranch.

44. Under a company's former medical insurance plan, employees were responsible for the first $500 of their medical expenses. Under the new cafeteria plan, employees can choose between receiving $500 in cash or having the company provide coverage for all medical expenses. Irene elected the expanded medical benefits. In 1993, she incurred $1,500 of medical expenses that were paid for under the plan. How much is Irene required to include in gross income?

45. Ed is employed by FUN Bowling Lanes, Inc. Determine Ed's gross income in each of the following situations:

a. Ed's children are allowed to use the lanes without charge. Each child can also bring a friend without charge. This benefit is available to all employees. During the year, the children bowled 200 games, and the usual charge was $1.50 per game. Friends of Ed's children bowled 150 games.
b. The company has a lunch counter. Ed is allowed to take home the leftover donuts each night. The company's cost was $400, and the value of the donuts Ed took home was $150.
c. The company pays Ed's subscription to *Bowling Lanes Management*, a monthly journal.

46. PQR Corporation would like you to review its employee fringe benefits program with regard to the effects of the plan on the company's president (Polly), who is also the majority shareholder:

a. All employees receive free tickets to State University football games. Polly is seldom able to attend the games and usually gives her tickets to her nephew. The cost of Polly's tickets for the year was $75.

b. The company pays all parking fees for its officers but not for other employees. The company paid $1,200 for Polly's parking for the year.
c. Employees are allowed to use the copy machine for personal purposes as long as the privilege is not abused. Polly is president of a trade association and made extensive use of the copy machine to prepare mailings to members of the association. The cost of the copies was $900.
d. The company is in the household moving business. Employees are allowed to ship goods without charge whenever there is excess space on a truck. Polly purchased a dining room suite for her daughter. Company trucks delivered the furniture to the daughter. Normal freight charges would have been $600.
e. The company has a storage facility for household goods. Officers are allowed a 20% discount on charges for storing their goods. All other employees are allowed a 10% discount. Polly's discounts for the year totaled $400.

47. Eli works for a company that operates a cruise ship. All employees are allowed to take a one-week cruise each year at no cost to the employee. The employee is provided with a room, meals, and general recreation on the ship. Determine the tax consequences of Eli accepting a trip under the following assumptions:

a. Eli must travel on a standby basis; that is, Eli can travel only if the ship is not completely booked. The room Eli occupies has maid service, and the sheets and towels are changed each day.
b. Eli takes his meals with the other customers who pay a fixed amount for the cruise that includes meals and lodging.
c. The recreation consists of the use of the pool, dancing, and bingo games.
d. All guests must pay for their drinks and snacks between meals, but Eli and the other employees are given a 20% discount.
e. Employees at Eli's level and above are provided with free parking at the pier. Parking for the week would cost $70. This group comprises about 25% of all employees of the company.

48. Pedro is a U.S. citizen and a production manager for MEX Company. On May 1, 1992, he was temporarily assigned to the Monterrey, Mexico, plant. On August 6, 1992, he returned to the United States for medical treatment. On September 1, 1992, he returned to his duties in Monterrey. Except for a two-week period in the United States (December 16–31, 1992), he worked in Monterrey until December 1, 1993, when he was transferred to Boston, Massachusetts. Pedro's salary was $4,000 per month in 1992 and $5,000 per month in 1993. His housing expense did not exceed the base amount. Compute Pedro's foreign earned income exclusion in 1992 and 1993.

49. Determine Hazel's gross income from the following receipts for the year:

Interest on U.S. government savings bonds	$750
Interest on state income tax refund	100
Gain on sale of Augusta County bonds	700
Interest on Augusta County bonds	900
Patronage dividend from Potato Growers Cooperative	1,500

The patronage dividend was received in March of the current year for amounts paid and deducted in the previous year as expenses of Hazel's profitable cash basis farming business.

50. Determine Jack's taxable income from the following items:

a. Jack owns 100 shares of BCD Company common stock. The company has a dividend reinvestment plan. Under the plan, Jack can receive an $18 cash dividend or an additional share of stock with a fair market value of $18. He elected to take the stock.
b. Jack owns 100 shares of NOP Corporation. The company declared a dividend, and Jack was to receive an additional share of the company's stock with a fair market value of $18. Jack did not have the option to receive cash. However, a

management group announced a plan to repurchase all available shares for $18 each. The offer was part of a takeover defense.

c. Jack collected $125 on a corporate debenture. The corporation had been in bankruptcy for several years. Jack had correctly deducted the cost of the bond in a prior year because the bankruptcy judge had informed the bondholders they would not receive anything in the final liquidation. Later the company collected on an unanticipated claim and had the funds to make partial payment on the bonds.

51. Lynn recently inherited $25,000. She is considering using the money to finance a college education for her 5-year-old child. Lynn does not expect her gross income to ever exceed $40,000 a year. She is very concerned with the safety of the principal and has decided to invest the $25,000 in Series EE U.S. government savings bonds. The bonds earn 8% interest each year. At the end of 13 years, when Lynn's child is 18 and ready to go to college, the bonds will be worth $68,000. This is the estimated cost of a 4-year college education at that time.

a. What will be the amount of the after-tax proceeds from the bonds at maturity, assuming Lynn purchases the bonds in her name but uses the proceeds for the child's college education?
b. Should the bonds be purchased in the child's name (with Lynn as custodian) or should Lynn purchase the bonds in her own name?

52. How does the tax benefit rule apply in the following cases?

a. In 1992, Wilma paid Vera $5,000 for locating a potential client. The deal fell through, and in 1993, Vera refunded the $5,000 to Wilma.
b. In 1992, Wilma paid an attorney $300 for services in connection with a title search. Because the attorney was negligent, Wilma incurred some additional costs in acquiring the land. In 1993, the attorney refunded his $300 fee to Wilma.
c. In 1993, Wilma received a $90 dividend with respect to 1993 premiums on her life insurance policy.
d. In 1993, a cash basis farmer received a $400 patronage dividend with respect to 1992 purchases of cattle feed.

53. Fran, who is in the 31% tax bracket, recently collected $100,000 on a life insurance policy she carried on her father. She currently owes $120,000 on her personal residence and $120,000 on business property. National Bank holds the mortgage on both pieces of property and has agreed to accept $100,000 in complete satisfaction of either mortgage. The interest rate on the mortgages is 8%, and both mortgages are payable over 10 years. Fran can also purchase Montgomery County school bonds yielding 8%. What would be the tax consequences of each of the following alternatives, assuming Fran currently deducts the mortgage interest on her tax return?

a. Retire the mortgage on the residence.
b. Retire the mortgage on the business property.
c. Purchase tax-exempt bonds but not pay off either mortgage.

Which alternative should Fran select?

54. RST Company is experiencing financial troubles and is considering negotiating the following with its creditors. Determine the tax consequences to RST of the following plan:

a. The Motor Finance Company will cancel $1,500 in accrued interest. RST had deducted the interest in the prior year. Motor Finance Company will also reduce the principal on the note by $1,000. The note financed the purchase of equipment from a local dealer.
b. The Trust Land Company, which sold RST land and buildings, will reduce the mortgage on the building by $15,000.
c. Ridge, the sole shareholder in the corporation, will cancel a $50,000 receivable from the corporation in exchange for additional stock.

CUMULATIVE PROBLEMS

55. Oliver W. Hand was divorced from Sandra D. Hand on May 12, 1992. On September 6, 1993, Oliver married Beulah Crane. Oliver and Beulah will file a joint return for 1993. Oliver's Social Security number is 262–60–3814. Beulah's number is 259–68–4184, and she will adopt "Hand" as her married name. The Hands live at 210 Mason Drive, Atlanta, GA 30304. Sandra's Social Security number is 219–74–1361.

Oliver is 49 and is employed by Atom, Inc., as an electrical engineer. His salary for 1993 was $55,000. Beulah is 30 and earned $35,000 as a marriage counselor in 1993. She was employed by Family Counselors, Inc.

The divorce agreement required Oliver to make 132 monthly payments to Sandra. The payments are $1,200 per month for 84 months, at which time the payments decrease to $1,000 per month. Oliver and Sandra have a 14-year-old daughter, Daisy Hand. If Daisy should die before she attains age 21, Oliver's remaining payments to Sandra would be reduced to $1,000 per month. Sandra was granted custody of Daisy and can document that she provided $2,000 of support for Daisy. Oliver made 12 payments in 1993. Oliver's employer provided him with group term life insurance coverage in the amount of $90,000 in 1993.

Beulah's employer provided Beulah with free parking in a parking garage adjacent to the office building where Beulah works. The monthly charge to the general public is $50.

Oliver received dividends of $40 on XYZ Corporation stock he owned before marriage, and Beulah received dividends of $50 on her separately owned MNO Corporation stock. They received dividends of $400 on jointly owned RST Corporation stock, which they acquired after marriage. Oliver and Beulah live in a common law state.

Combined itemized deductions for Oliver and Beulah in 1993 were as follows:

State income taxes withheld		
Oliver	$2,900	
Beulah	800	$3,700
Real estate taxes on residence		1,500
Home mortgage interest (paid to Atlanta Federal Savings and Loan)		4,020
Cash contributions to church		900

In 1993, Beulah received a refund of 1992 state income taxes of $600. She had deducted state income taxes withheld as an itemized deduction on her 1992 return. Oliver received a $400 refund on his 1992 state income taxes. He had used the standard deduction in 1992.

Additional information:

- Oliver's employer withheld Federal income tax of $7,650 and $4,253 of FICA (Social Security) tax. Beulah's employer withheld $2,900 of Federal income tax and $2,678 of FICA tax.

Part 1—Tax Computation

Compute the Hands' net tax payable (or refund due) for 1993. Suggested software (if available): *TurboTax* or *MacInTax* for tax return or WFT tax planning software.

Part 2—Tax Planning

Assume the Hands came to you in early December of 1993 seeking tax planning advice for 1993 and 1994. They provide you with the following information:

a. All the facts previously presented will be essentially the same in 1994 except for the items described in (b), (c), (d), and (e) below.

b. Oliver inherited $100,000 from his mother on December 1. He will use part of his inheritance to pay off the mortgage on the Hands' residence on January 3, 1994. Consequently, there will be no mortgage interest expense in 1994.

c. Oliver expects a 6% salary increase in 1994, and Beulah expects a 10% increase.

d. The Hands have pledged to contribute $2,400 to their church in 1994 (as opposed to $900 contributed in 1993). However, they could use Oliver's inherited funds to pay the pledge before the end of 1993 if you advise them to do so to achieve an overall tax savings.
e. The Hands acquired 100 shares of ABC Corporation stock on July 5, 1993, at a total cost of $2,000. The value of the stock has increased rapidly, and it is now worth $5,000. The Hands plan to sell the stock and ask whether they should sell it in 1993 or wait until 1994.

Advise the Hands as to the appropriate tax planning strategy for 1993 and 1994. Support your recommendations by computing their tax liabilities for 1993 and 1994 considering the various available alternatives. Suggested software (if available): WFT tax planning software.

56. Archie S. Monroe (Social Security number 363–33–1411) is 35 years old and is married to Annie B. Monroe (Social Security number 259–68–4284). The Monroes live at 215 Adams Dr., Thor, VA 24317. They file a joint return and have two dependent children (Barry and Betty). In 1993, Archie and Annie had the following transactions:

a. Salary received by Archie from Allen Steel Company (Archie is vice president).	$69,000
b. Interest received on jointly owned State of Nebraska bonds.	8,000
c. Group term life insurance premiums paid by Archie's employer (coverage of $60,000).	220
d. Annual increment in the value of Series E government savings bonds (the Monroes have not previously included the accrued amounts in gross income).	400
e. Taxable dividends received from Allen Steel Company, a U.S. corporation (the stock was jointly owned). Of the $5,900 in dividends, $1,000 was mailed on December 31, 1993, and received by Archie and Annie on January 4, 1994.	5,900
f. Alimony payments to Archie's former wife (Rosa T. Monroe, Social Security number 800–60–2580) under a divorce decree.	9,000
g. Itemized deductions:	
State income tax	1,750
Real estate tax on residence	900
Interest on personal residence (paid to Thor Federal Savings)	3,200
Cash contribution to church	700
h. Federal income tax withheld.	9,634

Part 1—Tax Computation

Compute the Monroes' net tax payable (or refund due) for 1993. Suggested software (if available): *TurboTax* or *MacInTax* or WFT tax planning software.

Part 2—Tax Planning

The Monroes plan to sell 200 shares of AXE, Inc., stock they purchased on July 12, 1982, at a cost of $18,000. The stock is worth $10,000 in December 1993, and the Monroes' broker predicts a continued decline in value. Annie plans to resume her career as a model in 1994, and her earnings will move the Monroes into the 31% bracket. How much Federal income tax will the Monroes save for 1993 if they sell the stock in 1993? Should they sell the stock in 1993 or 1994? Write a letter to the Monroes that contains your advice and prepare a memo for the tax files. Suggested software (if available): WFT tax planning software.

CHAPTER

DEDUCTIONS AND LOSSES: IN GENERAL

OBJECTIVES

Explain the importance of deductions *for* and *from* adjusted gross income.

Classify the deductions *for* and *from* adjusted gross income.

Define "ordinary," "necessary," and "reasonable" in relation to deductible business expenses.

Explain the differences between cash basis and accrual basis.

Discuss the following disallowance possibilities: public policy limitations, political activities, investigation of business opportunities, hobby losses, vacation home rentals, payment of others' expenses, personal expenditures, unrealized losses, capital expenditures, and transactions between related parties.

Explain the substantiation requirements that must be met to take a deduction.

Examine the nondeductibility of expenses and interest related to tax-exempt income.

Describe various tax planning techniques concerning the time value of deductions, unreasonable compensation, shifting deductions, hobby losses, and substantiation requirements.

OUTLINE

CLASSIFICATION OF DEDUCTIBLE EXPENSES

As discussed in Chapters 3 and 4, § 61 provides an all-inclusive definition of gross income. Deductions, however, must be specifically provided for by law. The courts have established the doctrine that an item is not deductible unless a specific provision in the tax law allows its deduction. Whether and to what extent deductions are allowed depends on legislative grace.[1]

It is important to classify deductible expenses as deductions *for* adjusted gross income (AGI) or deductions *from* AGI. Deductions *for* AGI can be claimed whether or not the taxpayer itemizes. Deductions *from* AGI result in a tax benefit only if they exceed the taxpayer's standard deduction. If itemized deductions (*from* AGI) are less than the standard deduction, they provide no tax benefit.

Deductions *for* AGI are also important in determining the *amount* of itemized deductions because many itemized deductions are limited to amounts in excess of specified percentages of AGI. Examples of itemized deductions that are limited by AGI are medical expenses and personal casualty losses.

Itemized deductions that are deductible only to the extent that they exceed a specified percentage of AGI are increased when AGI is decreased. Likewise, when AGI is increased, these itemized deductions are decreased.

EXAMPLE 1

Tina earns a salary of $20,000 and has no other income. She itemizes deductions during the current year. Medical expenses for the year are $1,800. Since medical expenses are deductible only to the extent they exceed 7.5% of AGI, Tina's medical expense deduction is $300 [$1,800 – (7.5% × $20,000)]. If Tina had a $2,000 deduction *for* AGI, her medical expense deduction would be $450 [$1,800 – (7.5% × $18,000)], which is $150 more. If the $2,000 deduction was *from* AGI, her medical expense deduction would remain $300 since AGI is unchanged. ◆

The preceding example illustrates how deductions *for* AGI can affect AGI and thus can affect itemized deductions. Changes in income recognition have a similar impact on AGI and, consequently, on itemized deductions.

A deduction *for* AGI is also more valuable to taxpayers who live in states that begin the tax computation with Federal AGI rather than with Federal taxable income. A lower base of Federal AGI results in lower state income taxes.

Deductions for Adjusted Gross Income

To understand how deductions of individual taxpayers are classified, it is necessary to examine the role of § 62. Section 62 merely classifies various deductions as deductions *for* AGI. It does not provide the authority for taking the deduction. For example, § 212 allows individuals to deduct expenses attributable to income-producing property. Section 62(a)(4) classifies § 212 expenses that are attributable to rents or royalties as deductions *for* AGI. Likewise, a deduction for trade or business expenses is allowed by § 162. These expenses are classified as deductions *for* AGI by § 62(a)(1), if the trade or business does not consist of the performance of services by the taxpayer as an employee.

1. *New Colonial Ice Co. v. Helvering*, 4 USTC ¶1292, 13 AFTR 1180, 54 S.Ct. 788 (USSC, 1934).

If a deduction is not listed in § 62, it is *not* a deduction for AGI; it is an itemized deduction. Following is a partial list of the items classified as deductions *for* AGI by § 62:

1. Expenses attributable to a trade or business carried on by the taxpayer. A trade or business does not consist of the performance of services by the taxpayer as an employee. Trade or business expenses include half of the self-employment tax paid. Tax return preparation fees related to the taxpayer's business as a sole proprietor are deductible. Also deductible are fees incurred in resolving tax deficiencies relating to the taxpayer's sole proprietorship.
2. Expenses incurred by a taxpayer in connection with the performance of services as an employee if the expenses are reimbursed, an adequate accounting is made to the employer, the employee is not allowed to keep any excess reimbursements, and other conditions are satisfied (see Chapter 9).
3. Deductions that result from losses on the sale or exchange of property by the taxpayer.
4. Deductions attributable to property held for the production of rents and royalties. Such deductions include expenses incurred in preparing tax schedules or resolving tax disputes relating to rent or royalty income or losses.
5. The deduction for payment of alimony allowed by § 215.
6. Certain contributions to pension, profit sharing, and annuity plans of self-employed individuals.
7. The deduction for certain retirement savings allowed by § 219 (e.g., IRAs).
8. A certain portion of lump-sum distributions from pension plans taxed under § 402(e).
9. The penalty imposed on premature withdrawal of funds from time savings accounts or deposits.

Items 1 through 5 are covered in detail in various chapters in the text.

Itemized Deductions

Section 63(d) defines itemized deductions as the deductions allowed other than "the deductions allowable in arriving at adjusted gross income." Deductions that are not deductions *for* AGI are itemized deductions.

Section 212 allows deductions for ordinary and necessary expenses paid or incurred for the following:

- The production or collection of income.
- The management, conservation, or maintenance of property held for the production of income.
- Expenses paid in connection with the determination, collection, or refund of any tax.

Section 62(a)(4) classifies § 212 expenses that are related to rent and royalty income as deductions *for* AGI. All other § 212 expenses are itemized deductions (deductions *from* AGI).

Investment-related expenses (e.g., safe deposit box rentals) are deductible as itemized deductions attributable to the production of investment income.

Taxpayers are allowed to deduct certain expenses that are primarily personal in nature. These expenses, which generally are not related to the production of income, are deductions *from* AGI (itemized deductions). Some of the more frequently encountered deductions in this category include the following:

- Contributions to qualified charitable organizations (not to exceed a specified percentage of AGI).
- Medical expenses (in excess of 7.5 percent of AGI).
- State and local taxes (e.g., real estate taxes and state and local income taxes).
- Personal casualty losses (in excess of an overall floor of 10 percent of AGI *and* a $100 floor per casualty).
- Certain personal interest (e.g., mortgage interest on a personal residence).

Some *miscellaneous* itemized deductions are deductible only to the extent that in the aggregate they exceed 2 percent of AGI. Other miscellaneous itemized deductions are fully deductible. Itemized deductions are discussed in detail in Chapter 10.

Trade or Business Expenses

Section 162(a) permits a deduction for all ordinary and necessary expenses paid or incurred in carrying on a trade or business. These include reasonable salaries paid for services, expenses for the use of business property, and one-half of self-employment taxes paid. Such expenses are deducted *for* AGI.

It is sometimes difficult to determine whether an expenditure is deductible as a trade or business expense. The term "trade or business" is not defined in the Code or Regulations, and the courts have not provided a satisfactory definition. It is usually necessary to ask one or more of the following questions to determine whether an item qualifies as a trade or business expense:

- Was the use of the particular item related to a business activity? For example, if funds are borrowed for use in a business, the interest is deductible as a business expense (as a deduction *for* AGI).
- Was the expenditure incurred with the intent to realize a profit or to produce income? For example, expenses in excess of the income from raising horses are not deductible if the activity is classified as a personal hobby rather than a trade or business.
- Were the taxpayer's operation and management activities extensive enough to indicate the carrying on of a trade or business?

Section 162 excludes the following items from classification as trade or business expenses:

- Charitable contributions or gifts.
- Illegal bribes and kickbacks and certain treble damage payments.
- Fines and penalties.

A bribe paid to a domestic official is not deductible if it is illegal under the laws of the United States. Foreign bribes are deductible unless they are unlawful under the Foreign Corrupt Practices Act of 1977.

Ordinary and Necessary Requirement. The terms "ordinary" and "necessary" are found in both §§ 162 and 212. Section 162 governs the deductibility of trade or business expenses. To be deductible, any trade or business expense must be ordinary and necessary. In addition, compensation for services must be "reasonable" in amount.

Many expenses that are necessary are *not* ordinary. The words "ordinary and necessary" are not defined in the Code or Regulations. The courts have held that an expense is necessary if a prudent businessperson would incur the same expense and the expense is expected to be appropriate and helpful in the taxpayer's business.[2]

EXAMPLE 2

Pat purchased a manufacturing concern that had just been adjudged bankrupt. Because the business had a poor financial rating, Pat satisfies some of the obligations to employees and outside salespeople incurred by its former owners. Pat had no legal obligation to pay these debts but felt this was the only way to keep salespeople and employees. The Second Court of Appeals found that the payments were necessary in that they were both appropriate and helpful.[3] However, the Court held that the payments were *not* ordinary but were in the nature of capital expenditures to build a reputation. Therefore, no deduction was allowed. ◆

An expense is ordinary if it is normal, usual, or customary in the type of business conducted by the taxpayer and is not capital in nature. However, an expense need not be recurring to be deductible as ordinary.

EXAMPLE 3

Juan engaged in a mail-order business. The post office judged that his advertisements were false and misleading. Under a fraud order, the post office stamped "fraudulent" on all letters addressed to his business and returned them to the senders. Juan spent $30,000 on legal fees in an unsuccessful attempt to force the post office to stop. The legal fees (though not recurring) were ordinary business expenses because they were normal, usual, or customary in the circumstances. ◆

The law requires that expenses bear a reasonable and proximate relationship to (1) the production or collection of income or to (2) the management, conservation, or maintenance of property held for the production of income.[4]

EXAMPLE 4

Wanda owns a small portfolio of investments, including 10 shares of Hawk, Inc., common stock worth $1,000. She incurred $350 in travel expenses to attend the annual shareholders' meeting at which she voted her 10 shares against the current management group. No deduction is permitted because a 10-share investment is insignificant in value in relation to the travel expenses incurred. ◆

Reasonableness Requirement. Code § 162(a)(1) refers to reasonableness solely with respect to salaries and other compensation for services. The courts, however, have held that for any business expense to be ordinary and necessary it must also be reasonable in amount.[5]

What constitutes reasonableness is a question of fact. If an expense is unreasonable, the excess amount is not allowed as a deduction. The question of reasonableness generally arises with respect to closely held corporations where there is no separation of ownership and management.

Transactions between the shareholders and the company may result in the disallowance of deductions for excessive salaries and rent expense paid by the

2. *Welch v. Helvering*, 3 USTC ¶1164, 12 AFTR 1456, 54 S.Ct. 8 (USSC, 1933).
3. *Dunn and McCarthy, Inc. v. Comm.*, 43–2 USTC ¶9688, 31 AFTR 1043, 139 F.2d 242 (CA–2, 1943).
4. Reg. § 1.212–1(d).
5. *Comm. v. Lincoln Electric Co.*, 49–2 USTC ¶9388, 38 AFTR 411, 176 F.2d 815 (CA–6, 1949).

corporation. The courts will view an unusually large salary in light of all relevant circumstances and may find that the salary is reasonable despite its size.[6] If excessive payments for salaries and rents are closely related to the percentage of stock owned by the recipients, the payments are generally treated as dividends, which are not deductible by the corporation. Deductions for reasonable salaries will not be disallowed solely because the corporation has paid insubstantial portions of its earnings as dividends to its shareholders.

EXAMPLE 5

Paloma Corporation, a closely held corporation, is owned equally by Lupe, Carlos, and Ramon. The company has been highly profitable for several years and has not paid dividends. Lupe, Carlos, and Ramon are key officers of the company, and each receives a salary of $200,000. Salaries for similar positions in comparable companies average only $100,000. Amounts paid to the owners in excess of $100,000 may be deemed unreasonable, and a total of $300,000 in salary deductions may be disallowed. The excess amounts may be treated as dividends rather than salary income to Lupe, Carlos, and Ramon because the payments are proportional to stock ownership. Salaries are deductible by the corporation but dividends are not. ◆

Business and Nonbusiness Losses of Individuals

Section 165 provides for a deduction for losses not compensated for by insurance. Deductible losses of individual taxpayers include those incurred in a trade or business or in a transaction entered into for profit. Individuals are also allowed to deduct losses that are the result of a casualty. Casualty losses include, but are not limited to, fire, storm, shipwreck, and theft (see Chapter 7 for a further discussion of this topic). Deductible personal casualty losses are reduced by $100 per casualty, and the aggregate of all casualty losses is reduced by 10 percent of AGI. A personal casualty loss is an itemized deduction. See Concept Summary 5–3 for the classification of expenses.

Reporting Procedures

All deductions *for* and *from* AGI wind up on pages 1 and 2 of Form 1040. All deductions *for* AGI are reported on page 1. The last line on page 1 is adjusted gross income.

The first item on page 2 is adjusted gross income. Itemized deductions (deductions *from* AGI) are entered next, followed by the deduction for dependency exemptions. The result is taxable income.

Most of the deductions *for* AGI on page 1 originate on supporting schedules. Examples include business expenses (Schedule C) and rent, royalty, partnership, and fiduciary deductions (Schedule E). Other deductions *for* AGI, such as IRAs, Keogh retirement plans, and alimony, are entered directly on page 1 of Form 1040.

All deductions *from* AGI on page 2 are carried over from Schedule A. Some Schedule A deductions originate on other forms. Examples include home mortgage interest, investment interest, noncash charitable contributions in excess of $500, casualty losses, moving expenses, and unreimbursed employee expenses.

Form 1040 becomes a summary of other schedules and forms, pulling together the detailed information from the other forms and schedules. See Concept Summary 5–1.

---

6. *Kennedy, Jr. v. Comm.*, 82–1 USTC ¶9186, 49 AFTR2d 82–628, 671 F.2d 167 (CA–6, 1982), *rev'g* 72 T.C. 793 (1979).

Deductions and Losses—Timing of Expense Recognition

Importance of Taxpayer's Method of Accounting

A taxpayer's method of accounting is a major factor in determining taxable income. The method used determines when an item is includible in income and when an item is deductible on the tax return. Usually, the taxpayer's regular method of record keeping is used for income tax purposes. The taxing authorities do not require uniformity among all taxpayers, but they do require that the

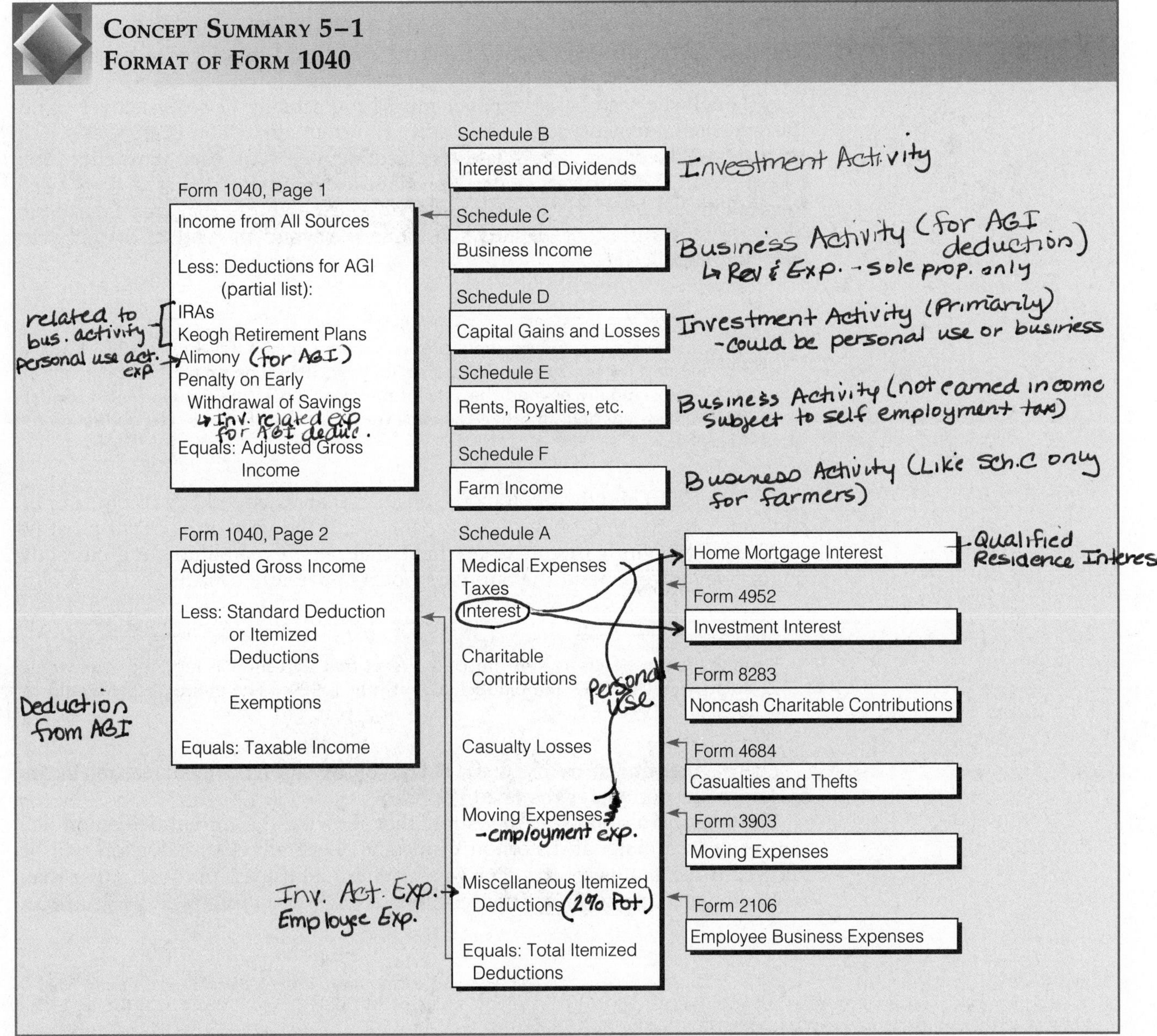

method used clearly reflect income and that items be handled consistently. The most common methods of accounting are the cash method and the accrual method.

Throughout the portions of the Code dealing with deductions, the phrase "paid or incurred" is used. *Paid* refers to the cash basis taxpayer who gets a deduction only in the year of payment. *Incurred* concerns the accrual basis taxpayer who obtains the deduction in the year in which the liability for the expense becomes certain (refer to Chapter 4).

Cash Method Requirements

The expenses of cash basis taxpayers are deductible only when they are actually or constructively paid with cash or other property. Promising to pay or issuing a note does not satisfy the *actually paid* requirement. However, the payment can be made with borrowed funds. At the time taxpayers charge expenses on their bank credit cards, they are allowed to claim the deduction. They are deemed to have simultaneously borrowed money from the credit card issuer and constructively paid the expenses.

Although the cash basis taxpayer must have actually or constructively paid the expense, payment does not assure a current deduction. Cash basis and accrual basis taxpayers cannot take a current deduction for capital expenditures, except through amortization or depreciation over the life of the asset. The Regulations set forth the general rule that an expenditure that creates an asset having a useful life that extends substantially beyond the end of the tax year must be capitalized.[7]

EXAMPLE 6

Kareem, a cash basis taxpayer, rents property from Chahon. On July 1, 1994, Kareem paid $2,400 rent for the 24 months ending June 30, 1996. The prepaid rent extends 18 months— substantially beyond the year of payment. Therefore, Kareem must capitalize the prepaid rent and amortize the expense on a monthly basis. His deduction for 1994 is $600. ◆

The Tax Court and the IRS took the position that an asset that will expire or be consumed by the end of the tax year following the year of payment must be prorated. The Ninth Circuit Court held that such expenditures are currently deductible, however, and the Supreme Court apparently concurs.[8]

EXAMPLE 7

Assume the same facts as in Example 6, except that Kareem was required to pay only 12 months rent in 1994. He paid $1,200 on July 1, 1994. The entire $1,200 would be deductible in 1994. ◆

The payment must be required, not a voluntary prepayment, to obtain the current deduction under the one-year rule.

The taxpayer also must demonstrate that allowing the current deduction will not result in a material distortion of income. Generally, the deduction will be allowed if the item is recurring or was made for a business purpose rather than to manipulate income. Deduction of prepaid interest is disallowed by § 461(g).

7. Reg. § 1.461–1(a).

8. *Zaninovich v. Comm.*, 80–1 USTC ¶9342, 45 AFTR2d 80–1442, 616 F.2d 429 (CA–9, 1980), *rev'g* 69 T.C. 605 (1978). Cited by the Supreme Court in *Hillsboro National Bank v. Comm.*, 83–1 USTC ¶9229, 51 AFTR2d 83–874, 103 S.Ct. 1134 (USSC, 1983).

Several categories of taxpayers are not allowed to use the cash method. See Chapter 15.

Accrual Method Requirements

The period in which an accrual basis taxpayer can deduct an expense is determined by applying the economic performance test. This test is met only when the service, property, or use of property giving rise to the liability is actually performed for, provided to, or used by the taxpayer.

Example 8

On December 15, 1993, a rusted water main broke and flooded the business premises of Chris, an accrual basis, calendar year taxpayer. An outside firm surveyed the damage and estimated the cleanup fee at $6,000. Chris signed a contract (paying 20% down) on December 20, 1993. Because of the holidays, the cleanup crew did not start work until January 2, 1994. Chris cannot deduct the $1,200 until 1994, when the services are performed. ◆

An exception to the economic performance requirements allows certain recurring items to be deducted if the following conditions are met:

- The items are treated consistently.
- Either they are not material in amount or accrual results in better matching of income and expenses.
- The all-events test is met. This test is met when all the events that determine the fact of the liability have occurred and the amount of the liability can be determined with reasonable accuracy.
- Economic performance occurs within a reasonable period but not more than 8½ months after year-end.

Example 9

Rick, an accrual basis, calendar year taxpayer, entered into a monthly maintenance contract during the year. He makes a monthly accrual at the end of every month for this service and pays the fee some time between the first and fifteenth of the following month when services are performed. The amount involved is immaterial, and all other tests are met. The December 1993 accrual is deductible even though the service is performed on January 12, 1994. ◆

Example 10

Rita, an accrual basis, calendar year taxpayer, shipped merchandise sold on December 30, 1993, via Greyhound Van Lines on January 2, 1994, and paid the freight charges at that time. Since Rita reported the sale of the merchandise in 1993, the shipping charge should also be deductible in 1993. This procedure results in a better matching of income and expenses. ◆

Reserves for estimated expenses (frequently employed for financial accounting purposes) generally are not allowed for tax purposes because the economic performance test cannot be satisfied.

Example 11

Bluebird Airlines is required by Federal law to test its engines after 3,000 flying hours. Aircraft cannot return to flight until the tests have been conducted. An unrelated aircraft maintenance company does all of the company's tests for $1,500 per engine. For financial reporting purposes, the company accrues an expense based upon $.50 per hour of flight and credits an allowance account. The actual amounts paid to the maintenance company are offset against the allowance account. For tax purposes, the economic performance test is not satisfied until the work has been done. ◆

Disallowance Possibilities

The tax law provides for the disallowance of certain types of expenses. Without specific restrictions in the tax law, taxpayers might attempt to deduct certain items that in reality are personal expenditures. For example, specific tax rules are provided to determine whether an expenditure is for trade or business purposes and therefore deductible, or related to a personal hobby and therefore nondeductible.

Certain disallowance provisions codify or extend prior court decisions. After the courts denied deductions for payments considered to be in violation of public policy, the tax law was changed to provide specific authority for the disallowance of these deductions. Detailed discussions of specific disallowance provisions in the tax law follow.

Public Policy Limitation

Justification for Denying Deductions. The courts developed the principle that a payment that is in violation of public policy is not a necessary expense and is not deductible.[9]

Although a bribe or fine may be appropriate, helpful, and even contribute to the profitability of an activity, the courts have held that to allow such expenses would frustrate clearly defined public policy. A deduction would dilute the effect of the penalty since the government would be indirectly subsidizing a taxpayer's wrongdoing.

Accordingly, the IRS was free to restrict deductions if, in its view, the expenses were contrary to public policy. But since the law did not explain which actions violated public policy, taxpayers often had to go to court to determine if their expense fell into this category.

Furthermore, the public policy doctrine could be arbitrarily applied in cases where no clear definition had emerged. To solve these problems, Congress enacted legislation that attempts to limit the use of the doctrine. Under this legislation, deductions are disallowed for certain specific types of expenditures that are considered contrary to public policy:

- Bribes and kickbacks (in the case of foreign bribes and kickbacks, only if the payments violate the U.S. Foreign Corrupt Practices Act of 1977).
- Fines and penalties paid to a government for violation of law.

Example 12

Brown Corporation, a moving company, consistently loads its trucks with weights in excess of the limits allowed by state law. The additional revenue more than offsets the fines levied. The fines are for a violation of public policy and are not deductible. ◆

- Two-thirds of the treble damage payments made to claimants resulting from violation of the antitrust law.

9. *Tank Truck Rentals, Inc. v. Comm.*, 58–1 USTC ¶9366, 1 AFTR2d 1154, 78 S.Ct. 507 (USSC, 1958).

No deduction is permitted for a kickback that is illegal under state law if the state law is generally enforced. The kickback must also subject the payer to a criminal penalty or the loss of license or privilege to engage in a trade or business.

Legal Expenses Incurred in Defense of Civil or Criminal Penalties. Generally, legal expenses are deductible *for* AGI as ordinary and necessary business expenses if incurred in connection with a trade or business. Legal expenses may also be deductible *for* AGI as expenses incurred in conjunction with rental property held for the production of income. Legal expenses are deductible *from* AGI if they are for fees for tax advice relative to the preparation of the taxpayer's income tax returns. These tax-related legal fees are itemized deductions (discussed in Chapter 10) that are deductible only to the extent that they exceed 2 percent of AGI.

Personal legal expenses are not deductible. Legal fees incurred in connection with a criminal defense are deductible if the crime is associated with the taxpayer's trade or business.[10] To deduct legal expenses, the taxpayer must be able to show that the origin and character of the claim are directly related to a trade or business or an income-producing activity. Otherwise, the legal expenses are personal and nondeductible.

Example 13

Debra, a financial officer of Blue Corporation, incurred legal expenses in connection with her defense in a criminal indictment for evasion of Blue's income taxes. Debra may deduct her legal expenses because she is deemed to be in the trade or business of being an executive. The legal action impairs her ability to conduct this business activity. ◆

Expenses Relating to an Illegal Business. Although the usual expenses of operating an illegal business (e.g., a numbers racket) are deductible, § 162 disallows a deduction for fines, bribes to public officials, illegal kickbacks, and other illegal payments.

An exception applies to expenses incurred in illegal trafficking in drugs. Drug dealers are not allowed a deduction for ordinary and necessary business expenses incurred in their business. In arriving at gross income from the business, however, dealers may reduce total sales by cost of goods sold. In this regard, no distinction is made between legal and illegal businesses.

Political Contributions and Lobbying Activities

Political Contributions. Generally, no business deduction is permitted for direct or indirect payments for political purposes. Historically, the government has been reluctant to accord favorable tax treatment to business expenditures for political purposes. Allowing deductions might encourage abuses and enable businesses to have undue influence upon the political process.

Lobbying Expenditures. A deduction is allowed for certain expenses incurred to influence legislation, provided that the proposed legislation is of direct interest to the taxpayer. A direct interest exists if the legislation will, or may reasonably be expected to, affect the trade or business of the taxpayer. Dues and expenses

---

10. *Comm. v. Tellier,* 66–1 USTC ¶9319, 17 AFTR2d 633, 86 S.Ct. 1118 (USSC, 1966).

paid to a labor union or trade association where the members have a common direct interest in proposed legislation can be deducted in part. The deduction is in proportion to the organization's allowable legislative activity. No deduction is allowed for expenses incurred to influence the public on legislative matters or for any political campaign.

Example 14

Teresa, a contractor, drove to her state capitol to testify against proposed legislation that would affect building codes. She believes that the proposed legislation is unnecessary and not in the best interest of her company. The expenses are deductible because the legislation is of direct interest to Teresa's company. If she later travels to another city to speak at a Lion's Club meeting concerning the legislation, her travel expenses are not deductible. The expenses are incurred to influence the public on legislative matters. ◆

Investigation of a Business

Investigation expenses are expenses paid or incurred to determine the feasibility of entering a new business or expanding an existing business. They include such costs as travel, engineering and architectural surveys, marketing reports, and various legal and accounting services. How such expenses are treated for tax purposes depends on a number of variables, including the following:

- The current business, if any, of the taxpayer.
- The nature of the business being investigated.
- The extent to which the investigation has proceeded.
- Whether the acquisition actually takes place.

If the taxpayer is in a business the same as or similar to that being investigated, all expenses in this connection are deductible in the year paid or incurred. The tax result is the same whether or not the taxpayer acquires the business being investigated.

Example 15

Terry, an accrual basis sole proprietor, owns and operates three motels in Georgia. In 1994, he incurs expenses of $8,500 in investigating the possibility of acquiring several additional motels located in South Carolina. The $8,500 is deductible in 1994 whether or not Terry acquires the motels in South Carolina. ◆

When the taxpayer is not in a business that is the same as or similar to the one being investigated, the tax result depends on whether the new business is acquired. If the business is not acquired, all investigation expenses generally are nondeductible.

If a taxpayer is in a different business than the one being investigated, and actually acquires the new business, the expenses must be capitalized. At the election of the taxpayer, the expenses may be amortized over a period of 60 months or more.

Hobby Losses

Business or investment expenses are deductible only if the taxpayer can show that the activity was entered into for the purpose of making a profit. Certain activities may have either profit-seeking and/or personal attributes, depending upon individual circumstances. An example is raising horses and operating a farm used as a weekend residence. Personal losses are not deductible, although losses attributable to profit-seeking activities may be deducted and used to offset a taxpayer's other income. For this reason, the tax law limits the deductibility of hobby losses.

General Rules. If an individual or an S corporation can show that an activity has been conducted with the intent to earn a profit, losses from the activity are fully deductible. The hobby loss rules apply only if the activity is not engaged in for profit. Hobby expenses are deductible only to the extent of hobby income.

The Regulations stipulate that the following nine factors should be considered in determining whether an activity is profit-seeking or a hobby:[11]

- Whether the activity is conducted in a businesslike manner.
- The expertise of the taxpayers or their advisers.
- The time and effort expended.
- The expectation that the assets of the activity will appreciate in value.
- The previous success of the taxpayer in the conduct of similar activities.
- The history of income or losses from the activity.
- The relationship of profits earned to losses incurred.
- The financial status of the taxpayer (e.g., if the taxpayer does not have substantial amounts of other income, this may indicate that the activity is engaged in for profit).
- Elements of personal pleasure or recreation in the activity.

Presumptive Rule of § 183. The Code provides a rebuttable presumption that an activity is profit-seeking if it shows a profit in at least three of five prior consecutive years. If the activity involves horses, a profit in at least two of seven consecutive prior years meets the presumptive test. If these profitability tests are met, the activity is presumed to be a trade or business rather than a personal hobby. The IRS bears the burden of proving that the activity is personal rather than trade or business related.

Example 16

Camille, an executive for a large corporation, is paid a salary of $200,000. Her husband is a collector of antiques. Several years ago, he opened an antique shop in a local shopping center and spends most of his time buying and selling antiques. He occasionally earns a small profit from this activity but more frequently incurs substantial losses. If the losses are business related, they are fully deductible against Camille's salary income on a joint return. In resolving this issue, consider the following:

- Initially determine whether the antique activity has met the three-out-of-five years profit test.
- If the presumption is not met, the activity may nevertheless qualify as a business if the taxpayer can show that the intent is to engage in a profit-seeking activity. It is not necessary to show actual profits.
- Attempt to fit the operation within the nine criteria prescribed in the Regulations and listed above. These criteria are the factors considered in trying to rebut the § 183 presumption. ◆

If an activity is deemed to be a hobby, expenses (other than those deductible under other provisions of the Code) are deductible only to the extent of the

---

11. Reg. §§ 1.183–2(b)(1) through (9).

income from the hobby. Hobby-related expenses must be deducted in the following order:

- Amounts deductible under other Code sections without regard to the nature of the activity, such as property taxes.
- Amounts deductible under other Code sections if the activity had been engaged in for profit, but only if those amounts do not affect adjusted basis. Examples include maintenance, utilities, and supplies.
- Amounts deductible under other Code sections if the activity had been engaged in for profit, which affect adjusted basis. Examples include depreciation, amortization, and depletion.

These expenses are deductible as itemized deductions to the extent they exceed 2 percent of AGI.

EXAMPLE 17

Jim, the vice president of an oil company, has AGI of $80,000. He decides to pursue painting in his spare time. He uses a home studio, comprising 10% of the home's square footage. During the current year, Jim incurs the following expenses:

Picture frames	$ 350
Art supplies	300
Fees paid to models	1,000
Home studio expenses:	
Total property taxes	900
Total home mortgage interest	10,000
Depreciation on 10% of home	500
Total home maintenance and utilities	3,600

During the year, Jim sold paintings for a total of $3,200. If the activity is held to be a hobby, he is allowed deductions as follows:

Gross income		$3,200
Deduct: Taxes and interest (10% of $10,900)		1,090
Remainder		$2,110
Deduct: Picture frames	$ 350	
Art supplies	300	
Models' fees	1,000	
Maintenance and utilities (10%)	360	$2,010
Remainder		100
Depreciation ($500, but limited to $100)		100
Net income		$ -0-

Jim includes the $3,200 of income in AGI, making his AGI $83,200. The taxes and interest are itemized deductions, deductible in full. The remaining $2,110 of expenses are reduced by 2% of his AGI ($1,664) so the net deduction is $446. Since the property taxes and home mortgage interest are deductible anyway, the net effect is a $2,754 ($3,200 less $446) increase in taxable income. ◆

EXAMPLE 18

If Jim's activity in Example 17 is held to be a business, he could deduct expenses totaling $2,510 ($2,010 plus $500 of depreciation) *for* AGI, in addition to the $1,090 of taxes and interest. All expenses would be trade or business expenses deductible *for* AGI. His reduction in AGI would be as follows:

Gross income		$3,200
Less: Taxes and interest	$1,090	
Other business expenses	2,010	
Depreciation	500	3,600
Reduction in AGI		$ (400)

◆

Rental of Vacation Homes

Restrictions on the deductions allowed for part-year rentals of personal vacation homes were written into the law to prevent taxpayers from deducting essentially personal expenses as rental losses. Many taxpayers who owned vacation homes had formerly treated the homes as rental property and generated rental losses as deductions *for* AGI. For example, a summer cabin would be rented for 2 months per year, used for vacationing for 1 month, and left vacant the rest of the year. The taxpayer would then deduct 11 months' depreciation, maintenance, etc., as rental expenses, resulting in a rental loss. Section 280A eliminates this treatment by allowing deductions on residences used primarily for personal purposes only to the extent of income generated. Only a break-even situation is allowed; no losses can be deducted.

There are three possible tax treatments for residences used for both personal and rental purposes. The treatment depends upon the relative time the residence is used for personal purposes versus rental use.

Primarily Personal Use. If the residence is rented for less than 15 days per year, it is treated as a personal residence. The rent income is excluded from income, and mortgage interest and real estate taxes are allowed as itemized deductions, as with any personal residence. No other expenses (e.g., depreciation, utilities, maintenance) are deductible.

Example 19

Dixie owns a vacation cottage on the lake. During the current year, she rented it for $1,600 for two weeks, lived in it two months, and left it vacant the remainder of the year. The year's expenses amounted to $6,000 interest expense, $500 property taxes, $1,500 utilities and maintenance, and $2,400 depreciation. Since the property was not rented for at least 15 days, the income is excluded, the interest and property tax expenses are itemized deductions, and the remaining expenses are nondeductible personal expenses. ◆

Primarily Rental Use. If the residence is not used for personal purposes for more than the greater of (1) 14 days or (2) 10 percent of the total days rented, the residence is treated as rental property. The expenses must be allocated between personal and rental days if there are any personal use days during the year. In that case, the deduction of the expenses allocated to rental days can exceed rent income and result in a rental loss. The loss may be deductible under the passive loss rules (discussed in Chapter 6).

Example 20

Assume Dixie in Example 19 rented the cottage for 120 days. The cottage is primarily rental if she did not use it for personal purposes for more than 14 days. ◆

Example 21

Assume Dixie in Example 19 rented the cottage for 200 days. She could use it for personal purposes for no more than 20 days (10% of the rental days) for it to be primarily rental. ◆

EXAMPLE 22

Assume that Dixie in Example 19 used the cottage for 12 days and rented it for 48 days for $4,800. Since she did not use the cottage for more than 14 days, the expenses must be allocated between personal and rental days. The cottage is treated as rental property.

	Percentage of Use	
	Rental 80%	**Personal 20%**
Income	$4,800	$ -0-
Expenses		
Interest ($6,000)	$4,800	$1,200
Property taxes ($500)	400	100
Utilities and maintenance ($1,500)	1,200	300
Depreciation ($2,400)	1,920	480
Total expenses	$8,320	$2,080
Rental loss	($3,520)	$ -0-

Dixie deducts the $3,520 rental loss *for* AGI (assuming she meets the passive loss rules, discussed in Chapter 6). She also has itemized interest of $1,200 and taxes of $100. The portion of utilities and maintenance and depreciation attributable to personal use is not deductible. ◆

Personal/Rental Use. If the residence is rented for 15 or more days *and* is used for personal purposes for more than the greater of (1) 14 days or (2) 10 percent of the total days rented, it is treated as a personal/rental residence. Expenses are allowed only to the extent of income.

EXAMPLE 23

Assume that Dixie in Example 19 rented the property for 30 days and lived in it for 30 days. The residence is classified as personal/rental property since she used it more than 14 days and rented it for more than 14 days. The expenses must be allocated, and the rental expenses are allowed only to the extent of rent income. ◆

If a residence is classified as personal/rental property, the expenses that are deductible anyway (e.g., real estate taxes) must be deducted first. If a positive subtotal results, otherwise nondeductible expenses (e.g., maintenance, utilities, insurance) are allowed next. Finally, depreciation is allowed if any positive balance remains.

Expenses must be allocated between personal and rental days before the limits are applied. The courts have held that taxes and interest, which accrue ratably over the year, are allocated on the basis of 365 days.[12] The IRS, however, disagrees and allocates taxes and interest on the basis of total days of use.[13] Other expenses (utilities, maintenance, depreciation, etc.) are allocated on the basis of total days used.

EXAMPLE 24

Sue rents her vacation home for 60 days and lives in the home for 30 days. The limitations on personal/rental residences apply. Sue's gross rent income is $10,000. For the entire year (not a leap year), the real estate taxes are $2,190; her mortgage interest

12. *Bolton v. Comm.*, 82–2 USTC ¶9699, 51 AFTR2d 83–305, 694 F.2d 556 (CA–9, 1982).

13. Prop.Reg. § 1.280A–3(d)(4).

expense is $10,220; utilities and maintenance expense equals $2,400; and depreciation is $9,000. Using the IRS approach, these amounts are deductible in this specific order:

Gross income	$10,000
Deduct: Taxes and interest (60/90 × $12,410)	8,273
Remainder to apply to rental operating expenses and depreciation	1,727
Deduct: Utilities and maintenance (60/90 × $2,400)	1,600
Balance	$ 127
Deduct: Depreciation (60/90 × $9,000 = $6,000 but limited to above balance)	127
Net income	$ -0-

The nonrental use portion of taxes and interest ($4,137 in this case) is deductible if the taxpayer elects to itemize (see Chapter 10). The personal use portion of utilities, maintenance, and depreciation is not deductible in any case. Also note that the basis of the property is not reduced by the $5,873 depreciation not allowed ($6,000 – $127) because of the above limitation. (See Chapter 12 for a discussion of the reduction in basis for depreciation allowed or allowable.) ◆

Example 25

Using the court's approach in allocating property taxes and interest, Sue, in Example 24, would have this result:

Gross income	$10,000
Deduct: Taxes and interest (60/365 × $12,410)	2,040
Remainder to apply to rental operating expenses and depreciation	$ 7,960
Deduct: Utilities and maintenance (60/90 × $2,400)	1,600
Balance	$ 6,360
Deduct: Depreciation (60/90 × $9,000, but limited to $6,360)	6,000
Net rent income	$ 360

Sue can deduct $10,370 of personal use interest and taxes ($12,410 paid – $2,040 deducted as expense in computing rent income). ◆

Note the contrasting results in Examples 24 and 25. The IRS's approach (Example 24) results in no rental gain or loss and an itemized deduction for taxes and interest of $4,137. In Example 25, Sue has net rent income of $360 and $10,370 of itemized deductions. The court's approach decreases her taxable income by $10,010 ($10,370 itemized deductions less $360 net rent income). The IRS's approach reduces her taxable income by only $4,137.

Example 26

Assume that Sue in Example 24 had not lived in the home at all during the year. The house is rental property. The rental loss is calculated as follows:

Gross income	$10,000
Expenses	
Taxes and interest	$12,410
Utilities and maintenance	2,400
Depreciation	9,000
Total expenses	$23,810
Rental loss	($13,810)

Whether any of the rental loss would be deductible depends upon whether Sue actively participated in the rental activity and met the other requirements for deducting passive losses (discussed in Chapter 6). ◆

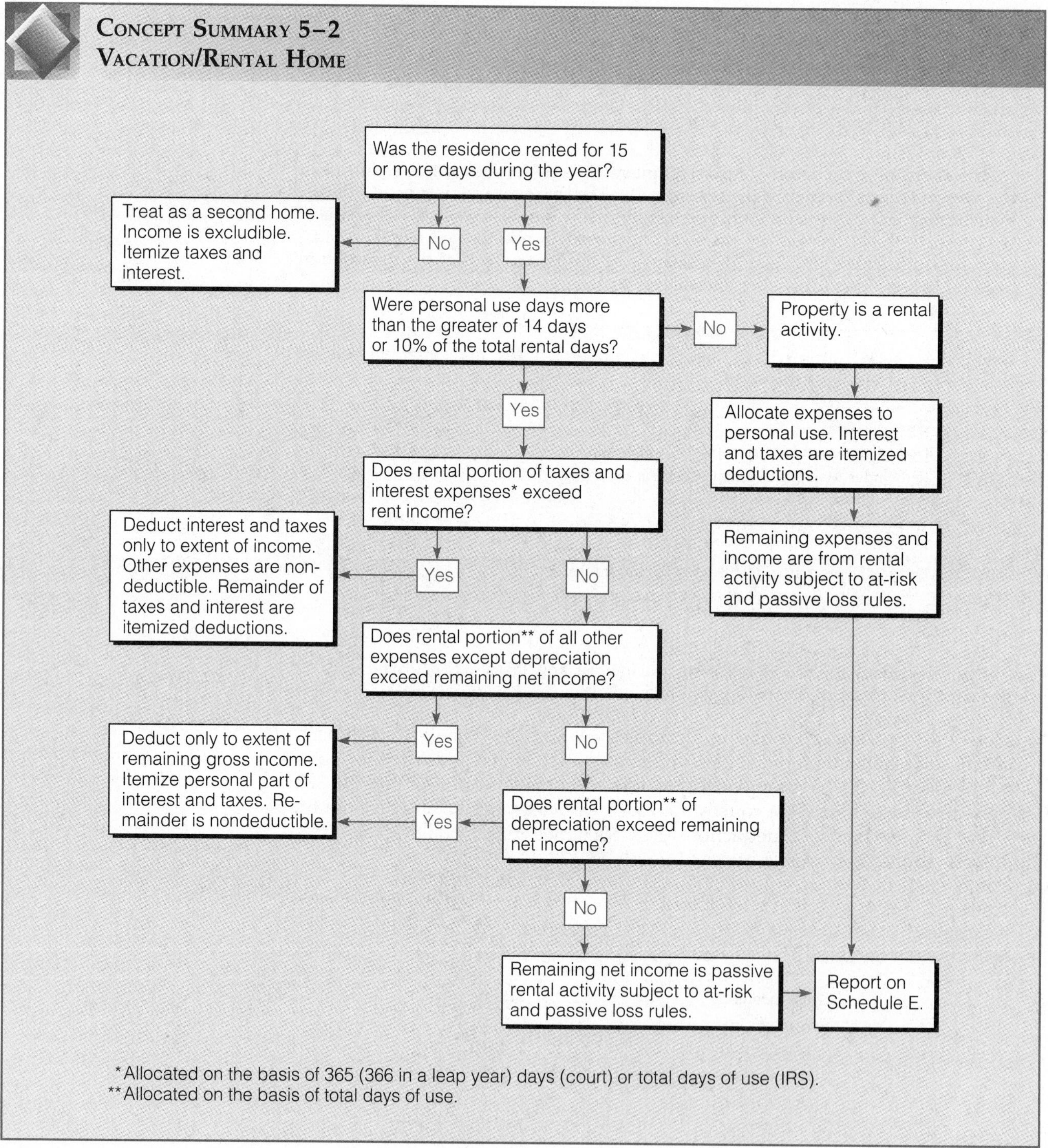
Concept Summary 5–2
Vacation/Rental Home
Was the residence rented for 15 or more days during the year?
No
Yes
Treat as a second home. Income is excludible. Itemize taxes and interest.
Were personal use days more than the greater of 14 days or 10% of the total rental days?
No
Property is a rental activity.
Allocate expenses to personal use. Interest and taxes are itemized deductions.
Remaining expenses and income are from rental activity subject to at-risk and passive loss rules.
Yes
Does rental portion of taxes and interest expenses* exceed rent income?
Yes
Deduct interest and taxes only to extent of income. Other expenses are non-deductible. Remainder of taxes and interest are itemized deductions.
No
Does rental portion** of all other expenses except depreciation exceed remaining net income?
Yes
Deduct only to extent of remaining gross income. Itemize personal part of interest and taxes. Remainder is nondeductible.
No
Does rental portion** of depreciation exceed remaining net income?
Yes
No
Remaining net income is passive rental activity subject to at-risk and passive loss rules.
Report on Schedule E.
*Allocated on the basis of 365 (366 in a leap year) days (court) or total days of use (IRS).
**Allocated on the basis of total days of use.

Expenditures Incurred for Taxpayer's Benefit or Taxpayer's Obligation

An expense must be incurred for the taxpayer's benefit or arise from the taxpayer's obligation. An individual cannot claim a tax deduction for the payment of the expenses of another individual.

EXAMPLE 27

During the current year, Sanjay pays the interest on his son, Vijay's, home mortgage. Neither Sanjay nor Vijay can take a deduction for the interest paid. Sanjay is not entitled to a deduction because the mortgage is not his obligation. Vijay cannot claim a deduction because he did not pay the interest. The tax result would have been more favorable had Sanjay made a cash gift to Vijay and let him pay the interest. Then Vijay could have deducted the interest, and Sanjay might not have been liable for any gift taxes, depending upon the amount involved. A deduction would have been created with no cash difference to the family. ◆

One exception to this rule applies to the payment of medical expenses for a dependent. Such expenses are deductible by the payer.

Disallowance of Personal Expenditures

Section 262 states that "except as otherwise expressly provided in this chapter, no deduction shall be allowed for personal, living, or family expenses." Thus, to justify a deduction, an individual must be able to identify a particular Section of the Code that sanctions the deduction (e.g., charitable contributions, § 170; medical expenses, § 213; moving expenses, § 217). Sometimes the character of a particular expenditure is not easily determined.

EXAMPLE 28

During the current year, Howard pays $1,500 in legal fees and court costs to obtain a divorce from his wife, Vera. Involved in the divorce action is a property settlement that concerns the disposition of income-producing property owned by Howard. In a similar situation, the Tax Court held that the taxpayer could not deduct any of the legal fees and court costs. "Although fees primarily related to property division concerning his income-producing property, they weren't ordinary and necessary expenses paid for conservation or maintenance of property held for production of income. Legal fees incurred in defending against claims that arise from a taxpayer's marital relationship aren't deductible expenses regardless of possible consequences on taxpayer's income-producing property."[14] ◆

The IRS has clarified the issue of the deduction of legal fees incurred in connection with a divorce.[15] To be deductible, an expense must relate solely to tax advice in a divorce proceeding. For example, legal fees attributable to the determination of dependency exemptions of children are deductible if the fees are distinguishable from the general legal fees incurred in obtaining a divorce. Other examples are the costs of creating a trust to make periodic alimony payments and the determination of tax consequences of a property settlement. Therefore, it is advisable to request an itemization of attorney's fees to substantiate a deduction for the tax-related amounts.

14. *Harry H. Goldberg,* 29 TCM 74, T.C.Memo., 1970–27.

15. Rev.Rul. 72–545, 1972–2 C.B. 179.

Disallowance of Deductions for Unrealized Losses

One of the basic concepts in the tax law is that a deduction can be taken only when a loss has actually been realized. A drop in the market price of securities held by the taxpayer does not result in a deductible loss until the securities are actually sold or exchanged at the lower price. Any deductible loss is limited to the taxpayer's basis in the asset.

Disallowance of Deductions for Capital Expenditures

The Code specifically disallows a deduction for "any amount paid out for new buildings or for permanent improvements or betterments made to increase the value of any property or estate."[16] The Regulations further define capital expenditures to include expenditures that add to the value or prolong the life of property or adapt the property to a new or different use.[17] Incidental repairs and maintenance of the property are not capital expenditures and can be deducted as ordinary and necessary business expenses. Repairing a roof is a deductible expense, but replacing a roof is a capital expenditure subject to depreciation deductions over its useful life. The tune-up of a delivery truck is an expense; a complete overhaul probably is a capital expenditure.

Exceptions. There are several exceptions to the general rule regarding capitalization of expenditures. Taxpayers can elect to expense certain mineral developmental costs and intangible drilling costs. Certain farm capital expenditures (such as soil and water conservation) and certain research and experimental expenditures may be expensed immediately.

In addition, § 179 permits an immediate write-off of certain amounts of depreciable property. These provisions are discussed more fully in Chapter 8.

Capitalization versus Expense. When an expenditure is capitalized rather than expensed, the deduction is at best deferred and at worst lost forever. Although an immediate tax benefit for a large cash expenditure is lost, the cost can be deducted in increments over a longer period of time. If the expenditure is for some improvement that has an ascertainable life, it can be capitalized and depreciated or amortized over that life. Costs that can be amortized include copyrights and patents. Many other expenditures, such as land and payments made for goodwill, cannot be amortized or depreciated. Goodwill has an indeterminate life, and land is not a depreciable asset since its value generally does not decline.

EXAMPLE 29

Stan purchased a prime piece of land located in an apartment-zoned area. He paid $500,000 for the property, which had an old but usable apartment building on it. Stan immediately had the building demolished at a cost of $100,000. The $500,000 purchase price and the $100,000 demolition costs must be capitalized, and the basis of the land is $600,000. Since land is a nondepreciable asset, no deduction is allowed. More favorable tax treatment might result if Stan rented the apartments in the old building for a period of time to attempt to establish that there was no intent to demolish the building. If Stan's attempt is successful, it might be possible to allocate a substantial portion of the original purchase price of the property to the building (a depreciable asset). When the building is later demolished, any remaining adjusted basis can be deducted as an ordinary (§ 1231) loss. (See Chapter 13 for a discussion of the treatment of § 1231 assets.) ◆

16. § 263(a)(1).

17. Reg. § 1.263(a)–1(b).

Capitalization Elections. The treatment of most capital expenditures is not elective. In certain cases, however, a taxpayer may elect to capitalize a particular item *or* to expense it immediately. Section 266 allows some taxpayers (but not individuals, S corporations, or personal holding companies) an opportunity to capitalize certain "taxes and carrying charges." The election applies to carrying charges, interest on indebtedness, and certain taxes (such as property and employer-paid payroll taxes) paid during the construction period on realty or personalty. It does not matter whether the property is business or nonbusiness in nature. A taxpayer may elect to capitalize some expenditures and not others, e.g., to capitalize property taxes and expense interest on the construction indebtedness. A new election may be made for each project. One could elect to capitalize expenditures on a factory being constructed and expense the same type of items on a constructed machine. On unimproved and unproductive real estate (land held for later sale, for example), a new election must be made for each year.

Section 263A requires individuals, S corporations, and personal holding companies to capitalize construction period interest and taxes, subject to specific rules for amortizing such amounts (see Chapter 8). This Code Section was intended both to match expenses with income in accordance with the traditional accounting principle and to restrict tax shelter opportunities for individuals.

Transactions between Related Parties

The Code places restrictions on the recognition of gains and losses between related parties. Without these restrictions, relationships created by birth, marriage, and business would provide endless possibilities for engaging in financial transactions that would produce tax savings with no real economic substance or change. For example, to create an artificial loss, a wife could sell property to her husband at a loss and deduct the loss on their joint return. Her husband then could hold the asset indefinitely, and the family would sustain no real economic loss. A complex set of laws has been designed to eliminate such possibilities.

Losses. Section 267 provides for the disallowance of any "losses from sales or exchanges of property . . . directly or indirectly" between related parties. When the property is subsequently sold to a nonrelated party, any gain recognized is reduced by the loss that was previously disallowed.

EXAMPLE 30

Freida sells common stock with a basis of $1,000 to her son, Bill, for $800. Bill sells the stock several years later for $1,100. Freida's $200 loss is disallowed upon the sale to Bill, and only $100 of gain is taxable to him upon the subsequent sale ($300 gain – $200 previously disallowed loss). ◆

EXAMPLE 31

Khalid sells common stock with a basis of $1,000 to his son, Rashad, for $800. Rashad sells the stock to an unrelated party for $900. Rashad's gain of $100 is not recognized because of Khalid's previously disallowed loss of $200. Note that the offset may result in only partial tax benefit upon the subsequent sale. If the property had not been transferred to Rashad, Khalid could have recognized a $100 loss upon the subsequent sale to the unrelated party ($1,000 basis – $900 selling price). ◆

EXAMPLE 32

Jaime sells common stock with a basis of $1,000 to an unrelated third party for $800. His son repurchased the same stock in the market on the same day for $800. The $200 loss is not allowed because the transaction is an indirect sale between related parties. ◆

Unpaid Expenses and Interest. Section 267 also prevents related taxpayers from engaging in tax avoidance schemes in which one related taxpayer uses the accrual method of accounting and the other is on the cash basis. An accrual basis closely held corporation, for example, could borrow funds from a cash basis individual shareholder. At the end of the year, the corporation would accrue and deduct the interest, but the cash basis lender would not recognize interest income since no interest had been paid. Section 267 specifically defers deduction by the accruing taxpayer until the recipient taxpayer must include it in income, that is, when the amount is actually paid to the cash basis taxpayer. The rule applies to interest as well as to other expenses, such as salaries and bonuses.

Relationships and Constructive Ownership. Section 267 operates to disallow losses and defer deductions only between related parties. Losses or deductions generated by similar transactions with an unrelated party are allowed. Related parties include the following:

- Brothers and sisters (whether whole, half, or adopted), a spouse, ancestors (parents, grandparents), and lineal descendants (children, grandchildren) of the taxpayer.
- A corporation owned more than 50 percent (directly or indirectly) by the taxpayer.
- Two corporations that are members of a controlled group.
- A series of other complex relationships between trusts, corporations, and individual taxpayers.

The law provides that constructive ownership rules are applied to determine whether the taxpayers are related. These rules state that stock owned by certain relatives or related entities is deemed to be owned by the taxpayer for purposes of applying the loss and expense deduction disallowance provisions. A taxpayer is deemed to own not only his or her stock but the stock owned by his or her lineal descendants, ancestors, brothers and sisters or half-brothers and half-sisters, and spouse. The taxpayer also is deemed to own his or her proportionate share of stock owned by any partnership, corporation, estate, or trust of which he or she is a shareholder, partner, or beneficiary. An individual is deemed to own any stock owned, directly or indirectly, by his or her partner. Constructive ownership by an individual of the partnership's and the other partner's shares does not extend to the individual's spouse or other relatives.

EXAMPLE 33

The stock of Sparrow Corporation is owned 20% by Ted, 30% by his father, 30% by his mother, and 20% by his sister. On July 1 of the current year, Ted loaned $10,000 to Sparrow Corporation at 8% annual interest, principal and interest payable on demand. For tax purposes, Sparrow uses the accrual basis and Ted uses the cash basis. Both are on a calendar year. Since Ted is deemed to own the 80% owned by his parents and sister, he constructively owns 100% of Sparrow Corporation. If the corporation accrues the interest within the taxable year, no deduction can be taken until payment is made to Ted. ◆

Substantiation Requirements

The tax law is built on a voluntary system. Taxpayers file their tax returns, report income and take deductions to which they are entitled, and pay their taxes through withholding or estimated tax payments during the year. The taxpayer has the burden of proof for substantiating expenses deducted on the returns and thus must retain adequate records. Upon audit, the IRS may disallow any undocumented or unsubstantiated deductions. This has resulted in numerous conflicts between taxpayers and the IRS.

Some events throughout the year should be documented as they occur. For example, it is generally advisable to receive a pledge payment statement from one's church, in addition to a canceled check, for proper documentation of a charitable contribution. Other types of deductible expenditures may require receipts or some other type of support.

Specific and *more stringent* rules for deducting travel, entertainment, and gift expenses are discussed in Chapter 9. Certain mixed-use (both personal and business) and *listed* property is also subject to the adequate records requirement (discussed in Chapter 8).

Expenses and Interest Relating to Tax-Exempt Income

Certain income, such as interest on municipal bonds, is tax-exempt. Section 212 allows the taxpayer to deduct expenses incurred for the production of income, but § 265 disallows deductions related to tax-exempt income. If it were not for the disallowance provisions of § 265, it might be possible to make money at the expense of the government by excluding interest income and deducting interest expense.

Judicial Interpretations. It is often difficult to show a direct relationship between borrowings and investment in tax-exempt securities. Suppose, for example, that a taxpayer borrows money, adds it to existing funds, buys inventory and stocks, then later sells the inventory and buys municipal bonds. A series of transactions such as these can completely obscure any connection between the loan and the tax-exempt investment. One solution would be to disallow interest on any debt to the extent that the taxpayer holds any tax-exempt securities. This approach would preclude individuals from deducting part of their home mortgage interest if they owned any municipal bonds. The law was not intended to go to such extremes. As a result, judicial interpretations have tried to be reasonable in disallowing interest deductions under § 265.

In one case,[18] a company used municipal bonds as collateral on short-term loans to meet seasonal liquidity needs. The Court disallowed the interest deduction on the grounds that the company could predict its seasonal liquidity needs. The company should anticipate the need to borrow the money to continue to carry the tax-exempt securities. The same company *was* allowed an interest deduction on a building mortgage, even though tax-exempt securities it owned could have been sold to pay off the mortgage. The Court reasoned that short-term liquidity position would have been impaired if the tax-exempt securities were sold. Furthermore, the Court ruled that carrying the tax-exempt securities bore no relationship to the long-term financing of a construction project.

In another case,[19] the Court disallowed an interest deduction to a company that refused to sell tax-exempt securities it had received from the sale of a major asset. The company's refusal to sell the tax-exempt securities necessitated large borrowings to finance company operations. The Court found that the primary reason that the company would not sell its bonds to reduce its bank debt was the tax savings. The bonds and the debt both arose from the same transaction and were therefore directly related.

Time Value of Tax Deductions

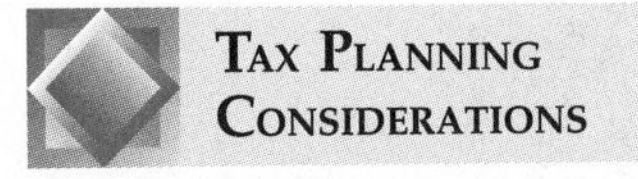
Tax Planning Considerations

Cash basis taxpayers often have the ability to make early payments for their expenses at the end of the tax year. This permits the payments to be deducted

18. *The Wisconsin Cheeseman, Inc. v. U.S.*, 68–1 USTC ¶9145, 21 AFTR2d 383, F.2d 420 (CA–7, 1968).

19. *Illinois Terminal Railroad Co. v. U.S.*, 67–1 USTC ¶9374, 19 AFTR2d 1219, 375 F.2d 1016 (Ct.Cls., 1967).

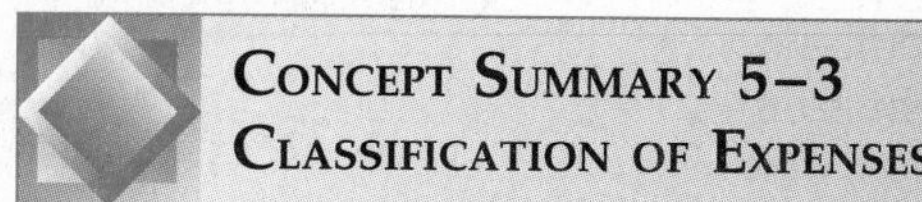

Concept Summary 5–3
Classification of Expenses

Expense Item	Deductible For AGI	Deductible From AGI	Not Deductible	Applicable Code §
Investment expenses				
Rent and royalty	X			§ 62(a)(4)
All other investments		X[4]		§ 212
Employee expenses				
Commuting expenses			X	§ 262
Travel and transportation[1]		X[4,5]		§ 162(a)(2)
Reimbursed expenses	X			§ 62(a)(2)(A)
Moving expenses		X		§ 217
Entertainment[1]		X[4,5]		§ 212
All other employee expenses[1]		X[4,5]		§ 212
Certain expenses of performing artists	X			§ 62(a)(2)(B)
Trade or business expenses	X			§ 162
Casualty losses				
Business	X			§ 165(c)(1)
Personal		X[6]		§ 165(c)(3)
Tax determination, Collection, or Refund expenses	X[8]	X[4]		§ 212
Bad debts	X			§ 166
Medical expenses		X[7]		§ 213
Charitable contributions		X		§ 170
Taxes				
Trade or business	X			§ 162
Personal taxes				
Real property		X		§ 164(a)(1)
Personal property		X		§ 164(a)(2)
State and local income		X		§ 164(a)(3)
Investigation of a business[2]	X			§ 162
Interest				
Business	X			§ 162
Personal[3]		X		§ 163(a)
All other personal expenses			X	§ 262

1. Deduction *for* AGI if reimbursed, an adequate accounting is made, and employee is required to repay excess reimbursements.
2. Provided certain criteria are met.
3. Subject to the excess investment interest provisions.
4. Subject (in the aggregate) to a 2%-of-AGI floor imposed by § 67.
5. Only 80% of meals and entertainment are deductible.
6. Subject to a 10%-of-AGI floor and a $100 floor.
7. Subject to a 7.5%-of-AGI floor.
8. Only that portion relating to business, rental, or royalty activities.

currently instead of in the following tax year. In view of the time value of money, a tax deduction this year may be worth more than the same deduction next year. Before employing this strategy, the taxpayer must consider next year's expected income and tax rates and whether a cash-flow problem may develop from early payments.

The time value of money as well as tax rate changes must be considered when an expense can be paid and deducted in either of two years.

EXAMPLE 34

Jena pledged $5,000 to her church's special building fund. She can make the contribution in December 1993 or January 1994. Jena is in the 31% tax bracket in 1993 and in the 28% bracket in 1994. She itemizes in both years. If she takes the deduction in 1993, she saves $254 ($1,550 – $1,296), due to the decrease in the tax rates and the time value of money.

	1993	1994
Contribution	5,000	5,000
Tax bracket	.31	.28
Tax savings	$1,550	$1,400
Discounted @ 8%	1.0	.926
Savings in present value	$1,550	$1,296

◆

EXAMPLE 35

Assume the same facts as in Example 34, except that Jena is in the 28% bracket in both 1993 and 1994. By taking the deduction in 1993, Jena saves $104 ($1,400 – $1,296), due to the time value of money.

	1993	1994
Contribution	$5,000	$5,000
Tax bracket	.28	.28
Tax savings	$1,400	$1,400
Discounted @ 8%	1.0	.926
Savings in present value	$1,400	1,296

◆

Unreasonable Compensation

In substantiating the reasonableness of a shareholder-employee's compensation, an internal comparison test is sometimes useful. If it can be shown that employees who are nonshareholders receive the same (or more) compensation as shareholder-employees in comparable positions, it is indicative that compensation is not unreasonable.

Another possibility is to demonstrate that the shareholder-employee has been underpaid in prior years. For example, the shareholder-employee may have agreed to take a less-than-adequate salary during the unprofitable formative years of the business, expecting the "postponed" compensation to be paid in later, more profitable years. The agreement should be documented, if possible, in the corporate minutes.

Keep in mind that in testing for reasonableness, the *total* pay package must be considered. All fringe benefits or perquisites, such as contributions by the corporation to a qualified pension plan, must be taken into account, even though those amounts are not immediately available to the covered employee-shareholder.

Shifting Deductions

Taxpayers should manage their obligations to avoid the loss of a deduction. Deductions can be shifted among family members, depending upon who makes the payment. For example, a father buys a condo for his daughter and puts the title in both names. The taxpayer who makes the payment gets the deduction for the property taxes. If the condo is owned by the daughter only and her father makes the payment, neither is entitled to a deduction.

Hobby Losses

To demonstrate that an activity has been entered into for the purpose of making a profit, a taxpayer should treat the activity as a business. The business should engage in advertising, use business letterhead stationery, and maintain a business phone.

If a taxpayer's activity earns a profit in three out of five consecutive years, the presumption is that the activity is engaged in for profit. It may be possible for a cash basis taxpayer to meet these requirements by timing the payment of expenses or the receipt of revenues. The payment of certain expenses incurred before the end of the year might be made in the following year, or the billing of year-end sales might be delayed so that collections are received in the following year.

Keep in mind that the three-out-of-five-years rule under § 183 is not absolute. All it does is shift the presumption. If a profit is not made in three out of five years, the losses may still be allowed if the taxpayer can show that they are due to the nature of the business. For example, success in artistic or literary endeavors can take a long time. Also, due to the present state of the economy, even full-time farmers and ranchers are often unable to show a profit. How can one expect a part-time farmer or rancher to do so?

Merely satisfying the three-out-of-five-years rule does not guarantee that a taxpayer is automatically home free. If the three years of profits are insignificant relative to the losses of other years, or if the profits are not from the ordinary operation of the business, the taxpayer is vulnerable. The IRS may still be able to establish that the taxpayer is not engaged in an activity for profit. If a taxpayer in such a situation can show conformity with the factors enumerated in the Regulations[20] or can show evidence of business hardships (e.g., injury, death, or illness), the government cannot override the presumptive rule of § 183.[21]

PROBLEM MATERIALS

DISCUSSION QUESTIONS

1. Tyson, who is single, had AGI of $30,000 and deductions of $5,000. Would it matter to him whether the deductions were *for* or *from* AGI? Why or why not?
2. If a taxpayer is audited and $1,000 of income is added to his AGI, will his tax increase (ignoring penalties and interest) be equal to $1,000 multiplied by his marginal tax bracket? Discuss.

---

20. Reg. §§ 1.183–2(b)(1) through (9).

21. *Faulconer, Sr. v. Comm.*, 84–2 USTC ¶9955, 55 AFTR2d 85–302, 748 F.2d 890 (CA–4, 1984), *rev'g* 45 TCM 1084, T.C. Memo. 1983–165.

3. Are the following items deductible *for* AGI, deductible *from* AGI, or nondeductible personal items?

   a. Unreimbursed travel expenses of an employee.
   b. Alimony payments.
   c. Charitable contributions.
   d. Medical expenses.
   e. Rental of safe deposit box in which stocks and bonds are kept.
   f. Repairs made on a personal residence.
   g. Expenses related to tax-exempt municipal bonds.

4. Are the following expenditures deductible *for* AGI, deductible *from* AGI, nondeductible personal items, or capital expenditures?

   a. Repairs made to a rental property.
   b. State income taxes.
   c. Investment advice subscriptions.
   d. Child support payments.
   e. New roof on rental property.
   f. New roof on personal residence.
   g. Mortgage interest on personal residence.

5. Define and contrast the "ordinary" and "necessary" tests for business expenses.
6. When Jason died, he left equal shares of stock to his four children, although he made it clear that he wanted Jill and John to run the company. This was quite all right with the other two children, who were to receive $100,000 each per year from the company and were free to pursue their own interests. Jill and John each received reasonable salaries of $250,000 and $210,000, respectively. They paid the other two children salaries of $100,000 each. What were they trying to accomplish from a tax standpoint? Will it work? If not, what are the tax consequences to the corporation and to the other two children?
7. Landry, a cash basis taxpayer, decides to reduce his taxable income for 1993 by buying $10,000 worth of supplies on December 28, 1993. The supplies will be used up in 1994. Can Landry deduct this expenditure in 1993? Would your answer differ if he bought the supplies because a supplier was going out of business and had given him a significant discount on the supplies?
8. Masie operates a drug-running operation. Which of the following expenses she incurs are deductible?

   a. Bribes paid to border guards.
   b. Salaries to employees.
   c. Price paid for drugs purchased for resale.
   d. Kickbacks to police.
   e. Rent on an office.

9. Kelly is an executive in Gray Corporation. She used insider information to buy Gray stock just before public announcement of the discovery of huge oil reserves on company-owned property. She was caught and incurred legal expenses and treble damage payments. Can Kelly deduct either expense?
10. What is the significance of one's present occupation in determining the deductibility of expenses incurred in investigating another business?
11. What factors should be considered in determining whether an activity is profit-seeking or a hobby? Discuss.
12. What is meant by the statement that § 183 is a "presumptive rule"?
13. Contrast the differing results obtained in a personal/rental situation by allocating property taxes and interest on the IRS's basis and the court's basis. Which method would the taxpayer prefer?
14. Discuss the tax treatment of the rental of a vacation home if it is:

    a. Rented 10 days during the year.
    b. Rented 130 days during the year; used personally for 12 days.
    c. Rented for 250 days; used personally for 40 days.

15. Explain what legal fees, if any, are deductible when incurred obtaining a divorce. Are they deductible *for* or *from* AGI?

16. Igor repaired the roof on his factory at a cost of $1,500 in the current year. During the same year, Raisa replaced the roof on her small rental house for $1,500. Both taxpayers are on the cash basis. Are their expenditures treated the same on their tax returns? Why or why not?

17. Helen owns 20% of Black Corporation; 20% of Black's stock is owned by Sara, Helen's mother; 15% is owned by Richard, Helen's brother; the remaining 45% is owned by unrelated parties. Helen is on the cash basis, and Black Corporation is on the accrual basis. On December 31, 1993, Black accrued Helen's salary of $5,000 and paid it on April 4, 1994. Both Black and Helen are on a calendar year. What are the tax effects to Black and Helen?

18. Discuss the reasons for the disallowance of losses between related parties. Would it make any difference if a parent sold stock to an unrelated third party and the child repurchased the same number of shares of the stock in the market the same day?

19. Tara sold 100 shares of Eagle Company stock to Frank, her brother, for $8,000. She had originally paid $7,100 for the stock. Frank later sold the stock for $6,000 on the open market. What are the tax consequences to Tara and Frank?

20. Would your answer to Question 19 differ if Tara had sold the stock to Frank for $6,500?

21. Robin Corporation is owned as follows:

Irene	20%
Paul, Irene's husband	20%
Sylvia, Irene's mother	15%
Ron, Irene's father	25%
Quinn, an unrelated party	20%

Irene and Paul each loaned Robin Corporation $10,000 out of their separate funds. On December 31, 1993, Robin accrued interest at 6% on both loans. The interest was paid on February 4, 1994. Robin is on the accrual basis, and Irene and Paul are on the cash basis. What is the tax treatment of this interest expense/income to Irene, Paul, and Robin?

22. Why are taxpayers required to substantiate their expenditures in order to obtain a deduction?

PROBLEMS

23. Ted filed his 1992 tax return, claiming two exemptions and itemizing his deductions as follows:

AGI (salary)			$20,000
Less: Itemized deductions:			
Medical expenses	$1,800		
Less: 7½% of AGI	1,500	$ 300	
Charitable contributions		1,900	
Interest		5,300	
Taxes		900	
Miscellaneous	$ 600		
Less: 2% of AGI	400	200	
Total itemized deductions			8,600
			$11,400
Less: 2 exemptions			4,600
Taxable income			$ 6,800

In 1993, Ted realized that he had forgotten to deduct his $2,000 IRA contribution for 1992. On an amended return (Form 1040X), what is his new AGI? Taxable income?

24. Peggy, who is single, has a sole proprietorship and keeps her books on the cash basis. Following is a summary of her receipts, disbursements, and other items related to her business account for 1994:

Receipts	
Sales	$28,000
Dividend received from AT&T	300
Interest on savings account	450
Long-term capital gain on sale of stock	1,200
Disbursements	
Rent on building used 75% for business and 25% for living quarters	6,000
Salary paid to part-time secretary	3,000
Taxes	
Gross receipts tax on sales	840
State income taxes	750
Charitable contributions	1,400
Insurance on business property (policy runs from October 1, 1994, to September 30, 1995)	1,200
Depreciation on business equipment	1,000
Business supplies	980

Calculate Peggy's AGI for 1994.

25. Andrew, a cash basis taxpayer, had the following income and expenses in his local trucking business:

Service fees collected	$322,000
Expenses:	
Salaries paid to drivers	185,000
Repairs and maintenance on trucks	15,000
Supplies	8,000
Fuel purchased	63,000
Fines for overloading trucks	4,200
Depreciation on trucks	30,600
Purchase price of two new trucks (paid $40,000 down and signed an installment note for the balance)	120,000
Interest paid on truck installment note	4,000
Tax return preparation fees (60% was for Schedule C preparation)	1,000
Protection money paid to local gang so trucks would not be vandalized	12,000

What is Andrew's net income from this business for tax purposes?

26. David runs an illegal numbers racket. His gross income was $500,000. He incurred the following expenses:

Illegal kickbacks	$20,000
Salaries	80,000
Rent	24,000
Utilities and telephone	9,000
Bribes to police	25,000
Interest	6,000
Depreciation on equipment	12,000

What is his net income from this business that is includible in taxable income? If the business was an illegal drug operation, would your answer differ?

27. Tim traveled to a neighboring state to investigate the purchase of two restaurants. His expenses included travel, legal, accounting, and miscellaneous expenses. The total was $12,000. He incurred the expenses in March and April 1994.

    a. What can he deduct in 1994 if he was in the restaurant business and did not acquire the two restaurants?
    b. What can he deduct in 1994 if he was in the restaurant business and acquired the two restaurants and began operating them on July 1, 1994?
    c. What can he deduct in 1994 if he did not acquire the two restaurants and was not in the restaurant business?
    d. What can he deduct in 1994 if he acquired the two restaurants but was not in the restaurant business when he acquired them?

28. Larry made a fortune in the stock market and retired at age 42. He bought a charming home in Vermont and incurred the following expenses in turning it into a country inn:

Repairs and maintenance	$14,000
Utilities	4,800
Depreciation	50,000
Interest on house mortgage	18,000
Property taxes	5,000
Supplies and food	20,000
All other expenses	10,000

    a. Assuming that Larry's endeavor was deemed a hobby and he had income of $30,000, what would he have to include in income? What could he deduct, assuming an AGI of $200,000 (not counting the $30,000 from the inn)?
    b. Assuming that Larry's endeavor was a bona fide business, how would your answer change?

29. Samantha is an executive with AGI of $100,000 before consideration of income or loss from her miniature horse business. Her income from the miniature horse activity comes from winning horse shows, stud fees, and sales of yearlings. Her home is on 20 acres, 18 of which she uses to pasture the horses and upon which she has erected stables, paddocks, fences, tack houses, and so forth. She uses an office in her home that is 10% of the square footage of the house.

    Samantha uses the office exclusively for keeping records of breeding lines, histories, and show and veterinary records. Her records show the following income and expenses for the current year:

Income from fees, prizes, and sales	$22,000
Expenses:	
Entry fees	1,000
Feed and veterinary bills	4,000
Supplies	900
Publications and dues	500
Travel to horse shows (no meals)	2,300
Salaries and wages of employees	8,000
Depreciation on horse equipment	3,000
Depreciation on horse farm improvements	7,000
Depreciation on 10% of home	1,000
Total home mortgage interest	24,000
Total property taxes on home	2,200
Total property taxes on horse farm improvements	800

    The mortgage interest is only on her home. The horse farm improvements are not mortgaged.

    How must Samantha treat the income and expenses of the operation if the miniature horse activity is held to be a hobby?

30. How would your answer in Problem 29 differ if the horse operation was held to be a business?

31. Louis makes macramé animals in his spare time. He sold $1,000 worth of animals during the year and incurred expenses as follows:

Supplies	$500
Depreciation on business property	800
Advertising	100

How are these items treated if the endeavor is a hobby? A business?

32. Matt is a promoter, real estate developer, and investor. Because he has inherited wealth, he can afford to be somewhat of a wheeler-dealer. He is single, age 41. During 1993, Matt incurred expenses in traveling to the state capitol to testify against proposed legislation for a green belt around the city because it interfered with some of his development plans. The expenses amounted to $900. He also spent $300 traveling to various locations to speak to civic groups against the proposed legislation.

He also incurred $1,600 of expense investigating the purchase of a computer franchising operation. He did not purchase the operation because he felt that his lack of expertise in that type of business was too big an obstacle to overcome.
Matt's other income and expenses for the year were as follows:

Income	
Interest	$ 80,000
Dividends	160,000
Short-term capital loss	(50,000)
Long-term capital gains	175,000
Other fees	24,000
Expenses	
Office expenses	17,000
Expenses incurred on land held for resale	6,000
Tax advice on stock investments	5,000
All other itemized deductions	34,000

Assume Matt's self-employment tax is $862. Calculate his taxable income for 1993.

33. In 1993, Anna rented her vacation home for 60 days, used it personally for 20 days, and left it vacant for 285 days. She had the following income and expenses:

Rent income	$ 6,000
Expenses	
Real estate taxes	2,000
Interest on mortgage	9,000
Repairs	1,000
Roof replacement	12,000
Depreciation	8,000

Compute Anna's net rent income or loss and the amounts she can itemize on her tax return, using the court's approach in allocating property taxes and interest.

34. How would your answer in Problem 33 differ using the IRS's method of allocating property taxes and interest?

35. How would your answer in Problem 34 differ if Anna had rented the house for 90 days and had used it personally for 12 days?

36. Chee, single, age 40, had the following income and expenses in 1993:

Income	
Salary	$43,000
Rental of vacation home (rented 60 days, used personally 60 days, vacant 245 days)	4,000
Municipal bond interest	2,000
Dividend from General Motors	400

Expenses	
Interest	
On home mortgage	8,400
On vacation home	4,745
On loan used to buy municipal bonds	3,100
Taxes	
Property tax on home	2,200
Property tax on vacation home	1,095
State income tax	3,300
Charitable contributions	1,100
Tax return preparation fee	300
Utilities and maintenance on vacation home	2,600
Depreciation related to rental of vacation home	3,500

Calculate Chee's taxable income for 1993 before personal exemptions.

37. Lee incurred the following expenses in the current tax year. Indicate, in the spaces provided, whether each expenditure is deductible *for* AGI, *from* AGI, or not deductible.

Expense Item	Deductible For AGI	Deductible From AGI	Not Deductible
1. Lee's personal medical expenses	____	____	____
2. Lee's dependent daughter's medical expenses	____	____	____
3. Real estate taxes on rental property	____	____	____
4. Real estate taxes on Lee's personal residence	____	____	____
5. Real estate taxes on daughter's personal residence	____	____	____
6. Lee's state income taxes	____	____	____
7. Interest on rental property mortgage	____	____	____
8. Interest on Lee's personal residence mortgage	____	____	____
9. Interest on daughter's personal residence mortgage	____	____	____
10. Interest on business loans	____	____	____
11. Charitable contributions	____	____	____
12. Depreciation on rental property	____	____	____
Utilities and maintenance on 13, 14 and 15:			
13. Rental property	____	____	____
14. Lee's home	____	____	____
15. Daughter's home	____	____	____
16. Depreciation on auto used in Lee's business	____	____	____
17. Depreciation on Lee's personal auto	____	____	____
18. Depreciation on daughter's personal auto	____	____	____

38. Janet sold stock (basis of $41,000) to her brother, Fred, for $32,000.

a. What are the tax consequences to Janet?

b. What are the tax consequences to Fred if he later sells the stock for $42,000? For $28,000? For $36,000?

39. What is Kim's constructive ownership of Wren Corporation, given the following information?

Shares owned by Kim	900
Shares owned by Sam, Kim's uncle	600
Shares owned by Barbara, Kim's partner	30
Shares owned by Green, a partnership owned by Kim and Barbara equally	300

Shares owned by Vera, Kim's granddaughter	570
Shares owned by unrelated parties	600

40. Chris has a brokerage account and buys on the margin, which resulted in interest expense of $8,000 during the year. The brokerage account generated income as follows:

Municipal interest	$30,000
Taxable dividends, interest, and capital gains	70,000

How much investment interest can Chris deduct?

CUMULATIVE PROBLEMS

41. Linda Maples, age 49, is single and lives at 321 Poplar Road, Springfield, IL 60740. Her Social Security number is 648–23–9981. Linda's husband died in 1991, and she has dependent twins, Joshua and Samantha, age 10. Joshua's Social Security number is 648–92–3471, and Samantha's is 648–92–3472.

Linda is an accountant and earned $65,000 in 1992. Her employer withheld $9,600 in Federal income tax, $1,300 in state income tax, and the correct amount of FICA tax.

Linda received $100,000 from her late husband's insurance policy in March and promptly invested it in mutual funds. On December 10, 1992, she sold 100 shares of Unco stock for $7,000. She had purchased the stock on March 8, 1992, for $8,000.

She had the following interest and dividends in 1992:

First National Bank savings account	$ 800
Total dividends from United Mutual Fund	5,000
Capital gains portion from United Mutual Fund	2,000

An examination of her records reveals the following:

- Linda made charitable contributions of $3,000 and gave used clothing worth $200 to the Salvation Army.
- Her deceased husband's employer gave her and the two children $5,000 each.
- Linda received a $300 state income tax refund in 1992. She and her husband had itemized on their joint return in 1991 and deducted the full amount.
- Linda paid unreimbursed medical expenses of $5,800 for herself and her children.
- Her deductible mortgage interest was $9,000, home property taxes were $900, and she had deductible personal property taxes of $150.
- Linda paid $500 for tax return preparation, $100 for a safe deposit box, and $580 for investment advice.
- She does not wish to contribute $1 to the Presidential Election Campaign Fund.

a. Calculate Linda's net tax payable or refund due for 1992. If you use tax forms, you will need Form 1040 and Schedules A, B, and D. Suggested software (if available): *TurboTax* or *MacInTax* for tax return solutions or WFT tax planning software.

b. Assuming that Linda's employer withholds the same amount of Federal income tax next year, what should she pay in estimated taxes?

42. John and Mary Jane are married, filing jointly. They are expecting their first child in early 1994. John's salary in 1993 was $40,000, from which $7,000 of Federal income tax and $2,500 of state income tax were withheld. Mary Jane made $35,000 and had $4,000 of Federal income tax and $2,000 of state income tax withheld.

They had $400 of savings account interest and $800 of dividends during the year.

They made charitable contributions of $2,000 during the year and paid an additional $200 in state income taxes in 1993 upon filing their 1992 state income tax return. Their deductible home mortgage interest was $8,200, and their property taxes came to $1,600. They had no other deductible expenses.

a. Calculate their tax (or refund) due for 1993. Suggested software (if available): WFT tax planning software.

b. Assume that they come to you for advice in December 1993. John has learned that he will receive a $20,000 bonus. He wants to know if he should take it in

December 1993 or in January 1994. Mary Jane will quit work in January to stay home with the baby. Their itemized deductions will decrease by $2,000 because Mary Jane will not have state income taxes withheld. Suggested software (if available): WFT tax planning software.

Chapter

Passive Activity Losses

Objectives

Discuss tax shelters and the reasons for at-risk and passive loss limitations.

Explain the at-risk limitation.

Examine the rationale for the passive loss limitations.

Identify taxpayers who are subject to the passive loss limits.

Describe how the passive loss rules limit deductions for losses.

Examine the definition of passive activities.

Analyze and apply the tests for material participation.

Consider special rules related to rental activities.

Examine the rules for identifying passive activities.

Discuss the rental real estate exception.

Determine the proper tax treatment upon the disposition of a passive activity.

Suggest tax planning strategies to minimize the effect of the passive loss limitations.

Outline

THE TAX SHELTER PROBLEM

Before Congress enacted legislation to reduce or eliminate their effectiveness, tax shelters were popular investments for tax avoidance purposes. The typical tax shelter relied heavily on nonrecourse financing[1] and generated large losses in the early years of the activity. Investors would offset these tax shelter losses against other types of income. At the very least, the tax shelter deductions deferred income taxes for the investor until the activity was sold. In the best of situations, additional tax savings were realized because sale of the activity produced capital gain, which was taxed at much lower rates than ordinary income. The following example illustrates what was possible *before* Congress enacted legislation to curb tax shelter abuses.

EXAMPLE 1

Bob, who earned a salary of $100,000, invested $20,000 for a 10% interest in a tax shelter. Through the use of $800,000 of nonrecourse financing, the partnership acquired assets worth $1,000,000. Depreciation, interest, and other deductions related to the activity resulted in a loss of $400,000, of which Bob's share was $40,000. Bob was allowed to deduct the $40,000 loss, even though he had invested and stood to lose only $20,000. ◆

A review of Example 1 shows that Bob took a *two-for-one* write-off ($40,000 deduction, $20,000 investment). In the heyday of tax shelters, promoters often promised *multiple* write-offs for the investor.

The first major provision aimed at the tax shelter strategy was the at-risk limitation enacted in 1976. The objective of the at-risk rule is to limit a taxpayer's tax shelter deductions to the amount at risk, that is, the amount the taxpayer stands to lose if the investment turns out to be a financial disaster. Under the current at-risk rules, the investor in Example 1 would not be allowed to deduct more than $20,000.[2] The remaining $20,000 would be suspended under the at-risk rules and would be deductible in the future if his at-risk amount increased.

The second major attack on tax shelters came in the Tax Reform Act of 1986. The passive loss limits in that legislation have nearly made the term *tax shelter* obsolete. Now such investments are generally referred to as passive investments, or *passive activities,* rather than tax shelters.

The passive loss rules require the taxpayer to segregate income and losses into three categories: active, passive, and portfolio. In general, the passive loss limits disallow the deduction of passive losses against active or portfolio income, even if the taxpayer is at risk for the amount of the loss. Refer again to Example 1. Under current law, the at-risk rules and passive loss limits work together to disallow the entire $40,000 loss in the year it is incurred. However, the *suspended* passive loss may be carried forward and deducted in the future if the taxpayer has passive income or disposes of the activity.

1. Nonrecourse debt is an obligation for which the endorser is not personally liable. An example of nonrecourse debt is a liability on real estate acquired by a partnership without the partnership or any of the partners assuming any liability for the mortgage. The acquired property generally is pledged as collateral for the loan.

2. If the investment is in a *passive activity,* the deduction is limited further under the passive loss rules.

At-Risk Limits

The at-risk provisions limit the deductibility of losses from business and income-producing activities. These provisions, which apply to individuals and closely held corporations, are designed to prevent a taxpayer from deducting losses in excess of the actual economic investment in an activity.

Under the at-risk rules, a taxpayer's deductible losses from an activity for any taxable year are limited to the amount the taxpayer has at risk at the end of the taxable year (the amount the taxpayer could actually lose in the activity). The initial amount considered at risk is generally the sum of the following:[3]

- The amount of cash and the adjusted basis of property contributed to the activity.
- Amounts borrowed for use in the activity for which the taxpayer is personally liable or has pledged as security property not used in the activity.

This amount generally is increased each year by the taxpayer's share of income and is decreased by the taxpayer's share of losses and withdrawals from the activity. Partners are jointly and severally liable for recourse debts of the partnership. Therefore, a partner's at-risk amount is increased when the partnership increases its debt, and decreased when the partnership reduces its debt.

A taxpayer generally is not considered at risk with respect to borrowed amounts if either of the following is true:

- The taxpayer is not personally liable for repayment of the debt (nonrecourse loans).
- The lender has an interest (other than as a creditor) in the activity (except to the extent provided in the Treasury Regulations).

Although taxpayers are generally not considered at risk for nonrecourse loans, there is an important exception. This exception provides that, in the case of an activity involving the holding of real property, a taxpayer is considered at risk for his or her share of any qualified nonrecourse financing that is secured by real property used in the activity.

The taxpayer also is not considered at risk for amounts for which he or she is protected against loss by guarantees, stop-loss arrangements, insurance (other than casualty insurance), or a similar arrangement.

Taxpayers can compute the deductible loss from an activity on Form 6198 (At-Risk Limitations). Form 6198 is required if the taxpayer

- has a loss from an activity that is covered by the at-risk rules and
- is not at-risk for some of his or her investment in the activity.

Any losses disallowed for any given taxable year by the at-risk rules may be deducted in the first succeeding year in which the rules do not prevent the deduction. However, if the losses are incurred in a passive activity, they are subject to the passive loss limitations.

3. § 465(b)(1).

EXAMPLE 2

In 1993, Sue invests $40,000 in an oil partnership (not a passive activity) that, through the use of nonrecourse loans, spends $60,000 on intangible drilling costs applicable to her interest. Sue's interest in the partnership is subject to the at-risk limits but is not subject to the passive loss limits. Since Sue has only $40,000 of capital at risk, she cannot deduct more than $40,000 against her other income and must reduce her at-risk amount to zero ($40,000 at-risk amount – $40,000 loss deducted). The nondeductible loss of $20,000 ($60,000 loss – $40,000 allowed) can be carried over to 1994. ◆

EXAMPLE 3

In 1994, Sue has taxable income of $15,000 from the oil partnership and invests an additional $5,000 in the venture. Her at-risk amount is now $20,000 ($0 beginning balance + $15,000 taxable income + $5,000 additional investment). This enables Sue to deduct the carried-over loss and again requires her to reduce her at-risk amount to zero ($20,000 at-risk amount – $20,000 carried-over loss). ◆

Recapture of previously allowed losses is required to the extent the at-risk amount is reduced below zero.[4] This rule applies if the amount at risk is reduced below zero by distributions to the taxpayer, by changes in the status of indebtedness from recourse to nonrecourse, or by the commencement of a guarantee or other similar arrangement that affects the taxpayer's risk of loss.

Generally, a taxpayer's amount at risk is separately determined for each activity. Nevertheless, activities are treated as one activity (aggregated) if they constitute a trade or business and either of the following is true:

- The taxpayer *actively participates* in the management of that trade or business.
- In the case of a trade or business carried on by a partnership or an S corporation, 65 percent or more of the entity's losses is allocable to persons who actively participate in the management of the trade or business.

All of the facts and circumstances must be examined to determine whether the taxpayer has met the *active participation* requirement. The following factors indicate active participation:

- Making decisions involving the operation or management of the activity.
- Performing services for the activity.
- Hiring and discharging employees.

These factors must be balanced against the factors that indicate lack of active participation:

- Lack of control in managing the operation of the activity.
- Having authority only to discharge the manager of the activity.
- Having a manager of the activity who is an independent contractor rather than an employee.

The active participation requirement differs from the active participation requirement that applies to real estate rental operations (discussed later under Real Estate Rental Activities).

4. § 465(e).

PASSIVE LOSS LIMITS

Taxpayers Subject to the Passive Loss Rules

The passive loss rules apply to individuals, estates, trusts, closely held C corporations, and personal service corporations.[5] Passive income or loss from investments in S corporations or partnerships (see Chapters 21 and 22) flows through to the owners, and the passive loss rules are applied at the owner level.

Before enactment of the passive loss limits, taxpayers were able to defer or avoid taxes by investing in tax shelters that produced losses. These losses were used to offset income from other sources.

EXAMPLE 4

Karen, a physician, earned $150,000 from her practice in 1985 (before the passive loss rules were enacted). She also received $10,000 in dividends and interest on various portfolio investments. During the year, she acquired a 20% interest in a tax shelter that produced a $300,000 loss not subject to the at-risk limits. In 1985, Karen would have been allowed to deduct her $60,000 share of the tax shelter loss, resulting in AGI of $100,000 ($150,000 salary + $10,000 dividends and interest – $60,000 tax shelter loss). ◆

Why would a taxpayer ever intentionally invest in an activity that would produce losses? There is a logical answer. Under the most favorable tax shelter scenario, the investor would take loss deductions for several years, then the tax shelter would be sold at a gain. Upon the sale of the tax shelter, the taxpayer would, in effect, report income to the extent of the previously deducted losses plus an additional gain due to appreciation of the investment. Deduction of the losses had the effect of deferring taxes. In addition, all or part of the gain would have been subject to the much lower capital gain rates that existed before TRA of 1986.

As a general rule, under current law taxpayers who are subject to the passive loss limitations cannot offset passive losses against active income or portfolio income.

EXAMPLE 5

Assume the same facts as in Example 4, except that the year is 1993 and that Karen does not materially participate in the operations of the activity. Her $60,000 share of the loss is a *passive loss* and is not deductible in 1993. It is treated as a *suspended loss,* which is carried over to the future. If Karen has passive income from this investment, or from other passive investments, in the future, she can offset the suspended loss against that passive income. If she does not have passive income to offset the suspended loss in the future, she will be allowed to offset the loss against other types of income when she eventually *disposes* of the passive activity. Karen's AGI in 1993 is $160,000 ($150,000 salary + $10,000 portfolio income), compared to $100,000 based on the same set of facts for tax year 1985. ◆

Personal Service Corporations. Application of the passive loss limitation to personal service corporations is intended to prevent taxpayers from sheltering personal service income by creating personal service corporations and acquiring passive activities at the corporate level.

5. § 469(a).

EXAMPLE 6

Five attorneys, who earn a total of $1,000,000 a year in their individual practices, form a personal service corporation. Shortly after its formation, the corporation invests in a passive activity that produces a $200,000 loss during the year. Because the passive loss rules apply to personal service corporations, the corporation may not deduct the $200,000 loss. ◆

Determination of whether a corporation is a *personal service corporation* is based on rather broad definitions. A personal service corporation is a corporation that meets *both* of the following conditions:

- The principal activity is the performance of personal services.
- Such services are substantially performed by owner-employees.

Personal service corporations include those in the fields of health, law, engineering, architecture, accounting, actuarial science, performing arts, and consulting.[6] A corporation is treated as a personal service corporation if more than 10 percent of the stock (by value) is held by owner-employees.[7] A shareholder is treated as an owner-employee if he or she is an employee or shareholder on *any day* during the testing period.[8] For these purposes, shareholder status and employee status do not even have to occur on the same day.

Closely Held Corporations. Application of the passive loss rules to closely held (non-personal service) corporations also is intended to prevent individuals from incorporating to avoid the passive loss limitation. A corporation is classified as a closely held corporation if, at any time during the taxable year, more than 50 percent of the value of its outstanding stock is owned, directly or indirectly, by or for not more than five individuals. Closely held corporations (other than personal service corporations) may offset passive losses against *active* income, but not against portfolio income.

EXAMPLE 7

Silver Corporation, a closely held C corporation, has $500,000 of passive losses from a rental activity, $400,000 of active income, and $100,000 of portfolio income. The corporation may offset $400,000 of the $500,000 passive loss against the $400,000 of active business income, but may not offset the remainder against the $100,000 of portfolio income. Thus, $100,000 of the passive loss is suspended ($500,000 passive loss – $400,000 offset against active income). ◆

Application of the passive loss limitation to closely held corporations also prevents individuals from transferring their portfolio investments to such corporations in order to offset passive losses against portfolio income.

Passive Activities Defined

Code § 469 specifies that the following types of activities are to be treated as passive:

- Any trade or business or income-producing activity in which the taxpayer does not materially participate.
- All rental activities, regardless of the level of the taxpayer's participation.

6. § 448(d).
7. § 469(j)(2).
8. § 269A(b)(2).

As originally enacted, § 469 required that a taxpayer participate on a *regular, continuous,* and *substantial* basis in order to be a material participant. In many situations, however, it was difficult or impossible to determine whether the taxpayer had met these vague material participation standards. Temporary Regulations under § 469,[9] issued in February 1988, help taxpayers cope with these material participation issues.

The Temporary Regulations provide seven tests that can be applied to determine whether a taxpayer is a material participant in an activity. One of these tests specifies that a taxpayer who participates more than 500 hours a year in a nonrental trade or business activity is a material participant.

EXAMPLE 8

Juan spends 40 hours a week, 50 weeks a year, operating a restaurant that he owns. He also owns a men's clothing store in another state that is operated by an employee. Because Juan participates for more than 500 hours during the year, the restaurant is treated as an active business. However, because he does not participate in the operations of the clothing store, it is a passive activity. ◆

The seven tests for material participation provided by the Temporary Regulations, including the test reflected in Example 8, are discussed in detail under Material Participation later in the chapter.

Although the Code specifies that *rental activities* are to be treated as passive, identifying passive rental activities can be complicated. The general rule is that an activity is a rental activity if customers are charged rental fees for the use of tangible property (real or personal).

EXAMPLE 9

Sara owns an apartment building and spends an average of 60 hours a week in its operation. The rental activity does not qualify under any of the six exceptions provided by the Temporary Regulations. Consequently, it is treated as a rental activity and is automatically classified as a passive activity, even though Sara spends more than 500 hours a year in its operation. ◆

Application of the passive loss limits to rental activities is complicated by the fact that some activities that involve rentals of real or personal property are not treated as rental activities for purposes of the passive loss provisions. The Temporary Regulations contain six exceptions that allow rental activities to escape *automatic* passive activity classification. The following example illustrates one of the exceptions.

EXAMPLE 10

Dan owns a videotape rental business. Because the average period of customer use is seven days or less, Dan's videotape business is not treated as a rental activity. ◆

The fact that Dan's videotape business in Example 10 is not treated as a rental activity does not necessarily mean that it is classified as a nonpassive activity. Instead the videotape business is treated as a trade or business activity subject to the material participation standards. If Dan is a material participant, the business is treated as active. If he is not a material participant, it is treated as a passive activity.

9. The Temporary Regulations are also Proposed Regulations. Temporary Regulations have the same effect as Final Regulations. Refer to Chapter 26 for a discussion of the different categories of regulations.

The six rental exceptions provided in the Temporary Regulations, including the exception illustrated in Example 10, are discussed in detail under Rental Activities later in the chapter.

Material Participation

If an individual taxpayer materially participates in a nonrental trade or business activity, any loss from that activity is treated as an active loss that can be offset against active income. If a taxpayer does not materially participate, however, the loss is treated as a passive loss, which can only be offset against passive income. Therefore, controlling whether a particular activity is treated as active or passive is an important part of the tax strategy of a taxpayer who owns an interest in one or more businesses. Consider the following examples.

EXAMPLE 11

Nora, a corporate executive, earns a salary of $200,000 per year. In addition, she owns a separate business in which she participates. The business produces a loss of $100,000 in 1993. If Nora materially participates in the business, the $100,000 loss is an active loss that may be offset against her active income from her corporate employer. If she does not materially participate, the loss is passive and is suspended. Nora may use the suspended loss in the future only if she has passive income or disposes of the activity. ◆

EXAMPLE 12

Kay, an attorney, earns $250,000 a year in her law practice. She also owns interests in two activities, A and B, in which she participates in 1993. Activity A, in which she does *not* materially participate, produces a loss of $50,000. Kay has not yet met the material participation standard for Activity B, which produces income of $80,000. However, she can meet the material participation standard if she spends an additional 50 hours in Activity B during the year. Should Kay attempt to meet the material participation standard for Activity B? If she continues working in Activity B and becomes a material participant, the $80,000 income from the activity is *active,* and the $50,000 passive loss from Activity A must be suspended. A more favorable tax strategy is for Kay to *not meet* the material participation standard for Activity B, thus making the income from that activity passive. This enables her to offset the $50,000 passive loss from Activity A against the passive income from Activity B. ◆

It is possible to devise numerous scenarios in which the taxpayer could control the tax outcome by increasing or decreasing his or her participation in different activities. Examples 11 and 12 demonstrate some of the possibilities. The conclusion reached in most analyses of this type is that taxpayers will benefit by having profitable activities classified as passive, so that any passive losses can be used to offset passive income. If the activity produces a loss, however, the taxpayer will benefit if it is classified as active so the loss is not subject to the passive loss limitations.

As discussed above, a nonrental trade or business in which a taxpayer owns an interest must be treated as a passive activity unless the taxpayer materially participates. The Staff of the Joint Committee on Taxation explained the importance of the material participation standard as follows:[10]

> Congress believed that there were several reasons why it was appropriate to examine the materiality of a taxpayer's participation in an activity in determining

10. *General Explanation of the Tax Reform Act of 1986 ("Blue Book"),* prepared by The Staff of the Joint Committee on Taxation, May 4, 1987, H.R. 3838, 99th Cong., p. 212.

> the extent to which such taxpayer should be permitted to use tax benefits from the activity. A taxpayer who materially participated in an activity was viewed as more likely than a passive investor to approach the activity with a significant nontax economic profit motive, and to form a sound judgment as to whether the activity had genuine economic significance and value. A material participation standard identified an important distinction between different types of taxpayer activities. It was thought that, in general, the more passive investor seeks a return on capital invested, including returns in the form of reductions in the taxes owed on unrelated income, rather than an ongoing source of livelihood. A material participation standard reduced the importance, for such investors, of the tax-reduction features of an investment, and thus increased the importance of the economic features in an investor's decision about where to invest his funds.

The Temporary Regulations provide seven tests for determining whether a taxpayer is a material participant. These tests are discussed below.

Tests Based on Current Participation. Material participation is achieved by meeting any one of seven tests provided in the Regulations. The first four tests are quantitative tests that require measurement, in hours, of the taxpayer's participation in the activity during the year.

1. *Does the individual participate in the activity for more than 500 hours during the year?*

The purpose of the 500-hour requirement is to restrict deductions from the types of trade or business activities Congress intended to treat as passive activities. The 500-hour standard for material participation was adopted for the following reasons:[11]

- Few investors in traditional tax shelters devote more than 500 hours a year to such an investment.
- The IRS believes that income from an activity in which the taxpayer participates for more than 500 hours a year should not be treated as passive.

2. *Does the individual's participation in the activity for the taxable year constitute substantially all of the participation in the activity of all individuals (including non-owner employees) for the year?*

EXAMPLE 13

Ned, a physician, operates a separate business in which he participates for 80 hours during the year. He is the only participant and has no employees in the separate business. Ned meets the material participation standards of Test 2. If he had employees, it would be difficult to apply Test 2 because the Temporary Regulations do not define the term *substantially all.* ◆

3. *Does the individual participate in the activity for more than 100 hours during the year, and is the individual's participation in the activity for the year not less than the participation of any other individual (including non-owner employees) for the year?*

EXAMPLE 14

Judy, a college professor, owns a separate business in which she participates 110 hours during the year. She has an employee who works 90 hours during the year. Judy meets

11. T.D. 8175, 1988–1 C.B. 191.

the material participation standard under Test 3, but probably does not meet it under Test 2 because her participation is only 55% of the total participation. It is unlikely that 55% would meet the *substantially all* requirement of Test 2. ◆

Tests 2 and 3 are included because the IRS recognizes that the operation of some activities does not require more than 500 hours of participation during the year.

4. *Is the activity a significant participation activity for the taxable year, and does the individual's aggregate participation in all significant participation activities during the year exceed 500 hours?*

A *significant participation* activity is one in which the individual's participation exceeds 100 hours during the year. This test treats taxpayers whose aggregate participation in several significant participation activities exceeds 500 hours as material participants. Test 4 thus accords the same treatment to an individual who devotes an aggregate of more than 500 hours to several significant participation activities as to an individual who devotes more than 500 hours to a single activity.

EXAMPLE 15

Mike owns five different businesses. He participated in each activity during the year as follows:

Activity	Hours of Participation
A	110
B	140
C	120
D	150
E	100

Activities A, B, C, and D are significant participation activities, and Mike's aggregate participation in those activities is 520 hours. Therefore, Activities A, B, C, and D are not treated as passive activities. Activity E is not a significant participation activity (not more than 100 hours), so it is not included in applying the 500-hour test. Activity E is treated as a passive activity, unless Mike meets one of the other material participation tests for that activity. ◆

EXAMPLE 16

Assume the same facts as in the previous example, except that Activity A does not exist. All of the activities are now treated as passive. Activity E is not counted in applying the more than 500-hour test, so Mike's aggregate participation in significant participation activities is 410 hours (140 in Activity B + 120 in Activity C + 150 in Activity D). He could meet the significant participation test for Activity E by participating for one more hour in the activity. This would cause Activities B, C, D, and E to be treated as nonpassive activities. Before deciding whether to participate for at least one more hour in Activity E, Mike should assess how the participation would affect his overall tax liability. ◆

Tests Based on Prior Participation. Tests 5 and 6 are based on material participation in prior years. Under these tests, a taxpayer who is no longer a participant in an activity can continue to be *classified* as a material participant. The IRS takes the position that material participation in a trade or business for a long period of time is likely to indicate that the activity represents the individual's principal livelihood, rather than a passive investment. Consequently, withdrawal from the activity, or reduction of participation to the point where it is not material, does not change the classification of the activity from active to passive.

5. *Did the individual materially participate in the activity for any 5 taxable years (whether consecutive or not) during the 10 taxable years that immediately precede the taxable year?*

Test 1 (the 500-hour test) is the only test that can be used in determining whether a taxpayer was a material participant in an activity for any taxable year beginning before 1987. Tests 2 through 7 are irrelevant for this purpose.[12]

Example 17

Dawn, who owns a 50% interest in a restaurant, was a material participant in the operations of the restaurant from 1987 through 1991. She retired at the end of 1991 and is no longer involved in the restaurant except as an investor. Dawn will be treated as a material participant in the restaurant in 1992. Even if she does not become involved in the restaurant as a material participant again, she will continue to be treated as a material participant in 1993, 1994, 1995, and 1996. In 1997 and later years, Dawn's share of income or loss from the restaurant will be classified as passive. ◆

6. *Is the activity a personal service activity, and did the individual materially participate in the activity for any three preceding taxable years (whether consecutive or not)?*

As indicated above, the material participation standards differ for personal service activities and other businesses. An individual who was a material participant in a personal service activity for *any three years* prior to the taxable year continues to be treated as a material participant after withdrawal from the activity.

Example 18

Evan, a CPA, retires from the EFG Partnership after working full-time in the partnership for 30 years. As a retired partner, he will continue to receive a share of the profits of the firm for the next 10 years, even though he will not participate in the firm's operations. Evan also owns an interest in a passive activity that produces a loss for the year. He continues to be treated as a material participant in the EFG Partnership, and his income from the partnership is active income. He is not allowed to offset the loss from his passive investment against the income from the EFG Partnership. ◆

Facts and Circumstances Test. Test 7 is a facts and circumstances test to determine whether the taxpayer has materially participated.

7. *Based on all the facts and circumstances, did the individual participate in the activity on a regular, continuous, and substantial basis during the year?*

The Temporary Regulations do not define what constitutes regular, continuous, and substantial participation except to say that a taxpayer's activities will *not* be considered material participation under Test 7 in the following three circumstances:[13]

---

12. Temp. and Prop.Reg. § 1.469–5T(j).

13. Temp. and Prop.Reg. § 1.469–5T(b)(2).

1. The taxpayer satisfies the participation standards (whether or not as a *material participant*) of any Code Section other than § 469.
2. The taxpayer manages the activity, unless

    - no other person receives compensation for management services, and
    - no individual spends more hours during the tax year managing the activity than does the taxpayer.

3. The taxpayer participates in the activity for 100 hours or less during the tax year.

A part of the Temporary Regulations has been reserved for further development of this test. Presumably, additional guidelines will be issued in the future. For the time being, taxpayers should rely on Tests 1 through 6 in determining whether the material participation standards have been met.

Participation Defined. Participation generally includes any work done by an individual in an activity that he or she owns. Participation does not include work if it is of a type not customarily done by owners *and* if one of its principal purposes is to avoid the disallowance of passive losses or credits. Also, work done in an individual's capacity as an investor (e.g., reviewing financial reports in a nonmanagerial capacity) is not counted in applying the material participation tests. Participation by an owner's spouse counts as participation by the owner.[14]

EXAMPLE 19

Tom, who is a partner in a CPA firm, owns a computer store that has operated at a loss during the year. In order to offset this loss against the income from his CPA practice, Tom would like to avoid having the computer business classified as a passive activity. Through December 15, he has worked 400 hours in the business in management and selling activities. During the last two weeks of December, he works 80 hours in management and selling activities and 30 hours doing janitorial chores. Also during the last two weeks in December, Tom's wife participates 40 hours as a salesperson. She has worked as a salesperson in the computer store in prior years, but has not done so during the current year. If any of Tom's work is of a type not customarily done by owners *and* if one of its principal purposes is to avoid the disallowance of passive losses or credits, it is not counted in applying the material participation tests. It is likely that Tom's 480 hours of participation in management and selling activities will count as participation, but the 30 hours spent doing janitorial chores will not. However, the 40 hours of participation by his wife will count, and Tom will qualify as a material participant under the more-than-500-hour rule (480 + 40 = 520). ◆

Limited Partners. A *limited* partner is one whose liability to third-party creditors of the partnership is limited to the amount the partner has invested in the partnership. A partnership must have at least one *general* partner, who is fully liable in an individual capacity for the debts of the partnership to third parties. Generally, a *limited partner* is not considered a material participant unless he or she qualifies under Test 1, 5, or 6 in the above list. However, a *general partner* may qualify as a material participant by meeting any of the seven tests. If an unlimited, or general, partner also owns a limited interest in the same limited partnership, all interests are treated as a general interest.[15]

---

14. Temp. and Prop.Reg. § 1.469–5T(f)(3).

15. Temp. and Prop.Reg. § 1.469–5T(e)(3)(ii).

Rental Activities

As discussed previously, § 469 specifies that all rental activities are to be treated as passive activities.[16] A rental activity is defined as any activity where payments are received principally for the use of tangible property.[17] However, Temporary Regulations provide that in certain circumstances activities involving rentals of real and personal property are *not* to be treated as rental activities.[18]

Activities covered by any of the following six exceptions in the Temporary Regulations are not *automatically* treated as passive activities. Instead, these activities are subject to the material participation tests.

1. *The average period of customer use for the property is seven days or less.*

Under this exception, activities involving the short-term use of tangible property such as automobiles, videocassettes, tuxedos, tools, and other such property are not treated as rental activities. The provision also applies to short-term rentals of hotel or motel rooms.

This exception is based on the presumption that a person who rents property for seven days or less is generally required to provide *significant services* to the customer. Providing such services supports a conclusion that the person is engaged in a service business rather than a rental business.

2. *The average period of customer use for the property is 30 days or less, and the owner of the property provides significant personal services.*

For longer-term rentals, the presumption that significant services are provided is not automatic, as it is in the case of the seven-day exception. Instead, the taxpayer must be able to *prove* that significant personal services are rendered in connection with the activity. Therefore, an understanding of what constitutes significant personal services is necessary in order to apply the rule.

Significant personal services include only services provided by *individuals.* This provision excludes such items as telephone and cable television services. Four additional categories of *excluded services* are not considered significant personal services:[19]

- Services necessary to permit the lawful use of the property.
- Services performed in connection with the construction of improvements to property.
- Services performed in connection with the performance of repairs that extend the property's useful life for a period substantially longer than the average period for which the property is used by customers.
- Services similar to those commonly provided in connection with long-term rentals of high-grade commercial or residential real property (including cleaning and maintenance of common areas, routine repairs, trash collection, elevator service, and security at entrances or perimeters).

3. *The owner of the property provides extraordinary personal services. The average period of customer use is of no consequence in applying this test.*

Extraordinary personal services are services provided by individuals where the customers' use of the property is incidental to their receipt of the services.

---

16. § 469(c)(2).
17. § 469(j)(8).
18. Temp. and Prop.Reg. § 1.469–1T(e)(3)(ii).
19. Temp. and Prop.Reg. § 1.469–1T(e)(3)(iv).

For example, a patient's use of a hospital bed is incidental to his or her use of medical services. Another example is the use of a boarding school's dormitory, which is incidental to the scholastic services received.

4. *The rental of the property is treated as incidental to a nonrental activity of the taxpayer.*

Rentals of real property incidental to a nonrental activity are not considered a passive activity. The Temporary Regulations provide that the following rentals are not passive activities:[20]

- *Property held primarily for investment.* This occurs where the principal purpose for holding the property is the expectation of gain from the appreciation of the property and the gross rent income is less than 2 percent of the lesser of (1) the unadjusted basis or (2) the fair market value of the property.

EXAMPLE 20

Anna invests in vacant land for the purpose of realizing a profit on its appreciation. She leases the land during the period it is held. The unadjusted basis is $250,000, and the fair market value is $350,000. The lease payments are $4,000 per year. Because gross rent income is less than 2% of $250,000, the activity is not a rental activity. ◆

- *Property used in a trade or business.* This occurs where the property is owned by a taxpayer who is an owner of the trade or business using the rental property. The property must also have been used in the trade or business during the year or during at least two of the five preceding taxable years. The 2 percent test above also applies in this situation.

EXAMPLE 21

A farmer owns land with an unadjusted basis of $250,000 and a fair market value of $350,000. He used it for farming purposes in 1991 and 1992. In 1993, he leased the land to another farmer for $4,000. The activity is not a rental activity. ◆

- *Property held for sale to customers.* If property is held for sale to customers and rented during the year, the rental of the property is not a rental activity.

EXAMPLE 22

An automobile dealer rents automobiles held for sale to customers to persons who are having their own cars repaired. The activity is not a rental activity. ◆

EXAMPLE 23

A taxpayer acquires land upon which to construct a shopping center. Before beginning construction, she rents it to a business for use as a parking lot. Since she did not acquire the land as an investment, nor use it in her trade or business, nor hold it for sale to customers, the rental is a rental activity. ◆

- *Lodging rented for the convenience of an employer.* If an employer provides lodging for an employee incidental to the employee's performance of services in the employer's trade or business, no rental activity exists.

20. Temp. and Prop.Regs. §§ 1.469–1T(e)(3)(vi)(B) through (E).

Example 24

Joe has a farming business. He rents houses on his property to migrant workers during the harvest season. Joe does not have a rental activity. ◆

- A partner who rents property to a partnership that is used in the partnership's trade or business does not have a rental activity.

Example 25

Betty, the owner of a business, transfers most of her business assets to a partnership retaining the land and building as her separate property. She then rents the property to the partnership. Betty does not have a rental activity. ◆

These rules were written to prevent taxpayers from converting active or portfolio income into a passive activity for the purpose of offsetting other passive losses.

In other cases, passive activity income is reclassified as nonpassive activity income. Such cases include significant participation activities, rentals of nondepreciable property, net investment income from passive equity-financed lending activities, net income from certain property rented incidental to development activities, and property rented to a nonpassive activity.[21]

5. *The taxpayer customarily makes the property available during defined business hours for nonexclusive use by various customers.*

Example 26

Pat is the owner-operator of a public golf course. Some customers pay daily greens fees each time they use the course, while others purchase weekly, monthly, or annual passes. The golf course is open every day from sunrise to sunset, except on certain holidays and on days when the course is closed due to weather conditions. Pat is not engaged in a rental activity, regardless of the average period customers use the course. ◆

6. *The property is provided for use in an activity conducted by a partnership, S corporation, or joint venture in which the taxpayer owns an interest.*

Example 27

Kim, a partner in the ABC Partnership, contributes the use of a building to the partnership. The partnership has net income of $30,000 during the year, of which Kim's share is $10,000. Unless the partnership is engaged in a rental activity, none of Kim's income from the partnership is income from a rental activity. ◆

Identification of Passive Activity

Identifying what constitutes an activity is a necessary first step in applying the passive loss limitations. Taxpayers who are involved in complex business operations need to be able to determine whether a given segment of their overall business operations constitutes a separate activity or is to be treated as part of a single activity. Proper treatment is necessary in order to determine whether income or loss from an activity is active or passive.

21. Temp. and Prop.Regs. §§ 1.469–2T(f)(2) through (7).

EXAMPLE 28

Ben owns a business with two separate departments. Department A generates net income of $120,000, and Department B generates a net loss of $95,000. Ben participates for 700 hours in the operations of Department A and for 100 hours in Department B. If Ben is allowed to treat both departments as a single activity, he is a material participant in the activity because his participation (700 + 100) exceeds 500 hours. Therefore, Ben can offset the $95,000 loss from Department B against the $120,000 income from Department A. ◆

EXAMPLE 29

Assume the same facts as in the previous example. If Ben is required to treat each department as a separate activity, he is a material participant in Department A (700 hours), and the $120,000 profit is active income. However, he is not a material participant in Department B (100 hours), and the $95,000 loss is a passive loss. Ben cannot offset the $95,000 passive loss from Department B against the $120,000 of active income from Department A. ◆

Upon disposition of a passive activity, a taxpayer is allowed to offset suspended losses from the activity against other types of income. Therefore, identifying what constitutes an activity is of crucial importance.

EXAMPLE 30

Linda owns a business with two departments. She participates for 200 hours in Department A, which had a net loss of $125,000 in the current year. Linda participates for 250 hours in Department B, which had a $70,000 net loss. She disposes of Department B during the year. She is allowed to treat the two departments as separate activities. Linda can offset the passive loss from Department B against other types of income in the following order: gain from disposition of the passive activity, other passive income, and nonpassive income. She has a suspended loss of $125,000 from Department A. ◆

It is not possible to apply the passive loss limitations without knowing what constitutes an activity. The IRS has issued Proposed Regulations that set forth rules for grouping a taxpayer's trade or business activities and rental activities for purposes of applying the passive loss limitations.[22] These Proposed Regulations, which apply to tax years ending after May 10, 1992, provide a *facts and circumstances test* to determine whether a taxpayer's activities constitute an appropriate economic unit. Taxpayers may use *any reasonable method* in applying the facts and circumstances test.

In general, one or more trade or business or rental activities of a taxpayer will be treated as a single activity if the activities constitute an *appropriate economic unit.* The following five factors are given the greatest weight in determining whether activities constitute an appropriate economic unit. It is not necessary to meet all of these conditions in order to treat multiple activities as a single activity.[23]

- Similarities and differences in types of business conducted in the various trade or business or rental activities.
- The extent of common control over the various activities.
- The extent of common ownership of the activities.
- Geographical location of the different units.
- Interdependencies among the activities.

22. Prop.Reg. § 1.469–4.

23. Prop.Reg. § 1.469–4(c)(2).

To determine the degree of interdependencies among the activities, it is necessary to consider the extent to which the activities[24]

- purchase or sell goods among themselves;
- involve products or services that are normally provided together;
- have the same customers;
- have the same employees; and
- are accounted for with a single set of books and records.

The following examples, adapted from the Proposed Regulations, illustrate the application of the general rules for grouping activities.[25]

EXAMPLE 31

George owns a clothing store and a video game parlor in Chicago. He also owns a clothing store and a video game parlor in Milwaukee. Reasonable methods of applying the facts and circumstances test may result in any of the following groupings:

- All four activities may be grouped into a single activity.
- The clothing stores may be grouped into an activity, and the video parlors may be grouped into a separate activity.
- The Chicago activities may be grouped into an activity, and the Milwaukee activities may be grouped into a separate activity.
- Each of the four activities may be treated as a separate activity. ◆

EXAMPLE 32

Sharon, an individual, is a partner in a business that sells snack items to drugstores. She also is a partner in a partnership that owns and operates a warehouse. Both partnerships, which are under common control, are located in the same industrial park. The predominant part of the warehouse business is warehousing items for the snack business, and it is the only warehousing business in which Sharon is involved. Sharon should treat the snack business and the warehousing business as a single activity. ◆

Taxpayers should carefully consider all tax factors in deciding how to group their activities. Once activities have been grouped, they cannot be regrouped unless the original grouping was clearly inappropriate or there has been a material change in facts and circumstances. If a regrouping is necessary for either of these reasons, the taxpayer is required to disclose to the IRS all information relevant to the regrouping.

Grouping Rental Activities. Two rules deal specifically with the grouping of rental activities. These provisions are designed to prevent taxpayers from grouping rental activities with other businesses in a way that would result in a tax advantage.

First, a rental activity may be grouped with a trade or business activity only if one activity is insubstantial in relation to the other. That is, the rental activity must be insubstantial in relation to the trade or business activity, or the trade or business activity must be insubstantial in relation to the rental activity. The Proposed Regulations provide no guidelines as to the meaning of insubstantial.[26]

Second, taxpayers may not treat an activity involving the rental of real property and an activity involving the rental of personal property as a single activity. There is an exception if the personal property is provided in connection

24. Prop.Reg. § 1.469–4(c)(2)(v).

25. Prop.Reg. § 1.469–4(c)(3).

26. Prop.Reg. § 1.469–4(d).

with the real property. This rule prevents taxpayers from deducting losses from the rental of personal property (e.g., furniture and appliances rented in connection with apartment rentals) under the $25,000 real estate rental exception discussed later in the chapter. It also prevents taxpayers from offsetting real property losses against personal property profits by grouping profitable personal property rentals with real estate rental activities that produce losses.[27]

Regrouping of Activities. Although the Proposed Regulations allow taxpayers great latitude in grouping activities, they grant the IRS the right to regroup activities when both of the following conditions exist:[28]

- The taxpayer's grouping fails to reflect one or more appropriate economic units.
- One of the primary purposes of the taxpayer's grouping is to avoid the passive loss limitations.

The following example, adapted from the proposed Regulations, illustrates a situation where the IRS would exercise its prerogative to regroup a taxpayer's activities.

Example 33

Baker, Edwards, Andrews, Clark, and Henson are physicians who operate their own separate practices. Each of the physicians owns interests in activities that generate passive losses, so they devise a plan to set up an entity that will generate passive income. They form the BEACH Partnership to acquire and operate X-ray equipment, and each receives a limited partnership interest. They select an unrelated person to operate the X-ray business as a general partner, and none of the limited partners participates in the activity. Substantially all of the services provided by BEACH are provided to the physicians who own limited partnership interests, and fees are set at a level that assures a profit for BEACH. Each physician treats his medical practice and his interest in the partnership as separate activities and offsets losses from passive investments against income from the partnership. The IRS would interpret the physicians' separate groupings as attempts to avoid the passive loss limitations and would regroup each medical practice and the services performed by the partnership as an appropriate economic unit. ◆

The Proposed Regulations also apply to partnerships and S corporations. These pass-through entities (see Chapter 21 and 22) must group their activities according to the same guidelines that apply to individuals. Taxpayers who own interests in pass-through entities are required to abide by the entity's grouping. Each partner or shareholder must then group activities from the pass-through entity with activities he or she conducts directly.

Classification of Income and Losses

The passive loss rules require the classification of income and losses into three categories: active, passive, and portfolio. *Active income* includes, but is not limited to, the following:

- Wages, salary, commissions, bonuses, and other payments for services rendered by the taxpayer.

27. Prop.Reg. § 1.469–4(e).

28. Prop.Reg. § 1.469–4(h).

- Profit from a trade or business in which the taxpayer is a material participant.
- Gain on the sale or other disposition of assets used in an active trade or business.
- Income from intangible property if the taxpayer's personal efforts significantly contributed to the creation of the property.
- Income from a qualified low-income housing project that is not subject to the passive loss limitations under transitional rules.

Portfolio income includes, but is not limited to, the following:

- Interest, dividends, annuities, and royalties not derived in the ordinary course of a trade or business.
- Gain or loss from the disposition of property that produces portfolio income or is held for investment purposes.

Code § 469 provides that income or loss from the following activities is treated as *passive:*

- Any trade or business or income-producing activity in which the taxpayer does not materially participate.
- Any rental activity, whether the taxpayer materially participates or not.

Although the Code defines rental activities as passive activities, an exception allows losses from certain real estate rental activities to be offset against nonpassive (active or portfolio) income. The exception is discussed under Real Estate Rental Activities later in the chapter.

Income Not Treated as Passive

Certain items of income and expense are not taken into account in computing passive activity losses.[29] Some of these income items are discussed in this section. Others are beyond the scope of this text. Deductions that are not treated as passive are covered in the following section.

Portfolio income of an activity is not included in computing the passive income or loss from the activity. This provision negates any tax benefit taxpayers would otherwise achieve by transferring assets that produce portfolio income to an activity that produces a passive loss. Thus, it is possible that an activity might produce a passive loss *and* portfolio income in the same year.

Example 34

Lou owns an activity that produces a passive loss of $15,000 during the year. He transfers to the activity corporate stock that produces portfolio income of $15,000. The passive loss cannot be offset against the portfolio income. Lou must report a passive loss of $15,000 and portfolio income of $15,000 from the activity. ◆

Portfolio income includes interest, annuities, royalties, dividends, and other items. However, such income is included in the passive loss computation if it is *derived* in the ordinary course of business.[30] For example, interest earned on loans made in the ordinary course of a trade or business of lending money is not treated as portfolio income. In addition, interest on accounts receivable arising

29. Temp. and Prop.Reg. § 1.469–2T(a)(2).

30. Temp. and Prop.Reg. § 1.469–2T(c)(3).

from the performance of services or the sale of property is not treated as portfolio income if the business customarily offers credit to customers.

Gains on dispositions of portfolio assets are also treated as portfolio income. The rules for determining whether other gain is to be treated as portfolio income are very complex and are beyond the scope of this text. Refer to the Temporary and Proposed Regulations for additional information.[31]

Compensation paid to or on behalf of an individual for services performed or to be performed is not treated as passive activity gross income.[32]

EXAMPLE 35

Mara owns 50% of the stock of Greene, Inc., an S corporation that owns rental real estate. Greene pays Mara a $10,000 salary for services she performs for the corporation in connection with managing the rental real estate. The corporation has a $30,000 passive loss on the property during the year. Mara must report compensation income of $10,000 and a passive loss of $15,000 ($30,000 × .50). ◆

The following are some of the other income items that are specifically excluded from the passive loss computation:[33]

- Gross income of an individual from intangible property (such as a patent, copyright, or literary, musical, or artistic composition) if the taxpayer's personal efforts significantly contributed to the creation of the property.
- Gross income attributable to a refund of any state, local, or foreign income, war profits, or excess profits tax.
- Gross income of an individual for a covenant not to compete.

Deductions Not Treated as Passive

The general rule is that a deduction is treated as a passive activity deduction if and only if the deduction arises in connection with the conduct of an activity that is a passive activity. The Temporary Regulations list several items that are not treated as passive activity deductions:[34]

- Any deduction for an expense that is clearly and directly allocable to portfolio income.
- Any deduction for a loss from the disposition of property of a type that produces portfolio income.
- Any deduction for a dividend if the dividend is not included in passive activity gross income.
- Any deduction for qualified residence interest or interest that is capitalized under a capitalization provision.
- Any miscellaneous itemized deduction that is disallowed by operation of the 2 percent floor.
- Any deduction allowed under § 170 for a charitable contribution.
- Any net operating loss carryforward allowed under § 172.
- Any capital loss carryforward allowed under § 1212(b).

EXAMPLE 36

Chris, who owns a sole proprietorship that is a passive activity, calculated a loss for the activity as follows:

31. Temp. and Prop.Reg. § 1.469–2T(c)(2).
32. Temp. and Prop.Reg. § 1.469–2T(c)(4).
33. Temp. and Prop.Reg. § 1.469–2T(c)(7).
34. Temp. and Prop.Reg. § 1.469–2T(d).

Operating income	$ 50,000
Dividends on stock held for investment	15,000
Total income	$ 65,000
– Expenses: Operating expenses (wages, rent, supplies, etc.)	(60,000)
Investment interest	(8,000)
– Loss on sale of stock held for investment	(5,000)
= Net loss	$ (8,000)

◆

EXAMPLE 37

In computing Chris's passive loss, the net loss of $8,000 in Example 36 must be modified because the computation included gross income and deductions that are not to be considered in computing a passive loss. The passive loss is computed as follows:

Operating income	$ 50,000
– Operating expenses (wages, rent, supplies, etc.)	(60,000)
= Passive loss	$(10,000)

◆

A comparison of Examples 36 and 37 shows that the portfolio income is not included in computing the passive loss, and that no deduction is taken for the investment interest or the loss on the portfolio investment.

Suspended Losses

The determination of whether a loss is suspended under the passive loss rule is made after application of the at-risk rules as well as other provisions relating to the measurement of taxable income. A loss that is not allowed for the year because the taxpayer is not at risk with respect to it is suspended under the at-risk provision and not under the passive loss rule.

A taxpayer's basis is reduced by deductions (e.g., depreciation) even if the deductions are not currently usable because of the passive loss rule.

EXAMPLE 38

Jack's adjusted basis in a passive activity is $10,000 at the beginning of 1991. His loss from the activity in 1991 is $4,000. Since Jack had no passive activity income, the $4,000 cannot be deducted. At year-end, Jack has an adjusted basis of $6,000 in the activity and a suspended loss of $4,000. ◆

EXAMPLE 39

Jack in Example 38 had a loss of $9,000 in the activity in 1992. Since the $9,000 exceeds his at-risk amount ($6,000) by $3,000, that $3,000 loss is disallowed by the at-risk rules. If Jack has no passive activity income, the remaining $6,000 is suspended under the passive activity rules. At year-end, he has a $3,000 loss suspended under the at-risk rules, $10,000 ($4,000 for 1991 plus $6,000 for 1992) of suspended passive losses, and an adjusted basis in the activity of zero. ◆

EXAMPLE 40

Jack in Example 39 realized a $1,000 gain in 1993. Because the $1,000 increases his at-risk amount, $1,000 of the $3,000 unused loss can be reclassified as a passive loss. If he has no other passive income, the $1,000 income is offset against $1,000 of (reclassified) suspended passive losses. At the end of 1993, Jack has no taxable passive income, $2,000 ($3,000 – $1,000) of unused losses under the at-risk rules, $10,000 ($10,000 + $1,000 of reclassified unused at-risk losses – $1,000 of passive losses offset against passive gains), and an adjusted basis in the activity of zero. ◆

EXAMPLE 41

In 1994, Jack had no gain or loss from the activity in Example 40. He contributed $5,000 more to the passive activity. Because the $5,000 increases his at-risk amount, the $2,000 of losses suspended under the at-risk rules is reclassified as a passive loss. Jack gets no passive loss deduction in 1994. At year-end, he has no losses suspended under the at-risk rules, $12,000 of suspended passive losses ($10,000 + $2,000 of reclassified suspended at-risk losses), and an adjusted basis of $3,000 ($5,000 additional investment – $2,000 of reclassified losses). ◆

Interest deductions attributable to passive activities are treated as passive activity deductions but are not treated as investment interest. (See Chapter 10 for a detailed discussion of investment interest.) As a result, these interest deductions are subject to limitation under the passive loss rule and not under the investment interest limitation.

Carryovers of Suspended Losses. To determine the suspended loss for an activity, passive activity losses must be allocated among all activities in which the taxpayer has an interest. The allocation to the activity is made by multiplying the disallowed passive activity loss from all activities by a fraction. The numerator of the fraction is the loss from the activity, and the denominator is the sum of the losses for the taxable year from all activities having losses.

EXAMPLE 42

Ted has investments in three passive activities (acquired in 1992) with the following income and losses for that year:

Activity A	($ 30,000)
Activity B	(20,000)
Activity C	25,000
Net passive loss	($ 25,000)
Allocated to:	
A ($25,000 × $30,000/$50,000)	$ 15,000
B ($25,000 × $20,000/$50,000)	10,000
Total suspended losses	($ 25,000)

◆

Suspended losses are carried over indefinitely and are offset against any passive income from the activities to which they relate in the immediately succeeding taxable year.[35]

EXAMPLE 43

Assume the same facts as in Example 42 and that Activity A produces $15,000 of income in 1993. The disallowed loss of $15,000 from 1992 for Activity A is offset against income from Activity A. ◆

Upon the taxable disposition of a passive activity, the suspended passive losses from that activity can be offset against the taxpayer's active and portfolio income. See Dispositions of Passive Interests later in the chapter.

35. § 469(b).

Passive Credits

Credits arising from passive activities are limited much like passive losses. They can be utilized only against regular tax attributable to passive income,[36] which is calculated by comparing the tax on all income (including passive income) with the tax on income excluding passive income.

EXAMPLE 44

A taxpayer owes $50,000 of tax, disregarding net passive income, and $80,000 of tax, considering both net passive and other taxable income (disregarding the credits in both cases). The amount of tax attributable to the passive income is $30,000.

Tax due (before credits) including net passive income	$ 80,000
Less: Tax due (before credits) without including net passive income	(50,000)
Tax attributable to passive income	$ 30,000

◆

The taxpayer in the preceding example, can claim a maximum of $30,000 of passive activity credits; the excess credits are carried over. These passive activity credits (such as the jobs credit, low-income housing credit, research activities credit, and rehabilitation credit) can be used against the *regular* tax attributable to passive income only. If a taxpayer has a net loss from passive activities during a given year, no credits can be used. Likewise, if a taxpayer has net passive income but the alternative minimum tax applies to that year, no passive activity credits can be used. (The alternative minimum tax is discussed in Chapter 14.) In addition, the unused passive losses are carried over.

When the passive activity that generates tax credits fits under the exception for real estate rental activities (discussed subsequently under Real Estate Rental Activities), the credits must be converted into *deduction equivalents.* The deduction equivalent is the deduction necessary to reduce one's tax liability by an amount equal to the credit. A taxpayer with $5,000 of credits and a tax bracket of 28 percent would have a deduction equivalent of $17,857 ($5,000 divided by 28 percent). See the subsequent discussion under Real Estate Rental Activities for examples calculating deduction equivalents.

Carryovers of Passive Credits. Tax credits attributable to passive activities can be carried forward indefinitely much like suspended passive losses. Unlike passive losses, however, passive credits can be lost forever when the activity is disposed of in a taxable transaction.

EXAMPLE 45

Alicia sells a passive activity for a gain of $10,000. The activity had suspended losses of $40,000 and suspended credits of $15,000. The $10,000 gain is offset by $10,000 of the suspended losses, and the remaining $30,000 of suspended losses is deductible against Alicia's active and portfolio income. The suspended credits are lost forever because the sale of the activity did not generate any tax. This is true even if Alicia has positive taxable income or is subject to the alternative minimum tax. ◆

36. § 469(d)(2).

EXAMPLE 46

If Alicia in Example 45 had realized a $100,000 gain on the sale of the passive activity, the $15,000 of suspended credits could have been used to the extent of regular tax attributable to the net passive income.

Gain on sale	$100,000
Less: Suspended losses	40,000
Net gain	$ 60,000

If the tax attributable to the net gain of $60,000 is $15,000 or more, the entire $15,000 of suspended credits can be used. If the tax attributable to the gain is less than $15,000, the excess of the suspended credit over the tax attributable to the gain is lost forever. ◆

When a taxpayer has adequate regular tax liability from passive activities to trigger the use of suspended credits, the credits lose their character as passive credits. They are reclassified as regular tax credits and made subject to the same limits as other credits (discussed in Chapter 11).

This reclassification of passive credits can occur when they cannot be used in the year of reclassification because the taxpayer is subject to the alternative minimum tax (discussed in Chapter 14). Tax credits cannot reduce the tax calculated under the alternative minimum tax rules; the credits are carried over under the general rules for tax credits. Form 8582–CR (Passive Activity Credit Limitations) is used to report passive activity credits.

EXAMPLE 47

During the year, Akeem had the following regular tax, alternative minimum tax, and credits:

Activity	Regular Tax	Alternative Minimum Tax	Tax Credits	Carried Over As Passive	Carried Over As Regular
Passive	$ 50	$150	$150	$100	$ 50
Active	500	450	150	–	150
	$550	$600	$300	$100	$200

Even though Akeem has to pay the alternative minimum tax of $600 since it exceeds the regular tax of $550, he can reclassify $50 of the suspended passive credits as regular credits because of the $50 of regular tax generated by passive income. He has suspended passive credits of $100 left over for use against future passive income tax. The $50 of reclassified credits can be used in a future year (together with the $150 of active credits) against tax attributable to active and portfolio income. The entire $200 of regular tax credit carryovers is subject to the general rules governing credits. (See Chapter 11.) ◆

Real Estate Rental Activities

The passive loss limits contain two exceptions related to real estate activities. These exceptions allow all or part of real estate rental losses to be offset against active or portfolio income, even though the activity is a passive activity.

The first exception provides favorable treatment for investors in low-income housing. Under a transition rule, losses from certain investments in low-income housing are not treated as passive losses for a period of up to seven years from the date of the original investment.

The second exception is more significant in that it is not restricted to low-income housing. This exception allows individuals to deduct up to $25,000 of losses on real estate rental activities against active and portfolio income.[37] The annual $25,000 deduction is reduced by 50 percent of the taxpayer's AGI in excess of $100,000. Thus, the entire deduction is phased out at $150,000. If married individuals file separately, the $25,000 deduction is reduced to zero unless they lived apart for the entire year. If they lived apart for the entire year, the loss amount is $12,500 each, and the phase-out begins at $50,000. AGI for purposes of the phase-out is calculated without regard to IRA deductions, Social Security benefits, and net losses from passive activities.

To qualify for the $25,000 exception, a taxpayer must meet the following requirements:[38]

- Actively participate in the real estate rental activity.
- Own 10 percent or more (in value) of all interests in the activity during the entire taxable year (or shorter period during which the taxpayer held an interest in the activity).

The difference between *active participation* and *material participation* is that the former can be satisfied without regular, continuous, and substantial involvement in operations as long as the taxpayer participates in the making of management decisions in a significant and bona fide sense. In this context, relevant management decisions include such decisions as approving new tenants, deciding on rental terms, and approving capital or repair expenditures.

The $25,000 allowance is available after all active participation rental losses and gains are netted and applied to other passive income. If a taxpayer has a real estate rental loss in excess of the amount that can be deducted under the real estate rental exception, that excess is treated as a passive loss.

Example 48

Diane, who has $90,000 of AGI before considering rental activities, has $85,000 of losses from a real estate rental activity in which she actively participates. She also actively participates in another real estate rental activity from which she has $25,000 of income. She has other passive income of $36,000. The net rental loss of $60,000 is offset by the $36,000 of passive income, leaving $24,000 that can be deducted against other income. ◆

The $25,000 offset allowance is an aggregate of both deductions and credits in deduction equivalents. The deduction equivalent of a passive activity credit is the amount of deductions that reduces the tax liability for the taxable year by an amount equal to the credit.[39] If the total deduction and deduction equivalent exceed $25,000, the taxpayer must allocate on a pro rata basis, first among the losses (including real estate rental activity losses suspended in prior years) and then to credits in the following order: (1) credits other than rehabilitation credits, (2) rehabilitation credits, and (3) low-income housing credits.

Example 49

Kevin is an active participant in a real estate rental activity that produces $8,000 of income, $26,000 of deductions, and $1,500 of credits. Kevin, who is in the 28% tax bracket, may deduct the net passive loss of $18,000 ($8,000 less $26,000). After

---

37. § 469(i).

38. § 469(i)(6).

39. § 469(j)(5).

deducting the loss, he has an available deduction equivalent of $7,000 ($25,000 less $18,000 passive loss). Therefore, the maximum amount of credits that he may claim is $1,960 ($7,000 × 28%). Since the actual credits are less than this amount, Kevin may claim the entire $1,500 credit. ◆

EXAMPLE 50

Kelly, who is in the 28% tax bracket, is an active participant in three separate real estate rental activities. She has $20,000 of losses from Activity A, $10,000 of losses from Activity B, and $4,200 of passive credits from Activity C. Kelly's deduction equivalent from the credits is $15,000 ($4,200 ÷ .28). Total passive deductions and deduction equivalents are $45,000 ($20,000 + $10,000 + $15,000) and therefore exceed the maximum allowable amount of $25,000. Kelly must allocate pro rata first from among losses and then from among credits. Deductions from Activity A are limited to $16,667 {$25,000 × [$20,000 ÷ ($20,000 + $10,000)]}, and deductions from Activity B are limited to $8,333 {$25,000 × [$10,000 ÷ ($20,000 + $10,000)]}.

Since the amount of passive deductions exceeds the $25,000 maximum, the deduction balance of $5,000 and passive credit of $4,200 must be carried forward. Kelly's suspended losses and credits by activity are as follows:

			Activity	
	Total	A	B	C
Allocated losses	$30,000	$ 20,000	$10,000	$ -0-
Allocated credits	4,200	-0-	-0-	4,200
Utilized losses	25,000	(16,667)	(8,333)	-0-
Suspended losses	5,000	3,333	1,667	-0-
Suspended credits	4,200	-0-	-0-	4,200 ◆

Further complications arise when passive rental activities generate both losses and credits. Recall that the phase-out of rental losses begins when the taxpayer's AGI reaches $100,000. For each two dollars by which AGI exceeds $100,000, one dollar of the $25,000 loss is disallowed. When the taxpayer's AGI reaches $150,000, no real estate rental loss is allowed.

Dispositions of Passive Interests

When a taxpayer disposes of his or her entire interest in a passive activity, the actual economic gain or loss on the investment finally can be determined. As a result, under the passive loss rules, upon a fully taxable disposition, any overall loss from the activity realized by the taxpayer is recognized and allowed against any income. Special rules apply to dispositions of certain property that disallow their classification as passive income. Included in these rules are dispositions of partnership interests and S corporation stock, partial interests in property, property used in more than one activity, and substantially appreciated property formerly used in a nonpassive activity.[40]

Since the purpose of the disposition rule is to allow the taxpayer's real economic losses to be deducted, credits (which are not related to the measurement of such loss) are not allowable just by reason of a disposition. Credits are allowed *only* when there is sufficient tax on passive income to absorb them.

A fully taxable disposition generally includes a sale of the property to a third party at arm's length and thus, presumably, for a price equal to the property's

40. Temp. and Prop.Regs. §§ 1.469–2T(c)(2)(i) through (iii).

fair market value. Gain recognized upon a transfer of an interest in a passive activity generally is treated as passive and is first offset by the suspended losses from that activity.

EXAMPLE 51

Kim sold an apartment building with an adjusted basis of $100,000 for $180,000. In addition, Kim has suspended losses associated with that specific apartment building of $60,000. The total gain, $80,000, and the taxable gain, $20,000, are calculated as follows:

Net sales price	$ 180,000
Less: Adjusted basis	(100,000)
Total gain	$ 80,000
Less: Suspended losses	(60,000)
Taxable gain (passive)	$ 20,000

◆

If current and suspended losses of the passive activity exceed the gain realized or if the sale results in a realized loss, the sum of

- any loss from the activity for the tax year (including losses suspended in the activity disposed of), plus
- any loss realized on the disposition

in excess of

- net income or gain for the tax year from all passive activities (without regard to the activity disposed of)

is treated as a loss that is not from a passive activity.

EXAMPLE 52

Dean sold an apartment building with an adjusted basis of $100,000 for $150,000. In addition, he has current and suspended losses of $60,000 associated with that specific apartment building and has no other passive activities. The total gain, $50,000, and the deductible loss, $10,000, are calculated as follows:

Net sales price	$ 150,000
Less: Adjusted basis	(100,000)
Total gain	$ 50,000
Less: Suspended losses	(60,000)
Deductible loss	$ (10,000)

The $10,000 deductible loss is offset against Dean's ordinary income and portfolio income. ◆

Disposition of a Passive Activity at Death. A transfer of a taxpayer's interest in an activity by reason of the taxpayer's death results in suspended losses being allowed (to the decedent) to the extent they exceed the amount, if any, of the step-up in basis allowed.[41] Suspended losses are lost to the extent of the amount of the basis increase. The losses allowed generally are reported on the final return of the deceased taxpayer.

41. § 469(g)(2).

EXAMPLE 53

A taxpayer dies with passive activity property having an adjusted basis of $40,000, suspended losses of $10,000, and a fair market value at the date of the decedent's death of $75,000. The step-up in basis (see Chapter 12) is $35,000 (fair market value at date of death in excess of adjusted basis). None of the $10,000 suspended loss is deductible by either the decedent or the beneficiary. The suspended losses ($10,000) did not exceed the step-up in basis ($35,000). ◆

EXAMPLE 54

A taxpayer dies with passive activity property having an adjusted basis of $40,000, suspended losses of $10,000, and a fair market value at the date of the decedent's death of $47,000. Since the basis increase under § 1014 would be only $7,000 ($47,000 – $40,000), the suspended losses allowed are limited to $3,000 ($10,000 suspended loss at time of death – $7,000 increase in basis). The $3,000 loss available to the decedent is reported on the decedent's final income tax return. ◆

Disposition of a Passive Activity by Gift. In a disposition of a taxpayer's interest in a passive activity by gift, the suspended losses are added to the basis of the property.[42]

EXAMPLE 55

A taxpayer makes a gift of passive activity property having an adjusted basis of $40,000, suspended losses of $10,000, and a fair market value at the date of the gift of $100,000. The taxpayer cannot deduct the suspended losses in the year of the disposition. The suspended losses transfer with the property and are added to the adjusted basis of the property. ◆

Installment Sale of a Passive Activity. An installment sale of a taxpayer's entire interest in a passive activity triggers the recognition of the suspended losses.[43] The losses are allowed in each year of the installment obligation in the ratio that the gain recognized in each year bears to the total gain on the sale.

EXAMPLE 56

Stan sold his entire interest in a passive activity for $100,000. His adjusted basis in the property was $60,000. If he uses the installment method, his gross profit ratio is 40% ($40,000/$100,000). If Stan received a $20,000 down payment, he would recognize a gain of $8,000 (40% of $20,000). If the activity had a suspended loss of $25,000, Stan would deduct $5,000 [($8,000 ÷ $40,000) × $25,000] of the suspended loss in the first year. ◆

Passive Activity Changes to Active. If a formerly passive activity becomes an active one, suspended losses are allowed to the extent of income from the now active business.[44] If any of the suspended loss remains, it continues to be treated as a loss from a passive activity. The excess suspended loss can be deducted from passive income or carried over to the next tax year and deducted to the extent of income from the now active business in the succeeding year(s). The activity must continue to be the same activity.

Nontaxable Exchange of a Passive Activity. In a nontaxable exchange of a passive investment, the taxpayer keeps the suspended losses, which generally

42. § 469(j)(6).
43. § 469(g)(3).
44. § 469(f).

become deductible when the acquired property is sold. If the activity of the old and new property are the same, suspended losses can be used.

EXAMPLE 57

A taxpayer exchanged a duplex for a limited partnership interest in a § 721 nonrecognition transaction (see Chapter 22 for details). The suspended losses from the duplex are not deductible until the limited partnership interest is sold. Two separate activities exist: a real estate rental activity and a limited partnership activity. If the taxpayer had continued to own the duplex and the duplex had future taxable income, the suspended losses would have become deductible before the time of disposition. ◆

EXAMPLE 58

In a § 1031 nontaxable exchange (see Chapter 12 for details), a taxpayer exchanged a duplex (rental activity) for an apartment building. The suspended losses from the duplex are deductible against future taxable income of the apartment building. The same rental activity exists for the apartment building. ◆

Transition Rules for Passive Losses (1987–1990)

The passive loss rules disallow 100 percent of losses on passive activities acquired after October 22, 1986. However, under transition rules the disallowance provisions for losses on passive activities acquired before October 23, 1986, were phased in over five years. If a taxpayer had a loss on a passive activity acquired before October 23, 1986 (the date TRA of 1986 was enacted), a percentage of the loss was deductible under the transition rules. Congress enacted the phase-in schedule to provide some relief to taxpayers who had committed their investment funds to passive activities prior to enactment of the passive loss limitations. The following table shows the percentages that applied during the five-year phase-in period.

Taxable Years Beginning in	Losses and Credits Allowed	Losses and Credits Disallowed
1987	65%	35%
1988	40%	60%
1989	20%	80%
1990	10%	90%
1991	0%	100%

Although the transition percentages do not allow the deduction of passive losses after 1990, it is necessary to understand how they affected taxpayers during the transition period. Losses suspended under the transition rules can be deducted in future years when the taxpayer has passive income or upon a taxable disposition of the activity that produced the loss. Thus, the transition rules will continue to affect the computation of passive gains and losses as long as a taxpayer continues to own any pre-October 23, 1986 activity with suspended losses incurred during the transition period.

EXAMPLE 59

Erin acquired a passive activity in 1984. In 1990, she realized a loss of $10,000 on this activity. Under the transition rules, $1,000 (10% of $10,000) was deductible in 1990. The $9,000 disallowed loss is a suspended loss that can be carried forward and deducted against passive income in later years. If Erin has no passive income in later years, the suspended loss can be deducted when she disposes of the passive activity in a fully taxable transaction (see Example 51). If she had acquired the passive activity after October 22, 1986, no deduction would have been allowed in 1990, and the entire $10,000 would have been suspended. ◆

EXAMPLE 60

Assume that Erin in Example 59 has another loss of $20,000 on the pre-enactment passive activity in 1992. Pre-enactment passive activity losses are not deductible in 1992. The entire $20,000 loss is suspended. ◆

If a taxpayer had both pre-enactment and post-enactment activities prior to 1991, the transition percentage was applied to the lesser of (1) the pre-enactment passive activity loss or (2) the net passive loss from pre-enactment and post-enactment activities.

EXAMPLE 61

Steve has two passive activity investments. Investment A was purchased in 1985 and Investment B was purchased in 1987. In 1990, Investment A generated a $10,000 loss, and Investment B generated an $8,000 gain. Steve's net passive loss was $2,000 ($10,000 loss – $8,000 gain). The allowable deduction was $200 (10% of $2,000). The remaining $1,800 would have been suspended and carried over. ◆

EXAMPLE 62

In Example 61, if Investment A had generated income of $10,000 and Investment B had generated an $8,000 loss, the net passive gain of $2,000 would have been included in income. ◆

EXAMPLE 63

In Example 61, assume Investment A (the pre-enactment activity) had generated a loss of $10,000 and Investment B had generated a loss of $8,000. The net passive loss was $18,000. Only $1,000 (10% of $10,000) could have been deducted in 1990. The remaining $17,000 ($8,000 post-enactment loss plus 90% of $10,000 pre-enactment loss) would have been suspended and carried over to the future. ◆

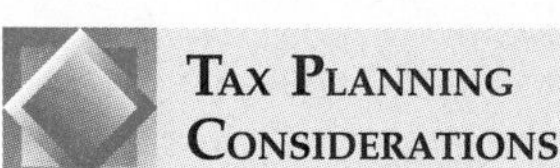
TAX PLANNING CONSIDERATIONS

Utilizing Passive Losses

Taxpayers who have passive activity losses (PALs) should adopt a strategy of generating passive activity income that can be sheltered by existing passive losses. One approach is to buy an interest in any passive activity that is generating income (referred to as passive income generators, or PIGs). Then the PAL can be offset against income from the PIG. From a tax perspective, it would be foolish to buy a loss-generating passive activity (PAL) unless one has other passive income (PIG) to shelter, or the activity is rental real estate that can qualify for the $25,000 exception.

A taxpayer with existing passive losses might consider buying rental property. If a large down payment is made and the straight-line method of ACRS (discussed in Chapter 8) is elected, a positive net income could be realized. The income would be sheltered by other passive losses, depreciation expense would be spread out evenly and preserved for future years, and depreciation recapture (discussed in Chapter 13) is avoided upon the sale of the property. Future gain realized upon the sale of the rental property could be sheltered by existing suspended passive losses.

Taxpayers with passive losses should consider all other trades or businesses in which they have an interest. If they show that they do not materially participate in the activity, the activity becomes a passive activity. Any income generated could be sheltered by existing passive losses and suspended losses. Family partnerships in which certain members do not materially participate would qualify. The silent partner in any general partnership engaged in a trade or business would also qualify.

PROBLEM MATERIALS

DISCUSSION QUESTIONS

1. Congress has passed two major provisions to inhibit taxpayers' ability to use tax shelters to reduce or defer Federal income tax. Explain.
2. Alice invested $50,000 for a 25% interest in a partnership in which she is not a material participant. The partnership borrowed $100,000 from a bank and used the proceeds to acquire a building. What is Alice's at-risk amount if the $100,000 was borrowed on a recourse loan?
3. Eric invested $40,000 for a 20% interest in a partnership in which he is not a material participant. The partnership borrowed $200,000 from a bank and used the proceeds to acquire machinery. What is Eric's at-risk amount if the $200,000 was borrowed on a nonrecourse loan?
4. List some events that increase and decrease an investor's at-risk amount, and discuss some strategies that a taxpayer can employ to increase the at-risk amount in order to claim a higher deduction for losses.
5. What constitutes a taxpayer's initial at-risk amount, and what causes increases and decreases in the amount at risk?
6. Roy invested $10,000 in a cattle-feeding operation that used nonrecourse notes to purchase $100,000 in feed, which was fed to the cattle and expensed. His share of the expense was $18,000. How much can Roy deduct?
7. Gray Corporation has $100,000 of active income and a $55,000 passive loss for the year. Under what circumstances is the corporation prohibited from deducting the loss? Under what circumstances is the corporation allowed to deduct the loss?
8. Hi-Tech Consulting, Inc., is a corporation owned by four engineers, all of whom work full-time for the corporation. The corporation has eight other full-time employees, all on the clerical staff. Hi-Tech provides consulting services to inventors. The corporation has invested in a passive activity that produced a $60,000 loss in 1993. Can Hi-Tech deduct the loss in 1993? Explain.
9. Jane owns an interest in a dress shop in which she works 450 hours during the year. She has three full-time employees in the dress shop. Jane also owns an apartment building in which she participates 1,200 hours during the year. She has no employees for the apartment activity. Is either activity a passive activity? Explain.
10. Discuss whether the passive loss rules apply to the following: individuals, closely held C corporations, S corporations, partnerships, and personal service corporations.
11. How is passive activity defined in the Code, and what aspects of the definition have been clarified by the Temporary Regulations?
12. What is the significance of the term *material participation?* Why is the extent of a taxpayer's participation in an activity important in determining whether a loss from the activity is deductible or nondeductible?
13. Manuel owns an interest in an activity that produces a $100,000 loss during the year. Would he generally prefer to have the activity classified as active or passive? Discuss.
14. Kim owns an interest in an activity that produces $100,000 of income during the year. Would Kim generally prefer to have the activity classified as active or passive? Discuss.

15. Laura owns an apartment building and a videotape rental business. She participates for more than 500 hours in the operations of each activity. Are the businesses active or passive?
16. Why did the IRS adopt the more-than-500-hour standard for material participation?
17. Keith, a physician, operates a separate business that he acquired in 1985. He participated for 90 hours in the business during the current year, and the business incurred a loss of $20,000. Under what circumstances will the loss be deductible as an ordinary loss?
18. Jan, an attorney, operates a separate business that she acquired in 1985. She has one part-time employee in the business. Jan participated for 130 hours in the business during the current year, and the business incurred a loss of $20,000. Under what circumstances will the loss be deductible as an ordinary loss?
19. Zelda, a professor, operates three separate businesses, all acquired in 1985. She participates for less than 500 hours in each business. Each business incurs a loss during the year. Are there any circumstances under which Zelda may treat the losses as active?
20. In 1992, Paul retired as a partner in a CPA firm he founded 30 years ago. He continues to share in the profits, although he no longer participates in the activities of the firm. Paul also owns an interest in a passive activity that he acquired in 1984. The passive activity produced a loss of $50,000 in 1993. Can Paul offset the passive loss against his income from the CPA firm?
21. Some types of work are counted in applying the material participation standards, and some types are not counted. Discuss and give examples of each type.
22. Some rental operations automatically are treated as passive activities, and others are treated as passive only if the owner does not meet the material participation standards. How can one differentiate between the two categories?
23. What are *significant personal services,* and what is their importance in determining whether a rental activity is treated as a passive activity?
24. What are *extraordinary personal services,* and what is their importance in determining whether a rental activity is treated as a passive activity?
25. Discuss which types of services are treated as significant personal services. Which types are not treated as significant personal services?
26. The Proposed Regulations set forth a *facts and circumstances test* for determining what constitutes an activity. Describe this test and comment on the significance of the term *appropriate economic unit.*
27. What factors are given the greatest weight in determining whether activities constitute an appropriate economic unit?
28. The Proposed Regulations prohibit grouping rental activities in certain circumstances. Discuss these rules and the reasons they exist.
29. Under what circumstances may the IRS regroup activities in a different way than the taxpayer has grouped them? Give an example of a situation to which the regrouping rule would be applied.
30. Discuss the following issues in connection with the calculation of passive losses:

    a. What constitutes a passive activity?
    b. What types of income are not treated as passive income?
    c. What types of deductions are not treated as passive deductions?

31. What is a suspended loss? Why is it important to allocate suspended losses in cases where a taxpayer has interests in more than one passive activity?
32. Upon a taxable disposition of a passive activity, the taxpayer can utilize any suspended losses and credits related to that activity. True or false? Explain.
33. Matt owns a small apartment building that sustained a loss during the year. Under what circumstances can Matt deduct a loss from the rental activity, and what limitations apply?

34. In connection with passive activities, what is a *deduction equivalent?* How is a deduction equivalent computed?
35. What is the difference between material participation and active participation under the passive loss rules?
36. Upon the taxable disposition of a passive activity, what happens to the suspended losses? The suspended credits?
37. Felicia owns a passive activity that she acquired in 1985. She incurred losses on the activity in 1987 through 1990. This is the only passive activity she has ever owned. How will these passive losses affect Felicia's taxable income when she disposes of the activity?
38. In 1990, Jay incurred a $100,000 loss on a passive activity that he acquired in 1985 and a $40,000 loss on a passive activity he acquired in 1988. How much was Jay allowed to deduct in 1990?
39. In 1990, April incurred a $100,000 loss on a passive activity that she acquired in 1985 and had $40,000 of income on a passive activity she acquired in 1988. How much was April allowed to deduct in 1990?

PROBLEMS

40. Kelly, who earned a salary of $200,000, invested $40,000 for a 20% working interest in an oil and gas limited partnership (not a passive activity) in 1992. Through the use of $800,000 of nonrecourse financing, the partnership acquired assets worth $1,000,000. Depreciation, interest, and other deductions related to the activity resulted in a loss of $150,000, of which Kelly's share was $30,000. Kelly's share of loss from the partnership was $15,000 in 1993. How much of the loss from the partnership can Kelly deduct?
41. In 1992, Fred invested $50,000 in a limited partnership that has a working interest in an oil well (not a passive activity). In 1992, his share of the partnership loss was $35,000. In 1993, his share of the partnership loss was $25,000. How much can Fred deduct in 1992 and 1993?
42. Brown Corporation, a personal service corporation, earned active income of $500,000 in 1993. The corporation received $60,000 in dividends during the year. In addition, Brown incurred a loss of $80,000 from an investment in a passive activity acquired in 1990. What is Brown's income for 1993 after considering the passive investment?
43. Green Corporation, a closely held, non-personal service corporation, earned active income of $50,000 in 1993. Green received $60,000 in dividends during the year. In addition, Green incurred a loss of $80,000 from an investment in a passive activity acquired in 1992. What is Green's net income for 1993 after considering the passive investment?
44. Bob, an attorney, earned $200,000 from his law practice in 1993. He received $45,000 in dividends and interest during the year. In addition, he incurred a loss of $50,000 from an investment in a passive activity acquired in 1990. What is Bob's net income for 1993 after considering the passive investment?
45. Tina acquired passive Activity A in January 1985 and Activity B in September 1986. Until 1992, Activity A was profitable. Activity A produced a loss of $100,000 in 1992 and a loss of $50,000 in 1993. Tina has passive income from Activity B of $10,000 in 1992 and $20,000 in 1993. After offsetting passive income, how much of the net losses may she deduct?
46. In 1985, Kay acquired an interest in a partnership in which she is not a material participant. The partnership was profitable until 1992. Kay's basis in her partnership interest at the beginning of 1992 was $50,000. In 1992, Kay's share of the partnership loss was $35,000. In 1993, her share of the partnership income was $15,000. How much can Kay deduct in 1992 and 1993?
47. Lee acquired a 20% interest in the ABC Partnership for $60,000 in 1985. The partnership was profitable until 1993, and Lee's basis in the partnership interest was $120,000 at the end of 1992. ABC incurred a loss of $400,000 in 1993 and reported

income of $200,000 in 1994. Assuming Lee is not a material participant in ABC, how much of his loss from ABC Partnership is deductible in 1993 and 1994, respectively?

48. Hazel has two investments in nonrental passive activities. Activity A, which was acquired in 1985, was profitable until 1992. Activity B was acquired in 1992. Hazel's share of the loss from Activity A was $10,000 in 1992, and her share of the loss from Activity B was $6,000. What was the total of Hazel's suspended losses from these activities as of the end of 1992?

49. Joe acquired an activity in 1990. The loss from the activity was $50,000 in 1993. He had AGI of $140,000 before considering the loss from the activity. The activity is an apartment building, and Joe is an active participant. What is his AGI after the loss is considered?

50. Beth acquired an activity in 1990. The loss from the activity was $50,000 in 1993. She had AGI of $140,000 before considering the loss from the activity. The activity is an apartment building, and Beth is not an active participant. What is her AGI after considering the activity?

51. Ray acquired an activity in 1990. The loss from the activity was $50,000 in 1993. He had AGI of $140,000 before considering the loss from the activity. The activity is a bakery, and Ray is not a material participant. What is his AGI after considering this activity?

52. Ann acquired an activity in 1990. The loss from the activity was $50,000 in 1993. She had AGI of $140,000 before considering the loss from the activity. The activity is a service station, and Ann is a material participant. What is her AGI after considering this activity?

53. Ken has a $40,000 loss from an investment in a partnership in which he does not participate. He paid $30,000 for his interest in the partnership. How much of the loss is disallowed by the at-risk rules? How much is disallowed by the passive loss rules?

54. In 1993, Sue invested $20,000 for an interest in a partnership in which she is a material participant. Her share of the partnership's loss for the year was $25,000. Discuss the tax treatment of Sue's share of the loss, and compute her at-risk amount.

55. Assume the same facts as in Problem 54 and that Sue's share of the partnership's income in 1994 is $15,000. What will be the net effect on her taxable income for 1994?

56. Soong, a physician, earned $200,000 from his practice in 1993. He also received $18,000 in dividends and interest on various portfolio investments. During the year, he paid $45,000 to acquire a 20% interest in a partnership that produced a $300,000 loss.

    a. Compute Soong's AGI assuming he does not participate in the operations of the partnership.
    b. Compute Soong's AGI assuming he is a material participant in the operations of the partnership.

57. White, Inc., earned $400,000 from operations in 1993. White also received $36,000 in dividends and interest on various portfolio investments. During the year, White paid $150,000 to acquire a 20% interest in a passive activity that produced a $200,000 loss.

    a. How will this affect White's taxable income, assuming the corporation is a personal service corporation?
    b. How will this affect White's taxable income, assuming the corporation is a closely held, non-personal service corporation?

58. Ahmad owns four activities. He participated for 120 hours in Activity A, 150 hours in Activity B, 140 hours in Activity C, and 100 hours in Activity D. Which of the following statements is correct?

    a. Activities A, B, C, and D are all significant participation activities.
    b. Activities A, B, and C are significant participation activities.
    c. Ahmad is a material participant with respect to Activities A, B, and C.
    d. Ahmad is a material participant with respect to Activities A, B, C, and D.
    e. None of the above.

59. Dena owns interests in five businesses and has full-time employees in each business. She participates for 100 hours in Activity A, 120 hours in Activity B, 130 hours in

Activity C, 140 hours in Activity D, and 125 hours in Activity E. Which of the following statements is correct?

- **a.** All five of Dena's activities are significant participation activities.
- **b.** Dena is a material participant with respect to all five activities.
- **c.** Dena is not a material participant in any of the activities.
- **d.** Dena is a material participant with respect to Activities B, C, D, and E.
- **e.** None of the above.

60. Maria, who owns a 50% interest in a restaurant, has been a material participant in the restaurant activity for the last 20 years. She retired from the restaurant at the end of 1992 and will not participate in the restaurant activity in the future. However, she continues to be a material participant in a retail store in which she is a 50% partner. The restaurant operations resulted in a loss for 1993, and Maria's share of the loss is $80,000. Her share of the income from the retail store is $150,000. She does not own interests in any other activities. Which of the following statements is correct?

- **a.** Maria cannot deduct the $80,000 loss from the restaurant because she is not a material participant.
- **b.** Maria can offset the $80,000 loss against the $150,000 of income from the retail store.
- **c.** Maria will not be able to deduct any losses from the restaurant until 1998.
- **d.** None of the above.

61. Greg, a syndicated radio talk show host from Cincinnati, earns a $400,000 salary in 1993. He works approximately 30 hours per week in this job, which leaves him time to participate in several businesses he acquired in 1993. He owns a movie theater and a drugstore in Cincinnati, a movie theater and a drugstore in Indianapolis, and a drugstore in Louisville. A preliminary analysis on December 1, 1993, shows projected profits and losses for the various businesses as follows:

	Profit (Loss)
Cincinnati movie theater (95 hours participation)	$ 56,000
Cincinnati drugstore (140 hours participation)	(89,000)
Indianapolis movie theater (90 hours participation)	34,000
Indianapolis drugstore (170 hours participation)	(41,000)
Louisville drugstore (180 hours participation)	(15,000)

Greg has full-time employees in each of the five businesses listed above. Consider all possible groupings for Greg's activities. Write a letter to him suggesting the grouping method and other strategies that will provide the greatest tax advantage. Greg does not know much about the tax law, so you should provide a concise, nontechnical explanation.

62. Leanne has investments in four passive activity partnerships purchased in 1984. In 1992, the income and losses were as follows:

Activity	Income (Loss)
A	$ 60,000
B	(60,000)
C	(30,000)
D	(10,000)

In 1993, she sold her interest in Activity D for a $20,000 gain. Activity D, which had been profitable until 1992, had a $3,000 loss in 1993. How will the sale of Activity D affect Leanne's taxable income in 1993?

63. Hal and Wanda are married with no dependents and live together in Ohio, which is not a community property state. Since Wanda has large medical expenses, they seek

your advice about filing separately to save taxes. Their income and expenses for 1993 are as follows:

Hal's salary	$60,000
Wanda's salary	20,000
Dividends and interest (joint)	1,500
Rental loss from actively managed units (joint)	(22,000)
Wanda's medical expenses	5,800
All other itemized deductions:*	
Hal	8,000
Wanda	2,000

*None subject to limitations.

Would Hal and Wanda pay less in taxes if they filed jointly or separately for 1993?

64. Ida, who has AGI of $80,000 before considering rental activities, is active in three separate real estate rental activities and is in the 28% tax bracket. She had $12,000 of losses from Activity A, $18,000 of losses from Activity B, and income of $10,000 from Activity C. She also had $2,100 of tax credits from Activity A. Calculate her deductions and credits allowed and the suspended losses and credits.

65. Chris, who owns a sole proprietorship that is a passive activity, calculated a loss for the activity as follows:

Operating income	$ 75,000
Dividends on stock held for investment	22,500
Total income	$ 97,500
Less: Expenses:	
Operating expenses (wages, rent, supplies, etc.)	(90,000)
Investment interest	(12,000)
Less: Loss on sale of stock held for investment	(7,500)
=Net loss	$(12,000)

Compute Chris's passive loss from the activity based on the above information.

66. Ella has $105,000 of losses from a real estate rental activity in which she actively participates. She has other rental income of $25,000 and other passive income of $32,000. How much rental loss can Ella deduct against active and portfolio income (ignoring at-risk rules and the phase-out rules)? Does she have any suspended losses to carry over?

67. Faye died owning an interest in a passive activity property with an adjusted basis of $80,000, suspended losses of $8,000, and a fair market value of $85,000. What can be deducted on her final income tax return?

68. In 1992, Nina gave her son a passive activity with an adjusted basis of $100,000. Fair market value of the activity was $180,000, and the activity had suspended losses of $25,000. In 1993, her son realized income from the passive activity of $12,000. What is the effect on Nina and her son in 1992 and 1993?

69. Ray, who owns a sole proprietorship that is a passive activity, calculated a loss for the activity as follows:

Operating income	$ 70,000
Dividends on stock held for investment	25,000
Total income	$ 95,000
Less: Expenses:	
Operating expenses (wages, rent, supplies, etc.)	(90,000)
Investment interest	(6,000)
Less: Loss on sale of stock held for investment	(4,000)
Net loss	$ (5,000)

Compute Ray's passive loss for the year.

70. Sam invested $150,000 in a passive activity in 1982. On January 1, 1992, his adjusted basis in the activity was $30,000. His share of the losses in the activity was as follows:

Year	Gain (Loss)
1992	$(40,000)
1993	(30,000)
1994	50,000

How much can Sam deduct in 1992 and 1993? What is his taxable income from the activity in 1994? Keep in mind the at-risk rules as well as the passive loss rules.

71. Stan acquired a passive activity in 1992 that generated tax credits of $2,000 and income of $4,000. The regular tax attributable to the income was $1,120. However, Stan paid taxes of $80,000 under the alternative minimum tax provisions. In 1993, the activity generated $1,000 of income upon which $280 of regular tax was due. Stan paid regular taxes that year of $40,000. When and how can he use the $2,000 of credits?

72. Tonya sold a passive activity in 1993 for $150,000. Her adjusted basis was $50,000. She used the installment method of reporting the gain. The activity had suspended losses of $12,000. Tonya received $60,000 in the year of sale. What is her gain? How much of the suspended losses can she deduct?

73. If Tonya in Problem 72 had no suspended losses, was in the 28% tax bracket, and had $10,000 of tax credits attributable to the activity, how much of the credits could she use in 1993?

CHAPTER

DEDUCTIONS AND LOSSES: CERTAIN BUSINESS EXPENSES AND LOSSES

OBJECTIVES

Determine the amount of the bad debt deduction.

Distinguish between business and nonbusiness bad debts and recognize the tax consequences of the distinction.

Examine the tax treatment for worthless securities and § 1244 stock.

Calculate the amount of loss for business use property.

Define the term "casualty" and compute the amount of casualty and theft losses.

Recognize the alternative tax treatments for research and experimental expenditures.

Discuss the rationale for the net operating loss deduction.

Recognize the impact of the carryback and carryover of a net operating loss.

Suggest tax planning considerations in deducting certain business expenses and losses.

OUTLINE

Working with the tax formula for individuals requires the proper classification of items that are deductible *for* adjusted gross income (AGI) and items that are deductions *from* AGI (itemized deductions). Business expenses and losses, discussed in this chapter, are reductions of gross income to arrive at the taxpayer's AGI. Expenses and losses attributable to rents and royalties are deducted *for* AGI. All other expenses and losses incurred in connection with a transaction entered into for profit are deducted *from* AGI. Deductible losses on personal use property are deducted as itemized deductions. Itemized deductions are deductions *from* AGI. While the general coverage of itemized deductions is in Chapter 10, casualty and theft losses on personal use property are discussed in this chapter.

BAD DEBTS

If a taxpayer sells goods or provides services on credit and the account receivable subsequently becomes worthless, a bad debt deduction is permitted only if income arising from the creation of the account receivable was previously included in income. No deduction is allowed, for example, for a bad debt arising from the sale of a product or service when the taxpayer is on the cash basis because no income is reported until the cash has been collected. Permitting a bad debt deduction for a cash basis taxpayer would amount to a double deduction because the expenses of the product or service rendered are deducted when payments are made to suppliers and employees or at the time of the sale.

EXAMPLE 1

Pat, an individual engaged in the practice of accounting, performed accounting services for Tracy for which he charged $8,000. Tracy never paid the bill, and his whereabouts are unknown.

If Pat is an accrual basis taxpayer, the $8,000 is included in income when the services are performed. When Pat determines that Tracy's account will not be collected, he expenses the $8,000 as a bad debt.

If Pat is a cash basis taxpayer, the $8,000 is not included in income until payment is received. When Pat determines that Tracy's account will not be collected, he cannot deduct the $8,000 as a bad debt expense since it was never recognized as income. ◆

A bad debt can also result from the nonpayment of a loan made by the taxpayer or from purchased debt instruments.

Specific Charge-Off Method

For tax years beginning after 1986, taxpayers (other than certain financial institutions) may use only the *specific charge-off* method in accounting for bad debts. The *reserve* method for computing deductions for bad debts is allowed only for certain financial institutions.

A taxpayer using the specific charge-off method may claim a deduction when a specific business debt becomes either partially or wholly worthless or when a specific nonbusiness debt becomes wholly worthless. For a business debt, the taxpayer must satisfy the IRS that the debt is partially worthless and must demonstrate the amount of worthlessness.

If a business debt previously deducted as partially worthless becomes totally worthless in a future year, only the remainder not previously deducted can be deducted in the future year.

In the case of total worthlessness, a deduction is allowed for the entire amount in the year the debt becomes worthless. The amount of the deduction depends on the taxpayer's basis in the bad debt. If the debt arose from the sale of services or products and the face amount was previously included in income, that amount is deductible. If the taxpayer purchased the debt, the deduction is equal to the amount the taxpayer paid for the debt instrument.

One of the more difficult tasks is determining if and when a bad debt is worthless. The loss is deductible only in the year of partial or total worthlessness for business debts and only in the year of total worthlessness for nonbusiness debts. Legal proceedings need not be initiated against the debtor when the surrounding facts indicate that doing so will not result in collection.

EXAMPLE 2

In 1991, Jill loaned $1,000 to Kay, who agreed to repay the loan in two years. In 1993, Kay disappeared after the note became delinquent. If a reasonable investigation by Jill indicates that she cannot find Kay or that a suit against her would not result in collection, Jill can deduct the $1,000 in 1993. ◆

Bankruptcy is generally an indication of at least partial worthlessness of a debt. Bankruptcy may create worthlessness before the settlement date. If this is the case, the deduction must be taken in the year of worthlessness, not in the later year upon settlement.

EXAMPLE 3

In Example 2, assume Kay filed for personal bankruptcy in 1992 and that the debt is a business debt. At that time, Jill learned that unsecured creditors (including Jill) were expected ultimately to receive 20¢ on the dollar. In 1993, settlement is made and Jill receives only $150. She should deduct $800 ($1,000 loan less $200 expected settlement) in 1992 and $50 in 1993 ($200 balance less $150 proceeds). Jill is not permitted to wait until 1993 to deduct the entire $850. ◆

If a receivable has been written off as uncollectible during the current tax year and is subsequently collected during the current tax year, the write-off entry is reversed.

If a receivable has been written off as uncollectible, collection of the receivable in a later tax year may result in income being recognized. Income will result if the deduction yielded a tax benefit in the year it was taken. See Example 37 in Chapter 4.

Business versus Nonbusiness Bad Debts

A *nonbusiness* bad debt is a debt unrelated to the taxpayer's trade or business either when it was created or when it became worthless. The nature of a debt

CONCEPT SUMMARY 7–1
SPECIFIC CHARGE-OFF METHOD

Expense deduction and account write-off	The expense arises and the write-off takes place when a specific business account becomes either partially or wholly worthless or when a specific nonbusiness account becomes wholly worthless.
Recovery of accounts previously written off	If the account recovered was written off during the current taxable year, the write-off entry is reversed. If the account recovered was written off during a previous taxable year, income is recognized subject to the tax benefit rule.

depends on whether the lender was engaged in the business of lending money or if there is a proximate relationship between the creation of the debt and the lender's trade or business. The use to which the borrowed funds are put by the debtor is of no consequence. Loans to relatives or friends are the most common type of nonbusiness bad debt.

EXAMPLE 4

José loaned his friend, Shontelle, $1,500. Shontelle used the money to start a business, which subsequently failed. Even though proceeds of the loan were used in a business, the loan is a nonbusiness bad debt because the business was Shontelle's, not José's. ◆

The distinction between a business bad debt and a nonbusiness bad debt is important. A business bad debt is deductible as an ordinary loss in the year incurred, whereas a nonbusiness bad debt is always treated as a short-term capital loss. Thus, regardless of the age of a nonbusiness bad debt, the deduction may be of limited benefit due to the capital loss limitations on deductibility in any one year. The maximum amount of a net short-term capital loss that an individual can deduct against ordinary income in any one year is $3,000 (see Chapter 13 for a detailed discussion). Although no deduction is allowed when a nonbusiness bad debt is partially worthless, the taxpayer is entitled to deduct the net amount of the loss upon final settlement.

The following examples are illustrations of business bad debts adapted from the Regulations.[1]

EXAMPLE 5

In 1992, Leif sold his business but retained a claim (note receivable) against Bob. The claim became worthless in 1993. Leif's loss is accorded business bad debt treatment because the debt was created in the conduct of his former trade or business even though he was holding the note as an investor and was no longer in a trade or business when the claim became worthless. ◆

EXAMPLE 6

In 1992, Leif died and left his business assets to his son, Sam. One of the business assets Sam inherited was a claim against Bob that becomes worthless in Sam's hands in 1993. Sam's loss is a business bad debt since he incurs the loss in the conduct of the trade or business in which he is engaged at the time the debt becomes worthless. ◆

The nonbusiness bad debt provisions do not apply to corporations. It is assumed that any loans made by a corporation are related to its trade or business. Therefore, any bad debts of a corporation are business bad debts.

Loans between Related Parties

Loans between related parties (especially family members) raise the issue of whether the loan was *bona fide* or a gift. The Regulations state that a bona fide debt arises from a debtor-creditor relationship based on a valid and enforceable obligation to pay a fixed or determinable sum of money. Thus, individual circumstances must be examined to determine whether transfers between related parties are gifts or loans. Some considerations are these:

- Was a note properly executed?
- Was there a reasonable rate of interest?

1. Reg. § 1.166–5(d).

- Was collateral provided?
- What collection efforts were made?
- What was the intent of the parties?

EXAMPLE 7

Lana loans $2,000 to her widowed mother for an operation. Lana's mother owns no property and is not employed, and her only income consists of Social Security benefits. No note is issued for the loan, no provision for interest is made, and no repayment date is mentioned. In the current year, Lana's mother dies leaving no estate. Assuming the loan is not repaid, Lana cannot take a deduction for a nonbusiness bad debt because the facts indicate that no debtor-creditor relationship existed. ◆

Loss of Deposits in Insolvent Financial Institutions

Qualified individuals can *elect* to deduct losses on deposits in qualified financial institutions as personal casualty losses in the year in which the amount of the loss can be reasonably estimated. If the taxpayer elects to treat a loss on a deposit as a personal casualty loss, no bad debt deduction for the loss will be allowed. As a personal casualty loss, the loss is subject to the $100 per event floor and the 10 percent of AGI aggregate floor. Both floors limiting casualty losses are explained later in the chapter. The amount of loss to be recognized under the election is the difference between (1) the taxpayer's basis in the deposit and (2) a reasonable estimate of the amount to be received.

If the individual does not elect to deduct the loss as a casualty loss, it will be treated as a nonbusiness bad debt and, hence, as a short-term capital loss. As a short-term capital loss, it will be subject to the capital loss limitation rules (see the discussion in Chapter 13).

WORTHLESS SECURITIES

A loss is allowed under § 165 for a security that becomes *completely* worthless during the year. Such securities are shares of stock, bonds, notes, or other evidence of indebtedness issued by a corporation or government. The losses generated are treated as capital losses deemed to have occurred on the *last day* of the taxable year. By treating the loss as having occurred on the last day of the taxable year, a loss that otherwise would have been classified as short term (if the date of worthlessness was used) may be classified as a long-term capital loss. Capital losses may be of limited benefit due to the $3,000 capital loss limitation.

EXAMPLE 8

Ali, a calendar year taxpayer, owns stock in ABC Corporation (a publicly held company). The stock was acquired as an investment on November 30, 1992, at a cost of $5,000. On April 1, 1993, the stock became worthless. Since the stock is deemed to have become worthless as of December 31 of 1993, Ali has a capital loss from an asset held for 13 months (a long-term capital loss). ◆

Securities in Affiliated Corporations

If securities of an affiliated corporation become worthless during the taxable year, the corporate taxpayer's loss will be treated as an *ordinary loss* rather than a capital loss. A corporation is treated as an affiliated corporation to the parent if two requirements are satisfied. First, the corporate shareholder must own at least

80 percent of the voting power of all classes of stock and at least 80 percent of each class of nonvoting stock of the affiliated company. Second, more than 90 percent of the gross receipts of the affiliate must be from sources other than royalties, rents, dividends, interest, annuities, and gains from sales or exchanges of stocks and securities.

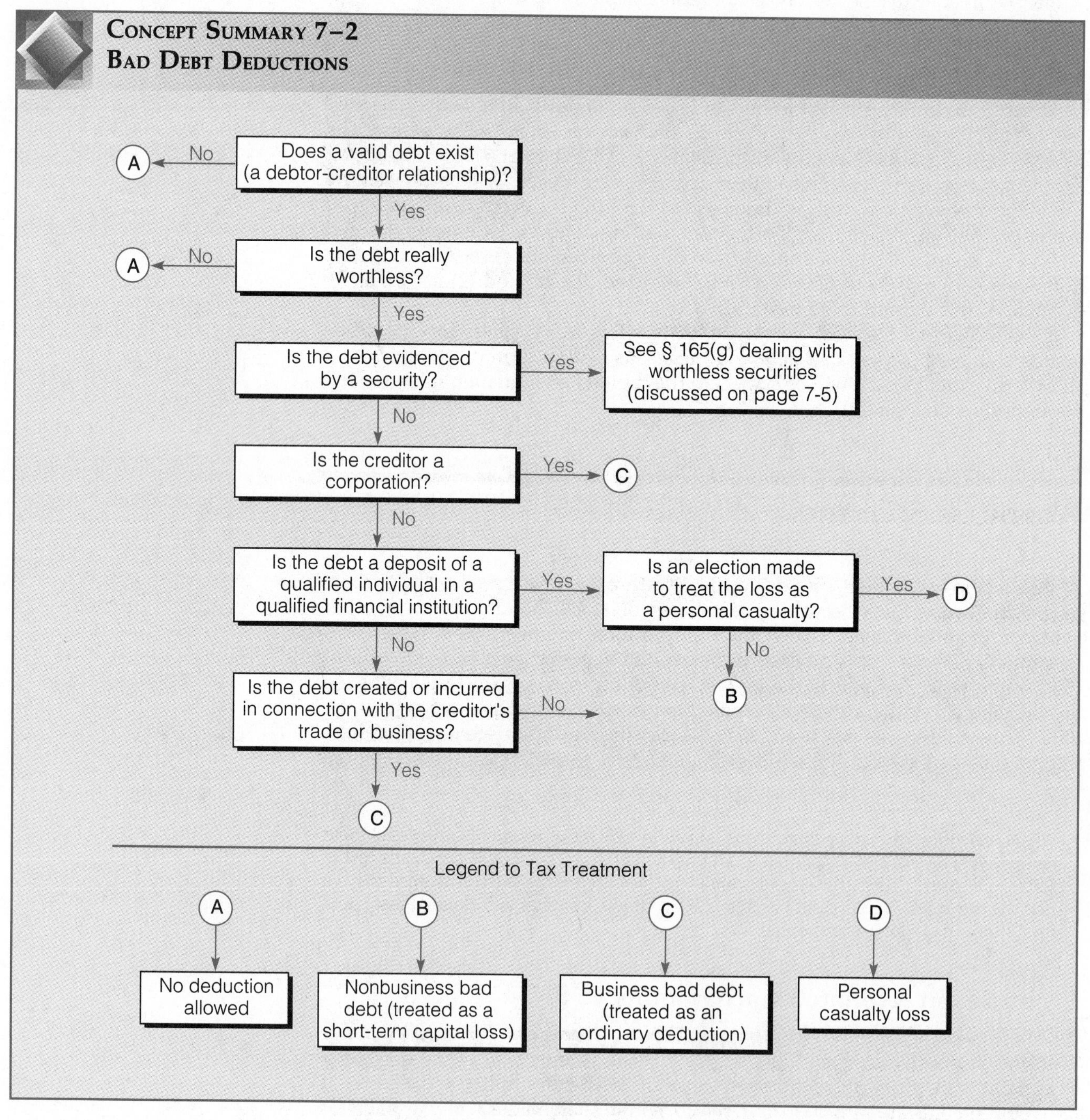

Small Business Stock

The general rule is that shareholders receive capital gain or loss treatment upon the sale or exchange of stock. However, it is possible to receive an ordinary loss deduction if the loss is sustained on small business stock—§ 1244 stock. This loss could arise from a sale of the stock or from the stock becoming worthless. Only *individuals*[2] who acquired the stock from the corporation are eligible to receive ordinary loss treatment under § 1244. The ordinary loss treatment is limited to $50,000 ($100,000 for married individuals filing jointly) per year. Losses on § 1244 stock in excess of the amounts treated as *ordinary* losses are treated as *capital* losses.

The corporation must meet certain requirements for the worthlessness of § 1244 stock to be treated as an *ordinary*—rather than a capital—loss. The major requirement is that the total amount of money and other property received by the corporation for stock as a contribution to capital (or paid-in surplus) does not exceed $1 million. The $1 million test is made at the time the stock is issued. Section 1244 stock can be common or preferred stock. Section 1244 applies only to losses. If § 1244 stock is sold at a gain, the Section has no application, and the gain will be capital gain.

Example 9

On July 1, 1991, Iris, a single individual, purchased 100 shares of XYZ Corporation common stock for $100,000. The XYZ stock qualifies as § 1244 stock. On June 20, 1993, Iris sells all of the XYZ stock for $20,000. Because the XYZ stock is § 1244 stock, Iris has $50,000 of ordinary loss and $30,000 of long-term capital loss. ◆

Losses of Individuals

An individual may deduct the following losses under § 165(c):

- Losses incurred in a trade or business.
- Losses incurred in a transaction entered into for profit.
- Losses caused by fire, storm, shipwreck, or other casualty or by theft.

An individual taxpayer may deduct losses to property used in the taxpayer's trade or business or losses to property used in a transaction entered into for profit. Examples include a loss on property used in a proprietorship, a loss on property held for rent, or a loss on stolen bearer bonds. Note that an individual's losses on property used in a trade or business or on transactions entered into for profit are not limited to losses caused by fire, storm, shipwreck, or other casualty or by theft.

A taxpayer suffering losses from damage to nonbusiness property can deduct only those losses attributable to fire, storm, shipwreck, or other casualty or theft. Although the meaning of the terms "fire, storm, shipwreck, and theft" is relatively free from dispute, the term "other casualty" needs further clarification. It means casualties analogous to fire, storm, or shipwreck. The term also includes accidental loss of property provided the loss qualifies under the same rules as any other casualty. These rules are that the loss must result from an event that is

2. The term "individuals" for this purpose includes a partnership but not a trust or an estate.

(1) identifiable; (2) damaging to property; and (3) sudden, unexpected, and unusual in nature.

A *sudden event* is one that is swift and precipitous and not gradual or progressive. An *unexpected event* is an event that is ordinarily unanticipated and occurs without the intent of the individual who suffers the loss. An *unusual event* is one that is extraordinary and nonrecurring, that does not commonly occur during the activity in which the taxpayer was engaged when the destruction occurred. Examples include hurricanes, tornadoes, floods, storms, shipwrecks, fires, auto accidents, mine cave-ins, sonic booms, and vandalism. Weather that causes damages (drought, for example) must be unusual and severe for the particular region. Damage must be to the taxpayer's property to qualify as a casualty loss.

A taxpayer can take a deduction for a casualty loss from an automobile accident only if the damage was not caused by the taxpayer's willful act or willful negligence.

EXAMPLE 10

Ted parks his car on a hill and fails to set the brake properly and to curb the wheels. As a result of Ted's negligence, the car rolls down the hill and is damaged. The repairs to the car should qualify for casualty loss treatment since Ted's act of negligence appears to be simple rather than willful. ◆

Events That Are Not Casualties

Not all "acts of God" are treated as casualty losses for income tax purposes. Because a casualty must be sudden, unexpected, and unusual, progressive deterioration (such as erosion due to wind or rain) is not a casualty because it does not meet the suddenness test.

Examples of nonsudden events that generally do not qualify as casualties include disease and insect damages. When termites caused damage over a period of several years, some courts have disallowed a casualty loss deduction.[3] On the other hand, some courts have held that termite damage over periods of up to 15 months after infestation constituted a sudden event and was, therefore, deductible as a casualty loss.[4] Despite the existence of some judicial support for the deductibility of termite damage as a casualty loss, the current position of the IRS is that termite damage is not deductible.[5]

Other examples of events that are not casualties are losses resulting from a decline in value rather than an actual loss of the property. No loss was allowed where the taxpayer's home declined in value as a result of a landslide that destroyed neighboring homes but did no actual damage to the taxpayer's home.[6] Similarly, a taxpayer was allowed a loss for the actual flood damage to his property but not for the decline in market value due to the property's being flood-prone.[7]

The Eleventh Court of Appeals has stated that loss of present value generated by a fear of future damage cannot be factored into the fair market value of the property. However, the Court has held that permanent buyer resistance, as

3. *Fay v. Helvering*, 41–2 USTC ¶9494, 27 AFTR 432, 120 F.2d 253 (CA–2, 1941); *U.S. v. Rogers*, 41–1 USTC ¶9442, 27 AFTR 423, 120 F.2d 244 (CA–9, 1941).

4. *Rosenberg v. Comm.*, 52–2 USTC ¶9377, 42 AFTR 303, 198 F.2d 46 (CA–8, 1952); *Shopmaker v. U.S.*, 54–1 USTC ¶9195, 45 AFTR 758, 119 F.Supp. 705 (D.Ct.Mo., 1953).

5. Rev.Rul. 63–232, 1963–2 C.B. 97.

6. *H. Pulvers v. Comm.*, 69–1 USTC ¶9222, 23 AFTR2d 69–678, 407 F.2d 838 (CA–9, 1969).

7. *S. L. Solomon*, 39 TCM 1282, T.C.Memo 1980–87.

evidenced by changes made to the neighborhood surrounding the taxpayer's home following a flood, does affect the fair market value and may be included in a determination as to what the fair market value is after the disaster.[8]

Theft Losses

Theft includes, but is not necessarily limited to, larceny, embezzlement, and robbery. Theft does not include misplaced items.

Theft losses are computed like other casualty losses (discussed in the following section), but the *timing* for recognition of the loss differs. A theft loss is deducted in the year of discovery, not the year of the theft (unless, of course, the discovery occurs in the same year as the theft). If, in the year of the discovery, a claim exists (e.g., against an insurance company) and there is a reasonable expectation of recovering the adjusted basis of the asset from the insurance company, no deduction is permitted. If, in the year of settlement, the recovery is less than the asset's adjusted basis, a partial deduction may be available. If the recovery is greater than the asset's adjusted basis, recognition of gain may be required.

EXAMPLE 11

Keith's new sailboat, which he uses for personal purposes, was stolen from the storage marina in December 1991. He discovered the loss on June 3, 1992, and filed a claim with his insurance company that was settled on January 30, 1993. Assuming there is a reasonable expectation of full recovery, no deduction is allowed in 1992. A partial deduction may be available in 1993 if the actual insurance proceeds are less than the lower of the adjusted basis or decline in fair market value of the asset. (Loss measurement rules are discussed later in this chapter.) ◆

When to Deduct Casualty Losses

General Rule. Generally, a casualty loss is deducted in the year the loss occurs. However, no casualty loss is permitted if a reimbursement claim with a *reasonable prospect of full recovery* exists.[9] If the taxpayer has a partial claim, only part of the loss can be claimed in the year of the casualty, and the remainder is deducted in the year the claim is settled.

EXAMPLE 12

Chee's new sailboat was completely destroyed by fire in 1993. Its cost and fair market value were $10,000. Chee's only claim against the insurance company was on a $7,000 policy that was not settled by year-end. The following year, 1994, Chee settled with the insurance company for $6,000. Chee is entitled to a $3,000 deduction in 1993 and a $1,000 deduction in 1994. If the sailboat were held for personal use, the $3,000 deduction in 1993 would be reduced first by $100 and then by 10% of Chee's 1993 AGI. The $1,000 deduction in 1994 would be reduced by 10% of Chee's 1994 AGI (see the following discussion of the $100 and 10% floors). ◆

If a taxpayer receives reimbursement for a casualty loss sustained and deducted in a previous year, an amended return is not filed for that year. Instead, the taxpayer must include the reimbursement in gross income on the return for the year in which it is received to the extent that the previous deduction resulted in a tax benefit.

---

8. *Finkbohner, Jr. v. U.S.*, 86–1 USTC ¶9393, 57 AFTR2d 86–1400, 788 F.2d 723 (CA–11, 1986).

9. Reg § 1.165–1(d)(2)(i).

EXAMPLE 13

Fran had a deductible casualty loss of $5,000 on her 1992 tax return. Fran's taxable income for 1992 was $60,000. In June 1993, Fran was reimbursed $3,000 for the prior year's casualty loss. Fran would include the entire $3,000 in gross income for 1993 because the deduction in 1992 produced a tax benefit. ◆

Disaster Area Losses. An exception to the general rule for the time of deduction is allowed for casualties sustained in an area designated as a disaster area by the President of the United States. In such cases, the taxpayer may *elect* to treat the loss as having occurred in the taxable year immediately preceding the taxable year in which the disaster actually occurred. The rationale for this exception is to provide immediate relief to disaster victims in the form of accelerated tax benefits.

If the due date, plus extensions, for the prior year's return has not passed, a taxpayer makes the election to claim the disaster area loss on the prior year's tax return. If the disaster occurs after the prior year's return has been filed, it is necessary to file either an amended return or a refund claim. In any case, the taxpayer must show clearly that such an election is being made.

Disaster loss treatment also applies in the case of a personal residence that has been rendered unsafe for use as a residence because of a disaster. This provision applies when, within 120 days after the President designates the area as a disaster area, the state or local government where the residence is located orders the taxpayer to demolish or relocate the residence.

Measuring the Amount of Loss

Amount of Loss. The rules for determining the amount of a loss depend in part on whether business use, income-producing use, or personal use property was involved. Another factor that must be considered is whether the property was partially or completely destroyed.

If business property or property held for the production of income (e.g., rental property) is *completely destroyed,* the loss is equal to the adjusted basis of the property at the time of destruction.

EXAMPLE 14

Vicki's automobile, which was used only for business purposes, was destroyed by fire. She had unintentionally allowed her insurance coverage to expire. The fair market value of the automobile was $9,000 at the time of the fire, and its adjusted basis was $10,000. Vicki is allowed a loss deduction of $10,000 (the basis of the automobile). The $10,000 loss is a deduction *for* AGI. ◆

A different measurement rule applies for *partial destruction* of business property and income-producing property and for *partial* or *complete destruction* of personal use property. In these situations, the loss is the *lesser* of the following:

1. The adjusted basis of the property.
2. The difference between the fair market value of the property before the event and the fair market value immediately after the event.

EXAMPLE 15

Kelly's uninsured automobile, which was used only for business purposes, was damaged in a wreck. At the date of the wreck, the fair market value of the automobile was $12,000, and its adjusted basis was $9,000. After the wreck, the automobile was appraised at $4,000. Kelly's loss deduction is $8,000 (the lesser of the adjusted basis or the decrease in fair market value). The $8,000 loss is a deduction *for* AGI. ◆

The deduction for the loss of property that is part business and part personal must be computed separately for the business portion and the personal portion.

Any insurance recovery reduces the loss for business, production of income, and personal use losses. In fact, a taxpayer may realize a gain if the insurance proceeds exceed the amount of the loss. Chapter 13 discusses the treatment of net gains and losses on business property and income-producing property.

A taxpayer will not be permitted to deduct a casualty loss for damage to insured personal use property unless he or she files a timely insurance claim with respect to the damage to the property. This rule applies to the extent that any insurance policy provides for full or partial reimbursement for the loss.

Generally, an appraisal before and after the casualty is needed to measure the amount of the loss. However, the *cost of repairs* to the damaged property is acceptable as a method of establishing the loss in value provided the following criteria are met:

- The repairs are necessary to restore the property to its condition immediately before the casualty.
- The amount spent for the repairs is not excessive.
- The repairs do not extend beyond the damage suffered.
- The repairs do not cause the value of the property to be higher after the repairs than it was immediately before the casualty.[10]

Reduction for $100 and 10 Percent of AGI. The amount of the loss for personal use property must be reduced by a $100 *per event* floor and a 10 percent of AGI *aggregate* floor. The $100 floor applies separately to each casualty and applies to the entire loss from each casualty. For example, if a storm damages both a taxpayer's residence and automobile, only $100 is subtracted from the total amount of the loss. The losses are then added together, and the total is reduced by 10 percent of the taxpayer's AGI. The resulting loss is the taxpayer's itemized deduction for casualty and theft losses.

EXAMPLE 16

Rocky, who had AGI of $30,000, was involved in an accident in which his motorcycle was completely destroyed. The motorcycle, which was used only for personal use, had a fair market value of $12,000 and an adjusted basis of $9,000. Rocky received $5,000 from his insurance company. Rocky's casualty loss deduction is $900 [$9,000 basis – $5,000 insurance – $100 floor – $3,000 (.10 × $30,000 AGI)]. The $900 casualty loss is an itemized deduction (*from* AGI). ◆

When a nonbusiness casualty loss is spread between two taxable years because of the *reasonable prospect of recovery* doctrine, the loss in the second year is not reduced by the $100 floor. This result occurs because this floor is imposed per event and has already reduced the amount of the loss in the first year. However, the loss in the second year is still subject to the 10 percent floor based on the taxpayer's second-year AGI (refer to Example 12).

Taxpayers who suffer qualified disaster area losses can elect to deduct the losses in the year preceding the year of occurrence. The disaster loss is treated as having occurred in the preceding taxable year. Hence, the 10 percent of AGI floor is determined by using the AGI of the year for which the deduction is claimed.

Multiple Losses. The rules for computing loss deductions where multiple losses have occurred are explained in Examples 17 and 18.

10. Reg. § 1.165–7(a)(2)(ii).

EXAMPLE 17

During the year, Tim had the following losses:

		Fair Market Value of Asset		
Asset	Adjusted Basis	Before the Casualty	After the Casualty	Insurance Recovery
A	$900	$600	$-0-	$400
B	300	800	250	100

Assets A and B were used in Tim's business at the time of the casualty. The following losses are allowed:

Asset A: $500. The complete destruction of a business asset results in a deduction of the adjusted basis of the property (reduced by any insurance recovery) regardless of the asset's fair market value.

Asset B: $200. The partial destruction of a business (or personal use) asset results in a deduction equal to the lesser of the adjusted basis ($300) or the decline in value ($550), reduced by any insurance recovery ($100). Both Asset A and Asset B losses are deductions *for* AGI. The $100 floor and the 10% of AGI floor do not apply because the assets are business assets. ◆

EXAMPLE 18

During the year, Emily had AGI of $20,000 and the following casualty losses:

		Fair Market Value of Asset		
Asset	Adjusted Basis	Before the Casualty	After the Casualty	Insurance Recovery
A	$ 900	$ 600	$ -0-	$ 200
B	2,500	4,000	1,000	-0-
C	800	400	100	250

Assets A, B, and C were held for personal use, and the losses to these three assets are from three different casualties. The loss for each asset is computed as follows:

Asset A: $300. The lesser of the adjusted basis of $900 or the $600 decline in value, reduced by the insurance recovery of $200, minus the $100 floor.

Asset B: $2,400. The lesser of the adjusted basis of $2,500 or the $3,000 decline in value, minus the $100 floor.

Asset C: $0. The lesser of the adjusted basis of $800 or the $300 decline in value, reduced by the insurance recovery of $250, minus the $100 floor.

Emily's itemized casualty loss deduction for the year is $700:

Asset A loss	$ 300
Asset B loss	2,400
Asset C loss	-0-
Total loss	$ 2,700
Less: 10% of AGI (10% × $20,000)	(2,000)
Itemized casualty loss deduction	$ 700

◆

Statutory Framework for Deducting Losses of Individuals

Casualty and theft losses incurred by an individual in connection with a trade or business are deductible *for* AGI. These losses are not subject to the $100 per event and the 10 percent of AGI limitations.

Casualty and theft losses incurred by an individual in a transaction entered into for profit are not subject to the $100 per event and the 10 percent of AGI limitations. If these losses are attributable to rents or royalties, the deduction is *for* AGI. However, if these losses are not connected with property held for the production of rents and royalties, they are deductions *from* AGI. More specifically, these losses are classified as other miscellaneous itemized deductions. An example of this type of loss would be the theft of a security. The aggregate of certain miscellaneous itemized deductions is subject to a 2 percent of AGI floor (explained in Chapter 10).

Casualty and theft losses attributable to personal use property are subject to the $100 per event and the 10 percent of AGI limitations. These losses are itemized deductions, but they are not subject to the 2 percent of AGI floor. The treatment of casualty gains and losses is summarized in Concept Summary 7–3.

Personal Casualty Gains and Losses

If a taxpayer has personal casualty and theft gains as well as losses, a special set of rules applies for determining the tax consequences. The term *personal casualty gain* means the recognized gain from a casualty or theft of personal use property. A *personal casualty loss* for this purpose is a casualty or theft loss of personal use property after the application of the $100 floor. A taxpayer who has both gains and losses for the taxable year must first net (offset) the personal casualty gains and personal casualty losses. If the gains exceed the losses, the gains and losses will be treated as gains and losses from the sale of capital assets. The capital gains and losses will be short term or long term, depending on the period the taxpayer held each of the assets. In the netting process, personal casualty and theft gains and losses are not netted with the gains and losses on business and income-producing property.

Concept Summary 7–3
Casualty Gains and Losses

	Business Use or Income-Producing Property	Personal Use Property
Event creating the loss	Any loss sustained.	Casualty or theft loss.
Amount	The lesser of the decline in fair market value or the adjusted basis, but always the adjusted basis if the property is totally destroyed.	The lesser of the decline in fair market value or the adjusted basis.
Insurance	Insurance proceeds received reduce the amount of the loss.	Insurance proceeds received (or for which there is an unfiled claim) reduce the amount of the loss.
$100 floor	Not applicable.	Applicable per event.
Gains and losses	Gains and losses are netted (see detailed discussion in Chapter 13).	Personal casualty and theft gains and losses are netted.
Gains exceeding losses		The gains and losses are treated as gains and losses from the sale of capital assets.
Losses exceeding gains		The gains—and the losses to the extent of gains—are treated as ordinary items in computing AGI. The losses in excess of gains, to the extent they exceed 10% of AGI, are itemized deductions.

EXAMPLE 19

During the year, Cliff had the following personal casualty gains and losses (after deducting the $100 floor):

Asset	Holding Period	Gain or (Loss)
A	Three months	($300)
B	Three years	(2,400)
C	Two years	3,200

Cliff would compute the tax consequences as follows:

Personal casualty gain	$ 3,200
Personal casualty loss ($300 + $2,400)	(2,700)
Net personal casualty gain	$ 500

Cliff would treat all of the gains and losses as capital gains and losses and would have the following:

Short-term capital loss (Asset A)	$ 300
Long-term capital loss (Asset B)	2,400
Long-term capital gain (Asset C)	3,200

◆

If personal casualty losses exceed personal casualty gains, all gains and losses are treated as ordinary items. The gains—and the losses to the extent of gains—will be treated as ordinary income and ordinary loss in computing AGI. Losses in excess of gains are deducted as itemized deductions to the extent the losses exceed 10 percent of AGI.

EXAMPLE 20

During the year, Hazel had AGI of $20,000 and the following personal casualty gain and loss (after deducting the $100 floor):

Asset	Holding Period	Gain or (Loss)
A	Three years	($2,700)
B	Four months	200

Hazel's tax consequences are computed as follows:

Personal casualty loss	($2,700)
Personal casualty gain	200
Net personal casualty loss	($2,500)

Hazel treats the gain and the loss as ordinary items. The $200 gain and $200 of the loss are included in computing AGI. Hazel's itemized deduction for casualty losses is computed as follows:

Casualty loss in excess of gain ($2,700 – $200)	$ 2,500
Less: 10% of AGI (10% × $20,000)	(2,000)
Itemized deduction	$ 500

◆

Research and Experimental Expenditures

Section 174 covers the treatment of *research and experimental expenditures.* The Regulations define research and experimental expenditures as follows:

> . . . all such costs incident to the development of an experimental or pilot model, a plant process, a product, a formula, an invention, or similar property, and the improvement of already existing property of the type mentioned. The term does not include expenditures such as those for the ordinary testing or inspection of materials or products for quality control or those for efficiency surveys, management studies, consumer surveys, advertising, or promotions.[11]

Expenses in connection with the acquisition or improvement of land or depreciable property are not research and experimental expenditures. Rather, they increase the basis of the land or depreciable property. However, depreciation on a building used for research may be a research and experimental expense. Only the depreciation that is a research and experimental expense (not the cost of the asset) is subject to the three alternatives discussed below.

The law permits the following three alternatives for the handling of research and experimental expenditures:

- Expensing in the year paid or incurred.
- Deferral and amortization.
- Capitalization.

If the costs are capitalized, a deduction is not available until the research project is abandoned or is deemed worthless. Since many products resulting from research projects do not have a definite and limited useful life, a taxpayer should ordinarily elect to write off the expenditures immediately or to defer and amortize them. It is generally preferable to elect an immediate write-off of the research expenditures because of the time value of the tax deduction.

The law also provides for a research activities credit. The credit amounts to 20 percent of certain research and experimental expenditures. (The credit is discussed more fully in Chapter 11.)

Expense Method

A taxpayer can elect to expense all of the research and experimental expenditures incurred in the current year and all subsequent years. The consent of the IRS is not required if the method is adopted for the first taxable year in which such expenditures were paid or incurred. Once the election is made, the taxpayer must continue to expense all qualifying expenditures unless a request for a change is made to, and approved by, the IRS. In certain instances, a taxpayer may incur research and experimental expenditures before actually engaging in any trade or business activity. In such instances, the Supreme Court has applied a liberal standard of deductibility and permitted a deduction in the year of incurrence.[12]

11. Reg. § 1.174–2(a)(1).

12. *Snow v. Comm.,* 74–1 USTC ¶9432, 33 AFTR2d 74–1251, 94 S.Ct. 1876 (USSC, 1974).

Deferral and Amortization Method

A taxpayer may elect to use the deferral and amortization method for research and experimental expenditures. Under this method, the expenditures are amortized ratably over a period of not less than 60 months. A deduction is allowed beginning with the month in which the taxpayer first realizes benefits from the experimental expenditure. The election is binding, and a change requires permission from the IRS.

EXAMPLE 21

Gold Corporation decided to develop a new line of adhesives. The project was begun in 1993. Gold incurred the following expenses in 1993 in connection with the project:

Salaries	$25,000
Materials	8,000
Depreciation on machinery	6,500

Gold incurred the following expenses in 1994 in connection with the project:

Salaries	$18,000
Materials	2,000
Depreciation on machinery	5,700

The benefits from the project will be realized starting in March 1995. If Gold Corporation elects a 60-month deferral and amortization period, there will be no deduction before March 1995, the month benefits from the project begin to be realized. The deduction for 1995 will be $10,867, computed as follows:

Salaries ($25,000 + $18,000)	$43,000
Materials ($8,000 + $2,000)	10,000
Depreciation ($6,500 + $5,700)	12,200
Total	$65,200
$65,200 × (10 months/60 months) =	$10,867

◆

The option to treat research and experimental expenditures as deferred expense is usually employed when a company does not have sufficient income to offset the research and experimental expenses. Rather than create net operating loss carryovers that might not be utilized because of the 15-year limitation on such carryovers, the deferral and amortization method may be used. The deferral of research and experimental expenditures should also be considered if the taxpayer expects higher tax rates in the future.

NET OPERATING LOSSES

The requirement that every taxpayer file an annual income tax return (whether on a calendar year or a fiscal year) may result in certain inequities for taxpayers who experience cyclical patterns of income or expense. Inequities result from the application of a progressive rate structure to taxable income determined on an annual basis. A net operating loss (NOL) in a particular tax year would produce no tax benefit if the Code did not provide for the carryback and carryforward of such losses to profitable years.

EXAMPLE 22

Juanita has a business that realizes the following taxable income or loss over a five-year period: Year 1, $50,000; Year 2, ($30,000); Year 3, $100,000; Year 4, ($200,000); and Year 5, $380,000. She is married, has no dependents, and files a joint return. Hubert, on the other hand, has a taxable income pattern of $60,000 every year. He, too, is married and files a joint return. Note that both Juanita and Hubert have total taxable income of $300,000 over the five-year period. Assume there is no provision for carrybacks or carryover of NOLs. Juanita and Hubert would have the following five-year tax bills:

Year	Juanita's Tax	Hubert's Tax
1	$ 9,203	$12,103
2	-0-	12,103
3	23,529	12,103
4	-0-	12,103
5	110,329	12,103
	$143,061	$60,515

The tax is computed using rates from the 1993 Tax Rate Schedule without regard to any NOL benefit.

Even though Juanita and Hubert realized the same taxable income ($300,000) over the five-year period, Juanita had to pay taxes of $143,061, while Hubert paid taxes of only $60,515. ◆

To provide partial relief from this inequitable tax treatment, a deduction is allowed for NOLs. This provision permits NOLs for any one year to be offset against taxable income of other years. The NOL provision is intended as a form of relief for business income and losses. Thus, only losses from the operation of a trade or business (or profession), casualty and theft losses, or losses from the confiscation of a business by a foreign government can create an NOL. In other words, a salaried individual with itemized deductions and personal exemptions in excess of gross income is not permitted to deduct the excess amounts as an NOL. On the other hand, a personal casualty loss is treated as a business loss and can therefore create (or increase) an NOL for an individual.

Carryback and Carryover Periods

General Rules. An NOL must be applied initially to the three taxable years preceding the year of the loss, unless the taxpayer elects not to carry the loss back at all. It is carried first to the third prior year, then to the second prior year, then to the immediately preceding tax year (or until used up). If the loss is not fully used in the carryback period, it must be carried forward to the first year after the loss year, and then forward to the second, third, etc., year after the loss year. The carryover period is 15 years. If a loss is sustained in 1993, it is used in this order: 1990, 1991, 1992, 1994 through 2008.

If the loss is being carried to a preceding year, an amended return is filed on Form 1040X, or a quick refund claim is filed on Form 1045. In any case, a refund of taxes previously paid is requested. When the loss is carried forward, the current return shows an NOL deduction for the prior year's loss.

Sequence of Use of NOLs. Where there are NOLs in two or more years, the rule is always to use the earliest year's loss first until it is completely absorbed. The later years' losses can then be used until they also are absorbed or lost. Thus, one year's return could show NOL carryovers from two or more years. Each loss is computed and applied separately.

Election to Forgo Carryback. A taxpayer can *irrevocably elect* not to carry back an NOL to any of the three prior years. In that case, the loss is available as a carryover for 15 years. A taxpayer would make the election if it is to his or her tax advantage. For example, a taxpayer might be in a low marginal tax bracket in the carryback years but expect to be in a high marginal tax bracket in future years. Therefore, it would be to the taxpayer's advantage to use the NOL to offset income in years when the tax rate is high rather than use it when the tax rate is relatively low.

Computation of the Net Operating Loss

Since the NOL provisions apply solely to business-related losses, certain adjustments must be made so that the loss more closely resembles the taxpayer's *economic* loss. The required adjustments for corporate taxpayers are usually insignificant because a corporation's tax loss is generally similar to its economic loss. However, in computing taxable income, individual taxpayers are allowed deductions for such items as personal and dependency exemptions and itemized deductions that do not reflect actual business-related economic losses. Detailed coverage of the NOL computation is beyond the scope of this text.

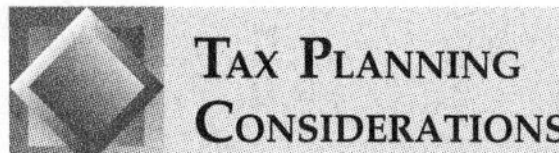

TAX PLANNING CONSIDERATIONS

Documentation of Related-Taxpayer Loans, Casualty Losses, and Theft Losses

Since non-bona fide loans between related taxpayers may be treated as gifts by the IRS, adequate documentation is needed to substantiate a bad debt deduction if the loan subsequently becomes worthless. Documentation should include proper execution of the note (legal form) and the establishment of a bona fide purpose for the loan. In addition, it is desirable to stipulate a reasonable rate of interest and a fixed maturity date.

Since a theft loss is not permitted for misplaced items, a loss should be documented by a police report and evidence of the value of the property (e.g., appraisals, pictures of the property, newspaper clippings). Similar documentation of the value of property should be provided to support a casualty loss deduction because the amount of loss is measured by the decline in fair market value of the property.

Casualty loss deductions must be reported on Form 4684.

Small Business Stock

Because § 1244 limits the amount of loss classified as ordinary loss on a yearly basis, a taxpayer might maximize the benefits of § 1244 by selling the stock in more than one taxable year. The result could be that the losses in any one taxable year would not exceed the § 1244 limits on ordinary loss.

EXAMPLE 23

Mitch, a single individual, purchased small business stock in 1991 for $150,000 (150 shares at $1,000 per share). On December 20, 1993, the stock is worth $60,000 (150 shares at $400 per share). Mitch wants to sell the stock at this time. He earns a salary of $80,000 a year, has no other capital transactions, and does not expect any in the future. If Mitch sells all of the small business stock in 1993, his recognized loss will be $90,000 ($60,000 – $150,000). The loss will be characterized as a $50,000 ordinary loss and a $40,000 long-term capital loss. In computing taxable income for 1993, Mitch could deduct the $50,000 ordinary loss but could deduct only $3,000 of the capital loss. The remainder of the capital loss could be carried over and used in future years subject to the $3,000 limitation if Mitch has no capital gains. If Mitch sells 82 shares in 1993, he will recognize an ordinary loss of $49,200 [82 × ($1,000 – $400)]. If Mitch then sells the remainder of the shares in 1994, he will recognize an ordinary loss of $40,800 [68 × ($1,000 – $400)]. Mitch could deduct the $49,200 ordinary loss in computing 1993 taxable income and the $40,800 ordinary loss in computing 1994 taxable income. ◆

Casualty Losses

A special election is available for taxpayers who sustain casualty losses in an area designated by the President as a disaster area. This election affects only the timing, not the calculation, of the deduction. The deduction can be taken in the year before the year in which the loss occurred. Thus, an individual can take the deduction on the 1992 return for a loss occurring between January 1 and December 31, 1993. The benefit, of course, is a faster refund (or reduction in tax). It will also be advantageous to carry the loss back if the taxpayer's tax rate in the carryback year is higher than the tax rate in the year of the loss.

To find out if an event qualifies as a disaster area loss, one can look in any of the major tax services, the Weekly Compilation of Presidential Documents, or the *Internal Revenue Bulletin.*

PROBLEM MATERIALS

DISCUSSION QUESTIONS

1. Gary, a cash basis taxpayer, is a CPA. He performed extensive tax work for Joe, for which he charged $10,000. Joe never paid for the work, and there is no possibility of Gary ever collecting any of the $10,000. Gary feels that he is entitled to a bad debt deduction of $10,000. Comment on Gary's tax position on this matter.
2. Discuss whether legal proceedings must be brought against a debtor in order to show that a debt is worthless.
3. Bill made a loan to a friend three years ago to help the friend purchase an automobile. Bill's friend has notified him that the car has been sold and the most he will be able to repay is 50% of the loan. Discuss the possibility of Bill taking a bad debt deduction for half of the loan.
4. Discuss the difference between business and nonbusiness bad debts. How is the distinction determined? How is each treated on the return?
5. What factors are to be considered in determining whether a bad debt arising from a loan between related parties is, in fact, a bad debt?
6. Discuss a taxpayer's options for the tax treatment of a loss incurred on a deposit in a qualified financial institution. Also note the consequences of each option.
7. Discuss the tax treatment of a worthless security of an affiliated corporation.
8. Discuss the ordinary loss limitations on the sale of stock and the advantages of such a characterization.
9. Dena, an individual and sole proprietor, discovers that her store has been extensively damaged by termites. Discuss whether she may take a deduction for the damage to her store.
10. What is a disaster area loss? Why might a taxpayer benefit from making the disaster area loss election?
11. Discuss the tax consequences of property being completely destroyed in determining the amount of a casualty loss.
12. Discuss the tax consequences of not making an insurance claim when insured personal use property is subject to a casualty or theft loss.

13. Mark's 10-year-old automobile was extensively damaged in a collision in which he was not at fault. The original cost of the automobile was $10,000, and the cost of repairing it was $5,000. Discuss any problems with using the $5,000 as the measurement of the loss.
14. Discuss the reduction of personal casualty losses by the $100 and 10% of AGI floors.
15. When casualty losses exceed casualty gains, the amount of the casualty loss subject to the 10% of AGI floor is only the casualty loss in excess of casualty gains. Discuss the significance of netting losses against gains in this manner rather than having the entire casualty loss subject to the 10% of AGI floor.
16. If a taxpayer is required to spread a personal casualty loss between two years under the reasonable prospect of recovery doctrine, how will the $100 per event floor and the 10% of AGI limitation be treated?
17. Zina, an individual, sustained a loss on an apartment building damaged by fire. She owns the building and rents apartments to tenants. Discuss the tax treatment of the loss on Zina's individual tax return.
18. Discuss the computation of a personal casualty loss.
19. Why do most taxpayers elect to write off research and experimental expenditures rather than capitalize and amortize such amounts? Would the capitalization and amortization approach be preferable in some situations?

PROBLEMS

20. Maria loaned Tara $20,000 on April 1, 1992. In 1993, Tara filed for bankruptcy. At that time, it was revealed that Tara's creditors could expect to receive 80¢ on the dollar. In February 1994, final settlement was made and Maria received $15,000. How much loss can Maria deduct and in which year? How is it treated on Maria's return?
21. In 1991, Jack loaned his mother $10,000. In 1993, his mother told him that she would try and pay him $1,000. In 1994, Jack's mother filed for bankruptcy and told Jack that she would be unable to pay him anything. Determine Jack's possible deductions with respect to the loan.
22. In 1992, Wilma deposited $20,000 with a commercial bank. On July 1, 1993, Wilma was notified that the bank was insolvent, and she subsequently received only 30% of the deposit. Wilma also has a salary of $50,000, long-term capital gain of $9,000, and itemized deductions (other than casualty and theft) of $7,000. Determine Wilma's possible deductions with respect to the deposit.
23. Seth, a married taxpayer filing a joint return, had the following items for the year 1993:

    - Salary of $150,000.
    - Gain of $30,000 on the sale of § 1244 stock he acquired three years ago.
    - Loss of $120,000 on the sale of § 1244 stock he acquired two years ago.
    - Stock acquired on December 15, 1992, for $5,000 became worthless on March 28, 1993.

    Determine Seth's AGI for 1993.
24. Joyce, a single taxpayer, had the following items for the current year:

    - Worthless stock of $5,000. The stock was acquired two years earlier and became worthless in June of the current year.
    - A nonbusiness bad debt of $10,000.
    - Gain of $27,000 on the sale of § 1244 stock acquired two years earlier.
    - Loss of $58,000 on the sale of § 1244 stock acquired three months earlier.
    - Salary of $70,000.

    Determine Joyce's AGI for the current year.
25. When Helen returned from a vacation in Hawaii on November 8, 1993, she discovered that a burglar had stolen her silver, stereo, and color television. In the process of removing these items, the burglar damaged some furniture that originally

cost $1,400. Helen's silver cost $3,640 and was valued at $6,500; the stereo system cost $8,400 and was valued at $6,200; the television cost $840 and was worth $560. Helen filed a claim with her insurance company and was reimbursed in the following amounts on December 20, 1993:

Silver	$2,800
Stereo	5,600
Television	490

The insurance company disputed the reimbursement claimed by Helen for the damaged furniture, but she protested and was finally paid $280 on January 30, 1994. The repairs to the furniture totaled $448. Helen's AGI for 1993 was $12,000, and it was $15,000 for 1994. How much can Helen claim as a casualty and theft loss? In which year?

26. Eduardo owned 50 acres of land in Florida that he farmed. A hurricane hit the area and destroyed a farm building and some farm equipment and damaged a barn. Applicable information is as follows:

Item	Adjusted Basis	FMV Before	FMV After	Insurance Proceeds
Building	$50,000	$65,000	$ –0–	$30,000
Equipment	35,000	29,000	–0–	27,000
Barn	80,000	90,000	70,000	5,000

a. How much is Eduardo's loss?

b. Assuming the loss occurred on August 24, 1994, and that the president designated the area as a disaster area, what options are available to Eduardo with respect to the timing of the loss deduction?

27. On June 15, 1993, Kirby was involved in an accident with his personal automobile. He had purchased the car new two years earlier for $14,000. At the time of the accident, the car was worth $12,000. After the accident, the car was appraised at $4,000. Kirby had an insurance policy that had a 20% deductible clause. Because Kirby was afraid that the policy would be canceled, he made no claim against the insurance policy for the damages to the car.

On September 17, 1993, Kirby was involved in an accident with his business automobile. The automobile had a fair market value of $10,000 before the accident, and it was worthless after the accident. Kirby had a basis in the car of $15,000 at the time of the accident. The car was covered by an insurance policy that insured the car for fair market value. Kirby made a claim and collected against the policy. He earned a salary of $60,000 and had other itemized deductions of $10,000 for the year. Determine taxable income for Kirby and his wife, who file a joint return for 1993.

28. Green Corporation, a manufacturing company, decided to develop a new line of fireworks. Because of the danger involved, Green purchased an isolated parcel of land for $300,000 and constructed a building for $400,000. The building was to be used for research and experimentation in creating the new fireworks. The project was begun in 1993. Green had the following expenses in 1993 in connection with the project:

Salaries	$80,000
Utilities	10,000
Materials	20,000
Insurance	30,000
Cost of market survey to determine profit potential for new fireworks line	15,000
Depreciation on the building	10,000

Green had the following expenses in 1994 in connection with the project:

Salaries	$90,000
Utilities	15,000
Materials	25,000
Insurance	24,000
Depreciation on the building	13,000

The benefits from the project will be realized starting in June of 1995.

a. If Green Corporation elects to expense research and experimental expenditures, determine the amount of the deduction for 1993, 1994, and 1995.
b. If Green Corporation elects a 60-month deferral and amortization period, determine the amount of the deduction for 1993, 1994, and 1995.

29. Nell, single and age 38, had the following income and expense items in 1993:

Nonbusiness bad debt	$ 6,000
Business bad debt	2,000
Nonbusiness long-term capital gain	4,000
Nonbusiness short-term capital loss	3,000
Salary	40,000
Interest income	1,000

Determine Nell's AGI for 1993.

30. Assume that in addition to the information in Problem 29, Nell had the following items in 1993:

Personal casualty gain on an asset held for four months	$10,000
Personal casualty loss on an asset held for two years	1,000

Determine Nell's AGI for 1993.

CUMULATIVE PROBLEMS

31. Ned Wilson, age 60, single, and retired, has no dependents. Ned lives at 231 Wander Lane, Salt Lake City, UT 84201. Ned's Social Security number is 985–12–3774. During 1993, Ned had the following income and expense items:

a. On January 27, 1992, Ned deposited $8,000 in a savings account at the ABC Financial Company. The savings account bore interest at 15%, compounded semiannually. Ned received a $600 interest payment on July 27, 1992, but received no interest payments thereafter. The finance company filed for bankruptcy on January 12, 1993. Ned received a $710 check in final settlement of his account from the bankruptcy trustee on December 20, 1993.
b. On January 1, 1993, a fire severely damaged a two-story building owned by Ned, who occupied the second story of the building as a residence and had recently opened a hardware store on the ground level. The following information is available with respect to the incident:

	Adjusted Basis	Fair Market Value Before	Fair Market Value After
Building	$64,000	$130,000	$50,000
Inventory	35,000	55,000	None
Store equipment	3,000	1,800	None
Home furnishings	12,600	6,000	800
Personal auto	8,900	7,800	7,600

Ned's fire insurance policy paid the following amounts for damages:

Building	$50,000 (policy maximum)
Inventory	33,000
Store equipment	None
Home furnishings	1,000 (policy maximum)
Personal auto	None

Assume all of the destroyed property was acquired on December 15, 1992.

c. On March 1, 1989, Ned loaned a neighboring businessman $15,000. The debtor died of a heart attack on June 21, 1993. Ned had no security and was unable to collect anything from the man's estate.
d. Ned received $72,000 of interest income from Salt Lake City Bank.
e. On March 3, 1993, Ned sold a piece of real estate he had been holding for speculation for $90,000. Ned had bought the land July 18, 1978, for $52,800.
f. Ned made a charitable contribution of $3,000.
g. Ned made four quarterly estimated tax payments of $4,500 each.

Part 1—Tax Computation

Compute Ned's 1993 Federal income tax payable (or refund due), assuming he deducts the lost deposit as a bad debt. Suggested software (if available): *TurboTax* or *MacInTax* for tax return or WFT tax planning software.

Part 2—Tax Planning

Determine whether Ned should elect to treat the deposit in ABC Financial Company as a casualty loss rather than as a bad debt. Suggested software (if available): *TurboTax* for tax return or WFT tax planning software.

32. Jane Smith, age 40, is single and has no dependents. She is employed part-time as a legal secretary by Legal Services, Inc. She owns and operates Typing Services located near the campus of San Jose State University at 1986 Campus Drive. She is a cash basis taxpayer. Jane lives at 2020 Oakcrest Road, San Jose, CA 95134. Jane's Social Security number is 123–89–6666. Jane indicates that she wishes to designate $1 to the Presidential Election Campaign Fund. During 1992, Jane had the following income and expense items:

a. $40,000 salary from Legal Services, Inc.
b. $15,000 gross receipts from her typing services business.
c. $300 cash dividend from Buffalo Mining Company, a Canadian corporation.
d. $1,000 Christmas bonus from Legal Services, Inc.
e. $10,000 life insurance proceeds on the death of her sister.
f. $5,000 check given to her by her wealthy aunt.
g. $100 won in a bingo game.
h. Expenses connected with the typing service:

Office rent	$5,000
Supplies	2,400
Utilities and telephone	3,680
Wages to part-time typists	4,000
Payroll taxes	600
Equipment rentals	3,000

i. $8,000 interest expense on a home mortgage (paid to San Jose Savings and Loan).
j. $5,000 fair market value of silverware stolen from her home by a burglar on October 12, 1992. Jane had paid $4,000 for the silverware on July 1, 1983. She was reimbursed $1,500 by her insurance company.
k. Jane had loaned $2,100 to a friend, Joan Jensen, on June 3, 1989. Joan declared bankruptcy on August 14, 1992, and was unable to repay the loan.
l. Legal Services, Inc., withheld Federal income tax of $5,000 and the appropriate amount of FICA tax.

Part 1—Tax Computation

Compute Jane Smith's 1992 Federal income tax payable (or refund due). If you use tax forms for your computations, you will need Forms 1040 and 4684 and Schedules A, C, and D. Suggested software (if available): *TurboTax* or *MacInTax* for tax return or WFT tax planning software.

Part 2—Tax Planning

In 1993, Jane plans to continue her job with Legal Services, Inc. Therefore, items a, d, and l will recur in 1993. Jane plans to continue her typing services business (refer to item b) and expects gross receipts of $20,000. She projects that all business expenses (refer to item h) will increase by 10%, except for office rent, which, under the terms of her lease, will remain the same as in 1992. Items e, f, g, j, and k will not recur in 1993. Items c and i will be approximately the same as in 1992.

Jane would like you to compute the minimum amount of estimated tax she will have to pay for 1993 so that she will not have to pay any additional tax upon filing her 1993 Federal income tax return. Write a letter to Jane that contains your advice and prepare a memo for the tax files. Suggested software (if available): *TurboTax* for tax return or WFT tax planning software.

CHAPTER

DEPRECIATION, COST RECOVERY, AMORTIZATION, AND DEPLETION

OBJECTIVES

Determine the amount of cost recovery under ACRS rules.

Determine the amount of cost recovery under modified ACRS rules (MACRS).

Explain the operation of the rules governing listed property.

Determine the amount of amortization for intangible assets.

Explain the alternative tax treatments for intangible drilling and development costs.

Determine the amount of depletion expense.

Explain the reporting procedures for depreciation and cost recovery.

Develop tax planning ideas for depreciation, cost recovery, and depletion.

OUTLINE

During the 1980s, the tax law underwent frequent, major changes. Few areas were subjected to greater change than the depreciation (cost recovery) provisions. The Economic Recovery Tax Act of 1981 replaced the existing *depreciation* system with an *accelerated cost recovery system (ACRS)*. The Tax Reform Act of 1986, in turn, replaced ACRS with a *modified accelerated cost recovery system (MACRS)*. These changes have produced something of a nightmare for taxpayers who own long-lived assets.

Example 1

Brown Corporation owns machinery purchased in 1980. The machinery has a 15-year useful life. The corporation also owns equipment purchased in 1985 that has a 10-year cost recovery life. In 1990, Brown purchased a computer, which has a 5-year cost recovery life. To compute the depreciation and cost recovery allowances for 1993, Brown Corporation must use the pre-ACRS depreciation rules for the machinery, the ACRS rules for the equipment, and the MACRS provisions for the computer. ◆

The situation reflected in Example 1 can be explained by a brief review of tax law changes that occurred in the 1980s. Before 1981, write-offs for long-lived assets were computed under the depreciation rules in § 167. Under this system, depreciation was computed under the declining-balance, sum-of-the-years' digits, or straight-line methods, as well as other special methods. These methods were similar to, but somewhat different from, the depreciation methods used in financial accounting.

The pre-1981 depreciation system was replaced by ACRS for property acquired after 1980. ACRS was one of many provisions enacted in the Economic Recovery Tax Act of 1981 that were intended to stimulate the economy. The following features of ACRS resulted in accelerated write-offs:

- Cost recovery periods were shorter than estimated useful lives required under the pre-1981 depreciation system.
- The use of salvage value, required under the § 167 depreciation system, was eliminated under ACRS.
- For many assets, the methods for computing ACRS deductions were more generous than the allowable methods for computing depreciation.

ACRS was in effect from 1981 through 1986, when it was replaced by MACRS for property acquired after 1986. MACRS cost recovery periods are generally longer than ACRS cost recovery periods, and MACRS methods, in most cases, are not as generous as the methods used in ACRS.

Concept Summary 8–1
Depreciation and Cost Recovery: Relevant Time Periods

System	Date Property Is Placed in Service
§ 167 depreciation (pre-ACRS)	Before January 1, 1981, and *certain* property placed in service after December 31, 1980.
Accelerated cost recovery system (ACRS)	After December 31, 1980, and before January 1, 1987.
Modified accelerated cost recovery system (MACRS)	After December 31, 1986.

The frequent changes in the depreciation and cost recovery provisions have increased complexity and made it more difficult for taxpayers to compute write-offs for long-lived assets. In addition, as Example 1 illustrated, many taxpayers are required to compute write-offs under the depreciation system, ACRS, and MACRS. ACRS and MACRS are covered in detail in this chapter. See IRS Publication 534 (Depreciation) for detailed coverage of the pre-1981 depreciation system.

Overview

Taxpayers may write off the cost of certain assets that are used in a trade or business or held for the production of income. A write-off may take the form of depreciation, depletion, or amortization. Tangible assets, other than natural resources, are *depreciated.* Natural resources, such as oil, gas, coal, and timber, are *depleted.* Intangible assets, such as copyrights and patents, are *amortized.* Generally, no write-off is allowed for an asset that does not have a determinable useful life.

ACRS and MACRS provide separate cost recovery tables for *realty* (real property) and *personalty* (personal property). Realty generally includes land and buildings permanently affixed to the land. Write-offs are not available for land because it does not have a determinable useful life. Cost recovery allowances for real property other than land are based on recovery lives specified in the law. For most types of realty, cost recovery allowances are specified in tables provided by the IRS.

Personalty is defined as any asset that is not realty. Personalty includes furniture, machinery, equipment, and many other types of assets. Do not confuse personalty (or personal property) with *personal use* property. Personal use property is any property (realty or personalty) that is held for personal use rather than for use in a trade or business or an income-producing activity. Write-offs are not allowed for personal use assets.

Accelerated Cost Recovery System (ACRS)

Under ACRS, the cost of an asset is recovered over a predetermined period that is generally shorter than the useful life of the asset or the period the asset is used to produce income. The system was designed to encourage investment, improve productivity, and simplify the law and its administration. However, the pre-ACRS depreciation rules continue to apply in the following situations:

- Property placed in service after 1980 whose life is not based on years (e.g., units-of-production method).
- The remaining depreciation on property placed in service by the taxpayer before 1981.
- Personal property acquired after 1980 if the property was owned or used during 1980 by the taxpayer or a related person (antichurning rule).
- Property that is amortized (e.g., leasehold improvements).

Personalty: Recovery Periods and Methods

Classification of Property: ACRS. ACRS recovery periods for personalty are 3, 5, 10, and 15 years. Property is classified by recovery period as follows:

3 years....................	Autos, light-duty trucks, R & D equipment, racehorses over 2 years old and other horses over 12 years old, and personalty with an ADR midpoint life of 4 years or less.[1]
5 years....................	Most other equipment except long-lived public utility property. Also includes single-purpose agricultural structures and petroleum storage facilities, which are designated as § 1245 property under the law.
10 years..................	Public utility property with an ADR midpoint life greater than 18 but not greater than 25 years, burners and boilers using coal as a primary fuel if used in a public utility power plant and if replacing or converting oil- or gas-fired burners or boilers, railroad tank cars, mobile homes, and realty with an ADR midpoint life of 12.5 years or less (e.g., theme park structures).
15 years..................	Public utility property with an ADR midpoint life exceeding 25 years (except certain burners and boilers using coal as a primary fuel).

Taxpayers who own 10-year or 15-year ACRS property continue to compute cost recovery allowances under the ACRS rules. However, all cost has already been recovered on any 3-year or 5-year ACRS property.

Taxpayers had the choice of using (1) the straight-line method over the regular or optional (see below) recovery period or (2) a prescribed accelerated method over the regular recovery period. These two methods are both part of the ACRS system, but the Code does not provide a convenient name for either method. Hereafter, the straight-line method will be referred to as the *optional* (or *elective*) *straight-line method.* The method using percentages prescribed in the Code will be referred to as the *statutory percentage method.* The rates in the cost recovery tables at the end of the chapter (prior to the Problem Materials) reflect all relevant methods and assumptions.

The rates to be used in computing the deduction under the statutory percentage method are shown in Table 8–1 and are based on the 150 percent declining-balance method, using the half-year convention and an assumption of zero salvage value. The half-year convention assumes all property is placed in service at mid-year and thus provides for a half-year's cost recovery.

EXAMPLE 2

XYZ Utilities acquired 10-year public utility property in 1985 at a cost of $100,000. The property was placed in service on August 12, 1985. XYZ's cost recovery allowance for 1993 is determined from Table 8–1 (see page 8–27). The cost recovery percentage for 1993 (recovery year 9) is 9%, and the cost recovery allowance is $9,000 ($100,000 cost × .09). ◆

Under ACRS, no cost recovery deduction is allowed in the year of disposition of personalty.

EXAMPLE 3

Assume the same facts as in the previous example and that the property is sold in December 1994. XYZ is not allowed a cost recovery deduction for the property in 1994. ◆

Reduction of Basis for Investment Tax Credit. For personalty placed in service after 1982 and before January 1, 1986, taxpayers were required to reduce the basis of the property for the ACRS write-off by one-half the amount of any investment

1. The Asset Depreciation Range (ADR) system specified ranges of useful life for various assets. Rev.Proc. 83–35, 1983–1 C.B. 745 is the source for these ADR midpoint lives.

tax credit taken on the property. Investment tax credit was not allowed on realty. (See Chapter 11 for details.)

Example 4

Transrail Company acquired a railroad tank car on September 4, 1985, for $100,000. The tank car is 15-year personalty, and Transrail claimed a $10,000 investment tax credit ($100,000 × 10% investment credit rate). The basis of the tank car was reduced by $5,000 (one-half of the $10,000 investment tax credit), and the basis for depreciation is $95,000. The cost recovery allowance for 1993 is $8,550 ($95,000 cost recovery basis × .09 rate for year nine). ◆

As an alternative to reducing the basis of the property, a taxpayer could elect to take a *reduced* investment tax credit. Under this election, the investment tax credit was 8 percent (rather than 10 percent) for recovery property other than three-year property and 4 percent (instead of 6 percent) for three-year property. In Example 4, if Transrail elected the reduced investment tax credit, its basis for cost recovery would be $100,000 rather than $95,000.

TRA of 1986 generally repealed the investment tax credit for property placed in service after December 31, 1985. Therefore, the reduction of basis for the investment tax credit does not apply to such property.

Classification of Property: MACRS. The general effect of TRA of 1986 was to lengthen asset lives. MACRS provides that the cost recovery basis of eligible personalty (and certain realty) is recovered over 3, 5, 7, 10, 15, or 20 years. Property is classified by recovery period under MACRS as follows:

3-year 200% class	ADR midpoints of 4 years and less.[2] Excludes automobiles and light trucks. Includes racehorses more than 2 years old and other horses more than 12 years old.
5-year 200% class	ADR midpoints of more than 4 years and less than 10 years, including automobiles, light trucks, qualified technological equipment, renewable energy and biomass properties that are small power production facilities, research and experimentation property, semiconductor manufacturing equipment, and computer-based central office switching equipment.
7-year 200% class	ADR midpoints of 10 years and more and less than 16 years, including single-purpose agricultural or horticultural structures and property with no ADR midpoint not classified elsewhere. Includes railroad track and office furniture, fixtures, and equipment.
10-year 200% class	ADR midpoints of 16 years and more and less than 20 years.
15-year 150% class	ADR midpoints of 20 years and more and less than 25 years, including sewage treatment plants, and telephone distribution plants and comparable equipment used for the two-way exchange of voice and data communications.
20-year 150% class	ADR midpoints of 25 years and more, other than real property with an ADR midpoint of 27.5 years and more, and including sewer pipes.

Accelerated depreciation is allowed for these six MACRS classes of property. Two hundred percent declining-balance is used for the 3-, 5-, 7-, and 10-year classes, with a switchover to straight-line depreciation when it yields a larger amount. One hundred and fifty percent declining-balance is allowed for the 15- and 20-year classes, with an appropriate straight-line switchover.

2. Rev.Proc. 87–56, 1987–2 C.B. 674 is the source for ADR midpoint lives.

Taxpayers may elect the straight-line method to compute cost recovery allowances for these classes of property. Certain property is not eligible for accelerated depreciation and must be depreciated under an alternative depreciation system (ADS). Both the straight-line election and ADS are discussed later in the chapter.

The original ACRS system gave the taxpayer a half-year of depreciation for the tax year an asset was placed in service but allowed the taxpayer to recover the balance of the depreciable basis over the years remaining in the property's recovery period. No cost recovery deduction was permitted for the year of disposition or retirement of the property. Thus, conceptually, the taxpayer was considered to have placed property in service at the beginning of the recovery period but was allowed only a half-year's worth of depreciation for the year property was placed in service.

By contrast, MACRS views property as placed in service in the middle of the first year. Thus, for example, the statutory recovery period for three-year property begins in the middle of the year an asset is placed in service and ends three years later. In practical terms, this means that taxpayers must wait an extra year to recover the total cost of depreciable assets. That is, the actual write-off

Concept Summary 8–2
Cost Recovery Periods: MACRS

Class of Property	Examples
3-year	Tractor units for use over-the-road. Any horse that is not a racehorse and is more than 12 years old at the time it is placed in service. Any racehorse that is more than 2 years old at the time it is placed in service. Breeding hogs. Special tools used in the manufacturing of motor vehicles such as dies, fixtures, molds, and patterns.
5-year	Automobiles and taxis. Light and heavy general-purpose trucks. Buses. Trailers and trailer-mounted containers. Typewriters, calculators, and copiers. Computers and peripheral equipment. Breeding and dairy cattle.
7-year	Office furniture, fixtures, and equipment. Breeding and work horses. Agricultural machinery and equipment. Single-purpose agricultural or horticultural structures. Railroad track.
10-year	Vessels, barges, tugs, and similar water transportation equipment. Assets used for petroleum refining, manufacture of grain and grain mill products, manufacture of sugar and sugar products, and manufacture of vegetable oils and vegetable oil products.
15-year	Land improvements. Assets used for industrial steam and electric generation and/or distribution systems. Assets used in the manufacture of cement. Assets used in pipeline transportation. Electric utility nuclear production plant. Municipal wastewater treatment plant.
20-year	Farm buildings except single-purpose agricultural and horticultural structures. Gas utility distribution facilities. Water utilities. Municipal sewer.

periods are 4, 6, 8, 11, 16, and 21 years. MACRS also allows for a half-year of cost recovery in the year of disposition or retirement.

The procedure for computing the cost recovery allowance under MACRS is the same as under the original ACRS method. The cost recovery basis is multiplied by the percentages that reflect the applicable cost recovery method and the applicable convention. The percentages are shown in Table 8–2.

EXAMPLE 5

Kareem acquired a five-year class asset on April 10, 1993, for $30,000. His cost recovery deduction for 1993 is $6,000 [$30,000 × .20 (Table 8–2)]. ◆

EXAMPLE 6

Assume the same facts as in Example 5, and that Kareem disposes of the asset on March 5, 1995. His cost recovery deduction for 1995 is $2,880 [$30,000 × ½ × .192 (Table 8–2)]. ◆

Mid-Quarter Convention. Under the original ACRS rules for personal property, the half-year convention was used no matter when property was acquired during the year. Thus, if a substantial dollar amount of assets was acquired late in the tax year, the half-year convention still applied. The law now contains a provision to curtail the benefits of such tax strategy. If more than 40 percent of the value of property other than eligible real estate is placed in service during the last quarter of the year, a *mid-quarter convention* applies. Property acquisitions are then grouped by the quarter they were acquired for cost recovery purposes. Acquisitions during the first quarter are allowed 10.5 months of cost recovery; the second quarter, 7.5 months; the third quarter, 4.5 months; and the fourth quarter, 1.5 months. The percentages are shown in Table 8–3.

EXAMPLE 7

Silver Corporation acquired the following five-year class property in 1993:

Property Acquisition Dates	Cost
February 15	$ 200,000
July 10	400,000
December 5	600,000
Total	$1,200,000

If Silver Corporation uses the statutory percentage method, the cost recovery allowances for the first two years are computed as indicated below. Since more than 40% ($600,000/$1,200,000) of the acquisitions are in the last quarter, the mid-quarter convention applies.

1993		
February 15	[$200,000 × .35 (Table 8–3)]	$ 70,000
July 10	($400,000 × .15)	60,000
December 5	($600,000 × .05)	30,000
Total		$160,000

1994		
February 15	[$200,000 × .26 (Table 8–3)]	$ 52,000
July 10	($400,000 × .34)	136,000
December 5	($600,000 × .38)	228,000
Total		$416,000

◆

EXAMPLE 8

Assume the same facts as in Example 7, except that Silver Corporation sells the $400,000 asset on November 30 of Year 2. The cost recovery allowance for Year 2 is computed as follows:

February 15	[$200,000 × .26 (Table 8–3)]	$ 52,000
July 10	[$400,000 × .34 × (3.5/4)]	119,000
December 5	($600,000 × .38)	228,000
Total		$399,000

◆

Realty: Recovery Periods and Methods

ACRS. Under the original ACRS rules, realty was assigned a 15-year recovery period. Real property other than low-income housing is depreciated using the 175 percent declining-balance method with a switchover to straight-line depreciation when it yields a larger amount. Low-income housing is depreciated using the 200 percent declining-balance method with an appropriate straight-line switchover. In either case, zero salvage value is assumed. Statutory percentages for real property are shown in Table 8–4, which contains rates for low-income housing as well as for other 15-year real estate. As explained later in the chapter, taxpayers were allowed to elect the straight-line method for real property.

The half-year convention does not apply to 15-year real property. As a result, Table 8–4 is structured differently from Tables 8–1 and 8–2. The cost recovery deduction for 15-year real property is based on the month the asset is placed in service rather than on the half-year convention.

EXAMPLE 9

Alicia purchased a warehouse for $100,000 on January 1, 1984. The cost recovery allowance for the years 1984 through 1993, using the statutory percentage method, is computed as follows (see Table 8–4 for percentages):

1984—$12,000 (12% × $100,000)
1985—$10,000 (10% × $100,000)
1986—$9,000 (9% × $100,000)
1987—$8,000 (8% × $100,000)
1988—$7,000 (7% × $100,000)
1989—$6,000 (6% × $100,000)
1990—$6,000 (6% × $100,000)
1991—$6,000 (6% × $100,000)
1992—$6,000 (6% × $100,000)
1993—$5,000 (5% × $100,000)

◆

EXAMPLE 10

Assume the same facts as in Example 9, except the property is low-income housing. Cost recovery deductions for 1984 through 1993 using the statutory percentage method, are as follows (see Table 8–4 for percentages):

1984—$13,000 (13% × $100,000)
1985—$12,000 (12% × $100,000)
1986—$10,000 (10% × $100,000)
1987—$9,000 (9% × $100,000)
1988—$8,000 (8% × $100,000)
1989—$7,000 (7% × $100,000)

1990—$6,000 (6% × $100,000)
1991—$5,000 (5% × $100,000)
1992—$5,000 (5% × $100,000)
1993—$5,000 (5% × $100,000) ◆

The Deficit Reduction Act of 1984 changed the ACRS recovery period for real property to 18 years. This recovery period applies generally to property placed in service after March 15, 1984. However, the 15-year recovery period was retained for low-income housing as well as for other real property placed in service before March 16, 1984.

Eighteen-year real property placed in service after June 22, 1984, is subject to a mid-month convention.[3] This means that real property placed in service at any time during a particular month is treated as if it were placed in service in the middle of the month. This allows for one-half month's cost recovery for the month the property is placed in service. If the property is disposed of before the end of the recovery period, one-half month's cost recovery is permitted for the month of disposition regardless of the specific date of disposition. Statutory percentages for 18-year real property with a mid-month convention are shown in Table 8–5.

EXAMPLE 11

Rex purchased a building for $300,000 and placed it in service on August 21, 1984. The first year's cost recovery using the statutory percentage method is $12,000 (4% × $300,000). (See Table 8–5 for percentages.) ◆

EXAMPLE 12

Assume the same facts as in Example 11 and that Rex disposes of the building on May 3, 1993. The cost recovery in the year of disposition is $5,625 ($300,000 × 5% × 4.5/12). ◆

Public Law 99–121 extended the recovery period for real property (except low-income housing) from 18 years to 19 years. This applies to property placed in service after May 8, 1985, and before 1987. Statutory percentages for 19-year real property are shown in Table 8–6. Because the percentages are determined using a mid-month convention, the computation of cost recovery is mechanically the same as illustrated for 18-year property with the mid-month convention.

MACRS. Under MACRS, the cost recovery period for residential rental real estate is 27.5 years, and the straight-line method is used for computing the cost recovery allowance. *Residential rental real estate* includes property where 80 percent or more of the gross rental revenues are from nontransient dwelling units (e.g., an apartment building). Hotels, motels, and similar establishments are not residential rental property. Low-income housing is classified as residential rental real estate. Nonresidential real estate has a recovery period of 31.5 years and is also depreciated using the straight-line method.

Some items of real property are not treated as real estate for purposes of MACRS. For example, single-purpose agricultural structures are in the seven-year MACRS class. Land improvements are in the 15-year MACRS class.

All eligible real estate is depreciated using the mid-month convention. Regardless of when during the month the property is placed in service, it is deemed to

3. A transitional rule, which provides for a full-month convention, is effective for property placed in service after March 15, 1984, and before June 23, 1984. A cost recovery table for realty placed in service during this period is not included in this chapter.

have been placed in service at the middle of the month. In the year of disposition, a mid-month convention is also used.

Cost recovery is computed by multiplying the applicable rate (Table 8–7) by the cost recovery basis.

EXAMPLE 13

Ann acquired a building on April 1, 1993, for $800,000. If the building is classified as residential rental real estate, the cost recovery for 1993 is $20,608 (.02576 × $800,000). If the building is classified as nonresidential real estate, the 1993 cost recovery allowance is $17,992 (.02249 × $800,000). (See Table 8–7 for percentages.) ◆

Straight-Line Election under ACRS and MACRS

ACRS. Under ACRS, taxpayers could *elect* to write off an asset using the straight-line method rather than the statutory percentage method. The straight-line recovery period could be the same as the prescribed recovery period under the statutory percentage method, or a longer period. The allowable straight-line recovery periods for each class of property are summarized as follows:

3-year property	3, 5, or 12 years
5-year property	5, 12, or 25 years
10-year property	10, 25, or 35 years
15-year property	15, 35, or 45 years
18-year real property and low-income housing (placed in service after March 15, 1984)	18, 35, or 45 years
19-year real property and low-income housing (placed in service after May 8, 1985)	19, 35, or 45 years

CONCEPT SUMMARY 8–3
STATUTORY PERCENTAGE METHOD UNDER ACRS AND MACRS

ACRS

	Personal Property	Real Property 15-Year	Real Property 18-Year	Real Property 19-Year
Convention	Half-year	Full-month	Mid-month	Mid-month
Cost recovery deduction in the year of disposition	None	Full-month for month of disposition	Half-month for month of disposition	Half-month for month of disposition

MACRS

	Personal Property	Real Property*
Convention	Half-year or mid-quarter	Mid-month
Cost recovery deduction in the year of disposition	Half-year for year of disposition or half-quarter for quarter of disposition	Half-month for month of disposition

*Straight-line method must be used.

If the straight-line option was elected for ACRS personal property, the half-year convention applied in computing the cost recovery deduction. The effect of electing the straight-line method for ACRS personalty is to extend the statutory recovery period by one year (e.g., three to four and five to six years). There is no cost recovery deduction in the year of the disposition of the property.

EXAMPLE 14

On May 6, 1985, ABC Utilities paid $20,000 for coal-fired boilers to replace gas-fired boilers (10-year property). ABC elected to compute the cost recovery allowance using the straight-line method and the regular cost recovery period. ABC's cost recovery allowance for 1985 was $1,000 ($20,000 basis × .10 straight-line rate × ½ year). The cost recovery allowance is $2,000 for 1993 ($20,000 basis × .10 straight-line rate) and $1,000 for 1995 ($20,000 basis × .10 straight-line rate × ½ year). These cost recovery allowances reflect the half-year convention for the first and last years of the cost recovery period. ◆

For each class of personal property, the straight-line election applies to *all* assets in a *particular class* that are placed in service during the year for which the election is made. The election applies for the entire recovery period of these assets. The election is not binding for personal property of the same class placed in service in another taxable year.

Under the straight-line option for 15-year *real* property, the first year's cost recovery deduction and the cost recovery deduction for the year of disposition are computed on the basis of the number of months the property was in service during the year.

EXAMPLE 15

Kate acquired a store building on October 1, 1983, at a cost of $150,000. She elected the straight-line method using a recovery period of 15 years. Her cost recovery deduction for 1983 was $2,500 [($150,000 ÷ 15) × 3/12]. ◆

EXAMPLE 16

Assume the same facts as in the previous example and that Kate disposed of the asset on September 30, 1993. Her cost recovery deduction for 1993 is $7,500 [($150,000 ÷ 15) × 9/12]. ◆

Under the straight-line option for 18-year or 19-year real property, the cost recovery allowances in the year the property was placed in service and in the year of disposition are computed in the same manner (except for the use of different rates) as under the statutory percentage method. Note that 18-year and 19-year real property use a mid-month convention, whereas 15-year real property uses a full-month convention. Table 8–8 contains the applicable percentages to be used under the straight-line option for 19-year real property. (The tables that contain the percentages for 18-year real property using the straight-line method over 18, 35, and 45 years and 19-year real property using the straight-line method over 35 and 45 years are not reproduced in this text.)

EXAMPLE 17

Ned acquired 19-year real property on October 1, 1986, at a cost of $150,000. He elected the straight-line method of cost recovery. Ned's cost recovery deduction for 1986 was $1,650 [$150,000 × 1.1% (Table 8–8)]. ◆

EXAMPLE 18

Assume the same facts as in the previous example and that Ned disposed of the asset on September 20, 1993. Ned's cost recovery deduction for 1993 (recovery year 8) is $5,631 [($150,000 × 5.3% × 8.5/12) (Table 8–8)]. ◆

MACRS. Although MACRS requires straight-line depreciation for all eligible real estate as previously discussed, the taxpayer may *elect* to use the straight-line method for personal property. The property is depreciated using the class life (recovery period) of the asset with a half-year convention or a mid-quarter convention, whichever is applicable. The election is available on a class-by-class and year-by-year basis. The percentages for the straight-line election with a half-year convention appear in Table 8–9.

EXAMPLE 19

Terry acquired a 10-year class asset on August 4, 1993, for $100,000. He elects the straight-line method of cost recovery. Terry's cost recovery deduction for 1993 is $5,000 ($100,000 × .050). His cost recovery deduction for 1994 is $10,000 ($100,000 × .100). (See Table 8–9 for percentages.) ◆

Election to Expense Assets

Section 179 permits taxpayers to elect to write off up to $10,000 of the acquisition cost of tangible personal property used in a trade or business. Amounts that are expensed under § 179 may not be capitalized and depreciated. The election is an annual election and applies to the acquisition cost of property placed in service that year.[4] The § 179 amount is per taxpayer, per year. On a joint return, the

CONCEPT SUMMARY 8–4
STRAIGHT-LINE ELECTION UNDER ACRS AND MACRS

ACRS

	Personal Property	Real Property 15-Year	Real Property 18-Year	Real Property 19-Year
Convention	Half-year	Full-month	Mid-month	Mid-month
Cost recovery deduction in the year of disposition	None	Full-month for month of disposition	Half-month for month of disposition	Half-month for month of disposition
Elective or mandatory	Elective	Elective	Elective	Elective
Breadth of election	Class by class	Property by property	Property by property	Property by property

MACRS

	Personal Property	Real Property
Convention	Half-year or mid-quarter	Mid-month
Cost recovery deduction in the year of disposition	Half-year for year of disposition or half-quarter for quarter of disposition	Half-month for month of disposition
Elective or mandatory	Elective	Mandatory
Breadth of election	Class by class	

4. § 179(b).

statutory amounts apply to the couple. If the taxpayers are married and file separate returns, each spouse is eligible for 50 percent of the statutory amount. The immediate expense election is only available for personalty used in a trade or business. It is not available for real property or property used for the production of income.

EXAMPLE 20

Kelly acquired machinery (five-year class) on February 1, 1993, at a cost of $40,000 and elected to expense $10,000 under § 179. Her statutory percentage cost recovery allowance for 1993 is $6,000 [($40,000 cost – $10,000 expensed) × .200]. (See Table 8–2 for percentage.) Kelly's total deduction for 1993 is $16,000 ($10,000 + $6,000). ◆

Annual Limitations. Two limitations apply to the amount deductible under § 179. First, the ceiling amount on the deduction is reduced dollar-for-dollar when property (other than eligible real estate) placed in service during the taxable year exceeds $200,000. Second, the amount expensed under § 179 cannot exceed the aggregate amount of taxable income derived from the conduct of any trade or business by the taxpayer. Taxable income of a trade or business is computed without regard to the amount expensed under § 179. Any § 179 amount in excess of taxable income is carried forward to future taxable years and added to other amounts eligible for expensing; it is subject to the ceiling rules for the carryforward years.

EXAMPLE 21

Jill owns a computer service and operates it as a sole proprietorship. In 1993, she will net $5,000 before considering any § 179 deduction. If Jill spends $204,000 on new equipment, her § 179 expense deduction is computed as follows:

§ 179 deduction before adjustment	$10,000
Less: Dollar limitation reduction ($204,000 – $200,000)	(4,000)
Remaining § 179 deduction	$ 6,000
Business income limitation	$ 5,000
§ 179 deduction allowed	$ 5,000
§ 179 deduction carryforward ($6,000 – $5,000)	$ 1,000

◆

Effect on Basis. The basis of the property for cost recovery purposes is reduced by the § 179 amount after it is adjusted for property placed in service in excess of $200,000. This adjusted amount does not reflect any business income limitation.

EXAMPLE 22

Assume the same facts as in the previous example and that the new equipment is five-year class property. Jill's statutory percentage cost recovery deduction for 1993 is $39,600 [($204,000 – $6,000) × .200]. (See Table 8–2 for percentage.) ◆

Conversion to Personal Use. Conversion of the expensed property to personal use at any time results in recapture income (see Chapter 13). A property is converted to personal use if it is not used predominantly in a trade or business. Regulations provide for the mechanics of the recapture.[5]

5. Reg. § 1.179–1(e).

Business and Personal Use of Automobiles and Other Listed Property

MACRS deductions for business and personal use of automobiles and other listed property are limited. If the listed property *is predominantly used* for business, the taxpayer is allowed to use the statutory percentage method to recover cost. In cases where the property is *not predominantly used* for business, the cost is recovered using a straight-line recovery.

Listed property includes the following:

- Any passenger automobile.
- Any other property used as a means of transportation.
- Any property of a type generally used for purposes of entertainment, recreation, or amusement.
- Any computer or peripheral equipment, with the exception of equipment used exclusively at a regular business establishment, including a qualifying home office.
- Any cellular telephone or other similar telecommunications equipment.
- Any other property specified in the Regulations.

Automobiles and Other Listed Property Used Predominantly in Business. For listed property to be considered as predominantly used in business, the percentage of business use must exceed 50 percent. The use of listed property for production of income does not qualify as business use for purposes of the more-than-50 percent test. However, if the more-than-50 percent test is met, both production of income and business use percentages are used to compute the cost recovery deduction.

EXAMPLE 23

On September 1, 1992, Shontelle places in service listed five-year recovery property. The property cost $10,000. If Shontelle uses the property 40% for business and 25% for the production of income, the property will not be considered as predominantly used for business. The cost would be recovered using straight-line cost recovery. If, however, Shontelle uses the property 60% for business and 25% for the production of income, the property will be considered as used predominantly for business, and the statutory percentage method may be used. Shontelle's cost recovery allowance for the year would be $1,700 ($10,000 × .200 × 85%). ◆

Specific methods for determining the percentage of business usage for listed property are provided in the Regulations. For automobiles, a mileage-based percentage is to be used. Other listed property is to use the most appropriate unit of time (e.g., hours) the property is actually used (rather than available for use).[6]

The law places special limitations on the cost recovery deduction for passenger automobiles. These statutory dollar limits were imposed on passenger automobiles because Congress believed the tax system was being used to underwrite automobiles whose cost and luxury far exceeded what was needed for their business use.

A *passenger automobile* is any four-wheeled vehicle manufactured for use on public streets, roads, and highways with an unloaded gross vehicle weight rating of 6,000 pounds or less. This definition specifically excludes vehicles used directly in the business of transporting people or property for compensation such

6. Reg. § 1.280F–6T(e).

as taxicabs, ambulances, hearses, and trucks and vans as prescribed by the Regulations.

The following limits apply to cost recovery deductions for passenger automobiles:

Year	Recovery Limitation
1	$2,760
2	4,400
3	2,650
Succeeding years until the cost is recovered	1,575

However, these limits are imposed before any percentage reduction for personal use. In addition, the limitation in the first year includes any amount the taxpayer elects to expense under § 179. If the passenger automobile is used partly for personal use, the personal use percentage is ignored for the purpose of determining the unrecovered cost available for deduction in later years.

Example 24

On July 1, 1993, Dan places in service an automobile that cost $15,000. The car is always used 80% for business and 20% for personal use. The cost recovery for the automobile would be as follows:

1993—$2,208	[$15,000 × 20% (limited to $2,760) × 80%]
1994—$3,520	[$15,000 × 32% (limited to $4,400) × 80%]
1995—$2,120	[$15,000 × 19.2% (limited to $2,650) × 80%]
1996—$1,260	[$15,000 × 11.52% (limited to $1,575) × 80%]
1997—$1,260	[$15,000 × 11.52% (limited to $1,575) × 80%]
1998—$1,260	[$2,040 unrecovered cost ($15,000 – $12,960*) (limited to $1,575) × 80%]
1999—$372	[$465 unrecovered cost ($15,000 – $14,535) × 80%]

*($2,760 + $4,400 + $2,650 + $1,575 + $1,575). Although the statutory percentage method appears to restrict the deduction to $691 [$15,000 × 5.76% (limited to $1,575) × 80%], the unrecovered cost of $2,040 (limited to $1,575) multiplied by the business usage percentage is deductible. At the start of 1996 (Year 4), there is an automatic switch to the straight-line depreciation method. Under this method, the unrecovered cost up to the maximum allowable limit ($1,575) is deductible in the last year of the recovery period (1998 or Year 6). Because the limit restricts the deduction, the remaining unrecovered cost is deductible in the next or succeeding year(s), subject to the maximum allowable yearly limit ($1,575), multiplied by the business usage percentage.

The total cost recovery for the years 1993–1999 is $12,000 (80% business usage × $15,000). ◆

The cost recovery limitations are maximum amounts. If the regular calculation produces a lesser cost recovery allowance, the lesser amount is used.

Example 25

On April 2, 1993, Gail placed in service an automobile that cost $10,000. The car is always used 70% for business and 30% for personal use. The cost recovery for 1993 is $1,400 ($10,000 × 20% × 70%), which is less than $1,932 ($2,760 × 70%). (See Table 8–11 for percentage.) ◆

Note that the cost recovery limitations apply *only* to passenger automobiles and not to other listed property.

Automobiles and Other Listed Property Not Used Predominantly in Business. The cost of listed property that does not pass the more-than-50 percent business usage test in the year the property is placed in service must be recovered using the straight-line method. Under MACRS, the straight-line method to be used is that required under the alternative depreciation system (ADS) (explained later in the chapter). This system requires a straight-line recovery period of five years for automobiles. However, even though the straight-line method is used, the cost recovery allowance for passenger automobiles cannot exceed the dollar limitations.

EXAMPLE 26

On July 27, 1993, Fred placed in service an automobile that cost $20,000. The auto is used 40% for business and 60% for personal use. The cost recovery allowance for 1993 is $800 [$20,000 × 10% (Table 8–11) × 40%]. ◆

EXAMPLE 27

Assume the same facts as in the previous example, except that the auto cost $50,000. The cost recovery allowance for 1993 is $1,104 [$50,000 × 10% = $5,000 (limited to $2,760) × 40%]. (See Table 8–11 for percentage.) ◆

If the listed property fails the more-than-50 percent business usage test, the straight-line method must be used for the remainder of the property's life. This applies even if at some later date the business usage of the property increases to more than 50 percent. However, even though the straight-line method must continue to be used, the amount of cost recovery will reflect the increase in business usage.

EXAMPLE 28

Assume the same facts as in Example 26, except that in 1994, Fred uses the auto 70% for business and 30% for personal use. Fred's cost recovery allowance for 1994 is $2,800 [$20,000 × 20% (Table 8–11) × 70%]. ◆

Change from Predominantly Business Use. If the business use percentage of listed property falls to 50 percent or lower after the year the property is placed in service, the property is subject to *cost recovery recapture.* The amount required to be recaptured and included in the taxpayer's return as ordinary income is the excess depreciation.

Excess depreciation is the excess of the cost recovery deduction taken in prior years using the statutory percentage method over the amount that would have been allowed if the straight-line method had been used since the property was placed in service.

EXAMPLE 29

Seth purchased a car on January 22, 1993, at a cost of $20,000. Business usage was 80% in 1993, 70% in 1994, 40% in 1995, and 60% in 1996. ACRS deductions in 1993 and 1994 are $2,208 (80% × $2,760) and $3,080 (70% × $4,400), respectively. Seth's excess depreciation to be recaptured as ordinary income in 1995 is $888, calculated as follows:

	1993
Statutory percentage allowance	$ 2,208
Straight-line ($20,000 × 10% × 80%)	(1,600)
Excess	$ 608

1994	
Statutory percentage allowance	$ 3,080
Straight-line ($20,000 × 20% × 70%)	(2,800)
1994 excess	$ 280
1993 excess	608
Total excess	$ 888

◆

After the business usage of the listed property drops below the more-than-50 percent level, the straight-line method must be used for the remaining life of the property.

EXAMPLE 30

Assume the same facts as in Example 29. Seth's cost recovery allowance for the years 1995 and 1996 would be $1,060 and $945, computed as follows:

1995—$1,060 [($20,000 × 20%) limited to $2,650 × 40%]
1996—$945 [($20,000 × 20%) limited to $1,575 × 60%] ◆

Leased Automobiles. A taxpayer who leases a passenger automobile must report an *inclusion amount* in gross income. The inclusion amount is computed from an IRS table for each taxable year the automobile is leased. This provision is intended to prevent taxpayers from circumventing the cost recovery dollar limitations by leasing, instead of purchasing, an automobile.

The dollar amount of the inclusion is based on the fair market value of the automobile and is prorated for the number of days the auto is used during the taxable year. The prorated dollar amount is then multiplied by the business and income-producing usage percentage to determine the amount to be included in gross income. The taxpayer deducts the lease payments, multiplied by the business and income-producing usage percentage. The net effect is that the annual deduction for the lease payment is reduced by the inclusion amount.

EXAMPLE 31

On April 1, 1991, Liz leases and places in service a passenger automobile worth $40,000. The lease is for a period of five years. During the taxable years 1993 and 1994, Liz uses the automobile 70% for business and 30% for personal use. Assuming the dollar amounts from the IRS table for 1993 and 1994 are $226 and $495, Liz must include $119 in gross income for 1993 and $347 for 1994, computed as follows:

1993—$226 × (275/365) × 70% = $119
1994—$495 × (365/365) × 70% = $347

In addition, Liz can deduct 70% of the lease payments each year because this is the business use percentage. ◆

Substantiation Requirements. Listed property is now subject to the substantiation requirements of § 274. This means that the taxpayer must prove the amount of expense or use, the time and place of use, the business purpose for the use, and the business relationship to the taxpayer of persons using the property. Substantiation will require adequate records or sufficient evidence corroborating the taxpayer's statement. However, these substantiation requirements do not apply to vehicles that, by reason of their nature, are not likely to be used more than a *de minimis* amount for personal purposes.

Alternative Depreciation System (ADS)

The *alternative depreciation system (ADS)* must be used for the following:

- To calculate the portion of depreciation treated as an alternative minimum tax (AMT) adjustment for purposes of the corporate and individual AMT (see Chapter 14).
- To compute depreciation allowances for property for which any of the following is true:
  - Used predominantly outside the United States.
  - Leased or otherwise used by a tax-exempt entity.
  - Financed with the proceeds of tax-exempt bonds.
  - Imported from foreign countries that maintain discriminatory trade practices or otherwise engage in discriminatory acts.
- To compute depreciation allowances for earnings and profits purposes (see Chapter 18).

In general, ADS depreciation is computed using straight-line recovery without regard to salvage value. However, for purposes of the AMT, depreciation of

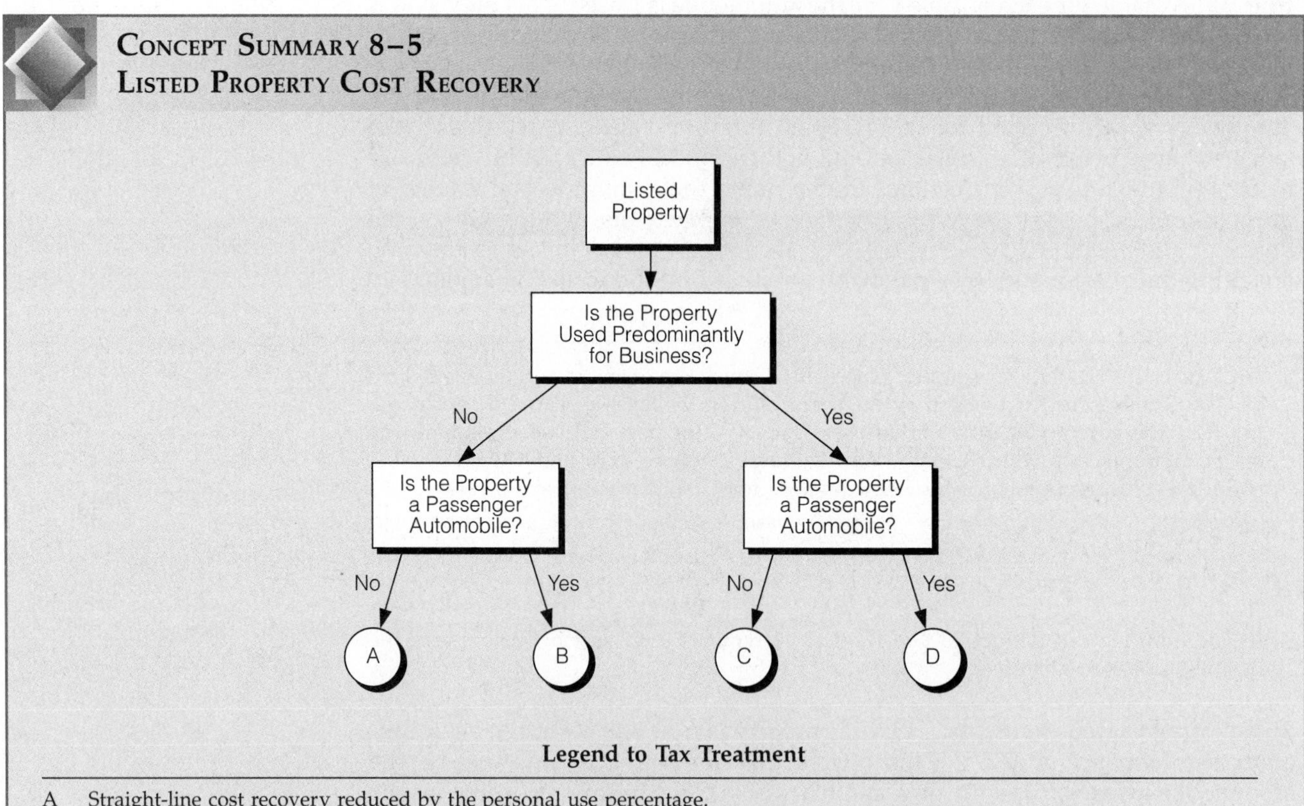
Concept Summary 8–5
Listed Property Cost Recovery
Listed Property
Is the Property Used Predominantly for Business?
No
Yes
Is the Property a Passenger Automobile?
Is the Property a Passenger Automobile?
No
Yes
No
Yes
A
B
C
D
Legend to Tax Treatment
A Straight-line cost recovery reduced by the personal use percentage.
B Straight-line cost recovery subject to the recovery limitations ($2,760, $4,400, $2,650, $1,575) and reduced by the personal use percentage.
C Statutory percentage cost recovery reduced by the personal use percentage.
D Statutory percentage cost recovery subject to the recovery limitations ($2,760, $4,400, $2,650, $1,575) and reduced by the personal use percentage.

personal property is computed using the 150 percent declining-balance method with an appropriate switch to the straight-line method.

The taxpayer must use the half-year or the mid-quarter convention, whichever is applicable, for all property other than eligible real estate. The mid-month convention is used for eligible real estate. The applicable ADS rates are found in Tables 8–10 (AMT depreciation), 8–11 (ADS half-year convention), and 8–12 (ADS mid-month convention).

The recovery periods under ADS are as follows:[7]

- The ADR midpoint life for property that does not fall into any of the following listed categories.
- Five years for qualified technological equipment, automobiles, and light-duty trucks.
- Twelve years for personal property with no class life.
- Forty years for all residential rental property and all nonresidential real property.

Taxpayers may *elect* to use the 150 percent declining-balance method to compute the regular tax rather than the 200 percent declining-balance method that is available for personal property. Hence, if the election is made, there will be no difference between the cost recovery for computing the regular tax and the AMT. However, taxpayers who make this election must use the ADS recovery periods in computing the cost recovery for the regular tax, and the ADS recovery periods generally are longer than the regular recovery periods under MACRS.

The following are examples of the classification of property by class life for the ADS recovery periods:[8]

3-year	Special tools used in the manufacture of motor vehicles, breeding hogs.
5-year	Automobiles, light general-purpose trucks.
7-year	Breeding and dairy cattle.
9.5-year	Computer-based telephone central office switching equipment.
10-year	Office furniture, fixtures, and equipment; railroad track.
12-year	Racehorses more than 2 years old at the time they are placed in service.

EXAMPLE 32

On March 1, 1993, Abby purchases computer-based telephone central office switching equipment for $80,000. If she uses statutory percentage cost recovery (assuming no § 179 election), the cost recovery for 1993 is $16,000 [$80,000 × 20% (Table 8–2, 5-year class property)]. If Abby elects to use ADS 150% declining-balance cost recovery (assuming no § 179 election), the cost recovery for 1993 is $6,312 [$80,000 × 7.89% (Table 8–10, 9.5-year class property)]. ◆

In lieu of depreciation under the regular MACRS method, taxpayers may *elect* straight-line under ADS for property that qualifies for the regular MACRS method. The election is available on a class-by-class and year-by-year basis for property other than eligible real estate. The election for eligible real estate is on a property-by-property basis.

7. The class life for certain properties described in §168(e)(3) are specially determined under §168(g)(3)(B).

8. Rev.Proc. 87–56, 1987–2 C.B. 674 is the source for the recovery periods.

AMORTIZATION

Intangible property used in a trade or business or in the production of income may be amortized if the property has a limited life that can be determined with a reasonable degree of accuracy.[9] Patents and copyrights are examples of intangible assets that have a definite limited life established by law and therefore can be amortized. Other examples of intangibles that have been found to have a useful life ascertainable with reasonable accuracy are covenants not to compete, customer lists, and sports player contracts.

Generally, intangible property is amortized using a straight-line method. The cost of the intangible property is divided by the useful life to determine the annual amortization deduction.

EXAMPLE 33

On January 2 of the current year, Copper Corporation was granted a 17-year patent. The costs associated with developing and acquiring the patent were $340,000. For the current year, Copper Corporation may amortize $20,000 ($340,000/17 years) of the cost of the patent. ◆

Intangibles that do not have a useful life ascertainable with reasonable accuracy, such as goodwill, may not be amortized. Case law further holds that to be amortizable, intangible property must have an ascertainable cost basis separate and distinct from goodwill.[10] Goodwill has been defined as the expectation that "the old customers will resort to the old place."[11] An intangible asset is separate and distinct from goodwill if the asset has a measurable value for a specific use.[12] While covenants not to compete may be amortizable, the close relationship between a covenant not to compete and the goodwill concept of old customers resorting to the old place creates a potential conflict. It can be argued that a covenant not to compete is merely a transfer of goodwill.

For the purchaser of a covenant not to compete, the cost represents an intangible asset that is amortizable over the fixed life of the covenant. From the standpoint of the seller of a covenant not to compete, the proceeds from the sale are ordinary income, similar to compensation for forgone personal services. For the purchaser of goodwill, the cost represents an intangible asset that is not amortizable. The seller of goodwill, on the other hand, is selling an asset that will result in the recognition of capital gain.

Because of the different tax treatments accorded to a covenant not to compete and goodwill, the purchaser and the seller have conflicting goals with regard to taxes. The purchaser would prefer the increased amortization deductions associated with a covenant not to compete. The seller would prefer the potentially lower capital gain taxes (through the use of the alternative tax for net capital gains) associated with the sale of goodwill. The courts have often relied on this tax conflict between a purchaser and a seller to support the economic reality of a covenant not to compete.[13] However, to assure the creation of an amortizable

---

9. Reg. § 1.167(a)–3.
10. *Citizens and Southern Corp.*, 91 T.C. 463 (1988), aff'd per curiam in an unpublished opinion (CA–2, March 22, 1990).
11. See the opinion cited in Footnote 10 at 480.
12. See the opinion cited in Footnote 10 at 516.
13. For example, see *Theophelis v. U.S.*, 751 F.2d 165 (CA–6, 1984) and *Better Beverages v. U.S.*, 619 F.2d 424 (CA–5, 1980).

asset, any agreement between a purchaser and seller should contain factors that weigh in favor of the independent economic significance or economic reality of the covenant not to compete. Examples of these factors are specific negotiations for the covenant, a specific allocation of the purchase price to the covenant, reasonable terms with respect to the covenant, and a reasonable price for the covenant.

DEPLETION

Natural resources (e.g., oil, gas, coal, gravel, timber) are subject to depletion, which is simply a form of depreciation applicable to natural resources. Land generally cannot be depleted.

The owner of an interest in the natural resource is entitled to deduct depletion. An owner is one who has an economic interest in the property.[14] An economic interest requires the acquisition of an interest in the resource in place and the receipt of income from the extraction or severance of that resource. Like depreciation, depletion is a deduction *for* adjusted gross income.

Although all natural resources are subject to depletion, oil and gas wells are used as an example in the following paragraphs to illustrate the related costs and issues.

In developing an oil or gas well, the producer must make four types of expenditures.

- Natural resource costs.
- Intangible drilling and development costs.
- Tangible asset costs.
- Operating costs.

Natural resources are physically limited, and the costs to acquire them (e.g., oil under the ground) are, therefore, recovered through depletion. Costs incurred in making the property ready for drilling such as the cost of labor in clearing the property, erecting derricks, and drilling the hole are *intangible drilling and development costs (IDC)*. These costs generally have no salvage value and are a lost cost if the well is dry. Costs for tangible assets such as tools, pipes, and engines are capital in nature. These costs must be capitalized and recovered through depreciation. Costs incurred after the well is producing are operating costs. These costs would include expenditures for such items as labor, fuel, and supplies. Operating costs are deductible when incurred (on the accrual basis) or when paid (on the cash basis).

The expenditures for depreciable assets and operating expenses pose no unusual problems for producers of natural resources. The tax treatment of depletable costs and IDC is quite a different matter.

Intangible Drilling and Development Costs (IDC)

IDC can be handled in one of two ways at the option of the taxpayer. They can be *either* charged off as an expense in the year in which they are incurred *or*

14. Reg. § 1.611–1(b).

capitalized and written off through depletion. The taxpayer makes the election in the first year such expenditures are incurred either by taking a deduction on the return or by adding them to the depletable basis. No formal statement of intent is required. Once made, the election is binding on both the taxpayer and the IRS for all such expenditures in the future. If the taxpayer fails to make the election to expense IDC on the original timely filed return the first year these expenditures are incurred, an automatic election to capitalize them has been made and is irrevocable.

As a general rule, it is more advantageous to expense IDC. The obvious benefit of an immediate write-off (as opposed to a deferred write-off through depletion) is not the only advantage. Since a taxpayer can use percentage depletion, which is calculated without reference to basis, the IDC may be completely lost as a deduction if they are capitalized.

Depletion Methods

There are two methods of calculating depletion: cost and percentage. Cost depletion can be used on any wasting asset (and is the only method allowed for timber). Percentage depletion is subject to a number of limitations, particularly for oil and gas deposits. Depletion should be calculated both ways, and generally the method that results in the *larger* deduction is used. The choice between cost and percentage depletion is an annual election.

Cost Depletion. *Cost depletion* is determined by using the adjusted basis of the asset. The basis is divided by the estimated recoverable units of the asset (e.g., barrels, tons) to arrive at the depletion per unit. The depletion per unit then is multiplied by the number of units *sold* (not the units produced) during the year to arrive at the cost depletion allowed. Cost depletion, therefore, resembles the units-of-production method of calculating depreciation.

EXAMPLE 34

On January 1, 1993, Pablo purchased the rights to a mineral interest for $1,000,000. At that time, the remaining recoverable units in the mineral interest were estimated to be 200,000. The depletion per unit is $5 [$1,000,000 (adjusted basis) ÷ 200,000 (estimated recoverable units)]. If during the year 60,000 units were mined and 25,000 were sold, the cost depletion would be $125,000 [$5 (depletion per unit) × 25,000 (units sold)]. ◆

If the taxpayer later discovers that the original estimate was incorrect, the depletion per unit for future calculations must be redetermined based on the revised estimate.

Percentage Depletion. *Percentage depletion* (also referred to as statutory depletion) is a specified percentage provided for in the Code. The percentage varies according to the type of mineral interest involved. A sample of these percentages is shown in Figure 8–1. The rate is applied to the gross income from the property, but in no event may percentage depletion exceed 50 percent of the taxable income from the property before the allowance for depletion.[15]

15. § 613(a). Special rules apply for certain oil and gas wells under § 613A. For example, the 50% ceiling is replaced with a 100% ceiling, and the percentage depletion may not exceed 65% of the taxpayer's taxable income from all sources before the allowance for depletion.

EXAMPLE 35

Assuming gross income of $100,000, a depletion rate of 22%, and other expenses relating to the property of $60,000, the depletion allowance is determined as follows:

Gross income	$100,000
Less: Other expenses	(60,000)
Taxable income before depletion	$ 40,000
Depletion allowance [the lesser of $22,000 (22% × $100,000) or $20,000 (50% × $40,000)]	(20,000)
Taxable income after depletion	$ 20,000

The adjusted basis of the property is reduced by $20,000, the depletion allowed. If the other expenses had been only $55,000, the full $22,000 could have been deducted, and the adjusted basis would have been reduced by $22,000. ◆

Note that percentage depletion is based on a percentage of the gross income from the property and makes no reference to cost. Thus, when percentage depletion is used, it is possible to deduct more than the original cost of the property. If percentage depletion is used, however, the adjusted basis of the property (for computing cost depletion) must be reduced by the amount of percentage depletion taken until the adjusted basis reaches zero.

Depreciation, ACRS, and MACRS

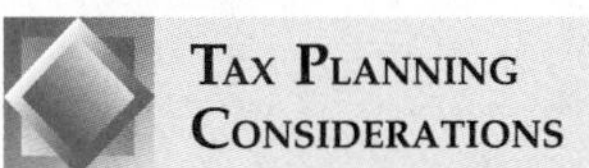

Depreciation schedules should be reviewed annually for possible retirements, abandonments, obsolescence, and changes in estimated useful lives.

FIGURE 8–1
Sample of Percentage Depletion Rates

22% Depletion	
Cobalt	Sulfur
Lead	Tin
Nickel	Uranium
Platinum	Zinc

15% Depletion	
Copper	Oil and gas
Gold	Oil shale
Iron	Silver

14% Depletion	
Borax	Magnesium carbonates
Calcium carbonates	Marble
Granite	Potash
Limestone	Slate

10% Depletion	
Coal	Perlite
Lignite	Sodium chloride

5% Depletion	
Gravel	Pumice
Peat	Sand

EXAMPLE 36

An examination of the depreciation schedule of Greene Company reveals the following:

- Asset A was abandoned when it was discovered that the cost of repairs would be in excess of the cost of replacement. Asset A had an adjusted basis of $3,000.
- Asset D was being depreciated over a period of 20 years, but a revised estimate showed that its estimated remaining life is only 2 years. Its original cost was $60,000, and it had been depreciated under the straight-line method for 15 years.
- Asset J became obsolete this year, at which point, its adjusted basis was $8,000.

The depreciation expense on Asset D should be $7,500 [$60,000 (cost) – $45,000 (accumulated depreciation) = $15,000 ÷ 2 (remaining estimated useful life)]. Assets A and J should be written off for an additional expense of $11,000 ($3,000 + $8,000). ◆

Because of the deductions for depreciation, interest, and ad valorem property taxes, investments in real estate can be highly attractive. In figuring the economics of such investments, one should be sure to take into account any tax savings that result.

EXAMPLE 37

In early January 1993, Vern (an individual in the 31% tax bracket) purchased residential rental property for $170,000 (of which $20,000 was allocated to the land and $150,000 to the building). Vern made a down payment of $25,000 and assumed the seller's mortgage for the balance. Under the mortgage agreement, monthly payments of $1,000 are required and are applied toward interest, taxes, insurance, and principal. Since the property was already occupied, Vern continued to receive rent of $1,200 per month from the tenant. Vern actively participates in this activity and hence comes under the special rule for a rental real estate activity with respect to the limitation on passive activity losses (refer to Chapter 6).

During the first year of ownership, Vern's expenses were as follows:

Interest	$10,000
Taxes	800
Insurance	1,000
Repairs and maintenance	2,200
Depreciation ($150,000 × .03485)	5,228
Total	$19,228

The deductible loss from the rental property is computed as follows:

Rent income ($1,200 × 12 months)	$14,400
Less expenses (see above)	(19,228)
Net loss	$(4,828)

But what is Vern's overall position for the year when the tax benefit of the loss is taken into account? Considering just the cash intake and outlay, it is summarized as follows:

Intake—		
Rent income	$14,400	
Tax savings [31% (income tax bracket) × $4,828 (loss from the property)]	1,497	$ 15,897
Outlay—		
Mortgage payments ($1,000 × 12 months)	$12,000	
Repairs and maintenance	2,200	(14,200)
Net cash benefit		$ 1,697

◆

It should be noted, however, that should Vern cease being an active participant in the rental activity, the passive activity loss rules would apply, and Vern could lose the current period benefit of the loss.

Depletion

Since the election to use the cost or percentage depletion method is an annual election, a taxpayer can use cost depletion (if higher) until the basis is exhausted and then switch to percentage depletion in the following years.

EXAMPLE 38

Assume the following facts for Melissa:

Remaining depletable basis	$ 11,000
Gross income (10,000 units)	100,000
Expenses (other than depletion)	30,000

Since cost depletion is limited to the basis of $11,000 and if the percentage depletion is $22,000 (assume a 22% rate), Melissa would choose the latter. Her basis is then reduced to zero. In future years, however, she can continue to take percentage depletion since percentage depletion is taken without reference to the remaining basis. ◆

Tables

Summary of Tables

Table 8–1	Original ACRS statutory percentage table for personalty. Applicable depreciation method: 150 percent declining-balance switching to straight-line. Applicable recovery periods: 3, 5, 10, 15 years. Applicable convention: half-year.
Table 8–2	Modified ACRS statutory percentage table for personalty. Applicable depreciation methods: 200 or 150 percent declining-balance switching to straight-line. Applicable recovery periods: 3, 5, 7, 10, 15, 20 years. Applicable convention: half-year.
Table 8–3	Modified ACRS statutory percentage table for personalty. Applicable depreciation method: 200 percent declining-balance switching to straight-line. Applicable recovery periods: 3, 5, 7 years. Applicable convention: mid-quarter.
Table 8–4	Original ACRS statutory percentage table for realty. Applicable depreciation methods: 200 or 175 percent declining-balance switching to straight-line. Applicable recovery period: 15 years. Applicable convention: full-month.
Table 8–5	Original ACRS statutory percentage table for realty. Applicable depreciation method: 175 percent declining-balance switching to straight-line. Applicable recovery period: 18 years. Applicable convention: mid-month.
Table 8–6	Original ACRS statutory percentage table for realty. Applicable depreciation method: 175 percent declining-balance switching to straight-line. Applicable recovery period: 19 years. Applicable convention: mid-month.
Table 8–7	Modified ACRS straight-line table for realty. Applicable depreciation method: straight-line. Applicable recovery periods: 27.5, 31.5 years. Applicable convention: mid-month.
Table 8–8	Original ACRS optional straight-line table for realty. Applicable depreciation method: straight-line. Applicable recovery period: 19 years. Applicable convention: mid-month.
Table 8–9	Modified ACRS optional straight-line table for personalty. Applicable depreciation method: straight-line. Applicable recovery periods: 3, 5, 7, 10, 15, 20 years. Applicable convention: half-year.
Table 8–10	Alternative minimum tax declining-balance table for personalty. Applicable depreciation method: 150 percent declining-balance switching to straight-line. Applicable recovery periods: 3, 5, 9.5, 10 years. Applicable convention: half-year.
Table 8–11	Alternative depreciation system straight-line table for personalty. Applicable depreciation method: straight-line. Applicable recovery periods: 5, 9.5, 12 years. Applicable convention: half-year.
Table 8–12	Alternative depreciation system straight-line table for realty. Applicable depreciation method: straight-line. Applicable recovery period: 40 years. Applicable convention: mid-month.

TABLE 8–1 **ACRS Statutory Percentages for Property Other Than 15-Year Real Property, 18-Year Real Property, or 19-Year Real Property Assuming Half-Year Convention**

For Property Placed in Service after December 31, 1980, and before January 1, 1987

The applicable percentage for the class of property is:

Recovery Year	3-Year	5-Year	10-Year	15-Year Public Utility
1	25	15	8	5
2	38	22	14	10
3	37	21	12	9
4		21	10	8
5		21	10	7
6			10	7
7			9	6
8			9	6
9			9	6
10			9	6
11				6
12				6
13				6
14				6
15				6

TABLE 8–2 **MACRS Accelerated Depreciation for Personal Property Assuming Half-Year Convention**

For Property Placed in Service after December 31, 1986

Recovery Year	3-Year (200% DB)	5-Year (200% DB)	7-Year (200% DB)	10-Year (200% DB)	15-Year (150% DB)	20-Year (150% DB)
1	33.33	20.00	14.29	10.00	5.00	3.750
2	44.45	32.00	24.49	18.00	9.50	7.219
3	14.81*	19.20	17.49	14.40	8.55	6.677
4	7.41	11.52*	12.49	11.52	7.70	6.177
5		11.52	8.93*	9.22	6.93	5.713
6		5.76	8.92	7.37	6.23	5.285
7			8.93	6.55*	5.90*	4.888
8			4.46	6.55	5.90	4.522
9				6.56	5.91	4.462*
10				6.55	5.90	4.461
11				3.28	5.91	4.462
12					5.90	4.461
13					5.91	4.462
14					5.90	4.461
15					5.91	4.462
16					2.95	4.461
17						4.462
18						4.461
19						4.462
20						4.461
21						2.231

*Switchover to straight-line depreciation.

TABLE 8–3 **MACRS Accelerated Depreciation for Personal Property Assuming Mid-Quarter Convention**

For Property Placed in Service after December 31, 1986 (Partial Table*)

3-Year

Recovery Year	First Quarter	Second Quarter	Third Quarter	Fourth Quarter
1	58.33	41.67	25.00	8.33
2	27.78	38.89	50.00	61.11

5-Year

Recovery Year	First Quarter	Second Quarter	Third Quarter	Fourth Quarter
1	35.00	25.00	15.00	5.00
2	26.00	30.00	34.00	38.00

7-Year

Recovery Year	First Quarter	Second Quarter	Third Quarter	Fourth Quarter
1	25.00	17.85	10.71	3.57
2	21.43	23.47	25.51	27.55

*The figures in this table are taken from the official tables that appear in Rev.Proc. 87–57, 1987–2 C.B. 687. Because of their length, the complete tables are not presented.

TABLE 8–4 ACRS Statutory Percentages for 15-Year Real Property

For Property Placed in Service after December 31, 1980, and before January 1, 1987
15-Year Real Property: Low-Income Housing

And the month in the first recovery year the property is placed in service is:

The applicable percentage is (use the column for the month in the first year the property is placed in service):

If the recovery year is:	1	2	3	4	5	6	7	8	9	10	11	12
1	13	12	11	10	9	8	7	6	4	3	2	1
2	12	12	12	12	12	12	12	13	13	13	13	13
3	10	10	10	10	11	11	11	11	11	11	11	11
4	9	9	9	9	9	9	9	9	10	10	10	10
5	8	8	8	8	8	8	8	8	8	8	8	9
6	7	7	7	7	7	7	7	7	7	7	7	7
7	6	6	6	6	6	6	6	6	6	6	6	6
8	5	5	5	5	5	5	5	5	5	5	6	6
9	5	5	5	5	5	5	5	5	5	5	5	5
10	5	5	5	5	5	5	5	5	5	5	5	5
11	4	5	5	5	5	5	5	5	5	5	5	5
12	4	4	4	5	4	5	5	5	5	5	5	5
13	4	4	4	4	4	4	5	4	5	5	5	5
14	4	4	4	4	4	4	4	4	4	5	4	4
15	4	4	4	4	4	4	4	4	4	4	4	4
16	–	–	1	1	2	2	2	3	3	3	4	4

For Property Placed in Service after December 31, 1980, and before March 16, 1984
15-Year Real Property (other than low-income housing)

If the recovery year is:	1	2	3	4	5	6	7	8	9	10	11	12
1	12	11	10	9	8	7	6	5	4	3	2	1
2	10	10	11	11	11	11	11	11	11	11	11	12
3	9	9	9	9	10	10	10	10	10	10	10	10
4	8	8	8	8	8	8	9	9	9	9	9	9
5	7	7	7	7	7	7	8	8	8	8	8	8
6	6	6	6	6	7	7	7	7	7	7	7	7
7	6	6	6	6	6	6	6	6	6	6	6	6
8	6	6	6	6	6	6	6	6	6	6	6	6
9	6	6	6	6	5	6	5	5	5	6	6	6
10	5	6	5	6	5	5	5	5	5	5	6	5
11	5	5	5	5	5	5	5	5	5	5	5	5
12	5	5	5	5	5	5	5	5	5	5	5	5
13	5	5	5	5	5	5	5	5	5	5	5	5
14	5	5	5	5	5	5	5	5	5	5	5	5
15	5	5	5	5	5	5	5	5	5	5	5	5
16	–	–	1	1	2	2	3	3	4	4	4	5

Table 8–5 ACRS Cost Recovery Table for 18-Year Real Property

For Property Placed in Service after June 22, 1984, and before May 9, 1985
18-Year Real Property (18-Year 175% Declining Balance)
(Assuming Mid-Month Convention)

If the recovery year is:	And the month in the first recovery year the property is placed in service is: 1	2	3	4	5	6	7	8	9	10	11	12
	The applicable percentage is (use the column for the month in the first year the property is placed in service):											
1	9	9	8	7	6	5	4	4	3	2	1	0.4
2	9	9	9	9	9	9	9	9	9	10	10	10.0
3	8	8	8	8	8	8	8	8	9	9	9	9.0
4	7	7	7	7	7	8	8	8	8	8	8	8.0
5	7	7	7	7	7	7	7	7	7	7	7	7.0
6	6	6	6	6	6	6	6	6	6	6	6	6.0
7	5	5	5	5	6	6	6	6	6	6	6	6.0
8	5	5	5	5	5	5	5	5	5	5	5	5.0
9	5	5	5	5	5	5	5	5	5	5	5	5.0
10	5	5	5	5	5	5	5	5	5	5	5	5.0
11	5	5	5	5	5	5	5	5	5	5	5	5.0
12	5	5	5	5	5	5	5	5	5	5	5	5.0
13	4	4	4	5	4	4	5	4	4	4	5	5.0
14	4	4	4	4	4	4	4	4	4	4	4	4.0
15	4	4	4	4	4	4	4	4	4	4	4	4.0
16	4	4	4	4	4	4	4	4	4	4	4	4.0
17	4	4	4	4	4	4	4	4	4	4	4	4.0
18	4	3	4	4	4	4	4	4	4	4	4	4.0
19	–	1	1	1	2	2	2	3	3	3	3	3.6

TABLE 8–6 ACRS Cost Recovery Table for 19-Year Real Property

For Property Placed in Service after May 8, 1985, and before January 1, 1987
19-Year Real Property (19-Year 175% Declining Balance)
(Assuming Mid-Month Convention)

And the month in the first recovery year the property is placed in service is:

If the recovery year is:	1	2	3	4	5	6	7	8	9	10	11	12
	The applicable percentage is (use the column for the month in the first year the property is placed in service):											
1	8.8	8.1	7.3	6.5	5.8	5.0	4.2	3.5	2.7	1.9	1.1	0.4
2	8.4	8.5	8.5	8.6	8.7	8.8	8.8	8.9	9.0	9.0	9.1	9.2
3	7.6	7.7	7.7	7.8	7.9	7.9	8.0	8.1	8.1	8.2	8.3	8.3
4	6.9	7.0	7.0	7.1	7.1	7.2	7.3	7.3	7.4	7.4	7.5	7.6
5	6.3	6.3	6.4	6.4	6.5	6.5	6.6	6.6	6.7	6.8	6.8	6.9
6	5.7	5.7	5.8	5.9	5.9	5.9	6.0	6.0	6.1	6.1	6.2	6.2
7	5.2	5.2	5.3	5.3	5.3	5.4	5.4	5.5	5.5	5.6	5.6	5.6
8	4.7	4.7	4.8	4.8	4.8	4.9	4.9	5.0	5.0	5.1	5.1	5.1
9	4.2	4.3	4.3	4.4	4.4	4.5	4.5	4.5	4.5	4.6	4.6	4.7
10	4.2	4.2	4.2	4.2	4.2	4.2	4.2	4.2	4.2	4.2	4.2	4.2
11	4.2	4.2	4.2	4.2	4.2	4.2	4.2	4.2	4.2	4.2	4.2	4.2
12	4.2	4.2	4.2	4.2	4.2	4.2	4.2	4.2	4.2	4.2	4.2	4.2
13	4.2	4.2	4.2	4.2	4.2	4.2	4.2	4.2	4.2	4.2	4.2	4.2
14	4.2	4.2	4.2	4.2	4.2	4.2	4.2	4.2	4.2	4.2	4.2	4.2
15	4.2	4.2	4.2	4.2	4.2	4.2	4.2	4.2	4.2	4.2	4.2	4.2
16	4.2	4.2	4.2	4.2	4.2	4.2	4.2	4.2	4.2	4.2	4.2	4.2
17	4.2	4.2	4.2	4.2	4.2	4.2	4.2	4.2	4.2	4.2	4.2	4.2
18	4.2	4.2	4.2	4.2	4.2	4.2	4.2	4.2	4.2	4.2	4.2	4.2
19	4.2	4.2	4.2	4.2	4.2	4.2	4.2	4.2	4.2	4.2	4.2	4.2
20	0.2	0.5	0.9	1.2	1.6	1.9	2.3	2.6	3.0	3.3	3.7	4.0

TABLE 8–7 **MACRS Straight-Line Depreciation for Real Property Assuming Mid-Month Convention***

For Property Placed in Service after December 31, 1986
27.5-Year Residential Real Property

The applicable percentage is (use the column for the month in the first year the property is placed in service):

Recovery Year(s)	1	2	3	4	5	6	7	8	9	10	11	12
1	3.485	3.182	2.879	2.576	2.273	1.970	1.667	1.364	1.061	0.758	0.455	0.152
2–18	3.636	3.636	3.636	3.636	3.636	3.636	3.636	3.636	3.636	3.636	3.636	3.636
19–27	3.637	3.637	3.637	3.637	3.637	3.637	3.637	3.637	3.637	3.637	3.637	3.637
28	1.970	2.273	2.576	2.879	3.182	3.485	3.636	3.636	3.636	3.636	3.636	3.636
29	0.000	0.000	0.000	0.000	0.000	0.000	0.152	0.455	0.758	1.061	1.364	1.667

31.5-Year Nonresidential Real Property

The applicable percentage is (use the column for the month in the first year the property is placed in service):

Recovery Year(s)	1	2	3	4	5	6	7	8	9	10	11	12
1	3.042	2.778	2.513	2.249	1.984	1.720	1.455	1.190	0.926	0.661	0.397	0.132
2–19	3.175	3.175	3.175	3.175	3.175	3.175	3.175	3.175	3.175	3.175	3.175	3.175
20–31	3.174	3.174	3.174	3.174	3.174	3.174	3.174	3.174	3.174	3.174	3.174	3.174
32	1.720	1.984	2.249	2.513	2.778	3.042	3.175	3.175	3.175	3.175	3.175	3.175
33	0.000	0.000	0.000	0.000	0.000	0.000	0.132	0.397	0.661	0.926	1.190	1.455

*The official tables contain a separate row for each year. For ease of presentation, certain years are grouped in these two tables. In some instances, this will produce a difference of .001 for the last digit when compared with the official tables.

TABLE 8–8 **ACRS Cost Recovery Table for 19-Year Real Property: Optional Straight-Line**

For Property Placed in Service after May 8, 1985, and before January 1, 1987
19-Year Real Property for Which an Optional 19-Year Straight-Line Method Is Elected (Assuming Mid-Month Convention)

If the recovery year is:	And the month in the first recovery year the property is placed in service is: 1	2	3	4	5	6	7	8	9	10	11	12
	The applicable percentage is (use the column for the month in the first year the property is placed in service):											
1	5.0	4.6	4.2	3.7	3.3	2.9	2.4	2.0	1.5	1.1	.7	.2
2	5.3	5.3	5.3	5.3	5.3	5.3	5.3	5.3	5.3	5.3	5.3	5.3
3	5.3	5.3	5.3	5.3	5.3	5.3	5.3	5.3	5.3	5.3	5.3	5.3
4	5.3	5.3	5.3	5.3	5.3	5.3	5.3	5.3	5.3	5.3	5.3	5.3
5	5.3	5.3	5.3	5.3	5.3	5.3	5.3	5.3	5.3	5.3	5.3	5.3
6	5.3	5.3	5.3	5.3	5.3	5.3	5.3	5.3	5.3	5.3	5.3	5.3
7	5.3	5.3	5.3	5.3	5.3	5.3	5.3	5.3	5.3	5.3	5.3	5.3
8	5.3	5.3	5.3	5.3	5.3	5.3	5.3	5.3	5.3	5.3	5.3	5.3
9	5.3	5.3	5.3	5.3	5.3	5.3	5.3	5.3	5.3	5.3	5.3	5.3
10	5.3	5.3	5.3	5.3	5.3	5.3	5.3	5.3	5.3	5.3	5.3	5.3
11	5.3	5.3	5.3	5.3	5.3	5.3	5.3	5.3	5.3	5.3	5.3	5.3
12	5.3	5.3	5.3	5.3	5.3	5.3	5.3	5.3	5.3	5.3	5.3	5.3
13	5.3	5.3	5.3	5.3	5.3	5.3	5.3	5.3	5.3	5.3	5.3	5.3
14	5.2	5.2	5.2	5.2	5.2	5.2	5.2	5.2	5.2	5.2	5.2	5.2
15	5.2	5.2	5.2	5.2	5.2	5.2	5.2	5.2	5.2	5.2	5.2	5.2
16	5.2	5.2	5.2	5.2	5.2	5.2	5.2	5.2	5.2	5.2	5.2	5.2
17	5.2	5.2	5.2	5.2	5.2	5.2	5.2	5.2	5.2	5.2	5.2	5.2
18	5.2	5.2	5.2	5.2	5.2	5.2	5.2	5.2	5.2	5.2	5.2	5.2
19	5.2	5.2	5.2	5.2	5.2	5.2	5.2	5.2	5.2	5.2	5.2	5.2
20	.2	.6	1.0	1.5	1.9	2.3	2.8	3.2	3.7	4.1	4.5	5.0

TABLE 8–9 **MACRS Straight-Line Depreciation for Personal Property Assuming Half-Year Convention***

For Property Placed in Service after December 31, 1986

ACRS Class	% First Recovery Year	Other Recovery Years: Years	Other Recovery Years: %	Last Recovery Year: Year	Last Recovery Year: %
3-year	16.67	2–3	33.33	4	16.67
5-year	10.00	2–5	20.00	6	10.00
7-year	7.14	2–7	14.29	8	7.14
10-year	5.00	2–10	10.00	11	5.00
15-year	3.33	2–15	6.67	16	3.33
20-year	2.50	2–20	5.00	21	2.50

*The official table contains a separate row for each year. For ease of presentation, certain years are grouped in this table. In some instances, this will produce a difference of .01 for the last digit when compared with the official table.

TABLE 8–10 **Alternative Minimum Tax: 150% Declining-Balance Assuming Half-Year Convention**

For Property Placed in Service after December 31, 1986
(Partial Table*)

Recovery Year	3-Year 150%	5-Year 150%	9.5-Year 150%	10-Year 150%
1	25.00	15.00	7.89	7.50
2	37.50	25.50	14.54	13.88
3	25.00**	17.85	12.25	11.79
4	12.50	16.66**	10.31	10.02
5		16.66	9.17**	8.74**
6		8.33	9.17	8.74
7			9.17	8.74
8			9.17	8.74
9			9.17	8.74
10			9.16	8.74
11				4.37

*The figures in this table are taken from the official table that appears in Rev.Proc. 87–57, 1987–2 C.B. 687. Because of its length, the complete table is not presented.
**Switchover to straight-line depreciation.

TABLE 8–11 **ADS Straight-Line for Personal Property Assuming Half-Year Convention**

For Property Placed in Service after December 31, 1986
(Partial Table*)

Recovery Year	5-Year Class	9.5-Year Class	12-Year Class
1	10.00	5.26	4.17
2	20.00	10.53	8.33
3	20.00	10.53	8.33
4	20.00	10.53	8.33
5	20.00	10.52	8.33
6	10.00	10.53	8.33
7		10.52	8.34
8		10.53	8.33
9		10.52	8.34
10		10.53	8.33
11			8.34
12			8.33
13			4.17

*The figures in this table are taken from the official table that appears in Rev.Proc. 87–57, 1987–2 C.B. 678. Because of its length, the complete table is not presented. The tables for the mid-quarter convention also appear in Rev.Proc. 87–57.

TABLE 8–12 **ADS Straight-Line for Real Property Assuming Mid-Month Convention**

For Property Placed in Service after December 31, 1986

Recovery Year	Month Placed in Service											
	1	2	3	4	5	6	7	8	9	10	11	12
1	2.396	2.188	1.979	1.771	1.563	1.354	1.146	0.938	0.729	0.521	0.313	0.104
2–40	2.500	2.500	2.500	2.500	2.500	2.500	2.500	2.500	2.500	2.500	2.500	2.500
41	0.104	0.312	0.521	0.729	0.937	1.146	1.354	1.562	1.771	1.979	2.187	2.396

PROBLEM MATERIALS

DISCUSSION QUESTIONS

1. Distinguish between depreciation, cost recovery, amortization, and depletion.
2. Discuss whether a taxpayer can depreciate personal property (personalty).
3. If a personal use asset is converted to business use, why is it necessary to compute depreciation on the lower of fair market value or adjusted basis at the date of conversion?
4. Discuss whether a parking lot that is used in a business can be depreciated.
5. Distinguish between the treatment of salvage value on tangible personal property placed in service before January 1, 1981, and on tangible personal property placed in service after December 31, 1980.
6. Discuss the half-year convention as it is used in the MACRS rules.
7. Discuss when the mid-quarter convention must be used.
8. Discuss the mid-month convention as it is used in the MACRS rules.
9. Discuss the applicable conventions if a taxpayer elects to use straight-line cost recovery for property placed in service after December 31, 1986.
10. If a taxpayer makes a straight-line election under MACRS, discuss the possibility of taking a cost recovery deduction, for personal and real property, in the year of disposition.
11. Discuss whether an election to use straight-line cost recovery under MACRS can be applied on an asset-by-asset basis.
12. Discuss the limitation on the § 179 amount that can be expensed and its impact on the basis of the property.
13. If a taxpayer does not pass the more-than-50% business use test on an automobile, discuss whether the statutory dollar limitations on cost recovery are applicable.
14. Discuss the tax consequences that result when a passenger automobile, which failed the more-than-50% business usage test during the first two years, satisfies the test for the third year.
15. Explain the reason for the inclusion amount for leased passenger automobiles.
16. Explain how an inclusion amount is determined for leased passenger automobiles.
17. What factors must exist for an intangible asset to be amortized?
18. Compare the tax treatment of the sale and purchase of a convenant not to compete with the tax treatment of the sale and purchase of goodwill.
19. Discuss the options for handling intangible drilling and development costs.
20. Briefly discuss the differences between cost depletion and percentage depletion.

PROBLEMS

21. Lori acquired a 10-year class asset on March 1, 1986, for $20,000. She did not elect immediate expensing under § 179. On October 5, 1993, she sold the asset.

    a. Determine Lori's cost recovery for 1986.
    b. Determine Lori's cost recovery for 1993.

22. Walt acquired a seven-year class asset on February 17, 1993, for $12,000. He did not elect immediate expensing under § 179. On January 2, 1998, he sold the asset.

    a. Determine Walt's cost recovery for 1993.
    b. Determine Walt's cost recovery for 1998.

23. Pedro acquired a 10-year class asset on April 4, 1993, for $150,000. He did not elect immediate expensing under § 179, but did elect the straight-line method. On June 2, 1999, he sold the asset.

    a. Determine Pedro's cost recovery for 1993.
    b. Determine Pedro's cost recovery for 1999.

24. Debra acquired a building for $300,000 (exclusive of land) on January 1, 1984. Calculate the cost recovery using the statutory percentage method for 1984 and 1993 if:

    a. The real property is low-income housing.
    b. The real property is a factory building.

25. On December 2, 1984, Wade purchased and placed in service a warehouse. The warehouse cost $800,000. He used the statutory percentage cost recovery method. On July 7, 1993, he sold the warehouse.

    a. Determine Wade's cost recovery for 1984.
    b. Determine Wade's cost recovery for 1993.

26. Tina, who is single, acquired a new copier (five-year class property) on March 2, 1993, for $28,000. What is the maximum amount that she can deduct in 1993 assuming the following:

    a. The taxable income derived from Tina's trade or business (without regard to the amount expensed under § 179) is $100,000.
    b. The taxable income derived from Tina's trade or business (without regard to the amount expensed under § 179) is $3,000.

27. Jack owns a small business that he operates as a sole proprietor. In 1993, he will net $9,000 of business income before consideration of any § 179 deduction. He spends $205,000 on new equipment in 1993. Jack also has $3,000 of § 179 deduction carryforwards from 1992. Determine his § 179 expense deduction for 1993 and the amount of any carryforward.

28. Olga is the proprietor of a small business. In 1993, her business income, before consideration of any § 179 deduction, is $5,000. She spends $203,000 on new equipment and furniture for 1993. If Olga elects to take the § 179 deduction on a desk that cost $15,000 (included in the $203,000), determine her total cost recovery for 1993 with respect to the desk.

29. On March 10, 1993, Yoon purchased three-year class property for $20,000. On December 15, 1993, he purchased five-year class property for $50,000.

    a. Calculate Yoon's cost recovery for 1993, assuming he does not make the § 179 election or use straight-line depreciation.
    b. Calculate Yoon's cost recovery for 1993, assuming he does elect to use § 179 and does not elect to use straight-line depreciation.

30. Pat acquires a warehouse on November 1, 1993, at a cost of $4,500,000. On January 30, 2005, he sells the warehouse. Calculate his cost recovery for 1993. For 2005.

31. On July 1, 1993, Wilma places in service a computer (five-year class property). The computer cost $20,000. She used the computer 65% for business. The remainder of the time, she used the computer for personal purposes. If Wilma does not elect § 179, determine her cost recovery deduction for the computer for 1993.

32. On February 16, 1993, Ron purchased and placed into service a new car. The purchase price was $18,000. He drove the car 12,000 miles during the remainder of the year, 9,000 miles for business and 3,000 miles for personal use. He used the statutory percentage method of cost recovery. Calculate the total deduction Ron may take for 1993 with respect to the car.

33. On June 5, 1993, Leo purchased and placed in service a $19,000 car. The business use percentage for the car is always 100%. Compute Leo's cost recovery deduction in 1999.

34. On June 14, 1993, Helen purchased and placed in service a new car. The purchase price was $16,000. The car was used 75% for business and 25% for personal use in both 1993 and 1994. In 1995, the car was used 40% for business and 60% for personal use. Compute the cost recovery deduction for the car in 1995 and the cost recovery recapture.

35. In 1993, Paul purchased a computer (five-year property) for $120,000. The computer was used 60% for business, 20% for income production, and 20% for personal use. In 1994, the usage changed to 40% for business, 30% for income production, and 30% for personal use. Compute the cost recovery deduction for 1994 and any cost recovery recapture. Assume Paul did not make a § 179 election on the computer in 1993.

36. Midway through 1993, Abdel leases and places in service a passenger automobile. The lease will run for five years, and the payments are $430 per month. During 1993, he uses the car 70% for business use and 30% for personal use. Assuming the dollar amount from the IRS table is $226, determine the tax consequences to Abdel from the lease for the year 1993.

37. Use the information given in Problem 36, but assume the dollar amount is $495. Abdel uses the car 60% for business use and 40% for personal use in 1994. Determine his tax consequences from the lease in 1994.

38. On March 5, 1993, Nell purchased office furniture and fixtures for $40,000. The assets are seven-year class property and have an ADS midpoint of 9.5 years. Determine Nell's cost recovery deduction for computing 1993 taxable income, using the alternative depreciation system and assuming she does not make a § 179 election.

39. In 1993 Muhammad purchased a light-duty truck for $12,000. The truck is used 100% for business. He did not make a § 179 election with respect to the truck. If Muhammad uses the statutory percentage method, determine his cost recovery deduction for 1993 for computing taxable income and for computing alternative minimum tax.

40. In June 1993, XYZ, Inc., purchased and placed in service railroad track costing $600,000.

   a. Calculate XYZ's cost recovery deduction for 1993 for computing taxable income, assuming XYZ does not make the § 179 election or use straight-line cost recovery.
   b. Calculate XYZ's cost recovery deduction for 1993 for computing taxable income, assuming XYZ does not make the § 179 election but does elect to use ADS 150% declining-balance cost recovery.

41. On January 1, 1993, Blue Corporation acquired all of the assets of Rick's proprietorship. Blue paid Rick $1,000,000. In the agreement, Rick signed a covenant not to compete with Blue for five years. The agreement stipulated that $100,000 of the purchase price was for the covenant not to compete. Blue Corporation also allocates $50,000 of the purchase price to goodwill. Determine the tax consequences (with respect to the covenant not to compete and the goodwill) of the purchase to Blue for 1993.

42. Wes acquired a mineral interest during the year for $5,000,000. A geological survey estimated that 250,000 tons of the mineral remained in the deposit. During the year,

80,000 tons were mined and 45,000 tons were sold for $6,000,000. Other expenses amounted to $4,000,000. Assuming the mineral depletion rate is 22%, calculate Wes's lowest taxable income.

43. Chris purchased an oil interest for $2,000,000. Recoverable barrels were estimated to be 500,000. During the year, 120,000 barrels were sold for $3,840,000, regular expenses (including depreciation) were $1,240,000, and IDC were $1,000,000. Calculate Chris's taxable income under the expensing and capitalization methods of handling IDC.

CUMULATIVE PROBLEMS

44. John Smith, age 31, is single and has no dependents. At the beginning of 1993, John started his own excavation business and named it Earth Movers. John lives at 1045 Center Street, Lindon, UT, and his business is located at 381 State Street, Lindon, UT. The zip code for both addresses is 84059. John's Social Security number is 321–09–6456, and the business identification number is 98–1234567. John is a cash basis taxpayer. During 1993, he had the following items in connection with his business:

Fees for services	$250,000
Building rental expense	30,000
Office furniture and equipment rental expense	5,000
Office supplies	1,500
Utilities	2,000
Salary for secretary	25,000
Salary for equipment operators	70,000
Payroll taxes	9,000
Fuel and oil for the equipment	20,000
Purchase of three front-end loaders on January 15, 1993, for $175,000. John made the election under § 179.	175,000
Purchase of a new dump truck on January 18, 1993	30,000

During 1993, John had the following additional items:

Interest income from First National Bank	$8,000
Dividends from Exxon	500
Quarterly estimated tax payments	10,000

Assuming John does not itemize his deductions, compute his Federal income tax payable (or refund due). Suggested software (if available): *TurboTax* or *MacInTax* for tax returns or WFT tax planning software.

45. Bob Brown, age 30, is single and has no dependents. He was employed as a barber until May 1992 by Hair Cuts, Inc. In June 1992, Bob opened his own styling salon, the Style Shop, located at 465 Willow Drive, St. Paul, MN 55455. Bob is a cash basis taxpayer. He lives at 1021 Snelling Avenue, St. Paul, MN 55455. His Social Security number is 321–56–7102. Bob does not wish to designate $1 to the Presidential Election Campaign Fund. During 1992, Bob had the following income and expense items:

a. $20,800 salary from Hair Cuts, Inc.
b. $2,400 Federal income tax withheld by Hair Cuts, Inc.
c. $600 cash dividend from General Motors.
d. $7,000 gross receipts from his own hair styling business.
e. Expenses connected with Bob's hair styling business:

- $100 laundry and cleaning
- $4,400 rent
- $700 supplies
- $600 utilities and telephone

f. Bob purchased and installed a fancy barber chair on June 3, 1992. The chair cost $6,400. Bob did not make the § 179 election.

g. Bob purchased and installed furniture and fixtures on June 5, 1992. These items cost $7,000. Bob did not make the § 179 election.

h. Bob had no itemized deductions.

Compute Bob Brown's 1992 Federal income tax payable (or refund due). If you use tax forms for your computations, you will need Forms 1040 and 4562 and Schedules B and C. Suggested software (if available): *TurboTax* or *MacInTax* for tax returns or WFT tax planning software.

CHAPTER

DEDUCTIONS: EMPLOYEE EXPENSES

OBJECTIVES

Discuss factors that determine whether an individual is self-employed or an employee.

Distinguish between self-employment and employee business expenses.

Determine which employee business expenses are deductions *for* adjusted gross income and which are deductions *from* adjusted gross income.

Identify miscellaneous itemized deductions subject to the 2 percent floor.

Distinguish between travel and transportation expenses.

Examine the requirements for deducting moving expenses and the limitations on the amount deductible.

Discuss when and how education expenses can be deducted.

Discuss the limitations on the deductibility of entertainment expenses.

Explain the deduction for contributions to Individual Retirement Accounts.

Develop tax planning ideas related to employee business expenses.

OUTLINE

Statistically, most students reading this text will become employees, as opposed to self-employed people. They will also frequently incur expenses in connection with their employment activities. Some of these expenses are deductible and some are not. Certain deductible expenses are subject to specific reductions and limitations. After determining which expenses are deductible and applying any limitations, the expenses must be classified as deductions *for* or deductions *from* adjusted gross income (AGI).

The rules for computing and classifying expenses incurred by self-employed individuals sometimes differ from those applicable to employees. It is important to determine whether an individual is an employee or is self-employed. Guidelines for making this determination are discussed in the following section. Subsequent sections examine the rules for computing and classifying employee business expenses.

CLASSIFICATION OF EMPLOYMENT-RELATED EXPENSES

Self-Employed versus Employee Status

In many instances, it is difficult to distinguish between an individual who is self-employed and one who is performing services as an employee. Expenses of self-employed individuals are deductible as trade or business expenses (*for* AGI).

EXAMPLE 1

Nadia, a self-employed CPA, incurred transportation expenses of $1,000 in connection with her business. The transportation expenses are deductions *for* AGI because they are expenses incurred by a self-employed individual. ◆

Expenses incurred by an employee in an employment relationship are subject to limitations. Only reimbursed employee expenses are deductible *for* AGI. All other deductible employee expenses are deducted *from* AGI.

EXAMPLE 2

Kendall, a CPA employed by Nadia, incurred unreimbursed transportation expenses of $1,000 in connection with his employment activities. Because Kendall is an employee, the transportation expenses are deductions *from* AGI (subject to a 2% floor discussed in Example 7). ◆

EXAMPLE 3

George, a CPA employed by Nadia, incurred entertainment expenses of $1,000 in connection with his employment activities. Nadia reimbursed George for these entertainment expenses under an accountable plan. The $1,000 of gross income is reduced by a $1,000 deduction *for* AGI. ◆

Because the treatment of expenses differs depending on employment status, as in the above examples, it is important to determine when an employer-employee relationship exists.

An employer-employee relationship exists when the employer has the right to specify the end result and the ways and means by which that result is to be attained. An employee is subject to the will and control of the employer with respect not only to what shall be done but also to how it shall be done. If the individual is subject to the direction or control of another only to the extent of the end result but not as to the means of accomplishment, an employer-employee relationship does not exist. An example is the preparation of a taxpayer's return by an independent CPA.

Certain factors may indicate an employer-employee relationship. They include (1) the right to discharge without legal liability the person performing the service, (2) the furnishing of tools or a place to work, and (3) payment based on time spent rather than the task performed. Each case is tested on its own merits, and the right to control the means and methods of accomplishment is the definitive test. Generally, physicians, lawyers, dentists, contractors, subcontractors, and others who offer services to the public are not classified as employees.

EXAMPLE 4

Denzel is a lawyer whose major client accounts for 60% of his billings. He does the routine legal work and income tax returns at the client's request. He is paid a monthly retainer in addition to amounts charged for extra work. Denzel is a self-employed individual. Even though he derives most of his income from one client, he still has the right to determine how the end result of his work is attained. ◆

EXAMPLE 5

Ellen is a lawyer hired by Denzel to assist him in the performance of services for the client mentioned in Example 4. Ellen is under Denzel's supervision; he reviews her work and pays her an hourly fee. Ellen is an employee of Denzel. ◆

EXAMPLE 6

Frank is a licensed practical nurse who works as a private duty nurse. He is under the supervision of the patient's doctor and is paid by the patient. Frank is not an employee of either the patient (who pays him) or the doctor (who supervises him). The ways and means of attaining the end result (care of the patient) are under his control. ◆

Real estate agents and direct sellers are classified as self-employed persons if two conditions are met. The first condition is that substantially all of their income for services must be directly related to sales or other output. The second condition is that their services must be performed under a written contract that specifies that they are not to be treated as employees for tax purposes.

A self-employed individual is required to file Schedule C of Form 1040, and all allowable expenses are deductions *for* AGI.

A special category of employees is also allowed to file Schedule C to report income and deduct expenses *for* AGI. These employees are called *statutory employees* because they are not common law employees under the rules explained above. The wages or commissions paid to statutory employees are subject to Social Security tax.

Deductions for or from AGI

The Code specifies that employee expenses reimbursed under an accountable plan are deductible *for* AGI. All unreimbursed employee expenses are deductions *from* AGI and can be deducted only if the employee-taxpayer itemizes deductions. Employment-related expenses of a qualified performing artist, which are deductible *for* AGI, are the one exception.

The distinction between deductions *for* and deductions *from* AGI is important. No benefit is received for an item that is deductible *from* AGI if a taxpayer's itemized deductions are less than the standard deduction. Refer to Chapter 5 for a detailed discussion of deductions *for* versus deductions *from* AGI.

Limitations on Itemized Deductions

Many itemized deductions, such as medical expenses and charitable contributions, are subject to limitations expressed as a percentage of AGI. These limitations may be expressed as floors or ceilings. For example, medical expenses are deductible only to the extent they exceed 7.5 percent of AGI. There is a 7.5 percent *floor.* Charitable contributions in excess of 50 percent of AGI are not deductible in the year of the contribution. There is a 50 percent ceiling on the deductibility of charitable contributions. These limitations are discussed more fully in Chapter 10.

Miscellaneous Itemized Deductions Subject to the 2 Percent Floor. Certain miscellaneous itemized deductions, including unreimbursed employee business expenses, must be aggregated and then reduced by 2 percent of AGI. Expenses subject to the 2 percent floor include the following:

- All § 212 expenses, except expenses related to the production of rent and royalty income (refer to Chapter 5).
- All unreimbursed employee expenses (after 20 percent reduction, if applicable).
- Professional dues and subscriptions.
- Union dues and work uniforms.
- Employment-related education expenses.
- Malpractice insurance premiums.
- Expenses of job hunting (including employment agency fees and resumé-writing expenses).
- Home office expenses of an employee or outside salesperson.
- Legal, accounting, and tax return preparation fees.
- Hobby expenses (up to hobby income).
- Investment expenses, including investment counsel fees, subscriptions, and safe deposit box rental.
- Custodial fees relating to income-producing property or an IRA or a Keogh plan.
- Any fees paid to collect interest or dividends.
- Appraisal fees establishing a casualty loss or charitable contribution.

Miscellaneous Itemized Deductions Not Subject to the 2 Percent Floor. Certain miscellaneous itemized deductions, including the following, are not subject to the 2 percent floor:

- Impairment-related work expenses of handicapped individuals.
- Federal estate tax on income in respect of a decedent.
- Certain adjustments when a taxpayer restores amounts held under a claim of right.
- Amortizable bond premium.
- Gambling losses (deductible only to the extent of gambling winnings).
- Deductions allowable in connection with personal property used in a short sale.
- Certain terminated annuity payments.
- Certain costs of cooperative housing corporations.

EXAMPLE 7

Ted, who has AGI of $20,000, has the following miscellaneous itemized deductions:

Gambling losses (to extent of gains)	$1,200
Tax return preparation fees	300
Unreimbursed employee transportation	200
Professional dues and subscriptions	260
Safe deposit box rental	30

Ted's itemized deductions are as follows:

Deduction not subject to 2% floor (gambling losses)		$1,200
Deductions subject to 2% floor ($300 + $200 + $260 + $30)	$790	
Less 2% of AGI	(400)	390
Total miscellaneous itemized deductions		$1,590

If Ted's AGI were $40,000, the floor would be $800 (2% of $40,000), and he could not deduct any expenses subject to the 2% floor. ◆

Percentage Reduction for Meals and Entertainment Expenses

Deductions for meals and entertainment (including entertainment facilities) are limited to 80 percent of allowable expenditures. The allowable expenditures are limited to reasonable amounts. "Lavish or extravagant" expenses are excluded before application of the 80 percent rule.

EXAMPLE 8

Rebecca spends $100 for deductible business entertainment. She is not reimbursed by her employer. Only $80 is allowed as a deduction. This $80 is combined with other miscellaneous itemized deductions subject to the 2% floor, and the total is reduced by 2% of AGI. ◆

EXAMPLE 9

Maria, who is self-employed, purchased two tickets to an entertainment event from a scalper and used the tickets to entertain a client. She paid $220 and the face value of the tickets was $100. Since $120 of the $220 is lavish or extravagant, Maria's deduction cannot exceed $80 (80% of $100). ◆

The 80 percent limit applies to the following items:

- Any expense for food or beverages.
- Any expense that constitutes entertainment, amusement, or recreation (or expense related to a facility used in connection with these activities).

Transportation expenses are not affected by this provision—only meals and entertainment. The 80 percent rule applies to taxes and tips relating to meals and entertainment. Cover charges, parking fees at an entertainment location, and room rental fees for a meal or cocktail party are also subject to the 80 percent rule.

EXAMPLE 10

Tandy pays a $20 cab fare to meet his client for dinner at The Ritz. The meal costs $90, and Tandy leaves a $15 tip. His deduction is $104 [($90 + $15) 80% + $20 cabfare]. ◆

The 80 percent rule is applied before application of the 2 percent floor previously discussed.

EXAMPLE 11

Lars incurs unreimbursed meal and entertainment expenses of $1,000 in the course of his job as a salesman. His AGI is $20,000, and he has no other expenses subject to the 2% floor. If Lars itemizes, his deduction is limited to $400, as follows:

Expenses (80% of $1,000)	$800
Less 2% of AGI	(400)
Deductible	$400

◆

It does not matter where or how meal and entertainment expenses are incurred. Only 80 percent of meals incurred in the course of travel away from home, in connection with moving expenses, or in connection with education expenses are deductible. The cost of meals furnished by an employer to employees on the employer's premises may be subject to the 80 percent rule in computing the employer's deduction.

Exceptions for Luxury Water Travel. If meals and entertainment incurred in the course of luxury water travel are not separately stated, the 80 percent rule does not apply. If meals and entertainment are separately stated or are clearly identifiable, the 80 percent rule is applied before the limitation on luxury water travel expenses (discussed later in the chapter).

Exceptions to the 80 Percent Rule. There are several exceptions to the 80 percent rule. Exceptions one and two apply where the full value of meals or entertainment is included in the compensation of employees or the income of independent contractors.

EXAMPLE 12

Margaret won an all-expense-paid pleasure trip to Europe for selling the most insurance in her company during the year. Xena, Margaret's employer, included the fair market value of the trip on Margaret's W–2 (Wage and Tax Statement). Xena need not allocate any of the cost to meals or entertainment. Xena deducts the entire amount. ◆

The third exception applies to meals and entertainment in a subsidized eating facility or where the *de minimis* fringe benefit rule is met (refer to Chapter 4).

EXAMPLE 13

General Hospital has an employee cafeteria on the premises for doctors, nurses, and other employees. Such employees need to be available during meal breaks for emergencies. The cafeteria operates at breakeven. The 80% rule does not apply. ◆

EXAMPLE 14

Brown Company gives a ham, a fruitcake, and a bottle of wine to each employee at year-end. Brown's costs for these items are not subject to the percentage reduction rule. The *de minimis* fringe benefit exclusion applies to business gifts of packaged foods and beverages. ◆

Exception four applies to fully reimbursed employee business meals and entertainment expenses. The 80 percent rule applies to the taxpayer making the reimbursement.

EXAMPLE 15

Ted is a salesman who paid for lunch with a customer. He made an adequate accounting to his employer, Yolanda, who reimbursed him. Ted omits both the reimbursement and the expense on his return. Yolanda (the employer) can deduct only 80% of the expenditure on her return. ◆

Exception five relates to traditional employer-paid recreation expenses for employees.

EXAMPLE 16

Black Company provides a yearly Christmas party and an annual spring picnic for its employees and their families. Black's reasonable costs for these events are fully deductible. ◆

The remaining exceptions are of limited applicability.

EMPLOYEE BUSINESS EXPENSES

The tax treatment of employee business expenses depends on whether the expenses are reimbursed or unreimbursed and whether the reimbursement is done under an accountable or a nonaccountable plan.

Accountable Plans

In General. An accountable plan requires the employee to satisfy both of the following requirements:

- Adequately account for (substantiate) the expenses. An employee renders an *adequate accounting* by submitting a record, with receipts and other substantiation, to the employer or by meeting the *deemed substantiation* rules discussed below.
- Return any excess reimbursement or allowance. An "excess reimbursement or allowance" is any amount that the employee does not adequately account for as an ordinary and necessary business expense.

Substantiation. The law provides that no deduction will be allowed for any travel, entertainment, business gift, or listed property (automobiles, computers) expenditure unless properly substantiated by adequate records. The records should contain the following information:

- The amount of the expense.
- The time and place of travel or entertainment (or date of gift).
- The business purpose of the expense.
- The business relationship of the taxpayer to the person entertained (or receiving the gift).

This means that taxpayers must maintain an account book or diary in which the above information is recorded at the time of the expenditure. Documentary evidence, such as itemized receipts, is required to support any expenditure for lodging while traveling away from home and for any other expenditure of $25 or more. If a taxpayer fails to keep adequate records, each expense must be established by a written or oral statement of the exact details of the expense and by other corroborating evidence.

EXAMPLE 17

Bertha has travel expenses substantiated only by canceled checks. The checks establish the date, place, and amount of the expenditure. Because neither the business relationship nor the business purpose is established, the deduction will be disallowed. ◆

EXAMPLE 18

Dwight has travel and entertainment expenses substantiated by a diary showing the time, place, and amount of the expenditure. His oral testimony provides the business relationship and business purpose; however, since he has no receipts, any expenditures of $25 or more will be disallowed. ◆

Deemed Substantiation. In lieu of reimbursing actual expenses for travel away from home, many employers reduce their paperwork by adopting a policy of reimbursing employees with a *per diem* allowance, a flat dollar amount per day of business travel. Of the substantiation requirements listed above, the *amount* of the expense is proved, or *deemed substantiated*, by using such a per diem allowance or reimbursement procedure. The amount of expenses that is deemed substantiated is equal to the lesser of the per diem allowance or the amount of the Federal per diem rate.

The regular Federal per diem rate for these purposes is the highest amount that the Federal government will pay to its employees for lodging and meals while in travel status away from home in a particular area. The rates are different for different locations.

To avoid the need to keep a current list of the per diem rate in effect for each city or locale, a simplified method called the high-low method can be used. This method specifies a limited number of high travel cost locations where the per diem is considered to be the same for all cities on the list. All other cities are considered to have the same, but lower, Federal per diem rate in effect.

The use of the standard Federal per diem for meals constitutes an adequate accounting. Employees and self-employed persons can use the standard meal allowance instead of deducting the actual cost of daily meals, even if not reimbursed. There is no standard lodging allowance, however. An employee who receives a reimbursement of not more than the standard mileage rate allowed for tax purposes will be treated as rendering an adequate accounting.

Only the amount of the expense is considered substantiated under the deemed substantiated method. The other substantiation requirements must be satisfied: place, date, and business purpose of the expense and the business relationship of the parties involved. Employees who are related to their employers under § 267(b) cannot use the per diem allowance or standard meal allowance as an adequate accounting. They must use the actual expense method. An employee who owns more than 10 percent of the employer corporation's stock is considered related to the corporation.

Nonaccountable Plans

A nonaccountable plan is one that does not require an adequate accounting or return of excess amounts. All reimbursements of expenses are reported in full as wages on the employee's Form W–2. Any allowable expenses are deductible in the same manner as unreimbursed expenses.

Unreimbursed Employee Expenses. Unreimbursed employee expenses are treated in a straightforward manner. Meals and entertainment expenses are subject to the 80 percent limit. Total unreimbursed employee business expenses are reported as miscellaneous itemized deductions subject to the 2 percent-of-AGI floor. If the employee could have received, but did not seek, reimbursement for whatever reason, none of the employment-related expenses are deductible.

Failure to Comply with Accountable Plan Requirements. An employer may have an accountable plan and require employees to return excess reimbursements or allowances, but an employee may fail to follow the rules of the plan. In that case, the expenses and reimbursements are subject to nonaccountable plan treatment.

Reporting Procedures

The reporting requirements range from no reporting at all (accountable plans when all requirements are met) to the use of some or all of three forms, Form W–2 (Wage and Tax Statement), Form 2106 (Employee Expenses), and Schedule A (Itemized Deductions), for nonaccountable plans and unreimbursed employee expenses. These reporting procedures are set out in Concept Summary 9–1.

Reimbursed employee expenses that are adequately accounted for under an accountable plan are deductible *for* AGI on Form 2106. Allowed excess expenses, expenses reimbursed under a nonaccountable plan, and unreimbursed expenses are deductible *from* AGI on Schedule A, subject to the 2 percent-of-AGI floor.

When a reimbursement under an accountable plan is paid in separate amounts relating to designated expenses such as meals or entertainment, no problem arises. The reimbursements and expenses are reported as such on the appropriate forms. If the reimbursement is made in a single amount, an allocation must be made to determine the appropriate portion of the reimbursement that applies to meals and entertainment and to other employee expenses.

EXAMPLE 19

Elizabeth, who is employed by Green Company, had AGI of $40,000. During the year, she incurred $2,000 of transportation and lodging expense and $1,000 of meals and entertainment expense, all fully substantiated. Elizabeth received $2,100 reimbursement under an accountable plan. The reimbursement rate that applies to meals and entertainment is 33.33% ($1,000 meals and entertainment expense/$3,000 total expenses). Thus, $700 ($2,100 × 33.33%) of the reimbursement applies to meals and entertainment, and $1,400 ($2,100 – $700) applies to transportation and lodging. Elizabeth's itemized deduction will consist of the $600 ($2,000 total – $1,400 reimbursement) of unreimbursed transportation and lodging expenses and $300 ($1,000 – $700) of unreimbursed meal and entertainment expenses as follows:

Transportation and lodging	$ 600
Meals and entertainment ($300 × 80%)	240
Total (reported on Form 2106)	$ 840
Less: 2% of $40,000 AGI	(800)
Deduction (reported on Schedule A)	$ 40

In summary, Elizabeth must report $3,000 of expenses and the $2,100 reimbursement on Form 2106 and $40 as a miscellaneous itemized deduction on Schedule A. ◆

The reporting procedures for self-employed persons, statutory employees, performing artists, and handicapped individuals with impairment-related work expenses were discussed previously in the chapter.

TRANSPORTATION EXPENSES

Qualified Expenditures

An employee may deduct unreimbursed employment-related transportation expenses as miscellaneous itemized deductions *from* AGI, subject to the 2 percent floor. Transportation expense includes only the cost of transporting the employee from one place to another when the employee is not away from home *in travel status.* Such costs include taxi fares, automobile expenses, tolls, and parking.

Commuting between home and one's place of employment is a personal, nondeductible expense. The fact that one employee drives 30 miles to work and another employee walks six blocks is of no significance.[1]

CONCEPT SUMMARY 9–1 REPORTING EMPLOYEE TRAVEL, TRANSPORTATION, AND MEAL AND ENTERTAINMENT EXPENSES AND REIMBURSEMENTS[1]

Type of Reimbursement or Other Expense Allowance Arrangement	Employer Reports on Form W–2	Employee Reports on Form 2106	Employee Claims on Schedule A
Accountable			
Adequate accounting and excess returned.	No	No	No
Per diem or mileage allowance (up to government rate). Adequate accounting and excess returned.	No	All expenses and reimbursements only if excess expenses are claimed.[4] Otherwise, form is not filed.	Expenses the employee can prove and that exceed the reimbursements received.[4]
Per diem or mileage allowance (exceeds government rate). Adequate accounting up to the government rate only and excess not returned.	Excess reported as income.[2] Amount up to the government rate is reported as fringe benefit.[3]	All expenses, and reimbursements equal to the government rate only if expenses in excess of the government rate are claimed.[4] Otherwise, form is not filed.	Expenses the employee can prove and that exceed the government rate.[4]
Nonaccountable			
Adequate accounting or return of excess either not required or required but not met.	Entire amount is reported as wages.[2]	All expenses.[4,5]	Expenses the employee can prove.[4,5]
No reimbursement.	Normal reporting of wages, etc.	All expenses.[4,5]	Expenses the employee can prove.[4,5]

1. Adapted from IRS chart on page 65 of *Tax Guide for Small Business,* (Publication 334, 1992).
2. Subject to income tax withholding and all employment taxes.
3. Not subject to withholding.
4. Any allowable expense is carried to line 19 of Schedule A and deducted as a miscellaneous itemized deduction, subject to the 2%-of-AGI limitation.
5. Meals and entertainment are subject to the 80% limitation.

---

1. *Tauferner v. U.S.,* 69–1 USTC ¶9241, 23 AFTR2d 69–1025, 407 F.2d 243 (CA–10, 1969).

EXAMPLE 20

Geraldo is employed by Sparrow Corporation. He drives 22 miles each way to work. One day Geraldo drove to a customer's office from his place of work. The drive was a 14-mile round trip to the customer's office. Geraldo can take a deduction for 14 miles of business transportation. The remaining 44 miles are a nondeductible commuting expense. ◆

Exceptions to Disallowance of Commuting Expenses. The general rule that disallows a deduction for commuting expenses has several exceptions. An employee who uses an automobile to transport heavy tools to work and who otherwise would not drive to work will be allowed a deduction, but only for the additional costs incurred to transport the work implements. Additional costs are those exceeding the cost of commuting by the same mode of transportation without the tools. For example, the rental of a trailer for transporting tools is deductible, but the expenses of operating the automobile are not deductible.[2] The Supreme Court has held that a deduction is permitted only when the taxpayer can show that the automobile would not have been used without the necessity to transport the tools or equipment.[3]

Another exception is provided for an employee who has a second job. The expenses of getting from one job to another are deductible. If the employee goes home between jobs, the deduction is based on the distance between jobs.

EXAMPLE 21

In the current year, Cynthia holds two jobs, a full-time job with Blue Corporation and a part-time job with Wren Corporation. During the 250 days that she works (adjusted for weekends, vacation, and holidays), Cynthia customarily leaves home at 7:30 A.M. and drives 30 miles to the Blue Corporation plant, where she works until 5:00 P.M. After dinner at a nearby cafe, Cynthia drives 20 miles to Wren Corporation and works from 7:00 to 11:00 P.M. The distance from the second job to Cynthia's home is 40 miles. Her deduction is based on 20 miles (the distance between jobs). ◆

It is sometimes difficult to distinguish between a nondeductible commuting expense and a deductible transportation expense necessary to the taxpayer's business. If the taxpayer is required to incur a transportation expense to travel between work stations, that expense is deductible.

EXAMPLE 22

Thomas, a general contractor, drove from his home to his office, then drove to three building sites to perform his required inspections, and finally drove home. The costs of driving to his office and driving home from the last inspection site are nondeductible commuting expenses. The other transportation costs are deductible. ◆

However, the commuting costs from home to the first work station and from the last work station to home are not deductible.

EXAMPLE 23

Vivian works for a firm in downtown Denver and commutes to work. She occasionally works in a customer's office. On one such occasion, Vivian drove directly to the customer's office, a round-trip distance from her home of 40 miles. She did not go into her office, which is a 52-mile round-trip. Her mileage is deductible. ◆

2. Rev.Rul. 75–380, 1975–2 C.B. 59.

3. *Fausner v. Comm.*, 73–2 USTC ¶9515, 32 AFTR2d 73–5202, 93 S.Ct. 2820 (USSC, 1973).

Also deductible is the reasonable travel cost between the general working area and a temporary work station outside that area. What constitutes the general working area depends on the facts and circumstances of each situation. Furthermore, if an employee customarily works on several temporary assignments in a localized area, that localized area becomes the regular place of employment. Transportation from home to these locations becomes a personal, nondeductible commuting expense.

EXAMPLE 24

Sven, a building inspector in Minneapolis, regularly inspects buildings for building code violations for his employer, a general contractor. During one busy season, the St. Paul inspector became ill, and Sven was required to inspect several buildings in St. Paul. The transportation expenses for the trips to St. Paul are deductible. ◆

Computation of Automobile Expenses

A taxpayer has two choices in computing automobile expenses. The actual operating cost, which includes depreciation, gas, oil, repairs, licenses, and insurance, may be used. Records must be kept that detail the automobile's personal and business use. Only the percentage allocable to business transportation and travel is allowed as a deduction. Complex rules for the computation of depreciation (discussed in Chapter 8) apply if the actual expense method is used.

Use of the automatic mileage method is the second alternative. For 1992 and 1993, the deduction is based on 28 cents per mile for all business miles.[4] Parking fees and tolls are allowed in addition to expenses computed using the automatic mileage method.

Generally, a taxpayer may elect either method for any particular year. However, the following restrictions apply:

- The vehicle must be owned by the taxpayer.
- If two or more vehicles are in use (for business purposes) at the *same* time (not alternately), a taxpayer may not use the automatic mileage method.
- A basis adjustment is required if the taxpayer changes from the automatic mileage method to the actual operating cost method. Depreciation is considered allowed for the first 15,000 business miles in accordance with the following schedule for the most recent five years:

Year	Rate per Mile
1993	11.5 cents
1992	11.5 cents
1991	11 cents
1990	11 cents
1989	11 cents

EXAMPLE 25

Tim purchased his automobile in 1990 for $9,000. It is used 90% for business purposes. Tim drove the automobile for 10,000 business miles in 1992; 8,500 miles in 1991; and 6,000 miles in 1990. At the beginning of 1993, the basis of the business portion is $5,355.

4. Rev.Proc. 92–104, I.R.B. No. 52, 24.

Cost ($9,000 × 90%)	$8,100
Less depreciation:	
1992 (10,000 miles × 11.5 cents)	(1,150)
1991 (8,500 miles × 11 cents)	(935)
1990 (6,000 × 11 cents)	(660)
Adjusted business basis 1/1/93	$5,355

- Use of the standard mileage rate in the first year the auto is placed in service is considered an election to exclude the auto from the ACRS method of depreciation (discussed in Chapter 8).
- A taxpayer may not switch to the automatic mileage method if the ACRS statutory percentage method or expensing under § 179 has been used.

Travel Expenses

Definition of Travel Expenses

An itemized deduction is allowed for unreimbursed travel expenses related to a taxpayer's employment, subject to the 2 percent floor. Travel expenses are more broadly defined in the Code than are transportation expenses. Travel expenses include transportation expenses and meals and lodging while away from home in the pursuit of a trade or business. Meals cannot be lavish or extravagant under the circumstances. Transportation expenses are deductible even though the taxpayer is not away from home. A deduction for travel expenses is available only if the taxpayer is away from his or her tax home. Travel expenses also include reasonable laundry and incidental expenses. To the extent that travel expenses are reimbursed, they are reported in the same manner discussed previously for employee expenses. The unreimbursed part is a miscellaneous itemized deduction subject to the 2 percent floor. Unreimbursed meals and entertainment expenses are subject to the 80 percent rule.

Away-from-Home Requirement

The crucial test for the deductibility of travel expenses is whether the employee is away from home overnight. "Overnight" need not be a 24-hour period, but it must be a period substantially longer than an ordinary day's work and must require rest, sleep, or a relief-from-work period.[5] A one-day or intracity business trip is not travel, and meals and lodging for such a trip are not deductible.

The employee must be away from home for a temporary period. If the taxpayer-employee is reassigned to a new post for an indefinite period of time, that new post becomes his or her tax home. *Temporary* indicates that the assignment's termination is expected within a reasonably short period of time. The position of the IRS is that the tax home is the business location, post, or station of the taxpayer. Thus, travel expenses are not deductible if a taxpayer is reassigned for an indefinite period and does not move his or her place of residence to the new location.

5. *U.S. v. Correll*, 68–1 USTC ¶9101, 20 AFTR2d 5845, 88 S.Ct. 445 (USSC, 1967); Rev.Rul. 75–168, 1975–1 C.B. 58.

EXAMPLE 26

Malcolm's employer opened a branch office in San Diego. Malcolm was assigned to the new office for three months to train a new manager and to assist in setting up the new office. He tried commuting from his home in Los Angeles for a week and decided that he could not continue driving several hours a day. He rented an apartment in San Diego, where he lived during the week. He spent weekends with his wife and children at their home in Los Angeles. Malcolm's rent, meals, laundry, incidentals, and automobile expenses in San Diego are deductible. To the extent that Malcolm's transportation expense related to his weekend trips home exceeds what his cost of meals and lodging would have been, the excess is personal and nondeductible. ◆

EXAMPLE 27

Assume that Malcolm in Example 26 was transferred to the new location to become the new manager permanently. His wife and children continued to live in Los Angeles until the end of the school year. Malcolm is no longer "away from home" because the assignment is not temporary. His travel expenses are not deductible. ◆

Determining the Tax Home. Under ordinary circumstances, there is no problem in determining the location of a taxpayer's tax home and whether or not the taxpayer is on a temporary work assignment away from that tax home. The tax home is the area in which the taxpayer derives his or her principal source of income or is based on the amount of time spent in each area when the taxpayer has more than one place of employment. Under other circumstances, however, this is a controversial problem that has found the IRS and various courts in conflict.[6] An example is the situation in which a construction worker cannot find work in the immediate area and takes work several hundred miles away, with the duration of that work uncertain.

An absence of more than one year from one's tax home automatically causes a change in the tax home.[7]

The following objective factors are to be used in determining whether the home that the taxpayer claims to be away from is the taxpayer's actual tax home:

- Whether the taxpayer has used the claimed home for lodging purposes while performing work in the vicinity immediately before the current job.
- Whether the taxpayer continues to maintain bona fide work contacts (such as job seeking, leave of absence, ongoing business) in the area during the alleged temporary employment.
- Whether the taxpayer's living expenses at the claimed home are duplicated because work requires the taxpayer to be away from home.
- Whether the taxpayer has a family member or members (marital or lineal only) currently residing at the claimed home or currently continues to use the claimed home frequently for the purposes of his or her own lodging.

Travel expenses are allowed if the taxpayer clearly demonstrates a realistic expectation as to the temporary nature of the job and satisfies all four of the above requirements. If the taxpayer clearly demonstrates the expectation that the job is of a temporary nature and satisfies two of the above requirements, the deductibility question will be decided on the basis of all the facts and circumstances of the case. If it is determined that the assignment is indefinite rather than temporary, no deduction will be allowed for the traveling expenses.

6. Rev.Rul. 73–529, 1973–2 C.B. 37.
7. Section 162(a) as amended by the Comprehensive National Energy Policy Act of 1992. The restriction applies to costs paid or incurred after December 31, 1992.

If an employee establishes a new home as the result of a work assignment or has no established tax home, living expenses are of a personal nature and are nondeductible.

Example 28

Howard is employed as a long-haul truck driver. He stores his clothes and other belongings at his parents' home and stops there for periodic visits. The rest of the time, Howard is on the road, sleeping in his truck and in motels. His meals, lodging, laundry, and incidental expenses are not deductible because he has no tax home from which he can be absent.[8] ◆

Disallowed and Limited Travel Expenses

The possibility always exists that taxpayers will attempt to treat vacation or pleasure travel as deductible business travel. To prevent such practices, the law contains limitations for certain travel expenses.

Nonbusiness Conventions. One tactic taxpayers used in an attempt to deduct the cost of vacations was to attend a tax or financial seminar at a vacation resort. They then took the travel expenses as a deduction under § 212, which allows deductions related to the production of income or determination of taxes.

As a remedy, the law disallows all deductions related to attending a convention, seminar, or similar meeting unless the expenses are related to a trade or business of the taxpayer. The restriction does not apply to trade or business conventions and seminars. For example, a CPA who is an employee of an accounting firm can deduct the expenses of attending a tax seminar. A stockbroker can deduct the cost of attending a convention concerning investments. A physician attending either the tax or the investment meeting can deduct nothing. If the lectures are videotaped, both the CPA and the stockbroker must attend convention sessions to view the videotaped materials along with other participants. This requirement does not disallow deductions for costs (other than travel, meals, and entertainment) of renting or using videotaped materials related to business.

Example 29

A CPA is unable to attend a convention at which current developments in taxation are discussed. She pays $200 for videotapes of the lectures and views them at home later. The $200 is a miscellaneous itemized deduction (subject to the 2% floor) if the CPA is an employee. If she is self-employed, the $200 is a deduction *for* AGI. ◆

Luxury Water Travel. Limits are placed on the deductibility of travel by water. The deduction is limited to twice the highest amount generally allowable for a day of travel for Federal employees serving in the United States.

Example 30

During the taxable year, the highest Federal per diem rate is $154. Martin took a six-day trip from New York to London on the *Queen Mary II* to meet with customers. The maximum deduction related to the water travel is $1,848 [($154 × 2) × 6 days]. ◆

If the expenses of luxury water travel include separately stated amounts for meals or entertainment, those amounts must be reduced by 20 percent before the application of this per diem limitation. If the meals and entertainment are not separately stated (or otherwise clearly identifiable), the 20 percent reduction does not apply.

8. *Moses Mitnick,* 13 T.C. 1 (1949).

The per diem rule does not apply to any expense allocable to a convention, seminar, or other meeting held on a cruise ship. The deduction for such a meeting is limited to $2,000 per individual per year. This deduction is restricted to ships registered in the United States and sailing to ports of call located within the United States or its possessions (e.g., Puerto Rico). Thus, a cruise on a ship of U.S. registry sailing to Bermuda does not qualify. A cruise on the same ship from Florida to Puerto Rico will qualify.

Educational Travel. No deduction is allowed for travel that by itself is deemed by the taxpayer to be educational. This does not apply to a deduction claimed for travel that is necessary to engage in an activity that gives rise to a business deduction relating to education.

EXAMPLE 31

Greta, a German teacher, travels to Germany to maintain general familiarity with the language and culture. No travel expense deduction is allowed. ◆

EXAMPLE 32

Jean-Claude, a scholar of French literature, travels to Paris to do specific library research that cannot be done elsewhere and to take courses that are offered only at the Sorbonne. The travel costs are deductible, assuming that the other requirements for deducting education expenses (discussed later in the chapter) are met. ◆

Combined Business and Pleasure Travel

To be deductible, travel expenses need not be incurred in the performance of specific job functions. An employee may deduct travel expenses incurred in attending a professional convention if attendance is connected with his or her services as an employee. For example, an employee of a law firm can deduct travel expenses incurred in attending a meeting of the American Bar Association.

Travel deductions have been used in the past by persons to claim a tax deduction for what was essentially a personal vacation. As a result, several provisions have been enacted to govern deductions associated with combined business and pleasure trips. If the business/pleasure trip is from one point in the United States to another point in the United States, the transportation expenses are deductible only if the trip is *primarily for business*. If the trip is primarily for pleasure, no transportation expenses can be taken as a deduction. Meals, lodging, and other expenses must be allocated between business and personal days.

EXAMPLE 33

Hana traveled from Seattle to New York primarily for business. She spent five days conducting business and three days sightseeing and attending shows. Her plane and taxi fare amounted to $560. Her meals amounted to $100 per day, and lodging and incidental expenses were $150 per day. She can deduct the transportation charges of $560 since the trip was primarily for business (five days of business versus three days of sightseeing). Meals are limited to $400 [5 days × ($100 × 80%)], and other expenses are limited to $750 (5 days × $150). All the travel expenses are miscellaneous itemized deductions subject to the 2% floor. ◆

EXAMPLE 34

Assume Hana goes to New York for a two-week vacation. While there, she spends several hours renewing acquaintances with people in her company's New York office. Her transportation expenses are not deductible. ◆

The incremental costs paid for travel of a taxpayer's relative cannot be deducted unless that person's presence has a bona fide business purpose.

Incidental services performed by family members do not constitute a bona fide business purpose.

When the trip is *outside the United States,* special rules apply. Transportation expenses must be allocated between business and personal expenses unless (1) the taxpayer is away from home for seven days or less or (2) less than 25 percent of the time was for personal purposes. No allocation is required if the taxpayer has no substantial control over arrangements for the trip or the desire for a vacation is not a major factor in taking the trip. If the trip is primarily for pleasure, no transportation charges are deductible. Days devoted to travel are considered business days. Weekends, legal holidays, and intervening days are considered business days, provided that both preceding and succeeding days were business days.

Example 35

Robert took a trip from New York to Japan primarily for business purposes. He was away from home from June 10 through June 19. He spent three days vacationing and seven days conducting business (including two travel days). His air fare was $2,500, his meals amounted to $100 per day, and lodging and incidental expenses were $160 per day. Since Robert was away from home for more than seven days and more than 25% of his time was devoted to personal purposes, only 70% (7 days business/10 days total) of the transportation is deductible. His deductions are as follows:

Transportation (70% × $2,500)		$1,750
Lodging ($160 × 7)		1,120
Meals ($100 × 7)	$700	
Less: 20%	(140)	560
Total		$3,430

◆

Example 36

Shelly, a fashion buyer for a large department store, travels to London primarily to view the spring collections. She is gone 10 days (including 2 days of travel). She spends 8 days (including travel time) engaged in business and 2 days sightseeing. Since less than 25% of the total time is spent vacationing, all her transportation expenses and all but 2 days of meals and lodging are deductible. ◆

Foreign Convention Expenses

Certain restrictions are imposed on the deductibility of expenses paid or incurred to attend conventions located outside the North American area. For this purpose, the North American area includes the United States, its possessions (including the Trust Territory of the Pacific Islands), Canada, and Mexico. The expenses will be disallowed unless it is established that the meeting is directly related to a trade or business of the taxpayer. Disallowance will also occur unless the taxpayer shows that it is as reasonable for the meeting to be held in a foreign location as within the North American area.

The foreign convention rules will not operate to bar a deduction to an employer if the expense is compensatory in nature. For example, a trip to Paris won by a top salesperson is included in the gross income of the employee and is fully deductible by the employer.

Moving Expenses

Moving expenses are deductible for moves in connection with the commencement of work (either as an employee or as a self-employed individual) at a new principal place of work. Both employees and self-employed individuals can deduct these expenses. Reimbursement from employers must be included in gross income. Moving expenses are itemized deductions but are *not* subject to the 2 percent floor. Meals included as moving expenses *are* subject to the 80 percent rule. To be eligible for a moving expense deduction, a taxpayer must meet two basic tests: distance and time.

Distance Test

The distance test requires the taxpayer's new job location to be at least 35 miles farther from the taxpayer's old residence than the old residence was from the former place of employment. In this regard, the location of the new residence is not relevant. This eliminates a moving deduction for taxpayers who purchase a new home in the same general area without changing their place of employment. Those who accept a new job in the same general area as the old job location are also eliminated.

EXAMPLE 37

Harry is permanently transferred to a new job location. The distance from Harry's former home to his new job (80 miles) exceeds the distance from his former home to his old job (30 miles) by at least 35 miles. Harry has met the distance requirements for a moving expense deduction. (See the following diagram.)

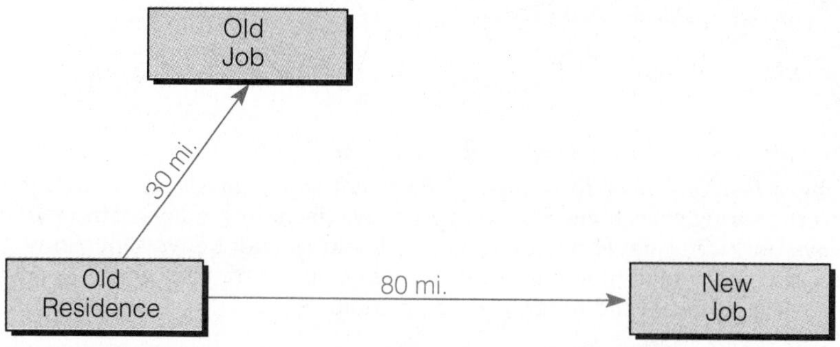

If Harry was not employed before the move, his new job must be at least 35 miles from his former residence. In this instance, the distance requirements would be met if Harry had not been previously employed. ◆

Time Requirements

To meet the time requirement, an employee must be employed on a full-time basis at the new location for 39 weeks in the 12-month period following the move. If the taxpayer is a self-employed individual, he or she must work in the new location for 78 weeks during the next two years. The first 39 weeks must be in the first 12 months. The taxpayer can work either as a self-employed individual or as an employee. The time requirement is suspended if the taxpayer dies, becomes disabled, or is discharged or transferred by the new employer through no fault of the employee.

A taxpayer might not be able to meet the 39-week requirement by the due date of the tax return for the year of the move. For this reason, two alternatives are allowed. The taxpayer can take the deduction in the year the expenses were incurred, even though the 39-week test has not been met. If the taxpayer later fails to meet the test, the income of the following year must be increased by an amount equal to the deduction previously claimed for moving expenses, or an amended return must be filed for the year of the move. The second alternative is to wait until the test is met and then file an amended tax return for the year of the move.

When Deductible

The general rule is that expenses of a cash basis taxpayer are deductible only in the year of payment. However, a taxpayer who receives reimbursement from his or her employer may elect to deduct the moving expenses in the year of reimbursement in the following circumstances:

- The moving expenses are incurred and paid in 1993, and the reimbursement is received in 1994.
- The moving expenses are incurred in 1993 and are paid by the employee in 1994 (on or before the due date including extensions for filing the 1993 return), and the reimbursement from the employer is received in 1993.

The election to deduct moving expenses in the year of reimbursement is made by claiming the deduction on the return or filing an amended return for that year.

The moving expense deduction is allowed regardless of whether the employee is transferred by the existing employer or is employed by a new employer. It is allowed if the employee moves to a new area and obtains employment or switches from self-employed status to employee status (and vice versa). The moving expense deduction is also allowed if an individual is unemployed before obtaining employment in a new area.

Classification of Moving Expenses

There are five classes of moving expenses, and different limitations and qualifications apply to each class. Direct moving expenses include the following:

1. *The expense of moving household and personal belongings.* This class includes fees paid to a moving company for packing, storing, and moving possessions and the rental of a truck if the taxpayer moves his or her own belongings. Also included is the cost of moving household pets. Reasonableness is the only limit on these direct expenses. Such expenses as refitting rugs or draperies and losses on the disposal of club memberships are not deductible as moving expenses.
2. *Travel to the new residence.* This includes the cost of transportation, meals, and lodging of the taxpayer and the members of the taxpayer's household en route. It does not include the cost of moving servants or others who are not members of the household. The taxpayer can elect to deduct actual auto expenses (no depreciation is allowed) or the automatic mileage method. In this case, moving expense mileage is limited to nine cents per mile for each car. These expenses are also limited by the reasonableness standard. For example, if one moves from Texas to Florida via Maine and takes six weeks to do so, the transportation, meals, and lodging must be allocated between personal and moving expenses.

Indirect moving expenses include the following:

3. *House-hunting trips.* Expenses of traveling (including meals and lodging) to the new place of employment to look for a home are deductible only if the

job has been secured in advance of the house-hunting trip. The dollar limitation is explained below.

4. *Temporary living expenses.* Meals and lodging expenses incurred while living in temporary quarters in the general area of the new job while waiting to move into a new residence are deductible. (The dollar limits are discussed below.) These living expenses are limited to any consecutive 30-day period beginning after employment is secured.
5. *Certain residential buying and selling expenses.* Buying and selling expenses include those that would normally be offset against the selling price of a home and those incurred in buying a new home. Examples are commissions, escrow fees, legal expenses, points paid to secure a mortgage, transfer taxes, and advertising. Also deductible are costs involved in settling an old lease or acquiring a new lease or both. Fixing-up expenses, damage deposits, prepaid rent, and the like are not deductible.

Indirect moving expenses are limited to a total of $3,000. Furthermore, house-hunting and temporary living expenses may not exceed $1,500 in the aggregate. Direct moving expenses, as discussed previously, are unlimited.

Moving Expense Limits

Classes 1[9] + 2	=	No limit
Classes 3 + 4	=	$1,500 limit
Classes 3 + 4 + 5	=	$3,000 limit

Generally, the above dollar limitations apply regardless of filing status. If both spouses change jobs and file separate returns, the limitations are $750 (instead of $1,500) and $1,500 (instead of $3,000). If only one spouse makes a job change, the spouse who makes the change is allowed the full amount. If both change jobs, do not live together, and work at job sites at least 35 miles apart, each spouse applies the $1,500 and the $3,000 limits. It does not matter whether they file jointly or separately.

EXAMPLE 38

James, an employee of Tanager Corporation, is hired by Robin Corporation at a substantial increase in salary. James is hired in February 1993 and is to report for work in March 1993. The new job requires a move from Los Angeles to New York City. In connection with the move, James incurs the following expenses:

February 1993 house-hunting trip (no meals)	$ 650
Temporary living expenses in New York City incurred by James and family from March 10 to 30, 1993, while awaiting the renovation of their new apartment (including $400 of meals)	1,000
Penalty for breaking lease on Los Angeles apartment	2,400
Charge for packing and moving household goods	4,200
Transportation and lodging expenses during move (March 5–10)	700
Meal expense during move	300

9. The numbers refer to the types of moving expenses outlined previously.

James can deduct the following amount:

Moving household goods			$4,200
Transportation and lodging			700
Meals ($300 × 80%)			240
House-hunting trip	$ 650		
Temporary living expenses [$600 + ($400 cost of meals × 80%)]	920		
	$1,570		
Limited to		$1,500	
Lease penalty		2,400	
		$3,900	
Limited to			3,000
Total itemized moving expense deduction			$8,140

Form 3903 is used to report the detailed calculations of the ceiling limitations and change in job locations. If the employee is reimbursed for the move, the reimbursement is included in salary income.

EDUCATION EXPENSES

General Requirements

An employee may deduct expenses incurred for education as ordinary and necessary business expenses provided the expenses were incurred for either of two reasons:

- To maintain or improve existing skills required in the present job.
- To meet the express requirements of the employer or the requirements imposed by law to retain his or her employment status.

Education expenses are not deductible if the education is for either of the following purposes:

- To meet the minimum educational standards for qualification in the taxpayer's existing job.
- To qualify the taxpayer for a new trade or business.

Fees incurred for professional qualification exams (the bar exam, for example) and fees for review courses (such as a CPA review course) are not deductible.[10] A deduction may be allowed for non-accounting courses that also maintain and improve an accountant's existing skills in a present job.[11] If the education incidentally results in a promotion or raise, the deduction still can be taken as long as the education maintained and improved existing skills and did not qualify a person for a new trade or business. A change in duties is not always fatal to the deduction if the new duties involve the same general work. For

10. Reg. § 1.212–1(f) and Rev.Rul. 69–292, 1969–1 C.B. 84.

11. *Howard Sherman Cooper*, 38 TCM 955, T.C.Memo. 1979–241.

example, the IRS has ruled that a practicing dentist's education expenses incurred to become an orthodontist are deductible.[12]

Requirements Imposed by Law or by the Employer for Retention of Employment

Teachers qualify under the provision that permits the deduction of education expenses if additional courses are required by the employer or are imposed by law. Many states require a minimum of a bachelor's degree and a specified number of additional courses to retain a teaching job. In addition, some public school systems have imposed a master's degree requirement and have required teachers to make satisfactory progress toward a master's degree in order to keep their positions.

If the required education is the minimum degree required for the job, no deduction is allowed. A taxpayer classified as an Accountant I who went back to school to obtain a bachelor's degree was not allowed to deduct the expenses. Although some courses tended to maintain and improve his existing skills in his entry-level position, the degree was the minimum requirement for his job.[13]

Maintaining or Improving Existing Skills

The "maintaining or improving existing skills" requirement in the Code has been difficult for both taxpayers and the courts to interpret. For example, a business executive may be permitted to deduct the costs of obtaining an M.B.A. on the grounds that the advanced management education is undertaken to maintain and improve existing management skills. The executive would be eligible to deduct the costs of specialized, nondegree management courses that were taken for continuing education or to maintain or improve existing skills. If the business executive incurred the expenses to obtain a law degree, the expenses would not be deductible because they constitute training for a new trade or business. The Regulations do not allow a self-employed accountant to deduct expenses relating to law school.[14]

Classification of Specific Items

Education expenses include books, tuition, typing, and transportation (e.g., from the office to night school) and travel (e.g., meals and lodging while away from home at summer school).

EXAMPLE 39

Bill, who holds a bachelor of education degree, is a secondary education teacher in the Los Angeles school system. The school board recently changed its minimum education requirement for new teachers by prescribing five years of college training instead of four. Under a grandfather clause, teachers who have only four years of college would continue to qualify if they show satisfactory progress toward a graduate degree. Bill enrolls at the University of California and takes three graduate courses. His unreimbursed expenses for this purpose are as follows:

---

12. Rev.Rul. 74–78, 1974–1 C.B. 44.

13. Reg. § 1.162–5(b)(2)(iii) Example (2); *Collin J. Davidson*, 43 TCM 743, T.C.Memo. 1982–119.

14. Reg. § 1.162–5(b)(3)(ii) Example (1).

Books and tuition	$2,600
Lodging while in travel status (June–August)	1,150
Meals while in travel status	800
Laundry while in travel status	220
Transportation	600

Bill has a miscellaneous itemized deduction subject to the 2% floor as follows:

Books and tuition	$2,600
Lodging	1,150
Meals (80% × $800)	640
Laundry	220
Transportation	600
	$5,210

◆

ENTERTAINMENT EXPENSES

Many taxpayers attempt to deduct personal entertainment expenses as business expenses. For this reason, Code § 274 restricts the deductibility of entertainment expenses. The law contains strict record-keeping requirements and provides restrictive tests for the deduction of certain types of entertainment expenses.

Classification of Expenses

Entertainment expenses are categorized as follows: those *directly related* to business and those *associated with* business. Directly related expenses are related to an actual business meeting or discussion. These expenses can be contrasted with entertainment expenses that are incurred to promote goodwill such as maintaining existing customer relations. To obtain a deduction for directly related entertainment, it is not necessary to show that actual benefit resulted from the expenditure as long as there was a reasonable expectation of benefit. To qualify as directly related, the expense should be incurred in a clear business setting. If there is little possibility of engaging in the active conduct of a trade or business due to the nature of the social facility, it may be difficult to qualify the expenditure as directly related to business.

Expenses associated with, rather than directly related to, business entertainment must serve a specific business purpose, such as obtaining new business or continuing existing business. These expenditures qualify only if the expenses directly precede or follow a bona fide business discussion. Entertainment occurring on the same day as the business discussion meets the test.

Restrictions upon Deductibility

Business Meals. Any business meal is deductible only if the following are true:

- The meal is directly related to or associated with the active conduct of a trade or business.
- The expense is not lavish or extravagant under the circumstances.
- The taxpayer (or an employee) is present at the meal.

A business meal with a business associate or customer is not deductible unless business is discussed before, during, or after the meal. This requirement is not intended to disallow the deduction for a meal consumed while away from home on business.

EXAMPLE 40

Lacy travels to San Francisco for a business convention. She pays for dinner with three colleagues and is not reimbursed by her employer. They do not discuss business. She can deduct 80% of the cost of her meal. However, she cannot deduct the cost of her colleagues' meals. ◆

The *clear business purpose* test requires that meals be directly related to or associated with the active conduct of a business. A meal is not deductible if it serves no business purpose.

The taxpayer or an employee must be present at the business meal for the meal to be deductible. An independent contractor who renders significant services to the taxpayer is treated as an employee for this purpose.

EXAMPLE 41

Lance, a party to a contract negotiation, buys dinner for other parties to the negotiation but does not attend the dinner. No deduction is allowed. ◆

Entertainment Facilities. Deducting the cost of maintaining an entertainment facility such as a hunting lodge, fishing camp, yacht, or country club lends itself to taxpayer manipulation. Such a facility could be used for personal vacations and entertainment as well as business. For this reason, the law allows a deduction only in limited situations and imposes stringent record-keeping requirements.

To obtain a deduction for the dues paid or incurred to maintain a club membership, a primary use test is imposed.[15] Unless the taxpayer can show that over 50 percent of the use of the facility was for business purposes, no deduction is permitted. In meeting the primary use test, the following rules govern:

- Consider only the days the facility is used. Days of nonuse do not enter into the determination.
- A day of both business and personal use counts as a day of business use.
- Business use includes entertainment that is associated with or directly related to business.

Even if the primary use test is satisfied, only the portion of the dues attributable to the directly related entertainment qualifies for the deduction.

EXAMPLE 42

Melvin, the sales manager of an insurance agency, is expected to incur entertainment expenses in connection with the sale of insurance. None of these expenses are reimbursed by his employer. During the year, Melvin paid the following amounts to the Leesville Country Club:

Annual dues	$1,200
Meals relating to business use	900
Meals and other charges relating to personal use	400
Other charges relating to business use	200

15. §§ 274(a)(2)(A) and (C).

Melvin used the club 120 days for purposes directly related to business and 80 days for personal use. He did not use the club at all during the remaining days of the year. Since Melvin used the facility for business more than 50% of the time (120 days out of 200 days), the primary use test is satisfied. The portion of the annual dues that Melvin can deduct is $720 (120/200 = 60% × $1,200). He is allowed a total deduction as follows:

Annual dues	$ 720
Business meals	900
Other business charges	200
Total	$1,820
Less 20%	(364)
Deductible	$1,456

Note that the $1,456 is a miscellaneous itemized deduction subject to the 2% floor. ◆

Ticket Purchases for Entertainment. A deduction for the cost of a ticket for an entertainment activity is limited to the face value of the ticket. This limitation is applied before the 80 percent rule. The face value of a ticket includes any tax. Under this rule, the excess payment to a scalper for a ticket is not deductible. Similarly, the fee to a ticket agency for the purchase of a ticket is not deductible.

Expenditures for the rental or use of a luxury skybox at a sports arena in excess of the face value of regular tickets are disallowed as deductions. If a luxury skybox is used for entertainment that is directly related to or associated with business, the deduction is limited to the face value of nonluxury box seats. All seats in the luxury skybox are counted, even when some seats are unoccupied.

The taxpayer may also deduct stated charges for food and beverages under the general rules for business entertainment. The deduction for skybox seats, food, and beverages is limited to 80 percent of cost.

EXAMPLE 43

In the current year, Black Co. pays $6,000 to rent a 10-seat skybox at City Stadium for three football games. Nonluxury box seats at each event range in cost from $25 to $35 a seat. In March, a Black Co. representative and five clients use the skybox for the first game. The entertainment follows a bona fide business discussion, and Black Co. spends $85 for food and beverages during the game. The deduction for the first sports event is as follows:

Food and beverages	$ 85
Deduction for seats ($35 × 10 seats)	350
Total entertainment expense	$ 435
80% limitation	×.80
Deduction	$ 348

◆

Business Gifts. Business gifts are deductible to the extent of $25 per donee per year. An exception is made for gifts costing $4 or less (e.g., pens with the employee's or company's name on them) or promotional materials. Such items are not treated as business gifts subject to the $25 limitation. In addition, incidental costs such as engraving of jewelry and nominal charges for giftwrapping, mailing, and delivery are not included in the cost of the gift in applying the limitation. The $25 limitation applies to both direct and indirect gifts. A gift is indirect if it is made to a person's spouse or other family member or to a corporation or partnership on behalf of the individual. All such gifts must be aggregated in applying the $25 limit. Excluded from the $25 limit are gifts or awards to employees, such as for length of service, that are under $400.[16] Gifts to superiors and employers are not deductible. It is necessary to maintain records substantiating the gifts.

OTHER EMPLOYEE EXPENSES

Office in the Home

Employees and self-employed individuals are not allowed a deduction for expenses of an office in the home unless a portion of the residence is used exclusively on a regular basis as either:

- The principal place of business for any trade or business of the taxpayer.
- A place of business used by clients, patients, or customers.

Employees must meet an additional test: the use must be for the convenience of the employer rather than merely being "appropriate and helpful."[17]

The precise meaning of "principal place of business" was recently resolved by the U.S. Supreme Court. In a divided opinion, the Court established a two-pronged test. First, determine the relative importance of the activities performed at each business location (i.e., inside and outside the personal residence). Second, compare the time spent at each business location.

EXAMPLE 44

Dr. Smith is a self-employed anesthesiologist. During the year, he spends 30 to 35 hours per week administering anesthesia and postoperative care to patients in three hospitals, none of which provides him with an office. He also spends two to three hours per day in a room in his home that he uses exclusively as an office. He does not meet patients there, but he performs a variety of tasks related to his medical practice (e.g., contacting surgeons, bookkeeping, reading medical journals). None of Dr. Smith's expenses of the office in the home are deductible because the hospital procedures (i.e., administering to patients) are more important than those done at home. Also, more business time is spent outside rather than inside the home. ◆

The exclusive use requirement means that a specific part of the home must be used solely for business purposes. A deduction, if permitted, will require an allocation of total expenses of operating the home between business and personal use based on floor space or number of rooms.

Even if the taxpayer meets the above requirements, the allowable home office expenses cannot exceed the gross income from the business less all other business expenses attributable to the activity. Furthermore, the home office expenses that must be deducted first are those that would be allowable as itemized deductions anyway (e.g., mortgage interest and real estate taxes). All home office expenses of an employee are miscellaneous itemized deductions subject to the 2 percent floor, except those (such as interest) that qualify as other

16. § 274(b)(1)(C). Section 274(b)(3)(C) allows a deduction for gifts to employees of up to $1,600 under a *qualified plan* as long as the average cost of all awards under the qualified plan does not exceed $400. Qualified plans are described in § 274(b)(3).

17. § 280(A)(c)(1).

personal itemized deductions. Home office expenses of a self-employed individual are trade or business expenses and are deductible *for* AGI.

Any disallowed home office expenses can be carried forward and used in future years subject to the same limitations.

Example 45

Rick is a certified public accountant employed by a regional CPA firm as a tax manager. He operates a separate business in which he refinishes furniture in his home. For this business, he uses two rooms in the basement of his home exclusively and regularly. The floor space of the two rooms constitutes 10% of the floor space of his residence. Gross income from the business totals $8,000. Expenses of the business (other than home office expenses) are $6,500. Rick incurs the following home office expenses:

Real property taxes on residence	$4,000
Interest expense on residence	7,500
Operating expenses of residence	2,000
Depreciation on residence (based on 10% business use)	250

Rick's deductions are determined as follows:

Business income		$ 8,000
Less: Other business expenses		(6,500)
		$ 1,500
Less: Allocable taxes ($4,000 × 10%)	$400	
Allocable interest ($7,500 × 10%)	750	(1,150)
		$ 350
Allocable operating expenses of the residence ($2,000 × 10%)		(200)
		$ 150
Allocable depreciation ($250, limited to remaining income)		(150)
		$ -0-

Rick has a carryover of $100 (the unused excess depreciation). Because he is self-employed, the allocable taxes and interest ($1,150), the other deductible office expenses ($200 + $150), and $6,500 of other business expenses are deductible *for* AGI. ◆

Form 8829 (Expenses for Business Use of Your Home) is used for computing the office in the home deduction.

The home office limitation cannot be circumvented by leasing part of one's home to an employer, using it as a home office, and deducting the expenses as a rental expense under § 212.

Miscellaneous Employee Expenses

Some deductible miscellaneous employee expenses include special clothing and its upkeep, union dues, and professional expenses. Also deductible are professional dues, professional meetings, and employment agency fees for seeking employment in the same trade or business, whether or not a new job is secured. The employee reports these expenses in the same manner as other employee business expenses discussed previously in the chapter.

To be deductible, special clothing must be both specifically required as a condition of employment and not generally adaptable for regular wear. For example, a police officer's uniform is not suitable for off-duty activities. An exception is clothing used to the extent that the clothing takes the place of regular clothing (e.g., military uniforms).

The current position of the IRS is that expenses incurred in seeking employment are deductible if the taxpayer is seeking employment in the same trade or business. The deduction is allowed whether or not the attempts to secure employment are successful. An unemployed taxpayer can take a deduction providing there has been no substantial lack of continuity between the last job and the search for a new one. No deduction is allowed for persons seeking their first job or seeking employment in a new trade or business.

The basic cost of one telephone in the home is not deductible, even if the telephone is used for business. Any long-distance or toll charges relating to business are deductible.

Contributions to Individual Retirement Accounts

Employees not covered by another qualified plan can establish their own tax-deductible Individual Retirement Accounts (IRAs). The contribution ceiling is the smaller of $2,000 (or $2,250 for spousal IRAs) or 100 percent of compensation. If the taxpayer or spouse is an active participant in another qualified plan, the IRA deduction limitation is phased out *proportionately* between certain AGI ranges. Refer to Figure 9–1.

AGI is calculated taking into account any § 469 passive activity losses and § 86 taxable Social Security benefits and ignoring any § 911 foreign income exclusion, § 135 savings bonds interest exclusion, and the IRA deduction. There is a $200 minimum allowable IRA deduction for individuals whose AGI is not above the phase-out range (see Figure 9–1).

EXAMPLE 46

In 1993, Mr. and Mrs. Quaid had compensation income of $27,000 and $20,000, respectively. Their AGI for 1993 was $47,000. Mr. Quaid was an active participant in his employer's qualified retirement plan. Mr. and Mrs. Quaid may *each* contribute $600 to an IRA. The deductible amount for each is reduced from $2,000 by $1,400 because of the phase-out mechanism:

$$\frac{\$7{,}000 \text{ (income above \$40,000)}}{\$10{,}000 \text{ (phase-out range)}} \times \$2{,}000 = \$1{,}400 \text{ reduction}$$

◆

EXAMPLE 47

An unmarried individual is an active participant in his employer's qualified retirement plan. With AGI of $34,500, he would normally have an IRA deduction limit of $100 ($2,000 – [($34,500 – $25,000)/$10,000 × $2,000]). However, because of the special floor provision, a $200 IRA deduction is allowable. ◆

To the extent that an individual is ineligible to make a deductible contribution to an IRA, *nondeductible contributions* can be made to separate accounts. The nondeductible contribution will be subject to the same dollar limits for deductible contributions of $2,000 of earned income ($2,250 for a spousal IRA). Income in the account accumulates tax-free until distributed. Only the account earnings will be taxed upon distribution. A taxpayer may elect to treat deductible IRA

FIGURE 9–1
Phase-Out of IRA Deduction

AGI Filing Status	Phase-Out Begins	Phase-Out Ends
Single and head of household	$25,000	$35,000
Married, filing joint return	40,000	50,000
Married, filing separate return	–0–	10,000

contributions as nondeductible. If an individual has no taxable income for the year after taking into account other deductions, the election will be beneficial. It is made on the individual's tax return for the taxable year to which the designation relates.

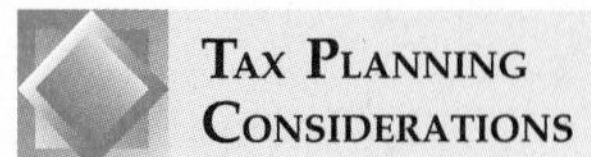

Self-Employed Individuals

Some taxpayers have the flexibility to be classified as either employees or self-employed individuals. Examples include real estate agents and direct sellers. These taxpayers should carefully consider all factors and not automatically assume that self-employment status is preferable.

It is advantageous to deduct one's business expenses *for* AGI and avoid the 2 percent floor. However, a self-employed individual may have higher expenses, such as local gross receipts taxes, license fees, franchise fees, personal property taxes, and occupation taxes. The record-keeping and filing requirements can be quite burdensome.

One of the most expensive considerations is the Social Security tax versus the self-employment tax. For an employee in 1993, for example, the Social Security tax applies at a rate of 6.2 percent on a base amount of wages of $57,600, and the Medicare (hospital insurance) tax applies at a rate of 1.45 percent on a base amount of $135,000. For self-employed persons, the rate, but not the base amount, for each tax doubles. Even though a deduction *for* AGI is allowed for one-half of the self-employment tax paid, an employee and a self-employed individual are not in the same tax position on equal amounts of earnings. For the application of these taxes to employees, see Chapter 1.

After analyzing all these factors, a taxpayer may decide that employee status is preferable to self-employed status.

Shifting Deductions between Employer and Employee

An employee can avoid the 2 percent floor for employee business expenses. Typically, an employee incurs travel and entertainment expenses in the course of employment. The employer gets the deduction if it reimburses the employee, and the employee gets the deduction *for* AGI. An adequate accounting must be made, and excess reimbursements must be returned to the employer.

Transportation and Travel Expenses

Adequate detailed records should be kept of all transportation and travel expenses. Since the regular mileage allowance is 28 cents per mile, a new, expensive automobile used primarily for business may generate a higher expense based on actual cost. The election to expense part of the cost of the automobile under § 179, ACRS depreciation, insurance, repairs and maintenance, automobile club dues, and interest on the auto loan may result in automobile expenses greater than the automatic mileage allowance.

If a taxpayer wishes to sightsee or vacation on a business trip, it would be beneficial to schedule business on both a Friday and a Monday to turn the weekend into business days for allocation purposes. It is especially crucial to schedule appropriate business days when foreign travel is involved.

Unreimbursed Employee Business Expenses

The 2 percent floor for unreimbursed employee business expenses offers a tax planning opportunity for married couples. If one spouse has high miscellaneous expenses subject to the floor, it may be beneficial for the couple to file separate returns. If they file jointly, the 2 percent floor will be based on the incomes of both. Filing separately will lower the reduction to 2 percent of only one spouse's income.

Other provisions of the law should be considered, however. For example, filing separately could cost a couple losses of up to $25,000 from self-managed rental units under the passive loss rules (discussed in Chapter 6).

Another possibility is to negotiate a salary reduction with one's employer in exchange for the 100 percent reimbursement of employee expenses. The employee will be better off because the 2 percent floor will not apply. The employer will be better off because certain expense reimbursements are not subject to Social Security and other payroll taxes.

Moving Expenses

Reimbursements of moving expenses must be included in gross income, and certain moving expenses may not be deductible because of the ceiling limitations. As a result, an employee may be required to pay additional income tax because of an employment-related move. Some employers reimburse their employees for these additional taxes, which are estimated and included in the employee's reimbursement.

Persons who retire and move to a new location incur personal nondeductible moving expenses. If the retired person accepts a full-time job in the new location before moving, the moving expenses become deductible.

Education Expenses

Education expenses are treated as nondeductible personal items unless the individual is employed or is engaged in a trade or business. A temporary leave of absence for further education is one way to reasonably assure that the taxpayer is still qualified, even if a full-time student. An individual was permitted to deduct education expenses even though he resigned from his job, returned to school full-time for two years, and accepted another job in the same field upon graduation. The Court held that the student had merely suspended active participation in his field.[18] If the time out of the field is too long, educational expense deductions will be disallowed. For example, a teacher who left the field for four years to raise her child and curtailed her employment searches and writing activities was denied a deduction. She was not actively engaged in the trade or business of being an educator.[19] To secure the deduction, an individual should be advised to arrange his or her work situation to preserve employee or business status.

Entertainment Expenses

Proper documentation of expenditures is essential because of the strict record-keeping requirements and the restrictive tests that must be met. For example, credit card receipts and canceled checks as the sole source of documentation may be inadequate to substantiate the business purpose and business relationship.[20] Taxpayers should maintain detailed records of amounts, time, place, business

18. *Stephen G. Sherman*, 36 TCM 1191, T.C.Memo. 1977–301.

19. *Brian C. Mulherin*, 42 TCM 834, T.C.Memo. 1984–454; *George A. Baist*, 56 TCM 778, T.C.Memo. 1988–554.

20. *Kenneth W. Guenther*, 54 TCM 382, T.C.Memo. 1987–440.

purpose, and business relationships. A credit card receipt details the place, date, and amount of the expense. A notation on the receipt of the names of the person(s) attending, the business relationship, and the topic of discussion should constitute proper documentation.

Associated with or goodwill entertainment is not deductible unless a business discussion is conducted immediately before or after the entertainment. Furthermore, there must be a business purpose for the entertainment. Taxpayers should arrange for a business discussion before or after such entertainment. They must provide documentation of the business purpose such as obtaining new business from a prospective customer.

Since a 50 percent test is imposed for the deductibility of country club dues, it may be necessary to accelerate business use or reduce personal use of a club facility. The 50 percent test is made on a daily use basis, so the taxpayer should maintain detailed records to substantiate business versus personal use.

Example 48

Sheila confers with her CPA on December 5 and finds that she has used the country club 30 days for business and 33 days for personal use. On the advice of her CPA, Sheila schedules four business lunches between December 5 and December 31 and refrains from using the club for personal purposes until January of the following year. Because of this action, Sheila will meet the 50% test and will be permitted a deduction for a portion of the club dues. ◆

Unreimbursed meals and entertainment are subject to the 80 percent rule in addition to the 2 percent floor. Negotiating a salary reduction, as previously discussed under Unreimbursed Employee Business Expenses, is even more valuable to the taxpayer.

Problem Materials

Discussion Questions

1. What difference does it make if an individual's expenses are classified as employment-related expenses or as expenses from self-employment?
2. What is the advantage to being a "statutory employee" as opposed to a regular common law employee?
3. How does the tax treatment of meals and entertainment differ from the treatment of other employee business expenses? Does the treatment differ if the expenses are reimbursed?
4. What constitutes an adequate accounting to an employer?
5. Fred is an executive with the Green Corporation and owns 30% of the company's common stock. Fred incurred employee business expenses during the year. How should he treat these expenses on his tax return if he was reimbursed in full under an accountable plan? How would your answer differ if the company did *not* have an accountable plan?
6. What tax return reporting procedures must be followed by an employee under the following circumstances?

   a. Expenses and reimbursements are equal under an accountable plan.
   b. Reimbursements at the appropriate Federal per diem rate exceed expenses, and an adequate accounting is made to the employer.
   c. Expenses exceed reimbursements under a nonaccountable plan.

7. Chris has two jobs. He drives 40 miles to his first job. The distance from the first job to the second is 32 miles. During the year, he worked 200 days at both jobs. On 150 days, he drove from his first job to the second job. On the remaining 50 days, he drove home (40 miles) and then to the second job (42 miles). How much can he deduct?
8. Janice incurred travel expenses while away from home on company business. These expenses were not reimbursed by her employer. Can she deduct the travel expenses? If so, where and how are they deducted?
9. Martin took a cruise in the Hawaiian Islands on a ship of U.S. registry to attend a business-related seminar. The cost was $3,000. What, if anything, can he deduct?
10. James takes a combined business and pleasure trip to Hawaii. What portion of the expenses is deductible?
11. Josephine took a combined business and pleasure trip to Europe. She traveled to London from New York on Friday, vacationed on Saturday and Sunday, conducted business on Monday, got snowed in at the airport on Tuesday, traveled to Paris on Wednesday, relaxed on Thursday (a legal holiday), conducted business on Friday, went sightseeing on Saturday and Sunday, picked up business samples and papers on Monday, and flew back to New York on Tuesday. What portion of her air fare can she deduct?
12. What are a taxpayer's two alternatives if she moves in November and cannot meet the 39-week test by the due date of filing her tax return? Which alternative is financially preferable if she meets the test in the following year? If she does not meet the test?
13. Distinguish between direct moving expenses and indirect moving expenses. Why is it important to classify such items properly?
14. What difference does it make for the purpose of the education deduction if a taxpayer is improving existing skills or acquiring new ones? On what general tax principle is the justification for this rule based?
15. Discuss the difference between entertainment that is *directly related to* business and entertainment that is *associated with* business.
16. Fred asks your advice on December 1 regarding the tax deductibility of his country club dues. To date, he has used the club 40 days for purposes directly related to business use, 42 days for purposes associated with business use, and 84 days for personal use. During December, members of Fred's family have planned to use the facility 4 more days for personal parties. No business use is planned in December. What would you advise him to do?
17. What limits are imposed on the deduction of expenses for tickets purchased for business entertainment? How are such expenses treated on an employee's return if they are reimbursed? Not reimbursed?
18. To what extent may a taxpayer take a deduction for business gifts to a business associate? To an employee? To a superior?
19. How are deductible home office expenses treated for tax purposes? Is the deduction *for* or *from* AGI?

PROBLEMS

20. Paige incurred the following expenses related to her employment as a chief executive officer:

Lodging while away from home	$2,800
Meals while away from home	1,200
Entertainment while away from home	2,000
Dues, subscriptions, and books	1,000
Transportation expenses	4,000

Paige's AGI was $100,000, and she received $6,600 under her employer's accountable plan. What are her deductions *for* and *from* AGI?

21. Kenneth received $4,400 in reimbursements under an accountable plan after he had made an adequate accounting to his employer. His expenses were as follows:

Transportation expenses	$3,200
Meals	1,400
Lodging and incidentals	2,300
Dues, phone, and subscriptions	100
Entertainment	1,000

How much can Kenneth deduct *for* and *from* AGI? Assume he had AGI of $50,000 and no other miscellaneous itemized deductions.

22. Patrick, an executive with Gray Corporation, incurred the following employee business expenses:

Lodging	$2,000
Meals	1,600
Transportation	2,400
Entertainment	1,500
Phone	500

Patrick received $5,600 under an accountable plan to cover the above expenses. He made an adequate accounting. In addition to incurring the above expenses, Patrick incurred expenses in attending a seminar on communications for executives. He paid $500 for transportation, $100 for meals, and $300 for fees and books. He was not reimbursed.

Patrick's salary was $50,000. He made a deductible contribution of $2,000 to his IRA. His only other income was interest of $800. He is 47 and single.

Calculate Patrick's AGI and itemized employee expenses.

23. Thelma, who is age 42 and single, earned a salary of $60,000. She had other income consisting of interest of $2,000, dividends of $1,600, and long-term capital gains of $4,000.

Thelma received reimbursements of $3,000 under an accountable plan. She incurred the following expenses during the year:

Transportation	$2,300
Meals	1,600
Dues and subscriptions	800
Entertainment of clients	300
Total	$5,000

Calculate Thelma's AGI and itemized employee business expenses.

24. Phyllis purchased a new automobile for $15,000 in 1990. She used it 80% for business purposes, driving 12,000 business miles in 1990, 10,000 business miles in 1991, 8,000 business miles in 1992, and 5,000 business miles in 1993.

She used the automatic mileage method for all years. What is the adjusted basis of the business portion of her automobile on January 1, 1994?

25. Hal, an investment counselor, attended a conference on the impact of the new tax law on investment choices. His unreimbursed expenses were as follows:

Air fare	$250
Lodging	500
Meals	300
Tuition and fees	400

a. How much can Hal deduct on his return? Are the expenses *for* or *from* AGI?
b. Would your answer differ if Hal were a self-employed physician?

26. Jane, an executive, traveled to England to confer with branch office officials of her company. Because an inner-ear birth defect prevents her from flying, she traveled to

England on the *Queen Elizabeth II.* The journey, which took six days and cost $2,400, was sold as a package deal with no breakdown of costs. How much can Jane deduct, assuming the U.S. government per diem amount is $150? Would your answer differ if the cost were broken down between transportation ($1,000) and meals and entertainment ($1,400)?

27. David, a professor of French history, went to France during the year to research documents available only in France. His time on the trip was spent entirely on business. No vacation days were involved, and David kept adequate records. David received no reimbursements for the following carefully documented expenses:

Air fare and other transportation	$1,600
Hotels	1,200
Meals	900

a. What can David deduct in 1993 if he has AGI of $30,000 and no other miscellaneous itemized deductions? Are the deductions *for* or *from* AGI?
b. Would your answer differ if David had gone to France to soak up the culture and brush up on his French?

28. Louis took a business trip from Chicago to Seattle. He spent two days in travel, conducted business for eight days, and visited friends for five days. He incurred the following expenses:

Air fare	$ 900
Lodging	2,100
Meals	1,500
Entertainment of clients	500

Louis received no reimbursements. What amount can he deduct?

29. Nadine took a business trip of 10 days. Seven days were spent on business (including travel time) and 3 days were personal. Her unreimbursed expenses were as follows:

Air fare	$3,000
Lodging (per day)	400
Meals (per day)	200
Entertainment of clients	600

a. How much can Nadine deduct if the trip is within the United States?
b. How much can she deduct if the trip is outside the United States?

30. Samuel traveled from New York to Helsinki primarily on business for his employer. He spent 16 days (including travel) on business and 4 days sightseeing. His expenses were as follows:

Air fare	$3,600
Meals	2,250
Lodging	2,850
Incidental expenses	300

Samuel was not reimbursed. How are these expenses reported assuming an AGI of $100,000?

31. Helen incurred the following expenses when she was transferred from San Francisco to Dallas:

Loss on the sale of old residence	$8,000
Moving company's charges	4,000
House-hunting trip	1,300
Temporary living expenses for 60 days (including meals of $1,000)	3,200
Broker's fees on residence sold	7,000
Charges for fitting drapes in new residence	1,500

a. How much can Helen deduct? Is the deduction *for* or *from* AGI?
b. What would be Helen's tax consequences if the employer reimbursed her for all of the expenses?

32. Upon his graduation from college in Texas, George was hired by a Los Angeles brokerage firm. His moving expenses were not reimbursed. How much can he deduct of the following expenses? Are the expenses deducted *for* or *from* his AGI of $25,000?

Loss of apartment deposit because of damage done by cat	$ 200
Apartment-hunting trip to Los Angeles (including meals of $500)	1,600
Cost of shipping cat to Los Angeles	100
Payment to apartment-locating service	150
Expense of renting and driving a truck to Los Angeles to move household goods	2,600
Lodging in Los Angeles for two weeks after arrival (apartment was not ready)	750
Meals for two weeks after arrival	512

33. Betty belongs to a country club that she uses for both business and personal purposes. Assuming none of her expenses are reimbursed, how much can she deduct on her tax return in the following two cases:

Annual dues		$5,000
Meals *directly related to* business		400
Meals *associated with* business		300
Personal meals and charges		2,000
Case (a) Days directly related to business	110	
Days associated with business	30	
Days for personal use	150	
Case (b) Days directly related to business	70	
Days associated with business	80	
Days for personal use	75	

34. Robert is an executive with a large manufacturing firm. He is 54 and married with two children. His compensation was $126,000. His wife is not employed outside the home. Robert took a trip from New York to London primarily for business. He was away from home 12 days, spending 8 days conducting business and 4 days vacationing. He incurred transportation expenses of $3,000, lodging expenses of $200 per day, meals of $60 per day, and expenses of $500 while entertaining clients. Robert belongs to a country club that he uses for both personal and business entertainment. His records reveal that he used the facility 57 days for purposes directly related to business, 14 days for purposes associated with business, and 93 days for personal use during the year. Expenses were as follows:

Annual dues	$6,000
Business meals	1,800
Business entertainment	965
Personal meals and charges	3,100

Robert received $8,600 in dividends and $3,400 in interest during the year. He receives a nonaccountable annual allowance of $10,000 to cover all of his employment expenses. Calculate Robert's AGI and his itemized employee business expenses.

35. Rita belongs to a country club that she uses for entertaining clients of her employer as well as for personal use. She incurred charges as follows:

Annual dues	$4,200
Business meals	3,000
Other business charges	700
Personal meals and charges	4,200

Rita kept careful records, which revealed the following use:

Days *associated with* business	60
Days *directly related to* business	50
Days for personal use	90

Sixty of the personal use days occurred on the same days that the club was used for entertainment directly related to business.

a. How much can Rita deduct if she received no reimbursements?
b. Would your answer differ if she made an adequate accounting and received a $2,000 reimbursement under an accountable plan?

36. Dennis is a single, 37-year-old executive who earned $60,000 in 1993. He also earned $2,000 in dividends and had interest of $1,800 credited to his savings account. An examination of Dennis's records revealed the following:

- He incurred education expenses to maintain and improve his existing skills. Tuition and books cost $580, transportation expenses amounted to $960, and parking fines totaled $80.
- He paid $1,200 in country club dues and $920 for meals for clients. The club was used 200 days for business and 50 days for personal use.
- He took a business trip to London. He flew there on a Thursday, conducted business on Friday, went sightseeing on Saturday and Sunday, conducted business on Monday and Tuesday, and flew home on Wednesday. His unreimbursed expenses amounted to $2,100 for air fare, $500 for meals, and $1,400 for lodging.

Calculate Dennis's AGI and his itemized employee deductions.

37. Camille is a professor who consults on the side. She uses one-fifth of her home exclusively for her consulting business, and clients regularly meet her there. Camille is single and under 65. Her AGI (before considering consulting income) is $40,000. Other relevant data follow:

Income from consulting business	$4,000
Consulting expenses other than home office	1,400
Total costs relating to home	
Interest and taxes	8,000
Utilities	1,400
Maintenance and repairs	900
Depreciation (business part only)	1,200

Calculate Camille's AGI for the year.

38. Ron is a self-employed wholesale jobber who had sales of $80,000 in 1993. He keeps meticulous business income and expense records.

His business expenses included an office in his home, used exclusively for his business. Expenses allocated to the home office on the basis of square footage were as follows:

Taxes and interest	$1,300
Utilities and maintenance	620
Office depreciation	1,200
Office supplies	380
Office furniture depreciation	700

Ron incurred the following business expenses:

Transportation	$6,000
Business meals	1,400
Business entertainment	900
Telephone, dues, and books	1,500
Other business expenses	2,000

Assume that Ron's self-employment tax is $8,869. He received interest of $2,000 and dividends of $1,000 during the year. Calculate his AGI for 1993.

39. Tom and Sally are married and file a joint return. Tom is a manager and earned a salary and bonus of $51,000 in 1993. He incurred employee business expenses of $800 for transportation and $400 for meals and entertainment. He was fully reimbursed under an accountable plan. He took a combined business and pleasure trip to New York. He spent five days conducting business and three days sightseeing. His air fare and taxi expense amounted to $1,200, meals averaged $60 per day, and lodging was $80 per day. He was not reimbursed for this trip.

Sally is a self-employed court reporter who works out of the home. One room is used regularly and exclusively for her business. She had receipts of $12,000 and incurred office expenses of $1,000 for depreciation, $300 for utilities, $150 for her business phone (a second line), and $500 for repairs and maintenance. She earned $200 in interest on her savings account and incurred other business expenses of $2,300. Assume that her self-employment tax is $1,095.

Calculate taxable income for Tom and Sally on a joint return, assuming all other itemized deductions totaled $5,100.

CUMULATIVE PROBLEMS

40. Sam Diamond is 38 and divorced with no dependents. His salary was $45,000, from which $4,900 was withheld for Federal income tax. The proper amount of FICA (Social Security) taxes and state income taxes of $1,600 were also withheld. Examination of his 1993 records revealed the following:

a. Sam had other receipts as follows:

Dividends on AT&T stock	$520
Interest credited to savings account	310
State income tax refund (he itemized in 1992)	220

b. Sam's itemized deductions were as follows:

Home mortgage interest	$8,600
Property taxes	890
Charitable contributions	720

c. Sam paid his former wife $2,400 for support of their child, Mary, who lives with her mother.

d. Sam received $5,000 in settlement of a damage claim resulting from a personal automobile accident.

e. He took a business trip during the year and was reimbursed $3,000 under an accountable plan by his employer. His expenses were as follows:

Transportation	$1,700
Meals	320
Lodging and incidentals	680
	$2,700

f. He drove a total of 8,000 business miles and uses the standard mileage rate to compute his automobile expense.

g. Sam incurred the following unreimbursed employee business expenses:

Business meals	$500
Publications and dues	250
Phone and miscellaneous	60
Business entertainment	290
Tuition and books for college course to maintain existing skills	612

Compute Sam's Federal taxable income for 1993. Suggested software (if available): *TurboTax* or *MacInTax* for tax return or WFT tax planning software.

41. George M. and Martha J. Jordan have no dependents and are both under age 65. George is a statutory employee of Consolidated Jobbers, and his Social Security number is 582–99–4444. Martha is an executive with General Corporation, and her Social Security number is 241–88–6642. The Jordans live at 321 Oak Street, Lincoln, NE 68024. They both want to contribute to the Presidential Election Campaign Fund.

In 1992, George earned $49,000 in commissions. His employer withholds FICA but not Federal income taxes. George paid $10,000 in estimated taxes. Martha earned $62,000, from which $9,000 was withheld for Federal income taxes. Neither George nor Martha received any expense reimbursements.

George uses his two-year-old car on sales calls and keeps a log of all miles driven. In 1992, he drove 36,000 miles, 25,554 of them for business. He made several out-of-state sales trips, incurring air fare of $1,600, meals of $800, and lodging costs of $750. He also spent $1,400 during the year taking customers to lunch.

Martha incurred the following expenses related to her work: taxi fares of $125, business lunches of $615, and a yearly commuter train ticket of $800. During the year, Martha received $1,200 in interest from the employees' credit union, $100,000 life insurance proceeds upon the death of her mother in December, and $500 in dividends from General Motors. She contributed $2,000 to her Individual Retirement Account. Neither George nor Martha is covered by an employee retirement plan. Martha gave a gift valued at $500 to the president of her firm upon his promotion to that position.

The Jordans had additional expenditures as follows:

Charitable contributions (cash)	$1,200
Medical and dental expenses	1,400
Real property taxes	1,200
Home mortgage interest	9,381
Tax return preparation fee	150

Part 1—Tax Computation

Compute the Jordans' Federal income tax payable or refund due, assuming they file a joint income tax return for 1992. You will need Form 1040, Form 2106, and Schedules A, B and C. Suggested software (if available): *TurboTax* or *MacInTax* for tax returns or WFT tax planning software.

Part 2—Tax Planning

Martha and George ask your help in deciding what to do with the $100,000 Martha inherited in 1992. They are considering three conservative investment alternatives: Suggested software (if available): *TurboTax* or WFT tax planning software.

- Invest in 8% long-term U.S. bonds.
- Invest in 7% Series EE bonds and elect to defer the interest earned.
- Invest in 6% municipal bonds.

a. Calculate the best alternative for next year. Assume that Martha and George will have the same income and deductions in 1993, except for the income from the investment they choose.

b. What other factors should the Jordans take into account?

c. Write a memo to the Jordans explaining their alternatives.

CHAPTER

DEDUCTIONS AND LOSSES: CERTAIN ITEMIZED DEDUCTIONS

OBJECTIVES

Distinguish between deductible and nondeductible personal expenses.

Define medical expenses and compute the medical expense deduction.

Contrast deductible taxes and nondeductible fees, licenses, etc.

Discuss rules relating to the Federal tax treatment of state income taxes.

Determine whether various types of interest are deductible.

Define charitable contributions and discuss related measurement problems and percentage limitations.

Enumerate the business and personal expenditures that are deductible either as miscellaneous itemized deductions or as other itemized deductions.

Explain the overall limitation on certain itemized deductions.

Identify tax planning procedures that can maximize the benefit of itemized deductions.

OUTLINE

GENERAL CLASSIFICATION OF EXPENSES

Personal expenditures are specifically disallowed as deductions by § 262. In contrast, business expenses that are incurred in the production or expectation of profit are deductions from gross income in arriving at adjusted gross income (AGI) and are reported on Schedule C of Form 1040. Certain nonbusiness expenses are also deductible in arriving at AGI (e.g., expenses attributable to rents and royalties and forfeited interest on a time savings deposit).

This chapter is principally concerned with expenses that are essentially personal in nature but are deductible because of legislative grace (e.g., charitable contributions, medical expenses, and certain state and local taxes). If the Code does not specifically state that a personal type of expense is deductible, no deduction is permitted. Allowable personal expenses are deductible *from* AGI in arriving at taxable income if the taxpayer elects to itemize. The election is appropriate when the total of the itemized deductions exceeds the standard deduction[1] based on the taxpayer's filing status. At this point, it may be helpful to review the computation in the tax formula for individuals that appears in Chapters 1 and 2.

MEDICAL EXPENSES

General Requirements

Medical expenses paid for the care of the taxpayer, spouse, and dependents are allowed as an itemized deduction to the extent the expenses are not reimbursed. The medical expense deduction is limited to the amount by which such expenses *exceed* 7.5 percent of the taxpayer's AGI.

EXAMPLE 1

During 1993, Iris had medical expenses of $3,800. If her AGI for the year is $40,000, the itemized deduction for medical expenses is limited to $800 [$3,800 – (7.5% × $40,000)]. ◆

Medical Expenses Defined

The term *medical care* includes expenditures incurred for the "diagnosis, cure, mitigation, treatment, or prevention of disease, or for the purpose of affecting any structure or function of the body."[2] A *partial* list of deductible and nondeductible medical items appears in Figure 10–1.

A medical expense does not have to relate to a particular ailment to be deductible. Since the definition of medical care is broad enough to cover preventive measures, the cost of periodic physical and dental exams qualifies even for a taxpayer in good health.

1. The total standard deduction is the sum of the basic standard deduction and the additional standard deduction (see Chapter 2). Chapter 2 also describes the situations in which a taxpayer is not eligible for the standard deduction.

2. § 213(d)(1)(A).

Under the Revenue Reconciliation Act of 1990, and effective for taxable years beginning after December 31, 1990, amounts paid for unnecessary *cosmetic surgery* are not deductible medical expenses.

EXAMPLE 2

In 1993, Art, a calendar year taxpayer, paid $11,000 to a plastic surgeon for a face lift. Art, age 75, merely wanted to improve his appearance. The $11,000 does not qualify as a medical expense since the surgery was unnecessary. ◆

If cosmetic surgery is deemed necessary, it is deductible as a medical expense. Cosmetic surgery is necessary when it ameliorates (1) a deformity arising from a congenital abnormality, (2) a personal injury, or (3) a disfiguring disease.

EXAMPLE 3

As a result of a serious automobile accident, Marge's face is disfigured. The cost of restorative cosmetic surgery is deductible as a medical expense. ◆

The deductibility of *nursing home expenses* depends on the medical condition of the patient and the nature of the services rendered.[3] If an individual enters a home for the aged for personal or family considerations and not because he or she requires medical or nursing attention, deductions are allowed only for the costs attributable to the medical and nursing care.

EXAMPLE 4

Norman has a chronic heart ailment. His family decided to place Norman in a nursing home equipped to provide medical and nursing care facilities. Total nursing home expenses amount to $15,000 per year. Of this amount, $4,500 is directly attributable to medical and nursing care. Since Norman is in need of significant medical and nursing care and is placed in the facility primarily for this purpose, all $15,000 of the nursing home costs are deductible (subject to the 7.5% floor). ◆

EXAMPLE 5

Assume the same facts as in Example 4, except that Norman does not have a chronic heart ailment. Norman enters the nursing home because he and his family feel that all

FIGURE 10–1
Illustration of Deductible and Nondeductible Medical Expenses

Deductible	Nondeductible
Medical (including dental, mental, and hospital) care	Funeral, burial, or cremation expenses
Prescription drugs	Nonprescription drugs (except insulin)
Special equipment	Bottled water
Wheelchairs	Toiletries, cosmetics
Crutches	Diaper service, maternity clothes
Artificial limbs	Programs for the *general* improvement of health
Eyeglasses (including contact lenses)	Weight reduction
Hearing aids	Health spas
Transportation for medical care	Stop-smoking clinics
Medical and hospital insurance premiums	Social activities (e.g., dancing and swimming lessons)
	Unnecessary cosmetic surgery

3. Reg. § 1.213–1(e)(1)(v).

of them would be more comfortable with this arrangement. Under these circumstances, only $4,500 of the expenses is deductible because the move was primarily for personal considerations. ◆

Tuition expenses of a dependent at a special school may be deductible as a medical expense. The cost of medical care can include the expenses of a special school for a mentally or physically handicapped individual. The deduction is allowed if a principal reason for sending the individual to the school is the school's special resources for alleviating the infirmities. In this case, the cost of meals and lodging, in addition to the tuition, is a proper medical expense deduction.[4]

EXAMPLE 6

Jason's daughter Marcia attended public school through the seventh grade. Because Marcia was a poor student, she was examined by a psychiatrist who diagnosed an organic problem that created a learning disability. Upon the recommendation of the psychiatrist, Marcia is enrolled in a private school so that she can receive individual attention. The school has no special program for students with learning disabilities and does not provide special medical treatment. The expense related to Marcia's attendance is not deductible as a medical expense. The cost of any psychiatric care, however, qualifies as a medical expense. ◆

Example 6 shows that the recommendation of a physician does not make the expenditure automatically deductible.

Capital Expenditures for Medical Purposes

Some examples of capital expenditures for medical purposes are swimming pools if the taxpayer does not have access to a neighborhood pool and air conditioners if they do not become permanent improvements (e.g., window units).[5] Other examples include dust elimination systems,[6] elevators,[7] and a room built to house an iron lung. These expenditures are medical in nature if they are incurred as a medical necessity upon the advice of a physician, the facility is used primarily by the patient alone, and the expense is reasonable.

Capital expenditures normally are adjustments to basis and are not deductible. However, both a capital expenditure for a permanent improvement and expenditures made for the operation or maintenance of the improvement may qualify as medical expenses. If a capital expenditure qualifies as a medical expense, the allowable cost is deductible in the year incurred. The tax law makes no provision for depreciating medical expenses as it does for other capital expenditures.

A capital improvement that ordinarily would not have a medical purpose qualifies as a medical expense if it is directly related to prescribed medical care and is deductible to the extent that the expenditure *exceeds* the increase in value of the related property. Appraisal costs related to capital improvements are also deductible, but not as medical expenses. These costs are expenses incurred in the determination of the taxpayer's tax liability.[8]

---

4. *Donald R. Pfeifer*, 37 TCM 816, T.C.Memo. 1978–189. Also see Rev.Rul. 78–340, 1978–2 C.B. 124.

5. Rev.Rul. 55–261, 1955–1 C.B. 307, modified by Rev.Rul. 68–212, 1968–1 C.B. 91.

6. *F. S. Delp*, 30 T.C. 1230 (1958).

7. *Riach v. Frank*, 62–1 USTC ¶9419, 9 AFTR2d 1263, 302 F.2d 374 (CA–9, 1962).

8. § 212(3).

EXAMPLE 7

Fred's physician advises him to install an elevator in his residence so that his wife, who is afflicted with heart disease, will not be required to climb the stairs. The cost of installing the elevator is $3,000, and the increase in the value of the residence is determined to be only $1,700. Therefore, $1,300 ($3,000 – $1,700) is deductible as a medical expense. Additional utility costs to operate the elevator and maintenance costs are deductible as medical expenses as long as the medical reason for the capital expenditure continues to exist. ◆

To enable a physically handicapped individual to live independently and productively, the full cost of certain home-related capital expenditures incurred qualifies as a medical expense. These expenditures are subject to the 7.5 percent floor only, and the increase in the home's value is deemed to be zero. Qualifying costs include expenditures for constructing entrance and exit ramps to the residence, widening hallways and doorways to accommodate wheelchairs, installing support bars and railings in bathrooms and other rooms, and adjusting electrical outlets and fixtures.[9]

Transportation and Lodging Expenses for Medical Treatment

Payments for transportation to and from a point of treatment for medical care are deductible as medical expenses (subject to the 7.5 percent floor). Transportation expenses for medical care include bus, taxi, train, or plane fare, charges for ambulance service, and out-of-pocket expenses for the use of an automobile. A mileage allowance of nine cents per mile[10] may be used instead of actual out-of-pocket automobile expenses. Whether the taxpayer chooses to claim out-of-pocket automobile expenses or the nine cents per mile automatic mileage option, related parking fees and tolls can also be deducted. The cost of meals while en route to obtain medical care is not deductible.

A deduction is also allowed for the transportation expenses of a parent who must accompany a child who is receiving medical care or for a nurse or other person giving medical assistance to a person who is traveling to get medical care and cannot travel alone.

A deduction is allowed for lodging while away from home for medical expenses if the following requirements are met:[11]

- The lodging is primarily for and essential to medical care.
- Medical care is provided by a doctor in a licensed hospital or a similar medical facility (e.g., a clinic).
- The lodging is not lavish or extravagant under the circumstances.
- There is no significant element of personal pleasure, recreation, or vacation in the travel away from home.

The deduction for lodging expenses included as medical expenses cannot exceed $50 *per* night for *each* person. The deduction is allowed not only for the patient but also for a person who must travel with the patient (e.g., a parent traveling with a child who is receiving medical care).

9. For a complete list of the items that qualify, see Rev.Rul. 87–106, 1987–2 C.B. 67.

10. Rev.Proc. 92–104, I.R.B. No. 52, 24.

11. § 213(d)(2).

EXAMPLE 8

Herman, a resident of Winchester, Kentucky, is advised by his family physician that Martha, Herman's dependent and disabled mother, needs specialized treatment for her heart condition. Consequently, Herman and Martha fly to Cleveland, Ohio, where Martha receives the therapy at a heart clinic on an out-patient basis. Expenses in connection with the trip are as follows:

Round trip airfare ($250 each)	$500
Lodging in Cleveland for two nights ($60 each per night)	240

Herman's medical expense deduction for transportation is $500, and his medical expense deduction for lodging is $200 ($50 per night per person). Because Martha is disabled, it is assumed that his accompaniment of her is justified. ◆

No deduction is allowed for the cost of meals unless they are part of the medical care and are furnished at a medical facility. When allowable, such meals are not subject to the 80 percent limit.

Amounts Paid for Medical Insurance Premiums

Medical insurance premiums are included with other medical expenses subject to the 7.5 percent floor. If amounts are paid under an insurance contract to cover loss of life, limb, sight, etc., no amount can be deducted unless the coverage for medical care is separately stated in the contract.

Medical insurance premiums paid by the taxpayer under a group plan or an individual plan are included as medical expenses. If an employer pays all or part of the taxpayer's medical insurance premiums, the amount paid by the employer is not included in gross income by the employee. Likewise, the premium is not included in the employee's medical expenses.

Special rules formerly applied to medical insurance premiums paid by *self-employed* taxpayers. Up to 25 percent of the premiums paid for medical insurance coverage were deductible as a business expense (*for* AGI). Any excess could be claimed as a medical expense. The business deduction could not exceed the net profit from the self-employment activity.[12] The deduction provision applied through June 30, 1992. Under H.R. 11 ("Revenue Act of 1992"), an extension of 12 months was authorized, but President Bush vetoed this legislation. Probabilities are strong that the deduction will be reinstated under the new administration. The extent to which it might be made retroactive is subject to conjecture.

Medical Expenses Incurred for Spouse and Dependents

In computing the medical expense deduction, a taxpayer may include medical expenses for a spouse and for a person who was a dependent at the time the expenses were paid or incurred. In determining dependency status for medical expense deduction purposes, neither the gross income nor the joint return tests (see Chapter 3) apply.

EXAMPLE 9

Ernie (age 22) is married and a full-time student at a university. During 1993, Ernie incurred medical expenses that were paid by Matilda (Ernie's mother). She provided more than half of Ernie's support for the year. Even if Ernie files a joint return with his

12. § 162(l).

wife, Matilda may claim the medical expenses she paid for him. Matilda would combine Ernie's expenses with her own in applying the 7.5% floor. ◆

Medical expenses paid on behalf of a former spouse are deductible if the parties were married when the expenditures were incurred. Also, medical expenses can be incorporated in the divorce decree and consequently may be deductible as alimony payments (*for* AGI).[13]

For divorced persons with children, a special rule applies to the noncustodial parent. The noncustodial parent may claim any medical expenses he or she pays even though the custodial parent claims the children as dependents. This rule applies if the dependency exemptions could have been shifted to the noncustodial parent by the custodial parent's waiver (refer to Chapter 2).

Example 10

Irv and Joan are divorced in 1992, and Joan is awarded custody of their child Keith. During 1993, Irv makes the following payments to Joan: $3,600 for child support and $2,500 for Keith's medical bills. Together, Irv and Joan provide more than half of Keith's support. Even though Joan claims Keith as a dependent, Irv can combine the medical expenses that he pays for Keith with his own. ◆

Year of Deduction

Regardless of a taxpayer's method of accounting, medical expenses are deductible only in the year *paid.* In effect, this places all individual taxpayers on a cash basis as far as the medical expense deduction is concerned. One exception, however, is allowed for deceased taxpayers. If the medical expenses are paid within one year from the day following the day of death, they can be treated as being paid at the time they were *incurred.*[14] Thus, such expenses may be reported on the final income tax return of the decedent or on earlier returns if incurred before the year of death.

No current deduction is allowed for payment of medical care to be rendered in the future unless the taxpayer is under an obligation to make the payment.[15] Whether an obligation to make the payment exists depends upon the policy of the physician or the institution furnishing the medical care.

Example 11

Upon the recommendation of his regular dentist, in late December 1993 Gary consults Dr. Smith, a prosthodontist, who specializes in crown and bridge work. Dr. Smith tells Gary that he can do the restorative work for $12,000. To cover his lab bill, however, Dr. Smith requires that 40% of this amount be prepaid. Accordingly, Gary pays Dr. Smith $4,800 in December 1993. The balance of $7,200 is paid when the work is completed in July 1994. Under these circumstances, the qualifying medical expenses are $4,800 for 1993 and $7,200 in 1994. The result would be the same even if Gary prepaid the full $12,000 in 1993. ◆

The IRS does allow a deduction for the portion of a lump-sum prepayment allocable to medical care made to a retirement home under a life care plan.[16]

Reimbursements

If medical expenses are reimbursed in the same year as paid, no problem arises. The reimbursement merely reduces the amount that would otherwise qualify for

13. This assumes the requirements of § 215 are met.

14. § 213(c).

15. *Robert S. Basset*, 26 T.C. 619 (1956).

16. Rev.Rul. 75–302, 1975–2 C.B. 86.

the medical expense deduction. But what happens if the reimbursement is received in a later year than the expenditure? Unlike casualty losses where reasonable prospect of recovery must be considered (refer to Chapter 7), the expected reimbursement is disregarded in measuring the amount of the deduction. Instead, the reimbursement is accounted for separately in the year in which it occurs.

As a general rule, when a taxpayer receives an insurance reimbursement for medical expenses deducted in a previous year, the reimbursement must be included in gross income in the year of receipt. However, taxpayers are not required to report more than the amount previously deducted as medical expenses. Thus, a taxpayer who did not itemize deductions in the year the expenses were paid is not required to include a reimbursement in gross income.

The tax benefit rule applies to reimbursements if the taxpayer itemized deductions in the previous year. In this case, the taxpayer may be required to report some or all of the medical expense reimbursement in income in the year the reimbursement is received. Under the tax benefit rule, the taxpayer must include the reimbursement in income up to the amount of the deductions that decreased income tax in the earlier year.

EXAMPLE 12

Homer has AGI of $20,000 for 1992. He was injured in a car accident and paid $1,300 for hospital expenses and $700 for doctor bills. Homer also incurred medical expenses of $600 for his dependent child. In 1993, Homer was reimbursed $650 by his insurance company for the medical expenses attributable to the car accident. His deduction for medical expenses in 1992 is computed as follows:

Hospitalization	$1,300
Bills for doctor's services	700
Medical expenses for dependent	600
Total	$2,600
Less: 7.5% of $20,000	(1,500)
Medical expense deduction (assuming Homer itemizes his deductions)	$1,100

Assume that Homer would have elected to itemize his deductions even if he had no medical expenses in 1992. If the reimbursement for medical care had occurred in 1992, the medical expense deduction would have been only $450 [$2,600 (total medical expenses) – $650 (reimbursement) – $1,500 (floor)], and Homer would have paid more income tax.

Since the reimbursement was made in a subsequent year, Homer would include $650 in gross income for 1993. If Homer had not itemized in 1992, he would not include the $650 reimbursement in 1993 gross income because he would have received no tax benefit in 1992. ◆

TAXES

Section 164 permits the deduction of certain state and local taxes paid or accrued by a taxpayer. The deduction was created to relieve the burden of multiple taxes upon the same source of revenue.

Deductibility as a Tax

A distinction must be made between a tax and a fee, since fees are not deductible unless incurred as an ordinary and necessary business expense or as an expense in the production of income.

The IRS has defined a tax as follows:

> A tax is an enforced contribution exacted pursuant to legislative authority in the exercise of taxing power, and imposed and collected for the purpose of raising revenue to be used for public or governmental purposes, and not as payment for some special privilege granted or service rendered. Taxes are, therefore, distinguished from various other contributions and charges imposed for particular purposes under particular powers or functions of the government. In view of such distinctions, the question whether a particular contribution or charge is to be regarded as a tax depends upon its real nature.[17]

Accordingly, fees for dog licenses, automobile inspection, automobile titles and registration, hunting and fishing licenses, bridge and highway tolls, drivers' licenses, parking meter deposits, postage, etc., are not deductible. These items, however, could be deductible if incurred as a business expense or for the production of income. Deductible and nondeductible taxes are summarized in Figure 10–2.[18]

Property Taxes, Assessments, and Apportionment of Taxes

Property Taxes. State, local, and foreign taxes on real property are generally deductible only by the person upon whom the tax is imposed. Cash basis taxpayers may deduct these taxes in the year of actual payment, and accrual basis taxpayers may deduct them in the year that fixes the right to deductibility.

Deductible personal property taxes must be *ad valorem* (assessed in relation to the value of the property). Therefore, a motor vehicle tax based on weight, model, year, and horsepower is not an ad valorem tax. However, a tax based on value and other criteria may qualify in part.

FIGURE 10–2
Deductible and Nondeductible Taxes

Deductible	Nondeductible
State, local, and foreign real property taxes	Federal income taxes
State and local personal property taxes	FICA taxes imposed on employees
State, local, and foreign income taxes	Employer FICA taxes paid on domestic household workers
The environmental tax	Estate, inheritance, and gift taxes
	General sales taxes
	Federal, state, and local excise taxes (e.g., gasoline, tobacco, spirits)
	Foreign income taxes if the taxpayer chooses the foreign tax credit option
	Taxes on real property to the extent such taxes are to be apportioned and treated as imposed on another taxpayer

17. Rev.Rul. 57–345, 1957–2 C.B. 132, and Rev.Rul. 70–622, 1970–2 C.B. 41.

18. Most deductible taxes are contained in § 164, while the nondeductible items are included in § 275.

EXAMPLE 13

A state imposes a motor vehicle registration tax on 4% of the value of the vehicle plus 40 cents per hundredweight. Belle, a resident of the state, owns a car having a value of $4,000 and weighing 3,000 pounds. Belle pays an annual registration fee of $172. Of this amount, $160 (4% of $4,000) is deductible as a personal property tax. The remaining $12, based on the weight of the car, is not deductible. ◆

Assessments for Local Benefits. As a general rule, real property taxes do not include taxes assessed for local benefits since such assessments tend to increase the value of the property (e.g., special assessments for streets, sidewalks, curbing, and other similar improvements). A taxpayer cannot deduct the cost of a new sidewalk (relative to a personal residence), even though the construction was required by the city and the sidewalk may have provided an incidental benefit to the public welfare.[19] Such assessments are added to the adjusted basis of the taxpayer's property.

Assessments for local benefits are deductible as a tax if they are made for maintenance or repair or for meeting interest charges with respect to the benefits. In such cases, the burden is on the taxpayer to show the allocation of the amounts assessed for the different purposes. If the allocation cannot be made, none of the amount paid is deductible.

Apportionment of Real Property Taxes between Seller and Purchaser. Real estate taxes for the entire year are apportioned between the buyer and seller on the basis of the number of days the property was held by each during the real property tax year. This apportionment is required whether the tax is paid by the buyer or the seller or is prorated according to the purchase agreement. The administrative convenience of the IRS is the rationale for the apportionment in that it helps in determining who is entitled to deduct the real estate taxes in the year of sale. In making the apportionment, the assessment date and the lien date are disregarded.

EXAMPLE 14

A county's real property tax year runs from April 1 to March 31. Susan, the owner on April 1, 1993, of real property located in the county, sells the real property to Bob on June 30, 1993. Bob owns the real property from June 30, 1993, through March 31, 1994. The tax for the real property tax year April 1, 1993, through March 31, 1994, is $730. The portion of the real property tax treated as imposed upon Susan, the seller, is $180 (90/365 × $730, April 1 through June 29, 1993), and $550 (275/365 × $730, June 30, 1993 through March 31, 1994) of the tax is treated as imposed upon Bob, the purchaser. Note that the allocable part of the real estate tax year applicable to the seller ends on the day before the sale, and the date of sale is included in the part of the year applicable to the purchaser. ◆

If the actual real estate taxes are not prorated between the buyer and seller as part of the purchase agreement, adjustments are required. The adjustments are necessary to determine the amount realized by the seller and the adjusted basis of the property to the buyer. If the buyer pays the entire amount of the tax, he or she has, in effect, paid the seller's portion of the real estate tax and has therefore paid more for the property than the actual purchase price. Thus, the amount of real estate tax that is apportioned to the seller (for Federal income tax purposes)

19. *Erie H. Rose*, 31 TCM 142, T.C.Memo. 1972–39; Reg. § 1.164–4(a).

and paid by the buyer is added to the buyer's adjusted basis. The seller must increase the amount realized on the sale by the same amount.

EXAMPLE 15

Seth sells real estate on October 3, 1993, for $50,000. The buyer, Wilma, pays the real estate taxes of $1,095 for the calendar year, which is the real estate property tax year. Of the real estate taxes, $825 is apportioned to and is deductible by the seller, Seth, and $270 of the taxes is deductible by Wilma. The buyer has, in effect, paid Seth's real estate taxes of $825 and has therefore paid $50,825 for the property. Wilma's basis is increased to $50,825, and the amount realized by Seth from the sale is increased to $50,825. ◆

The opposite result occurs if the seller (rather than the buyer) pays the real estate taxes. In this case, the seller reduces the amount realized from the sale by the amount that has been apportioned to the buyer. The buyer is required to reduce his or her adjusted basis by a corresponding amount.

EXAMPLE 16

Ruth sells real estate to Butch for $50,000 on October 3, 1993. While Ruth held the property, she paid the real estate taxes of $1,095 for the calendar year, which is the real estate property tax year. Although Ruth paid the entire $1,095 of real estate taxes, $270 of that amount is apportioned to Butch and is therefore deductible by him. The effect is that the buyer, Butch, has paid only $49,730 for the property. The amount realized by Ruth, the seller, is reduced by $270, and Butch reduces his basis in the property to $49,730. ◆

State and Local Income Taxes

The position of the IRS is that state and local income taxes imposed upon an individual are deductible only as itemized deductions (deduction *from*) even if the taxpayer's sole source of income is from a business, rents, or royalties.

Cash basis taxpayers are entitled to deduct state income taxes withheld by the employer in the year the taxes are withheld. In addition, estimated state income tax payments are deductible in the year the payment is made by cash basis taxpayers even if the payments relate to a prior or subsequent year.[20] If the taxpayer overpays state income taxes because of excessive withholdings or estimated tax payments, the refund received is included in gross income of the following year to the extent that the deduction reduced the tax liability in the prior year.

EXAMPLE 17

Leona, a cash basis, unmarried taxpayer, had $800 of state income tax withheld during 1993. Additionally in 1993, Leona paid $100 that was due when she filed her 1992 state income tax return and made estimated payments of $300 on her 1993 state income tax. When Leona files her 1993 Federal income tax return in April 1994, she elects to itemize deductions, which amount to $5,500, including the $1,200 of state income tax payments and withholdings, all of which reduce her tax liability.

As a result of overpaying her 1993 state income tax, Leona receives a refund of $200 early in 1994. She will include this amount in her 1994 gross income in computing her Federal income tax. It does not matter whether Leona received a check from the state for $200 or applied the $200 toward her 1994 state income tax. ◆

20. Rev.Rul. 71–190, 1971–1 C.B. 70. See also Rev.Rul. 82–208, 1982–2 C.B. 58, where a deduction is not allowed when the taxpayer cannot, in good faith, reasonably determine that there is additional state income tax liability.

INTEREST

A deduction for interest has been allowed since the income tax law was enacted in 1913. Despite its long history of congressional acceptance, the interest deduction continues to be one of the most controversial areas in the tax law.

The controversy has centered around the propriety of allowing the deduction of interest charges for the purchase of consumer goods and services and interest on borrowings used to acquire investments (investment interest). TRA of 1986 effectively put an end to this controversy by phasing out the deduction for personal interest and further limiting the deduction for investment interest after 1990. Even when interest is allowed as a deduction, limits are imposed on the deductibility of prepaid interest. In addition, no deduction is permitted for interest on debt incurred to purchase or carry tax-exempt securities.

Disallowed and Allowed Items

The Supreme Court has defined *interest* as compensation for the use or forbearance of money.[21] The general rule permits a deduction for all interest paid or accrued within the taxable year on indebtedness.[22] This rule is modified by other Code provisions that disallow or restrict certain interest deductions.

Personal (Consumer) Interest. *Personal interest* is any interest, with some exceptions as follows:

- Trade or business interest.
- Investment interest.
- Interest on passive activities.
- Home mortgage interest to a limited extent if it is qualified residence interest.

For this purpose, trade or business interest does not include interest on indebtedness to finance employee business expenses (e.g., interest on a loan to purchase an automobile used 80 percent for business). Such interest is personal interest. Personal, or consumer, interest also includes finance charges on department store and bank credit card purchases and on gasoline credit cards.[23] The term also includes late payment charges on utility bills[24] as well as interest on income tax deficiencies and assessments.

Beginning in 1991, personal interest is no longer deductible. The phase-out of the deduction took place over a five-year period.

Investment Interest. Taxpayers frequently borrow funds that they use to acquire investment assets. When the interest expense is large relative to the income from the investments, substantial tax benefits could result. Congress has therefore limited the deductibility of interest on funds borrowed for the purpose of purchasing or continuing to hold investment property. Investment interest expense is *now* limited to net investment income for the year.[25]

21. *Old Colony Railroad Co. v. Comm.*, 3 USTC ¶880, 10 AFTR 786, 52 S.Ct. 211 (USSC, 1932).
22. § 163(a).
23. Rev.Rul. 73–136, 1973–1 C.B. 68.
24. Rev.Rul. 74–187, 1974–1 C.B. 48.
25. § 163(d).

Investment income is gross income from interest, dividends, annuities, and royalties not derived in the ordinary course of a trade or business. It also includes net gain attributable to the disposition of property producing the types of income just enumerated or held for investment. Income from a passive activity and income from a real estate activity in which the taxpayer actively participates are not included in investment income.

Net investment income is the excess of investment income over investment expenses. Investment expenses are those deductible expenses directly connected with the production of investment income. Investment expenses *do not* include interest expense. When investment expenses fall into the category of miscellaneous itemized deductions that are subject to the 2 percent-of-AGI floor, some may not enter into the calculation of net investment income because of the floor.

EXAMPLE 18

Gina has AGI of $80,000, which includes dividends and interest income of $18,000. Besides investment interest expense, she paid $3,000 of city ad valorem property tax on stocks and bonds and had the following miscellaneous itemized expenses:

Safe deposit box rental (to hold investment securities)	$ 120
Investment counsel fee	1,200
Unreimbursed business travel	850
Uniforms	600

Before Gina can determine her investment expenses for purposes of calculating net investment income, those miscellaneous expenses that are not investment expenses are disallowed before any investment expenses are disallowed under the 2%-of-AGI floor. This is accomplished by selecting the *lesser* of the following:

1. The amount of investment expenses included in the total of miscellaneous itemized deductions subject to the 2%-of-AGI floor.
2. The amount of miscellaneous expenses deductible after the 2%-of-AGI rule is applied.

The amount under item 1 is $1,320 [$120 (safe deposit box rental) + $1,200 (investment counsel fee)]. The item 2 amount is $1,170 [$2,770 (total of miscellaneous expenses) – $1,600 (2% of $80,000 AGI)].

Then, Gina's investment expenses are calculated as follows:

Deductible miscellaneous deductions investment expense (the lesser of item 1 or item 2)	$1,170
Plus: Ad valorem tax on investment property	3,000
Total investment expenses	$4,170

Gina's net investment income is $13,830 ($18,000 investment income – $4,170 investment expenses). ◆

After net investment income is determined, deductible investment interest expense can be calculated. Investment interest expense does not include the following:

- Qualified residence interest (see below).
- Interest taken into account in computing income or loss from a passive activity (see Chapter 6).
- Interest that is otherwise nondeductible (e.g., interest on amounts borrowed to purchase or carry tax-exempt securities).

EXAMPLE 19

For 1993, Adam is a single person employed by a law firm. His investment activities for the year are as follows:

Net investment income	$30,000
Investment interest expense	44,000

Adam's investment interest deduction for 1993 is $30,000. ◆

The amount of investment interest disallowed is carried over to future years. In Example 19, therefore, the amount that is carried over to 1994 is $14,000 ($44,000 investment interest expense – $30,000 allowed). No limit is placed on the carryover period.

The investment interest expense deduction is determined by completing Form 4952 (see Appendix B).

Qualified Residence Interest. As previously stated, personal interest does not include qualified residence interest (interest on a home mortgage). *Qualified residence interest* is interest paid or accrued during the taxable year on indebtedness (subject to limitations) *secured* by any property that is a qualified residence of the taxpayer. Qualified residence interest falls into two categories: (1) interest on acquisition indebtedness and (2) interest on home equity loans. Before discussing each of these categories, however, the term qualified residence must be defined.

A *qualified residence* means the taxpayer's principal residence and one other residence of the taxpayer or spouse. The *principal residence* is one that meets the requirement for nonrecognition of gain upon sale under § 1034 (see Chapter 12). The *one other residence*, or second residence, refers to one that is used as a residence if not rented or, if rented, meets the requirements for a personal residence under the rental of vacation home rules (refer to Chapter 5). A taxpayer who has more than one second residence can make the selection each year of which one is the qualified second residence. A residence includes, in addition to a house in the ordinary sense, cooperative apartments, condominiums, and mobile homes and boats that have living quarters (sleeping accommodations and toilet and cooking facilities).

Although in most cases interest paid on a home mortgage would be fully deductible, there are limitations.[26] If the indebtedness is acquisition indebtedness, interest paid or accrued during the tax year on aggregate indebtedness of $1,000,000 ($500,000 for married persons filing separate returns) or less is qualified residence interest. *Acquisition indebtedness* refers to amounts incurred in acquiring, constructing, or substantially improving a qualified residence of the taxpayer.

Any indebtedness incurred on or before October 13, 1987, and secured by a qualified residence at all times thereafter is treated as acquisition indebtedness and is not subject to the $1,000,000 limitation (but does reduce the $1,000,000 limitation).

Qualified residence interest also includes interest on *home equity loans.* These loans utilize the personal residence of the taxpayer as security. Since tracing rules do not apply to home equity loans, the funds from these loans can be used for personal purposes (e.g., auto purchases, medical expenses). By making use of

26. § 163(h)(3).

home equity loans, therefore, what would have been nondeductible consumer interest becomes deductible qualified residence interest.

However, interest is deductible only on the portion of a home equity loan that does not exceed the *lesser of*:

- The fair market value of the residence, reduced by the acquisition indebtedness, *or*
- $100,000 ($50,000 for married persons filing separate returns).

EXAMPLE 20

Larry owns a personal residence with a fair market value of $150,000 and an outstanding first mortgage of $120,000. Larry issues a lien on the residence and in return borrows $15,000 to purchase a new family automobile. All interest on the $135,000 of debt is treated as qualified residence interest. ◆

EXAMPLE 21

Leon and Pearl, married taxpayers, took out a mortgage on their home for $200,000 in 1983. In March 1993, when the home had a fair market value of $400,000 and they owed $195,000 on the mortgage, Leon and Pearl took out a home equity loan for $120,000. They used the funds to purchase a boat to be used for recreational purposes. For 1993 on a joint return, Leon and Pearl can deduct all of the interest on the first mortgage since it is acquisition indebtedness. Of the $120,000 home equity loan, only the interest on the first $100,000 is deductible. The interest on the remaining $20,000 is not deductible because it exceeds the statutory ceiling of $100,000. ◆

Any interest paid on a mortgage secured by a third or more residences or paid on indebtedness that exceeds the allowable amounts is deductible according to the use of the proceeds. If the proceeds are used for personal purposes, the interest is nondeductible; if used for business, the interest is fully deductible. Interest on such proceeds used for investment purposes or in passive activities is subject to the limitations applicable to those activities.

Interest Paid for Services. It is common practice in the mortgage loan business to charge a fee for finding, placing, or processing a mortgage loan. Such fees are often called *points* and are expressed as a percentage of the loan amount. In periods of tight money, a borrower may have to pay points to obtain the necessary financing. To qualify as deductible interest, the points must be considered compensation to a lender solely for the use or forbearance of money. The points cannot be a form of service charge or payment for specific services if they are to qualify as deductible interest.[27]

Points must be capitalized and are amortized and deductible ratably over the life of the loan. A special exception permits the purchaser of a personal residence to deduct qualifying points in the year of payment.[28] The exception also covers points paid to obtain funds for home improvements. However, points paid to refinance an existing home mortgage cannot be immediately expensed but must be capitalized and amortized as interest expense over the life of the new loan.[29]

EXAMPLE 22

During 1993, Thelma purchased a new residence for $130,000 and paid points of $2,600 to obtain mortgage financing. At Thelma's election, the $2,600 can be claimed as an interest deduction for tax year 1993. ◆

27. Rev.Rul. 67–297, 1967–2 C.B. 87.

28. § 461(g)(2).

29. Rev.Rul. 87–22, 1987–1 C.B. 146.

EXAMPLE 23

Sandra purchased her residence four years ago, obtaining a 30-year mortgage at an annual interest rate of 12%. In 1993, Sandra refinances the mortgage in order to reduce the interest rate to 9%. To obtain the refinancing, she had to pay points of $2,600. The $2,600 paid comes under the usual rule applicable to points. The $2,600 must be capitalized and amortized over the life of the mortgage. ◆

Points paid by the seller are not deductible because the debt on which they are paid is not the debt of the seller. Points paid by the seller are treated as a reduction of the selling price of the property.

Prepayment Penalty. When a mortgage or loan is paid off in full in a lump sum before its term (early), the lending institution may require an additional payment of a certain percentage applied to the unpaid amount at the time of prepayment. This is known as a prepayment penalty and is considered to be interest (e.g., personal, qualified residence, investment) in the year paid.

Related Parties. Nothing prevents the deduction of interest paid to a related party as long as the payment actually took place and the interest meets the requirements for deductibility. Recall from Chapter 5 that a special rule for related taxpayers applies when the debtor uses the accrual basis and the related creditor is on the cash basis. If this rule is applicable, interest that has been accrued but not paid at the end of the debtor's tax year is not deductible until payment is made and the income is reportable by the cash basis recipient.

Tax-Exempt Securities. The tax law provides that no deduction is allowed for interest on debt incurred to purchase or carry tax-exempt securities.[30] A major problem for the courts has been to determine what is meant by the words *to purchase or carry.* Refer to Chapter 5 for a detailed discussion of these issues.

Restrictions on Deductibility and Timing Considerations

Taxpayer's Obligation. Allowed interest is deductible if the related debt represents a bona fide obligation for which the taxpayer is liable.[31] Thus, a taxpayer may not deduct interest paid on behalf of another individual. For interest to be deductible, both the debtor and creditor must intend for the loan to be repaid. Intent of the parties can be especially crucial between related parties such as a shareholder and a closely held corporation. A shareholder may not deduct interest paid by the corporation on his or her behalf.[32] Likewise, a husband may not deduct interest paid on his wife's property if he files a separate return, except in the case of qualified residence interest. If both husband and wife consent in writing, either the husband or the wife may deduct the allowed interest on the principal residence and one other residence.

Time of Deduction. Generally, interest must be paid to secure a deduction unless the taxpayer uses the accrual method of accounting. Under the accrual method, interest is deductible ratably over the life of the loan.

30. § 265(a)(2).

31. *Arcade Realty Co.,* 35 T.C. 256 (1960).

32. *Continental Trust Co.,* 7 B.T.A. 539 (1927).

EXAMPLE 24

On November 1, 1993, Ramon borrows $1,000 to purchase appliances for a rental house. The loan is payable in 90 days at 12% interest. On the due date in January 1994, Ramon pays the $1,000 note and interest amounting to $30. Ramon can deduct the accrued portion (2/3 × $30 = $20) of the interest in 1993 only if he is an accrual basis taxpayer. Otherwise, the entire amount of interest ($30) is deductible in 1994. ◆

Prepaid Interest. Accrual method reporting is imposed on cash basis taxpayers for interest prepayments that extend beyond the end of the taxable year.[33] Such payments must be allocated to the tax years to which the interest payments relate. These provisions are intended to prevent cash basis taxpayers from *manufacturing* tax deductions before the end of the year by prepaying interest. As previously noted, an exception allows immediate expensing of points paid to obtain funds to purchase or improve a personal residence.

Classification of Interest Expense

Whether interest is deductible *for* AGI or as an itemized deduction *(from)* depends on whether the indebtedness has a business, investment, or personal purpose. If the indebtedness is incurred in relation to a business (other than performing services as an employee) or for the production of rent or royalty income, the interest is deductible *for* AGI. However, if the indebtedness is incurred for personal use, such as qualified residence interest, any deduction allowed is reported on Schedule A of Form 1040 if the taxpayer elects to itemize. If the taxpayer is an employee who incurs debt in relation to his or her employment, the interest is considered to be personal, or consumer, interest. Business expenses appear on Schedule C of Form 1040, and expenses related to rents or royalties are reported on Schedule E.

If a taxpayer deposits money in a certificate of deposit (CD) that has a term of one year or less and the interest cannot be withdrawn without penalty, the full amount of the interest must still be included in income even though part of the interest is forfeited due to an early withdrawal. However, the taxpayer will be allowed a deduction *for* AGI for the forfeited amount.

For classification purposes, the IRS has issued complex tracing rules[34] to establish the use to which borrowed funds are put.

Interest on amounts borrowed in excess of $50,000 in total on life insurance policies covering the life of a self-employed taxpayer or an officer or employee of a corporation is nondeductible. This result occurs even though the borrowed funds are used in a trade or business.

CHARITABLE CONTRIBUTIONS

Section 170 permits individuals and corporations to deduct contributions made to qualified domestic organizations. Contributions to qualified charitable organizations serve certain social welfare needs and therefore relieve the government of the cost of providing these needed services to the community.

33. § 461(g)(1).

34. Reg. § 1.163–8T.

The charitable contribution provisions are among the most complex in the tax law. To determine the amount deductible as a charitable contribution, several important questions must be answered:

- What constitutes a charitable contribution?
- Was the contribution made to a qualified organization?
- When is the contribution deductible?
- What record-keeping and reporting requirements apply to charitable contributions?
- How is the value of donated property determined?
- What special rules apply to contributions of property that has increased in value?
- What percentage limitations apply to the charitable contribution deduction?

These questions are addressed in the sections that follow.

Criteria for a Gift

Section 170(c) defines a *charitable contribution* as a gift made to a qualified organization. The major elements needed to qualify a contribution as a gift are a donative intent, the absence of consideration, and acceptance by the donee. Consequently, the taxpayer has the burden of establishing that the transfer was made from motives of *disinterested generosity* as established by the courts.[35] This test is quite subjective and has led to problems of interpretation.

Benefit Received Rule. When a donor derives a tangible benefit from a contribution, he or she cannot deduct the value of the benefit.

EXAMPLE 25

Ralph purchases a ticket at $100 for a special performance of the local symphony (a qualified charity). If the price of a ticket to a symphony concert is normally $35, Ralph is allowed only $65 as a charitable contribution. ◆

An exception to this benefit rule provides for the deduction of an automatic percentage of the amount paid for the right to purchase athletic tickets from colleges and universities.[36] Under this exception, 80 percent of the amount paid to or for the benefit of the institution qualifies as a charitable contribution deduction.

EXAMPLE 26

Janet donates $500 to State University's athletic department. The payment guarantees that Janet will have preferred seating on the 50-yard line. Subsequently, Janet buys four $35 game tickets. Under the exception to the benefit rule, she is allowed a $400 (80% of $500) charitable contribution deduction for the taxable year.

If, however, Janet's $500 donation includes four $35 tickets, that portion [$140 ($35 × 4)] and the remaining portion of $360 ($500 – $140) are treated as separate amounts. Thus, Janet is allowed a charitable contribution deduction of $288 (80% of $360). ◆

Contribution of Services. No deduction is allowed for a contribution of one's services to a qualified charitable organization. However, unreimbursed expenses related to the services rendered may be deductible. For example, the cost of a uniform (without general utility) that is required to be worn while performing

35. *Comm. v. Duberstein*, 60–2 USTC ¶9515, 5 AFTR2d 1626, 80 S.Ct. 1190 (USSC, 1960).

36. § 170(l).

services may be deductible, as are certain out-of-pocket transportation costs incurred for the benefit of the charity. In lieu of these out-of-pocket costs for an automobile, a standard mileage rate of 12 cents per mile is allowed.[37] Deductions are permitted for transportation, reasonable expenses for lodging, and the cost of meals while away from home incurred in performing the donated services. The travel may not involve a significant element of personal pleasure, recreation, or vacation.[38]

EXAMPLE 27

Grace, a delegate representing her church in Miami, Florida, travels to a two-day national meeting in Denver, Colorado, in February. After the meeting, Grace spends two weeks at a nearby ski resort. Under these circumstances, none of the transportation, meals, or lodging is deductible since the travel involved a significant element of personal pleasure, recreation, or vacation. ◆

Nondeductible Items. In addition to the benefit received rule and the restrictions placed on contribution of services, the following items may *not* be deducted as charitable contributions:

- Dues, fees, or bills paid to country clubs, lodges, fraternal orders, or similar groups.
- Cost of raffle, bingo, or lottery tickets.
- Cost of tuition.
- Value of blood given to a blood bank.
- Donations to homeowners associations.
- Gifts to individuals.
- Rental value of property used by a qualified charity.

Qualified Organizations

To be deductible, a contribution must be made to one of the following organizations:[39]

- A state or possession of the United States or any subdivisions thereof.
- A corporation, trust, or community chest, fund, or foundation that is situated in the United States and is organized and operated exclusively for religious, charitable, scientific, literary, or educational purposes or for the prevention of cruelty to children or animals.
- A veterans' organization.
- A fraternal organization operating under the lodge system.
- A cemetery company.

The IRS publishes a list of organizations that have applied for and received tax-exempt status under § 501 of the Code.[40] This publication is updated frequently and may be helpful in determining if a gift has been made to a qualifying charitable organization.

Because gifts made to needy individuals are not deductible, a deduction will not be permitted if a gift is received by a donee in an individual capacity rather than as a representative of a qualifying organization.

---

37. § 170(i).

38. § 170(j).

39. § 170(c).

40. Although this *Cumulative List of Organizations,* IRS Publication 78 (available by purchase from the Superintendent of Documents, U.S. Government Printing Office, Washington, DC 20402), may be helpful, qualified organizations are not required to be listed. Not all organizations that qualify are listed in this publication (e.g., American Red Cross, University of Cleveland).

Time of Deduction

A charitable contribution generally is deducted in the year the payment is made. This rule applies to both cash and accrual basis individuals. An accrual basis corporation, however, is permitted a deduction in the year of accrual under the following conditions:

- The board of directors authorizes the payment during the taxable year, and
- The contribution is made within two and one-half months after the close of the taxable year.

The special exception for accrual basis corporations is illustrated in Example 6 in Chapter 16.

A contribution is ordinarily deemed to have been made on the delivery of the property to the donee. For example, if a gift of securities (properly endorsed) is made to a qualified charitable organization, the gift is considered complete on the day of delivery or mailing. However, if the donor delivers the certificate to his or her bank or broker or to the issuing corporation, the gift is considered complete on the date the stock is transferred on the books of the corporation.

A contribution made by check is considered delivered on the date of mailing. Thus, a check mailed on December 31, 1993, is deductible on the taxpayer's 1993 tax return. If the contribution is charged on a bank credit card, the date the charge is made determines the year of deduction. For a pay-by-phone account, the date shown on the statement issued by the financial institution is the date of payment.

Recordkeeping and Valuation Requirements

Recordkeeping Requirements. Cash contributions must be substantiated by one of the following:[41]

- A canceled check.
- A receipt, letter, or other written communication from the charitable organization (showing the name of the organization, the date, and the amount of the contribution).
- Other reliable written records (contemporaneous records or other evidence, such as buttons and tokens, given to contributors by the donee organization).

The records required for noncash contributions vary depending on the amount of the contribution. If the value of the contribution is $500 or less, it must be evidenced by a receipt from the charitable organization. The receipt must show the following:

- The name of the charitable organization.
- The date and location of the charitable contribution.
- A reasonably detailed description of the contributed property.

Generally, charitable organizations do not attest to the fair market value of the donated property. Nevertheless, the taxpayer must maintain reliable written evidence of the following information concerning the donation:

41. *Your Federal Income Tax,* IRS Publication 17 (1992), p. 185.

- The fair market value of the property and how that value was determined.
- The amount of the reduction in the value of the property (if required) for certain appreciated property and how that reduction was determined.
- Terms of any agreement with the charitable organization dealing with the use of the property and potential sale or other disposition of the property by the organization.
- A signed copy of the appraisal if the value of the property was determined by appraisal. Only for a contribution of art with an aggregate value of $20,000 or more must the appraisal be attached to the taxpayer's return.

Additional information is required if the value of the donated property is over $500 but not over $5,000. Also, the taxpayer must file Section A of Form 8283 (Noncash Charitable Contributions) for such contributions.

For noncash contributions with a claimed value in excess of $5,000 ($10,000 in the case of nonpublicly traded stock), the taxpayer must obtain a qualified appraisal and must file Section B of Form 8283. This schedule must show a summary of the appraisal and must be attached to the taxpayer's return. Failure to comply with these reporting rules may result in disallowance of the charitable contribution deduction. Additionally, significant overvaluation exposes the taxpayer to rather stringent penalties.

Valuation Requirements. Property donated to a charity is generally valued at fair market value at the time the gift is made. The Code and Regulations give very little guidance on the measurement of the fair market value except to say, "The fair market value is the price at which the property would change hands between a willing buyer and a willing seller, neither being under any compulsion to buy or sell and both having reasonable knowledge of relevant facts."

Limitations on Charitable Contribution Deduction

In General. The potential charitable contribution deduction is the total of all donations, both money and property, that qualify for the deduction. After this determination is made, the actual amount of the charitable contribution deduction that is allowed for individuals for the tax year is limited as follows:

- If the qualifying contributions for the year total 20 percent or less of AGI, they are fully deductible.
- If the qualifying contributions are more than 20 percent of AGI, the deductible amount may be limited to either 20 percent, 30 percent, or 50 percent of AGI, depending on the type of property given and the type of organization to which the donation is made.
- In any case, the maximum charitable contribution deduction may not exceed 50 percent of AGI for the tax year.

To understand the complex rules for computing the amount of a charitable contribution, it is necessary to understand the distinction between capital gain property and ordinary income property. In addition, it is necessary to understand when the 50 percent, 30 percent, and 20 percent limitations apply. If a taxpayer's contributions for the year exceed the applicable percentage limitations, the excess contributions may be carried forward and deducted during a five-year carryover period. These topics are discussed in the sections that follow.

Corporations are subject to an overall limitation of 10 percent of taxable income computed without regard to the contributions made and certain other adjustments. The rules applicable to contributions by corporations are discussed in detail in Chapter 16.

Ordinary Income Property. *Ordinary income property* is any property that, if sold, will result in the recognition of ordinary income. The term includes inventory for sale in the taxpayer's trade or business, a work of art created by the donor, and a manuscript prepared by the donor. It also includes, for purposes of the charitable contribution calculation, a capital asset held by the donor for less than the required holding period for long-term capital gain treatment. Property that results in the recognition of ordinary income due to the recapture of depreciation is ordinary income property.[42]

If ordinary income property is contributed, the deduction is equal to the fair market value of the property less the amount of ordinary income that would have been reported if the property were sold. In most instances, the deduction is limited to the adjusted basis of the property to the donor.

EXAMPLE 28

Tim owned stock in White Corporation that he donated to a local university on May 1, 1993. Tim had purchased the stock for $2,500 on March 3, 1993, and the stock had a value of $3,600 when he made the donation. Since he had not held the property long enough to meet the long-term capital gain requirement, Tim would have recognized a short-term capital gain of $1,100 if he had sold the property. Since short-term capital gain property is treated as ordinary income property for charitable contribution purposes, Tim's charitable contribution deduction is limited to the property's adjusted basis of $2,500 ($3,600 – $1,100 = $2,500). ◆

In Example 28, suppose the stock had a fair market value of $2,300 (rather than $3,600) when it was donated to charity. Because the fair market value now is less than the adjusted basis, the charitable contribution deduction is $2,300.

Capital Gain Property. *Capital gain property* is any property that would have resulted in the recognition of long-term capital gain or § 1231 gain if the property had been sold by the donor. As a general rule, the deduction for a contribution of capital gain property is equal to the fair market value of the property.

Two major exceptions preclude the deductibility of the appreciation on long-term capital gain property. One exception concerns certain private foundations. Private foundations are organizations that traditionally do not receive their funding from the general public (e.g., the Ford Foundation). Generally, foundations fall into two categories: operating and nonoperating. A private *operating* foundation is one that spends substantially all of its income in the active conduct of the charitable undertaking for which it was established.[43] Other private foundations are *nonoperating* foundations. However, if a private nonoperating foundation distributes the contributions it receives according to special rules within two and one-half months following the year of the contribution, the organization is treated the same as public charities and private operating foundations. Often, only the private foundation knows its status (operating or nonoperating) for sure, and the status can change from year to year.

If capital gain property is contributed to a private nonoperating foundation, the taxpayer must reduce the contribution by the long-term capital gain that

42. For a more complete discussion of the difference between ordinary income and capital gain property, see Chapter 16.

43. § 4942.

would have been recognized if the property had been sold at its fair market value. The effect of this provision is to limit the deduction to the property's adjusted basis.

Example 29

Walter purchases stock for $800 on January 1, 1975, and donates it to a private nonoperating foundation on June 21, 1993, when it is worth $2,000. Walter's charitable contribution is $800 ($2,000 – $1,200), the stock's basis. ◆

Example 30

Assume the same facts as in Example 29, except that the donation is to either a private operating foundation or a public charity. Now, Walter's charitable contribution is $2,000. ◆

A second exception applying to capital gain property relates to *tangible personalty.*[44] If tangible personalty is contributed to a public charity such as a museum, church, or university, the charitable deduction may have to be reduced. The amount of the reduction is the long-term capital gain that would have been recognized if the property had been sold for its fair market value. The reduction occurs *if* the property is put to an unrelated use. The term *unrelated use* means a use that is unrelated to the exempt purpose or function of the charitable organization.

A taxpayer in this instance must establish that the property is not in fact being put to an unrelated use by the donee. The taxpayer must also establish that at the time of the contribution it was reasonable to anticipate that the property would not be put to an unrelated use. For a contribution of personalty to a museum, if the work of art is the kind of art normally retained by the museum, it is reasonable for a donor to anticipate that the work of art will not be put to an unrelated use. This is the case even if the object is later sold or exchanged by the museum.[45]

Example 31

Myrtle contributes a Picasso painting, for which she paid $20,000, to a local museum. It had a value of $30,000 at the time of the donation. The museum displayed the painting for two years and subsequently sold it for $50,000. The charitable contribution is $30,000. It is not reduced by the unrealized appreciation since the painting was put to a related use even though it was later sold by the museum. ◆

As noted in Chapter 14, for purposes of the alternative minimum tax, the net untaxed appreciation on charitable contributions usually is a tax preference item.

Fifty Percent Ceiling. Contributions made to public charities may not exceed 50 percent of an individual's AGI for the year. Excess contributions may be carried over to the next five years. The 50 percent ceiling on contributions applies to the following types of public charities:

- A church or a convention or association of churches.
- An educational organization that maintains a regular faculty and curriculum.
- A hospital or medical school.

44. Tangible personalty is all property that is not realty (land and buildings) and does not include intangible property such as stock or securities.

45. Reg. § 1.170A–4(b)(3)(ii)(b).

- An organization supported by the government that holds property or investments for the benefit of a college or university.
- A Federal, state, or local governmental unit.
- An organization normally receiving a substantial part of its support from the public or a governmental unit.

The 50 percent ceiling also applies to contributions to the following organizations:

- All private operating foundations.
- Certain private nonoperating foundations that distribute the contributions they receive to public charities and private operating foundations within two and one-half months following the year they receive the contribution.
- Certain private nonoperating foundations in which the contributions are pooled in a common fund and the income and principal sum are paid to public charities.

Thirty Percent Ceiling. A 30 percent ceiling applies to contributions of cash and ordinary income property to private nonoperating foundations. The 30 percent ceiling also applies to contributions of appreciated capital gain property to 50 percent organizations unless the taxpayer makes a special election (see below).

In the event the contributions for any one tax year involve both 50 percent and 30 percent property, the allowable deduction comes first from the 50 percent property.

EXAMPLE 32

During 1993, Lisa made the following donations to her church: cash of $2,000 and unimproved land worth $30,000. Lisa had purchased the land four years ago for $22,000 and held it as an investment. Lisa's AGI for 1993 is $50,000. Disregarding percentage limitations, Lisa's potential deduction for 1993 is $32,000 [$2,000 (cash) + $30,000 (fair market value of land)]. Note that no reduction for the appreciation on the land is necessary since, if sold, it would have yielded a long-term capital gain.

In applying the percentage limitations, however, the *current* deduction for the land is limited to $15,000 [30% (limitation applicable to long-term capital gain property) × $50,000 (AGI)]. Thus, the total deduction for 1993 is $17,000 ($2,000 cash + $15,000 land). Note that the total deduction does not exceed $25,000, which is 50% of Lisa's AGI. ◆

Under a special election, a taxpayer may choose to forgo a deduction of the appreciation on capital gain property. Referred to as the *reduced deduction election,* this enables the taxpayer to move from the 30 percent limitation to the 50 percent limitation.

EXAMPLE 33

Assume the same facts as in Example 32, except that Lisa makes the reduced deduction election. Now the deduction for 1993 becomes $24,000 [$2,000 (cash) + $22,000 (basis in land)] because both donations fall under the 50% limitation. Thus, by making the election, Lisa has increased her charitable contribution deduction for 1993 by $7,000 [$24,000 – $17,000 (Example 32)]. ◆

Although the reduced deduction election appears attractive, it should be considered carefully. The election sacrifices a deduction for the appreciation on long-term capital gain property that might eventually be allowed. Note that in Example 32, the potential deduction was $32,000, yet in Example 33 only $24,000 is allowed. The reason the potential deduction is decreased by $8,000 ($32,000 – $24,000) is that no carryover is allowed for the amount sacrificed by the election.

Twenty Percent Ceiling. A 20 percent ceiling applies to contributions of appreciated long-term capital gain property to certain private nonoperating foundations.

Contribution Carryovers. Contributions that exceed the percentage limitations for the current year can be carried over for five years. In the carryover process, such contributions do not lose their identity for limitation purposes. Thus, if the contribution originally involved 30 percent property, the carryover will continue to be classified as 30 percent property in the carryover year.

Example 34

Assume the same facts as in Example 32. Because only $15,000 of the $30,000 value of the land was deducted in 1993, the balance of $15,000 may be carried over to 1994. But the carryover will still be treated as long-term capital gain property and is subject to the 30%-of-AGI limitation. ◆

In applying the percentage limitations, current charitable contributions must be claimed first before any carryovers can be considered. If carryovers involve more than one year, they are utilized in a first-in, first-out order.

Miscellaneous Itemized Deductions

According to § 262, no deduction is allowed for personal, living, or family expenses. However, a taxpayer may incur a number of expenditures related to employment. If an employee or outside salesperson incurs unreimbursed business expenses, including travel and transportation, the expenses are deductible as miscellaneous deductions.[46] Beyond unreimbursed employee expenses and those of an outside salesperson, certain other expenses fall into the special category of miscellaneous itemized deductions. Some are deductible only if, in total, they exceed 2 percent of the taxpayer's AGI. These miscellaneous itemized deductions include (but are not limited to) the following:

- Professional dues to membership organizations.
- Uniforms or other clothing that cannot be used for normal wear.
- Fees incurred for the preparation of one's tax return or fees incurred for tax litigation before the IRS or the courts.
- Job-hunting costs.
- Fee paid for a safe deposit box used to store papers and documents relating to taxable income-producing investments.
- Investment expenses that are deductible under § 212 as discussed in Chapter 5.
- Appraisal fees to determine the amount of a casualty loss or the fair market value of donated property.
- Hobby losses up to the amount of hobby income (see Chapter 5).

46. Actors and performing artists who meet certain requirements are not subject to this rule.

Certain employee business expenses that are reimbursed are not itemized deductions, but are deducted *for* AGI. Employee business expenses are discussed in depth in Chapter 9.

Other Miscellaneous Deductions

Certain expenses and losses do not fall into any category of itemized deductions already discussed but are nonetheless deductible.

- Moving expenses that meet the requirements for deductibility, discussed in Chapter 9.
- Casualty and theft losses, discussed in Chapter 7.
- Gambling losses up to the amount of gambling winnings.
- Impairment-related work expenses of a handicapped person.
- The unrecovered investment in an annuity contract when the annuity ceases by reason of death, discussed in Chapter 3.

The amount of each expense that is allowable as a deduction may be limited by the rules within a particular category (casualty and theft losses, moving expenses, gambling losses).

Moving expenses and casualty and theft losses are separate line items on Schedule A (Form 1040). The remaining expenses and losses are deductible as "Other Miscellaneous Deductions."

Comprehensive Example of Schedule A

Harry and Jean Brown, married filing jointly, had the following transactions for the current year:

■ Medicines that required a prescription	$ 430
■ Doctor and dentist bills paid and not reimbursed	2,120
■ Medical insurance premium payments	1,200
■ Contact lenses	175
■ Transportation for medical purposes (425 miles × 9 cents/mile + $4.75 parking)	43
■ State income tax withheld	620
■ Real estate taxes	1,580
■ Interest paid on qualified residence mortgage	2,840
■ Charitable contributions in cash	860
■ Transportation in performing charitable services (860 miles × 12 cents/mile + $15.80 parking and tolls)	119
■ Unreimbursed employee expenses (from a Form 2106)	870
■ Tax return preparation	150
■ Professional expenses (dues and publications)	135
■ Safe deposit box (used for keeping investment documents and tax records)	35

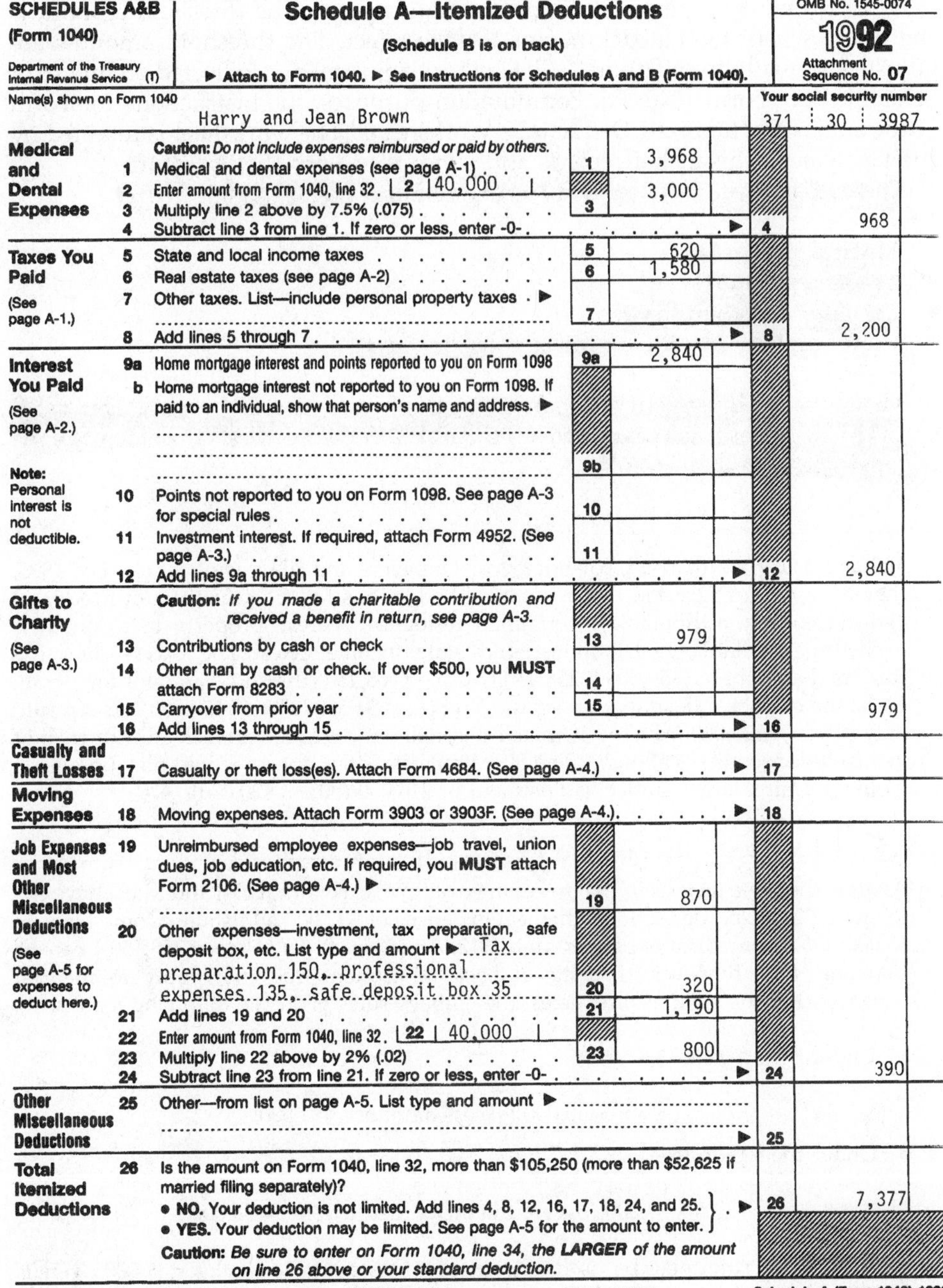

SCHEDULES A&B (Form 1040) — **Schedule A—Itemized Deductions** (Schedule B is on back) — OMB No. 1545-0074 — **1992**

Department of the Treasury Internal Revenue Service (T) ▶ Attach to Form 1040. ▶ See Instructions for Schedules A and B (Form 1040). Attachment Sequence No. 07

Name(s) shown on Form 1040: Harry and Jean Brown — Your social security number: 371 : 30 : 3987

Medical and Dental Expenses		Caution: *Do not include expenses reimbursed or paid by others.*				
	1	Medical and dental expenses (see page A-1)	1	3,968		
	2	Enter amount from Form 1040, line 32. 2 40,000				
	3	Multiply line 2 above by 7.5% (.075)	3	3,000		
	4	Subtract line 3 from line 1. If zero or less, enter -0- ▶			4	968
Taxes You Paid (See page A-1.)	5	State and local income taxes	5	620		
	6	Real estate taxes (see page A-2)	6	1,580		
	7	Other taxes. List—include personal property taxes ▶	7			
	8	Add lines 5 through 7 ▶			8	2,200
Interest You Paid (See page A-2.)	9a	Home mortgage interest and points reported to you on Form 1098	9a	2,840		
	b	Home mortgage interest not reported to you on Form 1098. If paid to an individual, show that person's name and address. ▶	9b			
Note: Personal interest is not deductible.	10	Points not reported to you on Form 1098. See page A-3 for special rules	10			
	11	Investment interest. If required, attach Form 4952. (See page A-3.)	11			
	12	Add lines 9a through 11 ▶			12	2,840
Gifts to Charity (See page A-3.)		Caution: *If you made a charitable contribution and received a benefit in return, see page A-3.*				
	13	Contributions by cash or check	13	979		
	14	Other than by cash or check. If over $500, you **MUST** attach Form 8283	14			
	15	Carryover from prior year	15			
	16	Add lines 13 through 15 ▶			16	979
Casualty and Theft Losses	17	Casualty or theft loss(es). Attach Form 4684. (See page A-4.) ▶			17	
Moving Expenses	18	Moving expenses. Attach Form 3903 or 3903F. (See page A-4.) ▶			18	
Job Expenses and Most Other Miscellaneous Deductions (See page A-5 for expenses to deduct here.)	19	Unreimbursed employee expenses—job travel, union dues, job education, etc. If required, you **MUST** attach Form 2106. (See page A-4.) ▶	19	870		
	20	Other expenses—investment, tax preparation, safe deposit box, etc. List type and amount ▶ Tax preparation 150, professional expenses 135, safe deposit box 35	20	320		
	21	Add lines 19 and 20	21	1,190		
	22	Enter amount from Form 1040, line 32. 22 40,000				
	23	Multiply line 22 above by 2% (.02)	23	800		
	24	Subtract line 23 from line 21. If zero or less, enter -0- ▶			24	390
Other Miscellaneous Deductions	25	Other—from list on page A-5. List type and amount ▶			25	
Total Itemized Deductions	26	Is the amount on Form 1040, line 32, more than $105,250 (more than $52,625 if married filing separately)? • **NO.** Your deduction is not limited. Add lines 4, 8, 12, 16, 17, 18, 24, and 25. • **YES.** Your deduction may be limited. See page A-5 for the amount to enter. ▶			26	7,377
		Caution: *Be sure to enter on Form 1040, line 34, the* ***LARGER*** *of the amount on line 26 above or your standard deduction.*				

For Paperwork Reduction Act Notice, see Form 1040 Instructions. Cat. No. 11330X **Schedule A (Form 1040) 1992**

The Browns' AGI is $40,000. The completed Schedule A for 1992 reports itemized deductions totaling $7,377.

Overall Limitation on Certain Itemized Deductions

The Revenue Reconciliation Act of 1990 established a cutback of certain itemized deductions of high-income taxpayers. The threshold amount for 1993 is $108,450

($54,225 for married persons filing a separate return). The threshold amount is the figure where the cutback begins to take effect. The threshold amounts are adjusted annually for inflation.[47] The cutback adjustment is reflected on line 26 of Schedule A of Form 1040. For computation purposes, the instructions for Form 1040 contain an "Itemized Deductions Worksheet." The worksheet is retained by the taxpayer for his or her records and is not filed with the tax return.

The cutback applies to all itemized deductions *except* the following:

- Medical expenses.
- Investment interest.
- Casualty and theft losses.
- Wagering losses to the extent of wagering gains.

The cutback adjustment is 3 percent of the excess of AGI over the threshold amount. In no case, however, may the cutback be more than 80 percent of the covered itemized deductions.

EXAMPLE 35

Hal and Mary are married, calendar year taxpayers and file a joint return. For 1993, they have AGI of $258,450. Their itemized deductions for the year amount to $20,000 and are entirely attributable to qualified residence interest, property taxes on their residence, charitable contributions, and state income taxes. The excess over the threshold amount is $150,000 [$258,450 (AGI) – $108,450 (threshold amount for 1993)]. Thus, the cutback adjustment under the 3% rule is $4,500 (3% of $150,000). As a result, only $15,500 [$20,000 (covered itemized deductions) – $4,500 (cutback adjustment)] of itemized deductions is allowed. The 80% limitation does not come into play because it would permit a larger cutback adjustment of $16,000 (80% × $20,000). ◆

EXAMPLE 36

Assume the same facts as in the preceding example, except that Hal and Mary have the following itemized deductions: medical expenses of $32,000 and state income taxes of $5,000. Of the medical expenses, only $12,616 [$32,000 – (7.5% × $258,450)] can be claimed. Note, however, that the cutback adjustment does not apply to medical expenses. For the state income taxes, the cutback rules yield the following results:

- Under the 3% rule—

  3% × $150,000 (excess amount) = $4,500

- Under the 80% rule—

  80% × $5,000 (covered itemized deductions) = $4,000

Thus, the 80% rule must be used since it provides a smaller cutback ($4,000 versus $4,500). Therefore, the total allowable itemized deductions are $13,616 [$12,616 (medical expenses) + $1,000 (state income taxes less cutback)]. ◆

The cutback adjustment is applied after taking into account other Code provisions that reduce the allowable deduction (e.g., the 2 percent-of-AGI floor that applies to miscellaneous itemized deductions).

---

47. § 68. The threshold amount for 1992 was $105,250 ($52,625 for married persons filing a separate return).

Effective Utilization of Itemized Deductions

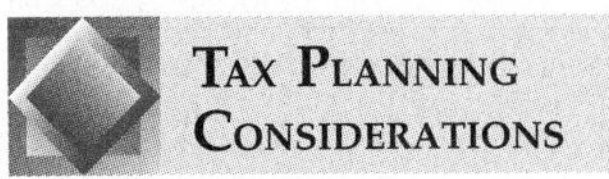

Since an individual may use the standard deduction in one year and itemize deductions in another year, it is frequently possible to obtain maximum benefit by shifting itemized deductions from one year to another. For example, if a taxpayer's itemized deductions and the standard deduction are approximately the same for each year of a two-year period, the taxpayer should use the standard deduction in one year and shift itemized deductions (to the extent permitted by law) to the other year. The individual could, for example, prepay a church pledge for a particular year or avoid paying end-of-the-year medical expenses to shift the deduction to the following year.

Utilization of Medical Deductions

When a taxpayer anticipates that medical expenses will approximate the percentage floor, much might be done to generate a deductible excess. Any of the following procedures can help build a deduction by the end of the year:

- Incur the obligation for needed dental work or have needed work carried out.[48] Orthodontic treatment, for example, may have been recommended for a member of the taxpayer's family.
- Have elective remedial surgery that may have been postponed from prior years (e.g., tonsillectomies, vasectomies, correction of hernias, hysterectomies).
- Incur the obligation for capital improvements to the taxpayer's personal residence recommended by a physician (e.g., an air filtration system to alleviate a respiratory disorder).

As an aid to taxpayers who may experience temporary cash-flow problems at the end of the year, the use of bank credit cards is deemed to be payment for purposes of timing the deductibility of charitable and medical expenses.

EXAMPLE 37

On December 13, 1993, Marge (a calendar year taxpayer) purchases two pairs of prescription contact lenses and one pair of prescribed orthopedic shoes for a total of $305. These purchases are separately charged to Marge's credit card. On January 6, 1994, Marge receives her statement containing these charges and makes payment shortly thereafter. The purchases are deductible as medical expenses in the year charged (1993) and not in the year the account is settled (1994). ◆

Recognizing which expenditures qualify for the medical deduction also may be crucial to exceeding the percentage limitations.

EXAMPLE 38

Mortimer employs Lana (an unrelated party) to care for his incapacitated and dependent mother. Lana is not a trained nurse but spends approximately one-half of the time performing nursing duties (e.g., administering injections and providing physical therapy) and the rest of the time doing household chores. An allocable portion of Lana's wages that Mortimer pays (including the employer's portion of FICA taxes) qualifies as a medical expense. ◆

48. Prepayment of medical expenses does not generate a current deduction unless the taxpayer is under an obligation to make the payment.

To assure a deduction for the entire cost of nursing home care for an aged dependent, it is helpful if the transfer of the individual to the home is for medical reasons and is recommended by a doctor. In addition, the nursing home facilities should be adequate to provide the necessary medical and nursing care. To assure a deduction for all of the nursing home expenses, it is necessary to show that the individual was placed in the home for required medical care rather than for personal or family considerations.

Proper documentation is required to substantiate medical expenses. The taxpayer should keep all receipts for credit card or other charge purchases of medical services and deductible drugs as well as all cash register receipts. In addition, medical transportation mileage should be recorded.

If a taxpayer or a dependent of the taxpayer must be institutionalized in order to receive adequate medical care, it may be good tax planning to make a lump-sum payment that will cover medical treatment for future periods. It is advisable to negotiate a contract with the institution so that the expense is fixed and the payment is not a mere deposit.

Protecting the Interest Deduction

Although the deductibility of prepaid interest by a cash basis taxpayer has been severely restricted, a notable exception allows a deduction for points paid to obtain financing for the purchase or improvement of a principal residence in the year of payment. However, such points must actually be paid by the taxpayer obtaining the loan and must represent a charge for the use of money. It has been held that points paid from the mortgage proceeds do not satisfy the payment requirement.[49] Also, the portion of the points attributable to service charges does not represent deductible interest.[50] Taxpayers financing home purchases or improvements usually should direct their planning toward avoiding these two hurdles to immediate deductibility.

In rare instances, a taxpayer may find it desirable to forgo the immediate expensing of points in the year paid. Instead, it could prove beneficial to capitalize the points and write them off as interest expense over the life of the mortgage.

EXAMPLE 39

Geraldine purchases a home on December 15, 1993, for $95,000 with $30,000 cash and a 15-year mortgage of $65,000 financed by the Greater Metropolis National Bank. Geraldine pays two points in addition to interest allocated to the period from December 15 until December 31, 1993, at an annual rate of 10%. Since Geraldine does not have enough itemized deductions to exceed the standard deduction for 1993, she should elect to capitalize the interest expense by amortizing the points over 15 years. In this instance, Geraldine would deduct $86.67 for 1994, as part of her qualified residence interest expense [$1,300 (two points) divided by 15 years], if she elects to itemize that year. ◆

Because personal (consumer) interest is not deductible, taxpayers should consider making use of home equity loans. Recall that these loans utilize the personal residence of the taxpayer as security. Since the tracing rules do not apply to home equity loans, the funds from these loans can be used for personal purposes (e.g., auto loans, education). By making use of home equity loans, therefore, what would have been nondeductible consumer interest becomes deductible qualified residence interest.

---

49. *Alan A. Rubnitz*, 67 T.C. 621 (1977).

50. *Donald L. Wilkerson*, 70 T.C. 240 (1978).

Assuring the Charitable Contribution Deduction

For a charitable contribution deduction to be available, the recipient must be a qualified charitable organization. Sometimes the mechanics of how the contribution is carried out can determine whether or not a deduction results.

EXAMPLE 40

Fumiko wants to donate $5,000 to her church's mission in Kobe, Japan. In this regard, she considers three alternatives:

1. Send the money directly to the mission.
2. Give the money to her church with the understanding that it is to be passed on to the mission.
3. Give the money directly to the missionary in charge of the mission who is currently in the United States on a fund-raising trip.

If Fumiko wants to obtain a deduction for the contribution, she should choose alternative 2. A direct donation to the mission (alternative 1) is not deductible because the mission is a foreign charity. A direct gift to the missionary (alternative 3) does not comply since an individual cannot be a qualified charity for income tax purposes.[51] ◆

When making noncash donations, the type of property chosen can have decided implications in determining the amount, if any, of the deduction.

EXAMPLE 41

Samantha wants to give $60,000 in value to her church in some form other than cash. In this connection, she considers four alternatives:

1. Stock held for two years as an investment with a basis of $100,000 and a fair market value of $60,000.
2. Stock held for five years as an investment with a basis of $10,000 and a fair market value of $60,000.
3. The rent-free use for a year of a building that normally leases for $5,000 a month.
4. A valuable stamp collection held as an investment and owned for 10 years with a basis of $10,000 and a fair market value of $60,000. The church plans to sell the collection if and when it is donated.

Alternative 1 is ill-advised as the subject of the gift. Even though Samantha would obtain a deduction of $60,000, she would forgo the potential loss of $40,000 that would be recognized if the property were sold.[52] Alternative 2 makes good sense since the deduction still is $60,000 and none of the $50,000 of appreciation that has occurred must be recognized as income. Alternative 3 yields no deduction at all and is not a wise choice. Alternative 4 involves tangible personalty that the recipient does not plan to use. As a result, the amount of the deduction is limited to $10,000, the stamp collection's basis.[53] ◆

For property transfers (particularly real estate), the ceiling limitations on the amount of the deduction allowed in any one year (50 percent, 30 percent, or 20 percent of AGI, as the case may be) could be a factor to take into account. With proper planning, donations can be controlled to stay within the limitations and therefore avoid the need for a carryover of unused charitable contributions.

---

51. *Thomas E. Lesslie,* 36 TCM 495, T.C.Memo. 1977–111.

52. *LaVar M. Withers,* 69 T.C. 900 (1978).

53. No reduction of appreciation is necessary in alternative 2 since stock is intangible property and not tangible personalty. As noted in Chapter 14, however, the untaxed appreciation usually is a tax preference item for purposes of the alternative minimum tax.

EXAMPLE 42

Andrew wants to donate a tract of unimproved land held as an investment to the University of Maryland (a qualified charitable organization). The land has been held for six years and has a current fair market value of $300,000 and a basis to Andrew of $50,000. Andrew's AGI for the current year is estimated to be $200,000, and he expects much the same for the next few years. In the current year, he deeds (transfers) an undivided one-fifth interest in the real estate to the university. ◆

What has Andrew in Example 42 accomplished for income tax purposes? In the current year, he will be allowed a charitable contribution deduction of $60,000 (⅕ × $300,000), which will be within the applicable limitation of AGI (30% × $200,000). Presuming no other charitable contributions for the year, Andrew has avoided the possibility of a carryover. In future years, Andrew can arrange donations of undivided interests in the real estate to stay within the bounds of the percentage limitations. The only difficulty with this approach is the need to revalue the real estate each year before the donation, since the amount of the deduction is based on the fair market value of the interest contributed at the time of the contribution.

It may be wise to avoid a carryover of unused charitable contributions, if possible, because that approach may be dangerous in several respects. First, the carryover period is limited to five years. Depending on the taxpayer's projected AGI rather than actual AGI, some of the amount carried over may expire without tax benefit after the five-year period has ended. Second, unused charitable contribution carryovers do not survive the death of the party making the donation and as a consequence are lost.

EXAMPLE 43

Tiffany dies in October 1993. In completing her final income tax return for 1993, Tiffany's executor determines the following information: AGI of $104,000 and a donation by Tiffany to her church of stock worth $60,000. Tiffany had purchased the stock two years ago for $50,000 and held it as an investment. Tiffany's executor makes the reduced deduction election and, as a consequence, claims a charitable contribution deduction of $50,000. With the election, the potential charitable contribution deduction of $50,000 ($60,000 – $10,000) is less than the 50% ceiling of $52,000 ($104,000 × 50%). If the executor had not made the election, the potential charitable contribution deduction of $60,000 would have been reduced by the 30% ceiling to $31,200 ($104,000 × 30%). No carryover of the $28,800 ($60,000 – $31,200) would have been available. ◆

PROBLEM MATERIALS

DISCUSSION QUESTIONS

1. Dan, a self-employed individual taxpayer, prepared his own income tax return for the past year and asked you to check it over for accuracy. Your review indicates that Dan failed to claim certain business entertainment expenses.
   a. Will the correction of this omission affect the amount of medical expenses Dan can deduct? Explain.
   b. Would it matter if Dan were employed rather than self-employed?
2. Ninfa is in perfect health. During the current year, however, she pays $450 for an annual physical exam and $80 for a dental checkup. Do these expenses qualify for the medical deduction? Why or why not?

3. Under what circumstances, if any, will the cost of cosmetic surgery qualify as a deductible medical expense?
4. What are the criteria for determining whether the cost of a nursing home can qualify as a medical expense?
5. Hugo has a history of heart disease. Upon the advice of his doctor, he installs an elevator in his residence so he does not have to climb stairs. Is this a valid medical expense? If it is, how much of the expense is deductible?
6. Vincent is employed as an accountant in New Orleans, Louisiana. One of Vincent's friends, Dr. Hill, practices general dentistry in Hot Springs, Arkansas. Once a year during the deer hunting season, Vincent travels to Hot Springs for his annual dental checkup. While there, Vincent makes use of Dr. Hill's deer lodge for hunting purposes. Do any of Vincent's travel expenses for the trip to Arkansas qualify for the medical expense deduction? Why or why not?
7. Leroy and Agnes were divorced in 1992, and Agnes was awarded custody of their daughter Meg. During tax year 1993, Leroy pays for all of Meg's medical expenses. Leroy contacts Agnes and suggests that he be awarded Meg as a dependent so he can claim the medical expenses he paid on her behalf. Is Leroy's understanding of the tax law correct? Explain.
8. If Ida's medical expense deduction was $500 in 1993 and the amount reduced her tax liability, how would a $300 insurance reimbursement be treated if received in 1994? Received in 1993? What if Ida had not itemized deductions in 1993 and received the $300 reimbursement in 1994?
9. Why would a taxpayer want to concentrate medical expenses in a particular tax year? Give *some* examples of how this can be accomplished.
10. When is a motor vehicle registration fee deductible for tax purposes?
11. The city of Galveston, Texas, assessed beachfront property owners for the construction of jetties to protect shorelines from the destructive effects of the ocean. Is this assessment deductible?
12. A seller of property pays real estate taxes apportioned to the buyer. What are the income tax consequences to each party?
13. If a taxpayer overpays his or her state income tax due to excessive withholdings or estimated tax payments, how is the refund check treated when received in the subsequent year? Are the excess amounts paid deductible in the current year?
14. Why has Congress imposed limitations on the deductibility of interest when funds are borrowed for the purpose of purchasing or continuing to hold investment property?
15. How can home equity loans be used to avoid the nondeductibility of interest on amounts borrowed to finance the purchase of consumer goods?
16. As to the deductibility of "points," comment on the following:

    a. Those paid by the seller.
    b. Those paid to finance the purchase of a rental house.
    c. Those relating to the rendering of personal services.
    d. When capitalization and amortization might be advisable.
    e. Points paid from the mortgage proceeds.

17. Discuss the special problems that arise with respect to the deductibility of interest on a debt between related parties. How does § 267 of the Code relate to this problem?
18. If a taxpayer withdraws amounts from a certificate of deposit prematurely and a penalty applies, what are the income tax consequences?
19. An accountant normally charges $100 an hour when preparing financial statements for clients. If the accountant performs accounting services for a church without charge, can she deduct the value of the donated services on her tax return?
20. John would like to attend the annual convention of his church, which is to be held in another state. Advise John on some of the tax implications that would result if he makes the trip.

21. What is ordinary income property? If inventory with an adjusted basis of $60 and fair market value of $100 is contributed to a public charity, how much is deductible?
22. What is capital gain property? What tax treatment is required if capital gain property is contributed to a private nonoperating foundation? To a public charity? What difference does it make if the contribution is tangible personalty and it is put to a use unrelated to the donee's business?
23. During 1993, Shirley donated five dresses to the Salvation Army. She had purchased the dresses three years ago at a cost of $1,200 and worn them as personal attire. Because the dresses are long-term capital assets, Shirley plans to deduct $1,200 on her 1993 income tax return. Comment on Shirley's understanding of the tax law governing charitable contributions.
24. In the year of her death, Sharon made significant charitable contributions of long-term capital gain property. In fact, the amount of the contributions exceeds 30% of her AGI. What might be a possible alternative for the executor of Sharon's estate who prepares her final income tax return?
25. In 1992, Vern had an excess charitable contribution that he could not deduct because of the percentage limitations. In 1993, Vern made further charitable contributions. In applying the percentage limitations for 1993, how are these transactions handled?
26. Regarding the cutback adjustment for certain itemized deductions, comment on the following:
    a. The threshold amount.
    b. Itemized deductions not covered.
    c. The 3% and 80% rules.

PROBLEMS

27. Bill and Nancy are married and together have AGI of $40,000. They have no dependents and filed a joint return in 1993. Each pays $800 for hospitalization insurance. During the year, they paid the following amounts for medical care: $4,100 in doctor and dentist bills and hospital expenses and $600 for prescribed medicine and drugs. They received an insurance reimbursement for hospitalization in December 1993 for $700. Determine the deduction allowable for medical expenses paid in 1993.
28. Dave is divorced and claims his father (Jesse) and his son (Sammy) as dependents. During the current year, he pays the following expenses:

Tuition (including room and board) to send Sammy to Prospect Military Academy	$12,000
To Dr. Brown (a child psychiatrist) for consultations with Sammy	2,500
Room and board at Happy Farms Assisted Living Home on behalf of Jesse	18,000
Doctor and hospital charges to correct Jesse's hernia	2,600

    Upon Dr. Brown's recommendation, Sammy was sent to Prospect Military Academy to alleviate a truancy problem. The academy provides no medical care but does impose strict discipline. Jesse moved to Happy Farms because he felt living with Dave was too dull. Disregarding percentage limitations, how much qualifies as a medical expense on Dave's tax return for:
    a. Sammy?
    b. Jesse?
29. Upon the advice of his physician, George, a heart patient, installs an elevator in his personal residence at a cost of $8,000. The elevator has a cost recovery period of five years. A neighbor who is in the real estate business charges George $60 for an appraisal that places the value of the residence at $60,000 before the improvement and $62,000 after. The value increases because George lives in a region where many older people retire and therefore would find the elevator an attractive feature in a

home. As a result of the operation of the elevator, George noticed an increase of $75 in his utility bills for the current year. Disregarding percentage limitations, which of the above expenditures qualify as a medical expense deduction?

30. Jerry lives in Arkansas and discovers that he has a rare disease that can be treated only with surgery by a surgeon in Germany. Jerry incurs $1,700 in airfare, $200 in meals taken at the medical facility, and $800 in lodging expenses for eight nights of lodging related to his medical care in Germany. What amount, if any, of these expenses is deductible?

31. During 1993, Agnew paid the following medical expenses:

On behalf of Sylvester (Agnew's son by a former marriage)	$9,000
On behalf of Roger (Agnew's uncle)	5,000
Hospital bill for an operation performed on Agnew in 1992	4,500

Of the $9,000 spent on Sylvester, $2,500 was for orthodontia services to be performed in 1994. The dentist required this amount as a deposit for the braces to be applied to Sylvester's teeth. Agnew could claim Sylvester as a dependent, but Sylvester's mother refuses to sign the custodial parent's waiver. Roger could be claimed as Agnew's dependent except for the gross income test. For these items, what amount qualifies as Agnew's medical expenses for 1993?

32. Fran is employed as a real estate broker. For calendar year 1993, Fran has $50,000 in wages from her job and pays $3,800 in medical insurance premiums. During the year, she paid the following other medical expenses:

Doctor and hospital bills for Herb and Georgia (Fran's parents)	$6,000
Doctor and dentist bills for Fran	3,200
Prescribed medicines for Fran	800
Nonprescribed insulin for Fran	350

Herb and Georgia would qualify as Fran's dependents except that they file a joint return. Fran's medical insurance policy does not cover them. Fran filed a claim for $2,100 for her own expenses with her insurance company in December 1993. She received the $2,100 reimbursement in January 1994. Discuss the tax treatment of these various expenses.

33. In Clay County, the real property tax year is the calendar year. The real property tax becomes a personal liability of the owner of real property on January 1 in the current real property tax year, 1993. The tax is payable on July 1, 1993. On May 1, 1993, Joe sells his house to Celia for $250,000. On July 1, 1993, Celia pays the entire real estate tax of $3,285 for the year ending December 31, 1993.

a. How much of the property taxes may Joe deduct?
b. How much of the property taxes may Celia deduct?

34. Assume the same facts as in Problem 33.

a. What is Celia's basis for the residence?
b. How much did Joe realize from the sale of the residence?

35. Roland uses the cash method of accounting and lives in a state that imposes an income tax (including withholding from wages). On April 14, 1993, he files his state return for 1992, paying an additional $900 in income taxes. During 1993, his withholdings for state income tax purposes amount to $3,100. On April 13, 1994, he files his state return for 1993 claiming a refund of $400. Roland receives the refund on August 3, 1994.

a. If Roland itemizes deductions, how much may he claim as a deduction for state income taxes on his Federal return for calendar year 1993 (filed in April 1994)?
b. How will the refund of $400 received in 1994 be treated for Federal income tax purposes?

36. In 1993, Myrna has $8,000 of investment income and the following miscellaneous deductions:

Unreimbursed employee business expenses (meals included at 80%)	$1,000
Tax return preparation fee	150
Investment expenses	600

For purposes of the investment interest expense limitation, what is the total of Myrna's net investment income in each of the following independent situations:

a. AGI of $30,000.
b. AGI of $70,000.
c. AGI of $100,000.

37. Clark is married and files a joint tax return for 1993. Clark has investment interest expense of $95,000 for a loan made to him in 1993 to purchase a parcel of unimproved land. His income from investments (dividends and interest) totaled $15,000. After reducing his miscellaneous deductions by the applicable 2% floor, the deductible portion amounted to $2,500. In addition to $1,100 of investment expenses included in miscellaneous deductions, Clark paid $3,000 of real estate taxes on the unimproved land. Clark also has $3,000 as a net long-term capital gain from the sale of another parcel of unimproved land. Calculate Clark's investment interest deduction for 1993.

38. Veronica borrowed $200,000 to acquire a parcel of land to be held for investment purposes. During 1993, she paid interest of $20,000 on the loan. She had AGI of $50,000 for the year. Other items related to Veronica's investments include the following:

Investment income	$10,200
Long-term gain on sale of stock	4,000
Investment counsel fees	1,500

Veronica is unmarried and elected to itemize her deductions. She had no miscellaneous deductions other than the investment counsel fees. Determine Veronica's investment interest deduction for 1993.

39. In 1993, Earl borrows $120,000 to purchase an airplane (to be used for pleasure purposes) by placing a lien on his personal residence. At this time, the first mortgage on the residence has a balance of $300,000, and the residence has a fair market value of $600,000. How should Earl determine his interest deduction?

40. Ted and his wife Alice own a personal residence in the city. For many years, they have owned a beach house 50 miles away. They do not rent out the beach house because they spend every weekend there. Last year, they purchased a condominium in Boulder, Colorado, for their son to live in while he attends college. During 1993, they paid the following mortgage interest (each mortgage is secured by the respective property): $7,800 on their personal residence, $5,500 on the beach house, and $9,000 on the condominium. How much can Ted and Alice deduct for the year as qualified residence interest?

41. Ron and Tom are equal owners in Robin Corporation. On July 1, 1993, each loans the corporation $30,000 at annual interest of 10%. Ron and Tom are brothers. Both shareholders are on the cash method of accounting, while Robin Corporation is on the accrual method. All parties use the calendar year for tax purposes. On June 30, 1994, Robin repays the loans of $60,000 together with the specified interest of $6,000.

a. How much of the interest can Robin Corporation deduct in 1993? In 1994?
b. When is the interest taxed to Ron and Tom?

42. In 1993 Peter pays $500 to become a charter member of State University's Athletic Council. The membership ensures that Peter will receive choice seating at all of State's home football games. Also in 1993, Peter pays $120 (the regular retail price) for season tickets for himself and his wife. For these items, how much qualifies as a charitable contribution?

43. Diego's child attends a parochial school operated by the church the family attends. Diego made a donation of $300 to the church in lieu of the normal registration fee of $100 for children of nonmembers. In addition, the regular tuition of $75 per week is paid to the school. Based on this information, what is Diego's charitable contribution?

44. Determine the amount of the charitable deduction allowed in each of the following situations:

    a. Donation of Wren Corporation stock (a publicly traded corporation) to taxpayer's church. The stock cost the taxpayer $2,000 four months ago and has a fair market value of $3,000 on the date of the donation.
    b. Donation of a painting to the Salvation Army. The painting cost the taxpayer $2,000 five years ago and has a fair market value of $3,500 on the date of the donation.
    c. The local branch of the American Red Cross uses a building rent-free for half of the current year. The building normally rents for $500 a month.
    d. Donation by a cash basis farmer to a church of a quantity of grain worth $900. The farmer raised the grain in the preceding year at a cost of $650, all of which was deducted for income tax purposes.

45. During 1993, Al made the following contributions to his church:

Cash	$20,000
Stock in Thrush Corporation (a publicly traded corporation)	30,000

The stock in Thrush Corporation was acquired as an investment three years ago at a cost of $10,000. Al's AGI for 1993 is $70,000.

    a. What is Al's charitable contribution deduction for 1993?
    b. How are excess amounts, if any, treated?

46. Mae died in 1993. Before she died, Mae made a gift of stock in Eagle Corporation (a publicly traded corporation) to her church. The stock was worth $35,000 and had been acquired as an investment two years ago at a cost of $30,000. In the year of her death, Mae had AGI of $60,000. In completing her final income tax return, how should Mae's executor handle the charitable contribution?

47. On December 30, 1993, Roberta purchased four tickets to a charity ball sponsored by the city of San Diego for the benefit of underprivileged children. Each ticket cost $200 and had a fair market value of $35. On the same day as the purchase, Roberta gave the tickets to the minister of her church for personal use by his family. At the time of the gift of the tickets, Roberta pledged $4,000 to the building fund of her church. The pledge was satisfied by check dated December 31, 1993, but not mailed until January 3, 1994.

    a. Presuming Roberta is a cash basis and calendar year taxpayer, how much can she deduct as a charitable contribution for 1993?
    b. Would the amount of the deduction be any different if Roberta is an accrual basis taxpayer? Explain.

48. Classify each of the following independent expenditures as nondeductible *(ND)* items, business *(dfor)* deductions, or itemized *(dfrom)* deductions. (*Note:* In many cases, it may be necessary to refer to the materials in earlier chapters of the text.)

    a. Interest allowed on home mortgage accrued by a cash basis taxpayer.
    b. State income taxes paid by a sole proprietor of a business.
    c. Subscription to the *Wall Street Journal* paid by a vice president of a bank and not reimbursed by her employer.
    d. Automobile mileage for attendance at weekly church services.
    e. Street-paving assessment paid to the county by a homeowner.
    f. Speeding ticket paid by the owner-operator of a taxicab.
    g. Interest and taxes paid by the owner of residential rental property.

h. Business entertainment expenses (properly substantiated) paid by a self-employed taxpayer.
i. State and Federal excise taxes on tobacco paid by a self-employed taxpayer who gave his clients cigars as Christmas presents. The business gifts were properly substantiated and under $25 each.
j. State and Federal excise taxes on cigarettes purchased by a heavy smoker for personal consumption.
k. Federal excise taxes (14.1 cents per gallon) on the purchase of gasoline for use in the taxpayer's personal automobile.
l. Theft loss of personal jewelry worth $300 but which originally cost $75.
m. Maternity clothing purchased by a taxpayer who is pregnant.
n. Medical expenses paid by an employer on behalf of an employee.
o. Qualified residence interest paid by a taxpayer on a loan obtained to build an artist studio in his personal residence. Assume that taxpayer's art activities are classified as a hobby.
p. Assume the same facts as in (o) except that the art activities are classified as a trade or business.

49. Some miscellaneous deductions are subject to the 2%-of-AGI floor while other deductions are not. In this connection, comment on the tax treatment of the following:

a. Job hunting costs.
b. Moving expenses.
c. Appraisal fees to determine the amount of a casualty loss.
d. Gambling losses up to the amount of gambling winnings.
e. Hobby loss up to the amount of hobby income.
f. Job uniforms not suited for normal wear.
g. Casualty and theft losses.
h. Medical expenses.

50. For calendar year 1993, Clyde and Trisha file a joint return reflecting AGI of $150,000. Their itemized deductions are as follows:

Medical expenses	$12,000
Casualty loss (not covered by insurance)	16,000
Interest on home mortgage	20,000
Property taxes on home	12,000
Charitable contributions	11,000
State income tax	8,000

After all necessary adjustments are made, what is the amount of itemized deductions Clyde and Trisha may claim?

51. Kareem and Veneia are married and file a joint return. For 1993, they have AGI of $305,520. Their itemized deductions for the year total $39,000 and consist of the following:

Medical expenses	$32,000
Interest on home mortgage	3,000
State income tax	4,000

After all necessary adjustments are made, what is the amount of itemized deductions Kareem and Veneia may claim?

CUMULATIVE PROBLEMS

52. Alice and Bruce Byrd are married taxpayers, ages 47 and 45, who file a joint return. Their Social Security numbers are 034–48–4382 and 016–50–9556, respectively. They live at 473 Revere Avenue, Ames, MA 01850. Alice is a receptionist for a dental clinic and earns an annual salary of $24,000. Bruce is the manager of several fast-food outlets owned and operated by Plymouth Corporation. His annual salary is $38,000.

The Byrds have two children, Cynthia (age 23 and S.S. no. 017–44–9126) and John (age 22 and S.S. no. 017–27–4148), who live with them. Both are full-time students at a nearby college. Bruce's mother, Myrtle Byrd (age 74 and S.S. no. 016–15–8266), also lives with them. Her sole source of income is a Social Security benefit, which she deposits in a savings account.

During 1992, a particularly harsh storm struck the Ames area. As a result, the Byrds suffered severe flood damage to the basement and foundation of their personal residence, which was purchased in 1985 at a cost of $80,000. Based on an appraisal, the fair market value of the house was $110,000 before the storm and $100,000 after. The Byrds' homeowner's insurance policy does not cover damage due to flooding. The cost of the appraisal was $300.

During 1992, the Byrds furnished one-third of the total support of Alice's widower father, Sam Harper (age 70 and S.S. no. 034–82–8583). Sam lives alone and receives the rest of his support from Alice's sister and brother (one-third each). They have signed a multiple support agreement allowing Alice to claim the father as a dependent for 1992.

The Byrds had the following expenses relating to their personal residence during 1992:

Property taxes	$1,800
Interest on home mortgage	6,000
Repairs to roof	1,000
Utilities	1,500
Fire and theft insurance	600

Medical expenses for 1992 include:

Medical insurance premiums	$2,400
Doctor bill incurred in 1991 and not paid until 1992	1,100
Operation for Sam Harper	3,200

The operation for Sam Harper represents the one-third Alice contributed toward her father's support.

Other relevant information follows:

- During 1992, Myrtle gave Alice and Bruce a tract of undeveloped land (basis of $30,000 and fair market value of $40,000), which she had inherited from her husband (Bruce's father).
- Alice and Bruce had $2,956 withheld from their salaries for state income taxes. When they filed their 1991 state return in 1992, they paid additional tax of $210.
- During 1992, Alice and Bruce attended a dinner dance sponsored by the Ames Police Disability Association (a qualified charitable organization). The Byrds paid $80 for the tickets. Cost of comparable entertainment would normally be $50. The Byrds contributed $1,200 to their church and gave used clothing (cost of $500 and fair market value of $100) to the Salvation Army. All donations are supported by receipts.
- In 1992, the Byrds received interest income of $390 from a savings account they maintained.
- Alice's employer requires that all female employees wear nurses' uniforms to work. During 1992, Alice spent $240 on new uniforms and $82 on laundry charges. Bruce paid $84 for an annual subscription to the *Journal of Franchise Management*. Neither Alice's nor Bruce's employers reimburse for employee expenses.
- Alice and Bruce had $5,532 ($2,586 for Alice and $2,946 for Bruce) of Federal income tax withheld in 1992 and paid no estimated Federal income tax. Neither Alice nor Bruce wishes to designate $1 to the Presidential Election Campaign Fund.

Compute net tax payable or refund due for Alice and Bruce Byrd for 1992. If they have overpaid, the amount is to be refunded. If you use tax forms for your computations, you will need Form 1040, Schedule A, and Form 4684. Suggested software (if available): *TurboTax* or *MacInTax* for tax return or WFT tax planning software.

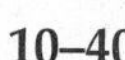

53. Sam Worthing, age 45, is married and has two dependent children. In 1993, he incurred the following:

Salary received from his employer, Geophysics, Inc.		$65,000
Cost of art supplies. Sam took up painting as a hobby and plans to sell the paintings to friends and art galleries but had no willing purchasers during 1993.		1,000
Contribution of shares of Xerox stock to his church (fair market value of $3,000, cost of $800, and acquired in 1976).		3,000
Sam's wife, Irene, had a diamond ring that was stolen in April 1993. A police report was filed, but her ring was not recovered. It is not covered by insurance. The ring had recently been appraised at $4,000, which was also its original cost.		4,000
Travel (meals included at 80%) and auto expenses incurred in connection with Sam's employment (none of which was reimbursed).		3,500
Sam and his family moved from Nashville to Boston during the year and incurred the following unreimbursed expenses:		
Moving van	$2,500	
House-hunting expenses (meals included at 80%)	2,000	
Sales commissions on the former house	3,500	8,000
Sam incurred and paid the following personal expenses:		
Medical and dental bills for the family		2,500
State and local income and property taxes		4,500

Determine the Worthings' AGI and taxable income for 1993, assuming that a joint return is filed and that there are no other items of income or expense. Suggested software (if available): *TurboTax* or *MacInTax* for tax return or WFT tax planning software.

CHAPTER

TAX CREDITS

OBJECTIVES

Discuss the use of tax credits as a tool of Federal tax policy.

Distinguish between refundable and nonrefundable credits.

Discuss carryover provisions and the priority system for determining the order in which credits are utilized.

Explain the various tax credits that apply to businesses and to individuals.

Identify tax planning opportunities related to tax credits.

OUTLINE

Tax credits are important factors in determining the final amount of tax that must be paid or the amount of refund a taxpayer receives. Tax credits have the general effect of directly reducing a taxpayer's tax liability. The chapter begins by discussing important tax policy considerations relevant to tax credits. Tax credits are categorized as being either refundable or nonrefundable. The distinction between refundable and nonrefundable credits is important because it may determine whether a taxpayer will receive a tax benefit from a particular credit.

Next an overview dealing with the priority of tax credits is presented. The remainder of the chapter examines the credits available to businesses and to individual taxpayers and the ways in which credits enter into the calculation of the tax liability.

TAX POLICY CONSIDERATIONS

Congress has generally used tax credits to achieve social or economic objectives or to provide equity for different types of taxpayers. For example, the investment tax credit was introduced in 1962. It was expected to encourage economic growth, improve the competitive position of American industry at home and abroad, and help alleviate the nation's balance of payments problem.[1] Since 1962, however, the investment tax credit has had a *checkered* history. It has been suspended, reinstated, repealed, reenacted, and finally repealed again in response to changing economic and political conditions. More specifically, under current law, the investment tax credit has been repealed for property placed in service after December 31, 1985. In repealing the credit, Congress was pursuing the goal of limiting the effect of taxes as a factor in business decisions. It will be interesting to see if Congress and the administration maintain this objective in light of current economic conditions (i.e., a sluggish economy).

A tax credit should not be confused with an income tax deduction. Certain expenditures of individuals are allowed as deductions from gross income in arriving at AGI (e.g., business expenses). Additionally, individuals are allowed to deduct certain nonbusiness and investment-related expenses *from* AGI. Whereas the tax benefit received from a tax deduction depends on the tax rate, a tax credit is not affected by the tax rate of the taxpayer.

EXAMPLE 1

Assume Congress wishes to encourage a certain type of expenditure. One way to accomplish this objective is to allow a tax credit of 25% for such expenditures. Another way to accomplish this objective is to allow an itemized deduction for the expenditures. Assume Abby's tax rate is 15%, while Bill's tax rate is 31%. In addition, assume that Carmen does not incur enough qualifying expenditures to itemize deductions. The following tax benefits are available to each taxpayer for a $1,000 expenditure:

	Abby	Bill	Carmen
Tax benefit if a 25% credit is allowed	$250	$250	$250
Tax benefit if an itemized deduction is allowed	150	310	–0–

1. Summary of remarks of the Secretary of the Treasury, quoted in S.Rept. 1881, 87th Cong., 2nd Sess., reported in 1962–3 C.B. 707.

As these results indicate, tax credits provide benefits on a more equitable basis than do tax deductions. Equally apparent is the fact that in this case the deduction approach will benefit only taxpayers who itemize deductions, while the credit approach benefits all taxpayers who make the specified expenditure. ◆

For many years, Congress used the tax credit provisions of the Code liberally in implementing tax policy. Although existing tax credits still carry out this objective, budget constraints and economic considerations have dictated the repeal of some credits (e.g., regular investment tax credit, political contributions credit). Nevertheless, such credits as those applicable to expenses incurred for child and dependent care and expenses related to making businesses more accessible still reflect social policy considerations. Other credits, such as those applicable to taxes paid on income generated in foreign countries, have been retained based on economic considerations. Finally, note that the use of tax credits as a tax policy tool continues to evolve as economic and political circumstances change, as illustrated by the recent enactment of several credits (e.g., the disabled access credit).

OVERVIEW AND PRIORITY OF CREDITS

Refundable versus Nonrefundable Credits

As illustrated in Figure 11–1, certain credits are refundable while others are nonrefundable. *Refundable credits* are paid to the taxpayer even if the amount of the credit (or credits) exceeds the taxpayer's tax liability.

EXAMPLE 2

Ted, who is single, had taxable income of $21,000 in 1993. His income tax from the 1993 Tax Rate Schedule is $3,150. During 1993, Ted's employer withheld income tax of $3,500. Ted is entitled to a refund of $350 ($3,500 – $3,150) because the credit for tax withheld on wages is a refundable credit. ◆

FIGURE 11–1
Partial Listing of Refundable and Nonrefundable Credits

Refundable Credits

Taxes withheld on wages
Earned income credit

Nonrefundable Credits

Credit for child and dependent care expenses
Credit for the elderly and disabled
Foreign tax credit
General business credit, which is the sum of the following:

- Investment tax credit, which includes
  - Regular investment tax credit
  - Tax credit for rehabilitation expenditures
  - Business energy credit
- Jobs credit*
- Research activities credit*
- Low-income housing credit*
- Disabled access credit

*These credits expired after June 30, 1992, but Congress is likely to reenact them in 1993.

Nonrefundable credits are not paid if they exceed the taxpayer's tax liability.

EXAMPLE 3

Tina is single, age 67, and retired. Her taxable income for 1993 is $1,320, and the tax on this amount is $198. Tina's tax credit for the elderly is $225. This credit can be used to reduce her net tax liability to zero, but it will not result in a refund, even though the credit ($225) exceeds Tina's tax liability ($198). This result occurs because the tax credit for the elderly is a nonrefundable credit. ◆

Some nonrefundable credits, such as the foreign tax credit, can be carried over and used in a later year if they exceed the amount allowable as a credit in a given year. Other nonrefundable credits, such as the tax credit for the elderly (refer to Example 3), are not subject to carryover provisions and are lost if they exceed the limitations. Because some credits are subject to carryover provisions while others are not, the order in which credits are offset against the tax liability is important. The Code provides that nonrefundable credits are to be offset against a taxpayer's income tax liability in the order shown in Figure 11–1 (see page 11–3).

General Business Credit

Two special rules apply to the general business credit. First, any unused credit must be carried back 3 years, then forward 15 years. Second, for any tax year, the general business credit is limited to the taxpayer's *net income tax* reduced by the greater of:

- The *tentative minimum tax.*
- 25 percent of *net regular tax liability* that exceeds $25,000 ($12,500 for married taxpayers filing separately unless one of the spouses is not entitled to the general business credit).

Before discussing the general business credit limitation, several terms need to be defined:

- *Net income tax* is the sum of the regular tax liability and the alternative minimum tax reduced by certain nonrefundable tax credits.
- *Tentative minimum tax* for this purpose is reduced by the foreign tax credit allowed.
- *Regular tax liability* is determined from the appropriate tax table or tax rate schedule, based on taxable income. However, the regular tax liability does not include certain taxes (e.g., alternative minimum tax).
- *Net regular tax liability* is the regular tax liability reduced by certain nonrefundable credits (e.g., credit for child and dependent care expenses, foreign tax credit).

EXAMPLE 4

Floyd's general business credit for 1993 is $70,000. His net income tax is $150,000, tentative minimum tax is $130,000, and net regular tax liability is $150,000. He has no other tax credits. Floyd's general business credit allowed for the tax year is computed as follows:

Net income tax	$150,000
Less: The greater of	
■ $130,000 (tentative minimum tax)	
■ $31,250 [25% × ($150,000 – $25,000)]	130,000
Amount of general business credit allowed for tax year	$ 20,000

Floyd then has $50,000 ($70,000 – $20,000) of unused general business credits that may be carried back or forward as discussed below. ◆

Treatment of Unused General Business Credits

Unused general business credits are initially carried back three years (first to the earliest year in the sequence) and are applied to reduce tax during these years. Thus, the taxpayer may receive a tax refund as a result of the carryback. Any remaining unused credits are then carried forward 15 years.

A FIFO method is applied to the carryovers, carrybacks, and utilization of credits earned during a particular year. The oldest credits are used first in determining the amount of the general business credit.

The FIFO method minimizes the potential for loss of a general business credit benefit due to the expiration of credit carryovers, since the earliest years are used before the current credit for the taxable year.

EXAMPLE 5

This example illustrates the use of general business credit carryovers.

■ General business credit carryovers		
1990	$ 4,000	
1991	6,000	
1992	2,000	
Total carryovers	$12,000	
■ 1993 general business credit		$ 40,000
■ Total credit allowed in 1993 (based on tax liability)	$50,000	
Less: Utilization of carryovers		
1990	(4,000)	
1991	(6,000)	
1992	(2,000)	
■ Remaining credit allowed	$38,000	
Applied against		
1993 general business credit		(38,000)
1993 unused amount carried forward to 1994		$ 2,000

◆

SPECIFIC BUSINESS-RELATED TAX CREDIT PROVISIONS

The business-related tax credits that form a single general business credit include the investment tax credit, jobs credit, research activities credit, low-income housing credit, and disabled access credit. Each is determined separately under its own set of rules and is explained here in the order listed.

Investment Tax Credit: Introduction

Since its original enactment in 1962, the investment tax credit (ITC) has been suspended, reinstated, repealed, and reenacted in response to varying economic conditions and political pressures. These changes in the tax laws have created a nightmare for tax practitioners. This phenomenon continued with the TRA of 1986, which repealed the *regular* credit for most property placed in service after 1985. However, other components of the ITC (*rehabilitation expenditures credit* and *business energy credit*) are still allowed in certain situations. In addition, practitioners will have to deal with carryover and recapture provisions related to the ITC for many years in the future. Because of all of these factors, an awareness of the pre-1986 ITC is necessary. Each of the ITC components is discussed below.

Regular Investment Tax Credit

Qualifying Property. Prior to the repeal by TRA of 1986, the ITC was allowed for most business tangible personal property (e.g., automobiles, machinery, furniture) and was not allowed for most real property (e.g., land, buildings).[2] In addition, before 1991 qualifying property also included *transition property.* Transition property was certain property placed in service after 1985 that satisfied several restrictive requirements.

Computation of Qualified Investment and Amount of the Credit. Because of the recapture provisions and the carryover provisions applicable to the ITC, it is necessary to understand how the credit was computed. The ITC was based on the aggregate amount, without limit, of qualifying new property and limited amounts of used property placed in service during the year.

The credit was based on the recovery period under ACRS (refer to Chapter 8 for details). To avoid a basis reduction, the taxpayer could have elected a reduced ITC rate. Rates for the full credit and the reduced credit were as follows:

Recovery Period (in years)	Full Credit Rate	Reduced Credit Rate
3	6%	4%
5, 10, or 15	10%	8%

EXAMPLE 6

If Susan had placed into service five-year property costing $100,000 that qualified for the ITC, her allowable credit would have been $10,000 ($100,000 × 10%), assuming she chose to use the full credit rate. If she chose the reduced credit rate, the ITC would have been $8,000 ($100,000 × 8%). ◆

Recapture of Investment Tax Credit. The amount of the ITC is based on the recovery period of the qualifying property (refer to Example 6). However, if property is disposed of (or ceases to be qualified ITC property) before the end of the recovery period, the taxpayer must recapture all or a portion of the ITC originally taken.[3] Generally, the amount of the ITC that is recaptured in the year of premature disposition (or disqualification as ITC property) is added to the taxpayer's regular tax liability for the recapture year.

The portion of the credit recaptured is a specified percentage of the credit that was taken by the taxpayer. This percentage is based on the period the ITC property was held by the taxpayer, as shown in Figure 11–2.

EXAMPLE 7

Assume Susan sells or gives away the property acquired in Example 6 after using it in her business for four and one-half years. She is required to recapture ITC of $2,000 ($10,000 × 20%). This recapture provision leads to an increase of $2,000 in her tax

2. § 49(e).

3. § 50(a).

liability. Susan could have avoided the ITC recapture entirely by postponing the property's disposition by six months. That is, no recapture would have been required had Susan held the property for five years or more. ◆

Reduction of Investment Tax Credit. In general, a 35 percent reduction of the ITC is required for ITC carryovers from pre-1986 years. This also applies to the regular ITC, regardless of when the property was placed in service.

EXAMPLE 8

In an earlier year, Gary placed property into service that qualified for the ITC. The property, five-year recovery property, cost $10,000 and generated a tentative ITC of $1,000 ($10,000 × 10%). However, Gary was not able to actually use the ITC until 1993. The $1,000 ITC carried forward to 1993 produces a credit of $650 [$1,000 – $350 (reduction amount)]. ◆

Tax Credit for Rehabilitation Expenditures

Taxpayers are allowed a tax credit for expenditures to rehabilitate industrial and commercial buildings and certified historic structures. This credit, which is an extension of the regular ITC, is intended to discourage businesses from moving from older, economically distressed areas (e.g., inner city) to newer locations and to encourage the preservation of historic structures.

Congress has changed the credit rates and the structures to which the credit applies from time to time to ensure that the credit accomplishes its intended purpose. The operating features of this credit follow:

Rate of the Credit for Rehabilitation Expenses	Nature of the Property
10%	Nonresidential buildings, other than certified historic structures, originally placed in service before 1936
20%	Residential and nonresidential certified historic structures

To qualify for the credit, a taxpayer is required to depreciate the costs of the rehabilitation using the straight-line method (refer to Chapter 8 for details on depreciation provisions). The basis of a rehabilitated building must be reduced by the full rehabilitation credit allowed.

EXAMPLE 9

Juan spent $60,000 to rehabilitate a building that had originally been placed in service in 1932. He is allowed a credit of $6,000 (10% of $60,000) for rehabilitation expenditures.

FIGURE 11–2
ITC Recapture

If the Property Is Held for	The Recapture Percentage Is: For 15-Year, 10-Year, and 5-Year Property	For 3-Year Property
Less than 1 year	100	100
One year or more but less than 2 years	80	66
Two years or more but less than 3 years	60	33
Three years or more but less than 4 years	40	0
Four years or more but less than 5 years	20	0
Five years or more	0	0

Juan then increases the basis of the building by $54,000 [$60,000 (rehabilitation expenditures) – $6,000 (credit allowed)] and must depreciate these capitalized expenditures using the straight-line method. If the building were a historic structure instead, the credit allowed would be $12,000 (20% of $60,000), and the building's depreciable basis would increase by $48,000 [$60,000 (rehabilitation expenditures) – $12,000 (credit allowed)]. ◆

To qualify for the credit, buildings must be substantially rehabilitated. A building has been *substantially rehabilitated* if qualified rehabilitation expenditures exceed the greater of (1) the adjusted basis of the property before the rehabilitation or (2) $5,000. Qualified rehabilitation expenditures do not include the cost of acquiring a building, the cost of facilities related to a building (such as a parking lot), and the cost of enlarging an existing building. Stringent rules apply concerning the retention of internal and external walls.

The rehabilitation credit must be recaptured if the rehabilitated property is disposed of prematurely or if it ceases to be qualifying property. The amount recaptured is based on a holding period requirement of five years. In addition, the recapture amount is *added* to the adjusted basis of the rehabilitation expenditures for purposes of determining the amount of gain or loss realized on the property's disposition.

EXAMPLE 10

On March 15, 1990, Rashad placed in service $30,000 of rehabilitation expenditures on a building qualifying for a 10% credit. A credit of $3,000 ($30,000 × 10%) was allowed, and the basis of the building was increased by $27,000 ($30,000 – $3,000). The building was sold on December 15, 1993. Rashad must recapture a portion of the rehabilitation credit based on the schedule for five-year property in Figure 11–2. Because Rashad held the rehabilitated property for more than three years but less than four, 40% of the credit, or $1,200, must be added to his 1993 tax liability. Also, the adjusted basis of the rehabilitation expenditures is increased by the $1,200 recaptured amount. ◆

Business Energy Credits

Since 1978, a business energy credit has been allowed to encourage the conservation of natural resources and the development of alternative energy sources (to oil and natural gas). Many of these credits have now expired. Among the most important business energy credits are those for solar energy property (10 percent rate) and geothermal property (10 percent rate).

Reporting the Investment Tax Credit

Reporting the ITC involves one or all of several forms:

- Form 3468, Investment Credit, is used for determining the amount of current-year credit.
- Form 4255, Recapture of Investment Credit, is used to determine the increase in tax from recapture.
- If the taxpayer also has any of the other business credits (e.g., the disabled access credit), Form 3800, General Business Credit, consolidates them for purposes of determining the current-year amount allowed. This form is also used when the taxpayer has carrybacks or carryforwards of general business credits from other years.

Jobs Credit

The jobs credit (also referred to as the targeted jobs credit) was enacted to encourage employers to hire individuals from one or more of the following target groups traditionally subject to high rates of unemployment:

- Vocational rehabilitation referrals.
- Economically disadvantaged youths (age 18 to 22).
- Economically disadvantaged Vietnam-era veterans.
- Recipients of certain Social Security supplemental income benefits.
- General assistance recipients.
- Youths (age 16 to 19) participating in cooperative education programs.
- Economically disadvantaged ex-convicts.
- Eligible work incentive employees.
- Qualified summer youth employees (age 16 and 17).

The credit is available for wages paid to employees in their first year of service. This provision expired for employees who started work after June 30, 1992, but Congress is expected to reenact it in 1993.

Computation of the Regular Jobs Credit. The regular jobs credit is equal to 40 percent of the first $6,000 of wages (per eligible employee) for the *first year* of employment. Thus, the credit is not available for any wages paid to an employee after his or her first year of employment. However, if the employee's first year of employment overlaps two of the employer's tax years, the employer may take the credit over two tax years. If the jobs credit is elected, the employer's tax deduction for wages is reduced by the amount of the credit. For an employer to qualify for the credit, an unemployed individual must be certified by a local jobs service office of a state employment security agency. The jobs credit is not available for wages paid to certain related parties.

Wages will be taken into account in computing the regular jobs credit only if paid to an individual who is employed for at least 90 days or has completed 120 hours of work. The equivalent thresholds for qualified summer youth employees (discussed below) are 14 days or 20 hours.

Example 11

In January 1992, Green Company hires four handicapped individuals (certified to be eligible employees for the jobs credit). Each of these employees is paid wages of $7,000 during the year. Green Company's jobs credit is $9,600 [($6,000 × 40%) × 4 employees]. If the tax credit is taken, Green must reduce its deduction for wages paid by $9,600. No credit is available for wages paid to these employees after their first year of employment. ◆

Example 12

On June 1, 1992, Maria, a calendar year taxpayer, hired a member of a targeted group and obtained the required certification. During the last seven months of 1992, this employee is paid $3,500. Maria is allowed a jobs credit of $1,400 ($3,500 × 40%). The employee continues to work for Maria in 1993 and is paid $7,000 through May 31. Because up to $6,000 of first-year wages are eligible for the credit, Maria is also allowed a 40% credit on $2,500 [$6,000 – $3,500 (wages paid in 1992)] of wages paid in 1993, or $1,000 ($2,500 × 40%). None of this employee's wages paid after May 31, the end of the first year of employment, are eligible for the jobs credit. Likewise, no credit is allowed for wages paid to persons newly hired after June 30, 1992. ◆

Computation of the Jobs Credit for Qualified Summer Youth Employees. The credit for qualified summer youth employees is allowed on wages for services during any 90-day period between May 1 and September 15 if the employee is hired by June 30, 1992. A qualified summer youth employee generally must be age 16 or 17 on the hiring date. The maximum wages eligible for the credit are $3,000 per summer youth employee. Thus, the maximum credit per employee for 1992 is $1,200 ($3,000 × .40). If the employee continues employment after the 90-day period as a member of another targeted group, the amount of wages subject to the regular jobs credit must be reduced by the wages paid to the employee as a qualified summer youth employee.

EXAMPLE 13

Blue Corporation employs Tim as a qualified summer youth employee beginning May 1, 1992. After 90 days, Tim continues his employment as a member of a second targeted group. He was paid $2,000 as a qualified summer youth employee. As a member of the second targeted group, Tim is paid another $5,000 during the year. Of the $7,000 total paid to Tim, only $6,000 qualifies for the jobs credit. This amount consists of the $2,000 wages paid under the qualified summer youth employee program plus $4,000 ($6,000 – $2,000) paid to him as a member of the other targeted group. Blue Corporation's jobs credit will be 40% of $6,000 ($2,000 + $4,000), or $2,400. ◆

Research Activities Credit

To encourage research and experimentation, usually described as research and development (R & D), a credit was allowed for certain qualifying expenditures paid or incurred through June 30, 1992. Like the jobs credit discussed above, this credit is expected to be reenacted by Congress in 1993. The research activities credit is the *sum* of two components: an incremental research activities credit and a basic research credit.

Incremental Research Activities Credit. The incremental research activities credit applies at a 20 percent rate to the *excess* of qualified research expenses for the current taxable year (the credit year) over the base amount. These components of the credit are explained below.

In general, research expenditures qualify if the research relates to discovering information technological in nature that is intended for use in the development of a new or improved business component of the taxpayer. Such expenses qualify fully if the research is performed in-house (by the taxpayer or employees). If the research is conducted by persons outside the taxpayer's business (under contract), only 65 percent of the amount paid qualifies for the credit.

EXAMPLE 14

Sungho incurs the following research expenditures for the tax year.

In-house wages, supplies, computer time	$50,000
Paid to XYZ Scientific Foundation for research	30,000

Sungho's qualified research expenditures are $69,500 [$50,000 + ($30,000 × 65%)]. ◆

Beyond the general guidelines discussed above, the Code does not give specific examples of qualifying research. However, the credit is *not* allowed for research that falls into certain categories, which include the following:

- Research conducted after commercial production of the business component begins.

- Surveys and studies such as market research, testing, and routine data collection.
- Research conducted *outside* the United States.
- Research in the social sciences, arts, or humanities.

The *base amount* for the credit year is determined by multiplying the taxpayer's fixed base percentage by the average gross receipts for the four preceding taxable years. The fixed base percentage depends on whether the taxpayer is an existing firm or a start-up company. For purposes of the incremental research activities credit, an *existing firm* is one that both incurred qualified research expenditures *and* had gross receipts during each of at least three years from 1984 to 1988. A *start-up company* is one that did not have both of the above during each of at least three years in the same 1984–1988 period.

For existing firms, the fixed base percentage is the ratio of total qualified research expenses for the 1984–1988 period to total gross receipts for this same period. Gross receipts are net of sales returns and allowances. The fixed base percentage cannot exceed a maximum ratio of .16, or 16 percent. Start-up companies are *assigned* a fixed base percentage ratio of .03, or 3 percent.

To calculate the incremental research activities credit available for 1992, the following template may be used:

1.	Calculate the fixed base percentage for the period 1984–1988 (aggregate research expenses ÷ aggregate gross receipts).	________
2.	Calculate the average gross receipts for the four preceding years.	________
3.	Multiply the line 2 amount by the lesser of the line 1 amount or 16%.	________
4.	Subtract from the qualified research expenditures for the current year the line 3 amount or, if greater, 50% of the current year's qualified research expenditures. This is the excess research expenditures incurred.	________
5.	Multiply the line 4 amount by 20%. This is the incremental research activities credit.	________

EXAMPLE 15

Jack, a calendar year taxpayer, has gross receipts (net of sales returns and allowances) and qualified research expenses as follows:

	Gross Receipts	Qualified Research Expenses
1984	$150,000	$25,000
1985	300,000	45,000
1986	400,000	30,000
1987	350,000	35,000
1988	450,000	50,000
1989	450,000	50,000
1990	500,000	55,000
1991	650,000	73,000
1992	700,000	80,000

Using the template above, calculate Jack's incremental research activities credit.

1.	Calculate the fixed base percentage for the period 1984–1988 (aggregate research expenses ÷ aggregate gross receipts). ($185,000 ÷ $1,650,000)	11.21%
2.	Calculate the average gross receipts for the four preceding years. [($450,000 + $450,000 + $500,000 + $650,000) ÷ 4]	$512,500

3.	Multiply the line 2 amount by the lesser of the line 1 amount or 16%. ($512,500 × 11.21%)	$57,451
4.	Subtract from the qualified research expenditures for the current year the line 3 amount or, if greater, 50% of the current year's qualified research expenditures. This is the excess research expenditures incurred. ($80,000 – $57,451)	$22,549
5.	Multiply the line 4 amount by 20%. This is the incremental research activities credit.	$ 4,510

◆

As indicated in the template, a special rule limits the credit available for taxpayers who have incurred small amounts of research and experimentation costs during the base period. The rule provides that in no event shall the base amount be less than 50 percent of qualified research expenses for the credit year.

EXAMPLE 16

Assume the same facts as in Example 15, except that qualified research and experimentation expenses in 1992 were $200,000. Incremental research and experimentation expenditures eligible for the credit are $100,000, and the tax credit is computed as follows:

1.	Calculate the fixed base percentage for the period 1984–1988 (aggregate research expenses ÷ aggregate gross receipts). ($185,000 ÷ $1,650,000)	11.21%
2.	Calculate the average gross receipts for the four preceding years. [($450,000 + $450,000 + $500,000 + $650,000) ÷ 4]	$512,500
3.	Multiply the line 2 amount by the lesser of the line 1 amount or 16%. ($512,500 × 11.21%)	$ 57,451
4.	Subtract from the qualified research expenditures for the current year the line 3 amount or, if greater, 50% of the current year's qualified research expenditures. This is the excess research expenditures incurred. ($200,000 – $100,000)	$100,000
5.	Multiply the line 4 amount by 20%. This is the incremental research activities credit.	$ 20,000

◆

Qualified research and experimentation expenditures not only are eligible for the 20 percent credit but also can be *expensed* in the year incurred.[4] In this regard, the taxpayer has two choices:

- Use the full credit and reduce the expense deduction for research expenses by 100 percent of the credit.
- Retain the full expense deduction and reduce the credit by the product of 50 percent times the maximum corporate tax rate.

As an alternative to the expense deduction, the taxpayer may capitalize the research expenses and amortize them over 60 months or more. In this case, the amount capitalized and subject to amortization is reduced by the full amount of the credit *only* if the credit exceeds the amount allowable as a deduction.

EXAMPLE 17

Assume the same facts as in Example 16, which shows that the potential incremental research activities credit is $20,000. The expense that the taxpayer can deduct currently and the credit are as follows:

4. § 174. Also refer to the discussion of rules for deduction of research and development expenditures in Chapter 7.

	Credit Amount	Deduction Amount
■ Full credit and reduced deduction		
$20,000 – $0	$20,000	
$200,00 – $20,000		$180,000
■ Reduced credit and full deduction		
$20,000 – [(.50 × $20,000) × .34]	16,600	
$200,000 – $0		200,000
■ Full credit and capitalize and elect to amortize costs over 60 months		
$20,000 – $0	20,000	
$200,000/60 × 12		40,000

◆

Basic Research Credit. Corporations (but not S corporations or personal service corporations) are allowed an additional 20 percent credit for basic research payments through June 30, 1992, in *excess* of a base amount. This credit is not available to individual taxpayers. *Basic research payments* are defined as amounts paid in cash (property transfers do not qualify) to a qualified basic research organization. However, two requirements must be met for the payments to qualify. First, the payments must be made under a written agreement between the corporation and the qualified organization. Second, the qualified organization must perform basic research.

Basic research is defined generally as any original investigation for the advancement of scientific knowledge not having a specific commercial objective. The definition excludes basic research conducted outside the United States and basic research in the social sciences, arts, or humanities. This reflects the intent of Congress to encourage high-tech research in the United States.

The calculation of this additional credit for basic research expenditures is complex and is based on expenditures in excess of a specially defined base amount. This amount in turn may be subject to cost of living adjustments. The portion of the basic research expenditures that does not exceed the base amount is not eligible for the basic research credit, but the amount does become a component of the regular credit for incremental research activities.

Example 18

Orange Corporation, a qualifying corporation, pays $75,000 to a university for basic research. Assume that Orange's specially calculated base amount is $50,000. The basic research activities credit allowed is $5,000 [($75,000 – $50,000) × 20%]. The $50,000 of current year basic research expenditures that are not eligible for the credit because they do not exceed the base amount are treated as contract research expenses for purposes of the regular incremental research activities credit. ◆

Low-Income Housing Credit

A credit is available to owners of qualified low-income housing projects. This credit expired after June 30, 1992, but Congress is expected to reenact it in 1993. The purpose of the low-income housing credit is to encourage building owners to make affordable housing available for low-income individuals. Generally, the credit applies only if the qualifying expenses within a 24-month period are (1) not less than 10 percent of the building's adjusted basis or (2) $3,000 or more per low-income unit, but special exceptions abound.

This credit is influenced by many nontax factors. For example, certification of the property by the appropriate state or local agency authorized to provide low-income housing credits is required. These credits are issued based on a nationwide allocation. Once issued, however, they remain in effect for the entire credit period. Additional units require new certification based on allocations in effect at that later time.

The amount of the credit is based on the qualified basis of the property. The qualified basis depends on the number of units rented to low-income tenants. Renters qualify as low-income tenants if their income does not exceed a specified percentage of the area median gross income. Area median gross income is determined under the United States Housing Act of 1937.

Once declared eligible, the property must meet the required conditions continuously throughout a 30-year compliance period, although the credit itself is allowed over a 10-year period. After an initial 15-year compliance period, a 15-year *extended low-income commitment period* can be terminated in certain cases.

The credit rate is set monthly by the IRS so that the annualized credit amounts have a present value of either 70 percent or 30 percent of the basis attributable to qualifying low-income units. Once determined, though, the percentage remains constant for that property.

The *qualified basis* is that portion of the basis of the entire property (eligible basis) that is rented to qualifying low-income tenants. The amount of credit is determined by multiplying the qualified basis by the applicable percentage.

EXAMPLE 19

Sarah spends $100,000 to build a qualified low-income housing project completed January 1, 1992. The entire project is rented to low-income families. The credit rate for this 70% present credit value property for January 1992 is 8.70%. Sarah may claim a credit of $8,700 ($100,000 × 8.70%) in 1992 and in each of the following nine years. Generally, first-year credits are prorated based on the date the project is placed in service. A full year's credit is taken in each of the next nine years, and any remaining first-year credit is claimed in the eleventh year. ◆

Recapture of a portion of the credit may be required if the number of units set aside for low-income tenants falls below a minimum threshold, if the taxpayer disposes of the property or the interest in it, or if the taxpayer's amount at risk decreases.

Disabled Access Credit

The disabled access credit is designed to encourage small business owners to make their businesses more accessible to disabled individuals. The credit is available for any eligible access expenditures paid or incurred by an eligible small business. The credit is calculated at the rate of 50 percent of the eligible expenditures that exceed $250 but do not exceed $10,250. Thus, the maximum amount for the credit is $5,000. This nonrefundable credit is part of the general business credit.

An *eligible small business* is one that during the previous year either:

- had gross receipts of $1 million or less for the previous year, or
- had no more than 30 full-time employees during the previous year.

An eligible business can be a sole proprietorship, partnership, regular corporation, or S corporation. However, in the case of a partnership or S corporation, the limitation on the eligible expenditures is determined at both the entity and the owner level.

Eligible access expenditures are generally any reasonable and necessary amount that is paid or incurred to make certain changes to facilities. These changes must involve the removal of architectural, communication, physical, or transportation barriers that would otherwise make a business inaccessible to disabled and handicapped individuals. Examples of qualifying projects include installing ramps, widening doorways, and adding raised markings on elevator control buttons. However, eligible expenditures do *not* include amounts that are paid or incurred in connection with any facility that is placed into service after November 5, 1990.

To the extent a disabled access credit is available, no deduction or credit is allowed under any other provision of the tax law. The adjusted basis for depreciation is reduced by the amount of the credit.

EXAMPLE 20

In 1993, Red, Inc., an eligible business, made $11,000 of capital improvements to business realty that had been placed in service in June 1990. The expenditures were intended to make Red's business more accessible to the disabled and were considered eligible expenditures for purposes of the disabled access credit. The amount of the credit is $5,000 [($10,250 – $250) × 50%]. Although $11,000 of eligible expenditures were incurred, only the excess of $10,250 over $250 qualifies for the credit. Further, the depreciable basis of the capital improvement is $6,000 because the basis must be reduced by the amount of the credit [$11,000 (cost) – $5,000 (amount of the credit)]. ◆

OTHER TAX CREDITS

Earned Income Credit

Taxpayers whose earned income is below a specified level may be eligible for an earned income credit. The credit has three components:

- Basic earned income credit.
- Supplemental young child credit.
- Supplemental health insurance credit.

Each of the components is discussed below.

Basic Earned Income Credit. In 1993, the basic earned income credit is determined by multiplying a maximum of $7,750 of earned income by the appropriate credit percentage (see Figure 11–3). Generally, earned income includes employee compensation and net earnings from self-employment but excludes items such as interest, dividends, pension benefits, and alimony. The credit percentage used in the calculation is based on the number of the

Tax Year	Number of Qualifying Children	Credit Percentage	Phase-out Percentage
1993	One child	18.5	13.21
	Two or more children	19.5	13.93
1994	One child	23.0	16.43
	Two or more children	25.0	17.86

FIGURE 11–3
Basic Earned Income Credit: Credit and Phase-out Percentage

taxpayer's qualifying children. Thus, in 1993, the maximum basic earned income credit for a taxpayer with one qualifying child is $1,434 ($7,750 × 18.5%) and $1,511 ($7,750 × 19.5%) for a taxpayer with two or more qualifying children. However, the maximum basic earned income credit is phased out completely if the taxpayer's earned income or AGI exceeds $23,050. To the extent that thegreater of earned income or AGI exceeds $12,200, the difference, multiplied by the appropriate phase-out percentage, is subtracted from the maximum basic earned income credit.

EXAMPLE 21

In 1993, Grace, who otherwise qualifies for the earned income credit, receives wages of $14,000 and has no other income. She has one qualifying child. Grace's earned income credit is $1,434 ($7,750 × 18.5%) reduced by $238 [($14,000 – $12,200) × 13.21%]. Thus, Grace's earned income credit is $1,196. ◆

Supplemental Young Child Credit. A taxpayer with a qualifying child who has not attained the age of one at the end of the taxpayer's tax year is allowed an additional earned income credit. The supplemental young child credit is calculated by simply increasing the credit percentage by 5 percentage points and increasing the phase-out percentage by 3.57 percentage points (see Figure 11–3). Thus, in 1993, the applicable credit percentages and phase-out rates are as follows:

Number of Qualifying Children	Credit Percentage	Phase-out Percentage
One child	23.5	16.78
Two or more children	24.5	17.50

However, a taxpayer who elects to supplement the basic earned income credit with the supplemental young child credit cannot also claim the child as a qualifying individual for purposes of the credit for child and dependent care expenses (see the discussion later in the chapter).

EXAMPLE 22

Assume the same facts as in the previous example, except that Grace has one child below the age of one at the end of 1993 and one additional qualifying child. Then the credit would be $1,899 ($7,750 × 24.5%) reduced by $315 [($14,000 – $12,200) × 17.50%]. Thus, Grace's total earned income credit, including the supplemental young child credit, would be $1,584. ◆

Supplemental Health Insurance Credit. In addition to the basic earned income credit, a credit may be claimed up to the amount of the cost of health insurance coverage on one or more qualifying children. To determine the supplemental credit, the same rules that apply in calculating the basic earned income credit are used except the credit percentage is 6 percent and the phase-out percentage is 4.285 percent of the excess of the taxpayer's AGI (or earned income, if greater) over $12,200. However, the credit claimed cannot exceed the actual amount of the qualified health insurance expenses incurred. These percentages apply regardless of the size of the taxpayer's family.

EXAMPLE 23

In 1993, Ivan, who otherwise qualifies for the earned income credit, receives wages of $14,000 and has no other income. However, he has paid qualifying health insurance premiums of $750 during the year, which includes coverage for his qualifying child. Ivan's supplemental health insurance credit is $465 ($7,750 × 6%) reduced by $77 [($14,000 – $12,200) × 4.285%]. Thus, Ivan's supplemental health insurance credit is $388. If Ivan has two or more qualifying children, the supplemental credit would be the same. ◆

To the extent a supplemental health insurance credit is claimed, qualifying medical care expenses must be reduced for purposes of the medical expense itemized deduction.

Earned Income Credit Table. It is not necessary to compute the credit as was done in Examples 21 through 23. As part of the tax simplification process, the IRS issues an Earned Income Credit Table for the determination of the appropriate amount of the earned income credit. This table and a worksheet are included in the instructions to both Form 1040 and Form 1040A.

Eligibility Requirements. To be *eligible* for the credit, the taxpayer must not only meet the earned income and AGI thresholds, but must also have a *qualifying child.* A qualifying child must meet the following tests:

- *Relationship test.* The individual must be a son, daughter, descendant of the taxpayer's son or daughter, stepson, stepdaughter, or an eligible foster child of the taxpayer.[5] A legally adopted child of the taxpayer is considered the same as a child by blood.
- *Residency test.* The qualifying child must share the taxpayer's principal place of abode, which must be located within the United States, for more than one-half of the taxpayer's tax year. Temporary absences (e.g., due to illness or education) are disregarded for purposes of this test. A foster child, however, must share the taxpayer's home for the entire year.
- *Age test.* The child must not have reached the age of 19 (24 in the case of a full-time student) as of the end of the tax year. In addition, a child who is permanently and totally disabled at any time during the year is considered to meet the age test.

Advance Payment. The earned income credit is a form of negative income tax (a refundable credit to the extent it exceeds the tax liability). An eligible individual may elect to receive advance payments of the earned income credit from his or her employer (rather than receiving the credit from the IRS upon filing the tax return). The amount that can be received in advance is limited to the basic credit amount that is available to a taxpayer with only one qualifying child. If the election is made, the taxpayer must file a certificate of eligibility (Form W–5) with his or her employer and *must* file a tax return for the year the income is earned.

Tax Credit for Elderly or Disabled Taxpayers

The credit for the elderly was originally enacted in 1954 as the retirement income credit to provide tax relief for those who were not receiving substantial benefits from tax-free Social Security payments.

---

5. § 32(c)(1). The credit can also be claimed by a custodial parent who is not entitled to a dependency exemption for a child. This situation develops when the exemption is released through a written agreement or in a pre-1985 divorce or separation.

EXAMPLE 24

Olaf is a retired taxpayer who received $8,000 of Social Security benefits as his only income in 1993. His Social Security benefits are excluded from gross income. Therefore, Olaf's income tax is $0. In 1993, Olga, a single taxpayer 66 years of age, has $8,000 of income from a pension plan funded by her former employer. Assuming Olga has no itemized deductions or deductions *for* AGI, her income tax for 1993 (before credits) is $158. The retirement income credit was enacted to mitigate this inequity. ◆

The credit for the elderly applies to the following:

- Taxpayers age 65 or older.
- Taxpayers under age 65 who are retired with a permanent and total disability and who have disability income from a public or private employer on account of the disability.

The *maximum* allowable credit is $1,125 (15% × $7,500 of qualifying income), but the credit will be less for a taxpayer who receives Social Security benefits or has AGI in excess of specified amounts. Under these circumstances, the base used in the credit computation is reduced. Many taxpayers receive Social Security benefits or have AGI high enough to reduce the base for the credit to zero.

The eligibility requirements and the tax computation are somewhat complicated. Consequently, an individual may elect to have the IRS compute his or her tax and the amount of the tax credit.

The credit is based on an initial amount (referred to as the *base amount*), which depends on the taxpayer's filing status (see Figure 11–4). To qualify for the credit, married taxpayers who live together must file a joint return. For taxpayers under age 65 who are retired on permanent and total disability, the base amounts could be less than those shown in Figure 11–4, because these amounts are limited to taxable disability income.

This initial base amount is *reduced* by (1) Social Security, Railroad Retirement, and certain excluded pension benefits and (2) one-half of the taxpayer's AGI in excess of $7,500 for a single taxpayer, a head of household, or a surviving spouse. The AGI factor is $10,000 for married taxpayers filing jointly. It is generally $5,000 for married taxpayers filing separately. The credit is equal to 15 percent of the base amount after subtracting the adjustments just described.

EXAMPLE 25

Paul and his wife Peggy are both over age 65 and received Social Security benefits of $2,400 in 1993. On a joint return, they reported AGI of $14,000.

Base amount		$ 7,500
Less: Social Security benefits	$2,400	
One-half of the excess of AGI of $14,000 over $10,000	2,000	(4,400)
Balance subject to credit		$ 3,100
Tax credit allowed ($3,100 × 15%)		$ 465

◆

FIGURE 11–4
Base Amounts for Tax Credit for the Elderly and Disabled

Status	Base Amount
Single, head of household, or surviving spouse	$5,000
Married, joint return, only one spouse qualifies	5,000
Married, joint return, both spouses qualify	7,500
Married, separate return, spouses live apart the entire year	3,750

The credit for the elderly may not offset any alternative minimum tax. Schedule R of Form 1040 is used to calculate and report the credit.

Foreign Tax Credit

Both individual taxpayers and corporations may claim a tax credit for foreign income tax paid on income earned and subject to tax in another country or a U.S. possession.[6] As an alternative, a taxpayer may claim a deduction instead of a credit. In most instances the tax credit is advantageous since it is a direct offset against the tax liability.

The purpose of the foreign tax credit (FTC) is to mitigate double taxation since income earned in a foreign country is subject to both U.S. and foreign taxes. However, the ceiling limitation formula may result in some form of double taxation or taxation at rates in excess of U.S. rates when the foreign tax rates are higher than the U.S. rates. This is a distinct possibility because U.S. tax rates are lower than those of many foreign countries.

Other special tax treatments applicable to taxpayers working outside the United States include the foreign earned income exclusion (refer to Chapter 5) and limitations on deducting expenses of employees working outside the United States (refer to Chapter 9). Recall from the earlier discussion that a taxpayer may not take advantage of *both* the FTC and the foreign earned income exclusion.

Computation. Taxpayers are required to compute the FTC based upon an overall limitation. The FTC allowed is the *lesser* of the foreign taxes imposed or the *overall limitation* determined according to the following formula:

$$\frac{\text{Foreign-source taxable income}}{\text{Worldwide taxable income}} \times \text{U.S. tax before FTC}$$

For individual taxpayers, worldwide taxable income in the overall limitation formula is determined *before* personal and dependency exemptions are deducted.

EXAMPLE 26

In 1993, Carlos, has $10,000 of income from Country Y, which imposes a 15% tax, and $20,000 from Country Z, which imposes a 50% tax. He has taxable income of $60,600 from within the United States, is married filing a joint return, and claims two dependency exemptions. Thus, although Carlos's taxable income for purposes of determining U.S. tax is $90,600, taxable income amounts used in the limitation formula are not reduced by personal and dependency exemptions. Thus, for this purpose, taxable income is $100,000 [$90,600 + (4 exemptions × $2,350)]. Assume that Carlos's U.S. tax before the credit is $20,615. The overall limitation is computed as follows:

$$\frac{\text{Foreign-source taxable income}}{\text{Worldwide taxable income}} = \frac{\$30{,}000}{\$100{,}000} \times \$20{,}615 = \$6{,}185$$

In this case, $6,185 is allowed as the FTC because this amount is less than the $11,500 of foreign taxes imposed [$1,500 (Country Y) + $10,000 (Country Z)]. ◆

Thus, the overall limitation may result in some of the foreign income being subjected to double taxation. Unused FTCs can be carried back two years and

6. Section 27 provides for the credit, but the qualifications and calculation procedure for the credit are contained in §§ 901–908.

forward five years. Form 1116, Computation of Foreign Tax Credit, is used by individuals to compute the limitation on the amount of FTC.

Only foreign income taxes, war profits taxes, and excess profits taxes (or taxes paid in lieu of such taxes) qualify for the credit. In determining whether or not a tax is an income tax, U.S. criteria are applied. Thus, value added taxes (VAT), severance taxes, property taxes, and sales taxes do not qualify because they are not regarded as taxes on income. Such taxes may be deductible, however.

Credit for Child and Dependent Care Expenses

A credit is allowed to taxpayers who incur employment-related expenses for child or dependent care.[7] The credit is a specified percentage of expenses incurred to enable the taxpayer to work or to seek employment. Expenses on which the credit is based are subject to limitations.

Eligibility. To be eligible for the credit, an individual must maintain a household for either of the following:

- A dependent under age 13.
- A dependent or spouse who is physically or mentally incapacitated.

Generally, married taxpayers must file a joint return to claim the credit. The credit may be claimed by the custodial parent for a nondependent child under age 13 if the noncustodial parent is allowed to claim the child as a dependent under a pre-1985 divorce agreement or under a waiver in the case of a post-1984 agreement.

Eligible Employment-Related Expenses. Eligible expenses include amounts paid for household services and care of a qualifying individual that are incurred to enable the taxpayer to be employed. Child and dependent care expenses include expenses incurred in the home, such as payments for a housekeeper. Out-of-the-home expenses incurred for the care of a dependent under the age of 13 also qualify for the credit. In addition, out-of-the-home expenses incurred for an older dependent or spouse who is physically or mentally incapacitated qualify for the credit if that person regularly spends at least eight hours each day in the taxpayer's household. This makes the credit available to taxpayers who keep handicapped older children and elderly relatives in the home instead of institutionalizing them. Out-of-the-home expenses incurred for services provided by a dependent care center will qualify only if the center complies with all applicable laws and regulations of a state or unit of local government.

Child care payments to a relative are eligible for the credit unless the relative is a dependent of the taxpayer or the taxpayer's spouse or is a child (under age 19) of the taxpayer.

EXAMPLE 27

Wilma is an employed mother of an eight-year-old child. She pays her mother, Rita, $1,500 per year to care for the child after school. Wilma does not claim Rita as a dependent. Wilma also pays her daughter Eleanor, age 17, $900 for the child's care during the summer. Of these amounts, only the $1,500 paid to Rita qualifies as employment-related child care expenses. ◆

Earned Income Ceiling. The total for qualifying employment-related expenses is limited to an individual's earned income. For married taxpayers, this limitation

7. § 21.

applies to the spouse with the *lesser* amount of earned income. Special rules are provided for taxpayers with nonworking spouses who are disabled or are full-time students. If a nonworking spouse is physically or mentally disabled or is a full-time student, he or she is *deemed* to have earned income. The deemed amount is $200 per month if there is one qualifying individual in the household, or $400 per month if there are two or more qualifying individuals in the household. In the case of a student-spouse, the student's income is *deemed* to be earned only for the months that the student is enrolled on a full-time basis at an educational institution.

Calculation of the Credit. In general, the credit is equal to a percentage of *unreimbursed* employment-related expenses up to $2,400 for one qualifying individual and $4,800 for two or more individuals. The credit rate varies between 20 percent and 30 percent, depending on the taxpayer's AGI. The following chart shows that the applicable percentage decreases as AGI increases:

Adjusted Gross Income		
Over	**But Not Over**	**Applicable Rate of Credit**
$ 0	$10,000	30%
10,000	12,000	29%
12,000	14,000	28%
14,000	16,000	27%
16,000	18,000	26%
18,000	20,000	25%
20,000	22,000	24%
22,000	24,000	23%
24,000	26,000	22%
26,000	28,000	21%
28,000	No limit	20%

EXAMPLE 28

Nancy, who has two children under age 13, worked full-time while her spouse, Ron, was attending college for 10 months during the year. Nancy earned $21,000 and incurred $5,000 of child care expenses. Ron is *deemed* to be fully employed and to have earned $400 for each of the 10 months (or a total of $4,000). Since Ron and Nancy have AGI of $21,000, they are allowed a credit rate of 24%. Ron and Nancy are limited to $4,000 in qualified child care expenses (the lesser of $4,800 or $4,000). They are entitled to a tax credit of $960 (24% × $4,000) for the year. ◆

Dependent Care Assistance Program. Recall from Chapter 4 that a taxpayer is allowed an exclusion from gross income for a limited amount reimbursed to the taxpayer for child or dependent care expenses. However, the taxpayer is not allowed both an exclusion from income and a child and dependent care credit on the same amount. The $2,400 and $4,800 ceilings for allowable child and dependent care expenses are reduced dollar for dollar by the amount of reimbursement.

EXAMPLE 29

Assume the same facts as in Example 28, except that of the $5,000 paid for child care, Nancy was reimbursed $2,500 by her employer under a qualified dependent care assistance program. Under the employer's plan, the reimbursement reduces her taxable wages. Thus, Ron and Nancy have AGI of $18,500 ($21,000 – $2,500), so the credit rate is 25%. The maximum amount of child care expenses for two or more dependents of $4,800 is reduced by the $2,500 reimbursement, resulting in a tax credit of $575 [25% × ($4,800 – $2,500)]. ◆

Reporting Requirements. The credit is claimed by completing and filing Form 2441, Credit for Child and Dependent Care Expenses (see Appendix B).

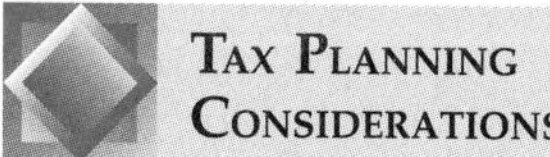

Foreign Tax Credit

A U.S. citizen or resident working abroad (commonly referred to as an *expatriate*) may elect to claim either a foreign tax credit or the foreign earned income exclusion. In cases where the income tax of a foreign country is higher than the U.S. income tax, the credit choice usually is preferable. If the reverse is true, electing the foreign earned income exclusion probably reduces the overall tax burden.

Unfortunately, the choice between the credit and the earned income exclusion is not without some restrictions. The election of the foreign earned income exclusion, once made, can be revoked for a later year. However, once revoked, the earned income exclusion will not be available for a period of five years unless the IRS consents to an earlier date. This will create a dilemma for expatriates whose job assignments over several years shift between low and high bracket countries.

EXAMPLE 30

In 1992, Ira, a calendar year taxpayer, is sent by his employer to Saudi Arabia (a low-tax country). For 1992, therefore, Ira elects the foreign earned income exclusion. In 1993, Ira's employer transfers him to France (a high-tax country). Accordingly, he revokes the foreign earned income exclusion election for 1993 and chooses instead to use the foreign income tax credit. If Ira is transferred back to Saudi Arabia (or any other low-tax country) within five years, he no longer may utilize the foreign earned income exclusion. ◆

Credit for Child and Dependent Care Expenses

A taxpayer may incur employment-related expenses that also qualify as medical expenses (e.g., a nurse is hired to provide in-the-home care for an ill and incapacitated dependent parent). Such expenses may be either deducted as medical expenses (subject to the 7.5 percent limitation) or utilized in determining the credit for child and dependent care expenses. If the dependent care expenses credit is chosen and the employment-related expenses exceed the limitation ($2,400, $4,800, or earned income, as the case may be), the excess may be considered a medical expense. If, however, the taxpayer chooses to deduct qualified employment-related expenses such as medical expenses, any portion that is not deductible because of the 7.5 percent limitation may not be used in computing the credit for child and dependent care expenses.

EXAMPLE 31

Alicia, a single individual, has the following tax position for tax year 1993:

Adjusted gross income		$30,000
Potential itemized deductions—		
Other than medical expenses	$2,500	
Medical expenses	6,000	$ 8,500

Concept Summary 11–1
Tax Credits

Credit	Computation	Comments
Tax withheld on wages (§ 31)	Amount is reported to employee on W–2 form.	Refundable credit.
Earned income (§ 32)	Amount is determined by reference to Earned Income Credit Table published by IRS. Computations of underlying amounts in Earned Income Credit Table are illustrated in Examples 21–23.	Refundable credit. A form of negative income tax to assist low-income taxpayers. Earned income and AGI must be less than specified threshold amount. Child must satisfy relationship, residency, and age requirements.
Child and dependent care (§ 21)	Rate ranges from 20% to 30% depending on AGI. Maximum base for credit is $2,400 for one qualifying individual, $4,800 for two or more.	Nonrefundable personal credit. No carryback or carryforward. Benefits taxpayers who incur employment-related child or dependent care expenses in order to work or seek employment. Eligible dependents include children under age 13 or dependent (any age) or spouse who is physically or mentally incapacitated.
Elderly and disabled (§ 22)	15% of sum of base amount minus reductions for (a) Social Security and other nontaxable benefits and (b) excess AGI. Base amount is fixed by law (e.g., $5,000 for a single taxpayer).	Nonrefundable personal credit. No carryback or carryforward. Provides relief for taxpayers not receiving substantial tax-free retirement benefits.
Foreign tax (§ 27)	Foreign income/total worldwide taxable income × U.S. tax = overall limitation. Lesser of foreign taxes imposed or overall limitation.	Nonrefundable credit. Unused credits may be carried back two years and forward five years. Purpose is to prevent double taxation of foreign income.
General business (§ 38)	May not exceed net income tax minus the greater of tentative minimum tax or 25% of net regular tax liability that exceeds $25,000.	Nonrefundable credit. Components include investment tax credit, jobs credit, research activities credit, low-income housing credit, and disabled access credit. Unused credit may be carried back 3 years and forward 15 years. FIFO method applies to carryovers, carrybacks, and credits earned during current year.
Investment (§ 46)	Qualifying investment times regular percentage, energy percentage, or rehabilitation percentage, depending on type of property. Part of general business credit and subject to its limitations.	Nonrefundable credit. Part of general business credit and therefore subject to same carryback, carryover, and FIFO rules. Regular credit repealed. Energy percentage is 10%. Regular rehabilitation rate is 10%; rate for certified historic structures is 20%.
Jobs credit (§ 51)	Regular credit is 40% of first $6,000 of wages paid to each eligible employee. Qualified summer youth employee (QSYE) credit is 40% of first $3,000 of wages paid to QSYE. Eligible employees must begin work by June 30, 1992.	Nonrefundable credit. Part of general business credit and therefore subject to same carryback, carryover, and FIFO rules. Purpose is to encourage employment of specified groups. QSYE generally must be age 16 or 17 on hiring date.

Credit	Computation	Comments
Research activities (§ 41)	Incremental credit is 20% of excess of computation year expenditures minus the base amount. Basic research credit is allowed to certain corporations for 20% of cash payments to qualified organizations that exceed a specially calculated base amount.	Nonrefundable credit. Part of general business credit and therefore subject to same carryback, carryover, and FIFO rules. Purpose is to encourage high-tech research in the United States.
Low-income housing (§ 42)	Appropriate rate times eligible basis (portion of project attributable to low-income units).	Nonrefundable credit. Part of general business credit and therefore subject to same carryback, carryover, and FIFO rules. Credit is available each year for 10 years. Recapture may apply.
Disabled access (§ 44)	Credit is 50% of eligible access expenditures that exceed $250, but do not exceed $10,250. Maximum credit is $5,000.	Nonrefundable credit. Part of general business credit and therefore subject to same carryback, carryover, and FIFO rules. Available only to eligible small businesses.

All of Alicia's medical expenses were incurred to provide nursing care for her disabled father while she was working. The father lives with Alicia and qualifies as her dependent. ◆

What should Alicia do in this situation? One approach would be to use $2,400 of the nursing care expenses to obtain the maximum dependent care credit allowed of $480 (20% × $2,400). The balance of these expenses should be claimed as medical expenses. After a reduction of 7.5 percent of AGI, this would produce a medical expense deduction of $1,350 [$3,600 (remaining medical expenses) – (7.5% × $30,000)].

Another approach would be to claim the full $6,000 as a medical expense and forgo the dependent care expenses credit. After the 7.5 percent adjustment of $2,250 (7.5% × $30,000), a deduction of $3,750 remains.

The choice, then, is between a credit of $480 plus a deduction of $1,350 or a credit of $0 plus a deduction of $3,750. Which is better, of course, depends on the relative tax savings involved.

One of the traditional goals of *family tax planning* is to minimize the total tax burden within the family unit. With proper planning and implementation, the child and dependent care credit can be used to help achieve this goal. For example, payments to certain relatives for the care of qualifying dependents and children qualify for the credit if the care provider is *not* a dependent of the taxpayer or the taxpayer's spouse or is *not* a child (under age 19) of the taxpayer. Thus, if the care provider is in a lower tax bracket than the taxpayer, the following benefits result:

- Income is shifted to a lower-bracket family member.
- The taxpayer qualifies for the credit for child and dependent care expenses.

In addition, the goal of minimizing the family income tax liability can be enhanced in some other situations, but only if the credit's limitations are recognized and avoided. For example, tax savings may still result even if the qualifying expenditures incurred by a cash basis taxpayer have already reached the annual ceiling ($2,400 or $4,800). To the extent that any additional payments can be shifted into future tax years, the benefit from the credit may be preserved on these excess expenditures.

EXAMPLE 32

Andre, a calendar year and cash basis taxpayer, has spent $2,400 by December 1 on qualifying child care expenditures for his dependent 11-year-old son. The $200 that is due the care provider for child care services rendered in December does not generate a tax credit benefit if the amount is paid in the current year because the $2,400 ceiling has been reached. However, if the payment can be delayed until the next year, the total credit over the two-year period for which Andre is eligible may be increased. ◆

A similar shifting of expenditures to a subsequent year may be wise if the potential credit otherwise generated would exceed the tax liability available to absorb the credit.

PROBLEM MATERIALS

DISCUSSION QUESTIONS

1. Would an individual taxpayer receive greater benefit from deducting an expenditure or from taking a credit equal to 25% of the expenditure?
2. What is a refundable credit? Give examples. What is a nonrefundable credit? Give examples.
3. What are the components of the general business credit?
4. Discuss the order in which credits are offset against the tax liability. Why is the order in which credits are utilized important?
5. Discuss the treatment of unused general business credits.
6. The investment tax credit is comprised of three components. Identify these components, and indicate whether the credit is available for qualifying expenditures made in 1992.
7. Vic is considering the purchase and renovation of an old building. He has heard about the tax credit for rehabilitation expenditures but does not know the specific rules applicable to the credit. He has asked you to explain the most important details to him. What will you tell him?
8. If property on which the tax credit for rehabilitation expenditures was claimed is prematurely disposed of or ceases to be qualified property, how is the tax liability affected in the year of the disposition or disqualification?
9. The jobs credit was enacted to encourage employers to hire individuals from one or more target groups. Identify the groups of individuals who have been targeted by this provision.
10. In 1992, TUV Corporation hired Chris, who is certified as a member of a targeted group for purposes of the jobs credit. Chris was paid $11,000 during the year. How much is TUV Corporation's deduction for wages paid to Chris during 1992?
11. What credit provisions that have been in the tax law were enacted to encourage technological development in the United States?
12. Explain the alternatives a taxpayer has in claiming the deduction and credit for research and experimentation expenditures.
13. During 1993, Rust Corporation made some structural changes to its facility to provide easier access for disabled persons. These changes cost $12,000 and were qualifying expenditures for purposes of the disabled access credit. Determine the amount of the disabled access credit and the depreciable basis for these capital improvements.

14. Which of the following taxpayers are eligible for the earned income credit for the tax year 1993?
    a. Bob and Bonnie are married and have a 15-year-old dependent child living with them. Bob earned $7,600 and Bonnie earned $7,000.
    b. Soong, a single parent, supports her 20-year-old daughter, who is a full-time college student. Soong earns $14,000 and has no other income.
    c. Manuel, an unmarried taxpayer, earns $12,000 and has no other income. He claims a dependency exemption for his aunt under a multiple support agreement.
15. What three tests must be met for a child to be considered a qualifying child for purposes of the earned income credit? Describe.
16. Individuals who receive substantial Social Security benefits are usually not eligible for the tax credit for the elderly because these benefits effectively eliminate the base upon which the credit is computed. Explain.
17. What purpose is served by the overall limitation to the foreign tax credit?
18. Do all foreign taxes qualify for the U.S. foreign tax credit? Explain.
19. In general, when would an individual taxpayer find it more beneficial to take advantage of the foreign earned income exclusion rather than the foreign tax credit in computing his or her income tax liability?
20. Pete is not concerned with the credit for child and dependent care expenses because his AGI is considerably in excess of $20,000. Is Pete under a misconception regarding the tax law? Explain.
21. Gary and Gail are married and have a dependent child eight years of age. Gary earned $15,000 during 1993. Gail, a full-time student for the entire year, was not employed. Gary and Gail believe they are not entitled to the credit for child and dependent care expenses because Gail was not employed. Is this correct? Explain your answer.
22. Polly and her spouse, Leo, file a joint return and expect to report AGI of $95,000 in 1993. Polly's employer offers a child and dependent care reimbursement plan that allows up to $2,500 of qualifying expenses to be reimbursed in exchange for a $2,500 reduction in the employee's salary. Because Polly and Leo have one minor child requiring child care that costs $2,500 each year, she is wondering if she should sign up for the program instead of taking advantage of the credit for child and dependent care expenses. What is your response?

PROBLEMS

23. Dan has a tentative general business credit of $110,000 for 1993. His net regular tax liability before the general business credit is $125,000; tentative minimum tax is $100,000. Compute Dan's allowable general business credit for 1993.
24. XYZ Corporation has the following general business credit carryovers:

1989	$ 60,000
1990	25,000
1991	10,000
1992	25,000
Total carryovers	$120,000

    If the general business credit generated by activities during 1993 equals $60,000 and the total credit allowed during the current year is $100,000 (based on tax liability), what amounts of the current general business credit and carryovers are utilized against the 1993 income tax liability? What is the amount of unused credit carried forward to 1994?
25. In 1985, Gus placed $100,000 of five-year assets and $60,000 of three-year assets into service in his business. All of the assets were new at the time and met the definition of qualified property for purposes of the regular investment tax credit. Because of limited tax exposure since 1985, Gus has been unable to utilize the credit until the

current year. Assuming that the full credit rates were used to compute the ITC, determine the amount of regular ITC that would be available as a carryover to the current tax year.

26. On August 1, 1990, Earl acquired and placed in service a pre-1936 office building. The cost was $250,000, of which $50,000 applied to the land. In order to keep tenants, Earl spent $250,000 renovating the building in 1993. The expenses were of the type that qualify for the rehabilitation credit. These improvements were placed in service on May 1.

   a. Compute Earl's rehabilitation tax credit for 1993.
   b. Determine cost recovery for the year.
   c. What is Earl's basis in the property at the end of 1993?

27. Diane acquires a qualifying historic structure for $250,000 (excluding the cost of land) in 1993 with full intentions of substantially rehabilitating the building. Compute the rehabilitation tax credit that is available to Diane and the impact on the depreciable basis if the following amounts are incurred for the rehabilitation project:

   a. $200,000
   b. $400,000

28. PQR Company hired six handicapped individuals (qualifying PQR for the jobs credit) in March 1992. Three of these individuals received wages of $7,000 each during 1992, while the other three received wages of $5,000 each.

   a. Calculate the amount of the jobs credit for 1992.
   b. Assume PQR Company paid total wages of $120,000 to its employees during the year. How much of this amount is deductible in 1992 if the jobs credit is elected?

29. On May 15, 1992, Gray Corporation hired four individuals (Anne, Barry, Cora, and David), all of whom qualified Gray Corporation for the jobs credit. Anne and Barry also were certified as qualified summer youth employees. David moved out of state in September, quitting his job after earning $4,000 in wages. Anne, Barry, and Cora continued as employees of Gray Corporation. During 1992, Cora earned $6,500. Anne and Barry each earned $3,500 during their first 90 days of employment. Beginning on August 15, Anne and Barry were certified for participation in the company's cooperative education program. In this capacity, Anne earned $2,000 to December 31 and $2,500 to the end of school on May 15, 1993. Barry also earned an additional $2,000 to December 31, at which time he quit school and left the program. Compute Gray Corporation's jobs credit, without regard to the tax liability ceiling limitation, for 1992. Also compute Gray's deduction for wages paid to Anne, Barry, Cora, and David during 1992. Will Gray receive any benefit in 1993?

30. Matt, a calendar year taxpayer, furnishes the following information. Gross receipts are net of returns and allowances.

	Gross Receipts	Qualified Research Expenses
1992	$180,000	$30,000
1991	170,000	50,000
1990	160,000	35,000
1989	120,000	45,000
1988	120,000	45,000
1987	135,000	40,000
1986	110,000	20,000
1985	95,000	–0–
1984	80,000	30,000

   a. Using the template provided in the text, determine Matt's incremental research activities credit for 1992.
   b. Matt is in the 28% tax bracket. He decides to deduct, not capitalize, the 1992 research expenses. Assuming Matt does not wish to capitalize and then amortize

the qualifying research expenditures, should he elect the full expense deduction and reduced credit or the full credit and reduced expense deduction?

31. Assume the same facts as in the previous problem, except that Matt incurs $60,000 of qualified research expenditures in 1992. Using the template in the text, compute the incremental research activities credit for 1992.

32. Rose Corporation is an eligible small business for purposes of the disabled access credit. During the year, Rose makes the following expenditures on a structure originally placed in service in 1984:

Removal of architectural barriers	$4,250
Acquired equipment for disabled persons	3,000
	$7,250

In addition $3,500 was expended on a building placed in service in the current year to ensure easy accessibility by disabled individuals. Calculate the amount of the disabled access credit available to Rose Corporation.

33. Which of the following individuals qualify for the earned income credit for 1993?

    a. Eduardo is single and has no dependents. His income consisted of $7,000 wages and taxable interest of $1,000.
    b. Kate maintains a household for a dependent 12-year-old son and is eligible for head-of-household tax rates. Her income consisted of $10,000 salary and $800 taxable interest.
    c. Keith is married and files a joint return with his wife. They have no dependents. Their combined income consisted of $8,000 salary and $600 taxable interest. Adjusted gross income is $8,600.

34. Irene, who qualifies for the earned income credit, has three qualifying children who live with her. Irene earns a salary of $13,500 during 1993.

    a. Calculate Irene's basic earned income credit for the year.
    b. If you learn that one of Irene's children is 6 months of age at the end of 1993, what is the maximum earned income credit available?

35. Vern, a widower, lives in an apartment with his three minor children (ages 3, 4, and 5) whom he supports. Vern earned $17,100 during 1993. He contributed $1,000 to an IRA and uses the standard deduction. Calculate the amount, if any, of Vern's earned income credit.

36. Joe, age 67, and Emily, age 66, are married retirees who received the following income and retirement benefits during 1993:

Fully taxable pension from Joe's former employer	$ 5,000
Dividends and interest	8,000
Social Security benefits	1,750
	$14,750

Assume Joe and Emily file a joint return, have no deductions *for* AGI, and do not itemize. Are they eligible for the tax credit for the elderly? If so, calculate the amount of the credit, assuming their actual tax liability (before credits) is $150.

37. Kim, a U.S. citizen and resident, owns and operates a novelty goods business. During 1993, she has taxable income of $100,000, made up as follows: $50,000 from foreign sources and $50,000 from U.S. sources. The standard deduction is used in calculating taxable income. The income from foreign sources is subject to foreign income taxes of $26,000. For 1993, Kim files a joint return claiming her three children as dependents. Assuming Kim chooses to claim the foreign taxes as an income tax credit, what is her income tax liability for 1993?

38. Pat and Jeri are husband and wife, and both are gainfully employed. They have three children under the age of 13. During 1993, Pat earned $20,000, while Jeri earned $4,900. In order for them to work, they paid $5,800 to various unrelated parties to

care for their children. Assuming Pat and Jeri file a joint return, what, if any, is their credit for child and dependent care expenses for 1993?

39. Jim and Jill are husband and wife and have two dependent children under the age of 13. Both Jim and Jill are gainfully employed and during 1993 earned salaries as follows: $12,000 (Jim) and $3,000 (Jill). To care for their children while they work, they pay Megan (Jim's mother) $3,600. Megan does not qualify as their dependent. Assuming Jim and Jill file a joint return, what, if any, is their credit for child and dependent care expenses?

CUMULATIVE PROBLEMS

40. Hal and Wanda Atkins, ages 38 and 36, are married and file a joint return. Their household includes Sam, their 10-year-old son, and Fred, who is Hal's 76-year-old father. Fred is very ill and has been confined to bed for most of the year. He has no income of his own and is fully supported by Hal and Wanda. The Atkins had the following income and expenses during 1992:

Hal's wages	$ 8,000
Wanda's salary	14,000
Interest from First National Bank	50
Unemployment compensation received by Hal, who was laid off for five months during the year	4,500
Dividends received on January 3, 1994; the corporation mailed the check on December 31, 1993	250
Amounts paid to Nora, Hal's niece, for household help and caring for Sam and Fred while Hal and Wanda were working	5,500
Unreimbursed travel expenses (including meals of $200) incurred by Wanda in connection with her job	1,250
Total itemized deductions (not including any potential deductions mentioned elsewhere in the problem)	4,700
Federal income taxes withheld by their employers	700

Compute net tax payable or refund due for Hal and Wanda for 1993. Suggested software (if available): *TurboTax* or *MacInTax* or WFT tax planning software.

41. James R. Jordan lives at 2322 Branch Road, Mesa, AZ 85202. He is a tax accountant with Mesa Manufacturing Company. He also writes computer software programs for tax practitioners and has a part-time tax practice. James, age 35, is single and has no dependents. His Social Security number is 111–35–2222. He wants to contribute one dollar to the Presidential Election Campaign Fund.

During 1992, James earned a salary of $45,680 from his employer. He received interest of $890 from Home Federal Savings and Loan and $435 from Home State Bank. He received dividends of $620 from Acme Corporation, $470 from Jason Corporation, and $360 from General Corporation.

James received a $1,600 income tax refund from the state of Arizona on May 12, 1992. On his 1991 Federal income tax return, he reported total itemized deductions of $6,700, which included $2,000 of state income tax withheld by his employer.

Fees earned from his part-time tax practice in 1992 totaled $4,200. He paid $500 to have the tax returns processed by a computerized tax return service.

On February 1, 1992, James bought 500 shares of Acme Corporation common stock for $17.60 a share. On July 16, he sold the stock for $15 a share.

James bought a used pickup truck for $3,000 on June 5, 1992. He purchased the truck from his brother-in-law, who was unemployed and was in need of cash. On November 2, 1992, he sold the truck to a friend for $3,400.

On January 2, 1982, James acquired 100 shares of Jason Corporation common stock for $30 a share. He sold the stock on December 19, 1992, for $75 a share.

During 1992, James received royalties of $15,000 on a software program he had written. He incurred the following expenditures in connection with his software writing activities:

Cost of microcomputer (100% business use)	$8,000
Cost of printer (100% business use)	2,000
Supplies	650
Fee paid to computer consultant	3,500

James elected to expense the maximum portion of the cost of the microcomputer and printer allowed under the provisions of § 179.

Although his employer suggested that James attend a convention on current developments in corporate taxation, James was not reimbursed for the travel expenses of $1,360 he incurred in attending the convention. The $1,360 included $200 for the cost of meals.

During 1992, James paid $300 for prescription medicines and $2,875 in doctor bills, hospital bills, and medical insurance premiums. His employer withheld state income tax of $1,954. James paid real property taxes of $1,766 on his home. Interest on his home mortgage was $3,845, and interest to credit card companies was $320. James contributed $20 each week to his church and $10 each week to the United Way. Professional dues and subscriptions totaled $350.

James's employer withheld Federal income taxes of $9,500 during 1992. James paid estimated taxes of $1,600. What is the amount of James Jordan's net tax payable or refund due for 1992? If James has a tax refund due, he wants to have it credited toward his 1993 income tax. If you use tax forms for your solution, you will need Forms 1040, 2106, and 4562 and Schedules A, B, C, D, and SE. Suggested software (if available): *TurboTax* or *MacInTax* for tax return or WFT tax planning software.

CHAPTER

PROPERTY TRANSACTIONS: DETERMINATION OF GAIN OR LOSS, BASIS CONSIDERATIONS, AND NONTAXABLE EXCHANGES

OBJECTIVES

Explain the computation of realized gain or loss on property dispositions.

Distinguish between realized and recognized gain or loss.

Explain how basis is determined for various methods of asset acquisition.

Present various loss disallowance provisions.

Describe provisions for postponing or excluding gain on the sale and replacement of a personal residence.

Discuss the rationale for nonrecognition (postponement) of gain in certain property transactions.

Identify the different types of nontaxable exchanges.

Examine the nonrecognition provisions available on the involuntary conversion of property and like-kind exchanges.

Discuss the provisions for permanent exclusion of gain on the sale of a personal residence for taxpayers age 55 and older.

Identify tax planning opportunities related to selected property transactions and the nonrecognition provisions discussed in the chapter.

OUTLINE

This chapter and the following chapter are concerned with the income tax consequences of property transactions (the sale or other disposition of property). The following questions are considered with respect to the sale or other disposition of property:

- Is there a realized gain or loss?
- If so, is the gain or loss recognized?
- If the gain or loss is recognized, is it ordinary or capital?
- What is the basis of any replacement property that is acquired?

This chapter is concerned with the determination of realized and recognized gain or loss and the basis of property. Chapter 13 covers the classification of the recognized gain or loss as ordinary or capital.

DETERMINATION OF GAIN OR LOSS

Realized Gain or Loss

Realized gain or loss is the difference between the amount realized from the sale or other disposition of property and the property's adjusted basis on the date of disposition. If the amount realized exceeds the property's adjusted basis, the result is a *realized gain*. Conversely, if the property's adjusted basis exceeds the amount realized, the result is a *realized loss*.

EXAMPLE 1

Tab sells Brown Corporation stock with an adjusted basis of $3,000 for $5,000. His realized gain is $2,000. If Tab had sold the stock for $2,000, he would have had a $1,000 realized loss. ◆

Sale or Other Disposition. The term *sale or other disposition* is defined broadly in the tax law and includes virtually any disposition of property. Thus, transactions such as trade-ins, casualties, condemnations, thefts, and bond retirements are treated as dispositions of property. The most common disposition of property is through a sale or exchange. The key factor in determining whether a disposition has taken place usually is whether an identifiable event has occurred[1] as opposed to a mere fluctuation in the value of the property.

EXAMPLE 2

Lori owns Tan Corporation stock that cost $3,000. The stock has appreciated in value by $2,000 since she purchased it. Lori has no realized gain, since mere fluctuation in value is not a disposition or identifiable event for tax purposes. Nor would she have a realized loss if the stock had declined in value by $2,000. ◆

Amount Realized. The *amount realized* from a sale or other disposition of property is the sum of any money received plus the fair market value of other property received. The amount realized also includes any real property taxes that are treated as imposed on the seller but paid by the buyer (refer to Chapter 10).

1. Reg. § 1.1001–1(c)(1).

The reason for including these taxes in the amount realized is that by paying the taxes, the purchaser is, in effect, paying an additional amount to the seller of the property.

The amount realized also includes any liability on the property disposed of, such as a mortgage debt, if the buyer assumes the mortgage or the property is sold subject to the mortgage.[2] The amount of the liability is included in the amount realized even if the debt is nonrecourse and the amount of the debt is greater than the fair market value of the mortgaged property.[3]

EXAMPLE 3

Barry sells property on which there is a mortgage of $20,000 to Cole for $50,000 cash. Barry's amount realized from the sale is $70,000 if Cole assumes the mortgage or takes the property subject to the mortgage. ◆

The *fair market value* of property received in a sale or other disposition has been defined by the courts as the price at which property will change hands between a willing seller and a willing buyer when neither is compelled to sell or buy.[4] Fair market value is determined by considering the relevant factors in each case. An expert appraiser is often required to evaluate these factors in arriving at fair market value. When the fair market value of the property received cannot be determined, the value of the property surrendered may be used.[5]

In calculating the amount realized, selling expenses such as advertising, commissions, and legal fees relating to the disposition are deducted. The amount realized is the net amount received directly or indirectly by the taxpayer from the disposition of property whether it is in the form of cash or other property.

Adjusted Basis. The *adjusted basis* of property disposed of is the property's original basis adjusted to the date of disposition. Original basis is the cost or other basis of the property on the date the property is acquired by the taxpayer. *Capital additions* increase and *recoveries of capital* decrease the original basis so that on the date of disposition the adjusted basis reflects the unrecovered cost or other basis of the property. Adjusted basis is determined as follows:

Cost (or other adjusted basis) on date of acquisition
\+ Capital additions
− Capital recoveries
= Adjusted basis on date of disposition

Capital Additions. Capital additions include the cost of capital improvements and betterments made to the property by the taxpayer. These expenditures are distinguishable from expenditures for the ordinary repair and maintenance of the property that are neither capitalized nor added to the original basis (refer to Chapter 5). The latter expenditures are deductible in the current taxable year if they are related to business or income-producing property. Amounts representing real property taxes treated as imposed on the seller but paid or assumed by

---

2. *Crane v. Comm.*, 47–1 USTC ¶9217, 35 AFTR 776, 67 S.Ct. 1047 (USSC, 1947). Although a legal distinction exists between the direct assumption of a mortgage and taking property subject to a mortgage, the tax consequences in calculating the amount realized are the same.
3. *Tufts v. Comm.*, 83–1 USTC ¶9328, 51 AFTR2d 83–1132, 103 S.Ct. 1826 (USSC, 1983).
4. *Comm. v. Marshman*, 60–2 USTC ¶9484, 5 AFTR2d 1528, 279 F.2d 27 (CA–6, 1960).
5. *U.S. v. Davis*, 62–2 USTC ¶9509, 9 AFTR2d 1625, 82 S.Ct. 1190 (USSC, 1962).

the buyer are part of the cost of the property. Any liability on property that is assumed by the buyer is also included in the buyer's original basis of the property. The same rule applies if property is acquired subject to a liability. Amortization of the discount on bonds increases the adjusted basis of the bonds.

Capital Recoveries. The following are examples of capital recoveries:

1. *Depreciation and cost recovery allowances.* The original basis of depreciable property is reduced by the annual depreciation charges (or cost recovery allowances) while the property is held by the taxpayer. The amount of depreciation that is subtracted from the original basis is the greater of the *allowed* or *allowable* depreciation on an annual basis. In most circumstances, the allowed and allowable depreciation amounts are the same (refer to Chapter 8).
2. *Investment tax credit.* For property placed in service after 1982 and before 1986, the taxpayer may be required to reduce the adjusted basis of the property by 50 percent of the available investment tax credit. This reduction in the adjusted basis of the property is required unless the taxpayer has elected to take a reduced investment tax credit (refer to Chapters 8 and 11).
3. *Casualties and thefts.* A casualty or theft may result in the reduction of the adjusted basis of property. The adjusted basis is reduced by the amount of the deductible loss. In addition, the adjusted basis is reduced by the amount of insurance proceeds received. However, the receipt of insurance proceeds may result in a recognized gain rather than a deductible loss. The gain increases the adjusted basis of the property.

EXAMPLE 4

An insured truck used in a trade or business is destroyed in an accident. The adjusted basis is $8,000, and the fair market value is $6,500. Insurance proceeds of $6,500 are received. The amount of the casualty loss is $1,500 ($6,500 insurance proceeds – $8,000 adjusted basis). The adjusted basis is reduced by the $1,500 casualty loss and the $6,500 of insurance proceeds received. ◆

EXAMPLE 5

An insured truck used in a trade or business is destroyed in an accident. The adjusted basis is $6,500, and the fair market value is $8,000. Insurance proceeds of $8,000 are received. The amount of the casualty gain is $1,500 ($8,000 insurance proceeds – $6,500 adjusted basis). The adjusted basis is increased by the $1,500 casualty gain and is reduced by the $8,000 of insurance proceeds received ($6,500 basis before casualty + $1,500 casualty gain – $8,000 insurance proceeds = $0 basis). ◆

4. *Certain corporate distributions.* A corporate distribution to a shareholder that is not taxable is treated as a return of capital, and it reduces the basis of the shareholder's stock in the corporation.[6] For example, if a corporation makes a cash distribution to its shareholders and has no earnings and profits, the distributions are treated as a return of capital. If the corporation does have earnings and profits but makes a distribution in excess of the earnings and profits, the excess distribution is treated as a return of capital. Once the basis of the stock is reduced to zero, the amount of any subsequent distributions is a capital gain if the stock is a capital asset.

6. § 1016(a)(4) and Reg. § 1.1016–5(a). See Chapter 18 for further discussion of corporate distributions.

EXAMPLE 6

Purple Corporation has accumulated earnings and profits of $140,000 at the beginning of 1993. For 1993, Purple generates current earnings and profits of $30,000. During 1993, the corporation makes cash distributions to its only shareholder, Maria, in the amount of $200,000. Maria's basis for her Purple Corporation stock is $20,000. Of the $200,000 cash distributed to her, $170,000 is classified as dividend income (to the extent of current earnings and profits of $30,000 and beginning accumulated earnings and profits of $140,000). The next $20,000 is treated as a return of capital and reduces Maria's basis for her Purple stock to zero. The remaining $10,000 is a capital gain. ◆

5. *Amortizable bond premium.* The basis in a bond purchased at a premium is reduced by the amortizable portion of the bond premium. Investors in taxable bonds may *elect* to amortize the bond premium, but the premium on tax-exempt bonds *must be* amortized. The amount of the amortized premium on taxable bonds is permitted as an interest deduction. Therefore, the election produces the opportunity for an annual interest deduction to offset ordinary income in exchange for a larger capital gain or smaller capital loss on the disposition of the bond. No such interest deduction is permitted for tax-exempt bonds.

The amortization deduction is allowed for taxable bonds because the premium is viewed as a cost of earning the taxable interest from the bonds. The reason the basis of taxable bonds is reduced is that the amortization deduction is a recovery of the cost or basis of the bonds. The basis of tax-exempt bonds is reduced even though the amortization is not allowed as a deduction. No amortization deduction is permitted on tax-exempt bonds, since the interest income is exempt from tax and the amortization of the bond premium merely represents an adjustment of the effective amount of such income.

EXAMPLE 7

Antonio purchases Gray Corporation taxable bonds with a face value of $100,000 for $110,000, thus paying a premium of $10,000. The annual interest rate is 7%, and the bonds mature 10 years from the date of purchase. The annual interest income is $7,000 (7% × $100,000). If Antonio elects to amortize the bond premium, the $10,000 premium is deducted over the 10-year period. His basis for the bonds is reduced each year by the amount of the amortization deduction. Note that if the bonds were tax-exempt, amortization of the bond premium and the basis adjustment would be mandatory. However, no deduction would be allowed for the amortization. ◆

Recognized Gain or Loss

Recognized gain is the amount of the realized gain included in the taxpayer's gross income. A *recognized loss,* on the other hand, is the amount of a realized loss that is deductible for tax purposes. As a general rule, the entire amount of a realized gain or loss is recognized.

Concept Summary 12–1 summarizes the realized gain or loss and recognized gain or loss concepts.

Nonrecognition of Gain or Loss

In certain cases, a realized gain or loss is not recognized upon the sale or other disposition of property. One of the exceptions to the recognition of gain or loss requirement involves nontaxable exchanges, which are covered later in this chapter. Additional exceptions include losses realized upon the sale, exchange, or condemnation of personal use assets (as opposed to business or income-producing property) and gains realized upon the sale of a residence by taxpayers 55 years of age or older (discussed later in this chapter). In addition, realized losses from the sale or exchange of business or income-producing property between certain related parties are not recognized.

Sale, Exchange, or Condemnation of Personal Use Assets. A realized loss from the sale, exchange, or condemnation of personal use assets (e.g., a personal residence or an automobile not used at all for business or income-producing purposes) is not recognized for tax purposes. An exception exists for casualty or theft losses from personal use assets (see Chapter 7). In contrast, any gain realized from the sale or other disposition of personal use assets is, generally, fully taxable. The following examples illustrate the tax consequences of the sale of personal use assets.

EXAMPLE 8

Freda sells an automobile, which is held exclusively for personal use, for $6,000. The adjusted basis of the automobile is $5,000. She has a realized and recognized gain of $1,000. ◆

EXAMPLE 9

Freda sells the automobile in Example 8 for $4,000. She has a realized loss of $1,000, but the loss is not recognized. ◆

Recovery of Capital Doctrine

Doctrine Defined. The *recovery of capital doctrine* pervades all the tax rules relating to property transactions and is very significant for these transactions. The doctrine derives its roots from the very essence of the income tax—a tax on income. Therefore, as a general rule, a taxpayer is entitled to recover the cost or other original basis of property acquired and is not taxed on that amount.

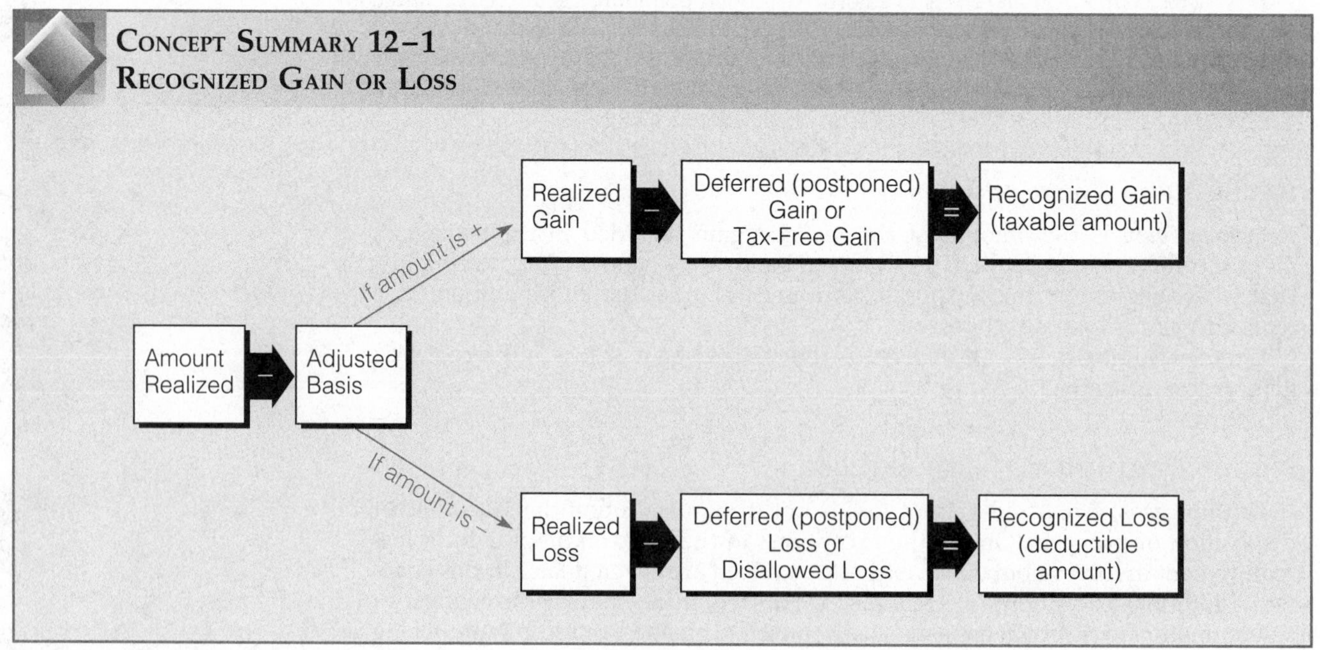

The cost or other original basis of depreciable property is recovered through annual depreciation deductions. The basis is reduced as the cost is recovered over the period the property is held. Therefore, when property is sold or otherwise disposed of, it is the adjusted basis (unrecovered cost or other basis) that is compared to the amount realized from the disposition to determine realized gain or loss.

Relationship of the Recovery of Capital Doctrine to the Concepts of Realization and Recognition. If a sale or other disposition results in a realized gain, the taxpayer has recovered more than the adjusted basis of the property. Conversely, if a sale or other disposition results in a realized loss, the taxpayer has recovered less than the adjusted basis.

The following general rules summarize the relationship between the recovery of capital doctrine and the realized and recognized gain and loss concepts:

Rule 1. A realized gain that is *never recognized* results in the *permanent recovery* of more than the taxpayer's cost or other basis for tax purposes. For example, all or a portion of the realized gain on the sale of a personal residence by taxpayers 55 years of age or older can be excluded from gross income under § 121.

Rule 2. A realized gain on which *recognition is postponed* results in the *temporary recovery* of more than the taxpayer's cost or other basis for tax purposes. For example, an exchange of like-kind property under § 1031, an involuntary conversion under § 1033, or a replacement of a personal residence under § 1034 are all eligible for postponement treatment.

Rule 3. A realized loss that is *never recognized* results in the *permanent recovery* of less than the taxpayer's cost or other basis for tax purposes. For example, a loss on the sale of an automobile held for personal use is not deductible.

Rule 4. A realized loss on which *recognition is postponed* results in the *temporary recovery* of less than the taxpayer's cost or other basis for tax purposes. For example, the realized loss on the exchange of like-kind property under § 1031 is postponed.

These rules are illustrated in discussions to follow in this chapter.

Basis Considerations

Determination of Cost Basis

The basis of property is generally the property's cost. Cost is the amount paid for the property in cash or other property. This general rule follows logically from the recovery of capital doctrine; that is, the cost or other basis of property is to be recovered tax-free by the taxpayer.

A *bargain purchase* of property is an exception to the general rule for determining basis. A bargain purchase may result when an employer transfers property to an employee at less than the property's fair market value (as compensation for services) or when a corporation transfers property to a shareholder at less than the property's fair market value (a dividend). The basis of property acquired in a bargain purchase is the property's fair market value. If the basis of the property were not increased by the bargain amount, the taxpayer would be taxed on this amount again at disposition.

EXAMPLE 10

Wade buys a machine from his employer for $10,000 on December 30, 1993. The fair market value of the machine is $15,000. Wade must include the $5,000 difference between cost and the fair market value of the machine in gross income for the taxable year 1993. The bargain element represents additional compensation to him. His basis for the machine is $15,000, the machine's fair market value. ◆

Identification Problems. Cost identification problems are frequently encountered in securities transactions. For example, the Regulations require that the taxpayer adequately identify the particular stock that has been sold.[7] A problem arises when the taxpayer has purchased separate lots of stock on different dates or at different prices and cannot adequately identify the lot from which a particular sale takes place. In this case, the stock is presumed to come from the first lot or lots purchased (a FIFO presumption).[8] When securities are left in the custody of a broker, it may be necessary to provide specific instructions and receive written confirmation as to which securities are being sold.

EXAMPLE 11

Polly purchases 100 shares of Olive Corporation stock on July 1, 1991, for $5,000 ($50 a share) and another 100 shares of the same stock on July 1, 1992, for $6,000 ($60 a share). She sells 50 shares of the stock on January 2, 1993. The cost of the stock sold, assuming Polly cannot adequately identify the shares, is $50 a share, or $2,500. This is the cost she will compare to the amount realized in determining the gain or loss from the sale. ◆

Allocation Problems. When a taxpayer acquires multiple assets in a lump-sum purchase, it is necessary to allocate the total cost among the individual assets. Allocation is necessary because some of the assets acquired may be depreciable (e.g., buildings) and others not (e.g., land). In addition, only a portion of the assets acquired may be sold, or some of the assets may be capital or § 1231 assets that receive special tax treatment upon subsequent sale or other disposition. The lump-sum cost is allocated on the basis of the fair market values of the individual assets acquired.

EXAMPLE 12

Harry purchases a building and land for $800,000. Because of the depressed nature of the industry in which the seller was operating, he was able to negotiate a very favorable purchase price. Appraisals of the individual assets indicate that the fair market value of the building is $600,000 and that of the land is $400,000. Harry's basis for the building is $480,000 ($600,000/$1,000,000 × $800,000), and his basis for the land is $320,000 ($400,000/$1,000,000 × $800,000). ◆

If a business is purchased and *goodwill* is involved, a special allocation rule applies. Initially, the purchase price is assigned to the assets, excluding goodwill, to the extent of their total fair market value. This assigned amount is allocated among the assets on the basis of the fair market value of the individual assets

7. Reg. § 1.1012–1(c)(1).

8. *Kluger Associates, Inc.*, 69 T.C. 925 (1978).

acquired. Goodwill is then assigned the residual amount of the purchase price. The resultant allocation is applicable to both the buyer and the seller.[9]

EXAMPLE 13

Rocky sells his business to Paul. They agree that the values of the individual assets are as follows:

Inventory	$ 50,000
Building	500,000
Land	200,000
Goodwill	150,000

After negotiations, Rocky and Paul agree on a sales price of $1 million. Applying the residual method with respect to goodwill results in the following allocation of the $1 million purchase price:

Inventory	$ 50,000
Building	500,000
Land	200,000
Goodwill	250,000

The residual method requires that all of the excess of the purchase price over the fair market value of the assets ($1,000,000 – $900,000 = $100,000) be allocated to goodwill. Without this requirement, the purchaser could allocate the excess pro rata to all of the assets, including goodwill, based on their respective fair market values. This would have resulted in only $166,667 [$150,000 + ($150,000 ÷ $900,000 × $100,000)] being assigned to goodwill. ◆

In the case of *nontaxable stock dividends,* the allocation depends upon whether the dividend is a common stock dividend on common stock or a preferred stock dividend on common stock. If the dividend is common on common, the cost of the original common shares is allocated to the total shares owned after the dividend. The holding period of the new shares includes the holding period of the old shares.

EXAMPLE 14

Susan owns 100 shares of Black Corporation common stock for which she paid $1,100. She receives a 10% common stock dividend, giving her a new total of 110 shares. Before the stock dividend, Susan's basis was $11 per share ($1,100 ÷ 100 shares). The basis of each share after the stock dividend is $10 ($1,100 ÷ 110 shares). ◆

If the dividend is preferred stock on common, the cost of the original common shares is allocated between the common and preferred shares on the basis of their relative fair market values on the date of distribution.

EXAMPLE 15

Fran owns 100 shares of Cardinal Corporation common stock for which she paid $1,000. She receives a stock dividend of 50 shares of preferred stock on her common stock. The fair market values on the date of distribution of the preferred stock dividend are $30 a share for common stock and $40 a share for preferred stock. Thus, the total

9. § 1060.

fair market value is $3,000 ($30 × 100) for common stock and $2,000 ($40 × 50) for preferred stock. The basis of Fran's common stock after the dividend is $600, or $6 a share ($3,000/$5,000 × $1,000), and the basis of the preferred stock is $400, or $8 a share ($2,000/$5,000 × $1,000). ◆

Gift Basis

When a taxpayer receives property as a gift, there is no cost to the recipient. Thus, under the cost basis provision, the donee's basis would be zero. However, this would violate the statutory intent that gifts are not subject to the income tax. With a zero basis, a sale by the donee would result in all of the amount realized being treated as realized gain. Therefore, a basis is assigned to the property received depending on the following:

- The date of the gift.
- The basis of the property to the donor.
- The amount of the gift tax paid.
- The fair market value of the property.

Gifts Prior to 1921. If property was acquired by gift before 1921, its basis for income tax purposes is its fair market value on the date of the gift.

Gift Basis Rules if No Gift Tax Is Paid. Property received by gift can be referred to as *dual basis* property; that is, the basis for gain and the basis for loss might not be the same amount. The present basis rules for gifts of property are as follows:

- If the donee subsequently disposes of gift property in a transaction that results in a gain, the basis to the donee is the same as the donor's adjusted basis.[10] The donee's basis in this case is referred to as the *gain basis*. Therefore, a *realized gain* results if the amount realized from the disposition exceeds the donee's gain basis.

EXAMPLE 16

Melissa purchased stock in 1992 for $10,000. She gave the stock to her son, Joe, in 1993, when the fair market value was $15,000. No gift tax is paid on the transfer, and Joe subsequently sells the property for $15,000. Joe's basis is $10,000, and he has a realized gain of $5,000. ◆

- If the donee subsequently disposes of gift property in a transaction that results in a loss, the basis to the donee is the lower of the donor's adjusted basis or fair market value on the date of the gift. The donee's basis in this case is referred to as the *loss basis*. Therefore, a *realized loss* results if the amount realized from the disposition is less than the donee's loss basis.

EXAMPLE 17

Burt purchased stock in 1992 for $10,000. He gave the stock to his son, Cliff, in 1993, when the fair market value was $7,000. No gift tax is paid on the transfer. Cliff later sells the stock for $6,000. Cliff's basis is $7,000 (fair market value is less than donor's adjusted basis of $10,000), and the loss from the sale is $1,000 ($6,000 amount realized − $7,000 basis). ◆

---

10. § 1015(a) and Reg. § 1.1015–1(a)(1). See Reg. § 1.1015–1(a)(3) for cases in which the facts necessary to determine the donor's adjusted basis are unknown. Refer to Example 22 for the effect of depreciation deductions by the donee.

The amount of the loss basis will differ from the amount of the gain basis only if at the date of the gift the adjusted basis of the property exceeds the property's fair market value. Note that the loss basis rule prevents the donee from receiving a tax benefit from the decline in value while the donor held the property. Therefore, in Example 17, Cliff has a loss of only $1,000 rather than a loss of $4,000. The $3,000 difference represents the decline in value while Burt held the property. However, the gain basis rule may eventually result in the donee's being subject to income tax on the appreciation that occurs while the donor held the property, as Example 16 illustrated.

If the amount realized from sale or other disposition is between the basis for loss and the basis for gain, no gain or loss is realized.

Example 18

Assume the same facts as in the previous example, except that Cliff sold the stock for $8,000. The application of the gain basis rule produces a loss of $2,000 ($8,000 – $10,000). The application of the loss basis rule produces a gain of $1,000 ($8,000 – $7,000). Therefore, Cliff recognizes neither a gain nor a loss because the amount realized is between the gain basis and the loss basis. ◆

Adjustment for Gift Tax. If gift taxes are paid by the donor, the donee's gain basis may exceed the adjusted basis of the property to the donor. This occurs only if the fair market value of the property at the date of the gift is greater than the donor's adjusted basis (the property has appreciated in value). The portion of the gift tax paid that is related to the appreciation is added to the donor's basis in calculating the donee's gain basis for the property. In this circumstance, the following formula is used for calculating the donee's gain basis:

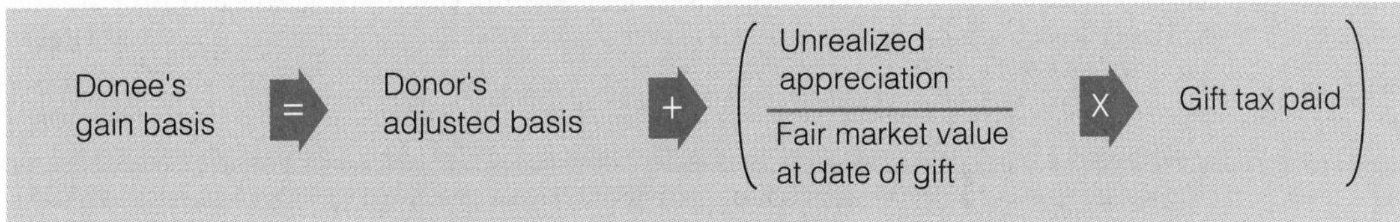

Example 19

Bonnie made a gift of stock to Peggy in 1993, when the fair market value of the stock was $40,000. Bonnie had purchased the stock in 1981 for $10,000. Because the unrealized appreciation is $30,000 ($40,000 fair market value – $10,000 adjusted basis) and the fair market value is $40,000, three-fourths ($30,000/$40,000) of the gift tax paid is added to the basis of the property. If Bonnie paid gift tax of $4,000, Peggy's basis in the property is $13,000 [$10,000 + $3,000 (¾ of the $4,000 gift tax)]. ◆

Example 20

Don made a gift of stock to Matt in 1993, when the fair market value of the stock was $40,000. Gift tax of $4,000 was paid by Don, who had purchased the stock in 1981 for $45,000. Because there is no unrealized appreciation at the date of the gift, none of the gift tax paid is added to Don's basis in calculating Matt's gain basis. Therefore, Matt's gain basis is $45,000. ◆

For *gifts made before 1977,* the full amount of the gift tax paid may be added to the donor's basis. However, the ceiling on this total is the fair market value of the property at the date of the gift. Thus, in Example 19, if the gift had been made before 1977, the basis of the property would be $14,000 ($10,000 + $4,000). In Example 20, the gain basis would still be $45,000 ($45,000 + $0).

Holding Period. The *holding period* for property acquired by gift begins on the date the donor acquired the property if the gain basis rule applies. The holding period starts on the date of the gift if the loss basis rule applies.[11] The significance of the holding period for capital assets is discussed in Chapter 13.

The following example summarizes the basis and holding period rules for gift property:

EXAMPLE 21

Jill acquires 100 shares of White Corporation stock on December 30, 1981, for $40,000. On January 3, 1993, when the stock has a fair market value of $38,000, Jill gives it to Dennis and pays gift tax of $4,000. There is no increase in basis for a portion of the gift tax paid because the property has not appreciated in value at the time of the gift. Therefore, Dennis's gain basis is $40,000. His basis for determining loss is $38,000 (fair market value) because the fair market value on the date of the gift is less than the donor's adjusted basis.

- If Dennis sells the stock for $45,000, he has a recognized gain of $5,000. The holding period for determining whether the capital gain is short term or long term begins on December 30, 1981, the date Jill acquired the property.
- If Dennis sells the stock for $36,000, he has a recognized loss of $2,000. The holding period for determining whether the capital loss is short term or long term begins on January 3, 1993, the date of the gift.
- If Dennis sells the property for $39,000, there is no gain or loss since the amount realized is less than the gain basis of $40,000 and more than the loss basis of $38,000. ◆

Basis for Depreciation. The basis for depreciation on depreciable gift property is the donee's gain basis. This rule is applicable even if the donee later sells the property at a loss and uses the loss basis rule in calculating the amount of the realized loss.

EXAMPLE 22

Vito gave a machine to Tina in 1993, when the adjusted basis was $32,000 (cost of $40,000 – accumulated depreciation of $8,000) and the fair market value was $26,000. No gift tax was paid. Tina's gain basis at the date of the gift is $32,000, and her loss basis is $26,000. During 1993, Tina deducts depreciation (cost recovery) of $10,240 ($32,000 × 32%). Therefore, at the end of 1993, Tina's gain basis is $21,760 ($32,000 – $10,240), and her loss basis is $15,760 ($26,000 – $10,240). ◆

Property Acquired from a Decedent

General Rules. The basis of property acquired from a decedent is generally the property's fair market value at the date of death (referred to as the *primary valuation amount*). The property's basis is the fair market value six months after the date of death if the executor or administrator of the estate *elects* the alternate valuation date for estate tax purposes. This amount is referred to as the *alternate valuation amount*. If an estate tax return does not have to be filed because the estate is below the threshold amount for being subject to the estate tax, the alternate valuation date and amount are not available. Even if an estate tax return is filed and the executor elects the alternate valuation date, the six-months-after-death date is available only for property that the executor has not distributed

11. Rev.Rul. 59–86, 1959–1 C.B. 209.

before this date. Any property distributed or otherwise disposed of by the executor during this six-month period will have an adjusted basis to the beneficiary equal to the fair market value on the date of distribution or other disposition.

For inherited property, both unrealized appreciation and decline in value are taken into consideration in determining the basis of the property for income tax purposes. Contrast this with the carryover basis rules for property received by gift.

The alternate valuation date can be elected only if the election results in the reduction of both the value of the gross estate and the estate tax liability below the amounts they would have been if the primary valuation date had been used. This provision prevents the alternate valuation election from being used to increase the basis of the property to the beneficiary for income tax purposes without simultaneously increasing the estate tax liability (because of estate tax deductions or credits).

Example 23

Linda and various other family members inherited property from Linda's father, who died in 1993. At date of death, her father's adjusted basis for the property she inherited was $35,000. The property's fair market value at date of death was $50,000. The alternate valuation date was not elected. Linda's basis for income tax purposes is $50,000. This is commonly referred to as a *stepped-up basis.* ◆

Example 24

Assume the same facts as in Example 23, except the property's fair market value at date of death was $20,000. Linda's basis for income tax purposes is $20,000. This is commonly referred to as a *stepped-down basis.* ◆

Example 25

Nancy inherited all the property of her father, who died in 1993. Her father's adjusted basis for the property at date of death was $35,000. The property's fair market value was $750,000 at date of death and $760,000 six months after death. The alternate valuation date cannot be elected because the value of the gross estate has increased during the six-month period. Nancy's basis for income tax purposes is $750,000. ◆

Example 26

Assume the same facts as in Example 25, except the property's fair market value six months after death was $745,000. If the executor elects the alternate valuation date, Nancy's basis for income tax purposes is $745,000. ◆

Example 27

Assume the same facts as in the previous example, except the property is distributed four months after the date of the decedent's death. At the distribution date, the property's fair market value is $747,500. Since the executor elected the alternate valuation date, Nancy's basis for income tax purposes is $747,500. ◆

The Code contains a provision designed to eliminate a tax avoidance technique referred to as *deathbed gifts.* If the time period between the date of the gift of appreciated property and the date of the donee's death is not longer than one year, the stepped-up basis rule for inherited property may not apply. The adjusted basis of such property inherited by the donor or his or her spouse from the donee shall be the same as the decedent's adjusted basis for the property rather than the fair market value at the date of death or the alternate valuation date.

EXAMPLE 28

Ned gives stock to his uncle, Vern, in 1993. Ned's basis for the stock is $1,000, and the fair market value is $9,000. No gift tax is paid. Eight months later, Ned inherits the stock from Vern. At the date of Vern's death, the fair market value of the stock is $12,000. Ned's adjusted basis for the stock is $1,000. ◆

Survivor's Share of Property. Both the decedent's share and the survivor's share of *community property* have a basis equal to fair market value on the date of the decedent's death.[12] This result applies to the decedent's share of the community property because the property flows to the surviving spouse from the estate (fair market value basis for inherited property). Likewise, the surviving spouse's share of the community property is deemed to be acquired by bequest, devise, or inheritance from the decedent. Therefore, it will also have a basis equal to fair market value.

EXAMPLE 29

Floyd and Vera reside in a community property state. They own community property (200 shares of Greene Corporation stock) that was acquired in 1974 for $100,000. Assume that Floyd dies in 1993, when the securities are valued at $300,000. One-half of the Greene stock is included in his estate. If Vera inherits Floyd's share of the community property, the basis for determining gain or loss is $300,000 [$150,000 (Vera's share of one-half of the community property) + $150,000 (½ × $300,000, the value of Greene stock at the date of Floyd's death)] for the 200 shares of Greene stock. ◆

In a *common law* state, only one-half of jointly held property of spouses (tenants by the entirety or joint tenants with rights of survivorship) is includible in the estate.[13] In such a case, no adjustment of the basis is permitted for the excluded property interest (the surviving spouse's share).

EXAMPLE 30

Assume the same facts as in the previous example, except that the property is jointly held by Floyd and Vera who reside in a common law state. Also assume that Floyd purchased the property and made a gift of one-half of the property when the stock was acquired, with no gift tax being paid. Only one-half of the Greene stock is included in Floyd's estate. Vera's basis for determining gain or loss in the excluded half is not adjusted upward for the increase in value to date of death. Therefore, Vera's basis is $200,000 ($50,000 + $150,000). ◆

Holding Period of Property Acquired from a Decedent. The holding period of property acquired from a decedent is *deemed to be long term* (held for the required long-term holding period). This provision applies regardless of whether the property is disposed of at a gain or a loss.

Disallowed Losses

Related Taxpayers. Section 267 provides that realized losses from sales or exchanges of property, directly or indirectly, between certain related parties are not recognized. This loss disallowance provision applies to several types of related-party transactions. The most common involve (1) members of a family and (2) transactions between an individual and a corporation in which the

12. § 1014(b)(6).

13. § 2040(a).

individual owns, directly or indirectly, more than 50 percent in value of the corporation's outstanding stock. Refer to Chapter 5 for a detailed discussion of the related-party provisions.

Wash Sales. Section 1091 stipulates that in certain cases, a realized loss on the sale or exchange of stock or securities is not recognized. Specifically, if a taxpayer sells or exchanges stock or securities and within 30 days before *or* after the date of the sale or exchange acquires substantially identical stock or securities, any loss realized from the sale or exchange is not recognized. The term *acquire* means acquire by purchase or in a taxable exchange and includes an option to purchase substantially identical securities. *Substantially identical* means the same in all important particulars. Corporate bonds and preferred stock are normally not considered substantially identical to the corporation's common stock. However, if the bonds and preferred stock are convertible into common stock, they may be considered substantially identical under certain circumstances. Attempts to avoid the application of the wash sales rules by having a related taxpayer repurchase the securities have been unsuccessful. The wash sales provisions do *not* apply to gains.

Recognition of the loss is disallowed because the taxpayer is considered to be in substantially the same economic position after the sale and repurchase as before the sale and repurchase. This disallowance rule does not apply to taxpayers engaged in the business of buying and selling securities. Investors, however, are not allowed to create losses through wash sales to offset income for tax purposes.

Realized loss that is not recognized is added to the basis of the substantially identical stock or securities whose acquisition resulted in the nonrecognition of loss. In other words, the basis of the replacement stock or securities is increased by the amount of the unrecognized loss. If the loss were not added to the basis of the newly acquired stock or securities, the taxpayer would never recover the entire basis of the old stock or securities.

The basis of the new stock or securities includes the unrecovered portion (i.e., the unrecognized loss) of the basis of the formerly held stock or securities. Therefore, the holding period of the new stock or securities begins on the date of acquisition of the old stock or securities.

EXAMPLE 31

Bhaskar owns 100 shares of Silver Corporation stock (adjusted basis of $20,000), 50 shares of which he sells for $8,000. Ten days later, he purchases 50 shares of the same stock for $7,000. Bhaskar's realized loss of $2,000 ($8,000 amount realized – $10,000 adjusted basis of 50 shares) is not recognized because it resulted from a wash sale. His basis in the newly acquired stock is $9,000 ($7,000 purchase price + $2,000 unrecognized loss from the wash sale). ◆

The taxpayer may acquire less than the number of shares sold in a wash sale. In this case, the loss from the sale is prorated between recognized and unrecognized loss on the basis of the ratio of the number of shares acquired to the number of shares sold.

Conversion of Property from Personal Use to Business or Income-Producing Use

As discussed previously, losses from the sale of personal use assets are not recognized for tax purposes, but losses from the sale of business and income-producing assets are deductible. Can a taxpayer convert a personal use asset that has declined in value to business or income-producing use and then sell the asset to recognize a business or income-producing loss? The tax law prevents this by specifying that the *original basis for loss* on personal use assets converted to business or income-producing use is the lower of the property's adjusted basis or fair market value on the date of conversion. The *gain basis* for converted property is the property's adjusted basis on the date of conversion. The tax law is not concerned with gains on converted property because gains are recognized regardless of whether property is business, income producing, or personal use.

EXAMPLE 32

Diane's personal residence has an adjusted basis of $75,000 and a fair market value of $60,000. She converts the personal residence to rental property. Her basis for loss is $60,000 (lower of $75,000 adjusted basis or fair market value of $60,000). The $15,000 decline in value is a personal loss and can never be recognized for tax purposes. Her basis for gain is $75,000. ◆

The basis for loss is also the basis for depreciating the converted property.[14] This is an exception to the general rule that provides that the basis for depreciation is the gain basis (e.g., property received by gift). This exception prevents the taxpayer from recovering a personal loss indirectly through depreciation of the higher original basis. After the property is converted, both its basis for loss and its basis for gain are adjusted for depreciation deductions from the date of conversion to the date of disposition. These rules apply only if a conversion from personal to business or income-producing use has actually occurred.

EXAMPLE 33

At a time when his personal residence (adjusted basis of $40,000) is worth $50,000, Keith converts one-half of it to rental use. The property is not MACRS recovery property. At this point, the estimated useful life of the residence is 20 years and there is no estimated salvage value. After renting the converted portion for five years, he sells the property for $44,000. All amounts relate only to the building; the land has been accounted for separately. Keith has a $2,000 realized gain from the sale of the personal use portion of the residence and a $7,000 realized gain from the sale of the rental portion. These gains are computed as follows:

	Personal Use	Rental
Original basis for gain and loss—adjusted basis on date of conversion (fair market value is greater than the adjusted basis)	$20,000	$20,000
Depreciation—five years	None	5,000
Adjusted basis—date of sale	$20,000	$15,000
Amount realized	22,000	22,000
Realized gain	$ 2,000	$ 7,000

As discussed later in this chapter, Keith may be able to defer recognition of part or all of the $2,000 gain from the sale of the personal use portion of the residence under § 1034. The $7,000 gain from the rental portion is recognized. ◆

EXAMPLE 34

Assume the same facts as in the previous example, except that the fair market value on the date of conversion is $30,000 and the sales proceeds are $16,000. Keith has a $12,000

14. Reg. § 1.167(g)–1.

realized loss from the sale of the personal use portion of the residence and a $3,250 realized loss from the sale of the rental portion. These losses are computed as follows:

	Personal Use	Rental
Original basis for loss—fair market value on date of conversion (fair market value is less than the adjusted basis)	*	$15,000
Depreciation—five years	None	3,750
Adjusted basis—date of sale	$20,000	$11,250
Amount realized	8,000	8,000
Realized loss	$12,000	$ 3,250

*Not applicable.

The $12,000 loss from the sale of the personal use portion of the residence is not recognized. The $3,250 loss from the rental portion is recognized. ◆

Summary of Basis Adjustments

Some of the more common items that either increase or decrease the basis of an asset appear in Concept Summary 12–2.

A number of specific techniques for determining basis have been presented. Although the various techniques are responsive to and mandated by transactions occurring in the marketplace, they do possess enough common characteristics to be categorized as follows:

- The basis of the asset may be determined by reference to the asset's cost.
- The basis of the asset may be determined by reference to the basis of another asset.
- The basis of the asset may be determined by reference to the asset's fair market value.
- The basis of the asset may be determined by reference to the basis of the asset to another taxpayer.

NONTAXABLE EXCHANGES

A taxpayer who is going to replace a productive asset (e.g., machinery) used in a trade or business may structure the transactions as a sale of the old asset and the purchase of a new asset. Using this approach, any realized gain on the asset sale is recognized. The basis of the new asset is its cost. Conversely, the taxpayer may be able to trade the old asset for the new asset. This exchange of assets may qualify for nontaxable exchange treatment.

The tax law recognizes that nontaxable exchanges result in a change in the *form* but not in the *substance* of the taxpayer's relative economic position. The replacement property received in the exchange is viewed as substantially a continuation of the old investment. Additional justification for nontaxable exchange treatment is that this type of transaction does not provide the taxpayer with the wherewithal to pay the tax on any realized gain. The nonrecognition provisions do not apply to realized losses from the sale or exchange of personal use assets. Such losses are not recognized because they are personal in nature and not because of any nonrecognition provision.

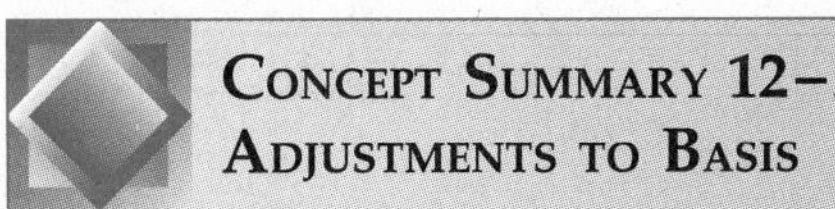

Concept Summary 12–2
Adjustments to Basis

Item	Effect	Refer to Chapter	Explanation
Amortization of bond discount.	Increase	13	Amortization is mandatory for certain taxable bonds and elective for tax-exempt bonds.
Amortization of bond premium.	Decrease	12	Amortization is mandatory for tax-exempt bonds and elective for taxable bonds.
Amortization of covenant not to compete.	Decrease	13	Covenant must be for a definite and limited time period.
Amortization of intangibles.	Decrease	8	Not all intangibles can be amortized (e.g., goodwill).
Assessment for local benefits.	Increase	10	To the extent not deductible as taxes (e.g., assessment for streets and sidewalks that increase the value of the property versus one for maintenance or repair or for meeting interest charges).
Bad debts.	Decrease	7	Only the specific charge-off method is permitted.
Capital additions.	Increase	12	Certain items, at the taxpayer's election, can be capitalized or deducted (e.g., selected indirect moving expenses and medical expenses).
Casualty.	Decrease	7	For a casualty loss, the amount of the adjustment is the summation of the deductible loss and the insurance proceeds received. For a casualty gain, the amount of the adjustment is the insurance proceeds received reduced by the recognized gain.
Condemnation.	Decrease	12	See casualty explanation.
Cost recovery.	Decrease	8	§ 168 is applicable to tangible assets placed in service after 1980 whose useful life is expressed in terms of years.
Depletion.	Decrease	8	Use the greater of cost or percentage depletion. Percentage depletion can still be deducted when the basis is zero.
Depreciation.	Decrease	8	§ 167 is applicable to tangible assets placed in service before 1981 and to tangible assets not depreciated in terms of years.
Easement.	Decrease		If the taxpayer does not retain any use of the land, all of the basis is allocable to the easement transaction. However, if only part of the land is affected by the easement, only part of the basis is allocable to the easement transaction.
Improvements by lessee to lessor's property.	Increase	4	Adjustment occurs only if the lessor is required to include the fair market value of the improvements in gross income under § 109.
Imputed interest.	Decrease	15	Amount deducted is not part of the cost of the asset.
Investment tax credit.	Decrease	11	Amount is 50% (100% for transition property) of the investment tax credit. If the election to reduce the investment tax credit is made, no adjustment is required.
Investment tax credit recapture.	Increase	11	Amount is 50% (100% for transition property) of the investment tax credit recaptured. If the election to reduce the investment tax credit was made, no adjustment is required.
Limited expensing under § 179.	Decrease	8	Occurs only if the taxpayer elects § 179 treatment.

Item	Effect	Refer to Chapter	Explanation
Medical capital expenditure permitted as a medical expense.	Decrease	10	Adjustment is the amount of the deduction (the effect on basis is to increase it by the amount of the capital expenditure net of the deduction).
Moving capital expenditure permitted as a moving expense.	Decrease	9	Adjustment is for the amount the taxpayer elects to deduct as an indirect moving expense (the effect on basis is to increase it by the amount of the capital expenditure net of the deduction).
Real estate taxes; apportionment between the buyer and seller.	Increase or decrease	10	To the extent the buyer pays the seller's pro rata share, the buyer's basis is increased. To the extent the seller pays the buyer's pro rata share, the buyer's basis is decreased.
Rebate from manufacturer.	Decrease		Since the rebate is treated as an adjustment to the purchase price, it is not included in the buyer's gross income.
Stock dividend.	Decrease	4	Adjustment occurs only if the stock dividend is nontaxable. While the basis per share decreases, the total stock basis does not change.
Stock rights.	Decrease	12	Adjustment occurs only for nontaxable stock rights and only if the fair market value of the rights is at least 15% of the fair market value of the stock or, if less than 15%, the taxpayer elects to allocate the basis between the stock and the rights.
Theft.	Decrease	7	See casualty explanation.

In a *nontaxable exchange,* realized gains or losses are not recognized. However, the nonrecognition is usually temporary. The recognition of gain or loss is *postponed* (deferred) until the property received in the nontaxable exchange is subsequently disposed of in a taxable transaction. This is accomplished by assigning a carryover basis to the replacement property.

EXAMPLE 35

Debra exchanges property with an adjusted basis of $10,000 and a fair market value of $12,000 for property with a fair market value of $12,000. The transaction qualifies for nontaxable exchange treatment. Debra has a realized gain of $2,000 ($12,000 amount realized – $10,000 adjusted basis). Her recognized gain is $0. Her basis in the replacement property is a carryover basis of $10,000. Assume the replacement property is nondepreciable. If Debra subsequently sells the replacement property for $12,000, her realized and recognized gain will be the $2,000 gain that was postponed (deferred) in the nontaxable transaction. If the replacement property is depreciable, the carryover basis of $10,000 is used in calculating depreciation. ◆

In some nontaxable exchanges, only part of the property involved in the transaction qualifies for nonrecognition treatment. If the taxpayer receives cash or other nonqualifying property, part or all of the realized gain from the exchange is recognized. In these instances, gain is recognized because the taxpayer has changed or improved his or her relative economic position and has the wherewithal to pay income tax to the extent of cash or other property received.

It is important to distinguish between a nontaxable disposition, as the term is used in the statute, and a tax-free transaction. First, a direct exchange is not required in all circumstances (e.g., replacement of involuntarily converted property or sale and replacement of a personal residence). Second, as previously mentioned, the term *nontaxable* refers to postponement of recognition via a carryover basis. In a tax-free transaction, the nonrecognition is permanent (e.g., see the discussion later in the chapter of the § 121 election by a taxpayer age 55 or over to exclude gain on the sale of a residence). Therefore, the basis of any property acquired does not depend on the basis of the property disposed of by the taxpayer.

Like-Kind Exchanges—§ 1031

Section 1031 provides for nontaxable exchange treatment if the following requirements are satisfied:

- The form of the transaction is an exchange.
- Both the property transferred and the property received are held either for productive use in a trade or business or for investment.
- The property is like-kind property.

Like-kind exchanges include business for business, business for investment, investment for business, or investment for investment property. Property held for personal use, inventory, and partnership interests (both limited and general) do not qualify under the like-kind exchange provisions. Securities, even though held for investment, do not qualify for like-kind exchange treatment.

The nonrecognition provision for like-kind exchanges is *mandatory* rather than elective. That is, a taxpayer who wants to recognize a realized gain or loss will have to structure the transaction in a form that does not satisfy the statutory requirements for a like-kind exchange. This topic is discussed further under Tax Planning Considerations.

Like-Kind Property

"The words 'like-kind' refer to the nature or character of the property and not to its grade or quality. One kind or class of property may not . . . be exchanged for property of a different kind or class."[15]

Although the term *like-kind* is intended to be interpreted very broadly, three categories of exchanges are not included. First, livestock of different sexes do not qualify as like-kind property. Second, real estate can be exchanged only for other real estate, and personalty can be exchanged only for other personalty. For example, the exchange of a machine (personalty) for an office building (realty) is not a like-kind exchange. *Real estate* includes principally rental buildings, office and store buildings, manufacturing plants, warehouses, and land. It is immaterial whether real estate is improved or unimproved. Thus, unimproved land can be exchanged for an apartment house. *Personalty* includes principally machines, equipment, trucks, automobiles, furniture, and fixtures. Third, real property located in the United States exchanged for foreign real property (and vice versa) does not qualify as like-kind property.

15. Reg. § 1.1031(a)–1(b).

Example 36

Wade made the following exchanges during the taxable year:

a. Inventory for a machine used in business.
b. Land held for investment for a building used in business.
c. Stock held for investment for equipment used in business.
d. A business truck for a business truck.
e. An automobile used for personal transportation for an automobile used in business.
f. Livestock for livestock of a different sex.
g. Land held for investment in New York for land held for investment in London.

Exchanges (b), investment real property for business real property, and (d), business personalty for business personalty, qualify as exchanges of like-kind property. Exchanges (a), inventory; (c), stock; (e), personal use automobile (not held for business or investment purposes); (f), livestock of different sexes; and (g), U.S. and foreign real estate, do not qualify. ◆

A special provision applies if the taxpayers involved in the exchange are related parties under § 267(b). To qualify for like-kind exchange treatment, the taxpayer and the related party must not dispose of the like-kind property received in the exchange within the two-year period following the date of the exchange. If an early disposition does occur, the postponed gain is recognized as of the date of the early disposition. Dispositions due to death, involuntary conversions, and certain non-tax avoidance transactions are not treated as early dispositions.

Regulations dealing with § 1031 like-kind exchange treatment were finalized in April 1991.[16] These Regulations provide that if the exchange transaction involves the multiple assets of a business (e.g., a television station for another television station), the determination of whether the property qualifies as like-kind will not be made at the business level. Instead, the underlying assets must be evaluated.

The Regulations also provide for greater specificity in determining whether depreciable tangible personal property is of a like-kind or class. Such property held for productive use in a business is of a like class only if the exchanged property is within the same *general business asset class* (as specified by the IRS in Revenue Procedure 87–57 or as subsequently modified) or the same *product class* (as specified by the Department of Commerce). Property included in a general business asset class is evaluated under this system rather than under the product class system.

The following are examples of general business asset classes:

- Office furniture, fixtures, and equipment.
- Information systems (computers and peripheral equipment).
- Airplanes.
- Automobiles and taxis.
- Buses.
- Light general-purpose trucks.
- Heavy general-purpose trucks.

The new Regulations make it more difficult for depreciable tangible personal property to qualify for § 1031 like-kind exchange treatment. For example, the

16. Reg. §§ 1.1031(a)–2 and (j)(1).

exchange of office equipment for a computer does not qualify as the exchange of like-kind property. Even though both assets are depreciable tangible personal property, they are not like-kind property. The assets are in different general business asset classes.

Exchange Requirement

The transaction must actually involve a direct exchange of property to qualify as a like-kind exchange. The sale of old property and the purchase of new property, even though like-kind, is generally not an exchange. However, if the two transactions are mutually dependent, the IRS may treat them as a like-kind exchange. For example, if the taxpayer sells an old business machine to a dealer and purchases a new one from the same dealer, like-kind exchange treatment could result.

The taxpayer may want to avoid nontaxable exchange treatment. Recognition of gain gives the taxpayer a higher basis for depreciation (see Example 64). To the extent that such gains would, if recognized, either receive favorable capital gain treatment or be passive activity income that could offset passive activity losses, it may be preferable to avoid the nonrecognition provisions through an indirect exchange transaction. For example, a taxpayer may sell property to one individual and subsequently purchase similar property from another individual. The taxpayer may also want to avoid nontaxable exchange treatment so that a realized loss can be recognized.

Boot

If the taxpayer in a like-kind exchange gives or receives some property that is not like-kind property, recognition may occur. Property that is not like-kind property, including cash, is referred to as *boot.* Although the term "boot" does not appear in the Code, tax practitioners commonly use it rather than using "property that is not like-kind property."

The *receipt* of boot will trigger recognition of gain if there is realized gain. The amount of the recognized gain is the *lesser* of the boot received or the realized gain (realized gain serves as the ceiling on recognition).

Example 37

Emily and Fran exchange machinery, and the exchange qualifies as like-kind under § 1031. Since Emily's machinery (adjusted basis of $20,000) is worth $24,000 and Fran's machine has a fair market value of $19,000, Fran also gives Emily cash of $5,000. Emily's recognized gain is $4,000, the lesser of the realized gain ($24,000 amount realized – $20,000 adjusted basis = $4,000) or the fair market value of the boot received ($5,000). ◆

Example 38

Assume the same facts as in the previous example, except that Fran's machine is worth $21,000 (not $19,000). Under these circumstances, Fran gives Emily cash of $3,000 to make up the difference. Emily's recognized gain is $3,000, the lesser of the realized gain ($24,000 amount realized – $20,000 adjusted basis = $4,000) or the fair market value of the boot received ($3,000). ◆

The receipt of boot does not result in recognition if there is realized loss.

Example 39

Assume the same facts as in Example 37, except the adjusted basis of Emily's machine is $30,000. Emily's realized loss is $6,000 ($24,000 amount realized – $30,000 adjusted basis = $6,000 realized loss). The receipt of the boot of $5,000 does not trigger recognition. Therefore, the recognized loss is $0. ◆

The *giving* of boot usually does not trigger recognition. If the boot given is cash, any realized gain or loss is not recognized.

Example 40

Fred and Gary exchange equipment in a like-kind exchange. Fred receives equipment with a fair market value of $25,000 and transfers equipment worth $21,000 (adjusted basis of $15,000) and cash of $4,000. Fred's realized gain is $6,000 ($25,000 amount realized – $15,000 adjusted basis – $4,000 cash). However, none of the realized gain is recognized. ◆

If, however, the boot given is appreciated or depreciated property, gain or loss is recognized to the extent of the differential between the adjusted basis and the fair market value of the boot. For this purpose, *appreciated or depreciated property* is defined as property whose adjusted basis is not equal to the fair market value.

Example 41

Assume the same facts as in the previous example, except that Fred transfers equipment worth $10,000 (adjusted basis of $12,000) and boot worth $15,000 (adjusted basis of $9,000). His realized gain appears to be $4,000 ($25,000 amount realized – $21,000 adjusted basis). Since realization previously has served as a ceiling on recognition, it appears that the recognized gain is $4,000 (lower of realized gain of $4,000 or amount of appreciation on boot of $6,000). However, the recognized gain actually is $6,000 (full amount of the appreciation on the boot). In effect, Fred must calculate the like-kind and boot parts of the transaction separately. That is, the realized loss of $2,000 on the like-kind property is not recognized ($10,000 fair market value – $12,000 adjusted basis), and the $6,000 realized gain on the boot is recognized ($15,000 fair market value – $9,000 adjusted basis). ◆

Basis and Holding Period of Property Received

If an exchange does not qualify as nontaxable under § 1031, gain or loss is recognized, and the basis of property received in the exchange is the property's fair market value. If the exchange qualifies for nonrecognition, the basis of property received must be adjusted to reflect any postponed (deferred) gain or loss. The *basis of like-kind property* received in the exchange is the property's fair market value less postponed gain or plus postponed loss. If the exchange partially qualifies for nonrecognition (if recognition is associated with boot), the basis of like-kind property received in the exchange is the property's fair market value less postponed gain or plus postponed loss. The *basis* of any *boot* received is the boot's fair market value.

If there is a postponed loss, nonrecognition creates a situation in which the taxpayer has recovered *less* than the cost or other basis of the property exchanged in an amount equal to the unrecognized loss. If there is a postponed gain, the taxpayer has recovered *more* than the cost or other basis of the property exchanged in an amount equal to the unrecognized gain.

Example 42

Jaime exchanges a building (used in his business) with an adjusted basis of $30,000 and fair market value of $38,000 for land with a fair market value of $38,000. The land is to be held as an investment. The exchange qualifies as like-kind (an exchange of business real property for investment real property). Thus, the basis of the land is $30,000 (the land's fair market value of $38,000 less the $8,000 postponed gain on the building). If the land is later sold for its fair market value of $38,000, the $8,000 postponed gain is recognized. ◆

EXAMPLE 43

Assume the same facts as in the previous example, except that the building has an adjusted basis of $48,000 and fair market value of only $38,000. The basis in the newly acquired land is $48,000 (fair market value of $38,000 plus the $10,000 postponed loss on the building). If the land is later sold for its fair market value of $38,000, the $10,000 postponed loss is recognized. ◆

The Code provides an alternative approach for determining the basis of like-kind property received:

Adjusted basis of like-kind property surrendered
\+ Adjusted basis of boot given
\+ Gain recognized
– Fair market value of boot received
– Loss recognized
= Basis of like-kind property received

This approach is logical in terms of the recovery of capital doctrine. That is, the unrecovered cost or other basis is increased by additional cost (boot given) or decreased by cost recovered (boot received). Any gain recognized is included in the basis of the new property. The taxpayer has been taxed on this amount and is now entitled to recover it tax-free. Any loss recognized is deducted from the basis of the new property. The taxpayer has received a tax benefit on that amount.

The *holding period* of the property surrendered in the exchange carries over and *tacks on* to the holding period of the like-kind property received. The logic of this rule is derived from the basic concept of the new property as a continuation of the old investment. The boot received has a new holding period (from the date of exchange) rather than a carryover holding period.

Depreciation recapture potential carries over to the property received in a like-kind exchange. See Chapter 13 for a discussion of this topic.

The following comprehensive example illustrates the like-kind exchange rules.

EXAMPLE 44

Vicki exchanged the following old machines for new machines in five independent like-kind exchanges:

Exchange	Adjusted Basis of Old Machine	Fair Market Value of New Machine	Adjusted Basis of Boot Given	Fair Market Value of Boot Received
1	$4,000	$9,000	$ -0-	$ -0-
2	4,000	9,000	3,000	-0-
3	4,000	9,000	6,000	-0-
4	4,000	9,000	-0-	3,000
5	4,000	3,500	-0-	300

Vicki's realized and recognized gains and losses and the basis of each of the like-kind properties received are as follows:

Exchange	Realized Gain (Loss)	Recognized Gain (Loss)	Old Adjusted Basis	+	Boot Given	+	Gain Recognized	–	Boot Received	=	New Basis
			New Basis Calculation								
1	$ 5,000	$ -0-	$4,000	+	$ -0-	+	$ -0-	–	$ -0-	=	$ 4,000*
2	2,000	-0-	4,000	+	3,000	+	-0-	–	-0-	=	7,000*
3	(1,000)	(-0-)	4,000	+	6,000	+	-0-	–	-0-	=	10,000**
4	8,000	3,000	4,000	+	-0-	+	3,000	–	3,000	=	4,000*
5	(200)	(-0-)	4,000	+	-0-	+	-0-	–	300	=	3,700**

*Basis may be determined in gain situations under the alternative method by subtracting the gain not recognized from the fair market value of the new property,
$9,000 – $5,000 = $4,000 for exchange 1.
$9,000 – $2,000 = $7,000 for exchange 2.
$9,000 – $5,000 = $4,000 for exchange 4.

**In loss situations, basis may be determined by adding the loss not recognized to the fair market value of the new property,
$9,000 + $1,000 = $10,000 for exchange 3.
$3,500 + $200 = $3,700 for exchange 5.

The basis of the boot received is the boot's fair market value. ◆

If a taxpayer either assumes a liability or takes property subject to a liability, the amount of the liability is treated as boot given. For the taxpayer whose liability is assumed or whose property is taken subject to the liability, the amount of the liability is treated as boot received. Example 45 illustrates the effect of such a liability. In addition, the example illustrates the tax consequences for both parties involved in the like-kind exchange.

EXAMPLE 45

Jane and Leo exchange real estate investments. Jane gives up property with an adjusted basis of $250,000 (fair market value $400,000) that is subject to a mortgage of $75,000 (assumed by Leo). In return for this property, Jane receives property with a fair market value of $300,000 (adjusted basis $200,000) and cash of $25,000.

- Jane's realized gain is $150,000. She gave up property with an adjusted basis of $250,000. She received $400,000 from the exchange ($300,000 fair market value of like-kind property + $100,000 boot received). The boot received consists of the cash of $25,000 received from Leo and Jane's mortgage of $75,000 that Leo assumes.
- Jane's recognized gain is $100,000. The realized gain of $150,000 is recognized to the extent of boot received.
- Jane's basis in the real estate received from Leo is $250,000. This basis can be computed by subtracting the postponed gain ($50,000) from the fair market value of the real estate received ($300,000). It can also be computed by adding the recognized gain ($100,000) to the adjusted basis of the real estate given up ($250,000) and subtracting the boot received ($100,000).
- Leo's realized gain is $100,000. He gave up property with an adjusted basis of $200,000 + boot of $100,000 ($75,000 mortgage assumed + $25,000 cash) or a total of $300,000. He received $400,000 from the exchange (fair market value of like-kind property received).
- Leo has no recognized gain because he did not receive any boot. The entire realized gain of $100,000 is postponed.
- Leo's basis in the real estate received from Jane is $300,000. This basis can be computed by subtracting the postponed gain ($100,000) from the fair market value of the real estate received ($400,000). It can also be computed by adding the boot given ($75,000 mortgage assumed by Leo + $25,000 cash) to the adjusted basis of the real estate given up ($200,000).[17] ◆

17. Example (2) of Reg. § 1.1031(d)–2 illustrates a special situation where both the buyer and the seller transfer liabilities that are assumed or property is acquired subject to a liability by the other party.

INVOLUNTARY CONVERSIONS—§ 1033

General Scheme

Section 1033 provides that a taxpayer who suffers an involuntary conversion of property may postpone recognition of *gain* realized from the conversion. The objective of this provision is to provide relief to the taxpayer who has suffered hardship and does not have the wherewithal to pay the tax on any gain realized from the conversion. Postponement of realized gain is permitted to the extent that the taxpayer reinvests the amount realized from the conversion in replacement property. The rules for nonrecognition of gain are as follows:

- If the amount reinvested in replacement property *equals or exceeds* the amount realized, realized gain is *not recognized.*
- If the amount reinvested in replacement property is *less than* the amount realized, realized gain *is recognized* to the extent of the deficiency.

If a *loss* occurs on an involuntary conversion, § 1033 does not modify the normal rules for loss recognition. That is, if realized loss otherwise would be recognized, § 1033 does not change the result.

Involuntary Conversion Defined

An *involuntary conversion* results from the destruction (complete or partial), theft, seizure, requisition or condemnation, or the sale or exchange under threat or imminence of requisition or condemnation of the taxpayer's property. To prove the existence of a threat or imminence of condemnation, the taxpayer must obtain confirmation that there has been a decision to acquire the property for public use. In addition, the taxpayer must have reasonable grounds to believe the property will be taken.[18] The property does not have to be sold to the authority threatening to condemn it to qualify for § 1033 postponement. If the taxpayer satisfies the confirmation and reasonable grounds requirements, he or she can sell the property to another party.[19] Likewise, the sale of property to a condemning authority by a taxpayer who acquired the property from its former owner with the knowledge that the property was under threat of condemnation also qualifies as an involuntary conversion under § 1033.[20]

Although most involuntary conversions are casualties or condemnations, the definition includes some special situations. Involuntary conversions, for example, include livestock destroyed by or on account of disease or exchanged or sold because of disease or solely on account of drought. A voluntary act, such as a taxpayer destroying his or her own property by arson, is not an involuntary conversion.[21]

Computing the Amount Realized

The amount realized from the condemnation of property usually includes only the amount received as compensation for the property.[22] Any amount received that is designated as severance damages by both the government and the

18. Rev.Rul. 63–221, 1963–2 C.B. 332, and *Joseph P. Balistrieri*, 38 TCM 526, T.C.Memo. 1979–115.

19. Rev.Rul. 81–180, 1981–2 C.B. 161.

20. Rev.Rul. 81–181, 1981–2 C.B. 162.

21. Rev.Rul. 82–74, 1982–1 C.B. 110.

22. *Pioneer Real Estate Co.*, 47 B.T.A. 886 (1942), *acq.* 1943 C.B. 18.

taxpayer is not included in the amount realized. *Severance awards* usually occur when only a portion of the entire property is condemned (e.g., a strip of land is taken to build a highway). Severance damages are awarded because the value of the taxpayer's remaining property has declined as a result of the condemnation. Such damages reduce the basis of the property. However, if either of the following requirements is satisfied, the nonrecognition provision of § 1033 applies to the severance damages:

- Severance damages are used to restore the usability of the remaining property.
- The usefulness of the remaining property is destroyed by the condemnation, and the property is sold and replaced at a cost equal to or exceeding the sum of the condemnation award, severance damages, and sales proceeds.

EXAMPLE 46

The government condemns a portion of Ron's farmland to build part of an interstate highway. Because the highway denies his cattle access to a pond and some grazing land, Ron receives severance damages in addition to the condemnation proceeds for the land taken. He must reduce the basis of the property by the amount of the severance damages. If the amount of the severance damages received exceeds the adjusted basis, Ron recognizes gain. ◆

EXAMPLE 47

Assume the same facts as in the previous example, except that Ron used the proceeds from the condemnation and the severance damages to build another pond and to clear woodland for grazing. Therefore, all the proceeds are eligible for § 1033 treatment. Thus, there is no possibility of gain recognition as the result of the amount of the severance damages received exceeding the adjusted basis. ◆

Replacement Property

The requirements for replacement property generally are more restrictive than those for like-kind property under § 1031. The basic requirement is that the replacement property be similar or related in service or use to the involuntarily converted property.

Different interpretations of the phrase *similar or related in service or use* apply if the involuntarily converted property is held by an *owner-user* rather than an *owner-investor* (e.g., lessor). A taxpayer who uses the property in his or her trade or business is subject to a more restrictive test in terms of acquiring replacement property. For an owner-user, the *functional use test* applies, and for an owner-investor, the *taxpayer use test* applies.

Taxpayer Use Test. The taxpayer use test for owner-investors provides the taxpayer with more flexibility in terms of what qualifies as replacement property than does the functional use test for owner-users. Essentially, the properties must be used by the taxpayer (the owner-investor) in similar endeavors. For example, rental property held by an owner-investor qualifies if replaced by other rental property, regardless of the type of rental property involved. The test is met when an investor replaces a manufacturing plant with a wholesale grocery warehouse if both properties are held for the production of rental income.[23] The replacement of a rental residence by a personal residence does not meet the test.[24]

23. *Loco Realty Co. v. Comm.*, 62–2 USTC ¶9657, 10 AFTR2d 5359, 306 F.2d 207 (CA–8, 1962).

24. Rev.Rul. 70–466, 1970–2 C.B. 165.

Functional Use Test. Under this test, the taxpayer's use of the replacement property and of the involuntarily converted property must be the same. Replacing a manufacturing plant with a wholesale grocery warehouse, whether rented or not, does not meet this test. As indicated above, the IRS applies the taxpayer use test to owner-investors. However, the functional use test still applies to owner-users (e.g., a manufacturer whose manufacturing plant is destroyed by fire is required to replace the plant with another facility of similar functional use). Replacing a rental residence with a personal residence does not meet this test.

Special Rules. Under one set of circumstances, the broader replacement rules for like-kind exchanges are substituted for the narrow replacement rules normally used for involuntary conversions. This beneficial provision applies if business real property or investment real property is condemned. Therefore, the taxpayer has substantially more flexibility in selecting replacement property. For example, improved real property can be replaced with unimproved real property.

The rules concerning the nature of replacement property are illustrated in Concept Summary 12–3.

Time Limitation on Replacement

The taxpayer normally has a two-year period after the close of the taxable year in which any gain is realized from the involuntary conversion to replace the property (the latest date).[25] This rule affords as much as three years from the date of realization of gain to replace the property if the realization of gain took place on the first day of the taxable year.[26] If the involuntary conversion involved the condemnation of real property used in a trade or business or held for

Concept Summary 12–3
Replacement Property Tests

Type of Property and User	Like-Kind Test	Taxpayer Use Test	Functional Use Test
Land used by a manufacturing company is condemned by a local government authority.	X		
Apartment and land held by an investor are sold due to the threat or imminence of condemnation.	X		
An investor's rented shopping mall is destroyed by fire; the mall may be replaced by other rental properties (e.g., an apartment building).		X	
A manufacturing plant is destroyed by fire; replacement property must consist of another manufacturing plant that is functionally the same as the property converted.			X
Personal residence of taxpayer is condemned by a local government authority; replacement property must consist of another personal residence.			X

25. §§ 1033(a)(2)(B) and (g)(4) and Reg. §§ 1.1033(a)–2(c)(3) and (f)–1(b).

26. The taxpayer can apply for an extension of this time period anytime before its expiration [Reg. § 1.1033(a)–2(c)(3)]. Also, the period for filing the application for extension can be extended if the taxpayer shows reasonable cause.

investment, a three-year period is substituted for the normal two-year period. In this case, the taxpayer can actually have as much as four years from the date of realization of gain to replace the property.

Example 48

Megan's warehouse is destroyed by fire on December 16, 1992. The adjusted basis is $325,000. Megan receives $400,000 from the insurance company on January 10, 1993. She is a calendar year taxpayer. The latest date for replacement is December 31, 1995 (the end of the taxable year in which realized gain occurred plus two years). The critical date is not the date the involuntary conversion occurred, but rather the date of gain realization. ◆

Example 49

Assume the same facts as in the previous example, except Megan's warehouse is condemned. The latest date for replacement is December 31, 1996 (the end of the taxable year in which realized gain occurred plus three years). ◆

The earliest date for replacement typically is the date the involuntary conversion occurs. However, if the property is condemned, it is possible to replace the condemned property before this date. In this case, the earliest date is the date of the threat or imminence of requisition or condemnation of the property. The purpose of this provision is to enable the taxpayer to make an orderly replacement of the condemned property.

Example 50

Assume the same facts as in Example 49. Megan can replace the warehouse before December 16, 1992 (the condemnation date). The earliest date for replacement is the date of the threat or imminence of requisition or condemnation of the warehouse. ◆

Nonrecognition of Gain

Nonrecognition of gain can be either mandatory or elective, depending upon whether the conversion is direct (into replacement property) or into money.

Direct Conversion. If the conversion is directly into replacement property rather than into money, nonrecognition of realized gain is *mandatory.* In this case, the basis of the replacement property is the same as the adjusted basis of the converted property. Direct conversion is rare in practice and usually involves condemnations. The following example illustrates the application of the rules for direct conversions.

Example 51

Lupe's property with an adjusted basis of $20,000 is condemned by the state. Lupe receives property with a fair market value of $50,000 as compensation for the property taken. Since the nonrecognition of realized gain is mandatory for direct conversions, Lupe's realized gain of $30,000 is not recognized, and the basis of the replacement property is $20,000 (adjusted basis of the condemned property). ◆

Conversion into Money. If the conversion is into money, "at the election of the taxpayer the gain shall be recognized only to the extent that the amount realized upon such conversion ... exceeds the cost of such other property or such stock."[27] This is the usual case, and nonrecognition (postponement) is *elective.*

27. § 1033(a)(2)(A) and Reg. § 1.1033(a)–2(c)(1).

The basis of the replacement property is the property's cost less postponed (deferred) gain. If the election to postpone gain is made, the holding period of the replacement property, includes the holding period of the converted property.

Section 1033 applies *only to gains* and *not to losses.* Losses from involuntary conversions are recognized if the property is held for business or income-producing purposes. Personal casualty losses are recognized, but condemnation losses related to personal use assets (e.g., a personal residence) are neither recognized nor postponed.

Examples 52 and 53 illustrate the application of the involuntary conversion rules.

EXAMPLE 52

Walt's building (used in his trade or business), with an adjusted basis of $50,000, is destroyed by fire in 1993. Walt is a calendar year taxpayer. In 1993, he receives an insurance reimbursement for the loss in the amount of $100,000. Walt invests $80,000 in a new building.

- Walt has until December 31, 1995, to make the new investment and qualify for the nonrecognition election.
- Walt's realized gain is $50,000 ($100,000 insurance proceeds received – $50,000 adjusted basis of old building).
- Assuming the replacement property qualifies as similar or related in service or use, Walt's recognized gain is $20,000. He reinvested $20,000 less than the insurance proceeds received ($100,000 proceeds – $80,000 reinvested). Therefore, his realized gain is recognized to that extent.
- Walt's basis in the new building is $50,000. This is the building's cost of $80,000 minus the postponed gain of $30,000 (realized gain of $50,000 – recognized gain of $20,000).
- The computation of realization, recognition, and basis would apply even if Walt was a real estate dealer and the building destroyed by fire was part of his inventory. Unlike § 1031, § 1033 does not generally exclude inventory. ◆

EXAMPLE 53

Assume the same facts as in the previous example, except that Walt receives only $45,000 (instead of $100,000) of insurance proceeds. He has a realized and recognized loss of $5,000. The basis of the new building is the building's cost of $80,000. If the destroyed building was held for personal use, the recognized loss is subject to other limitations. The loss of $5,000 is limited to the decline in fair market value of the property, and the amount of the loss is reduced first by $100 and then by 10% of adjusted gross income (refer to Chapter 7). ◆

Involuntary Conversion of a Personal Residence

The tax consequences of the involuntary conversion of a personal residence depend upon whether the conversion is a casualty or condemnation and whether a realized loss or gain results.

Loss Situations. If the conversion is a condemnation, the realized loss is not recognized. Loss from the condemnation of a personal use asset is never recognized. If the conversion is a casualty (a loss from fire, storm, etc.), the loss is recognized subject to the personal casualty loss limitations.

Gain Situations. If the conversion is a condemnation, the gain may be postponed under either § 1033 or § 1034. That is, the taxpayer may elect to treat the condemnation as a sale under the deferral of gain rules relating to the sale of a personal residence under § 1034 (presented subsequently). If the conversion is a casualty, the gain is postponed only under the involuntary conversion provisions.

Reporting Considerations

An election to postpone gain normally is made on the return for the taxable year in which gain is realized. The taxpayer should attach to the return a statement that includes supportive details. If the property has not been replaced before filing the tax return, the taxpayer should also attach a supporting statement to the return for the taxable year in which the property is replaced.

If the property either is not replaced within the prescribed time period or is replaced at a cost less than anticipated, an amended return must be filed for the taxable year in which the election was made. A taxpayer who has elected § 1033 postponement and makes an appropriate replacement may not later revoke the election. In addition, once the taxpayer has designated qualifying property as replacement property, he or she cannot later change the designation.[28] If no election is made on the return for the taxable year in which gain is realized, an election may still be made within the prescribed time period by filing a claim for credit or refund.[29]

Involuntary conversions from casualty and theft are reported first on Form 4684, Casualties and Thefts. Casualty and theft losses on personal use property for the individual taxpayer are carried from Form 4684 to Schedule A of Form 1040. For other casualty and theft items, the Form 4684 amounts are generally reported on Form 4797, Sales of Business Property, unless Form 4797 is not required. In the latter case, the amounts are reported directly on the tax return involved.

Except for personal use property, recognized gains and losses from involuntary conversions other than by casualty and theft are reported on Form 4797. As stated previously, if the property involved in the involuntary conversion (other than by casualty and theft) is personal use property, any realized loss is not recognized. Any realized gain is treated as gain on a voluntary sale.

SALE OF A RESIDENCE—§ 1034

A realized loss from the sale of a personal residence is not recognized because the residence is personal use property. A realized gain, however, is subject to taxation. The tax law includes two provisions under which all or part of the realized gain is either postponed or excluded from taxation. The first of these, § 1034, is discussed below. The second, § 121, is discussed later in the chapter.

Section 1034 provides for the *mandatory* nonrecognition of gain from the sale or exchange of a personal residence if the sales proceeds are reinvested in a replacement residence within a prescribed time period. Both the old and new residences must qualify as the taxpayer's principal residence. A houseboat or house trailer qualifies if it is used by the taxpayer as a principal residence.[30]

The reason for not recognizing gain when a residence is replaced by a new residence within the prescribed time period (discussed below) is that the new residence is viewed as a continuation of the investment. Also, if the proceeds

28. Rev.Rul. 83–39, 1983–1 C.B. 190.

29. Reg. § 1.1033(a)–2(c)(2).

30. Reg. § 1.1034–1(c)(3)(i).

from the sale are reinvested, the taxpayer does not have the wherewithal to pay tax on the realized gain. Beyond these fundamental concepts, Congress, in enacting § 1034, was concerned with the hardship of involuntary moves and the socially desirable objective of encouraging the mobility of labor.

Replacement Period

For the nonrecognition treatment to apply, the old residence must be replaced by a new residence within a period *beginning two years before* the sale of the old residence and *ending two years after* the sale. This four-year period applies regardless of whether the new residence is purchased or constructed. In addition to *acquiring* the residence during this period, the taxpayer must *occupy* and use the new residence as the principal residence during this same time period. Both the IRS and the courts have strictly construed the occupancy requirement, and even circumstances beyond a taxpayer's control do not excuse noncompliance.[31]

EXAMPLE 54

Gail sells her personal residence from which she realizes a gain of $50,000. Construction of a new residence begins immediately after the sale. However, unstable soil conditions and a trade union strike cause unforeseen delays. The new residence ultimately is completed and occupied by Gail 25 months after the sale of the old residence. Since the occupancy requirement has not been satisfied, § 1034 is inapplicable, and Gail must recognize a gain of $50,000 on the sale of the old residence. ◆

Taxpayers might be inclined to make liberal use of § 1034 as a means of speculating when the price of residential housing is rising. Without any time restriction on its use, § 1034 would permit deferral of gain on multiple sales of principal residences, each one of which would result in an economic profit. The Code curbs this approach by precluding the application of § 1034 to any sales occurring within two years of its last use.

EXAMPLE 55

After Seth sells his principal residence (the first residence) in March 1992 for $150,000 (realized gain of $60,000), he buys and sells the following (all of which qualify as principal residences):

	Date of Purchase	Date of Sale	Amount Involved
Second residence	April 1992		$160,000
Second residence		May 1993	180,000
Third residence	June 1993		200,000

Because multiple sales have occurred within a period of two years, § 1034 does not apply to the sale of the second residence. Thus, the realized gain of $20,000 [$180,000 (selling price) – $160,000 (purchase price)] must be recognized. ◆

The two-year rule precluding multiple use of § 1034 could create a hardship where a taxpayer is transferred by his or her employer and has little choice in the matter. For this reason, § 1034 was amended to provide an exception to the two-year rule when the sale results from a change in the location of employment. To qualify for the exception, a taxpayer must meet the distance and length-of-employment requirements specified for the deduction of moving expenses under § 217.

31. *James A. Henry*, 44 TCM 844, T.C.Memo. 1982–469; and *William F. Peck*, 44 TCM 1030, T.C.Memo. 1982–506.

EXAMPLE 56

Assume the same facts as in the previous example, except that in February 1993, Seth's employer transfers him to a job in another state. Consequently, the sale of the second residence and the purchase of the third residence were due to the relocation of employment. If Seth satisfies the distance and length-of-employment requirements of § 217, no gain is recognized on the sale of the first and second residences. ◆

Principal Residence

Both the old and new residences must qualify as the taxpayer's principal residence. Whether property is the taxpayer's principal residence depends ". . . upon all the facts and circumstances in each case."[32]

EXAMPLE 57

Mitch sells his principal residence and moves to Norfolk, Virginia, where he is employed. He decides to rent an apartment in Norfolk because of its proximity to his place of employment. He purchases a beach house in Virginia Beach that he occupies most weekends. Mitch does not intend to live in the beach house other than on weekends. The apartment in Norfolk is his principal place of residence. Therefore, the purchase of the beach house does not qualify as an appropriate replacement. ◆

If the old residence ceases to be the taxpayer's principal residence before its sale, the nonrecognition provision does not apply. For example, if the taxpayer abandons the old residence before its sale, the residence no longer qualifies as a principal residence.[33] If the old residence is converted to other than personal use (e.g., rental) before its sale, the nonrecognition provision does not apply. If the residence is only partially converted to business use, gain from the sale of the personal use portion still qualifies for nonrecognition. It is possible to convert part of a principal residence to business use and later to convert that part back to being part of the principal residence (e.g., a home office).[34]

Temporarily renting out the old residence before sale does not necessarily terminate its status as the taxpayer's principal residence,[35] nor does temporarily renting out the new residence before it is occupied by the taxpayer. An issue associated with temporarily renting out the old residence while attempting to sell it is whether a taxpayer is entitled to deduct expenses in excess of income relating to the rental of a residence before its sale. That is, is the old residence subject to the loss deduction rules for hobby loss activities? If it is, the deductions associated with the rental activity are limited to the rent income generated. The Tax Court concluded that since the property was considered to be the taxpayer's principal residence and as a result qualifies for § 1034 postponement of gain, the property was subject to the hobby loss limitations. The Court of Appeals reversed the Tax Court and held that the hobby loss provisions did not apply.[36]

Nonrecognition of Gain Requirements

Realized gain from the sale of the old residence is not recognized if the taxpayer reinvests an amount *at least equal* to the adjusted sales price of the old residence. Realized gain is recognized to the extent the taxpayer does not reinvest an amount at least equal to the adjusted sales price in a new residence. Therefore,

32. Reg. § 1.1034–1(c)(3).

33. *Richard T. Houlette*, 48 T.C. 350 (1967), and *Stolk v. Comm.*, 64–1 USTC ¶9228, 13 AFTR2d 535, 326 F.2d 760 (CA–2, 1964).

34. Rev.Rul. 82–26, 1982–1 C.B. 114.

35. *Robert W. Aagaard*, 56 T.C. 191 (1971), *acq.* 1971–2 C.B. 1; *Robert G. Clapham*, 63 T.C. 505 (1975); Rev.Rul. 59–72, 1959–1 C.B. 203; and Rev.Rul. 78–146, 1978–1 C.B. 260.

36. *Bolaris v. Comm.*, 85–2 USTC ¶9822, 56 AFTR2d 85–6472, 776 F.2d 1428 (CA–9, 1985).

the amount not reinvested is treated similarly to boot received in a like-kind exchange.

The *adjusted sales price* is the amount realized from the sale of the old residence less fixing-up expenses. The *amount realized* is calculated by reducing the selling price by the selling expenses. *Selling expenses* include items such as advertising the property for sale, real estate broker commissions, legal fees in connection with the sale, and loan placement fees paid by the taxpayer as a condition of arranging financing for the buyer. To the extent that the selling expenses are deducted as moving expenses, they are not allowed as deductions in the computation of the amount realized (refer to Chapter 9).

Fixing-up expenses are personal in nature and are incurred by the taxpayer to assist in the sale of the old residence. Fixing-up expenses include such items as ordinary repairs, painting, and wallpapering. To qualify as a fixing-up expense, the expense must (1) be incurred for work performed during the 90-day period ending on the date of the contract of sale, (2) be paid within 30 days after the date of the sale, and (3) not be a capital expenditure.

Although selling expenses are deductible in calculating the amount realized, fixing-up expenses are not. Therefore, fixing-up expenses do not have an impact on the calculation of realized gain or loss. However, since fixing-up expenses are deductible in calculating the adjusted sales price, they do have the potential for producing tax benefit in that they reduce the amount of the reinvestment required to qualify for nonrecognition treatment. Conversely, if a replacement residence is not acquired, the fixing-up expenses produce no tax benefit.

Reducing the amount of the required reinvestment by the amount of fixing-up expenses is another application of the wherewithal to pay concept. To the extent that the taxpayer has expended part of the funds received from the sale in preparing the old residence for sale, he or she does not have the funds available to reinvest in the new residence.

As previously mentioned, fixing-up expenses are not considered in determining realized gain. They are considered only in determining how much realized gain is to be postponed. In addition, fixing-up expenses have no direct effect on the basis of the new residence. Indirectly, though, through their effect on postponed gain, they can bring about a lesser basis for the new residence. The effects of fixing-up expenses on the computation of gain realized and recognized and on basis are illustrated in Concept Summary 12–4 and in Example 58.

Capital Improvements

Capital improvements are added to the adjusted basis of a personal residence. The adjusted basis is used in computing gain or loss on a subsequent sale or other disposition of the property. In calculating the cost of a replacement residence (for determining the nonrecognition of gain under § 1034), only capital improvements made during a certain time period are counted. The time period begins two years before the date of sale of the old residence and ends two years after that date (the time period during which the old residence can be replaced).[37]

If the taxpayer receives a residence by gift or inheritance, the residence will not qualify as a replacement residence. However, if the taxpayer makes substantial capital expenditures (e.g., reconstruction or additions) to the property within the replacement time period, these expenditures do qualify.

---

37. *Charles M. Shaw,* 69 T.C. 1034 (1978); Reg. § 1.1034–1(c)(4)(ii); and Rev.Rul. 78–147, 1978–1 C.B. 261.

Basis and Holding Period of the New Residence

The *basis* of the new residence is the cost of the new residence less the realized gain not recognized (postponed gain). If there is any postponed gain, the *holding period* of the new residence includes the holding period of the old residence.

Concept Summary 12–4 summarizes the sale of residence concepts. Example 58 illustrates these concepts and the application of the nonrecognition provision.

EXAMPLE 58

Veneia, age 47, sells her personal residence (adjusted basis of $136,000) for $244,000. She receives only $229,400 after paying a brokerage fee of $14,600. Ten days before the sale, Veneia incurred and paid for qualified fixing-up expenses of $3,400. Two months later, she acquires a new residence. Determine the gain, if any, Veneia must recognize and the basis of the new residence under each of the following circumstances:

1. The new residence costs $230,000.
2. The new residence costs $210,000.
3. The new residence costs $110,000.

		1	2	3
Step 1:	Sales price	$244,000	$244,000	$244,000
	–Selling expenses	(14,600)	(14,600)	(14,600)
	=Amount realized	$229,400	$229,400	$229,400

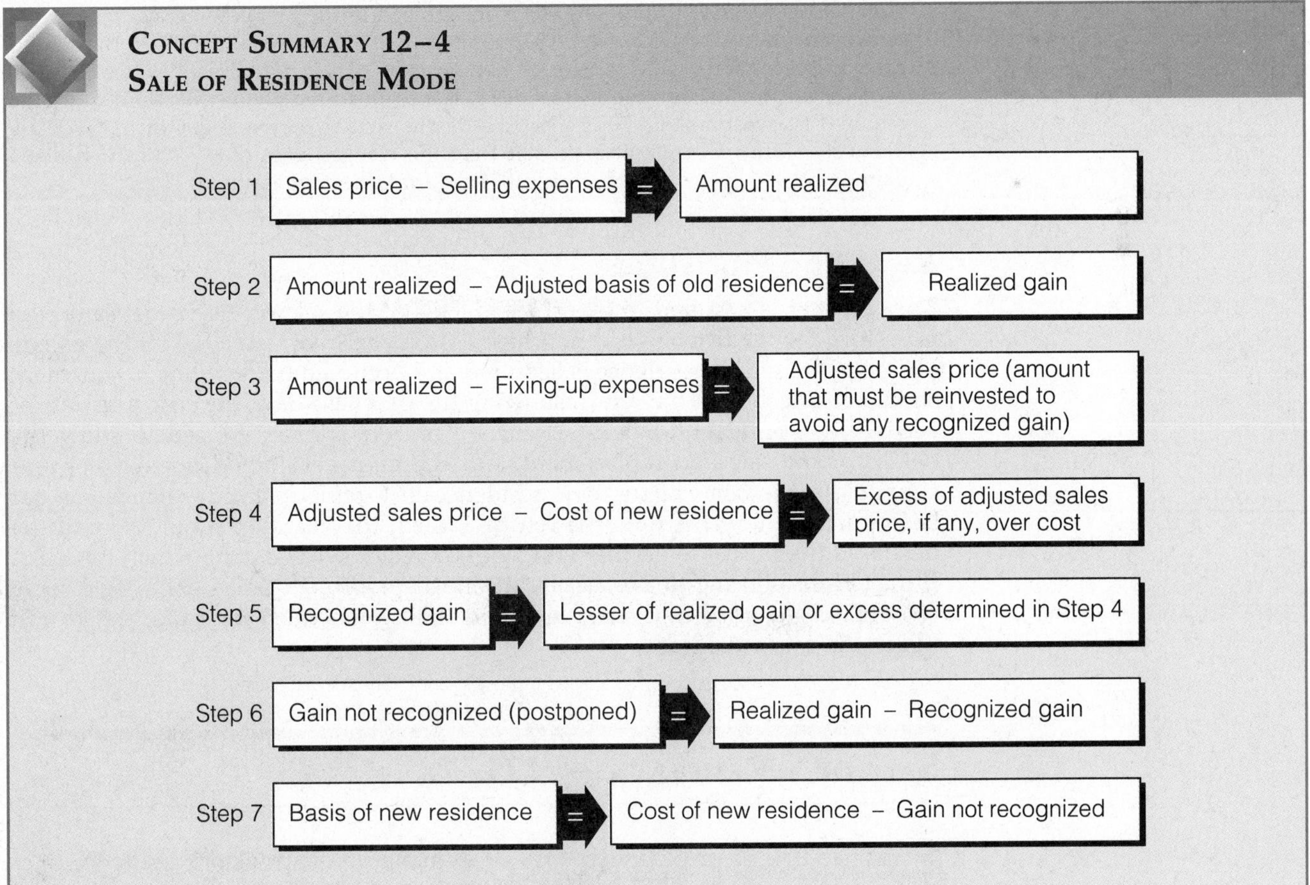

CONCEPT SUMMARY 12–4
SALE OF RESIDENCE MODE
Step 1
Sales price – Selling expenses
=
Amount realized
Step 2
Amount realized – Adjusted basis of old residence
=
Realized gain
Step 3
Amount realized – Fixing-up expenses
=
Adjusted sales price (amount that must be reinvested to avoid any recognized gain)
Step 4
Adjusted sales price – Cost of new residence
=
Excess of adjusted sales price, if any, over cost
Step 5
Recognized gain
=
Lesser of realized gain or excess determined in Step 4
Step 6
Gain not recognized (postponed)
=
Realized gain – Recognized gain
Step 7
Basis of new residence
=
Cost of new residence – Gain not recognized

		1	2	3
Step 2:	Amount realized	$ 229,400	$ 229,400	$ 229,400
	–Adjusted basis	(136,000)	(136,000)	(136,000)
	=Realized gain	$ 93,400	$ 93,400	$ 93,400
Step 3:	Amount realized	$ 229,400	$ 229,400	$ 229,400
	–Fixing-up expenses	(3,400)	(3,400)	(3,400)
	=Adjusted sales price	$ 226,000	$ 226,000	$ 226,000
Step 4:	Adjusted sales price	$ 226,000	$ 226,000	$ 226,000
	–Cost of new residence	(230,000)	(210,000)	(110,000)
	=Excess of ASP over cost	$ -0-	$ 16,000	$ 116,000
Step 5:	Recognized gain (lesser of Step 2 or Step 4)	$ -0-	$ 16,000	$ 93,400
Step 6:	Realized gain	$ 93,400	$ 93,400	$ 93,400
	–Recognized gain	(-0-)	(16,000)	(93,400)
	=Postponed gain	93,400	(77,400)	$ -0-
Step 7:	Cost of new residence	$ 230,000	$ 210,000	$ 110,000
	–Postponed gain	(93,400)	(77,400)	(-0-)
	=Basis of new residence	$ 136,600	$ 132,600	$ 110,000

None of the realized gain of $93,400 is recognized in the first case because the actual reinvestment of $230,000 exceeds the required reinvestment of $226,000. In the second case, the recognized gain is $16,000 because the required reinvestment of $226,000 exceeds the actual reinvestment of $210,000 by this amount. In the third case, the required reinvestment of $226,000 exceeds the actual reinvestment of $110,000 by $116,000. Since this amount is greater than the realized gain of $93,400, the realized gain of $93,400 is recognized, and § 1034 deferral does not apply. ◆

Reporting Procedures

The taxpayer is required to report the details of the sale of the residence on the tax return for the taxable year in which gain is realized, even if all of the gain is postponed. If a new residence is acquired and occupied before filing, a statement should be attached to the return showing the purchase date, the cost, and date of occupancy. Form 2119, Sale or Exchange of Your Home, is used to show the details of the sale and replacement, and the taxpayer should retain a copy as support for the basis of the new residence. If a replacement residence has not been purchased by the time the return is filed, the taxpayer should submit the details of the purchase on the return of the taxable year during which it occurs. If the old residence is not replaced within the prescribed time period, or if some recognized gain results, the taxpayer must file an amended return for the year in which the sale took place.

SALE OF A RESIDENCE—§ 121

Taxpayers age 55 or older who sell or exchange their principal residence may *elect to exclude* up to $125,000 ($62,500 for married individuals filing separate returns) of realized gain from the sale or exchange. The election can be made *only once.* This provision differs from § 1034 where nonrecognition is mandatory and may occur many times during a taxpayer's lifetime. Section 121 also differs from § 1034 in that it does not require the taxpayer to purchase a new residence. The excluded gain is never recognized, whereas the realized gain not recognized under § 1034 is postponed by subtracting it from the cost of the new residence in calculating the adjusted basis.

This provision is the only case in the tax law where a realized gain from the disposition of property that is not recognized is excluded rather than merely postponed. The provision allows the taxpayer a permanent recovery of more than the cost or other basis of the residence tax-free.

Congress enacted § 121 simply to relieve older citizens of the large tax they might incur from the sale of a personal residence. The dollar and age limitations restrict the benefit of § 121 to taxpayers who presumably have a greater need for increased tax-free dollars.

Exclusion Requirements

The taxpayer must be at least age 55 before the date of the sale and have *owned* and *used* the residence as a principal residence for at least *three years* during the *five-year* period ending on the date of sale. The ownership and use periods do not have to be the same period of time. Short temporary absences (e.g., vacations) count as periods of use. If the residence is owned jointly by husband and wife, only one of the spouses is required to meet these requirements if a joint return is filed for the taxable year in which the sale took place.

In determining whether the ownership and use period requirements are satisfied, transactions affecting prior residences may be relevant. If a former residence is involuntarily converted and any gain is postponed under § 1033, the holding period of the former residence is added to the holding period of the replacement residence for § 121 purposes. However, if the realized gain is postponed under § 1034 (sale of residence provision), the holding period of the former residence is not added to the holding period of the replacement residence for § 121 purposes. In this instance, the holding period of the replacement residence begins with the acquisition date of the replacement residence.

EXAMPLE 59

Cole has lived in his residence since 1984. The residence is involuntarily converted in July 1993. He purchases a replacement residence in August 1993. When the replacement residence is subsequently sold, Cole includes the holding period of the involuntarily converted residence in determining whether he can satisfy the ownership and use requirements. ◆

EXAMPLE 60

Assume the same facts as in the previous example, except that Cole's residence was not involuntarily converted. Instead, he sold it so that he could move into a larger house. When the replacement residence is subsequently sold, Cole is not permitted to include the holding period of the old residence in determining whether he can satisfy the ownership and use requirements. ◆

Relationship to Other Provisions

The taxpayer can treat an involuntary conversion of a principal residence as a sale for purposes of § 121. Any gain not excluded under § 121 is then subject to postponement under § 1033 or § 1034 (condemnation only), assuming the requirements of those provisions are met.

Any gain not excluded under § 121 from the sale of a residence is subject to postponement under § 1034, assuming the requirements of that provision are met. Examples 61 and 62 illustrate this relationship.

Making and Revoking the Election

The election not to recognize gain under § 121 may be made or revoked at any time before the statute of limitations expires. Therefore, the taxpayer generally has until the *later* of (1) three years from the due date of the return for the year the gain is realized or (2) two years from the date the tax is paid to make or revoke the election. The election is made by attaching a signed statement (showing all the details of the sale) to the return for the taxable year in which the sale took place. Form 2119 is used for this purpose. The election is revoked by filing a signed statement (showing the taxpayer's name, Social Security number, and taxable year for which the election was made) indicating the revocation.

Computation Procedure

The following examples illustrate the application of both the § 121 and § 1034 provisions.

EXAMPLE 61

Keith sells his personal residence (adjusted basis of $32,000) for $205,000, of which he receives only $195,400 after the payment of selling expenses. Ten days before the sale, he incurred and paid for qualified fixing-up expenses of $6,400. Keith is age 55 and elects the exclusion of gain under § 121. He does not acquire a replacement residence. ◆

EXAMPLE 62

Assume the same facts as in the previous example, except that Keith acquires a new residence for $40,000 within the prescribed time period.

The solutions to Examples 61 and 62 are as follows:

	Example 61	Example 62
Amount realized ($205,000 – $9,600)	$ 195,400	$ 195,400
Adjusted basis	(32,000)	(32,000)
Realized gain	$ 163,400	$ 163,400
§ 121 exclusion	(125,000)	(125,000)
Realized gain after exclusion	$ 38,400	$ 38,400
Amount realized	$ 195,400	$ 195,400
Fixing-up expenses	(6,400)	(6,400)
Adjusted sales price	$ 189,000	$ 189,000
§ 121 exclusion	(125,000)	(125,000)
Adjusted sales price after exclusion	$ 64,000	$ 64,000
Cost of new residence	(–0–)	(40,000)
Excess of adjusted sales price after the exclusion over reinvestment	$ 64,000	$ 24,000
Recognized gain (lower of realized gain after exclusion or above excess)	$ 38,400	$ 24,000
Realized gain after exclusion	$ 38,400	$ 38,400
Recognized gain	(38,400)	(24,000)
Postponed gain	$ –0–	$ 14,400
Cost of new residence	$ –0–	$ 40,000
Postponed gain	(–0–)	(14,400)
Basis of new residence	$ –0–	$ 25,600

◆

Comparing the results of Examples 61 and 62 provides insight into the relationship between § 1034 and § 121. If Keith had not made the election to postpone gain under § 121 in Example 61, his recognized gain would have been $163,400 (the realized gain). Thus, the election resulted in the permanent exclusion of the $125,000 of realized gain by reducing the recognized gain to $38,400. Further documentation of the permanent nature of the § 121 exclusion is provided in the calculation of the basis of the new residence in Example 62. The $40,000 cost of the residence is reduced only by the postponed gain of $14,400. That is, it is not reduced by the amount of the § 121 exclusion. To postpone all of the $38,400 realized gain after the exclusion, Keith would have needed to reinvest $64,000 (the adjusted sales price after the exclusion). Also, note that the Example 61 results demonstrate that the realized gain after the exclusion is the ceiling on recognition.

Other Nonrecognition Provisions

The typical taxpayer experiences the sale of a residence or an involuntary conversion more frequently than the other types of nontaxable exchanges. Several additional nonrecognition provisions that are not as common are treated briefly in the remainder of this chapter.

Exchange of Stock for Property—§ 1032

Under this Section, a corporation does not recognize gain or loss on the receipt of money or other property in exchange for its stock (including treasury stock). In other words, a corporation does not recognize gain or loss when it deals in its own stock. This provision is consistent with the financial accounting treatment of such transactions.

Certain Exchanges of Insurance Policies—§ 1035

Under this provision, no gain or loss is recognized from the exchange of certain insurance contracts or policies. The rules relating to exchanges not solely in kind and the basis of the property acquired are the same as under § 1031. Exchanges qualifying for nonrecognition include the following:

- The exchange of life insurance contracts.
- The exchange of a life insurance contract for an endowment or annuity contract.
- The exchange of an endowment contract for another endowment contract that provides for regular payments beginning at a date not later than the date payments would have begun under the contract exchanged.
- The exchange of an endowment contract for an annuity contract.
- The exchange of annuity contracts.

Exchange of Stock for Stock of the Same Corporation—§ 1036

A shareholder does not recognize gain or loss on the exchange of common stock solely for common stock in the same corporation or from the exchange of preferred stock for preferred stock in the same corporation. Exchanges between individual shareholders as well as between a shareholder and the corporation are included. The rules relating to exchanges not solely in kind and the basis of the property acquired are the same as under § 1031. For example, a nonrecognition exchange occurs when common stock with different rights, such as voting for nonvoting, is exchanged. A shareholder usually recognizes gain or loss from the exchange of common for preferred or preferred for common, even though the stock exchanged is in the same corporation.

Certain Reacquisitions of Real Property—§ 1038

Under this provision, no loss is recognized from the repossession of real property sold on an installment basis. Gain is recognized to a limited extent.

Transfers of Property between Spouses or Incident to Divorce—§ 1041

Section 1041 provides that transfers of property *between spouses or former spouses incident to divorce* are nontaxable transactions. Therefore, the basis to the recipient is a carryover basis. To be treated as incident to the divorce, the transfer must be related to the cessation of marriage or occur within one year after the date on which the marriage ceases.

Section 1041 also provides for nontaxable exchange treatment on property transfers *between spouses during marriage.* The basis to the recipient spouse is a carryover basis.

Sale of Stock to Stock Ownership Plans or Certain Cooperatives—§ 1042

Section 1042 provides that the realized gain will be postponed if the taxpayer (or his or her executor) sells qualified securities to a qualified entity and, within a specified time period, purchases qualified replacement property. Qualified entities include an employee stock ownership plan (ESOP) and an eligible worker-owned cooperative. To qualify for this treatment, several statutory requirements must be satisfied.

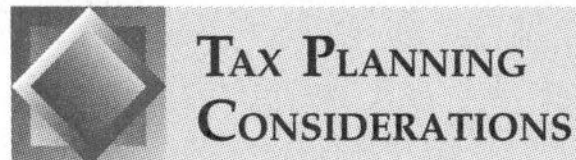

Tax Planning Considerations

Cost Identification and Documentation Considerations

When multiple assets are acquired in a single transaction, the contract price must be allocated for several reasons. First, some of the assets may be depreciable while others are not. From the different viewpoints of the buyer and the seller, this may produce a tax conflict that needs to be resolved. That is, the seller prefers a high allocation for nondepreciable assets, whereas the purchaser prefers a high allocation for depreciable assets (see Chapter 13). Second, the seller needs to know the amount realized on the sale of the capital assets and the ordinary income assets so that the recognized gains and losses can be classified as capital or ordinary. For example, an allocation to goodwill or to a covenant not to compete (see Chapter 13) produces different tax consequences to the seller. Third, the buyer needs the adjusted basis of each asset to calculate the realized gain or loss on the sale or other disposition of each asset.

Selection of Property for Making Gifts

A donor can achieve several tax advantages by making gifts of appreciated property. Income tax on the unrealized gain that would have occurred had the donor sold the property is avoided by the donor. A portion of this amount can be permanently avoided because the donee's adjusted basis is increased by part or all of the gift tax paid by the donor. Even without this increase in basis, the income tax liability on the sale of the property by the donee can be less than the income tax liability that would have resulted from the donor's sale of the property. This reduced income tax liability occurs if the donee is in a lower tax bracket than the donor. In addition, any subsequent appreciation during the time the property is held by the lower tax bracket donee results in a tax savings on the sale or other disposition of the property. Such gifts of appreciated property can be an effective tool in family tax planning.

Taxpayers should generally not make gifts of depreciated property (property that, if sold, would produce a realized loss) because the donor does not receive an income tax deduction for the unrealized loss element. In addition, the donee receives no benefit from this unrealized loss upon the subsequent sale of the property because of the loss basis rule. The loss basis rule provides that the donee's basis is the lower of the donor's basis or fair market value at the date of the gift. If the donor anticipates that the donee will sell the property upon receiving it, the donor should sell the property and take the loss deduction, assuming the loss is deductible. The donor can then give the proceeds from the sale to the donee.

Selection of Property for Making Bequests

A decedent's will should generally make bequests of appreciated property. Doing so enables both the decedent and the heir to avoid income tax on the unrealized gain because the recipient takes the fair market value as his or her basis.

Taxpayers generally should not make bequests of depreciated property (property that, if sold, would produce a realized loss) because the decedent does not receive an income tax deduction for the unrealized loss element. In addition, the heir will receive no benefit from this unrealized loss upon the subsequent sale of the property.

Example 63

On the date of her death, Marta owned land held for investment purposes. The land had an adjusted basis of $600,000 and a fair market value of $100,000. If she had sold the property before her death, the recognized loss would have been $500,000. If Ramon inherits the property and sells it for $60,000, the recognized loss will be $40,000 (the decline in value since Marta's death). In addition, regardless of the period of time Ramon holds the property, the holding period is long term (see Chapter 13). ◆

From an income tax perspective, it is preferable to transfer appreciated property as a bequest rather than as a gift.[38] This results because inherited property receives a step-up in basis, whereas the donee has a carryover basis for property received by gift. However, in making this decision, the estate tax consequences of the bequest should be weighed against the gift tax consequences of the gift.

Wash Sales. The wash sales provisions can be avoided if the security is replaced within the statutory time period with a similar rather than a substantially

38. Consideration must also be given to the estate tax consequences of the bequest versus the gift tax consequences of the gift.

identical security. For example, the sale of Bethlehem Steel common stock and a purchase of Inland Steel common stock would not be treated as a wash sale. Such a procedure can enable the taxpayer to use an unrealized capital loss to offset a recognized capital gain. The taxpayer can sell the security before the end of the taxable year, offset the recognized capital loss against the capital gain, and invest the sales proceeds in a similar security.

Because the wash sales provisions do not apply to gains, it may be desirable to engage in a wash sale before the end of the taxable year. This recognized capital gain may be used to offset capital losses or capital loss carryovers from prior years. Since the basis of the replacement stock or securities will be the purchase price, the taxpayer in effect has exchanged a capital gain for an increased basis for the stock or securities.

Like-Kind Exchanges

Since application of the like-kind provisions is mandatory rather than elective, in certain instances it may be preferable to avoid qualifying for § 1031 nonrecognition. If the like-kind provisions do not apply, the end result may be the recognition of capital gain in exchange for a higher basis in the newly acquired asset. Also, the immediate recognition of gain may be preferable in certain situations. Examples where immediate recognition is beneficial include the following:

- Taxpayer has unused net operating loss carryovers.
- Taxpayer has unused general business credit carryovers.
- Taxpayer has suspended or current passive activity losses.
- Taxpayer expects his or her effective tax rate to increase in the future.

EXAMPLE 64

Alicia disposes of a machine (used in her business) with an adjusted basis of $3,000 for $4,000. She also acquires a new business machine for $9,000. If § 1031 applies, the $1,000 realized gain is not recognized, and the basis of the new machine is reduced by $1,000 (from $9,000 to $8,000). If § 1031 does not apply, a $1,000 gain is recognized and may receive favorable capital gain treatment to the extent that the gain is not recognized as ordinary income due to the depreciation recapture provisions (see Chapter 13). In addition, the basis for depreciation on the new machine is $9,000 rather than $8,000 since there is no unrecognized gain. ◆

Another time for avoiding the application of § 1031 nonrecognition treatment is when the adjusted basis of the property being disposed of exceeds the fair market value.

EXAMPLE 65

Assume the same facts as in the previous example, except the fair market value of the machine is $2,500. If § 1031 applies, the $500 realized loss is not recognized. To recognize the loss, Alicia should sell the old machine and purchase the new one. The purchase and sale transactions should be with different taxpayers. ◆

On the other hand, the like-kind exchange procedure can be utilized to control the amount of recognized gain.

EXAMPLE 66

Rex has property with an adjusted basis of $40,000 and a fair market value of $100,000. Sandra wants to buy Rex's property, but Rex wants to limit the amount of recognized gain on the proposed transaction. Sandra acquires other like-kind property (from an outside party) for $80,000. She then exchanges this property and $20,000 cash for Rex's property. Rex has a realized gain of $60,000 ($100,000 amount realized – $40,000 adjusted basis). His recognized gain is only $20,000, the lower of the boot received of $20,000 or the realized gain of $60,000. His basis for the like-kind property is $40,000 ($40,000 adjusted basis + $20,000 gain recognized – $20,000 boot received). If Rex had sold the property to Sandra for its fair market value of $100,000, the result would have been a $60,000 recognized gain ($100,000 amount realized – $40,000 adjusted basis) to Rex. It is permissible for Rex to identify the like-kind property that he wants Sandra to purchase.[39] ◆

Involuntary Conversions

In certain cases, a taxpayer may prefer to recognize gain from an involuntary conversion. Keep in mind that § 1033, unlike § 1031 (dealing with like-kind exchanges), generally is an elective provision.

EXAMPLE 67

Ahmad has a $40,000 realized gain from the involuntary conversion of an office building. He reinvests the entire proceeds of $450,000 in a new office building. Ahmad, however, does not elect to postpone gain under § 1033 because of an expiring net operating loss carryover that is offset against the gain. Therefore, none of the realized gain of $40,000 is postponed. By not electing § 1033 postponement, Ahmad's basis in the replacement property is the property's cost of $450,000 rather than $410,000 ($450,000 reduced by the $40,000 realized gain). ◆

Sale of a Personal Residence

Replacement Period Requirements. Several problems arise in avoiding the recognition of gain on the sale of a principal residence. Most of these problems can be resolved favorably through appropriate planning procedures. However, a few represent situations where the taxpayer has to accept the adverse tax consequences and possesses little, if any, planning flexibility. One pitfall concerns the failure to reinvest *all* of the proceeds from the sale of the residence into a new principal residence.

EXAMPLE 68

Rita sells her principal residence in January 1991 for $150,000 (adjusted basis of $40,000). Shortly thereafter, she purchases for $100,000 a 50-year-old house in a historical part of the community and uses it as her principal residence. Rita intends to significantly renovate the property over a period of time and make it more suitable to her living needs. In December 1993, she enters into a contract with a home improvement company to carry out the renovation at a cost of $60,000. It is clear that only $100,000 of the proceeds from the sale of the old residence has been reinvested in a new principal residence on a *timely* basis. Of the realized gain of $110,000, therefore, $50,000 ($150,000 adjusted sales price – $100,000 reinvested) must be recognized.[40] ◆

Principal Residence Requirement. Section 1034 will not apply unless the property involved is the taxpayer's principal residence. A potential hurdle arises in cases where the residence has been rented and therefore has not been occupied

39. *Franklin B. Biggs*, 69 T.C. 905 (1978); Rev.Rul. 57–244, 1957–1 C.B. 247; Rev.Rul. 73–476, 1973–2 C.B. 300; *Starker vs. U.S.*, 79–2 USTC ¶9541, 44 AFTR2d 79–5525, 602 F.2d 1341 (CA–9, 1979); and *Baird Publishing Co.*, 39 T.C. 608 (1962).

40. It has been assumed that § 121 did not apply.

by the taxpayer for an extended period of time. Depending on the circumstances, the IRS may contend that the taxpayer has abandoned the property as his or her principal residence. The *key* to the abandonment issue is whether or not the taxpayer intended to reoccupy the property and use it as a principal residence upon returning to the locale. If the residence is, in fact, not reoccupied, the taxpayer should have a good reason to explain why it is not.

EXAMPLE 69

Lori's employer transfers her to another office out of the state on a three-year assignment. It is the understanding of the parties that the assignment is temporary, and upon its completion, she will return to the original job site. During her absence, Lori rents her principal residence and lives in an apartment at the new location. She has every intention of reoccupying her residence. However, when she returns from the temporary assignment, she finds that the residence no longer suits her needs. Specifically, the public school located nearby where she had planned to send her children has been closed. As a consequence, Lori sells the residence and replaces it with one more conveniently located to a public school. Under these circumstances, it would appear that she is in an excellent position to show that she has not abandoned the property as her principal residence. She can satisfactorily explain why she did not reoccupy the residence before its sale.[41] ◆

The principal residence requirement can cause difficulty when a taxpayer works in two places and maintains more than one household. In such cases, the principal residence will be the location where the taxpayer lives most of the time.[42]

EXAMPLE 70

Hubert is a vice president of Green Corporation and in this capacity spends about an equal amount of time in the company's New York City and Miami offices. He owns a house in each location and expects to retire in about five years. At that time, he plans to sell his New York home and use some of the proceeds to make improvements on the Miami property. Both homes have appreciated in value since their acquisition, and Hubert expects the appreciation to continue. From a tax planning standpoint, he should be looking toward the use of §§ 121 and 1034 to shelter some or all of the gain he will realize on the future sale of the New York City home.[43] To do this, he should arrange his affairs so as to spend more than six months each year at that location. Upon its sale, therefore, the New York home will be his principal residence. ◆

Section 121 Considerations. Older individuals who may be contemplating a move from their home to an apartment should consider the following possibilities for minimizing or deferring taxes:

- Wait until age 55 to sell the residence and elect under § 121 to exclude up to $125,000 of the realized gain.
- Sell the personal residence under an installment contract to spread the gain over several years.[44]
- Sell the personal residence and purchase a condominium instead of renting an apartment, thereby permitting further deferral of the unrecognized gain.

The use of § 121 should be carefully considered. Although the use avoids the immediate recognition of gain, the election expends the full $125,000 allowed.

41. Rev.Rul. 78–146, 1978–1 C.B. 260. Compare *Rudolph M. Stucchi*, 35 TCM 1052, T.C.Memo. 1976–242.

42. Rev.Rul. 77–298, 1977–2 C.B. 308.

43. If Hubert qualifies, § 121 would allow the first $125,000 of gain to be nontaxable. Further gain recognition might be avoided under § 1034 to the extent the sales proceeds are applied toward improvements on the Miami home.

44. § 453(a). See the discussion of the installment method in Chapter 15.

EXAMPLE 71

In 1993 Kate, age 55, sells her personal residence for an amount that yields a realized gain of $5,000. Presuming she does not plan to reinvest the sales proceeds in a new principal residence (take advantage of the deferral possibility of § 1034), should she avoid the recognition of this gain by utilizing § 121? Electing § 121 means that Kate will waste $120,000 of her lifetime exclusion. ◆

In this connection, the use of § 121 by one spouse precludes the other spouse from later taking advantage of the exclusion.

EXAMPLE 72

Assume the same facts as in the previous example, except that Kate was married to Wes at the time of the sale. Later, they are divorced and Wes marries Alice. If Kate has used the § 121 exclusion, it is unavailable to Wes and Alice even though either one of them may otherwise qualify. When Kate made the election for the 1993 sale, it was necessary for Wes to join with her in making the election even if the residence was owned separately by Kate. For Wes and Alice to be able to make the § 121 election, Wes and Kate must revoke their prior election. Another planning approach is for Alice to sell her residence before marrying Wes and to elect the exclusion on that sale. ◆

A taxpayer who is eligible to elect § 121 exclusion treatment may choose not to do so in order to remain eligible to elect it in the future. In arriving at this decision, consideration must be given to the probability that the taxpayer will satisfy the three-out-of-five-year ownership and use period requirements associated with a residence sale in the future. As previously mentioned, the holding period for the occupancy and use requirements does carry over for a § 1033 involuntary conversion but does not carry over for a § 1034 sale.

Taxpayers should maintain records of both the purchase and sale of personal residences since the sale of one residence results in an adjustment of the basis of the new residence if the deferral provisions of § 1034 apply. Form 2119 should be filed with the tax return and a copy retained as support for the basis of the new residence. Detailed cost records should be retained for an indefinite period.

PROBLEM MATERIALS

DISCUSSION QUESTIONS

1. Upon the sale or other disposition of property, what four questions should be considered for income tax purposes?
2. In addition to sales and exchanges, what are some other transactions that are treated as dispositions of property?
3. Carol and Dave each purchase 100 shares of stock of Burgundy, Inc., a publicly owned corporation, in July for $10,000 each. Carol sells her stock on December 31 for $14,000. Since Burgundy, Inc.'s stock is listed on a national exchange, Dave is able to ascertain that his shares are worth $14,000 on December 31. Does the tax law treat the appreciation in value of the stock differently for Carol and Dave? Explain.
4. If a taxpayer sells property for cash, the amount realized consists of the net proceeds from the sale. For each of the following, indicate the effect on the amount realized:

   a. The property is sold on credit.
   b. A mortgage on the property is assumed by the buyer.
   c. The purchaser pays property taxes that are treated as imposed on the seller.

5. If the buyer pays real property taxes that are treated as imposed on the seller, what are the effects on the seller's amount realized and the buyer's adjusted basis for the property? If the seller pays real property taxes that are treated as imposed on the buyer, what are the effects on the seller's amount realized and the buyer's adjusted basis for the property?
6. Tom is negotiating to buy some land from Sandra. Under the first option, he will give Sandra $70,000 and assume her mortgage on the land for $30,000. Under the second option, Tom will give Sandra $100,000, and she will immediately pay off the mortgage. Tom would like his basis for the land to be as high as possible. Given this objective, which option should Tom select?
7. Edith purchases land from Mike. She gives Mike $40,000 in cash and agrees to pay him an additional $80,000 one year later plus interest at 12%.

   a. What is Edith's adjusted basis for the land at the date purchased?
   b. What is Edith's adjusted basis for the land one year later?

8. Federico owns a machine that he uses in his trade or business. He sells the machine on the last day of his taxable year. If the machine was placed in service before 1981 (i.e., subject to § 167 depreciation), what effect does the depreciation in the year of sale have on the adjusted basis of the machine? If the machine was placed in service after 1980 (i.e., subject to § 168 ACRS or MACRS), what effect does cost recovery in the year of sale have on the adjusted basis of the machine? What would the results be if the asset were a building rather than a machine?
9. Chris and Jeff each own an automobile used exclusively in his respective trade or business. The adjusted basis of each automobile is $17,000, and the fair market value is $11,000. Both automobiles are destroyed in accidents. Chris's automobile is insured, and he receives insurance proceeds of $11,000. Dave's automobile is uninsured. Explain how the adjusted basis for each automobile is reduced to zero, even though one is insured and the other is uninsured.
10. Abby owns stock in Orange Corporation and Blue Corporation. She receives a $1,000 distribution from both corporations. The instructions from Orange Corporation state that the $1,000 is a dividend. The instructions from Blue Corporation state that the $1,000 is not a dividend. What could cause the instructions to differ as to the tax consequences?
11. A taxpayer who acquires a taxable bond at a premium may elect to amortize the premium, whereas a taxpayer who acquires a tax-exempt bond at a premium must amortize the premium. Why would a taxpayer make the amortization election for taxable bonds? What effect does the mandatory amortization of tax-exempt bonds have on taxable income?
12. Why are gains from the sale or exchange of personal use assets recognized when such losses are never recognized?
13. Explain the relationship between the recovery of capital doctrine and (a) realized gain and (b) recognized gain or loss.
14. How is the basis of the property determined in a bargain purchase, and why is this method used?
15. Discuss the residual method as it applies to goodwill in the lump-sum purchase of a business. Why must this method be used for goodwill rather than the normal allocation method based on the fair market value of the individual assets acquired?
16. Gary makes a gift of an appreciated building to Carmen, who dies three months later. Gary inherits the building from Carmen. During the period that Carmen held the building, she deducted depreciation and made a capital expenditure. What effect might these items have on Gary's basis for the inherited building?
17. Immediately before his death in 1993, Kirby sells securities (adjusted basis of $100,000) for their fair market value of $20,000. The sale was not to a related party. The securities were community property, and Kirby is survived by his wife, Zina, who inherited all of his property.

    a. Did Kirby act wisely? Why or why not?
    b. Suppose the figures are reversed (sale for $100,000 of property with an adjusted basis of $20,000). Would the sale be wise? Why or why not?

18. What is the holding period for property received by gift? What is the holding period for inherited property?
19. What is a wash sale? Why isn't a realized loss recognized on a wash sale? How is the recovery of capital doctrine maintained?
20. What is the basis for property converted from personal use to business or income-producing use when there is a loss? When there is a gain? Why is there a difference? How does conversion affect depreciation and why?
21. In general, what is a nontaxable exchange? Are nontaxable exchanges ever taxed? If so, how?
22. Distinguish between a loss that is not recognized on a nontaxable exchange and a loss that is not recognized on the sale or exchange of a personal use asset.
23. Why would a taxpayer want to avoid like-kind exchange treatment?
24. Which of the following qualify as like-kind exchanges under § 1031?

    a. Improved for unimproved real estate.
    b. Crane (used in business) for inventory.
    c. Rental house for truck (used in business).
    d. Business equipment for securities.
    e. Delicatessen for bakery (both used for business).
    f. Personal residence for apartment building (held for investment).
    g. Rental house for land (both held for investment).
    h. Ten shares of stock in Blue Corporation for 10 shares of stock in Red Corporation.

25. If a taxpayer exchanges a personal use car for another car to be held for personal use, any realized loss is not recognized. However, if realized gain occurs, the realized gain is recognized. Why?
26. Why does the receipt of boot in a like-kind exchange trigger the recognition of realized gain but not the recognition of realized loss?
27. In a like-kind exchange, the basis of the property received is the same as the adjusted basis of the property transferred. If boot is received, what effect does the boot have on the basis of the like-kind property received? If boot is given, what effect does the boot have on the basis of the like-kind property received?
28. Taxpayer's warehouse is destroyed by fire. What are the different tax options available to the taxpayer (a) if he has a realized gain and (b) if he has a realized loss?
29. Bob is notified by the city public housing authority on October 5, 1993, that his apartment building is going to be condemned as part of an urban renewal project. On October 12, 1993, Carol offers to buy the building from Bob. Bob sells the building to Carol on October 30, 1993. Condemnation occurs on February 1, 1994, and Carol receives the condemnation proceeds from the city. Assume both Bob and Carol are calendar year taxpayers.

    a. What is the earliest date that Bob can dispose of the building and qualify for § 1033 postponement treatment?
    b. Does the sale to Carol qualify as a § 1033 involuntary conversion?
    c. What is the latest date that Carol can acquire qualifying replacement property and qualify for postponement of the realized gain?
    d. What type of property will be qualifying replacement property?

30. Discuss the justification for nonrecognition of gain on the sale or exchange of a principal residence. Discuss the justification for disallowance of loss.
31. Peggy has owned and occupied a house as her principal residence for 10 years. She purchases a new residence in March 1993. She initially listed her old residence with a realtor in January 1993. Needing the cash flow, she rents the old residence to Joe for a six-month period beginning in March. She sells the old residence to Paul upon the expiration of the rental period in September. Does the sale of the old residence in September qualify as the sale of a principal residence?
32. Define each of the following associated with the sale of a residence:

    a. Amount realized.
    b. Adjusted sales price.
    c. Fixing-up expenses.

33. If the taxpayer elects to deduct selling expenses on the sale of his or her principal residence as indirect moving expenses, what effect does this election have on the realized and recognized gain or loss on the sale of the residence?

PROBLEMS

34. Kareem bought a rental house at the beginning of 1988 for $80,000, of which $10,000 is allocated to the land and $70,000 to the building. Early in 1990, he had a tennis court built in the backyard at a cost of $5,000. Kareem has deducted $32,200 for depreciation on the house and $1,300 for depreciation on the court. At the beginning of 1993, he sells the house and tennis court for $125,000 cash.

    a. What is Kareem's realized gain or loss?
    b. If an original mortgage of $20,000 is still outstanding and the buyer assumes the mortgage in addition to the cash payment, what is Kareem's realized gain or loss?
    c. If the buyer takes the property subject to the mortgage, what is Kareem's realized gain or loss?

35. Nell owns a personal use automobile that has an adjusted basis of $8,000. The fair market value of the automobile is $4,500.

    a. Calculate the realized and recognized loss if Nell sells the automobile for $4,500.
    b. Calculate the realized and recognized loss if Nell exchanges the automobile for another automobile worth $4,500.
    c. Calculate the realized and recognized loss if the automobile is stolen and Nell receives insurance proceeds of $4,500.

36. Mitch's automobile, which is used exclusively in his business, is stolen. The adjusted basis is $22,000, and the fair market value is $23,000. His AGI is $45,000.

    a. If Mitch receives insurance proceeds of $22,500, what effect do the theft and the receipt of the insurance proceeds have on the adjusted basis of the automobile?
    b. If the automobile is not insured, what effect do the theft and the absence of insurance have on the adjusted basis of the automobile?

37. Lynn and Debra each own 50% of the stock of a corporation. The earnings and profits of the corporation are $30,000. Lynn's adjusted basis for the stock is $40,000. Lynn and Debra each receive a cash distribution of $70,000 from the corporation.

    a. What effect does the distribution have on the adjusted basis of Lynn's stock?
    b. What effect would the distribution have on the adjusted basis of Lynn's stock if the earnings and profits of the corporation were $180,000?
    c. In (a) and (b), what is the effect on Lynn's gross income?

38. Chee paid $270,000 for bonds with a face value of $250,000 at the beginning of 1989. The bonds mature in 10 years and pay 9% interest per year.

    a. If Chee sells the bonds for $255,000 at the beginning of 1993, does she have a realized gain or loss? If so, how much?
    b. If Chee trades the bonds at the beginning of 1994 for stock worth $262,500, does she have a realized gain or loss? If so, how much?

39. Which of the following would definitely result in a recognized gain or loss?

    a. Kay sells her lakeside cabin, which has an adjusted basis of $10,000, for $15,000.
    b. Adam sells his personal residence, which has an adjusted basis of $15,000, for $10,000.
    c. Carl's personal residence is on the site of a proposed airport and is condemned by the city. He receives $55,000 for the house, which has an adjusted basis of $65,000.
    d. Olga's land is worth $40,000 at the end of the year. She had purchased the land six months earlier for $25,000.
    e. Jack gives stock to his niece. His adjusted basis is $8,000, and the fair market value is $5,000.

40. Hubert's personal residence is condemned as part of an urban renewal project. His adjusted basis for the residence is $160,000. He receives condemnation proceeds of $150,000 and invests the proceeds in stock.

   a. Calculate Hubert's realized and recognized gain or loss.
   b. If the condemnation proceeds are $180,000, what are Hubert's realized and recognized gain or loss?
   c. What are Hubert's realized and recognized gain or loss in (a) if the house was rental property?

41. Walt buys a watch from his employer for $2,500. The fair market value of the watch is $6,000. Assuming that the excess $3,500 represents compensation for services rendered:

   a. What is Walt's basis for the watch?
   b. Why?

42. Paula purchases the assets of a sole proprietorship from Seth. The adjusted basis of each of the assets on Seth's books and the fair market value of each asset as agreed to by Paula and Seth are as follows:

Asset	Seth's Adjusted Basis	FMV
Accounts receivable	$ -0-	$ 10,000
Notes receivable	15,000	20,000
Machinery and equipment	85,000	100,000
Building	100,000	300,000
Land	200,000	350,000

The purchase price is $900,000. Determine Paula's basis for each of the assets of the sole proprietorship.

43. Rick received various gifts over the years. He has decided to dispose of the following assets that he received as gifts:

   a. In 1920, he received a Rolls Royce worth $22,000. The donor's adjusted basis for the auto was $16,000. Rick sells the auto for $45,000 in 1993.
   b. In 1945, he received land worth $20,000. The donor's adjusted basis was $32,000. Rick sells the land for $87,000 in 1993.
   c. In 1950, he received stock in Gold Company. The donor's adjusted basis was $1,000. The fair market value on the date of the gift was $3,000. Rick sells the stock for $3,500 in 1993.
   d. In 1961, he received land worth $12,000. The donor's adjusted basis was $25,000. Rick sells the land for $9,000 in 1993.
   e. In 1990, he received stock worth $30,000. The donor's adjusted basis was $40,000. Rick sells the stock in 1993 for $37,000.

What is the realized gain or loss from each of the preceding transactions? Assume in each of the gift transactions that no gift tax was paid.

44. Ron receives a gift of property (after 1976) that has a fair market value of $100,000 on the date of gift. The donor's adjusted basis for the property was $40,000. Assume the donor paid gift tax of $15,000 on the gift.

   a. What is Ron's basis for gain and loss and for depreciation?
   b. If Ron had received the gift of property before 1977, what would his basis be for gain and loss and for depreciation?

45. Ira is planning to make a charitable contribution of stock worth $20,000 to the Boy Scouts. The stock he is considering contributing has an adjusted basis of $15,000. A friend has suggested that Ira sell the stock and contribute the $20,000 in proceeds rather than contribute the stock.

   a. Should Ira follow the friend's advice? Why?
   b. Assume the fair market value is only $13,000. In this case, should Ira follow the friend's advice? Why?
   c. Rather than make a charitable contribution to the Boy Scouts, Ira is going to make a gift to Nancy, his niece. Advise Ira regarding (a) and (b).

46. Dena inherits property from Mary, her mother. Mary's adjusted basis for the property is $100,000, and the fair market value is $725,000. Six months after Mary's death, the fair market value is $740,000. Dena is the sole beneficiary of Mary's estate.

a. Can the executor of Mary's estate elect the alternate valuation date?
b. What is Dena's basis for the property?

47. Earl's estate includes the following assets available for distribution to Robert, one of Earl's beneficiaries:

	Earl's Adjusted Basis	FMV at Date of Death	FMV at Alternate Valuation Date
Cash	$10,000	$ 10,000	$ 10,000
Stock	40,000	125,000	60,000
Apartment building	60,000	300,000	325,000
Land	75,000	100,000	110,000

The fair market value of the stock six months after Earl's death was $60,000. However, believing that the stock would continue to decline in value, the executor of the estate distributed the stock to Robert one month after Earl's death. Robert immediately sold the stock for $85,000.

a. Determine Robert's basis for the assets if the primary valuation date and amount apply.
b. Determine Robert's basis for the assets if the executor elects the alternate valuation date and amount.

48. Dan bought a hotel for $720,000 in January 1990. In January 1993, he died and left the hotel to Ed. Dan had deducted $42,000 of cost recovery on the hotel before his death. The fair market value in January 1993 was $780,000.

a. What is the basis of the property to Ed?
b. If the land is worth $240,000, what is Ed's basis for cost recovery?

49. Kim purchased 100 shares of White Corporation common stock on June 6, 1992, for $20,000. He sold the stock on January 6, 1993, for $30,000. On January 28, 1993, he purchased another 100 shares of White Corporation common stock for $28,000.

a. What are Kim's realized and recognized gain or loss on January 6, 1993?
b. What is Kim's basis for the stock he purchased on January 28, 1993?
c. What would be your answer for (a) and (b) if Kim's cost of the stock on June 6, 1992, had been $35,000?

50. Surendra's personal residence originally cost $150,000 (ignore land). After living in the house for five years, he converts it to rental property. At the date of conversion, the fair market value of the house is $130,000.

a. Calculate Surendra's basis for loss for the rental property.
b. Calculate Surendra's basis for depreciation for the rental property.
c. Calculate Surendra's basis for gain for the rental property.

51. Bonnie owns a personal computer that she uses exclusively in her business. The adjusted basis is $3,000. Bonnie transfers the personal computer and cash of $2,000 to Don for a laser printer worth $6,000 that she will use in her business.

a. Calculate Bonnie's recognized gain or loss on the exchange.
b. Calculate Bonnie's basis for the printer.

52. Diego exchanges an automobile used exclusively in his business for a light-duty truck that will be used in his business. The adjusted basis for the automobile is $12,000, and the fair market value of the truck is $10,000.

a. Calculate Diego's recognized gain or loss on the exchange.
b. Calculate Diego's basis for the truck.

53. Tom owns land and building with an adjusted basis of $125,000 and a fair market value of $275,000. He exchanges the land and building for land with a fair market value of $175,000 that he will use as a parking lot. In addition, Tom receives stock worth $100,000.

   a. What is Tom's realized gain or loss?
   b. His recognized gain or loss?
   c. The basis of the land and the stock received?

54. Olga owns a machine that she uses in her business. The adjusted basis is $60,000, and the fair market value is $90,000. She exchanges it for another machine worth $55,000. Olga also receives cash of $35,000.

   a. Calculate Olga's realized and recognized gain or loss on the exchange.
   b. Calculate Olga's basis for the new machine.

55. Ed owns investment land with an adjusted basis of $35,000. Polly has offered to purchase the land from Ed for $175,000 for use in a real estate development. The amount offered by Polly is $10,000 in excess of what Ed perceives as the fair market value of the land. Ed would like to dispose of the land to Polly but does not want to incur the tax liability that would result. He identifies an office building with a fair market value of $175,000 that he would like to acquire. Polly purchases the office building and then exchanges the office building for Ed's land.

   a. Calculate Ed's realized and recognized gain on the exchange and his basis for the office building.
   b. Calculate Polly's realized and recognized gain on the exchange and her basis in the land.

56. What is the basis of the new property in each of the following exchanges?

   a. Apartment building held for investment (adjusted basis $150,000) for lakefront property held for investment (fair market value $200,000).
   b. Land and building used as a barber shop (adjusted basis $30,000) for land and building used as a grocery store (fair market value $350,000).
   c. Office building (adjusted basis $30,000) for bulldozer (fair market value $42,000), both held for business use.
   d. IBM common stock (adjusted basis $14,000) for Exxon common stock (fair market value $18,000).
   e. Rental house (adjusted basis $90,000) for land held for investment (fair market value $115,000).

57. Gus exchanges real estate held for investment plus stock for real estate to be held for investment. The stock transferred has an adjusted basis of $10,000 and a fair market value of $6,000. The real estate transferred has an adjusted basis of $15,000 and a fair market value of $22,000. The real estate acquired has a fair market value of $28,000.

   a. What is Gus's realized gain or loss?
   b. His recognized gain or loss?
   c. The basis of the newly acquired real estate?

58. Helen exchanges a machine (adjusted basis of $30,000 and fair market value of $55,000) and undeveloped land held for investment (adjusted basis of $100,000 and fair market value of $325,000) for land worth $320,000 to be used in her business. The undeveloped land has a mortgage of $60,000 that the other party to the exchange assumes.

   a. What is Helen's realized gain or loss?
   b. Her recognized gain or loss?
   c. The basis of the newly acquired real estate?

59. Carmen converted her personal residence to rental property on January 1, 1992. At that time, the adjusted basis was $70,000, and the fair market value was $100,000. During the interim rental period, Carmen deducted cost recovery of $5,576. The

rental property is condemned on December 31, 1993, in connection with an urban renewal project, and Carmen receives condemnation proceeds of $62,000.

a. What is the adjusted basis at the condemnation date?
b. What is the recognized gain or loss on the condemnation?

60. For each of the following involuntary conversions, indicate whether the property acquired qualifies as replacement property:

a. Frank owns a shopping mall that is destroyed by a tornado. The space in the mall was rented to various tenants. He uses the insurance proceeds to build a shopping mall in a neighboring community where no property has been damaged by tornadoes.
b. Ivan owns a warehouse that he uses in his business. The warehouse is destroyed by fire. Due to economic conditions in the area, Ivan decides not to rebuild the warehouse. Instead, he uses the insurance proceeds to build a warehouse to be used in his business in another state.
c. Ridge's personal residence is condemned as part of a local government project to widen the highway from two lanes to four lanes. He uses the condemnation proceeds to purchase another personal residence.

61. Do the following qualify for involuntary conversion treatment?

a. Purchase of a sporting goods store as a replacement for a bookstore (used in a business) that was destroyed by fire.
b. Sale of a home because a neighbor converted his residence into a nightclub.
c. Purchase of an airplane to replace a shrimp boat (used in a business) that was wrecked by a hurricane.
d. Taxpayer's residence destroyed by a tornado and replaced with another residence.
e. Purchase of an apartment building to replace a rental house by an investor. The rental house was destroyed by a flood.

62. Lynn's office building, which is used in her business, is destroyed by a hurricane in September 1993. The adjusted basis is $225,000. Lynn receives insurance proceeds of $350,000 in October 1993.

a. Calculate Lynn's realized gain or loss, recognized gain or loss, and basis for the replacement property if she acquires an office building for $390,000 in October 1993.
b. Calculate Lynn's realized gain or loss, recognized gain or loss, and basis for the replacement property if she acquires a warehouse for $330,000 in October 1993.
c. Calculate Lynn's realized gain or loss and recognized gain or loss if she does not acquire replacement property.

63. Carlos's warehouse, which has an adjusted basis of $325,000 and a fair market value of $490,000, is condemned by an agency of the Federal government to make way for a highway interchange. The initial condemnation offer is $450,000. After substantial negotiations, the agency agrees to transfer to Carlos a surplus warehouse that he believes is worth $490,000.

a. What are the recognized gain or loss and the basis of the replacement warehouse if Carlos's objective is to recognize as much gain as possible?
b. What are the recognized gain or loss and the basis of the replacement warehouse if Carlos's objective is to minimize gain recognition?

64. Rental property owned by Freda, a calendar year taxpayer, is destroyed by a tornado on January 1, 1993. Freda had originally paid $150,000 for the property, of which $125,000 was allocated to the building and $25,000 was allocated to the land. During the time Freda owned the property, ACRS deductions of $46,250 were taken. ACRS deductions of $57,500 would have been taken, except that Freda chose to forgo deductions of $11,250 one year when her tax return showed a net operating loss. Freda receives insurance proceeds of $60,000 in November 1993. As a result of

continuing negotiations with the insurance company, Freda receives additional proceeds of $35,000 in August 1994.

a. What is Freda's adjusted basis for the property?
b. What is Freda's realized gain or loss on the involuntary conversion in 1993? In 1994?
c. What is the latest date that Freda can replace the involuntarily converted property to qualify for § 1033 postponement?
d. What is the latest date that Freda can replace the involuntarily converted property to qualify for § 1033 postponement if the form of the involuntary conversion is a condemnation?

65. Tina, age 42, has lived in her residence for three years. Her adjusted basis is $130,000. Knowing that she is going to move to another city, she lists her residence for sale in February 1991. When she moves in May 1991, she purchases another residence for $190,000. Due to market conditions, she does not sell her original residence until July 1993. The selling price is $225,000, selling expenses are $13,000, and fixing-up expenses are $4,000.

a. What is Tina's realized gain or loss?
b. Her recognized gain or loss?
c. The basis of the new residence?

66. What are the realized, recognized, and postponed gain or loss, the new basis, and the adjusted sales price for each of the following? Assume that none of the taxpayers is 55 years of age or older.

a. Susan sells her residence for $90,000. The adjusted basis was $55,000. The selling expenses were $5,000. The fixing-up expenses were $3,000. She did not reinvest in a new residence.
b. Rocky sells his residence for $170,000. The adjusted basis was $120,000. The selling expenses were $4,000. The fixing-up expenses were $6,000. He reinvested $160,000 in a new residence.
c. Veneia sells her residence for $65,000. The adjusted basis was $35,000. The selling expenses were $1,000. The fixing-up expenses were $2,000. She reinvested $40,000.
d. Barry sells his residence for $70,000. The adjusted basis was $65,000. The selling expenses were $6,000. He reinvested $80,000.
e. Carl sells his residence for $100,000, and his mortgage is assumed by the buyer. The adjusted basis was $80,000; the mortgage, $50,000. The selling expenses were $4,000. The fixing-up expenses were $2,000. He reinvested $120,000.

67. On January 15, 1993, Kelly, a 48-year-old widow, buys a new residence for $180,000. On March 1, 1993, she sells for an adjusted sales price of $197,000 her old residence, which had an adjusted basis of $110,000. No fixing-up expenses are incurred. Between April 1 and June 30, 1993, she constructs an addition to her new house at a cost of $20,000.

a. What is Kelly's realized gain or loss?
b. Kelly's recognized gain or loss?
c. Kelly's basis for the new residence?

CUMULATIVE PROBLEMS

68. Ada Johnson, age 28, is single and has no dependents. Her Social Security number is 444–11–3333, and she resides at 210 Avenue G, Kentwood, LA 70444. Her salary in 1993 was $52,000. She incurred unreimbursed expenses of $1,800 for travel and $500 for entertainment in connection with her job as an assistant personnel director. In addition, she had the following items of possible tax consequence in 1993:

a. Itemized deductions (not including any potential deductions mentioned previously), $12,000.

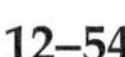

b. Proceeds from the October 8, 1993, sale of land inherited from her father on June 15, 1993 (fair market value on June 15 was $35,000; her father's adjusted basis was $15,000), $55,000.

c. Proceeds from the November 1, 1993, sale of 50 shares of JKL Corporation stock received as a gift from her father on October 5, 1976, when the fair market value of the stock was $6,000 (her father's adjusted basis in the stock was $5,500, and he paid gift tax of $800 on the transfer), $9,500.

d. Proceeds from the November 5, 1993, sale of her personal automobile, for which she had paid $4,500 in 1985, $3,100.

e. Proceeds from the December 3, 1993, sale of 10 shares of MNO Corporation stock to her brother (she had paid $85 per share for the stock on February 7, 1993), $600.

f. Dividends received from a domestic corporation, $480.

Part 1—Tax Computation

Ada's employer withheld Federal income tax of $14,880. Compute Ada's net tax payable or refund due for 1993. Suggested software (if available): *TurboTax, MacInTax* or WFT tax planning software.

Part 2—Tax Planning

As of the beginning of 1994, Ada is promoted to the position of personnel director. The promotion will result in a salary increase. Her new position will result in an estimated increase in her expenses for travel from $1,800 to $4,000 and in her expenses for entertainment from $500 to $4,000. Her employer has offered her the following options.

a. Salary increase of $20,000.

b. Salary increase of $12,000 and reimbursement for all travel and entertainment expenses not in excess of $8,000.

Ada estimates that her itemized deductions (excluding any potential deductions for travel and entertainment) will remain at $12,000. She anticipates that no dividends will be received and no proceeds from asset sales will be received.

Calculate Ada's tax liability for 1994 under both option (a) and option (b) so she can decide which option to select. Suggested software (if available): *TurboTax, MacInTax* or WFT tax planning software.

69. Tammy Walker, age 37, is a self-employed accountant. Tammy's Social Security number is 333–40–1111. Her address is 101 Glass Road, Richmond, VA 23236. Her income and expenses associated with her accounting practice for 1993 are as follows:

Revenues (cash receipts during 1993)	$186,000
Expenses:	
Salaries	$ 83,000
Office supplies	1,100
Postage	500
Depreciation of equipment	25,000
Telephone	650
	$110,250

Since Tammy is a cash basis taxpayer, she does not record her receivables as revenue until she receives cash payment. At the beginning of 1993, her accounts receivable were $17,000, and the balance had decreased to $8,000 by the end of the year. The balance on December 31, 1993, would have been $13,500, except that an account for $5,500 had become uncollectible in November.

Tammy used one room in her 10-room house as an office (400 square feet out of a total square footage of 4,000). She paid the following expenses related to the house during 1993:

Utilities	$4,000
Insurance	800
Property taxes	4,000
Repairs	1,400

Tammy had purchased the house on September 1, 1992, for $200,000. She sold her previous house on November 15, 1992, for $105,000. Her selling expenses had been $9,000, and qualified fixing-up expenses were $1,100. Tammy and her former husband, Lou, had purchased the house in 1990 for $80,000. Tammy had received Lou's 50% ownership interest as part of their divorce settlement in August 1991. Tammy had not used any part of the former residence as a home office.

Tammy has one child, Thomas, age 17. Thomas lives with his father during the summer and with Tammy for the rest of the year. Tammy can document that she spent $8,000 during 1993 for the child's support. The father normally provides about $2,000 per year, but this year he gave the child a new car for Christmas. The cost of the car was $18,000. The divorce decree is silent regarding the dependency exemption for the child.

Under the terms of the divorce decree, Tammy is to receive alimony of $800 per month. The payments will terminate at Tammy's death or if she should remarry.

Tammy provides part of the support of her mother, age 67. The total support for 1993 for her mother was as follows:

Social Security benefits	$4,800
From Tammy	1,900
From Bob, Tammy's brother	1,300
From Susan, Tammy's sister	2,000

Bob and Susan have both indicated their willingness to sign a multiple support waiver form if it will benefit Tammy.

Tammy's deductible itemized deductions during 1993, excluding any itemized deductions related to the house, were $11,000. She made estimated tax payments of $22,000.

Part 1—Tax Computation

Compute Tammy's lowest net tax payable or refund due for 1993. Suggested software (if available): *TurboTax* or *MacInTax* for tax return or WFT tax planning software.

Part 2—Tax Planning

Tammy and her former husband have been discussing the $800 alimony he pays her each month. Due to a health problem of his new wife, he does not feel that he can afford to continue to pay the $800 each month. He is in the 15% tax bracket. If Tammy will agree to decrease the amount by 25%, he will agree that the amount paid is not alimony for tax purposes. Assume that the other data used in calculating Tammy's taxable income for 1993 will apply for her 1994 tax return. Write a letter to Tammy that contains your advice on whether she should agree to her former husband's proposal. Also prepare a memo for the tax files. Suggested software (if available): WFT tax planning software.

CHAPTER

PROPERTY TRANSACTIONS: CAPITAL GAINS AND LOSSES, SECTION 1231, AND RECAPTURE PROVISIONS

OBJECTIVES

Discuss the rationale for separate reporting of capital asset transactions.

Define a capital asset, apply the definition, and examine its statutory expansions.

Discuss the rules relating to capital gain treatment and retirement of corporate obligations.

Discuss and apply the holding period rules for determining whether capital gain or loss is long term or short term.

Explain the differences in the tax treatment of capital gains and losses of corporate versus noncorporate taxpayers.

Define § 1231 assets and compute § 1231 gains and losses.

Discuss §§ 1245 and 1250 recapture and certain other recapture provisions.

Explain the treatment of gains and losses from dispositions of passive activity property.

Discuss tax planning opportunities arising from the sale or exchange of capital assets.

Develop tax planning ideas related to §§ 1231, 1245, and 1250.

OUTLINE

General Considerations

Rationale for Separate Reporting of Capital Gains and Losses

The tax law requires capital gains and losses to be separated from other types of gains and losses. There are two reasons for this treatment. First, long-term capital gains may be taxed at a lower rate than ordinary gains. An *alternative tax computation* is used to determine the tax when taxable income includes net long-term capital gain. Capital gains and losses must therefore be matched with one another to see if a net long-term capital gain exists. The alternative tax computation is discussed in the Tax Treatment of Capital Gains and Losses of Noncorporate Taxpayers portion of this chapter.

Why else does the Code require separate reporting of gains and losses and a determination of their tax character? The second reason is that a net capital loss is only deductible up to $3,000 per year. Excess loss over the annual limit carries over and may be deductible in a future tax year. Capital gains and losses must be matched with one another to see if a net capital loss exists.

For these reasons, capital gains and losses must be distinguished from other types of gains and losses. Much of this chapter describes the intricate rules for determining what type of gains and losses the taxpayer has.

As a result of the need to distinguish and separately match capital gains and losses, the individual tax forms include extensive reporting requirements for capital gains and losses. This chapter will help you understand the principles underlying the forms.

In addition to the capital gains provisions, this chapter is concerned with § 1231 provisions, which apply to the sale or exchange of business properties and to certain involuntary conversions. The chapter also covers the recapture provisions that treat as ordinary income certain gains that otherwise would be treated as long-term capital gain. The impact of the passive loss provisions (refer to Chapter 6) on the taxation of property gains and losses is discussed briefly in the chapter.

General Scheme of Taxation

Recognized gains and losses must be properly classified. Proper classification depends upon three characteristics:

- The tax status of the property.
- The manner of the property's disposition.
- The holding period of the property.

The three possible tax statuses are capital asset, § 1231 asset, or ordinary asset. Property disposition may be by sale, exchange, casualty, theft, or condemnation. The two holding periods are one year or less (short term) and more than one year (long term).

Capital gains and losses usually result from the disposition of a capital asset. The most common disposition is a sale of the asset. Capital gains and losses can also result from the disposition of § 1231 assets. Except in very limited circumstances, capital gains and losses cannot result from the disposition of ordinary assets.

CAPITAL ASSETS

Definition of a Capital Asset

Personal use assets and investment assets are the most common capital assets owned by individual taxpayers. Personal use assets usually include items such as clothing, recreation equipment, a residence, and automobiles. Investment assets usually include corporate stocks and bonds, government bonds, and vacant land. Remember, however, that losses from the sale or exchange of personal use assets are not recognized. Therefore, the classification of such losses as capital losses can be ignored.

Due to the historical preferential treatment of capital gains, taxpayers have preferred that gains be capital gains rather than ordinary gains. As a result, a great many statutes, cases, and rulings have accumulated in the attempt to define what is and what is not a capital asset. Capital assets are not directly defined in the Code. Instead, § 1221 defines what is *not* a capital asset. A capital asset is property held by the taxpayer (whether or not it is connected with the taxpayer's business) that is *not* any of the following:

- Inventory or property held primarily for sale to customers in the ordinary course of a business. The Supreme Court, in *Malat v. Riddell,* defined *primarily* as meaning *of first importance* or *principally.*[1]
- Accounts and notes receivable acquired from the sale of inventory or acquired for services rendered in the ordinary course of business.
- Depreciable property or real estate used in a business.
- Certain copyrights; literary, musical, or artistic compositions; or letters, memoranda, or similar property held by (1) a taxpayer whose efforts created the property; (2) in the case of a letter, memorandum, or similar property, a taxpayer for whom it was produced; or (3) a taxpayer in whose hands the basis of such property is determined, for purposes of determining gain from a sale or exchange, in whole or part by reference to the basis of the property in the hands of a taxpayer described in (1) or (2).
- U.S. government publications that are (1) received by a taxpayer from the U.S. government other than by purchase at the price at which they are offered for sale to the public or (2) held by a taxpayer whose basis, for purposes of determining gain from a sale or exchange, is determined by reference to a taxpayer described in (1).

The Code defines what is *not* a capital asset. From the preceding list, it is apparent that inventory, accounts and notes receivable, and most fixed assets of a business are not capital assets. The following discussion provides further detail on each part of the capital asset definition.

Inventory. What constitutes inventory is determined by the taxpayer's business.

EXAMPLE 1

Green Company buys and sells used cars. Its cars are inventory. Its gains from sale of the cars are ordinary income. ◆

1. 66–1 USTC ¶9317, 17 AFTR2d 604, 86 S.Ct. 1030 (USSC, 1966).

EXAMPLE 2

Soong sells his personal use automobile at a $500 gain. The automobile is a personal use asset and, therefore, a capital asset. The gain is a capital gain. ◆

Accounts and Notes Receivable. Collection of an accrual basis account receivable usually does not result in a gain or loss because the amount collected equals the receivable's basis. However, the sale of an accrual basis receivable may result in a gain or loss because it will probably be sold for more or less than its basis. A cash basis account receivable has no basis. Sale of such a receivable will generate a gain. Collection of a cash basis receivable generates ordinary income rather than a gain. A gain usually requires a sale of the receivable. See the discussion of Sale or Exchange later in this chapter.

EXAMPLE 3

Wren Company has accounts receivable of $100,000. Because it needs working capital, it sells the receivables for $83,000 to a financial institution. Wren would have a $17,000 ordinary loss if it were an accrual basis taxpayer. Revenue of $100,000 would have been recorded and a $100,000 basis would have been established when the receivable was created. Wren Company would have $83,000 of ordinary income if it were a cash basis taxpayer because it would not have recorded any revenue earlier and thus the receivable has no tax basis. ◆

Business Fixed Assets. Depreciable personal property and real estate (both depreciable and nondepreciable) used by a business are not capital assets. Thus *business fixed assets* are generally not capital assets. The Code has a very complex set of rules pertaining to such property. One of these rules is discussed below under Real Property Subdivided for Sale. This chapter also discusses the potential capital gain treatment under § 1231 for business fixed assets.

Copyrights and Creative Works. Generally, the person whose efforts led to the copyright or creative work has an ordinary asset, not a capital asset. *Creative works* include the works of authors, composers, and artists. Also, the person for whom a letter, memorandum, or other similar property was created has an ordinary asset. Finally, a person receiving a copyright, creative work, letter, memorandum, or similar property by gift from the creator or the person for whom the work was created has an ordinary asset.

EXAMPLE 4

Wanda is a part-time music composer. A music publisher purchases one of her songs for $5,000. She has a $5,000 ordinary gain from the sale of an ordinary asset. ◆

EXAMPLE 5

Ed received a letter from the President of the United States in 1944. In the current year, he sells the letter to a collector for $300. Ed has a $300 ordinary gain from the sale of an ordinary asset (because the letter was created for him). ◆

EXAMPLE 6

Isabella gives a song she composed to her son. The son sells the song to a music publisher for $5,000. The son has a $5,000 ordinary gain from the sale of an ordinary asset. ◆

(Patents are subject to special statutory rules discussed later in the chapter.)

U.S. Government Publications. U.S. government publications received from the U.S. government (or its agencies) for a reduced price are not capital assets. This prevents a taxpayer from later donating the publications to charity and claiming a charitable contribution equal to the fair market value of the publications. A charitable contribution of a capital asset generally yields a deduction equal to the fair market value. A charitable contribution of an ordinary asset generally yields a deduction equal to less than the fair market value. If such property is received by gift from the original purchaser, the property is not a capital asset to the donee. (For a more comprehensive explanation of charitable contributions of property, refer to Chapter 10.)

Effect of Judicial Action

Court decisions play an important role in the definition of capital assets. Because the Code only lists categories of what are *not* capital assets, judicial interpretation is sometimes required to determine whether a specific item fits into one of those categories. The Supreme Court follows a literal interpretation of the categories.[2] For instance, corporate stock is not mentioned in § 1221. Thus, corporate stock is usually a capital asset. However, what if corporate stock is purchased for resale to customers? Then it is *inventory* and is not a capital asset because inventory is one of the categories in § 1221. (See the discussion of Dealers in Securities below.) A Supreme Court decision was required to make the distinction between capital asset and noncapital asset status when a taxpayer who did not normally acquire stock for resale to customers acquired stock with the intention of resale. The Court decided that since the stock was not acquired primarily for sale to customers (the taxpayer did not sell the stock to its regular customers), the stock was a capital asset.

Often the outcome of the capital asset determination hinges on whether the asset is held for investment purposes (capital asset) or business purposes (ordinary asset). The taxpayer's *use* of the property often provides objective evidence.

EXAMPLE 7

Ramon's business buys an expensive painting. If the painting is used to decorate his office and is not of investment quality, the painting is depreciable and, therefore, not a capital asset. If Ramon's business is buying and selling paintings, the painting is inventory and, therefore, an ordinary asset. If the painting is of investment quality and the business purchased it for investment, the painting is a capital asset, even though it serves a decorative purpose in Ramon's office. *Investment quality* generally means that the painting is expected to appreciate in value. ◆

Statutory Expansions

Because of the uncertainty associated with the capital asset definition, Congress has enacted several Code Sections to clarify the definition. These statutory expansions of the capital asset definition are discussed in the following sections.

Dealers in Securities. As a general rule, securities (stocks, bonds, and other financial instruments) held by a dealer are considered to be inventory and are

2. *Arkansas Best v. Comm.*, 88–1 USTC ¶9210, 61 AFTR2d 88–655, 108 S.Ct. 971 (USSC, 1988).

not, therefore, subject to capital gain or loss treatment. A *dealer in securities* is a merchant (e.g., a brokerage firm) that regularly engages in the purchase and resale of securities to customers. The dealer must identify any securities being held for investment. Generally, if a dealer clearly identifies certain securities as held for investment purposes by the close of business on the date of acquisition, gain from the sale of the securities will be capital gain. However, the gain will not be capital gain if the dealer ceases to hold the securities for investment prior to the sale. Losses are capital losses if at any time the securities have been clearly identified by the dealer as held for investment.[3]

Real Property Subdivided for Sale. Substantial real property development activities may result in the owner being considered a dealer for tax purposes. Income from the sale of real estate lots is treated as the sale of inventory (ordinary income) if the owner is considered to be a dealer. However, § 1237 allows real estate investors capital gain treatment if they engage in *limited* development activities. To be eligible for § 1237 treatment, the following requirements must be met:

- The taxpayer may not be a corporation.
- The taxpayer may not be a real estate dealer.
- No substantial improvements may be made to the lots sold. *Substantial* generally means more than a 10 percent increase in the value of a lot. Shopping centers and other commercial or residential buildings are considered substantial, while filling, draining, leveling, and clearing operations are not.
- The taxpayer must have held the lots sold for at least five years, except for inherited property. The substantial improvements test is less stringent if the property is held at least 10 years.

If the preceding requirements are met, all gain is capital gain until the tax year in which the *sixth* lot is sold. Sales of contiguous lots to a single buyer in the same transaction count as the sale of one lot. In the tax year the sixth lot is sold, some of the gain may be ordinary income. Five percent of the revenue from lot sales is potential ordinary income. That potential ordinary income is offset by any selling expenses from the lot sales. Practically, sales commissions often are at least 5 percent of the sales price, so none of the gain is treated as ordinary income.

If the requirements for § 1237 treatment are not met (e.g., the seller is a corporation), the gain still may not necessarily be ordinary income. The gain may be capital gain under § 1221 or § 1231 if the requirements of either of these sections are met.

Section 1237 does not apply to losses. A loss from the sale of subdivided real property is an ordinary loss unless the property qualifies as a capital asset under § 1221.

EXAMPLE 8

Ahmed owns a large tract of land and subdivides it for sale. Assume he meets all the requirements of § 1237 and during the tax year sells the first 10 lots to 10 different

3. §§ 1236(a) and (b) and Reg. § 1.1236–1(a). Section 107(b)(1) of the Deficit Reduction Act of 1984 authorizes the Treasury to impose earlier identification deadlines than the close of the business day. The Treasury could also provide by Regulations for a method of identification other than the taxpayer's records. At this writing, such Regulations have not been issued.

buyers for $10,000 each. Ahmed's basis in each lot sold is $3,000, and he incurs total selling expenses of $4,000 on the sales. Ahmed's gain is computed as follows:

Selling price (10 × $10,000)		$100,000	
Basis (10 × $3,000)		(30,000)	
Excess over basis		$ 70,000	
Five percent of selling price	$ 5,000		
Selling expenses	(4,000)		
Amount of ordinary income			$ 1,000
Five percent of selling price	$ 5,000		
Excess of expenses over 5% of selling price	-0-	(5,000)	
Capital gain			65,000
Total gain ($70,000 – $4,000 selling expenses)			$66,000

◆

SALE OR EXCHANGE

Recognition of capital gain or loss usually requires a sale or exchange of a capital asset. The Code uses the term *sale or exchange,* but does not define it. Generally, a sale of property involves the receipt of money by the seller and/or the assumption by the purchaser of the seller's liabilities related to the property. An exchange involves the transfer of property for other property. Thus, an involuntary conversion (casualty, theft, or condemnation) is not a sale or exchange. In several situations, the determination of whether a sale or exchange has taken place has been clarified by the enactment of Code sections that specifically provide for sale or exchange treatment.

Recognized gains or losses from the cancellation, lapse, expiration, or any other termination of a right or obligation with respect to personal property (other than stock) that is or would be a capital asset in the hands of the taxpayer are capital gains or losses.[4] See the discussion under Options later in the chapter for more details.

Worthless Securities

Occasionally, securities such as stock and, especially, bonds may become worthless due to the insolvency of their issuer. If such a security is a capital asset, the loss is deemed to have occurred as the result of a sale or exchange on the *last day* of the tax year.[5] This last-day rule may have the effect of converting what otherwise would have been a short-term capital loss into a long-term capital loss. See Treatment of Capital Losses later in this chapter.

Section 1244 allows an ordinary deduction on disposition of stock at a loss. The stock must be that of a small business company, and the ordinary deduction is limited to $50,000 ($100,000 for married individuals filing jointly) per year. For a more detailed discussion, refer to Chapter 7.

4. § 1234A.

5. § 165(g)(1).

Special Rule—Retirement of Corporate Obligations

A debt obligation (e.g., a bond or note payable) may have a tax basis in excess of or less than its redemption value because it may have been acquired at a premium or discount. Consequently, the collection of the redemption value may result in a loss or gain. Generally, the collection of a debt obligation is *not* a sale or exchange. Therefore, any loss or gain cannot be a capital loss or gain because no sale or exchange has taken place. However, if the debt obligation was issued by a corporation or certain government agencies, the collection of the redemption value is treated as a sale or exchange.[6]

EXAMPLE 9

Fran acquires $1,000 of XYZ Corporation bonds for $980 in the open market. If the bonds are held to maturity, the $20 difference between Fran's collection of the $1,000 maturity value and her cost of $980 is treated as capital gain. If the obligation had been issued to Fran by an individual instead of by a corporation, her $20 gain would be ordinary since she did not sell or exchange the debt. ◆

Options

Frequently, a potential buyer of property wants some time to make the purchase decision, but wants to control the sale and/or the sale price in the meantime. Options are used to achieve these objectives. The potential purchaser (grantee) pays the property owner (grantor) for an option on the property. The grantee then becomes the option holder. The option usually sets a price at which the grantee can buy the property and expires after a specified period of time.

Sale of an Option. A grantee may sell or exchange the option rather than exercising it or letting it expire. Generally, the grantee's sale or exchange of an option results in capital gain or loss if the option property is (or would be) a capital asset to the grantee.[7]

EXAMPLE 10

Rosa wants to buy some vacant land for investment purposes. She cannot afford the full purchase price. Instead, she convinces the landowner (grantor) to sell her the right to purchase the land for $100,000 anytime in the next two years. Rosa (grantee) pays $3,000 to obtain this option to buy the land. The option is a capital asset for her because if she actually purchased the land, the land would be a capital asset. Three months after purchasing the option, Rosa sells it for $7,000. She has a $4,000 short-term capital gain on this sale since she held the option for one year or less. ◆

Failure to Exercise Options. If an option holder (grantee) fails to exercise the option, the lapse of the option is considered a sale or exchange on the option expiration date. Thus, the loss is a capital loss if the property subject to the option is (or would be) a capital asset in the hands of the grantee.

The grantor of an option on stocks, securities, commodities, or commodity futures receives short-term capital gain treatment upon the expiration of the option. Options on property other than stocks, securities, commodities, or commodity futures result in ordinary income to the grantor when the option expires. For example, an individual investor who owns stock (a capital asset) may sell a call option, entitling the buyer of the option to acquire the stock at a

6. § 1271.

7. § 1234(a) and Reg. § 1.1234–1(a)(1). See the Glossary of Tax Terms in Appendix C for a definition of "stock options."

specified price higher than the value at the date the option is granted. The writer of the call receives a premium (e.g., 10 percent) for writing the option. If the price of the stock does not increase during the option period, the option will expire unexercised. Upon the expiration of the option, the grantor must recognize short-term capital gain. These provisions do not apply to options held for sale to customers (e.g., the inventory of a securities dealer).

Exercise of Options by Grantee. If the option is exercised, the amount paid for the option is added to the optioned property's selling price. This increases the gain (or reduces the loss) to the grantor resulting from the sale of the property. The grantor's gain or loss is capital or ordinary depending on the tax status of the property. The grantee adds the cost of the option to the basis of the property purchased.

EXAMPLE 11

On September 1, 1988, Wes purchases 100 shares of Robin Company stock for $5,000. On April 1, 1993, he writes a call option on the stock, giving the grantee the right to buy the stock for $6,000 during the following six-month period. Wes (the grantor) receives a call premium of $500 for writing the call.

- If the call is exercised by the grantee on August 1, 1993, Wes has $1,500 ($6,000 + $500 – $5,000) of long-term capital gain from the sale of the stock. The grantee has a $6,500 ($500 option premium + $6,000 purchase price) basis for the stock.
- Assume that Wes decides to sell his stock prior to exercise for $6,000 and enters into a closing transaction by purchasing a call on 100 shares of Robin Company stock for $5,000. Since the Robin stock is selling for $6,000, Wes must pay a call premium of $1,000. He recognizes a $500 short-term capital loss [$1,000 (call premium paid) – $500 (call premium received)] on the closing transaction. On the actual sale of the Robin stock, Wes has a long-term capital gain of $1,000 [$6,000 (selling price) – $5,000 (cost)]. The grantee is not affected by Wes's closing transaction. The original option is still in existence, and the grantee's tax consequences will depend on the action he or she takes—exercising the option, letting the option expire, or selling the option.
- Assume that the original option expired unexercised. Wes has a $500 short-term capital gain equal to the call premium received for writing the option. This gain is not recognized until the option expires. The grantee has a loss from expiration of the option. The nature of the loss will depend upon whether the option was a capital asset or an ordinary asset. ◆

Patents

Rationale for Capital Gain Treatment. The sale of a patent may result in long-term capital gain treatment whether the patent is a capital asset or not.[8] The encouragement of technological progress is the primary reason for this provision. Ironically, authors, composers, and artists are not eligible for capital gain treatment on their creations because such works are not capital assets. The Code allows special treatment for patents, but not for copyrights. Presumably, Congress chose not to use the tax law to encourage cultural endeavors. The following example illustrates the special treatment for patents.

EXAMPLE 12

Mei-Yen, a druggist, invents a pill-counting machine, which she patents. In consideration of a lump-sum payment of $200,000 plus $10 per machine sold, she assigns the

8. § 1235.

patent to Drug Products, Inc. Assuming Mei-Yen has transferred all substantial rights, the question of whether the transfer is a sale or exchange of a capital asset is not relevant. She automatically has a long-term capital gain from both the lump-sum payment and the $10 per machine royalty to the extent these proceeds exceed her basis for the patent. ◆

Statutory Requirements. The following are key issues for the transfer of patent rights:

- Whether the patent is a capital asset.
- Whether the transfer is a sale or exchange.
- Whether all substantial rights to the patent (or an undivided interest in it) are transferred.

Section 1235 resolves whether the transfer is a sale or exchange of a capital asset. The statute provides that

> a transfer ... of property consisting of all substantial rights to a patent, or an undivided interest therein which includes a part of all such rights, by any holder shall be considered the sale or exchange of a capital asset held for [the long-term holding period], regardless of whether or not payments in consideration of such transfer are (1) payable periodically over a period generally coterminous with the transferee's use of the patent, or (2) contingent on the productivity, use, or disposition of the property transferred.[9]

If the transfer meets the requirements, any gain or loss is *automatically* a long-term capital gain or loss regardless of whether the patent is a capital asset,

CONCEPT SUMMARY 13–1
OPTIONS

Event	Effect on Grantor	Effect on Grantee
Option is granted.	Receives value and has a contract obligation (a liability).	Pays value and has a contract right (an asset).
Option expires.	Has a short-term capital gain if the option property is stocks, securities, commodities, or commodity futures. Otherwise, gain is ordinary income.	Has a loss (capital loss if option property would have been a capital asset for the grantee).
Option is exercised.	Amount received for option increases proceeds from sale of the option property.	Amount paid for option becomes part of basis of the option property purchased.
Option is sold or exchanged by grantee.	Result depends upon whether option later expires or is exercised (see above).	Could have gain or loss (capital gain or loss if option property would have been a capital asset for the grantee).

9. § 1235(a) and Reg. § 1.1235–1(a).

whether the transfer is a sale or exchange, or how long the patent was held by the transferor.

Substantial Rights. To receive favorable capital gain treatment, all *substantial rights* to the patent (or an undivided interest in it) must be transferred. All substantial rights to a patent means all rights (whether or not then held by the grantor) that are valuable at the time the patent rights (or an undivided interest in the patent) are transferred. All substantial rights have not been transferred when the transfer is limited geographically within the issuing country or is for a period that is less than the remaining life of the patent.[10] The circumstances of the entire transaction, rather than merely the language used in the transfer instrument, are to be considered in deciding whether all substantial rights have been transferred.

EXAMPLE 13

Assume Mei-Yen, the druggist in Example 12, only licensed Drug Products, Inc., to manufacture and sell the invention in Michigan. She retained the right to license the machine elsewhere in the United States. Mei-Yen has retained a substantial right and is not eligible for automatic long-term capital gain treatment. ◆

Holder Defined. The *holder* of a patent must be an *individual* and usually is the creator of the invention. A holder may also be an individual who purchases the patent rights from the creator before the patented invention is reduced to practice. However, the creator's employer and certain parties related to the creator do not qualify as holders. Thus, in the common situation where an employer has all rights to an employee's inventions, the employer is not eligible for long-term capital gain treatment. More than likely, the employer will have an ordinary asset because the patent was developed as part of its business.

Franchises, Trademarks, and Trade Names

A mode of operation, a widely recognized brand name (trade name), and a widely known business symbol (trademark) are all valuable assets. These assets may be licensed (commonly known as franchising) by their owner for use by other businesses. Many fast-food restaurants are franchises. The franchisee usually pays the owner (franchisor) an initial fee plus a contingent fee. The contingent fee is often based upon the franchisee's sales volume.

For Federal income tax purposes, a *franchise* is an agreement that gives the franchisee the right to distribute, sell, or provide goods, services, or facilities within a specified area.[11] A franchise transfer includes granting a franchise, transfers by one franchisee to another person, or renewal of a franchise.

A franchise transfer is generally not a sale or exchange of a capital asset. Section 1253 provides that

> a transfer of a franchise, trademark, or trade name shall not be treated as a sale or exchange of a capital asset if the transferor retains any significant power, right, or continuing interest with respect to the subject matter of the [transfer].

Significant Power, Right, or Continuing Interest. *Significant powers, rights, or continuing interests* include control over assignment, quality of products and services, sale or advertising of other products or services, and the right to require

10. Reg. § 1.1235–2(b)(1).

11. § 1253(b)(1).

that substantially all supplies and equipment be purchased from the transferor. Also included are the right to terminate the franchise at will and the right to substantial contingent payments. Most modern franchising operations involve some or all of these powers, rights, or continuing interests.

In the unusual case where no significant power, right, or continuing interest is retained by the transferor, a sale or exchange may occur, and capital gain or loss treatment may be available. For capital gain or loss treatment to be available, the asset transferred must qualify as a capital asset.

Example 14

Orange, Inc., a franchisee, sells the franchise to a third party. Payments to Orange are not contingent, and all significant powers, rights, and continuing interests are transferred. The gain on the sale (payments – adjusted basis) is a capital gain to Orange. ◆

Noncontingent Payments. When the transferor retains a significant power, right, or continuing interest, the transferee's noncontingent payments to the transferor will be ordinary income to the transferor. The payments will be deductible by the transferee as ordinary deductions. However, the timing of the deduction will depend upon the form of the payment.

A noncontingent payment up to $100,000 is capitalized and may be amortized by the franchisee over the shorter of the franchise period or 10 years. The payment period is not relevant to the "shorter of" determination since only the *franchise period* and 10 years are compared. Payment may be made in a lump sum or be spread out over several payments that comprise part of the total to be paid. Noncontingent payments exceeding $100,000 must be capitalized and may be amortized over 25 years. Both types of amortization are subject to recapture as ordinary income under § 1245.

Example 15

Gray Company signs a 15-year franchise agreement with DOH Donuts. Gray (the franchisee) makes payments of $3,000 per year for the first 8 years of the franchise agreement—a total of $24,000. Gray cannot deduct $3,000 per year as the payments are made. Instead, Gray may amortize the $24,000 total over 10 years since that is shorter than the 15-year franchise period. Thus, Gray may deduct $2,400 per year for each of the first 10 years of the franchise period. The same result would occur if Gray made a $24,000 lump-sum payment at the beginning of the franchise period. Assuming DOH Donuts (the franchisor) retains significant powers, rights, or a continuing interest, it will have ordinary income when it receives the payments from Gray. ◆

Contingent Payments. Whether or not the transferor retains a significant power, right, or continuing interest, contingent franchise payments are ordinary income for the franchisor and an ordinary deduction for the franchisee. For this purpose, a payment qualifies as a contingent payment only if the following requirements are met:

- The contingent amounts are paid as part of a series of payments that are paid at least annually throughout the term of the transfer agreement.
- The payments are substantially equal in amount or are payable under a fixed formula.

Example 16

TAK, a spicy chicken franchisor, transfers an eight-year franchise to Otis. TAK retains a significant power, right, or continuing interest. Otis, the franchisee, agrees to pay TAK

15% of sales. This contingent payment is ordinary income to TAK and a business deduction for Otis as the payments are made. ◆

Sports Franchises. Professional sports franchises (e.g., the Chicago Bulls) are not covered by § 1253.[12] However, § 1056 restricts the allocation of sports franchise acquisition costs to player contracts. Player contracts are usually one of the major assets acquired with a sports franchise. These contracts last only for the time stated in the contract. Therefore, owners of sports franchises would like to allocate franchise acquisition costs disproportionately to the contracts so that the acquisition costs will be amortizable over the contracts' lives. Section 1056 prevents this by generally limiting the amount that can be allocated to player contracts to no more than 50 percent of the franchise acquisition cost. In addition, the seller of a sports franchise has ordinary income under § 1245 for the portion of the gain allocable to the disposition of player contracts.[13]

Lease Cancellation Payments

The tax treatment of payments received for canceling a lease depends on whether the recipient is the lessor or the lessee and whether the lease is a capital asset or not.[14]

Lessee Treatment. Lease cancellation payments received by a lessee are treated as an exchange.[15] Thus, these payments will be capital gains if the lease is a capital asset or ordinary income if the asset is an ordinary asset. Generally, a lessee's lease is a capital asset if the property (either personalty or realty) is used for the lessee's personal use (e.g., as his or her residence). A lessee's lease is an ordinary asset if the property is used in the lessee's trade or business.[16]

EXAMPLE 17

Mark owns an apartment building that he is going to convert into an office building. Vicki is one of the apartment tenants and receives $1,000 from Mark to cancel the lease. Vicki has a capital gain of $1,000 (which will be long term or short term depending upon how long she has held the lease). Mark has an ordinary deduction of $1,000. ◆

Lessor Treatment. Payments received by a lessor for a lease cancellation are always ordinary income because they are considered to be in lieu of rental payments.[17]

EXAMPLE 18

Floyd owns an apartment building near a university campus. Hvi-Fen, one of the tenants, is graduating early and offers Floyd $800 to cancel the lease. Floyd accepts the offer. Floyd has ordinary income of $800. Hvi-Fen has a nondeductible payment since the apartment was personal use property. ◆

---

12. § 1253(e).
13. See the discussion of recapture provisions later in the chapter.
14. See the Glossary of Tax Terms in Appendix C for definitions of the terms "lessor" and "lessee."
15. § 1241 and Reg. § 1.1241–1(a).
16. Reg. § 1.1221–1(a).
17. *Hort v. Comm.*, 41–1 USTC ¶9354, 25 AFTR 1207, 61 S.Ct. 757 (USSC, 1941).

HOLDING PERIOD

Property must be held more than one year to qualify for long-term capital gain or loss treatment.[18] Property not held for the required long-term period will result in short-term capital gain or loss. To compute the holding period, start counting on the day after the property was acquired and include the day of disposition.

EXAMPLE 19

Marge purchases a capital asset on January 15, 1992, and sells it on January 16, 1993. Marge's holding period is more than one year. If Marge had sold the asset on January 15, 1993, the holding period would have been exactly one year, and the gain or loss would have been short term. ◆

To be held for more than a year, a capital asset acquired on the last day of any month must not be disposed of until on or after the first day of the thirteenth succeeding month.[19]

EXAMPLE 20

Leo purchases a capital asset on February 28, 1992. If Leo sells the asset on February 28, 1993, the holding period is one year, and he will have a short-term capital gain or loss. If Leo sells the asset on March 1, 1993, the holding period is more than one year, and he will have a long-term capital gain or loss. If he sells the asset on February 29, 1993, the holding period is short term because the asset was purchased on the last day of a month and was not disposed of on or after the first day of the thirteenth succeeding month. ◆

Review of Special Holding Period Rules

There are several special holding period rules.[20] The application of these rules depends on the type of asset and how it was acquired.

Nontaxable Exchanges. The holding period of property received in a like-kind exchange includes the holding period of the former asset if the property that has been exchanged is a capital asset or a § 1231 asset. In certain nontaxable transactions involving a substituted basis, the holding period of the former property is *tacked on* to the holding period of the newly acquired property.

EXAMPLE 21

Vern exchanges a business truck for another truck in a like-kind exchange. The holding period of the exchanged truck tacks on to the holding period of the new truck. ◆

EXAMPLE 22

Alicia sells her personal residence and acquires a new residence. If the transaction qualifies for nonrecognition of gain on the sale of a residence, the holding period of the new residence includes the holding period of the former residence. ◆

Certain Nontaxable Transactions Involving a Carryover of Another Taxpayer's Basis. A former owner's holding period is tacked on to the present owner's

18. § 1222.
19. Rev.Rul. 66–7, 1966–1 C.B. 188.
20. § 1223.

holding period if the transaction is nontaxable and the basis of the property to the former owner carries over to the new owner.

EXAMPLE 23

Kareem acquires 100 shares of GHI Corporation stock for $1,000 on December 31, 1989. He transfers the shares by gift to Megan on December 31, 1992, when the stock is worth $2,000. Megan's holding period begins with the date the stock was acquired by Kareem. Kareem's basis of $1,000 becomes the basis for determining gain or loss on a subsequent sale by Megan. ◆

EXAMPLE 24

Assume the same facts as in Example 23, except that the fair market value of the shares is only $800 on the date of the gift. The holding period begins on the date of the gift if Megan sells the stock for a loss. The value of the shares at the date of the gift is used in the determination of basis. If she sells the shares for $500 on April 1, 1993, Megan has a $300 recognized capital loss, and the holding period is from December 31, 1992, to April 1, 1993 (thus, the loss is short term). ◆

Certain Disallowed Loss Transactions. Under several Code provisions, realized losses are disallowed. When a loss is disallowed, the holding period does not carry over. Losses can be disallowed under § 267 (sale or exchange between related taxpayers), § 707(b)(1) (sale or exchange involving controlled partnerships), and § 262 (sale or exchange of personal use assets) as well as other Code sections. When taxpayers acquire property in a disallowed loss transaction, a new holding period begins, and their basis is equal to the purchase price.

EXAMPLE 25

Janet sells her personal residence at a loss. She may not deduct the loss because it arises from the sale of personal use property. Janet purchases a replacement residence for more than the selling price of her former residence. She has a basis equal to the cost of the replacement residence, and her holding period begins when she acquires the replacement residence. ◆

Inherited Property. The holding period for inherited property is treated as long term no matter how long the property is actually held by the heir. The holding period of the decedent or the decedent's estate is not relevant for determining the heir's holding period.

EXAMPLE 26

Shandra inherits Blue Company stock from her father. She receives the stock on April 1, 1993, and sells it on November 1, 1993. Even though the stock was not held more than one year, Shandra receives long-term capital gain or loss treatment on the sale. ◆

Special Rules for Short Sales

The holding period of property sold short is determined under special rules provided in § 1233. A *short sale* occurs when a taxpayer sells borrowed property and repays the lender with substantially identical property either held on the date of the sale or purchased after the sale. Short sales usually involve corporate stock. The seller's objective is to make a profit in anticipation of a decline in the price of the stock. If the price declines, the seller in a short sale recognizes a profit equal to the difference between the sales price of the borrowed stock and the price paid for the replacement stock.

A *short sale against the box* occurs when the stock is borrowed from a broker by a seller who already owns the same stock. The *box* is the safe deposit box where stock owners routinely used to keep stock certificates. Although today stockbrokers generally keep stock certificates for their customers, the terminology short sale against the box is still used.

Example 27

Chris does not own any shares of Brown Corporation. However, he sells 30 shares of Brown. The shares are borrowed from Chris's broker and must be replaced within 45 days. Chris has a short sale because he was short the shares he sold. He will *close* the short sale by purchasing Brown shares and delivering them to his broker. If the original 30 shares were sold for $10,000 and Chris later purchases 30 shares for $8,000, he will have a gain of $2,000. Chris's hunch that the price of Brown stock would decline was correct. He was able to profit from selling high and buying low. If Chris had to purchase Brown shares for $13,000 to close the short sale, he would have a loss of $3,000. In this case, Chris has sold low and bought high—not the result he wanted! Chris also would be making a short sale against the box if he borrowed shares from his broker to sell and then closed the short sale by delivering other Brown shares he owned at the time he made the short sale. ◆

A short sale gain or loss is a capital gain or loss to the extent that the short sale property constitutes a capital asset of the taxpayer. The gain or loss is not recognized until the short sale is closed. Generally, the holding period of the short sale property is determined by how long the property used to close the short sale was held. However, if the taxpayer holds *substantially identical property* (e.g., other shares of the same stock), the short-term or long-term character of the short sale gain or loss may be affected:

- If substantially identical property has *not* been held for the long-term holding period on the short sale date, the short sale *gain or loss* is short term.
- If substantially identical property has *been* held for the long-term holding period on the short sale date, the short sale *gain* is long term if the substantially identical property is used to close the short sale and short term if the property is not used to close the short sale.
- If substantially identical property has *been* held for the long-term holding period on the short sale date, the short sale *loss* is long term whether or not the substantially identical property is used to close the short sale.
- If substantially identical property is acquired *after* the short sale date and on or before the closing date, the short sale *gain or loss* is short term.

Concept Summary 13–2 summarizes the short sale rules.

The short sale rules are intended to prevent the conversion of short-term capital gains into long-term capital gains and long-term capital losses into short-term capital losses. The following examples illustrate the application of the short sale rules.

Example 28

On January 4, 1993, Donald purchases five shares of Gold Corporation common stock for $100. On April 14, 1993, he engages in a short sale of five shares of the same stock for $150. On August 15, Donald closes the short sale by repaying the borrowed stock with the five shares purchased on January 4. He has a $50 short-term capital gain from the short sale because he had not held substantially identical shares for the long-term holding period on the short sale date. ◆

Example 29

Assume the same facts as in the previous example, except that Donald closes the short sale on January 30, 1994, by repaying the borrowed stock with five shares purchased on January 29, 1994, for $200. The stock used to close the short sale was not the property purchased on January 4, 1993, but since Donald held short-term property at the April 14, 1993, short sale date, the gain or loss from closing the short sale is short term. He has a $50 short-term loss ($200 cost of stock purchased January 29, 1994, and a short sale selling price of $150). ◆

Example 30

Assume the same facts as in the previous example. On January 31, 1994, Donald sells for $200 the stock purchased January 4, 1993. His holding period for that stock begins January 30, 1994, because the holding period portion of the short sale rules applies to

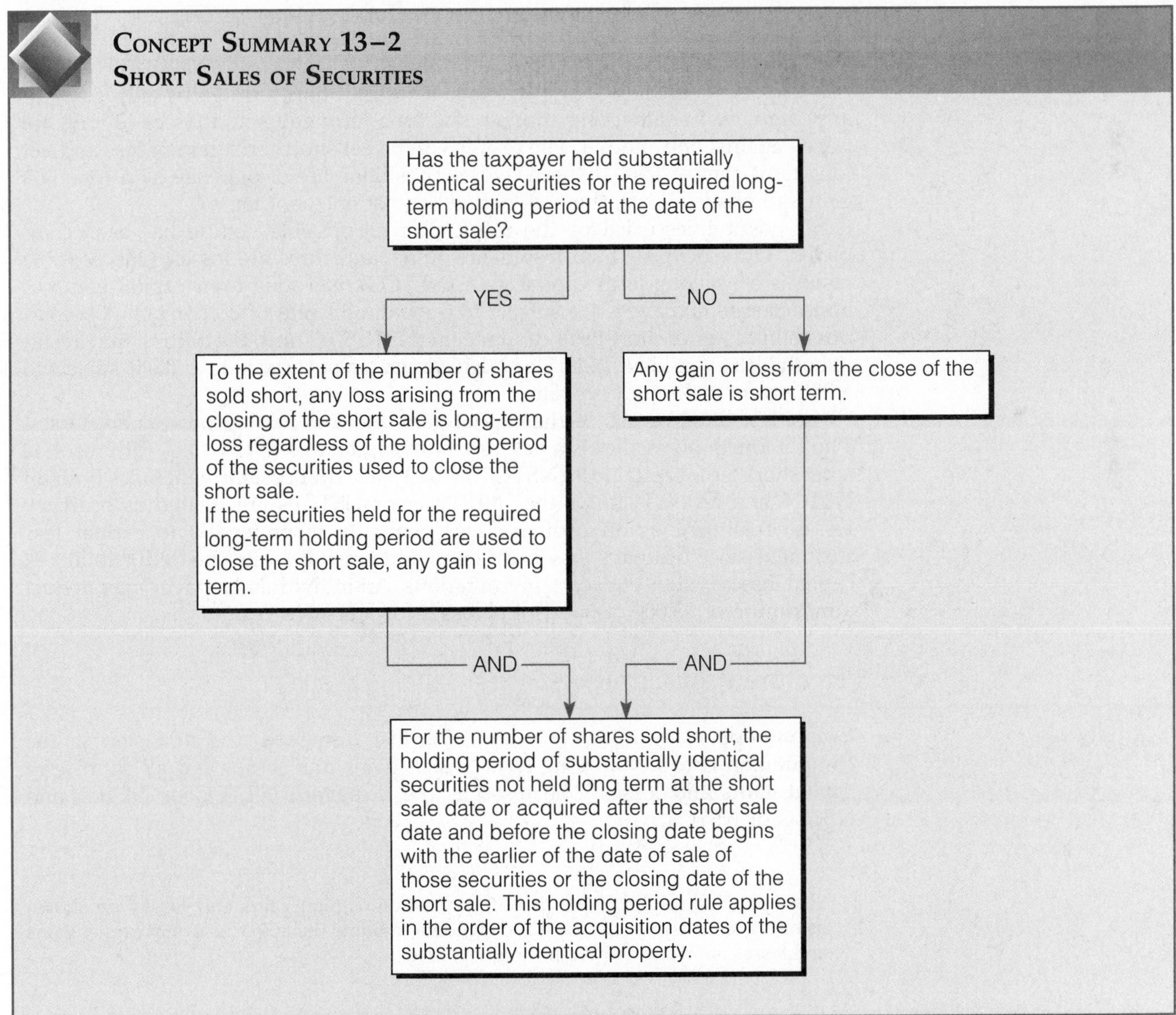
Concept Summary 13–2
Short Sales of Securities
Has the taxpayer held substantially identical securities for the required long-term holding period at the date of the short sale?
YES
NO
To the extent of the number of shares sold short, any loss arising from the closing of the short sale is long-term loss regardless of the holding period of the securities used to close the short sale.
If the securities held for the required long-term holding period are used to close the short sale, any gain is long term.
Any gain or loss from the close of the short sale is short term.
AND
AND
For the number of shares sold short, the holding period of substantially identical securities not held long term at the short sale date or acquired after the short sale date and before the closing date begins with the earlier of the date of sale of those securities or the closing date of the short sale. This holding period rule applies in the order of the acquisition dates of the substantially identical property.

the substantially identical property in order of acquisition. Donald has a short-term gain of $100 ($100 cost of stock purchased January 4, 1993, and a selling price of $200). ◆

EXAMPLE 31

On January 2, 1993, Rita purchases five shares of Gold Corporation common stock for $100. She purchases five more shares of the same stock on April 14, 1993, for $200. On January 17, 1994, she sells short five shares of the same stock for $150. On September 30, 1994, she repays the borrowed stock with the five shares purchased on April 14, 1993, and sells the five shares purchased on January 2, 1993, for $200. Rita has a $50 long-term capital loss from the short sale because she held substantially identical shares for more than one year on the date of the short sale. Rita has a $100 long-term capital gain from the sale of the shares purchased on January 2, 1993. ◆

TAX TREATMENT OF CAPITAL GAINS AND LOSSES OF NONCORPORATE TAXPAYERS

All taxpayers net their capital gains and losses. Short-term gains and losses (if any) are netted against one another, and long-term gains and losses (if any) are netted against one another. The results will be net short-term gain or loss and net long-term gain or loss. If these two net positions are of opposite sign (one is a gain and one is a loss), they are netted against one another.

Six possibilities exist for the result after all possible netting has been completed. Three of these final results are gains, and three are losses. One possible result is a net long-term capital gain (NLTCG). Net long-term capital gains of noncorporate taxpayers are subject to a maximum rate of 28 percent. A second possibility is a net short-term capital gain (NSTCG). Third, the netting may result in both NLTCG and NSTCG. The NLTCG portion of these net results is subject to a 28 percent maximum tax rate.

The last three results of the capital gain and loss netting process are losses. Thus, a fourth possibility is a net long-term capital loss (NLTCL). A fifth result is a net short-term capital loss (NSTCL). Finally, a sixth possibility includes both an NLTCL and an NSTCL. Neither NLTCLs nor NSTCLs are treated as ordinary losses. Treatment as an ordinary loss generally is preferable to capital loss treatment since ordinary losses are deductible in full while the deductibility of capital losses is subject to certain limitations. An individual taxpayer may deduct a maximum of $3,000 of net capital losses for a taxable year.[21]

Treatment of Capital Gains

Computation of Net Capital Gain. As just discussed, the first step in the computation is to net all long-term capital gains and losses and all short-term capital gains and losses. The result is the taxpayer's NLTCG or NLTCL and NSTCG or NSTCL.

EXAMPLE 32

Some possible results of the *first step* in netting capital gains and losses are shown below. Assume that each case is independent (assume the taxpayer's only capital gains and losses are those shown in the given case).

21. § 1211(b).

Case	STCG	STCL	LTCG	LTCL	Result of Netting	Description of Result
A	$8,000	($5,000)			$ 3,000	NSTCG
B	2,000	(7,000)			(5,000)	NSTCL
C			$9,000	($1,000)	8,000	NLTCG
D			8,800	(9,800)	(1,000)	NLTCL

◆

The *second step* in netting capital gains and losses requires offsetting any positive and negative amounts that remain after the first netting step. This procedure is illustrated in the following examples.

EXAMPLE 33

Assume that Sanjay had all the capital gains and losses specified in Cases B and C in Example 32:

Case C ($9,000 LTCG – $1,000 LTCL)	$ 8,000	NLTCG
Case B ($2,000 STCG – $7,000 STCL)	(5,000)	NSTCL
Excess of NLTCG over NSTCL	$ 3,000	NCG

◆

The excess of NLTCG over NSTCL is defined as *net capital gain (NCG).* There is a $3,000 net capital gain (NCG) in Example 33.

Alternative Tax on NCG. When taxable income includes NCG, an alternative tax computation is available. This computation taxes the NCG component of taxable income at a maximum tax rate of 28 percent. When taxable income including the NCG does not put the taxpayer into the 31 percent rate bracket, the alternative tax computation does not yield a tax benefit.

The *NCG alternative tax* is the summation of the following computations. It is illustrated in Example 34.

1. The tax computed using the regular rates on the greater of:
   a. Taxable income less the NCG, or
   b. The amount of taxable income taxed at a rate below 28 percent, plus
2. Twenty-eight percent of taxable income in excess of taxable income used in (1).

EXAMPLE 34

Tim, an unmarried taxpayer, has taxable income (TI) of $175,000. The TI includes NCG of $50,000. Tim's regular tax liability for 1993 is $49,772 [($22,100 × 15%) + 28%($53,500 – $22,100) + 31%($175,000 – $53,500)]. His alternative tax on the NCG is calculated as follows:

1. Tax on greater of:	
a. TI less NCG ($175,000 – $50,000)	$34,272
b. TI taxed below 28% ($22,100), plus	
2. 28% of TI exceeding TI used in (1) [28% × ($175,000 – $125,000)]	14,000
Alternative tax on TI including NCG	$48,272

The NCG alternative tax saves Tim $1,500 ($49,772 – $48,272) in 1993. ◆

EXAMPLE 35

Assume that Nora had all the capital gains and losses specified in Cases A and D in Example 32:

Case A ($8,000 STCG – $5,000 STCL)	$ 3,000	NSTCG
Case D ($8,800 LTCG – $9,800 LTCL)	(1,000)	NLTCL
Excess of NSTCG over NLTCL	$ 2,000	

◆

There is no special name for the excess of NSTCG over NLTCL, nor is there any special tax treatment. The nature of the gain is short term, and the gain is treated the same as ordinary gain and is included in Nora's gross income.

Treatment of Capital Losses

Computation of Net Capital Loss. A *net capital loss (NCL)* results if capital losses exceed capital gains for the year. An NCL may be all long term, all short term, or part long and part short term.[22] The characterization of an NCL as long or short term is important in determining the capital loss deduction (discussed later in this chapter).

EXAMPLE 36

Three different individual taxpayers have the following capital gains and losses during the year:

Taxpayer	LTCG	LTCL	STCG	STCL	Result of Netting	Description of Result
Robert	$1,000	($2,800)	$1,000	($500)	($1,300)	NLTCL
Carlos	1,000	(500)	1,000	(2,800)	(1,300)	NSTCL
Troy	400	(1,200)	500	(1,200)	(1,500)	NLTCL ($800)
						NSTCL ($700)

Robert's NCL of $1,300 is all long term. Carlos's NCL of $1,300 is all short term. Troy's NCL is $1,500, $800 of which is long term and $700 of which is short term. ◆

Treatment of Net Capital Loss. An NCL is deductible from gross income to the extent of $3,000 per tax year.[23] Capital losses exceeding the loss deduction limits may be carried forward indefinitely.[24] Notice that NCG is taxed at a maximum rate of 28 percent, but NCL is deductible only to the extent of $3,000. Thus, although there may or may not be beneficial treatment for capital gains, capital losses receive *unfavorable* treatment in terms of the $3,000 annual limitation on deducting NCL against ordinary income. If the NCL includes both long-term and short-term capital loss, the short-term capital loss is counted first toward the $3,000 annual limitation.

---

22. Section 1222(10) defines an NCL as the net loss after the capital loss deduction. However, that definition confuses the discussion of NCL. Therefore, NCL is used here to mean the result after netting capital gains and losses and before considering the capital loss deduction. The capital loss deduction is discussed under Treatment of Net Capital Loss in this chapter.

23. § 1211(b)(1). Married persons filing separate returns are limited to a $1,500 deduction per taxable year.

24. § 1212(b).

Example 37

Burt has an NCL of $5,000, of which $2,000 is STCL and $3,000 is LTCL. He has a capital loss deduction of $3,000 ($2,000 of STCL and $1,000 of LTCL) with an LTCL carryforward of $2,000. ◆

Carryovers. Taxpayers are allowed to carry over unused capital losses indefinitely. The STCL and LTCL carried over retain their character as STCL or LTCL.

Example 38

In 1992, Yoon incurred $1,000 of STCL and $11,000 of LTCL. In 1993, he has a $400 LTCG.

- Yoon's NCL for 1992 is $12,000. He deducts $3,000 ($1,000 STCL and $2,000 LTCL). Yoon has $9,000 of LTCL carried forward to 1993.
- Yoon combines the $9,000 LTCL carryforward with the $400 LTCG for 1993. He has an $8,600 NLTCL for 1993. He deducts $3,000 of LTCL in 1993 and carries forward $5,600 of LTCL to 1994. ◆

When a taxpayer has both a capital loss deduction and negative taxable income, a special computation of the capital loss carryover is required. Specifically, the capital loss carryover is the NCL minus the lesser of the following:

- The capital loss deduction claimed on the return.
- The negative taxable income increased by the capital loss deduction claimed on the return and the personal and dependency exemption deduction.

Without this provision, some of the tax benefit of the capital loss deduction would be wasted when the deduction drives taxable income below zero.

Example 39

In 1993, Joanne has a $13,000 NCL (all long term), a $2,350 personal exemption deduction, and $4,000 negative taxable income. The negative taxable income includes a $3,000 capital loss deduction. The capital loss carryover to 1994 is $11,650 computed as follows:

Concept Summary 13–3
Noncorporate Taxpayer's Treatment of Net Capital Gain or Loss

Net Capital Gain Treatment Summarized	
1. All long-term capital gain	28% alternative tax is available, but is not always beneficial.
2. All short-term capital gain	Taxable as ordinary income.
3. Part long-term and part short-term capital gain	Short-term capital gain portion taxable as ordinary income. 28% alternative tax is available for long-term capital gain portion, but is not always beneficial.
Net Capital Loss Treatment Summarized	
4. All long-term capital loss	Deduction is *for* AGI and limited to $3,000 per year. Portion of loss not used carries forward indefinitely.
5. All short-term capital loss	Deduction is *for* AGI and limited to $3,000 per year. Portion of loss not used carries forward indefinitely.
6. Part long-term and part short-term capital loss	Short-term losses used first to make $3,000 deduction.

- The $4,000 negative taxable income is treated as a negative number, but the capital loss deduction and personal exemption deduction are treated as positive numbers.
- $13,000 – the lesser of $3,000 (capital loss deduction) or $1,350 [– $4,000 (negative taxable income) + $3,000 (capital loss deduction) + $2,350 (personal exemption deduction)] = $13,000 – $1,350 = $11,650 carryover. ◆

TAX TREATMENT OF CAPITAL GAINS AND LOSSES OF CORPORATE TAXPAYERS

The treatment of a corporation's net capital gain or loss differs from the rules for individuals. Briefly, the differences are as follows:

- There is an NCG alternative tax rate of 34 percent. However, since the maximum corporate tax rate is 34 percent, the alternative tax is not beneficial.
- Capital losses offset only capital gains. Capital losses cannot be deducted against ordinary taxable income (whereas individuals are allowed a $3,000 deduction).[25]
- There is a three-year carryback and a five-year carryover period for NCLs.[26] Corporate carryovers and carrybacks are always treated as short term, regardless of their original nature.

EXAMPLE 40

Gray Corporation has a $15,000 NLTCL for the current year and $57,000 of ordinary taxable income. Gray may not offset the $15,000 NLTCL against its ordinary income by taking a capital loss deduction. The $15,000 NLTCL becomes a $15,000 STCL for carryback and carryover purposes. This amount may be offset by capital gains in the three-year carryback period or, if not absorbed there, offset by capital gains in the five-year carryforward period. ◆

The rules applicable to corporations are discussed in greater detail in Chapter 16.

SECTION 1231 ASSETS

Relationship to Capital Assets

Depreciable personal property and real property used in business are not capital assets. Thus, the recognized gains from the disposition of such property (principally machinery, equipment, buildings, and land) would appear to be ordinary income rather than capital gain. Due to § 1231, however, *net gain* from the disposition of such property is sometimes *treated* as *long-term capital gain.* A long-term holding period requirement must be met; the disposition must generally be from a sale, exchange, or involuntary conversion; and certain recapture provisions must be satisfied for this result to occur. Section 1231 may

25. § 1211(a).

26. § 1212(a)(1).

also apply to involuntary conversions of capital assets. Since an involuntary conversion is not a sale or exchange, such a disposition would not normally result in a capital gain.

If the disposition of depreciable property and real property used in business results in a *net loss*, § 1231 treats the loss as an *ordinary loss* rather than as a capital loss. Ordinary losses are fully deductible *for* adjusted gross income (AGI). Capital losses are offset by capital gains, and, if any loss remains, the loss is deductible to the extent of $3,000 per year for individuals and is not deductible in the loss year by regular corporations. It seems, therefore, that § 1231 provides the *best* of both potential results: net gain may be treated as long-term capital gain, and net loss is treated as ordinary loss.

EXAMPLE 41

Roberto sells business land and building at a $5,000 gain and business equipment at a $3,000 loss. Both properties were held for the long-term holding period. Roberto's net gain is $2,000, and that net gain may (depending on various recapture rules discussed later in this chapter) be treated as a long-term capital gain under § 1231. ◆

EXAMPLE 42

Samantha sells business equipment at a $10,000 loss and business land at a $2,000 gain. Both properties were held for the long-term holding period. Samantha's net loss is $8,000, and that net loss is an ordinary loss. ◆

The rules regarding § 1231 treatment do not apply to *all* business property. Important in this regard are the holding period requirements and the fact that the property must be either depreciable property or real estate used in business. Nor is § 1231 necessarily limited to business property. Transactions involving certain capital assets may fall into the § 1231 category. Thus, § 1231 singles out only some types of business property.

As discussed previously, for 1991 and later years, there is a beneficial tax rate for long-term capital gains. Section 1231 requires netting of § 1231 gains and losses. If the result is a gain, it may be treated as a long-term capital gain. The net gain is added to the "real" long-term capital gains (if any) and netted with capital losses (if any). Thus, the net § 1231 gain may eventually be taxed at the alternative long-term capital gain rate or help avoid the unfavorable net capital loss result. The § 1231 gain and loss netting may result in a loss. In this case, the loss is an ordinary loss and is deductible *for* AGI. Finally, § 1231 assets are treated the same as capital assets for purposes of the appreciated property charitable contribution provisions (refer to Chapter 10).

Justification for Favorable Tax Treatment

The favorable capital gain/ordinary loss treatment sanctioned by § 1231 can be explained by examining several historical developments. Before 1938, business property was included in the definition of capital assets. Thus, if such property was sold for a loss (not an unlikely possibility during the depression years), a capital loss resulted. If, however, the property was depreciable and could be retained for its estimated useful life, much (if not all) of its costs could be recovered in the form of depreciation. Because the allowance for depreciation was fully deductible whereas capital losses were not, the tax law favored those who did not dispose of an asset. Congress recognized this inequity when it removed business property from the capital asset classification. During the period 1938–1942, therefore, all such gains and losses were ordinary gains and losses.

With the advent of World War II, two developments in particular forced Congress to reexamine the situation regarding business assets. First, the sale of business assets at a gain was discouraged because the gain would be ordinary income. Gains were common because the war effort had inflated prices. Second, taxpayers who did not want to sell their assets often were required to because of government acquisitions through condemnation. Often the condemnation awards resulted in large gains to the taxpayers who were forced to part with their property and deprived them of the benefits of future depreciation deductions. Of course, the condemnations constituted involuntary conversions, the gain from which could be deferred through timely reinvestment in property that was "similar or related in service or use." But where was such property to be found in view of wartime restrictions and other governmental condemnations? The end product did not seem equitable: a large ordinary gain due to government action and no possibility of deferral due to government restrictions.

In recognition of these conditions, in 1942 Congress eased the tax bite on the disposition of some business property by allowing preferential capital gain treatment. Thus, the present scheme of § 1231 and the dichotomy of capital gain/ordinary loss treatment evolved from a combination of economic considerations existing in 1938 and 1942.

Property Included

Section 1231 property includes the following:

- Depreciable or real property used in business or for the production of income (principally machinery and equipment, buildings, and land).
- Timber, coal, or domestic iron ore to which § 631 applies.
- Livestock held for draft, breeding, dairy, or sporting purposes.
- Unharvested crops on land used in business.
- Certain nonpersonal use capital assets.

Property Excluded

Section 1231 property does *not* include the following:

- Property not held for the long-term holding period. Since the benefit of § 1231 is long-term capital gain treatment, the holding period must correspond to the more-than-one-year holding period that applies to capital assets. Livestock must be held at least 12 months (24 months in some cases). Unharvested crops do not have to be held for the required long-term holding period, but the land must be held for the long-term holding period.
- Property where casualty losses exceed casualty gains for the taxable year. If a taxpayer has a net casualty loss, the individual casualty gains and losses are treated as ordinary gains and losses.
- Inventory and property held primarily for sale to customers.
- Copyrights; literary, musical, or artistic compositions, etc.; and certain U.S. government publications.
- Intangible assets such as accounts receivable and notes receivable.

Special Rules for Nonpersonal Use Capital Assets

Nonpersonal use property disposed of by casualty or theft may receive § 1231 treatment. Nonpersonal use property includes capital assets held for the production of income, such as an investment painting or investment land. Nonpersonal use property also includes business property. The casualty or theft *long-term* gains and losses from nonpersonal use property are combined (see Concept Summary 13–4). If the result is a gain, the gains and losses are treated as § 1231 transactions. If the result is a loss, § 1231 does not apply. Instead, the gains are treated as ordinary (even though some of them may initially be capital gains), the business losses are deductible *for* AGI, and the other losses (even though some of them may initially be capital losses) are deductible *from* AGI as miscellaneous losses subject to the 2 percent-of-AGI limitation. Thus, a nonpersonal use capital asset that is disposed of by casualty or theft may or may not be a § 1231 asset, depending on the result of the netting process. For simplicity, the rest of this chapter will use the term *casualty* to mean casualty *or* theft.

Personal use property casualty gains and losses are not subject to the § 1231 rules. If the result of netting these gains and losses is a gain, the net gain is a capital gain. If the netting results in a loss, the net loss is a deduction *from* AGI to the extent it exceeds 10 percent of AGI.

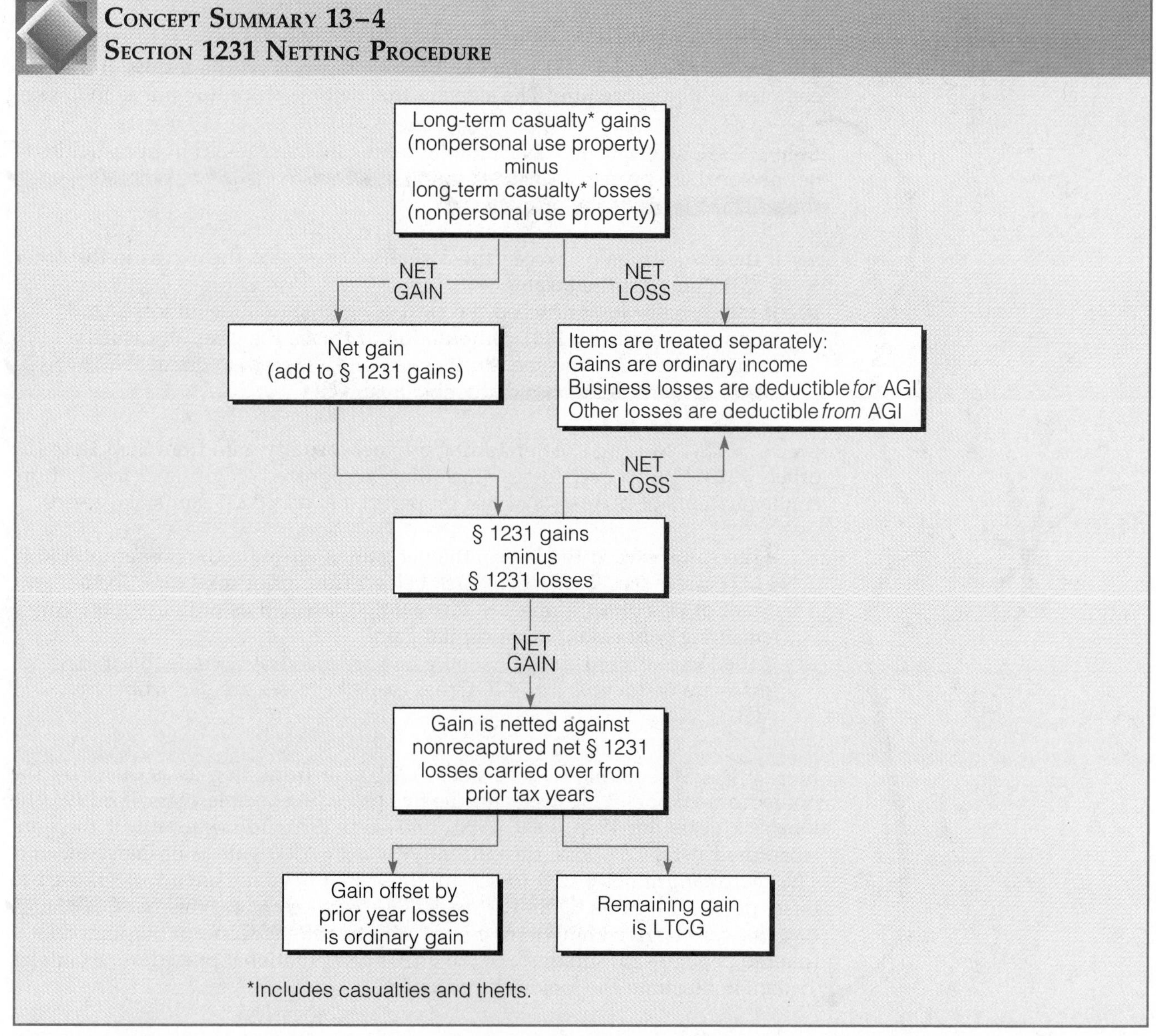

Casualties, thefts, and condemnations are *involuntary conversions.* Notice that condemnation gains and losses are not included in the netting processes discussed above. Long-term *recognized* condemnation gains and losses from the disposition of property held for business use and for the production of income are treated as § 1231 gains and losses. Involuntary conversion gains may be deferred if conversion proceeds are reinvested, but involuntary conversion losses are recognized (refer to Chapter 12) regardless of whether the conversion proceeds are reinvested.

This variation in treatment between casualty and condemnation gains and losses sheds considerable light on what § 1231 is all about. Section 1231 has no effect on whether realized gain or loss is recognized. Instead, it merely dictates how such gain or loss might be *classified* (ordinary or capital) under certain conditions.

Gains and losses from *condemnations* of personal use property are not subject to the § 1231 rules. The gains are capital gains and the losses are nondeductible because they arise from the disposition of personal use property.

General Procedure for § 1231 Computation

The tax treatment of § 1231 gains and losses depends on the results of a rather complex *netting* procedure. The steps in this netting procedure are as follows.

Step 1: Casualty Netting. Net all long-term gains and losses from casualties of nonpersonal use property. Casualty gains result when insurance proceeds exceed the adjusted basis of the property.

a. If the casualty gains exceed the casualty losses, add the excess to the other § 1231 gains for the taxable year.
b. If the casualty losses exceed the casualty gains, exclude all losses and gains from further § 1231 computation. If this is the case, all casualty gains are ordinary income. Business casualty losses are deductible *for* AGI. Other casualty losses are deductible *from* AGI.

Step 2: § 1231 Netting. After adding any net casualty gain from Step 1a to the other § 1231 gains and losses (including recognized gains and losses from condemnations of nonpersonal use property), net all § 1231 gains and losses.

a. If the gains exceed the losses, the net gain is offset by the nonrecaptured § 1231 losses (see § 1231 Lookback below) from prior tax years. To the extent of this offset, the net § 1231 gain is classified as ordinary gain. Any remaining gain is long-term capital gain.
b. If the losses exceed the gains, all gains are ordinary income. Business losses are deductible *for* AGI. Other casualty losses are deductible *from* AGI.

Step 3: § 1231 Lookback. The net § 1231 gain from Step 2a is offset by the nonrecaptured net § 1231 losses for the five preceding taxable years. For 1993, the lookback years are 1988, 1989, 1990, 1991, and 1992. To the extent of the nonrecaptured net § 1231 loss, the current-year net § 1231 gain is ordinary income. The *nonrecaptured* net § 1231 losses are those that have not already been used to offset net § 1231 gains. Only the net § 1231 gain exceeding this net § 1231 loss carryforward is given long-term capital gain treatment. Concept Summary 13–4 (refer to page 13–25) summarizes the § 1231 computational procedure. Examples 45 and 46 illustrate the lookback procedure.

Examples 43 through 46 illustrate the application of the § 1231 computation procedure.

EXAMPLE 43

During 1993, Ross had $125,000 of AGI before considering the following recognized gains and losses:

Capital Gains and Losses	
Long-term capital gain	$3,000
Long-term capital loss	(400)
Short-term capital gain	1,000
Short-term capital loss	(200)

Casualties	
Theft of diamond ring (owned four months)	$ (800)*
Fire damage to personal residence (owned 10 years)	(400)*
Gain from insurance recovery on accidental destruction of business truck (owned two years)	200

§ 1231 Gains and Losses from Depreciable Business Assets Held Long Term	
Asset A	$ 300
Asset B	1,100
Asset C	(500)

Gains and Losses from Sale of Depreciable Business Assets Held Short Term	
Asset D	$ 200
Asset E	(300)

*As adjusted for the $100 floor on personal casualty losses.

Ross had no net § 1231 losses in tax years before 1993.

Disregarding the recapture of depreciation and passive loss offset possibilities (discussed later in the chapter), Ross's gains and losses receive the following tax treatment:

- The diamond ring and the residence are personal use assets. Therefore, these casualties are not § 1231 transactions. The $800 (ring) plus $400 (residence) losses are potentially deductible *from* AGI. However, the total loss of $1,200 does not exceed 10% of AGI. Thus, only the business casualty remains. The $200 gain is added to the § 1231 gains.
- The gains from § 1231 transactions (Assets A, B, and C and the business casualty gain) exceed the losses by $1,100 ($1,600 – $500). This excess is a long-term capital gain and is added to Ross's other long-term capital gains.
- Ross's net long-term capital gain is $3,700 ($3,000 + $1,100 from § 1231 transactions – $400 long-term capital loss). His net short-term capital gain is $800 ($1,000 – $200). The result is capital gain net income of $4,500. The $3,700 net long-term capital gain portion is eligible for the 28% alternative tax, and the $800 net short-term capital gain is subject to tax as ordinary income.[27]

---

27. Ross's taxable income (unless the itemized deductions and the personal exemption and dependency deductions are extremely large) will put him in the 31% tax bracket. Thus, the 28% alternative tax computation will yield a lower tax. Refer to Example 34.

- Ross treats the gain and loss from Assets D and E (depreciable business assets held for less than the long-term holding period) as ordinary gain and loss.

Results of the Gains and Losses on Ross's Tax Computation

NLTCG	$ 3,700
STCG	800
Ordinary gain from sale of Asset D	200
Ordinary loss from sale of Asset E	(300)
AGI from other sources	125,000
AGI	$129,400

- Ross will have personal casualty losses of $1,200 [$800 (diamond ring) + $400 (personal residence)]. A personal casualty loss is deductible only to the extent it exceeds 10% of AGI. Thus, none of the $1,200 is deductible ($129,400 × 10% = $12,940). ◆

EXAMPLE 44

Assume the same facts as in Example 43, except the loss from Asset C was $1,700 instead of $500.

- The treatment of the casualty losses is the same as in Example 43.
- The losses from § 1231 transactions now exceed the gains by $100 ($1,700 – $1,600). As a result, the gains from Assets A and B and the business casualty gain are ordinary income, and the loss from Asset C is a deduction *for* AGI (a business loss). The same result can be achieved by simply treating the $100 net loss as a deduction *for* AGI.
- Capital gain net income is $3,400 ($2,600 long term + $800 short term). The $2,600 net long-term capital gain portion is eligible for the 28% alternative tax, and the $800 net short-term capital gain is subject to tax as ordinary income.

Results of the Gains and Losses on Ross's Tax Computation

NLTCG	$ 2,600
STCG	800
Net ordinary loss on Assets A, B, and C and business casualty gain	(100)
Ordinary gain from sale of Asset D	200
Ordinary loss from sale of Asset E	(300)
AGI from other sources	125,000
AGI	$128,200

- None of the personal casualty losses will be deductible since $1,200 does not exceed 10% of $128,200. ◆

EXAMPLE 45

Assume the same facts as in Example 43, except that Ross has a $700 nonrecaptured net § 1231 loss from 1992.

- The treatment of the casualty losses is the same as in Example 43.
- The 1993 net § 1231 gain of $1,100 is treated as ordinary income to the extent of the 1992 nonrecaptured § 1231 loss of $700. The remaining $400 net § 1231 gain is a long-term capital gain and is added to Ross's other long-term capital gains.
- Ross's net long-term capital gain is $3,000 ($3,000 + $400 from § 1231 transactions – $400 long-term capital loss). His short-term capital gain is still $800

($1,000 – $200). The result is capital gain net income of $3,800. The $3,000 net long-term capital gain portion is eligible for the 28% alternative tax, and the $800 net short-term capital gain is subject to tax as ordinary income.

Results of the Gains and Losses on Ross's Tax Computation

NLTCG	$ 3,000
STCG	800
Ordinary gain from recapture of § 1231 losses	700
Ordinary gain from sale of Asset D	200
Ordinary loss from sale of Asset E	(300)
AGI from other sources	125,000
AGI	$129,400

- None of the personal casualty losses will be deductible since $1,200 does not exceed 10% of $129,400. ◆

EXAMPLE 46

Assume the same facts as in Example 43, except that in 1991 Ross had a net § 1231 loss of $2,700 and in 1992 a net § 1231 gain of $300.

- The treatment of the casualty losses is the same as in Example 43.
- The 1991 net § 1231 loss of $2,700 will have been carried over to 1992 and been offset against the 1992 net § 1231 gain of $300. Thus, the $300 gain will have been ordinary income, and $2,400 of nonrecaptured 1991 net § 1231 loss will carry over to 1993. The 1993 net § 1231 gain of $1,100 will be offset against this loss, resulting in $1,100 of ordinary income. The nonrecaptured net § 1231 loss of $1,300 ($2,400 – $1,100) carries over to 1994.
- Capital gain net income is $3,400 ($2,600 net long-term capital gain + $800 net short-term capital gain). The $2,600 net long-term capital gain portion is eligible for the 28% alternative tax, and the $800 net short-term capital gain is subject to tax as ordinary income.

Results of the Gains and Losses on Ross's Tax Computation

NLTCG	$ 2,600
STCG	800
Ordinary gain from recapture of § 1231 losses	1,100
Ordinary gain from sale of Asset D	200
Ordinary loss from sale of Asset E	(300)
AGI from other sources	125,000
AGI	$129,400

- None of the personal casualty losses will be deductible since $1,200 does not exceed 10% of $129,400. ◆

SECTION 1245 RECAPTURE

Now that the basic rules of § 1231 have been introduced, it is time to add some complications. The Code contains two major *recapture* provisions— §§ 1245 and 1250. These provisions cause *gain* to be treated *initially* as ordinary gain. Thus, what may appear to be a § 1231 gain is ordinary gain instead. These recapture provisions may also cause a gain in a nonpersonal use casualty to be *initially* ordinary gain rather than casualty gain. Classifying gains (and losses) properly initially is important because improper initial classification may lead to incorrect mixing and matching of gains and losses. This section discusses the § 1245 recapture rules, and the next section discusses the § 1250 recapture rules.

Section 1245 prevents taxpayers from receiving the dual benefits of depreciation deductions that offset ordinary income plus § 1231 long-term capital gain treatment on the disposition of the depreciated property. Section 1245 applies primarily to non-real estate property such as machinery, trucks, and office furniture. Section 1245 requires recognized gain to be treated as ordinary income to the extent of depreciation taken on the property disposed of. Section 1245 does not apply if property is disposed of at a loss. Generally, the loss will be a § 1231 loss unless the form of the disposition is a casualty.

EXAMPLE 47

Alice purchased a $100,000 business machine and deducted $70,000 depreciation before selling it for $80,000. If it were not for § 1245, the $50,000 would be § 1231 gain ($80,000 – $30,000 adjusted basis). Section 1245 prevents this potentially favorable result by treating as ordinary income (not as § 1231 gain) any gain to the extent of depreciation taken. In this example, the entire $50,000 gain would be ordinary income. ◆

Section 1245 provides, in general, that the portion of recognized gain from the sale or other disposition of § 1245 property that represents depreciation (including § 167 depreciation, § 168 cost recovery, and § 179 immediate expensing) is recaptured as ordinary income. Thus, in Example 47, $50,000 of the $70,000 depreciation taken is recaptured as ordinary income when the business machine is sold. Only $50,000 is recaptured rather than $70,000 because Alice is only required to recognize § 1245 recapture ordinary gain equal to the lower of the depreciation taken or the gain recognized. In Example 47, the recognized gain is lower than the depreciation taken.

The method of depreciation (e.g., accelerated or straight-line) does not matter. All depreciation taken is potentially subject to recapture. Thus, § 1245 recapture is often referred to as *full recapture.* Any remaining gain after subtracting the amount recaptured as ordinary income will usually be § 1231 gain. The remaining gain would be casualty gain if it were disposed of in a casualty event. If the business machine in Example 47 had been disposed of by casualty and the $80,000 received had been an insurance recovery, Alice would still have a gain of $50,000, and the gain would still be recaptured by § 1245 as ordinary gain. The § 1245 recapture rules apply before there is any casualty gain. Since all the $50,000 gain is recaptured, no casualty gain arises from the casualty.

Although § 1245 applies primarily to non-real estate property, it does apply to certain real estate. Nonresidential real estate acquired after 1980 and before 1987 and for which accelerated depreciation (the statutory percentage method of the accelerated cost recovery system) is used is subject to the § 1245 recapture rules. Such property includes 15-year, 18-year, and 19-year nonresidential real estate.

The following examples illustrate the general application of § 1245.

EXAMPLE 48

On January 1, 1993, Gary sold for $13,000 a machine acquired several years ago for $12,000. He had taken $10,000 of depreciation on the machine.

- The recognized gain from the sale is $11,000. This is the $13,000 amount realized less the adjusted basis of $2,000 ($12,000 cost – $10,000 depreciation taken).
- Depreciation taken is $10,000. Therefore, since § 1245 recapture gain is the lower of depreciation taken or gain recognized, $10,000 of the $11,000 recognized gain is ordinary income, and the remaining $1,000 gain is § 1231 gain.

- The § 1231 gain of $1,000 is also equal to the excess of the sales price over the original cost of the property ($13,000 – $12,000 = $1,000 § 1231 gain). ◆

EXAMPLE 49

Assume the same facts as in the previous example, except the asset is sold for $9,000 instead of $13,000.

- The recognized gain from the sale is $7,000. This is the amount realized of $9,000 less the adjusted basis of $2,000.
- Depreciation taken is $10,000. Therefore, since the $10,000 depreciation taken exceeds the recognized gain of $7,000, the entire $7,000 recognized gain is ordinary income.
- The § 1231 gain is zero. There is no § 1231 gain because the selling price ($9,000) does not exceed the original purchase price ($12,000). ◆

EXAMPLE 50

Assume the same facts as in Example 48, except the asset is sold for $1,500 instead of $13,000.

- The recognized loss from the sale is $500. This is the amount realized of $1,500 less the adjusted basis of $2,000.
- Since there is a loss, there is no depreciation recapture. All of the loss is § 1231 loss. ◆

If § 1245 property is disposed of in a transaction other than a sale, exchange, or involuntary conversion, the maximum amount recaptured is the excess of the property's fair market value over its adjusted basis. See the discussion under Considerations Common to §§ 1245 and 1250 later in the chapter.

Section 1245 Property

Generally, § 1245 property includes all depreciable personal property (e.g., machinery and equipment), including livestock. Buildings and their structural components generally are not § 1245 property. The following property is *also* subject to § 1245 treatment:

- Amortizable personal property such as patents, copyrights, and leaseholds of § 1245 property. Professional baseball and football player contracts are § 1245 property.
- Amortization of reforestation expenditures and expensing of costs to remove architectural and transportation barriers to the handicapped and elderly.
- Section 179 immediate expensing of depreciable tangible personal property costs.
- Elevators and escalators acquired before January 1, 1987.
- Certain depreciable tangible real property (other than buildings and their structural components) employed as an integral part of certain activities such as manufacturing and production. For example, a natural gas storage tank where the gas is used in the manufacturing process is § 1245 property.
- Pollution control facilities, railroad grading and tunnel bores, on-the-job training, and child care facilities on which amortization is taken.
- Single-purpose agricultural and horticultural structures and petroleum storage facilities (e.g., a greenhouse or silo).
- As noted above, 15-year, 18-year, and 19-year nonresidential real estate for which accelerated cost recovery is used is subject to the § 1245 recapture rules, although it is technically not § 1245 property. Such property would have been placed in service after 1980 and before 1987.

EXAMPLE 51

James acquired nonresidential real property on January 1, 1986, for $100,000. He used the statutory percentage method to compute the ACRS depreciation. He sells the asset on January 15, 1993, for $120,000. The amount and nature of James's gain are determined as follows:

Amount realized			$120,000
Adjusted basis			
Cost		$100,000	
Less cost recovery:	1986	(8,800)	
	1987	(8,400)	
	1988	(7,600)	
	1989	(6,900)	
	1990	(6,300)	
	1991	(5,700)	
	1992	(5,200)	
	1993	(196)	
January 15, 1993, adjusted basis			(50,904)
Gain realized and recognized			$ 69,096

The gain of $69,096 is treated as ordinary income to the extent of *all* depreciation taken because the property is 19-year nonresidential real estate for which accelerated depreciation was used. Thus, James reports ordinary income of $49,096 ($8,800 + $8,400 + $7,600 + $6,900 + $6,300 + $5,700 + $5,200 + $196) and § 1231 gain of $20,000 ($69,096 – $49,096). ◆

Observations on § 1245

- In most instances, the total depreciation taken will exceed the recognized gain. Therefore, the disposition of § 1245 property usually results in ordinary income rather than § 1231 gain. Thus, generally, no § 1231 gain will occur unless the § 1245 property is disposed of for more than its original cost. Refer to Example 48.
- Recapture applies to the total amount of depreciation allowed or allowable regardless of the depreciation method used.
- Recapture applies regardless of the holding period of the property. Of course, the entire recognized gain would be ordinary income if the property were held for less than the long-term holding period, because § 1231 would not apply.
- Section 1245 does not apply to losses, which receive § 1231 treatment.
- As discussed later in the chapter, gains from the disposition of § 1245 assets may also be treated as passive gains.

SECTION 1250 RECAPTURE

Generally, *§ 1250 property* is depreciable real property (principally buildings and their structural components) that is not subject to § 1245.[28] Intangible real property, such as leaseholds of § 1250 property, is also included.

28. As previously discussed, in one limited circumstance, § 1245 does apply to nonresidential real estate. If the nonresidential real estate was placed in service after 1980 and before 1987 and accelerated depreciation was used, the § 1245 recapture rules rather than the § 1250 recapture rules apply.

The recapture rules under § 1250 are substantially less punitive than the § 1245 recapture rules since only the amount of additional depreciation is subject to recapture. To have additional depreciation, accelerated depreciation must have been taken on the asset. Straight-line depreciation (except for property held one year or less) is not recaptured. Since real property placed in service after 1986 can only be depreciated using the straight-line method, there will be no § 1250 depreciation recapture on such property.

Section 1250 was enacted in 1964 for depreciable real property and has been revised many times. The provision prevents taxpayers from receiving the benefits of both *accelerated* depreciation (or cost recovery) deductions and subsequent long-term capital gain treatment upon the disposition of real property. If straight-line depreciation is taken on the property, § 1250 does not apply. Nor does § 1250 apply if the real property is sold at a loss. The loss will generally be a § 1231 loss unless the property is disposed of by casualty.

Section 1250 as originally enacted required recapture of a percentage of the additional depreciation deducted by the taxpayer. *Additional depreciation* is the excess of accelerated depreciation actually deducted over depreciation that would have been deductible if the straight-line method had been used. Since only the additional depreciation is subject to recapture, § 1250 recapture is often referred to as *partial recapture.*

Post-1969 additional depreciation on nonresidential real property is subject to 100 percent recapture (see Example 52). Post-1969 additional depreciation on residential property may be subject to less than 100 percent recapture (see Example 53).

The following discussion describes the computational steps prescribed in § 1250 and reflected on Form 4797 (Gains and Losses from Sales or Exchanges of Assets Used in a Trade or Business and Involuntary Conversions).

If § 1250 property is disposed of in a transaction other than a sale, exchange, or involuntary conversion, the maximum amount recaptured is the excess of the property's fair market value over the adjusted basis. For example, if a corporation distributes property to its shareholders as a dividend, the property will have been disposed of at a gain if the fair market value is greater than the adjusted basis. The maximum amount of § 1250 recapture will be the amount of the gain.

Computing Recapture on Nonresidential Real Property

For § 1250 property other than residential rental property, the potential recapture is equal to the amount of additional depreciation taken since December 31, 1969. This nonresidential real property includes buildings such as offices, warehouses, factories, and stores. (The definition of and rules for residential rental housing are discussed later in the chapter.) The lower of the potential § 1250 recapture amount or the gain recognized is ordinary income. The following general rules apply:

- Post-1969 additional depreciation is depreciation taken in excess of straight-line after December 31, 1969.
- If the property is held for one year or less (usually not the case), all depreciation taken, even under the straight-line method, is additional depreciation.
- Special rules apply to dispositions of substantially improved § 1250 property. These rules are rather technical, and the reader should consult the examples in the Regulations for illustrations of their application.[29]

---

29. § 1250(f) and Reg. § 1.1250–5.

The following procedure is used to compute recapture on nonresidential real property under § 1250:

- Determine the recognized gain from the sale or other disposition of the property.
- Determine post-1969 additional depreciation.
- The lower of the recognized gain or the post-1969 additional depreciation is ordinary income.
- If any recognized gain remains (total recognized gain less recapture), it is § 1231 gain. However, it would be casualty gain if the disposition was by casualty.

The following example shows the application of the § 1250 computational procedure.

EXAMPLE 52

On January 3, 1980, Larry acquired a new building at a cost of $200,000 for use in his business. The building had an estimated useful life of 50 years and no estimated salvage value. Depreciation has been taken under the 150% declining-balance method through December 31, 1992. Information pertinent to depreciation taken follows:

Year	Undepreciated Balance (Beginning of the Year)	Current Depreciation Provision	Straight-Line Depreciation	Additional Depreciation
1980	$200,000	$ 6,000	$ 4,000	$ 2,000
1981	194,000	5,820	4,000	1,820
1982	188,180	5,645	4,000	1,645
1983	182,535	5,476	4,000	1,476
1984	177,059	5,312	4,000	1,312
1985	171,747	5,152	4,000	1,152
1986	166,595	4,998	4,000	998
1987	161,597	4,848	4,000	848
1988	156,749	4,702	4,000	702
1989	152,047	4,561	4,000	561
1990	147,486	4,425	4,000	425
1991	143,061	4,292	4,000	292
1992	138,769	4,163	4,000	163
Total 1980–1992		$65,394	$52,000	$13,394

On January 2, 1993, Larry sold the building for $180,000. Compute the amount of his § 1250 ordinary income and § 1231 gain.

- Larry's recognized gain from the sale is $45,394. This is the difference between the $180,000 amount realized and the $134,606 adjusted basis ($200,000 cost – $65,394 depreciation taken).
- Post-1969 additional depreciation is $13,394.
- The amount of post-1969 ordinary income is $13,394. Since the post-1969 additional depreciation of $13,394 is less than the recognized gain of $45,394, the entire gain is not recaptured.
- The remaining $32,000 ($45,394 – $13,394) gain is § 1231 gain. ◆

Computing Recapture on Residential Rental Housing

Section 1250 recapture applies to the sale or other disposition of residential rental housing. Property qualifies as *residential rental housing* only if at least 80 percent of gross rent income is rent income from dwelling units.[30] The rules are the same as for other § 1250 property, except that only the post-1975 additional depreciation may be recaptured in full. The post-1969 through 1975 recapture percentage is 100 percent less one percentage point for each full month the property is held over 100 months.[31] Therefore, the additional depreciation for periods after 1975 is initially applied against the recognized gain, and these amounts may be recaptured in full as ordinary income. If any of the recognized gain is not absorbed by the recapture rules pertaining to the post-1975 period, the remaining gain is § 1231 gain.

EXAMPLE 53

Assume the same facts as in the previous example, except the building is residential rental housing.

- Post-1975 ordinary income is $13,394 (post-1975 additional depreciation of $13,394).
- The remaining $32,000 ($45,394 – $13,394) gain is § 1231 gain. ◆

Under § 1250, when straight-line depreciation is used, there is no § 1250 recapture potential unless the property is disposed of in the first year of use. Before 1987, accelerated depreciation on real estate generally was available. For real property placed in service after 1986, however, only straight-line depreciation is allowed. Therefore, the § 1250 recapture rules do not apply to such property unless it is disposed of in the first year of use.

EXAMPLE 54

Sanjay acquires a residential rental building on January 1, 1992, for $300,000. He receives an offer of $450,000 for the building in 1993 and sells it on December 23, 1993.

- Sanjay takes $20,909 [($300,000 × .03485) + ($300,000 × .03636 × 11.5/12) = $20,909] of total depreciation for 1992 and 1993, and the adjusted basis of the property is $279,091 ($300,000 – $20,909).
- Sanjay's gain is $170,909 ($450,000 – $279,091).
- All of the gain is § 1231 gain. ◆

Section 1250 Recapture Situations

The § 1250 recapture rules apply to the following property for which accelerated depreciation was used:

- Residential real estate acquired before 1987.
- Nonresidential real estate acquired before 1981.
- Real property used predominantly outside the United States.
- Certain government-financed or low-income housing described in § 1250(a)(1)(B).

Concept Summary 13–5 compares and contrasts the § 1245 and § 1250 depreciation recapture rules.

30. § 168(e)(2)(A) and Reg. § 1.167(j)–3(b)(1)(i). Note that there may be residential, nonrental housing (e.g., a bunkhouse on a cattle ranch). Such property is commonly regarded as "nonresidential real estate." The rules for such property were discussed in the previous section.

31. §§ 1250(a)(1) and (2) and Reg. § 1.1250–1(d)(1)(i)(c). Since the post-1969 through 1975 recapture percentage is 100% less one percentage point for each full month the property is held over 100 months, this approach now yields a zero percentage no matter when the property was acquired in the 1969–1975 period. For instance, if a building was acquired on January 3, 1975, and sold on January 3, 1993, it would have been held 216 months. The recapture percentage is zero because 100% – (216% – 100%) is less than zero.

CONSIDERATIONS COMMON TO §§ 1245 AND 1250

Exceptions

Recapture under §§ 1245 and 1250 does not apply to the following transactions.

Gifts. The recapture potential carries over to the donee.[32]

EXAMPLE 55

Wade gives his daughter, Helen, § 1245 property with an adjusted basis of $1,000. The amount of recapture potential is $700. Helen uses the property in her business and claims further depreciation of $100 before selling it for $1,900. Helen's recognized gain is $1,000 ($1,900 amount realized – $900 adjusted basis), of which $800 is recaptured as ordinary income ($100 depreciation taken by Helen + $700 recapture potential carried over from Wade). The remaining gain of $200 is § 1231 gain. Even if Helen used the property for personal purposes, the $700 recapture potential would still be carried over. ◆

Death. Although not a very attractive tax planning approach, death eliminates all recapture potential.[33] In other words, any recapture potential does not carry over from a decedent to an estate or heir.

CONCEPT SUMMARY 13–5
COMPARISON OF § 1245 AND § 1250 DEPRECIATION RECAPTURE

	§ 1245	§ 1250
Property affected	All depreciable personal property, but also nonresidential real property acquired after December 31, 1980, and before January 1, 1987, for which accelerated cost recovery was used. Also includes miscellaneous items such as § 179 expense and amortization of patents and copyrights.	Residential real property acquired after December 31, 1980, and before January 1, 1987, on which accelerated cost recovery was taken. Nonresidential real property acquired after December 31, 1969, and before January 1, 1976, on which accelerated depreciation was taken. Residential and nonresidential real property acquired after December 31, 1975, and before January 1, 1981, on which accelerated depreciation was taken.
Depreciation recaptured	Potentially all depreciation taken. If the selling price is greater than or equal to the original cost, all depreciation is recaptured. If the selling price is between the adjusted basis and the original cost, only some depreciation is recaptured.	Additional depreciation (the excess of accelerated cost recovery over straight-line cost recovery or the excess of accelerated depreciation over straight-line depreciation).
Limit on recapture	Lower of depreciation taken or gain recognized.	Lower of additional depreciation or gain recognized.
Treatment of gain exceeding recapture gain	Usually § 1231 gain.	Usually § 1231 gain.
Treatment of loss	No depreciation recapture; loss is usually § 1231 loss.	No depreciation recapture; loss is usually § 1231 loss.

32. §§ 1245(b)(1) and 1250(d)(1) and Reg. §§ 1.1245–4(a)(1) and 1.1250–3(a)(1).

33. §§ 1245(b)(2) and 1250(d)(2).

EXAMPLE 56

Assume the same facts as in the previous example, except Helen receives the property as a result of Wade's death. The $700 recapture potential from Wade is extinguished. Helen has a basis for the property equal to the property's fair market value (assume $1,700) at Wade's death. Helen will have a $300 gain when the property is sold because the selling price ($1,900) exceeds the property's adjusted basis ($1,700 original basis to Helen – $100 depreciation) by $300. Because of § 1245, $100 is ordinary income. The remaining gain of $200 is § 1231 gain. ◆

Charitable Transfers. The recapture potential reduces the amount of the charitable contribution deduction under § 170.[34]

EXAMPLE 57

Kanisha donates to her church § 1245 property with a fair market value of $10,000 and an adjusted basis of $7,000. Assume that the amount of recapture potential is $2,000 (the amount of recapture that would occur if the property were sold). Her charitable contribution deduction (subject to the limitations discussed in Chapter 10) is $8,000 ($10,000 fair market value – $2,000 recapture potential). ◆

Certain Nontaxable Transactions. These are transactions in which the transferor's adjusted basis of property carries over to the transferee.[35] The recapture potential also carries over to the transferee.[36] Included in this category are transfers of property pursuant to

- Nontaxable incorporations under § 351.
- Certain liquidations of subsidiary companies under § 332.
- Nontaxable contributions to a partnership under § 721.
- Nontaxable reorganizations.

Gain may be recognized in these transactions if boot is received. If gain is recognized, it is treated as ordinary income to the extent of the recapture potential or recognized gain, whichever is lower.[37]

Like-Kind Exchanges (§ 1031) and Involuntary Conversions (§ 1033). Realized gain will be recognized to the extent of boot received under § 1031. Realized gain also will be recognized to the extent the proceeds from an involuntary conversion are not reinvested in similar property under § 1033. Such recognized gain is subject to recapture as ordinary income under §§ 1245 and 1250. The remaining recapture potential, if any, carries over to the property received in the exchange.

EXAMPLE 58

Anita exchanges § 1245 property with an adjusted basis of $300 for § 1245 property with a fair market value of $6,000. The exchange qualifies as a like-kind exchange under § 1031. Anita also receives $1,000 cash (boot). Her realized gain is $6,700 ($7,000 amount realized – $300 adjusted basis of property). Assuming the recapture potential is $7,500, Anita recognizes gain of $1,000 because she received boot of $1,000. The remaining recapture potential of $6,500 carries over to the like-kind property received. ◆

---

34. § 170(e)(1)(A) and Reg. § 1.170A–4(b)(1). In certain circumstances, § 1231 gain also reduces the amount of the charitable contribution. See § 170(e)(1)(B).

35. §§ 1245(b)(3) and 1250(d)(3) and Reg. §§ 1.1245–4(c) and 1.1250–3(c).

36. Reg. §§ 1.1245–2(a)(4) and –2(c)(2) and 1.1250–2(d)(1) and (3) and –3(c)(3).

37. §§ 1245(b)(3) and 1250(d)(3) and Reg. §§ 1.1245–4(c) and 1.1250–3(c). Some of these special corporate problems are discussed in Chapter 16. Partnership contributions are discussed in Chapter 22.

SPECIAL RECAPTURE PROVISIONS

Special Recapture for Corporations

Corporations (other than S corporations) selling depreciable real estate may have ordinary income in addition to that required by § 1250. The *ordinary gain adjustment* is 20 percent of the excess of the § 1245 potential recapture over the § 1250 recapture.[38] The result is a decrease in the § 1231 gain corresponding to this increase in ordinary income.

EXAMPLE 59

Brown Corporation purchased a residential building on January 1, 1986, for $100,000. Accelerated depreciation of $49,096 was taken before the building was disposed of on January 15, 1993. The straight-line depreciation for the same period would have been $37,021. The selling price was $120,000. Section 1250 would recapture $12,075 ($49,096 – $37,021). Section 1245 would have recaptured the entire $49,096. The ordinary gain adjustment is computed as follows:

Section 1245 recapture (lower of depreciation taken or total gain)	$ 49,096
Less: Gain recaptured by § 1250	(12,075)
Excess of § 1245 gain over § 1250 gain	$ 37,021
Percentage that is ordinary gain	20%
Ordinary gain adjustment	$ 7,404
Section 1231 gain [$120,000 selling price – ($100,000 cost – $49,096 depreciation taken) = $69,096; $69,096 gain – $12,075 § 1250 gain – $7,404 ordinary gain adjustment]	$ 49,617

◆

Gain from Sale of Depreciable Property between Certain Related Parties

When the sale or exchange of property, which in the hands of the *transferee* is depreciable property (principally machinery, equipment, and buildings, but not land), is between certain related parties, any gain recognized is ordinary income.[39] This provision applies to both direct and indirect sales or exchanges. A *related party* is an individual and his or her controlled corporation or partnership or a taxpayer and any trust in which the taxpayer (or the taxpayer's spouse) is a beneficiary.

EXAMPLE 60

Isabella sells a personal use automobile (therefore nondepreciable) to her controlled corporation. The automobile, which was purchased two years ago, cost $5,000 and is sold for $7,000. The automobile is to be used in the corporation's business. If the related-party provision did not exist, Isabella would realize a $2,000 long-term capital gain. The income tax consequences would be favorable because her controlled corporation is entitled to depreciate the automobile based upon the purchase price of $7,000. Under the related-party provision, Isabella's $2,000 gain is ordinary income. ◆

38. § 291(a)(1).

39. § 1239.

The related-party provision was enacted to prevent certain related parties from enjoying the dual benefits of long-term capital gain treatment (transferor) and a step-up in basis for depreciation (transferee). Recapture under §§ 1245 and 1250 applies first before recapture under the related-party provision.

Control means ownership of more than 50 percent in value of the corporation's outstanding stock or more than 50 percent of the capital interest or profits interest of a partnership. In determining the percentage of stock owned or partnership interest owned, the taxpayer must include the stock or partnership interest owned by related taxpayers as determined under the constructive ownership rules of § 267(c).

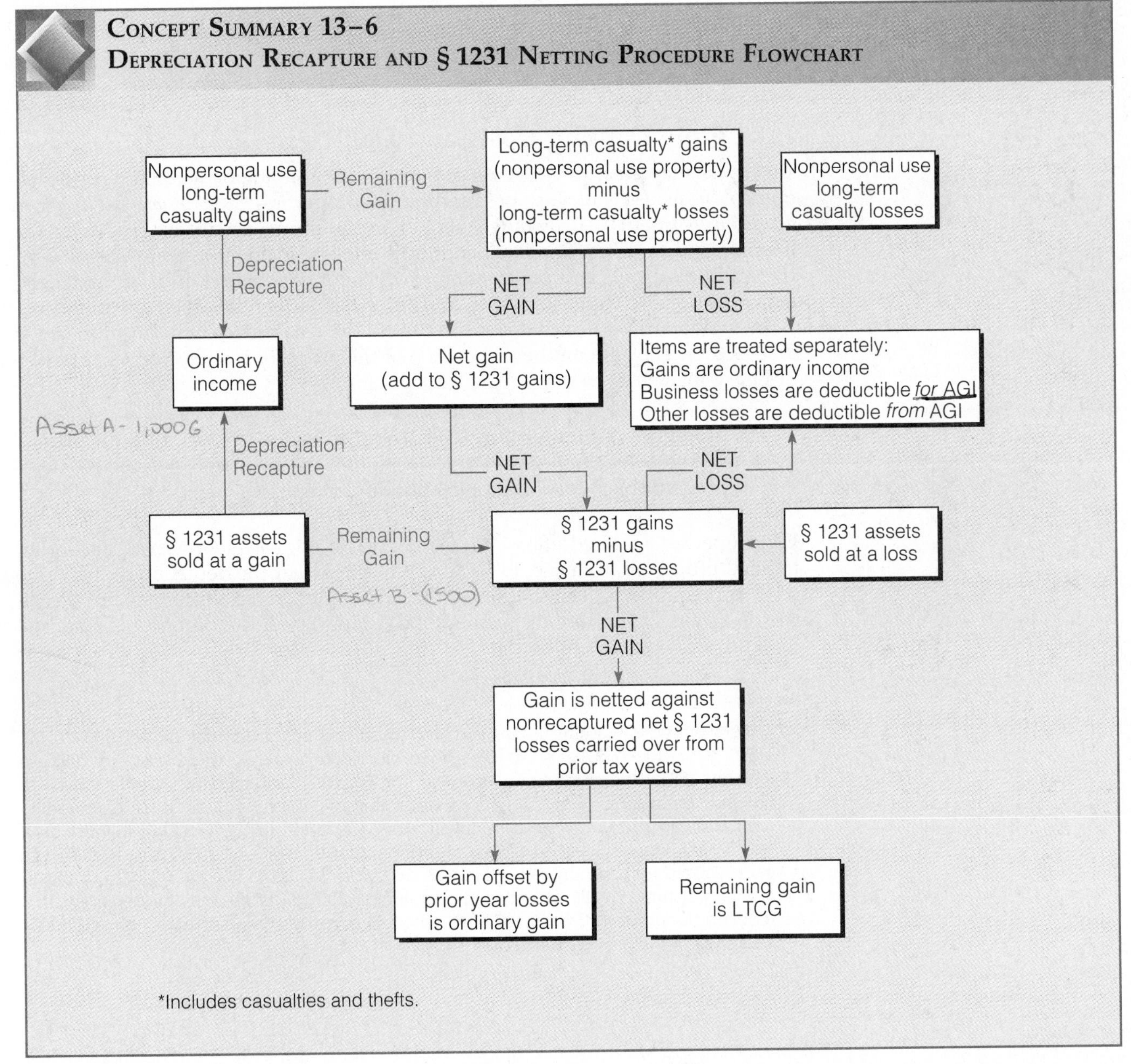

Section 267(a)(1) disallows a loss on the sale of property between certain related taxpayers. Therefore, a sale of property between certain related parties may result in ordinary income (if the property is depreciable in the hands of the transferee) or a nondeductible loss.

The related-party provision applies regardless of whether the transfer is from a shareholder or partner to the entity or from the entity to a shareholder or partner. Ordinary income treatment also applies to transfers between two corporations controlled by the same shareholder.

EXAMPLE 61

Soong, the sole shareholder of WWW Enterprises, Inc., sells a building (adjusted basis of $40,000) for $100,000 to the corporation for use in its business. Since Soong had depreciated the building using the straight-line method, none of the depreciation will be recaptured under § 1250. Nevertheless, the related-party provision applies to convert Soong's $60,000 § 1231 gain to ordinary income. The basis of the building to WWW Enterprises is $100,000 (the building's cost). ◆

Intangible Drilling Costs and Depletion

Taxpayers may elect to either *expense or capitalize* intangible drilling and development costs for oil, gas, or geothermal properties.[40] *Intangible drilling and development costs* (*IDC*) include operator expenditures for wages, fuel, repairs, hauling, and supplies. These expenditures must be incident to and necessary for the drilling of wells and preparation of wells for production. In most instances, taxpayers elect to expense IDC to maximize tax deductions during drilling.

Intangible drilling costs are subject to § 1254 recapture when the property is disposed of. The gain on the disposition of the property is subject to recapture as ordinary income as follows:

- For properties acquired before 1987, the IDC expensed after 1975 in excess of what cost depletion would have been had the IDC been capitalized.
- For properties acquired after 1986, the IDC expensed.

For properties acquired after 1986, depletion on oil, gas, geothermal, and other mineral properties is subject to recapture to the extent the depletion reduced the basis of the property. The combined IDC and depletion recapture may not exceed the recognized gain from disposition of the property. If the property is disposed of at a loss, no recapture occurs.

EXAMPLE 62

Mike acquired a working interest in certain oil and gas properties for $50,000 during 1992. He incurred $10,000 of IDC. Mike elected to expense these costs in 1992. In January 1993, the properties were sold for $60,000. Disregard any depreciation on tangible depreciable properties and assume that cost depletion would have amounted to $2,000 had the IDC been capitalized. Also, depletion of the working interest itself was $7,000. Thus, the basis of Mike's working interest is $43,000 ($50,000 – $7,000). His gain realized and recognized is $17,000 ($60,000 – $43,000). The gain is recaptured as ordinary income to the extent of the expensed IDC ($10,000) and the depletion that reduced the property's basis ($7,000), which is equal to the recognized gain ($17,000). Therefore, $17,000 is recaptured. ◆

40. § 263(c).

Special rules are provided for determining recapture upon the sale or other disposition of a portion or an undivided interest in oil, gas, geothermal, and other mineral properties.

Passive Activity Losses

Passive activity losses may result in current losses that are not deductible against nonpassive activity income.[41] If there is insufficient current passive income to absorb the passive losses, the losses are *suspended* until sufficient passive income is available to absorb them. (Passive activity losses are discussed in Chapter 6.) When a passive activity is disposed of, the suspended and current-year losses of that activity are fully deductible. However, they also reduce the recognized gain, if any, from disposition of the activity. Any remaining gain is then available to allow other passive activity current and suspended losses to be currently deductible. The recognized gain still receives treatment under the normal property disposition rules discussed earlier in this chapter. If a passive activity is disposed of at a recognized loss, the loss is treated under the normal property disposition provisions. Thus, recognized *gains* from passive activity dispositions have a dual purpose: to allow deductibility of passive losses to the extent of the gain and to be treated under the normal property disposition rules. Recognized *losses* from passive activity dispositions do not have a dual purpose.

Example 63

Mei-Yen disposes of a passive activity during 1993 at a $36,000 gain. The passive activity asset was a § 1231 asset, and the gain is a § 1231 gain. However, Mei-Yen has a current passive loss of $6,000 from this activity, no suspended losses from the activity, and $21,000 of current losses from another passive activity. The $36,000 gain allows the $6,000 and $21,000 passive losses to be fully deductible in 1992 as deductions *for* AGI. For purposes of computing Mei-Yen's net § 1231 gain, the full $36,000 of § 1231 gain is used. ◆

Example 64

Assume the same facts as in the previous example, except that Mei-Yen has a $36,000 § 1231 loss rather than a gain. The § 1231 loss would be included in Mei-Yen's net § 1231 computation. The $6,000 current loss from the passive activity disposed of would be deductible in full as a deduction *for* AGI. The $21,000 loss from the other passive activity would not be deductible. ◆

Reporting Procedures

Noncapital gains and losses are reported on Form 4797, Sales of Business Property. Before filling out Form 4797, however, Form 4684, Casualties and Thefts, must be completed to determine whether or not any casualties will enter into the § 1231 computation procedure. Recall that gains from casualties may be recaptured by § 1245 or § 1250. These gains will not appear on Form 4684. Only

41. § 469.

long-term nonrecaptured nonpersonal use property casualty gains are netted against long-term nonpersonal use property casualty losses to determine whether there is a net gain to transfer to Part I of Form 4797.

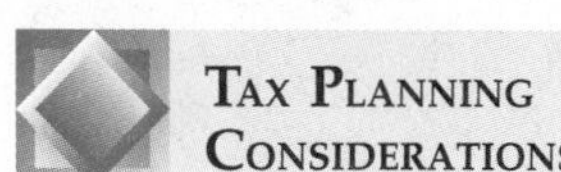

Importance of Capital Asset Status

Why is capital asset status important when net long-term capital gain is subject to a maximum 28 percent tax rate? The 3 percent difference between the maximum 31 percent regular tax rate and the maximum 28 percent net long-term capital gain tax rate may generate significant tax savings for taxpayers in the highest regular tax bracket who can receive income in the form of long-term capital gains.

Capital asset status is also important because capital gains must be offset by capital losses. If a net capital loss results, the maximum deduction is $3,000 per year.

Consequently, capital gains and losses must be segregated from other types of gains and losses and must be reported separately in Schedule D of Form 1040.

Planning for Capital Asset Status

It is important to keep in mind that capital asset status often is a question of objective evidence. Thus, property that is not a capital asset to one party may qualify as a capital asset to another party.

EXAMPLE 65

Diane, a real estate dealer, transfers by gift a tract of land to Jeff, her son. The land was recorded as part of Diane's inventory (it was held for resale) and was therefore not a capital asset to her. Jeff, however, treats the land as an investment. The land is a capital asset in Jeff's hands, and any later taxable disposition of the property by Jeff will yield a capital gain or loss. ◆

If proper planning is carried out, even a dealer may obtain long-term capital gain treatment on the sale of the type of property normally held for resale.

EXAMPLE 66

Jim, a real estate dealer, segregates tract A from the real estate he regularly holds for resale and designates the property as being held for investment purposes. The property is not advertised for sale and is disposed of several years later. The negotiations for the sale were initiated by the purchaser and not by Jim. Under these circumstances, it would appear that any gain or loss from the sale of tract A should be a capital gain or loss.[42] ◆

When a business is being sold, one of the major decisions usually concerns whether a portion of the sales price is goodwill. For the seller, goodwill generally represents the disposition of a capital asset. Goodwill has no basis and represents a residual portion of the selling price that cannot be allocated reasonably to the known assets. The amount of goodwill thus represents capital gain. The buyer purchasing goodwill has a capitalizable, nonamortizable asset—a very disadvantageous situation.

---

42. *Toledo, Peoria & Western Railroad Co.*, 35 TCM 1663, T.C.Memo. 1976–366.

The buyer would prefer that the residual portion of the purchase price be allocated to a covenant not to compete (a promise that the seller will not compete against the buyer by conducting a business similar to the one that the buyer has purchased). Payments for a covenant not to compete are ordinary income to the seller, but are ordinary deductions for the buyer over the life of the covenant.

The case law requires a covenant not to compete to be clearly specified in the sales contract.[43] Otherwise, unallocated payments will be regarded as payments for goodwill.[44] The parties should therefore bargain for the nature of this portion of the sales price and clearly specify its nature in the sales contract.

Example 67

Marcia is buying Jack's dry cleaning proprietorship. An appraisal of the assets indicates that a reasonable purchase price would exceed the value of the known assets by $30,000. If the purchase contract does not specify the nature of the $30,000, the amount will be goodwill, and Jack will have a long-term capital gain of $30,000. Marcia will have a nonamortizable $30,000 asset. If Marcia is paying the extra $30,000 to prevent Jack from conducting another dry cleaning business in the area, Jack will have $30,000 of ordinary income. Marcia will have a $30,000 deduction over the life of the covenant if the contract specifies the purpose for the payment. ◆

Effect of Capital Asset Status in Transactions Other Than Sales

The nature of an asset (capital or ordinary) is important in determining the tax consequences that result when a sale or exchange occurs. It may, however, be just as significant in circumstances other than a taxable sale or exchange. When a capital asset is disposed of, the result is not always a capital gain or loss. Rather, in general, the disposition must be a sale or exchange. Collection of a debt instrument having a basis less than the face value results in an ordinary gain rather than a capital gain even though the debt instrument is a capital asset. The collection is not a sale or exchange. Sale of the debt shortly before the due date for collection will not produce a capital gain.[45] If selling the debt in such circumstances could produce a capital gain but collecting could not, the narrow interpretation of what constitutes a capital gain or loss will be frustrated. Another illustration of the sale or exchange principle involves a donation of certain appreciated property to a qualified charity. Recall that in certain circumstances, the measure of the charitable contribution is fair market value when the property, if sold, would have yielded a long-term capital gain [refer to Chapter 10 and the discussion of § 170(e)].

Example 68

Sharon wants to donate a tract of unimproved land (basis of $40,000 and fair market value of $200,000) held for the required long-term holding period to State University (a qualified charitable organization). However, she currently is under audit by the IRS for capital gains she reported on certain real estate transactions during an earlier tax year. Although Sharon is not a licensed real estate broker, the IRS agent conducting the audit is contending that she has achieved dealer status by virtue of the number and frequency of the real estate transactions she has conducted. Under these circumstances, Sharon would be well-advised to postpone the donation to State University until her status is clarified. If she has achieved dealer status, the unimproved land may be

43. See, for example, *James A. Patterson*, 49 TCM 670, T.C.Memo. 1985–53.

44. § 1060(a)(2).

45. *Comm. v. Percy W. Phillips*, 60–1 USTC ¶9294, 5 AFTR2d 855, 275 F.2d 33 (CA–4, 1960).

inventory (refer to Example 66 for another possible result), and her charitable contribution deduction would be limited to $40,000. If not, and if the land is held as an investment, her deduction is $200,000 (the fair market value of the property). ◆

Stock Sales

The following rules apply in determining the date of a stock sale:

- The date the sale is executed is the date of the sale. The execution date is the date the broker completes the transaction on the stock exchange.
- The settlement date is the date the cash or other property is paid to the seller of the stock. This date is *not* relevant in determining the date of sale.

EXAMPLE 69

Lupe, a cash basis taxpayer, sells stock that results in a gain. The sale was executed on December 29, 1992. The settlement date is January 7, 1993. The date of sale is December 29, 1992 (the execution date). The holding period for the stock sold ends with the execution date. ◆

Maximizing Benefits

Ordinary losses generally are preferable to capital losses because of the limitations imposed on the deductibility of net capital losses and the requirement that capital losses be used to offset capital gains. The taxpayer may be able to convert what would otherwise have been capital loss to ordinary loss. For example, business (but not nonbusiness) bad debts, losses from the sale or exchange of small business investment company stock, and losses from the sale or exchange of small business company stock all result in ordinary losses.[46]

Although capital losses can be carried over indefinitely, *indefinite* becomes definite when a taxpayer dies. Any loss carryovers not used by the taxpayer are permanently lost. That is, no tax benefit can be derived from the carryovers subsequent to death.[47] Therefore, the potential benefit of carrying over capital losses diminishes when dealing with older taxpayers.

It is usually beneficial to spread gains over more than one taxable year. In some cases, this can be accomplished through the installment sales method of accounting.

Year-End Planning

The following general rules can be applied for timing the recognition of capital gains and losses near the end of a taxable year:

- If the taxpayer already has recognized over $3,000 of capital loss, sell assets to generate capital gain equal to the excess of the capital loss over $3,000.

EXAMPLE 70

Kevin has already incurred a $6,000 LTCL. He should generate $3,000 of capital gain. The gain will offset $3,000 of the loss. Thus, the remaining loss of $3,000 can be deducted against ordinary income. ◆

---

46. §§ 166(d), 1242, and 1244. Refer to the discussion in Chapter 7.

47. Rev.Rul. 74–175, 1974–1 C.B. 52.

- If the taxpayer already has recognized capital gain, sell assets to generate capital loss equal to the capital gain. The gain will not be taxed, and the loss will be fully *deductible* against the gain.

Timing of § 1231 Gain

Although §§ 1245 and 1250 recapture much of the gain from the disposition of business property, sometimes § 1231 gain is still substantial. For instance, land held as a business asset will generate either § 1231 gain or § 1231 loss. If the taxpayer already has a capital loss for the year, the sale of land at a gain should be postponed so that the net § 1231 gain is not netted against the capital loss. The capital loss deduction will therefore be maximized for the current tax year, and the capital loss carryforward (if any) may be offset against the gain when the land is sold. If the taxpayer already has a § 1231 loss, § 1231 gains might be postponed to maximize the ordinary loss deduction this year. However, the carryforward of nonrecaptured § 1231 losses will make the § 1231 gain next year an ordinary gain.

EXAMPLE 71

Mark has a $2,000 net STCL for 1993. He could sell business land for a $3,000 § 1231 gain. He will have no other capital gains and losses or § 1231 gains and losses in 1993 or 1994. He has no nonrecaptured § 1231 losses from prior years. Mark is in the 28% tax bracket in 1993 and 1994. If he sells the land in 1993, he will have a $1,000 net LTCG ($3,000 § 1231 gain – $2,000 STCL) and will pay a tax of $280 ($1,000 × 28%). If he sells the land in 1994, he will have a 1993 tax savings of $560 ($2,000 capital loss deduction × 28% tax rate on ordinary income). In 1994, he will pay tax of $840 ($3,000 gain × 28%). By postponing the sale for a year, Mark will have the use of $840 ($560 + $280). ◆

EXAMPLE 72

Beth has a $15,000 § 1231 loss in 1993. She could sell business equipment for a $20,000 § 1231 gain and a $12,000 § 1245 gain. She is in the 28% tax bracket in 1993 and 1994. She has no nonrecaptured § 1231 losses from prior years. If Beth sells the equipment in 1993, she will have a $5,000 net § 1231 gain and $12,000 of ordinary gain. Her tax would be $4,760 [($5,000 § 1231 gain × 28%) + ($12,000 ordinary gain × 28%)].

If Beth postpones the equipment sale until 1994, she would have a 1993 ordinary loss of $15,000 and tax savings of $4,200 ($15,000 × 28%). In 1994, she would have $5,000 of § 1231 gain (the 1993 § 1231 loss carries over and recaptures $15,000 of the 1994 § 1231 gain as ordinary income) and $27,000 of ordinary gain. Her tax would be $8,960 [($5,000 § 1231 gain × 28%) + ($27,000 ordinary gain × 28%)]. By postponing the equipment sale, Beth has the use of $8,960 ($4,200 + $4,760). ◆

Timing of Recapture

Since recapture is usually not triggered until the property is sold or disposed of, it may be possible to plan for recapture in low-bracket or in loss years. If a taxpayer has net operating loss carryovers that are about to expire, the recognition of ordinary income from recapture may be advisable to absorb the loss carryovers.

EXAMPLE 73

Ahmad has a $15,000 net operating loss carryover that will expire this year. He owns a machine that he plans to sell in the early part of next year. The expected gain of $17,000 from the sale of the machine will be recaptured as ordinary income under § 1245. Ahmad sells the machine before the end of this year and offsets $15,000 of the ordinary income against the net operating loss carryover. ◆

Postponing and Shifting Recapture

It is also possible to postpone recapture or to shift the burden of recapture to others. For example, recapture is avoided upon the disposition of a § 1231 asset if the taxpayer replaces the property by entering into a like-kind exchange. In this instance, recapture potential is merely carried over to the newly acquired property (refer to Example 58).

Recapture can be shifted to others through the gratuitous transfer of § 1245 or § 1250 property to family members. A subsequent sale of such property by the donee will trigger recapture to the donee rather than the donor (refer to Example 55). This procedure would be advisable only if the donee is in a lower income tax bracket than the donor.

Avoiding Recapture

The immediate expensing election (§ 179) is subject to § 1245 recapture. If the election is not made, the § 1245 recapture potential will accumulate more slowly (refer to Chapter 8). Since using the immediate expense deduction complicates depreciation and book accounting for the affected asset, not taking the deduction may make sense even though the time value of money might indicate it should be taken.

Disposing of Passive Activities

Taxpayers with suspended or current passive activity losses may wish to dispose of passive activities. The current and suspended losses of the activity disposed of will be fully deductible. If there is a recognized loss on the disposition, the loss will not be subject to the passive activity loss limitations. Rather, it will be classified and treated as a normal property disposition loss (refer to Example 64). If there is a recognized gain on the disposition, the gain will first absorb the current and suspended losses of the activity disposed of, and any remaining gain will absorb losses from other passive activities. The gain will also be treated under the normal property disposition rules (refer to Example 63).

PROBLEM MATERIALS

DISCUSSION QUESTIONS

1. Why does the tax law require that capital gains and losses be separated from other types of gains and losses?
2. What are the most common capital assets owned by individual taxpayers?
3. Todd owns the following assets. Which of them are capital assets?
   a. Ten shares of Standard Motors common stock.
   b. A copyright on a song Todd wrote.
   c. A U.S. government savings bond.
   d. A note Todd received when he loaned $100 to a friend.
   e. A very rare copy of "Your Federal Income Tax" (a U.S. government publication that Todd purchased many years ago from the U.S. Government Printing Office).
   f. Todd's personal use automobile.
   g. A letter Todd received from a former U.S. President. He received the letter because he had complained to the President about the President's foreign policy.

4. Are business fixed assets capital assets?
5. Why do court decisions play an important role in the definition of capital assets?
6. In what circumstances may real estate held for resale receive capital gain treatment?
7. A loan made by a taxpayer is a nonbusiness receivable. If the loan is not paid because the debtor defaults, what are the tax consequences?
8. Recognition of capital gain or loss usually requires a sale or exchange of a capital asset. Define "sale" and "exchange."
9. A corporate bond is worthless due to a bankruptcy on May 10. At what date does the tax loss occur? (Assume the bond was held by an individual for investment purposes.)
10. Mequoia, a real estate dealer, purchased for $25,000 a one-year option on 40 acres of farmland. If Mequoia is able to get the property rezoned for single-family residential development, she will exercise the option and purchase the land for $800,000. The rezoning effort is unsuccessful, and the option expires. How should the $25,000 be treated?
11. If a grantee of an option exercises the option, do the grantor's proceeds from the sale of the option property increase? Why?
12. When does the transfer of a patent result in long-term capital gain? Short-term capital gain? Ordinary income?
13. What is a franchise? In practice, does the transfer of a franchise usually result in capital gain or loss treatment? Why or why not?
14. When are lease cancellation payments received by a lessee capital in nature? When are lease cancellation payments received by a lessor capital in nature?
15. Taxpayer is the lessee and the lease is on the taxpayer's residence. Taxpayer makes a payment to the lessor to cancel the lease. Why is the payment nondeductible?
16. In determining the long-term holding period, how is the day of acquisition counted? The day of disposition?
17. Helen exchanges a computer used in her business for another computer that she will use in her business. The transaction qualifies as a like-kind exchange. She had held the computer given up in the exchange for four years. The computers are § 1231 assets. What is the holding period of the computer received in the exchange on the day of its acquisition?
18. Juan purchased corporate stock for $10,000 on April 10, 1992. On July 14, 1993, when the stock was worth $17,000, he gave it to his son, Miguel. When does Miguel's holding period for the stock begin?
19. John inherits stock on July 17, 1993. John's father had purchased the stock on April 10, 1992, for $12,000. The stock was worth $15,000 when the father died on December 20, 1992. The stock was worth $18,000 when John received it on July 17, 1993. When does John's holding period for the stock begin?
20. What is the general rule used to determine the holding period of property sold short? What is an exception to this rule, and why was the exception enacted?
21. Is there any reason a taxpayer would prefer to recognize a loss as a capital loss rather than as an ordinary loss?
22. Differentiate between the capital loss carryover rules for unused capital losses of individuals and corporations.
23. What types of transactions involving capital assets are included under § 1231? Why wouldn't they qualify for long-term capital gain treatment without § 1231?
24. Do casualty gains from disposition of personal use assets receive § 1231 treatment?
25. Are recognized long-term business asset condemnation gains treated as § 1231 gains? (Ignore the possibility of depreciation recapture.)
26. If the result of the netting of § 1231 gains and losses is a net loss, how is the net loss treated?
27. How does the *lookback* rule change the character of a current-year net § 1231 gain?
28. Fully depreciated business equipment purchased for $75,000 was stolen from Max. It was not recovered, and the insurance reimbursement was $10,000. Is this $10,000 gain subject to depreciation recapture? Why?

29. Differentiate between the types of property covered by §§ 1245 and 1250.
30. If depreciable real property is sold at a loss after being held long term, does § 1250 apply?
31. Do any of the recapture provisions apply to real property that is owned by a U.S. taxpayer, but used in Italy?
32. If a taxpayer has a § 1231 gain from disposition of a passive activity, what may happen to the gain before it is treated under the normal § 1231 gain and loss netting process?

PROBLEMS

33. Nancy had three property transactions during the year. She sold a vacation home used for personal purposes at a $35,000 gain. The home had been held for five years and had never been rented. She also sold an antique clock for $3,500 that she had inherited from her grandmother. The clock was valued in her grandmother's estate at $5,000. Nancy owned the clock for only four months. She sold these assets to finance her full-time occupation as a songwriter. Near the end of the year, she sold one of the songs she had written two years earlier. She received cash of $15,000 and a royalty interest in revenues derived from the merchandising of the song. She had no tax basis for the song. Nancy had no other income and $18,000 in deductible songwriting expenses. Assume the maximum tax rate applies to Nancy. Assuming the year is 1993, what is her AGI?
34. Rashad is the owner of a sole proprietorship. The business is on the cash basis of accounting and has $40,000 of account receivables. Rashad is desperate for cash, so he sells the receivables to a collection agency for $23,000. How should he treat this sale of the receivables? How would the answer differ if Rashad was on the accrual basis of accounting?
35. Lucy is a dealer in securities. She purchased $10,000 of stock several years ago. She designated it as held for investment by the end of the day she acquired it. Two years later, she decided that she no longer wanted to hold the stock for investment and, therefore, redesignated it as held for sale in the ordinary course of her business. During the current year, she sold the stock for $35,000.

    a. What are the amount and nature of her gain from disposition of the stock?
    b. Assume the stock was sold for $8,000. What are the amount and nature of the loss from disposition of the stock?

36. Abby sells real estate lots, but meets all the conditions of § 1237. In 1993, she sells six lots, one lot each to Bob, Carl, Don, and Ed and two adjacent lots to Frank. The sales price of each lot is $20,000. Abby's basis is $15,000 for each lot. Sales expenses are $500 per lot.

    a. What are the realized and recognized gain?
    b. Explain the nature of the gain (ordinary income or capital gain).
    c. Would your answers change if the two lots sold to Frank were not adjacent? If so, how?

37. Masram lends $15,000 to his close friend, Bart, on January 29, 1992. Masram is not in the business of making loans. On February 10, 1993, Bart is adjudicated bankrupt, and Masram receives only $1,000 as the first and only payment on the loan. What are the amount and nature of Masram's loss?
38. Marta is looking for vacant land to buy. She would hold the land as an investment. For $1,000, she is granted an 11-month option on January 1, 1993, to buy 10 acres of vacant land for $25,000. The owner (who is holding the land for investment) paid $10,000 for the land several years ago.

    a. Does the landowner have gross income when he receives $1,000 for granting the option?
    b. Does Marta have an asset when the option is granted?
    c. If the option lapses, does the landowner have a recognized gain? If so, what type of gain? Does Marta have a recognized loss? If so, what type of loss?

d. If Marta exercises the option and pays an additional $25,000 for the land, how much recognized gain does the seller have? What type of gain? What is Marta's tax basis for the property?

39. In each of the following independent situations, determine whether the sale at a gain of all substantial rights in a patent qualifies for capital gain treatment:

a. The creator (an individual) sells the patent to a manufacturing company. The creator is not an employee of the manufacturing company.
b. A manufacturing company owns a patent developed by one of its employees. It has been using the patent in its manufacturing process. The company sells the patent along with the assets of the manufacturing process.
c. An investor (an individual) buys a patent that has not been reduced to practice from the creator (also an individual). After holding it for three months, the investor sells it to a retail company.

40. Rocky purchases a seven-year franchise from Wearever Mufflers for $60,000. The $60,000 is payable at the rate of $12,000 per year for each of the first five years. Wearever retained significant powers and rights in the franchise agreement. How much may Rocky deduct in the first franchise year? How much and what type of income must Wearever report in the first franchise year?

41. Freys, Inc., sells a 12-year franchise to Reynaldo. The franchise contains many restrictions on how Reynaldo may operate his store. For instance, Reynaldo cannot use less than Grade 10 Idaho potatoes, must fry the potatoes at a constant 410 degrees, dress store personnel in Freys-approved uniforms, and have a Freys sign that meets detailed specifications on size, color, and construction. When the franchise contract is signed, Reynaldo makes a noncontingent $40,000 payment to Freys. During the same year, Reynaldo pays Freys $25,000—14% of his sales. How does Freys treat each of these payments? How does Reynaldo treat each of the payments?

42. Evelyn acquires 200 Copper Corporation common shares at $10 per share on October 13, 1987. On August 10, 1992, she gives the shares to her son, Bob. At the time of the gift, the shares are worth $40 each. On May 11, 1993, Bob sells the shares for $45 each. What is Bob's gain? Is it short or long term?

43. Dennis sells short 100 shares of ARC stock at $20 per share on January 15, 1993. He buys 200 shares of ARC stock on April 1, 1993, at $25 per share. On May 2, 1993, he closes the short sale by delivering 100 of the shares purchased April 1.

a. What are the amount and nature of Dennis's loss upon closing the short sale?
b. When does the holding period for the remaining 100 shares begin?
c. If Dennis sells (at $27 per share) the remaining 100 shares on January 20, 1994, what will be the nature of his gain or loss?

44. Elaine (single with no dependents) has the following transactions in 1993:

Adjusted gross income (exclusive of capital gains and losses)	$80,000
Long-term capital gain	12,000
Long-term capital loss	(5,000)
Short-term capital gain	1,000
Short-term capital loss	(1,900)

What is Elaine's net capital gain or loss?

45. Betty is a head of household with three dependents. In 1993, she had an $18,000 loss from the sale of a personal residence. She also purchased a patent from an individual inventor for $8,000 and resold it in two months for $7,000. The patent had not yet been reduced to practice. Betty purchased the patent as an investment. Additionally, she had the following capital gains and losses from stock transactions:

Long-term capital loss	($3,000)
Long-term capital loss carryover from 1992	(12,000)
Short-term capital gain	21,000
Short-term capital loss	(6,000)

What is Betty's net capital gain or loss?

46. In 1993, Wilbur (single with no dependents) engaged in various stock transactions. He purchased RST, Inc., common stock on January 10, for $8,000. The price began to plummet almost immediately. Wilbur sold the stock short on March 31, 1993, for $3,000. On June 11, 1993, he closed the short sale by delivering identical stock that he had purchased on June 10, 1993, for $10,000. On June 11, 1993, the price of the RST stock was $12,000. A very favorable first-quarter earnings report (contrary to rumored large losses) accounted for the swings in the stock price. Wilbur also had the following other stock transaction results: $500 STCG, $6,300 STCL, $700 LTCL, $43,500 LTCG. He has $210,000 of taxable income from sources other than those previously mentioned. The taxable income has already been adjusted the appropriate amount for the phase-out of the personal exemption deduction. What is Wilbur's net capital gain or loss? What is his total tax liability?

47. For several years, Keith had rented an apartment for $3,000 per month. In 1993, a fire destroyed the apartment building. Under local law, the landlord was required to find comparable housing for Keith within five days. The landlord offered him $10,000 in lieu of suitable housing and in cancellation of the remaining two years of his lease. Keith accepted. Keith's belongings were destroyed in the fire. All the belongings had been owned more than one year. His insurance covered everything for replacement value. Keith received a check for $76,000. He prepared the following schedule to aid in your analysis:

Item	Adjusted Basis	FMV	Insurance Award	Action Taken	Amount Spent
Clothing	$25,000	$ 3,000	$25,000	Replaced	$40,000
Piano	8,000	12,000	10,000	Not replaced	—
Furniture	45,000	33,000	41,000	Replaced	38,000

Keith wishes to defer gains if possible. His salary is $120,000. What is his net capital gain or loss? His AGI? His basis for the replacement assets?

48. For 1993, Ahmad completes the following stock transactions:

	Date Acquired	Cost	Date Sold	Selling Price
1,000 shares ABC	1/6/93	$4,000	8/2/93	$8,000
200 shares DEF	7/1/82	8,800	9/18/93	9,400
3,500 shares GHI	5/2/93	7,000	11/2/93	8,900
5,000 shares JKL	8/5/93	9,700	12/15/93	5,000

What is Ahmad's includible gain or deductible loss resulting from these stock sales?

49. Consuela, a head of household, with two dependents, has the following 1993 transactions:

Adjusted gross income (exclusive of capital gains and losses)	$125,250
Long-term capital loss	(5,000)
Long-term capital gain	20,000
Short-term capital loss carryover	(2,000)

a. What is Consuela's net capital gain or loss?
b. What is Consuela's taxable income assuming she does not itemize and has one personal exemption?
c. What is Consuela's tax on taxable income?

50. Purple Corporation has $16,800 of long-term capital loss for 1993 and $5,000 of other taxable income. What are Purple's 1993 taxable income and the amount (if any) of its capital loss carryover?

51. Bob owns a farming sole proprietorship. During the year, he sold a milk cow that he had owned for 13 months and a workhorse that he had owned for 56 months. The

cow had an adjusted basis of $800 and was sold for $550. The horse had an adjusted basis of $350 and was sold for $1,000. Bob also has a $200 long-term capital loss from the sale of corporate stock. He has $55,000 of other AGI (not associated with the items above) for the year. Bob has no net § 1231 losses from previous years. What is the nature of the gains or losses from the disposition of the farm animals, and what is Bob's AGI for the year?

52. Vicki has the following net § 1231 results for each of the years shown. What would be the nature of the net gains in 1992 and 1993?

Tax Year	Net § 1231 Loss	Net § 1231 Gain
1988	$ 5,000	
1989	17,000	
1990	35,000	
1991		$10,000
1992		30,000
1993		25,000

53. Troy, who owns and operates a farm business, had the following transactions during 1993:

- Damage from the wreck of a business machine held more than one year due to hurricane ($15,000 loss).
- Sale of a mechanical rake bought on April 1 and sold on September 1 ($600 loss).
- Sale of farmland with unharvested crops, held four years ($12,000 gain).
- Insurance recovery on theft of a family brooch owned for 10 years ($10,000 gain).
- Fire in silo on December 6, purchased May 8 ($1,000 loss).
- Sale of grist mill owned 11 years ($3,000 loss).
- Sale of 15 shares of ABC Corporation stock held four months ($1,800 gain).

a. How is each transaction treated?
b. What is Troy's 1993 AGI?

54. Rose Company owns two lathes. Lathe A was purchased several years ago for $15,000, has a $10,000 adjusted basis, and was sold in 1993 for $11,000. Lathe B was purchased several years ago for $8,000, has a $6,000 adjusted basis, and was sold in 1993 for $4,500. What are the amount and nature of the recognized gain or loss from the disposition of each asset?

55. Tan Corporation sold machines A and B during the current year. The machines had been purchased for $180,000 and $240,000, respectively. The machines were purchased eight years ago and were depreciated to zero. Machine A was sold for $40,000, and machine B for $260,000. What amount of gain is recognized by Tan, and what is the nature of the gain?

56. On June 1, 1990, HIJ Enterprises (not a corporation) acquired a retail store for $400,000. The store was 31.5-year real property, and the statutory percentage cost recovery method was used. The store was sold on June 21, 1993, for $390,000. Depreciation taken totaled $38,000. What are the amount and nature of HIJ's gain or loss from disposition of the store?

57. On January 1, 1983, Esteban acquired a $600,000 residential building for use in his rental activity. He took $450,000 of cost recovery on the building before disposing of it for $800,000 on January 1, 1993. For the period he held the building, straight-line cost recovery would have been $400,000. What are the amount and nature of Esteban's gain from disposition of the property?

58. Dave is the sole proprietor of a trampoline shop. During 1993, the following transactions occurred:

- Unimproved land adjacent to the store was condemned by the city on February 1. The condemnation proceeds were $25,000. The land, acquired in 1982, had an allocable basis of $15,000. Dave has additional parking across the street and plans to use the condemnation proceeds to build his inventory.

- A truck used to deliver trampolines was sold on January 2 for $3,500. The truck was purchased on January 2, 1989, for $6,000. On the date of sale, the adjusted basis was $2,509.
- Dave sold an antique rowing machine at an auction. Net proceeds were $3,900. The rowing machine was purchased as used equipment 17 years ago for $5,200 and is fully depreciated.
- Dave sold an apartment building for $200,000 on September 1. The rental property was purchased on September 1, 1990, for $150,000 and was being depreciated over a 27.5-year life using the straight-line method. At the date of sale, the adjusted basis was $124,783. This is Dave's only passive activity loss, and he has no current or suspended losses from this activity.
- Dave's personal yacht was stolen September 5. The yacht had been purchased in August at a cost of $25,000. The fair market value immediately preceding the theft was $20,000. Dave's yacht was insured for 50% of the original cost, and he received $12,500 on December 1.
- Dave sold a Buick on May 1 for $9,600. The vehicle had been used exclusively for personal purposes. It was purchased on September 1, 1988, for $10,800.
- An adding machine used by Dave's bookkeeper was sold on June 1. Net proceeds of the sale were $135. The machine was purchased on June 2, 1989, for $350. It was being depreciated over a five-year life employing the straight-line method. The adjusted basis on the date of sale was $95.
- Dave's trampoline stretching machine (owned two years) was stolen on May 5, but the business's insurance company will not pay any of the machine's value because he failed to pay the insurance premium. The machine had a fair market value of $8,000 and an adjusted basis of $6,000 at the time of theft.
- Dave had AGI of $4,000 from sources other than those described above.

  a. For each transaction, what are the amount and nature of recognized gain or loss?
  b. What is Dave's 1993 AGI?

59. On January 1, 1986, Cora acquired depreciable real property for $100,000. She used accelerated depreciation to compute the asset's cost recovery. The asset was sold for $89,000 on January 3, 1993, when its adjusted basis was $50,904. Straight-line depreciation for the period of time the asset was held would have been $38,554.

    a. What are the amount and nature of the gain if the real property was residential?
    b. What are the amount and nature of the gain if the real property was nonresidential?

60. Paul owned a § 1245 asset with an adjusted basis of $5,000. He had deducted depreciation of $6,000 ($5,000 adjusted basis + $6,000 depreciation = $11,000 original cost). On May 1, 1991, when the fair market value was $22,500, Paul made a gift of the asset to his daughter, Caroline. She used the asset in her business for two years (deducting an additional $2,000 of depreciation). On November 7, 1993, Caroline sold the asset for $36,000.

    a. What is Caroline's basis for the asset on November 7, 1993?
    b. What are the amount and character of Caroline's recognized gain?
    c. How would your answers in (a) and (b) differ if Caroline had received the asset as a result of Paul's death?

61. Orange Corporation sells depreciable equipment for $59,000 to its sole shareholder, Jane. Orange had a $45,000 adjusted basis for the equipment and had originally paid $85,000 for it. Jane will use the equipment in her home for her personal use. The $59,000 sale price is the property's fair market value at the time of the sale. What are the consequences of this sale for Orange? For Jane?

62. June sold an apartment building she had owned for three years for $35,000. The building had an adjusted basis of $40,000 and was sold to June's brother at its FMV. The furniture in the building was sold to an unrelated party, and a $28,000 § 1245 gain resulted. June sold the land to her brother for a loss of $20,000. She had other

income of $78,000 and $75,000 of expenses deductible for AGI. What is June's 1993 AGI? Assume the real estate was not a passive activity and June had no nonrecaptured § 1231 losses.

63. In 1993, Martha disposes of passive activity A for a $15,000 § 1245 gain and a $30,000 § 1231 gain. Martha has no suspended losses from this activity but has a current operating loss of $3,000. She also has a current operating loss of $8,700 from passive activity B, but has no suspended losses from that activity. Martha has no other property transactions during 1993 and has no nonrecaptured § 1231 losses. What is the treatment of the gains from the disposition of activity A?

64. Refer to the facts of Problem 63. Assume that Martha has a $45,000 § 1231 loss rather than a gain from the disposition of the passive activity. What is the treatment of the loss from the disposition of activity A?

CUMULATIVE PROBLEMS

65. Nikki Hassad is a graduate student at State University. She is single and has no dependents. During 1993, she had $25,500 wages from a full-time job she held until returning to school in August. Nikki received a $3,000 scholarship from State University and used all of the scholarship money to pay for tuition and fees. In June 1993, she won $35,000 with an instant lottery ticket and immediately invested in various stocks. The following table summarizes her stock transactions for 1993:

	Date Acquired	Cost	Date Sold	Selling Price
150 shares Clay	7/2/93	$5,000	12/11/93	$6,200
100 shares Gold	7/2/93	5,000	11/6/93	3,300
120 shares Iron	7/2/93	3,100	10/8/93	8,000
25 shares Sand	7/2/93	1,900		
100 shares Uranium	6/16/91	2,000	12/11/93	9,600

Nikki does not have many itemized deductions, so she will take the standard deduction. Her Social Security number is 393–86–4502, and she lives at 518 Marigold Lane, Okemos, MI 48864. She had $5,600 of Federal income tax withheld on her wages and $7,000 of Federal income tax withheld on her lottery winnings. She also made Federal estimated income tax payments of $3,500.

Compute Nikki's lowest legal tax liability for 1993. Suggested software (if available): *TurboTax* or *MacInTax* for tax return or WFT tax planning software.

66. Margaret Gill, age 33, is single with two dependents. She does not wish to have $1 go to the Presidential Election Campaign. Margaret is an insurance adjuster. She resides at 2510 Grace Avenue, Richmond, VA 23100. Her Social Security number is 566–88–1000. The following information is for Margaret's 1992 tax year. She earned a $40,000 salary. Margaret received $35,000 of alimony and $40,000 of child support from her former husband. The children are Susan Gill (age 11, Social Security number 396–42–8909) and Jason Gill (age 9, Social Security number 396–43–9090). Both children lived with Margaret all year. On March 1, 1982, she purchased 500 shares of People's Power Company for $10,000. She sold those shares on October 14, 1992, for $8,500 after receiving nontaxable dividends totaling $2,600 (including $700 in 1992). She also received $300 in taxable dividends in 1992 from People's Power Company. On November 7, 1983, Margaret purchased 1,000 shares of Violet Corporation for $22,000. On February 12, 1992, she received an additional 100 shares in a nontaxable 10% stock dividend. On February 13, 1992, she sold those 100 shares for $2,500. During 1992, she paid $6,000 in deductible home mortgage interest, $1,200 in property taxes, $2,000 in state income taxes, $600 in sales tax, $2,300 in charitable contributions, and $1,500 in professional dues and subscriptions. Her employer withheld Federal income tax of $12,200. Compute Margaret's net tax payable or refund due for 1992. If you use tax forms for your computations, you will need Form 1040 and Schedules A, B, and D. Suggested software (if available): *TurboTax* or *MacInTax* for tax returns or WFT tax planning software.

67. Glen and Diane Okumura are married, file a joint return, and live at 39 Kaloa Street, Honolulu, Hawaii 56790. Glen's Social Security number is 777–88–2000, and Diane's is 888–77–1000. The Okumuras have two dependent children, Amy (age 15) and John (age 9). Glen works for the Hawaii Public Works Department, and Diane owns a retail dress shop. The Okumuras had the following transactions during 1993:

a. Glen earned $57,000 in wages and had Federal income tax withholding of $14,000.
b. Diane had net income of $98,000 from the dress shop and made Federal income tax estimated payments of $104,000.
c. The Okumuras sold a small apartment building for $465,000 on November 15, 1993. The building was acquired in October 1987 for $300,000; cost recovery was $86,820. The apartment building was a passive activity, with a $2,000 1993 operating loss, and $4,500 of prior-year suspended passive activity losses.
d. Diane sold a delivery truck used in her business. The truck cost $35,000, $21,700 of cost recovery had been taken, and it was sold for $18,000.
e. The Okumuras received $13,000 in dividends on various domestic corporation stock that they own.
f. The Okumuras sold stock for a $15,000 long-term capital gain and other stock at a $6,000 short-term capital loss.
g. The Okumuras had the following itemized deductions: $1,000 unreimbursed medical expenses; $10,500 personal use property taxes; $7,000 qualified residence interest; $3,000 consumer interest; $1,500 of Glen's unreimbursed employee business expenses; $535 of investment-related expenses; and $6,300 of state income taxes paid.

Compute the Okumuras' 1993 net tax payable or refund due. (Ignore self-employment tax.) Suggested software (if available): *TurboTax* or *MacInTax* for tax return or WFT tax planning software.

CHAPTER

ALTERNATIVE MINIMUM TAX

OBJECTIVES

Examine the rationale for the individual alternative minimum tax.

Apply the formula for computing alternative minimum taxable income.

Discuss the role of adjustments in the computation of the alternative minimum tax and explain the adjustments required.

Differentiate tax preferences from alternative minimum tax adjustments and discuss specific tax preferences.

Explain the formula for computation of alternative minimum taxable income to arrive at the alternative minimum tax.

Describe the role of the alternative minimum tax credit in the alternative minimum tax structure.

Introduce the corporate alternative minimum tax.

OUTLINE

Once gross income has been determined and various deductions accounted for, the income tax liability can be computed. Generally, the computation procedure requires only familiarity with use of the Tax Table or Tax Rate Schedules. Some taxpayers, however, may be subject to taxes in addition to the regular income tax. One such additional tax is the alternative minimum tax (AMT). Any taxpayer who is subject to the regular income tax may be subject to the AMT. This chapter explains the provisions of the AMT and the determination of tax liability under its terms.

The individual AMT is discussed in the first part of the chapter. The corporate AMT is similar to the individual AMT, but differs from it in several important ways. Details of the corporate AMT are covered in the last part of the chapter.

INDIVIDUAL ALTERNATIVE MINIMUM TAX

The tax law contains many incentives that are intended to influence the economic and social behavior of taxpayers (refer to Chapter 1). Some of the more prominent incentives designed to influence *economic* behavior permit rapid write-offs of certain costs, including the following:

- Accelerated depreciation write-offs for realty (buildings) and personalty (e.g., machinery and equipment).
- Immediate expensing of intangible drilling costs, circulation expenditures, mining exploration and development costs, and research and development expenditures.

Tax incentives designed to provide relief for taxpayers also include provisions that allow for deferral of income. For example, in limited circumstances, taxpayers may use the completed contract method instead of the percentage of completion method for income tax purposes.

Other tax incentives that are intended to influence social or economic behavior include the following:

- Charitable contribution deductions based on the fair market value of appreciated long-term capital gain property.
- Deduction of certain personal expenditures, including state and local taxes and miscellaneous itemized deductions.
- Exclusion of interest received on debt obligations of state and local governmental units.

Statistical data compiled by the Department of the Treasury revealed that some taxpayers with large economic incomes were able to minimize or even avoid the payment of income tax by taking advantage of the incentive provisions that Congress had enacted. Although these taxpayers were reducing taxes legally through various investments that resulted in preferential treatment for income tax purposes, Congress was distressed by the resulting inequity.

To ensure that taxpayers who benefit from such special provisions pay at least some amount of tax, Congress enacted a special tax, called the *alternative minimum tax (AMT)*, that applies to corporations, individuals, trusts, and estates. Because it is referred to as a *minimum* tax, it is easy to misinterpret the nature of the tax. The AMT is *not* beneficial to taxpayers. Instead of saving (or minimizing) tax dollars through special computation procedures, it can result in additional tax liability.

In expanding the scope of the AMT in TRA of 1986, Congress expressed the following concerns about the ability of some taxpayers to avoid the income tax:

> [T]he minimum tax should serve one overriding objective: to ensure that no taxpayer with substantial economic income can avoid significant tax liability by using exclusions, deductions, and credits. Although these provisions may provide incentives for worthy goals, they become counterproductive when taxpayers are allowed to use them to avoid virtually all tax liability. The ability of high-income taxpayers to pay little or no tax undermines respect for the entire tax system and, thus, for the incentive provisions themselves. In addition, even aside from public perceptions . . . it is inherently unfair for high-income taxpayers to pay little or no tax due to their ability to utilize tax preferences.[1]

Overview of the Alternative Minimum Taxable Income (AMTI) Computation

The original minimum tax and previous versions of the AMT were based on tax preferences. For example, if a taxpayer deducted percentage depletion in excess of the basis of a mineral property, the excess depletion was treated as a tax preference and became a part of the minimum tax base. The *current* AMT is based on preferences *and* adjustments to regular taxable income.

Taxable income is the starting point for computing the AMT. AMT adjustments to taxable income arise because Congress has prescribed AMT treatment for certain income and deduction items that differs from the regular income tax treatment of these items. The alternative minimum taxable income (AMTI) computation requires adjustments to reflect these differences between income tax and AMT treatment of the specified items. Tax preferences are then added and the total is labeled AMTI. The first step in the calculation of the AMT is the determination of AMTI, as shown in Figure 14–1 (see page 14–4).

In order to comprehend the structure of the AMT, it is important to understand the nature of adjustments and preferences.

Adjustments. As shown in the AMTI formula in Figure 14–1, taxable income is increased by *positive adjustments* and decreased by *negative adjustments.* Many of the positive adjustments arise as a result of timing differences related to deferral of income or acceleration of deductions. When these timing differences reverse, *negative adjustments* are made.

Taxable income
Plus: Positive AMT adjustments
Minus: Negative AMT adjustments
Equals: Taxable income after AMT adjustments
Plus: Tax preferences
Equals: Alternative minimum taxable income

Figure 14–1
Alternative Minimum Taxable Income (AMTI) Formula

1. *General Explanation of the Tax Reform Act of 1986 ("Blue Book"),* prepared by The Staff of the Joint Committee on Taxation, May 4, 1987, H.R. 3838, 99th Cong., pp. 432–433.

Adjustments to taxable income that arise as a result of timing differences related to the acceleration of deductions for regular tax purposes include the following:

- Difference between MACRS depreciation deducted for income tax purposes and ADS (alternative depreciation system) depreciation deductible for AMT purposes.
- Difference between the amount allowed under *immediate expensing* provisions applicable for income tax purposes and the amount that would be allowed if the expenditures were *amortized* as prescribed for AMT purposes.

In addition, there are timing differences that relate to deferrals allowed for regular tax purposes but not for AMT purposes. Included in this category of adjustments is the difference between income reported under the completed contract method for income tax purposes and income that would be reported under the percentage of completion method prescribed for AMT purposes.

Several other adjustments do not relate to timing differences. These "adjustments" are like preferences in that they are always positive, never negative (they always increase and never decrease AMTI). Included in this category of adjustments are the following:

- Itemized deductions allowed for regular tax purposes but not for AMT purposes (e.g., state and local taxes and miscellaneous itemized deductions).
- The standard deduction if the taxpayer does not itemize.
- The deduction for personal and dependency exemptions.

These adjustments, and their effect on AMTI, are discussed in detail under AMT Adjustments.

Refer to Figure 14–1 and note the subtotal "Taxable income after AMT adjustments." It would be possible to compute this amount by direct application of the AMT provisions. In the direct method, gross income, computed by applying the AMT rules applicable to income items, would be reduced by deductions computed by applying the appropriate AMT rules. This method, however, would entail much duplication of effort. Instead of computing "Taxable income after AMT adjustments" directly, it is less cumbersome to start with regular taxable income and adjust that figure to reflect differences in the income tax rules and the AMT rules. From a procedural perspective, this means that it is necessary to compute taxable income on Form 1040 before computing AMTI on Form 6251.

Preferences. Some deductions allowed to taxpayers for regular income tax purposes provide extraordinary tax savings. Congress has chosen to single out these items, which are referred to as tax preferences. The AMT is designed to take back all or part of the tax benefits derived through the use of preferences in the computation of taxable income for regular income tax purposes. This is why taxable income, which is the starting point in computing AMTI, is increased by tax preference items. The effect of adding these preference items is to disallow for AMT purposes those preferences that were allowed in the regular income tax computation. Tax preferences include the following items:

- Percentage depletion in excess of the property's adjusted basis.
- Excess intangible drilling costs reduced by 65 percent of the net income from oil, gas, and geothermal properties.

- Net appreciation on contributed long-term capital gain property.
- Interest on certain private activity bonds.
- Excess of accelerated over straight-line depreciation on real property placed in service before 1987.
- Excess of accelerated over straight-line depreciation on *leased* personal property placed in service before 1987.
- Excess of amortization allowance over depreciation on pre-1987 certified pollution control facilities.

These preferences are discussed in detail under AMT Preferences.

AMT Adjustments

Circulation Expenditures. For income tax purposes, circulation expenditures, other than those the taxpayer elects to charge to a capital account, may be expensed in the year incurred.[2] Included are expenditures made to establish, maintain, or increase the circulation of a newspaper, magazine, or other periodical.

Circulation expenditures are not deductible in the year incurred for AMT purposes. In computing AMTI, these expenditures must be capitalized and amortized ratably over the three-year period beginning with the year in which the expenditures were made.[3]

The AMT adjustment for circulation expenditures is the amount expensed for income tax purposes minus the amount that can be amortized for AMT purposes. The adjustment can be either positive or negative, as shown in Example 1 below. The *nature* of AMT adjustments can be understood by examining the adjustments required for circulation expenditures.

Example 1

In 1993, Ted incurs $24,000 of deductible circulation expenditures and deducts this amount for income tax purposes. For AMT purposes, the circulation expenditures must be deducted over a three-year period. This results in a deduction for AMT purposes of $8,000 ($24,000 ÷ 3). Ted's schedule of positive and negative adjustments is as follows:

Year	Income Tax Deduction	AMT Deduction	AMT Adjustment
1993	$24,000	$ 8,000	+$16,000
1994	–0–	8,000	–8,000
1995	–0–	8,000	–8,000
Total	$24,000	$24,000	$ –0–

◆

As discussed previously, it is necessary to realize that taxable income computed for income tax purposes is the starting point in the AMTI computation. Adjustments are required to reconcile differences in the rules for computing taxable income and the rules for computing AMTI (refer to Figure 14–1).

Example 2

Assume the same facts as in Example 1. In addition, assume that Ted's regular taxable income for 1993 was $100,000 and that he had no other AMT adjustments and no tax preferences. In arriving at regular taxable income, Ted was allowed to deduct circulation expenditures of $24,000. However, for AMT purposes, Ted is allowed to deduct

2. § 173(a).

3. § 56(b)(2)(A)(i).

only $8,000. Therefore, his taxable income after adjustment to reflect the AMT rules (rather than the income tax rules) is $116,000 ($100,000 + $16,000 positive adjustment for circulation expenditures). ◆

The AMT adjustments for circulation expenditures can be avoided if the taxpayer elects to write off the expenditures over a three-year period for regular income tax purposes.[4]

Direction of Adjustments. It is necessary to determine not only the amount of an adjustment, but also whether the adjustment is positive or negative. Careful study of Example 1 reveals the following pattern with regard to deductions:

- If the deduction allowed for income tax purposes exceeds the deduction allowed for AMT purposes, the difference is a positive adjustment.
- If the deduction allowed for AMT purposes exceeds the deduction allowed for income tax purposes, the difference is a negative adjustment.

Conversely, the direction of an adjustment attributable to an income item can be determined as follows:

- If the income reported for income tax purposes exceeds the income reported for AMT purposes, the difference is a negative adjustment.
- If the income reported for AMT purposes exceeds the income reported for income tax purposes, the difference is a positive adjustment.

Depreciation of Post-1986 Real Property. For real property placed in service after 1986, AMT depreciation is computed under the alternative depreciation system (ADS), which uses the straight-line method over a 40-year life. The depreciation lives for regular tax purposes are 27.5 years for residential rental property and 31.5 years for all other real property. The difference between AMT depreciation and regular tax depreciation is treated as an adjustment in computing the AMT. The differences will be positive during the regular tax life of the asset because the cost is written off over a shorter period for regular tax purposes. For example, during the 31.5-year income tax life of real property, the regular tax depreciation will exceed the AMT depreciation, because AMT depreciation is computed over a 40-year period.

Table 8–7 is used to compute regular income tax depreciation on real property placed in service after 1986. For AMT purposes, depreciation on real property placed in service after 1986 is computed under the ADS (refer to Table 8–12).

EXAMPLE 3

In January 1993, Sara placed in service a nonresidential building that cost $100,000. Depreciation for 1993 for income tax purposes is $3,042 ($100,000 cost × 3.042% from Table 8–7). For AMT purposes, depreciation is $2,396 ($100,000 cost × 2.396% from Table 8–12). In computing AMTI for 1993, Sara has a positive adjustment of $646 ($3,042 income tax depreciation – $2,396 AMT depreciation). ◆

After real property has been held for the entire depreciation period for income tax purposes, income tax depreciation will be zero. However, the depreciation period under the ADS is 41 years due to application of the half-year convention,

4. § 59(e)(2)(A).

so depreciation will continue for AMT purposes. This will cause negative adjustments after the property has been fully depreciated for income tax purposes.

EXAMPLE 4

Assume the same facts as in the previous example, and compute the AMT adjustment for 2025 (the thirty-third year of the asset's life). Income tax depreciation will be zero (refer to Table 8–7). AMT depreciation will be $2,500 ($100,000 cost × 2.500% from Table 8–12). Therefore, Sara will have a negative AMT adjustment of $2,500 ($0 income tax depreciation – $2,500 AMT depreciation). ◆

After real property has been fully depreciated for income tax and AMT purposes, the positive and negative adjustments that have been made for AMT purposes will net to zero.

Depreciation of Post-1986 Personal Property. For most personal property placed in service after 1986, the modified ACRS (MACRS) deduction for regular income tax purposes is based on the 200 percent declining-balance method with a switch to straight-line when that method produces a larger depreciation deduction for the asset. Refer to Table 8–2 for computing income tax depreciation.

For AMT purposes, the taxpayer must use the ADS. This method is based on the 150 percent declining-balance method with a similar switch to straight-line for all personal property. Refer to Table 8–10 for percentages to be used in computing AMT depreciation.

All personal property placed in service after 1986 may be taken into consideration in computing one net adjustment. Using this netting process, the AMT adjustment for a tax year is the difference between the total MACRS depreciation for all personal property computed for regular tax purposes and the total ADS depreciation computed for AMT purposes. When the total of MACRS deductions exceeds the total of ADS deductions, the amount of the adjustment is positive. When the total of ADS deductions exceeds the total of MACRS deductions, the adjustment for AMTI is negative.

The MACRS deduction for personal property will be larger than the ADS deduction in the early years of an asset's life, but the ADS deduction will be larger in the later years. This is so because ADS lives (based on class life) are longer than MACRS lives (based on recovery period).[5] Over the ADS life of the asset, the same amount of depreciation will be deducted for both regular tax and AMT purposes. In the same manner as other timing adjustments, the AMT adjustments for depreciation will net to zero over the ADS life of the asset.

The taxpayer may elect to use ADS for regular income tax purposes.[6] If this election is made, no AMT adjustment is required because the depreciation deduction will be the same for both income tax and AMT purposes.

Pollution Control Facilities. For regular tax purposes, the cost of certified pollution control facilities may be amortized over a period of 60 months. For AMT purposes, the cost of these facilities placed in service after 1986 must be depreciated under ADS over the appropriate class life, determined as explained above for depreciation of post-1986 property. The required adjustment for AMTI

5. Class lives and recovery periods are established for all assets in Rev.Proc. 87–56, 1987–2 C.B. 674.

6. § 168(g)(7).

is equal to the difference between the amortization deduction allowed for regular tax purposes and the depreciation deduction computed under ADS. The adjustment may be positive or negative.

Mining Exploration and Development Costs. In computing taxable income, taxpayers are allowed to deduct certain mining exploration and development expenditures. The deduction is allowed for expenditures paid or incurred during the taxable year for exploration[7] (ascertaining the existence, location, extent, or quality of a deposit or mineral) and for development of a mine or other natural deposit, other than an oil or gas well. Mining development expenditures are those paid or incurred after the existence of ores and minerals in commercially marketable quantities has been disclosed.[8]

For AMT purposes, however, mining exploration and development costs must be capitalized and amortized ratably over a 10-year period.[9] The AMT adjustment for mining exploration and development costs that are expensed is equal to the amount expensed minus the allowable expense if the costs had been capitalized and amortized ratably over a 10-year period. This provision does not apply to costs relating to an oil or gas well.

EXAMPLE 5

In 1993, Eve incurs $150,000 of mining exploration expenditures and deducts this amount for income tax purposes. For AMT purposes, these mining exploration expenditures must be amortized over a 10-year period. Eve must make a positive adjustment for AMTI of $135,000 ($150,000 allowed for income tax – $15,000 for AMT) for 1992, the first year. In each of the next nine years for AMT purposes, Eve is required to make a negative adjustment of $15,000 ($0 allowed for regular tax – $15,000 for AMT). ◆

To avoid the AMT adjustments for mining exploration and development costs, a taxpayer may elect to write off the expenditures over a 10-year period for regular income tax purposes.[10]

Research and Experimental Expenditures. For income tax purposes, research and experimental expenditures (refer to Chapter 7) may be deducted by the taxpayer in the year paid or incurred.[11] However, for AMT purposes, such expenditures must be capitalized and amortized ratably over a 10-year period.[12] For research and experimental expenditures that are expensed, the AMT adjustment is equal to the amount expensed minus the amount that would have been allowed if the expenditures had been capitalized and amortized ratably over a 10-year period. The AMT adjustment for research and experimental expenditures can be avoided if the taxpayer elects to write the expenditures off over a 10-year period.

EXAMPLE 6

Ann incurs research and experimental expenditures of $100,000 in 1993 and elects to expense that amount for regular tax purposes. Since research and experimental expenditures must be amortized over a 10-year period for AMT purposes, Ann's AMT deduction is $10,000 each year ($100,000 ÷ 10 years) for 1993 and the succeeding nine

7. § 617(a).
8. § 616(a).
9. § 56(a)(2).
10. §§ 59(e)(2)(D) and (E).
11. § 174(a).
12. § 56(b)(2)(A)(ii). For tax years beginning after 1990, a special rule applies to individuals who materially participate in an activity. They are not required to capitalize and amortize research and experimental expenditures generated by the activity.

years. Ann has a positive adjustment for 1993 of $90,000 ($100,000 allowed for regular tax – $10,000 allowed for AMT purposes). The adjustment reverses in each of the following nine years ($0 deduction for regular tax – $10,000 for AMT purposes = $10,000 negative adjustment). ◆

Passive Activity Losses. Losses on passive activities acquired *after* October 22, 1986, are not deductible in computing either the income tax or the AMT. This does not, however, eliminate the possibility of adjustments attributable to passive activities.

The rules for computing taxable income differ from the rules for computing AMTI. It follows, then, that the rules for computing a loss for income tax purposes differ from the AMT rules for computing a loss. Therefore, any *passive loss* computed for income tax purposes may differ from the passive loss computed for AMT purposes.

The Staff of the Joint Committee on Taxation provides this interpretation of the provisions related to AMT passive losses:

> . . . where a Code provision refers to a 'loss' of the taxpayer from an activity, for purposes of the alternative minimum tax the existence of a loss is determined with regard to the items that are includable and deductible for minimum tax, not regular tax, purposes. . . . With respect to the passive loss provision, for example, section 58 provides expressly that, in applying the limitation for minimum tax purposes, all minimum tax adjustments to income and expense *are made* and regular tax deductions that are items of tax preference *are disregarded.*[13]

This explanation by the Staff of the Joint Committee leads to the interpretations in Examples 7 and 8.

EXAMPLE 7

Soong acquired two passive activities in 1993. Activity A had net passive income of $10,000, and no AMT adjustments or preferences were connected with the activity. Activity B had gross income of $28,000 and operating expenses (not affected by AMT adjustments or preferences) of $20,000. Soong claimed MACRS depreciation of $20,000 for Activity B; depreciation under the ADS would have been $15,000. In addition, Soong deducted $10,000 of percentage depletion in excess of basis. The following comparison illustrates the differences in the computation of the passive loss for income tax and AMT purposes.

	Income Tax	AMT
Gross income	$28,000	$28,000
Deductions:		
Operating expenses	$20,000	$20,000
Depreciation	20,000	15,000
Depletion	10,000	-0-
Total deductions	$50,000	$35,000
Passive loss	$22,000	$ 7,000

Because the adjustment for depreciation ($5,000) applies and the preference for depletion ($10,000) is not taken into account in computing AMTI, the regular tax passive activity loss of $22,000 for Activity B must be reduced by these amounts, resulting in a passive activity loss for AMT purposes of $7,000, as shown. ◆

13. *General Explanation of the Tax Reform Act of 1986 ("Blue Book")*, prepared by The Staff of the Joint Committee on Taxation, May 4, 1987, H.R. 3838, 99th Cong., p. 448.

For income tax purposes, Soong would offset the $10,000 of net passive income from Activity A with $10,000 of the passive loss from Activity B. For AMT purposes, he would offset the $10,000 of net passive income from Activity A with the $7,000 passive activity loss allowed from Activity B, resulting in passive activity income of $3,000. Thus, in computing AMTI, Soong must make a positive passive loss adjustment of $3,000 [$10,000 (passive activity loss allowed for regular tax) – $7,000 (passive activity loss allowed for the AMT)]. To avoid duplication, the AMT adjustment for depreciation and the preference for depletion are *not* separately reported. They are accounted for in determining the AMT passive loss adjustment. This reporting procedure also applies to tax shelter farm activities.

EXAMPLE 8

Assume the same facts as in the previous example. For regular tax purposes, Soong has a suspended passive loss of $12,000 [$22,000 (amount of loss) – $10,000 (used in 1993)]. This suspended passive loss can offset passive income in the future or can offset active or portfolio income when Soong disposes of the loss activity (refer to Chapter 7). For AMT purposes, Soong's suspended passive loss is $0 [$7,000 (amount of loss) – $7,000 (amount used in 1993)]. ◆

Passive Farm Losses. A passive farm loss is defined as any loss from a tax shelter farming activity (a farming syndicate or any other activity consisting of farming unless the taxpayer materially participates in the activity). The limitations on passive farm losses are more severe than the limitations on nonfarm passive losses. Each farming activity is treated separately for purposes of applying the limitation, and passive losses from one farming activity cannot be netted against passive income from a different farming activity. For AMT purposes, the passive farm loss limitations are applied before application of the general passive loss limitations. Thus, even though passive income from a farming activity cannot be offset by passive losses from other farming activities, such income can be offset by passive loss from nonfarm activities.[14]

If a nonfarm passive activity results in a suspended loss, the suspended loss can offset passive income from other nonfarm activities. However, if a farm passive activity results in a suspended loss, the suspended loss can offset income only from the *same* activity in a subsequent year for AMT purposes. This rule does not apply, however, in the year of termination of the taxpayer's entire interest in the farm shelter activity. In this case, the amount of loss is allowed in determining AMTI and is not treated as a loss from a tax shelter farm activity.[15]

Use of Completed Contract Method of Accounting. For any long-term contract entered into after March 1, 1986, taxpayers are required to use the percentage of completion method for AMT purposes. However, in limited circumstances, taxpayers can use the completed contract method for income tax purposes (see Chapter 15).[16] Thus, the taxpayer will recognize a different amount of income for income tax purposes than for AMT purposes. The resulting AMT adjustment is equal to the difference between income reported under the percentage of completion method and the amount reported using the completed contract

14. *General Explanation of the Tax Reform Act of 1986 ("Blue Book")*, prepared by The Staff of the Joint Committee on Taxation, May 4, 1987, H.R. 3838, 99th Cong., pp. 446–447.

15. § 58(c)(2).

16. See Chapter 15, Accounting Periods and Methods, for a detailed discussion of the completed contract and percentage of completion methods of accounting.

method. The adjustment can be either positive or negative, depending on the amount of income recognized under the different methods.

An AMT adjustment on long-term contracts can be avoided by using the percentage of completion method for regular income tax purposes rather than the completed contract method.

Incentive Stock Options. Employers grant incentive stock options (ISOs) to help attract new personnel and retain those who are already employed. At the time an ISO is granted, the employer corporation sets an option price for the corporation's stock. If the value of the stock increases during the option period, the employee can obtain stock at a favorable price by exercising the option. Employees generally face certain restrictions as to when they can dispose of stock acquired under an ISO (e.g., a condition as to length of employment may be imposed). Therefore, the stock may not be freely transferable until a specified period has passed. The exercise of an ISO does not increase regular taxable income.[17] However, for AMT purposes, the excess of the fair market value of stock over the exercise price is treated as an adjustment in the first taxable year in which the rights in the stock are freely transferable or are not subject to a substantial risk of forfeiture.

Example 9

In 1991, Manuel exercised an ISO that had been granted by his employer, Gold Corporation. Manuel acquired 1,000 shares of Gold stock for the option price of $20 per share. The stock became freely transferable in 1993. The fair market value of the stock at the date of exercise was $50 per share. For AMT purposes, Manuel has a positive gain or loss adjustment (see discussion below) for 1993 of $30,000 ($50,000 fair market value – $20,000 option price). The transaction does not affect regular taxable income in 1991 or 1993. ◆

No adjustment is required if the taxpayer exercises the option and disposes of the stock in the same year. Nor is there an adjustment if the amount realized on the disposition is less than the value of the option at the time it was exercised.

The income tax basis of stock acquired through the exercise of ISOs is different from the AMT basis. The income tax basis of such stock is equal to its cost, while the AMT basis is equal to the fair market value on the date the options were exercised. Consequently, the gain or loss upon disposition of the stock will be different for income tax purposes and AMT purposes.

Example 10

Assume the same facts as in the previous example and that Manuel sells the stock for $60,000 in 1995. His gain for income tax purposes will be $40,000 ($60,000 amount realized – $20,000 income tax basis). For AMT purposes, the gain will be $10,000 ($60,000 amount realized – $50,000 AMT basis). Therefore, Manuel will have a $30,000 negative adjustment in computing AMT in 1995 ($40,000 income tax gain – $10,000 AMT gain). Note that the $30,000 negative adjustment upon disposition in 1995 offsets the $30,000 positive adjustment upon exercise of the ISO in 1993. ◆

Adjusted Gain or Loss. When property is sold during the year or a casualty occurs to business or income-producing property, gain or loss reported for regular income tax may be different from gain or loss determined for the AMT.

---

17. § 421(a).

This is so because the adjusted basis of the property for AMT purposes must reflect any current and prior AMT adjustments for the following:

- Depreciation.
- Circulation expenditures.
- Research and experimental expenditures.
- Mining exploration and development costs.
- Amortization of certified pollution control facilities.

A negative gain or loss adjustment is required if:

- the gain for AMT purposes is less than the gain for income tax purposes;
- the loss for AMT purposes is more than the loss for income tax purposes; or
- a loss is computed for AMT purposes and a gain is computed for income tax purposes.

Otherwise, the AMT gain or loss adjustment is positive.

EXAMPLE 11

In January 1993, Kate paid $100,000 for a duplex acquired for rental purposes. Income tax depreciation in 1993 was $3,485 ($100,000 cost × 3.485% from Table 8–7). AMT depreciation was $2,396 ($100,000 cost × 2.396% from Table 8–12). For AMT purposes, Kate made a positive adjustment of $1,089 ($3,485 income tax depreciation – $2,396 AMT depreciation). ◆

EXAMPLE 12

Kate sold the duplex on December 20, 1994, for $105,000. Income tax depreciation for 1994 is $3,485 [($100,000 cost × 3.636% from Table 8–7) × (11.5/12)]. AMT depreciation for 1994 is $2,396 [($100,000 cost × 2.500% from Table 8–12) × (11.5/12)]. Kate's AMT adjustment for 1994 is $1,089 ($3,485 income tax depreciation – $2,396 AMT depreciation). ◆

Because depreciation on the duplex differs for income tax and AMT purposes, the adjusted bases also will differ. Consequently, the gain or loss on disposition of the duplex will be different for income tax and AMT purposes.

EXAMPLE 13

The adjusted basis of Kate's duplex for income tax purposes is $93,030 ($100,000 cost – $3,485 depreciation for 1993 – $3,485 depreciation for 1994). For AMT purposes, the adjusted basis is $95,208 ($100,000 cost – $2,396 depreciation for 1993 – $2,396 depreciation for 1994). The income tax gain is $11,970 ($105,000 amount realized – $93,030 income tax basis). The AMT gain is $9,792 ($105,000 amount realized – $95,208 AMT basis). Because the income tax and AMT gain on the sale of the duplex differ, Kate must make a negative AMT adjustment of $2,178 ($11,970 income tax gain – $9,792 AMT gain). Note that this negative adjustment offsets the $2,178 total of the two positive adjustments for depreciation ($1,089 in 1993 + $1,089 in 1994). ◆

Alternative Tax Net Operating Loss Deduction. In computing taxable income, taxpayers are allowed to deduct net operating loss (NOL) carryovers and carrybacks (refer to Chapter 7). The income tax NOL must be modified, however, in computing AMTI. The starting point in computing the alternative tax NOL is the regular NOL computed for income tax purposes. The alternative tax net operating loss (ATNOL), however, is determined by applying AMT adjustments and ignoring tax preferences. Thus, preferences that have been deducted in computing the income tax NOL will be added back, thereby reducing or eliminating the ATNOL.

EXAMPLE 14

In 1993, Adam incurs an NOL of $100,000. Adam has no AMT adjustments, but his deductions include tax preferences of $18,000. His ATNOL carryover to 1994 is $82,000 ($100,000 regular tax NOL – $18,000 tax preferences deducted in computing the NOL). ◆

In Example 14, if the adjustment was not made to the income tax NOL, the $18,000 in tax preference items deducted in 1993 would have the effect of reducing AMTI in the year the 1993 NOL is utilized. This would weaken the entire concept of the AMT.

If a taxpayer has an ATNOL that is carried back or over to another year, the ATNOL must be used against AMTI in the carryback or carryover year even if the regular tax, rather than the AMT, applies.

EXAMPLE 15

Matt's ATNOL for 1994 (carried over from 1993) is $10,000. AMTI before considering the ATNOL is $25,000. If Matt's regular income tax exceeds the AMT, the AMT does not apply. Nevertheless, Matt's ATNOL of $10,000 is "used up" in 1994 and is not available for carryover to a later year. ◆

For income tax purposes, the NOL can be carried back 3 years and forward 15 years. However, the taxpayer may elect to forgo the three-year carryback. These rules generally apply to the ATNOL as well, except that the election to forgo the three-year carryback is not available for the ATNOL unless it was elected with respect to the income tax NOL.

Itemized Deductions. Taxes (state, local, foreign income, and property taxes) and miscellaneous itemized deductions that are subject to the 2 percent of AGI floor are not allowed in computing AMT. A positive AMT adjustment in the total amount of the income tax deduction for each is required. Moreover, if the taxpayer's gross income includes the recovery of any tax deducted as an itemized deduction for income tax purposes, a negative AMT adjustment in the amount of the recovery is allowed for AMTI purposes. For example, state, local, and foreign income taxes can be deducted for income tax purposes, but cannot be deducted in computing AMTI. Because of this, any refund of such taxes from a prior year is not included in AMTI. Therefore, a negative adjustment is made if an income tax refund has been included in computing regular taxable income. Under the tax benefit rule, a tax refund is included in taxable income to the extent that the taxpayer obtained a tax benefit by deducting the tax in a prior year.

Itemized deductions that are allowed for AMT purposes include the following:

- Casualty losses.
- Gambling losses.
- Charitable contributions.
- Medical expenses in excess of 10 percent of AGI.
- Estate tax on income in respect of a decedent.
- Qualified interest.

The 3 percent floor that applies to income tax itemized deductions of certain high-income taxpayers (refer to Chapter 10) does not apply in computing AMT. The effect of the 3 percent floor is to disallow a portion of the taxpayer's itemized deductions for income tax purposes. Because this floor does not apply for AMT purposes, taxable income, which is the starting point for computing AMTI, must be reduced by the amount of the disallowed deductions. Although this reduction has the same effect on AMTI as a negative adjustment, it is not shown on Form 6251 as such. Instead, it is shown on a separate line as a subtraction from taxable income.

Medical Expenses. The rules for determining the AMT deductions for medical expenses are sufficiently complex to require further explanation. For income tax purposes, medical expenses are deductible to the extent they exceed 7.5 percent of AGI. However, for AMT purposes, medical expenses are deductible only to the extent they exceed 10 percent of AGI.

EXAMPLE 16

Norm, who had AGI of $100,000 in 1993, incurred medical expenses of $12,000 during the year. For income tax purposes, he can deduct $4,500 [$12,000 medical expenses – .075($100,000 AGI)]. In computing the AMT, he can deduct only $2,000 [$12,000 medical expenses – .10($100,000 AGI)]. Because taxable income is the starting point in computing AMTI, Norm must make a positive adjustment of $2,500 ($4,500 income tax deduction – $2,000 AMT deduction). ◆

Interest in General. The AMT itemized deduction allowed for interest expense includes only qualified housing interest and investment interest to the extent of net investment income that is included in the determination of AMTI.

In computing regular taxable income, taxpayers who itemize can deduct the following types of interest (refer to Chapter 10):

- Qualified residence interest.
- Investment interest, subject to the investment interest limitations (discussed under Investment Interest).

Housing Interest. Under current income tax rules, taxpayers who itemize can deduct qualified *residence* interest on up to two residences. However, the deduction is limited to interest on acquisition indebtedness up to $1 million and home equity indebtedness up to $100,000. Acquisition indebtedness is debt that is incurred in acquiring, constructing, or substantially improving a qualified residence of the taxpayer and secured by the residence of the taxpayer. Home equity indebtedness is indebtedness secured by a qualified residence of the taxpayer, but does not include acquisition indebtedness.

EXAMPLE 17

Gail, who used the proceeds of a mortgage to acquire a personal residence, paid mortgage interest of $112,000 in 1993. Of this amount, $14,000 was attributable to acquisition indebtedness in excess of $1 million. For income tax purposes, Gail may deduct mortgage interest of $98,000 ($112,000 total – $14,000 disallowed). ◆

The mortgage interest deduction for AMT purposes is limited to *qualified housing interest*, rather than *qualified residence interest*. Qualified housing interest includes only interest incurred to acquire, construct, or substantially improve the taxpayer's principal residence. It also includes such interest on one other dwelling used for personal purposes. When additional mortgage interest is incurred (e.g., through a home equity loan), interest paid will be deductible as qualified housing interest for AMT purposes only if:

- The proceeds are used to acquire or substantially improve a qualified residence.

- Interest on the prior loan was qualified housing interest.
- The amount of the loan was not increased.

A positive AMT adjustment is required in the amount of the difference between qualified *residence* interest allowed as an itemized deduction for regular tax purposes and qualified *housing* interest allowed in the determination of AMTI.

Investment Interest. Investment interest is deductible for income tax purposes and for AMT purposes to the extent of qualified net investment income.

EXAMPLE 18

For the year, Jill had net investment income of $16,000 before deducting investment interest. She incurred investment interest expense of $30,000 during the year. Her investment interest deduction is $16,000. ◆

Even though investment interest is deductible for both income tax and AMT purposes, an adjustment is required if the amount of investment interest deductible for income tax purposes differs from the amount deductible for AMT purposes. There are at least two situations where such an adjustment may arise.

First, interest income on bonds issued by state and local governments is tax-exempt for income tax purposes. Therefore, any interest expense paid or incurred to purchase or carry such bonds is not deductible (refer to Chapter 5). As a result, the income tax base is not affected by either the income or the expense related to the state or local government bonds. For AMT purposes, however, the interest on these bonds is treated as a tax preference and is included in the AMT base. Consequently, any interest expense paid or incurred to purchase or carry the private activity bonds is deductible as investment interest for AMT purposes and is limited to the amount of net investment income included in the AMT base.

Second, an adjustment will arise if proceeds from a home equity loan are used to purchase investments. Interest on a home equity loan is deductible as qualified residence interest for income tax purposes, but is not deductible for AMT purposes unless the proceeds are used to acquire or substantially improve a qualified residence. For AMT purposes, however, interest on a home equity loan is deductible as investment interest expense if proceeds from the loan are used for investment purposes.

To determine the AMT adjustment for interest expense, it is necessary to compute the investment interest deduction for both income tax and AMT purposes. This computation is illustrated in the following example.

EXAMPLE 19

Tom had $20,000 interest income from corporate bonds, $12,000 interest income from private activity bonds, and $5,000 dividends from preferred stock. He reported the following amounts of investment income for income tax and AMT purposes:

	Income Tax	AMT
Corporate bond interest	$20,000	$20,000
Private activity bond interest	–0–	12,000
Preferred stock dividends	5,000	5,000
Net investment income	$25,000	$37,000

Tom incurred investment interest expense of $10,000 related to the corporate bonds and $7,000 related to the private activity bonds. He also incurred $4,000 interest on a home equity loan and used the proceeds of the loan to purchase preferred stock. This $4,000 is deductible as mortgage interest. His investment interest expense for income tax and AMT purposes is computed below:

	Income Tax	AMT
To carry corporate bonds	$10,000	$10,000
To carry private activity bonds	–0–	7,000
On home equity loan to carry preferred stock	–0–	4,000
Total investment interest expense	$10,000	$21,000

Investment interest expense is deductible to the extent of net investment income. Because the amount deductible for income tax purposes ($10,000) differs from the amount deductible for AMT purposes ($21,000), an AMT adjustment is required. The adjustment is computed as follows:

AMT deduction for investment interest expense	$21,000
Income tax deduction for investment interest expense	10,000
Negative AMT adjustment	$11,000

◆

Other Adjustments. The standard deduction is not allowed as a deduction in computing AMTI. Although a person who does not itemize will rarely be subject to the AMT, it is possible. In that case, the taxpayer is required to enter a positive adjustment for the standard deduction in computing the AMT.

The exemption amount deducted for income tax purposes is not allowed in computing AMT. Therefore, taxpayers must enter a positive AMT adjustment for the exemption amount claimed in computing the income tax. A separate exemption (discussed later in the chapter) is allowed for AMT purposes. To allow both the income tax exemption amount and the AMT exemption amount would result in extra benefits for taxpayers.

EXAMPLE 20

Eli, who is single, has no dependents and does not itemize deductions. He earned a salary of $106,050 in 1993. Based on this information, Eli's taxable income for 1993 is $100,000 ($106,050 – $3,700 standard deduction – $2,350 exemption). ◆

EXAMPLE 21

Assume the same facts as in Example 20. In addition, assume Eli's tax preferences for the year totaled $150,000. His AMTI is $256,050 ($100,000 taxable income + $3,700 adjustment for standard deduction + $2,350 adjustment for exemption + $150,000 tax preferences). ◆

AMT Preferences

Percentage Depletion. Congress originally enacted the percentage depletion rules to provide taxpayers with incentives to invest in the development of specified natural resources. Percentage depletion is computed by multiplying a rate specified in the Code times the gross income from the property (refer to Chapter 8). The percentage rate is based on the type of mineral involved. The basis of the property is reduced by the amount of percentage depletion taken until the basis reaches zero. However, once the basis of the property reaches zero, taxpayers are allowed to continue taking percentage depletion deductions. Thus, over the life of the property, depletion deductions may greatly exceed the cost of the property.

The percentage depletion preference is equal to the excess of the regular tax deduction for percentage depletion over the adjusted basis of the property at the end of the taxable year. Basis is determined without regard to the depletion deduction for the taxable year. This preference item is figured separately for each piece of property for which the taxpayer is claiming depletion.

EXAMPLE 22

Kim owns a mineral property that qualifies for a 22% depletion rate. The basis of the property at the beginning of the year was $10,000. Gross income from the property for the year was $100,000. For regular tax purposes, Kim's percentage depletion deduction (assume it is not limited by taxable income from the property) is $22,000. For AMT purposes, Kim has a tax preference of $12,000 ($22,000 – $10,000). ◆

For tax years beginning after 1992, the percentage depletion preference does not apply to independent oil producers and royalty owners.

Intangible Drilling Costs. In computing the income tax, taxpayers are allowed to deduct certain intangible drilling and development costs in the year incurred, although such costs are normally capital in nature. The deduction is allowed for costs incurred in connection with oil and gas wells and geothermal wells. A geothermal deposit is defined as a geothermal reservoir consisting of natural heat that is stored in rock or in an aqueous liquid or vapor.[18]

For AMT purposes, excess intangible drilling costs (IDC) for the year are treated as a preference.[19] The preference for excess IDC is computed as follows:

Intangible drilling costs expensed in the year incurred
Minus: Deduction if IDC were capitalized and amortized over 10 years
Equals: Excess of IDC expense over amortization
Minus: 65% of net oil and gas income
Equals: Tax preference item

EXAMPLE 23

Ben, who incurred IDC of $50,000 during the year, elected to expense that amount. His net oil and gas income for the year was $60,000. Ben's tax preference for IDC is $6,000 [($50,000 IDC – $5,000 amortization) – (.65 × $60,000 income)]. ◆

For tax years beginning after 1992, the preference for excess IDC applies only to a limited extent to independent oil producers.

Charitable Contributions of Appreciated Property. For income tax purposes, taxpayers who contribute certain appreciated long-term capital gain property to a qualified charity are allowed to compute their itemized deduction based on the fair market value of the property (refer to Chapter 10). If the property is greatly appreciated, a generous tax benefit can result because the unrealized appreciation is not taxable.

EXAMPLE 24

Maria contributed Whyte Corporation stock to the United Fund, a qualified charitable organization. Her basis in the stock was $5,000, and its fair market value at the date of

18. § 613(e).
19. The Revenue Reconciliation Act of 1990 provided an AMT deduction for taxpayers who incur IDC attributable to qualified exploratory costs. Coverage of these extremely complex rules is beyond the scope of this text.

contribution was $100,000. Maria's charitable contribution deduction is based on the $100,000 fair market value, even though she has never included the $95,000 of appreciation in income. ◆

For AMT purposes, the contribution of appreciated long-term capital gain property to charity results in a tax preference item. Unrealized gain on such property is offset by unrealized loss on other long-term capital gain property contributed to charity. Thus, only the net amount of appreciation on all long-term capital gain properties contributed to charity becomes a preference.

EXAMPLE 25

Adam made two property contributions of long-term assets to charity during the year. Asset A had a fair market value of $60,000 and an adjusted basis of $25,000. Asset B had a fair market value of $40,000 and an adjusted basis of $56,000. Adam's tax preference on the contributions is $19,000 ($35,000 appreciation on Asset A – $16,000 decline in value on Asset B). ◆

Interest on Private Activity Bonds. Income from private activity bonds is not included in taxable income, and expenses related to carrying such bonds are not deductible for income tax purposes. However, interest on private activity bonds is included as a preference in computing AMTI. Therefore, expense incurred in carrying the bonds is allowed as an investment interest expense in computing AMTI (refer to Example 19).

Depreciation. For real property and leased personal property placed in service before 1987, there is an AMT preference for the excess of accelerated depreciation over straight-line depreciation.

EXAMPLE 26

Joe is a landlord who owns an apartment building acquired on January 2, 1986, for $450,000, with $50,000 of the cost allocated to the land. The building is 19-year property. Joe did not elect the straight-line method for cost recovery purposes. Under the pre-1987 rules applicable to the property, Joe will have an AMT preference item if accelerated depreciation (Table 8–6) exceeds straight-line depreciation (Table 8–8). However, straight-line exceeds accelerated depreciation for 1993, which is the eighth year in the cost recovery period. Consequently, there is no preference item on the property. Joe's cost recovery allowances are computed as follows:

Accelerated depreciation (Table 8–6) ($400,000 × .047 rate for year 8)	$18,800
Straight-line depreciation ($400,000 × .053 rate for year 8)	21,200
Excess of straight-line over accelerated depreciation	$ 2,400

◆

Examination of the cost recovery tables for pre-1987 real property (refer to Chapter 8) reveals that from the eighth year on, accelerated depreciation will exceed straight-line depreciation. Consequently, after 1992 taxpayers will no longer have preferences attributable to pre-1987 real property.

Accelerated depreciation on pre-1987 leased personal property was computed using specified ACRS percentages (refer to Table 8–1, Chapter 8). AMT depreciation was based on the straight-line method, which was computed using the half-year convention, no salvage value, and a longer recovery period.[20] As a

20. The specified lives for AMT purposes are 5 years for 3-year property 8 years for 5-year property, 15 years for 10-year property, and 22 years for 15-year property.

result, in the early years of the asset's life, the cost recovery allowance used in computing income tax was greater than the straight-line depreciation deduction allowed in computing AMT. The excess depreciation was treated as a tax preference item.

EXAMPLE 27

Paul acquired personal property on January 1, 1986, at a cost of $30,000. The property, which was placed in service as leased personal property on January 1, was 10-year ACRS property. Paul's 1986 depreciation deduction for regular tax purposes was $2,400 ($30,000 cost × 8% rate from Table 8–1). For AMT purposes, the asset was depreciated over the AMT life of 15 years using the straight-line method with the half-year convention. Thus, AMT depreciation for 1986 was $1,000 [($30,000 ÷ 15) × ½ year convention]. Paul's tax preference for 1986 was $1,400 ($2,400 – $1,000). ACRS depreciation for 1993 is $2,700 ($30,000 × .09 ACRS rate), and straight-line depreciation is $2,000 ($30,000 ÷ 15). Therefore, the tax preference for 1993 is $700 ($2,700 – $2,000). Paul's tax preferences for excess depreciation are summarized below:

Year	ACRS Allowance	AMT Deduction	Preference
1986	$2,400	$1,000	$1,400
1987	4,200	2,000	2,200
1988	3,600	2,000	1,600
1989	3,600	2,000	1,600
1990	3,000	2,000	1,000
1991	3,000	2,000	1,000
1992	2,700	2,000	700

◆

The preference item for excess depreciation on leased personal property is figured separately for each piece of property. No preference is reported in the year the property is disposed of.

Amortization of Certified Pollution Control Facilities. For income tax purposes, § 169 of the Code provides an election that allows taxpayers to amortize the cost of certified pollution control facilities over a period of 60 months. For pre-1987 facilities, excess amortization is a tax preference item. Excess amortization equals the amortization deducted by the taxpayer minus the amount that would have been deducted if the asset were depreciated over its longer useful life or cost recovery period.

Other Components of the AMT Formula

Alternative minimum taxable income is a somewhat confusing term. For income tax purposes, once *taxable income* has been computed, it is possible to compute the income tax. However, even after *AMTI* has been computed, the AMT cannot be computed until the *AMT base* has been determined. It is necessary to deduct the AMT exemption to arrive at the AMT base. This procedure is shown in the AMT formula in Figure 14–2 on the following page.

Exemption Amount. The initial exemption amount is $40,000 for married taxpayers filing joint returns, $30,000 for single taxpayers, and $20,000 for married taxpayers filing separate returns. However, the exemption is phased out at a rate of 25 cents on the dollar when AMTI exceeds the levels listed below:

- $112,500 for single taxpayers.
- $150,000 for married taxpayers filing jointly.
- $75,000 for married taxpayers filing separately.

The following example explains the calculation of the phase-out of the AMT exemption.

EXAMPLE 28

Grace, who is single, has AMTI of $192,500 for the year. Her $30,000 initial exemption amount is reduced by $20,000 [($192,500 – $112,500) × .25 phase-out rate]. Grace's AMT exemption is $10,000 ($30,000 exemption – $20,000 reduction). ◆

The following table shows the beginning and end of the AMT exemption phase-out range for each filing status.

Status	Exemption	Phase-Out Begins at	Phase-Out Ends at
Married, joint	$40,000	$150,000	$310,000
Single or head of household	30,000	112,500	232,500
Married, separate	20,000	75,000	155,000

AMT Rate. The rate for the individual AMT is a flat 24 percent (21 percent before 1991).

Regular Tax Liability. The AMT is equal to the tentative minimum tax minus the *regular tax liability.* The regular tax liability is equal to the amount of tax from the Tax Table or Tax Rate Schedules increased by any tax from Form 4970 and decreased by any foreign tax credit allowable for income tax purposes. Because only the foreign tax credit is allowed as a reduction of the tentative minimum tax, taxpayers who pay AMT lose the benefit of all other non-refundable credits.

In an AMT year, the taxpayer's total tax liability is equal to the tentative minimum tax. The tentative minimum tax consists of two components: the regular tax liability and the AMT. The disallowance of credits does not affect a taxpayer's total liability in an AMT year. However, it does decrease the amount

FIGURE 14–2
Alternative Minimum Tax Formula

Regular taxable income
Plus or minus: Adjustments
Equals: Taxable income after AMT adjustments
Plus: Tax preferences
Equals: Alternative minimum taxable income
Minus: Exemption
Equals: Alternative minimum tax base
Times: 24% rate
Equals: Tentative minimum tax before foreign tax credit
Minus: Alternative minimum tax foreign tax credit
Equals: Tentative minimum tax
Minus: Regular tax liability*
Equals: Alternative minimum tax (if amount is positive)

*This is the regular tax liability for the year reduced by any allowable foreign tax credit. It does not include any tax on lump-sum distributions from pension plans, any investment tax credit recapture, or any low-income credit recapture. See § 55(c).

of the AMT and, as a consequence, reduces the minimum tax credit available to be carried forward. Thus, for AMT purposes, the government denies all the credits (except the foreign tax credit) that apply in computing the income tax liability. Furthermore, the foreign tax credit cannot offset more than 90 percent of the tentative minimum tax.

It is also possible that taxpayers who have adjustments and preferences but *do not pay* AMT will lose the benefit of some or all of their nonrefundable credits. This occurs because nonrefundable credits may be claimed only to the extent that the regular tax liability exceeds the tentative minimum tax.

EXAMPLE 29

Vern has total nonrefundable credits of $10,000, regular tax liability of $33,000, and tentative minimum tax of $25,000. He can claim only $8,000 of the nonrefundable credits in the current year. The disallowed $2,000 credit will be lost unless a carryover provision applies. ◆

Illustration of the AMT Computation

The following example illustrates the computation of the AMT.

EXAMPLE 30

Hans, who is single, had taxable income for 1993 as follows:

Salary		$ 92,000
Interest		8,000
Adjusted gross income		$100,000
Less itemized deductions:		
Medical expenses ($17,500 – 7.5% of $100,000 AGI)[a]	$10,000*	
State income taxes	4,000	
Interest[b]		
Home mortgage (for qualified housing)	20,000*	
Investment interest	3,300*	
Contributions	5,000*	
Casualty losses ($14,000 – 10% of $100,000)	4,000	(46,300)
		$ 53,700
Less exemption		(2,350)
Taxable income		$ 51,350

[a]Total medical expenses were $17,500, reduced by 7.5% of AGI, resulting in an itemized deduction of $10,000. However, for AMT purposes, the reduction is 10%, which leaves an AMT itemized deduction of $7,500 ($17,500 – 10% of $100,000 AGI). Therefore, an adjustment of $2,500 ($10,000 – $7,500) is required for medical expenses disallowed for AMT purposes.

[b]In this illustration, all interest is deductible in computing AMTI. Qualified housing interest is deductible. Investment interest ($3,300) is deductible to the extent of net investment income included in the minimum tax base. For this purpose, the $8,000 of interest income is treated as net investment income.

Deductions marked by an asterisk are allowed as *alternative tax itemized deductions,* and AMT adjustments are required for the other itemized deductions. Thus, adjustments are required for state income taxes and for medical expenses to the extent the medical expenses that are deductible for income tax purposes are not deductible in computing AMT (see note a above). In addition to the items that affected taxable income, Hans had $35,000 interest on private activity bonds (an exclusion preference). Alternative minimum taxable income is computed as follows:

Taxable income	$ 51,350
Plus: Adjustments	
State income taxes	4,000
Medical expenses	2,500
Personal exemption	2,350
Plus: Tax preference (interest on private activity bonds)	35,000
Equals: Alternative minimum taxable income	$ 95,200
Minus: AMT exemption	30,000
Equals: Minimum tax base	$ 65,200
Times: AMT rate	.24
	$ 15,648
Minus: Regular tax on taxable income	(11,604)
Equals: Alternative minimum tax	$ 4,044

◆

AMT Credit

As discussed previously, timing differences will give rise to adjustments to the minimum tax base. In later years, the timing differences will reverse, as was illustrated in several of the preceding examples. To provide equity for the taxpayer when timing differences reverse, the regular tax liability may be reduced by a tax credit for prior years' minimum tax liability attributable to timing differences. The minimum tax credit may be carried over indefinitely. Therefore, there is no need to keep track of when the minimum tax credit arose.

EXAMPLE 31

Assume the same facts as in Example 1. Also assume that in 1993, Ted paid AMT as a result of the $16,000 adjustment arising from the circulation expenditures. In 1994, $8,000 of the timing difference reverses, resulting in regular taxable income that is $8,000 greater than AMTI. Because Ted has already paid AMT as a result of the write-off of circulation expenditures, he is allowed an AMT credit in 1994. ◆

The AMT credit is applicable only for the AMT that results from timing differences. It is not available in connection with exclusions, which include the following:

- The standard deduction.
- Personal exemptions.
- Medical expenses, to the extent deductible for income tax purposes but not deductible in computing AMT.
- Other itemized deductions not allowable for AMT purposes, including miscellaneous itemized deductions, taxes, and interest expense.
- Excess percentage depletion.
- Tax-exempt interest on specified private activity bonds.
- The charitable contribution preference.

EXAMPLE 32

Don, who is single, has zero taxable income for 1993. He also has positive timing adjustments of $300,000 and exclusions of $100,000. His AMTI is $400,000 because his AMT exemption is phased out completely due to the level of AMTI. Don's tentative AMT is $96,000 ($400,000 × 24% AMT rate). ◆

To determine the amount of AMT credit to carry over, the AMT must be recomputed reflecting only the exclusions and the AMT exemption amount.

Example 33

Assume the same facts as in the previous example. If he had had no positive timing adjustments for the year, Don's tentative AMT liability would have been $16,800 [($100,000 exclusions – $30,000 exemption) × 24% AMT rate]. Don may carry over an AMT credit of $79,200 ($96,000 AMT – $16,800 related to exclusions). ◆

Concept Summary 14–1 presents an expanded version of the AMT formula, with brief descriptions of the components of the formula. Form 8801 should be used to calculate the credit for prior year minimum tax.

Concept Summary 14–1
Expanded Alternative Minimum Tax Formula

Taxable income

Plus: Income tax NOL deduction

Plus or minus: Adjustments to taxable income that are required to compute AMTI, including the following:

Standard deduction (if taxpayer did not itemize).

Personal and dependency exemption amounts.

Itemized deductions allowed for income tax purposes but not for AMT:

Medical expenses deducted for income tax purposes minus amount deductible for AMT.

Miscellaneous itemized deductions in excess of 2% of AGI.

Taxes (includes state and local income taxes, real estate taxes, and personal property taxes).

Refund of taxes deducted in previous year if such taxes were not allowed for AMT (enter as negative amount).

Mortgage interest that is not qualified housing interest.

Difference between investment interest expense allowed for income tax purposes and deduction allowed for AMT.

Excess of ACRS over ADS depreciation on real property placed in service after 1986 (AMT alternative period is 40 years vs. regular tax periods of 27.5 years for residential rental property and 31.5 years for all other rental property).

Excess of ACRS depreciation over alternative depreciation on all personal property placed in service after 1986 (AMT requires 150% declining-balance method, switching to straight-line, over the asset's ADR midpoint or class life).

Circulation expenditures (AMT requires amortization over three years vs. immediate expensing allowed for income tax).

Research and experimentation expenditures (AMT requires amortization over 10 years vs. immediate expensing allowed for income tax).

Mining and exploration expenditures (AMT requires amortization over 10 years vs. immediate expensing allowed for income tax).

Income on long-term contracts (AMT requires percentage of completion method; completed contract method is allowed in limited circumstances for income tax purposes).

Pollution control facilities placed in service after 1986 (AMT requires ADS depreciation using the ADR class life; the straight-line method, 60-month amortization is allowed for income tax purposes).

Adjusted gain or loss:

Incentive stock options (excess of fair market value over option price is a positive adjustment in the year the options are freely transferable or not subject to a substantial risk of forfeiture).

Dispositions of assets (if gain or loss for AMT purposes differs from gain or loss for income tax purposes—refer to Examples 11 through 13).

Tax shelter farm loss if the farm activity is not a passive activity (difference between the amount reported for AMT purposes and income tax purposes).

Passive activity loss (recompute gains and losses for AMT by taking into account all AMT adjustments, preferences, and AMT prior year unallowed losses that apply to the activity; enter difference between AMT amounts and income tax gains and losses).

Beneficiary's share of AMTI from an estate or trust.

Plus: Preferences that must be added to compute AMTI, including the following:

Net appreciation on contribution of long-term capital gain property (considering all contributions, whether the property has appreciated or declined in value).

Tax-exempt interest on private activity bonds issued on or after August 7, 1986.

Percentage depletion in excess of the property's adjusted basis.

Excess of accelerated over straight-line depreciation on real property placed in service before 1987.

Excess of accelerated over straight-line depreciation on leased personal property placed in service before 1987.

Excess intangible drilling costs (IDC) minus 65% of the net income from oil, gas, and geothermal properties (AMT requires amortization over 120 months vs. immediate expensing of IDC allowed for income tax purposes).

Equals: AMTI before deduction of ATNOL.

Minus: Allowable ATNOL (which cannot exceed 90% of AMTI before deduction of ATNOL).

Equals: AMTI.

Minus: Exemption ($40,000 for married joint, $30,000 for single, $20,000 for married separate; exemption is subject to phase-out rules).

Equals: Alternative minimum tax base.

Times: 24% rate.

Equals: Tentative minimum tax before allowable AMT foreign tax credit.

Minus: Allowable AMT foreign tax credit (may not reduce tentative minimum tax before allowable AMT foreign tax credit by more than 90%).

Equals: Tentative minimum tax.

Minus: Regular income tax liability before credits (other than foreign tax credit allowed for income tax purposes).

Equals: Alternative minimum tax (if positive).

Corporate Alternative Minimum Tax

The AMT applicable to corporations is similar to that applicable to noncorporate taxpayers. However, there are several important differences:

- The corporate AMT rate is 20 percent versus 24 percent for noncorporate taxpayers.
- The AMT exemption for corporations is $40,000 reduced by 25 percent of the amount by which AMTI exceeds $150,000.
- Tax preferences applicable to noncorporate taxpayers are also applicable to corporate taxpayers, but some adjustments differ (see below).

Although there are computational differences, the objective of the corporate AMT is identical to the objective of the noncorporate AMT: to force taxpayers who are more profitable than their taxable income reflects to pay additional tax. The formula for determining the corporate AMT appears in Figure 14–3.

AMT Adjustments

Adjustments Applicable to Individuals and Corporations. The following adjustments that were discussed in connection with the individual AMT also apply to the corporate AMT:

- Excess of ACRS over ADS depreciation on real and personal property placed in service after 1986.
- Mining and exploration expenditures (AMT requires amortization over 10 years versus immediate expensing allowed for income tax purposes).
- Income on long-term contracts (AMT requires percentage of completion method; completed contract method is allowed in limited circumstances for income tax purposes).

- Pollution control facilities placed in service after 1986 (AMT requires ADS depreciation over the asset's ADR life; 60-month amortization is allowed for income tax purposes).
- Dispositions of assets (if gain or loss for AMT purposes differs from gain or loss for income tax purposes).
- Allowable ATNOL (which cannot exceed 90 percent of AMTI before deduction for ATNOL).

Adjustments Applicable Only to Corporations. Three AMT adjustments are applicable only to corporations:

- The Merchant Marine capital construction fund adjustment.
- The adjustment for special deductions allowed to Blue Cross/Blue Shield organizations.
- The adjusted current earnings (ACE) adjustment.

The first two adjustments apply to specific types of corporations and are not discussed in detail in the chapter. On the other hand, the *ACE* adjustment generally applies to all corporations[21] and is expected to have a significant impact on both tax and financial accounting.

Capital Construction Funds of Shipping Companies. Amounts deposited in capital construction funds established under the Merchant Marine Act of 1936 are deductible for income tax purposes but not for AMT purposes. Also, earnings on such funds are excludible for income tax purposes, but are not excludible in computing the AMT.

Special Deduction for Blue Cross and Blue Shield Organizations. Section 833(b) allows Blue Cross, Blue Shield, and certain other organizations a special deduction for high-risk coverages. This deduction is allowed for income tax purposes but not for AMT purposes.

Ace Adjustment. Corporations are subject to an AMT adjustment equal to 75 percent of the excess of ACE over AMTI before the ACE adjustment. Historically,

Figure 14–3
AMT Formula for Corporations

Taxable income
Plus: Income tax NOL deduction
Plus or minus: AMT adjustments
Plus: Tax preferences
Equals: Alternative minimum taxable income (AMTI) before ATNOL deduction
Minus: ATNOL deduction (limited to 90% of AMTI before ATNOL deduction)
Equals: AMTI
Minus: Exemption
Equals: Alternative minimum tax base
Times: 20% rate
Equals: AMT before AMT foreign tax credit
Minus: AMT foreign tax credit (limited to 90% of AMT before AMT foreign tax credit)
Equals: Tentative alternative minimum tax
Minus: Regular tax liability before credits minus regular foreign tax credit
Equals: Alternative minimum tax (AMT) if positive

21. The ACE adjustment does not apply to S corporations, regulated investment companies, real estate investment trusts, or REMICs. § 56(g)(6).

the government has not required conformity between tax accounting and financial accounting. For many years, the only *direct* conformity requirement was that if the LIFO method was used for tax accounting, it also had to be used for financial accounting.[22] Through the ACE adjustment, Congress is *indirectly* imposing a conformity requirement on corporations. While a corporation may still choose to use different methods for tax and financial accounting purposes, it may no longer be able to do so without incurring AMT as a result of the ACE adjustment. Thus, a corporation may incur AMT not only because of specifically targeted adjustments and preferences, but also as a result of any methods that cause ACE to exceed AMTI before the ACE adjustment.

The ACE adjustment can be either a positive or a negative amount. AMTI is increased by 75 percent of the excess of ACE over unadjusted AMTI. Or AMTI is reduced by 75 percent of the excess of unadjusted AMTI over ACE. The negative adjustment is limited to the aggregate of the positive adjustments under ACE for prior years, reduced by the previously claimed negative adjustments. See Concept Summary 14–2 (page 14–27). Thus, the ordering of the timing differences is crucial because any lost negative adjustment is permanent. Unadjusted AMTI is AMTI without the ACE adjustment or the ATNOL.[23]

EXAMPLE 34

A calendar year corporation has the following data:

	1992	1993	1994
Pre-adjusted AMTI	$3,000	$3,000	$3,100
Adjusted current earnings	4,000	3,000	2,000

Because ACE exceeds unadjusted AMTI by $1,000 in 1992, $750 (75% × $1,000) will be included as a positive adjustment to AMTI. No adjustment is necessary for 1993. Because unadjusted AMTI exceeds ACE by $1,100 in 1994, there is a potential negative adjustment to AMTI of $825. Since total increases to AMTI for prior years equal $750 and there are no negative adjustments, only $750 of the potential negative adjustment will reduce AMTI for 1994. Further, $75 of the negative amount is lost forever. Prior book income adjustments are ignored for limitation purposes. ◆

ACE should not be confused with current earnings and profits. Although many items are treated in the same manner, certain variations exist. For example, Federal income taxes, deductible in computing earnings and profits, are not deductible in determining ACE.

The starting point for computing ACE is AMTI, which is defined as regular taxable income after AMT adjustments (other than the ATNOL and ACE adjustments) and tax preferences. The resulting figure is then adjusted for the following items to arrive at ACE:

- *Exclusion items.* An exclusion item is an income item (net of related expenses) that is included in earnings and profits, but will never be included in regular taxable income or AMTI (except on liquidation disposal of a business). An example would be interest income from tax-exempt bonds. Exclusion expense items do not include fines and penalties, disallowed golden parachute payments, and the disallowed portion of meal and entertainment expense.

22. § 472(c).

23. §§ 56(g)(1) and (2).

- *Depreciation.* The depreciation expense is calculated using the ADS. Thus, depreciation is computed using the straight-line method without regard to salvage value. The half-year or mid-quarter convention is used for all property other than eligible real estate. The mid-month convention is used for eligible real estate. The recovery periods are 5 years for automobiles, 12 years for property with no class life, and 40 years for all residential rental property and nonresidential real property. These methods are reflected in the appropriate depreciation tables in Chapter 8.
- *Disallowed items.* Any deduction that is never deductible in computing earnings and profits is not allowed in computing ACE. Thus, the dividends received deduction and the NOL deduction are not allowed. However, since the starting point for ACE is AMTI before the NOL, no adjustment is necessary for the NOL. One exception does allow the 100 percent dividends received deduction if the payer corporation and recipient corporations are not members of the same affiliated group. Another exception allows the 80 percent dividends received deduction when there is at least 20 percent

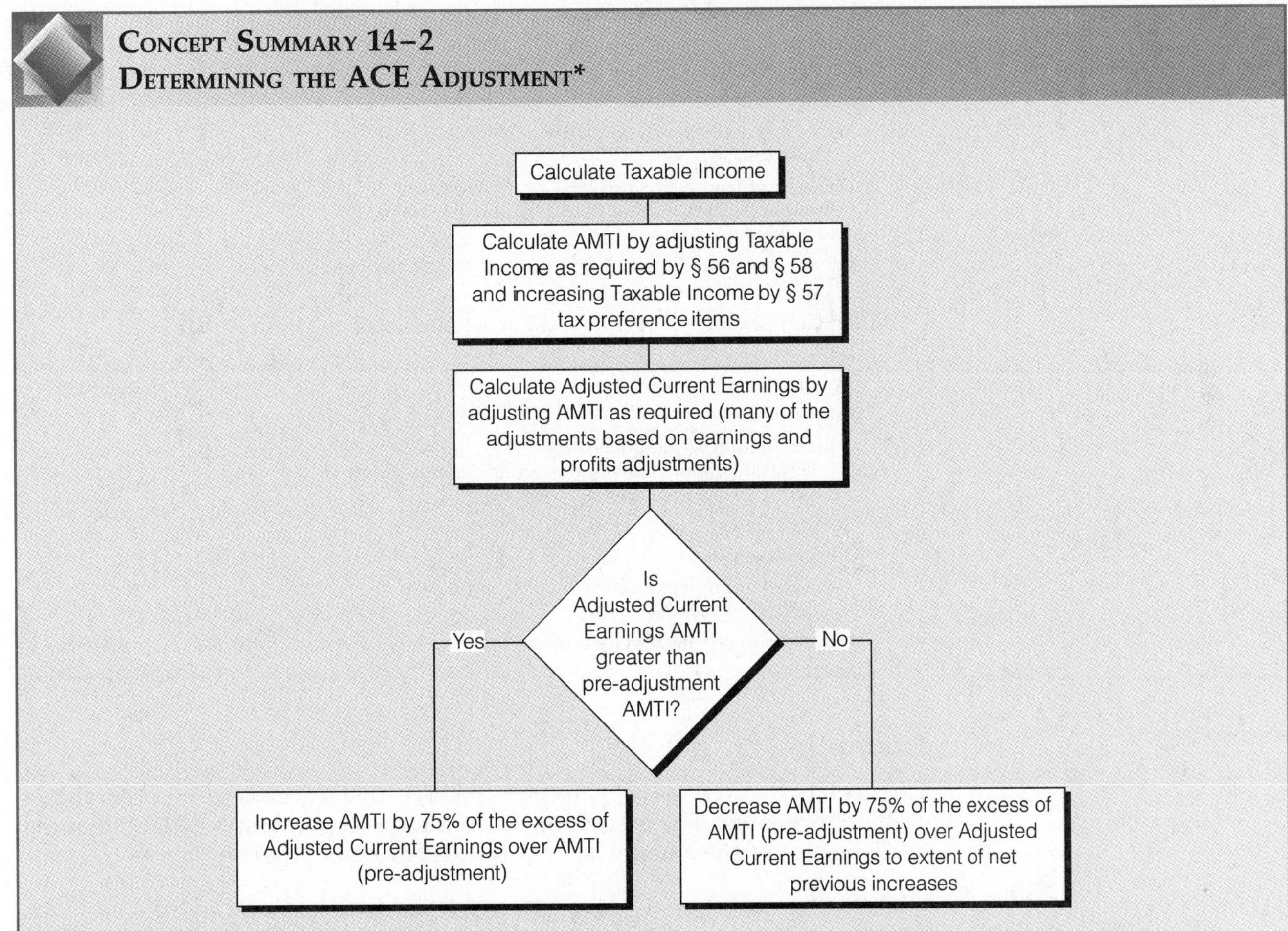
Concept Summary 14–2
Determining the ACE Adjustment*
Calculate Taxable Income
Calculate AMTI by adjusting Taxable Income as required by § 56 and § 58 and increasing Taxable Income by § 57 tax preference items
Calculate Adjusted Current Earnings by adjusting AMTI as required (many of the adjustments based on earnings and profits adjustments)
Is Adjusted Current Earnings AMTI greater than pre-adjustment AMTI?
Yes
No
Increase AMTI by 75% of the excess of Adjusted Current Earnings over AMTI (pre-adjustment)
Decrease AMTI by 75% of the excess of AMTI (pre-adjustment) over Adjusted Current Earnings to extent of net previous increases

*Adapted from "Corporate Alternative Minimum Tax: The Impact of Current Earnings Adjustment on Oil and Gas Companies" by Gallun and Zachry, which appeared in the September 1989 issue of the *Oil and Gas Tax Quarterly* published and copyrighted in 1989 by Matthew Bender & Co., and appears here with their permission.

ownership of the payer corporation. Note that these exceptions do not cover dividends received from corporations where the ownership percentage is less than 20 percent.

- *Other adjustments.* The following adjustments required for regular earnings and profits purposes are necessary: intangible drilling costs, construction period carrying charges, circulation expenditures, LIFO inventory adjustments, installment sales, and long-term contracts.[24]
- *Special rules.* Other special rules apply to disallowed losses on the exchange of debt pools, acquisition expenses of life insurance companies, depletion, and certain ownership changes.

Tax Preferences

AMTI includes designated tax preference items. In some cases, this has the effect of subjecting nontaxable income to the AMT. Tax preference items that apply to individuals also apply to corporations.

EXAMPLE 35

The following information applies to Brown Corporation (a calendar year taxpayer) for 1993:

Taxable income	$200,000
Mining exploration costs	50,000
Percentage depletion claimed (the property has a zero adjusted basis)	70,000
Donation of land held since 1980 as an investment (basis of $40,000 and fair market value of $50,000) to a qualified charity	50,000
Interest on City of Elmira (Michigan) private activity bonds	20,000

Brown Corporation's AMTI for 1993 is determined as follows:

Taxable income		$200,000
Adjustments:		
Excess mining exploration costs [$50,000 (amount expensed) – $5,000 (amount allowed over a 10-year amortization period)]		45,000
Tax preferences:		
Excess depletion	$70,000	
Untaxed appreciation on charitable contribution ($50,000 – $40,000)	10,000	
Interest on private activity bonds	20,000	100,000
AMTI		$345,000

◆

Exemption

The tentative AMT is 20 percent of AMTI that exceeds the corporation's exemption amount. The exemption amount for a corporation is $40,000 reduced by 25 percent of the amount by which AMTI exceeds $150,000.

EXAMPLE 36

Blue Corporation has AMTI of $180,000. The exemption amount is reduced by $7,500 [25% × ($180,000 – $150,000)], and the amount remaining is $32,500 ($40,000 – $7,500).

24. §§ 312(n)(1) through (6).

Thus, Blue Corporation's alternative minimum tax base (refer to Figure 14–3) is $147,500 ($180,000 − $32,500). ◆

Note that the exemption phases out entirely when AMTI reaches $310,000.

Other Aspects of the AMT

Foreign tax credits can be applied against only 90 percent of tentative AMT liability. The 90 percent limit does not apply to certain corporations meeting specified requirements for tax years beginning after March 31, 1990.

All of a corporation's AMT is available for carryover as a minimum tax credit. This is so regardless of whether the adjustments and preferences originate from timing differences or exclusions.

EXAMPLE 37

In Example 35, the AMTI exceeds $310,000, so no exemption is allowed. The tentative minimum tax would be $69,000 (20% of $345,000). Assuming the regular tax liability is $61,250, the AMT liability is $7,750 ($69,000 − $61,250). The amount of the minimum tax credit carryover is $7,750, which is all of the current year's AMT. ◆

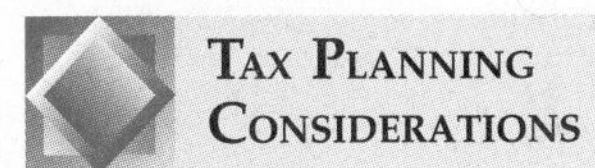

Avoiding Preferences and Adjustments

Several strategies and elections are available to help taxpayers avoid having preferences and adjustments.

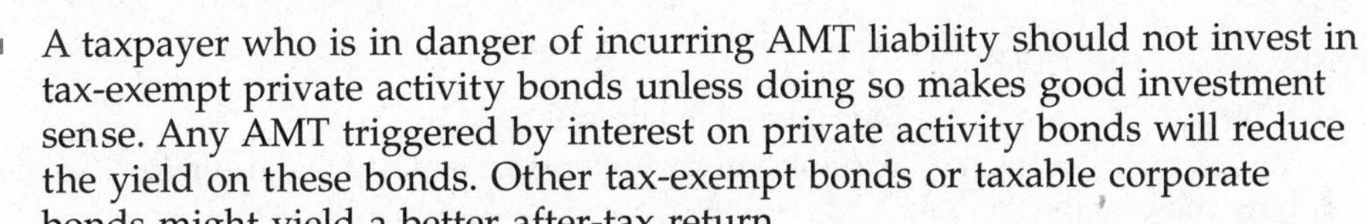

- A taxpayer who is in danger of incurring AMT liability should not invest in tax-exempt private activity bonds unless doing so makes good investment sense. Any AMT triggered by interest on private activity bonds will reduce the yield on these bonds. Other tax-exempt bonds or taxable corporate bonds might yield a better after-tax return.
- A taxpayer may elect to expense certain costs in the year incurred or to capitalize and amortize the costs over some specified period. The decision should be based on the present discounted value of after-tax cash flows under the available alternatives. Costs subject to elective treatment include circulation expenditures, mining exploration and development costs, and research and experimental expenditures.

Controlling the Timing of Preferences and Adjustments

The AMT exemption often will keep items of tax preference from being subject to the AMT. To use the AMT exemption effectively, taxpayers should avoid bunching preferences and positive adjustments in any one year. To avoid bunching preferences and adjustments, taxpayers should attempt to control the timing of those items when possible. For example, a contribution of appreciated long-term capital gain property will result in a tax preference item. Usually, however, the taxpayer can control the timing of such contributions. Therefore, before making a substantial contribution of appreciated long-term capital gain property, the taxpayer should assess his or her position relative to the AMT.

Taking Advantage of the AMT/Regular Tax Rate Differential

A taxpayer who cannot avoid triggering the AMT in a given year can usually save taxes by taking advantage of the rate differential between the AMT and the regular tax.

EXAMPLE 38

Peter, who expects to be in the 31% tax bracket in 1994, is subject to the AMT in 1993. He is considering selling a parcel of land at a gain of $100,000. If he sells the land in 1994, he will have to pay tax of $28,000 ($100,000 gain × .28 alternative capital gains rate). However, if he sells the land in 1993, he will pay tax of $24,000 ($100,000 gain × .24 AMT rate). Thus, accelerating the sale into 1993 will save Peter $4,000 in tax. ◆

EXAMPLE 39

Cora, who expects to be in the 31% tax bracket in 1994, is subject to the AMT in 1993. She is going to contribute $10,000 in cash to her alma mater, State University. If she makes the contribution in 1994, she will save tax of $3,100 ($10,000 contribution × .31 regular tax rate). However, if she makes the contribution in 1993, she will save tax of $2,400 ($10,000 contribution × .24 AMT rate). Thus, deferring the contribution until 1994 will save Cora $700 in tax. ◆

This deferral/acceleration strategy should be considered for any income or expenses where the taxpayer can control the timing. This strategy applies to corporations as well as to individuals.

PROBLEM MATERIALS

DISCUSSION QUESTIONS

1. Why did Congress enact the alternative minimum tax?
2. Two elements in the AMT formula are tax preferences and AMT adjustments. Explain how these elements differ.
3. Adjustments that are considered in computing the AMT can be either positive or negative. Give an example of an AMT adjustment, including amounts. Explain the rationale behind the concept of positive and negative adjustments.
4. Why is it necessary for individual taxpayers to compute taxable income on Form 1040 *before* computing AMTI on Form 6251?
5. Bob incurred $45,000 of circulation expenditures in 1992 and expensed that amount. Compute Bob's AMT adjustments for 1992, 1993, and 1994 and indicate whether the adjustments are positive or negative.
6. During the year, Fran earned $25,000 interest on private activity bonds and incurred interest expense of $14,000 in connection with the bonds. How will this affect Fran's AMT for the year?
7. Tom, who owns and operates a sole proprietorship, acquired machinery and placed it in service in February 1993. If Tom has to pay AMT in 1993, he will be required to make an AMT adjustment for depreciation on the machinery. True or false? Explain.
8. How can an individual taxpayer avoid having an AMT adjustment for research and experimental expenditures?
9. How does the AMT treatment of losses from passive farm activities differ from the treatment of losses from nonfarm passive activities?
10. Certain taxpayers have the option of using either the percentage of completion method or the completed contract method for reporting profit on long-term contracts. What impact could the AMT have on this decision?
11. Megan, a corporate executive, plans to exercise an incentive stock option granted by her employer to purchase 500 shares of the corporation's stock for an option price of $75 per share. The stock is currently selling for $110 per share. Explain the possible consequences of this action on Megan's regular tax and AMT.

12. Ramon acquired stock under an incentive stock option plan in 1990. All conditions of employment were satisfied in 1992, and the stock became freely transferable. Ramon sold the stock in 1993. Discuss the possible effects on taxable income and AMTI in each of the three years (1990, 1992, 1993).
13. Could computation of the AMT ever require an adjustment for the standard deduction? Explain.
14. Abby, who had AGI of $200,000, incurred medical expenses of $25,000 during the year. Compute her medical expense deductions for income tax and AMT purposes. How much is Abby's AMT adjustment, and is it positive or negative?
15. The following itemized deductions are allowed for income tax purposes: medical expenses, state and local income taxes, real estate taxes, personal property taxes, home mortgage interest, investment interest, charitable contributions of cash, charitable contributions of long-term capital gain property, casualty losses, moving expenses, unreimbursed employee business expenses, and gambling losses. Which of these itemized deductions will result in an AMT adjustment?
16. In computing the alternative tax itemized deduction for interest, it is possible that some interest allowed as an itemized deduction for income tax purposes will not be allowed. Explain.
17. What is the purpose of the AMT credit? Briefly describe how the credit is computed.
18. Discuss tax planning strategies for minimizing the AMT.
19. Lee, an equipment dealer who will be subject to the AMT in 1993, has an opportunity to make a large sale of equipment in December 1993 or January 1994. Discuss tax planning strategies Lee should consider in connection with the sale.
20. Discuss the similarities and differences between the individual AMT and the corporate AMT.
21. Some observers believe the ACE adjustment will cause corporations to change some of the methods they use for financial accounting and tax accounting purposes. Comment.
22. Is it ever advisable for a taxpayer to accelerate income into an AMT year? Explain and give an example of how this acceleration might be accomplished.
23. Is it ever advisable for a taxpayer to defer deductions from an AMT year into a non-AMT year where the regular income tax applies? Explain and give an example of how such a deferral might be accomplished.

PROBLEMS

24. Lance is a landlord who owns two apartment buildings. He acquired Longwood Acres on February 21, 1986, for $350,000, with $50,000 of the cost allocated to the land. He acquired Colony Square on April 5, 1990, for $500,000, and $100,000 of the cost was allocated to land. Neither apartment complex is low-income housing. Lance elected to write off the cost of each building as fast as possible. What is the effect of depreciation (cost recovery) on Lance's AMTI for 1993?
25. Jim owns and operates Jimco, a sole proprietorship. On January 3, Jimco acquired a warehouse for $120,000 and allocated $20,000 of the cost to land. Jim claimed depreciation at the MACRS rate of 3.042%. The ADS rate for the first recovery year is 2.396%. Compute Jim's AMT adjustment for depreciation on the warehouse, and indicate whether the adjustment is positive or negative.
26. In January 1993, Helen acquired and placed in service a nonresidential building costing $220,000 and allocated $20,000 of the cost to land. For regular tax purposes, Helen depreciated the building over a 31.5-year period. Compute Helen's AMT adjustment for depreciation on the building, and indicate whether the adjustment is positive or negative.
27. Vera sold an apartment building in October 1993 for $210,000. She had acquired the building in April 1990 for $200,000 and had deducted MACRS depreciation of $25,453 ($5,152 in 1990, $7,272 in 1991, $7,272 in 1992, and $5,757 in 1993). What adjustments must be made in computing Vera's AMTI in each year (1990, 1991, 1992, and 1993)?

28. Tim owns and operates Tim's Auto Parts (TAP), a sole proprietorship. On January 3, TAP acquired a warehouse for $110,000 and claimed MACRS depreciation. Compute Tim's AMT adjustment for depreciation on the warehouse. Refer to the appropriate depreciation tables in Chapter 8 and allocate $10,000 of the cost to land.

29. In 1993, Gary incurred $150,000 of mining and exploration expenditures. He elects to deduct the expenditures as quickly as the tax law allows for income tax purposes.

   a. How will Gary's treatment of mining and exploration expenditures affect his income tax and AMT computations for 1993?
   b. How can Gary avoid having AMT adjustments related to the mining and exploration expenditures?

30. Freda acquired a passive activity in 1993. Gross income from operations of the activity was $150,000. Operating expenses, not including depreciation, were $135,000. Income tax depreciation of $37,500 was computed under the MACRS (post-1986 ACRS). AMT depreciation, computed under the alternative depreciation system (ADS), was $24,000. Compute Freda's passive loss for income tax purposes and for AMT purposes.

31. In 1991, Diego exercised an incentive stock option, acquiring 1,000 shares of stock at an option price of $90 per share. The fair market value of the stock at the date of exercise was $112 per share. In 1993, the rights in the stock become freely transferable and are not subject to a substantial risk of forfeiture. How do these transactions affect Diego's AMTI in 1991 and 1992?

32. Otis is a vice president of Greene Corporation. He acquired 1,000 shares of Greene stock in 1991 under the corporation's incentive stock option plan for an option price of $43 per share. At the date of exercise, the fair market value of the stock was $65 per share. The stock became freely transferable in 1992, and Otis sold the 1,000 shares for $69 per share in 1993. How do these transactions affect Otis's AMTI in 1991, 1992, and 1993?

33. In 1991, Lori exercised an incentive stock option that had been granted by her employer, Black Corporation. Lori acquired 100 shares of Black stock for the option price of $175 per share. The rights in the stock become freely transferable and not subject to a substantial risk of forfeiture in 1993. The fair market value of the stock at the date of exercise was $210 per share. Lori sells the stock for $320 per share in 1994. What is the amount of her AMT adjustment in 1994?

34. Vito owns and operates a news agency (as a sole proprietorship). During 1992, he incurred expenses of $36,000 to increase circulation of newspapers and magazines that his agency distributes. For income tax purposes, he elected to expense the $36,000 in 1992. In addition, he incurred $21,000 in circulation expenditures in 1993 and again elected expense treatment. What AMT adjustments will be required in 1992 and 1993 as a result of the circulation expenditures?

35. Ken, who is single and has no dependents, had AGI of $100,000 in 1993. Ken's potential itemized deductions were as follows:

Medical expenses (before percentage limitation)	$15,000
State income taxes	3,000
Real estate taxes	7,000
Mortgage (qualified housing and residence) interest	9,000
Cash contributions to various charities	4,000
Unreimbursed employee expenses (before percentage limitation)	4,300

What is the amount of Ken's AMT adjustment for itemized deductions for 1993?

36. During the current year, Yoon earned $10,000 dividends on corporate stock and incurred $13,000 of investment interest expense related to his stock holdings. Yoon also earned $5,000 interest on private activity bonds during the year and incurred

interest expense of $3,500 in connection with the bonds. How much investment interest expense can Yoon deduct for income tax and AMT purposes for the year?

37. During 1993, Ed contributed $10,000 cash plus 50 shares of stock to his alma mater, State College. Ed had acquired the stock in 1985 at a cost of $8,000. Fair market value of the stock at the date of contribution was $17,000. Ed also contributed stock worth $4,800 to the United Church. He had acquired the stock for $7,000 in 1985. How much is his tax preference for 1993 as a result of these contributions?

38. Mr. and Mrs. Jackson own a personal residence in the city. The Jacksons also own a cabin at Willow Lake. They use the cabin as a vacation home. In March 1992, they borrowed $50,000 on a home equity loan and used the proceeds to pay off credit card obligations and other debt. During 1993, the Jacksons paid the following amounts of interest:

On the personal residence	$16,000
On the cabin	4,000
On the home equity loan	4,500

What amount, if any, must the Jacksons recognize as an AMT adjustment in 1993?

39. Bill, who is single with no dependents, had AGI of $100,000 in 1993. His AGI included net investment income of $14,000 and gambling income of $1,100. Bill incurred the following expenses during the year, all of which resulted in itemized deductions for income tax purposes:

Medical expenses (before 7.5% of AGI floor)	$11,000
State income taxes	3,200
Personal property tax	1,000
Real estate tax	8,400
Interest on personal residence	12,200
Interest on vacation home (never rented to others)	3,800
Interest on home equity loan (proceeds were used to buy a new automobile)	2,700
Investment interest expense	3,300
Charitable contribution	5,000
Casualty loss (after $100 floor, before 10%-of-AGI floor)	13,000
Unreimbursed employee expenses (before 2%-of-AGI floor)	2,400
Gambling losses	900

What is the amount of Bill's AMT adjustment for itemized deductions in 1993, and is it positive or negative?

40. Sam had AGI of $80,000 in 1993. During the year, he donated corporate stock in Gold, Brown, and Silver Corporations to various public charities. Relevant information about the stock follows:

	Gold	Brown	Silver
FMV at date of donation	$5,000	$7,000	$9,900
Basis of stock	6,500	4,600	2,000
Year of acquisition	1989	1993	1990

What is the amount of Sam's tax preference for charitable contributions for 1993?

41. Peggy, who is single and has no dependents, had taxable income of $102,000 and tax preferences of $72,500 in 1993. She did not itemize deductions for income tax purposes. Compute Peggy's AMT exemption for 1993.

42. Carl, who is single, has no dependents and does not itemize deductions. He had taxable income of $79,900 in 1993. His tax preferences totaled $90,000. What is Carl's AMTI for 1993?

43. Tara, who is single, has no dependents and does not itemize. She has the following items relative to her tax return for 1993:

Bargain element from the exercise of an incentive stock option (no restrictions apply to the stock)	$ 35,000
Accelerated depreciation on equipment acquired before 1987 (straight-line depreciation would have yielded $26,000)	41,000
Percentage depletion in excess of property's adjusted basis	60,000
Taxable income for regular tax purposes	101,000

a. Determine Tara's AMT adjustments and preferences for 1993.
b. Calculate the AMT (if any) for 1993.

44. Beth, who is single, has the following items for 1993:

Income:	
Salary	$105,000
Interest from bank	12,000
Interest on corporate bonds	7,000
Dividends	6,000
Short-term capital gain	8,000
Expenses:	
Unreimbursed employee business expenses (no meals or entertainment)	4,000
Total medical expenses	24,000
State income taxes	6,500
Real property taxes	6,800
Home mortgage (qualified housing) interest	7,200
Casualty loss on vacation home:	
Decline in value	20,000
Adjusted basis	70,000
Insurance proceeds	12,000
Tax preferences	116,000

Compute Beth's tax liability for 1993 before credits or prepayments.

45. Anna incurred an income tax net operating loss of $40,000 in 1993. She had positive AMT adjustments of $8,700 resulting from itemized deductions not allowed for AMT purposes. Her business deductions included tax preferences of $9,200. What is Anna's alternative tax net operating loss (ATNOL) carryover to 1994?

46. During the course of your interview with Jim, who is one of your tax clients, you obtain the following information:

a. Jim, age 52, is single and has no dependents. He is independently wealthy and lives in Aspen, Colorado. In 1993, he earned $32,000 as a ski instructor.
b. Jim's savings account at First National Bank was credited with $18,000 of interest during the year. In addition, he received $20,000 of dividends from General Motors and $49,000 interest on private activity bonds.
c. On March 15, 1993, Jim sold 1,000 shares of Widgets, Inc., stock for $60 per share. He had acquired 1,500 shares of Widgets stock on April 1, 1992, at a cost of $31 per share.
d. An examination of Jim's personal financial documents yields the following information:

- IRA contribution, $2,000 (Jim is not covered by his employer's pension plan).
- State income taxes withheld and estimated payments, $2,160.
- Real estate taxes on his residence, $9,600.
- Home mortgage interest, $22,100.
- Credit card interest, $800.
- Cash contributions to qualified (50% limit) charities, $13,000.

- Professional dues and subscriptions, $900.
- Tax return preparation fee, $2,400.

e. In 1985, Jim acquired an Aspen apartment complex, which he manages. Rental income in 1993 was $240,000. Expenses were $275,000.
f. In 1993, Jim invested in MNO Realty, a limited partnership. His share of the partnership's loss in 1993 was $200,000.
g. Jim's employer withheld $3,500 of Federal income tax in 1993. In addition, Jim made estimated payments of $4,500.

Analyze Jim's tax information and compute his tax liability for 1993. Suggested software (if available): WFT tax planning software.

47. The following itemized deductions were reported on Eve's Schedule A for 1993. On the basis of this information and the additional information in the notes below, determine the effect of Eve's itemized deductions on AMTI.

Medical expenses (before 7.5% floor)	$12,000
State income taxes	4,600
Real estate taxes	2,400
Mortgage (qualified housing) interest	5,400
Investment interest	2,100
Charitable contributions	8,600
Casualty loss	1,100
Unreimbursed employee expenses (before 2% floor)	2,800
Gambling losses	1,500

Additional information:

a. Eve's AGI for 1993 was $100,000.
b. Eve reported $800 of interest income and $1,500 of dividends for the year.
c. Eve earned $1,300 interest on private activity bonds.
d. Eve contributed $2,100 cash to various charitable organizations. She also contributed 100 shares of stock to her church. She paid $40 per share for the stock in 1972, and it was worth $65 per share at the date of contribution.

48. Lynn is single and has no dependents. Based on the financial information presented below, compute Lynn's AMT for 1993.

Income:	
Salary	$33,000
Taxable interest on corporate bonds	1,800
Dividend income	1,900
Business income	64,000
Expenditures:	
Medical expenses	$12,000
State income taxes	6,000
Real estate taxes	8,500
Mortgage (qualified housing) interest	9,200
Investment interest	5,500
Cash contributions to various charities	2,900

Additional information:

a. The $64,000 business income is from Acme Office Supplies Company, a sole proprietorship Lynn owns and operates. Acme claimed MACRS depreciation of $3,175 on real property used in the business. ADS depreciation on the property would have been $2,500.
b. Lynn received interest of $27,000 on City of Columbus private activity bonds.

49. Hal and Wilma filed a joint return in 1993. They have no dependents. Based on the items below and other relevant financial information presented in notes (a) through (e), compute Hal and Wilma's AMT for the year.

Income:	
Hal's salary	$40,000
Dividend income (jointly owned stock)	5,500
Wilma's business income	30,000
Expenditures:	
State income taxes	$ 1,500
Real estate taxes	4,800
Mortgage interest	8,600
Investment interest	7,000
Charitable contributions	28,000

Additional information:

a. Wilma's business income was derived from a news agency (sole proprietorship) she owns and operates. During 1993, Wilma incurred expenses of $30,000 to increase circulation of newspapers and magazines her agency distributes. She elected to expense these expenditures for income tax purposes.
b. Hal and Wilma earned $12,000 interest on State of New York bonds they acquired in 1988. These bonds are classified as private activity bonds.
c. Hal and Wilma contributed corporate stock to Wilma's alma mater, State University. They had acquired the stock in 1975 at a cost of $4,000. Fair market value of the stock at the date of contribution was $25,000.

50. Juan owns a mineral property that had a basis of $17,000 at the beginning of the year. The property qualifies for a 22% depletion rate. Gross income from the property was $100,000 for the year, and net income was $48,000. What is Juan's tax preference for excess depletion?

51. Rita incurred and expensed intangible drilling costs (IDC) of $70,000 during 1993. Her net oil and gas income was $60,000. What is the amount of Rita's tax preference item for IDC?

52. Pat, who is single and has no dependents, had a salary of $90,000 in 1993. She had interest and dividend income of $6,000, gambling income of $4,000, and $40,000 interest income from private activity bonds. Pat presents the following additional information:

Medical expenses	$12,000
State income taxes	4,100
Real estate taxes	2,800
Mortgage interest on residence	3,100
Investment interest expense	1,800
Gambling losses	5,100

Compute Pat's tentative minimum tax for 1993 (rounded to the nearest dollar).

53. Jack is single, has no dependents, and does not itemize. He provides you with the following information for 1993:

Short-term capital loss	$ 5,000
Long-term capital gain	25,000
Municipal bond interest received on private activity bonds acquired in 1989	9,000
Dividends from General Motors	1,500
Excess of FMV over cost of incentive stock options (the rights became freely transferable and not subject to a substantial risk of forfeiture in 1993)	35,000
Fair market value of corporate stock contributed to charity (basis = $5,000)	30,000

What is the total amount of Jack's tax preference items and AMT adjustments for 1993?

54. Bonnie, who is single, had taxable income of $0 in 1993. She has positive timing adjustments of $200,000 and exclusion items of $100,000 for the year. What is the amount of Bonnie's AMT credit for carryover to 1994?

55. Rosa, who is single, had taxable income of $100,000 for 1993. She had positive AMT adjustments of $50,000; negative AMT adjustments of $15,000; and tax preference items of $57,500.

    a. Compute Rosa's AMTI.
    b. Assume the same facts as in (a). Compute Rosa's tentative minimum tax.

56. White Corporation, a calendar year taxpayer, has AMTI of $300,000 for 1993. What is White Corporation's tentative minimum tax for 1993?

57. Browne Corporation, a calendar year taxpayer, has AMTI of $600,000 for 1993 before adjustment for adjusted current earnings (ACE). Browne's ACE is $1,500,000. What is its tentative minimum tax for 1993?

58. In each of the following independent situations, determine the tentative AMT:

	AMTI (before the exemption amount)
Quincy Corporation	$150,000
Redland Corporation	160,000
Tanzen Corporation	320,000

59. Gray Corporation (a calendar year corporation) reports the following information for the years listed below:

	1992	1993	1994
Unadjusted AMTI	$3,000	$2,000	$5,000
Adjusted current earnings	4,000	3,000	2,000

    Compute the adjusted current earnings adjustment for each year.

60. For 1993, Brown Corporation (a calendar year taxpayer) had the following transactions:

Taxable income	$100,000
Depreciation for regular tax purposes on realty in excess of ADS (placed in service in 1988)	150,000
Excess amortization of certified pollution control facilities	10,000
Tax-exempt interest on municipal bonds (funds were used for nongovernmental purposes)	30,000
Untaxed appreciation on property donated to charity	8,000
Percentage depletion in excess of the property's basis	60,000

    a. Determine Brown Corporation's AMTI for 1993.
    b. Determine the alternative minimum tax base (refer to Figure 14–3).
    c. Determine the tentative minimum tax.
    d. What is the amount of the AMT?

CUMULATIVE PROBLEMS

61. Ned, who is single and age 46, has no dependents. In 1993, he earned a salary of $65,000 as vice president of ABC Manufacturing Corporation. Over the years, he has invested wisely and owns several thousand shares of stock and an apartment complex.

In January 1993, Ned sold 500 shares of stock for a gain of $12,000. He had owned the stock 11 months. Ned received dividends of $800 on the stock he retained.

On May 20, 1990, Ned exercised his rights under ABC's incentive stock option plan. For an option price of $26,000, he acquired stock worth $53,000. The stock became freely transferable in 1993.

On September 15, Ned contributed 100 shares of JKL Corporation stock to the American Red Cross. The basis of the stock was $32 per share, and its fair market value was $70 per share.

Gross rent income from the apartment complex, which was acquired in 1982, was $150,000. Deductible expenses for the complex were $180,000. Ned actively participates in the management of the complex.

Ned received $24,000 interest on private activity bonds in 1993. His itemized deductions were as follows: state and local income taxes, $4,100; property taxes on residence, $3,900; mortgage interest on home (qualified housing), $16,500.

Compute Ned's lowest legal tax liability, before prepayments or credits, for 1993.

62. Ron, age 38, is single and has no dependents. He is independently wealthy as a result of having inherited sizable holdings in real estate and corporate stocks and bonds. Ron is a minister at First Methodist Church, but he accepts no salary from the church. However, he does reside in the church's parsonage free of charge. The rental value of the parsonage is $400 a month. The church also provides him a cash grocery allowance of $100 a week. Examination of Ron's financial records provides the following information for 1993:

a. On January 16, 1993, Ron sold 2,000 shares of stock for a gain of $10,000. The stock was acquired four months ago.
b. He received $85,000 of interest on private activity bonds in 1993.
c. He received gross rent income of $145,000 from an apartment complex he owns and manages.
d. Expenses related to the apartment complex, which he acquired in 1983, were $230,000.
e. Ron's dividend and interest income on a savings account totaled $26,000.
f. Ron had the following itemized deductions *from* AGI:
   - $3,000 fair market value of stock contributed to Methodist church (basis of stock was $1,000).
   - $3,000 interest on consumer purchases.
   - $1,600 state and local taxes.
   - $7,000 medical expenses (before 7.5% floor).
   - $1,000 casualty loss (in excess of the $100 floor and the 10% limitation).

Compute Ron's tax, including AMT if applicable, before prepayments or credits, for 1993.

63. Robert M. and Jane R. Armstrong live at 1802 College Avenue, Carmel, Indiana, 46302. They are married and file a joint return for 1992. The Armstrongs have two dependent children, Ellen J. and Sean M., who are 10-year-old twins. Ellen's Social Security number is 333-42-3368 and Sean's is 333-42-3369.

Robert (224-36-9987) is a factory foreman, and Jane (443-56-3421) is a computer systems analyst. The Armstrongs' W-2 forms for 1992 reflect the following information:

	Robert	Jane
Salary (Indiana Foundry, Inc.)	$45,000	
Salary (Carmel Computer Associates)		$70,000
Federal income tax withheld	6,600	13,600
Social Security wages	45,000	55,500
Social Security withheld	2,790	3,441
Medicare wages	45,000	70,000
Medicare tax withheld	653	1,015
State wages	45,000	70,000
State income tax withheld	1,350	2,100

In addition to their salaries, the Armstrongs had the following income items in 1992:

Interest income (Carmel Sanitation District Bonds)	$10,200
Interest income (Carmel National Bank)	800
Dividend income (Able Computer Corporation)	2,200
Gambling income	2,000

Jane inherited $200,000 from her grandfather in January and invested the money in the Carmel Sanitation District Bonds, which are private activity bonds.

The Armstrongs incurred the following expenses during 1992:

Medical expenses (doctor and hospital bills)	$15,000
Real property tax on personal residence	2,600
Mortgage interest on personal residence (reported on Form 1098)	3,600
Investment interest expense	1,200
Contributions	10,300
Gambling losses	1,500

On March 1, Robert and Jane contributed Ace stock to the Carmel Salvation Army, a public charity. They had acquired the stock on February 9, 1979, for $1,500. The stock was listed on the New York Stock Exchange at a value of $10,300 on the date of the contribution.

Use Forms 1040, 4952, 6251, and 8283 and Schedules A and B to compute the AMT for Robert and Jane Armstrong for 1992. Suggested software (if available): *TurboTax* or *MacInTax*.

CHAPTER

ACCOUNTING PERIODS AND METHODS

OBJECTIVES

Explain the tax year provisions and the requirements for adopting and changing the tax year.

Describe the rules of income and expense recognition for the cash and accrual methods of tax accounting.

Analyze the procedures for changing accounting methods.

Explain and illustrate the installment method of accounting.

Explain the alternative methods of accounting for long-term contracts.

Analyze the imputed interest rules applicable to installment sales.

Identify tax planning opportunities related to accounting periods and accounting methods.

OUTLINE

Earlier chapters discussed the types of income subject to tax (gross income and exclusions) and allowable deductions. This chapter focuses on the related issue of the periods in which income and deductions are reported. Generally, a taxpayer's income and deductions must be assigned to particular 12-month periods—calendar years or fiscal years.

Income and deductions are placed within particular years through the use of tax accounting methods. The basic accounting methods are the cash method, accrual method, and hybrid method. Other special purpose methods are available for specific circumstances or types of transactions, such as the installment method and the methods used for long-term construction contracts.

An entire subchapter of the Code, Subchapter E, is devoted to accounting periods and accounting methods. Over the long run, the accounting period used by a taxpayer will not affect the aggregate amount of reported taxable income. However, taxable income for any particular year may vary significantly due to the use of a particular reporting period. Also, through the choice of accounting methods or accounting periods, it is possible to postpone the recognition of taxable income and to enjoy the benefits from deferring the related tax. This chapter discusses the taxpayer's alternatives for accounting periods and accounting methods.

Accounting Periods

In General

A taxpayer who keeps adequate books and records may be permitted to elect to use a *fiscal year,* a 12-month period ending on the *last day* of a month other than December. Otherwise, a *calendar year* must be used. Frequently, corporations can satisfy the record-keeping requirements and elect to use a fiscal year. Often the fiscal year conforms to a natural business year (e.g., a summer resort's fiscal year may end on September 30, after the close of the season). Individuals seldom use a fiscal year because they do not maintain the necessary books and records and because complications can arise as a result of changes in the tax law (e.g., often the transition rules and effective dates differ for fiscal year taxpayers).

Generally, a taxable year may not exceed 12 calendar months. However, if certain requirements are met, a taxpayer may elect to use an annual period that varies from 52 to 53 weeks. In that case, the year-end must be on the same day of the week (e.g., the Tuesday falling closest to October 31 or the last Tuesday in October). The day of the week selected for ending the year will depend upon business considerations. For example, a retail business that is not open on Sundays may end its tax year on a Sunday so that it can take an inventory without interrupting business operations.

Example 1

Wade is in the business of selling farm supplies. His natural business year terminates at the end of October with the completion of harvesting. At the end of the fiscal year, Wade must take an inventory, which is most easily accomplished on a Tuesday. Therefore, Wade could adopt a 52–53 week tax year ending on the Tuesday closest to October 31. If Wade selects this method, the year-end date may fall in the following month if that Tuesday is closer to October 31. The tax year ending in 1993 will contain 52 weeks beginning on Wednesday, November 4, 1992, and ending on Tuesday, November 2, 1993. The tax year ending in 1994 will have 52 weeks beginning on Wednesday, November 3, 1993, and ending on Tuesday, November 1, 1994. ◆

Partnerships and S Corporations. When a partner's tax year and the partnership's tax year differ, the partner will enjoy a deferral of income. This results because the partner reports his or her share of the partnership's income and deductions for the partnership's tax year ending within or with the partner's tax year. For example, if the tax year of the partnership ends on January 31, a calendar year partner will not report partnership profits for the first 11 months of the partnership tax year until the following year. Therefore, partnerships are subject to special tax year requirements.

In general, the partnership tax year must be the same as the tax year of the majority interest partners. The *majority interest partners* are the partners who own a greater than 50 percent interest in the partnership capital and profits. If the majority owners do not have the same tax year, the partnership must adopt the same tax year as its principal partners. A *principal partner* is a partner with a 5 percent or more interest in the partnership capital or profits.

EXAMPLE 2

The RST Partnership is owned equally by Rose Corporation, Silver Corporation, and Tom. The partners have the following tax years.

Partner	Tax Year Ending
Rose	June 30
Silver	June 30
Tom	December 31

The partnership's tax year must end on June 30. If Silver Corporation's as well as Tom's year ended on December 31, the partnership would be required to adopt a calendar year. ◆

If the principal partners do not all have the same tax year and no majority of partners have the same tax year, the partnership must use a year that results in the *least aggregate deferral* of income.[1] Under the least aggregate deferral method, the different tax years of the principal partners are tested to determine which produces the least aggregate deferral. This is calculated by first multiplying the combined percentages of the principal partners with the same tax year by the months of deferral for the test year. Once this is done for each set of principal partners with the same tax year, the resulting products are summed to produce the aggregate deferral. After calculating the aggregate deferral for each of the test years, the test year with the smallest summation (the least aggregate deferral) is the tax year for the partnership.

EXAMPLE 3

The DE Partnership is owned equally by Diane and Emily. Diane's fiscal year ends on March 31, and Emily's fiscal year ends on August 31. The partnership must use the partner's fiscal year that will result in the least aggregate deferral of income. Therefore, the fiscal years ending March 31 and August 31 must both be tested.

Test for Fiscal Year Ending March 31

Partner	Year Ends	Profit %	Months of Deferral	Product
Diane	3–31	50	0	0
Emily	8–31	50	5	2.5
Aggregate deferral months				2.5

1. Temp. Reg. § 1.706–1T(a)(2).

Thus, with a year ending March 31, Emily would be able to defer her half of the income for five months. That is, Emily's share of the partnership income for the fiscal year ending March 31, 1994, would not be included in her income until August 31, 1994.

Test for Fiscal Year Ending August 31

Partner	Year Ends	Profit %	Months of Deferral	Product
Diane	3–31	50	7	3.5
Emily	8–31	50	0	0
Aggregate deferral months				3.5

Thus, with a year ending August 31, Diane would be able to defer her half of the income for seven months. That is, Diane's share of the partnership income for the fiscal year ending August 31, 1994, would not be included in her income until March 31, 1995.

The year ending March 31 must be used because it results in the least aggregate deferral of income. ◆

Generally, S corporations must adopt a calendar year. However, partnerships and S corporations may *elect* an otherwise *impermissible year* under any of the following conditions:

- A business purpose for the year can be demonstrated.
- The partnership's or S corporation's year results in a deferral of not more than three months' income, and the entity agrees to make required tax payments.
- The entity retains the same year as was used for the fiscal year ending in 1987, provided the entity agrees to make required tax payments.

Business Purpose. The only business purpose for a fiscal year that the IRS has acknowledged is the need to conform the tax year to the natural business year of a business.[2] Generally, only seasonal businesses have a natural business year. For example, the natural business year for a department store may end on January 31, after Christmas returns have been processed and clearance sales have been completed.

Required Tax Payments. Under this system, tax payments are due from the partnership or S corporation by April 15 of each tax year. The amount due is computed by applying the highest individual tax rate plus 1 percent to an estimate of the deferral period income. The deferral period runs from the close of the fiscal year to the end of the calendar year. Estimated income for this period is based on the average monthly earnings for the previous fiscal year. The amount due is reduced by the amount of required tax payments for the previous year.

EXAMPLE 4

Brown, Inc., an S corporation, elected a fiscal year ending September 30. Bob is the only shareholder. For the fiscal year ending September 30, 1993, Brown earned $100,000. The required tax payment for the previous year was $5,000. The corporation must pay $3,000 by April 15, 1994, calculated as follows:

$$(\$100{,}000 \times 3/12 \times 32\%^{*}) - \$5{,}000 = \$3{,}000$$

*Maximum § 1 rate of 31% + 1%.

◆

2. Rev.Rul. 87–57, 1987–2 C.B. 117.

Personal Service Corporations (PSCs). A PSC is a corporation whose shareholder-employees provide personal services (e.g., medical, dental, legal, accounting, engineering, actuarial, consulting, or performing arts). Generally, a PSC must use a calendar year. However, a PSC can *elect* a fiscal year under any of the following conditions:

- A business purpose for the year can be demonstrated.
- The PSC year results in a deferral of not more than three months' income; the corporation pays the shareholder-employee's salary during the portion of the calendar year after the close of the fiscal year; and the salary for that period is at least proportionate to the shareholder-employee's salary received for the fiscal year.
- The PSC retains the same year it used for the fiscal year ending in 1987, provided it satisfies the latter two requirements in the preceding option.

EXAMPLE 5

Nancy's corporation paid her a salary of $120,000 during its fiscal year ending September 30, 1993. The corporation cannot satisfy the business purpose test for a fiscal year. The corporation can continue to use its fiscal year without any negative tax effects, provided Nancy receives at least $30,000 (3 months/12 months × $120,000) as salary during the period October 1 through December 31, 1993. ◆

If the salary test is not satisfied, the PSC can retain the fiscal year, but the corporation's deduction for salary for the fiscal year is limited to the following:

$$A + A(F/N)$$

Where A = Amount paid after the close of the fiscal year.
F = Number of months in fiscal year minus number of months from the end of the fiscal year to the end of the ongoing calendar year.
N = Number of months from the end of the fiscal year to the end of the ongoing calendar year.

EXAMPLE 6

Assume the corporation in the previous example paid Nancy $10,000 of salary during the period October 1 through December 31, 1993. The deduction for Nancy's salary for the corporation's fiscal year ending September 30, 1993, is thus limited to $40,000 calculated as follows:

$$\$10{,}000 + \left[\$10{,}000\left(\frac{12-3}{3}\right)\right] = \$10{,}000 + \$30{,}000 = \$40{,}000$$

◆

Making the Election

A taxpayer elects to use a calendar or fiscal year by the timely filing of his or her initial tax return. For all subsequent years, the taxpayer must use this same period unless approval for change is obtained from the IRS.

Changes in the Accounting Period

A taxpayer must obtain consent from the IRS before changing the tax year. This power to approve or not to approve a change is significant in that it permits the IRS to issue authoritative administrative guidelines that must be met by taxpayers who wish to change their accounting period. An application for permission to change tax years must be made on Form 1128, Application for Change in

Accounting Period. The application must be filed on or before the fifteenth day of the second calendar month following the close of the short period that results from the change in accounting period.

EXAMPLE 7

Beginning in 1993, Gold Corporation, a calendar year taxpayer, would like to switch to a fiscal year ending March 31. The corporation must file Form 1128 by May 15, 1993. ◆

IRS Requirements. The IRS will not grant permission for the change unless the taxpayer can establish a substantial business purpose for the request. One substantial business purpose is to change to a tax year that coincides with the *natural business year* (the completion of an annual business cycle). The IRS applies an objective gross receipts test to determine if the entity has a natural business year. At least 25 percent of the entity's gross receipts for the 12-month period must be realized in the final 2 months of the 12-month period for three consecutive years.

EXAMPLE 8

A Virginia Beach motel had gross receipts as follows:

	1991	1992	1993
July–August receipts	$ 300,000	$250,000	$ 325,000
September 1–August 31 receipts	1,000,000	900,000	1,250,000
Receipts for 2 months divided by receipts for 12 months	30.0%	27.8%	26.0%

Since it satisfies the natural business year test, the motel will be allowed to use a fiscal year ending August 31. ◆

The IRS usually establishes certain conditions that the taxpayer must accept if the approval for change is to be granted. In particular, if the taxpayer has a net operating loss for the short period, the IRS may require that the loss be carried forward and allocated equally over the 6 following years. As you may recall (refer to Chapter 7), net operating losses are ordinarily carried back for 3 years and forward for 15 years.

EXAMPLE 9

XYZ Corporation changed from a calendar year to a fiscal year ending September 30. The short-period return for the nine months ending September 30, 1993, reflected a $60,000 net operating loss. The corporation had taxable income for 1990, 1991, and 1992. As a condition for granting approval, the IRS requires XYZ to allocate the $60,000 loss over the next six years, rather than carrying the loss back to the three preceding years (the usual order for applying a net operating loss). Thus, XYZ Corporation will reduce its taxable income by $10,000 each year ending September 30, 1994, through September 30, 1999. ◆

Taxable Periods of Less Than One Year

A *short year* (or short period) is a period of less than 12 calendar months. A taxpayer may have a short year for (1) the first income tax return, (2) the final income tax return, or (3) a change in the tax year. If the short period results from a change in the taxpayer's annual accounting period, the taxable income for the period must be *annualized*. Due to the progressive tax rate structure, taxpayers could reap benefits from a short-period return if some adjustments were not required. Thus, the taxpayer is required to do the following:

1. Annualize the short-period income.

$$\text{Annualized income} = \text{Short-period income} \times \frac{12}{\text{Number of months in the short period}}$$

2. Compute the tax on the annualized income.
3. Convert the tax on the annualized income to a short-period tax.

$$\text{Short-period tax} = \text{Tax on annualized income} \times \frac{\text{Number of months in the short period}}{12}$$

EXAMPLE 10

Gray Corporation obtained permission to change from a calendar year to a fiscal year ending September 30, beginning in 1993. For the short period January 1 through September 30, 1993, the corporation's taxable income was $48,000. The relevant tax rates and the resultant short-period tax are as follows:

Amount of Taxable Income	Tax Calculation
Not over $50,000	15% of taxable income
Over $50,000 but not over $75,000	$7,500 plus 25% of taxable income in excess of $50,000

Annualized income ($48,000 × 12/9)	$64,000
Tax on annualized income [$7,500 + .25($64,000 – $50,000)]	$11,000
Short-period tax = ($11,000 × 9/12)	$ 8,250
Annualizing the income increased the tax by $1,050:	
Tax with annualizing	$ 8,250
Tax without annualizing ($48,000 × .15)	7,200
Increase in tax from annualizing	$ 1,050

◆

Rather than annualize the short-period income, the taxpayer can elect to (1) calculate the tax for a 12-month period beginning on the first day of the short period and (2) convert the tax in (1) to a short-period tax as follows:

$$\frac{\text{Taxable income for short period}}{\text{Taxable income for the 12-month period}} \times \text{Tax on the 12 months of income}$$

EXAMPLE 11

Assume Gray Corporation's taxable income for the calendar year 1993 was $60,000. The tax on the full 12 months of income would have been $10,000 [$7,500 + .25($60,000 – $50,000)]. The short-period tax would be $8,000 ($48,000/$60,000 × $10,000). Thus, if the corporation utilized this option, the tax for the short period would be $8,000 (rather than $8,250, as calculated in Example 10). ◆

For individuals, annualizing requires some special adjustments:

- Deductions must be *itemized* for the short period (the standard deduction is not allowed).
- Personal and dependency exemptions must be prorated.

Fortunately, individuals rarely change tax years.

Mitigation of the Annual Accounting Period Concept

Several provisions in the Code are designed to give the taxpayer relief from the seemingly harsh results that may be produced by the combined effects of an arbitrary accounting period and a progressive rate structure. For example, under the net operating loss carryback and carryover rules, a loss in one year can be carried back and offset against taxable income for the preceding 3 years. Unused net operating losses are then carried over for 15 years. In addition, the Code provides special relief provisions for casualty losses stemming from a disaster and for the reporting of insurance proceeds from destruction of crops.[3]

Restoration of Amounts Received under a Claim of Right. The court-made *claim of right doctrine* applies when the taxpayer receives property as income and treats it as his or her own but a dispute arises over the taxpayer's rights to the income.[4] According to the doctrine, the taxpayer must include the amount as income in the year of receipt. The rationale for the doctrine is that the Federal government cannot await the resolution of all disputes before exacting a tax. As a corollary to the doctrine, if the taxpayer is later required to repay the funds, generally a deduction is allowed in the year of repayment.[5]

EXAMPLE 12

In 1993, Pedro received a $5,000 bonus computed as a percentage of profits. In 1994, Pedro's employer determined that the 1993 profits had been incorrectly computed, and Pedro had to refund the $5,000 in 1994. Pedro was required to include the $5,000 in his 1993 income, but he can claim a $5,000 deduction in 1994. ◆

In Example 12 the transactions were a wash; that is, the income and deduction were the same ($5,000). Suppose, however, Pedro was in the 31 percent tax bracket in 1993 but in the 15 percent bracket in 1994. Without some relief provision, the mistake would be costly to Pedro. He paid $1,550 tax in 1993 (.31 × $5,000), but the deduction reduced his tax liability in 1994 by only $750 (.15 × $5,000). The Code does provide the needed relief in such cases. Under § 1341, when income that has been taxed under the claim of right doctrine must later be repaid, in effect, the taxpayer gets to apply to the deduction the tax rate of the year that will produce the greater tax benefit. Thus, in Example 12, the repayment in 1994 would reduce Pedro's 1994 tax liability by the greater 1993 rate (.31) applied to the $5,000. However, relief is provided only in cases where the tax is significantly different; that is, when the deduction for the amount previously included in income exceeds $3,000.

ACCOUNTING METHODS

Permissible Methods

Section 446 requires the taxpayer to compute taxable income using the method of accounting regularly employed in keeping his or her books, provided the

3. §§ 165(i) and 451(d). Refer to Chapter 7.
4. *North American Oil Consolidated v. Burnet*, 3 USTC ¶943, 11 AFTR 16, 52 S.Ct. 613 (USSC, 1932).
5. *U.S. v. Lewis*, 51–1 USTC ¶9211, 40 AFTR 258, 71 S.Ct. 522 (USSC, 1951).

method clearly reflects income. The Code recognizes the following as generally permissible methods:

- The cash receipts and disbursements method.
- The accrual method.
- A hybrid method (a combination of cash and accrual).

The Regulations under § 446 refer to these alternatives as *overall methods* and add that the term *method of accounting* includes not only the overall method of accounting of the taxpayer but also the accounting treatment of any item.

Generally, any of the three methods of accounting may be used if the method is consistently employed and clearly reflects income. However, the taxpayer is required to use the accrual method for sales and cost of goods sold if inventories are an income-producing factor to the business. Other situations in which the accrual method is required are discussed later. Special methods are also permitted for installment sales, long-term construction contracts, and farmers.

A taxpayer who has more than one trade or business may use a different method of accounting for each trade or business activity. Furthermore, a different method of accounting may be used to determine income from a trade or business than is used to compute nonbusiness items of income and deductions.

EXAMPLE 13

Linda operates a grocery store and owns stock and bonds. The sales and cost of goods sold from the grocery store must be computed by the accrual basis because inventories are material. However, Linda can report her dividends and interest under the cash method. ◆

The Code grants the IRS broad powers to determine whether the taxpayer's accounting method *clearly reflects income.* Thus, if the method employed does not clearly reflect income, the IRS has the power to prescribe the method to be used by the taxpayer.

Cash Receipts and Disbursements Method—Cash Basis

Most individuals and many businesses use the cash basis to report income and deductions. The popularity of this method can largely be attributed to its simplicity and flexibility.

Under the cash method, income is not recognized until the taxpayer actually receives, or constructively receives, cash or its equivalent. Cash is constructively received if it is available to the taxpayer. Deductions are generally permitted in the year of payment. Thus, year-end accounts receivable, accounts payable, and accrued income and deductions are not included in the determination of taxable income.

In many cases, a taxpayer using the cash method can choose the year in which a deduction is claimed simply by postponing or accelerating the payment of expenses. For fixed assets, however, the cash basis taxpayer claims deductions through depreciation or amortization, the same as an accrual basis taxpayer does. In addition, prepaid expenses must be capitalized and amortized if the life of the asset extends substantially beyond the end of the tax year. Most courts have applied the one-year rule to determine whether capitalization and amortization are required. According to this rule, capitalization is required only if the asset has a life that extends beyond the tax year following the year of payment.

Restrictions on Use of the Cash Method. Using the cash method to measure income from a merchandising or manufacturing operation would often yield a distorted picture of the results of operations. Income for the period would largely be a function of when payments were made for goods or materials. Thus, the Regulations prohibit the use of the cash method (and require the accrual method) to measure sales and cost of goods sold if inventories are material to the business.[6]

The prohibition on the use of the cash method if inventories are material and the rules regarding prepaid expenses (discussed above) are intended to assure that annual income is clearly reflected. However, certain taxpayers may not use the cash method of accounting for Federal income tax purposes regardless of whether inventories are material. The accrual basis must be used to report the income earned by (1) a corporation (other than an S corporation), (2) a partnership with a corporate partner, and (3) a tax shelter. This accrual basis requirement has three exceptions:

- A farming business.
- A qualified personal service corporation (e.g., a corporation performing services in health, law, engineering, architecture, accounting, actuarial science, performing arts, or consulting).
- An entity that is not a tax shelter whose average annual gross receipts for the most recent three-year period are $5,000,000 or less.

Farming. Although inventories are material to farming operations, the IRS long ago created an exception to the general rule which allows farmers to use the cash method of accounting. The purpose of the exception is to relieve the small farmer from the bookkeeping burden of accrual accounting. However, tax shelter promoters recognized, for example, that by deducting the costs of a crop in one tax year and harvesting the crop in a later year, income could be deferred from tax. Thus, §§ 447 and 464 were enacted to prevent certain farming corporations and limited partnerships (farming syndicates) from using the cash method.

Farmers who are allowed to use the cash method of accounting must nevertheless capitalize their costs of raising trees when the preproduction period is greater than two years. Thus, a cash basis apple farmer must capitalize the cost of raising trees until the trees produce in merchantable quantities. Cash basis farmers can elect not to capitalize these costs, but if the election is made, the alternative depreciation system (refer to Chapter 8) must be used for all farming property.

Generally, the cost of purchasing an animal must be capitalized. However, the cash basis farmer's cost of raising the animal can be expensed.

Accrual Method

All Events Test for Income. Under the accrual method, an item is generally included in gross income for the year in which it is earned, regardless of when the income is collected. An item of income is earned when (1) all the events have occurred to fix the taxpayer's right to receive the income and (2) the amount of income (the amount the taxpayer has a right to receive) can be determined with reasonable accuracy.[7]

EXAMPLE 14

Andre, a calendar year taxpayer who uses the accrual basis of accounting, was to receive a bonus equal to 6% of Blue Corporation's net income for its fiscal year ending

6. Reg. § 1.446–1(a)(4)(i).

7. Reg. § 1.451–1(a). Refer to Chapter 3 for further discussion of the accrual basis.

each June 30. For the fiscal year ending June 30, 1993, Blue had net income of $240,000, and for the six months ending December 31, 1993, the corporation's net income was $150,000. Andre will report $14,400 (.06 × $240,000) for 1993 because his rights to the amount became fixed when Blue's year closed. However, Andre would not accrue income based on the corporation's profits for the last six months of 1993 since his right to the income does not accrue until the close of the corporation's tax year. ◆

In a situation where the accrual basis taxpayer's right to income is being contested and the income has not yet been collected, generally no income is recognized until the dispute has been settled.[8] Before the settlement, "all of the events have not occurred that fix the right to receive the income."

All Events and Economic Performance Tests for Deductions. An *all events test* applies to accrual basis deductions. A deduction cannot be claimed until (1) all the events have occurred to create the taxpayer's liability and (2) the amount of the liability can be determined with reasonable accuracy. Once these requirements are satisfied, the deduction will be permitted only if economic performance has occurred.

The *economic performance test* addresses situations in which the taxpayer has either of the following obligations:

1. To pay for services or property to be provided in the future.
2. To provide services or property (other than money) in the future.

When services or property are to be provided to the taxpayer in the future (situation 1), economic performance occurs when the property or services are actually provided by the other party.

EXAMPLE 15

An accrual basis, calendar year taxpayer, JKL, Inc., promoted a boxing match held in the company's arena on December 31, 1993. CLN, Inc., had contracted to clean the arena for $5,000, but did not actually perform the work until January 1, 1994. JKL, Inc., did not pay the $5,000 until 1995. Although financial accounting would require JKL, Inc., to accrue the $5,000 cleaning expense in 1993 to match the revenues from the fight, the economic performance test was not satisfied until 1994, when CLN, Inc., performed the service. Thus, JKL, Inc., must deduct the expense in 1994. ◆

If the taxpayer is obligated to provide property or services (situation 2), economic performance occurs (and thus the deduction is allowed) in the year the taxpayer provides the property or services.

EXAMPLE 16

Copper Corporation, an accrual basis taxpayer, is in the strip mining business. According to the contract with the landowner, the company must reclaim the land. The estimated cost of reclaiming land mined in 1993 was $500,000, but the land was not actually reclaimed until 1995. The all events test was satisfied in 1993. The obligation existed, and the amount of the liability could be determined with reasonable accuracy. However, the economic performance test was not satisfied until 1995. Therefore, the deduction is not allowed until 1995. ◆

The economic performance test is waived if the *recurring item exception* applies. Year-end accruals can be deducted if all the following conditions are met:

8. *Burnet v. Sanford & Brooks Co.*, 2 USTC ¶636, 9 AFTR 603, 51 S.Ct. 150 (USSC, 1931).

- The obligation exists and the amount of the liability can be reasonably estimated.
- Economic performance occurs within a reasonable period (but not later than 8 ½ months after the close of the taxable year).
- The item is recurring in nature and is treated consistently by the taxpayer.
- Either the accrued item is not material, or accruing it results in a better matching of revenues and expenses.

EXAMPLE 17

Green Corporation often sells goods that are on hand but cannot be shipped for another week. Thus, the sales account usually includes revenues for some items that have not been shipped at year-end. Green Corporation is obligated to pay shipping costs. Although the company's obligation for shipping costs can be determined with reasonable accuracy, economic performance is not satisfied until Green (or its agent) actually delivers the goods. However, accruing shipping costs on sold items will better match expenses with revenues for the period. Therefore, the company should be allowed to accrue the shipping costs on items sold but not shipped at year-end. ◆

The economic performance test as set forth in the Code does not address all possible accrued expenses. That is, in some cases the taxpayer incurs costs even though no property or services were received. In these instances, according to proposed Regulations, economic performance generally is not satisfied until the liability is paid. The following liabilities are cases in which payment is generally the only means of satisfying economic performance:

1. Workers' compensation.
2. Torts.
3. Breach of contract.
4. Violation of law.
5. Rebates and refunds.
6. Awards, prizes, and jackpots.
7. Insurance, warranty, and service contracts.
8. Taxes.

EXAMPLE 18

Yellow Corporation sold defective merchandise that injured a customer. Yellow admitted liability in 1993, but did not pay the claim until January 1994. The customer's tort claim cannot be deducted until it is paid. ◆

However, items (5) through (8) above are eligible for the aforementioned recurring item exception.

EXAMPLE 19

PQR Corporation filed its 1993 state income tax return in March 1994. At the time the return was filed, PQR was required to pay an additional $5,000. The state taxes are eligible for the recurring item exception. Thus, the $5,000 of state income taxes can be deducted on the corporation's 1993 Federal tax return. The deduction is allowed because all the events had occurred to fix the liability as of the end of 1993, the payment was made within 8 ½ months after the end of the tax year, the item is recurring in nature, and allowing the deduction in 1993 produces a good matching of revenues and expenses. ◆

Reserves. Generally, the all events and economic performance tests will prevent the use of reserves (e.g., for product warranty expense) frequently used in financial accounting to match expenses with revenues. However, small banks are allowed to use a bad debt reserve. Furthermore, an accrual basis taxpayer in a service business is permitted to not accrue revenue that appears uncollectible based on experience. In effect, this approach indirectly allows a reserve.

Hybrid Method

A *hybrid method* of accounting involves the use of more than one method. For example, a taxpayer who uses the accrual basis to report sales and cost of goods sold but uses the cash basis to report other items of income and expense is employing a hybrid method. The Code permits the use of a hybrid method provided the taxpayer's income is clearly reflected.[9] A taxpayer who uses the accrual method for business expenses must also use the accrual method for business income (a cash method may not be used for income items if the taxpayer's expenses are accounted for under the accrual method).

It may be preferable for a business that is required to report sales and cost of goods sold on the accrual method to report other items of income and expense under the cash method. The cash method permits greater flexibility in the timing of income and expense recognition.

Change of Method

The taxpayer, in effect, makes an election to use a particular accounting method when an initial tax return is filed using that method. If a subsequent change in method is desired, the taxpayer must obtain the permission of the IRS. The request for change is made on Form 3115, Application for Change in Accounting Method. Generally, the form must be filed within the first 180 days of the taxable year of the desired change.

As previously mentioned, the term *accounting method* encompasses not only the overall accounting method used by the taxpayer (the cash or accrual method) but also the treatment of any material item of income or deduction. Thus, a change in the method of deducting property taxes from a cash basis to an accrual basis that results in a deduction for taxes in a different year constitutes a change in an accounting method. Another example of accounting method change is a change involving the method or basis used in the valuation of inventories. However, a change in treatment resulting from a change in underlying facts does not constitute a change in the taxpayer's method of accounting. For example, a change in employment contracts so that an employee accrues one day of vacation pay for each month of service rather than 12 days of vacation pay for a full year of service is a change in the underlying facts and, thus, is not an accounting method change.

Correction of an Error. A change in accounting method should be distinguished from the *correction of an error.* The taxpayer can correct an error (by filing amended returns) without permission, and the IRS can simply adjust the taxpayer's liability if an error is discovered on audit of the return. Some examples of errors are incorrect postings, errors in the calculation of tax liability or tax credits, deductions of business expense items that are actually personal, and omissions of income and deductions. Unless the taxpayer or the IRS corrects the error within the statute of limitations, the taxpayer's total lifetime taxable income will be overstated or understated by the amount of the error.

---

9. § 446(c).

Change from an Incorrect Method. An *incorrect accounting method* is the consistent (year-after-year) use of an incorrect rule to report an item of income or expense. The incorrect accounting method generally will not affect the taxpayer's total lifetime income (unlike the error). That is, an incorrect method has a self-balancing mechanism. For example, deducting freight on inventory in the year the goods are purchased, rather than when the inventory is sold, is an incorrect accounting method. The total cost of goods sold over the life of the business is not affected, but the year-to-year income is incorrect.

If a taxpayer is employing an incorrect method of accounting, permission must be obtained from the IRS to change to a correct method. An incorrect method is not treated as a mechanical error that can be corrected by merely filing an amended tax return.

The tax return preparer as well as the taxpayer will be subject to penalties if the tax return is prepared using an incorrect method of accounting and permission for a change to a correct method has not been requested.

Net Adjustments Due to Change in Accounting Method. In the year of a change in accounting method, some items of income and expense may have to be adjusted to prevent the change from distorting taxable income.

EXAMPLE 20

In 1993, White Corporation, with consent from the IRS, switched from the cash to the accrual basis for reporting sales and cost of goods sold. The corporation's accrual basis gross profit for the year was computed as follows:

Sales		$100,000
Beginning inventory	$ 15,000	
Purchases	60,000	
Less: Ending inventory	(10,000)	
Cost of goods sold		(65,000)
Gross profit		$ 35,000

At the end of the previous year, White Corporation had accounts receivable of $25,000 and accounts payable for merchandise of $34,000. The accounts receivable from the previous year in the amount of $25,000 were never included in gross income since White was on the cash basis and did not recognize the uncollected receivables. In the current year, the $25,000 was not included in the accrual basis sales since the sales were made in a prior year. Therefore, a $25,000 adjustment to income is required to prevent the receivables from being omitted from income.

The corollary of the failure to recognize a prior year's receivables is the failure to recognize a prior year's accounts payable. The beginning of the year's accounts payable was not included in the current or prior year's purchases. Thus, a deduction for the $34,000 was not taken in either year and is therefore included as an adjustment to income for the period of change.

An adjustment is also required to reflect the $15,000 beginning inventory that White deducted (due to the use of a cash method of accounting) in the previous year. In this instance, the cost of goods sold during the year of change was increased by the beginning inventory and resulted in a double deduction.

The net adjustment due to the change in accounting method is computed as follows:

Beginning inventory (deducted in prior and current year)	$ 15,000
Beginning accounts receivable (omitted from income)	25,000
Beginning accounts payable (omitted from deductions)	(34,000)
Net increase in taxable income	$ 6,000

◆

Disposition of the Net Adjustment. Generally, if the IRS *requires* the taxpayer to change an accounting method, the net adjustment is added to or subtracted from the income for the year of the change. In cases of positive (an increase in income) adjustments in excess of $3,000, the taxpayer is allowed to calculate the tax by spreading the adjustment over one or more previous years.

To encourage taxpayers to *voluntarily* change from incorrect methods and to facilitate changes from one correct method to another, the IRS generally allows the taxpayer to spread the adjustment into future years. Assuming the taxpayer files a timely request for change (Form 3115), the allocation periods in Concept Summary 15–1 generally apply.

SPECIAL ACCOUNTING METHODS

Generally, accrual basis taxpayers recognize income when goods are sold and shipped to the customer. Cash basis taxpayers generally recognize income from a sale on the collection of cash from the customer. The tax law provides special accounting methods for certain installment sales and long-term contracts. These special methods were enacted, in part, to assure that the tax will be due when the taxpayer is best able to pay the tax.

Installment Method

Under the general rule for computing the gain or loss from the sale of property, the taxpayer recognizes the entire amount of gain or loss upon the sale or other disposition of the property.

EXAMPLE 21

Mark sells property to Fran for $10,000 cash plus Fran's note (fair market value and face amount of $90,000). Mark's basis for the property was $15,000. Gain or loss is computed under either the cash or accrual basis as follows:

Amount realized	
Cash down payment	$ 10,000
Note receivable	90,000
	$100,000
Basis in the property	(15,000)
Realized gain	$ 85,000

◆

CONCEPT SUMMARY 15–1
ADJUSTMENT PERIODS

Change	Type of Adjustment	Allocation Period
Incorrect to correct method	Positive	Three years—year of change and the two succeeding years
Incorrect to correct method	Negative	Year of change
Correct to correct	Positive	Six years—year of change and the five succeeding years
Correct to correct	Negative	Six years—year of change and the five succeeding years

In Example 21, the general rule for recognizing gain or loss requires Mark to pay a substantial amount of tax on the gain in the year of sale even though he received only $10,000 cash. Congress enacted the installment sales provisions to prevent this sort of hardship by allowing the taxpayer to spread the gain from installment sales over the collection period. The *installment method* is a very important planning tool because of the tax deferral possibilities.

Eligibility and Calculations. The installment method applies to *gains* (but not losses) from the sale of property where the seller will receive at least one payment *after* the year of sale. For many years, practically all gains from the sale of property were eligible for the installment method. However, in recent years, the Code has been amended to *deny* the use of the installment method for the following:[10]

- Gains on property held for sale in the ordinary course of business.
- Depreciation recapture under § 1245 or § 1250.
- Gains on stocks or securities traded on an established market.

As an exception to the first item, the installment method may be used to report gains from sales of the following:

- Time-share units (e.g., the right to use real property for two weeks each year).
- Residential lots (if the seller is not to make any improvements).
- Any property used or produced in the trade or business of farming.

The Nonelective Aspect. Regardless of the taxpayer's method of accounting, as a general rule, eligible sales *must* be reported by the installment method. A special election is required to report the gain by any other method of accounting (see the discussion in a subsequent section of this chapter).

Computing the Gain for the Period. The gain reported on each sale is computed by the following formula:

$$\frac{\text{Total gain}}{\text{Contract price}} \times \text{Payments received} = \text{Recognized gain}$$

The taxpayer must compute each variable as follows:

1. *Total gain* is the selling price reduced by selling expenses and the adjusted basis of the property. The selling price is the total consideration received by the seller, including notes receivable from the buyer, and the seller's liabilities assumed by the buyer.
2. *Contract price* is the selling price less the seller's liabilities that are assumed by the buyer. Generally, the contract price is the amount, other than interest, the seller will receive from the purchaser.
3. *Payments received* are the collections on the contract price received in the tax year. This generally is equal to the cash received less the interest income collected for the period. If the buyer pays any of the seller's expenses, the seller regards the amount paid as a payment received.

10. §§ 453(b), (i), and (l).

EXAMPLE 22

The seller is not a dealer, and the facts are as follows:

Sales price (amount realized)		
Cash down payment	$ 1,000	
Seller's mortgage assumed	3,000	
Notes payable to the seller	13,000	$ 17,000
Selling expenses		(500)
Seller's basis		(10,000)
Total gain		$ 6,500

The contract price is $14,000 ($17,000 – $3,000). Assuming the $1,000 is the only payment in the year of sale, the recognized gain in that year is computed as follows:

$$\frac{\$6{,}500 \text{ (total gain)}}{\$14{,}000 \text{ (contract price)}} \times \$1{,}000 = \$464 \begin{array}{l}\text{(gain recognized}\\ \text{in year of sale)}\end{array}$$

◆

If the sum of the seller's basis and selling expenses is less than the liabilities assumed by the buyer, the difference must be added to the contract price and to the payments (treated as *deemed payments*) received in the year of sale. This adjustment to the contract price is required so that the ratio of total gain to contract price will not be greater than one. The adjustment also accelerates the reporting of income from the deemed payments.

EXAMPLE 23

Assume the same facts as in Example 22, except that the seller's basis in the property is only $2,000. The total gain, therefore, is $14,500 [$17,000 – ($2,000 + $500)]. Payments in the year of sale are $1,500 and are calculated as follows:

Down payment	$1,000
Excess of mortgage assumed over seller's basis and expenses ($3,000 – $2,000 – $500)	500
	$1,500

The contract price is $14,500 [$17,000 (selling price) – $3,000 (seller's mortgage assumed) + $500 (excess of mortgage assumed over seller's basis and selling expenses)]. The gain recognized in the year of sale is computed as follows:

$$\frac{\$14{,}500 \text{ (total gain)}}{\$14{,}500 \text{ (contract price)}} \times \$1{,}500 = \$1{,}500$$

In subsequent years, all amounts the seller collects on the note principal ($13,000) will be recognized gain ($13,000 × 100%). ◆

As previously discussed, gains attributable to ordinary income recapture under §§ 1245 and 1250 are *ineligible* for installment reporting. Therefore, the § 1245 or § 1250 gain realized must be recognized in the year of sale, and the installment sale gain is the remaining gain.

EXAMPLE 24

Olaf sold an apartment building for $50,000 cash and a $75,000 note due in two years. Olaf's basis in the property was $25,000, and $40,000 ordinary income was recaptured under § 1250.

Olaf's realized gain is $100,000 ($125,000 – $25,000), and the $40,000 recapture must be recognized in the year of sale. Of the $60,000 remaining § 1231 gain, $24,000 must be recognized in the year of sale:

$$\frac{\S\ 1231\ \text{gain}}{\text{Contract price}} \times \text{Payments received}$$

$$= \frac{\$125{,}000 - \$25{,}000 - \$40{,}000}{\$125{,}000} \times \$50{,}000$$

$$= \frac{\$60{,}000}{\$125{,}000} \times \$50{,}000 = \$24{,}000$$

The remaining realized gain of $36,000 ($60,000 – $24,000) will be recognized as the $75,000 note is collected. ◆

Other Amounts Considered as Payments Received. Congress and the IRS have added the following items to be considered as payments received in the year of sale:[11]

- Purchaser's evidence of indebtedness payable on demand and certain other readily tradable obligations (e.g., bonds traded on a stock exchange).
- Purchaser's evidence of indebtedness secured by cash or its equivalent.

In the absence of the first adjustment, the seller will have control over the year the gain is reported—whenever he or she demands payment or sells the tradable obligations. The seller receiving the obligations secured by cash can often post them as collateral for a loan and have the cash from the sale. Thus, there would be no justification for deferring the tax.

Imputed Interest. Sections 483 and 1274 provide that if a deferred payment contract for the sale of property with a selling price greater than $3,000 does not contain a reasonable interest rate, a reasonable rate is imputed. The imputing of interest effectively restates the selling price of the property to equal the sum of the payments at the date of the sale and the discounted present value of the future payments. The difference between the present value of a future payment and the payment's face amount is taxed as interest income, as discussed in the following paragraphs. Thus, the imputed interest rules prevent sellers of capital assets from increasing the selling price to reflect the equivalent of unstated interest on deferred payments and thereby converting ordinary (interest) income into long-term capital gains. In addition, the imputed interest rules are important because they affect the timing of income recognition.

Generally, if the contract does not charge at least the Federal rate, interest will be imputed at the Federal rate. The Federal rate is the interest rate the Federal government pays on new borrowing and is published monthly by the IRS.[12]

As a general rule, the buyer and seller must account for interest on the accrual basis with semiannual compounding. Requiring the use of the accrual basis assures that the seller's interest income and the buyer's interest expense are reported in the same tax year. Under pre-1984 law, the cash basis seller did not report interest income until it was actually collected, but an accrual basis buyer could deduct the interest as it accrued. The following example illustrates the calculation and amortization of imputed interest.

---

11. § 453(f)(4) and Temp.Reg. § 15a.453–1(e).

12. § 1274(d)(1). There are three Federal rates: short-term (not over three years), mid-term (over three years but not over nine years), and long-term (over nine years).

Example 25

Peggy, a cash basis taxpayer, sold land on January 1, 1993, for $100,000 cash and $3,000,000 due on December 31, 1994, with 5% interest payable December 31, 1993, and December 31, 1994. At the time of the sale, the Federal rate was 8% (compounded semiannually). Because Peggy did not charge at least the Federal rate, interest will be imputed at 8% (compounded semiannually).

Date	Payment	Present Value (at 8%) on 1/1/1993	Imputed Interest
12/31/1993	$ 150,000	$ 138,750	$ 11,250
12/31/1994	3,150,000	2,693,250	456,750
	$3,300,000	$2,832,000	$468,000

Thus, the selling price will be restated to $2,932,000 ($100,000 + $2,832,000) rather than $3,100,000 ($100,000 + $3,000,000), and Peggy will recognize interest income in accordance with the following amortization schedule:

Year	Beginning Balance	Interest Income (at 8%)*	Received	Ending Balance
1993	$2,832,000	$231,091	$ 150,000	$2,913,091
1994	2,913,091	236,909	3,150,000	-0-

*Compounded semiannually.

◆

Congress has created several exceptions regarding the rate at which interest is imputed and the method of accounting for the interest income and expense. The general rules and exceptions are summarized in Concept Summary 15–2.

Related-Party Sales of Nondepreciable Property. If the Code did not contain special rules, a taxpayer could make an installment sale of property to a related party (e.g., a family member) who would obtain a basis in the property equal to the purchase price (the fair market value of the property). Then, the purchasing family member could immediately sell the property to an unrelated party for cash with no recognized gain or loss (the amount realized would equal the basis). The related-party purchaser would not pay the installment note to the selling family member until a later year or years. The net result would be that the family has the cash, but no taxable gain is recognized until the intrafamily transfer of the cash (the purchasing family member makes payments on the installment note).

Under special rules designed to combat this scheme, the proceeds from the subsequent sale (the second sale) by the purchasing family member are treated as though they were used to pay the installment note due the selling family member (the first sale). As a result, the recognition of gain from the original sale between the related parties is accelerated.[13]

However, even with these special rules, Congress did not eliminate the benefits of all related-party installment sales.

- Related parties include the first seller's brothers, sisters, ancestors, lineal descendants, controlled corporations, and partnerships, trusts, and estates in which the seller has an interest.
- There is no acceleration if the second disposition occurs more than two years after the first sale.

13. § 453(e).

Thus, if the taxpayer can sell the property to a relative who is not a "related party" or to a patient family member, the intrafamily installment sale is still a powerful tax planning tool. Other exceptions also can be applied in some circumstances.

Related-Party Sales of Depreciable Property. The installment method cannot be used to report a gain on the sale of depreciable property to a controlled entity. The purpose of this rule is to prevent the seller from deferring gain (until collections are received) while the related purchaser is enjoying a stepped-up basis for depreciation purposes.

The prohibition on the use of the installment method applies to sales between the taxpayer and a partnership or corporation in which the taxpayer holds a more-than-50 percent interest. Constructive ownership rules are used in applying the ownership test (e.g., the taxpayer is considered to own stock owned by a spouse and certain other family members). However, if the taxpayer can establish that tax avoidance was not a principal purpose of the transaction, the installment method can be used to report the gain.

CONCEPT SUMMARY 15–2
INTEREST ON INSTALLMENT SALES

	Imputed Interest Rate
General rule	Federal rate
Exceptions	
■ Principal amount not over $2.8 million.[1]	Lesser of Federal rate or 9%
■ Sale of land (with a calendar year ceiling of $500,000) between family members (the seller's spouse, brothers, sisters, ancestors, or lineal descendants).[2]	Lesser of Federal rate or 6%

	Method of Accounting for Interest	
	Seller's Interest Income	Buyer's Interest Expense
General rule[3]	Accrual	Accrual
Exceptions		
■ Total payments under the contract are $250,000 or less.[4]	Taxpayer's overall method	Taxpayer's overall method
■ Sale of a farm (sales price of $1 million or less).[5]	Taxpayer's overall method	Taxpayer's overall method
■ Sale of a principal residence.[6]	Taxpayer's overall method	Taxpayer's overall method
■ Sale for a note with a principal amount of not over $2 million, the seller is on the cash basis, the property sold is not inventory, and the buyer agrees to report expense by the cash method.[7]	Cash	Cash

1. § 1274A. This amount is adjusted annually for inflation. For 1993, the amount is $3,332,400.
2. §§ 1274(c)(3)(F) and 483(e).
3. §§ 1274(a) and 1272(a)(3).
4. §§ 1274(c)(3)(C) and 483.
5. §§ 1274(c)(3)(A) and 483.
6. §§ 1274(c)(3)(B) and 483.
7. § 1274A(c). This amount is adjusted annually for inflation. For 1993, the amount is $2,380,300.

EXAMPLE 26

Ali purchased an apartment building from her controlled corporation, Emerald Corporation. Ali was short of cash at the time of the purchase (December 1993), but was to collect a large cash payment in January 1994. The agreement required Ali to pay the entire arm's length price in January 1994. Ali had good business reasons for acquiring the building. Emerald Corporation should be able to convince the IRS that tax avoidance was not a principal purpose for the installment sale because the tax benefits are not overwhelming. The corporation will report all of the gain in the year following the year of sale, and the building must be expensed over 27.5 years (the cost recovery period). ◆

Disposition of Installment Obligations

Generally, a taxpayer must recognize the deferred profit from an installment sale when the obligation is transferred to another party or otherwise relinquished. The rationale for accelerating the gain is that the deferral should continue for no longer than the taxpayer owns the installment obligation.

The gift or cancellation of an installment note will be treated as a taxable disposition by the donor. The amount realized from the cancellation is the face amount of the note if the parties (obligor and obligee) are related to each other.

EXAMPLE 27

Liz cancels a note issued by Tina (Liz's daughter) that arose in connection with the sale of property. At the time of the cancellation, the note had a basis to Liz of $10,000, a face amount of $25,000, and a fair market value of $20,000. Presuming the initial sale by Liz qualified as an installment sale, the cancellation would result in gain of $15,000 ($25,000 – $10,000) to Liz. ◆

Certain exceptions to the recognition of gain provisions are provided for transfers of installment obligations pursuant to tax-free incorporations under § 351, contributions of capital to a partnership, certain corporate liquidations, transfers due to the taxpayer's death, and transfers between spouses or incident to divorce. In such instances, the deferred profit is merely shifted to the transferee, who is responsible for the payment of tax on the subsequent collections of the installment obligations.

Interest on Deferred Taxes

With the installment method, the seller earns interest on the receivable. The receivable includes the deferred gain. Thus, one could argue that the seller is earning interest on the deferred taxes. Some commentators reason that the government is, in effect, making interest-free loans to taxpayers who report gains by the installment method. Following the argument that the amount of the deferred taxes is a loan, in some situations, the taxpayer is required to pay interest on the deferred taxes.[14]

Electing Out of the Installment Method

A taxpayer can *elect not to use* the installment method. The election is made by reporting on a timely filed return the gain computed by the taxpayer's usual method of accounting (cash or accrual). However, the Regulations provide that

14. See § 453A for details.

the amount realized by a cash basis taxpayer cannot be less than the value of the property sold. This rule differs from the usual cash basis accounting rules (discussed earlier),[15] which measure the amount realized in terms of the fair market value of the property received. The net effect of the Regulations is to allow the cash basis taxpayer to report his or her gain as an accrual basis taxpayer. The election is frequently applied to year-end sales by taxpayers who expect to be in a higher tax bracket in the following year.

Example 28

On December 31, 1993, Jaime sold land to Veneia for $20,000 (fair market value). The cash was to be paid on January 4, 1994. Jaime is a cash basis taxpayer, and his basis in the land is $8,000. Jaime has a large casualty loss and very little other income in 1993. Thus, his marginal tax rate in 1993 is 15%. He expects his rate to increase to 31% in 1994.

The transaction constitutes an installment sale because a payment will be received in a tax year after the tax year of disposition. Veneia's promise to pay Jaime is an installment obligation, and under the Regulations, the value of the installment obligation is equal to the value of the property sold ($20,000). If Jaime elects out of the installment method, he would shift $12,000 of gain ($20,000 – $8,000) from the expected 31% rate in 1994 to the 15% rate in 1993. The expected tax savings of $1,920 [(.31 – .15) ($12,000)] may exceed the benefit of the tax deferral available with the installment method. ◆

Permission of the IRS is required to revoke an election not to use the installment method.

Long-Term Contracts

A *long-term contract* is a building, installation, construction, or manufacturing contract that is entered into but not completed within the same tax year. However, a *manufacturing* contract is long term *only* if the contract is to manufacture (1) a unique item not normally carried in finished goods inventory or (2) items that normally require more than 12 calendar months to complete. An item is *unique* if it is designed to meet the customer's particular needs and is not suitable for use by others. A contract to perform services (e.g., auditing or legal services) is not considered a contract for this purpose and thus cannot qualify as a long-term contract.

Example 29

Rocky, a calendar year taxpayer, entered into two contracts during the year. One contract was to construct a building foundation. Work was to begin in October 1992 and was to be completed by June 1993. The contract is long term because it will not be entered into and completed in the same tax year. The fact that the contract requires less than 12 calendar months to complete is not relevant because the contract is not for manufacturing. The second contract was for architectural services to be performed over two years. These services will not qualify for long-term contract treatment because the taxpayer will not build, install, construct, or manufacture a product. ◆

Generally, the taxpayer must accumulate all of the direct and indirect costs incurred under a contract. This means the production costs must be accumulated

15. Refer to Chapter 3.

and allocated to individual contracts. Furthermore, mixed services costs, costs that benefit contracts as well as the general administrative operations of the business, must be allocated to production. Concept Summary 15–3 lists the types of costs that must be accumulated and allocated to contracts. The taxpayer must develop reasonable bases for cost allocations.

CONCEPT SUMMARY 15–3
CONTRACT COSTS, MIXED SERVICES COSTS, AND CURRENT EXPENSE ITEMS FOR CONTRACTS

	Contracts Eligible for the Completed Contract Method	Other Contracts
Contract costs		
Direct materials (a part of the finished product).	Capital	Capital
Indirect materials (consumed in production but not in the finished product, e.g., grease and oil for equipment).	Capital	Capital
Storage, handling, and insurance on materials.	Expense	Capital
Direct labor (worked on the product).	Capital	Capital
Indirect labor (worked in the production process but not directly on the product, e.g., a construction supervisor).	Capital	Capital
Fringe benefits for direct and indirect labor (e.g., vacation, sick pay, unemployment, and other insurance).	Capital	Capital
Pension costs for direct and indirect labor:		
■ Current cost.	Expense	Capital
■ Past service costs.	Expense	Capital
Depreciation on production facilities:		
■ For financial statements.	Capital	Capital
■ Tax depreciation in excess of financial statements.	Expense	Capital
Depreciation on idle facilities.	Expense	Expense
Property taxes, insurance, rent, and maintenance on production facilities.	Capital	Capital
Bidding expenses—successful.	Expense	Capital
Bidding expenses—unsuccessful.	Expense	Expense
Interest to finance real estate construction.	Capital	Capital
Interest to finance personal property:		
■ Production period of one year or less.	Expense	Expense
■ Production period exceeds one year and costs exceed $1,000,000.	Capital	Capital
■ Production period exceeds two years.	Capital	Capital
Mixed services costs:		
■ Personnel operations.	Expense	Allocate
■ Data processing.	Expense	Allocate
■ Purchasing.	Expense	Allocate
Selling, general, and administrative expenses (including an allocated share of mixed services).	Expense	Expense
Losses.	Expense	Expense

EXAMPLE 30

ABC, Inc., uses detailed cost accumulation records to assign labor and materials to its contracts in progress. The total cost of fringe benefits is allocated to a contract on the following basis:

$$\frac{\text{Labor on the contract}}{\text{Total salaries and labor}} \times \text{Total cost of fringe benefits}$$

Similarly, storage and handling costs for materials are allocated to contracts on the following basis:

$$\frac{\text{Contract materials}}{\text{Materials purchases}} \times \text{Storage and handling costs}$$

The cost of the personnel operations, a mixed services cost, is allocated between production and general administration based on the number of employees in each function. The personnel cost allocated to production is allocated to individual contracts on the basis of the formula used to allocate fringe benefits. ◆

The accumulated costs are deducted when the revenue from the contract is recognized. Generally, two methods of accounting are used in varying circumstances to determine when the revenue from a contract is recognized:

- The completed contract method.
- The percentage of completion method.

The completed contract method may be used for (1) home construction contracts (contracts in which at least 80 percent of the estimated costs are for dwelling units in buildings with four or fewer units) and (2) certain other real estate construction contracts. Other real estate contracts can qualify for the completed contract method if the following requirements are satisfied:

- The contract is expected to be completed within the two-year period beginning on the commencement date of the contract.
- The contract is performed by a taxpayer whose average annual gross receipts for the three taxable years preceding the taxable year in which the contract is entered into do not exceed $10 million.

All other contractors must use the percentage of completion method.

Completed Contract Method. Under the *completed contract method,* no revenue from the contract is recognized until the contract is completed and accepted. However, a taxpayer may not delay completion of a contract for the principal purpose of deferring tax.

In some instances, the original contract price may be disputed, or the buyer may want additional work to be done on a long-term contract. If the disputed amount is substantial (it is not possible to determine whether a profit or loss will ultimately be realized on the contract), the Regulations provide that no amount of income or loss is recognized until the dispute is resolved. In all other cases, the profit or loss (reduced by the amount in dispute) is recognized in the current period on completion of the contract. However, additional work may need to be performed with respect to the disputed contract. In this case, the difference between the amount in dispute and the actual cost of the additional work will be recognized in the year the work is completed rather than in the year in which the dispute is resolved.[16]

Example 31

Ted, a calendar year taxpayer utilizing the completed contract method of accounting, constructed a building for Khalid under a long-term contract. The gross contract price was $500,000. Ted finished construction in 1993 at a cost of $475,000. When Khalid examined the building, he insisted that it be repainted or the contract price be reduced. The estimated cost of repainting is $10,000. Since under the terms of the contract, Ted is assured of a profit of at least $15,000 ($500,000 – $475,000 – $10,000) even if the dispute is ultimately resolved in favor of Khalid, Ted must include $490,000 ($500,000 – $10,000) in gross income and is allowed deductions of $475,000 for 1993.

In 1994, Ted and Khalid resolve the dispute, and Ted repaints certain portions of the building at a cost of $6,000. Ted must include $10,000 in 1994 gross income and may deduct the $6,000 expense in that year. ◆

Example 32

Assume the same facts as in the previous example, except the estimated cost of repainting the building is $50,000. Since the resolution of the dispute completely in Khalid's favor would mean a net loss on the contract for Ted ($500,000 – $475,000 – $50,000 = $25,000 loss), he does not recognize any income or loss until the year the dispute is resolved. ◆

Frequently, a contractor receives payment at various stages of completion. For example, when the contract is 50 percent complete, the contractor may receive 50 percent of the contract price less a retainage. The taxation of these payments is generally governed by Regulation § 1.451–5 "advance payments for goods and long-term contracts" (discussed in Chapter 3). Generally, contractors are permitted to defer the advance payments until the payments are recognized as income under the taxpayer's method of accounting.

Percentage of Completion Method. The percentage of completion method must be used to account for long-term contracts unless the taxpayer qualifies for one of the two exceptions that permit the completed contract method to be used (home construction contracts and certain other real estate construction contracts). Under the *percentage of completion method,* a portion of the gross contract price is included in income during each period as the work progresses. The revenue accrued each period is computed as follows:

$$\frac{C}{T} \times P$$

Where C = Contract costs incurred during the period.
T = Estimated total cost of the contract.
P = Contract price.

All of the costs allocated to the contract during the period are deductible from the accrued revenue. Because T in this formula is an estimate that frequently differs from total actual costs, which are not known until the contract has been completed, the profit on a contract for a particular period may be overstated or understated.

16. Reg. § 1.451–3(d)(2)(ii)–(vii), Example (2).

EXAMPLE 33

Tan, Inc., entered into a contract that was to take two years to complete, with an estimated cost of $2,250,000. The contract price was $3,000,000. Costs of the contract for 1993, the first year, totaled $1,350,000. The gross profit reported by the percentage of completion method for 1993 was $450,000 [($1,350,000/$2,250,000 × $3,000,000) – $1,350,000]. The contract was completed at the end of 1994 at a total cost of $2,700,000. In retrospect, 1993 profit should have been $150,000 [($1,350,000/$2,700,000 × $3,000,000) – $1,350,000]. Thus, taxes were overpaid for 1993. ◆

A *de minimis* rule enables the contractor to delay the recognition of income for a particular contract under the percentage of completion method. If less than 10 percent of the estimated contract costs have been incurred by the end of the taxable year, the taxpayer can elect to defer the recognition of income and the related costs until the taxable year in which cumulative contract costs are at least 10 percent of the estimated contract costs.

Lookback Provisions. In the year a contract is completed, a *lookback* provision requires the recalculation of annual profits reported on the contract under the percentage of completion method. Interest is paid to the taxpayer if taxes were overpaid, and interest is payable by the taxpayer if there was an underpayment.

EXAMPLE 34

Assume Tan, Inc., in Example 33, was in the 34% tax bracket in both years and the relevant interest rate was 10%. For 1993, the company paid excess taxes of $102,000 [($450,000 – $150,000) × .34]. When the contract is completed at the end of 1994, Tan, Inc., should receive interest of $10,200 for one year on the tax overpayment ($102,000 × .10). ◆

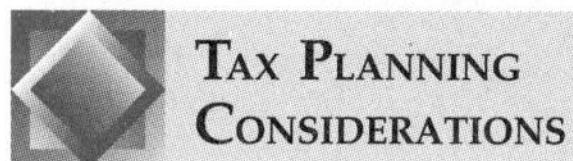

Taxable Year

Under the general rules for tax years, partnerships and S corporations frequently will be required to use a calendar year. However, if the partnership or S corporation can demonstrate a business purpose for a fiscal year, the IRS will allow the entity to use the requested year. The advantage to a fiscal year is that the calendar year partners and S corporation shareholders may be able to defer from tax the income earned from the close of the fiscal year until the end of the calendar year. Tax advisers for these entities should apply the IRS's gross receipts test described in Revenue Procedure 87–32 to determine if permission for the fiscal year will be granted.

Cash Method of Accounting

The cash method of accounting gives the taxpayer considerable control over the recognition of expenses and some control over the recognition of income. This method can be used by proprietorships, partnerships, and small corporations (gross receipts of $5 million or less) that provide services (inventories are not material to the service business). Farmers (except certain farming corporations) can also use the cash method.

Installment Method

Unlike the accrual and cash methods, the installment method results in an interest-free loan (of deferred taxes) from the government. Thus, the installment method is a powerful tax planning tool and should be considered when a sale of eligible property is being planned. Note, however, that the provision that requires interest to be paid on the deferred taxes on certain installment obligations reduces this benefit.

Related Parties. Intrafamily installment sales can still be a useful family tax planning tool. If the related party holds the property more than two years, a subsequent sale will not accelerate the gain from the first disposition. Patience and forethought are rewarded.

The 6 percent limitation on imputed interest on sales of land between family members enables the seller to convert ordinary income into capital gain or make what is, in effect, a nontaxable gift. If the selling price is raised to adjust for the low interest rate charges on an installment sale, the seller has more capital gain but less ordinary income than would be realized from a sale to an unrelated party. If the selling price is not raised and the specified interest of 6 percent is charged, the seller enables the relative to have the use of the property without having to pay for its full market value. As an additional benefit, the bargain sale is not a taxable gift.

Disposition of Installment Obligations. A disposition of an installment obligation is also a serious matter. Gifts of the obligations will accelerate income to the seller. The list of taxable and nontaxable dispositions of installment obligations should not be trusted to memory. In each instance where transfers of installment obligations are contemplated, the practitioner should conduct research to be sure he or she knows the consequences.

PROBLEM MATERIALS

DISCUSSION QUESTIONS

1. Megan recently began conducting an office supply business as a corporation. Vito began conducting his law practice through a corporation. Neither corporation has made an S election. What tax year alternatives are available to Megan's business that are not available to the Vito's business?
2. Why would a C corporation want to use a tax year other than a calendar year?
3. What do you think of a proposal to change the tax law to allow S corporations and partnerships to select a tax year independent of the tax years of the shareholders and partners? The justification for the change is that supposedly it would allow tax accountants to spread their work more evenly throughout the year.
4. Dan is an orthopedic surgeon who practices in a ski area. He recently incorporated his practice and elected S corporation treatment. Dan's brother has recommended that the corporation elect a year ending April 30, right after the close of the ski season. What is your advice to Dan?
5. Jack is a cash basis taxpayer. In 1992, when Jack was in the 31% marginal tax bracket, he received $25,000 for services provided for Jane. In 1993, Jack discovered that he had overcharged Jane by $4,000 in 1992. Therefore, he immediately refunded Jane the $4,000. As a result of some unusually large expenses in 1993, Jack's taxable income for the year was only $5,000. What special tax treatment is afforded the $4,000 payment?
6. Quinn is the sole shareholder of an accrual basis S corporation, Red, Inc. If Quinn forms another S corporation, Purple, Inc., does the fact that Red uses the accrual method mean that Purple is required to use the accrual method?

7. GHI Corporation is a retailer, and its annual gross receipts have never exceeded $5 million. NOP Corporation is a retailer whose gross receipts have never been less than $5 million for a tax year. GHI and NOP are C corporations and have been in existence for more than four years. What accounting method options are available to each corporation for the following types of income and deductions?

   a. Inventories.
   b. Accrued payroll taxes.
   c. Sales of merchandise.
   d. Income from repair services.

8. Rita buys and sells produce. Her annual gross receipts are less than $5 million. Approximately 30% of her sales are on account. Rita sells all of her inventory each day. Thus, she has no beginning or ending inventory each year. Is Rita required to use the accrual method of accounting?
9. Earl, a certified public accountant, recently obtained a new client. The client is a retail grocery store that has used the cash method to report its income since it began doing business. Will Earl incur any liability if he prepares the tax return in accordance with the cash method and does not advise the client of the necessity of seeking the IRS's permission to change to the accrual method?
10. In December 1993, a cash basis taxpayer paid January through June 1994 management fees in connection with his rental properties. The fees were $4,000 per month. Compute the 1993 expense under the following assumptions:

   a. The fees were paid by an individual who derived substantially all of his income from the properties.
   b. The fees were paid by a tax-shelter partnership.

11. Compare the cash basis and accrual basis of accounting as applied to the following:

   a. Fixed assets.
   b. Prepaid rent income.
   c. Prepaid interest expense.
   d. A note received for services performed if the market value and face amount of the note differ.

12. When are reserves for estimated expenses allowed for tax purposes? What is the role of the matching concept in tax accounting?
13. What difference does it make whether the taxpayer or the IRS initiates the change in accounting method?
14. Generally, what is the deadline for a taxpayer filing a request for a change from an incorrect accounting method?
15. Generally, what incentives are provided to encourage a taxpayer to change voluntarily from an incorrect method of accounting?
16. What difference does it make whether the taxpayer is deemed to have used an incorrect accounting method versus having committed an error?
17. Irene has made Sara an offer on the purchase of a capital asset. Irene will pay (1) $200,000 cash or (2) $50,000 cash and a 9% installment note for $150,000 guaranteed by City Bank of New York. If Sara sells for $200,000 cash, she will invest the after-tax proceeds in certificates of deposit yielding 9% interest. Sara's cost of the asset is $25,000. Why would Sara prefer the installment sale?
18. Which of the following are eligible for installment reporting? Assume some payments are received after the year of sale and the sales are for gains.

   a. Fully depreciated equipment sold for $50,000. The original cost of the equipment was $75,000.
   b. Sale of a tractor by a farm equipment dealer.
   c. Sale of stock in a family-controlled corporation.
   d. Sale of residential lots.

19. Juan, a cash basis taxpayer, sold land in December 1993. At the time of the sale, he received $10,000 cash and a note for $90,000 due in 90 days. Juan expects to be in a much higher tax bracket in 1994. Can he report the entire gain in 1993?
20. On June 1, 1991, Father sold land to Son for $100,000. Father reported the gain by the installment method, with the gain to be spread over five years. In May 1993, Son received an offer of $150,000 for the land, to be paid over three years. What would be the tax consequences of Son's sale?
21. In 1992, Bhaskar sold a building to his 100% controlled corporation. The entire purchase price is to be paid in 1993. When should Bhaskar report the gain on the sale of the building?
22. Abby sold stock in a closely held corporation for $7 million. She received a $1 million down payment and was to receive the balance of the sales price over the next 10 years. Should Abby elect not to use the installment method so that she can avoid having to pay interest on the deferred taxes?

PROBLEMS

23. Red, White, and Blue are unrelated corporations engaged in real estate development. The three corporations formed a joint venture (treated as a partnership) to develop a tract of land. Assuming the venture does not have a natural business year, what tax year must the joint venture adopt under the following circumstances?

		Tax Year Ending	Interest in Joint Venture
a.	Red	September 30	60%
	White	June 30	20%
	Blue	March 31	20%
b.	Red	September 30	30%
	White	June 30	40%
	Blue	January 31	30%

24. Zack conducted his professional practice through Zack, Inc. The corporation uses a fiscal year ending September 30 even though the business purpose test for a fiscal year cannot be satisfied. For the year ending September 30, 1993, the corporation paid Zack a salary of $150,000, and during the period January through September 1993, the corporation paid him a salary of $120,000.

    a. How much salary should Zack receive during the period October 1 through December 31, 1993?
    b. Assume Zack received only $30,000 salary during the period October 1 through December 31, 1993. What would be the consequences to Zack, Inc.?

25. PQR Corporation is in the business of sales and home deliveries of fuel oil and currently uses a calendar year for reporting its taxable income. However, PQR's natural business year ends April 30. For the short period, January 1, 1993, through April 30, 1993, the corporation earned $32,000. Assume the corporate tax rates are as follows: 15% on taxable income of $50,000 or less, 25% on taxable income over $50,000 but not over $75,000, and 34% on taxable income over $75,000.

    a. What must PQR Corporation do to change its taxable year?
    b. Compute PQR Corporation's tax for the short period.

26. Jim, a cash basis taxpayer, owned a building that he leased to Edith. In 1993, Edith prepaid the 1994 rent. During 1994, the building was destroyed by fire. Under the lease agreement, Jim was required to refund $6,000 to Edith. Also, in June 1993, Jim paid the insurance premium on the property for the next 12 months. After the building was destroyed in 1994, Jim got a $600 refund on the insurance premium. He was in the 31% marginal tax bracket in 1993 and in the 15% marginal tax bracket in 1994. What are the effects of the refunds on Jim's 1994 tax liability?

27. Compute the taxpayer's income or deductions for 1993 using (1) the cash basis and (2) the accrual basis for each of the following:

   a. In 1993, the taxpayer purchased new equipment for $100,000. The taxpayer paid $25,000 in cash and gave a $75,000 interest-bearing note for the balance. The equipment has an ACRS life of five years, the mid-year convention applies, and the § 179 election was not made.
   b. In December 1993, the taxpayer collected $10,000 for January rents. In January 1994, the taxpayer collected $2,000 for December 1993 rents.
   c. In December 1993, the taxpayer paid office equipment insurance premiums of $30,000 for January–June 1994.

28. Which of the following businesses must use the accrual method of accounting?

   a. A corporation with annual gross receipts of $12 million from equipment rentals.
   b. A partnership (not a tax shelter) engaged in farming and with annual gross receipts of $8 million.
   c. A corporation that acts as an insurance agent with annual gross receipts of $1 million.
   d. A manufacturer with annual gross receipts of $600,000.
   e. A retailer with annual gross receipts of $250,000.

29. Determine when Helen, an accrual basis taxpayer, should record the expenses in each of the following cases:

   a. A customer returned defective merchandise to Helen in December 1993. The customer claimed the goods did not meet specifications and threatened to sue Helen for breach of contract. Helen admitted liability in 1993, but did not pay the damages until January 1994.
   b. A customer slipped and fell on the business premises in 1993. Helen admitted liability, and a settlement was reached late in the year. Under the terms of the settlement, Helen was to pay the customer's medical expenses. By the end of 1993, the total medical expenses associated with the injury were determined. However, some of the expenses were for doctor visits that were to be spread over an 18-month period, and payments would not be made until the time of the visits.
   c. In March 1994, Helen filed her 1993 state income tax return and paid the balance due on 1993 state income taxes.

30. In 1993, the taxpayer was required to switch from the cash to the accrual basis of accounting for sales and cost of goods sold. Taxable income for 1993 computed under the cash basis was $40,000. Relevant account balances were as follows:

	Beginning of the Year	End of the Year
Accounts receivable	$24,000	$30,000
Accounts payable	9,000	8,000
Inventory	7,000	4,000

Compute the following:

   a. The adjustment due to the change in accounting method.
   b. The accrual basis taxable income for 1993.

31. In 1993, the taxpayer changed from the cash to the accrual basis of accounting for sales, cost of goods sold, and accrued expenses. Taxable income for 1993 computed under the cash method was $45,000. Relevant account balances are as follows:

	Beginning of the Year	End of the Year
Accounts receivable	$ 5,000	$11,000
Accounts payable	–0–	–0–
Accrued expenses	2,000	3,000
Inventory	10,000	16,000

a. Compute the accrual basis taxable income for 1993 and the adjustment due to the change in accounting method.
b. Assuming the change was voluntary, how will the adjustment due to the change be treated?

32. Floyd, a cash basis taxpayer, has agreed to sell land to Beige, Inc., a well-established and highly profitable company. Beige is willing to (1) pay $100,000 cash or (2) pay $25,000 cash and the balance ($75,000) plus interest at 10% (the Federal rate) in two years. Floyd is in the 35% marginal tax bracket (combined Federal and state) for all years and believes he can reinvest the sales proceeds and earn a 14% before-tax rate of return.

    a. Should Floyd accept the deferred payments option if his basis in the land is $10,000?
    b. Do you think your results would change if Floyd's basis in the land is $90,000?

33. Kay, who is not a dealer, sold an apartment house to Polly during 1993. The closing statement for the sale is as follows:

Total selling price		$100,000
Add: Polly's share of property taxes (6 months) paid by Kay		2,500
Less: Kay's 11% mortgage assumed by Polly	$55,000	
Polly's refundable binder ("earnest money") paid in 1992	1,000	
Polly's 11% installment note given to Kay	30,000	
Kay's real estate commissions and attorney's fees	7,500	(93,500)
Cash paid to Kay at closing		$ 9,000
Cash due from Polly = $9,000 + $7,500 expenses		$ 16,500

During 1993, Kay collected $4,000 in principal on the installment note and $2,000 interest. Her basis in the property was $70,000 [$85,000 – $15,000 (depreciation)], and there was $9,000 in potential depreciation recapture under § 1250. The Federal rate is 9%.

    a. Compute the following:
        1. Total gain.
        2. Contract price.
        3. Payments received in the year of sale.
        4. Recognized gain in the year of sale and the character of such gain.
        (*Hint:* Think carefully about the manner in which the property taxes are handled before you begin your computations.)
    b. Same as (a)(2) and (3), except Kay's basis in the property was $45,000.

34. On June 30, 1993, Kelly sold property for $250,000 cash on the date of sale and a $750,000 note due on September 30, 1994. No interest was stated in the contract. The present value of the note (using 13.2%, which was the Federal rate) was $640,000. Kelly's basis in the property was $400,000, and $40,000 of the gain was depreciation recapture under § 1245. Expenses of the sale totaled $10,000, and Kelly was not a dealer in the property sold.

    a. Compute Kelly's gain to be reported in 1993.
    b. Compute Kelly's interest income for 1994.

35. On July 1, 1992, a cash basis taxpayer sold land for $800,000 due on the date of the sale and $6,000,000 principal and $741,600 interest (6%) due on June 30, 1994. The seller's basis in the land was $1 million. The Federal short-term rate was 8%, compounded semiannually.

    a. Compute the seller's interest income and gain in 1992, 1993, and 1994.
    b. Same as (a), except that the amount due in two years was $2 million principal and $508,800 interest and the purchaser will use the cash method to account for interest.

36. On December 30, 1993, Father sold land to Son for $10,000 cash and a 7% installment note with a face amount of $190,000. In 1994, after paying $30,000 on the principal of the note, Son sold the land. In 1995, Son paid Father $25,000 on the note principal. Father's basis in the land was $50,000. Assuming Son sold the land for $250,000, compute Father's taxable gain in 1994.

37. George sold land to an unrelated party in 1992. His basis in the land was $40,000, and the selling price was $100,000: $25,000 payable at closing and $25,000 (plus 10% interest) due January 1, 1993, 1994, and 1995. What would be the tax consequences of the following? [Treat each part independently and assume (1) George did not elect out of the installment method and (2) the installment obligations have values equal to their face amounts.]

   a. In 1993, George gave to his daughter the right to collect all future payments on the installment obligations.
   b. In 1993, after collecting the payment due on January 1, George transferred the installment obligation to his 100% controlled corporation in exchange for additional shares of stock.
   c. On December 31, 1993, George received the payment due on January 1, 1994. On December 15, 1994, George died, and the remaining installment obligation was transferred to his estate. The estate collected the amount due on January 1, 1995.

38. The DGE Construction Company reports its income by the completed contract method. At the end of 1993, the company completed a contract to construct a building at a total cost of $980,000. The contract price was $1,200,000. However, the customer refused to accept the work and would not pay anything on the contract because he claimed the roof did not meet specifications. DGE's engineers estimated it would cost $140,000 to bring the roof up to the customer's standards. In 1994, the dispute was settled in the customer's favor; the roof was improved at a cost of $170,000, and the customer accepted the building and paid the $1,200,000.

   a. What would be the effects of the above on DGE's taxable income for 1993 and 1994?
   b. Same as (a), except DGE had $1,100,000 accumulated cost under the contract at the end of 1993.

39. Rust Company is a real estate construction company with average annual gross receipts of $3 million. Rust uses the completed contract method, and the contracts require 18 months to complete. Which of the following costs would be allocated to construction in progress by Rust?

   a. The payroll taxes on direct labor.
   b. The current services pension costs for employees whose wages are included in direct labor.
   c. Accelerated depreciation on equipment used on contracts.
   d. Sales tax on materials assigned to contracts.
   e. The past service costs for employees whose wages are included in direct labor.
   f. Bidding expenses for contracts awarded.

40. Indicate the accounting method that should be used to compute the income from the following contracts:

   a. A contract to build six jet aircraft.
   b. A contract to build a new home. The contractor's average annual gross receipts are $15 million.
   c. A contract to manufacture 3,000 pairs of boots for a large retail chain. The manufacturer has several contracts to produce the same boot for other retailers.
   d. A contract to pave a parking lot. The contractor's average annual gross receipts are $2 million.

41. STO Company makes gasoline storage tanks. Everything produced is under contract (that is, the company does not produce until it gets a contract for a product). The company makes three basic models. However, the tanks must be adapted to each

individual customer's location and needs (e.g., the location of the valves, the quality of the materials and insulation). Discuss the following issues relative to the company's operations:

a. An examining IRS agent contends that each of the company's contracts is to produce a "unique product." What difference does it make whether the product is unique rather than a "shelf item"?
b. Producing one of the tanks takes over one year from start to completion, and the total price is in excess of $1 million. What costs must be capitalized for this contract that are not subject to capitalization for a contract with a shorter duration and lower cost?
c. What must STO do with the costs of bidding on contracts?
d. STO frequently makes several cost estimates for a contract, using various estimates of materials costs. These costs fluctuate almost daily. Assuming the company must use the percentage of completion method to report the income from the contract, what will be the consequence if STO uses the highest estimate of a contract's costs and the actual cost is closer to the lowest estimated cost?

42. The AAA Construction Company reports its income by the percentage of completion method. In 1993, the company entered into a contract to build a warehouse for $1,500,000. AAA estimated that the total cost of the contract would be $900,000. At the end of 1993, the company had $750,000 of accumulated costs for the contract, and the architect estimated that it would cost an additional $210,000 to complete the contract. In 1994, the contract was completed at a total cost of $1,050,000.

a. Determine AAA's profit on the contract that should be reported for 1993.
b. Determine AAA's profit on the contract that should be reported for 1994.
c. Under the lookback provisions, what are the consequences to AAA of having incorrectly estimated the costs of the contract?

CHAPTER

CORPORATIONS: INTRODUCTION, OPERATING RULES, AND RELATED CORPORATIONS

OBJECTIVES

Summarize the income tax treatment of various forms of conducting a business.

Determine when an entity will be treated as a corporation for Federal income tax purposes.

Review the general income tax provisions applicable to individuals.

Discuss the tax rules unique to corporations.

Illustrate the computation of the corporate income tax.

Describe the procedural aspects of filing and reporting for corporate taxpayers.

Describe the tax rules unique to multiple corporations that are controlled by the same shareholders.

Introduce some fundamental concepts relating to consolidated returns.

Evaluate the corporate form as a means of conducting a trade or business.

OUTLINE

TAX TREATMENT OF VARIOUS BUSINESS FORMS

Business operations can be conducted in a number of different forms. Among the various possibilities are the following:

- Sole proprietorships.
- Partnerships.
- Trusts and estates.
- S corporations (also known as Subchapter S corporations).
- Regular corporations (also called Subchapter C or C corporations).

For Federal income tax purposes, the distinctions among these forms of business organization are very important. The following discussion of the tax treatment of sole proprietorships, partnerships, and regular corporations highlights these distinctions. Trusts and estates are covered in Chapter 27, and S corporations are discussed in Chapter 21.

Sole Proprietorships

A sole proprietorship is not a taxable entity separate from the individual who owns the proprietorship. The owner of a sole proprietorship reports all business transactions of the proprietorship on Schedule C of Form 1040. The net profit or loss from the proprietorship is then transferred from Schedule C to Form 1040, which is used by the taxpayer to report taxable income. The proprietor reports all of the net profit from the business, regardless of the amount actually withdrawn during the year.

Income and expenses of the proprietorship retain their character when reported by the proprietor. For example, ordinary income of the proprietorship is treated as ordinary income when reported by the proprietor, and capital gain is treated as capital gain.

EXAMPLE 1

George is the sole proprietor of George's Record Shop. Gross income of the business in 1994 is $200,000, and operating expenses are $110,000. George also sells a capital asset held by the business for a $10,000 long-term capital gain. During 1994, he withdraws $60,000 from the business for living expenses. George reports the income and expenses of the business on Schedule C, resulting in net profit (ordinary income) of $90,000. Even though he withdrew only $60,000, George reports all of the $90,000 net profit from the business on Form 1040, where he computes taxable income for the year. He also reports a $10,000 long-term capital gain. ◆

Partnerships

Partnerships are not subject to the income tax. However, a partnership is required to file Form 1065, which reports the results of the partnership's business activities. Most income and expense items are aggregated in computing the net profit of the partnership on Form 1065. Any income and expense items that are not aggregated in computing the partnership's net income are reported separately to the partners. Some examples of separately reported income items are interest income, dividend income, and long-term capital gain. Examples of separately reported expenses include charitable contributions and expenses related to interest and dividend income. Partnership reporting is discussed in detail in Chapter 22.

The partnership net profit (loss) and the separately reported items are allocated to each partner according to the partnership's profit sharing agreement, and the partners receive separate K–1 schedules from the partnership. Schedule K–1 reports each partner's share of the partnership net profit (loss) and separately reported income and expense items. Each partner reports these items on his or her own tax return.

EXAMPLE 2

Jim and Bob are equal partners in JayBee Enterprises, a calendar year partnership. During the year, JayBee Enterprises had $500,000 gross income and $350,000 operating expenses. In addition, the partnership sold land that had been held for investment purposes for a long-term capital gain of $60,000. During the year, Jim withdrew $40,000 from the partnership and Bob withdrew $45,000. The partnership's Form 1065 reports net profit of $150,000 ($500,000 income – $350,000 expenses). The partnership also reports the $60,000 long-term capital gain as a separately stated item on Form 1065. Jim and Bob both receive a Schedule K–1 reporting net profit of $75,000 and separately stated long-term capital gain of $30,000. Each partner reports net profit of $75,000 and long-term capital gain of $30,000 on his own return. ◆

Regular Corporations

Regular corporations are governed by Subchapter C of the Internal Revenue Code. Thus, they are frequently referred to as C corporations. Unlike proprietorships and partnerships, C corporations are taxpaying entities. This results in what is known as a *double tax effect.* A C corporation reports its income and expenses on Form 1120 (or Form 1120–A, the corporate short form). The corporation computes tax on the net income reported on the corporate tax return using the rate schedule applicable to corporations (refer to the rate schedule inside the front cover of this text). When a corporation distributes its income, the corporation's shareholders report dividend income on their own tax returns. Thus, income that has already been taxed at the corporate level is also taxed at the shareholder level.

EXAMPLE 3

Thompson Corporation files Form 1120, which reports net profit of $100,000. The corporation pays tax of $22,250. This leaves $77,750, all of which is distributed as a dividend to Carla, the sole shareholder of the corporation. Carla, who has $250,000 income from other sources and is in the 31% tax bracket, pays income tax of $24,103 on the distribution. The combined tax on the corporation's net profit is $46,353. ◆

EXAMPLE 4

Assume the same facts as in Example 3, except that the business is organized as a sole proprietorship. Carla reports the $100,000 net profit from the business on her tax return and pays tax of $31,000 ($100,000 net profit × 31% marginal rate). Therefore, operating the business as a sole proprietorship results in tax savings of $15,353 ($46,353 tax from Example 3 – $31,000). ◆

Shareholders in closely held corporations frequently attempt to avoid double taxation by paying out all the profit of the corporation as salary to themselves.

EXAMPLE 5

Orange Corporation has net income of $180,000 during the year ($300,000 revenue – $120,000 operating expenses). Emilio is the sole shareholder of Orange Corporation. In an effort to avoid tax at the corporate level, Emilio has Orange pay him a salary of $180,000, which results in zero taxable income for the corporation. ◆

Will the strategy described in Example 5 effectively avoid double taxation? The answer depends on whether the compensation paid to the shareholder is reasonable. Section 162 of the Code provides that compensation is deductible only to the extent that it is reasonable in amount. The IRS is aware that many taxpayers use this strategy to bail out corporate profits and, in an audit, looks closely at compensation expense. If the IRS believes that compensation is too high based on the amount and quality of services performed by the shareholder, the compensation deduction of the corporation is reduced to a reasonable amount. Compensation that is determined to be unreasonable is usually treated as a constructive dividend to the shareholder and is not deductible by the corporation.

EXAMPLE 6

Assume the same facts as in Example 5, and that the IRS determines that $80,000 of the amount paid to Emilio is unreasonable compensation. As a result, $80,000 of the corporation's compensation deduction is disallowed and treated as a constructive dividend to Emilio. Orange has taxable income of $80,000. Emilio would report salary of $100,000 and a taxable dividend of $80,000. The net effect is that $80,000 is subject to double taxation. ◆

The excessive compensation issue is discussed in more detail in Chapter 18.

Comparison of Corporations and Other Forms of Doing Business. Comparison of the tax results in Examples 3 and 4 might lead to the conclusion that incorporation is not a wise tax strategy. In some cases that would be a correct conclusion, but in others it would not. While corporate taxes are generally higher than individual taxes, in many situations tax and nontax factors combine to make the corporate form of doing business the only reasonable choice.

While a detailed comparison of sole proprietorships, partnerships, S corporations, and C corporations as forms of doing business must be made, it is appropriate at this point to consider some of the tax and nontax factors that favor corporations over proprietorships.

Consideration of tax factors requires an examination of the corporate rate structure. The income tax rate schedule applicable to corporations is reproduced below.

Taxable Income	Tax Rate
■ $50,000 or less	15%
■ Over $50,000 but not over $75,000	25%
■ Over $75,000	34%
■ Additional tax on $100,000 to $335,000	5%

As this schedule shows, corporate rates on taxable income up to $75,000 are lower than individual rates for persons in the 28 and 31 percent brackets. Therefore, corporate tax will be lower than individual tax. When dividends are paid, however, the double taxation problem occurs. This leads to an important question: Will incorporation ever result in Federal income tax savings? The following example illustrates a situation where this occurs.

EXAMPLE 7

Ned, an individual in the 31% tax bracket, owns a business that produces net profit of $50,000 each year. Ned has significant income from other sources, so he does not withdraw any of the profit from the business. If the business is operated as a proprietorship, Ned's Federal income tax on the net profit of the business is $15,500 ($50,000 × 31%). However, if the business is operated as a corporation and pays no dividends, the tax will be $7,500 ($50,000 × 15%). Operating as a corporation saves $8,000 of Federal income tax each year. If Ned invests the $8,000 tax savings each year for several years, it is possible that a positive cash flow will result, even though Ned will be required to pay tax on dividends distributed by the corporation some time in the future. ◆

The preceding example deals with a specific set of facts. The conclusions reached in this situation cannot be extended to all decisions about a form of business organization. Each specific set of facts and circumstances requires a thorough analysis of the tax factors.

Another tax consideration involves the nature of dividend income. All income and expense items of a proprietorship retain their character when reported on the proprietor's tax return. In the case of a partnership, several separately reported items (e.g., charitable contributions and long-term capital gains) retain their character when passed through to the partners. However, the tax attributes of income and expense items of a corporation are lost as they pass through the corporate entity to the shareholders.

EXAMPLE 8

During the current year, Wilberg Company receives tax-exempt interest, which is distributed to its owners. If Wilberg Company is a regular corporation, the distribution to the shareholders constitutes a dividend. The fact that it originated from tax-exempt interest is of no consequence. On the other hand, if Wilberg Company is a partnership or an S corporation, the tax-exempt interest retains its identity and passes through to the individual partners or owners. ◆

Losses of a C corporation are treated differently than losses of a proprietorship, partnership, or S corporation. A loss incurred by a proprietorship may be deductible by the owner, because all income and expense items are reported by the proprietor. Partnership losses are passed through the partnership entity and may be deductible by the partners, and S corporation losses are passed through to the shareholders. C corporation losses, however, have no effect on the taxable income of the shareholders. Income from a C corporation is reported when the shareholders receive dividends. C corporation losses are not reported by the shareholders.

Nontax Considerations. Nontax considerations will sometimes override tax considerations and lead to a conclusion that a business should be operated as a corporation. The following are some of the more important nontax considerations:

- Sole proprietors and general partners in partnerships face the danger of *unlimited liability.* That is, creditors of the business may file claims not only against the assets of the business but also against the personal assets of proprietors or general partners. Shareholders are protected against claims against their personal assets by state corporate law.
- The corporate form of business organization can provide a vehicle for raising large amounts of capital. Most major businesses in the United States are operated as corporations.
- Shares of stock in a corporation are freely transferable, whereas a partner's sale of his or her partnership interest is subject to approval by the other partners.

- Shareholders may come and go, but a corporation can continue to exist. This *continuity of life* is a distinct advantage of the corporate form of doing business.

The tax consequences of operating a business in the regular corporate form fall within Subchapter C of the Code and are the subject of this chapter and Chapters 17 through 19. Corporations that either accumulate earnings unreasonably or meet the definition of a personal holding company may be subject to further taxation. These so-called penalty taxes are imposed in addition to the corporate income tax and are discussed in Chapter 20.

Clearly, the form of organization chosen to carry on a trade or business has significant Federal income tax consequences. Though tax considerations may not control the choice, it could be unfortunate if they are not taken into account.

WHAT IS A CORPORATION?

The first step in any discussion of the Federal income tax treatment of corporations must be definitional. Specifically, what is a corporation? At first glance, the answer to this question appears to be quite simple: Merely look to the appropriate state law to determine whether the entity has satisfied the requirements for corporate status. Have articles of incorporation been drawn up and filed with the state regulatory agency? Has a charter been granted? Has stock been issued to shareholders? These are all points to consider.

Compliance with state law, although important, may not tell the full story as to whether an entity will be recognized as a corporation for tax purposes. On the one hand, a corporation qualifying under state law may be disregarded as a taxable entity if it is a mere "sham." On the other hand, an organization not qualifying as a regular corporation under state law may be taxed as a corporation under the *association* approach. These two possibilities are discussed in the following sections.

Disregard of Corporate Entity

In most cases, the IRS and the courts will recognize a corporation legally constituted under state law. In exceptional situations, however, the corporate entity may be disregarded because it lacks substance.[1] The key to such treatment is the degree of business activity conducted at the corporate level. The more the corporation is involved in trade or business activities, the less likely it will be treated as a sham and disregarded as a separate entity.[2]

Depending on the circumstances, either the IRS or the taxpayers may attempt to disregard the corporate entity. More often than not, the IRS may try to disregard (or "collapse") a corporation to make its income taxable directly to the

1. The reader should bear in mind that the textual discussion relates to the classification of an entity for *Federal* income tax purposes. State corporate income taxes or other corporate taxes (e.g., franchise taxes) may still be imposed. An entity may quite possibly be treated as a corporation for state tax purposes and not for Federal, and vice versa. This will become even more apparent when dealing with S corporations (Chapter 21) because some states do not recognize S corporation status.

2. A classic case in this area is *Paymer v. Comm.*, 45–2 USTC ¶9353, 33 AFTR 1536, 150 F.2d 334 (CA–2, 1945). Here, two corporations were involved. The Court chose to disregard one corporate entity but to recognize the other.

shareholders. In other situations, a corporation may try to avoid the corporate income tax or permit its shareholders to take advantage of excess corporate deductions and losses.[3]

Theoretically, the disregard-of-corporate-entity approach should be equally available to both the IRS and the taxpayers. From a practical standpoint, however, taxpayers have enjoyed considerably less success than has the IRS. Courts generally conclude that since the taxpayers created the corporation in the first place, they should not be permitted to later disregard it in order to avoid taxes.

Associations Taxed as Corporations

The definition of a corporation in § 7701(a)(3) includes "associations, joint stock companies, and insurance companies." What Congress intended by including associations in the definition has never been entirely clear. To some extent, judicial decisions have clarified the status of associations and the relationship between associations and corporations.

The designation given to the entity under state law is not controlling. In one case, an entity that was a business trust under state law was deemed to be an association (and therefore taxable as a corporation) for Federal income tax purposes.[4] In another case, a partnership of physicians was held to be an association and, therefore, subject to the Federal income tax rules applicable to corporations. This result occurred even though state law applicable to the tax year in question prohibited the practice of medicine in the corporate form.[5]

Whether an entity will be considered an association for Federal income tax purposes depends upon the number of corporate characteristics it possesses. According to court decisions and Regulation § 301.7701–2(a), corporate characteristics include the following:

1. Associates.
2. An objective to carry on a business and divide the gains.
3. Continuity of life.
4. Centralized management.
5. Limited liability.
6. Free transferability of interests.

The Regulations state that an unincorporated organization shall not be classified as an association unless it possesses more corporate than noncorporate characteristics. In making the determination, the characteristics common to both corporate and noncorporate business organizations shall be disregarded.

Both corporations and partnerships generally have associates (shareholders and partners) and an objective to carry on a business and divide the gains. In testing whether a particular partnership is an association, these criteria would be disregarded.

It then becomes a matter of determining whether the partnership possesses a majority of the remaining corporate characteristics (items 3 through 6). Does the partnership terminate upon the withdrawal or death of a partner (no continuity of life)? Is the management of the partnership centralized, or do all partners

3. An election under Subchapter S would generally accomplish this if the parties qualify and the election is made on a timely basis. See Chapter 21.

4. *Morrissey v. Comm.*, 36–1 USTC ¶9020, 16 AFTR 1274, 56 S.Ct. 289 (USSC, 1936).

5. *U.S. v. Kintner*, 54–2 USTC ¶9626, 47 AFTR 995, 216 F.2d 418 (CA–9, 1954).

participate? Are all partners individually liable for the debts of the partnership, or is the liability of some limited to their actual investment in the partnership (a limited partnership)? May a partner freely transfer his or her interest without the consent of the other partners?

Courts have ruled that any partnership lacking two or more of these characteristics will not be classified as an association. Conversely, any partnership having three or more of these characteristics will be classified as an association.

For trusts, the first two characteristics are considered in testing for association status. The conventional type of trust often does not have associates and usually restricts its activities to handling investments rather than carrying on a trade or business. These characteristics, however, are common to corporations. Consequently, whether a trust qualifies as an association depends upon the satisfaction of the first two corporate characteristics.

From a taxpayer's standpoint, the desirability of association status turns on the tax implications involved. In some cases, the parties may find it advantageous to have the entity taxed as a corporation, while in others they may not. These possibilities are explored at length under Tax Planning Considerations in this chapter.

AN INTRODUCTION TO THE INCOME TAXATION OF CORPORATIONS

An Overview of Corporate versus Individual Income Tax Treatment

In a discussion of how corporations are treated under the Federal income tax, a useful approach is to compare their treatment with that applicable to individual taxpayers.

Similarities. Gross income of a corporation is determined in much the same manner as it is for individuals. Thus, gross income includes compensation for services rendered, income derived from a business, gains from dealings in property, interest, rents, royalties, and dividends—to name only a few items [§ 61(a)]. Both individuals and corporations are entitled to exclusions from gross income. However, corporate taxpayers are allowed fewer exclusions. Interest on municipal bonds is excluded from gross income whether the bondholder is an individual or a corporate taxpayer.

Gains and losses from property transactions are handled similarly. For example, whether a gain or loss is capital or ordinary depends upon the nature of the asset in the hands of the taxpayer making the taxable disposition. In defining what is not a capital asset, § 1221 makes no distinction between corporate and noncorporate taxpayers.

In the area of nontaxable exchanges, corporations are like individuals in that they do not recognize gain or loss on a like-kind exchange (§ 1031) and may defer recognized gain on an involuntary conversion of property (§ 1033). The nonrecognition of gain provisions dealing with the sale of a personal residence (§§ 121 and 1034) do not apply to corporations. Both corporations and individuals are vulnerable to the disallowance of losses on sales of property to related parties

[§ 267(a)(1)] or on wash sales of securities (§ 1091). The wash sales rules do not apply to individuals who are traders or dealers in securities or to corporations that are dealers if the securities are sold in the ordinary course of the corporation's business.

Upon the sale or other taxable disposition of depreciable property, the recapture rules (e.g., §§ 1245 and 1250) generally make no distinction between corporate and noncorporate taxpayers. However, § 291(a) does cause a corporation to have more recapture on § 1250 property. This difference is discussed later in the chapter.

The business deductions of corporations also parallel those available to individuals. Deductions are allowed for all ordinary and necessary expenses paid or incurred in carrying on a trade or business under the general rule of § 162(a). Specific provision is made for the deductibility of interest, certain taxes, losses, bad debts, accelerated cost recovery, charitable contributions, net operating losses, research and experimental expenditures, and other less common deductions. No deduction is permitted for interest paid or incurred on amounts borrowed to purchase or carry tax-exempt securities. The same holds true for expenses contrary to public policy and certain unpaid expenses and interest between related parties.

Some of the tax credits available to individuals can also be claimed by corporations. This is the case with the foreign tax credit. Not available to corporations are certain credits that are personal in nature, such as the child care credit, the credit for the elderly, and the earned income credit.

Dissimilarities. The income taxation of corporations and individuals also differs significantly. As noted earlier, different tax rates apply to corporations (§ 11) and to individuals (§ 1). Corporate tax rates are discussed in more detail later in the chapter (see Examples 26 and 27).

All allowable corporate deductions are treated as business deductions. Thus, the determination of adjusted gross income (AGI), so essential for individual taxpayers, has no relevance to corporations. Taxable income is computed simply by subtracting from gross income all allowable deductions and losses. Corporations thus need not be concerned with itemized deductions or the standard deduction. Likewise, the deduction for personal and dependency exemptions is not available to corporations.

Because corporations can have only business deductions and losses, they are not subject to the $100 floor on the deductible portion of casualty and theft losses. Also inapplicable is the provision limiting the deductibility of nonbusiness casualty losses to the amount in excess of 10 percent of AGI.

Specific Provisions Compared

In comparing the tax treatment of individuals and corporations, the following areas warrant special discussion:

- Accounting periods and methods.
- Capital gains and losses.
- Recapture of depreciation.
- Passive losses.
- Charitable contributions.
- Net operating losses.
- Special deductions available only to corporations.

Accounting Periods and Methods

Accounting Periods. Corporations generally have the same choices of accounting periods as do individual taxpayers. Like an individual, a corporation may choose a calendar year or a fiscal year for reporting purposes. Corporations, however, enjoy greater flexibility in the selection of a tax year. For example, corporations usually can have different tax years from those of their shareholders. Also, newly formed corporations (as new taxpayers) usually may choose any approved accounting period without having to obtain the consent of the IRS. Personal service corporations (PSCs) and S corporations, however, are subject to severe restrictions in the use of fiscal years. The rules applicable to S corporations are discussed in Chapter 21.

A PSC, often an association treated as a corporation (refer to the earlier discussion in this chapter), has as its principal activity the performance of personal services. Such services must be substantially performed by owner-employees and must be in the fields of health, law, engineering, architecture, accounting, actuarial science, performing arts, or consulting.[6] Barring certain exceptions, PSCs must adopt a calendar year for tax purposes. The exceptions that permit the use of a fiscal year are discussed in Chapter 15.[7]

Accounting Methods. As a general rule, the cash method of accounting is unavailable to regular corporations.[8] Exceptions apply in the following situations:

- S corporations.
- Corporations engaged in the trade or business of farming and timber.
- Qualified PSCs.
- Corporations with average annual gross receipts of $5 million or less. (In applying the $5 million or less test, the corporation uses the average of the three prior taxable years.)

Both individuals and corporations that maintain inventory for sale to customers are required to use the accrual method of accounting for determining sales and cost of goods sold.

Capital Gains and Losses

Capital gains and losses result from the taxable sales or exchanges of capital assets. Whether these gains and losses are long term or short term depends upon the holding period of the assets sold or exchanged. Each year a taxpayer's long-term capital gains and losses are combined, and the result is either a *net* long-term capital gain or a *net* long-term capital loss. A similar aggregation is made with short-term capital gains and losses, the result being a *net* short-term capital gain or a *net* short-term capital loss. The following combinations and results are possible:

1. A net long-term capital gain and a net short-term capital loss. These are combined, and the result is either a net capital gain or a net capital loss.

---

6. § 448(d).
7. §§ 444 and 280H.
8. § 448.

2. A net long-term capital gain and a net short-term capital gain. No further combination is made.
3. A net long-term capital loss and a net short-term capital gain. These are combined, and the result is either capital gain net income or a net capital loss.
4. A net long-term capital loss and a net short-term capital loss. No further combination is made.

Capital Gains. Before the TRA of 1986, long-term capital gains (combination 2 and, possibly, combination 1) enjoyed favorable tax treatment. Individuals were allowed a 60 percent deduction, which meant that only 40 percent of net capital gains were subject to the income tax. For corporations, the gains were subject to the lower of the applicable corporate rate or an alternative rate of 28 percent.

TRA of 1986 eliminated the capital gains deduction, and capital gains did not receive preferential treatment during 1988, 1989, and 1990. However, for years after 1990, the tax rate on long-term capital gains of individuals is limited to a maximum of 28 percent, as opposed to the 31 percent maximum rate applicable to ordinary income.

Capital Losses. Net capital losses (refer to combinations 3 and 4 and, possibly, to combination 1) of corporate and noncorporate taxpayers receive different income tax treatment. Generally, *noncorporate taxpayers* (e.g., individuals) can deduct up to $3,000 of such net losses against other income.[9] Any remaining capital losses can be carried forward to future years until absorbed by capital gains or by the $3,000 deduction.[10] Carryovers do not lose their identity but remain either long term or short term.

Example 9

Smithson, an individual, incurs a net long-term capital loss of $7,500 for calendar year 1993. Assuming adequate taxable income, Smithson may deduct $3,000 of this loss on his 1993 return. The remaining $4,500 ($7,500 – $3,000) of the loss is carried to 1994 and years thereafter until it is offset against future capital gains or deducted against ordinary income (subject to the $3,000 maximum per year). The $4,500 will be carried forward as a long-term capital loss. ◆

Unlike individuals, corporate taxpayers are not permitted to claim any net capital losses as a deduction against ordinary income. Capital losses, therefore, can be used only to offset capital gains. Corporations may, however, carry back net capital losses to three preceding years, applying them first to the earliest year in point of time. Carryforwards are allowed for a period of five years from the year of the loss. When carried back or forward, a corporation's long-term capital loss is treated as a short-term capital loss.

Example 10

Assume the same facts as in Example 9, except that Smithson is a corporation. None of the $7,500 long-term capital loss incurred in 1993 can be deducted in that year. Smithson Corporation may, however, carry back the loss to years 1990, 1991, and 1992 (in this order) and offset it against any capital gains recognized in these years. If the carryback does not exhaust the loss, the loss may be carried forward to calendar years 1994, 1995, 1996, 1997, and 1998 (in this order). Either a carryback or a carryforward of

9. The limitations on capital losses for both corporate and noncorporate taxpayers are contained in § 1211.

10. Carryback and carryover rules for both corporate and noncorporate taxpayers are found in § 1212.

the long-term capital loss converts it to a short-term capital loss. Carryback of a capital loss generates a refund of taxes previously paid on the capital gain against which the carryback is offset. ◆

Recapture of Depreciation

Depreciation recapture for § 1245 property is computed in the same manner for individuals and for corporations. However, corporations may have more depreciation recapture than individuals. Corporations that sell *depreciable real estate* that is § 1250 property are subject to additional recapture of depreciation under § 291(a)(1). This provision requires recapture of 20 percent of the excess of any amount that would be treated as ordinary income under § 1245 over the amount treated as ordinary income under § 1250. The amount of ordinary income under § 291 is computed as shown in Figure 16–1.

EXAMPLE 11

Franklin Corporation purchased an office building on January 3, 1984, for $300,000. Accelerated depreciation was taken in the amount of $211,250 before the building was sold on January 5, 1993, for $250,000. Straight-line depreciation would have been $181,667 (using a 15-year recovery period under ACRS). The corporation's depreciation recapture and § 1231 gain are computed as follows:

Determine realized gain:	
Sales price	$250,000
Less: Adjusted basis [$300,000 (cost of building) – $211,250 (ACRS depreciation)]	88,750
Realized gain	$161,250

Because the building is 15-year real estate, it is treated as § 1245 recovery property. The gain of $161,250 is recaptured to the extent of all depreciation taken. Thus, all gain is ordinary income under § 1245, and there is no § 1231 gain. ◆

EXAMPLE 12

Assume the building in Example 11 is residential rental property, making it § 1250 property. Gain recaptured under § 1250 is $29,583 ($211,250 depreciation taken – $181,667 straight-line depreciation). However, for a corporate taxpayer, § 291(a)(1) causes additional § 1250 ordinary income of $26,333, computed as follows:

Ordinary income if property were § 1245 property	$161,250
Less: Gain recaptured under § 1250	29,583
Excess § 1245 gain	$131,667
Percentage that is ordinary gain	20%
Additional § 1250 gain	$ 26,333
Ordinary income ($29,583 + $26,333)	$ 55,916
Section 1231 gain ($161,250 – $29,583 – $26,333)	105,334
Total gain	$161,250

◆

FIGURE 16–1
Computation of Depreciation Recapture under § 291

Ordinary income under § 1245	$xx,xxx
Less: Ordinary income under § 1250	(x,xxx)
Equals: Excess ordinary income under § 1245 as compared to ordinary income under § 1250	$ x,xxx
Apply § 291 percentage	× 20%
Equals: Amount of ordinary income under § 291	$ xxx

EXAMPLE 13

Assume the building in Example 12 is commercial property and straight-line depreciation was used. An individual would report all gain as § 1231 gain. However, under § 291 a corporate taxpayer would recapture as ordinary income 20% of the depreciation that would be ordinary income if the property were § 1245 property.

First, determine realized gain:	
Sales price	$250,000
Less: Adjusted basis [$300,000 (cost of building) – $181,667 (straight-line depreciation)]	118,333
Realized gain	$131,667
Second, determine § 291 gain:	
Ordinary income if property were § 1245 property	$131,667
Less: Ordinary income under § 1250	-0-
Excess ordinary income under § 1245	$131,667
Apply § 291 percentage	20%
Ordinary income under § 291	$ 26,333

For a corporate taxpayer, $26,333 of the $131,667 gain would be ordinary, and $105,334 would be § 1231 gain. ◆

Passive Losses

The passive loss rules apply to noncorporate taxpayers and to closely held C corporations and personal service corporations (PSCs). For S corporations and partnerships, passive income or loss flows through to the owners, and the passive loss rules are applied at the owner level. The passive loss rules are applied to closely held corporations and to PSCs to prevent taxpayers from incorporating to avoid the passive loss limitations (refer to Chapter 6).

A corporation is closely held if, at any time during the taxable year, more than 50 percent of the value of the corporation's outstanding stock is owned, directly or indirectly, by or for not more than five individuals. A corporation is classified as a PSC for purposes of the passive loss provisions if it meets the following requirements:

- The principal activity of the corporation is the performance of personal services.
- Such services are substantially performed by owner-employees.
- More than 10 percent of the stock (in value) is held by owner-employees. *Any* stock held by an employee on *any* one day causes the employee to be an owner-employee.

The general passive activity loss rules apply to PSCs. Passive activity losses cannot be offset against either active income or portfolio income. The application of the passive activity rules is not as harsh for closely held corporations. They may offset passive losses against active income, but not against portfolio income.

EXAMPLE 14

Brown, Inc., a closely held corporation, has $300,000 of passive losses from a rental activity, $200,000 of active business income, and $100,000 of portfolio income. The corporation may offset $200,000 of the $300,000 passive loss against the $200,000 active business income, but may not offset the remainder against the $100,000 of portfolio income. ◆

Individual taxpayers are not allowed to offset passive losses against *either* active or portfolio income.

Charitable Contributions

Both corporate and noncorporate taxpayers may deduct charitable contributions if the recipient is a qualified charitable organization. Generally, a deduction will be allowed only for the year in which the payment is made. However, an important exception is made for *accrual basis corporations.* They may claim the deduction in the year *preceding* payment if two requirements are met. First, the contribution must be authorized by the board of directors by the end of that year. Second, it must be paid on or before the fifteenth day of the third month of the next year.[11]

EXAMPLE 15

On December 28, 1993, Blue Company, a calendar year, accrual basis partnership, authorizes a $5,000 donation to the Atlanta Symphony Association (a qualified charitable organization). The donation is made on March 14, 1994. Because Blue Company is a partnership, the contribution can be deducted only in 1994.[12] ◆

EXAMPLE 16

Assume the same facts as in Example 15, except that Blue Company is a corporation. Presuming the December 28, 1993, authorization was made by its board of directors, Blue may claim the $5,000 donation as a deduction for calendar year 1993. If no authorization was made, the deduction may still be claimed for calendar year 1994. ◆

Property Contributions. The amount that can be deducted for a noncash charitable contribution depends on the type of property contributed. Property must be identified as long-term capital gain property or ordinary income property. *Long-term capital gain property* is property that, if sold, would result in long-term capital gain for the taxpayer. Such property generally must be a capital asset and must be held for the long-term holding period (more than one year). *Ordinary income property* is property that, if sold, would result in ordinary income for the taxpayer.

The deduction for a charitable contribution of long-term capital property is generally measured by fair market value.

EXAMPLE 17

In 1993, Brown Corporation donated a parcel of land (a capital asset) to Oakland Community College. Brown acquired the land in 1987 for $60,000, and the fair market value on the date of the contribution was $100,000. The corporation's charitable contribution deduction (subject to a percentage limitation discussed later) is measured by the asset's fair market value of $100,000, even though the $40,000 appreciation on the land has never been included in income. ◆

In two situations, a charitable contribution of long-term capital gain property is measured by the basis of the property, rather than fair market value. If the corporation contributes *tangible personal property* and the charitable organization puts the property to an unrelated use, the appreciation on the property is not

---

11. § 170(a)(2).
12. Each calendar year partner will report an allocable portion of the charitable contribution deduction as of December 31, 1994 (the end of the partnership's tax year). See Chapter 22.

deductible. Unrelated use is defined as use that is not related to the purpose or function that qualifies the organization for exempt status under § 501.

EXAMPLE 18

White Corporation donates a painting worth $200,000 to Western States Art Museum (a qualified organization), which exhibits the painting. White had acquired the painting in 1980 for $90,000. Because the museum put the painting to a related use, White is allowed to deduct $200,000, the fair market value of the painting. ◆

EXAMPLE 19

Assume the same facts as in the previous example, except that White Corporation donates the painting to the American Cancer Society, which sells the painting and deposits the $200,000 proceeds in the organization's general fund. White's deduction is limited to the $90,000 basis because it contributed tangible personal property that was put to an unrelated use by the charitable organization. ◆

The deduction for charitable contributions of long-term capital gain property to certain *private nonoperating foundations* is also limited to the basis of the property.

Ordinary income property is property that, if sold, would result in ordinary income. Examples of ordinary income property include inventory and capital assets that have not been held long term. In addition, § 1231 property (depreciable property used in a trade or business) is treated as ordinary income property to the extent of any ordinary income recaptured under § 1245 or § 1250. As a general rule, the deduction for a contribution of ordinary income property is limited to the basis of the property. However, *corporations* enjoy two special exceptions where 50 percent of the appreciation (but not to exceed twice the basis) on property is allowed on certain contributions. The first exception concerns inventory if the property is used in a manner related to the exempt purpose of the donee. Also, the charity must use the property solely for the care of the ill, the needy, or infants.

EXAMPLE 20

Yellow Corporation, a grocery chain, donates canned goods to the Salvation Army to be used to feed the needy. Yellow's basis in the canned goods was $2,000, and the fair market value was $3,000. Yellow's deduction is $2,500 [$2,000 basis + 50%($3,000 – $2,000)]. ◆

The second exception involves gifts of scientific property to colleges and certain scientific research organizations for use in research, provided certain conditions are met.[13] As was true of the inventory exception, 50 percent of the appreciation on such property is allowed as an additional deduction.

Limitations Imposed on Charitable Contribution Deductions. Like individuals, corporations are subject to percentage limits on the charitable contribution deduction. For any one year, a corporate taxpayer's contribution deduction is limited to 10 percent of taxable income. For this purpose, taxable income is computed without regard to the charitable contribution deduction, any net operating loss carryback or capital loss carryback, and the dividends received deduction. Any contributions in excess of the 10 percent limitation may be

13. These conditions are set forth in § 170(e)(4). For the inventory exception, see § 170(e)(3).

carried forward to the five succeeding tax years. Any carryforward must be added to subsequent contributions and will be subject to the 10 percent limitation. In applying this limitation, the current year's contributions must be deducted first, with excess deductions from previous years deducted in order of time.[14]

EXAMPLE 21

During 1993, Orange Corporation (a calendar year taxpayer) had the following income and expenses:

Income from operations	$140,000
Expenses from operations	110,000
Dividends received	10,000
Charitable contributions made in May 1993	5,000

For purposes of the 10% limitation *only*, Orange Corporation's taxable income is $40,000 ($140,000 – $110,000 + $10,000). The dividends received deduction (see page 16–17) is not considered in computing income for this purpose. Consequently, the allowable charitable deduction for 1993 is $4,000 (10% × $40,000). The $1,000 unused portion of the contribution can be carried forward to 1994, 1995, 1996, 1997, and 1998 (in that order) until exhausted. ◆

EXAMPLE 22

Assume the same facts as in Example 21. In 1994, Orange Corporation has taxable income (for purposes of the 10% limitation) of $50,000 and makes a charitable contribution of $4,500. The maximum deduction allowed for 1994 would be $5,000 (10% × $50,000). The first $4,500 of the allowed deduction must be allocated to the contribution made in 1994, and $500 of the $1,000 unused contribution is carried over from 1993. The remaining $500 of the 1993 contribution may be carried over to 1995 (and later years, if necessary). ◆

Net Operating Losses

As for individuals, the net operating loss (NOL) of a corporation may be carried back 3 years and forward 15 to offset taxable income for those years. However, a corporation does not adjust its tax loss for the year for capital losses as do individual taxpayers, because a corporation is not permitted a deduction for net capital losses. Nor does a corporation make adjustments for nonbusiness deductions as do individual taxpayers. Further, a corporation is allowed to include the dividends received deduction (discussed below) in computing its NOL.[15]

EXAMPLE 23

In 1993, Green Corporation has gross income (including dividends) of $200,000 and deductions of $300,000 excluding the dividends received deduction. Green Corporation had received taxable dividends of $100,000 from Exxon stock. Green has an NOL computed as follows:

Gross income (including dividends)		$200,000
Less: Business deductions	$300,000	
Dividends received deduction (70% of $100,000)*	70,000	(370,000)
Taxable income (or loss)		($170,000)

*See the discussion of the dividends received deduction in the next section of this chapter.

14. The carryover rules relating to all taxpayers are in § 170(d).
15. The modifications required to arrive at the amount of NOL that can be carried back or forward are in § 172(d).

The NOL is carried back three years to 1990. (Green Corporation may *elect* to forgo the carryback option and instead carry the loss forward.) Assume Green had taxable income of $40,000 in 1990. The carryover to 1991 is computed as follows:

Taxable income for 1990	$ 40,000
Less: NOL carryback	(170,000)
Taxable income for 1990 after NOL carryback (carryover to 1991)	($ 130,000)

◆

Deductions Available Only to Corporations

Dividends Received Deduction. The purpose of the dividends received deduction is to prevent triple taxation. Without the deduction, income paid to a corporation in the form of a dividend would be taxed to the recipient corporation with no corresponding deduction to the distributing corporation. Later, when the recipient corporation paid the income to its individual shareholders, the income would again be subject to taxation with no corresponding deduction to the corporation. The dividends received deduction alleviates this inequity by causing only some or none of the dividend income to be taxable to the recipient corporation.

As the following table illustrates, the amount of the dividends received deduction depends upon the percentage of ownership the recipient corporate shareholder holds in a domestic corporation making the dividend distribution.[16]

Percentage of Ownership by Corporate Shareholder	Deduction Percentage
Less than 20%	70%
20% or more (but less than 80%)	80%
80% or more*	100%

*The payor corporation must be a member of an affiliated group with the recipient corporation.

The dividends received deduction is limited to a percentage of the taxable income of a corporation. For this purpose, taxable income is computed without regard to the NOL, the dividends received deduction, and any capital loss carryback to the current tax year. The percentage of taxable income limitation corresponds to the deduction percentage. Thus, if a corporate shareholder owns less than 20 percent of the stock in the distributing corporation, the dividends received deduction is limited to 70 percent of taxable income. However, the taxable income limitation does not apply if the corporation has an NOL for the current taxable year.[17]

In working with these myriad rules, the following steps are useful:

1. Multiply the dividends received by the deduction percentage.
2. Multiply the taxable income by the deduction percentage.
3. Limit the deduction to the lesser of step 1 or step 2, unless subtracting the amount derived in step 1 from 100 percent of taxable income *generates* an NOL. If so, use the amount derived in step 1. This is referred to as the NOL rule.

---

16. § 243(a).

17. § 246(b).

EXAMPLE 24

Red, White, and Blue Corporations are three unrelated calendar year corporations. For 1993 they have the following transactions:

	Red Corporation	White Corporation	Blue Corporation
Gross income from operations	$ 400,000	$ 320,000	$ 260,000
Expenses from operations	(340,000)	(340,000)	(340,000)
Dividends received from domestic corporations (less than 20% ownership)	200,000	200,000	200,000
Taxable income before the dividends received deduction	$ 260,000	$ 180,000	$ 120,000

In determining the dividends received deduction, use the three-step procedure described above:

	Red	White	Blue
Step 1 (70% × $200,000)	$140,000	$140,000	$140,000
Step 2			
70% × $260,000 (taxable income)	$182,000		
70% × $180,000 (taxable income)		$126,000	
70% × $120,000 (taxable income)			$ 84,000
Step 3			
Lesser of step 1 or step 2	$140,000	$126,000	
Deduction generates an NOL			$140,000

White Corporation is subject to the 70% of taxable income limitation. It does not qualify for NOL rule treatment since subtracting $140,000 (step 1) from $180,000 (100% of taxable income) does not yield a negative figure. Blue Corporation qualifies for NOL rule treatment because subtracting $140,000 (step 1) from $120,000 (100% of taxable income) yields a negative figure. In summary, each corporation has a dividends received deduction for 1993: $140,000 for Red Corporation, $126,000 for White Corporation, and $140,000 for Blue Corporation. ◆

Deduction of Organizational Expenditures. Expenses incurred in connection with the organization of a corporation normally are chargeable to a capital account. That they benefit the corporation during its existence seems clear. But how can they be amortized when most corporations possess unlimited life? The lack of a determinable and limited estimated useful life would therefore preclude any tax write-off. Code § 248 was enacted to solve this problem.

Under § 248, a corporation may elect to amortize organizational expenditures over a period of 60 months or more. The period begins with the month in which the corporation begins business.[18] Organizational expenditures *subject to the election* include the following:

- Legal services incident to organization (e.g., drafting the corporate charter, bylaws, minutes of organizational meetings, terms of original stock certificates).

18. The month in which a corporation begins business may not be immediately apparent. See Reg. § 1.248–1(a)(3). For a similar problem in the Subchapter S area, see Chapter 21.

- Necessary accounting services.
- Expenses of temporary directors and of organizational meetings of directors or shareholders, and fees paid to the state of incorporation.

Expenditures that *do not qualify* include those connected with issuing or selling shares of stock or other securities (e.g., commissions, professional fees, and printing costs) or with the transfer of assets to a corporation. Such expenditures reduce the amount of capital raised and are not deductible at all.

To qualify for the election, the expenditures must be *incurred* before the end of the taxable year in which the corporation begins business. In this regard, the corporation's method of accounting is of no consequence. Thus, an expense incurred by a cash basis corporation in its first tax year qualifies even though it is not paid until a subsequent year.

The election is made in a statement attached to the corporation's return for its first taxable year. The return and statement must be filed no later than the due date of the return (including any extensions). The statement must set forth the description and amount of the expenditures involved. Also, it should include the date the expenditures were incurred, the month in which the corporation began business, and the number of months (not less than 60) over which the expenditures are to be deducted ratably.

If the election is not made on a timely basis, organizational expenditures cannot be deducted until the corporation ceases to do business and liquidates. These expenditures will be deductible if the corporate charter limits the life of the corporation.

EXAMPLE 25

Black Corporation, an accrual basis taxpayer, was formed and began operations on May 1, 1993. The following expenses were incurred during its first year of operations (May 1 through December 31, 1993):

Expenses of temporary directors and of organizational meetings	$500
Fee paid to the state of incorporation	100
Accounting services incident to organization	200
Legal services for drafting the corporate charter and bylaws	400
Expenses incident to the printing and sale of stock certificates	300

Assume Black Corporation makes a timely election under § 248 to amortize qualifying organizational expenses over a period of 60 months. The monthly amortization is $20 [($500 + $100 + $200 + $400) ÷ 60 months], and $160 ($20 × 8 months) is deductible for tax year 1993. Note that the $300 of expenses incident to the printing and sale of stock certificates does not qualify for the election. These expenses cannot be deducted at all but reduce the amount of the capital realized from the sale of stock. ◆

DETERMINING THE CORPORATE INCOME TAX LIABILITY

Corporate Income Tax Rates

Although corporate income tax rates have fluctuated widely over past years, the general trend has been a reduction in the rates. Refer to the inside front cover of the text for a schedule of current corporate income tax rates.

EXAMPLE 26

Gold Corporation, a calendar year taxpayer, has taxable income of $90,000 for 1993. Its income tax liability is $18,850, determined as follows:

$50,000 × 15%	$ 7,500
$25,000 × 25%	6,250
$15,000 × 34%	5,100
Tax liability	$18,850

◆

For a corporation that has taxable income in excess of $100,000 for any taxable year, the amount of the tax is increased by the lesser of (1) 5 percent of the excess or (2) $11,750. In effect, the additional tax means a 39 percent rate for every dollar of taxable income from $100,000 to $335,000.[19]

EXAMPLE 27

Silver Corporation, a calendar year taxpayer, has taxable income of $335,000 for 1993. Its income tax liability is $113,900, determined as follows:

$50,000 × 15%	$ 7,500
$25,000 × 25%	6,250
$260,000 × 34%	88,400
$235,000 × 5%	11,750
Tax liability	$113,900

Note that the tax liability of $113,900 is 34% of $335,000. Thus, due to the 5% additional tax on taxable income between $100,000 and $335,000, the benefit of the lower rates on the first $75,000 of taxable income completely phases out at $335,000. ◆

Qualified PSCs are taxed at a flat 34 percent rate on all taxable income. Thus, they do not enjoy the tax savings of the 15 percent (on the first $50,000) and 25 percent (on the next $25,000) lower brackets applicable to other corporations. For this purpose, a PSC is a corporation that is substantially employee owned. Also, it must engage in one of the following activities: health, law, engineering, architecture, accounting, actuarial science, performing arts, or consulting.

Alternative Minimum Tax

Corporations are subject to an alternative minimum tax (AMT) that is structured similar to the AMT applicable to individuals. The AMT for corporations, as for individuals, involves a broader tax base than does the regular tax. Like an individual, a corporation is required to apply a minimum tax rate to the expanded base and to pay the difference between the AMT tax liability and the regular tax. Many of the adjustments and tax preference items necessary to arrive at alternative minimum taxable income (AMTI) are the same for individuals and corporations. Although the objective of the AMT is the same for individual and corporate taxpayers, the rate and exemptions are different. Refer to Chapter 14 for a detailed discussion of the corporate AMT.

19. § 11(b).

Tax Liability of Related Corporations

Related corporations are subject to special rules for computing the income tax, the accumulated earnings credit, the AMT exemption, and the environmental tax exemption.[20] If these restrictions did not exist, the shareholders of a corporation could gain significant tax advantages by splitting a single corporation into *multiple* corporations. The next two examples illustrate the potential *income tax* advantage of multiple corporations.

EXAMPLE 28

Gray Corporation annually yields taxable income of $300,000. The corporate tax on $300,000 is $100,250, computed as follows:

$50,000 × 15%	$ 7,500
$25,000 × 25%	6,250
$225,000 × 34%	76,500
$200,000 × 5%	10,000
Tax liability	$100,250

◆

EXAMPLE 29

Assume that Gray Corporation in the previous example is divided equally into four corporations. Each corporation would have taxable income of $75,000, and the tax for each would be computed as follows:

$50,000 × 15%	$ 7,500
$25,000 × 25%	6,250
Tax liability	$13,750

The total liability for the four corporations would be $55,000 ($13,750 × 4). The savings would be $45,250 ($100,250 – $55,000). ◆

To preclude the advantages that could be gained by using multiple corporations, the tax law requires special treatment for *controlled groups* of corporations. A comparison of Examples 28 and 29 reveals that the income tax savings that could be achieved by using multiple corporations result from having more of the total income taxed at lower rates. To close this potential loophole, the law provides that controlled groups are limited to taxable income in the first two tax brackets (the 15 percent and 25 percent brackets) as though they were one corporation. Thus, in Example 29, under the controlled corporation rules, only $12,500 (one-fourth of the first $50,000 of taxable income) for each of the four related corporations would be taxed at the 15 percent rate. The 25 percent rate would apply to the next $6,250 (one-fourth of the next $25,000) of taxable income of each corporation. This equal allocation of the $50,000 and $25,000 amounts is required unless all members of the controlled group consent to an apportionment plan providing for an unequal allocation.

Similar limitations apply to the election to expense certain depreciable assets under § 179 (see Chapter 8), to the $250,000 accumulated earnings credit (see Chapter 20) for controlled groups, and to the $40,000 exemption amount for purposes of computing the AMT (see Chapter 14).

Controlled Groups

A controlled group of corporations includes parent-subsidiary groups, brother-sister groups, combined groups, and certain insurance companies. Groups of the

20. § 1561(a).

first three types are discussed in the following sections. Insurance groups are not discussed in this text.

Parent-Subsidiary Controlled Group. A parent-subsidiary controlled group consists of one or more *chains* of corporations connected through stock ownership with a common parent corporation. The ownership connection can be established through either a *voting power test* or a *value test.* The voting power test requires ownership of stock possessing at least 80 percent of the total voting power of all classes of stock entitled to vote.[21]

EXAMPLE 30

Black Corporation owns 80% of White Corporation. Black and White Corporations are members of a parent-subsidiary controlled group. Black is the parent corporation, and White is the subsidiary. ◆

The parent-subsidiary relationship illustrated in Example 30 is easy to recognize because Black Corporation is the direct owner of White Corporation. Real-world business organizations are often much more complex, sometimes including numerous corporations with chains of ownership connecting them. In these complex corporate structures, determining whether the controlled group classification is appropriate becomes more difficult. The ownership requirements can be met through direct ownership (refer to Example 30) or through indirect ownership, as illustrated in the two following examples.

EXAMPLE 31

Red Corporation owns 80% of the voting stock of White Corporation, and White Corporation owns 80% of the voting stock of Blue Corporation. Red, White, and Blue Corporations constitute a controlled group in which Red is the common parent and White and Blue are subsidiaries. The same result would occur if Red Corporation, rather than White Corporation, owned the Blue Corporation stock. This parent-subsidiary relationship is diagrammed below in Figure 16–2. ◆

EXAMPLE 32

Brown Corporation owns 80% of the stock of Green Corporation, which owns 30% of Blue Corporation. Brown also owns 80% of White Corporation, which owns 50% of Blue Corporation. Brown, Green, Blue and White Corporations constitute a parent-subsidiary controlled group in which Brown is the common parent and Green, Blue and White are subsidiaries. This parent-subsidiary relationship is diagrammed in Figure 16–3 on the following page. ◆

FIGURE 16–2
Controlled Groups—Parent-Subsidiary Corporations

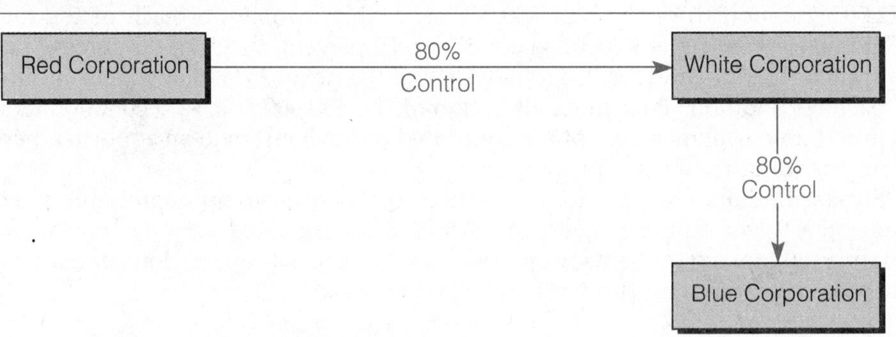

Red is the common parent of a parent-subsidiary controlled group consisting of Red, White, and Blue Corporations.

21. § 1563(a)(1).

The value test requires ownership of at least 80 percent of the total value of all shares of all classes of stock of each of the corporations, except the parent corporation, by one or more of the other corporations.

Brother-Sister Corporations. A brother-sister controlled group *may* exist if two or more corporations are owned by five or fewer *persons* (individuals, estates, or trusts). Brother-sister status will apply if such a shareholder group meets an 80 percent total ownership test *and* a 50 percent common ownership test.[22]

- The *total* ownership test is met if the shareholder group possesses stock representing at least 80 percent of the total combined voting power of all classes of stock entitled to vote, *or* at least 80 percent of the total value of shares of all classes of stock of each corporation.
- The *common* ownership test is met if the shareholder group owns more than 50 percent of the total combined voting power of all classes of stock entitled to vote, *or* more than 50 percent of the total value of shares of all classes of stock of each corporation.

In applying the common ownership test, the stock held by each person is considered only to the extent that the stock ownership is *identical* for each corporation. That is, if a shareholder owns 30 percent of Silver Corporation and 20 percent of Gold Corporation, such shareholder has identical ownership of 20 percent of each corporation.

EXAMPLE 33

The outstanding stock of Hawk, Eagle, Crane, and Dove Corporations, each of which has only one class of stock outstanding, is owned by the following unrelated individuals:

	Corporations				Identical
Individuals	Hawk	Eagle	Crane	Dove	Ownership
Allen	40%	30%	60%	60%	30%
Barton	50%	20%	30%	20%	20%
Carter	10%	30%	10%	10%	10%
Dixon		20%		10%	
Total	100%	100%	100%	100%	60%

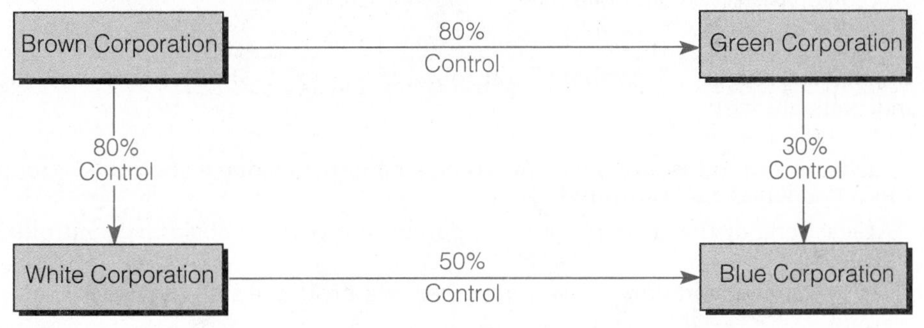

FIGURE 16–3
Controlled Groups—Parent-Subsidiary Corporations

22. § 1563(a)(2).

Five or fewer individuals (Allen, Barton, and Carter) with more than a 50% common ownership own at least 80% of all classes of stock in Hawk, Eagle, Crane, and Dove. They own 100% of Hawk, 80% of Eagle, 100% of Crane, and 90% of Dove. Consequently, Hawk, Eagle, Crane, and Dove are regarded as members of a brother-sister controlled group. ◆

EXAMPLE 34

Changing the facts in Example 33, assume the ownership is as follows:

	Corporations				
Individuals	Hawk	Eagle	Crane	Dove	Identical Ownership
Allen	20%	10%	5%	60%	5%
Barton	10%	20%	60%	5%	5%
Carter	10%	70%	35%	25%	10%
Dixon	60%			10%	
Total	100%	100%	100%	100%	20%

In this instance, the identical ownership is only 20%. Consequently, the four corporations are not members of a brother-sister controlled group. However, Eagle and Crane would be brother-sister corporations because both the total ownership and the common ownership tests are met. Allen, Barton, and Carter own 100% of each corporation, and common ownership exceeds 50% (5% by Allen, 20% by Barton, and 35% by Carter). ◆

EXAMPLE 35

The outstanding stock of Black Corporation and Brown Corporation, each of which has only one class of stock outstanding, is owned as follows:

	Corporations		
Individuals	Black	Brown	Identical Ownership
Rossi	55%	100%	55%
Smith	45%		
Total	100%	100%	55%

Although the 50% common ownership test is met, the 80% test is not since there is no common ownership in Brown Corporation. Are Black and Brown brother-sister corporations? No, according to the U.S. Supreme Court.[23] ◆

Combined Groups. A combined controlled group exists if all of the following conditions are met:

- Each corporation is a member of either a parent-subsidiary controlled group or a brother-sister controlled group.
- At least one of the corporations is a parent of a parent-subsidiary controlled group.
- The parent corporation is also a member of a brother-sister controlled group.

23. *U.S. v Vogel Fertilizer Co.*, 82–1 USTC ¶9134, 49 AFTR2d 82–491, 102 S.Ct. 821 (USSC, 1982). See also Reg. § 1.1563–1(a)(3), which was amended to comply with the conclusions reached in *Vogel.*

Example 36

Robert owns 80% of all classes of stock of Red and Orange Corporations. Red Corporation, in turn, owns 80% of all classes of stock of Blue Corporation. Orange owns all the stock of Green Corporation. Red, Blue, Orange, and Green are members of the same combined group. As a result, Red, Blue, Orange, and Green are limited to taxable income in the first two tax brackets and the $250,000 accumulated earnings credit as though they were one corporation. This is also the case for the election to expense certain depreciable business assets under § 179 and the $40,000 exemption for purposes of computing the AMT. ◆

Procedural Matters

Filing Requirements for Corporations

A corporation must file a Federal income tax return whether it has taxable income or not.[24] A corporation that was not in existence throughout an entire annual accounting period is required to file a return for the fraction of the year during which it was in existence. In addition, a corporation must file a return even though it has ceased to do business if it has valuable claims for which it will bring suit. A corporation is relieved of filing income tax returns only when it ceases to do business and retains no assets.

The corporate return is filed on Form 1120 unless the corporation is a small corporation entitled to file the shorter Form 1120–A. A corporation may file Form 1120–A if it meets all the following requirements:

- Gross receipts or sales do not exceed $500,000.
- Total income (gross profit plus other income including gains on sales of property) does not exceed $500,000.
- Total assets do not exceed $500,000.
- The corporation is not involved in a dissolution or liquidation.
- The corporation is not a member of a controlled group under §§ 1561 and 1563.
- The corporation does not file a consolidated return.
- The corporation does not have ownership in a foreign corporation.
- The corporation does not have foreign shareholders who directly or indirectly own 50 percent or more of its stock.

Corporations electing under Subchapter S (see Chapter 21) file on Form 1120S. Forms 1120, 1120–A, and 1120S are reproduced in Appendix B.

The return must be filed on or before the fifteenth day of the third month following the close of a corporation's tax year. Corporations can receive an automatic extension of six months for filing the corporate return by filing Form 7004 by the due date for the return.[25] However, the IRS may terminate the extension by mailing a 10-day notice to the corporation.

A corporation must make payments of estimated tax unless its tax liability can reasonably be expected to be less than $500. For tax years beginning after June 30, 1992, and before 1997, the required annual payment (which includes any estimated AMT liability) is the lesser of (1) 97 percent of the corporation's final tax or (2) 100 percent of the tax for the preceding year (if that was a 12-month tax

24. § 6012(a)(2).

25. § 6081.

Concept Summary 16–1
Income Taxes of Individuals and Corporations Compared

	Individuals	Corporations
Computation of gross income	§ 61.	§ 61.
Computation of taxable income	§ 62 and §§ 63(b) through (h).	§ 63(a). Concept of AGI has no relevance.
Deductions	Trade or business (§ 162); nonbusiness (§ 212); some personal and employee expenses (generally deductible as itemized deductions).	Trade or business (§ 162).
Charitable contributions	Limited in any tax year to 50% of AGI; 30% for long-term capital gain property unless election is made to reduce fair market value of gift.	Limited in any tax year to 10% of taxable income computed without regard to the charitable contribution deduction, NOL, and dividends received deduction.
	Excess charitable contributions carried over for five years.	Same as for individuals.
	Amount of contribution is the fair market value of the property; if lower, ordinary income property will be limited to adjusted basis; capital gain property will be treated as ordinary income property if certain tangible personalty is donated to a nonuse charity or a private nonoperating foundation is the donee.	Same as individuals, but exceptions allowed for certain inventory and for scientific property where one-half of the appreciation will be allowed as a deduction.
	Time of deduction is the year in which payment is made.	Time of deduction is the year in which payment is made unless accrual basis taxpayer. Accrual basis corporation can take deduction in year preceding payment if contribution was authorized by board of directors by end of year and contribution is paid by fifteenth day of third month of following year.
Casualty losses	$100 floor on personal casualty and theft losses; personal casualty losses deductible only to extent losses exceed 10% of AGI.	Deductible in full.
Depreciation recapture under § 1250	Recaptured to extent accelerated depreciation exceeds straight-line.	20% of excess of amount that would be recaptured under § 1245 over amount recaptured under § 1250 is additional ordinary income under § 291.
Net operating loss	Adjusted for several items, including nonbusiness deductions over nonbusiness income and personal exemptions.	Generally no adjustments.
	Carryback period is 3 years and carryforward period is 15 years.	Same as for individuals.
Dividends received deduction	None.	70%, 80%, or 100% of dividends received depending on percentage of ownership by corporate shareholder.
Net capital gains	Taxed in full. Tax rate cannot exceed 28% for tax years beginning after 1990.	Taxed in full.
Capital losses	Only $3,000 of capital loss per year can offset ordinary income; loss is carried forward indefinitely to offset capital gains or ordinary income up to $3,000; carryovers retain their character as long term or short term.	Can offset only capital gains; carried back three years and forward five; carryovers and carrybacks are short-term losses.
Passive losses	Passive activity losses cannot be offset against either active income or portfolio income.	Passive loss rules apply to closely held C corporations and personal service corporations.
		For personal service corporations, the rule is the same as for individuals.
		For closely held corporations, passive losses may offset active income but not portfolio income.

	Individuals	Corporations
Tax rates	Mildly progressive with three rates (15%, 28%, and 31%).	Mildly progressive with three rates (15% 25%, and 34%); lower brackets phased out between $100,000 and $335,000 of taxable income.
Alternative minimum tax (see Chapter 14)	Applied at a 24% rate to AMTI; exemption allowed depending on filing status (e.g., $40,000 for married filing jointly); exemption phase-out begins when AMTI reaches a certain amount (e.g., $150,000 for married filing jointly).	Applied at a 20% rate on AMTI; $40,000 exemption allowed but phase-out begins when AMTI reaches $150,000; adjustments and tax preference items are similar to those applicable to individuals but also include 75% of adjusted current earnings over AMTI.

year and the return filed showed a tax liability). Estimated payments can be made in four installments due on or before the fifteenth day of the fourth month, the sixth month, the ninth month, and the twelfth month of the corporate taxable year. The full amount of the unpaid tax is due on the due date of the return.

Failure to make the required estimated tax prepayments results in a nondeductible penalty being imposed on the corporation. The penalty is avoided, however, if any of various exceptions apply.[26]

Reconciliation of Taxable Income and Financial Net Income

Schedule M–1 on the last page of Form 1120 is used to reconcile net income as computed for financial accounting purposes with taxable income reported on the corporation's income tax return. The starting point on Schedule M–1 is net income per books (financial accounting net income). Additions and subtractions are entered for items that affect net income per books and taxable income differently. The following items are entered as additions (see lines 2 through 5 of Schedule M–1):

- Federal income tax liability (deducted in computing net income per books but not deductible in computing taxable income).
- The excess of capital losses over capital gains (deducted for financial accounting purposes but not deductible by corporations for income tax purposes).
- Income that is reported in the current year for tax purposes that is not reported in computing net income per books (e.g., prepaid income).
- Various expenses that are deducted in computing net income per books but not allowed in computing taxable income (e.g., charitable contributions in excess of the 10 percent ceiling applicable to corporations).

The following subtractions are entered on lines 7 and 8 of Schedule M–1:

- Income reported for financial accounting purposes but not included in taxable income (e.g., tax-exempt interest).
- Expenses deducted on the tax return but not deducted in computing net income per books (e.g., a charitable contributions carryover deducted in a

26. See § 6655 for the penalty involved and the various exceptions to it.

prior year for financial accounting purposes but deductible in the current year for tax purposes).

The result is taxable income (before the NOL deduction and the dividends received deduction).

EXAMPLE 37

During the current year, Brown Corporation had the following transactions:

Net income per books (after tax)	$92,400
Taxable income	50,000
Federal income tax liability (15% × $50,000)	7,500
Interest income from tax-exempt bonds	5,000
Interest paid on loan, the proceeds of which were used to purchase the tax-exempt bonds	500
Life insurance proceeds received as a result of the death of a key employee	50,000
Premiums paid on key employee life insurance policy	2,600
Excess of capital losses over capital gains	2,000

For book and tax purposes, Brown Corporation determines depreciation under the straight-line method. Brown's Schedule M–1 for the current year is as follows:

Schedule M-1 Reconciliation of Income (Loss) per Books With Income per Return (See instructions.)

1 Net income (loss) per books	92,400	7 Income recorded on books this year not included on this return (itemize): Tax-exempt interest $ 5,000 Life insurance proceeds on key employee $50,000	55,000
2 Federal income tax	7,500		
3 Excess of capital losses over capital gains	2,000		
4 Income subject to tax not recorded on books this year (itemize):		8 Deductions on this return not charged against book income this year (itemize): a Depreciation $ b Contributions carryover $	
5 Expenses recorded on books this year not deducted on this return (itemize): a Depreciation $ b Contributions carryover $ c Travel and entertainment $ Int. on tax-exempt bonds $500 Prem. on key employee ins. $2,600	3,100	9 Add lines 7 and 8	55,000
6 Add lines 1 through 5	105,000	10 Income (line 28, page 1)—line 6 less line 9	50,000

◆

Schedule M–2 reconciles unappropriated retained earnings at the beginning of the year with unappropriated retained earnings at year-end. Beginning balance plus net income per books, as entered on line 1 of Schedule M–1, less dividend distributions during the year equals ending retained earnings. Other sources of increases or decreases in retained earnings are also listed on Schedule M–2.

EXAMPLE 38

Assume the same facts as in Example 37. Brown Corporation's beginning balance in unappropriated retained earnings is $125,000. During the year, Brown distributed a cash dividend of $30,000 to its shareholders. Based on these further assumptions, Brown's Schedule M–2 for the current year is as follows:

Schedule M-2 Analysis of Unappropriated Retained Earnings per Books (Line 25, Schedule L)

1 Balance at beginning of year	125,000	5 Distributions: a Cash	30,000
2 Net income (loss) per books	92,400	b Stock	
3 Other increases (itemize):		c Property	
		6 Other decreases (itemize):	
		7 Add lines 5 and 6	30,000
4 Add lines 1, 2, and 3	217,400	8 Balance at end of year (line 4 less line 7)	187,400

◆

Consolidated Returns

Requirements. Corporations that are members of a parent-subsidiary affiliated group, as defined in § 1504(a) of the Code, may file a consolidated income tax return for a taxable year. An affiliated group for this purpose is one or more chains of includible corporations connected through stock ownership with a common parent but only if both the following requirements are met:

1. The common parent owns stock that represents at least 80 percent of the total voting power *and* 80 percent of the total value of stock of at least one of the includible corporations.
2. Stock representing at least 80 percent of the total voting power *and* 80 percent of the total value of stock in each of the includible corporations (except the common parent) is owned directly by one or more of the includible corporations.

Each corporation that has been a member of the group during any part of the taxable year for which the consolidated return is to be filed must consent by filing Form 1122. It may also consent by the actual filing of a consolidated return on Form 1120 with an affiliations schedule on Form 851 that includes all the member corporations. Once a consolidated return is filed, the controlled group must continue to file consolidated returns unless it secures permission from the IRS to discontinue filing such returns. Applications to discontinue should be made to the IRS by the ninetieth day preceding the return's due date. A corporation that ceases to be a member of a consolidated group must generally wait five years before it can again file on a consolidated basis.

The privilege of filing a consolidated return is based on the concept that the affiliated group constitutes a single taxable entity despite the existence of technically separate businesses. By filing a consolidated return, the corporations can eliminate intercompany profits and losses on the principle that tax liability should be based on transactions with outsiders rather than on intragroup affairs.

The filing of consolidated returns is available only to parent-subsidiary affiliated groups; it is not available to brother-sister corporations.

Advantages and Disadvantages of Filing a Consolidated Return. Filing a consolidated return offers distinct advantages. Income of a profitable company is offset by losses of another. Capital losses of one corporation can offset capital gains of another. Without this possibility, net capital losses cannot be deducted in the year incurred, as noted previously.

Filing a consolidated return also has certain disadvantages. Losses on intercompany transactions must be deferred. Accounting for consolidated taxable income and deferral of intercompany transactions can be perplexing. Another problem is that the consolidated returns filed for tax purposes and the consolidated financial statements may not include the same corporations. For example, most foreign corporations cannot be consolidated for Federal income tax purposes but should be consolidated when preparing financial statements. This variance will cause some compliance problems in computing the taxable income and the AMT of the group.

Corporate versus Noncorporate Forms of Business Organization

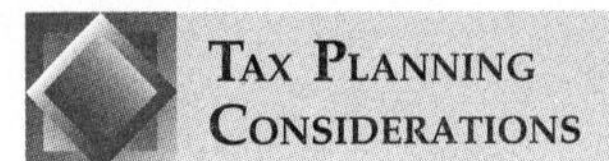

The decision to use the corporate form in conducting a trade or business must be weighed carefully. Besides the nontax considerations associated with the corporate form (limited liability, continuity of life, free transferability of interest, centralized management), tax ramifications will play an important role in any such decision. Close attention should be paid to the following:

1. Operating as a regular corporate entity (C corporation) results in the imposition of the corporate income tax. Corporate taxable income will be taxed twice—once as earned by the corporation and again when distributed to the shareholders. Since dividends are not deductible, a closely held corporation has a strong incentive to structure corporate distributions in a deductible form. Thus, profits can be bailed out by the shareholders in the form of salaries, interest, or rents. Such procedures lead to a multitude of problems, one of which, the reclassification of debt as equity, is discussed in Chapter 17. The problems of unreasonable salaries and rents are covered in Chapter 18 in the discussion of constructive dividends.
2. Assuming the current tax rates remain in effect, the top rates favor the noncorporate taxpayer over the corporate taxpayer. For example, the top rate for individuals currently is 31 percent. For corporations, the top rate is 34 percent. The differential is less pronounced, however, if a shareholder has a top rate of 31 percent and a corporation limits its taxable income to $100,000 to avoid the phase-out of the 15 percent and 25 percent lower brackets. Here, the time value of the taxes saved (by not distributing dividends and postponing the effect of the double tax that otherwise results) could make operating a business in the corporate form advantageous (refer to Example 7).
3. Corporate-source income loses its identity as it passes through the corporation to the shareholders. Thus, preferential tax treatment of certain items by the corporation (e.g., interest on municipal bonds) does not carry over to the shareholders.
4. As noted in Chapter 18, it may be difficult for shareholders to recover some or all of their investment in the corporation without an ordinary income result. Most corporate distributions are treated as dividends to the extent of the corporation's earnings and profits.
5. Corporate losses cannot be passed through to the shareholders.[27]
6. The liquidation of a corporation will normally generate tax consequences to both the corporation and its shareholders (see Chapter 19).
7. The corporate form provides shareholders with the opportunity to be treated as employees for tax purposes if the shareholders render services to the corporation. Such status makes a number of attractive tax-sheltered fringe benefits available. They include, but are not limited to, group term life insurance (§ 79), the $5,000 death benefit [§ 101(b)(1)], and excludible meals and lodging (§ 119). These benefits are not available to partners and sole proprietors.

The Association Route

Consideration 7 in the preceding section led to the popularity of the professional association. The major tax incentive was to cover the shareholder-employees under a qualified pension plan. Professionals, particularly physicians, who were not permitted to form regular corporations because of prohibitions under state

27. Points 1, 2, and 5 could be resolved through a Subchapter S election (see Chapter 21), assuming the corporation qualifies for the election. In part, the same can be said for point 3.

law or professional ethics restrictions, created organizations with sufficient corporate attributes to be classified as associations. The position of the IRS on the status of these professional associations (whether or not they should be treated as corporations for tax purposes) vacillated over a period of years. After a series of judicial losses, however, the IRS has accepted their association status, assuming certain conditions are satisfied.

In recent years, the popularity of the association approach has diminished significantly. Changes in the tax law have curtailed the deferral opportunities of qualified pension and profit sharing plans available to employees. At the same time, rules for H.R. 10 (Keogh) plans available to self-employed taxpayers have been liberalized. By placing the two types of plans on a parity with each other, one of the major incentives to achieve employee status through association status was eliminated.

Operating the Corporation

Tax planning to reduce corporate income taxes should occur before the end of the tax year. Effective planning can cause income to be shifted to the next tax year and can produce large deductions by incurring expenses before year-end. Particular attention should be focused on the following.

Charitable Contributions. Recall that accrual basis corporations may claim a deduction for charitable contributions in the year preceding payment. The contribution must be authorized by the board of directors by the end of the tax year and paid on or before the fifteenth day of the third month of the following year. Even though the contribution may not ultimately be made, it might well be authorized. A deduction cannot be thrown back to the previous year (even if paid within the two and a half months) if it has not been authorized.

Timing of Capital Gains and Losses. A corporation should consider offsetting profits on the sale of capital assets by selling some of the depreciated securities in the corporate portfolio. In addition, any already realized capital losses should be carefully monitored. Recall that corporate taxpayers are not permitted to claim any net capital losses as deductions against ordinary income. Capital losses can be used only as an offset against capital gains. Further, net capital losses can only be carried back three years and forward five. Gains from the sales of capital assets should be timed to offset any capital losses. The expiration of the carryover period for any net capital losses should be watched carefully so that sales of appreciated capital assets occur before that date.

Net Operating Losses. In some situations, electing to forgo an NOL carryback and utilizing the carryforward option may generate greater tax savings. When deciding whether to forgo the carryback options, take into account three considerations. First, the time value of the tax refund that is lost by not using the carryback procedure should be calculated. Second, the election to forgo an NOL carryback is irrevocable. Thus, one cannot later choose to change if the predicted high profits do not materialize. Third, consider the future increases (or decreases) in corporate income tax rates that can reasonably be anticipated. This last consideration is the most difficult to work with. Although corporate tax rates have remained relatively stable in past years, projected budget deficits do little to assure taxpayers that future rates will remain constant.

Dividends Received Deduction. The dividends received deduction is normally limited to the lesser of 70 percent of the qualifying dividends or 70 percent of taxable income. An exception is made when the full deduction yields an NOL. In close situations, therefore, the proper timing of income or deductions to generate an NOL may yield a larger dividends received deduction.

Organizational Expenditures. To qualify for the 60-month amortization procedure of § 248, only organizational expenditures incurred in the first taxable year of the corporation can be considered. This rule could prove to be an unfortunate trap for corporations formed late in the year.

EXAMPLE 39

Green Corporation is formed in December 1993. Qualified organizational expenditures are incurred as follows: $2,000 in December 1993 and $3,000 in January 1994. If Green uses the calendar year for tax purposes, only $2,000 of the organizational expenditures can be written off over a period of 60 months. ◆

The solution to the problem posed by Example 39 is for Green Corporation to adopt a fiscal year that ends beyond January 31. All organizational expenditures will then have been incurred before the close of the first taxable year.

Shareholder-Employee Payment of Corporate Expenses. In a closely held corporate setting, shareholder-employees often pay corporate expenses (e.g., travel and entertainment) for which they are not reimbursed by the corporation. The IRS often disallows the deduction of these expenses by the shareholder-employee since the payments are voluntary on his or her part. If the deduction is more beneficial at the shareholder-employee level, a corporate policy against reimbursement of such expenses should be established. Proper planning in this regard would be to decide before the beginning of each tax year where the deduction would do the most good. Corporate policy on reimbursement of such expenses could be modified on a year-to-year basis depending upon the circumstances.

In deciding whether corporate expenses should be kept at the corporate level or shifted to the shareholder-employee, the treatment of unreimbursed employee expenses must be considered. First, since employee expenses are itemized deductions, they will be of no benefit to the taxpayer who chooses the standard deduction option. Second, these expenses will be subject to the 2 percent-of-AGI floor. No such limitation will be imposed if the corporation claims the expenses.

Related Corporations

Controlled Groups. Recall that § 1561 was designed to prevent shareholders from operating a business as multiple corporations to obtain lower tax brackets and multiple accumulated earnings tax credits or AMT exemptions. Corporations in which substantially all the stock is held by five or fewer persons are subject to the provisions of § 1561. Dividing ownership so that control of each corporation does not lie with individuals having common control of all corporations avoids the prohibitions of § 1561.

PROBLEM MATERIALS

DISCUSSION QUESTIONS

1. Jill owns 100% of Black Company, which had operating income of $100,000 and operating expenses of $140,000 in 1993. In addition, Black Company had a long-term

capital loss of $15,000. Based on this information, what is the tax treatment in each of the following situations?

a. Black Company is a corporation and pays no dividends during the year.
b. Black Company is a proprietorship.

2. Gray Company had $80,000 net profit from operations in 1993 and paid Pat Gray, its sole shareholder, a dividend of $50,000. Pat has a large amount of income from other sources and is in the 31% marginal tax bracket. Would Pat's tax situation be better or worse if Gray Company were a proprietorship and Pat withdrew $50,000 from the business during the year?
3. Redd Company incurred a $50,000 net loss from operations in 1993. Kim Redd, its sole shareholder, has a large amount of income from other sources and is in the 31% marginal tax bracket. Would Kim's tax situation be better or worse if Redd Company were a proprietorship rather than a corporation?
4. Under what circumstances may a corporation legally constituted under state law be disregarded for Federal income tax purposes?
5. Ann and Fran, who are sisters, own adjacent parcels of land they inherited from their parents. They form Twin Properties, Inc., and transfer the land to the corporation. At the date of transfer, each parcel of land is worth $25,000. Ann wants to have the corporation hold the land until it appreciates to $100,000 and then sell it. Fran wants to have the corporation subdivide the property, put in streets and a sewer system, and then sell the lots. What are the Federal income tax implications of the two plans?
6. Why might the IRS attempt to disregard a legally constituted corporate entity? Why might the shareholders attempt such a move?
7. Under what circumstances might the owners of a business wish to have the business classified as an association? To have it not so classified?
8. In testing for association status, what criteria are considered in the case of partnerships? In the case of trusts?
9. Compare the income tax treatment of corporations and individuals in the following respects:

a. Applicable tax rates.
b. AGI determination.
c. Deduction for casualty losses.
d. Allowable tax credits.
e. Recapture of depreciation.
f. Dividends received from domestic corporations.
g. Net operating losses.

10. A taxpayer realized a net long-term capital gain of $10,000 during the year. How is the gain treated if the taxpayer is a corporation? An individual?
11. A taxpayer incurred a net long-term capital loss of $5,000 during the year. How is the loss treated if the taxpayer is a corporation? An individual?
12. Red Corporation owns 85% of the stock of Blue Corporation, which pays Red a dividend of $100,000. Red Corporation also owns 15% of the stock of Green Corporation, which pays Red a $20,000 dividend. How much dividend income will Red Corporation report for the year?
13. A taxpayer sells a warehouse for a gain of $50,000. The warehouse has been depreciated as 15-year property under ACRS. Depreciation recapture will be higher if the taxpayer is a corporation than if the taxpayer is an individual. Explain.
14. Compare the tax treatment of corporate and noncorporate taxpayers' charitable contributions with respect to the following:

a. The year of the deduction for an accrual basis taxpayer.
b. The percentage limitations on the maximum deduction allowed for any one year.
c. The amount of the deduction allowed for the donation of certain inventory.

15. In connection with organizational expenditures, comment on the following:

a. Those that qualify for amortization.
b. Those that do not qualify for amortization.

c. The period over which amortization can take place.
d. Expenses incurred but not paid by a cash basis corporation.
e. Expenses incurred by a corporation in its second year of operation.
f. The alternative if no election to amortize is made.
g. The timing of the election to amortize.

16. Lavender Corporation, a PSC, had taxable income of $100,000 in 1993. Aqua Corporation had taxable income of $335,000 for the year, and Silver Corporation's 1993 taxable income was $500,000. Only Aqua Corporation's Federal income tax can be calculated by multiplying taxable income times 34%. True or false? Explain.

17. Silver Corporation, which owns stock in Gold Corporation, had net operating income of $100,000 for the year. Gold pays Silver a dividend of $20,000. Under what circumstances can Silver take a dividends received deduction of $14,000? A dividends received deduction of $20,000?

18. Dan, Grace, Paul, and Tammy each own shares in Eagle, Hawk, Dove, and Robin Corporations, but the ownership is distributed in such a way that the four corporations do not constitute a controlled group. It will be advantageous from a Federal income tax viewpoint if the shareholders restructure ownership in a way that will cause the four corporations to be considered a controlled group. True or false? Explain.

19. What is the difference between a brother-sister controlled group and a parent-subsidiary controlled group?

20. What are the conditions for filing a Form 1120–A?

21. Taxable income and financial accounting income for a corporation are seldom the same amount. Discuss some common reasons for differences and how these differences affect the reconciliation of taxable income and financial accounting income on Schedule M–1 of Form 1120.

22. What groups of corporations may file consolidated returns?

23. What are the advantages and disadvantages of filing a consolidated return?

PROBLEMS

24. Mike owns 100% of White Company, which had net operating income of $60,000 in 1993 ($100,000 operating income – $40,000 operating expenses). In addition, White Company had a long-term capital gain of $10,000. Mike has sufficient income from other activities to place him in the 31% marginal tax bracket before considering results from White Company. Using this information, explain the tax treatment under the following circumstances:

a. White Company is a corporation and pays no dividends during the year.
b. White Company is a corporation and pays Mike $70,000 of dividends during the year.
c. White Company is a corporation and pays Mike a $70,000 salary during the year.
d. White Company is a proprietorship and Mike withdraws $0 during the year.
e. White Company is a proprietorship and Mike withdraws $70,000 during the year.

25. Rust Corporation and Al and Bob form a limited partnership on January 1 to construct office buildings. Rust Corporation is the general partner, and Al and Bob are both limited partners. The partnership agreement provides that Rust will have sole management of the business. Al's and Bob's liabilities for debts of the partnership will be limited to their investments. The partnership agreement provides that the partnership will not end upon the death of any of the partners. The agreement also provides that both Al or Bob may sell their interests without the consent of the other parties. Al and Bob invest $50,000 each in the partnership. Rust Corporation, which has a net worth of only $20,000, invests $10,000. The partnership secures

a loan from the bank to help finance the initial cost of construction. How will the partnership be classified for tax purposes? Explain.

26. In the current year, Hicks, a calendar year taxpayer, suffers a casualty loss of $9,000. How much of the casualty loss will be a tax deduction to Hicks under the following circumstances?

    a. Hicks is an individual and has AGI of $20,000. The casualty loss was a personal loss. Hicks recovered insurance of $3,000.
    b. Hicks is a corporation. Hicks recovered insurance of $3,000.

27. In 1993, a business sells a capital asset, which it had held for two years, at a loss of $15,000. How much of the capital loss may be deducted in 1993, and how much is carried back or forward under the following circumstances?

    a. The business was a sole proprietorship owned by Kim. Kim had a short-term capital gain of $3,000 and a long-term capital gain of $2,000 in 1993. Kim had ordinary net income from the proprietorship of $60,000.
    b. The business is incorporated. The corporation had a short-term capital gain of $3,000 and a long-term capital gain of $2,000. Its ordinary net income from the business was $60,000.

28. White Corporation realized net short-term capital gains of $10,000 and net long-term capital losses of $90,000 during 1993. Taxable income from other sources was $400,000. Prior years' transactions included the following:

1989	Net long-term capital gains	$40,000
1990	Net short-term capital gains	20,000
1991	Net long-term capital gains	30,000
1992	Net long-term capital gains	20,000

    a. How are the capital gains and losses treated on the 1993 tax return?
    b. Compute the capital loss carryback to the carryback years.
    c. Compute the amount of capital loss carryover, if any, and designate the years to which the loss may be carried.

29. Starling Corporation acquired residential rental property on January 3, 1984, for $100,000. The property was depreciated using the accelerated method and a 15-year recovery period under ACRS. Depreciation in the amount of $70,417 was claimed. Straight-line depreciation for the period would have been $63,333. Starling sold the property on January 1, 1993, for $110,000. What is the gain on the sale, and how is it taxed?

30. Assume the property in Problem 29 was a commercial building and Starling Corporation used the straight-line method of depreciation with a 15-year recovery period under ACRS. What would be the gain on the sale, and how would it be taxed?

31. In 1993, Green Corporation has passive losses from a rental activity of $140,000. It has active business income of $900,000 and $60,000 of portfolio income. What is Green's taxable income for 1993 under the following circumstances?

    a. Green Corporation is a closely held corporation.
    b. Green Corporation is a personal service corporation.

32. During the current year, Sanchez Corporation, a calendar year taxpayer, had the following income and expenses:

Income from operations	$450,000
Expenses from operations	330,000
Qualifying dividends from domestic corporations	30,000
NOL carryover from prior year	9,000

On June 3, Sanchez Corporation made a contribution to a qualified charitable organization of $21,000 in cash (not included in any of the above items).

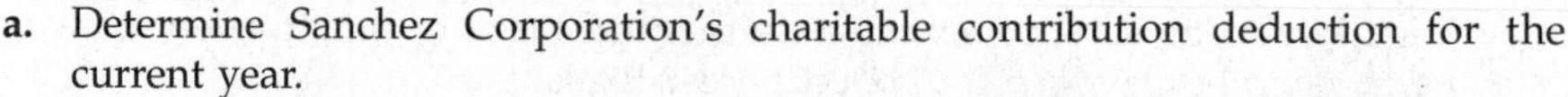

a. Determine Sanchez Corporation's charitable contribution deduction for the current year.
b. What happens to any excess charitable contribution deduction not allowable for the current year?

33. Pursuant to a resolution adopted by its board of directors, Blue Corporation, a calendar year, accrual basis taxpayer, authorizes a $50,000 donation to City University (a qualified charitable organization) on December 20, 1992. The donation is made on March 10, 1993. Is the corporation correct in claiming a deduction (subject to statutory limitations) in 1992? What if the donation were made on April 10, 1993?

34. During 1993, a corporation has $200,000 of gross income and $250,000 in allowable business deductions. Included in gross income is $60,000 in qualifying dividends from domestic corporations (less than 20% owned).

a. Determine the corporation's NOL for 1993.
b. What happens to the loss if the corporation was newly created in 1993? In 1990?

35. In each of the following independent situations, determine the dividends received deduction. Assume that none of the corporate shareholders owns 20% or more of the stock in the corporations paying the dividends.

	Red Corporation	White Corporation	Blue Corporation
Income from operations	$ 700,000	$ 800,000	$ 700,000
Expenses from operations	(600,000)	(900,000)	(740,000)
Qualifying dividends	100,000	200,000	200,000

36. Green Corporation was formed on December 1, 1993. Qualifying organizational expenses were incurred and paid as follows:

Incurred and paid in December 1993	$10,000
Incurred in December 1993 but paid in January 1994	5,000
Incurred and paid in February 1994	3,000

Assume Green Corporation makes a timely election under § 248 to amortize organizational expenditures over a period of 60 months. What amount may be amortized in the corporation's first tax year under each of the following assumptions?

a. Green Corporation adopts a calendar year and the cash basis of accounting for tax purposes.
b. Same as (a), except that Green Corporation chooses a fiscal year of December 1 through November 30.
c. Green Corporation adopts a calendar year and the accrual basis of accounting for tax purposes.
d. Same as (c), except that Green Corporation chooses a fiscal year of December 1 through November 30.

37. Topaz Corporation, an accrual basis taxpayer, was formed and began operations on July 1, 1993. The following expenses were incurred during the first tax year of operations (July 1 through December 31, 1993):

Expenses of temporary directors and of organizational meetings	$ 5,000
Fee paid to the state of incorporation	600
Accounting services incident to organization	1,200
Legal services for drafting the corporate charter and bylaws	2,800
Expenses incident to the printing and sale of stock certificates	1,000
	$10,600

Assume Topaz Corporation makes an appropriate and timely election under § 248.

a. What is the maximum organizational expense Topaz may write off for tax year 1993?
b. What would have been the result if a proper election had not been made?

38. In each of the following independent situations, determine the corporation's income tax liability. Assume that all corporations use a calendar year for tax purposes and that the tax year involved is 1993.

	Taxable Income
Wren Corporation	$ 45,000
Thrush Corporation	140,000
Gull Corporation	420,000
Oriole Corporation	65,000

39. A regular corporation did not distribute any dividends in tax year 1993. It had no capital gains or losses. What is its 1993 income tax liability under the following independent situations?

a. Its taxable income was $30,000.
b. Its taxable income was $70,000.
c. Its taxable income was $130,000.
d. Its taxable income was $2 million.
e. Same as (a) except that the corporation distributed $20,000 in dividends to its sole shareholder.
f. Same as (a) except that the corporation had a $20,000 capital loss.

40. Red Corporation owns 80% of the total combined voting power of all classes of stock entitled to vote in White Corporation. White owns 20% of the stock in Blue Corporation. Red owns 90% of Green Corporation, while the latter owns 60% of Blue Corporation. Which corporations are part of a controlled group?

41. The outstanding stock of Starling, Robin, Crow, Grouse, and Swallow Corporations is owned by the following unrelated individual and corporate shareholders:

	Corporations				
Shareholders	Starling	Robin	Crow	Grouse	Swallow
Albert	20%		5%	10%	
Burke	30%		40%	50%	
Clark	20%		15%	10%	
Dave	10%		20%	10%	
Starling Corporation		90%			
Grouse Corporation					85%

Which, if any, of the above corporations are members of a controlled group?

42. For 1993, Acme Corporation, an accrual basis, calendar year taxpayer, had net income per books of $172,750 and the following special transactions:

Life insurance proceeds received upon the death of the corporation president	$100,000
Premiums paid on the life insurance policy on the president	10,000
Prepaid rent received and properly taxed in 1992 but credited as rent income in 1993	15,000
Rent income received in 1993 ($10,000 is prepaid and relates to 1994)	25,000
Interest income on tax-exempt bonds	5,000
Interest on loan to carry tax-exempt bonds	3,000
ACRS depreciation in excess of straight-line (straight-line was used for book purposes)	4,000
Capital loss in excess of capital gains	6,000
Federal income tax liability for 1993	22,250

Using Schedule M–1 of Form 1120 (the most recent version available), compute Acme Corporation's taxable income for 1993.

43. Using the legend provided, classify each of the following statements:

Legend

I = Applies only to individual taxpayers.
C = Applies only to corporate taxpayers.
B = Applies to both individual and corporate taxpayers.
N = Applies to neither individual nor corporate taxpayers.

a. A net capital loss can be carried back.
b. Net long-term capital losses are carried back or forward as short-term capital losses.
c. A $4,000 net short-term capital loss in the current year can be deducted against ordinary income only to the extent of $3,000.
d. The carryforward period for net capital losses is five years.
e. The alternative minimum tax does not apply.
f. Net operating losses are not allowed to be carried back.
g. The credit for the elderly applies.
h. The carryback period for excess charitable contributions is three years.
i. Excess charitable contributions can be carried forward indefinitely.
j. On the disposition of certain depreciable real estate, more ordinary income may result.
k. Percentage limitations may restrict the amount of charitable deductions that can be claimed in any one tax year.
l. Casualty losses are deductible in full.
m. More adjustments are necessary to arrive at an NOL deduction.

Chapter

Corporations: Organization and Capital Structure

Objectives

Describe the tax consequences of incorporating a new or existing business.

Explain how to deal with subsequent property transfers to a controlled corporation.

Describe the capital structure of a corporation and explain what it means for tax purposes.

Discuss the advantages and disadvantages of preferring debt over an equity investment.

Describe the nature and treatment of shareholder debt and stock losses.

Outline

Chapter 16 dealt with three principal areas fundamental to working with corporations: (1) the recognition of an entity as a corporation for Federal income tax purposes, (2) the tax rules applicable to the day-to-day operation of a corporation, and (3) the filing and reporting procedures governing corporations.

Chapter 17 addresses more sophisticated problems in dealing with corporations:

- The tax consequences to the shareholders and the corporation upon the organization of the corporation.
- Once the corporation has been formed, the tax result that ensues when shareholders make later transfers of property.
- The capital structure of a corporation, including the treatment of capital contributions by nonshareholders and shareholders and the handling of investor losses suffered by shareholders.

ORGANIZATION OF AND TRANSFERS TO CONTROLLED CORPORATIONS

In General

Unless special provisions in the Code apply, a transfer of property to a corporation in exchange for stock is a sale or exchange of property and constitutes a taxable transaction. Gain or loss is measured by the difference between the tax basis of the property transferred and the value of the stock received. Section 351 provides that gain or loss is not recognized upon the transfer of property to a corporation solely in exchange for stock if the persons transferring the property are in control of the corporation immediately after the transfer.

The nonrecognition of gain or loss reflects the principle of continuity of the taxpayer's investment. The taxpayer's economic status has not really changed. The investment in certain properties carries over to the investment in corporate stock. Since the taxpayer has received only stock in the new corporation, he or she is hardly in a position to pay a tax on any realized gain. As noted later, when the taxpayer receives property other than stock (i.e., boot) from the corporation, realized gain may be recognized.

The same principle governs the nonrecognition of gain or loss on like-kind exchanges under § 1031. The nonrecognition concept causes gain to be postponed until a substantive change in the taxpayer's investment occurs (a sale to or a taxable exchange with outsiders). This approach is justified under the wherewithal to pay concept.

EXAMPLE 1

Ron is considering incorporating his donut shop. He is concerned about his potential liability for the shop's obligations in case he encounters financial difficulties in the future. Ron realizes that if he incorporates his shop, he will be liable only for the debts of the business that he has personally guaranteed. If Ron incorporates, he will transfer the following assets to the corporation:

	Tax Basis	Fair Market Value
Cash	$10,000	$ 10,000
Furniture and fixtures	20,000	60,000
Building	40,000	100,000
	$70,000	$170,000

Ron will receive stock in the newly formed corporation worth $170,000 in exchange for the assets. Without the nonrecognition provisions of § 351, Ron would recognize a taxable gain of $100,000 on the transfer. Under § 351, however, Ron does not recognize any gain because his economic status has not really changed. Ron's investment in the assets of his unincorporated donut shop carries over to his investment in the incorporated donut shop. Thus, § 351 provides for tax neutrality on the initial incorporation of Ron's donut shop. ◆

If the transferor shareholders receive money or property other than stock, § 351(b) provides that gain is recognized to the extent of the lesser of the gain realized or the boot received (the amount of money and the fair market value of other property received). The gain is characterized according to the type of asset transferred.[1] Loss is never recognized. The nonrecognition of gain or loss is accompanied by a carryover of basis.[2]

EXAMPLE 2

Abby and Bill form White Corporation. Abby transfers property with an adjusted basis of $30,000, fair market value of $60,000, for 50% of the stock. Bill transfers property with an adjusted basis of $70,000, fair market value of $60,000, for the remaining 50% of the stock. The transfer qualifies under § 351. Abby has an unrecognized gain of $30,000, and Bill has an unrecognized loss of $10,000. Both have a carryover basis in the stock in White Corporation. Abby has a basis of $30,000 in her stock, and Bill has a basis of $70,000 in his stock. ◆

Section 351 is mandatory. If a transaction falls within its provisions, neither gain nor loss is recognized on the transfer (except that realized gain is recognized to the extent of boot received), and there is a carryover of basis.

There are three requirements for nonrecognition of gain or loss: (1) *property* is transferred for (2) *stock* and (3) the transferors must be in *control* of the transferee corporation.

Transfer of Property

Questions have arisen concerning what constitutes property for purposes of § 351. The Code specifically excludes services rendered from the definition of property. With this exception, the definition of property is comprehensive. Unrealized receivables from a cash basis taxpayer and installment obligations are considered property, for example. The transfer of an installment obligation in a transaction qualifying under § 351 is not a disposition of the installment obligation. Thus, the transferor does not recognize gain. Secret processes and formulas, as well as secret information in the general nature of a patentable inventory, also qualify as property under § 351.

1. Rev.Rul. 68–55, 1968–1 C.B. 140.

2. §§ 358(a) and 362(a). See the discussion preceding Example 20.

Services are not considered to be property under § 351 for a critical reason. A taxpayer must report as income the fair market value of property received as compensation for services rendered.[3] Thus, if a taxpayer receives stock in a corporation as consideration for rendering services to the corporation, the taxpayer has taxable income. The amount of income is the fair market value of the stock received. The taxpayer's basis in the stock then is the fair market value of the stock.

EXAMPLE 3

Ann and Bob form Brown Corporation and transfer the following property to it:

	Property Transferred		
	Basis to Transferor	Fair Market Value	Number of Shares Issued
From Ann:			
Personal services rendered to Brown	$ -0-	$20,000	200
From Bob:			
Installment obligation	5,000	40,000	
Inventory	10,000	30,000	800
Secret process	-0-	10,000	

The value of each share in Brown Corporation is $100. Ann has income of $20,000 on the transfer because services do not qualify as "property." She has a basis of $20,000 in her 200 shares of stock in Brown. Bob has no gain on the transfer because all the property he transferred to Brown qualifies as "property" under § 351. Bob has a basis of $15,000 in his stock in Brown. ◆

Stock

If property is transferred to a corporation in exchange for any property other than stock, the property constitutes boot. The boot is taxable to the transferor shareholder to the extent of any realized gain. The Regulations state that the term "stock" does not include stock rights and stock warrants.[4] Generally, however, the term "stock" needs no clarification. It includes both common stock and preferred stock.

Currently, securities (i.e., long-term debt) constitute boot under § 351. Thus, a shareholder who receives securities in exchange for the transfer of appreciated property to a controlled corporation must recognize gain.

Control of the Transferee Corporation

To qualify as a nontaxable transaction under § 351, the transferor must be in control of the transferee corporation immediately after the exchange. Control means that the person or persons transferring the property must have an 80 percent stock ownership in the transferee corporation. The transferor shareholders must own stock possessing at least 80 percent of the total combined *voting power* of all classes of stock entitled to vote and at least 80 percent of the total *number* of shares of all other classes of stock.[5]

3. §§ 61 and 83.
4. Reg. § 1.351–1(a)(1)(ii).
5. § 368(c).

Control Immediately after the Transfer. Control can apply to a single person or to several individuals if they are all parties to an integrated transaction. Section 351 requires control "immediately after the exchange." The Regulations provide that when more than one person is involved, the exchange does not necessarily require simultaneous exchanges by two or more persons. However, the rights of the parties (e.g., those transferring property to the corporation) must be previously set out and determined. Also, the agreement to transfer property should be executed ". . . with an expedition consistent with orderly procedure."[6]

If two or more persons transfer property to a corporation for stock, the transfers should occur close together in time and should be made in accordance with an agreement among the parties.

Example 4

Jack exchanges property, basis of $60,000 and fair market value of $100,000, for 70% of the stock of Gray Corporation. The other 30% is owned by Jane, who acquired it several years ago. The fair market value of Jack's stock is $100,000. Jack recognizes a taxable gain of $40,000 on the transfer. ◆

Example 5

Lana, Leo, and Lori incorporate their respective businesses and form Green Corporation. Lana exchanges her property for 300 shares in Green on January 5, 1993. Leo exchanges his property for 400 shares of Green Corporation stock on January 10, 1993, and Lori exchanges her property for 300 shares in Green on March 5, 1993. The three exchanges are part of a prearranged plan. The nonrecognition provisions of § 351 apply to all the exchanges. ◆

Stock need not be issued to the transferring parties in proportion to the interest each held in the transferred property. However, when stock received is not proportionate to the value of the property transferred, the transaction could be treated as a gift from one transferor to the other.

Example 6

Hazel and Hal organize a corporation with 500 shares of stock. Hazel transfers property with a fair market value of $10,000 for 100 shares, and Hal transfers property with a fair market value of $5,000 for 400 shares. The transaction qualifies under § 351; however, if Hazel did in fact make a gift to Hal, the transfer might be subject to a gift tax (see Chapter 26). ◆

Control is not lost if stock received by shareholders in a § 351 exchange is sold or given to persons who are not parties to the exchange shortly after the transaction. A different result might materialize if a plan for the ultimate sale or gift of the stock existed before the exchange.

Example 7

Lee and Pat form Black Corporation. They transfer appreciated property to the corporation with each receiving 50 shares of the stock. Shortly after the formation, Lee gives 25 shares to his son. Because Lee was not committed to make the gift, he is considered to own his original shares of the Black stock "immediately after the exchange." The requirements of § 351 are met, and neither Lee nor Pat is taxed on the exchange. ◆

---

6. Reg. § 1.351–1.

Transfers for Property and Services. Section 351 treatment is lost if stock is transferred to persons who did not contribute property, causing those who did to lack control immediately after the exchange.

EXAMPLE 8

Kate transfers property with a fair market value of $60,000 and a basis of $5,000 for 600 shares of stock in newly formed Wren Corporation. Kevin receives 400 shares in Wren for services rendered to the corporation. Each share of stock is worth $100. Both Kate and Kevin have taxable gain on the transaction. Kevin is not part of the control group because he did not transfer "property" for stock. He has taxable income of $40,000 (400 shares × $100). Kate has a taxable gain of $55,000 [$60,000 (fair market value of the stock in Wren) − $5,000 (basis in the transferred property)]. She is taxed on the exchange because she received only 60% of the stock in Wren Corporation. ◆

A person who performs services for the corporation in exchange for stock and also transfers some property is treated as a member of the transferring group. That person is taxed on the value of the stock issued for services. In this case, all the stock received by the person transferring both property and services is counted in determining whether the transferors acquired control of the corporation.

EXAMPLE 9

Assume the same facts as in Example 8, except that Kevin transfers property with a fair market value of $30,000 (basis of $3,000) in addition to the services rendered to the corporation (valued at $10,000). Now Kevin becomes a part of the control group. Kate and Kevin together received 100% of the stock in Wren Corporation. Consequently, § 351 is applicable to the exchanges. Kate has no recognized gain. Kevin does not recognize gain on the transfer of the property but has taxable income to the extent of the value of the shares issued for services rendered. Thus, Kevin has income of $10,000. ◆

Transfers for Services and Nominal Property. To be a member of the group and aid in qualifying all transferors under the 80 percent test, the person contributing services must transfer property having more than a relatively small value compared to the services performed. Stock issued for property whose value is relatively small compared to the value of the stock already owned (or to be received for services rendered) will not be treated as issued in return for property. This will be the result when the primary purpose of the transfer is to qualify the transaction under § 351 for concurrent transferors.[7]

EXAMPLE 10

Olga and Otis transfer property to Redbird Corporation, each in exchange for one-third of the stock. Olaf receives the other one-third of the stock for services rendered. The transaction will not qualify under § 351 because Olaf is not a member of the group transferring property and Olga and Otis together received only 66⅔% of the stock. The post-transfer control requirement is not met.

Assume instead that Olaf also transfers property. Then he is a member of the group, and the transaction qualifies under § 351. Olaf is taxed on the value of the stock issued for services, but the remainder of the transaction is tax-free. However, if the property transferred by Olaf is of relatively small value in comparison to the stock he receives for his services, and the primary purpose for including the property is to cause the transaction to be tax-free for Olga and Otis, the exchange does not qualify under § 351. Gain or loss is recognized by all parties. ◆

7. Reg. § 1.351–1(a)(1)(ii).

The IRS generally requires that before a transferor who receives stock for both property and services can be included in the control group, the value of the property transferred must be at least 10 percent of the value of the services provided.[8] If the value of the property transferred is less than this amount, the IRS will not issue an advance ruling that the exchange meets the requirements of § 351.

Example 11

Sara and Rick form White Corporation. Sara transfers land (fair market value $100,000, basis of $20,000) for 50% of the stock in White. Rick transfers equipment (fair market value $50,000, adjusted basis of $10,000) and provides services worth $50,000 for 50% of the stock. Rick's stock in White Corporation is counted in determining control for purposes of § 351; thus, the transferors own 100% of the stock in White. All of Rick's stock, not just the shares received for the equipment, is counted in determining control because the property he transferred has more than a nominal value in comparison to the value of the services rendered. Sara does not recognize gain on the transfer of the land. She will have a basis of $20,000 in the White Corporation stock. Rick, however, must recognize income of $50,000 on the transfer. Even though the transfer of the equipment qualifies under § 351, his transfer of services for stock does not. ◆

Example 12

Assume the same facts as in Example 11 except that the equipment has a fair market value of only $1,000 (basis of $400) and the services Rick provided were valued at $99,000. The transfers do not qualify under § 351. Sara does not have the requisite 80% control. Thus, she has a taxable gain of $80,000 [$100,000 (fair market value of the land) – $20,000 (basis in the land)]. B has income of $99,000 for services rendered plus gain of $600 on the transfer of the equipment. ◆

Transfers to Existing Corporations. Once a corporation is in operation, § 351 also applies to any later transfers of property for stock by either new or former shareholders.

Example 13

Sam and Seth formed Blue Corporation three years ago. Both Sam and Seth transferred appreciated property to Blue in exchange for 50 shares each in the corporation. The original transfers qualified under § 351, and neither Sam nor Seth was taxed on the exchange. In the current year, Sam transfers property (fair market value $90,000, adjusted basis of $5,000) for 50 additional shares in Blue Corporation. Sam has a taxable gain of $85,000 on the transfer. The exchange does not qualify under § 351 because Sam does not have 80% control of Blue. (Sam will have 100 shares of the 150 shares outstanding, or a 66⅔% ownership.) ◆

Due to the 80 percent control rule, it is difficult for a transfer by a new shareholder to qualify for nonrecognition of gain under § 351.

Assumption of Liabilities–§ 357

Without § 357 of the Code, the transfer of mortgaged property to a controlled corporation could trigger gain to the extent of the mortgage whether the corporation assumed the mortgage or took property subject to it. This is the rule in nontaxable like-kind exchanges under § 1031. Liabilities assumed by the other party are considered the equivalent of cash and treated as boot. Section 357(a) provides, however, that when the acquiring corporation assumes a liability or

8. Rev.Proc. 77–37, 1977–2 C.B. 568.

takes property subject to a liability in a § 351 transaction, the transfer does not result in boot to the transferor shareholder. Nevertheless, liabilities assumed by the transferee corporation are treated as boot in determining the basis of the stock received. The basis of the stock received is reduced by the amount of the liabilities assumed by the corporation.

Example 14

Vera transfers property with an adjusted basis of $60,000, fair market value of $100,000, to Gray Corporation for 100% of the stock in Gray. The property is subject to a liability of $25,000 that Gray assumes. The exchange is tax-free under §§ 351 and 357. However, the basis to Vera of the stock in Gray Corporation is $35,000 [$60,000 (basis of property transferred) – $25,000 (amount of mortgage)]. ◆

The rule of § 357(a) has two exceptions. Section 357(b) provides that if the principal purpose of the assumption of the liabilities is to avoid tax *or* if there is no bona fide business purpose behind the exchange, the liabilities are treated as boot. Further, § 357(c) provides that if the sum of the liabilities exceeds the adjusted basis of the properties transferred, the excess is taxable gain.

Tax Avoidance or No Bona Fide Business Purpose Exception. Unless liabilities are incurred shortly before incorporation, § 357(b) generally poses few problems. A tax avoidance purpose for transferring liabilities to a controlled corporation seems unlikely in view of the basis adjustment noted above. Since the liabilities transferred reduce the basis of the stock received, any realized gain is deferred and not avoided. The gain materializes when and if the stock is disposed of in a taxable sale or exchange.

Satisfying the bona fide business purpose is not difficult if the liabilities were incurred in connection with the transferor's normal course of conducting a trade or business. But the bona fide business purpose requirement can cause difficulty if the liability is taken out shortly before the property is transferred and the proceeds are utilized for personal purposes. This type of situation is analogous to a cash distribution by the corporation, which is taxed as boot.

Example 15

Dan transfers real estate (basis of $40,000 and fair market value of $90,000) to a controlled corporation in return for stock in the corporation. Shortly before the transfer, Dan mortgages the real estate and uses the $20,000 proceeds to meet personal obligations. Along with the real estate, the mortgage is transferred to the corporation. In this case, it appears that the assumption of the mortgage lacks a bona fide business purpose. The amount of the liability is boot, and Dan has a taxable gain of $20,000 on the transfer.[9] ◆

The effect of the application of § 357(b) is to taint *all* liabilities transferred even though some are supported by a bona fide business purpose.

Example 16

Tim, an accrual basis taxpayer, incorporates his sole proprietorship. Among the liabilities transferred to the new corporation are trade accounts payable of $100,000 and a MasterCard bill of $5,000. Tim had used the MasterCard to purchase a wedding anniversary gift for his wife. Under these circumstances, all of the $105,000 liabilities are boot. ◆

9. § 351(b).

Liabilities in Excess of Basis Exception. Unlike § 357(b), § 357(c) has posed numerous problems in § 351 transfers. Much litigation has centered around this provision in recent years, particularly with respect to cash basis taxpayers who incorporate their businesses. Section 357(c) states that if the sum of liabilities assumed and the liabilities to which transferred property is subject exceeds the total of the adjusted bases of the properties transferred, the excess is taxable gain. Without this provision, if liabilities exceed basis in property exchanged, a taxpayer would have a negative basis in the stock received in the controlled corporation. Section 357(c) precludes the negative basis possibility by treating the excess over basis as gain to the transferor.

EXAMPLE 17

Andre transfers assets with an adjusted tax basis of $40,000 to a newly formed corporation in exchange for 100% of the stock. The corporation assumes liabilities on the transferred properties in the amount of $50,000. Without § 357(c), Andre's basis in the stock of the new corporation would be a negative $10,000 [$40,000 (basis of property transferred) + $0 (gain recognized) – $0 (boot received) – $50,000 (liabilities assumed)]. Section 357(c) causes him to recognize a gain of $10,000. As a result, the stock will have a zero basis in Andre's hands, determined as follows:

Basis in the property transferred	$40,000
Add: Gain recognized	10,000
Less: Boot received	–0–
Less: Liabilities assumed	50,000
Basis in the stock received	$ –0–

Thus, no negative basis results. ◆

Accounts payable of a cash basis taxpayer that give rise to a deduction and amounts payable under § 736(a) (payments to a retiring partner or payments in liquidation of a deceased partner's interest) are not considered to be liabilities for purposes of § 357(c).

EXAMPLE 18

Tina, a cash basis taxpayer, incorporates her sole proprietorship. In return for all of the stock of the new corporation, she transfers the following items:

	Adjusted Basis	Fair Market Value
Cash	$10,000	$10,000
Unrealized accounts receivable (amounts due to Tina but not yet paid to her)	–0–	40,000
Trade accounts payable	–0–	30,000
Note payable	5,000	5,000

Unrealized accounts receivable and trade accounts payable have a zero basis. Under the cash method of accounting, no income is recognized until the receivables are collected, and no deduction materializes until the payables are satisfied. The note payable has a basis because it was issued for consideration received.

The accounts receivable and the trade accounts payable are disregarded. Thus, Tina has only transferred cash ($10,000) and a note payable ($5,000) and does not have a problem of liabilities in excess of basis. ◆

The definition of liabilities under § 357(c) excludes obligations that would have been deductible to the transferor had he or she paid those obligations before the transfer. Consequently, Tina in Example 18 has no gain.

If §§ 357(b) and (c) both apply to the same transfer, § 357(b) predominates.[10] This could be significant because § 357(b) does not create gain on the transfer, as does § 357(c), but merely converts the liability to boot. Thus, the realized gain limitation continues to apply to § 357(b) transactions.

EXAMPLE 19

Chris forms Robin Corporation by transferring land with a basis of $100,000, fair market value of $1,000,000. The land is subject to a mortgage of $300,000. One month prior to incorporating Robin, Chris borrows $200,000 for personal purposes and gives the lender a second mortgage on the land. Robin Corporation issues stock worth $500,000 to Chris and assumes the mortgages on the land. Section 357(c) applies to the transfer because the mortgages on the property ($500,000) exceed the basis of the property ($100,000). Thus, Chris has a gain of $400,000 under § 357(c). Section 357(b) also applies to the transfer because Chris borrowed $200,000 just prior to the transfer and used the amount for personal purposes. Under § 357(b), Chris has boot of $500,000 in the amount of the liabilities (*all* of which are treated as boot). She has realized gain of $900,000 [$1,000,000 (fair market value of the land) – $100,000 (basis in the land)]. Gain is recognized to the extent of the boot of $500,000. Note that § 357(b) predominates over § 357(c). ◆

Basis Determination

Recall that § 351(a) postpones gain until the taxpayer's investment changes substantially. Postponement of the realized gain results in a carryover of basis under §§ 358(a) and 362(a).

Section 358(a). For a taxpayer transferring property to a corporation in a § 351 transaction, the basis of stock received in the transfer is the same as the basis the taxpayer had in the property transferred, increased by any gain recognized on the exchange and decreased by boot received. For basis purposes, boot received includes any liabilities transferred by the shareholder to the corporation.

Section 362(a). The basis of properties received by the corporation is determined under § 362(a). The basis to the corporation is the basis in the hands of the transferor increased by the amount of any gain recognized to the transferor shareholder.

The basis rules are summarized in Figures 17–1 and 17–2 and illustrated in Examples 20 and 21.

FIGURE 17–1
Shareholder's Basis in Stock Received

Adjusted basis of property transferred	$xx,xxx
Plus: Gain recognized	x,xxx
Minus: Boot received (including any liabilities transferred)	(x,xxx)
Equals: Basis of stock received	$xx,xxx

FIGURE 17–2
Corporation's Basis in Properties Received

Adjusted basis of property transferred	$xx,xxx
Plus: Gain recognized by transferor shareholder	xxx
Equals: Basis of property to corporation	$xx,xxx

10. § 357(c)(2)(A).

EXAMPLE 20

Maria and Ned form Brown Corporation. Maria transfers land (basis of $30,000 and fair market value of $70,000); Ned invests cash ($60,000). They each receive 50 shares in Brown Corporation, worth $1,200 per share, but Maria also receives $10,000 cash from Brown. The transfers of property, the realized and recognized gain on the transfers, and the basis of the stock in Brown Corporation to Maria and Ned are as follows:

	A	B	C	D	E	F
	Basis of Property Transferred	FMV of Stock Received	Boot Received	Realized Gain (B + C – A)	Recognized Gain (Lesser of C or D)	Basis of Stock in Brown (A – C + E)
From Maria:						
Land	$30,000	$60,000	$10,000	$40,000	$10,000	$30,000
From Ned:						
Cash	60,000	60,000	–0–	–0–	–0–	60,000

Brown Corporation has a basis of $40,000 in the land. The basis to Brown is Maria's basis of $30,000 plus her recognized gain of $10,000. ◆

EXAMPLE 21

Assume the same facts as in Example 20, except that Maria's basis in the land is $68,000 (instead of $30,000). Because recognized gain cannot exceed realized gain, the transfer generates only $2,000 of gain to Maria. The realized and recognized gain and the basis of the stock in Brown Corporation to Maria are as follows:

	A	B	C	D	E	F
	Basis of Property Transferred	FMV of Stock Received	Boot Received	Realized Gain (B + C – A)	Recognized Gain (Lesser of C or D)	Basis of Stock in Brown (A – C + E)
Land	$68,000	$60,000	$10,000	$2,000	$2,000	$60,000

◆

Stock Issued for Services Rendered. Section 1032 provides that a corporation's disposition of stock for property is not a taxable exchange. A transfer of shares for services is also not a taxable transaction to a corporation.[11] Can a corporation deduct the fair market value of the stock it issues in consideration of services as a business expense? Yes, unless the services are such that the payment is characterized as a capital expenditure.

EXAMPLE 22

Carol and Carl form White Corporation. Carol transfers cash of $500,000 for 100 shares of White Corporation stock. Carl transfers property with a fair market value of $480,000 (basis of $90,000), and agrees to serve as manager of the corporation for one year; in return, Carl receives 100 shares of stock in White. The value of Carl's services to White Corporation is $20,000. The transfers qualify under § 351. Carl is not taxed on the transfer of the appreciated property. However, Carl has income of $20,000, the value of the services he will render to White Corporation. White has a basis of $90,000 in the property it acquired from Carl. It has a business deduction under § 162 of $20,000 for the value of services Carl will render. ◆

11. Reg. § 1.1032–1(a).

EXAMPLE 23

Assume, in Example 22, that Carl receives the 100 shares of White stock in consideration for the appreciated property and for providing legal services in organizing the corporation. The value of Carl's legal services is $20,000. Carl has no gain on the transfer of the property but has income of $20,000 for the value of the services rendered. White Corporation has a basis of $90,000 in the property it acquired from Carl and must capitalize the $20,000 as organizational expenses. ◆

Holding Period for Shareholder and Transferee Corporation. The shareholder's holding period for stock received for a capital asset or for § 1231 property includes the holding period of the property transferred to the corporation. The holding period of the property is "tacked on" to the holding period of the stock. The holding period for stock received for any other property (e.g., inventory or property held primarily for sale) begins on the day after the exchange. The transferee corporation's holding period for property acquired in a § 351 transfer is the holding period of the transferor shareholder regardless of the character of the property to the transferor.

Recapture Considerations

Recapture of Accelerated Cost Recovery (Depreciation). In a pure § 351(a) nontaxable transfer (no boot involved) to a controlled corporation, the recapture of accelerated cost recovery rules do not apply.[12] Moreover, any recapture potential of the property carries over to the corporation as it steps into the shoes of the transferor-shareholder for purposes of basis determination.

EXAMPLE 24

Paul transfers equipment (basis of $30,000 and fair market value of $100,000) to a controlled corporation in return for additional stock. If Paul had sold the equipment, it would have yielded a gain of $70,000, all of which would be recaptured as ordinary income under § 1245. If the transfer comes within § 351(a), Paul has no recognized gain and no accelerated cost recovery to recapture. If the corporation later disposes of the equipment in a taxable transaction, it will have to take into account the § 1245 recapture potential originating with Paul. ◆

Tax Benefit Rule. A taxpayer may have to take into income the recovery of an item previously expensed. Such income, however, is limited to the amount of the deduction that actually produced a tax saving. The relevance of the tax benefit rule to transfers to controlled corporations under § 351 was first raised in connection with accounts receivable and the reserve for bad debts.

EXAMPLE 25

Wanda, an accrual basis taxpayer, incorporates her sole proprietorship. In return for all of the stock of the corporation, she transfers, among other assets, accounts receivable with a face amount of $100,000 and a reserve for bad debts of $10,000 (book value of $90,000). Wanda had previously deducted the addition to the reserve. The $10,000 deduction resulted in a tax benefit to Wanda. ◆

The IRS took the position that § 351 did not insulate the transfer from the tax benefit rule. Since Wanda had previously deducted the reserve for bad debts and

12. §§ 1245(b)(3) and 1250(d)(3).

the reserve was no longer necessary, she should take the full $10,000 into income. In *Nash v. U.S.*,[13] the Supreme Court disagreed. Operating on the assumption that the stock Wanda received must be worth only $90,000 (the book value of the receivables), the Court compared the situation to a sale. No gain would have resulted if Wanda had sold the receivables for $90,000. Why should it matter that they were transferred to a controlled corporation under § 351?

The Supreme Court decision in *Nash* does not imply that the tax benefit rule is inapplicable to transfers to controlled corporations when no gain is recognized. Returning to the facts in Example 25, suppose Wanda was one of several transferors and the value of the stock she received exceeded the book value of the receivables ($90,000). Could the excess be subject to income recognition by virtue of the application of the tax benefit rule? The courts have not specifically addressed this question.

CAPITAL STRUCTURE OF A CORPORATION

Capital Contributions

The receipt of money or property in exchange for capital stock (including treasury stock) produces neither gain nor loss to the recipient corporation. Nor does a corporation's gross income include shareholders' contributions of money or property to the capital of the corporation. Additional funds received from shareholders through voluntary pro rata payments are not income to the corporation. This is the case even though there is no increase in the outstanding shares of stock of the corporation. The payments represent an additional price paid for the shares held by the shareholders and are treated as additions to the operating capital of the corporation.

Contributions by nonshareholders, such as land contributed to a corporation by a civic group or a governmental group to induce the corporation to locate in a particular community, are also excluded from the gross income of a corporation. Property that is transferred to a corporation by a nonshareholder for services rendered or for merchandise is taxable income to the corporation.

EXAMPLE 26

A television company charges its customers an initial fee to hook up to a new television system installed in the area. These payments are used to finance the total cost of constructing the television facilities. The customers will make monthly payments for the television service. The initial payments are used for capital expenditures, but they represent payments for services to be rendered by the television company. As such, they are taxable income and not contributions to capital by nonshareholders. ◆

The basis of property received by a corporation from a shareholder as a contribution to capital is the basis of the property in the hands of the shareholder increased by any gain recognized to the shareholder. The basis of property transferred to a corporation by a nonshareholder as a contribution to capital is zero.

13. 70–1 USTC ¶9405, 25 AFTR2d 1177, 90 S.Ct.1550 (USSC, 1970).

If a corporation receives money as a contribution to capital from a nonshareholder, a special rule applies. The basis of any property acquired with the money during a 12-month period beginning on the day the contribution was received is reduced by the amount of the contribution. The excess of money received over the cost of new property is used to reduce the basis of other property held by the corporation. The excess is applied to reduce the basis of property in the following order:

- Depreciable property.
- Property subject to amortization.
- Property subject to depletion.
- All other remaining properties.

The basis of property within each category is reduced in proportion to the relative bases of the properties.

EXAMPLE 27

A city donates land to Brown Corporation as an inducement for Brown to locate in the city. The receipt of the land does not produce taxable income. However, the land's basis to the corporation is zero. Assume the city also pays Brown $10,000 in cash. The money is not taxable income to the corporation. However, if Brown purchases property with the $10,000 within the next 12 months, the basis of the property is reduced by $10,000. ◆

Debt in the Capital Structure

Advantages of Debt. Shareholders must be aware of the difference between debt and equity in the capital structure. The advantages of receiving long-term debt are numerous. Interest on debt is deductible by the corporation, while dividend payments are not. Further, the shareholders are not taxed on loan repayments unless the repayments exceed basis. As long as a corporation has earnings and profits (see Chapter 18), an investment in stock cannot be withdrawn tax-free. Withdrawals will be deemed to be taxable dividends to the extent of earnings and profits of the distributing corporation.

EXAMPLE 28

Wade transfers cash of $100,000 to a newly formed corporation for 100% of the stock. In the first year of operations, the corporation has net income of $40,000. This income is credited to the earnings and profits account of the corporation. If the corporation distributes $9,500 to Wade, the distribution is a taxable dividend with no corresponding deduction to the corporation. Assume Wade transfers cash of $50,000 for stock. In addition, he loans the corporation $50,000, transferring cash of $50,000 to the corporation for a note in the amount of $50,000. The note is payable in equal annual installments of $5,000 and bears interest at the rate of 9%. At the end of the year, the corporation pays Wade $4,500 interest, which is tax deductible. The $5,000 principal repayment on the loan is not taxed to Wade. ◆

Reclassification of Debt as Equity ("Thin Capitalization" Problem). In certain instances, the IRS contends that debt is really an equity interest and denies the shareholders the tax advantages of debt financing. If the debt instrument has too many features of stock, it may be treated as a form of stock. In that case, the principal and interest payments are considered dividends. Under § 385, the IRS has the authority to characterize corporate debt wholly as equity or as part debt and part equity.

Section 385 lists several factors that *may* be used to determine whether a debtor-creditor relationship or a shareholder-corporation relationship exists. The thrust of § 385 is to authorize the Treasury to prescribe Regulations that provide more definite guidelines for determining when debt should be reclassified as equity. To date, the Treasury has not drafted acceptable Regulations. Consequently, taxpayers must rely on judicial decisions to determine whether a true debtor-creditor relationship exists.

Together, Congress through § 385 and the courts have identified the following factors to be considered in resolving the thin capitalization problem:

- Whether the debt instrument is in proper form. An open account advance is more easily characterized as a contribution to capital than a loan evidenced by a properly written note executed by the shareholder.
- Whether the debt instrument bears a reasonable rate of interest and has a definite maturity date. When a shareholder advance does not provide for interest, the return expected is that inherent in an equity interest (e.g., a share of the profits or an increase in the value of the shares). Likewise, a lender unrelated to the corporation will usually be unwilling to commit funds to the corporation for an indefinite period of time (i.e., no definite due date).
- Whether the debt is paid on a timely basis. A lender's failure to insist upon timely repayment (or satisfactory renegotiation) indicates that the return sought does not depend upon interest income and the repayment of principal.
- Whether payment is contingent upon earnings. A lender ordinarily will not advance funds that are likely to be repaid only if the venture is successful.
- Whether the debt is subordinated to other liabilities. Subordination tends to eliminate a significant characteristic of the creditor-debtor relationship. Creditors should have the right to share with other general creditors in the event of the corporation's dissolution or liquidation. Subordination also destroys another basic attribute of creditor status—the power to demand payment at a fixed maturity date.
- Whether holdings of debt and stock are proportionate. When debt and equity obligations are held in the same proportion, shareholders are, apart from tax considerations, indifferent as to whether corporate distributions are in the form of interest or dividends.
- Whether funds loaned to the corporation are used to finance initial operations or capital asset acquisitions. Funds used to finance initial operations or to acquire capital assets the corporation needs to operate are generally obtained through equity investments.
- Whether the corporation has a high ratio of shareholder debt to shareholder equity. Thin capitalization occurs when shareholder debt is high relative to shareholder equity. This indicates the corporation lacks reserves to pay interest and principal on debt when corporate income is insufficient to meet current needs. In determining a corporation's debt-equity ratio, courts have looked at the relation of the debt both to the book value of the corporation's assets and to their actual fair market value.

For the most part, the principles used to classify debt as equity developed in connection with closely held corporations. Here, the holders of the debt are also shareholders. The rules have often proved inadequate for dealing with such problems in large, publicly traded corporations.

Investor Losses

The choice between debt and equity financing leads to a consideration of the tax treatment of worthless stock and securities versus the treatment of bad debts.

Stock and Security Losses. If stocks and bonds are capital assets in the hands of the holder, losses from their worthlessness are governed by § 165(g)(1). Under this provision, a capital loss materializes as of the last day of the taxable year in which the stocks or bonds become worthless. No deduction is allowed for a mere decline in value. The burden of proving complete worthlessness is on the taxpayer claiming the loss. One way to recognize partial worthlessness is to dispose of the stocks or bonds in a taxable sale or exchange. But even then, the loss is disallowed under § 267(a)(1) if the sale or exchange is to a related party.

When the stocks or bonds are not capital assets, worthlessness yields an ordinary loss. For example, if the stocks or bonds are held by a broker for resale to customers in the normal course of business, they are not capital assets. Usually, however, stocks and bonds are held as investments and are capital assets.

Under certain circumstances involving stocks and bonds of affiliated corporations, an ordinary loss is allowed upon worthlessness. The possibility of an ordinary loss on the stock of small business corporations (§ 1244) is discussed later in the chapter.

Business versus Nonbusiness Bad Debts. In addition to the possible worthlessness of stocks and bonds, the financial end of a corporation can lead to bad debt deductions. These deductions can be either business bad debts or nonbusiness bad debts. The distinction between the two types of deductions is important for tax purposes in the following respects:

- Business bad debts are deducted as ordinary losses while nonbusiness bad debts are treated as short-term capital losses. A business bad debt can generate a net operating loss while a nonbusiness bad debt cannot.
- A deduction is allowed for the partial worthlessness of a business debt. Nonbusiness debts can be written off only when they become entirely worthless.
- Nonbusiness bad debt treatment is limited to noncorporate taxpayers. All of the bad debts of a corporation qualify as business bad debts.

When is a debt business or nonbusiness? Unfortunately, since the Code sheds little light on the matter, the distinction has been left to the courts. In a leading decision, the Supreme Court somewhat clarified the picture when it held that if individual shareholders loan money to a corporation in their capacity as investors, any resulting bad debt is classified as nonbusiness.[14] Nevertheless, the Court did not preclude the possibility of a shareholder-creditor's incurring a business bad debt.

If a loan is made in some capacity that qualifies as a trade or business, nonbusiness bad debt treatment is avoided. For example, has the loan been made to protect the shareholder's employment with the corporation? Employee status is a trade or business, and a loss on a loan made for this purpose qualifies for business bad debt treatment.[15] Shareholders also receive business bad debt treatment if they are in the trade or business of loaning money or of buying, promoting, and selling corporations.

---

14. *Whipple v. Comm.*, 63–1 USTC ¶9466, 11 AFTR2d 1454, 83 S.Ct. 1168 (USSC, 1963).

15. *Trent v. Comm.*, 61–2 USTC ¶9506, 7 AFTR2d 1599, 291 F.2d 669 (CA–2, 1961).

Section 1244 Stock. Section 1244 permits *ordinary loss* treatment for losses on the sale or worthlessness of stock of so-called small business corporations. By placing shareholders on a more nearly equal basis with proprietors and partners in terms of the tax treatment of losses, the provision encourages investment of capital in small corporations. Gain on the sale of § 1244 stock remains capital. Consequently, the shareholder has nothing to lose and everything to gain by complying with § 1244.

Only a *small business corporation* can issue qualifying § 1244 stock. The total amount of stock that can be offered under the plan to issue § 1244 stock cannot exceed $1,000,000. For these purposes, property received in exchange for stock is valued at its adjusted basis, reduced by any liabilities assumed by the corporation or to which the property is subject. The fair market value of the property is not considered. The $1,000,000 limitation is determined by property and money received for the stock as a contribution to capital and as paid-in capital on the date the stock is issued. Consequently, even though a corporation fails to meet these requirements when the stock later is sold, the stock can still qualify as § 1244 stock if the requirements were met on the date the stock was issued.

The amount of ordinary loss deductible in any one year on § 1244 stock is limited to $50,000 (or $100,000 for husband and wife filing a joint return). If the amount of the loss sustained in the taxable year exceeds these amounts, the remainder is considered a capital loss.

Example 29

A taxpayer acquires § 1244 stock at a cost of $100,000. He sells the stock for $10,000 in one tax year. He has an ordinary loss of $50,000 and a capital loss of $40,000. On a joint return, the entire $90,000 loss is ordinary. ◆

Only the original holder of § 1244 stock, whether an individual or a partnership, qualifies for ordinary loss treatment. If the stock is sold or donated, it loses its § 1244 status.

If a partnership is involved, the individual must have been a partner at the time the partnership acquired the stock. In addition, the partnership must not distribute the stock to the partners. Each partner's share of partnership tax attributes includes the share of the loss the partnership sustains on the stock.

Example 30

Rita and Quinn are partners in the RQ Partnership. The partnership acquires 100 shares of § 1244 stock in Brown Corporation at a cost of $100,000. A few months later the partnership distributes 25 shares to Rita and 25 shares to Quinn. Brown Corporation suffers financial difficulties and files for bankruptcy two years later. The Brown stock is worthless. RQ Partnership can claim an ordinary loss of $50,000 (the cost of the remaining 50 shares in Brown), which is then passed to Rita and Quinn as ordinary loss. However, Rita and Quinn have a capital loss of $25,000 each on the shares distributed to them by RQ Partnership. The 50 shares the partnership distributed to Rita and Quinn lose their § 1244 status. Rita and Quinn were not the original holders of the stock. If RQ Partnership had not distributed the stock to Rita and Quinn, it would have claimed an ordinary loss of $100,000, which would have passed to Rita and Quinn as ordinary loss. Thus, Rita and Quinn could each have claimed ordinary loss of $50,000 on their individual returns. ◆

Recall the advantages of issuing some debt to shareholders in exchange for cash contributions to a corporation. A disadvantage of issuing debt is that it does not qualify under § 1244. Should the debt become worthless, the taxpayer generally has a short-term capital loss rather than the ordinary loss for § 1244 stock.

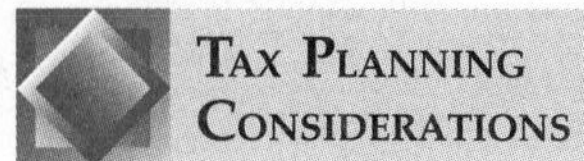

TAX PLANNING CONSIDERATIONS

Working with § 351

Effective tax planning with transfers of property to corporations involves a clear understanding of § 351 and its related Code provisions. The most important question in planning is simply: Does compliance with the requirements of § 351 yield the desired tax result?

Utilizing § 351. In using § 351(a), ensure that all parties transferring property (which includes cash) receive control of the corporation. Simultaneous transfers are not necessary, but a long period of time between transfers is vulnerable if the transfers are not properly documented as part of a single plan. To do this, the parties should document and preserve evidence of their intentions. Also, it is helpful to have some reasonable explanation for any delay in the transfers.

To meet the requirements of § 351, mere momentary control on the part of the transferor may not suffice if loss of control is compelled by a prearranged agreement.

EXAMPLE 31

For many years, Zelda operated a business as a sole proprietor employing Zina as manager. To dissuade Zina from quitting and going out on her own, Zelda promised her a 30% interest in the business. To fulfill this promise, Zelda transfers the business to newly formed Black Corporation in return for all its stock. Immediately thereafter, Zelda transfers 30% of the stock to Zina. Section 351 probably would not apply to the transfer by Zelda to Black Corporation. It appears that Zelda was under an obligation to relinquish control. If this is not the case and the loss of control was voluntary on Zelda's part, momentary control would suffice.[16] ◆

Be sure that later transfers of property to an existing corporation satisfy the control requirement if recognition of gain is to be avoided. In this connection, a transferor's interest cannot be counted if the value of stock received is relatively small compared with the value of stock already owned. Further, the primary purpose of the transfer may not be to qualify other transferors for § 351 treatment.[17]

To keep the matter in perspective, be in a position to recognize when § 351 is not relevant.

EXAMPLE 32

The stock in Green Corporation is held equally by Ted and Vicki (father and daughter). Ted transfers real estate (basis of $40,000 and fair market value of $100,000) to Green Corporation. Ted receives no additional stock in Green as a result of the transfer. He has made a capital contribution, and § 351 is of no consequence. The transfer causes no gain to Ted, but other tax consequences can result.[18] Ted should increase his basis in his Green stock. ◆

Avoiding § 351. Section 351(a) provides for the nonrecognition of gain on transfers to controlled corporations. As such, it is often regarded as a relief provision favoring taxpayers. In some situations, however, avoiding § 351(a) may

---

16. Compare *Fahs v. Florida Machine and Foundry Co.*, 48–2 USTC ¶9329, 36 AFTR 1151, 168 F.2d 957 (CA–5, 1948), with *John C. O'Connor*, 16 TCM 213, T.C.Memo. 1957–50, *aff'd.* in 58–2 USTC ¶9913, 2 AFTR2d 6011, 260 F.2d 358 (CA–6, 1958).

17. Reg. § 1.351–1(a)(1)(ii). Refer to Example 10 of this chapter. The stock attribution rules of § 318 (see Chapter 18) do not apply to § 351 transfers.

18. The daughter has benefited from Ted's capital contribution (her shares are, as a result, worth more). Therefore, a gift has taken place, and Ted's capital contribution could lead to the imposition of a gift tax liability. In this connection, see Chapter 26.

produce a more advantageous tax result. The transferors might prefer to recognize gain on the transfer of property if they cannot be particularly harmed by the gain. For example, they may be in low tax brackets, or the gain may be a capital gain from which substantial capital losses can be offset. The corporation will then have a stepped-up basis in the transferred property.

Another reason a particular transferor might wish to avoid § 351 concerns possible loss recognition. Recall that § 351 refers to the nonrecognition of both gains and losses. A transferor who wishes to recognize loss has several alternatives:

- Sell the property to the corporation for its stock. The IRS could attempt to collapse the "sale," however, by taking the approach that the transfer really falls under § 351(a). If the sale is disregarded, the transferor ends up with a realized, but unrecognized, loss.
- Sell the property to the corporation for other property or boot. Because the transferor receives no stock, § 351 is inapplicable.
- Transfer the property to the corporation in return for securities. Recall that § 351 does not apply to a transferor who receives securities. In both this and the previous alternatives, watch for the possible disallowance of the loss under § 267.

Suppose the loss property is to be transferred to the corporation and no loss is recognized by the transferor due to § 351(a). This could present an interesting problem in terms of assessing the economic realities involved.

EXAMPLE 33

Iris and Ivan form Wren Corporation with the following investment: property by Iris (basis of $40,000 and fair market value of $50,000) and property by Ivan (basis of $60,000 and fair market value of $50,000). Each receives 50% of the Wren stock. Has Ivan acted wisely in settling for only 50% of the stock? At first, it would appear so, since he and Iris each invested property of the same value ($50,000). But what about tax considerations? Due to basis carryover, the corporation now has a basis of $40,000 in Iris's property and $60,000 in Ivan's property. In essence, Iris has shifted a possible $10,000 gain to the corporation while Ivan has transferred a $10,000 potential loss. With this in mind, an equitable allocation of the Wren stock would call for Ivan to receive a greater percentage interest than Iris. ◆

Other Considerations in Incorporating a Business

When a business is incorporated, the organizers must determine which assets and liabilities should be transferred to the corporation. A transfer of assets that produces passive income (rents, royalties, dividends, and interest) can cause the corporation to be a personal holding company in a tax year when operating income is low. Thus, the corporation could be subject to the personal holding company penalty tax (see the discussion in Chapter 20).

A transfer of the accounts payable of a cash basis taxpayer prevents the taxpayer from taking a tax deduction when the accounts are paid. These payables should generally be retained.

Leasing some property to the corporation may be a more attractive alternative than transferring ownership. Leasing provides the taxpayer with the opportunity of withdrawing money from the corporation without the payment being characterized as a dividend. If the property is donated to a family member in a lower tax bracket, the lease income can be shifted as well. If the depreciation and other deductions available in connection with the property are larger than the lease income, the taxpayer would retain the property until the income exceeds the deductions.

Shareholder debt in a corporation can be given to family members in a lower tax bracket. This technique also causes income to be shifted without a loss of control of the corporation.

Debt in the Capital Structure

The advantages of debt as opposed to equity have previously been emphasized. The main hurdle to overstressing debt is the thin capitalization problem. In avoiding the problem, consider the following observations:

- Preserve the formalities of the debt. This includes providing for written instruments, realistic interest rates, and specified due dates.
- If possible, have the corporation repay the debt when it becomes due. If this is not possible, have the parties renegotiate the arrangement. Try to proceed as a third-party (i.e., nonshareholder) creditor would. It is not unusual, for example, for bondholders of publicly held corporations to extend due dates when default occurs. The alternative is to foreclose and perhaps seriously impair the amount the creditors will recover.
- Avoid provisions in the debt instrument that make the debt convertible to equity in the event of default. These provisions are standard practice when nonshareholder creditors are involved. They make no sense if the shareholders are also the creditors.

EXAMPLE 34

Gail, Gary, and Grace are equal shareholders in White Corporation. Each transfers cash of $100,000 to White in return for its bonds. The bond agreement provides that the holders will receive additional voting rights in the event White defaults on its bonds. The voting rights provision is worthless and merely raises the issue of thin capitalization. Gail, Gary, and Grace already control White Corporation, so what purpose is served by increasing their voting rights? The parties probably used a "boiler plate" bond agreement that was designed for third-party lenders (e.g., banks and financial institutions). ◆

- Pro rata holding of debt is difficult to avoid. For example, if each of the shareholders owns one-third of the stock, then each will want one-third of the debt. Nevertheless, some variation is possible.

EXAMPLE 35

Assume the same facts as Example 34 except that only Gail and Gary acquire the bonds. Grace leases property to White Corporation at an annual rent that approximates the yield on the bonds. Presuming the rent passes the arm's length test (i.e., what unrelated parties would charge), all parties reach the desired result. Gail and Gary withdraw corporate profits in the form of interest income, and Grace is provided for with rent income. White Corporation can deduct both the interest and the rent payments. ◆

- Try to keep the debt-equity ratio within reasonable proportions. A frequent problem arises when the parties first form the corporation. Often the amount invested in capital stock is the minimum required by state law. For example, if the state of incorporation permits a minimum of $1,000, limiting the investment to this amount does not provide much safety for later debt financing by the shareholders.
- The nature of the business can have an effect on what is an acceptable debt-equity ratio. Capital-intensive industries (e.g., manufacturing, transportation) characteristically rely heavily on debt financing. Consequently, larger debt should be tolerated.

Investor Losses

In connection with § 1244, be aware that there is a danger of losing § 1244 attributes. Recall that only the original holder of § 1244 stock is entitled to ordinary loss treatment. If a corporation is formed to shift income within the family group by transferring shares of stock to family members, the benefits of § 1244 are lost.

EXAMPLE 36

Norm incorporates his business by transferring property with a basis of $100,000 for 100 shares of stock. The stock qualifies as § 1244 stock. Norm later gives 50 shares each to his children, Susan and Paul. Eventually, the business fails, and the corporation becomes bankrupt. The shares of stock become worthless. If Norm had retained the stock, he would have had an ordinary loss deduction of $100,000 (assuming he filed a joint return). Susan and Paul, however, have a capital loss of $50,000 each because the § 1244 attributes were lost. ◆

PROBLEM MATERIALS

DISCUSSION QUESTIONS

1. In terms of justification and effect, § 351 (transfer to corporation controlled by transferor) and § 1031 (like-kind exchanges) are much alike. Explain.
2. Under what circumstances will gain and/or loss be recognized on a § 351 transfer?
3. What does the term "property" include for purposes of § 351?
4. Does the receipt of securities (i.e., long-term debt) in exchange for the transfer of appreciated property to a controlled corporation cause recognition of gain?
5. In arriving at the basis of stock received by a shareholder in a § 351 transfer, describe the effect of the following:

   a. The receipt of other property (boot) in addition to stock by the shareholder.
   b. Transfer of a liability to the corporation, along with the property, by the shareholder.
   c. The shareholder's basis in the property transferred to the corporation.

6. How does a corporation determine its basis in property received pursuant to a § 351 transfer?
7. What is the control requirement of § 351? Describe the effect of the following in satisfying this requirement:

   a. A shareholder renders services to the corporation for stock.
   b. A shareholder both renders services and transfers property to the corporation for stock.
   c. A shareholder has only momentary control after the transfer.
   d. A long period of time elapses between the transfers of property by different shareholders.

8. Matt and Megan form White Corporation. They transfer appreciated property to the corporation with each receiving 50 shares of the stock in White Corporation. If Matt gives his shares to his daughter immediately after the exchange, will the exchange qualify under § 351?
9. At a point when Robin Corporation has been in existence for six years, shareholder Ted transfers real estate (adjusted basis of $20,000 and fair market value of $100,000) to the corporation for additional stock. At the same time, Peggy, the other shareholder, purchases one share of stock for cash. After the two transfers, the percentage of stock ownership is as follows: 79% by Ted and 21% by Peggy.

a. What were the parties trying to accomplish?
b. Will it work? Explain.
c. Would the result change if Ted and Peggy are father and daughter?

10. Assume the same facts as in Question 9, except that Ted receives nothing from Robin Corporation for the transfer of the real estate to the corporation. Does this change the tax result as to Ted?

11. Before incorporating her apartment rental business, Beth takes out second mortgages on several of the units. She uses the mortgage funds to make capital improvements to her personal residence. Along with all of the rental units, Beth transfers the mortgages to the newly formed corporation in return for all of its stock. Discuss the tax consequences of these procedures to Beth.

12. In structuring the capitalization of a corporation, what are the advantages of utilizing debt rather than equity?

13. In determining whether the debt of a corporation should be reclassified as stock, comment on the relevance of the following:

a. The loan is on open account.
b. The loan is a demand loan.
c. Although the loan has a definite maturity date, the corporation has not made payments on a timely basis.
d. Payments on the loan are contingent upon corporate earnings.
e. The corporation's shareholders loaned funds to the corporation in the same proportion as their shareholdings, and the debt was used to purchase a new building.
f. The corporation has a debt-equity ratio of 5:1.

14. Assuming § 1244 does not apply, what is the tax treatment of stock that has become worthless?

15. Wilma, an unmarried individual taxpayer, had invested $75,000 in the stock of White Corporation, which recently declared bankruptcy. Although Wilma is distressed over the loss of her investment, she is somewhat consoled by the fact that the $75,000 will be an ordinary (rather than a capital) loss. Is Wilma fully apprised of the tax result? Why or why not?

PROBLEMS

16. Grace and Helen form Robin Corporation with the following investment:

	Property Transferred		
	Basis to Transferor	Fair Market Value	Number of Shares Issued
From Grace—			
Cash	$20,000	$ 20,000	
Installment obligation	70,000	180,000	40
From Helen—			
Cash	70,000	70,000	
Machinery	60,000	90,000	60
Patent	2,000	140,000	

The installment obligation has a face amount of $180,000 and was acquired last year from the sale of land held for investment purposes (adjusted basis of $70,000).

a. How much gain, if any, must Grace recognize?
b. What will be Grace's basis in the Robin Corporation stock?
c. What will be Robin Corporation's basis in the installment obligation?
d. How much gain, if any, must Helen recognize?
e. What will be Helen's basis in the Robin Corporation stock?
f. What will be Robin Corporation's basis in the machinery and patent?

g. How would your answer change if Grace received common stock and Helen received preferred stock?
h. How would your answer change if Helen were a partnership?

17. Hans, Irene, Jim, and Jack form Bluebird Corporation with the following investment:

	Property Transferred		
	Basis to Transferor	Fair Market Value	Number of Shares Issued
From Hans—			
Personal services rendered to Bluebird Corporation	$ -0-	$ 10,000	10
From Irene—			
Equipment	115,000	100,000	90*
From Jim—			
Cash	20,000	20,000	
Unrealized accounts			50
receivable	-0-	30,000	
From Jack—			
Land & building	70,000	150,000	
Mortgage on land			50
& building	100,000	100,000	

*Irene receives $10,000 in cash in addition to the 90 shares.

The mortgage transferred by Jack is assumed by Bluebird Corporation. The value of each share of Bluebird stock is $1,000.

a. What, if any, is Hans's recognized gain or loss?
b. What basis will Hans have in the Bluebird stock?
c. How much gain or loss must Irene recognize?
d. What basis will Irene have in the Bluebird stock?
e. What basis will Bluebird Corporation have in the equipment?
f. What, if any, is Jim's recognized gain or loss?
g. What basis will Jim have in the Bluebird stock?
h. What basis will Bluebird Corporation have in the unrealized accounts receivable?
i. How much gain or loss must Jack recognize?
j. What basis will Jack have in the Bluebird stock?
k. What basis will Bluebird Corporation have in the land and building?

18. Diego, Leo, Abdul, and Soong form Brown Corporation with the following investment:

	Property Transferred		
	Basis to Transferor	Fair Market Value	Number of Shares Issued
From Diego—			
Inventory	$10,000	$32,000	30*
From Leo—			
Equipment ($10,000 of depreciation taken by Leo in prior years)	15,000	33,000	30**
From Abdul—			
Secret process	5,000	30,000	30
From Soong—			
Cash	10,000	10,000	10

*Diego receives $2,000 in cash in addition to the 30 shares.
**Leo receives $3,000 in cash in addition to the 30 shares.

Assume the value of each share of Brown stock is $1,000.

a. What, if any, is Diego's recognized gain or loss? How is any such gain or loss treated?
b. What basis will Diego have in the Brown stock?
c. What basis will Brown Corporation have in the inventory?
d. How much gain or loss must Leo recognize? How is the gain or loss treated?
e. What basis will Leo have in the Brown stock?
f. What basis will Brown Corporation have in the equipment?
g. What, if any, is Abdul's recognized gain or loss?
h. What basis will Abdul have in the Brown stock?
i. What basis will Brown Corporation have in the secret process?
j. How much income, if any, must Soong recognize?
k. What basis will Soong have in the Brown stock?

19. Antonio, José, and Shontelle incorporate their respective businesses and form Gray Corporation. Antonio exchanges his property, basis of $50,000 and value of $200,000, for 200 shares in Gray Corporation on March 1, 1993. José exchanges his property, basis of $70,000 and value of $300,000, for 300 shares in Gray Corporation on April 15, 1993. Shontelle transfers her property, basis of $90,000 and value of $500,000, for 500 shares in Gray Corporation on May 10, 1993.

    a. If the three exchanges are part of a prearranged plan, what gain will each of the parties recognize on the exchanges?
    b. Assume Antonio and José exchanged their property for stock in 1990. Shontelle transfers her property for 500 shares in 1993. The transfer is not part of a prearranged plan with Antonio and José to incorporate their businesses. What gain will Shontelle recognize on the transfer?

20. Ramon organized Bluebird Corporation 10 years ago by contributing property worth $500,000, basis of $100,000, for 2,000 shares of stock in Bluebird, representing 100% of the stock in the corporation. Ramon later gave each of his children, José and Juan, 500 shares of stock in Bluebird Corporation. In the current year, Ramon transfers property worth $160,000, basis of $50,000, to Bluebird for 500 shares in the corporation. What gain, if any, will Ramon recognize on this transfer?

21. Gail and Gary form Wren Corporation. Gail transfers property worth $140,000 (basis of $50,000) for 70 shares in Wren Corporation. Gary receives 30 shares for property worth $55,000 (basis of $10,000) and for legal services in organizing the corporation; the services are worth $5,000.

    a. What gain, if any, will the parties recognize on the transfer?
    b. What basis will Gail and Gary have in the stock in Wren Corporation?
    c. What basis will Wren Corporation have in the property and services it received from Gail and Gary?

22. Assume in Problem 21 that the property Gary transfers to Wren Corporation is worth $5,000 (basis of $1,000) and his services in organizing the corporation are worth $55,000. What are the tax consequences to Gail, Gary, and Wren Corporation?

23. Earl forms Black Corporation by transferring land with a basis of $50,000, fair market value of $300,000. The land is subject to a mortgage of $150,000. Two weeks prior to incorporating Black, Earl borrows $50,000 for personal purposes and gives the lender a second mortgage on the land. Black Corporation issues stock worth $100,000 to Earl and assumes the mortgages on the land.

    a. What are the tax consequences to Earl and to Black Corporation?
    b. Assume that Earl does not borrow the $50,000 prior to incorporating Black. Earl transfers the land to Black Corporation for all the stock in Black. Black Corporation then borrows $50,000 and gives the lender a mortgage on the land. Black Corporation distributes the $50,000 to Earl. What are the tax consequences to Earl and to Black Corporation?

24. Polly and Pete form Jaybird Corporation. Polly transfers property, basis of $50,000 and value of $400,000, for 50 shares in Jaybird Corporation. Pete transfers property,

basis of $20,000 and value of $370,000, and agrees to serve as manager of Jaybird for one year; in return Pete receives 50 shares in Jaybird. The value of Pete's services to Jaybird is $30,000.

a. What gain will Polly and Pete recognize on the exchange?
b. What basis will Jaybird Corporation have in the property transferred by Polly and Pete? How will Jaybird treat the value of the services Pete renders?

25. Assume in Problem 24 that Pete receives the 50 shares of Jaybird stock in consideration for the appreciated property and for providing legal services in organizing the corporation. The value of Pete's services is $30,000.

a. What gain does Pete recognize?
b. What basis will Jaybird Corporation have in the property transferred by Pete? How will Jaybird treat the value of the services Pete renders?

26. A city donates land to Brown Corporation as an inducement for Brown to locate there. The land is worth $100,000. The city also donates $50,000 in cash to Brown.

a. What income, if any, must Brown recognize as a result of the transfer of land and cash to it by the city?
b. What basis will Brown have in the land?
c. If Brown purchases property six months later with the $50,000 cash, what basis will it have in the property?

27. Sara forms Black Corporation with an investment of $200,000 cash, for which she receives $20,000 in stock and $180,000 in 8% interest-bearing bonds maturing in nine years. Several years later, Sara loans the corporation an additional $50,000 on open account. Black Corporation subsequently becomes insolvent and is adjudged bankrupt. During the corporation's existence, Sara was paid an annual salary of $40,000. How might Sara's losses be treated for tax purposes?
28. Sam, a single taxpayer, acquired stock in a corporation that qualified as a small business corporation under § 1244, at a cost of $100,000 three years ago. He sells the stock for $10,000 in the current tax year. How will the loss be treated for tax purposes?
29. Assume that Sam in Problem 28 gave the stock to his brother a few months after he acquired it. The stock was worth $100,000 on the date of the gift. Sam's brother sells the stock for $10,000 in the current tax year. How will the loss be treated for tax purposes?
30. Eduardo transfers property with a basis of $40,000 and a fair market value of $20,000 to Gray Corporation in exchange for shares of § 1244 stock. (Assume the transfer qualifies under § 351.)

a. What is the basis of the stock to Eduardo?
b. What is the basis of the stock for purposes of § 1244 to Eduardo?
c. If Eduardo sells the stock for $10,000 two years later, how will the loss be treated for tax purposes?

CHAPTER

CORPORATIONS: DISTRIBUTIONS NOT IN COMPLETE LIQUIDATION

OBJECTIVES

Examine various types of corporate distributions not in complete liquidation of the corporation.

Explain the concept of earnings and profits and its importance in measuring dividend income.

Discuss the tax consequences of a property dividend to the recipient shareholder and to the corporation making the distribution.

Describe the nature and treatment of constructive dividends.

Differentiate between taxable and nontaxable stock dividends.

Describe the various stock redemptions that qualify for sale or exchange treatment and thereby avoid dividend treatment.

OUTLINE

A working knowledge of the rules pertaining to corporate distributions is essential for anyone dealing with the tax problems of corporations and their shareholders. The form of such distributions is important because it can produce varying tax results to shareholders. Cash or property dividends are taxed as ordinary income to the recipient shareholder, while stock redemptions generally receive capital gain or loss treatment after allowing the shareholder to recover basis in the redeemed stock. Stock dividends may not be taxed at all.

TAXABLE DIVIDENDS—IN GENERAL

Distributions by a corporation to its shareholders are presumed to be dividends unless the parties can prove otherwise. Section 316 treats such distributions as ordinary dividend income to a shareholder. Dividend income results to the extent of the distribution's pro rata share of earnings and profits (E & P) of the distributing corporation accumulated since February 28, 1913, or to the extent of corporate E & P for the current year.

EXAMPLE 1

Brown Corporation had accumulated E & P of $40,000 at the beginning of the tax year. During the current year, Brown has net earnings of $50,000 (current E & P). At the end of the tax year, Brown distributes $70,000 cash to its sole shareholder, Bill. Bill will have ordinary dividend income of $70,000. Although Brown's current E & P was only $50,000, the remaining $20,000 of the $70,000 distribution is also a taxable dividend. Brown Corporation had accumulated E & P at the beginning of the year in excess of that amount. ◆

Under § 301(c), the portion of a corporate distribution that is not taxed as a dividend (because of insufficient E & P) is nontaxable to the extent of the shareholder's basis in the stock. This reduces the stock basis accordingly. The excess of the distribution over the shareholder's basis is treated as a capital gain if the stock is a capital asset.

EXAMPLE 2

At the end of the year, Black Corporation (a calendar year taxpayer) has E & P of $30,000. On this date, the corporation distributes cash of $40,000 to its two *equal* shareholders, Bob and Bonnie. The adjusted basis of the shareholders' stock investment is $8,000 for Bob and $4,000 for Bonnie. The $40,000 distribution should be accounted for as follows:

	Bob	Bonnie
Amount distributed	$ 20,000	$ 20,000
Portion from E & P (taxed as a dividend)	–15,000	–15,000
	$ 5,000	$ 5,000
Return of capital (reduction of basis)	–5,000	–4,000
	$ –0–	$ 1,000
Capital gain	–0–	–1,000
	$ –0–	$ –0–

Thus, of the $20,000 Bob receives, $15,000 is dividend income and $5,000 is a nontaxable return of capital. After the distribution, Bob has a basis in the Black Corporation stock of $3,000 ($8,000 original adjusted basis – $5,000 return of capital). As to Bonnie, the result is $15,000 of dividend income, $4,000 of nontaxable return of capital, and $1,000 of capital gain. After the distribution, Bonnie has a basis in the Black stock of $0 ($4,000 original adjusted basis – $4,000 return of capital). ◆

Since E & P is the key to dividend treatment of corporate distributions, its significance cannot be emphasized enough. Beginning in 1990, E & P assumed added importance. A concept based on adjusted E & P replaced pretax book income in the determination of adjusted current earnings for purposes of the alternative minimum tax (refer to the discussion in Chapter 14).

Earnings and Profits (E & P)

The Code does not define the term *earnings and profits.* Although § 312 lists certain transactions that affect E & P, it stops short of a complete definition. E & P does possess similarities to the accounting concept of retained earnings (earnings retained in the business). However, E & P and retained earnings are often not the same. For example, a stock dividend is treated as a capitalization of retained earnings for financial accounting purposes (i.e., it is debited to the retained earnings account and credited to a capital stock account), but it does not decrease E & P. Similarly, the elimination of a deficit in a "quasi-reorganization" increases retained earnings but does not increase E & P.

Several observations are helpful in understanding the concept of E & P. First, E & P might well be described as the factor that fixes the upper limit on the amount of dividend income shareholders would have to recognize as a result of a distribution by the corporation. In this sense, E & P represents the corporation's economic ability to pay a dividend without impairing its capital. The effect of a specific transaction on the E & P account may be determined simply by considering whether or not the transaction increases or decreases the corporation's capacity to pay a dividend.

Computation of E & P

Barring certain important exceptions, E & P is increased by earnings for the taxable year computed in the same manner as taxable income is determined. If the corporation uses the cash method of accounting in computing taxable income, it must also use this method to determine the changes in E & P.[1]

E & P is increased for all items of income. Interest on municipal bonds, for example, though not taxed to the corporation, increases the corporation's E & P. Gains and losses from property transactions generally affect the determination of E & P only to the extent they are recognized for tax purposes. Thus, a gain on an involuntary conversion not recognized by the corporation because the insurance proceeds are suitably reinvested does not affect E & P. However, the E & P account can be affected by both deductible and nondeductible items. Consequently, excess capital losses, expenses incurred to produce tax-exempt income, and Federal income taxes all reduce E & P. Such items do not enter into the calculation of taxable income.

The E & P account can be reduced only by cost depletion, even though the corporation may be using percentage (statutory) depletion for income tax

1. Regulations relating to E & P begin at Reg. § 1.312–6.

purposes. E & P cannot be reduced by accelerated depreciation.[2] However, if a depreciation method such as units-of-production or machine hours is used, the adjustment to E & P is determined on this basis.

The alternative depreciation system must be used for purposes of computing E & P. If cost recovery is figured under MACRS, E & P must be computed using the straight-line recovery method over a recovery period equal to the asset's Asset Depreciation Range (ADR) midpoint life. Later, when the asset is sold, the increase or decrease in E & P is determined by using the adjusted basis of the asset for E & P purposes.

A corporation's E & P for the year in which it sells property on the installment basis is increased by the amount of any deferred gain. This is accomplished by treating all principal payments as having been received in the year of sale.[3]

Intangible drilling costs and mineral exploration and development costs are required to be capitalized for purposes of computing E & P. Once capitalized, these expenditures can be charged to E & P over a specified period: 60 months for intangible drilling costs and 120 months for mine exploration and development costs.[4]

EXAMPLE 3

A corporation sells property (basis of $10,000) to its sole shareholder for $8,000. Because of § 267 (disallowance of losses on sales between related parties), the $2,000 loss cannot be deducted in arriving at the corporation's taxable income. But since the overall economic effect of the transaction is a decrease in the corporation's assets by $2,000, the loss reduces the current E & P for the year of sale. ◆

EXAMPLE 4

A corporation pays a $10,000 premium on a key employee life insurance policy (the corporation is the owner and beneficiary of the policy) covering the life of its president. As a result of the payment, the cash surrender value of the policy is increased by $7,000. Although none of the $10,000 premium is deductible for tax purposes, current E & P is reduced by $3,000 (the excess of the premium paid over the increase in the cash surrender value). ◆

EXAMPLE 5

A corporation collects $100,000 on a key employee life insurance policy. At the time the policy matured on the death of the insured employee, it possessed a cash surrender value of $30,000. None of the $100,000 is included in the corporation's taxable income, but $70,000 is added to the current E & P account. ◆

EXAMPLE 6

During 1993, a corporation makes charitable contributions, $12,000 of which cannot be deducted in arriving at the taxable income for the year because of the 10% limitation. However, the $12,000 is carried over to 1994 and fully deducted in that year. The excess charitable contribution reduces the corporation's current E & P for 1993 by $12,000 and increases its current E & P for 1994, when the deduction is allowed, by a like amount. The increase in E & P in 1994 is necessary because the charitable contribution carryover reduces the taxable income for that year (the starting point for computing E & P) and already has been taken into account in determining the E & P for 1993. ◆

EXAMPLE 7

On January 2, 1991, White Corporation purchased for $30,000 equipment with an ADR midpoint life of 10 years that was then depreciated under MACRS. The asset was sold

2. § 312(k).
3. § 312(n)(5).
4. § 312(n)(2).

on July 2, 1993, for $27,000. For purposes of determining taxable income and E & P, cost recovery claimed on the machine and the machine's adjusted basis are summarized as follows:

	Cost Recovery	Adjusted Basis
Taxable income		
1991: $30,000 × 14.29%	$4,287	$25,713
1992: $30,000 × 24.49%	7,347	18,366
1993: $30,000 × 17.49% × ½ (half-year for year of disposal)	2,624	15,742
E & P		
1991: $30,000 ÷ 10-year recovery period × ½ (half-year for first year of service)	$1,500	$28,500
1992: $30,000 ÷ 10-year recovery period	3,000	25,500
1993: $30,000 ÷ 10-year recovery period × ½ (half-year for year of disposal.)	1,500	24,000

Gain on the sale for purposes of determining taxable income and the increase (decrease) in E & P are computed as follows:

	Taxable Income	E & P
$27,000 – $15,742 adjusted basis	$11,258	
$27,000 – $24,000 adjusted basis		$3,000

◆

EXAMPLE 8

In 1993, Cardinal Corporation, a calendar year taxpayer, sells unimproved real estate (basis of $20,000) for $100,000. Under the terms of the sale, beginning in 1994, Cardinal will receive two annual payments of $50,000 each with interest of 9%. Cardinal does not elect out of the installment method. Although Cardinal's taxable income for 1993 will not reflect any of the gain from the sale, the corporation must increase E & P for 1993 by $80,000 (the deferred profit component). ◆

Summary of E & P Adjustments

Recall that E & P serves as a measure of the earnings of the corporation that are treated as available for distribution as taxable dividends to the shareholders. Initially, E & P is increased by the corporation's taxable income. However, adjustments must be made to taxable income for various transactions in determining the corporation's current E & P. These adjustments are reviewed in Concept Summary 18–1. Other items that affect E & P, such as property dividends and stock redemptions, are covered later in the chapter and are not included in Concept Summary 18–1.

The Source of the Distribution

In determining the source of a dividend distribution, the dividend is deemed to have been made first from current E & P and then from E & P accumulated since February 28, 1913.

EXAMPLE 9

At the beginning of the current year, Brown Corporation has a deficit of $30,000 in accumulated E & P. For the year, it has current E & P of $10,000 and distributes $5,000 to its shareholders. The $5,000 distribution is treated as a taxable dividend since it is deemed to have been made from current E & P. This is the case even though Brown still has a deficit in accumulated E & P at the end of the current year. ◆

Distributions made during the year may exceed the current year's E & P. In this case, the portion of each distribution considered to have been made from current E & P is the percentage that the total E & P for the year bears to the total distributions for that year. This allocation can be important if any of the shareholders sell their stock during the year and total current distributions exceed current E & P.

Distinguishing between Current and Accumulated E & P

Accumulated E & P is the total of all previous years' current E & P as computed on the first day of each taxable year. The computation is made in accordance with the tax law in effect during that year. The factors that affect the computation of the current E & P for any one year have been discussed previously. Why must current and accumulated E & P be distinguished when it is clear that distributions are taxable if and to the extent that current *and* accumulated E & P exist?

1. When there is a deficit in accumulated E & P and a positive amount in current E & P, distributions are regarded as dividends to the extent of the current E & P. Refer to Example 9.
2. Current E & P is allocated on a pro rata basis to the distributions made during the year; accumulated E & P is applied (to the extent necessary) in chronological order beginning with the earliest distributions.

Concept Summary 18–1
E & P Adjustments

Nature of the Transaction	Effect on Taxable Income in Arriving at Current E & P
Tax-exempt income.	Add
Federal income taxes.	Subtract
Disallowed loss on sale between related parties.	Subtract
Payment of premiums on insurance policy on life of corporate officer.	Subtract
Collection of proceeds of insurance policy on life of corporate officer.	Add
Excess charitable contribution (over 10% limitation).	Subtract
Deduction of excess charitable contribution in succeeding taxable year (increase E & P because deduction reduces taxable income while E & P was reduced in a prior year).	Add
Realized gain (not recognized) on an involuntary conversion.	No effect
Percentage depletion (only cost depletion can reduce E & P).	Add
Accelerated depreciation (E & P is reduced only by straight-line, units-of-production, or machine hours depreciation).	Add
Deferred gain on installment sale (all gain is added to E & P in year of sale).	Add
Intangible drilling costs deducted currently (reduce E & P in future years by amortizing costs over 60 months).	Add
Mining exploration and development costs (reduce E & P in future years by amortizing costs over 120 months).	Add

3. Unless and until the parties can show otherwise, it is presumed that any distribution is covered by current E & P.
4. When a deficit in current E & P (a current loss) and a positive balance in accumulated E & P exist, the accounts are netted at the date of distribution. If the resulting balance is zero or a deficit, the distribution is a return of capital. If a positive balance results, the distribution is a dividend to the extent of the balance. Any loss is allocated ratably during the year unless the parties can show otherwise.

The following examples illustrate distinctions 3 and 4.

EXAMPLE 10

Green Corporation uses a fiscal year of July 1 through June 30 for tax purposes. Carmen, Green Corporation's only shareholder, uses a calendar year. As of July 1, 1993, Green had a zero balance in its accumulated E & P account. For fiscal year 1993–94, the corporation has suffered a $5,000 operating loss. On August 1, 1993, Green distributed $10,000 to Carmen. The distribution represents dividend income to Carmen and must be reported as such when she files her income tax return for calendar year 1993 on or before April 15, 1994. Because Carmen cannot prove until June 30, 1994, that the corporation had a deficit for fiscal year 1993–94, she must assume the $10,000 distribution was fully covered by current E & P. When Carmen learns of the deficit, she can file an amended return for 1993 showing the $10,000 as a return of capital. ◆

EXAMPLE 11

At the beginning of the current year, Gray Corporation (a calendar year taxpayer) has accumulated E & P of $10,000. During the year, the corporation incurs a $15,000 net loss from operations that accrued ratably. On July 1, Gray distributes $6,000 in cash to Hal, its sole shareholder. To determine how much of the $6,000 cash distribution represents dividend income to Hal, the balance of both accumulated and current E & P as of July 1 must be determined and netted. This is necessary because of the deficit in current E & P.

	Source of Distribution	
	Current E & P	**Accumulated E & P**
January 1		$10,000
July 1 (½ of $15,000 net loss)	($7,500)	2,500
July 1 distribution—$6,000:		
Dividend income: $2,500		
Return of capital: $3,500		

The balance in E & P on July 1 is $2,500. Thus, of the $6,000 distribution, $2,500 is taxed as a dividend, and $3,500 represents a return of capital. ◆

PROPERTY DIVIDENDS—IN GENERAL

The previous discussion assumed that all distributions by a corporation to its shareholders were in the form of cash. Although most corporate distributions are cash, a corporation may distribute property as a dividend for various reasons. The shareholders may want a particular property that is held by the corporation. The corporation may be strapped for cash, but may not want to forgo distributing a dividend to its shareholders.

Generally, the distribution of property as a dividend is treated in the same manner as a cash distribution. However, the value of property distributed and the basis of that property to the corporation are seldom the same. Consequently, the distribution of a property dividend involves additional tax considerations. The following questions must be asked when property is distributed as a dividend:

1. What is the amount of the dividend distributed to the shareholder?
2. What is the basis of the property received by the shareholder?
3. Does the corporation recognize gain or loss upon the distribution?
4. What is the effect of the property distribution on the E & P of the corporation?

Property Dividends—Effect on the Shareholder

When a corporation distributes property rather than cash to a shareholder, the amount distributed is measured by the fair market value of the property on the date of distribution. Section 301(c) applies to such distributions. Thus, the portion of the distribution covered by existing E & P is a dividend, and any excess is treated as a return of capital until basis is recovered.

If the fair market value of the property distributed exceeds the corporation's E & P and the shareholder's basis in the stock investment, a capital gain results. The amount distributed is reduced by any liabilities to which the distributed property is subject immediately before and immediately after the distribution and by any liabilities of the corporation assumed by the shareholder.[5] The basis in the distributed property is the fair market value of the property on the date of the distribution.

EXAMPLE 12

Robin Corporation has E & P of $60,000. It distributes land with a fair market value of $50,000 (adjusted basis of $30,000) to its sole shareholder, Carlos. The land is subject to a liability of $10,000, which Carlos assumes. Carlos has a taxable dividend of $40,000 ($50,000 fair market value – $10,000 liability). The basis of the land to Carlos is $50,000. ◆

EXAMPLE 13

Ten percent of Bluebird Corporation is owned by Redbird Corporation. Bluebird Corporation has ample E & P to cover any distributions made during the year. One distribution made to Redbird Corporation consists of a vacant lot with an adjusted basis of $5,000 and a fair market value of $3,000. Redbird has a taxable dividend of $3,000, and its basis in the lot is $3,000. ◆

Property that has depreciated in value is usually not a suitable subject for distribution as a property dividend. Note what has happened in Example 13. The loss of $2,000 (adjusted basis $5,000, fair market value $3,000) disappears. Bluebird Corporation could have preserved the loss for itself if it had sold the lot and then distributed the $3,000 proceeds.

Property Dividends—Effect on the Corporation

A property distribution by a corporation to its shareholders poses two questions. Does the distribution result in recognized gain or loss to the corporation making the distribution? What effect will the distribution have on the corporation's E & P?

5. § 301(b)(2).

Recognition of Gain or Loss. All distributions of appreciated property cause gain to the distributing corporation.[6] In effect, the corporation that distributes a property dividend is treated as if it had sold the property to the shareholder for its fair market value. However, the distributing corporation does not recognize loss on distributions of property with a tax basis in excess of fair market value.

EXAMPLE 14

Wren Corporation distributes land (basis of $10,000 and fair market value of $30,000) to an individual shareholder. Wren Corporation recognizes a gain of $20,000. ◆

EXAMPLE 15

Assume the property in Example 14 has a fair market value of $10,000 and a basis of $30,000. Wren Corporation does not recognize a loss on the distribution. ◆

If the distributed property is subject to a liability in excess of basis or the shareholder assumes such a liability, a special rule applies. The fair market value of the property for purposes of determining gain on the distribution is treated as not being less than the amount of the liability.

EXAMPLE 16

Assume the land in Example 14 is subject to a liability of $35,000. Wren Corporation recognizes a gain of $25,000 on the distribution. ◆

Effect of Corporate Distributions on E & P. In the event of a corporate distribution, the E & P account is reduced by the amount of money distributed or by the *greater* of the fair market value or the adjusted basis of property distributed, less the amount of any liability on the property.[7] E & P is increased by gain recognized on appreciated property distributed as a property dividend.

EXAMPLE 17

Brown Corporation distributes property (basis of $10,000 and fair market value of $20,000) to Alicia, its shareholder. Brown recognizes a gain of $10,000, which is added to its E & P, and which is reduced by $20,000, the fair market value of the property. Alicia has dividend income of $20,000. ◆

EXAMPLE 18

Assume the same facts as in Example 17, except that the fair market value of the property is $15,000 and the adjusted basis in the hands of Brown Corporation is $20,000. Because the loss is not recognized and the adjusted basis is greater than fair market value, E & P is reduced by $20,000. Alicia reports dividend income of $15,000. ◆

EXAMPLE 19

Assume the same facts as in Example 18, except that the property is subject to a liability of $6,000. E & P is now reduced by $14,000 ($20,000 adjusted basis – $6,000 liability). Alicia has a dividend of $9,000 ($15,000 amount of the distribution – $6,000 liability), and her basis in the property is $15,000. ◆

Under no circumstances can a distribution, whether cash or property, either generate a deficit in E & P or add to a deficit in E & P. Deficits can arise only through corporate losses.

6. Section 311 covers the taxability of a corporation on distribution.

7. §§ 312(a), (b), and (c).

EXAMPLE 20

Green Corporation had accumulated E & P of $10,000 at the beginning of the current tax year. During the year, it had current E & P of $15,000. At the end of the year, it distributed cash of $30,000 to its sole shareholder, Hans. Green Corporation's E & P at the end of the year will be zero. The beginning E & P of $10,000 is increased by current E & P of $15,000 and is reduced by $25,000 because of the dividend distribution. The remaining $5,000 of the distribution to Hans does not reduce E & P because a distribution cannot generate a deficit in E & P. ◆

EXAMPLE 21

Assume Green Corporation in Example 20 had an operating loss of $15,000 during the tax year (rather than current E & P of $15,000). Its E & P at the end of the year will be a deficit of $5,000. The operating loss generates a $5,000 deficit in E & P, computed as follows: $10,000 (beginning E & P) – $15,000 (operating loss) = $5,000 deficit in E & P. The $30,000 distribution to Hans does not increase the deficit in E & P because a distribution cannot add to a deficit. ◆

CONSTRUCTIVE DIVIDENDS

A distribution by a corporation to its shareholders can be treated as a dividend for Federal income tax purposes even though it is not formally declared or designated as a dividend. Also, it need not be issued pro rata to all shareholders. Nor must the distribution satisfy the legal requirements of a dividend as set forth by applicable state law. The key factor determining dividend status is whether there is a measurable economic benefit conveyed to the shareholder. This benefit, often described as a *constructive dividend,* is distinguishable from actual corporate distributions of cash and property in form only.

Constructive dividend situations usually arise in the context of closely held corporations. Here, the dealings between the parties are less structured, and, frequently, formalities are not preserved. The constructive dividend serves as a substitute for actual distributions. Usually, it is intended to accomplish some tax objective not available through the use of direct dividends. The shareholders may be attempting to bail out corporate profits in a form deductible to the corporation. Recall that dividend distributions do not provide the distributing corporation with an income tax deduction, although they do reduce E & P. Alternatively, the shareholders may be seeking benefits for themselves while avoiding the recognition of income. Constructive dividends are, in reality, disguised dividends.

Do not conclude that all constructive dividends are deliberate attempts to avoid actual and formal dividends. Often, constructive dividends are inadvertent. Consequently, a dividend result may come as a surprise to the parties. For this reason, if for none other, an awareness of the various constructive dividend situations is essential to protect the parties from unanticipated tax consequences.

Types of Constructive Dividends

The most frequently encountered types of constructive dividends are summarized below.

Shareholder Use of Corporate-Owned Property. A constructive dividend can occur when a shareholder uses corporation property for personal purposes at no cost. Personal use of corporate-owned automobiles, airplanes, yachts, fishing camps, hunting lodges, and other entertainment facilities is commonplace in some closely held corporations. The shareholder has dividend income to the extent of the fair rental value of the property for the period of its personal use.

Bargain Sale of Corporate Property to a Shareholder. Shareholders often purchase property from a corporation at a cost below the fair market value of the property. These bargain sales produce dividend income to the extent of the difference between the property's fair market value on the date of sale and the amount the shareholder paid for the property. These situations might be avoided by appraising the property on or about the date of the sale. The appraised value should become the price to be paid by the shareholder.

Bargain Rental of Corporate Property. A bargain rental of corporate property by a shareholder also produces dividend income. Here the measure of the constructive dividend is the excess of the property's fair rental value over the rent actually paid. Again, appraisal data should be used to avoid any questionable situations.

Payments for the Benefit of a Shareholder. If a corporation pays an obligation of a shareholder, the payment is treated as a constructive dividend. The obligation involved need not be legally binding on the shareholder; it may, in fact, be a moral obligation. Forgiveness of shareholder indebtedness by the corporation can create an identical problem. Excessive rentals paid by a corporation for the use of shareholder property are also treated as constructive dividends.

Excessive Compensation. A salary payment to a shareholder-employee that is deemed to be unreasonable is frequently treated as a constructive dividend and therefore is not deductible by the corporation. In determining the reasonableness of salary payments, the following factors are considered:

- The employee's qualifications.
- A comparison of salaries with dividend distributions.
- The prevailing rates of compensation for comparable positions in comparable business concerns.
- The nature and scope of the employee's work.
- The size and complexity of the business.
- A comparison of salaries paid with both gross and net income.
- The taxpayer's salary policy toward all employees.
- For small corporations with a limited number of officers, the amount of compensation paid the employee in question in previous years.

Loans to Shareholders. Advances to shareholders that are not bona fide loans are also deemed to be constructive dividends. Whether an advance qualifies as a bona fide loan is a question of fact to be determined in light of the particular circumstances. Factors considered in determining whether the advance is a bona fide loan include the following:

- Whether the advance is on open account or is evidenced by a written instrument.
- Whether the shareholder furnished collateral or other security for the advance.
- How long the advance has been outstanding.
- Whether any payments have been made, excluding dividend sources.
- The shareholder's financial capability to repay the advance.
- The shareholder's use of the funds (e.g., payment of routine bills versus nonrecurring, extraordinary expenses).

- The regularity of the advances.
- The dividend-paying history of the corporation.

If a corporation succeeds in proving that an advance to a shareholder is a bona fide loan, the advance is not deemed to be a constructive dividend. But getting past this hurdle does not eliminate all constructive dividend treatment. The shareholder will still have a constructive dividend in the amount of any forgone interest. Interest-free or below-market loans by a corporation to a shareholder cause the shareholder to have a constructive dividend to the extent of *imputed interest,* which is the difference between the rate the Federal government pays on new borrowings, compounded semiannually, and the interest charged on the loan. The corporation is deemed to have made a dividend distribution to the shareholder to the extent of the forgone interest. The shareholder is then deemed to have made an interest payment to the corporation for the same amount. Although the shareholder may be permitted to deduct the deemed interest payment, the corporation has interest income. No corresponding deduction is allowed since the imputed interest element is a constructive dividend.

EXAMPLE 22

Bluebird Corporation loans its principal shareholder, Sanjay, $100,000 on January 2, 1993. The loan is interest-free. On December 31, 1993, Bluebird is deemed to have made a dividend distribution to Sanjay in the amount of the imputed interest on the loan, determined by using the Federal rate and compounded semiannually. Assume the Federal rate is 10%. Bluebird Corporation is deemed to have paid a dividend to Sanjay in the amount of $10,250.

Although Sanjay has dividend income of $10,250, he may be permitted to offset the income with a $10,250 deemed interest payment to Bluebird. Bluebird Corporation has deemed interest income of $10,250, but has no corresponding deduction. The deemed payment from Bluebird to Sanjay is a nondeductible dividend. ◆

Loans to a Corporation by Shareholders. Shareholder loans to a corporation may be reclassified as equity because the debt has too many features of stock. Any interest and principal payments made by the corporation to the shareholder are treated as constructive dividends.

Tax Treatment of Constructive Dividends

Constructive distributions possess the same tax attributes as actual distributions. Thus, a corporate shareholder would be entitled to the dividends received deduction of § 243. The constructive distribution would be a taxable dividend only to the extent of the corporation's current and accumulated E & P. The task of proving that the distribution constitutes a return of capital because of inadequate E & P rests with the taxpayer.

STOCK DIVIDENDS AND STOCK RIGHTS

Stock Dividends—§ 305

A shareholder's proportionate interest in a corporation does not change upon receipt of a stock dividend. Accordingly, such distributions were initially accorded tax-free treatment. The current provisions of § 305 are based on the proportionate interest concept.

Stock dividends are not taxable if they are pro rata distributions of stock, or stock rights, on common stock. Section 305(b) contains five exceptions to the general rule that stock dividends are nontaxable. These exceptions deal with various disproportionate distribution situations. If stock dividends are not taxable, the corporation's E & P is not reduced.[8] If the stock dividends are taxable, the distributing corporation treats the distribution in the same manner as any other taxable property dividend.

If a stock dividend is taxable, basis to the shareholder-distributee is fair market value, and the holding period starts on the date of receipt. If a stock dividend is not taxable, § 307 requires that the basis of the stock on which the dividend is distributed be reallocated. If the dividend shares are identical to these formerly held shares, basis in the old stock is reallocated by dividing the taxpayer's cost in the old stock by the total number of shares. If the dividend stock is not identical to the underlying shares (e.g., a stock dividend of preferred on common), basis is determined by allocating the cost of the formerly held shares between the old and new stock according to the fair market value of each. The holding period includes the holding period of the formerly held stock.[9]

EXAMPLE 23

Gail bought 1,000 shares of stock two years ago for $10,000. In the current tax year, she receives 10 shares of common stock as a nontaxable stock dividend. Gail's basis of $10,000 is divided by 1,010. Each share of stock has a basis of $9.90 instead of the pre-dividend $10 basis. ◆

EXAMPLE 24

Assume Gail received, instead, a nontaxable preferred stock dividend of 100 shares. The preferred stock has a fair market value of $1,000, and the common stock, on which the preferred is distributed, has a fair market value of $19,000. After the receipt of the stock dividend, the basis of the common stock is $9,500, and the basis of the preferred is $500, computed as follows:

Fair market value of common	$19,000
Fair market value of preferred	1,000
	$20,000
Basis of common: 19/20 × $10,000	$ 9,500
Basis of preferred: 1/20 × $10,000	$ 500

◆

Stock Rights

The rules for determining taxability of stock rights are identical to those for determining taxability of stock dividends. If the rights are taxable, the recipient has income to the extent of the fair market value of the rights. The fair market value then becomes the shareholder-distributee's basis in the rights. If the rights are exercised, the holding period for the new stock is the date the rights (whether taxable or nontaxable) are exercised. The basis of the new stock is the basis of the rights plus the amount of any other consideration given.

If stock rights are not taxable and the value of the rights is less than 15 percent of the value of the old stock, the basis of the rights is zero. However, the shareholder may elect to have some of the basis in the formerly held stock allocated to the rights.[10] If the fair market value of the rights is 15 percent or more

8. § 312(d)(1).
9. § 1223(5).
10. § 307(b)(1).

of the value of the old stock and the rights are exercised or sold, the shareholder *must* allocate some of the basis in the formerly held stock to the rights.

Assume the value of the stock rights is less than 15 percent of the value of the stock and the shareholder makes an election to allocate basis to the rights. The election is made by attaching a statement to the shareholder's return for the year in which the rights are received.

EXAMPLE 25

A corporation with common stock outstanding declares a nontaxable dividend payable in rights to subscribe to common stock. Each right entitles the holder to purchase one share of stock for $90. One right is issued for every two shares of stock owned. Fred owns 400 shares of stock purchased two years ago for $15,000. At the time of the distribution of the rights, the market value of the common stock is $100 per share, and the market value of the rights is $8 per right. Fred receives 200 rights. He exercises 100 rights and sells the remaining 100 rights three months later for $9 per right. Fred need not allocate the cost of the original stock to the rights because the value of the rights is less than 15% of the value of the stock ($1,600 ÷ $40,000 = 4%).

If Fred does not allocate his original stock basis to the rights, his basis in the new stock is $9,000 ($90 × 100). Sale of the rights would produce long-term capital gain of $900 ($9 × 100). The holding period of the rights starts with the date the original 400 shares of stock were acquired. The holding period of the new stock begins on the date the stock was purchased.

If Fred elects to allocate basis to the rights, his basis in the rights is $577, computed as follows: $1,600 value of rights ÷ $41,600 value of rights and stock × $15,000 = $577. His basis in the stock is $14,423 [($40,000 ÷ $41,600) × $15,000 = $14,423]. When he exercises the rights, his basis in the new stock will be $9,288.50 ($9,000 cost + $288.50 basis in 100 rights). Sale of the rights would produce a long-term capital gain of $611.50 ($900 selling price – $288.50 basis in the remaining 100 rights). ◆

STOCK REDEMPTIONS

Overview

In a stock redemption, a corporation purchases its stock from a shareholder. The reacquired stock can be canceled, held as treasury stock, or otherwise disposed of. Redemptions take place for various reasons. Some of the more common reasons are summarized below:

1. A shareholder may wish to withdraw some or all of his or her investment in the corporation. Perhaps the shareholder wants to take advantage of other investment opportunities or retire or disagrees with current management policies.
2. The corporation may want to reacquire some of its stock to pass on to key nonshareholder employees or to fund employee stock ownership plans.
3. The corporation may feel that its own stock is an attractive investment. Thus, it chooses to "invest in itself."

Reason 1 above arises most often in the context of a closely held corporation. Because no market may exist for the stock, the withdrawing shareholder's choices are limited to selling the stock to the other shareholders or to the corporation. If the other shareholders lack the funds to purchase the stock, the withdrawing shareholder must resort to the corporation in order to sell the stock.

Presuming a shareholder sells all or part of his or her stock investment to the issuing corporation, what tax consequences result? Two possibilities exist. First, the transaction will be classified as a dividend if it does not qualify for *exchange* treatment under the law. In this regard, the *Internal Revenue Code* controls, and the classification of the transaction under state law is immaterial. Second, if exchange treatment requirements are satisfied, the shareholder will recognize *gain or loss* equal to the difference between the consideration received and the basis of the stock redeemed. This gain or loss will usually be capital because stock held as an investment is a capital asset.

EXAMPLE 26

Tom redeems stock (basis of $40,000) in Blue Corporation for its fair market value of $100,000. Tom acquired the stock five years ago as an investment. If the redemption *does not* qualify as an exchange and assuming Blue Corporation has adequate E & P, the $100,000 Tom receives is dividend income. If the redemption *does* qualify as an exchange, the result is as follows:

Redemption proceeds	$100,000
Less: Basis in the stock redeemed	40,000
Long-term capital gain	$ 60,000

◆

In Example 26 note the advantage of having the redemption qualify for exchange treatment. By allowing Tom to recover the basis in the stock, $40,000 of income is avoided. Thus, stock redemptions should be structured to satisfy the exchange requirements of the tax law. In addition, the maximum rate on capital gain is 28 percent, compared to 31 percent on ordinary income.

Under the Code, the following major types of stock redemptions qualify for exchange treatment and, as a result, avoid dividend income consequences:

- Distributions not essentially equivalent to a dividend [§ 302(b)(1)].
- Distributions substantially disproportionate in terms of shareholder effect [§ 302(b)(2)].
- Distributions in complete termination of a shareholder's interest [§ 302(b)(3)].
- Distributions to pay a shareholder's death taxes (§ 303).

Stock Attribution Rules

To obtain exchange treatment, most redemptions require a reduction in the redeeming shareholder's relative ownership in the corporation. To deter related parties from using certain qualifying stock redemptions, § 318 imposes constructive ownership of stock (stock attribution) rules. In testing for exchange treatment, a shareholder may be required to take into account stock owned by related parties. Related parties include immediate family, specifically spouses, children, grandchildren, and parents. Attribution also takes place *from* and *to* partnerships, estates, trusts, and corporations (50 percent or more ownership required in the case of corporations).

EXAMPLE 27

Lori owns 30% of the stock in Black Corporation, the other 70% being held by her children. For purposes of § 318, Lori is treated as owning 100% of the stock in Black Corporation. She owns 30% directly and, because of the family attribution rules, 70% indirectly. ◆

EXAMPLE 28

Chris owns 50% of the stock in Gray Corporation. The other 50% is owned by a partnership in which Chris has a 20% interest. Chris is deemed to own 60% of Gray Corporation: 50% directly and, because of the partnership interest, 10% indirectly. ◆

The stock attribution rules of § 318 do not apply to stock redemptions to pay death taxes. Under certain conditions, the *family* attribution rules (refer to Example 27) do not apply to stock redemptions in *complete termination* of a shareholder's interest.

Redemptions Not Essentially Equivalent to a Dividend—§ 302(b)(1)

Section 302(b)(1) provides that a redemption qualifies for exchange treatment if it is "not essentially equivalent to a dividend." There are few objective tests to determine when a redemption is or is not essentially equivalent to a dividend. Section 302(b)(1) was added to provide specifically for redemptions of preferred stock. Often, shareholders have no control over the redemption when corporations call in such stock. Some courts interpreted § 302(b)(1) to mean that a redemption would receive exchange treatment if there was a business purpose for the redemption and there was no tax avoidance scheme to bail out dividends at favorable tax rates. The real question was whether the stock attribution rules of § 318(a) applied to this provision.

These issues were resolved by the U.S. Supreme Court in *U.S. v. Davis.*[11] First, the Court found that the presence or absence of a business purpose was not determinative in the application of § 302(b)(1). For a redemption to be not essentially equivalent to a dividend, there must be "a meaningful reduction of the shareholder's proportionate interest in the corporation." Second, the attribution rules of § 318(a) must be considered in resolving the meaningful reduction test.

What the Supreme Court had in mind when it promulgated the meaningful reduction test has been the subject of much controversy. It should be clear, however, that a meaningful reduction requires a smaller change in ownership than is needed for a § 302(b)(2) redemption (see the discussion below of substantially disproportionate redemptions). Likewise, a shareholder who maintains voting control of the corporation after the redemption is not apt to qualify under § 302(b)(1).

Currently, a redemption will qualify under § 302(b)(1) as not being "essentially equivalent to a dividend" when there has been a meaningful reduction of the shareholder's proportionate interest in the redeeming corporation. The facts and circumstances of each case will determine whether a distribution in redemption of stock is essentially equivalent to a dividend within the meaning of § 302(b)(1). A decrease in the redeeming shareholder's voting control appears to be the most significant indicator of a meaningful reduction, but reductions in the rights of redeeming shareholders to share in corporate earnings or to receive corporate assets upon liquidation are also considered. The "meaningful reduction" test is applied whether common stock or preferred stock is being redeemed.

11. 70–1 USTC ¶9289, 25 AFTR2d 70–827, 90 S.Ct. 1041 (USSC, 1970).

Example 29

Pat owns 58% of the common stock of Green Corporation. After a redemption of part of Pat's stock, he owns 51% of the Green stock. Pat continues to have dominant voting rights in Green; thus, the redemption is treated as "essentially equivalent to a dividend," and Pat has ordinary income equal to the entire amount of the distribution. ◆

Example 30

Brown Corporation redeems 2% of the stock of Maria, a minority shareholder. Before the redemption, Maria owned 10% of Brown Corporation. In this case, the redemption may qualify as "not essentially equivalent to a dividend." Maria experiences a reduction in her voting rights, her right to participate in current earnings and accumulated surplus, and her right to share in net assets upon liquidation. ◆

If a redemption is treated as an ordinary dividend, the shareholder's basis in the stock redeemed attaches to the remaining stock. According to the Regulations, this basis will attach to other stock held by the taxpayer (or to stock he or she owns constructively).[12]

Example 31

Fran and Floyd, wife and husband, each own 50 shares in Gray Corporation, representing 100% of the stock of Gray. All the stock was purchased for $50,000. The corporation redeems Floyd's 50 shares. Assuming the rules governing the complete termination of a shareholder's interest under § 302(b)(3) do not apply, the redemption will be treated as a taxable dividend. Floyd's basis in the stock, $25,000, will attach to Fran's stock so she will have a basis of $50,000 in the 50 shares she currently owns in Gray. ◆

Substantially Disproportionate Redemptions—§ 302(b)(2)

A redemption of stock qualifies for capital gain treatment under § 302(b)(2) if two conditions are met:

1. The distribution must be substantially disproportionate. To be substantially disproportionate, the shareholder must own, after the distribution, less than 80 percent of his or her total interest in the corporation before the redemption. For example, if a shareholder has a 60 percent ownership in a corporation that redeems part of the stock, the redemption is substantially disproportionate only if the percentage of ownership after the redemption is less than 48 percent (80 percent of 60 percent).
2. The shareholder must own, after the distribution, less than 50 percent of the total combined voting power of all classes of stock entitled to vote.

Figure 18–1 provides a graphic presentation of a redemption qualifying under § 302(b)(2).

In determining the percentage of ownership of the shareholder, it must be remembered that the constructive ownership rules of § 318(a) apply.

12. Reg. § 1.302–2(c).

FIGURE 18–1
Redemption Qualifying under § 302(b)(2)

Setting

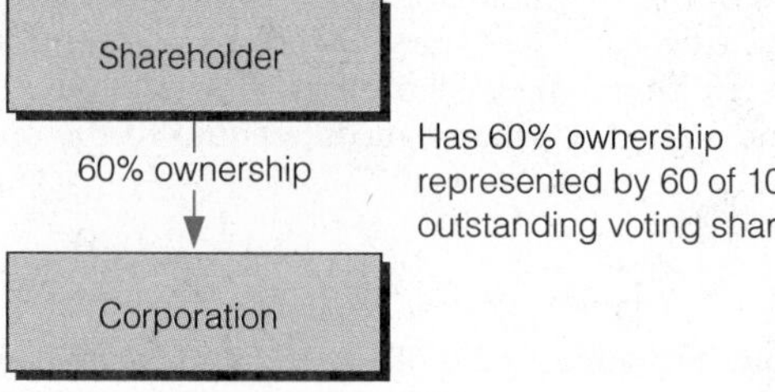

Shareholder
60% ownership
Corporation
Has 60% ownership represented by 60 of 100 outstanding voting shares

Redemption

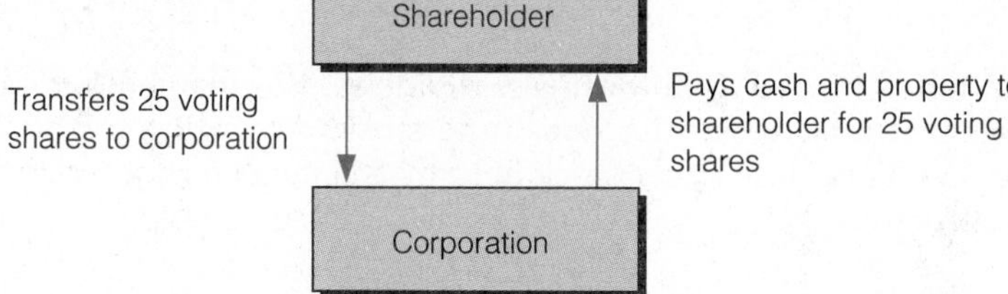

Shareholder
Transfers 25 voting shares to corporation
Pays cash and property to shareholder for 25 voting shares
Corporation

After Redemption

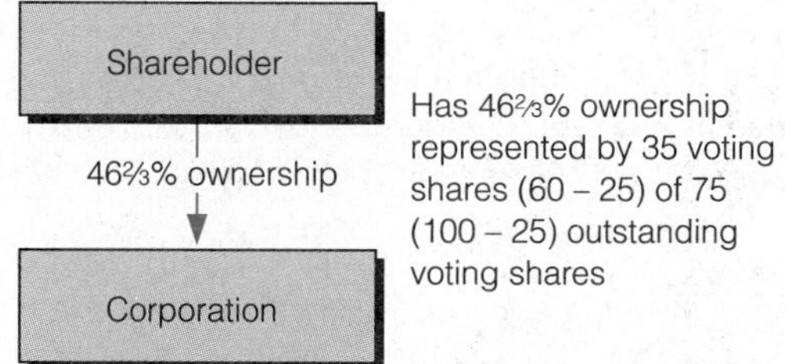

Shareholder
46⅔% ownership
Corporation
Has 46⅔% ownership represented by 35 voting shares (60 – 25) of 75 (100 – 25) outstanding voting shares

Results Redemption is a qualified redemption under § 302(b)(2). It meets both conditions of § 302(b)(2):

1. Shareholder owns less than 50% of the total combined voting power in the corporation.
2. Shareholder owns less than 80% of the 60% ownership held prior to the redemption (80% x 60% = 48%).

EXAMPLE 32

Bob, Carl, and Dan, unrelated individuals, own 30 shares, 30 shares, and 40 shares, respectively, in Black Corporation. Black has E & P of $200,000. The corporation redeems 20 shares of Dan's stock for $30,000. Dan paid $200 a share for the stock two years ago.

Dan's ownership in Black Corporation before and after the redemption is as follows:

	Total Shares	Dan's Ownership	Ownership Percentage	80% of Original Ownership
Before redemption	100	40	40%	32% (80% × 40%)
After redemption	80	20	25% (20 ÷ 80)	

Dan's 25% ownership after the redemption meets both tests of § 302(b)(2). It is less than 50% of the total voting power and less than 80% of his original ownership. The distribution qualifies as a stock redemption. Dan has a long-term capital gain of $26,000 [$30,000 – $4,000 (20 shares × $200)]. ◆

EXAMPLE 33

Given the situation in Example 32, assume instead that Carl and Dan are father and son. The redemption described previously would not qualify for exchange treatment. Dan is deemed to own the stock of Carl, so after the redemption, he would have 50 shares of a total of 80 shares, more than 50% ownership. He would also fail the 80% test.

Dan's ownership in Black Corporation is computed as follows:

	Total Shares	Dan's Direct Ownership	Carl's Ownership	Dan's Deemed Ownership	Ownership Percentage	80% of Original Ownership
Before redemption	100	40	30	70	70%	56% (80% × 70%)
After redemption	80	20	30	50	62.5% (50 ÷ 80)	

Dan's deemed ownership of 62.5% fails to meet either of the tests of § 302(b)(2). It is more than 50% ownership and more than 80% of his original ownership. Thus, the distribution does not qualify as a stock redemption. Dan has a taxable dividend of $30,000. ◆

Redemptions in Complete Termination of a Shareholder's Interest—§ 302(b)(3)

If a shareholder terminates his or her entire stock ownership in a corporation through a stock redemption, the redemption will qualify for exchange treatment. Such a complete termination may not meet the substantially disproportionate rules of § 302(b)(2) if the constructive ownership rules are applied. The difference in the two provisions is that the constructive ownership rules of § 318(a)(1) do not apply to § 302(b)(3). This occurs only if the following conditions are met: (1) the former shareholder has no interest, other than that of a creditor, in the corporation after the redemption (including an interest as an officer, director, or employee) for at least 10 years, and (2) the former shareholder files an agreement to notify the IRS of any acquisition within the 10-year period and to retain all necessary records pertaining to the redemption during this time period. A shareholder can reacquire an interest in the corporation by bequest or inheritance, but in no other manner.

The required agreement should be in the form of a separate statement signed by the shareholder and attached to the return for the year in which the redemption occurred. The agreement should state that the shareholder agrees to notify the appropriate District Director within 30 days of reacquiring an interest in the corporation within the 10-year period following the redemption.

EXAMPLE 34

The stock of Green Corporation is held as follows: 40 shares by Kevin (basis of $30,000), 30 shares by Keith (Kevin's son), and 30 shares by Helen (Kevin's wife). At a time when each share is worth $2,000, Green Corporation redeems Kevin's 40 shares for $80,000. Although Kevin filed the necessary agreement with the IRS, he remains an employee of Green at a salary of $12,000. Section 302(b)(3) does not apply to this redemption because of Kevin's continued employment status. Consequently, and to the extent of Green Corporation's E & P, the distribution proceeds are a dividend to Kevin. ◆

Redemptions to Pay Death Taxes—§ 303

Section 303 provides an executor the opportunity to redeem stock in a closely held corporation when the stock represents a substantial amount of the gross estate of the shareholder-decedent. The purpose of the redemption is to provide the estate with liquidity. Stock in a closely held corporation is generally not marketable. However, it could be redeemed if § 302 would not cause ordinary dividend treatment. Section 303, to an extent, alleviates this problem.

Section 303 is an exception to § 302(b). If a stock redemption qualifies under § 303, the rules of § 302(b) do not apply. The distribution will qualify as a stock redemption regardless of whether it is substantially disproportionate or is not essentially equivalent to a dividend.

In a § 303 redemption, the redemption price generally equals the basis of the stock. Under § 1014, the income tax basis of property owned by a decedent becomes the property's fair market value on the date of death (or alternate valuation date if available and if elected). When this so-called step-up or step-down in basis that occurs at death (refer to Chapter 12) equals the redemption price, the exchange is free of any income tax consequences to the shareholder's estate.

Section 303 applies to a distribution made with respect to stock of a corporation when the value of the stock in the gross estate of a decedent exceeds 35 percent of the value of the adjusted gross estate. (For a definition of "gross estate" and "adjusted gross estate," see the Glossary of Tax Terms in Appendix C.)

EXAMPLE 35

The adjusted gross estate of Juan, decedent, is $900,000. The death taxes and funeral and administration expenses of the estate total $200,000. Included in the estate is stock in White Corporation, a closely held corporation, valued at $340,000. Juan had acquired the stock years ago at a cost of $60,000. White Corporation redeems $200,000 of the stock from Juan's estate. The redemption qualifies under § 303 and would not be a dividend to Juan's estate. Section 1014 applies to give the stock a step-up in basis. Consequently, there is no tax on the redemption. ◆

In determining whether the value of stock in a corporation exceeds 35 percent of the value of the adjusted gross estate of a decedent, the stock of two or more corporations may be treated as the stock of a single corporation. Stock in corporations in which the decedent held a 20 percent or more interest is treated as stock in a single corporation for purposes of § 303.[13]

EXAMPLE 36

The adjusted gross estate of a decedent is $300,000. The gross estate includes stock in Brown and Black Corporations valued at $100,000 and $80,000, respectively. Unless the two corporations are treated as a single corporation, § 303 does not apply to a redemption of the stock. Assume the decedent owned all the stock of Brown Corporation and 80% of the stock of Black. Section 303 applies because 20% or more of the value of the stock of both corporations may be included in the decedent's estate. The 35% test is met when the Brown and Black stock are treated as that of a single corporation. ◆

The use of § 303 is subject to time limitations. Section 303 applies only to redemptions made within 90 days after the expiration of the period of limitations for the assessment of the Federal estate tax. If a timely petition for a redetermi-

13. § 303(b)(2)(B).

nation of an estate tax deficiency is filed with the U.S. Tax Court, the applicable period for a § 303 redemption is extended to 60 days after the decision of the Court becomes final.[14]

Section 303 applies to the extent of the sum of the estate, inheritance, legacy, and succession taxes imposed by reason of the decedent's death. Also allowed are the funeral and administration expenses deductible to the estate.[15]

Effect on the Corporation Redeeming Its Stock

Having considered some of the different types of stock redemptions that will receive exchange treatment, what is the tax effect to the corporation redeeming its stock? If the corporation uses property to carry out the redemption, is gain or loss recognized on the distribution? Furthermore, what effect does the redemption have on the corporation's E & P? These matters are discussed in the following paragraphs.

CONCEPT SUMMARY 18–2
CORPORATE DISTRIBUTIONS

1. Without a special provision, corporate distributions are taxed as dividend income to the recipient shareholders to the extent of the distributing corporation's E & P accumulated since February 28, 1913, or to the extent of current E & P. Any excess is treated as a return of capital to the extent of the shareholder's basis in the stock and, thereafter, as capital gain. See §§ 301 and 316.
2. Property distributions are considered dividends (taxed as noted in item 1) in the amount of their fair market value. The amount deemed distributed is reduced by any liabilities on the property distributed. The shareholder's basis in the property is the fair market value.
3. Earnings and profits of a corporation are increased by corporate earnings for the taxable year computed in the same manner as the corporation computes its taxable income. As a general rule, the account is increased for all items of income, whether taxed or not, and reduced by all items of expense, whether deductible or not. See § 312. Refer to Concept Summary 18–1 for a summary of the effect of certain transactions on taxable income in arriving at current E & P.
4. A corporation recognizes gain, but not loss, on distributions of property to its shareholders. E & P of the distributing corporation is reduced by the amount of money distributed or by the greater of the fair market value or the adjusted basis of property distributed less the amount of any liability applicable to the distributed property.
5. As a general rule, stock dividends or stock rights (representing stock in the distributing corporation) are not taxed, with certain exceptions.
6. Stock redemptions that qualify under § 302(b) are given exchange treatment. Section 302(b) requires that such distributions either be substantially disproportionate or not be essentially equivalent to a dividend. In making a determination of substantially disproportionate or not essentially equivalent to a dividend under §§ 302(b)(1), (2), and (3), the rules of § 318(a) determining the constructive ownership of stock apply, unless the shareholder redeems all of his or her interest in the corporation and does not reacquire (other than by bequest or inheritance) any interest (except as a creditor) for 10 years after the redemption.
7. If stock included in a decedent's estate represents more than 35% of the adjusted gross estate, it may upon redemption qualify for exchange treatment separate and apart from § 302(b). Section 303 provides automatic exchange treatment on the redemption of such stock.
8. A corporation is taxed on the appreciation of property distributed in redemption of its stock.
9. In a stock redemption, the E & P account of the distributing corporation is reduced in proportion to the amount of the corporation's outstanding stock that is redeemed.

---

14. § 303(b)(1).

15. § 303(a).

Recognition of Loss by the Corporation. The purchase of stock, including the repurchase by an issuing corporation of its own stock, is generally treated as a capital transaction that does not give rise to a loss. All expenses a corporation incurs in redeeming its stock are nonamortizable capital expenditures. Stock purchase premiums are not deductible. Also not deductible are payments to a shareholder for an agreement not to reacquire stock in the corporation for a specified time as well as legal, accounting, transfer agent, brokerage, and appraisal fees.

Recognition of Gain by the Corporation. Section 311 provides that corporations are taxed on all distributions of appreciated property whether in the form of a property dividend or a stock redemption.

Example 37

To carry out a redemption, Bluebird Corporation transfers land (basis of $80,000, fair market value of $300,000) to a shareholder's estate. Bluebird has a recognized gain of $220,000 ($300,000 – $80,000). ◆

Effect on Earnings and Profits. A stock redemption reduces the E & P account of a corporation in an amount not in excess of the ratable share of the distributing corporation's E & P that is attributable to the stock redeemed.[16]

Example 38

Green Corporation has 100 shares of stock outstanding. It redeems 30 shares for $100,000 at a time when it has paid-in capital of $120,000 and E & P of $150,000. The charge to E & P is 30% of the amount in the E & P account ($45,000), and the remainder of the redemption price ($55,000) is a reduction of the capital account. ◆

Other Corporate Distributions

Partial liquidations of a corporation, if in compliance with the statutory requirements of § 302(e), will result in exchange treatment to the shareholders. Distributions of stock and securities of a controlled corporation to the shareholders of the parent corporation will be free of any tax consequences if they fall under § 355. Both of these types of corporate distributions are similar to stock redemptions and dividend distributions in some respects but are not discussed here because of their limited applicability.

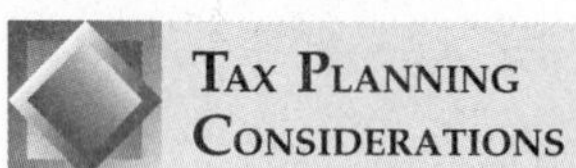

Tax Planning Considerations

Corporate Distributions

In connection with the discussion of corporate distributions, the following points need reinforcement:

- Because E & P is the measure of dividend income, its periodic determination is essential to corporate planning. Thus, an E & P account should be established and maintained, particularly if the possibility exists that a corporate distribution might represent a return of capital.
- Accumulated E & P is the sum of all past years' current E & P. There is no statute of limitations on the computation of E & P. The IRS could, for

16. § 312(n)(7).

example, redetermine a corporation's current E & P for a tax year long since passed. Such a change would affect accumulated E & P and would have a direct impact on the taxability of current distributions to shareholders.

- Taxpayers should be aware that manipulating distributions to avoid or minimize dividend exposure is possible.

Example 39

After several unprofitable years, Brown Corporation has a deficit in accumulated E & P of $100,000 as of January 1, 1993. Starting in 1993, Brown expects to generate annual E & P of $50,000 for the next four years and would like to distribute this amount to its shareholders. The corporation's cash position (for dividend purposes) will correspond to the current E & P generated. Compare the following possibilities:

1. On December 31 of 1993, 1994, 1995, and 1996, Brown Corporation distributes a cash dividend of $50,000.
2. On December 31 of 1994 and 1996, Brown Corporation distributes a cash dividend of $100,000.

The two alternatives are illustrated as follows:

Year	Accumulated E & P (First of Year)	Current E & P	Distribution	Amount of Dividend
		Alternative 1		
1993	($100,000)	$50,000	$50,000	$50,000
1994	(100,000)	50,000	50,000	50,000
1995	(100,000)	50,000	50,000	50,000
1996	(100,000)	50,000	50,000	50,000
		Alternative 2		
1993	($100,000)	$50,000	$ -0-	$ -0-
1994	(50,000)	50,000	100,000	50,000
1995	(50,000)	50,000	-0-	-0-
1996	-0-	50,000	100,000	50,000

Alternative 1 leads to an overall result of $200,000 in dividend income since each $50,000 distribution is fully covered by current E & P. Alternative 2, however, results in only $100,000 of dividend income to the shareholders. The remaining $100,000 is a return of capital. Why? At the time Brown Corporation made its first distribution of $100,000 on December 31, 1994, it had a deficit of $50,000 in accumulated E & P (the original deficit of $100,000 is reduced by the $50,000 of current E & P from 1993). Consequently, the $100,000 distribution yields a $50,000 dividend (the current E & P for 1994) and $50,000 as a return of capital. As of January 1, 1995, Brown's accumulated E & P now has a deficit balance of $50,000 (a distribution cannot increase a deficit in E & P). Add in $50,000 of current E & P from 1995, and the balance as of January 1, 1996, is zero. Thus, the second distribution of $100,000 made on December 31, 1996, also yields $50,000 of dividends (the current E & P for 1996) and $50,000 as a return of capital. ◆

Constructive Dividends

Tax planning can be particularly effective in avoiding constructive dividend situations. Shareholders should try to structure their dealings with the corporation on an arm's length basis. For example, reasonable rent should be paid for the use of corporate property, and a fair price should be paid for its purchase. The parties should make every effort to support the amount involved with appraisal data or market information obtained from reliable sources at or close to the time of the transaction. Dealings between shareholders and a closely held corporation should be as formal as possible. In the case of loans to shareholders, for example, the parties should provide for an adequate rate of interest, written evidence of the debt, and a realistic repayment schedule that is both arranged and followed.

If corporate profits are to be bailed out by the shareholders in a form deductible to the corporation, a balanced mix of the possible alternatives could lessen the risk of disallowance by the IRS. Rent for the use of shareholder property, interest on amounts borrowed from shareholders, or salaries for services rendered by shareholders are all feasible substitutes for dividend distributions. But overdoing any one approach may attract the attention of the IRS. Too much interest, for example, might mean the corporation is thinly capitalized, and some of the debt is really equity investment.

Much can be done to protect against the disallowance of corporate deductions for compensation that is determined to be unreasonable in amount. Example 40 is an illustration, all too common in a family corporation, of what *not* to do.

EXAMPLE 40

Black Corporation is wholly owned by Cole. Corporate employees and annual salaries include Mrs. Cole ($15,000), Cole, Jr. ($10,000), Cole ($80,000), and Ed ($40,000). The operation of Black Corporation is shared about equally between Cole and Ed (an unrelated party). Mrs. Cole (Cole's wife) performed significant services for the corporation during the corporation's formative years but now merely attends the annual meeting of the board of directors. Cole, Jr. (Cole's son), is a full-time student and occasionally signs papers for the corporation in his capacity as treasurer. Black Corporation has not distributed a dividend for 10 years, although it has accumulated substantial E & P. What is wrong with this situation?

- Mrs. Cole's salary seems vulnerable unless proof is available that some or all of her $15,000 annual salary is payment for services rendered to the corporation in prior years (i.e., she was underpaid for those years).[17]
- Cole, Jr.'s, salary is also vulnerable; he does not appear to earn the $10,000 paid to him by the corporation. True, neither Cole, Jr., nor Mrs. Cole is a shareholder, but each one's relationship to Cole is enough of a tie-in to raise the unreasonable compensation issue.
- Cole's salary appears susceptible to challenge. Why is he receiving $40,000 more than Ed when it appears they share equally in the operation of the corporation?
- Black Corporation has not distributed dividends for 10 years, although it is capable of distributing dividends. ◆

Stock Redemptions

Stock redemptions offer several possibilities for tax planning:

- The § 302(b)(1) variety (not essentially equivalent to a dividend) provides minimal utility and should be relied upon only as a last resort. Instead, the redemption should be structured to fit one of the safe harbors. These include § 302(b)(2) (substantially disproportionate), § 302(b)(3) (complete termination), and § 303 (to pay death taxes).
- For a family corporation in which all of the shareholders are related to each other, the only hope of a successful redemption may lie in the use of § 302(b)(3) or § 303. But in using § 302(b)(3), be careful that the family stock attribution rules are avoided. Here, strict compliance with § 302(c)(2) (i.e., the withdrawing shareholder does not continue as an employee of the

17. See, for example, *R. J. Nicoll Co.*, 59 T.C. 37 (1972).

corporation, etc., and does not reacquire an interest in the corporation within 10 years) is crucial.

- The alternative to a successful stock redemption is dividend treatment of the distribution under § 301. But do not conclude that a dividend is always undesirable from a tax standpoint. Suppose the distributing corporation has little, if any, E & P. Or the distributee-shareholder is another corporation. In the latter situation, dividend treatment may be preferred because of the availability of the dividends received deduction.
- When using the § 303 redemption, the amount to be sheltered from dividend treatment is the sum of death taxes and certain estate administration expenses. Nevertheless, a redemption in excess of the limitation does not destroy the applicability of § 303.
- The timing and sequence of a redemption should be carefully handled.

EXAMPLE 41

Bluejay Corporation's stock is held as follows: Abby (60 shares), Antonio (20 shares), and Ali (20 shares). Abby, Antonio, and Ali are not related to each other. The corporation redeems 24 of Abby's shares. Shortly thereafter, it redeems 5 of Antonio's shares. Does Abby's redemption qualify as substantially disproportionate? Taken in isolation, it would appear to meet the requirements of § 302(b)(2)—the 80% and 50% tests have been satisfied. Yet, if the IRS takes into account the later redemption of Antonio's shares, Abby has not satisfied the 50% test; she still owns $^{36}/_{71}$ of the corporation after both redemptions.[18] A greater time lag between the two redemptions places Abby in a better position to argue against collapsing the series of redemptions into one. ◆

PROBLEM MATERIALS

DISCUSSION QUESTIONS

1. What is meant by the term *earnings and profits?*
2. How do nontaxable items of income and nondeductible expenditures affect the E & P account?
3. Describe the effect of a distribution in a year when the distributing corporation has any of the following:
   - **a.** A deficit in accumulated E & P and a positive amount in current E & P.
   - **b.** A positive amount in accumulated E & P and a deficit in current E & P.
   - **c.** A deficit in both current and accumulated E & P.
   - **d.** A positive amount in both current and accumulated E & P.
4. Five years ago, a corporation determined its current E & P to be $100,000. In the current year, it makes a distribution of $200,000 to its shareholders. The IRS contends that the current E & P of the corporation five years ago was really $150,000.
   - **a.** Can the IRS successfully make this contention?
   - **b.** What difference would the additional $50,000 in E & P make?
5. If a corporation is chartered in a state that prohibits the payment of dividends that impair paid-in capital, is it possible for the corporation to pay a dividend that is a return of capital for tax purposes and yet comply with state law? Discuss.

18. § 302(b)(2)(D).

6. The suggestion is made that any distributions to shareholders by a calendar year corporation should take place on January 1 before the corporation has generated any current E & P. Assess the validity of this suggestion.
7. White Corporation has a deficit in E & P of $10,000 on January 1, 1993. Without considering a land sale in 1993, White Corporation has a tax loss of $20,000 that increases the deficit in E & P by that amount. White Corporation sold a tract of land on December 15, 1993, in consideration of a $200,000 note to be paid in five equal installments, the first installment due and payable on December 15, 1994. The land had a tax basis to White Corporation of $50,000. Because White did not elect out of the installment method, it did not include any of the $150,000 gain on the sale of the land in its taxable income for 1993. If the corporation distributes $30,000 to its shareholder, Bob, on December 24, 1993, how must Bob report the $30,000 for tax purposes? Bob has a basis of $60,000 in his stock in White Corporation.
8. What are the tax consequences to a corporation that distributes property to a shareholder that is subject to a liability in excess of the fair market value of the property?
9. A corporation distributed property (adjusted basis of $100,000 and fair market value of $80,000) to its shareholders. Has the corporation acted wisely? Why or why not?
10. Does the distributing corporation recognize gain or loss when it distributes property as a dividend to its shareholders? Explain.
11. When are stock dividends taxable?
12. How are nontaxable stock rights handled for tax purposes? Taxable stock rights?
13. Gray Corporation sells its plant and equipment to its shareholders. Shortly thereafter, Gray enters into a long-term lease for the use of these assets. In connection with the possible tax ramifications of these transactions, consider the following:
    a. The sale of the assets for less than their adjusted basis to Gray Corporation.
    b. The amount of rent Gray Corporation has agreed to pay.
14. Why is it important that an advance from a corporation to a shareholder be categorized as a bona fide loan? In resolving this issue, comment on the relevance of the following factors:
    a. The corporation has never paid a dividend.
    b. The advance is on open account.
    c. The advance provides for 2% interest.
    d. No date is specified for the repayment of the advance.
    e. The shareholder used the advance to pay personal bills.
    f. The shareholder repays the advance immediately after the transaction is questioned by the IRS on audit of the corporate income tax return.
15. How can shareholders bail out corporate profits in a manner that will provide the corporation with a deduction? What are the risks involved?
16. Whether compensation paid to a corporate employee is reasonable is a question of fact to be determined from the surrounding circumstances. How would the resolution of this problem be affected by each of the following factors?
    a. The employee is not a shareholder but is related to the sole owner of the corporate employer.
    b. The employee-shareholder never completed high school.
    c. The employee-shareholder is a full-time college student.
    d. The employee-shareholder was underpaid for her services during the formative period of the corporate employer.
    e. The corporate employer pays a nominal dividend each year.
    f. Year-end bonuses are paid to all shareholder-employees.
17. Lana wants to retire and sell her shares in Brown Corporation to Brown's remaining shareholders, Jack and Ivan. Why is it more preferable tax-wise for Brown Corporation to redeem Lana's shares than for Jack and Ivan to purchase her shares?
18. When does a redemption qualify under § 302(b)(1) as being "not essentially equivalent to a dividend"?

19. Under what circumstances does § 303 apply to a stock redemption? What is the tax effect of the application of § 303?
20. "A § 303 stock redemption usually results in no gain or loss being recognized by the estate." Evaluate this statement.
21. A corporation distributes $100,000 to a shareholder in complete redemption of the shareholder's stock. Can the corporation reduce its E & P by this amount? Explain.

PROBLEMS

22. At the beginning of the year, White Corporation (a calendar year taxpayer) has accumulated E & P of $50,000. Its current E & P is $30,000. During the year, White distributes $90,000 ($45,000 each) to its equal shareholders, Wanda and Wilma. Wanda has a basis of $8,000 in her stock, and Wilma has a basis of $2,000 in her stock. How will the $90,000 distribution be treated for tax purposes?
23. In 1993, Brown Corporation received dividend income of $50,000 from a corporation in which Brown holds a 5% interest. Brown Corporation also received interest income of $10,000 from municipal bonds. The municipality used the proceeds from the sale of the bonds to construct a needed facility to house city documents and to provide office space for several city officials. Brown Corporation borrowed funds to purchase the municipal bonds and paid $9,000 in interest on the loan in 1993. Brown Corporation's taxable income exclusive of the items noted above was $60,000. The $60,000 also represents current E & P.

    a. What is Brown Corporation's taxable income for 1993 after considering the dividend income, the interest from the municipal bonds, and the interest paid on the indebtedness to purchase the municipals?
    b. What is Brown Corporation's E & P as of December 31, 1993, if its E & P account balance was $15,000 as of January 1, 1993?

24. Complete the following schedule for each case.

	Accumulated E & P Beginning of Year	Current E & P	Cash Distributions (All on Last Day of Year)	Amount Taxable	Return of Capital
a.	$40,000	($10,000)	$50,000	$ ____	$ ____
b.	(50,000)	30,000	40,000	____	____
c.	30,000	50,000	70,000	____	____
d.	60,000	(20,000)	45,000	____	____
e.	Same as (d), except the distribution of $45,000 is made on June 30 and the corporation uses the calendar year for tax purposes.			____	____

25. Complete the following schedule for each case.

	Accumulated E & P Beginning of Year	Current E & P	Cash Distributions (All on Last Day of Year)	Amount Taxable	Return of Capital
a.	$75,000	$20,000	$60,000	$ ____	$ ____
b.	20,000	40,000	45,000	____	____
c.	(90,000)	50,000	30,000	____	____
d.	60,000	(55,000)	40,000	____	____
e.	Same as (d), except the distribution of $40,000 is made on June 30 and the corporation uses the calendar year for tax purposes.			____	____

26. Chris, the sole shareholder of Cardinal Corporation, had a basis of $10,000 in the stock in Cardinal Corporation that he sold to Terry on July 30, 1993, for $60,000. Cardinal had accumulated E & P of $25,000 on January 1, 1993, and current E & P (for 1993) of $20,000. During 1993, Cardinal Corporation made the following distributions: $40,000 cash to Chris on July 1, 1993, and $40,000 cash to Terry on December 30, 1993. How will the distributions be taxed to Chris and to Terry? What gain will Chris recognize on the sale of his stock to Terry?

27. Thrush Corporation had accumulated E & P of $20,000 at the beginning of the current tax year. During the current tax year, it had current E & P of $30,000. At the end of the year, it distributed cash of $70,000 to its sole shareholder, Yoon. What is Thrush Corporation's E & P at the end of the year?

28. Indicate in each of the following independent situations the effect on taxable income and E & P, stating the amount of any increase (or decrease) as a result of the transaction. (In determining the effect on E & P, assume E & P has already been increased by current taxable income.)

Transaction	Taxable Income Increase (Decrease)	E & P Increase (Decrease)
a. Receipt of $15,000 tax-exempt income	______	______
b. Payment of $15,150 Federal income taxes	______	______
c. Collection of $100,000 on life insurance policy on corporate president	______	______
d. Charitable contribution, $30,000, with $20,000 allowable as a deduction in the current tax year	______	______
e. Deduction of remaining $10,000 charitable contribution in succeeding year	______	______
f. Realized gain on involuntary conversion of $200,000 ($30,000 of gain is recognized)	______	______

29. Indicate in each of the following independent situations the effect on taxable income and E & P, stating the amount of any increase (or decrease) as a result of the transaction. (In determining the effect on E & P, assume E & P has already been increased by current taxable income.)

Transaction	Taxable Income Increase (Decrease)	E & P Increase (Decrease)
a. Intangible drilling costs incurred on January 1 of the current year and deductible from current taxable income in the amount of $50,000	______	______
b. Sale of unimproved real estate, basis of $200,000, fair market value of $800,000 (no election out of installment method; payments in year of sale total $40,000)	______	______
c. Accelerated depreciation of $70,000 (straight-line would have been $40,000)	______	______
d. Sale of equipment to 100% owned corporation (adjusted basis was $120,000 and selling price was $50,000)	______	______

30. A corporation sells property (basis of $50,000) to its sole shareholder for $10,000 on December 30, 1993. Prior to this transaction, the corporation's E & P account was $45,000. The corporation also distributes cash of $10,000 to its sole shareholder on December 31, 1993. Assuming no other transactions occurred that affected E & P for 1993, how will the shareholder report the $10,000 distribution? The shareholder has a basis of $20,000 in his stock in the corporation.

31. Redbird Corporation sells property, adjusted basis of $200,000, fair market value of $180,000, to its sole shareholder for $160,000. How much loss can Redbird deduct as

a result of this transaction? What is the effect on the corporation's E & P for the year of sale?

32. Brown Corporation, with E & P of $300,000, distributes property with a fair market value of $70,000, adjusted tax basis of $100,000, to Black, a corporate shareholder. The property is subject to a liability of $15,000, which Black assumes.

    a. What is the amount of dividend income to Black?
    b. What is Black's basis in the property received?
    c. How does the distribution affect Brown Corporation's E & P account?

33. Green Corporation owns 15% of the stock of Gray Corporation. Gray Corporation, with E & P of $80,000 on December 20, 1993, distributes land with a fair market value of $30,000 and a basis of $60,000 to Green Corporation. The land is subject to a liability of $20,000, which Green Corporation assumes.

    a. How is Green Corporation taxed on the distribution?
    b. What is Gray Corporation's E & P after the distribution?

34. A corporation distributes land (basis of $30,000 and fair market value of $90,000) to its sole shareholder, Antonio. The property is subject to a liability of $98,000, which Antonio assumes. The corporation has E & P of $50,000 prior to the distribution.

    a. What gain does the corporation recognize on the distribution?
    b. What is the amount of Antonio's dividend income on the distribution?

35. At the beginning of its taxable year 1993, White Corporation had E & P of $50,000. White sold an asset at a loss of $50,000 on June 30, 1993. It incurred a total deficit of $55,000 for the calendar year 1993. Assume White Corporation made a distribution of $15,000 to its sole shareholder, Wes, on July 1, 1993. How will Wes be taxed on the $15,000?

36. The stock in Black Corporation is owned equally by Pat and Brown Corporation. On January 1, 1993, Black had a deficit of $50,000. Its current E & P (for taxable year 1993) was $35,000. In 1993, Black distributed cash of $15,000 to both Pat and Brown Corporation. How will Pat and Brown Corporation be taxed on the distribution? What will be the accumulated E & P of Black Corporation at the end of 1993?

37. Brown Corporation declared a dividend permitting its shareholders to elect to receive $10 per share or 2 additional shares of stock in the corporation for every 10 shares currently held. Brown has only common stock outstanding. Stock in Brown Corporation has a fair market value of $50 per share. All shareholders elect to receive stock. Will the shareholders have any taxable gain on the receipt of the stock?

38. Robin Corporation has two classes of common stock outstanding, Class A and Class B. During the current year, Robin distributed a preferred stock dividend to the Class A shareholders and a common stock dividend to the Class B shareholders. Is either of these distributions a taxable dividend to the shareholders? Explain.

39. Isabella paid $30,000 for 15 shares of stock in White Corporation five years ago. In November 1992, she received a nontaxable stock dividend of 5 additional shares in White Corporation. She sells the 5 shares in March 1993 for $10,000. What is her gain, and how is it taxed?

40. Bluejay Corporation declares a nontaxable dividend payable in rights to subscribe to common stock. One right and $60 entitle the holder to subscribe to one share of stock. One right is issued for each share of stock owned. Carmen, a shareholder, owns 100 shares of stock that she purchased two years ago for $3,000. At the date of distribution of the rights, the market value of the stock was $80 per share, and the market value of the rights was $20 per right. Carmen received 100 rights. She exercises 60 rights and purchases 60 additional shares of stock. She sells the remaining 40 rights for $750. What are the tax consequences of these transactions to Carmen?

41. Brown Corporation has 400 shares of common stock outstanding. Bob owns 150 of the shares, Bob's mother owns 50 shares, Bob's brother owns 40 shares, and Bob's son owns 60 shares. Black Corporation owns 50 shares. Bob owns 70% of the stock in Black Corporation.

a. In applying the stock attribution rules of § 318, how many shares does Bob own in Brown Corporation?
b. Assume Bob owns only 30% of Black Corporation. How many shares does Bob own, directly or indirectly, in Brown Corporation?
c. Assume Bob owns 30% of BZ Partnership. The partnership owns 50 shares in Brown Corporation. How many shares does Bob own in Brown Corporation assuming the same facts as in (a) above?

42. Robin Corporation has 1,000 shares of common stock outstanding. The shares are owned by unrelated shareholders as follows: Leo, 400 shares; Lori, 400 shares; and Lana, 200 shares. The corporation redeems 100 shares of the stock owned by Lana for $45,000. Lana paid $100 per share for her stock two years ago. The E & P of Robin Corporation was $400,000 on the date of redemption. What is the tax effect to Lana of the redemption?

43. In Problem 42, assume Leo is the father of Lana. How would this affect the tax status of the redemption? What if Leo were Lana's brother instead of her father?

44. Hal and Hans own all the stock in Green Corporation. Each has a basis of $50,000 in his 50 shares. Green Corporation has accumulated E & P of $360,000. Hal wishes to retire in the current year and wants to sell his stock for $150,000, the fair market value. Hans would like to purchase Hal's shares and, thus, become the sole shareholder in Green Corporation, but Hans is short of funds. What are the tax consequences to Hal, to Hans, and to Green Corporation under the following circumstances?

a. Green Corporation distributes cash of $150,000 to Hans, and he uses the cash to purchase Hal's shares.
b. Green Corporation redeems all of Hal's shares for $150,000.

45. The adjusted gross estate of Dave, decedent, is $1,000,000. Dave's estate will incur death taxes and funeral and administration expenses of $120,000. Dave's gross estate includes stock in Redbird Corporation (fair market value of $120,000, basis to Dave of $10,000) and stock in Bluebird Corporation (fair market value of $200,000, basis to Dave of $50,000). Dave owned 25% of the stock in Redbird Corporation and 40% of the stock in Bluebird Corporation. If Redbird redeems all of Dave's stock from his estate, will the redemption qualify under § 303? Why or why not?

46. The gross estate of Debra, decedent, includes stock in Black Corporation and White Corporation valued at $150,000 and $250,000, respectively. Debra's adjusted gross estate is $900,000. She owned 30% of the Black stock and 60% of the White stock. Death taxes and funeral and administration expenses for Debra's estate were $100,000. Debra had a basis of $60,000 in the Black stock and $90,000 in the White stock. What are the tax consequences to Debra's estate if Black Corporation redeems one-third of her stock for $50,000 and White Corporation redeems one-fifth of her stock for $50,000?

47. On January 1, 1993, Green Corporation had paid-in capital of $60,000 and E & P of $90,000. Green had no current E & P (for 1993) as its deductions equaled its income for 1993. The 450 shares in Green Corporation are owned equally by Andre, Beth, and Carol, unrelated individuals, each of whom paid $10,000 in 1985 for their stock in Green. On June 1, 1993, Green Corporation redeemed all Carol's stock for $100,000 in a redemption that qualified under § 302(b)(3). On November 10, 1993, Green Corporation paid $45,000 to Andre and $45,000 to Beth. What are the tax consequences of the stock redemption to Carol, and the cash distributions to Andre and Beth?

48. Wren Corporation has 500 shares of stock outstanding. It redeems 50 shares for $90,000 when it has paid-in capital of $300,000 and E & P of $400,000. What is the reduction in the E & P of Wren Corporation as a result of the redemption?

Chapter

Corporations: Distributions in Complete Liquidation and an Overview of Reorganizations

Objectives

Contrast property dividends and stock redemptions with distributions in complete liquidation of a corporation.

Review the tax effect on the shareholders of a corporation being liquidated.

Review the tax effect of a complete liquidation on the corporation being liquidated.

Recognize the tax planning opportunities available to minimize the income tax in the complete liquidation of a corporation.

Present an overview of corporate reorganizations.

Outline

LIQUIDATIONS—IN GENERAL

When a stock redemption occurs or a dividend is distributed, the assumption usually is that the corporation will continue as a separate entity. With a complete liquidation, corporate existence terminates. A complete liquidation, like a qualified stock redemption, receives exchange treatment. However, the tax effects of a liquidation vary somewhat from those of a stock redemption.

The Liquidation Process

A complete liquidation exists for tax purposes when a corporation ceases to be a going concern. The corporation continues solely to wind up affairs, pay debts, and distribute any remaining assets to shareholders.[1] Legal dissolution under state law is not required for the liquidation to be complete for tax purposes. A transaction will be treated as a liquidation even if the corporation retains a nominal amount of assets to pay remaining debts and preserve its legal status.[2]

A liquidation may occur for several reasons. The corporate business may have been unsuccessful. But even when a business has been profitable, the shareholders may nonetheless decide to terminate the corporation to acquire its assets.

A liquidation occurs when another person or corporation wants to purchase the assets of the corporation. The purchaser may buy the stock of the shareholders and then liquidate the corporation to acquire the assets. On the other hand, the purchaser may buy the assets directly from the corporation. After the assets are sold, the corporation distributes the sales proceeds to its shareholders and liquidates. The different means used to liquidate a corporation produce varying tax results.

Liquidations and Other Distributions Compared

A property distribution, whether in the form of a dividend or a stock redemption, produces gain (but not loss) to the distributing corporation. For the shareholder, the fair market value of a property dividend produces ordinary income to the extent of the corporation's E & P. On the other hand, a stock redemption qualifying under § 302 or § 303 results in exchange treatment.

The tax effects to the corporation in a complete liquidation are similar to those in a stock redemption in that a liquidation also yields exchange treatment. Still a complete liquidation produces somewhat different tax consequences. With certain exceptions, a liquidating corporation recognizes gain *and* loss upon distribution of its assets. The shareholders receive exchange treatment on receipt of the property from the liquidating corporation. The distribution of assets is treated as payment for the shareholder's stock and results in either a gain or a loss.

Liquidations and stock redemptions parallel each other as to the effect of E & P. For the corporation undergoing liquidation, E & P has no tax impact on the gain or loss to be recognized by the shareholders. Section 301 (governing dividend distributions) specifically does not apply to complete liquidations.[3]

1. Reg. § 1.332–2(c).
2. Rev.Rul. 54–518, 1954–2 C.B. 142.
3. § 331(b).

EXAMPLE 1

Green Corporation, with E & P of $40,000, makes a cash distribution of $50,000 to its sole shareholder. Assume the shareholder's basis in the Green stock is $20,000 and the stock is held as an investment. If the distribution is not in complete liquidation or if it does not qualify as a stock redemption, the shareholder recognizes dividend income of $40,000 (the amount of Green's E & P) and treats the remaining $10,000 of the distribution as a return of capital. If the distribution is pursuant to a complete liquidation or qualifies as a stock redemption, the shareholder has a recognized capital gain of $30,000 [$50,000 (the amount of the distribution) – $20,000 (the basis in the stock)]. In the latter case, Green Corporation's E & P is of no consequence to the tax result. ◆

In the event the distribution results in a *loss* to the shareholder, an important distinction can exist between stock redemptions and liquidations. The distinction arises because § 267 (disallowance of losses between related parties) applies to stock redemptions but generally not to liquidations.

EXAMPLE 2

The stock of Robin Corporation is owned equally by three brothers, Rex, Sam, and Ted. When Ted's basis in his stock investment is $40,000, the corporation distributes $30,000 to him in cancellation of all his shares. If the distribution is a stock redemption, the $10,000 realized loss is not recognized. Ted and Robin Corporation are related parties because Ted is deemed to own more than 50% in value of the corporation's outstanding stock. Ted's direct ownership is limited to 33 ⅓%, but through his brothers, he owns indirectly another 66 ⅔% for a total of 100%. If the distribution qualifies as a complete liquidation, Ted's $10,000 realized loss is recognizable. ◆

With reference to the basis of noncash property received from the corporation, the rules governing liquidations and stock redemptions are identical. Section 334(a) specifies that the basis of such property distributed in a complete liquidation under § 331 shall be the fair market value on the date of distribution.

The tax consequences of a complete liquidation of a corporation are examined in this chapter from the standpoint of the effect on the distributing corporation and on the shareholder. Tax rules differ when a controlled subsidiary is liquidated. Thus, the rules relating to the liquidation of a controlled subsidiary receive separate treatment.

LIQUIDATIONS—EFFECT ON THE DISTRIBUTING CORPORATION

For a corporation in the process of complete liquidation, §§ 336 and 337 control the tax results. The general rules relating to complete liquidations are covered in § 336, where gain or loss is recognized to the distributing corporation. Loss is not recognized, however, for certain distributions of disqualified property and some distributions to related shareholders. Under § 337, a subsidiary corporation does not recognize gain or loss for distributions to a parent corporation that owns 80 percent or more of the stock of the subsidiary.

Background

Originally, a corporate distribution of property, whether a liquidating or a nonliquidating distribution, produced neither gain nor loss to the distributing corporation. This nonrecognition concept was referred to as the *General Utilities* doctrine.[4] Over the years, however, statutory and judicial modifications and interpretations significantly increased the number of recognition situations. For example, depreciation and the investment tax credit were recaptured on distributed assets. Further, under the tax benefit rule, a corporation had to include in income any assets distributed to the shareholders for which it had previously claimed a deduction. In addition, the assignment of income doctrine was applied to distributions in liquidation and to sales by the liquidating corporation. Gain resulted from the distribution or sale of LIFO inventory and installment notes receivable. The sale of inventory produced income to the corporation unless the inventory was sold in bulk to one person in one transaction. Due to the many modifications, a liquidating corporation was not shielded from recognition of *all* income.

With the many statutory and judicial inroads, not much was left of the *General Utilities* doctrine when it was repealed in 1986. Only a few transfers still insulated the liquidating corporation from a recognition result. The protected transfers included distributions in kind and sale of investment assets (e.g., marketable securities and land), distributions in kind and bulk sales of non-LIFO inventory, and the § 1231 element for assets used in a trade or business. With the repeal of the *General Utilities* doctrine, a liquidating corporation, as a general rule, recognizes all gains and most losses on distributions of property.

General Rule

Section 336 provides that a liquidating corporation recognizes gain or loss on the distribution of property in complete liquidation. The property is treated as if it were sold to the distributee at the fair market value. Section 336, which repealed the *General Utilities* doctrine, strengthens the notion of double taxation that is inherent in operating a business in the corporate form. As a result, liquidating distributions are subject to tax at both the corporate level and the shareholder level.

When property distributed in a complete liquidation is subject to a liability of the liquidating corporation, the deemed fair market value of that property cannot be less than the amount of the liability.

EXAMPLE 3

As part of a complete liquidation, Warbler Corporation distributes to its shareholders land held as an investment (basis of $200,000, fair market value of $300,000). The land is subject to a liability of $350,000. Warbler Corporation has a gain of $150,000 on the distribution. ◆

Limitation on Losses. As a general rule, losses on the distribution of property in a complete liquidation are recognized. There are two exceptions, however. The first exception applies to certain distributions to related parties as defined under § 267. The second exception prevents a loss deduction on certain distributions of property with a built-in loss that was contributed to the corporation shortly before the adoption of a plan of liquidation. In this instance, the built-in loss may be disallowed as a deduction upon liquidation even if the distribution is to an unrelated party.

Because the abolition of the *General Utilities* doctrine opens the door for recognition of losses in a liquidation, Congress was concerned that taxpayers

4. The doctrine was attributed to the 1935 Supreme Court decision in *General Utilities & Operating Co. v. Helvering,* 36–1 USTC ¶9012, 16 AFTR 1126, 56 S.Ct. 185 (USSC, 1935).

might attempt to create artificial losses at the corporate level. Taxpayers could accomplish this by contributing property with built-in losses to the corporation before a liquidation. Recall from Chapter 17 that in § 351 transfers (nontaxable transfers to a corporation in exchange for stock when the transferor is in control of the corporation) and contributions to capital, the transferor's income tax basis carries over to the transferee corporation. Thus, a taxpayer might transfer high-basis, low–fair market value property to a corporation contemplating liquidation in the hope that the built-in losses would neutralize expected gains from appreciated property distributed or sold in the liquidation process.

Section 336(d) closes the possibility of utilizing built-in losses to neutralize the gain upon liquidation. The deductibility of losses is limited in related-party situations (those covered by § 267) and in certain sales and distributions of built-in loss property. A corporation and a shareholder are related parties if the shareholder owns (directly or indirectly) more than 50 percent in value of the corporation's outstanding stock.

In a related-party situation, losses are disallowed on distributions to the related parties in either of the following cases: (1) the distribution is *not* pro rata or (2) the property distributed is *disqualified property.* Disqualified property is property acquired by the liquidating corporation in a § 351 transaction or as a contribution to capital during a five-year period ending on the date of the distribution.

EXAMPLE 4

Bluebird Corporation's stock is held equally by three brothers. One year before Bluebird's liquidation, the shareholders transfer property (basis of $150,000, fair market value of $100,000) to Bluebird Corporation in return for stock (a § 351 transaction). In liquidation, the corporation transfers the property (still worth $100,000) to the brothers. Because § 267 applies (each brother owns directly and indirectly 100% of the stock) and disqualified property is involved, none of the $50,000 realized loss is recognized by Bluebird Corporation. ◆

EXAMPLE 5

Assume that Bluebird Corporation stock is owned by Lee and Terry, who are unrelated. Lee owns 80% and Terry owns 20% of the stock in the corporation. Bluebird has the following assets (none of which was acquired in a § 351 transaction or as a contribution to capital) that are distributed in complete liquidation of the corporation:

	Adjusted Basis	Fair Market Value
Cash	$600,000	$600,000
Equipment	150,000	200,000
Building	400,000	200,000

Assume Bluebird Corporation distributes the equipment to Terry and the cash and the building to Lee. Bluebird recognizes a gain of $50,000 on the distribution of the equipment. The loss of $200,000 on the building will be disallowed. This is because the distribution is not pro rata, and the loss property is distributed to a related party. ◆

EXAMPLE 6

Assume that Bluebird Corporation in Example 5 distributed the cash and equipment to Lee and the building to Terry. Again, Bluebird recognizes the $50,000 gain on the equipment. However, it can now recognize the $200,000 loss on the building. The loss property is not distributed to a related party since Terry does not own more than 50% of the stock in Bluebird Corporation. ◆

The loss limitation provisions are extended to distributions to *unrelated* parties when loss property is transferred to a corporation shortly before the corporation is liquidated. This second exception to the general rule that a corporation can recognize losses on a complete liquidation is imposed to prevent the doubling of losses, or the so-called *stuffing* of a corporation.

EXAMPLE 7

Nora, a shareholder in White Corporation, transfers property with a basis of $10,000, fair market value of $3,000, to the corporation in a transaction that qualifies under § 351. Nora's basis in the additional stock acquired in White Corporation, in exchange for the property, is $10,000. White Corporation's basis in the property also is $10,000. A few months after the transfer, White Corporation adopts a plan of complete liquidation. Upon liquidation, White distributes the property to Nora. If White were permitted a loss deduction of $7,000, there would be a double loss because Nora would also recognize a loss of $7,000 upon receipt of the property [$10,000 (basis in Nora's stock) – $3,000 (fair market value of the property)]. To prevent the doubling of losses, § 336(d) prohibits White Corporation from taking a loss on the distribution even if Nora is an unrelated party. ◆

Losses are disallowed on a distribution to shareholders who are not related parties when the property distributed was acquired in a § 351 transaction or as a contribution to capital. Furthermore, the property must have been contributed as part of a plan whose principal purpose was to recognize loss by the corporation in connection with the liquidation. Such a purpose will be presumed if the transfer occurs within two years of the adoption of the liquidation plan.

The prohibition against a loss deduction on distributions to unrelated parties is broader than the first exception, which disallows losses on certain distributions to related parties. The prohibition applies regardless of whether the shareholder is a related party under § 267. At the same time, however, the prohibition is narrower than the first exception since it applies only to property that had a built-in loss upon acquisition by the corporation and only as to the amount of the built-in loss.

EXAMPLE 8

On January 2, 1993, in a transaction that qualifies under § 351, Brown Corporation acquires property with a basis of $10,000, fair market value of $3,000. Brown adopts a plan of liquidation on July 1, 1993, and distributes the property to Rick, an unrelated party, on November 10, 1993, when the property is worth $1,000. Brown Corporation can recognize a loss of $2,000, the difference between the value of the property on the date of acquisition and the fair market value of the property on the date of distribution. Only the built-in loss of $7,000 [$10,000 (basis) – $3,000 (fair market value on date of acquisition)] is disallowed. ◆

EXAMPLE 9

Assume the property in Example 8 had a fair market value of $12,000 on the date Brown Corporation acquired it. However, the property has a fair market value of only $2,000 when Brown distributes the property upon the complete liquidation of the corporation. If the distribution is to an unrelated shareholder, Brown will recognize the entire $8,000 loss [$10,000 (basis) – $2,000 (fair market value on date of distribution)]. However, if the distribution is to a related party, Brown cannot recognize any of the loss because the property is disqualified property (i.e., property acquired in a § 351 transaction within five years of the distribution). When the distribution is to a related party, the loss is disallowed even though the decline in value occurred entirely during the period the corporation held the property. In addition, the loss limitation applies even though the property's fair market value was more than its basis when it was transferred to the corporation. However, if the property is distributed to an unrelated party, only the built-in loss (i.e., the loss that occurred prior to the transfer to the corporation) is disallowed. ◆

For loss recognition purposes in a liquidation, the basis of disqualified property that is later sold or distributed to an unrelated party is reduced by the amount the property's basis on the contribution date exceeds the property's fair market value on that date.[5] Any subsequent decline in value to the point of the liquidating distribution results in a deductible loss as long as the property is not distributed to a related party.

The loss limitation can apply regardless of how long the corporation has held the property prior to liquidation. If the property is held for two years or less, a tax avoidance purpose is presumed. Still, if there is a clear and substantial relationship between the contributed property and the business of the corporation, a loss will be permitted on the distribution of the property to an unrelated party. When there was a business reason for transferring the loss property to the liquidating corporation, a loss will also be permitted on the sale of the property.

EXAMPLE 10

Cardinal Corporation's stock is held 60% by Manuel and 40% by Jack. One year before Cardinal's liquidation, property (basis of $150,000, fair market value of $100,000) is transferred to the corporation as a contribution to capital. There is no business reason for the transfer. In liquidation, Cardinal transfers the property (now with a fair market value of $90,000) to Jack. Because the distribution is to an unrelated party, the basis is reduced to $100,000 for liquidation purposes [$150,000 (carryover basis under § 362) – $50,000 (difference between carryover basis of $150,000 and fair market value of $100,000)]. A loss of $10,000 ($100,000 – $90,000) can be recognized. If the property is distributed to Manuel, a related party, even the $10,000 loss is disallowed. ◆

EXAMPLE 11

Assume in Example 10, that the property is transferred to Cardinal Corporation because a bank required the additional capital investment as a condition to making a loan to the corporation. Because there is a business purpose for the transfer, presumably the loss of $50,000 is recognized if the property is distributed to Jack in liquidation. If the property is distributed to Manuel, a related party, the loss is disallowed. ◆

Rules governing distributions of loss property by a liquidating corporation are summarized in Figure 19–1.

Expenses of Liquidation. A corporation may deduct the general expenses involved in liquidating as business expenses under § 162. Examples include the legal and accounting cost of drafting a liquidation plan and the cost of revoking the corporate charter. Liquidation expenses relating to the disposition of corporate assets are also deductible. Expenses relating to the sale of corporate assets, including a brokerage commission for the sale of real estate and a legal fee to clear title, are offset against the selling price of the assets.

EXAMPLE 12

During its liquidation, Wren Corporation incurs the following expenses:

General liquidation expenses	$12,000
Legal expenses incurred in distributing property	200
Sales commissions to sell inventory	3,000
Brokerage fee on sale of real estate	8,000

5. § 336(d)(2).

Wren can deduct $12,200 ($12,000 + $200). The $3,000 commission and the $8,000 brokerage fee are applied against the selling price of the inventory and the real estate. ◆

LIQUIDATIONS—EFFECT ON THE SHAREHOLDER

The tax consequences to the shareholders of a corporation in the process of liquidation are governed by the general rule under § 331 and two exceptions under §§ 332 and 338. Both exceptions relate to the liquidation of a subsidiary.

The General Rule under § 331

In the case of a complete liquidation, the general rule under § 331(a) provides for exchange treatment. Since § 1001(c) requires the recognition of gain or loss on the sale or exchange of property, the end result is to treat the shareholder as having sold his or her stock to the corporation being liquidated. The difference between the fair market value of the assets received from the corporation (less the

FIGURE 19–1
Distributions of Loss Property by a Liquidating Corporation

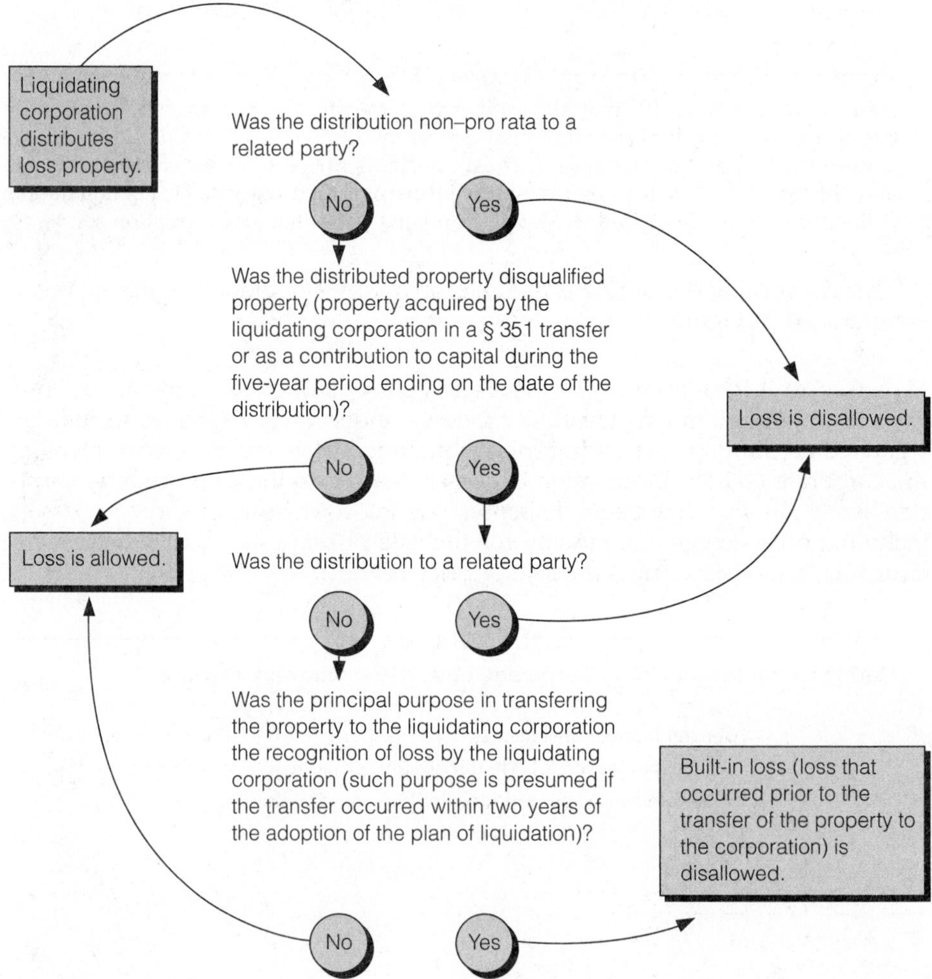

income tax paid by the corporation) and the adjusted basis of the stock surrendered is the amount of gain or loss recognized. If the stock is a capital asset in the hands of the shareholder, capital gain or loss results. The burden of proof is on the taxpayer to furnish evidence of the adjusted basis of the stock. In the absence of such evidence, the stock is deemed to have a zero basis, and the full amount of the liquidation proceeds becomes the amount of the gain recognized.[6]

Section 334(a) provides that under the general rule of § 331, the income tax basis to the shareholder of property received in a liquidation is the property's fair market value on the date of distribution. The rule follows the same approach taken with stock redemptions that qualify for exchange treatment.

Special Rule for Certain Installment Obligations

Section 453(h) provides some relief from the bunching of gain that occurs when a liquidating corporation sells its assets. The liquidating corporation must recognize all gain on such sales. The shareholders' gain on the receipt of notes obtained by the corporation on the sale of its assets may be deferred to the point of collection.[7] The shareholders must allocate their bases in the stock among the various assets received from the corporation.

EXAMPLE 13

After adopting a plan of complete liquidation, Black Corporation sells its only asset, unimproved land held as an investment. The land has appreciated in value and is sold to Ed (an unrelated party) for $100,000. Under the terms of the sale, Black Corporation receives cash of $25,000 and Ed's notes for the balance of $75,000. The notes are payable over 10 years ($7,500 per year) and carry a 9% rate of interest. Immediately after the sale, Black Corporation distributes the cash and notes to Earl, the sole shareholder. Earl has an adjusted basis of $20,000 in the Black stock, and the installment notes have a value equal to the face amount ($75,000). These transactions have the following tax result:

- Black Corporation recognizes gain on the sale of the land, measured by the difference between the $100,000 selling price and the basis Black had in the land.
- Earl may defer the gain on the receipt of the notes to the point of collection.
- Earl must allocate the adjusted basis in the stock ($20,000) between the cash and the installment notes. Using the relative fair market value approach, 25% [$25,000 (amount of cash)/$100,000 (total distribution)] of $20,000 (adjusted basis in the stock), or $5,000, is allocated to the cash, and 75% [$75,000 (FMV of notes)/$100,000 (total distribution)] of $20,000 (adjusted basis in the stock), or $15,000, is allocated to the notes.
- Earl must recognize $20,000 [$25,000 (cash received) – $5,000 (allocated basis of the cash)] in the year of the liquidation.
- Since Earl's gross profit on the notes is $60,000 [$75,000 (contract price) – $15,000 (allocated basis of the notes)], the gross profit percentage is 80% [$60,000 (gross profit)/$75,000 (contract price)]. Earl must report a gain of $6,000 [$7,500 (amount of note) × 80% (gross profit percentage)] on the collection of each note over the next 10 years. The interest element is accounted for separately. ◆

If the shareholder receives distributions in more than one taxable year, basis reallocations may require the filing of amended returns.[8]

6. *John Calderazzo*, 34 TCM 1, T.C.Memo. 1975–1.

7. Section 453(h) does not apply to the sale of inventory property and property held by the corporation primarily for sale to customers in the ordinary course of its trade or business unless such property is sold in bulk to one person.

8. § 453(h)(2). For an example of such a possibility, see the Finance Committee Report on H.R. 6883 (reported with amendments on September 26, 1980), the Installment Sales Revision Act of 1980.

Special rules apply if the installment obligations arise from sales between certain related parties.[9]

LIQUIDATIONS—PARENT-SUBSIDIARY SITUATIONS

Section 332 is an exception to the general rule that the shareholder recognizes gain or loss on a corporate liquidation. If a parent corporation liquidates a subsidiary corporation in which it owns at least 80 percent of the voting stock, no gain or loss is recognized for distributions to the parent.[10]

The requirements for applying § 332 are as follows:

- The parent must own at least 80 percent of the voting stock of the subsidiary and at least 80 percent of the total value of the subsidiary's stock.
- The subsidiary must distribute all of its property in complete redemption of all of its stock within the taxable year or within three years from the close of the tax year in which a plan was adopted and the first distribution occurred.
- The subsidiary must be solvent.[11]

If these requirements are met, § 332 becomes mandatory.

When a series of distributions occurs in the liquidation of a subsidiary corporation, the parent corporation must own the required amount of stock (at least 80 percent) on the date a plan of liquidation is adopted and at all times until all property has been distributed.[12] If the parent fails to qualify at any time, the provisions for nonrecognition of gain or loss do not apply to any distribution.

Tax Treatment When a Minority Interest Exists

A distribution to a minority shareholder in a § 332 liquidation is treated in the same manner as one made pursuant to a nonliquidating redemption. The distributing corporation recognizes gain (but not loss) on the property distributed to the minority shareholder.

EXAMPLE 14

The stock of Brown Corporation is held as follows: 80% by Black Corporation and 20% by Meg. Brown Corporation is liquidated on December 10, 1993, pursuant to a plan adopted on January 10, 1993. At the time of its liquidation, Brown has assets with a basis of $100,000 and fair market value of $500,000. Brown must recognize gain of $80,000 [($500,000 fair market value − $100,000 basis) × 20% minority interest]. The remaining gain of $320,000 is sheltered by § 337(a). ◆

The minority shareholder is subject to the general rule of § 331. Accordingly, the difference between the fair market value of the assets distributed and the basis of the minority shareholder's stock is the amount of gain or loss recognized. The tax basis of property received by the minority shareholder is the property's fair market value on the date of distribution.[13]

9. §§ 453(h)(1)(C) and (D). For this purpose, related parties are defined in § 1239(b).
10. § 332(a).
11. Reg. §§ 1.332–2(a) and (b).
12. The date of the adoption of a plan of complete liquidation could be crucial in determining whether § 332 applies. See, for example, *George L. Riggs, Inc.*, 64 T.C. 474 (1975).
13. § 334(a).

Indebtedness of Subsidiary to Parent

If a subsidiary satisfies a debt owed to the parent with appreciated property, it must recognize gain on the transaction unless § 332 applies. When § 332 applies, the subsidiary does not recognize gain or loss upon the transfer of properties to the parent. This is the case even if some properties are transferred to satisfy the subsidiary's indebtedness to the parent.[14]

EXAMPLE 15

Green Corporation owes $20,000 to its parent, Gray Corporation. It satisfies the obligation by transferring land worth $20,000 with a tax basis of $8,000. Normally, Green recognizes a gain of $12,000 on the transaction. However, if the transfer is made pursuant to a liquidation under § 332, Green does not recognize a gain. ◆

The special provision noted above will not apply to the parent corporation. The parent corporation recognizes realized gain or loss on the satisfaction of indebtedness, even if property is received during liquidation of the subsidiary.

EXAMPLE 16

Redbird Corporation purchased bonds of its subsidiary Bluebird at a discount. Upon liquidation of the subsidiary pursuant to § 332, Redbird receives payment in the face amount of the bonds. The transaction has no tax effect on Bluebird Corporation. However, Redbird Corporation recognizes gain in the amount of the difference between its basis in the bonds and the amount received in payment. ◆

If a parent corporation does not receive at least partial payment for its stock in a subsidiary corporation upon liquidation of the subsidiary, § 332 will not apply.[15] The parent corporation has a bad debt deduction for the difference between the value of any properties received from the subsidiary and its basis in the subsidiary debt.

If the subsidiary is insolvent, the parent corporation will also have a loss deduction for its worthless stock in the subsidiary. The loss is ordinary if more than 90 percent of the subsidiary's gross receipts for all tax years were from sources other than passive sources.[16] Otherwise, the loss is a capital loss.

EXAMPLE 17

Brown Corporation paid $100,000 for all the stock of Black Corporation 15 years ago. At present, Black has a deficit of $600,000 in E & P and is insolvent. If Brown liquidates Black, § 332 will not apply because Black is insolvent. Brown Corporation has a loss deduction for its worthless stock in Black Corporation. If more than 90% of Black's gross receipts for all tax years were from sources other than passive sources, the loss is ordinary. Otherwise, it is a capital loss. Assume Brown also loaned Black Corporation $50,000. Since the assets are not sufficient to pay the liability, Brown also has a loss on the note. Upon liquidation, the basis of Black's assets to Brown is the fair market value. Brown's loss is measured by the fair market value of Black's assets less the liabilities payable to third parties less Brown's basis in the Black stock and note. ◆

Basis of Property Received by the Parent Corporation—The General Rule of § 334(b)(1)

Unless a parent corporation makes an election under § 338, property received in a complete liquidation of its subsidiary under § 332 has the same basis it had in the hands of the subsidiary.[17] The parent's basis in stock of the liquidated

14. § 337(b).
15. Reg. § 1.332–2(b).
16. § 165(g) and Reg. § 1.165–5.
17. § 334(b)(1) and Reg. § 1.334–1(b).

subsidiary disappears. This is true even if some of the property is transferred to the parent in satisfaction of debt owed the parent by the subsidiary.

EXAMPLE 18

Wren, the parent corporation, has a basis of $20,000 in stock in Robin Corporation, a subsidiary in which it owns 85% of all classes of stock. Wren Corporation purchased the stock of Robin Corporation 10 years ago. In the current year, Wren liquidates Robin Corporation and acquires assets with a fair market value of $50,000 and a tax basis to Robin of $40,000. Wren Corporation has a basis of $40,000 in the assets, with a potential gain upon sale of $10,000. Wren's original $20,000 basis in Robin's stock disappears. ◆

EXAMPLE 19

White Corporation has a basis of $60,000 in stock in Gray Corporation, a subsidiary acquired 10 years ago. It liquidates Gray Corporation and receives assets with a fair market value of $50,000 and a tax basis to Gray of $40,000. White Corporation has a basis of $40,000 in the assets it acquired from Gray. If it sells the assets for $50,000, it has a gain of $10,000 in spite of the fact that its basis in the Gray stock was $60,000. White's loss will never be recognized. ◆

Because the parent corporation takes the subsidiary's basis in its assets, the carryover rules of § 381 apply. The parent acquires a net operating loss of the subsidiary, any investment credit carryover, capital loss carryover, and a carryover of the subsidiary's E & P. Section 381 applies to most tax-free reorganizations and to a tax-free liquidation under § 332 if the subsidiary's bases in its assets carry over to the parent.

Basis of Property Received by the Parent Corporation—The Exception of § 338

Background. Under the general rule of § 332(b)(1), problems developed when a subsidiary was liquidated shortly after acquisition by a parent corporation.

1. When the basis of the subsidiary's assets was more than the purchase price of the stock, the parent received a step-up in basis in the assets at no tax cost. If, for example, the parent paid $100,000 for the subsidiary's stock and the basis of the assets transferred to the parent was $150,000, the parent enjoyed a $50,000 benefit without any gain recognition. The $50,000 increase in basis of the subsidiary's assets could have led to additional depreciation deductions and either more loss or less gain upon the later disposition of the assets by the parent.
2. If the basis of the subsidiary's assets was below the purchase price of the stock, the parent suffered a step-down in basis in the assets with no attendant tax benefit. Return to Example 19, but change the situation slightly so that the subsidiary's stock is not held for 10 years. Instead, the subsidiary is liquidated shortly after acquisition. The basic inequity of the "no loss" situation now develops. But why would a corporation pay more for the stock in another corporation than the latter's basis in the assets? One reason is that the basis of the assets is not necessarily related to the fair market value. The acquiring corporation may not have the option of purchasing the assets of the acquired corporation rather than its stock. The shareholders in the acquired corporation may prefer to sell their stock rather than the assets of the corporation.

In the landmark decision of *Kimbell-Diamond Milling Co. v. Comm.*,[18] the courts finally resolved these problems. When a parent corporation liquidates a subsidiary shortly after acquiring its stock, the parent is really purchasing the assets of the subsidiary. Consequently, the basis of the assets should be the cost of the stock. Known as the *single transaction* approach, the basis determination is not made under the general rule of § 334(b)(1). The *Kimbell-Diamond* problem ultimately led to the enactment of § 338.

Requirements for Application. Section 338 provides that an acquiring corporation may *elect* to treat the acquisition of stock in an acquired corporation as a purchase of the acquired corporation's assets. The election must be made by the fifteenth day of the ninth month beginning after the month in which the qualified stock purchase occurs. The election is irrevocable.

A purchasing corporation makes a *qualified stock purchase* if it acquires at least 80 percent of the voting power and at least 80 percent of the value of the acquired corporation within a 12-month period beginning with the first purchase of stock. The stock must be acquired in a taxable transaction (i.e., § 351 and other nonrecognition provisions do not apply). An acquisition of stock by any member of an affiliated group, including the purchasing corporation, is considered to be an acquisition by the purchasing corporation.

Tax Consequences. If the parent makes a qualified election under § 338, the purchasing corporation has a basis in the subsidiary's assets equal to its basis in the subsidiary's stock. The subsidiary need not be liquidated.

Under § 338, the acquired corporation is deemed to have sold its assets for an amount equal to the purchasing corporation's grossed-up basis in the subsidiary's stock. This must be adjusted for liabilities of the subsidiary corporation. The grossed-up basis is the basis in the subsidiary stock multiplied by a fraction. The numerator of the fraction is 100 percent. The denominator is the percentage of value of the subsidiary's stock held by the purchasing corporation on the acquisition date.[19] The amount is allocated among the subsidiary's assets using the residual method described below.

The election of § 338 produces gain or loss to the subsidiary being purchased. The subsidiary is treated as having sold all of its assets at the close of the acquisition date in a single transaction at the fair market value.[20] The subsidiary is then treated as a new corporation that purchased all of the assets as of the beginning of the day after the acquisition date.

Example 20

White Corporation has an $800,000 basis in its assets and liabilities totaling $500,000. It has E & P of $200,000 and assets with a fair market value of $2,000,000. Black Corporation purchases 80% of the stock of White on March 10, 1993, for $1,200,000 [($2,000,000 less liabilities of $500,000) × 80%]. Because the purchase price of the White stock exceeds White's basis in its assets, and to eliminate White's E & P, Black may choose to elect § 338 treatment by December 15, 1993. White need not be liquidated for § 338 to apply. If Black elects § 338, the tax consequences are as follows:

- White is deemed to have sold its assets for an amount equal to the grossed-up basis in the White stock.

---

18. 14 T.C. 74 (1950), *aff'd.* in 51–1 USTC ¶9201, 40 AFTR 328, 187 F.2d 718 (CA–5, 1951), *cert. den.* 72 S.Ct. 50 (USSC, 1951).

19. § 338(b)(4).

20. § 338(a).

- The grossed-up basis in the White stock is computed as follows: the basis of the White stock is multiplied by a fraction, with 100% the numerator and 80% the denominator. The basis of the White stock, $1,200,000, is multiplied by 100/80. The result is $1,500,000, which is adjusted for White's liabilities of $500,000 for a deemed selling price of $2,000,000.
- The selling price of $2,000,000 less the basis of White's assets of $800,000 produces a recognized gain to White Corporation of $1,200,000. ◆

In that Black did not purchase 100 percent of the White stock, different results occur depending on whether or not White is liquidated. If White is not liquidated, it is treated as a new corporation as of March 11, 1993. The basis of White's assets is $2,000,000, and the E & P is eliminated. If White Corporation is liquidated, Black Corporation has a basis of $1,600,000 in White's assets, representing 80 percent of White's assets. White's E & P does not carry over to Black.

Note the results of the § 338 election. The assets of White Corporation receive a stepped-up basis but at a substantial tax cost. White Corporation must recognize all of its realized gain. Any tax liability White incurs on its recognized gain, causes Black Corporation to reduce the amount paid for White's assets.

Allocation of Purchase Price. The new stepped-up basis of the assets of a subsidiary when a § 338 election is in effect is allocated among the assets by use of the *residual method.*[21] The amount of the purchase price that exceeds the aggregate fair market values of the tangible and identifiable intangible assets must be allocated to goodwill or going concern value. Neither goodwill nor going concern value can be amortized for tax purposes.

EXAMPLE 21

For $4,000,000, Black Corporation acquires all of the stock of White Corporation and elects to liquidate under § 338. If the fair market value of White's physical assets is $3,500,000, Black must allocate $500,000 of the purchase price either to goodwill or to going concern value. ◆

In Example 21, none of the purchase price would have to be allocated to goodwill or going concern value if the physical assets were worth $4,000,000. However, the burden of proof of showing no residual amount is on the taxpayer and not on the IRS.

Consistency Requirement. A consistency requirement under § 338 prevents the acquiring corporation from choosing which of the acquired subsidiary corporations are to be covered by the § 338 election. The consistency period is a one-year period before and after the acquisition of the subsidiary. During this time, the parent is deemed to have made an election under § 338 if it makes a direct purchase of assets from the subsidiary or from an affiliate of the subsidiary.[22] Exceptions exist, such as for asset purchases in the ordinary course of a business.

EXAMPLE 22

Black Corporation purchases all of the stock of White Corporation within a 12-month period. During that 12-month period, Black purchases all of the assets of Gray Corporation, a subsidiary of White Corporation. Black is deemed to have made a § 338 election as to White Corporation even though it did not actually make such an election. ◆

21. § 1060.
22. § 338(e).

In addition, during the consistency period, tax treatment of acquisitions of stock of two or more other companies that are members of an affiliated group must be consistent.[23]

Example 23

Black Corporation purchases all the stock in White Corporation and makes a timely election under § 338. If White Corporation owns all the stock in Gray Corporation, the § 338 election also applies to Gray. This results even if Black Corporation never made an election as to Gray. If Black does not make an election as to White Corporation, however, it cannot make the election as to Gray Corporation. ◆

A Comparison of §§ 334(b)(1) and 338. Under the general rule of § 334(b)(1), a subsidiary's basis in its assets carries over to the parent corporation upon liquidation. A subsidiary liquidation under §§ 332 and 334(b)(1) is completely tax-free (except for any minority interest). A liquidation under § 338, while tax-free to the parent, is taxable to the subsidiary. The subsidiary assets will have a stepped-up basis.

If a liquidation under § 332 qualifies under § 338 and a timely election is made, the holding period of the property received by the parent corporation begins on the date the parent acquired the subsidiary's stock. If the corporation is not liquidated, the holding period of the assets to the subsidiary starts anew on the day after the acquisition date.[24] In a liquidation under § 334(b)(1), the holding period of the subsidiary carries over to the parent.

A Summary of the Liquidation Rules. Sections 336, 337, and 338 set out the tax effects to a corporation that is liquidated. Section 336 provides the general rule that gain or loss is recognized. There are exceptions for loss recognition when distributions are not made pro rata to related parties or when disqualified property is distributed.

Section 337 applies when a subsidiary corporation in which the parent has at least an 80 percent stock ownership is liquidated. Under § 337, the subsidiary corporation will not recognize gain or loss on distributions to the parent. When distributions are made to a minority interest, § 336 provides that the subsidiary corporation will recognize gain, but not loss. Section 338 sets out an exception to § 337. If control (at least 80 percent) of a subsidiary corporation is acquired within a 12-month period, an election can be made under § 338. In that event, the subsidiary corporation recognizes gain or loss.

Sections 331 and 332 set out the tax effects of a corporate liquidation to the shareholders. Section 331 provides the general rule that the shareholders have gain or loss on the liquidation. Section 332 applies to a parent corporation shareholder when § 337 is applicable. Under § 332, a parent corporation shareholder does not recognize gain or loss upon liquidation of its subsidiary.

Sections 334 and 338 provide the rules governing basis of assets acquired in a corporate liquidation. Section 334 provides the general rule that basis of the acquired assets will be the fair market value of the assets. An exception applies when a subsidiary is liquidated. A parent corporation holding at least an 80 percent stock ownership in the subsidiary will have a carryover basis in the subsidiary's assets. Section 338 applies only when an election is made in connection with the acquisition of at least an 80 percent interest in a subsidiary

23. § 338(f).

24. § 338(a).

corporation within a 12-month period. When an election is made under § 338, the basis of the assets of the subsidiary is the basis the parent had in the stock of the subsidiary.

The rules regarding liquidations are summarized in Concept Summary 19–1.

CORPORATE REORGANIZATIONS

A corporate combination or realignment, usually referred to as a reorganization, can be either a taxable or a nontaxable transaction. Assuming a business combination is taxable, § 1001 of the Code provides that the seller's gain or loss is measured by the difference between the amount realized and the basis of property surrendered. The purchaser's basis for the property received is the amount paid for the property, and the holding period begins on the date of purchase.

Certain exchanges are specifically excepted from tax recognition by the Code. For example, § 1031 provides that no gain or loss shall be recognized if property held for productive use or for investment is exchanged solely for ". . . property of

CONCEPT SUMMARY 19–1
SUMMARY OF LIQUIDATION RULES

Effect on the Shareholder	Basis of Property Received	Effect on the Corporation
§ 331—The general rule provides for capital gain treatment on the difference between the FMV of property received and the basis of the stock in the corporation. Gain on installment obligations resulting from sales of noninventory property or inventory property sold in bulk to one person by the corporation may, however, be deferred to the point of collection.	§ 334(a)—Basis of assets received by the shareholder will be the FMV on the date of distribution (except for installment obligations in which gain is deferred to the point of collection).	§ 336—Gain or loss is recognized for distributions in kind and for sales by the liquidating corporation. Losses are not recognized for distributions to related parties (shareholders who own, directly or indirectly, more than 50% of the corporation's stock) if the distribution is not pro rata or if disqualified property is distributed. Losses may be disallowed on distributions of disqualified property even if made to unrelated parties.
§ 332—Liquidation of a subsidiary in which the parent owns 80% of the voting stock and 80% of the value of the subsidiary stock. No gain or loss is recognized to the parent corporation. Subsidiary must distribute all of its property within the taxable year or within three years from the close of the taxable year in which the plan is adopted.	§ 334(b)(1)—Property has the same basis as it had in the hands of the subsidiary. Parent's basis in the stock disappears. Carryover rules of § 381 apply.	§ 337—No gain or loss is recognized by the subsidiary on distributions to an 80% or more parent. Gain (but not loss) is recognized on distributions to minority shareholders.
	§ 338—Basis of assets is the basis that the parent held in the stock in the subsidiary. Basis is allocated to assets using the residual method. Carryover rules of § 381 do not apply. Subsidiary need not be liquidated.	

a like kind . . . ." Section 1033, if elected by the taxpayer, provides for partial or complete nonrecognition of gain if property destroyed, seized, or stolen is compulsorily or involuntarily converted into similar property. Further, § 351 provides for nonrecognition of gain upon the transfer of property to a controlled corporation. Finally, §§ 361 and 368 provide for nonrecognition of gain in certain corporate reorganizations. The Regulations state the underlying assumption behind the nonrecognition of gain or loss as follows:

> . . . the new property is substantially a continuation of the old investment still unliquidated; and, in the case of reorganizations, . . . the new enterprise, the new corporate structure, and the new property are substantially continuations of the old still unliquidated.[25]

Summary of the Different Types of Reorganizations

Section 368(a) of the Code specifies seven corporate restructures or reorganizations that will qualify as nontaxable exchanges. The planner of a nontaxable business realignment must determine in advance that the proposed transaction falls specifically within one of these seven types. If the transaction fails to qualify, it will not be granted special tax treatment.

Section 368(a)(1) states that the term *reorganization* means the following:

A. A statutory merger or consolidation.
B. The acquisition by one corporation, in exchange solely for all or a part of its voting stock, of stock of another corporation. The exchange also can be solely for all or part of the voting stock of a corporation that is in control of the acquiring corporation. Immediately after the acquisition, the acquiring corporation must have control of the other corporation.
C. The acquisition by one corporation, in exchange solely for all or a part of its voting stock, of substantially all of the properties of another corporation. The exchange also can be solely for all or part of the voting stock of a corporation that is in control of the acquiring corporation. In determining whether the exchange is solely for stock, the assumption by the acquiring corporation of a liability of the other is disregarded. Likewise, the fact that the property acquired is subject to a liability is disregarded.
D. A transfer by a corporation of all or a part of its assets to another corporation if immediately after the transfer the transferor, or one or more of its shareholders, or any combination thereof, is in control of the corporation to which the assets are transferred. "One or more of the shareholders" includes persons who were shareholders immediately before the transfer. Pursuant to the plan, stock and securities of the corporation to which the assets are transferred must be distributed in a transaction that qualifies under § 354, § 355, or § 356.
E. A recapitalization.
F. A mere change in identity, form, or place of organization.
G. A transfer by a corporation of all or a part of its assets to another corporation in a bankruptcy or receivership proceeding. Pursuant to the plan, stock and securities of the transferee corporation must be distributed in a transaction that qualifies under § 354, § 355, or § 356.

---

25. Reg. § 1.1002–1(c).

These seven types of tax-free reorganizations are designated by their identifying letters: "Type A," "Type B," "Type C," and so on. Basically, excepting the recapitalization (E), the change in form (F), and the insolvent corporation (G) provisions, a tax-free reorganization is (1) a statutory merger or consolidation, (2) an exchange of stock for voting stock, (3) an exchange of assets for voting stock, or (4) a divisive reorganization (the so-called spin-off, split-off, or split-up).

General Consequences of Tax-Free Reorganizations

Generally, the security holders of the various corporations involved in tax-free reorganizations do not recognize gain or loss on the exchange of their stock and securities[26] except when they receive cash or other consideration in addition to stock and securities.[27] As far as securities (long-term debt) are concerned, gain is not recognized if securities are surrendered in the same principal amount (or a greater principal amount) as the principal amount of the securities received.

If additional consideration is received, gain is recognized but not more than the sum of money and the fair market value of other property received. If the distribution has the effect of the distribution of a dividend, any recognized gain is a taxable dividend to the extent of the shareholder's share of the corporation's E & P. The remainder is treated as an exchange of property.[28] The tax basis of stock and securities received by a shareholder pursuant to a tax-free reorganization will be the same as the basis of those surrendered, decreased by the amount of boot received and increased by the amount of gain and dividend income, if any, recognized on the transaction.

EXAMPLE 24

Quinn exchanges stock he owns in Target Corporation for stock in Acquiring Corporation plus $2,000 cash. The exchange is pursuant to a tax-free reorganization of both corporations. Quinn paid $10,000 for the stock in Target two years ago. The stock in Acquiring possesses a fair market value of $12,000. Quinn has a realized gain of $4,000 ($12,000 + $2,000 – $10,000), which is recognized to the extent of the boot received, $2,000. Assume the distribution has the effect of a dividend. If Quinn's share of E & P in Target is $1,000, that amount is a taxable dividend. The remaining $1,000 is treated as a gain from the exchange of property. Quinn's basis in the Acquiring stock is $10,000 ($10,000 basis in stock surrendered – $2,000 boot received + $2,000 gain and dividend income recognized). ◆

EXAMPLE 25

Assume Quinn's basis in the Target stock was $15,000. Quinn has a realized loss of $1,000 on the exchange, none of which is recognized. His basis in the Acquiring stock is $13,000 ($15,000 basis in stock surrendered – $2,000 boot received). ◆

Because there is a substituted basis in tax-free reorganizations, the unrecognized gain or loss will be recognized when the new stock or securities are disposed of in a taxable transaction.

The acquired corporation does not recognize any gain or loss on the exchange of property pursuant to a tax-free reorganization.[29] If the acquired corporation

26. The term "securities" includes bonds and long-term notes. Short-term notes are not considered to be securities. The problem of drawing a line between short-term and long-term notes is, to say the least, troublesome. Some courts include notes with a 5-year maturity date as long term; others, 10 years.

27. § 356(a).

28. § 356(a)(2).

29. § 361(a).

receives cash or other property in the exchange, as well as stock or securities in the acquiring corporation, the acquired corporation recognizes gain on the other property only if it fails to distribute the property to its shareholders. If the acquired corporation distributes boot received in a tax-free reorganization, the shareholders, and not the corporation, are taxed on any recognized gain occasioned by the receipt of boot.[30]

The acquiring corporation also does not recognize gain or loss. Property received from the acquired corporation retains the basis it had in the hands of the acquired corporation, increased by the amount of gain recognized by the acquired corporation on the transfer.[31]

If a corporate exchange qualifies as a tax-free reorganization under one of these seven types, the tax consequences described are automatic regardless of the intent of the parties involved.

Effect of a Liquidating Distribution on the Corporation

With the repeal of the *General Utilities* doctrine, liquidating distributions are taxed at both the corporate and the shareholder level. When a corporation liquidates, it can, as a general rule, deduct losses on assets that have declined in value. These assets should not be distributed in the form of a property dividend before liquidation. If such assets are distributed as property dividends, the corporation receives no tax benefit from the potential loss. With certain exceptions, losses are recognized in complete liquidations.

Effect of a Liquidating Distribution on the Shareholder

Under the general rule of § 331, shareholders have recognized gain or loss equal to the difference between the liquidation proceeds and the basis of the stock given up. In cases of a large gain, a shareholder may consider shifting the gain to others. One approach is to give the stock to family members or donate it to charity. Whether this procedure will be successful depends on the timing of the transfer. If the donee of the stock is not in a position to prevent the liquidation of the corporation, the donor is deemed to have made an anticipatory assignment of income. As a result, the gain is still taxed to the donor. Hence, advance planning is crucial in arriving at the desired tax result.

Recall that § 453(h) provides some relief from the general rule of § 331 that the shareholder recognizes all gain upon receiving the liquidation proceeds. Assume corporate assets are sold after a plan of liquidation has been adopted. The assets are purchased with installment notes. The shareholders receiving the notes as liquidation distributions may be able to report the gain on the installment method. In that case, some gain can be deferred until the notes are collected.

The use of § 332 for the liquidation of a subsidiary is not elective. Nevertheless, some flexibility may be available:

- Whether § 332 applies depends on the 80 percent stock ownership test. Assuming the transaction has some substance, § 332 may be avoided if a parent corporation reduces its stock ownership in the subsidiary below this percentage. On the other hand, the opposite approach may be desirable.

30. § 361(b). If the acquired corporation has sufficient E & P and the shareholders receive pro rata distributions as boot, the boot is treated as a dividend and taxed as ordinary income and not as capital gain. See *Shimberg v. U.S.*, 78–2 USTC ¶9607, 42 AFTR2d 78–5575, 577 F.2d 283 (CA–5, 1978).

31. § 362(b).

A parent can make § 332 applicable by acquiring enough additional stock in the subsidiary to meet the 80 percent test.

- Once § 332 becomes effective, less latitude is allowed in determining the parent's basis in the subsidiary's assets. If § 334(b)(1) applies, the subsidiary's basis carries over to the parent. If § 338 applies and a timely election is made, the parent's basis becomes the cost of the stock. If the subsidiary is not liquidated, the basis of the assets to the subsidiary is the parent's cost of the stock. Presumably, § 338 can be avoided by failing to make a timely election.
- If a timely election is made under § 338, the parent corporation's basis in the stock of the subsidiary is allocated among the assets of the subsidiary.

Problem Materials

Discussion Questions

1. Compare stock redemptions and liquidations with other corporate distributions in terms of the following:
   a. Recognition of gain to the shareholder.
   b. Recognition of gain or loss by the distributing corporation.
   c. Effect on the distributing corporation's E & P.
2. Compare stock redemptions with liquidations in terms of the following:
   a. Possible disallowance of a loss (§ 267) to a shareholder.
   b. Basis of noncash property received from the corporation.
3. What losses are not recognized by the liquidating corporation in a complete liquidation?
4. Can losses ever be recognized in a complete liquidation if disqualified property is involved? Explain.
5. Discuss the tax treatment of liquidation expenses in connection with the following:
   a. General liquidation expenses.
   b. Expenses relating to a distribution of assets in kind.
   c. Expenses relating to a sale of assets.
6. May a shareholder use the installment method to report gain on a complete liquidation? Explain.
7. Explain the tax consequences to a shareholder of a corporation in the process of liquidation under the general rule of § 331.
8. In terms of the applicability of § 332, describe the effect of each of the following:
   a. The adoption of a plan of complete liquidation.
   b. The period of time in which the corporation must liquidate.
   c. The amount of stock held by the parent corporation.
   d. The solvency of the subsidiary being liquidated.
9. What are the tax consequences of a § 332 liquidation when a minority interest is involved?
10. Could a liquidation of one corporation involve §§ 331 and 332?
11. What are the requirements for the application of § 338?
12. Under what circumstances could the application of § 338 be beneficial to the parent corporation? Detrimental?

13. Compare §§ 334(b)(1) and 338 with respect to the following:

    a. Carryover to the parent of the subsidiary's corporate attributes.
    b. Recognition by the subsidiary of gain or loss on distributions to its parent.

14. "The E & P of the corporation being liquidated will disappear."

    a. Do you agree with this statement?
    b. Why or why not?

15. Is it possible to have a complete liquidation where the existence of the corporation being liquidated is not terminated? Elaborate.

PROBLEMS

16. Robin Corporation distributes to its shareholders land held as an investment (basis of $100,000, fair market value of $600,000) pursuant to a complete liquidation. The land is subject to a liability of $700,000. How much gain does Robin Corporation have on a distribution of the land?

17. Black Corporation's stock is held equally by three sisters, Abby, Bonnie, and Carol. The three sisters owned, as tenants in common, a tract of land on which a warehouse needed by the corporation was located. The land and warehouse had a basis of $325,000 and fair market value of $100,000. Three years prior to liquidation, the sisters transferred the land and warehouse to the corporation in return for stock. At the time of the liquidation, the land and warehouse had a fair market value of $60,000 and a tax basis of $322,000. In liquidation, Black Corporation transferred the land and warehouse equally to Abby, Bonnie, and Carol as tenants in common. How much loss would Black Corporation recognize on the distribution?

18. Brown Corporation has the following assets:

	Basis to Brown Corporation	Fair Market Value
Cash	$ 900,000	$ 900,000
Inventory	300,000	900,000
Equipment	3,180,000	1,800,000
Building	200,000	2,280,000
Land	720,000	120,000

The inventory had been purchased by Brown Corporation; the remaining assets were acquired seven years ago. Brown adopted a plan of liquidation in January 1993 and distributed its assets that same year to its shareholders, Lynn (70%) and Pat (30%). Lynn and Pat are unrelated. What are the tax consequences to Brown Corporation under the following independent circumstances:

    a. The assets are distributed to Lynn and Pat in proportion to their stock interests (70% interest in each asset to Lynn and 30% interest in each asset to Pat).
    b. The equipment, building, and land are distributed to Lynn, and the cash and inventory are distributed to Pat.
    c. The equipment is distributed to Pat, and the remaining assets are distributed to Lynn.
    d. What is the result in (a) if the equipment had been transferred to Brown Corporation in a § 351 transaction 10 months before the liquidation when the equipment had a basis of $3,180,000 and a fair market value of $1,980,000?

19. Green Corporation acquired land in a § 351 exchange in 1991. The land had a basis of $600,000 and a fair market value of $650,000 on the date of the transfer. Green Corporation has two shareholders, Isabella and Gary, who are unrelated. Isabella owns 80% of the stock in the corporation, and Gary owns 20%. Green adopts a plan of liquidation in 1993. On this date, the value of the land has decreased to $200,000.

In distributing the land either to Isabella or to Gary, or to both, as part of the liquidating distributions from Green Corporation, should Green:

a. distribute all the land to Isabella?
b. distribute all the land to Gary?
c. distribute 80% of the land to Isabella and 20% to Gary?
d. distribute 50% of the land to Isabella and 50% to Gary?
e. sell the land and distribute the proceeds of $200,000 proportionately to Isabella and to Gary?

20. Assume in Problem 19 that the plan of liquidation is not adopted until 1994. In addition, assume the land had a fair market value of $500,000 on the date of its transfer to the corporation. Its fair market value on the date of the liquidation has decreased to $200,000. How would your answers to Problem 19 change?

21. The stock of Brown Corporation is held as follows: 85% by Black Corporation and 15% by Fred. Brown Corporation is liquidated on October 1, 1993, pursuant to a plan of liquidation adopted on January 15, 1993. At the time of its liquidation, Brown's assets had a basis of $2 million and a fair market value of $18 million. Black Corporation has a basis of $800,000 in its Brown Corporation stock. The basis of the Brown stock to Fred is $80,000.

a. How much gain, if any, must Brown Corporation recognize on the liquidation?
b. How much gain, if any, is recognized on the receipt of property from Brown Corporation by Black Corporation? By Fred?

22. At the time of its liquidation under § 332, Cardinal Corporation had the following assets and liabilities:

	Basis to Cardinal Corporation	Fair Market Value
Cash	$120,000	$120,000
Marketable securities	90,000	240,000
Unimproved land	150,000	300,000
Unsecured bank loan	(30,000)	(30,000)
Mortgage on land	(90,000)	(90,000)

Wren Corporation, the sole shareholder of Cardinal Corporation, has a basis of $360,000 in its stock investment. At the time of its liquidation, Cardinal's E & P was $200,000.

a. How much gain (or loss) will Cardinal Corporation recognize if it distributes all of its assets and liabilities to Wren Corporation?
b. How much gain (or loss) will Wren Corporation recognize?
c. If § 334(b)(1) applies, what will be Wren's basis in the marketable securities it receives from Cardinal Corporation?
d. What will be Wren's basis in the unimproved land?

23. Black Corporation, owned by two individual shareholders, has a basis of $450,000 (fair market value of $1,000,000) in its assets and E & P of $80,000. Its liabilities total $100,000. If the assets were sold, all gain would be long-term capital gain or § 1231 gain. White Corporation purchases 20% of all the stock of Black Corporation for $180,000 on March 1, 1993; 15% for $135,000 on September 20, 1993; and 60% for $540,000 on December 1, 1993, for a total consideration of $855,000.

a. Is White Corporation entitled to make an election under § 338?
b. Assume White Corporation may make an election under § 338. Should White do so? When must White make the election?
c. What are the tax consequences to Black Corporation and to White Corporation if White makes a valid election under § 338 but does not liquidate Black?

d. What is the tax result if Black Corporation is liquidated four months after a valid § 338 election? Eve, who holds the 5% minority interest in Black Corporation, has a $10,000 basis in her stock in Black. What is the tax result to Eve upon the liquidation?

24. Green Corporation paid $5,400,000 for all the stock of Gray Corporation 10 years ago. Gray Corporation's balance sheet is as follows:

Assets	
Cash	$ 135,000
Inventory	405,000
Machinery	270,000
Equipment	1,080,000
Land	1,350,000
	$ 3,240,000

Liabilities and Shareholders' Equity	
Accounts payable	$ 2,160,000
Payable to Green Corporation	3,240,000
Common stock	5,400,000
Deficit	(7,560,000)
	$ 3,240,000

What are the tax consequences to Green Corporation if it liquidates Gray Corporation?

CHAPTER

CORPORATE ACCUMULATIONS

OBJECTIVES

Explain the purpose of the accumulated earnings tax and the personal holding company tax.

Define the "reasonable needs of the business" and explain their role in avoiding the accumulated earnings tax.

Explain the mechanics of the accumulated earnings tax.

Define the requirements for personal holding company status.

Discuss the mechanics of the personal holding company tax.

Compare the accumulated earnings tax with the personal holding company tax and show how each of these taxes can be avoided or controlled.

OUTLINE

Chapter 21 discusses one major technique for minimizing the tax liability of closely held corporations: the S corporation election. However, some corporations that fall into the closely held category either may not qualify for the election or may find it unattractive. How can these other taxpayers transmit corporate earnings to the shareholders while generating a deduction for the corporation? One method is to reduce the amount of equity capital invested in a controlled corporation by increasing the debt obligations. In other words, convert dividends into interest payments deductible by the corporation. This method has limits. The Internal Revenue Service may contend that the capital structure is unrealistic and the debt is not valid. For these reasons, the IRS may disallow the corporate deduction for interest expense (refer to Chapter 17).

An alternative possibility is to convert the earnings of the closely held corporation into compensation to the officers, generally the major shareholders. The compensation is a deductible expense. If it were not for the reasonableness requirement, officer-shareholders could withdraw all corporate profits as salaries and eliminate the corporate tax (refer to Chapter 18). However, the reasonableness requirement prevents a corporation from deducting as salaries what are actually nondeductible dividends.

Another approach involves the lease of shareholder-owned property to the corporation. The corporation (the lessee) deducts the lease payment from gross income and saves taxes at the corporate level. The shareholders must recognize the rental payments as ordinary income. But there is an overall tax savings, because the corporation obtains deductions for what are essentially dividend payments. However, the IRS may classify the payments as disguised dividends and disallow the rental deductions (refer to Chapter 18).

A fourth method is to accumulate the earnings at the corporate level. A temporary or permanent accumulation of earnings in a corporation results in a deferral of the second tax at the shareholder level. The corporation can invest in instruments that produce tax-free income (e.g., state and local bonds) or buy stock in other domestic corporations to take advantage of the dividends received deduction. A *modest* tax benefit could result from accumulations at the corporate level. This benefit could occur because dividend income would be converted into long-term capital gain. Under current law, long-term capital gains of noncorporate taxpayers cannot be taxed at a rate in excess of 28 percent. Dividend income is ordinary income and can be taxed at a rate as high as 31 percent. Congress took steps to stem corporate accumulations as early as the first income tax law enacted under the Sixteenth Amendment. Today, in addition to the usual corporate income tax, an extra tax is imposed on earnings accumulated beyond the reasonable needs of the business. Also, a penalty tax may be imposed on undistributed personal holding company income.

This chapter demonstrates how the accumulation of earnings can occur without leading to adverse tax consequences—the imposition of additional taxes.

PENALTY TAX ON UNREASONABLE ACCUMULATIONS

One method of optimizing the distribution of corporate earnings is to accumulate the earnings until the most advantageous time to distribute them to the shareholders. If the board of directors is aware of the tax problems of the shareholders, it can channel earnings into the shareholders' pockets with a minimum of tax cost by using any of several mechanisms. The corporation can distribute dividends only in years when the major shareholders are in lower tax brackets. Alternatively, dividend distributions might be curtailed, causing the value of the stock to increase in a manner similar to a savings account. Later, the shareholders can sell their stock in the year of their choice at an amount that reflects the increased retained earnings. The capital gain may be taxed at a lower rate (28 percent versus 31 percent), or the capital gain could be postponed to years when the shareholders have capital losses to offset the gains. Alternatively, the shareholders can retain their shares. Upon death, the estate or heirs will receive a step-up in basis equal to the fair market value of the stock on the date of death or, if elected, on the alternate valuation date. The increment in value represented by the step-up in basis will be largely attributable to the earnings retained by the corporation and will not be subject to income taxation.

Accumulating corporate earnings always entails problems, however. A penalty tax may be imposed on accumulated taxable earnings, or a personal holding company tax may be levied on certain accumulated passive income. Consider first the accumulated earnings tax. The tax law is framed to discourage the retention of earnings that are unrelated to the business needs of the company. Earnings retained in the business to avoid the imposition of the tax that would have been imposed on distributions to the shareholder are subject to a penalty tax.

Example 1

Velvia operated a consulting business as a sole proprietor in 1992. Assume she is in the 28% tax bracket in 1993, and she incorporates her business at the beginning of the year. Her business earns $120,000 in 1993, before her salary of $60,000. Since $60,000 of the income is accumulated, $6,800 of taxes are "saved" ($16,800 individual tax versus $10,000 corporate tax on the $60,000 accumulated). This accumulated savings could occur each year with the corporation reinvesting the saved taxes. Thus, without an accumulated earnings tax or personal holding company tax, Velvia could use her corporation like a savings account. For example, the corporation could take advantage of the dividends received deduction for dividend-paying stocks. With the top individual tax rate (31% for 1993) below the top corporate tax rate (34% for 1993), it is less attractive to hold investment property in a C corporation than in a flow-through entity (partnership, S corporation, or sole proprietorship). Further, the earnings are still at the corporate level, and Velvia might be in a higher individual rate when the accumulated earnings are distributed. ◆

The Element of Intent

Although the penalty tax is normally applied against closely held corporations, a corporation is not exempt from the tax merely because its stock is widely held.[1] For example, a Second Court of Appeals decision[2] imposed the tax upon a widely held corporation with over 1,500 shareholders. However, a much smaller group of shareholders actually controlled the corporation. As a practical matter, a widely held corporation that is not under the legal or effective control of a small group is unlikely to be suspected of accumulating earnings for the purpose of tax avoidance.

The key to imposition of the tax is not the number of the shareholders in the corporation but whether a shareholder group controls corporate policy. If such a group does exist and withholds dividends to protect its own tax position, an accumulated earnings tax (§ 531) problem might materialize.

1. § 532(c).

2. *Trico Products v. Comm.*, 43–2 USTC ¶9540, 31 AFTR 394, 137 F.2d 424 (CA–2, 1943).

When a corporation is formed or used to shield its shareholders from individual taxes by accumulating rather than distributing earnings and profits, the "bad" purpose for accumulating earnings is considered to exist under § 532(a). This subjective test, in effect, asks, Did the corporation and/or shareholder(s) *intend* to retain the earnings in order to avoid the tax on dividends? According to the Supreme Court, the tax avoidance motive need *not* be the dominant or controlling purpose to trigger application of the penalty tax; it need only be a contributing factor to the retention of earnings.[3] The accumulation of funds beyond the corporation's reasonable needs is determinative of the existence of a "bad" purpose, unless the contrary can be proven by the preponderance of the evidence. The fact that the business is a mere holding or investment company is *prima facie* evidence of this tax avoidance purpose.[4]

Imposition of the Tax and the Accumulated Earnings Credit

Contrary to its name, the penalty tax is not levied on the corporate accumulated earnings balance. It is imposed on the current year's *addition* to this balance not needed for a reasonable business purpose. The tax is not imposed upon S corporations, personal holding companies, foreign personal holding companies, tax-exempt organizations, or passive foreign investment companies. The tax is in addition to the regular corporate tax and the 20 percent alternative minimum tax. Currently, the tax rate is 28 percent.

Most corporations are allowed a minimum $250,000 credit against accumulated taxable income, even when earnings are accumulated beyond reasonable business needs. However, certain personal service corporations in health, law, engineering, architecture, accounting, actuarial science, performing arts, and consulting are limited to a $150,000 accumulated earnings credit. Moreover, a nonservice corporation (other than a holding or investment company) may retain more than $250,000 (and a service organization may retain more than $150,000) of accumulated earnings if the company can justify that the accumulation is necessary to meet the *reasonable needs of the business.*[5]

The accumulated earnings credit is the greater of the following:

1. The current earnings and profits (E & P) for the tax year that are needed to meet the reasonable needs of the business (see the subsequent discussion) *less* the net long-term capital gain for the year (net of any tax). In determining the reasonable needs for any one year, the accumulated E & P of past years must be taken into account.
2. The amount by which $250,000 exceeds the accumulated E & P of the corporation at the close of the preceding tax year (designated the *minimum credit*).

EXAMPLE 2

Yellow Corporation, a calendar year manufacturing concern, has accumulated E & P of $120,000 as of December 31, 1992. For 1993, it has no capital gains and has current E & P of $140,000. A realistic estimate places Yellow's reasonable needs of the business for 1993 at $200,000. The allowable credit is the greater of (1) or (2).

3. *U.S. v. The Donruss Co.*, 69–1 USTC ¶9167, 23 AFTR2d 69–418, 89 S.Ct. 501 (USSC, 1969).

4. § 533. See, for example, *H. C. Cockrell Warehouse Corp.*, 71 T.C. 1036 (1979).

5. §§ 535(c) and 537 and Reg. § 1.537–1.

	(1)	(2)
Reasonable needs	$200,000	
Minimum credit		$250,000
Accumulated E & P	120,000	120,000
Potential credit	$ 80,000	$130,000

Thus, the credit becomes $130,000 (the greater of $80,000 or $130,000). ◆

Several observations can be made about the accumulated earnings credit. First, the minimum credit of $250,000 is of no consequence as long as the prior year's ending balance in accumulated E & P is $250,000 or more. Second, when the credit is based on reasonable needs, the credit is the amount that exceeds accumulated E & P. Third, a taxpayer must choose between the reasonable needs credit (item 1) or the minimum credit (item 2). Combining the two in the same year is not permissible. Fourth, although the § 531 tax is not imposed on accumulated E & P, the amount of the credit depends upon the balance of this account as of the end of the preceding year.

Reasonable Needs of the Business

If a corporation's funds are invested in assets essential to the needs of the business, the IRS will have a difficult time imposing the accumulated earnings tax. "Thus, the size of the accumulated earnings and profits or surplus is not the crucial factor; rather it is the reasonableness and nature of the surplus."[6] What are the reasonable business needs of a corporation? This is precisely the point that leads to difficulty and creates controversy with the IRS.

Justifiable Needs—In General. The reasonable needs of a business include the business's reasonably anticipated needs.[7] These anticipated needs must be specific, definite, and feasible. A number of court decisions illustrate that indefinite plans referred to only briefly in corporate minutes merely provide a false feeling of security for the taxpayer.[8]

The Regulations list some legitimate reasons that could indicate that a corporation is accumulating earnings to meet the reasonable needs of the business. Earnings may be allowed to accumulate to provide for bona fide expansion of the business enterprise or replacement of plant and facilities as well as to acquire a business enterprise through the purchase of stock or assets. Provision for the retirement of bona fide indebtedness created in connection with the trade or business (e.g., the establishment of a sinking fund for the retirement of bonds issued by the corporation) is a legitimate reason for accumulating earnings under ordinary circumstances. Providing necessary working capital for the business (e.g., to acquire inventories) and providing for investment or loans to suppliers or customers (if necessary to maintain the business of the corporation) are valid grounds for accumulating earnings.[9] Funds may be retained for self-insurance[10] and realistic business contingencies (e.g., lawsuits, patent infringements).[11] Accumulations to avoid an unfavorable competitive position[12]

---

6. *Smoot Sand & Gravel Corp. v. Comm.*, 60–1 USTC ¶9241, 5 AFTR2d 626, 274 F.2d 495 (CA–4, 1960).
7. § 537(a)(1).
8. See, for example, *Fine Realty, Inc. v. U.S.*, 62–2 USTC ¶9758, 10 AFTR2d 5751, 209 F.Supp. 286 (D.Ct. Minn., 1962).
9. Reg. § 1.537–2(b).
10. *Halby Chemical Co., Inc. v. U.S.*, 67–2 USTC ¶9500, 19 AFTR2d 1589 (Ct.Cls., 1967).
11. *Dielectric Materials Co.*, 57 T.C. 587 (1972).
12. *North Valley Metabolic Laboratories*, 34 TCM 400, T.C.Memo, 1975–79.

and to carry key employee life insurance policies[13] are justifiable. Accumulation to provide for the loss of a key customer or client is a reasonable need of the business.[14]

The reasonable business needs of a company also include the postdeath § 303 redemption requirements of a corporation.[15] Accumulations for such purposes are limited to the amount needed (or reasonably anticipated to be needed) to redeem stock included in the gross estate of the decedent-shareholder.[16] This amount may not exceed the sum of the death taxes and funeral and administration expenses allowable under §§ 2053 and 2106.[17]

Section 537(b) provides that reasonable accumulations to pay future product liability losses represent a reasonable anticipated need of the business. Guidelines for the application of this allowance are prescribed in Proposed Regulations.

Justifiable Needs—Working Capital Requirements for Inventory Situations. For many years, the penalty tax on accumulated earnings was based upon the concept of retained earnings. The courts generally looked at retained earnings alone to determine whether there was an unreasonable accumulation. However, a corporation may have a large retained earnings balance and yet possess no liquid assets with which to pay dividends. Therefore, the emphasis should more appropriately be placed upon the liquidity of a corporation. Does the business have liquid assets *not* needed that could be used to pay dividends? The courts did not begin to use this liquidity approach until 1960, however.

Over the years, greater recognition has been placed on the liquidity needs of the corporation. The reasonable needs of the business can be divided into two categories:

1. Working capital needed for day-to-day operations.
2. Expenditures of a noncurrent nature (extraordinary expenses).

The operating cycle of a business is the average time interval between the acquisition of materials (or services) entering the business and the final realization of cash. The courts seized upon the operating cycle because it had the advantage of objectivity for purposes of determining working capital. A normal business has two distinct cycles:

1. Purchase of inventory → the production process → finished goods inventory
2. Sale of merchandise → accounts receivable → cash collection

A systematic operating cycle formula was developed in *Bardahl Manufacturing Co.* and *Bardahl International Corp.*[18] The technique became known as the *Bardahl* formula. This formula is not a precise tool and is subject to various interpretations.

The following is the standard formula used to determine the reasonable working capital needs for a corporation:

---

13. *Emeloid Co. v. Comm.*, 51–1 USTC ¶66,013, 40 AFTR 674, 189 F.2d 230 (CA–3, 1951). Key employee life insurance is a policy on the life of a key employee that is owned by and made payable to the employer. Such insurance enables the employer to recoup some of the economic loss that could materialize upon the untimely death of the key employee.

14. *EMI Corporation*, 50 TCM 569, T.C.Memo. 1985–386, and *James H. Rutter*, 52 TCM 326, T.C.Memo. 1986–407.

15. The § 303 redemption to pay death taxes and administration expenses of a deceased shareholder is discussed in Chapter 18.

16. §§ 537(a)(2) and (b)(1).

17. § 303(a).

18. *Bardahl Manufacturing Co.*, 24 TCM 1030, T.C.Memo. 1965–200; *Bardahl International Corp.*, 25 TCM 935, T.C.Memo. 1966–182. See also *Apollo Industries, Inc. v. Comm.*, 66–1 USTC ¶9294, 17 AFTR2d 518, 358 F.2d 867 (CA–1, 1966).

$$\text{Inventory cycle} = \frac{\text{Average inventory}}{\text{Cost of goods sold}}$$

Plus

$$\text{Accounts receivable cycle} = \frac{\text{Average accounts receivable}}{\text{Net sales}}$$

Minus

$$\text{Accounts payable cycle} = \frac{\text{Average accounts payable}^{19}}{\text{Purchases}}$$

Equals

A decimal percentage

The formula assumes that working capital needs are computed on a yearly basis. However, this may not provide the most favorable result. A business that experiences seasonally based high and low cycles illustrates this point. For example, a construction company can justify a greater working capital need if computations are based on a cycle that includes the winter months only and not on an annual average.[20] In the same vein, an incorporated CPA firm would choose a cycle during the slow season.

Both of the original *Bardahl* decisions used the so-called peak cycle approach. Here, the inventory and accounts receivable figures are the amounts for the month-end during which the total amounts in inventory and accounts receivable are the greatest. In fact, the *Bardahl International* decision specifically rejects the average cycle approach. However, some courts have rejected the peak cycle approach,[21] which probably should be used where the business of the corporation is seasonal.[22] Using peak amounts increases the numerators of the inventory and receivable fractions, while the denominators stay the same. The turnover periods increase, which, in turn, increases the operating cycle percentage. A higher percentage produces a larger necessary accumulation of working capital. This makes a corporation less likely to be subject to the accumulated earnings tax.

The decimal percentage derived above, when multiplied by the cost of goods sold plus general, administrative, and selling expenses (not including unpaid Federal income taxes and depreciation),[23] equals the working capital needs of the business. Paid estimated Federal income taxes are treated as operating expenses, but profit sharing contributions and charitable contributions are not operating expenses.

If the statistically computed working capital needs plus any extraordinary expenses are more than the current year's net working capital, no penalty tax is imposed. Working capital is the excess of current assets over current liabilities. This amount is the relatively liquid portion of the total business capital that is a buffer for meeting obligations within the normal operating cycle of the business.

However, if working capital needs plus any extraordinary expenses are less than the current year's net working capital, the possibility of the imposition of a penalty tax does exist.[24]

---

19. The accounts payable cycle was developed in *Kingsbury Investments, Inc.*, 28 TCM 1082, T.C. Memo. 1969–205.
20. See *Audits of Construction Contracts*, AICPA, 1965, p. 25.
21. See, for example, *W. L. Mead, Inc.*, 34 TCM 924, T.C.Memo. 1975–215.
22. *Magic Mart, Inc.*, 51 T.C. 775 (1969).
23. In *W. L. Mead, Inc.*, cited in Footnote 21, the Tax Court allowed depreciation to be included in the expenses of a service firm with no inventory. Likewise, in *Doug-Long, Inc.*, 72 T.C. 158 (1979), the Tax Court allowed a truckstop to include quarterly estimated tax payments in operating expenses.
24. *Electric Regulator Corp. v. Comm.*, 64–2 USTC ¶9705, 14 AFTR2d 5447, 336 F.2d 339 (CA–2, 1964) used "quick assets" (current assets less inventory).

In *Bardahl Manufacturing Co.*, the costs and expenses used in the formula were those of the following year, whereas in *Bardahl International Corp.*, costs and expenses of the current year were used. Use of the subsequent year's expected costs seems to be the more equitable approach, but a taxpayer may not use the higher of the current year or next year's costs over a number of years.

The IRS normally takes the position that the operating cycle should be reduced by the accounts payable cycle. The IRS maintains that the payment of these expenses may be postponed by various credit arrangements that will reduce the operating capital requirements. However, a number of court decisions have omitted such a reduction. Some courts use all payables, while other courts use only material and trade payables. In any case, a corporate tax planner should not have to rely on creditors to avoid the accumulated earnings penalty tax. The corporation with the most acute working capital problem will probably have a large accounts payable balance. If the formula for determining reasonable working capital needs is used, a large accounts payable balance will result in a sizable reduction in the maximum working capital allowable before the tax is imposed. For tax planning purposes, a corporation should hold accounts payable at a reduced level.

EXAMPLE 3

Quinn, an accountant for a local appliance store, is asked by the store's president to determine if the corporation is susceptible to the accumulated earnings tax. Quinn calculates, as a fraction of the year, the inventory cycle (.08), the receivables cycle (.12), and the payables cycle (.13). The three ratios are combined to determine the operating cycle ratio of .07 (.08 + .12 – .13). Since the operating expenses are $525,000, Quinn calculates the working capital needs to be $36,750 (.07 × $525,000).

Next Quinn calculates the actual working capital, using current assets at fair market value less current liabilities. Thus, $285,000 less $200,000 results in $85,000 of actual working capital. Comparing actual working capital ($85,000) with the working capital needs of $36,750, Quinn determines that the corporation has excess working capital of $48,250. If this appliance store has no other reasonable business needs, the corporation may be subject to the accumulated earnings tax. ◆

Justifiable Needs—Working Capital Requirements for Noninventory Situations. In a service business, inventories are not purchased, and part of the operating cycle in the *Bardahl* formula is missing. However, a service business incurs certain costs such as salaries and overhead for a period of time before billing customers for services. Some courts have used a rough rule of thumb to determine an inventory equivalent cycle. Under certain circumstances, a human resource accounting (HRA) approach may be used to determine the working capital needs of a noninventory corporation. The use of an HRA approach is based on the contention that the strength of a service business—and its major asset—is its highly educated, skilled technicians. Such individuals must be available both to attract clients and to execute projects efficiently. In the event of a business downturn, it would be foolish to abruptly discharge highly paid specialists, recruited and trained at considerable expense. The business decline might prove to be of brief duration.

One court[25] allowed an engineering firm to add to the IRS's *Bardahl*-calculated operating reserve the reasonable professional and technical payroll for an additional period of two months (or 60 days). The Court felt that this extra

---

25. *Simons-Eastern Co. v. U.S.*, 73–1 USTC ¶9279, 31 AFTR2d 73–640, 354 F.Supp. 1003 (D.Ct.Ga., 1972). See also *Delaware Trucking Co., Inc.*, 32 TCM 105, T.C.Memo. 1973–29, and *Magic Mart, Inc.*, cited in Footnote 22.

amount would "... allow sufficient reserve for one cycle of full operation plus a reasonable period (60 days) of curtailed operation to recapture business or, in the alternative, to face up to hard decisions on reducing the scope of the entire operation or abandoning it." Further, the Court expressed its opinion that a multiple of reasonable professional and technical salaries is a useful method for determining the amount to be included in an operating reserve. However, the Court did not indicate why it selected two months as the magic number. It can be anticipated that the courts will continue to evolve a *Bardahl*-like formula for noninventory corporations.

No Justifiable Needs. Certain situations do *not* call for the accumulation of earnings. For example, accumulating earnings to make loans to shareholders or brother-sister corporations is not considered within the reasonable needs of the business.[26] Accumulations to retire stock without curtailment of the business and for unrealistic business hazards (e.g., depression of the U.S. economy) are invalid reasons for accumulating funds.[27] The same holds true for accumulations made to carry out investments in properties or securities unrelated to the corporation's activity.[28]

Concept Summary 20–1 reviews the previous discussion regarding what does and does not constitute a reasonable need of the business.

Measuring the Accumulation. Should the cost or fair market value of assets be used to determine whether a corporation has accumulated E & P beyond its reasonable needs? This issue remains unclear. The Supreme Court has indicated

CONCEPT SUMMARY 20–1
REASONABLE BUSINESS NEEDS

Legitimate Reasons	Invalid Reasons
Expansion of a business.	Loans to shareholders.
Replacement of capital assets.	Loans to brother-sister corporations.
Replacement of plant.	Future depression.
Acquisition of a business.	Unrealistic contingencies.
Working capital needs.	Investment in assets unrelated to the business.
Product liability loss.	Retirement of stock without a curtailment of the business.
Loans to suppliers or customers.	
Redemption under § 303 to pay death taxes and administration expenses of a shareholder.	
Realistic business hazards.	
Loss of a major customer or client.	
Reserve for actual lawsuit.	
Protection of a family business from takeover by outsiders.	
Debt retirement.	
Self-insurance.	

26. See *Young's Rubber Corp.*, 21 TCM 1593, T.C.Memo. 1962–300.

27. *Turnbull, Inc. v. Comm.*, 67–1 USTC ¶9221, 19 AFTR2d 609, 373 F.2d 91 (CA–5, 1967), and Reg. § 1.537–2(c)(5).

28. Reg. § 1.537–2(c)(4).

that fair market value is to be used when dealing with marketable securities.[29] Although the Court admitted that the concept of E & P does not include unrealized appreciation, it asserted that the current asset ratio must be considered in determining if accumulated earnings are reasonable. Thus, the Court looked to the economic realities of the situation and held that fair market value is to be used with respect to readily marketable securities. The Court's opinion did not address the proper basis for valuation of assets other than marketable securities. However, the IRS may assert that this rule should be extended to include other assets. Therefore, tax advisers and corporate personnel should regularly check all security holdings to guard against accumulations caused by the appreciation of investments.

EXAMPLE 4

Robin Company had accumulated E & P of approximately $2,000,000. Five years ago, the company invested $150,000 in various stocks and bonds. At the end of the current tax year, the fair market value of these securities approximates $2,500,000. Two of Robin's shareholders, father and son, own 75% of the stock. If these securities are valued at cost, current assets minus current liabilities are deemed to be equal to the reasonable needs of the business. However, if the marketable securities are valued at their $2,500,000 fair market value, the value of the liquid assets greatly exceeds the corporation's reasonable needs. Under the Supreme Court's economic reality test, the fair market value is used. Consequently, the corporation is subject to the § 531 penalty tax. ◆

Mechanics of the Penalty Tax

The taxable base for the accumulated earnings tax is a company's *accumulated taxable income (ATI)*. Taxable income of the corporation is modified as follows:[30]

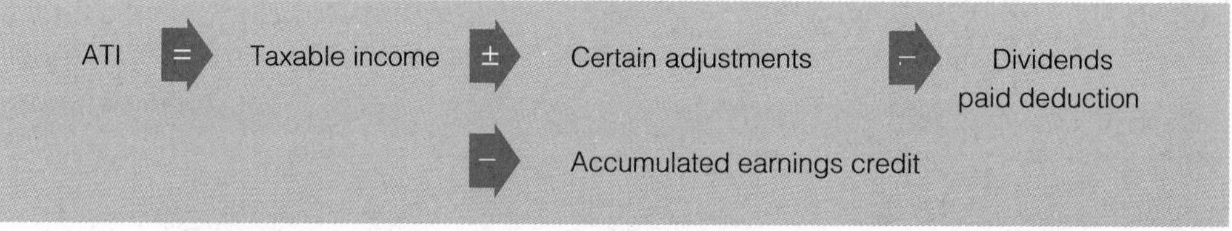

For a corporation that is not a mere holding or investment company, the "certain adjustments" include the following items as deductions:

1. Corporate income tax accrued.
2. Charitable contributions in excess of 10 percent of adjusted taxable income.
3. Capital loss adjustment.[31]
4. Excess of net long-term capital gain over net short-term capital loss, diminished by the capital gain tax and reduced by net capital losses from earlier years.

and the following items as additions:

5. Capital loss carryovers and carrybacks.
6. Net operating loss deduction.
7. Dividends received deduction.

29. *Ivan Allen Co. v. U.S.*, 75–2 USTC ¶9557, 36 AFTR2d 75–5200, 95 S.Ct. 2501 (USSC, 1975).

30. § 535(a).

31. This deduction (item 3) and item 4 are either/or deductions since a corporation will not have both in the same year. For the capital loss adjustment, see § 535(b)(5).

The purpose of each of these adjustments is to produce an amount that more closely represents the dividend-paying capacity of the corporation. For example, the corporate income tax is deducted from taxable income since the corporation does not have this money to pay dividends. Conversely, the dividends received deduction is added to taxable income since the deduction has no impact upon the ability to pay a dividend. Note that item 4, in effect, allows a corporation to accumulate any capital gains without a penalty tax.

Payment of dividends reduces the amount of accumulated taxable income subject to the penalty tax. The dividends paid deduction includes any dividends paid during the tax year that the shareholders must report as ordinary income *and* any dividends paid within 2½ months after the close of the tax year.[32] A nontaxable stock dividend under § 305(a) does not affect the dividends paid deduction. Further, a shareholder may file a consent statement to treat as a dividend the amount specified in the statement. A *consent dividend* is taxed to the shareholder even though it is not actually distributed. The shareholder treats the consent dividend as a contribution to the capital of the corporation (paid-in capital).[33]

EXAMPLE 5

A nonservice closely held corporation that had no capital gains or losses in prior years has the following financial transactions for calendar year 1993:

Taxable income	$300,000
Tax liability	100,250
Excess charitable contributions	22,000
Short-term capital loss	(40,000)
Dividends received (less than 20% owned)	100,000
Research and development expenses	46,000
Dividends paid in 1993	40,000
Accumulated earnings (1/1/93)	220,000

Presuming the corporation is subject to the § 531 tax and has *no* reasonable business needs that justify its accumulations, the accumulated taxable income is calculated as follows:

Taxable income		$300,000
Plus: 70% dividends received deduction		70,000
		$370,000
Less: Tax liability	$100,250	
Excess charitable contributions	22,000	
Net short-term capital loss adjustment	40,000	
Dividends paid	40,000	
Accumulated earnings minimum credit ($250,000 – $220,000)	30,000	(232,250)
Accumulated taxable income		$137,750

Thus, the accumulated earnings penalty tax for 1993 is $38,570 ($137,750 × 28%). ◆

32. §§ 535(a), 561(a), and 563(a).

33. §§ 565(a) and (c)(2). The consent dividend procedure is appropriate if the corporation is not in a position to make a cash or property distribution to its shareholders. The dividends paid deduction is discussed more fully later in the chapter.

EXAMPLE 6

In Example 5, assume that the reasonable needs of the business of § 535(c) amount to $270,000 in 1993. The current year's accumulated earnings are now reduced by $50,000, rather than the $30,000 of accumulated earnings minimum credit. Accumulated taxable income is $117,750, and the penalty tax is $32,970. Note that the first $220,000 of accumulated earnings *cannot* be omitted in determining whether taxable income for the current year is reasonably needed by the enterprise. ◆

PERSONAL HOLDING COMPANY PENALTY TAX

The personal holding company (PHC) tax was enacted to discourage the sheltering of certain types of passive income in corporations owned by high tax bracket individuals. These "incorporated pocketbooks" were frequently found in the entertainment and construction industries. For example, a taxpayer could shelter the income from securities in a corporation, which would pay no dividends, and allow the corporation's stock to increase in value. Like the accumulated earnings tax, the purpose of the PHC tax is to force the distribution of corporate earnings to the shareholders. However, in any one year, the IRS cannot impose both the PHC tax and the accumulated earnings tax.[34]

EXAMPLE 7

Considerable tax savings could be achieved by incorporating a "pocketbook" if § 541 did not exist. Assume that investments that yield $50,000 a year are transferred to a corporation by a 31% income tax bracket shareholder. A tax savings of $8,000 will occur each year if no dividends are paid to the shareholder. With no corporation, there would be a total tax liability of $15,500, but with a corporation the tax liability is only $7,500 in 1993 (15% × $50,000). Further, if the yield of $50,000 is in the form of dividends, the corporate tax will be even less because of the dividends received deduction. ◆

Whether a corporation will be included within the statutory definition of a PHC for any particular year depends upon the facts and circumstances during that year.[35] Therefore, PHC status may be conferred even in the absence of any avoidance intent on the part of the corporation. In one situation,[36] a manufacturing operation adopted a plan of complete liquidation, sold its business, and invested the proceeds of the sale in U.S. Treasury bills and certificates of deposit. During the liquidating corporation's last tax year, 100 percent of the corporation's adjusted ordinary gross income was interest income. Since the corporation was owned by one shareholder, the corporation was a PHC, even though in the process of liquidation.

Certain types of corporations are expressly excluded from PHC status in § 542(c):

- Tax-exempt organizations under § 501(a).
- Banks and domestic building and loan associations.
- Life insurance companies.
- Surety companies.
- Foreign personal holding companies.

34. § 532(b)(1) and Reg. § 1.541–1(a).

35. *Affiliated Enterprises, Inc. v. Comm.*, 44–1 USTC ¶9178, 32 AFTR 153, 140 F.2d 647 (CA–10, 1944).

36. *Weiss v. U.S.*, 75–2 USTC ¶9538, 36 AFTR2d 75–5186 (D.Ct. Ohio, 1975). See also *O'Sullivan Rubber Co. v. Comm.*, 41–2 USTC ¶9521, 27 AFTR 529, 120 F.2d 845 (CA–2, 1941).

- Lending or finance companies.
- Foreign corporations.
- Small business investment companies.

Without these exceptions, the business world could not perform necessary activities without a high rate of taxation. For example, a legitimate finance company should not be burdened by the PHC tax because it is performing a valuable business function of loaning money. In contrast, in the case of a classic incorporated pocketbook, the major purpose is to shelter the investment income from possible higher individual tax rates.

Definition of a Personal Holding Company

Two tests are incorporated within the PHC provisions:

1. Was more than 50 percent of the *value* of the outstanding stock owned by five or fewer individuals at any time during the *last half* of the taxable year?
2. Is a substantial portion (60 percent or more) of the corporate income (adjusted ordinary gross income) composed of passive types of income such as dividends, interest, rents, royalties, or certain personal service income?

If the answer to *both* of these questions is yes, the corporation is classified as a PHC. Once classified as a PHC, the corporation must pay a penalty tax in addition to the regular corporate income tax. The penalty tax rate is 28 percent.

Stock Ownership Test. To meet the stock ownership test, more than 50 percent *in value* of the outstanding stock must be owned, directly or indirectly, by or for not more than five individuals sometime during the last half of the tax year. Thus, if the corporation has 9 or fewer shareholders, it automatically meets this test. If 10 unrelated individuals own *equal* portions of the value of the outstanding stock, the stock ownership requirement is not met. However, if these 10 individuals do not hold equal value, the test is met.

The ownership test is based on fair market value and not on the number of shares outstanding. Fair market value is determined in light of all the circumstances and is based on the company's net worth, earning and dividend-paying capacity, appreciation of assets, and other relevant factors. If there are two or more classes of stock outstanding, the total value of all the stock is allocated among the various classes according to the relative value of each class.

In determining the stock ownership of an individual, broad constructive ownership rules apply. Under § 544, the following attribution rules determine indirect ownership:

1. Any stock owned by a corporation, partnership, trust, or estate is considered to be owned proportionately by the shareholders, partners, or beneficiaries.
2. The stock owned by the members of an individual's family (brothers, sisters, spouse, ancestors, and lineal descendants) or by the individual's partner is considered to be owned by the individual.
3. If an individual has an option to purchase stock, the stock is regarded as owned by that person.
4. Convertible securities are treated as outstanding stock.

EXAMPLE 8

During the last half of the tax year, Press Corporation has 1,000 shares of outstanding stock, 499 of which are held by various individuals having no relationship to one another and none of whom are partners. The remaining 501 shares are held by seven shareholders as follows:

Dana	100
Dana's spouse	50
Dana's brother	20
Dana's sister	70
Dana's father	120
Dana's son	80
Dana's daughter	61

Under the family attribution rules of § 544(a)(2), Dana owns 501 shares of Press for purposes of determining stock ownership in a PHC. ◆

Attribution rules 2, 3, and 4 are applicable only for the purpose of classifying a corporation as a PHC and cannot be used to avoid the application of the PHC provisions. Basically, the broad constructive ownership rules make it difficult for a closely held corporation to avoid application of the stock ownership test.

Gross Income Test. The gross income test is met if 60 percent or more of the corporation's adjusted ordinary gross income (AOGI) consists of certain passive income items (PHC income). AOGI is calculated by subtracting certain items from gross income (as defined by § 61).[37] The adjustments required to arrive at AOGI appear in Concept Summary 20–2.

In Concept Summary 20–2, the deductions from gross income results in the intermediate concept, ordinary gross income (OGI), whose use is noted subsequently. The starting point, gross income, is not necessarily synonymous with gross receipts. In fact, for transactions in stocks, securities, and commodities, the term "gross income" includes only the excess of gains over any losses.[38]

CONCEPT SUMMARY 20–2
ADJUSTED ORDINARY GROSS INCOME DETERMINATION

Gross income

Less: **a.** Capital gains.
b. Section 1231 gains.

Equals: Ordinary gross income (OGI).

Less: **a.** Depreciation, property taxes, interest expense, and rental expenses directly related to gross income from rents (not to exceed the income from rents).
b. Depreciation, property and severance taxes, interest expense, and rental expenses directly related to gross income from mineral, oil, and gas royalties (not to exceed gross income from the royalties).
c. Interest on a condemnation award, a judgment, a tax refund, and an obligation of the United States held by a dealer.

Equals: Adjusted ordinary gross income (AOGI).

37. §§ 543(b)(1) and (2).

38. Reg. § 1.542–2. See also Reg. § 1.543–2(b) where net gain on transactions in stocks and securities is not reduced by a net loss on commodities futures transactions.

PHC income includes income from dividends; interest; royalties; annuities;[39] rents; mineral, oil, and gas royalties; copyright royalties; produced film rents; computer software royalties; and amounts from certain personal service contracts.

EXAMPLE 9

Crow Corporation has four shareholders, and its AOGI is $95,000, consisting of gross income of $40,000 from a merchandising operation, interest income of $15,000, dividend income of $25,000, and adjusted income of $15,000 from rents. Total passive income is $55,000 ($15,000 + $25,000 + $15,000). Since 60% of AOGI ($57,000) is greater than the passive income ($55,000), the corporation is not a PHC. ◆

EXAMPLE 10

Assume in Example 9 that the corporation received $21,000 in interest income rather than $15,000. Total passive income is now $61,000 ($21,000 + $25,000 + $15,000). Since 60% of AOGI (60% × $101,000 = $60,600) is less than the passive income of $61,000, the corporation is a PHC. ◆

Most passive types of income such as dividends, interest, royalties, and annuities cause few classification problems. Certain income items, however, may or may not be classified as PHC income. Special rules apply to rent income, mineral, oil, and gas royalties, and personal service contracts.

Rent Income. Although rent income is normally classified as PHC income, it can be excluded from that category if two tests are met. The first test is met if a corporation's adjusted income from rents is 50 percent or more of the corporation's AOGI. The second test is satisfied if the total dividends for the tax year are equal to or greater than the amount by which the nonrent PHC income exceeds 10 percent of OGI.[40] Dividends for this purpose include those actually paid, those considered as paid on the last day of the tax year, and consent dividends (see the later discussion of the dividends paid deduction). The taxpayer must meet *both* tests for the rent income to be excluded from PHC income. (See Figure 20–3 later in the chapter.)

With respect to the 50 percent test, *adjusted income from rents* is defined as gross income from rents reduced by the deductions allowable under § 543(b)(3). The deductions are depreciation, property taxes, interest, and rent. Generally, compensation is not included in the term "rents" and is not an allowable deduction. The final amount included in AOGI as adjusted income from rents cannot be less than zero.

EXAMPLE 11

Assume that Hero Corporation has rent income of $10,000 and the following business deductions:

Depreciation on rental property	$1,000
Interest on mortgage	2,500
Real property taxes	1,500
Salaries and other business expenses (§ 162)	3,000

The adjusted income from rents included in AOGI is $5,000 ($10,000 – $1,000 – $2,500 – $1,500). Salaries and other § 162 expenses do not affect the calculation of AOGI. ◆

39. § 543(a)(1).

40. § 543(a)(2).

A company deriving its income primarily from rental activities can avoid PHC status by merely distributing as dividends the amount of nonrent PHC income that exceeds 10 percent of its OGI.

EXAMPLE 12

During the tax year, Now Corporation receives $15,000 in rent income, $4,000 in dividends, and a $1,000 long-term capital gain. Corporate deductions for depreciation, interest, and real estate taxes allocable to the rent income are $10,000. The company pays a total of $2,500 in dividends to its eight shareholders. To determine whether the rent income is PHC income, OGI, AOGI, and adjusted income from rents must be calculated.

Rent income	$15,000
Dividends	4,000
Long-term capital gain	1,000
Gross income	$20,000
Deduct: Gains from sale or disposition of capital assets	(1,000)
OGI	$19,000
Deduct: Depreciation, interest, and real estate taxes	(10,000)
AOGI	$ 9,000

First, adjusted income from rents must be 50% or more of AOGI.

Rent income	$15,000
Deduct: Depreciation, interest, and real estate taxes	(10,000)
Adjusted income from rents	$ 5,000
50% of AOGI	$ 4,500

Now Corporation has satisfied the first test.

Second, total dividends paid for the year are $2,500. This figure must be equal to or greater than the amount by which nonrent PHC income exceeds 10% of OGI.

Nonrent PHC income	$4,000
Less: 10% of OGI	(1,900)
Excess	$2,100

Because Now Corporation meets both tests, the adjusted income from rents is not PHC income. ◆

Mineral, Oil, and Gas Royalties. As with rent income, adjusted income from mineral, oil, and gas royalties can be excluded from PHC income if certain tests are met.[41] First, adjusted income from the royalties must constitute 50 percent or more of AOGI. Second, nonroyalty PHC income may not exceed 10 percent of OGI. Note that this 10 percent test is not accompanied by the dividend escape clause previously described in relation to rent income. Therefore, corporations receiving income from mineral, oil, or gas royalties must be careful to minimize nonroyalty PHC income. Furthermore, adjusted income from rents and copyright royalties are considered to be nonroyalty PHC income whether or not treated as

41. § 543(a)(3).

such by §§ 543(a)(2) and (4). Third, the company's business expenses under § 162 (other than compensation paid to shareholders) must be at least 15 percent of AOGI.

EXAMPLE 13

Pert Corporation has gross income of $4,000, which consists of gross income of $2,500 from oil royalties, $400 of dividends, and $1,100 from the sale of merchandise. The total deductions for depletion, interest, and property and severance taxes allocable to the gross income from oil royalties equal $1,000. Deductions allowable under § 162 are $450. Pert Corporation's adjusted income from oil royalties will not be PHC income if the three tests are met. Therefore, OGI, AOGI, and adjusted income from oil royalties must be determined:

Oil royalties income	$2,500
Dividends	400
Sale of merchandise	1,100
Gross income (*and* OGI)	$4,000
Deduct: Depletion, interest, and property and severance taxes	(1,000)
AOGI	$3,000

Adjusted income from oil royalties must be 50% or more of AOGI.

Oil royalties income	$2,500
Deduct: Depletion, interest, and property and severance taxes	(1,000)
Adjusted income from oil royalties	$1,500
50% of AOGI	$1,500

The first test is met. Since nonroyalty PHC income is $400 (composed solely of the $400 of dividends) and this amount is not more than 10% of OGI, the second test is also satisfied. The third requirement is satisfied if deductible expenses under § 162 amount to at least 15% of AOGI.

§ 162 expenses	$450
15% of $3,000 (AOGI)	$450

Pert Corporation's adjusted income from oil royalties is not PHC income. ◆

As in the case of income from mineral, oil, and gas royalties and rents, copyright royalties and produced film rents are not categorized as PHC income if certain tests are met.[42]

Royalties received from licensing computer software are excluded from the definition of PHC income if the following conditions are satisfied:[43]

- The corporation must be actively engaged in the business of developing computer software.
- The royalties must be at least 50 percent of OGI.
- Business-related deductions must equal or exceed 25 percent of OGI.
- Passive income (other than computer software royalties) in excess of 10 percent of OGI must be distributed as a dividend.

42. §§ 543(a)(4) and (5).

43. § 543(d).

Personal Service Contracts. Any amount from personal service contracts is classified as PHC income only if (1) some person other than the corporation has the right to designate, by name or by description, the individual who is to perform the services and (2) the person so designated owns, directly or indirectly, 25 percent or more in value of the outstanding stock of the corporation at some time during the taxable year.[44]

EXAMPLE 14

Blair, Cody, and Dana (all attorneys) are equal shareholders in Canary Company, a professional association engaged in the practice of law. Irene, a new client, retains Canary Company to pursue a legal claim. Under the terms of the retainer agreement, Irene designates Blair as the attorney who will perform the legal services. The suit is successful, and 30% of the judgment Irene recovers is paid to Canary as a fee. Since the parties have met all of the requirements of § 543(a)(7), the fee received by Canary is PHC income.[45] ◆

The result reached in Example 14 could have been avoided if the retainer agreement had not specifically named Blair as the party to perform the services.

Calculation of the PHC Tax

To this point, the discussion has focused on the determination of PHC status. Once a corporation is classified as a PHC, the amount upon which the penalty tax is imposed must be computed. The tax base is called undistributed PHC income (UPHC income). Basically, this amount is taxable income, subject to certain adjustments, minus the dividends paid deduction. After the adjustments, UPHC income more clearly represents the corporation's dividend-paying capacity. Concept Summary 20–3 shows how this amount is determined.

CONCEPT SUMMARY 20–3
UNDISTRIBUTED PHC INCOME DETERMINATION

Taxable income

Plus:
- a. Dividends received deduction.
- b. Net operating loss (NOL), other than the NOL from the preceding year (computed without the dividends received deduction).
- c. Certain business expenses and depreciation attributable to nonbusiness property owned by the corporation that exceed the income derived from such property (unless the taxpayer proves that the rent was the highest obtainable and the rental business was a bona fide business activity).*

Less:
- a. Federal income tax accrual (other than the PHC tax and the accumulated earnings tax).
- b. Excess charitable contributions beyond the 10% corporate limitation (with a maximum of the 20%, 30%, or 50% limitation imposed on individuals).**
- c. Excess of long-term capital gain over short-term capital loss (net of tax).

Equals: Adjusted taxable income.

Less: Dividends paid deduction.

Equals: Undistributed PHC income.

*§ 545(b).
**Reg. § 1.545–2.

---

44. § 543(a)(7). For an application of the "right to designate," see *Thomas P. Byrnes, Inc.*, 73 T.C. 416 (1979).

45. The example presumes Canary Company will be treated as a corporation for Federal tax purposes. As noted in Chapter 16, this is the usual result of professional association status.

Dividends Paid Deduction. Since the purpose of the PHC penalty tax is to force a corporation to pay dividends, five types of dividends paid deductions reduce the amount subject to the penalty tax (see Figure 20–1). First, dividends actually paid during the tax year ordinarily reduce UPHC income.[46] However, such distributions must be pro rata. They must exhibit no preference to any shares of stock over shares of the same class or to any class of stock over other classes outstanding. The prohibition is especially harsh when portions of an employee-shareholder's salary are declared unreasonable and classified as a disguised or constructive dividend. In the case of a dividend of appreciated property, the dividends paid deduction is the fair market value of the property (not the adjusted basis to the distributing corporation).

EXAMPLE 15

Three individuals are equal shareholders in a PHC. A property dividend with an adjusted basis of $20,000 (FMV of $30,000) is paid to the three shareholders in the following proportion: 25%, 35%, and 40%. This is not a pro rata distribution, and the dividends are not deductible from UPHC income. ◆

A 2½-month grace period exists following the close of the tax year. Dividends paid during this period may be treated as paid during the tax year just closed. However, the amount allowed as a deduction from UPHC income cannot exceed

FIGURE 20–1
Dividends Paid Deductions

Type of Dividend	Availability	Timing	Statutory Location	Effect on Shareholders
Current year	Both § 531 and § 541	By end of year.	§ 561(a)(1)	Reduction in ATI and UPHC income.
Two and one-half month grace period	Both § 531 and § 541	On or before the 15th day of the 3rd month after end of year.	§§ 563(a) and (b)	Reduction in ATI and UPHC income.
Consent dividend	Both § 531 and § 541	Not later than due date of the corporate tax return.	§ 565(a)	Treated as a dividend as of end of tax year and given back as a contribution to capital.
Dividend carryover	§ 541	Not later than due date of the corporate tax return.	§ 564	Reduction in UPHC income.
Deficiency dividend	§ 541	Within 90 days after determination of PHC tax deficiency.	§ 547	Treated as if dividend paid in offending year. No impact on interest and penalties.

46. §§ 561(a)(1) and 562.

either (1) the UPHC income for the tax year or (2) 20 percent of the total dividends distributed during the tax year.[47] Reasonable cause may not be used to overcome the 20 percent limitation, even if the taxpayer relied upon incorrect advice given by an accountant.[48]

The *consent dividend* procedure involves a hypothetical distribution of the corporate income to be taxed to the shareholders. Since the consent dividend is taxable, a dividends paid deduction is allowed. The shareholder's basis in his or her stock is increased by the consent dividend (a contribution to capital), and a subsequent actual distribution of the consent dividend might be taxed. The consent election is filed by the shareholders at any time not later than the due date of the corporate tax return. The consent dividend is considered distributed by the corporation on the last day of the tax year and is included in the gross income of the shareholder in the tax year in which or with which the tax year of the corporation ends. The disadvantage of this special election is that the shareholders must pay taxes on dividends they do not actually receive. However, if cash is not available for dividend distributions, the consent dividend route is a logical alternative.

EXAMPLE 16

Chad Corporation, a calendar year taxpayer solely owned by Tamara, is a PHC. Dividends of $30,000 must be paid to avoid the PHC tax, but the company has a poor cash position. Tamara elects the consent dividend treatment under § 565 and is taxed on $30,000 of dividends. Her basis in Chad Corporation stock is increased by $30,000 as a result of this special election. Thus, Chad does not incur the PHC tax, but Tamara is taxed even though she receives no cash from the corporation with which to pay the tax. ◆

Even after a corporation has been classified as a PHC, a delayed dividend distribution made in a subsequent tax year can avoid the PHC penalty tax. This *deficiency dividend* provision allows a dividend to be paid within 90 days after the determination of the PHC tax deficiency for a prior tax year.[49] A determination occurs when a decision of a court is final, a closing agreement under § 7121 is signed, or a written agreement is signed between the taxpayer and a District Director. The dividend distribution *cannot be made* before the determination or after the running of the 90-day time period. Furthermore, the deficiency dividend procedure does not relieve the taxpayer of interest, additional amounts, or assessable penalties computed with respect to the PHC tax.

A dividend carryover from two prior years may be available to reduce the UPHC income. When the dividends paid by a company in its prior years exceed the company's UPHC income for those years, the excess may be deducted in the current year. See § 564(b) for the computation of this dividend carryover.

Personal Holding Company Planning Model. Some of the complex PHC provisions may be developed into a flow chart format. Figures 20–2 and 20–3 provide a PHC planning model and the rules for the rent exclusion test.

Computations Illustrated. After the appropriate adjustments are made to corporate taxable income and the sum of the dividends paid is subtracted, the

47. §§ 563(b) and 543(a)(2)(B)(ii).
48. *Kenneth Farmer Darrow,* 64 T.C. 217 (1975).
49. § 547.

resulting figure is UPHC income. This is multiplied by the 28% penalty tax rate to obtain the PHC tax. Although the tax revenue from the PHC tax is small, the consequences of this confiscatory tax can be severe. Taxpayers should monitor their corporations and take the necessary steps to avoid the tax.

EXAMPLE 17

Bluebird Corporation had the following items of income and expense in the current year:

Dividend income (less than 20% owned)	$ 40,000
Rent income	150,000
Depreciation expense	40,000
Mortgage interest	30,000
Real estate taxes	30,000
Salaries	20,000
Dividends paid (three shareholders)	20,000
Corporate income tax liability (§ 11)	6,300

FIGURE 20–2 **Personal Holding Company Planning Model**

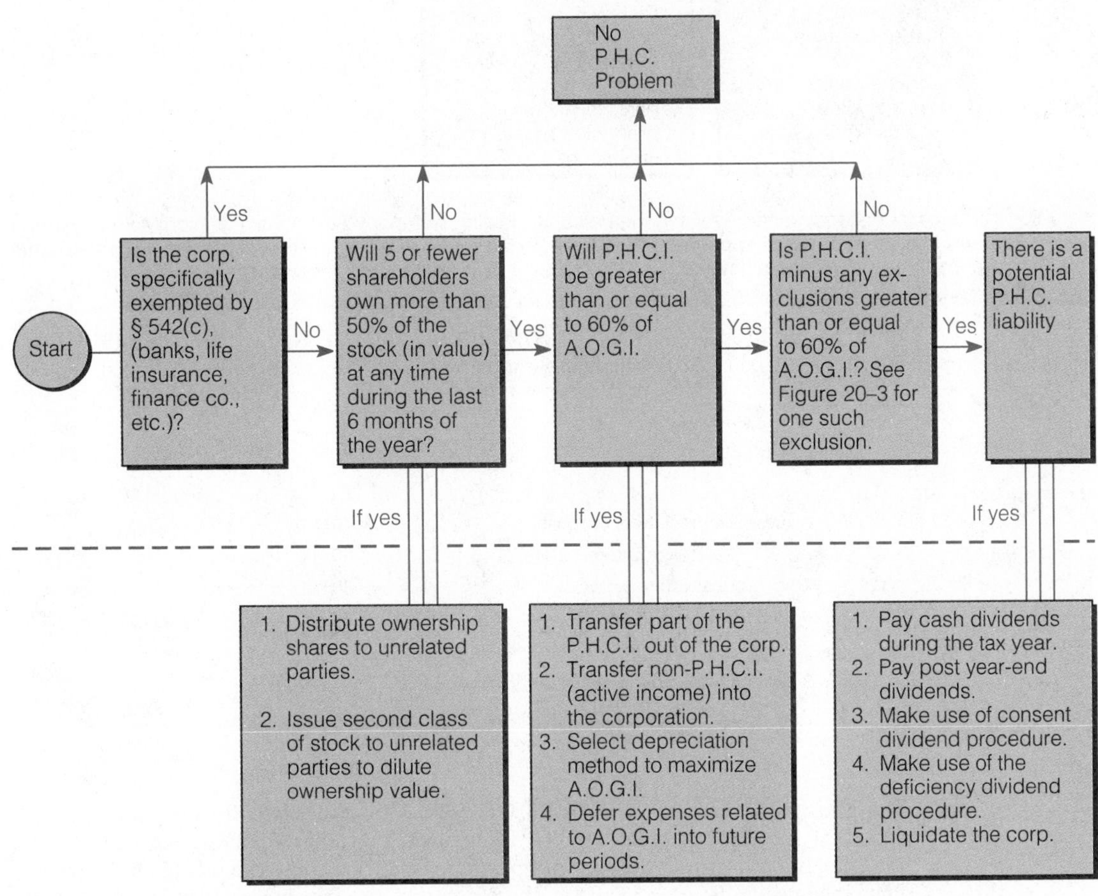

From "Understanding and Avoiding the Personal Holding Company Tax: A Tax Planning Model," by Pratt and Whittenburg, which appeared in the June 1975 issue of *Taxes — the Tax Magazine* published and copyrighted 1975 by Commerce Clearing House, Inc., and appears here with their permission.

FIGURE 20–3 **Rent Exclusion Test**

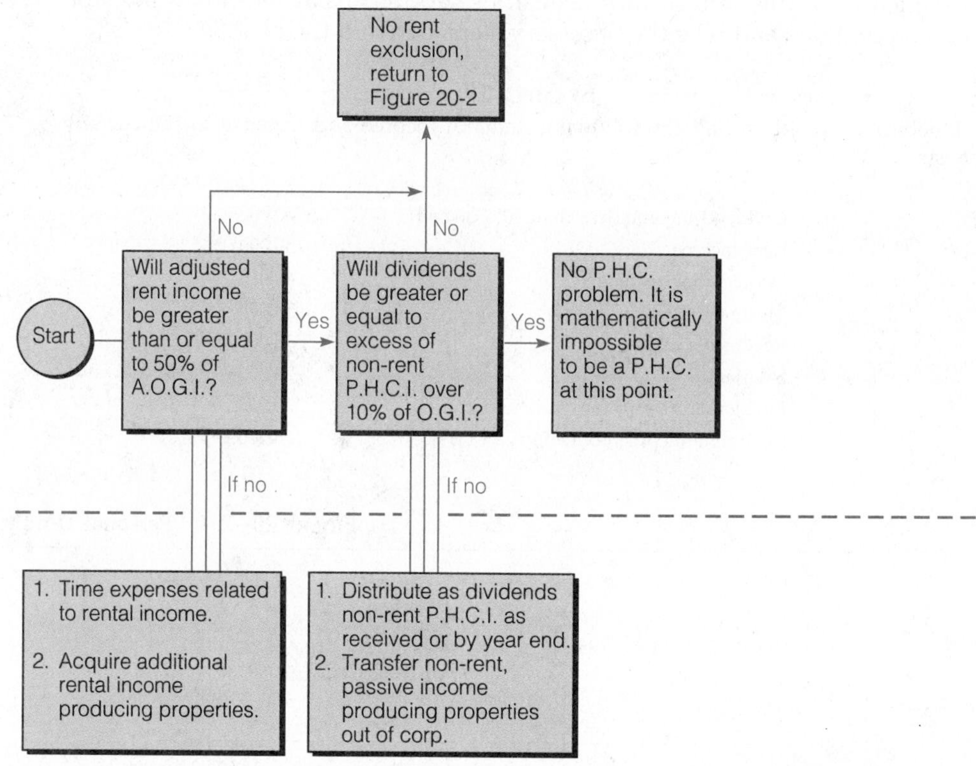

From "Understanding and Avoiding the Personal Holding Company Tax: A Tax Planning Model," by Pratt and Whittenburg, which appeared in the June 1975 issue of *Taxes — the Tax Magazine* published and copyrighted 1975 by Commerce Clearing House, Inc., and appears here with their permission.

OGI is $190,000 ($40,000 + $150,000), and AOGI is $90,000 ($190,000 – $40,000 – $30,000 – $30,000). Taxable income is $42,000, computed as follows:

Rent income		$150,000
Dividend income		40,000
		$190,000
Less: Depreciation expense	$40,000	
Mortgage interest	30,000	
Real estate taxes	30,000	
Salaries	20,000	(120,000)
		$ 70,000
Less: Dividends received deduction ($40,000 × 70%)		(28,000)
Taxable income		$ 42,000

The adjusted income from rents is $50,000 ($150,000 – $100,000). Bluebird does meet the 50% rent income test since $50,000 is greater than 50% of AOGI ($90,000 × 50% = $45,000). But the corporation did not pay at least $21,000 of dividends ($40,000 nonrent PHC income – $19,000 = $21,000). Therefore, the 10% rent income test is not met, and the rent income is classified as PHC income. Since all income is passive, Bluebird Corporation is a PHC. The PHC tax of $12,236 is calculated as follows:

Taxable income	$ 42,000
Plus: Dividends received deduction ($40,000 × 70%)	28,000
	$ 70,000
Less: § 11 tax	(6,300)
	$ 63,700
Less: Dividends paid	(20,000)
UPHC income	$ 43,700
	×.28
PHC tax liability	$ 12,236

◆

EXAMPLE 18

Assume that in Example 17, dividends of $22,000 (instead of $20,000) are paid to the shareholders. In this case, the rent income is not PHC income because the 10% test is met ($22,000 is equal to or greater than the nonrent PHC income in excess of 10% of OGI). Thus, an increase of $2,000 in the dividends paid in Example 17 avoids the $12,236 PHC tax liability. ◆

COMPARISON OF §§ 531 AND 541

A review of several important distinctions between the penalty tax on the unreasonable accumulation of earnings (§ 531) and the tax on PHCs (§ 541) sets the stage for the presentation of tax planning considerations applicable to both taxes.

- Unlike § 531, no element of intent is necessary for the imposition of the § 541 (PHC) tax. This makes § 541 a real trap for the unwary.
- The imposition of the § 541 tax is not affected by the past history of the corporation. Thus, it could be just as applicable to a newly formed corporation as to one that has been in existence for many years. This is not the case with the § 531 tax. Past accumulations have a direct bearing on the determination of the accumulated earnings credit. In this sense, younger corporations are less vulnerable to the § 531 tax since complete insulation generally is guaranteed until accumulations exceed $250,000.
- Although both taxes pose threats for closely held corporations, the stock ownership test of § 542(a)(2) makes this threat very explicit with regard to the § 541 tax. However, publicly held corporations can be subject to the § 531 tax if corporate policy is dominated by certain shareholders who are using the corporate form to avoid income taxes on dividends through the accumulation of corporate profits.[50]
- Sufficient dividend distributions can eliminate both taxes. In the case of § 531, however, such dividends must be distributed on a timely basis. Both taxes allow a 2½-month grace period and provide for the consent dividend procedure.[51] Only the § 541 tax allows the deficiency dividend procedure.

---

50. § 532(c).

51. Under the § 531 tax, dividends paid within the first 2½ months of the succeeding year *must* be carried back to the preceding year. In the case of the § 541 tax, the carryback is optional—some or all of the dividends can be deducted in the year paid. The 20% limit on carrybacks applicable to § 541 [see § 563(a)] does not cover § 531 situations.

- Differences in reporting procedures arise because the § 541 tax is a self-assessed tax while the § 531 tax is not. For example, if a corporation is a PHC, it must file a Schedule PH along with its Form 1120 (the corporate income tax return) for the year involved. Failure to file the Schedule PH can result in the imposition of interest and penalties and also brings into play a special six-year statute of limitations for the assessment of the § 541 tax.[52] On the other hand, the § 531 tax is assessed by the IRS and consequently requires no reporting procedures on the part of the corporate taxpayer.

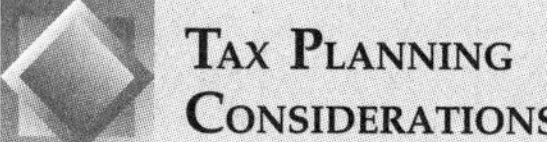

TAX PLANNING CONSIDERATIONS

Even with corporate rates higher than individual rates, a corporation can invest accumulated funds in tax-free vehicles or purchase high-yield corporate stocks to take advantage of the dividends received deduction. Thus, the threat of the accumulated earnings tax and the PHC tax continues to be a prime concern of many corporations.

The § 531 Tax

Justifying the Accumulations. The key defense against imposition of the § 531 tax is to show that the accumulations are necessary to meet the reasonable needs of the business. Several points should be kept in mind:

- To the extent possible, the justification for the accumulation should be documented. If, for example, the corporation plans to acquire additional physical facilities for use in its trade or business, the minutes of the board of directors' meetings should reflect the decision. Furthermore, the documentation should take place during the period of accumulation. This planning may require some foresight on the part of the taxpayer. Meaningful planning to avoid a tax problem should not be based on what happens after the issue has been raised by an agent as the result of an audit. In the case of a profitable closely held corporation that accumulates some or all of its profits, the parties should operate under the assumption that § 531 is always a potential issue. Recognizing a tax problem at an early stage is the first step in a satisfactory resolution.
- Multiple reasons for making an accumulation are not only permissible but invariably advisable. Suppose, for example, a manufacturing corporation plans to expand its plant. It would not be wise to stop with the cost of the expansion as the only justification for all accumulations. What about further justification based on the corporation's working capital requirements as determined under the *Bardahl* formula or some variation? Other reasons for making the accumulation may be present and should be recognized.
- The reasons for the accumulation should be sincere and, once established, pursued to the extent feasible.

EXAMPLE 19

In 1988, the directors of Wind Corporation decide to accumulate $1,000,000 to fund the replacement of Wind's plant. Five years pass, and no steps are taken to begin construction. ◆

52. § 6501(f). See also Chapter 25.

Example 20

In 1988, the directors of Youth Corporation decide to accumulate $1,000,000 to fund the replacement of Youth's plant. In the ensuing five-year period, the following steps are taken: a site selection committee is appointed (1988); a site is chosen (1989); the site (land) is purchased (1990); an architect is retained, and plans are drawn up for the new plant (1992); bids are requested and submitted for the construction of the new plant (1993). ◆

Compare Examples 19 and 20. Youth Corporation is in a much better position to justify the accumulation. Even though the plant has not yet been replaced some five years after the accumulations began, the progress toward its ultimate construction speaks for itself. Wind Corporation may be hard pressed to prove the sincerity of its objective for the accumulations in light of its failure to follow through on the projected replacement.

- The amount of the accumulation should be realistic under the circumstances.

Example 21

Diamond Corporation plans to replace certain machinery at an estimated cost of $500,000. The original machinery was purchased for $300,000 and, because of $250,000 in depreciation deducted for tax purposes, has a present book value of $50,000. How much of an accumulation can be justified for the replacement to avoid the § 531 tax? Initially, $500,000 seems to be the appropriate amount since this is the estimated replacement cost of the machinery. But what about the $250,000 in depreciation that Diamond already deducted? If it is counted again as part of a reasonable accumulation, a double tax benefit results. Only $250,000 ($50,000 unrecovered cost of the old machinery + $200,000 additional outlay necessary) can be justified as the amount for an accumulation.[53] ◆

Example 22

During the current year, a competitor files a $2,000,000 patent infringement suit against Gem Corporation. Competent legal counsel advises Gem that the suit is groundless. Under such conditions, the corporation can hardly justify accumulating $2,000,000 because of the pending lawsuit. ◆

- Since the § 531 tax is imposed on an annual basis, justification for accumulations may vary from year to year.[54]

Example 23

For calendar years 1992 and 1993, Red Corporation was able to justify large accumulations owing to a pending additional income tax assessment. In early 1994, the assessment is settled and paid. After the settlement, Red Corporation can no longer consider the assessment as a reasonable anticipated need of the business. ◆

Danger of Loans to Shareholders. The presence of loans made by a corporation to its shareholders often raises the § 531 issue. If this same corporation has a poor dividend-paying record, it becomes particularly vulnerable. The avowed goal of the § 531 tax is to force certain corporations to distribute dividends. If a

53. *Battelstein Investment Co. v. U.S.*, 71–1 USTC ¶9227, 27 AFTR2d 71–713, 442 F.2d 87 (CA–5, 1971).

54. Compare *Hardin's Bakeries, Inc. v. Martin, Jr.*, 67–1 USTC ¶9253, 19 AFTR2d 647, 293 F.Supp. 1129 (D.Ct.Miss., 1967), with *Hardin v. U.S.*, 70–2 USTC ¶9676, 26 AFTR2d 70–5852 (D.Ct. Miss., 1970), *aff'd., rev'd., rem'd.* by 72–1 USTC ¶9464, 29 AFTR2d 72–1446, 461 F.2d 865 (CA–5, 1972).

corporation can spare funds for loans to shareholders, it certainly has the capacity to pay dividends. Unfortunately, the presence of such loans can cause other tax problems for the parties.

EXAMPLE 24

During the year in question, Quail Corporation made advances of $120,000 to its sole shareholder, Tom. Although prosperous and maintaining substantial accumulations, Quail has never paid a dividend. Under these circumstances, the IRS could move in either of two directions. It could assess the § 531 tax against Quail for its unreasonable accumulation of earnings. Alternatively, the IRS could argue that the advances were not bona fide loans but, instead, taxable dividends. The dual approach places the taxpayers in a difficult position. If, for example, they contend that the advance was a bona fide loan, Tom avoids dividend income but Quail becomes vulnerable to the imposition of the § 531 tax.[55] On the other hand, a concession that the advance was not a loan hurts Tom but helps Quail avoid the penalty tax. ◆

Role of Dividends. The relationship between dividend distributions and the § 531 tax can be further clarified. First, can the payment of enough dividends completely avoid the § 531 tax? The answer must be yes due to the operation of § 535. This provision defines accumulated taxable income as *taxable income* (adjusted by certain items) *minus the sum of the dividends paid deduction and the accumulated earnings credit.* Since the § 531 tax is imposed on accumulated taxable income, no tax is due if the dividends paid and the accumulated earnings credit are large enough to offset taxable income. The payment of sufficient *taxable* dividends, therefore, avoids the tax.[56] Second, can the payment of *some* dividends completely avoid the § 531 tax? As the question is worded, the answer must be *no.* Theoretically, even significant dividend distributions will not insulate a corporation from the tax. From a practical standpoint, however, the payment of dividends indicates that the corporation is not being used exclusively to shield its shareholders from tax consequences. To the extent that this reflects the good faith of the parties and the lack of tax avoidance motivation, it is a factor the IRS considers with regard to the § 531 issue.

Avoiding the § 541 Tax

The classification of a corporation as a PHC requires the satisfaction of *both* the stock ownership and the gross income tests. Failure to meet either of these tests avoids PHC status and the § 541 tax.

- The stock ownership test can be handled through a dispersion of stock ownership. In this regard, however, watch the application of the stock attribution rules.
- Remember the following relationship when working with the gross income test:

$$\frac{\text{PHC income}}{\text{AOGI}} = 60\% \text{ or more}$$

Decreasing the numerator (PHC income) or increasing the denominator (AOGI) of the fraction reduces the resulting percentage. Keeping the percentage below 60

55. *Ray v. U.S.*, 69–1 USTC ¶9334, 23 AFTR2d 69–1141, 409 F.2d 1322 (CA–6, 1969).

56. As noted earlier, nontaxable stock dividends issued under § 305(a) do not affect the dividends paid deduction.

percent precludes classification as a PHC. To control PHC income, investments in low-yield growth securities are preferable to those that generate heavy interest or dividend income. Capital gains from the sale of such securities will not affect PHC status since they are not included in either the numerator or the denominator of the fraction. Investments in tax-exempt securities are attractive because the interest income, like capital gains, has no effect in applying the gross income test.

- Income from personal service contracts may, under certain conditions, be PHC income. Where a 25 percent or more owner of a PHC is specifically designated in a retainer agreement as the party to perform the services, the personal service contract income will be PHC income. See Example 14 earlier in this chapter.
- Rent income may or may not be PHC income. The relative amount of rent income is the key consideration. If

$$\frac{\text{Adjusted income from rents}}{\text{AOGI}} = 50\% \text{ or more}$$

and nonrent PHC income less 10 percent of OGI is distributed as a dividend, rent income is not PHC income. Maximizing adjusted income from rents clearly improves the situation for taxpayers. Since adjusted income from rents represents gross rents less attributable expenses, a conservative approach in determining such expenses is helpful. The taxpayer should minimize depreciation (e.g., choose straight-line over accelerated cost recovery method). This approach to the handling of expenses attributable to rental property is confusing to many taxpayers because it contradicts what is normally done to reduce income tax consequences.

PHC status need not carry tragic tax consequences if the parties are aware of the issue and take appropriate steps. Since the tax is imposed on UPHC income, properly timed dividend distributions neutralize the tax and avoid interest and penalties. Also, as long as a corporation holds PHC status, the § 531 tax cannot be imposed.

Example 25

Hawk Corporation is owned entirely by two sisters, Rose and Suzy (ages 86 and 88, respectively). Hawk Corporation's major assets consist of investments in low-yield and high-growth securities, unimproved real estate, and tax-exempt bonds, all of which have a realizable value of $500,000. Each sister has a basis of $50,000 in the Hawk stock. ◆

The liquidation of Hawk Corporation (a frequent solution to undesired PHC status) would be disastrous to the two sisters. As noted in the discussion of § 331 in Chapter 19, a liquidation results in the recognition of a capital gain of $400,000. In this case, therefore, it is preferable to live with PHC status. Considering the nature of the assets held by Hawk Corporation, this may not be difficult to do. Keep in mind that the interest from the tax-exempt bonds is not PHC income. Should Hawk Corporation wish to sell any of its investments, the long-term capital gain that results is not PHC income. The PHC tax on any other income (the dividends from the securities) can be controlled through enough dividend distributions to reduce UPHC income to zero. Furthermore, as long as Hawk remains a PHC, it is insulated from the § 531 tax (the imposition of which would be highly probable in this case).

The liquidation of Hawk Corporation should await the deaths of Rose and Suzy and should be carried out by their estates or heirs. By virtue of the application of § 1014 (refer to Chapter 12), the income tax basis in the stock is stepped up to the fair market value of the stock on the date of death. Much, if not all, of the capital gain potential currently existing at the shareholder level is eliminated.

PROBLEM MATERIALS

DISCUSSION QUESTIONS

1. List some valid business reasons for accumulating funds in a closely held corporation.
2. Explain the purpose(s) underlying the creation of the accumulated earnings penalty tax and the PHC tax.
3. A merger of two corporations could result in the imposition of the accumulated earnings tax on the surviving corporation. Is this possible? Explain.
4. Explain the *Bardahl* formula. How could it be improved?
5. Can the IRS impose both the PHC tax and the accumulated earnings tax upon a construction company?
6. ATI = Taxable income − Certain adjustments + Dividends paid deduction − Accumulated earnings credit. Please comment.
7. In making the "certain adjustments" (refer to Question 6) necessary in arriving at ATI, which of the following items should be added (+), should be subtracted (−), or will have no effect (NE) on taxable income?

   a. A nontaxable stock dividend distributed by the corporation to its shareholders.
   b. Corporate income tax incurred and paid.
   c. Charitable contributions paid in the amount of 10% of taxable income.
   d. Deduction of an NOL carried over from a prior year.
   e. The dividends received deduction.

8. Ms. Janson (a widow) and Mr. Kimbell (a bachelor) are both shareholders in Hillary Corporation (closely held). If they elope during the year, what possible effect, if any, could it have on Hillary Corporation's vulnerability to the PHC tax?
9. Nixon Corporation is a consulting firm. Its entire outstanding stock is owned by three individuals. Nixon enters into a contract with Claudia Corporation to perform certain consulting services in consideration of which Claudia is to pay Nixon $35,000. The individual who is to perform the services is not designated by name or description in the contract, and no one but Nixon has the right to designate such person. Does the $35,000 constitute PHC income?
10. Which of the following income items could be PHC income?

    a. Annuities.
    b. Interest.
    c. Rent income.
    d. Sales of inventory.
    e. Dividends.
    f. Mineral royalties.
    g. Copyright royalties.
    h. Produced film rents.
    i. Gain from sale of farmland.

11. Deion, a shareholder in Cimena Corporation, dies, and under his will, the stock passes to his children. If Cimena Corporation is a PHC, what effect, if any, will Deion's death have on the continuation of this status?

12. The election to capitalize (rather than to depreciate) certain expenses to rental property could make a difference in determining whether or not the corporate lessor is a PHC. How could this be so?
13. If the 50% test as to rents is satisfied, the PHC tax cannot be imposed upon the corporation. Do you agree? Why or why not?
14. The payment of enough dividends can avoid either the accumulated earnings tax or the PHC tax. Explain.
15. Explain the deficiency dividend procedure for purposes of the accumulated earnings tax.
16. Relate the following points to the avoidance of the accumulated earnings tax:
    a. Documentation of justification for the accumulation.
    b. Multiple justifications for the accumulation.
    c. Follow-up on the established justification for the accumulation.
    d. Loans by the corporation to its shareholders.
    e. The corporation's record of substantial dividend payments.
17. Relate the following points to the avoidance of the PHC tax:
    a. Sale of stock to outsiders.
    b. An increase in AOGI.
    c. A decrease in PHC income.
    d. Long-term capital gains recognized by the corporation.
    e. Corporate investment in tax-exempt bonds.
    f. Income from personal service contracts.
    g. The choice of straight-line depreciation for rental property owned by the corporation.
18. Compare the accumulated earnings tax to the PHC tax on the basis of the following items:
    a. The element of intent.
    b. Applicability of the tax to a newly created corporation.
    c. Applicability of the tax to a publicly held corporation.
    d. The 2½-month rule with respect to the dividends paid deduction.
    e. The availability of the deficiency dividend procedure.
    f. Procedures for reporting and paying the tax.

PROBLEMS

19. A calendar year consulting corporation has accumulated E & P of $90,000 on January 1, 1993. For the calendar year 1993, the corporation has taxable income of $100,000. This corporation has no reasonable needs that justify an accumulation of its E & P. Calculate the amount vulnerable to the accumulated earnings penalty tax.
20. Smoltz Corporation, a manufacturing company, retained $90,000 for its reasonable business needs in 1993. The company had a long-term capital gain of $30,000, a net short-term capital gain of $30,000, and a net short-term capital loss of $25,000, with a resulting capital gain tax of $1,250. The accumulated E & P at the end of 1992 was $260,000. On January 28, 1993, Smoltz paid a taxable dividend of $90,000. Calculate any accumulated earnings credit for 1993.
21. A retail corporation had accumulated E & P of $250,000 on January 1, 1993. Its taxable income for the year 1993 was $75,000. The corporation paid no dividends during the year. There were no other adjustments to determine accumulated taxable income. Assume a court determined that the corporation is subject to the accumulated earnings tax and that the reasonable needs of the business required E & P in the total amount of $266,500. Determine the accumulated earnings tax and explain your calculations.

22. A construction corporation is accumulating a significant amount of E & P. Although the corporation is closely held, it is not a PHC. The following facts relate to the tax year 1993:

Taxable income	$450,000
Federal income tax	153,000
Dividend income from a qualified domestic corporation (less than 20% owned)	40,000
Dividends paid in 1993	70,000
Consent dividends	35,000
Dividends paid on 2/1/94	5,000
Accumulated earnings credit	10,000
Excess charitable contributions (the portion in excess of the amount allowed as a deduction in computing the corporate income tax)	9,000
Net capital loss adjustment	4,000

Compute the accumulated earnings tax, if any.

23. The following facts relate to a closely held accounting services corporation's 1993 tax year:

Net taxable income	$400,000
Federal income taxes	136,000
Excess charitable contributions	20,000
Capital loss adjustment	30,000
Dividends received (less than 20% owned)	140,000
Dividends paid	40,000
Accumulated earnings, 1/1/93	130,000

Assume that this is not a PHC. Calculate any accumulated earnings tax.

24. A wholly owned motor freight corporation has permitted its earnings to accumulate. The company has no inventory but wishes to use the *Bardahl* formula to determine the amount of operating capital required for a business cycle. The following facts are relevant:

Yearly revenues	$3,300,000
Average accounts receivable	300,000
Yearly expenses	3,500,000
Average accounts payable	213,000

a. Determine the turnover rate of average accounts receivable.
b. Determine the number of days in the accounts receivable cycle.
c. Determine the expenses for one accounts receivable cycle.
d. Determine the number of days in the accounts payable cycle.
e. Determine the operating capital needed for one business cycle.
f. Explain why the time allowed a taxpayer for the payment of accounts payable should be taken into consideration in applying the *Bardahl* formula.

25. Nap Corporation is having accumulated earnings problems but has no accounts receivable. Otis, the corporate controller, provides you with the following information:

Year-end balances:	
Current assets	
Cash	$25,000
Inventory (average)	72,000
	$97,000
Current liabilities	17,000
Working capital available	$80,000

Income statement:		
Gross sales		$330,000
Less: Sales returns and allowances		30,000
		$300,000
Less: Cost of goods sold	$170,000	
Sales and administrative expenses	50,000	
Depreciation	15,000	
Income taxes	9,000	244,000
Net income		$ 56,000

Calculate the working capital *required* for the corporation if purchases total $120,000.

26. The stock of Party Corporation is owned as follows:

Sand Corporation (wholly owned by Karl)	100 shares
Karl's wife	100 shares
Karl's partner	100 shares
Karl's wife's sister	100 shares
Abe	50 shares
Betty	30 shares
Charles	20 shares
Unrelated individuals with 10 or fewer shares	500 shares
Total	1,000 shares

Do five or fewer individuals own more than 50% of Party Corporation?

27. A corporation has gross income of $20,000, which consists of $11,000 of rent income and $9,000 of dividend income. The corporation has $3,000 of rent income adjustments and pays $8,000 of dividends to its nine shareholders.

    a. Calculate adjusted income from rents.
    b. Calculate AOGI.
    c. Is the so-called 50% test met? Show calculations.
    d. Is the 10% rent income test met? Show calculations.
    e. Is the corporation a PHC?

28. Assume one change in the situation in Problem 27. Rent income adjustments are decreased from $3,000 to $2,000. Answer the same questions as in Problem 27.

29. Clear Corporation has gross income of $175,000, which consists of gross income from rent of $110,000, $40,000 from the sale of merchandise, dividends of $15,000, and income from annuities of $10,000. Deductions directly related to the rent income total $30,000.

    a. Calculate OGI.
    b. Calculate AOGI.
    c. Calculate adjusted income from rent.
    d. Does the rent income constitute PHC income? Explain.
    e. Is this corporation a PHC (assuming there are seven shareholders)?

30. Daryl is the sole owner of a corporation. The following information is relevant to the corporation's tax year just ended:

Capital gain	$ 20,000
Dividend income	30,000
Rent income	130,000
Rent expenses	40,000
Section 162 business expenses	15,000
Dividends paid	12,000

    a. Calculate OGI.
    b. Calculate AOGI.

c. Calculate adjusted income from rents.
d. Calculate nonrent PHC income.
e. Does this corporation meet the 50% rent income test? Explain.
f. Does this corporation meet the 10% rent income test? Explain.
g. Is this company a PHC?
h. Would your answers change if $15,000 of dividends are paid?

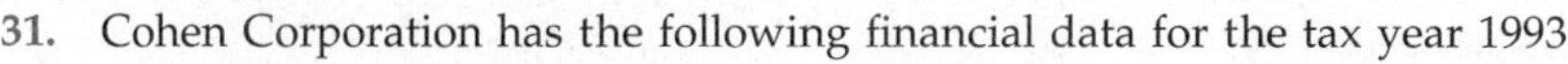

31. Cohen Corporation has the following financial data for the tax year 1993:

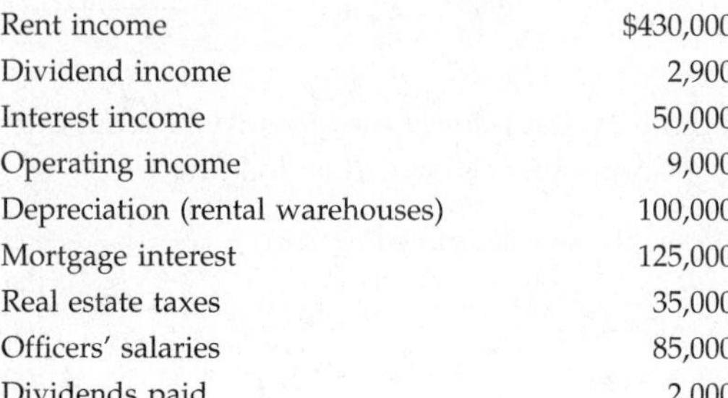

Rent income	$430,000
Dividend income	2,900
Interest income	50,000
Operating income	9,000
Depreciation (rental warehouses)	100,000
Mortgage interest	125,000
Real estate taxes	35,000
Officers' salaries	85,000
Dividends paid	2,000

a. Calculate OGI.
b. Calculate AOGI.
c. Does Cohen Corporation's adjusted income from rents meet the 50% or more of AOGI test?
d. Does Cohen Corporation meet the 10% dividend test?
e. How much in dividends could Cohen Corporation pay within the 2½-month grace period during 1994?
f. If the 1993 corporate income tax return has not been filed, what would you suggest for Cohen Corporation?

32. Using the legend provided, classify each of the following statements accordingly:

Legend

A = Relates only to the tax on unreasonable accumulation of earnings (the § 531 tax)
P = Relates only to the PHC tax (the § 541 tax)
B = Relates to both the § 531 tax and the § 541 tax
N = Relates to neither the § 531 tax nor the § 541 tax

a. The tax is applied to taxable income of the corporation after adjustments are made.
b. The tax is a self-assessed tax.
c. An accumulation of funds for reasonable business purposes will help avoid the tax.
d. A consent dividend mechanism can be used to avoid the tax.
e. If the stock of the corporation is equally held by 10 unrelated individuals, the tax cannot be imposed.
f. Any charitable deduction in excess of the 10% limitation is allowed as a deduction before the tax is imposed.
g. Gains from the sale or disposition of capital assets are not subject to the tax.
h. A sufficient amount of rent income will cause the tax not to be imposed.
i. A life insurance company would not be subject to the tax.
j. A corporation with only dividend income would avoid the tax.

33. Indicate in each of the following independent situations whether the corporation involved is a PHC (assume the stock ownership test is met):

	Able Corporation	Bacon Corporation	Cacey Corporation	Don Corporation
Sales of merchandise	$ 8,000	$ -0-	$ -0-	$ 2,500
Capital gains	-0-	-0-	-0-	1,000
Dividend income	15,000	5,000	1,000	2,500
Gross rent income	10,000	5,000	9,000	15,000
Expenses related to rents	8,000	2,500	8,000	10,000
Dividends paid	-0-	-0-	-0-	500
Personal holding company? (Circle Y for yes or N for no.)	Y N	Y N	Y N	Y N

34. Indicate in each of the following independent situations whether the corporation involved is a PHC (assume the stock ownership test is met):

	Eel Corporation	Foy Corporation	Get Corporation	Hit Corporation
Sales of merchandise	$ -0-	$3,000	$ -0-	$ -0-
Capital gains	-0-	-0-	1,000	-0-
Interest income	20,000	4,800	2,000	60,000
Gross rent income	80,000	1,200	20,000	50,000
Expenses related to rents	60,000	1,000	10,000	-0-
Dividends paid	12,000	-0-	-0-	20,000
Personal holding company? (Circle Y for yes or N for no.)	Y N	Y N	Y N	Y N

35. Calculate in each of the following independent situations the PHC tax liability in 1993:

	Pear Corporation	Quake Corporation
Taxable income	$140,000	$580,000
Dividends received deduction	37,000	70,000
Contributions in excess of 10%	3,000	10,000
Federal income taxes	37,850	197,200
Net capital gain	70,000	40,000
Capital gain tax	25,350	13,600
NOL under § 172		12,000
Current year dividends	12,000	120,000
Consent dividends		20,000
Two and one-half month dividends	4,000	

CHAPTER

S CORPORATIONS

OBJECTIVES

Provide an in-depth discussion of the rules governing S status.

Describe the corporations that qualify for the S election.

Discuss how the election must be made and, once made, how it can be lost.

Explain the effect of the S election on the corporation and its shareholders.

Describe the situations where S status is desirable or undesirable.

OUTLINE

GENERAL CONSIDERATIONS

Subchapter S of the Internal Revenue Code of 1986 allows for the unique treatment of certain corporations for Federal income tax purposes.[1] This election essentially results in the S corporation receiving tax treatment that resembles that of a partnership, but the entity is still a corporation under state law and for many other tax purposes. Special provisions pertain to the entity, however, under the operational provisions of §§ 1361 through 1379. Since individual tax rates are now generally lower than corporate rates, both Subchapter S and Subchapter K (partnerships) of the Code have taken on an added importance. Most businesses should reevaluate the desirability of using a C corporation as the means of conducting a trade or business.

An S corporation is largely a tax-reporting, rather than a tax-paying, entity. In this respect, the entity is treated much like a partnership. As in the partnership conduit concept, the taxable income of an S corporation flows through to the shareholders, regardless of whether the income is distributed in the form of actual dividends. There is, in general, no S corporation corporate-level tax, and the income is taxed to the shareholders immediately.

EXAMPLE 1

Assume that a flow-through business entity earns $300,000, the applicable marginal individual tax rate is 31%, the applicable marginal corporate tax rate is 34%, and all after-tax income is distributed currently. The entity's available after-tax earnings compared with those of a similar C corporation are as follows:

	C Corporation	S Corporation or Partnership
Earnings	$ 300,000	$300,000
Less: Corporate tax	(102,000)	–0–
Available for distribution	$ 198,000	$300,000
Less: Tax at shareholder level	(61,380)	(93,000)
Available after-tax earnings	$ 136,620	$207,000

The flow-through business entity generates an extra $70,380 of after-tax earnings ($207,000 – $136,620) compared with a similar C corporation. Moreover, the flow-through business entity avoids the corporate alternative minimum tax and the alternative minimum taxable income ACE adjustment (refer to Chapter 14). The C corporation might be able to reduce this disadvantage by paying out its earnings as compensation, rents, or interest expense. Tax at the owner level also can be avoided by not distributing after-tax earnings. ◆

An S corporation is not subject to the alternative minimum tax, accumulated earnings tax, or personal holding company tax. Certain S corporations may, however, be subject to an excess passive investment income tax, a built-in gains tax, or a capital gains tax.

Gains and losses of C corporations do not flow through to the shareholders. However, gains and losses of an S corporation *are* allocated to the shareholders, who report them on their individual tax returns. The nature of a closely held

---

1. Under the tax law, a Subchapter S corporation is called an "S corporation." A regular corporation that has not elected S status is designated a "C corporation." C corporations are those governed by Subchapter C of the Code (§§ 301–386).

sports organization makes an S election advantageous. H. R. "Bum" Bright, for example, purchased the Dallas Cowboys in 1984 for $85 million. Before the sale of the Cowboys to Jerry Jones in 1989, the team's record plummeted along with attendance. With an S election, Bright could have taken advantage of these losses on his personal tax return, except that he had a similar run of bad luck as the largest shareholder in First Republic Bank Corporation.

Other corporate transactions that flow through separately under the conduit concept include net long-term capital gains and losses, charitable contributions, tax-exempt interest, foreign tax credits, and business credits. Each shareholder of an S corporation separately takes into account his or her pro rata share of certain items of income, deductions, and credits. The character of any item of income, expense, gain, loss, or credit is determined at the corporate level. These tax items pass through as such to each shareholder, based on the prorated number of days during the relevant S year that each shareholder held stock in the corporation.

Subchapter S in Perspective

Subchapter S permits certain corporations to avoid the corporate income tax and enables them to pass through operating losses to their shareholders. It represents an attempt to achieve a measure of tax neutrality in resolving the issue of whether a business should be conducted as a sole proprietorship, partnership, or corporation.

In dealing with Subchapter S, certain observations should be kept in mind:

- S corporation status is an elective provision. Failure to make the election will mean that the rules applicable to the taxation of C corporations and shareholders will apply (refer to Chapter 16).
- S corporations are regular corporations in the legal sense. The S election affects only the Federal income tax consequences of electing corporations. A few states, including Louisiana and New Jersey, do not recognize the S election, and S corporations in these states are subject to the state corporate income tax and whatever other state corporate taxes are imposed.
- Federal income tax law treats S corporations neither as partnerships nor as regular corporations. The tax treatment is almost like partnership taxation, but it involves a unique set of tax rules. However, Subchapter C controls unless Subchapter S otherwise provides an applicable tax effect.
- Because Subchapter S is an elective provision, both the IRS and the courts have generally demanded strict compliance with the applicable Code requirements. Any unanticipated deviation from the various governing requirements may therefore lead to an undesirable and often unexpected tax result (e.g., the loss of the S election).

Although not generally regarded as a taxable entity, an S corporation may be subject to the following taxes.

- Preelection built-in gains tax.
- Passive investment income penalty tax.

An S corporation is *not* subject to the following taxes.

- Corporate income tax.
- Accumulated earnings tax.
- Personal holding company tax.
- Alternative minimum tax (AMT).
- Environmental excise tax on AMT income.

QUALIFICATION FOR S CORPORATION STATUS

Definition of a Small Business Corporation

A small business corporation must possess the following characteristics.[2]

- Is a domestic corporation (is incorporated or organized in the United States).
- Is not otherwise ineligible for the election.
- Has no more than 35 shareholders.
- Has as its shareholders only individuals, estates, and certain trusts.
- Issues only one class of stock.
- Does not have any nonresident alien shareholders.

Ineligible Corporation. Banks, insurance companies, Puerto Rico or possession corporations, and members of an affiliated group (as defined in § 1504) are not eligible to make an S election. Thus, an S corporation cannot own 80 percent or more of the stock of another corporation. Under certain conditions, however, a corporation can establish one or more *inactive* affiliates, in the event that such companies may be needed in the future. The *affiliated group* prohibition does not apply as long as none of the affiliated corporations engages in business or produces gross income.

Number of Shareholders Limitation. An electing corporation is limited to 35 shareholders. This number corresponds to the private placement exemption under Federal securities law. In testing for the 35-shareholder limitation, a husband and wife are treated as one shareholder as long as they remain married. Furthermore, the estate of a husband or wife and the surviving spouse are treated as one shareholder.

EXAMPLE 2

Harry and Wilma (husband and wife) jointly own 10 shares in Oriole, Inc., an S corporation, with the remaining 90 shares outstanding owned by 34 other unmarried persons. Harry and Wilma are divorced; pursuant to the property settlement approved by the court, the 10 shares held by Harry and Wilma are divided between them (5 to each). Before the divorce settlement, Oriole had only 35 shareholders. After the settlement, it has 36 shareholders and no longer qualifies as a small business corporation. ◆

Type of Shareholder Limitation. All of an S corporation's shareholders must be either individuals, estates, or certain trusts. Stated differently, none of the shareholders may be partnerships, corporations, or nonqualifying trusts. The justification for this limitation is related to the 35-shareholder restriction. If, for example, a partnership with 40 partners could be a shareholder, could it not be said that the corporation has at least 40 owners? If this interpretation were permitted, the 35-shareholder restriction could easily be circumvented by indirect ownership. Keep in mind, though, that an S corporation can be a partner in

2. § 1361(b)(1). Note that the definition of "small" for purposes of Subchapter S relates chiefly to the number of shareholders and not to the size of the corporation.

a partnership and can own stock of another corporation or all the stock of an inactive subsidiary corporation.

Nonresident Alien Prohibition. An S corporation cannot have a nonresident alien as a shareholder. In a community property jurisdiction where one of the spouses is married to a nonresident alien, this rule can be a trap for the unwary. A resident alien or a nonresident U.S. citizen can be an S corporation shareholder, however.

One Class of Stock Limitation. An S corporation can have only one class of stock issued and outstanding.[3] Congress apparently felt that the capital structure of a small business corporation should be kept relatively simple. Allowing more than one class of stock (e.g., common and preferred) would complicate the pass-through of various corporate tax attributes to the shareholders. Authorized and unissued stock or treasury stock of another class does not disqualify the corporation. Likewise, unexercised stock options, warrants, and convertible debentures do not constitute a second class of stock, and differences in voting rights among shares of common stock are permitted.

Essentially, an S corporation has one class of stock unless deliberate actions are taken to circumvent the requirement. Facts and circumstances determine the proper tax treatment of business transactions. For example, a second class of stock does not exist where the IRS recharacterizes a payment of excessive compensation as a dividend distribution.

Making the Election

If the corporation satisfies the definition of a small business corporation, the next step to achieving S status is a valid election. Key factors include who must make the election and when the election must be made.

Who Must Elect. The election is made by filing Form 2553, and *all* shareholders must consent.[4] For this purpose, both husband and wife must file consents even if their stock is held as joint tenants, tenants in common, tenants by the entirety, or community property. Since a husband and wife are generally considered as one shareholder for purposes of the 35-shareholder limitation, this inconsistency in treatment has led to considerable taxpayer grief—particularly in community property states where the spouses may not realize that their stock is jointly owned as a community asset.

The consent of a minor shareholder can be made by the minor or a legal or natural guardian (e.g., parent). If the stock is held under a state Uniform Gifts to Minors Act, the custodian of the stock may consent for the minor but only if the custodian is also the minor's legal or natural guardian. The minor is not required to issue a new consent when he or she comes of age and the custodianship terminates.[5]

When the Election Must Be Made. To be effective for the following year, the election can be made at any time during the current year. To be effective for the current year, the election must be made on or before the fifteenth day of the third month of that year. An election can be effective for a short tax year of less than two months and fifteen days, even if it is not made until the following tax year.[6]

---

3. § 1361(b)(1)(D).

4. § 1362(a)(2).

5. Rev.Rul. 71–287, 1971–2 C.B. 317.

6. § 1362(b).

EXAMPLE 3

In 1993, Xexus Corporation, a calendar year C corporation, decides to become an S corporation beginning January 1, 1994. An election made at any time during 1993 will accomplish this objective. If, however, the election is made in 1994, it must be made on or before March 15, 1994. An election after March 15, 1994, will not make Xexus an S corporation until 1995. ◆

Although no statutory authority exists for obtaining an extension of time for filing an election or consent, a shareholder may obtain an extension of time to file a consent if a timely election is filed, reasonable cause is given, and the interests of the government are not jeopardized.

An election cannot be made for an entity that does not yet exist.[7] In the case of a newly created corporation, the question may arise as to when the 2½-month election period begins to run. Under the law, the first month begins at the earliest occurrence of any of the following events: (1) when the corporation has shareholders, (2) when it acquires assets, or (3) when it begins doing business.

EXAMPLE 4

Several individuals acquire assets on behalf of Table Corporation on June 29, 1993, and begin doing business on July 3, 1993. They subscribe to shares of stock, file articles of incorporation for Table, and become shareholders on July 7, 1993. The S election must be filed no later than 2½ months from June 29, 1993 (on or before September 12) to be effective for 1993. ◆

Even if the 2½-month rule is met, a current election will not be valid until the following year under either of the following conditions:

- The eligibility requirements were not met during any part of the taxable year before the date of election.
- Persons who were shareholders during any part of the taxable year before the election date, but were not shareholders when the election was made, did not consent.

These rules prevent the allocation of income or losses to preelection shareholders who either were ineligible to hold S corporation stock or did not consent to the election.

EXAMPLE 5

As of January 15, 1993, the stock of Robin Corporation (a calendar year C corporation) was held equally by three individual shareholders: Yoon, Velvia, and Zelda. On that date, Zelda sold her interest to Yoon and Velvia. On March 14, 1993, Yoon and Velvia make the S election by filing Form 2553. Robin cannot become an S corporation until 1994. Although the election filing was timely, Zelda did not consent. Had all individuals who were shareholders (Yoon, Velvia, and Zelda) signed Form 2553 during the year, S status would have taken effect as of January 1, 1993. ◆

Once an election is made, it need not be renewed; it remains in effect unless otherwise lost.

7. See, for example, *T. H. Campbell & Bros., Inc.*, 34 TCM 695, T.C.Memo. 1975–149.

Loss of the Election

An S election can be lost in any of the following ways.

- A new shareholder owning more than one-half of the stock affirmatively refuses to consent to the election.
- Shareholders owning a majority of shares (voting and nonvoting) voluntarily revoke the election.
- The number of shareholders exceeds the maximum allowable limitation.
- A class of stock other than voting or nonvoting common stock is created.
- A subsidiary (other than a nonoperating entity) is acquired.
- The corporation fails the passive investment income limitation.
- A nonresident alien becomes a shareholder.

Voluntary Revocation. Section 1362(d)(1) permits a voluntary revocation of the election if shareholders owning a majority of shares consent. A revocation filed up to and including the fifteenth day of the third month of the tax year is effective for the entire tax year, unless a prospective effective date is specified. A revocation made after the fifteenth day of the third month of the tax year is effective on the first day of the following tax year. However, if a prospective date is specified, the termination is effective as of the specified date.

EXAMPLE 6

The shareholders of Termite Corporation, a calendar year S corporation, elect to revoke the election on January 5, 1993. Assuming the election is duly executed and its filing is timely, Termite becomes a regular corporation for calendar year 1993. If, on the other hand, the election is not made until June 1993, Termite is not a C corporation until calendar year 1994. ◆

A revocation that designates a prospective effective date results in the splitting of the year into a short S corporation taxable year and a short C corporation taxable year. The day *before* the day on which the revocation occurs is treated as the last day of a short S corporation taxable year, and the day on which the revocation occurs is treated as the first day of the short regular corporate taxable year. The corporation allocates the income or loss for the entire year on a pro rata basis.

EXAMPLE 7

Assume the same facts as in Example 6, except that Termite designates July 1, 1993, as the revocation date. Accordingly, June 30, 1993, is the last day of the S corporation taxable year. The C taxable year runs from July 1, 1993, to December 31, 1993. Any income or loss for the entire year is allocated between the short years on a prorated basis. ◆

Rather than making a pro rata allocation, the corporation can elect (with the consent of *all* who were shareholders at any time during the S short year) to report the income or loss on each return on the basis of income or loss as shown on the corporate permanent records. Under this method, items are attributed to the short S and C corporation years according to the time they were incurred (as reflected in the entity's accounting records).[8]

---

8. §§ 1362(e)(1), (2), and (3).

Cessation of Small Business Corporation Status. A corporation not only must be a small business corporation to make the S election but also must continue to qualify as such to keep the election. In other words, meeting the definition of a small business corporation is a continuing requirement for maintaining S status. In the case of an involuntary termination, the loss of the election applies as of the date on which the disqualifying event occurs.

EXAMPLE 8

Tamra Corporation has been a calendar year S corporation for three years. On August 13, 1993, one of its 35 unmarried shareholders sells *some* of her stock to an outsider. Tamra now has 36 shareholders, and it ceases to be a small business corporation. For 1993, Tamra is an S corporation through August 12, 1993, and a C corporation from August 13 through December 31, 1993. ◆

Passive Investment Income Limitation. The Code provides a passive investment income limitation for S corporations that possess accumulated earnings and profits (AEP) from years in which the entity was a C corporation. If such a corporation has passive income in excess of 25 percent of its gross receipts for three consecutive taxable years, the S election is terminated as of the beginning of the fourth year.[9]

EXAMPLE 9

For 1990, 1991, and 1992, Bacon Corporation, a calendar year S corporation, derived passive income in excess of 25% of its gross receipts. If Bacon holds AEP from years in which it was a C corporation, its S election is terminated as of January 1, 1993. ◆

An S corporation could acquire such damaging C corporation earnings and profits from a regular corporation where earnings and profits carry over in a reorganization (e.g., due to a merger). They could also have been earned in years before the S election. S corporations themselves never generate earnings and profits.

Although passive investment income appears to parallel that of personal holding company income (refer to Chapter 20), the two types of income are not identical. For example, long-term capital gain from the sale of securities is passive investment income but is not personal holding company income. Moreover, there are no relief provisions for rent income similar to the personal holding company rules. The inclusion of gains from the sale of securities within the definition of passive investment income generally has made it difficult, if not impossible, for corporations that deal chiefly in security transactions to achieve S status if C corporation earnings and profits exist.

Rents present a unique problem. Although they are classified by the Code as passive investment income, rents do not fall into this category if the corporation (landlord) renders significant services to the occupant (tenant).

EXAMPLE 10

Tepee Corporation owns and operates an apartment building. Although the corporation provides utilities for the building, maintains the lobby in the building, and furnishes trash collection for the tenants, this does not constitute the rendering of significant services for the occupants.[10] Thus, the rents paid by the tenants of the building are passive investment income to Tepee. ◆

9. § 1362(d)(3)(A)(ii).

10. Reg. § 1.1372–4(b)(5)(vi); *Bramlette Building Corp., Inc.*, 52 T.C. 200 (1969), *aff'd.* in 70–1 USTC ¶9361, 25 AFTR2d 70–1016, 424 F.2d 751 (CA–5, 1970).

Example 11

Assume the same facts as in Example 10, with one addition—Tepee also furnishes maid services to its tenants. Now the services rendered are significant, in that they go beyond what one might normally expect the landlord of an apartment building to provide. Under these circumstances, the rent income no longer constitutes passive investment income. ◆

Reelection after Termination. After the election has been terminated, five years must pass before a new election can be made. The Code does, however, allow the IRS to make exceptions to this rule and permit an earlier reelection by the corporation in two situations.

- There is a more-than-50 percent change in ownership after the first year for which the termination is applicable.
- The event causing the termination was not reasonably within the control of the S corporation or its majority shareholders.

Operational Rules

An S corporation is largely a tax-reporting, rather than a tax-paying, entity. In this respect, the entity is treated much like a partnership. As in the partnership conduit concept, the taxable income of an S corporation flows through to the shareholders, whether or not the income is distributed in the form of actual dividends. Likewise, losses of the entity are allocated to the shareholders, who deduct them on their individual tax returns. Other corporate transactions that flow through separately under the conduit concept include net long-term capital gains and losses, charitable contributions, tax-exempt interest, foreign tax credits, and business credits.

As under the partnership rules, each shareholder of an S corporation takes into account separately his or her pro rata share of certain items of income, deductions, and credits. Under § 1366(b), the character of any item of income, expense, gain, loss, or credit is determined at the corporate level and then is retained at the shareholder level. The tax items pass through to each shareholder, based on the prorated number of days during the relevant S year that each held stock in the corporation.

Choice of Tax Year

Since S corporation shareholders report their shares of S items as of the entity's year-end, the selection of a corporate tax year is an important tax decision. An S corporation may use a calendar year or a fiscal year; for tax deferral purposes, a corporate fiscal year ending January 31 and a calendar year shareholder would be ideal.

Under current law, however, S corporations must conform to the taxable years of their shareholders (the calendar year in most instances). There are two exceptions to this general rule. First, an S corporation may use a taxable year for which it can establish a business purpose.[11] Second, an S corporation may make

11. § 1378(a).

a one-time election under § 444 to keep or establish a fiscal year, provided that a corporate-level payment is made on any income deferred by the shareholders.

An S corporation can establish an acceptable business purpose for a fiscal year in three ways.

- The fiscal year is a natural business year.
- The fiscal year serves an acceptable business purpose.
- An existing S corporation meets certain grandfathering requirements.[12]

Meeting the natural business year exception involves a simple quantitative test. If 25 percent or more of a corporation's gross receipts for the 12-month period is recognized in the last 2 months of that period, and the requirement has been met for three consecutive 12-month periods, the S corporation may adopt, retain, or change to a noncalendar year. If the entity is to establish a natural business year, it must have at least a 47-month gross receipts history.

EXAMPLE 12

An S corporation's gross receipts total $100,000 for each of the last three calendar years. If the corporation recognizes at least $25,000 of the gross receipts in April and May for three consecutive years, the S corporation may adopt, retain, or change to a May 31 year-end. The following diagram illustrates the test for the May 31 year-end.

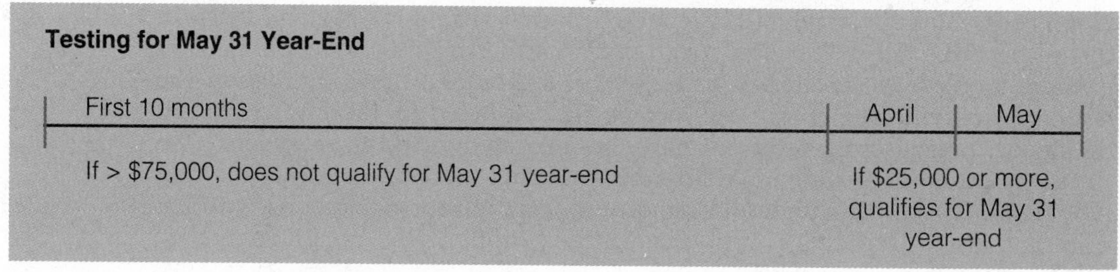

◆

Other business purposes may be used to establish the acceptability of a fiscal year to the IRS. However, the fiscal year must be close to the entity's natural business year (e.g., the entity barely fails the 25 percent test). The IRS lists the following factors that do *not* constitute a valid business purpose.[13]

- The use of a particular fiscal year for regulatory or financial accounting purposes.
- The hiring practices of a particular corporation.
- Tax deferral for the shareholders.
- Use of a fiscal year for administrative purposes (e.g., awarding bonuses or promotions).
- Use of model years, price lists, or other items that change on a noncalendar annual basis.

In general, a taxable year under the § 444 election may not result in a deferral period of more than three months. However, an S corporation in existence before 1987 may elect to retain its previous taxable year for years after 1986, even though such a year results in a deferral period exceeding three months.

12. Rev.Proc. 87–32, 1987–2 C.B. 396.

13. Rev.Rul. 87–57, 1987–2 C.B. 117.

The penalty for a fiscal year under § 444 is that the S corporation must make a required payment on April 15 for any tax year for which the election is in effect. This required payment is equal to the highest rate of tax under § 1 plus one percentage point. Thus, for election years beginning in 1992, the required payment rate is 32 percent (31% + 1%). These payments are not deductible by the S corporation (or by any person) for Federal income tax purposes. They are refundable deposits that do not earn interest and do not pass through to the S shareholders.[14]

EXAMPLE 13

Zebra was a C corporation in 1986 with a September 30 fiscal year. During 1987, Zebra elects S status and is unable to meet the business purpose exception for maintaining a fiscal year. For Zebra to maintain a fiscal year, it must elect under § 444 and make a required payment under § 7519 by April 15. A failure to make this payment will result in the termination of the § 444 election, effective for the year in which the failure occurred.

An electing corporation need not make a required payment until the amount for the current and all preceding election years exceeds $500. If Zebra had made an S election in 1986, § 444 would not be available. However, the entity would be allowed to change to a taxable year under § 444 by treating the deferral period of the tax year being changed as the same as the deferral period of the last tax year of the C corporation. ◆

The payment required from an S corporation under a § 444 election should approximate the tax that would be payable if a calendar year were used. Although the § 444 election is complex, an S corporation may have valid business reasons for selecting a fiscal year. A company may have difficulty closing the books, preparing statements, and issuing its Schedules K–1 on a timely basis under a calendar year.

Computation of Taxable Income

Subchapter S taxable income or loss is generally determined in a manner similar to the tax rules that apply to partnerships, except that the amortization of organization expenditures under § 248 is an allowable deduction. Also, an S corporation can deduct salaries and payroll taxes. Finally, S corporations must recognize any gains (but not losses) on distributions of appreciated property to the shareholders.

Certain deductions not allowable for a partnership are not allowable for an S corporation, including the standard deduction, personal exemptions, alimony deductions, personal moving expenses, and expenses for the care of certain dependents. Furthermore, provisions of the Code applicable only to the computation of taxable income of corporations, such as the dividends received deduction, do not apply.[15]

In general, S corporation items are divided into (1) nonseparately computed income or losses and (2) separately stated income, losses, deductions, and credits that uniquely could affect the tax liability of any shareholders. In essence, nonseparate items are lumped together into an undifferentiated amount that constitutes Subchapter S taxable income or loss. For example, any net gains from the recapture provisions of § 1245 and §§ 1250 through 1255 constitute nonseparately computed income, as does any § 291 recapture amount.

14. § 7519.

15. § 703(a)(2).

Each shareholder is allocated a pro rata portion of this nonseparately computed amount. If a shareholder dies during the year, the share of the pro rata items up to the date of death must be reported on the final individual income tax return. Tax accounting and other elections are generally made at the corporate level, except for elections that shareholders may make separately (e.g., foreign tax credit election).

The following items, among others, are separately stated on Schedule K of Form 1120S, and each shareholder takes into account his or her pro rata share (the share is passed through on a Schedule K–1).[16]

- Tax-exempt income.[17]
- Long-term and short-term capital gains and losses.
- Section 1231 gains and losses.
- Charitable contributions.
- Passive gains, losses, and credits under § 469.
- Certain portfolio income.
- Section 179 expense deduction.
- Tax preferences and adjustments.
- Depletion.
- Foreign income or losses.
- Wagering gains or losses.
- Nonbusiness income or loss (§ 212).
- Recoveries of tax benefit items.
- Intangible drilling costs.
- Investment interest, income, and expenses.
- Total property distributions.
- Total dividend distributions from accumulated earnings and profits.

This pro rata method assigns an equal amount of each of the S items to each day of the year. If a shareholder's interest changes during the year, this per-day method assigns the shareholder a pro rata share of each item for *each* day the stock is owned.

S Corporation item  Percentage of shares owned  Percentage of year owned  Amount of item to be reported

This per-day method must be used unless the shareholder disposes of his or her entire interest in the entity.[18]

If a shareholder's interest is completely terminated during the tax year, all shareholders may elect to treat the S taxable year as two taxable years, with the first year ending on the date of the termination. Under this election, an interim closing of the books is undertaken, and the owners report their shares of the S corporation items as they occurred during the year.

16. §§ 1366(a) and (b).

17. Tax-exempt income passes through to the shareholders and increases their tax basis in the stock. A subsequent distribution does not result in taxation of the tax-exempt income.

18. §§ 1366(a)(1) and 1377(a)(1).

EXAMPLE 14

The following is the income statement for Beakon, an S corporation.

Sales		$40,000
Less: Cost of sales		(23,000)
Gross profit on sales		$17,000
Less: Interest expense	$1,200	
Charitable contributions	400	
Advertising expenses	1,500	
Other operating expenses	2,000	(5,100)
		$11,900
Plus: Tax-exempt income	$ 300	
Dividend income	200	
Long-term capital gain	500	
	$1,000	
Less: Short-term capital loss	(150)	850
Net income per books		$12,750

Subchapter S taxable income for Beakon is calculated as follows, using net income for book purposes as a starting point.

Net income per books			$12,750
Separately computed items:			
Deduct: Tax-exempt interest		$ 300	
Dividend income		200	
Long-term capital gain		500	
		($1,000)	
Add: Charitable contributions	$400		
Short-term capital loss	150	550	
Net effect of separately computed items			(450)
Subchapter S taxable income			$12,300

The $12,300 of Subchapter S taxable income, as well as the separately computed items, are divided among the shareholders, based upon their stock ownership. ◆

EXAMPLE 15

Assume in Example 14 that shareholder Pat owned 10% of the stock for 100 days and 12% for the remaining 265 days. Using the required per-day allocation method, Pat's share of the S corporation items is as follows.

	Schedule K Totals	Pat's Share 10%	Pat's Share 12%	Pat's Schedule K–1 Totals
Subchapter S taxable income	$12,300	$337	$1,072	$1,409
Tax-exempt interest	300	8	26	34
Dividend income	200	5	17	22
LTCG	500	14	44	58
Charitable contributions	400	11	35	46
STCL	150	4	13	17

Pat's share of the Subchapter S taxable income is the total of $12,300 × .10 × 100/365 plus $12,300 × .12 × 265/365, or $1,409. Pat's Schedule K–1 totals would flow through to his Form 1040. ◆

EXAMPLE 16

If, in Example 15, Pat dies after owning the stock 100 days, his share of the S corporation items is reported on the final Form 1040. Thus, only the items in the column labeled 10% in Example 15 would be reported on Pat's final tax return. S corporation items that occur after his death would most likely appear on the Form 1041 (the estate's income tax return). ◆

Tax Treatment of Distributions to Shareholders

The amount of any distribution to an S corporation shareholder is equal to the cash plus the fair market value of any other property distributed. Either of two sets of distribution rules applies, depending upon whether the electing corporation has accumulated earnings and profits (e.g., from Subchapter C years).

A distribution by an S corporation having no accumulated earnings and profits (AEP) is not includible in gross income to the extent that it does not exceed the shareholder's adjusted basis in stock. When the amount of the distribution exceeds the adjusted basis of the stock, the excess is treated as a gain from the sale or exchange of property (capital gain in most cases).

EXAMPLE 17

Peacon, Inc., a calendar year S corporation, has no AEP. During the year, Juan, a shareholder of the corporation, receives a cash dividend of $12,200 from Peacon. Juan's basis in his stock is $9,700. From the cash distribution, Juan recognizes a capital gain of $2,500, the excess of the distribution over the stock basis ($12,200 – $9,700). The remaining $9,700 is tax-free, but it reduces Juan's basis in his stock to zero. ◆

An S corporation should maintain an *accumulated adjustments account (AAA)*. Essentially, the AAA is a cumulative total of undistributed net income items for S corporation taxable years beginning after 1982. The AAA is adjusted in a similar fashion to the shareholder's stock basis, except there is no adjustment for tax-exempt income and related expenses or for Federal taxes attributable to a C corporation tax year. Further, any decreases in stock basis have no impact on the AAA when the AAA balance is negative.

The AAA is a corporate account, whereas the shareholder's basis in his or her stock investment is calculated at the shareholder level. Therefore, the AAA (unlike the stock basis) can have a negative balance. All losses decrease the AAA balance, even those in excess of the shareholder's stock basis. However, distributions may not make AAA negative or increase a negative balance.

The AAA is determined at the end of the year of a distribution rather than at the time the distribution is made. When more than one distribution occurs in the same year, a pro rata portion of each distribution is treated as having been made out of the AAA. The AAA is important in maintaining the treatment of a property distribution as tax-free. This AAA procedure provides the mechanism for taxing the income of an S corporation only once.

A shareholder has a proportionate interest in the AAA, regardless of the size of his or her stock basis. However, since the AAA is a corporate account, there is no connection between the prior accumulated S corporation income and any particular shareholder. Thus, the benefits of the AAA can be shifted from one shareholder to another shareholder. For example, when one S shareholder transfers stock to another shareholder, any AAA on the purchase date is fully available to the purchaser. Similarly, issuing additional stock to a new shareholder in an S corporation having AAA dilutes the account relative to the existing shareholders.

The treatment of a distribution from an S corporation with AEP is summarized as follows.

1. Distributions are tax-free up to the amount in the AAA (limited to stock basis).
2. Any previously taxed income (PTI)[19] in the corporation under prior rules can be distributed on a tax-free basis. However, PTI probably cannot be distributed in property rather than cash [according to Regulation § 1.1375–4(b), effective under prior law].
3. The remaining distribution constitutes a dividend to the extent of AEP. With the consent of all of its shareholders, an S corporation can elect to have a distribution treated as made from AEP rather than from the AAA. This is known as an *AAA bypass* election. Otherwise, no adjustments are made to AEP during S years except for distributions taxed as dividends; investment tax credit recapture applicable to the corporation; and adjustments from redemptions, liquidations, reorganizations, and divisions. For example, AEP can be acquired in a reorganization.
4. Any residual amount is applied against the shareholder's remaining basis in his or her stock. This amount is considered to be a return of capital, which is not taxable. In this context, basis is reduced by the fair market value of the distributed asset.
5. Distributions that exceed the shareholder's tax basis in the stock are taxable as capital gains.

EXAMPLE 18

Tower, a calendar year S corporation, distributes a $1,200 cash dividend to its only shareholder, Otis, on December 31, 1993. Otis's basis in his stock is $100 on January 1, 1993, and the corporation has no AEP. For 1993, Tower had $1,000 of nonseparately computed income from operations, $500 capital loss, and $400 of tax-exempt income.

Otis must report $1,000 of income and $500 of capital loss. The tax-exempt income retains its character and is not taxed to Otis. His stock basis is increased by the $400 tax-exempt income and the $1,000 taxable income, and it is decreased by the $500 capital loss. The results of current operations affect the shareholder's basis before the application of the distribution rule.

Immediately before the cash dividend, Otis's stock basis is $1,000. Thus, $1,000 of the cash dividend is tax-free ($500 from the AAA and $500 from the remaining stock basis). Since Otis's stock basis drops to zero, the additional $200 of the distribution is a $200 gain from the sale or exchange of stock ($1,200 – $1,000). Otis's AAA and stock basis are both zero as of December 31, 1993, determined as follows:

	Corporate AAA	Otis's Stock Basis
Balance, 1/1/93	$ -0-	$ 100
Income	1,000	1,000
Capital loss	(500)	(500)
Tax-exempt income	—	400
Subtotal	$ 500	$ 1,000
Distribution	(500)	(1,000)
Balance, 12/31/93	$ -0-	$ -0-

◆

19. §§ 1368(c)(1) and (e)(1). Before 1983, an account similar to an AAA was called previously taxed income (PTI). Any S corporations in existence before 1983 may have PTI, which, at this point, can be distributed tax-free.

EXAMPLE 19

Assume the same facts as in Example 18, except that Tower had Subchapter C AEP of $750. Tower has an AAA of $500 ($1,000 – $500), which does not include the tax-exempt income. Otis's basis in the stock immediately before the distribution is $1,000 since his basis is increased by the tax-exempt income. Therefore, Otis is not taxed on the first $500, which is a recovery of the AAA. The next $700 is a taxable dividend from the AEP account. (Refer to the first column, step 3, of Concept Summary 21–1.) Otis's basis in the stock is $500 ($1,000 – $500). Although the taxable portion of the distribution does not reduce Otis's basis in the stock, the nontaxable AAA distribution does. ◆

Schedule M–2. Schedule M–2 on page 4 of Form 1120S (see below) contains a column labeled "Other adjustments account." Essentially, this account includes items not used in the calculation of the AAA, such as tax-exempt income and any related nondeductible expenses. However, distributions from this account are not taxable. Once the earnings and profits account reaches zero, distributions fall under the two-tier system: (1) nontaxable to the extent of basis, then (2) capital gain. Moreover, there is no need for an "other adjustments account" when a corporation has no AEP.

EXAMPLE 20

During 1993, Sparrow, an S corporation, records the following items.

AAA, beginning of year	$ 8,500
Previously taxed income, beginning of year	6,250
Ordinary income	25,000
Tax-exempt interest	4,000
Key-employee life insurance proceeds received	5,000
Payroll penalty expense	2,000
Charitable contributions	3,000
Unreasonable compensation	5,000
Premiums on key-employee life insurance	2,000
Distributions to shareholders	16,000

Sparrow's Schedule M–2 for the current year appears as follows.

Schedule M-2 **Analysis of Accumulated Adjustments Account, Other Adjustments Account, and Shareholders' Undistributed Taxable Income Previously Taxed** (See instructions.)

	(a) Accumulated adjustments account	(b) Other adjustments account	(c) Shareholders' undistributed taxable income previously taxed
1 Balance at beginning of tax year	8,500		6,250
2 Ordinary income from page 1, line 21	25,000		
3 Other additions		9,000**	
4 Loss from page 1, line 21	( )		
5 Other reductions	(10,000*)	(2,000)	
6 Combine lines 1 through 5	23,500	7,000	
7 Distributions other than dividend distributions	16,000	-	
8 Balance at end of tax year. Subtract line 7 from line 6	7,500	7,000	6,250

*$2,000 (payroll penalty) + $3,000 (charitable contributions) + $5,000 (unreasonable compensation).
**$4,000 (tax-exempt interest) + $5,000 (life insurance proceeds). ◆

Any distribution of *cash* by the corporation with respect to the stock during a post-termination transition period of approximately one year is applied against and reduces the adjusted basis of the stock to the extent that the amount of the distribution does not exceed the AAA.[20] Thus, a terminated S corporation should

20. §§ 1371(e) and 1377(b).

make a cash distribution during the one-year period following termination to the extent of all previously undistributed net income items for all S tax years.

EXAMPLE 21

The sole shareholder of Pistol, Inc., a calendar year S corporation during 1992, elects to terminate the S election, effective January 1, 1993. As of the end of 1992, Pistol has an AAA of $1,300. Pistol's sole shareholder, Quinn, can receive a nontaxable distribution of cash during a post-termination transition period of approximately one year to the extent of Pistol's AAA. Although a cash dividend of $1,300 during 1993 would be nontaxable to Quinn, it would reduce the adjusted basis of his stock. ◆

Alternative Minimum Tax. An S corporation is not directly subject to the alternative minimum tax (AMT). Under the conduit approach, all tax preference and adjustment items flow through the S corporation to be included in the shareholders' AMT calculations. The allocation of these items is based upon the pro rata daily allocation method, unless the corporation has elected the interim closing-of-the-books method. Each shareholder includes the proper portion of each tax preference and adjustment item in his or her AMT calculations. For a list of tax preference and adjustment items, see Chapter 14.

An S corporation has the advantage of calculating tax preference and adjustment items using individual, rather than corporate, rules. Thus, the S corporation has no accumulated current earnings (ACE) adjustment. For corporations with large ACE adjustments, an S election can be quite attractive. Recall, though, that the 24 percent individual AMT rate is 3 percent higher than the corporate rate.

EXAMPLE 22

During 1993, an S corporation has a positive adjustment for mining exploration costs of $45,000, an excess depletion tax preference of $70,000, and untaxed appreciation on a charitable contribution of stock of $10,000. The ACE adjustment is $80,000. If Gina is a 10% shareholder, she is assigned 10% of $45,000, $70,000, and $10,000 as tax preference and adjustment items ($4,500 + $7,000 + $1,000), but she has no ACE adjustment. ◆

CONCEPT SUMMARY 21–1
CLASSIFICATION PROCEDURES FOR DISTRIBUTIONS FROM AN S CORPORATION*

Where Earnings and Profits Exist

1. Distributions are tax-free to the extent of the accumulated adjustments account.**
2. Any PTI from pre-1983 tax years can be distributed tax-free.
3. The remaining distribution constitutes ordinary dividend from accumulated earnings and profits.***
4. Any residual amount is applied as a tax-free reduction in basis of stock.
5. Excess is treated as gain from the sale or exchange of stock (capital gain in most cases).

Where No Earnings and Profits Exist

1. Distributions are nontaxable to the extent of adjusted basis in stock.
2. Excess distributions are treated as gain from the sale or exchange of property (capital gain in most cases).

*A distribution of appreciated property by an electing corporation results in a gain that first is allocated to and reported by the shareholders.

**Once stock basis reaches zero, any distribution from the AAA is treated as a gain from the sale or exchange of stock. Thus, basis is an upper limit on what a shareholder may receive tax-free.

***An AAA bypass election is available to pay out AEP before reducing the AAA [§ 1368(e)(3)].

Corporate Treatment of Certain Property Distributions

An S corporation recognizes gain on any distribution of appreciated property (other than in a reorganization) in the same manner as if the asset had been sold to the shareholder at its fair market value.[21] The corporate gain is passed through to the shareholders. There is an important reason for this rule. Without it, property might be distributed tax-free (other than for certain recapture items) and later sold without income recognition to the shareholder, because the stepped-up basis equals the asset's fair market value.

The S corporation does not recognize a loss for assets that are worth less than their basis. Furthermore, when such property is distributed, the shareholder's basis in the asset is equal to the asset's fair market value. Thus, the potential loss is postponed until the shareholder sells the stock of the S corporation. Since loss property receives a step-down in basis without any loss recognition by the S corporation, such dividend distributions should be avoided.

The character of gain—capital gain or ordinary income—depends upon the type of asset being distributed.

EXAMPLE 23

Blue, Inc., an S corporation for 10 years, distributes a tract of land held as an investment to its majority shareholder. The land was purchased for $22,000 many years ago and is currently worth $82,000. Blue recognizes a capital gain of $60,000, which increases the AAA by $60,000. Then the property dividend reduces AAA by $82,000 (the fair market value). The tax consequences are the same for appreciated property, whether it is distributed to the shareholders and they dispose of it, or the corporation sells the property and distributes the proceeds to the shareholders.

If the land had been purchased for $80,000 many years ago and was currently worth $30,000, the $50,000 realized loss would not be recognized at the corporate level, and the shareholder would receive a $30,000 basis in the land. The $50,000 realized loss disappears from the corporate level. Since loss is not recognized on the distribution of property that has declined in value, the AAA is not reduced. For the loss on the property to be recognized, the S corporation must sell the property. ◆

EXAMPLE 24

Assume the same facts as in Example 23, except that Blue is a regular corporation or a partnership. Assume the partner's basis in the partnership is $25,000. The tax consequences may be summarized as follows:

	Appreciated Property		
	C Corporation	**S Corporation**	**Partnership**
Entity gain/loss	$60,000	$60,000	$ –0–
Owner's gain/loss	60,000	60,000	–0–
Owner's basis	82,000	82,000	25,000

	Property That Has Declined in Value		
	C Corporation	**S Corporation**	**Partnership**
Entity gain/loss	$ –0–	$ –0–	$ –0–
Owner's gain/loss	–0–	–0–	–0–
Owner's basis	30,000	30,000	25,000

◆

21. § 1363(d).

Shareholder's Tax Basis

The calculation of the initial tax basis of stock in an S corporation is similar to that for the basis of stock in a regular corporation and depends upon the manner in which the shares are acquired (e.g., gift, inheritance, purchase). Once the initial tax basis is determined, various transactions during the life of the corporation affect the shareholder's basis in the stock. Although each shareholder is required to compute his or her own basis in the S shares, neither Form 1120S nor Schedule K–1 provides a place for deriving this amount.

A shareholder's basis is increased by further stock purchases and capital contributions. Operations during the year also cause the following upward adjustments to basis.[22]

- Nonseparately computed income.
- Separately stated income items (e.g., nontaxable income).
- Depletion in excess of basis in the property.

Next, the following items cause a downward adjustment to basis (but not below zero) in this order.

- Nondeductible expenses of the corporation.
- Nonseparately computed loss.
- Separately stated loss and deduction items.
- Distributions not reported as income by the shareholder (AAA distributions).

A shareholder's basis in the stock can never be reduced below zero. Any further downward adjustment (losses or deductions) is applied to reduce (but not below zero) the shareholder's basis in any indebtedness from the electing corporation. Once the basis of any debt is reduced, subsequent net income items increase it (only up to the original amount). The adjustment is made *before* any increase to the basis in the stock.[23]

EXAMPLE 25

Stacey, a sole shareholder, has a $7,000 stock basis and a $2,000 basis in a loan that she made to a calendar year S corporation at the beginning of 1993. Subchapter S net income during 1993 is $8,200. The corporation incurred a short-term capital loss of $2,300 and received $2,000 of tax-exempt interest income. Cash of $15,000 is distributed to Stacey on November 15, 1993. As a result, Stacey's basis in her stock is zero, and her loan basis is $1,900 ($2,000 – $100) at the end of 1993:

Beginning basis in the stock	$ 7,000
Separately computed income	8,200
Short-term capital loss	(2,300)
Tax-exempt interest income	2,000
	$ 14,900
Distribution received (to extent of basis)	(14,900)
Final basis in the stock	$ -0-

Because stock basis cannot be reduced below zero, the $100 excess distribution reduces Stacey's loan basis. ◆

22. § 1367(a).

23. § 1367(b)(2).

Treatment of Losses

Net Operating Loss. One major advantage of an S election is the ability to pass through any net operating loss (NOL) of the corporation directly to the shareholders. A shareholder can deduct an NOL for the year in which the S corporation's tax year ends. The corporation is not entitled to any deduction for the NOL. The individual shareholder's loss is a deduction *for* AGI. A shareholder's basis in the stock is reduced to the extent of any pass-through of the NOL, and the shareholder's AAA is reduced by the same deductible amount.[24]

Net operating losses are allocated among shareholders in the same manner as income is. NOLs are allocated on a daily basis to all shareholders.[25] Transferred shares are considered to be held by the transferee (not the transferor) on the date of the transfer.

EXAMPLE 26

An S corporation incurs a $20,000 NOL for the current year. At all times during the tax year, the stock was owned equally by the same 10 shareholders. Each shareholder is entitled to deduct $2,000 *for* AGI for the tax year in which the corporate tax year ends. ◆

Deductions for an S corporation's NOL pass-through cannot exceed a shareholder's adjusted basis in the stock plus the basis of any loans made by the shareholder to the corporation. If a taxpayer is unable to prove the tax basis, the NOL pass-through can be denied. In essence, a shareholder's stock or loan basis cannot go below zero. As noted previously, once a shareholder's adjusted stock basis has been eliminated by an NOL, any excess NOL is used to reduce the shareholder's basis for any loans made to the corporation (but never below zero). The basis for loans is established by the actual advances made to the corporation, and not by indirect loans.[26] If the shareholder's basis is insufficient to allow a full flow-through and there is more than one type of loss (e.g., in the same year, the taxpayer incurs both a passive loss and a net capital loss), the flow-through amounts are determined on a pro rata basis.

If a shareholder has acquired stock at different times and for varying amounts, a separate-share approach is required. Thus, if the amount of a loss attributable to a share of stock exceeds its basis, any excess is applied to reduce the basis of the shareholder's other shares, in proportion to their remaining bases.

Except in the Eleventh Circuit, the fact that a shareholder has guaranteed a loan made to the corporation by a third party has no effect upon the shareholder's loan basis unless payments actually have been made as a result of that guarantee. If the corporation defaults on an indebtedness and the shareholder makes good on the guarantee, the shareholder's indebtedness basis is increased to that extent. Such a subsequent increase in basis has no influence on the results of a prior year in which an NOL exceeded a shareholder's adjusted basis.

A shareholder's share of an NOL may be greater than both the basis in the stock and the basis of the indebtedness. A shareholder is entitled to carry a loss forward to the extent that the loss for the year exceeds both the stock basis and the loan basis. Any loss carried forward may be deducted *only* by the same shareholder if and when the basis in the stock of or loans to the corporation is restored.[27]

24. §§ 1368(a)(1)(A) and (e)(1)(A).
25. § 1377(a)(1).
26. *Ruth M Prashker*, 59 T.C. 172 (1972); *Frederick G. Brown v. U.S.*, 83–1 USTC ¶9364, 52 AFTR2d 82–5080, 706 F.2d 75 (CA–6, 1983).
27. § 1366(d).

Any loss carryover remaining at the end of a one-year post-termination transition period is lost forever.[28] The post-termination transition period ends on the later of (1) one year after the effective date of the termination of the S election or the due date for the last S return (whichever is later) or (2) 120 days after the determination that the corporation's S election had terminated for a previous year. Thus, a shareholder who has a loss carryover should increase the stock or loan basis and flow through the loss before disposing of the stock.

Example 27

Dana has a stock basis of $4,000 in an S corporation. He has loaned $2,000 to the corporation and has guaranteed another $4,000 loan made to the corporation by a local bank. Although his share of the S corporation's NOL for the current year is $9,500, Dana may deduct only $6,000 of the NOL on his individual tax return. Dana may carry forward $3,500 of the NOL, to be deducted when the basis in his stock or loan to the corporation is restored. Dana has a zero basis in both the stock and loan after the flow-through of the $6,000 NOL. ◆

Net operating losses from C corporation years cannot be utilized at the corporate level (except with respect to built-in gains), nor can they be passed through to the shareholders. Further, the carryforward period continues to run during S status.[29] Consequently, it may not be appropriate for a corporation that has unused NOLs to make the S election. When a corporation is expecting losses in the future, an S election should be made before the loss year.

If a loan's basis has been reduced and is not restored, income is recognized when the loan is repaid. If the corporation issued a note as evidence of the debt, the repayment constitutes an amount received in exchange for a capital asset, and the amount that exceeds the shareholder's basis is entitled to capital gain treatment.[30] However, if the loan is made on open account, the repayment constitutes ordinary income to the extent that it exceeds the shareholder's basis for the loan. Each repayment must be prorated between the gain portion and the repayment of the debt. Thus, a note should be given to ensure capital gain treatment for the income that results from a loan's repayment.

Concept Summary 21–2
Treatment of Losses

Step 1. Allocate total loss to the shareholder on a daily basis, based upon stock ownership.

Step 2. If the shareholder's loss exceeds his or her stock basis, apply any excess to the adjusted basis of indebtedness to the shareholder. Losses from distributions do not reduce debt basis.

Step 3. Where loss exceeds the debt basis, any excess is suspended and carried over to succeeding tax years.

Step 4. In succeeding tax years, any net increase (resulting from *all* positive and negative basis adjustments) restores the debt basis first, up to its original amount.

Step 5. Once debt basis is restored, any net increase remaining is used to increase stock basis.

Step 6. Any suspended loss from a previous year reduces stock basis first and debt basis second.

Step 7. If the S election terminates, any suspended loss carryover may be deducted during the post-termination transition period to the extent of the *stock* basis at the end of this period. Any loss remaining at the end of the transition period is lost forever.

---

28. § 1377(b).
29. § 1371(b).
30. *Joe M. Smith*, 48 T.C. 872 (1967), *aff'd.* and *rev'd.* in 70–1 USTC ¶9327, 25 AFTR2d 70–936, 424 F.2d 219 (CA–9, 1970), and Rev.Rul. 64–162, 1964–1 C.B. 304.

Since the basis rule requires that corporate income be used to restore debt basis before it can be used to restore stock basis, a double tax can be imposed on current income. Any current income distributed, after both debt and stock basis have been reduced to zero, is taxed as capital gain because it is considered return of capital, but only to the extent of stock basis. To avoid this double tax, shareholders should consider forgiving debt that the S corporation owes them. Such a forgiveness is considered a contribution of capital, with a resulting increase in the shareholder's stock basis.

Passive Losses and Credits. There are three major classes of income and losses: active, portfolio, and passive. Section 469 provides that net passive losses and credits are not deductible and must be carried over to a year when there is passive income. S corporations are not directly subject to these limits, but shareholders who do not materially participate in operating the business will be able to apply the corporate losses and credits only against income from other passive activities. In other words, flow-through income and deductions from an S corporation are regarded as arising from a passive activity unless the shareholder materially participates in the corporate business. For example, a passive loss at the S corporation level could not be offset against the earned income of a nonparticipating shareholder. Regular, continuous, and substantial involvement in the S corporation is necessary to meet the material participation requirement.

EXAMPLE 28

Heather is a 50% owner of an S corporation engaged in a passive activity (refer to Chapter 6). A nonparticipating shareholder, she receives a salary of $6,000 for services as a result of the passive activity. This deduction creates a $6,000 passive loss at the corporate level. Heather has $6,000 of earned income as a result of the salary. The $6,000 salary creates a $6,000 deduction/passive loss, which flows through to the shareholders. Heather's $3,000 share of the loss may not be deducted against the $6,000 earned income. Earned income is not taken into account in computing the income or loss from a passive activity. ◆

At-Risk Rules. The at-risk rules generally apply to S corporation shareholders. Essentially, the amount at risk is determined separately for each shareholder. The amount of the corporation losses that are passed through and deductible by the shareholders is not affected by the amount the corporation has at risk. A shareholder usually is considered at risk with respect to an activity to the extent of cash and the adjusted basis of other property contributed to the electing corporation, any amount borrowed for use in the activity that the taxpayer is personally liable for paying from personal assets, and the net fair market value of personal assets that secure nonrecourse borrowing.

Tax on Preelection Built-in Gains

Because Congress was concerned that certain C corporations would elect S status to avoid the corporate income tax on the sale or exchange of appreciated property (avoiding a tax on such built-in gains), it completely revamped § 1374. A regular corporation converting to S corporation status after 1986 generally incurs a corporate-level tax on any built-in gains when the S corporation disposes of an asset in a taxable disposition within 10 years after the date on which the S election took effect.

General Rules. The built-in gains tax is applied to any unrealized gain attributable to appreciation in the value of an asset (e.g., real estate, cash basis receivables, goodwill) or other income items while held by the C corporation. The highest corporate tax rate (applicable to that type of income) is applied to the lesser of (1) the recognized built-in gains of the S corporation for the tax year or (2) the amount that would be the taxable income of the corporation for that tax year if it were a C corporation. Any built-in gain that escapes taxation due to the taxable income limitation is carried forward to future tax years. Then it is treated as recognized built-in gain. Thus, given a low or negative taxable income in any year when built-in gain assets are sold, the taxpayer defers the payment of the built-in gains penalty tax liability. The total amount of gain that must be recognized is limited to the aggregate net built-in gains of the corporation at the time it converted to S status. Thus, it may be advisable to obtain an independent appraisal when converting a C corporation to an S corporation. Certainly, a memorandum should be prepared listing the fair market values of all assets, along with the methods used to arrive at the values.

Example 29

Marble is a former C corporation whose first S corporation year began on January 1, 1993. At that time, it had two assets: X, with a value of $1,000 and a basis of $400, and Y, with a value of $400 and a basis of $600. Thus, net unrealized built-in gains as of January 1, 1993, are $400. If Marble sells asset X for $1,000 during 1993, while retaining asset Y, the recognized built-in gain is limited to $400. ◆

Example 30

Assume the same facts as in Example 29, except that taxable income in 1993 is $300. The new built-in gains tax is assessed only on $300. However, the $100 recognized built-in gain that circumvents the tax in 1993 is carried forward and treated as recognized built-in gain in 1994. There is no statutory limit on the carryforward period, but the gain will effectively expire at the end of the 10-year recognition period applicable to all built-in gains (except for installment sales after March 25, 1990).[31] ◆

Gains on sales or distributions of all assets by an S corporation are presumed to be built-in gains unless the taxpayer can establish that the appreciation accrued after the conversion. This built-in gains tax is avoided if the S election was made before 1987.[32]

Any tax imposed on built-in gain reduces proportionately the amount of built-in gain that passes through to the shareholder. Post-conversion appreciation is subject to the regular S corporation pass-through rules.

Example 31

Monkey Corporation elects S status, effective for calendar year 1992. As of January 1, 1992, one of Monkey's assets has a basis of $50,000 and a fair market value of $110,000. Early in 1993, the asset is sold for $135,000. Monkey incurs a realized gain of $85,000, of which $60,000 is subject to the § 1374 penalty tax of 34%. The entire $85,000 gain is subject to the corporate pass-through rules (reduced by the built-in gains tax itself), but only $25,000 of the gain fully bypasses the corporate income tax. ◆

Normally, tax attributes of a C corporation do not carry over to a converted S corporation. For purposes of the tax on built-in gains, however, certain carryovers are allowed. An S corporation can offset any gain by related attributes from prior C corporation years, such as unexpired NOLs or capital losses. In a similar manner, alternative minimum tax credit carryovers (arising in a C corporation tax year) and business credit carryforwards are allowed to offset the built-in gains tax.

31. § 1374(d)(7); Notice 90–27, 1990–1 C.B. 336.

32. § 1362.

EXAMPLE 32

Assume the same facts as in Example 31, except that Monkey also had a $10,000 NOL carryover when it elected S status. The NOL reduces Monkey's built-in gain from $60,000 to $50,000. Thus, only $50,000 is subject to the built-in gains penalty tax. ◆

EXAMPLE 33

An S corporation has a built-in gain of $100,000 and taxable income of $90,000. The built-in gains tax liability is calculated as follows.

Lesser of taxable income and built-in gain	$90,000
Less: NOL carryforward from C year	(12,000)
Capital loss carryforward from C year	(8,000)
Tax base	$70,000
Highest corporate tax rate	.34
Tentative tax	$23,800
Less: Business credit carryforward from C year	(4,000)
AMT credit carryforward from C year	(3,000)
Built-in gains tax liability	$16,800

The $10,000 realized (but not taxed) built-in gain in excess of taxable income may be carried forward to the next year, as long as the next year is within the 10-year recognition period. ◆

Concept Summary 21–3 summarizes the calculation of the built-in gains tax.

LIFO Recapture Tax. When a corporation uses the FIFO method for its last year before making the S election, any built-in gain is recognized and taxed as the inventory is sold. This is not true for a LIFO-basis corporation, unless it invades the LIFO layer during the 10-year period. To preclude deferral of gain recognition under LIFO, the law requires a LIFO recapture amount upon making an S election.

A C corporation using LIFO for its last year before making an S election must include in income the excess of the inventory's value under FIFO over the LIFO value. The increase in tax liability resulting from LIFO recapture is payable in four equal installments, with the first payment due on or before the due date for

CONCEPT SUMMARY 21–3
CALCULATION OF BUILT-IN GAINS TAX LIABILITY

Step 1. Select the smaller of built-in gains or taxable income.*

Step 2. Deduct unexpired net operating losses and capital losses from a C corporation tax year.

Step 3. Multiply the tax base obtained in step 2 by the top corporate tax rate.

Step 4. Deduct any business credit carryforwards and alternative minimum tax credit carryovers arising in a C corporation tax year from the amount obtained in step 3.

Step 5. The corporation pays any tax resulting in step 4.

*Any net recognized built-in gain in excess of taxable income may be carried forward to the next year, as long as the next year is within the 10-year recognition period.

the corporate return for the last C corporation year (without regard to any extensions). The remaining three installments must be paid on or before the due dates of the succeeding corporate returns. No interest is due if payments are made by the due dates. The basis of the LIFO inventory is adjusted to take into account this LIFO recapture amount.

EXAMPLE 34

Engelage Corporation converts from a C corporation to an S corporation at the beginning of 1994. Engelage used the LIFO inventory method in 1993 and had an ending LIFO inventory of $110,000 (with a FIFO value of $190,000). Engelage must add $80,000 of LIFO recapture amount to its 1993 taxable income, resulting in an increased tax liability of $27,200 ($80,000 × 34%). Thus, Engelage must pay one-fourth of the tax (or $6,800) with its 1993 corporate tax return. The three succeeding installments of $6,800 each must be paid with Engelage's next three tax returns. ◆

Passive Investment Income Penalty Tax

A tax is imposed on the excess passive income of S corporations that possess accumulated earnings and profits from Subchapter C years. The tax rate is the highest corporate rate for the year. It is applied to the portion of the corporation's net passive income that bears the same ratio to the total net passive income for the tax year as excess gross passive income bears to the total gross passive income for the year. However, the amount subject to the tax may not exceed the taxable income of the corporation.[33]

Excess net passive income

Passive investment income in excess of 25% of gross receipts for the year
---
Passive investment income for the year

Net passive investment income for the year

For this purpose, passive investment income means gross receipts derived from royalties, rents, dividends, interest, annuities, and sales and exchanges of stocks and securities. Only the net gain from the disposition of capital assets (other than stocks and securities) is taken into account in computing gross receipts. Net passive income means passive income reduced by any deductions directly connected with the production of that income. Any passive income tax reduces the amount the shareholders must take into income.

The excess net passive income cannot exceed the corporate taxable income for the year before considering any NOL deduction or the special deductions allowed by §§ 241–250 (except the organizational expense deduction of § 248).

EXAMPLE 35

At the end of 1993, Barnhardt Corporation, an electing S corporation, has gross receipts totaling $264,000 (of which $110,000 is passive investment income). Expenditures directly connected to the production of the passive investment income total $30,000. Therefore, Barnhardt has net passive investment income of $80,000 ($110,000 – $30,000), and its passive investment income for tax year 1993 exceeds 25% of its gross receipts by $44,000 ($110,000 passive investment income less $66,000). Excess net passive income (ENPI) is $32,000, calculated as follows.

33. §§ 1374(d)(4), and 1375(a) and (b).

$$\text{ENPI} = \frac{\$44{,}000}{\$110{,}000} \times \$80{,}000 = \$32{,}000$$

Barnhardt Corporation's passive investment income tax for 1993 is \$10,880 (\$32,000 × 34%). ◆

Fringe Benefit Rules

An S corporation cannot deduct its expenditures for providing certain fringe benefits to any employee-shareholder owning more than 2 percent of the stock of the S corporation. The constructive ownership rules of § 318 (refer to Chapter 18) are applicable in applying the 2 percent ownership test.[34] Such a shareholder-employee is restricted from receiving the following benefits, among others.

- Excludible group term life insurance.
- The \$5,000 death benefit exclusion.
- The exclusion from income of amounts paid for an accident and health plan.
- The exclusion from income of meals and lodging furnished for the convenience of the employer.
- Worker's compensation payments on behalf of the shareholder-employee.

EXAMPLE 36

Purple, Inc., an S corporation, pays for the medical care of two shareholder-employees during the current year. Tina, a shareholder owning 2% of the stock, receives \$1,700 for this purpose. Soo, a shareholder owning 20% of the stock, receives \$3,100. Purple deducts the \$1,700 as a business expense. The \$3,100 paid on behalf of Soo is not deductible by the corporation because she owns more than 2% of the stock. Soo can deduct the \$3,100 herself, but only to the extent that personal medical expenses are allowable as an itemized deduction under § 213. ◆

Other Operational Rules

Oil and Gas Producers. Oil and gas producers seldom choose S status. The election by a C corporation of Subchapter S is treated as a transfer of oil and gas properties under § 613A(c)(13)(C). Therefore, as of the date of the election, neither the shareholders nor the electing corporation is allowed to claim percentage depletion on production from proven oil or gas wells.

Miscellaneous Rules. Other possible effects of various Code provisions on S corporations include the following:

- An S corporation is required to make estimated tax payments with respect to any recognized built-in gain, excess passive investment income, and investment tax credit recapture.
- An S corporation may own stock in another corporation, but an S corporation may not have a corporate shareholder. An S corporation is not eligible for a dividends received deduction.

34. §§ 1372(a) and (b).

- An S corporation is not subject to the 10 percent of taxable income limitation applicable to charitable contributions made by a C corporation.
- Foreign taxes paid by an electing corporation will pass through to the shareholders and should be claimed as either a deduction or a credit (subject to the applicable limitations).[35]
- Any family member who renders services or furnishes capital to an electing corporation must be paid reasonable compensation. Otherwise, the IRS can make adjustments to reflect the value of the services or capital.[36] This rule may make it more difficult for related parties to shift Subchapter S taxable income to children or other family members.
- Although § 1366(a)(1) provides for a flow-through of S items to a shareholder, it does not apply to self-employment income. Thus, a shareholder's portion of S income is not self-employment income and is not subject to the self-employment tax. Compensation for services rendered to an S corporation is, however, subject to FICA taxes.

EXAMPLE 37

Cody and Dana each own one-third of a fast-food restaurant, and their 14-year-old son owns the other shares. Both parents work full-time in the restaurant operations, but the son works infrequently. Neither parent receives a salary during 1993, when the taxable income of the S corporation is $160,000. The IRS can require that reasonable compensation be paid to the parents to prevent the full one-third of the $160,000 from being taxed to the son. Otherwise, this would be an effective technique to shift earned income to a family member to reduce total family tax burden. With the procedure for taxing the unearned income of children, this shifting technique becomes much more valuable. Furthermore, low or zero salaries can reduce self-employment taxes due to the Federal government. ◆

- The depletion allowance is computed separately by each shareholder. Each shareholder is treated as having produced his or her pro rata share of the production of the electing corporation, and each is allocated a respective share of the adjusted basis of the electing corporation as to oil or gas property held by the corporation.[37]
- An S corporation is placed on the cash method of accounting for purposes of deducting business expenses and interest owed to a cash basis related party (including a shareholder who owns at least 2 percent of the stock in the corporation).[38] Thus, the timing of the shareholder's income and the corporate deduction must match.
- The S election is not recognized by the District of Columbia and several states, including Connecticut, Michigan, New Hampshire, New Jersey, and Tennessee. Thus, some or all of the entity's income may be subject to a state-level income tax.

When the Election Is Advisable

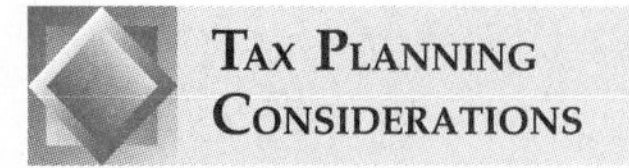

Effective tax planning with S corporations begins with the determination of whether the election is appropriate. In light of changes made by TRA of 1986, the taxpayer may wish to reevaluate the desirability of using a C corporation as a

35. § 1373(a).
36. § 1366(e). In addition, beware of an IRS search for the "real owner" of the stock, under Reg. § 1.1373–1(a)(2).
37. § 613A(c)(13).
38. § 267(b).

means of conducting a trade or business. In this context, one should consider the following factors.

- Are losses from the business anticipated? If so, the S election may be highly attractive because these losses pass through to the shareholders.
- What are the tax brackets of the shareholders? If the shareholders are in high individual income tax brackets, it may be desirable to avoid S corporation status and have profits taxed to the corporation at lower rates (e.g., 15 percent or 25 percent).
- When the immediate pass-through of Subchapter S taxable income is avoided, the shareholders may later receive the corporation's profits as capital gain income through stock redemptions, some liquidating distributions, or sales of stock to others, or as dividend distributions in low-tax-bracket years. Or the profits may be negated by a partial or complete step-up in basis upon the death of the shareholder. On the other hand, if the shareholders are in low individual income tax brackets, the pass-through of corporate profits has less effect, and the avoidance of the corporate income tax becomes the paramount consideration. Under these circumstances, the S election could be highly attractive. Although an S corporation usually escapes Federal taxes, it may not be immune from state and local taxes imposed on corporations or from several Federal penalty taxes.
- Does a C corporation have an NOL carryover from a prior year? Such a loss cannot be used in an S year (except for purposes of the § 1374 tax). Even worse, S years count in the 15-year carryover limitation. Thus, even if the S election is made, one might consider terminating the election before the carryover limitation expires. Such a termination would permit the loss to be utilized by (what is again) a C corporation.
- Both individuals and C corporations are subject to the alternative minimum tax. Many of the tax preference and adjustment items are the same, but some apply only to corporate taxpayers, while others are limited to individuals. The minimum tax adjustment relating to accumulated current earnings could create havoc with some C corporations (refer to Chapter 14). S corporations themselves are not subject to this tax.
- Some C corporations must convert from the cash method to the accrual method of accounting (refer to Chapter 15).
- S corporations and partnerships have lost most of the flexibility in the choice of their accounting period (see also Chapter 22).
- By taxing C corporations on nonliquidating and liquidating distributions of appreciated property (refer to Chapters 18 and 19), the effect of double taxation is reinforced.

The choice of the form of doing business often is dictated by other factors. For example, many businesses cannot qualify for the S election or would find the partnership form more practical. Therefore, freedom of action based on tax considerations may not be an attainable goal.

Making a Proper Election

Once the parties have decided the election is appropriate, it becomes essential to ensure that the election is made properly.

- Make sure all shareholders consent. If any doubt exists concerning the shareholder status of an individual, it would be wise to have that party issue a consent anyway. Too few consents will be fatal to the election; the same cannot be said for too many consents.

- Be sure that the election filing is timely and proper. Either hand carry the election to an IRS office or send it by certified or registered mail. A copy of the election should become part of the corporation's permanent files.
- Regarding the above, be careful to ascertain when the timely election period begins to run for a newly formed corporation. Remember that an election made too soon (before the corporation is in existence) is worse than one made too late. If serious doubts exist concerning when this period begins, more than one election might be considered as a practical means of guaranteeing the desired result.

Preserving the Election

Recall how an election can be lost and that a five-year waiting period generally is imposed before another S election is available. To preserve an S election, the following points should be kept in mind.

- As a starting point, make sure all parties concerned are aware of the various violations that lead to the loss of an election.
- Watch for possible disqualification as a small business corporation. For example, the divorce of a shareholder, accompanied by a property settlement, could violate the 35-shareholder limitation. The death of a shareholder could result in a nonqualifying trust becoming a shareholder. The latter circumstance might be avoided by utilizing a buy-sell agreement or binding the deceased shareholder's estate to turn in the stock to the corporation for redemption or, as an alternative, to sell it to the surviving shareholders.
- Make sure a new majority shareholder (including the estate of a deceased shareholder) does not file a refusal to continue the election.
- Watch for the passive investment income limitation. Avoid a consecutive third year with excess passive income if a corporation has accumulated Subchapter C earnings and profits. In this connection, assets that produce passive investment income (e.g., stocks and bonds, certain rental assets) might be retained by the shareholders in their individual capacities and thereby kept out of the corporation.
- Do not transfer stock to a nonresident alien.
- Do not create an active affiliate or issue a second class of stock.

Planning for the Operation of the Corporation

Operating an S corporation to achieve optimum tax savings for all parties involved requires a great deal of care and, most important, an understanding of the applicable tax rules.

AAA Considerations. Although the corporate-level accumulated adjustments account (AAA) is used primarily by an S corporation with accumulated earnings and profits (AEP) from a Subchapter C year, all S corporations should maintain an accurate record of the AAA. Because there is a grace period for distributing the AAA after termination of the S election, the parties must be in a position to determine the balance of the account.

EXAMPLE 38

Nobles, Inc., is an S corporation during 1992, with no AEP from a Subchapter C year. Over the years, no attempt was made to maintain an accurate accounting for the AAA.

In 1993, the S election is terminated, and Nobles has a grace period for distributing the AAA tax-free to its shareholders. A great deal of time and expense may be necessary to reconstruct the AAA balance in 1993. ◆

Tax-exempt income is not included in gross income and does not increase AAA. For an S corporation with AEP, tax-exempt income is a bad investment. Any subsequent distribution of tax-exempt income exceeds the AAA balance and is treated as dividend income to the extent of any AEP.

Where AEP is present, a negative AAA may cause double taxation of S corporation income. With a negative AAA, a distribution of current income restores the negative AAA balance to zero, but is considered to be a distribution in excess of AAA, taxable as a dividend to the extent of AEP.

The AAA bypass election may be used to avoid the accumulated earnings tax or personal holding company tax in the year preceding the first tax year under Subchapter S. This bypass election allows the AEP to be distributed instead.

Example 39

Zebra, Inc., is an S corporation during 1992, with a significant amount in its AEP account. The shareholders are subject to low income tax rates for 1993 and expect to terminate the election in that year. Since the new C corporation may be subject to the accumulated earnings penalty tax in 1993, the shareholders may wish to use the AAA bypass election to distribute some or all of the AEP. Of course, any distributions of the AEP account in 1992 would be taxable to the shareholders. ◆

A net loss allocated to a shareholder reduces the AAA. This required adjustment should encourage an electing corporation to make annual distributions of net income to avoid having an AAA reduced by a future net loss.

Salary Structure. The amount of salary paid to a shareholder-employee of an S corporation can have varying tax consequences and should be considered carefully. Larger amounts might be advantageous if the maximum contribution allowed under the retirement plan has not been reached. Smaller amounts may be beneficial if the parties are trying to shift taxable income to lower-bracket shareholders, lessen payroll taxes, curtail a reduction of Social Security benefits, or reduce losses that do not pass through because of the basis limitation. Many of the problems that arise in this area can be solved with proper planning. Most often, this planning involves making before-the-fact projections of the tax positions of the relevant parties.

The IRS can require that reasonable compensation be paid to family members who render services or provide capital to the S corporation. The IRS, though, can adjust the items taken into account by family-member shareholders to reflect the value of services or capital they have provided.

Loss Considerations. A net loss in excess of tax basis may be carried forward and deducted only by the same shareholder in succeeding years. Thus, before disposing of the stock, a shareholder should increase the basis of the stock/loan that will flow through the loss. The next shareholder does not obtain the carryover loss.

Any unused carryover loss in existence upon the termination of the S election may be deducted only in the next tax year and is limited to the individual's *stock* basis (not loan basis) in the post-termination year.[39] The shareholder may wish to purchase more stock to increase the tax basis in order to absorb the loss.

---

39. § 1366(d)(3).

The NOL provisions create a need for sound tax planning during the last election year and the post-termination transition period. If it appears that the S corporation is going to sustain an NOL or use up any loss carryover, each shareholder's basis should be analyzed to determine if it can absorb the share of the loss. If basis is insufficient to absorb the loss, further investments should be considered before the end of the post-termination transition year. These investments can be accomplished through additional stock purchases from the corporation or from other shareholders to increase basis. This action will ensure the full benefit from the NOL or loss carryover.

Example 40

A calendar year C corporation has an NOL of $20,000 in 1992. The corporation makes a valid S election in 1993 and has another $20,000 NOL in that year. At all times during 1993, the stock of the corporation was owned by the same 10 shareholders, each of whom owned 10% of the stock. Tim, one of the 10 shareholders, has an adjusted basis of $1,800 at the beginning of 1993. None of the 1992 NOL may be carried forward into the S year. Although Tim's share of the 1993 NOL is $2,000, his deduction for the loss is limited to $1,800 in 1993 with a $200 carryover. ◆

Managing the Built-in Gains Tax. A taxable income limitation encourages an S corporation to create deductions or accelerate deductions in the years that built-in gains are recognized. Although the postponed built-in gain is carried forward to future years, the time value of money makes the postponement beneficial. For example, payment of compensation, rather than a distribution, creates a deduction that reduces taxable income and postpones the built-in gains tax.

Example 41

Mundy, Inc., an S corporation, has built-in gain of $110,000 and taxable income of $120,000 before payment of salaries to its two shareholders. If Mundy pays at least $110,000 in salaries to the shareholders (rather than a distribution), taxable income will drop to zero, and the built-in gains tax will be postponed. Thus, Mundy needs to keep the salaries as high as possible to postpone the built-in gains tax in future years and to reap the time value of money benefit. Of course, paying the salaries may increase the payroll tax burden if the salaries are below FICA and FUTA limits. ◆

Giving built-in gain property to a charitable organization does not trigger the built-in gains tax. However, the built-in gain may be a preference item at the shareholder level for purposes of the alternative minimum tax. To reduce or eliminate the built-in gains tax, built-in *loss* property may be sold in the same year that built-in gain property is sold. Generally, the taxpayer should sell built-in loss property in a year when an equivalent amount of built-in gain property is sold. Otherwise, the built-in loss could be wasted.

Example 42

Green Corporation elects S status effective for calendar year 1992. As of January 1, 1992, Green's only asset has a basis of $40,000 and a fair market value of $100,000. If this asset is sold for $120,000 in 1993, Green recognizes an $80,000 gain, of which $60,000 is subject to the corporate built-in gains tax. The other $20,000 of gain is subject to the S corporation pass-through rules and bypasses the corporate income tax.

Unless Green can show otherwise, any appreciation existing at the sale or exchange is presumed to be preconversion built-in gain. Therefore, Green incurs a taxable gain of $80,000 unless it can prove that the $20,000 gain developed after the effective date of the election. ◆

Controlling Adjustments and Preference Items. The individual alternative minimum tax (AMT) now affects more taxpayers because the tax base has expanded and the difference between regular tax rates and the individual AMT rate has been narrowed. In an S corporation setting, tax adjustments and preferences flow through proportionately to the shareholders. In computing the individual AMT, a shareholder treats these adjustments and preferences as if they were directly realized.

A flow-through of tax adjustments and preferences can be a tax disaster for a shareholder who is an "almost-AMT" taxpayer. Certain steps can be taken to protect such a shareholder from being pushed into the AMT. For example, a large donation of appreciated property by an S corporation could adversely affect an "almost-AMT" taxpayer. Certain adjustment and preference items are subject to elections that can remove them from the shareholder's AMT computation. Positive adjustments can be removed from a shareholder's AMTI base if the S corporation elects to capitalize and amortize certain expenditures over a prescribed period of time. These include excess intangible drilling and development expenditures, research and experimental costs, mining exploration and development expenditures, and circulation expenses.

Other corporate choices can protect an "almost-AMT" shareholder. Using the percentage of completion method of accounting (rather than the completed contract method) can be beneficial to certain shareholders. However, many of these decisions and elections may generate conflicts of interest when some shareholders are not so precariously situated and would not suffer from the flow-through of adjustments and tax preference items.

Allocation of Tax Items. If a shareholder dies or stock is transferred during the taxable year, tax items may be allocated under the pro rata approach or the per-books method. Unless the per-books method is elected, a shareholder's pro rata share of tax items is determined by assigning an equal portion of each item to each day of the tax year, and then dividing that portion pro rata among the shares outstanding on the transfer day. With the consent of all persons who were shareholders during the entire taxable year, an S corporation can elect to allocate tax items according to the permanent records using normal tax accounting rules.

The allocation is made as if the taxable year consists of two taxable years. The first portion ends on the date of termination. On the day the shares are transferred, the shares are considered owned by the shareholder who acquired them. The selected method may be beneficial to the terminating shareholder and harmful to the acquiring shareholder. A per-books election might result in a higher allocation of losses to a taxpayer who is better able to utilize the losses. In the case of the death of a shareholder, a per-books election prevents the income and loss allocation to a deceased shareholder from being affected by postdeath events.

EXAMPLE 43

Alicia, the owner of all of the shares of an S corporation, transfers all of the stock to Bhaskar at the middle of the tax year. There is a $100,000 NOL for the entire tax year, but $30,000 of the loss occurs during the first half of the year. Without a per-books election, $50,000 of the loss would be allocated to Alicia, with $50,000 allocated to Bhaskar. If the corporation makes the per-books election, Bhaskar will receive $70,000 of the loss. Of course, Bhaskar may have a difficult time convincing Alicia to consent to the election. ◆

EXAMPLE 44

Mountain, a calendar year S corporation, is equally owned by Joey and Karl. Joey dies on June 29 (not a leap year). Mountain has income of $250,000 for January 1 through June 29 and $750,000 for the remainder of the year. Without the per-books election, the income is allocated by assigning an equal portion of the annual income of $1 million to each day (or $2,739.73 per day) and allocating the daily portion among the shareholders. Joey is allocated 50% of the daily income for the 180 days from January 1 to June 29, or $246,575.70 ($2,739.73 ÷ 2 × 180). Joey's estate is allocated 50% of the income for the 185 days from June 30 to December 31, or $253,425.02 ($2,739.73 ÷ 2 × 185).

If the per-books election is made, the income of $250,000 from January 1 to June 29 is divided equally between Joey and Karl, so that each is allocated $125,000. The income of $750,000 from June 30 to December 31 is divided equally between Joey's estate and Karl, or $375,000 to each. ◆

Termination Aspects. If the shareholders of an S corporation decide to terminate the election voluntarily, they should make sure that the disqualifying act possesses substance. When the intent of the parties is obvious and the act represents a technical noncompliance rather than a real change, the IRS may be able to disregard it and keep the parties in S status.[40]

Liquidation of an S Corporation. S corporations are subject to the same liquidation rules applicable to C corporations (refer to Chapter 19). The distribution of appreciated property to S shareholders in complete liquidation is treated as if the property were sold to the shareholders in a taxable transaction. Unlike a C corporation, however, the S corporation incurs no incremental tax on the liquidation gains because the gains flow through to the shareholders, subject only to the built-in gains tax of § 1374. Any corporate gain increases the shareholder's stock basis by a like amount and reduces any gain realized by the shareholder when he or she receives the liquidation proceeds. Thus, an S corporation usually avoids the double tax that is imposed on C corporations.

PROBLEM MATERIALS

DISCUSSION QUESTIONS

1. What are the major advantages and disadvantages of an S election?
2. Which of the following items could be considered to be disadvantageous (or potential hazards) for S elections?
   - **a.** The dividends received deduction is lost.
   - **b.** The foreign tax credit is not available.
   - **c.** Net operating loss at the corporate level cannot be utilized.
   - **d.** Constructive dividends are not actually distributed.
   - **e.** A locked-in AAA occurs after termination.
   - **f.** An AAA is a personal right that cannot be transferred.
   - **g.** Basis in stock is increased by constructive dividends.
   - **h.** A trust is treated as a shareholder.
   - **i.** Salaries of certain shareholders are not high enough.
3. On February 23, 1993, the two 50% shareholders of a calendar year corporation decide to elect to be an S corporation. One of the shareholders had purchased her stock from a previous shareholder on January 18, 1993. Discuss any potential problems.
4. Peggy is the sole owner of a calendar year S corporation that manufactures water heaters. On March 9, Peggy realizes that the corporation is going to make a very large profit. Discuss how Peggy can terminate her corporation's S election.

---

40. See *Clarence L. Hook,* 58 T.C. 267 (1972).

5. In which of the following situations is a termination of a calendar year S corporation's election effective as of the first day of the following tax year?
   a. A partnership becomes a shareholder on April 2.
   b. There is a failure of the passive investment income limitation.
   c. A new 45% shareholder affirmatively refuses to consent to the S election.
   d. Shareholders owning 57% of the outstanding stock file a formal revocation on February 23.
   e. A second class of stock is issued on March 3.
   f. The electing corporation becomes a member of an affiliated group on March 10.
6. An S corporation recently had its S election involuntarily terminated. Must the corporation wait five years before making a new election?
7. Karen is considering creating an S corporation for her interior decorating business. She has a friend who has an S corporation with a January 31 fiscal year. She wishes to adopt a similar fiscal year. Advise Karen.
8. In the current year, an S corporation distributes land worth $88,000 to a shareholder. The land cost $22,000 three years ago. Discuss any tax impact on the corporation or the shareholder from this distribution. The corporation has no accumulated earnings and profits, and the stock basis is $102,000.
9. Yoon's basis in his S corporation is $5,500, and he anticipates that his share of the NOL for this year will be $7,400. The tax year is not closed. Advise Yoon.
10. How do the passive loss limitations in § 469 affect an S corporation?
11. One of your clients is considering electing S corporation status. Texas, Inc., is a six-year-old company with two equal shareholders who paid $30,000 each for their stock. In 1993, Texas has a $90,000 NOL carryforward. Estimated income is $40,000 for 1994 and approximately $25,000 for each of the next three years. Should Texas make an S election for 1993?

PROBLEMS

12. An S corporation's profit and loss statement for 1993 shows net profits (book income) of $90,000. The corporation has three equal shareholders. From supplemental data, you obtain the following information about the corporation for 1993.

Selling expense	$11,500
Tax-exempt interest	2,000
Dividends received	9,000
Section 1231 gain	6,000
Section 1245 gain	10,000
Recovery of bad debts	3,400
Capital losses	6,000
Salary to owners (each)	9,000
Cost of goods sold	95,000

   a. Compute Subchapter S taxable income or (loss) for 1993.
   b. What would be one of the shareholders' portion of taxable income (or loss)?
13. Polly has been the sole shareholder of a calendar year S corporation since 1981. At the end of 1993, Polly's stock basis is $15,500, and she receives a distribution of $17,000. Corporate-level accounts are as follows.

AAA	$6,000
PTI	9,000
AEP	500

   How is Polly taxed on the distribution?
14. Paul owned 10% of the outstanding stock of a calendar year S corporation. Paul sold all of his stock to Quincey on July 1, 1993. At the end of 1993, the total AAA was $800,000 before considering any distributions, and the amount in the AEP account

was $800,000. The S corporation made a distribution of $600,000 to the shareholders on April 1, 1993, which included a distribution of $60,000 to Paul. On October 1, 1993, another distribution of $600,000 was made to the shareholders, including $60,000 to Quincey. Determine the amounts taxable to Paul and Quincey.

15. A calendar year S corporation has $60,000 of AEP. Lara, the sole shareholder, has an adjusted basis of $50,000 in her stock with zero in the AAA. Determine the tax aspects if a $60,000 salary is paid to Lara.

16. Assume the same facts as in Problem 15, except that Lara receives a dividend of $60,000.

17. Using the following legend, classify the transaction as a plus (+) or minus (–) on Schedule M–2 of Form 1120S.

Legend

PTI	=	Shareholders' undistributed taxable income previously taxed
AAA	=	Accumulated adjustments account
OAA	=	Other adjustments account
NA	=	No direct impact on Schedule M–2

a. Receipt of tax-exempt interest income.
b. Unreasonable compensation determined.
c. Ordinary income.
d. Distribution of nontaxable income (PTI) from 1981.
e. Nontaxable life insurance proceeds.
f. Expenses related to tax-exempt securities.
g. Charitable contributions.
h. Gifts in excess of $25.
i. Nondeductible fines.
j. Organizational expenses.

18. Adam and Bonnie form an S corporation, with Adam contributing cash of $100,000 for a 50% interest and Bonnie contributing appreciated ordinary income property with an adjusted basis of $10,000 and a FMV of $100,000.

a. Determine Bonnie's initial basis in her stock, assuming that she receives a 50% interest.
b. The S corporation sells the property for $100,000. Determine Adam's and Bonnie's stock basis after the sale.
c. Determine Adam's and Bonnie's gain or loss if the company is liquidated.

19. Money, Inc., a calendar year S corporation, has two unrelated shareholders, each owning 50% of the stock. Both shareholders have a $400,000 stock basis as of January 1, 1993. At the beginning of 1993, Money has AAA of $300,000 and AEP of $600,000. During 1993, Money has operating income of $100,000. At the end of the year, Money distributes securities worth $1 million, with an adjusted basis of $800,000. Determine the tax effects of these transactions.

20. Assume the same facts as in Problem 19, except that the two shareholders consent under § 1368(e)(3) to distribute AEP first.

21. An S corporation's Form 1120S shows taxable income of $70,000 for 1993. Peter, an individual, owns 40% of the stock throughout the year. The following information is obtained from the corporate records.

Salary paid to Peter	$52,000
Tax-exempt insurance proceeds	3,000
Charitable contributions	6,000
Dividends received from a foreign corporation	5,000
Long-term capital loss	6,000
Section 1250 gain	11,000
Refund of prior state income taxes	5,000
Cost of goods sold	72,000

Short-term capital loss	7,000
Administrative expenses	18,000
Short-term capital gains	14,000
Advertising expenses	11,000
Peter's beginning stock basis	$21,000
Peter's additional stock purchases	7,000
Beginning AAA	19,000
Peter's loan to corporation	20,000

a. Compute book income or loss.
b. Compute Peter's ending stock basis.
c. Calculate ending corporate AAA.

22. At the beginning of 1993, Malcolm, a 50% shareholder of a calendar year S corporation, has a stock basis of $22,000. During the year, the corporation has taxable income of $32,000. The following data are obtained from supplemental sources.

Dividends received	$12,000
Tax-exempt interest	18,000
Short-term capital gain	6,000
Section 1250 gain	10,000
Section 1231 gain	7,000
Charitable contributions	5,000
Political contributions	8,000
Long-term capital loss	12,000
Dividends to Malcolm	6,000
Advertising expense	13,000
Beginning AAA	42,000

a. Compute Malcolm's ending stock basis.
b. Compute ending AAA.

23. In the following independent statements, indicate whether the transaction will increase (+), decrease (−), or have no effect (NE) on the adjusted basis of a shareholder's stock in an S corporation.

a. Tax-exempt income.
b. Long-term capital gain.
c. Net operating loss.
d. Section 1231 gain.
e. Excess of percentage depletion over the basis of the property.
f. Separately computed income.
g. Nontaxable return-of-capital distribution by the corporation.
h. Charitable contributions.
i. Business gift in excess of $25.
j. Section 1245 gain.
k. Dividends received by the S corporation.
l. Short-term capital loss.
m. Recovery of a bad debt.
n. Long-term capital loss.

24. A calendar year S corporation has a taxable loss of $80,000 and a capital loss of $20,000 for 1994. Muhammad owns 40% of the corporate stock and has a $21,000 basis in the stock. Determine the amount of the taxable loss and capital loss, if any, that flow through to Muhammad.

25. Norm owns 30% of the stock of an S corporation throughout 1993 and lends the corporation $6,000 during the year. Norm's stock basis in the corporation at the end of the year is $22,000. If the corporation sustains a $110,000 operating loss during

the year, what amount, if any, is Norm entitled to deduct with respect to the operating loss?

26. Tina is the sole owner of a C corporation, which incurred a $47,000 NOL in 1992. An S election became effective January 1993, and the S corporation incurred another $56,000 NOL. During 1993, Tina loaned the company $20,000, and her stock basis (before considering the NOL) was $40,000.

    a. Determine the tax consequences of these events.
    b. What are the tax effects if the S corporation repays half of the loan in 1994?

27. Bud is a 30% shareholder of an S corporation that has a $120,000 NOL for a nonleap year. On February 3, Bud sells all of his stock to Carol for $63,000. Carol owns her stock for the rest of the year. Bud's stock basis at the beginning of the year was $52,000.

    a. What amount, if any, of the NOL will pass through to Bud and Carol?
    b. What gain, if any, is taxable to Bud on the sale of his stock?

28. During February 1989, Water, Inc., a C corporation, elects to become an S corporation at a time when its building and land are worth $2.2 million. The adjusted basis of the land is $200,000, and the adjusted basis of the building is $400,000. The company has some securities valued as of February at $260,000 (with an $80,000 cost basis). You are the accountant for a 40% shareholder. What happens at both the corporate and shareholder levels in the following events (show calculations)?

    a. In November 1993, Water, Inc., moves into a new building and sells the land and old building for $2.3 million (total tax basis of $500,000).
    b. In February 1994, the company sells one-half of the securities for $145,000.

29. Netural Corporation converts to S corporation status effective for tax year 1991. As of January 1, 1991, Netural's assets were appraised as follows:

	Adjusted Basis	Fair Market Value
Cash	$ 25,000	$ 25,000
Accounts receivable	120,000	110,000
Marketable securities	25,000	90,000
Inventory (FIFO)	80,000	95,000
Machinery	60,000	22,000
Building	300,000	363,000
Land	140,000	180,000
Goodwill	–0–	150,000
Accounts payable	–0–	110,000

In the following situations, calculate any built-in gains tax, assuming the highest corporate tax rate is 34%.

    a. During 1991, Netural Corporation collects $104,000 of the accounts receivable ($120,000 basis) and sells $135,000 of the inventory ($80,000 basis).
    b. Assume that the corporation has an overall $2,000 NOL for 1991. Would your answer change?
    c. In 1994, Netural sells the marketable securities for $97,000 and the machinery for $19,000 ($55,000 current tax basis).

30. Bandana Corporation converts to S corporation status for 1994. Bandana used the LIFO inventory method in 1993 and had an ending LIFO inventory of $800,000 ($960,000 FIFO value). Calculate any resulting taxes assuming the highest corporate tax rate is 34%.

CHAPTER

PARTNERSHIPS

OBJECTIVES

Define a partnership and identify its governing concepts.

Explain the computational process for partnership income (loss).

Discuss the tax effects of a partnership formation, including property contributions.

Illustrate how debt affects the adjusted basis of partners' interests.

Explain how partnership organization and syndication costs are treated.

Specify how a partnership tax year is determined.

Explain the tax problems involved when a partner engages in transactions with the partnership.

Explain the tax effects of nonliquidating distributions.

Provide insights as to when and how a partnership can best be used.

OUTLINE

OVERVIEW OF PARTNERSHIP TAXATION

This chapter and the previous chapter analyze two entity structures that, in many cases, offer certain advantages over the regular corporate structure. These entities are partnerships and S corporations, which are called *flow-through* or *pass-through* entities because the owners of the trade or business elect to avoid treating the enterprise as a separate taxable entity. Instead, the owners are taxed on a proportionate share of the entity's taxable income at the end of each of its taxable years, regardless of the amount of cash or property distributions the owners received from the entity during the year. The entity serves as an information provider to the IRS and its owners with respect to the proportionate income shares of its owners, and the tax falls directly upon the owners of the enterprise.

Consider certain aspects of corporate taxation to see why a flow-through entity might be more desirable in certain cases. The greatest disadvantage of the regular corporate structure is *double taxation.* Corporate income is taxed at the entity level, currently at rates up to 34 percent. Any after-tax income that is distributed to corporate owners is taxed again as a dividend at the owner level. The Code does provide certain techniques for reducing this second level of taxation, such as the *dividends received deduction,* which is available to a corporate shareholder of another corporation. When the *dividend-receiving* corporation makes a distribution to *its* noncorporate owners, however, the double taxation situation occurs anyway.

Corporations and their shareholders may also use *income-splitting* techniques to reduce the possibility of double taxation. For example, in arriving at taxable income, the corporate entity may deduct reasonable salary payments to shareholders who provide services to the corporation, interest paid to shareholders who lend money to the corporation, and rent paid to shareholders who allow the corporation to use property they own personally. In this case, taxation occurs only at the shareholder level when the shareholder reports the salary, interest, or rent income. Even after these deductions, though (especially for larger or publicly held corporations), some income may remain at the corporate level. This income is subject to double taxation when it is distributed.

A second disadvantage of the corporate form lies in the current rate structure: currently, the highest corporate Federal tax rate is 34 percent, and the highest individual tax rate is 31 percent. Even without the effects of double taxation, income is taxed at lower rates at the individual owner level than at the corporate level.

The partnership entity form is an especially advantageous alternative in many cases. Its administrative and filing requirements are relatively simple, and it offers certain planning opportunities not available to other entity forms. Both the C and S corporate structures are subject to rigorous allocation and distribution requirements (generally, each allocation or distribution is proportionate to the ownership interest of the shareholder). A partnership, though, may adjust its allocations of income and cash flow each year according to the needs of the owners, as long as certain standards (discussed later in this chapter) are met. Also, any previously unrealized income (such as appreciation of corporate assets) of an S or C corporation is taxed at the entity level when the corporation liquidates, but a partnership generally may liquidate tax-free. Finally, many states impose reporting and licensing requirements on corporate entities, including S corporations. These include franchise or capital stock tax returns that may require annual assessments and costly professional preparation assistance. Partnerships, on the other hand, frequently have no reporting requirements beyond Federal and state informational tax returns.

For smaller business operations, a partnership enables several owners to combine their resources at low cost. It also offers simple filing requirements, the taxation of income at lower individual tax rates, and the ability to discontinue operations relatively inexpensively.

For larger business operations, a partnership offers a unique ability to raise capital with low filing and reporting costs (compared to corporate bond issuances, for example). Special allocations of income and cash-flow items are available in all partnerships to meet the objectives of the owners.

Since partnerships and S corporations are so widespread, a study of related tax problems will prove useful to students, business owners, and consultants. This chapter primarily addresses partnership formations, operations, and nonliquidating distributions. Dispositions of partnership interests, partnership liquidating distributions, and optional basis adjustments are beyond the coverage of this text.

Concept Summary 22–6 (beginning on page 22–43) provides a comparative analysis of the forms by which business can be conducted.

What Is a Partnership?

A partnership is an association of two or more persons to carry on a trade or business, with each contributing money, property, labor, or skill, and with all expecting to share in profits and losses.[1] For Federal income tax purposes, a partnership includes a syndicate, group, pool, joint venture, or other unincorporated organization, through which any business, financial operation, or venture is carried on. The entity must not be otherwise classified as a corporation, trust, or estate. If a partnership is used for the following purposes, however, it may elect to be excluded from the partnership rules:

- Investment motivations, rather than the active conduct of a trade or business.
- Joint production, extraction, or use of property.
- Underwriting, selling, or distributing a specific security issue.[2]

When a partnership is used to conduct a service business, such as accounting, law, or medicine, very likely it will be a *general partnership,* so that creditors can collect the amounts owed from both partnership assets and the assets of owner/partners. On the other hand, the *limited partnership* form will likely be used for acquiring capital in activities such as real estate development. A limited partnership is comprised of a general partner and numerous limited partners. Unless special rules apply, only the general partners are liable to creditors; each limited partner's risk of loss is restricted to his or her equity investment in the entity.

Partnership Taxation and Reporting

A partnership is not a taxable entity.[3] Rather, the taxable income or loss of the partnership flows through to the partners at the end of the entity's tax year.[4]

---

1. § 7701(a)(2).

2. § 761(a).

3. § 701.

4. § 702.

Each partner reports his or her allocable share of the partnership's income or loss for the year. As a result, the partnership itself pays no Federal income tax on its income; instead, the partners' individual tax liabilities are affected by the activities of the entity.

EXAMPLE 1

Adam is a 40% partner in the ABC Partnership. Both Adam's and the partnership's tax years end on December 31. In 1993, the partnership generates $200,000 of ordinary taxable income. However, because the partnership needs capital for expansion and debt reduction, Adam makes no cash withdrawals during 1993. He meets his living expenses by reducing his investment portfolio. Adam is taxed on his $80,000 allocable share of the partnership's 1993 income, even though he received no distributions from the entity during 1993. This allocated income is included in Adam's gross income. ◆

EXAMPLE 2

Assume the same facts as in Example 1, except the partnership recognizes a 1993 taxable loss of $100,000. Adam's 1993 AGI is reduced by $40,000 because his proportionate share of the loss flows through to him from the partnership. He claims a $40,000 partnership loss for the year. ◆

Many items of partnership income or expense retain their identity as they flow through to the partners. When preparing a personal tax return, then, a partner may have to take into account several items rather than a single share of net partnership ordinary income or loss. Generally, any item that might affect two or more partners' tax liabilities in different ways is reported separately to the partners.[5]

Ordinary partnership income or loss includes only the income and expenses related to partnership trade or business activities. These income and expense items are netted to produce a single income or loss amount that is passed through to the partners. Other items (such as rent income and expense, capital gains or losses, interest income, and charitable contributions) are reported separately by the partnership. Each partner will combine the share of these partnership items with any income the partner may have earned outside the partnership. Any tax limitations or separate calculations (for example, net capital gain or loss, or deductible charitable contributions) are determined at the partner level.

EXAMPLE 3

Beth is a 25% partner in the BR Partnership. The cash basis entity collected sales income of $60,000 during 1993 and incurred $15,000 in business expenses. In addition, it sold a corporate bond for a $9,000 long-term capital gain. Finally, the partnership made a $1,000 contribution to the local Performing Arts Fund drive. The fund is a qualifying charity. BR and all of its partners use a calendar tax year.

For 1993, Beth is allocated ordinary taxable income of $11,250 [($60,000 – $15,000) × 25%] from the partnership. She also is allocated a flow-through of a $2,250 long-term capital gain and a $250 charitable contribution deduction. The ordinary income increases Beth's gross income, and the capital gain and charitable contribution are combined with her other similar activities for the year as though she had incurred them herself. These items could be treated differently on the individual tax returns of the various partners (e.g., because a partner may be subject to a percentage limitation on charitable contribution deductions for 1993), so they are not included in the computation of ordinary partnership income. Instead, the items flow through to the partners separately. ◆

5. § 703(a)(1).

Other items that are allocated separately to the partners[6] include recognized gains and losses from property transactions; dividend income; tax preferences and adjustments for the alternative minimum tax; expenditures that qualify for the jobs credit and the foreign tax credit; and expenses that would be itemized by the partners or other nonbusiness deductions.

Even though it is not a taxpaying entity, a partnership must file an information tax return, Form 1065. Look at Form 1065 in Appendix B, and refer to these forms during the following discussion. The partnership reports the results of its trade or business activities on Form 1065, page 1. Schedule K (page 3 of Form 1065) accumulates all items that must be separately reported to the partners, including net trade or business income or loss (from page 1). The amounts on Schedule K are allocated to all the partners. Each partner receives a Form K–1, which shows the share of all partnership items.

Example 4

The BR Partnership in Example 3 reports its $60,000 sales income on Form 1065, page 1, line 1. The $15,000 of business expenses are reported in the appropriate amounts on page 1, line 2 or lines 9–20. Partnership ordinary income of $45,000 is shown on page 1, line 22, and on Schedule K, line 1. The $9,000 capital gain and the $1,000 charitable contribution are reported only on Schedule K, lines 4e and 8, respectively.

Beth receives a Schedule K–1 from the partnership that shows her shares of partnership ordinary income of $11,250, long-term capital gain of $2,250, and charitable contributions of $250 on lines 1, 4e, and 8, respectively. She then combines these amounts with similar items from sources other than BR in her personal tax return. For example, if she has a $5,000 long-term capital loss from a stock transaction in 1993, her overall net capital loss is $2,750. She then evaluates this net amount to determine the amount she may deduct on her Form 1040. ◆

As this example shows, partnership accounting income is different from ordinary income reported on page 1 of Form 1065. Schedule K accumulates all partnership tax items and arrives at a total amount on line 23a. Schedule M–1, page 4, shows a reconciliation of accounting income and the total of partnership tax items on Schedule K (line 23a). Schedule L generally shows an accounting-basis balance sheet, and Schedule M–2 reconciles beginning and ending partner's capital accounts.

Partner's Ownership Interest in a Partnership

Each partner owns a *capital interest* and a *profits interest* in the partnership. A capital interest is measured by a partner's *capital sharing ratio,* which is the partner's percentage ownership of the capital of the partnership. A partner's capital interest can be determined in several ways. The most widely accepted method measures the capital interest as the percentage of net assets (assets remaining after payment of all partnership liabilities) a partner would receive on immediate liquidation of the partnership.

A profits interest is simply the partner's percentage allocation of current partnership operating results. Profit and loss sharing ratios are specified in the partnership agreement and are used to determine each partner's allocation of partnership ordinary taxable income and separately stated items.[7] The partnership can change its profit and loss allocations at any time simply by amending the partnership agreement.

6. § 702(a).

7. § 704(a).

Each partner's Schedule K–1 shows the profit, loss, and capital sharing ratios. In many cases, the three ratios will be the same. A partner's capital sharing ratio will generally equal the profit and loss sharing ratios if profit and loss allocations, for each year of the partnership's existence, have been in the same proportion as the partner's initial contributions to the partnership.

The partnership agreement may, in some cases, provide that certain amounts are either *specially allocated* to certain partners or allocated in a different proportion from general profit and loss sharing ratios. These items are separately reported to the partner receiving the allocation. For a special allocation to be recognized for tax purposes, it must produce economic consequences in addition to tax savings for the partner receiving the allocation.[8]

EXAMPLE 5

When the George-Helen Partnership was formed, George contributed cash and Helen contributed some City of Iuka bonds that she had held for investment purposes. The partnership agreement allocates all of the tax-exempt interest income from the bonds to Helen as an inducement for her to remain a partner. This is generally an acceptable special allocation for income tax purposes; it reflects the differing economic circumstances that underlie the partners' contributions to the capital of the entity. Since Helen would have received the exempt income if she had not joined the partnership, she can retain the tax-favored treatment via the special allocation. ◆

EXAMPLE 6

Assume the same facts as in Example 5. Three years after it was formed, the George-Helen Partnership purchased some City of Butte bonds. The municipal bond interest income flows through to the partners as a separately stated item, so that it retains its tax-exempt status. The partnership agreement allocates all of this income to George because he is subject to a higher marginal income tax bracket than is Helen. This allocation is not effective for income tax purposes because it has no purpose other than the reduction of the partners' income tax liability. ◆

Each partner has a basis in the partnership interest, just as each would have a tax basis in any asset owned. When income flows through to a partner from the partnership, the partner's basis in the partnership interest increases accordingly. When a loss flows through to a partner, basis is reduced.

EXAMPLE 7

Paul contributes $20,000 cash to acquire a 30% capital and profits interest in the Red Robin Partnership. In its first year of operations, the partnership earns ordinary income of $40,000. Paul's initial basis is the $20,000 he paid for the interest. He reports ordinary income of $12,000 (30% × $40,000 partnership income) on his individual return and increases his basis by the same amount, to $32,000. ◆

In allowing increases and decreases in a partner's basis in a partnership interest, the Code ensures that only one level of tax arises on the income or loss from partnership operations. In Example 7, if Paul sold his interest at the end of the first year for $32,000, he would have no gain or loss. If the Code did not provide for an adjustment of a partner's basis, Paul's basis would be $20,000, and he would be taxed on the gain of $12,000 in addition to being taxed on his $12,000

8. § 704(b).

share of income. In other words, without the basis adjustment, partnership income would be subject to double taxation.

As the following sections discuss in detail, a partner's basis is important for determining the treatment of distributions from the partnership to the partner and the deductibility of partnership losses.

A partner's basis is not reflected anywhere on the Schedule K–1. Instead, each partner should maintain a personal record of adjustments to basis. Schedule K–1 does reflect a reconciliation of a partner's capital account, but the ending capital account balance is rarely the same amount as the partner's basis. Just as the tax and accounting bases of a specific asset may differ, a partner's *capital account* and *basis* may not be equal for a variety of reasons. For example, a partnership may use generally accepted accounting principles (GAAP) in computing depreciation expense, which may differ from MACRS used for tax purposes. A partner's basis also includes the partner's share of partnership liabilities. These liabilities are not reported as part of the partner's capital account but are included in question B at the top of the partner's Schedule K–1.

Conceptual Basis for Partnership Taxation

The unique tax treatment of partners and partnerships can be traced to two legal concepts that evolved long ago: the *aggregate* or *conduit concept* and the *entity concept.* Both concepts have been used in civil and common law, and their influence can be seen in practically every partnership tax rule.

Aggregate or Conduit Concept. The aggregate or conduit concept treats the partnership as a channel through which income, credits, deductions, and the like flow to the partners for their own tax consideration. Under this concept, the partnership is regarded as a collection of taxpayers joined in an agency relationship with one another. The imposition of the income tax on individual partners reflects the influence of this doctrine. The aggregate concept has influenced the tax treatment of other pass-through entities, such as S corporations (Chapter 21) and trusts and estates (Chapter 27).

Entity Concept. The entity concept treats partners and partnerships as separate units and gives the partnership its own tax "personality" by (1) requiring a partnership to file an information tax return and (2) treating partners as separate and distinct from the partnership in certain transactions between a partner and the entity. A partner's recognition of capital gain or loss on the sale of the partnership interest illustrates this doctrine.

Combined Concepts. Rules that contain a blend of both the entity and aggregate concepts include provisions concerning the formation, operation, and liquidation of a partnership.

Formation of a Partnership: Tax Effects

Partner's Gain or Loss on Contributions to Entity

When a taxpayer transfers property to an entity in exchange for valuable consideration, a taxable exchange normally results. Typically, both the taxpayer and the entity will realize and recognize gain or loss on the exchange. The gain or loss recognized by the transferor is the difference between the fair market value of the consideration received and the adjusted basis of the property transferred.

Generally, however, neither the partner nor the partnership recognizes the realized gain or loss when a partner contributes property to a partnership in exchange for a partnership interest. Instead, the realized gain or loss is deferred.[9] The following diagram illustrates the transaction resulting in the formation of a partnership:

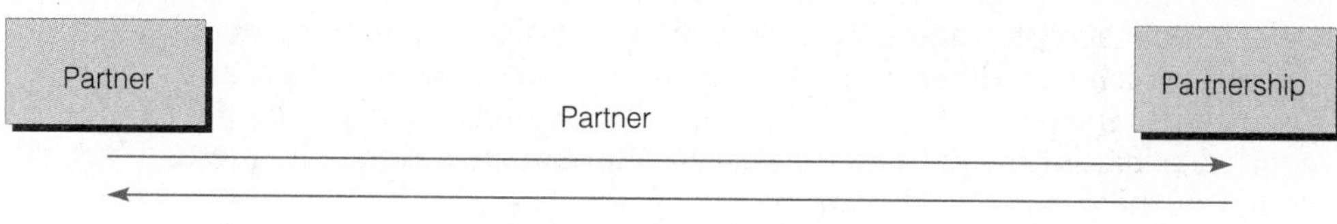

There are two reasons for this nonrecognition treatment. First, forming a partnership allows investors to combine their assets toward greater economic goals than could be achieved separately. Only the form of ownership, rather than the amount owned by each investor, has changed. Requiring that gain be recognized on such transfers would make the formation of some partnerships economically unfeasible (e.g., where two existing proprietorships are combined to form one larger business). Congress is not interested in hindering the creation of valid economic entities by requiring gain recognition when a partnership is created. Second, because the partnership interest received is typically not a liquid asset, the partner may not easily be able to find the cash to pay the tax. Thus, the deferral of the gain recognizes the economic realities of the business world and follows the wherewithal to pay principle of taxation.

EXAMPLE 8

Alicia transfers two assets to the Wren Partnership on the day the entity is created, in exchange for a 60% profit and loss interest. This 60% partnership interest is worth $60,000. She contributes cash of $40,000 and retail display equipment (basis to her as a sole proprietor, $8,000; fair market value, $20,000). Since an exchange has occurred between two entities, Alicia will *realize* a $12,000 gain on this transaction. The gain realized is the fair market value of the partnership interest of $60,000 less the basis of the assets that she surrendered to the partnership [$40,000 (cash) + $8,000 (equipment)].

Under § 721, Alicia *does not recognize* the $12,000 realized gain in the year of contribution. Alicia might have been pressed for cash if she had been required to recognize the $12,000 gain. All that she received from the partnership was an illiquid partnership interest; she received no cash with which to pay any resulting tax liability. ◆

EXAMPLE 9

Assume the same facts as in Example 8, except that the equipment Alicia contributed to the partnership had an adjusted basis of $25,000. She has a $5,000 realized loss [$60,000 – ($40,000 + $25,000)], but she cannot deduct any of this loss. Realized losses, as well as realized gains, are deferred by § 721.

9. § 721.

If it were not essential that the partnership receive Alicia's display equipment rather than similar equipment purchased from an outside supplier, Alicia should have sold the equipment to a third party. This would have allowed her to deduct a $5,000 loss in the year of the sale. Alicia then could have contributed $60,000 cash (including the proceeds from the sale) for her interest in the partnership, and the partnership would have funds to purchase similar equipment. ◆

EXAMPLE 10

Assume the same facts as in Example 8. Five years after the partnership was created, Alicia contributes another piece of equipment to the entity from her sole proprietorship. This property has a basis of $35,000 and a fair market value of $50,000. Alicia can defer the recognition of this $15,000 realized gain. Section 721 is effective whenever a partner makes a contribution to the capital of the partnership. ◆

The nonrecognition provisions of § 721 will not apply where:

- appreciated stocks are contributed to an investment partnership;
- the transaction is essentially an exchange of properties;
- the transaction is a disguised sale of properties; or
- the partnership interest is received in exchange for services rendered to the partnership by the partner.

Investment Partnership. If the transfer consists of appreciated stocks and securities and the partnership is an investment partnership, it is likely that the realized gain on the stocks and securities will be recognized by the contributing partner at the time of contribution.[10] This provision prevents multiple investors from using the partnership form to diversify their investment portfolios on a tax-free basis.

Exchange. The nonrecognition provisions of § 721 will not defer the tax on a transaction that is essentially an exchange of properties.[11]

EXAMPLE 11

Shontelle owns land and Bob owns stock. Shontelle would like to have Bob's stock, and Bob wants Shontelle's land. If Shontelle and Bob both contribute their property to a newly formed SB Partnership in exchange for interests in the partnership, the tax on the transaction would appear to be deferred under § 721. The tax on a subsequent distribution by the partnership of the land to Bob and the stock to Shontelle would also appear to be deferred under § 731 (discussed later in the chapter). According to a literal interpretation of the statutes, no taxable exchange has occurred. Shontelle and Bob will find, however, that this type of tax subterfuge is not permitted. The IRS will disregard the passage of the properties through the partnership and will hold, instead, that Shontelle and Bob exchanged the land and stock directly. Thus, the transactions will be treated as any other taxable exchange. ◆

Disguised Sale. A similar result occurs in a *disguised sale* of properties. A disguised sale is deemed to occur where a partner contributes property to a partnership and soon thereafter receives a distribution from the partnership. This distribution could be viewed as a payment by the partnership for purchase of the property.[12]

---

10. § 721(b).

11. Reg. § 1.731–1(c)(3).

12. § 707(a)(2)(B).

EXAMPLE 12

Kim transfers property to the KLM Partnership. The property has an adjusted basis of $10,000 and a fair market value of $30,000. Soon thereafter, the partnership makes a distribution of $30,000 to Kim. Under the distribution rules of § 731 (discussed later in the chapter), the distribution would not be taxable to Kim if the basis for her partnership interest prior to the distribution was greater than the amount distributed. However, the transaction appears to be a thin disguise of a purchase-sale transaction, rather than a contribution and distribution. Therefore, Kim must recognize gain of $20,000 on transfer of the property, and the partnership is deemed to have purchased the property for $30,000. ◆

Services. A final exception to the nonrecognition provision of § 721 occurs when a partner receives his or her interest in the partnership as compensation for services rendered to the partnership. This is not a tax-deferred transaction. Services are not included in the definition of property that can be transferred to a partnership on a tax-free basis. Instead, the partner performing the services recognizes ordinary compensation income equal to the fair market value of the partnership interest received.[13]

The partnership may deduct the amount included in the partner's income if the services are of a deductible nature. If the services are not deductible to the partnership, they must be capitalized to an asset account. For example, architectural plans created by a partner will be capitalized to the structure built with those plans. Alternatively, day-to-day management services performed by a partner for the partnership are usually deductible by the partnership.

EXAMPLE 13

When they formed the BCD Partnership, Bill, Carl, and Dave each received a one-third interest in the entity. Dave became a one-third partner to compensate him for the accounting and tax planning services that he rendered during the formation of the partnership. The value of a one-third interest in the partnership (for each of the parties) is $20,000. Dave must recognize $20,000 of compensation income. This treatment resembles the results that would occur if the partnership had paid Dave $20,000 for his services and he had immediately contributed that amount to the entity for a one-third ownership interest. ◆

Tax Issues Relative to Contributed Property

When a partner contributes an asset to the capital of a partnership, the entity assigns a carryover basis to the property.[14] The entity's basis in the asset is equal to the basis the partner held in the property prior to its transfer to the partnership. Thus, two assets are created out of one when a partnership is formed, namely, the property in the hands of the new entity and the new asset (the partnership interest) in the hands of the partner. Both assets are assigned a basis that is derived from the partner's existing basis in the contributed property. This basis is increased by the amount of any gain that the partner recognized as a result of the formation of an *investment company partnership.*

These rules are logical in view of what Congress was attempting to accomplish in this deferral transaction. As noted earlier, gain or loss is deferred when property is contributed to a partnership in exchange for a partnership interest. This deferral is implemented through the calculation of the partnership's basis in the transferred property and the partner's basis for the partnership interest. These bases are the amounts necessary to allow for the recognition of the

13. § 83(a).

14. § 723.

deferred gain or loss if the property or the partnership interest is subsequently disposed of in a taxable transaction. This treatment is similar to the treatment of assets transferred to a controlled corporation[15] and the treatment of like-kind exchanges.[16]

EXAMPLE 14

On June 1, 1993, José transfers property to the JKL Partnership in exchange for a one-third interest in the partnership. The property has an adjusted basis to José of $10,000 and a fair market value on June 1, of $30,000. José's realized gain on the exchange is $20,000 ($30,000 – $10,000), but under § 721, none of the gain is recognized. José's basis for his partnership interest is the amount necessary to recognize the $20,000 deferred gain if he subsequently sells the interest for its $30,000 fair market value. This amount, $10,000, is referred to as "substituted" basis. The basis of the property contributed to the partnership is the amount necessary to allow for the recognition of the $20,000 deferred gain if the property were subsequently sold for its $30,000 fair market value. This amount, also $10,000, is referred to as "carryover" basis. ◆

The holding period for the contributed asset also carries over to the partnership. Thus, the partnership's holding period for the asset includes the period during which the partner owned the asset individually.

Depreciation Method and Period. If depreciable property is contributed to the partnership, the partnership is usually required to use the same cost recovery method and life used by the partner. The partnership merely "steps into the shoes" of the partner and continues the same cost recovery calculations. If the property is not MACRS or ACRS property, the partnership must treat the property as used property for depreciation purposes. The partnership may not immediately expense any part of the basis of § 179 property it receives from the transferor partner.

Receivables, Inventory, and Losses. To prevent the conversion of ordinary income into capital gain, gain or loss is treated as ordinary when the partnership disposes of either of the following:[17]

- Contributed receivables that were unrealized in the contributing partner's hands at the contribution date. Such receivables include the right to receive payment for goods or services delivered (or to be delivered).
- Contributed property that was inventory in the contributor's hands on the contribution date, *if the disposal occurs within five years of this date.* Inventory includes all property except capital and real or depreciable business assets.

To prevent the conversion of a capital loss into an ordinary loss, capital treatment is assigned to a loss on the disposal of contributed property that was capital loss property in the contributor's hands on the contribution date, *if the disposal occurs within five years of this date.* The capital loss is limited to the "built-in" loss on the date of contribution.

EXAMPLE 15

Tyrone operates a cash basis retail electronics and television store as a sole proprietor. Ramon is an enterprising individual who likes to invest in small businesses. On

15. § 351.

16. § 1031.

17. § 724. For this purpose, § 724(d)(2) waives the holding period requirement in defining § 1231 property.

January 2 of the current year, Tyrone and Ramon form the TR Partnership. Their partnership contributions are as follows:

	Adjusted Basis	Fair Market Value
From Tyrone:		
Receivables	$ -0-	$ 2,000
Land used as parking lot*	1,200	5,000
Inventory	2,500	5,000
From Ramon:		
Cash	10,000	10,000

*Parking lot had been held for five months at contribution date.

Within 30 days of forming the partnership, TR collects the receivables and sells the inventory for $5,000 cash. It uses the land for the next 10 months as a parking lot, then sells it for $3,500 cash. TR realized the following income in the current year from these transactions:

- Ordinary income of $2,000 from collecting receivables.
- Ordinary income of $2,500 from sale of inventory.
- Section 1231 gain of $2,300 from sale of land.

The land takes a carryover holding period. Thus, it is treated as having been held 15 months at the sale date. ◆

EXAMPLE 16

Assume the same facts as Example 15, except for the following:

- The land contributed by Tyrone was held for investment and had a fair market value of $800 at the contribution date.
- TR used the land as a parking lot for 11 months and sold it for $650.

TR realizes the following income and loss from these transactions:

- Ordinary income of $2,000 from collecting receivables.
- Ordinary income of $2,500 from sale of inventory.
- Capital loss of $400 from sale of land.
- Section 1231 loss of $150 from sale of land.

Since the land was sold within five years of the contribution date, the built-in $400 loss is a capital loss. The post-contribution loss of $150 is a § 1231 loss, since TR used the property in its business. ◆

Throughout this chapter, reference is made to the partnership's inside basis and a partner's outside basis. *Inside basis* refers to the aggregate adjusted basis of *partnership* assets, as determined from the partnership's tax accounts. *Outside basis* represents the aggregate of each partner's basis in the partnership interest. Each partner owns a share of the partnership's inside basis and should maintain the records of outside basis. In many cases—especially on formation of the partnership—the total of all partners' outside bases will equal the partnership's inside bases for all its assets. Differences between inside and outside basis arise when a partner's interest is sold to another person for more or less than the selling partner's share of the inside basis of partnership assets. The buying partner's outside basis equals the price paid for the interest, but the share of the entity's inside basis is the same amount as the seller's share of the inside basis.

Concept Summary 22–1 reviews the rules that apply to partnership asset contribution and basis adjustments.

Tax Accounting Elections

A newly formed partnership must make numerous tax accounting elections. These elections are formal decisions on how a particular transaction or tax attribute should be handled. Most of these elections must be made by the partnership rather than by the partners individually.[18] The *partnership* makes the elections for the following items:

- Inventory method.
- Cost or percentage depletion method, excluding oil and gas wells.
- Accounting method (cash, accrual, or hybrid).
- Capitalizing or expensing of fixed assets.
- Cost recovery methods and assumptions.
- Tax year.
- Amortization of organizational costs and amortization period.
- Amortization of start-up expenditures and amortization period.
- Section 179 deductions for certain tangible personal property.
- Nonrecognition treatment for involuntary conversions gains.

Each partner is bound by the decisions made by the partnership relative to these elections. If the partnership fails to make an election, a partner cannot compensate for this error by making the election individually.

CONCEPT SUMMARY 22–1
PARTNERSHIP FORMATION AND BASIS COMPUTATION

1. The *entity concept* treats partners and partnerships as separate units. The nature and amount of gains and losses are determined at the partnership level.
2. The *aggregate concept* is used to connect partners and partnerships. It allows income, gains, losses, credits, deductions, etc. to flow through to the partners for separate tax reporting.
3. Sometimes both the *aggregate* and *entity* concepts apply, but one usually dominates. When land used as a parking lot is sold for a gain within five years of its contribution date, and the land was held by the contributing partner as inventory, the resulting gain is ordinary (aggregate concept).
4. Generally, partners or partnerships do not recognize gain or loss when property is contributed for capital interests.
5. Partners contributing property for partnership interests generally take the contributed property's adjusted basis for their *outside basis* in their partnership interest. The partners are said to take a substituted basis in their partnership interest.
6. The partnership will generally continue to use the contributing partner's basis for the *inside basis* in property it receives. The contributed property is said to take a carryover basis.
7. The holding period of a partner's interest includes that of contributed property when the property was a § 1231 asset or capital asset in the partner's hands. Otherwise, the holding period starts on the day the interest is acquired. The holding period of an interest acquired by a cash contribution starts at acquisition.
8. The partnership's holding period for contributed property includes the contributing partner's holding period.

18. § 703(b).

Though most elections must be made by the partnership, the partners are required to make three specific elections individually.[19] These elections involve relatively narrow tax issues. Each *partner* individually makes the election on the following issues:

- Income from discharge of indebtedness.
- Cost or percentage depletion method for oil and gas wells.
- Deductions and credits for foreign countries and U.S. possessions.

Organization and Syndication Costs

Amounts paid or incurred to organize a partnership or promote the sale of a partnership interest are not deductible. However, the Code permits a ratable amortization of some of these costs.[20]

Organization Costs. The partnership may elect to amortize organization costs ratably over a period of 60 months or more, starting with the month in which it began business. The election must be made by the due date (including extensions) of the partnership return for the year it began business.

Organization costs include expenditures that are (1) incident to the creation of the partnership; (2) chargeable to a capital account; and (3) of a character that, if incident to the creation of a partnership with an ascertainable life, would be amortized over that life. These expenditures include accounting fees and legal fees incident to the partnership's formation. To be amortizable, the expenditures must be incurred within a period that starts a reasonable time before the partnership begins business. The period ends with the due date (without extensions) of the tax return for the initial tax year.

Cash method partnerships are not allowed to deduct *in the year incurred* the portion of organization costs that are paid after the end of the first year. The partnership can deduct, in the year of payment, the portion of the expenditures that would have been deductible in a prior year, if they had been paid before that year's end.

EXAMPLE 17

The calendar year Bluejay Partnership was formed on May 1 of the current year and immediately started business. Bluejay incurred $720 in legal fees for drafting the partnership agreement and $480 in accounting fees for tax advice of an organizational nature. The legal fees were paid in October of the current year. The accounting fees were paid in January of the following year. The partnership selected the cash method of accounting and elected to amortize its organization costs.

On its first tax return, Bluejay deducts $96 of organization costs [($720 legal fees/60 months) × 8 months]. No deduction was taken for the accounting fees since the partnership selected the cash method and the fees were paid the following year. On its tax return for next year, Bluejay deducts organization costs of $304 {[($720 legal fees/60 months) × 12 months] + [($480 accounting fees/60 months) × 20 months]}. Note that the second-year deduction ($304) includes the $64 of accounting fees [($480/60) × 8] that could have been deducted on Bluejay's first tax return if they had been paid by the end of that year. ◆

Costs incurred for the following items are not organization costs:

19. §§ 703(b)(1), (2), and (3).

20. § 709.

- Acquiring assets for the partnership.
- Transferring assets to the partnership.
- Admitting partners, other than at formation.
- Removing partners, other than at formation.
- Negotiating operating contracts.
- Syndication costs.

Syndication Costs. Syndication costs are capitalized, but unlike organization costs, no amortization election is available. Syndication costs include the following expenditures incurred for promoting and marketing partnership interests:

- Brokerage fees.
- Registration fees.
- Legal fees paid to the underwriter, placement agent, and issuer for security advice or advice on the adequacy of tax disclosures in the prospectus or placement memo for securities law purposes.
- Accounting fees related to offering materials.
- Printing costs of prospectus, placement memos, and other selling materials.

Taxable Year of the Partnership

Partnership taxable income (and any separately stated items) flows through to each partner at the end of the *partnership's* taxable year. A *partner's* taxable income for a given year, then, will include the distributive share of partnership income for any *partnership* taxable year that ended within the partner's tax year.

When all partners use the calendar year, it would be beneficial in present value terms for a profitable partnership to adopt a fiscal year ending with January 31. Why? As Figure 22–1 illustrates, when the adopted year ends on January 31, the reporting of income from the partnership and payment of related taxes can be deferred an additional 11 months. For instance, income earned by the partnership in September 1993 is not taxed to the partners until January 31, 1994. It is reported in the partner's tax return for the year ended December 31, 1994, which is not due until April 15, 1995. Even though each partner may be required to file quarterly tax returns and make estimated tax payments, some deferral is still possible.

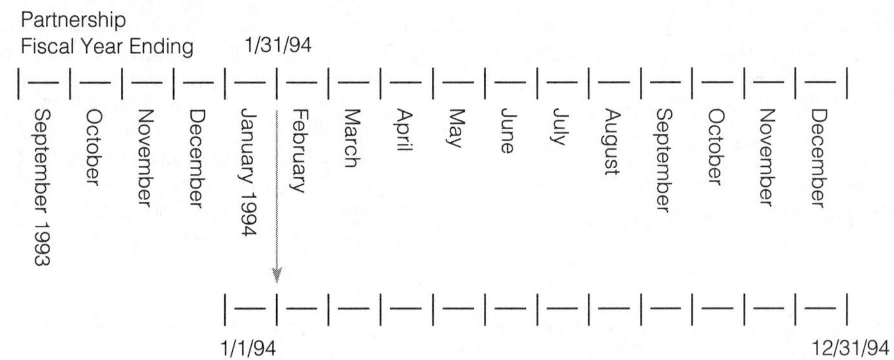

FIGURE 22–1
Deferral Benefit When Fiscal Year Is Used and All Partners Are on the Calendar Year

Required Taxable Years. To prevent excessive deferral of taxation of partnership income, Congress and the IRS have adopted a series of rules that prescribe the *required* taxable year an entity must adopt if no alternative tax years (discussed below) are available. Three rules are presented in Figure 22–2.[21] The partnership must consider each rule, in order. If a year-end is available under a given rule, the partnership must use that year-end.

The first two rules are relatively self-explanatory. Under the *least aggregate deferral rule,* the partnership tests the year-ends that are used by the various partners to determine the weighted-average deferral of partnership income. The year-end that offers the least amount of deferral is the *required tax year* for the partnership.

EXAMPLE 18

Anne and Bonnie will be equal partners in the AB Partnership. Anne uses the calendar year, and Bonnie uses a fiscal year ending August 31. Neither Anne nor Bonnie will be a majority partner. Although Anne and Bonnie are both principal partners, they do not have the same tax year. Therefore, the general rules indicate that the partnership's required tax year must be determined by the "least aggregate deferral" method. The following computations support August 31 as AB's tax year, since the 2.0 product using that year-end is less than the 4.0 product when December 31 is used.

Test for 12/31 Year-End

Partner	Year Ends	Profit Interest		Months of Deferral		Product
Anne	12/31	50%	×	–0–	=	0.0
Bonnie	8/31	50%	×	8	=	4.0
Aggregate number of deferral months						4.0

Test for 8/31 Year-End

Partner	Year Ends	Profit Interest		Months of Deferral		Product
Anne	12/31	50%	×	4	=	2.0
Bonnie	8/31	50%	×	–0–	=	0.0
Aggregate number of deferral months						2.0

◆

Alternative Tax Years. If the required tax year described above is undesirable to the entity, three other alternative tax years may be available:

- Establish to the IRS's satisfaction that a *business purpose* exists for a different tax year (a natural business year at the end of a peak season or shortly

FIGURE 22–2
Required Tax Year of Partnership

In Order, Partnership Must Use	Requirements
Majority partners' tax year	■ A majority partner owns more than 50% of capital *and* profits.
	■ All majority partners must have a common tax year.
Principal partners' tax year	■ All partners who own 5% or more of capital *or* profits are principal partners.
	■ All principal partners must have a common tax year.
Year with smallest amount of income deferred	■ "Least aggregate deferral" method (Example 18).

21. § 706(b).

thereafter, such as a Maine or Minnesota fishing resort that closes every fall). It is difficult to obtain IRS approval when using the business purpose exception unless the 25 percent, two-month test described next can be satisfied.

- Follow IRS procedures to obtain approval for using a *natural business tax year.* The IRS has stated that a natural business year exists when 25 percent or more of the partnership's gross receipts were recognized during the last 2 months of the same 12-month period for three consecutive years.[22] New partnerships cannot use this justification because they lack the required three-year history.
- Elect a tax year so that taxes on partnership income are deferred for not more than *three months* from the *required* tax year. Then, have the partnership maintain with the IRS a prepaid, non-interest-bearing deposit of estimated deferred taxes.

To use the three-month-or-less deferral rule, the partnership must file an election on Form 8716 by the *earlier of* the following:

- The fifteenth day of the fifth month following the month that includes the first day of the tax year for which the election is effective (e.g., for a June 30 fiscal year, this is November 15).
- The due date (without extensions) of the partnership return resulting from the election.

Required tax deferral deposits are computed on partnership income at the highest individual tax rate plus one percentage point. The first payment is due on April 15 (plus extensions) of the calendar year following the calendar year in which the first tax year begins. Future payments are also due on April 15 (plus extensions). When the required tax deferral deposit increases, the partnership makes additional payments. When it decreases, the partnership can get a refund. In summary, the partnership maintains an annually adjusted prepaid tax deferral balance with the IRS.[23]

Operations of the Partnership

An individual, corporation, trust, estate, or partnership can become a partner in a partnership. Since a partnership is a tax-reporting, rather than a taxpaying, entity for purposes of its Federal (and state) income tax computations, the partnership's income, deductions, credits, and alternative minimum tax (AMT) preferences and adjustments can ultimately be reported and taxed on any of a number of income tax forms (e.g., Forms 1040 [individuals], 1041 [fiduciaries], 1120 [C corporations], and 1120S [S corporations]).

A partnership is subject to all other taxes, in the same manner as any other business. Thus, the partnership files returns and pays the outstanding amount of pertinent sales taxes, property taxes, and Social Security, unemployment, and other payroll taxes.

---

22. Rev.Proc. 74–33, 1974–2 C.B. 489; Rev.Rul. 87–57, 1987–2 C.B. 117; and Rev.Proc. 87–32, 1987–1 C.B. 396.

23. §§ 444 and 7519.

Measuring and Reporting Income

The partnership's Form 1065 organizes and reports the transactions of the entity for the tax year, and each of the partnership's tax items is reported on Schedule K of that return. Each partner, and the IRS, receives a Schedule K–1 that reports the partner's allocable share of partnership income, credits, and preferences for the year. As required by § 6031, Form 1065 is due on the fifteenth day of the fourth month following the close of the partnership's tax year; for a calendar year partnership, this is April 15.

Income Measurement. The measurement and reporting of partnership income require a two-step approach. Certain items must be segregated and reported separately on the partnership return and each partner's Schedule K–1.

Items that are not separately reported are netted at the partnership level. Items passed through separately include the following:

- Short- and long-term capital gains and losses.
- Section 1231 gains and losses.
- Charitable contributions.
- Portfolio income items (dividends, interest, and royalties).
- Immediately expensed tangible personal property (§ 179).
- Items allocated differently from the general profit and loss ratio.
- Recovery of items previously deducted (tax benefit items).
- AMT preference and adjustment items.
- Passive activity items (rental real estate income or loss).
- Expenses related to portfolio income.
- Intangible drilling and development costs.
- Taxes paid to foreign countries and U.S. possessions.
- Nonbusiness and personal items (e.g., alimony, medical, and dental).[24]

The reason for separately reporting the preceding items is rooted in the aggregate or conduit concept. These items affect various exclusions, deductions, and credits at the partner level and must pass through without loss of identity so that the proper tax for each partner may be determined.[25]

A partnership is not allowed the following deductions:

- Personal exemptions.
- Taxes paid to foreign countries or U.S. possessions.
- Net operating losses.
- Alimony, medical expense, moving expense, and individual retirement savings.
- Depletion of oil and gas interests.
- Dividends received deduction.

EXAMPLE 19

Tiwanda is a one-third partner in the TUV Partnership. This year, the entity entered into the following transactions:

Fees received	$100,000
Salaries paid	30,000
Cost recovery deductions	11,000

24. § 702(a).

25. § 702(b).

Supplies, repairs	3,000
Payroll taxes paid	9,000
Contribution to art museum	5,000
Short-term capital gain recognized	12,000
Net income from passive rental operations	7,000
Dividends received	1,500
City of Albuquerque bond interest received	2,300
AMT adjustment (installment sale)	(44,000)
Payment of partner Vern's alimony obligations	4,000

The entity experienced a $20,000 net loss from operations last year, its first year of business.

The two-step computational process that is used to determine partnership income is applied in the following manner:

Nonseparately Stated Items (Ordinary Income)	
Fee income	$100,000
Salary deduction	(30,000)
Cost recovery deductions	(11,000)
Supplies, repairs	(3,000)
Taxes paid	(9,000)
Ordinary income	$ 47,000

Separately Stated Items	
Charitable contribution	$ 5,000
Short-term capital gain	12,000
Passive income (net rent income)	7,000
Portfolio income (dividends received)	1,500
Exempt income (bond interest)	2,300
AMT adjustment (installment sale)	(44,000)

Each of the separately stated items passes through proportionately to each partner and is included on the appropriate schedule or netted with similar items that the partner generated for the year. Thus, in determining what her tax liability will be on her Form 1040, Tiwanda includes a $1,667 charitable contribution, a $4,000 short-term capital gain, $2,333 of passive rent income, $500 of dividend income, and a $14,667 negative adjustment in computing alternative minimum taxable income. Tiwanda treats these items as if she had generated them herself. In addition, Tiwanda reports $15,667 as her share of the partnership's ordinary income, the combination of the nonseparately stated items.

The partnership is not allowed a deduction for last year's $20,000 net operating loss—this item was passed through to the partners' own income tax returns for the previous year. Moreover, no deduction is allowed for personal expenditures (payment of Vern's alimony), and no personal exemption is allowed on the Form 1065. ◆

Withdrawals. Capital withdrawals by partners during the year do not affect the partnership's income measuring and reporting process. These items are treated as distributions made on the last day of the partnership's tax year. Thus, in Example 19 above, the payment of Vern's alimony by the partnership is treated as a distribution from the partnership to Vern. When withdrawals exceed the partners' shares of partnership income, the excess is taxed under the distribution rules (discussed later in the chapter).[26]

---

26. §§ 731(a)(1) and 733.

Penalties. Each partner's share of partnership items should be reported on his or her individual tax return in the same manner as presented on the Form 1065. If a partner treats an item differently, the IRS must be notified of the inconsistent treatment.[27] A partnership with 10 or fewer partners, where each partner's share of partnership items is the same for all items, is automatically excluded from this rule.[28] If a partner fails to comply with this requirement because of negligence or intentional disregard of rules or regulations, a negligence penalty may be added to the tax due.

To encourage the filing of a partnership return, a penalty is imposed on the partnership of $50 per month (or fraction thereof), but not to exceed five months, for failure to file a complete and timely information return without reasonable cause.[29] Every general partner is personally liable for the penalty.

Partnership Allocations

Each previous example in this chapter has assumed that the partner has the same percentage interest in capital, profits, and losses. Thus, a partner who owns a 25 percent interest in partnership capital has been assumed to own 25 percent of partnership profits and 25 percent of partnership losses.

Economic Effect. A partner does not have to have identical percentage shares of all capital, profits, and losses. The partnership agreement can provide that any partner may share capital, profits, and losses in different ratios. For example, a partner could have a 25 percent capital sharing ratio, yet be allocated 30 percent of the profits and 20 percent of the losses of the partnership. Such *special* allocations are permissible if they follow certain rules contained in the Regulations under § 704(b).[30] Although these rules are too complex to discuss in detail, the general outline of one of these rules—the *economic effect* test—can be easily understood.

In general, the economic effect test requires the following:

1. An allocation of income to a partner must increase the partner's capital account, and an allocation of deduction or loss must decrease the partner's capital account.
2. When the partner's interest is liquidated, the partner must receive assets that have a fair market value equal to the balance in the capital account.
3. A partner with a negative capital account must restore that account upon liquidation of the interest. Restoration of a negative capital account can best be envisioned as a contribution of cash to the partnership equal to the negative balance.

These requirements are designed to ensure that a partner bears the economic burden of a loss or deduction allocation and receives the economic benefit of an income or gain allocation.

EXAMPLE 20

Eli and Sanjay each contribute $20,000 cash to the newly formed ES Partnership. The partnership uses the cash to acquire a depreciable asset for $40,000. The partnership agreement provides that the depreciation will be allocated 90% to Eli and 10% to

---

27. § 6222.
28. § 6231(a)(1)(B).
29. § 6098.
30. Reg. § 1.704–1(b).

Sanjay. Other items of partnership income, gain, loss, or deduction will be allocated equally between the partners. Upon liquidation of the partnership, property will be distributed to the partners in accordance with their capital account balances. Any partner with a negative capital account must restore the capital account upon liquidation. Assume the first-year depreciation on the equipment is $4,000. Also, assume nothing else happens in the first year that affects the partners' capital accounts.

Eli's capital account will be $16,400 ($20,000 – $3,600), and Sanjay's capital account will have a balance of $19,600 ($20,000 – $400) after the first year of partnership operations. The Regulations require that a hypothetical sale of the asset for its $36,000 adjusted basis on the last day of the year and an immediate liquidation of the partnership should result in Eli and Sanjay receiving distributions equal to their capital accounts. According to the partnership agreement, Eli would receive $16,400, and Sanjay would receive $19,600 of the cash in a liquidating distribution. Eli, therefore, bears the economic burden of $3,600 depreciation since he contributed $20,000 to the partnership and would receive only $16,400 upon liquidation. Likewise, Sanjay's economic burden is $400 since he would receive only $19,600 of his original $20,000 investment. The agreement, therefore, has economic effect.

If the partnership agreement had provided that Eli and Sanjay should each receive $18,000 of the liquidation proceeds, the "special" allocation of the depreciation would be defective. The IRS would require that the depreciation be allocated equally ($2,000 each) to the two partners to reflect the $2,000 economic burden borne by each partner. ◆

Precontribution Gain or Loss. Despite the flexibility that "special allocations" can provide, allocations of income, gain, loss, and deductions relative to contributed property may not be so allocated under the rules described above. Instead, precontribution gain or loss must be allocated among the partners to take into account the variation between the basis of the property and its fair market value on the date of contribution.[31] For nondepreciable property, this means that *built-in* gain or loss on the date of contribution must be allocated to the contributing partner when the property is eventually disposed of by the partnership in a taxable transaction.

EXAMPLE 21

Seth and Tim formed the equal profit and loss sharing ST Partnership. Seth contributed cash of $10,000, and Tim contributed land purchased two years ago and held for investment. The land had an adjusted basis of $6,000 and fair market value of $10,000 at the contribution date. For accounting purposes, the partnership recorded the land at its fair market value of $10,000. For tax purposes, the partnership took a carryover basis in the land of $6,000. After using the land as a parking lot for five months, ST sold it for $10,600. No other transactions took place.

The accounting and tax gain from the land sale are computed as follows:

	Accounting	Tax
Amount realized	$10,600	$10,600
Adjusted basis	10,000	6,000
Gain realized	$ 600	$ 4,600
Gain at contribution date to Tim	–0–	4,000
Remaining gain (split equally)	$ 600	$ 600

Seth recognizes $300 of the gain ($600 postcontribution gain ÷ 2), and Tim recognizes $4,300 [$4,000 built-in gain + ($600 ÷ 2)]. ◆

31. § 704(c)(1)(A).

Concept Summary 22–2 reviews the tax reporting rules for partnership activities.

Basis of Partnership Interest

Previously, this chapter discussed how to compute a partner's adjusted basis when the partnership is formed. It was noted that the partner's adjusted basis in the newly formed partnership usually equals (1) the adjusted basis in any property contributed to the partnership plus (2) the fair market value of any services the partner performed for the partnership.

A partnership interest also may be acquired after the partnership has been formed. The method of acquisition controls how the partner's adjusted basis is computed. If the partnership interest is purchased from another partner, the purchasing partner's basis is the amount paid (cost basis) for the partnership interest. The basis of a partnership interest acquired by gift is generally the donor's basis for the interest plus, in certain cases, some or all of the transfer (gift) tax paid by the donor. The basis of a partnership interest acquired through inheritance is usually the fair market value of the interest on the date the partner dies.

After the partnership begins its activities, or after a transferee partner is admitted to the partnership, the partner's basis is adjusted for numerous items. The following operating results *increase* a partner's adjusted basis:

- The partner's proportionate share of partnership income (including capital gains and tax-exempt income).
- The partner's proportionate share of any increase in partnership liabilities.

The following operating results *decrease* the partner's adjusted basis in the partnership:

CONCEPT SUMMARY 22–2
TAX REPORTING OF PARTNERSHIP ACTIVITIES

Event	Partnership Level	Partner Level
1. Compute partnership ordinary income.	Form 1065, line 22, page 1.	Schedule K–1 (Form 1065), line 1, page 1.
	Schedule K, Form 1065, line 1, page 3.	Each partner's share is passed through for separate reporting.
		Each partner's basis is increased.
2. Compute partnership ordinary loss.	Form 1065, line 22, page 1.	Schedule K–1 (Form 1065), line 1, page 1.
	Schedule K, Form 1065, line 1, page 3.	Each partner's share is passed through for separate reporting.
		Each partner's basis is decreased.
		The amount of a partner's loss deduction may be limited.
		Losses that may not be deducted are carried forward for use in future years.
3. Separately reported items like portfolio income, capital gain and loss, and § 179 deductions.	Schedule K, Form 1065, various lines, page 3.	Schedule K–1 (Form 1065), various lines, pages 1 and 2. Each partner's share is passed through for separate reporting.
4. Net earnings from self-employment.	Schedule K, Form 1065, line 15, page 3.	Schedule K–1 (Form 1065), line 15, page 2.

- The partner's proportionate share of partnership deductions and losses (including capital losses).
- The partner's proportionate share of nondeductible expenses.
- The partner's proportionate share of any decrease in partnership liabilities.[32]

Under no circumstances can the partner's adjusted basis for the partnership interest be reduced below zero.

Increasing the partner's adjusted basis for his or her share of partnership taxable income is logical since the partner has already been taxed on the income. By increasing the partner's basis, the Code ensures that the partner will not be taxed again on the income when he or she sells the interest or receives a distribution from the partnership.

It is also logical that the tax-exempt income should increase the partner's basis. If the income is exempt in the current period, it should not contribute to the recognition of gain when the partner either sells the interest or receives a distribution.

EXAMPLE 22

Yoon is a one-third partner in the Hammer Partnership. His proportionate share of the partnership income during the current year consists of $20,000 of ordinary taxable income and $10,000 of tax-exempt income. None of the income is distributed to Yoon. The adjusted basis of Yoon's partnership interest before adjusting for his share of income is $35,000, and the fair market value of the interest before considering the income items is $50,000.

The unrealized gain inherent in Yoon's investment in the partnership is $15,000 ($50,000 – $35,000). Yoon's proportionate share of the income items should increase the fair market value of the interest to $80,000 ($50,000 + $20,000 + $10,000). By increasing the adjusted basis of Yoon's partnership interest to $65,000 ($35,000 + $20,000 + $10,000), the Code ensures that the unrealized gain inherent in Yoon's partnership investment remains at $15,000. This makes sense because the $20,000 of ordinary taxable income is taxed to Yoon this year and should not be taxed again when he either sells his interest or receives a distribution. Similarly, the exempt income is exempt this year and should not increase Yoon's gain when he either sells his interest or receives a distribution from the partnership. ◆

Decreasing the partner's adjusted basis for his or her share of deductible losses, deductions, and noncapitalizable, nondeductible expenditures is logical for the same reasons. An item that is deductible currently should not contribute to creating a loss when the partnership interest is sold or a distribution is received from the partnership. Similarly, a noncapitalizable, nondeductible expenditure should never be deductible nor contribute to a loss when a subsequent sale or distribution transaction occurs.

Liability Sharing. A partner's adjusted basis is also affected by the share of partnership debt. Under § 752, increases in a partner's share of debt are treated as contributions by the partner to the partnership. Decreases in a partner's share of debt are treated as distributions from the partnership to the partner. Partnership debt includes any partnership obligation that creates an asset; results in a deductible expense; or results in a nondeductible, noncapitalizable item at the partnership level. This definition includes most debt that would be considered a liability under financial accounting rules except for accounts payable of a cash basis partnership and certain contingent liabilities.

---

32. §§ 705 and 752.

Under § 752, an increase in a partner's share of partnership debt is treated as a contribution by the partner to the partnership. A partner's share of debt increases as a result of (1) increases in outstanding partnership debt and (2) the assumption of a partner's individual debt by the partnership. A decrease in a partner's share of partnership debt is treated as a distribution from the partnership to the partner. A partner's share of debt decreases as a result of (1) decreases in outstanding partnership debt and (2) the assumption of partnership debt by a partner.

EXAMPLE 23

Jim and Becky contribute property to form the JB Partnership. Jim contributes cash of $30,000. Becky contributes land with an adjusted basis and fair market value of $45,000, subject to a liability of $15,000. The partnership borrows $50,000 to finance construction of a building on the contributed land. At the end of the first year, the accrual basis partnership owes $3,500 in trade accounts payable to various vendors. Assume no other operating activities occurred.

Partnership debt sharing rules are discussed later in this section, but assuming for simplicity that Jim and Becky share equally in liabilities, the partners' bases in their partnership interests are determined as follows:

Jim's Basis		Becky's Basis	
Contributed cash	$30,000	Basis in contributed land	$45,000
Share of construction loan	25,000	Less: Debt assumed by partnership	(15,000)
Share of trade accounts payable	1,750	Share of construction loan	25,000
Share of debt on land (assumed by partnership)	7,500	Share of trade accounts payable	1,750
		Share of debt on land (assumed by partnership)	7,500
	$64,250		$64,250

In this case, it is reasonable that the parties have an equal basis after contributing their respective properties, because each is a 50% owner, and they contributed property with identical bases and identical *net* fair market values. ◆

Decreases in liabilities can result in extremely negative tax consequences, so liability balances should be reviewed carefully near the partnership's year-end to ensure no unanticipated tax liabilities will arise to the partners. The following example illustrates the situation.

EXAMPLE 24

Assume the same facts as in Example 23, except the partnership reported an ordinary loss of $100,000 in its first year of operations. In the absence of loss deduction limitations, Jim and Becky would each deduct a $50,000 ordinary loss, and their bases in their respective partnership interests would be reduced to $14,250 (including a $34,250 share of liabilities).

In the second year, the partnership generated no taxable income or loss from operations, but was able to repay the $50,000 construction loan (assume from accounts receivable reported in the prior year). The $25,000 reduction of each partner's share of partnership liabilities is treated as a distribution by the partnership to each partner. A distribution in excess of basis generally results in a capital gain (in this case $10,750) to each partner. In other words, the partners must pay tax on $10,750 of capital gain even though the partnership reported no taxable income. This gain can be thought of as a recapture of loss deductions the partners claimed during the first year, but such gains can cause cash-flow difficulties to partners who are unaware that such a gain may occur. ◆

Two types of partnership debt exist. *Recourse debt* is partnership debt for which the partnership or at least one of the partners is personally liable. This liability can exist, for example, through the operation of state law or through personal guarantees that a partner makes to the creditor. Personal liability of a party related to a partner (under attribution rules) is treated as the personal liability of the partner. *Nonrecourse debt* is debt for which no party is personally liable. Lenders of nonrecourse debt generally require that collateral be pledged against the loan. Upon default, the lender can claim only the collateral, not the partners' personal assets.

How liabilities are shared among the partners depends upon when the liability was incurred. For most debt created before January 29, 1989, the rules are relatively straightforward. Recourse debt is shared among the partners in accordance with their loss sharing ratios while nonrecourse debt is shared among the partners in accordance with the way they share partnership profits. Although questions can arise about the calculation of the profit or loss sharing ratios and the treatment of personal guarantees of debt, the rules for sharing this earlier debt are generally easy to apply.

The rules for sharing partnership debt created after January 29, 1989, are much more complex. A complete analysis of these rules is beyond the scope of this text. The basic principles contained in these rules, however, can be easily understood.

Recourse debt created after January 29, 1989, is shared in accordance with a *constructive liquidation* scenario. Under this scenario, the following events are deemed to occur:

1. Most partnership assets (including cash) become worthless.
2. The worthless assets are sold at fair market value ($0), and losses on the deemed sales are determined.
3. Losses are allocated to the partners according to their loss sharing ratios. These losses reduce the partners' capital accounts.
4. Any partner with a (deemed) negative balance in the capital account is treated as contributing cash to the partnership to restore that negative balance to zero.
5. The cash deemed contributed by the partners with negative capital balances is used to pay the liabilities of the partnership.
6. The partnership is deemed to be liquidated immediately, and any remaining cash is distributed to partners with positive capital account balances.

The amount of each partner's cash contribution that is deemed to be used (in step 5 above) in payment of partnership recourse liabilities is the amount that the partner shares in partnership recourse liabilities.

EXAMPLE 25

On January 1 of the current year, Nina and Otis each contribute $20,000 cash to the newly created NO General Partnership. Each partner has a 50% interest in partnership capital, profits, and losses. The first year of partnership operations resulted in the following balance sheet as of December 31:

	Basis	Fair Market Value
Cash	$12,000	$12,000
Receivables	7,000	7,000
Land and buildings	50,000	50,000
	$69,000	$69,000
Recourse payables	$30,000	$30,000
Nina, capital	19,500	19,500
Otis, capital	19,500	19,500
	$69,000	$69,000

The recourse debt is shared in accordance with the constructive liquidation scenario. All of the partnership assets (including cash) are deemed to be worthless and are sold for that worthless amount. This creates a loss of $69,000 ($12,000 + $7,000 + $50,000), which is allocated equally between the two partners. The $34,500 loss allocated to each partner creates negative capital accounts of $15,000 each for Nina and Otis. If the partnership were actually liquidated, each partner would contribute $15,000 cash to the partnership; the cash would be used to pay the partnership recourse payables; and the partnership would be liquidated. Because each partner would be required to contribute $15,000 to pay the liabilities, each shares in $15,000 of the recourse payables. Accordingly, Nina and Otis will each have an adjusted basis for their partnership interests of $34,500 ($19,500 + $15,000) on December 31. ◆

EXAMPLE 26

Assume the same facts as in Example 25, except that the partners will allocate partnership losses 60% to Nina and 40% to Otis. The constructive liquidation scenario will result in the $69,000 loss being allocated $41,400 to Nina and $27,600 to Otis. As a result Nina's capital account will have a negative balance of $21,900, and Otis's account will have a negative balance of $8,100. Each partner will be deemed to contribute cash equal to these negative capital accounts, and the cash would be used to pay the recourse liabilities under the liquidation scenario. Accordingly, Nina and Otis will share $21,900 and $8,100, respectively, in the recourse debt. ◆

Nonrecourse debt is allocated in three stages. First, an amount of debt equal to the amount of *minimum gain* is allocated to partners who will share in minimum gain. Although the calculation of minimum gain is complex, it approximates the amount of nonrecourse liability on a property in excess of the basis of the property. If the lender foreclosed on the property, the result would be a deemed sale for the mortgage price. A gain would arise in the amount of the liability in excess of basis in the property—hence, minimum gain. Allocation of minimum gain should be addressed in the partnership agreement; specific guidelines are cumbersome and beyond the scope of this text.

Second, any debt related to a *precontribution gain or loss* under § 704(c) is allocated to the partner who contributed the property to the partnership, as shown in Example 27.

Third, any remaining nonrecourse debt is allocated to the partners in accordance with either their profit sharing ratios or the manner in which they share in nonrecourse deductions. The partnership agreement should specify which allocation method is used. In cases where there are no special allocations of deductions such as depreciation, maintenance, or repair expenses for the property securing the nonrecourse debt, allocations under the two methods would be the same.

EXAMPLE 27

Ted contributes an asset to the TK Partnership in exchange for a one-third interest in the capital, profits, and losses of the partnership. The asset has an adjusted basis to Ted of $24,000 and a fair market value on the contribution date of $50,000. The asset is encumbered by a nonrecourse note (created January 1, 1992) of $35,000. The Regulations provide that the first $11,000 of the nonrecourse debt is allocated to Ted under § 704(c) principles. The § 704(c) amount is the excess of the $35,000 nonrecourse debt transferred over the $24,000 adjusted basis of the contributed property. The remaining $24,000 nonrecourse debt is shared according to the profit sharing ratio, of which Ted's share is $8,000. Therefore, Ted shares in $19,000 ($11,000 + $8,000) of the nonrecourse debt.

Ted's basis in his partnership interest is determined as follows:

Substituted basis of contributed property	$24,000
Less: Liability assumed by partnership	(35,000)
Plus: Allocation of § 704(c) debt	11,000

Basis before remaining allocation	$ -0-
Plus: Allocation of remaining nonrecourse debt	8,000
Basis in partnership interest	$8,000

The § 704(c) allocation of nonrecourse debt prevents Ted from receiving a deemed distribution in excess of the basis in property contributed. Without this required allocation of nonrecourse debt, in some cases, a contributing partner would be required to recognize gain on a contribution of property encumbered by nonrecourse debt to a partnership. This special allocation of debt does not apply for recourse debt. ◆

Other Factors Affecting Basis Calculations. The partner's basis is also affected by (1) postacquisition contributions of cash or property to the partnership; (2) postacquisition distributions of cash or property from the partnership; and (3) special calculations that are designed to allow the full deduction of percentage depletion for oil and gas wells. Postacquisition contributions of cash or property affect basis in the same manner as contributions made upon the creation of the partnership. Postacquisition distributions of cash or property reduce basis.

EXAMPLE 28

Ed is a one-third partner in the Maple Partnership. On January 1, 1993, Ed's basis in his partnership interest was $50,000. During 1993, the calendar year, accrual basis partnership generated ordinary taxable income of $200,000. It also received $60,000 of interest income from City of Buffalo bonds. It paid $2,000 in nondeductible bribes to local law enforcement officials, so that the police would not notify the IRS about the products that the entity had imported without paying the proper $15,000 in tariffs. On July 1, 1993, Ed contributed $20,000 cash and a computer (zero basis to him) to the partnership. Ed's monthly draw from the partnership is $3,000; this is not a guaranteed payment. The only liabilities that the partnership has incurred are trade accounts payable. On January 1, 1993, the trade accounts payable totaled $45,000; this account balance was $21,000 on January 1, 1994.

Ed's basis in the partnership on December 31, 1993, is $112,000, computed as follows:

Beginning balance	$ 50,000
Share of ordinary partnership income	66,667
Share of exempt income	20,000
Share of nondeductible expenditures	(667)
Ed's basis in noncash capital contribution	-0-
Additional cash contributions	20,000
Capital withdrawals	(36,000)
Share of net decrease in partnership liabilities	(8,000)
	$112,000

◆

EXAMPLE 29

Assume the same facts as in Example 28. If Ed withdraws cash of $112,000 from the partnership on January 1, 1994, the withdrawal reduces his basis to zero. He has recognized his share of the partnership's corresponding income throughout his association with the entity, via the annual flow-through of his share of the partnership's income and expense items. In addition, the $20,000 municipal bond interest retains its nontaxable character in this distribution. Ed receives such assets as a part of his capital withdrawal because his basis was increased in 1993 when the partnership received the interest income. ◆

Generally, a partner is required to compute the adjusted basis only at the end of the partnership year. This spares the partner the inconvenience of making day-to-day calculations of basis. When a partnership interest is sold, exchanged, or retired, however, the partner must compute the adjusted basis as of the date the transaction occurs. Computation of the gain or loss requires an accurate calculation of the partner's adjusted basis on the transaction date.

Partner's Adjusted Basis—Special Rule. Sometimes partners may not be able to calculate the adjusted basis of their interest according to the rules outlined above. The partnership records may have been lost, or the partnership interest may have been received from a donor who failed to maintain accurate records. Fortunately, a special rule comes to the rescue. The rule states that a partner's adjusted basis may be simply the proportionate dollar interest in the adjusted basis of partnership property. It may be used when:

1. the partner cannot practicably compute the basis under the general rules outlined above; or
2. the IRS is satisfied that the calculation of basis under the special rule will not vary substantially from the basis that would have been computed under the general rules.[33]

EXAMPLE 30

Pam received a gift of a partnership interest from her father 10 years ago. Pam is going to sell her partnership interest during the current year and asks her tax adviser how to calculate her adjusted basis for the interest. The tax adviser determines that it is impossible to compute her adjusted basis in the more direct manner preferred by the Code. Pam has never calculated her adjusted basis previously, and her father's records were destroyed in a fire several years before his recent death. Pam does know, however, that her one-third interest in the adjusted basis of partnership property is $25,000. Therefore, under the special rule, Pam's adjusted basis for her partnership interest is deemed to be $25,000. ◆

Figure 22–3 summarizes the rules for computing a partner's basis in a partnership interest.

FIGURE 22–3
Partner's Basis in Partnership Interest

Initial basis. Price paid for interest or gift or inherited basis (including share of partnership debt). Price paid can be amount contributed to partnership or amount paid to another partner or former partner.

+ Since interest acquired, partner's share of partnership's
  - Debt increase
  - Income items
  - Exempt income items
  - Excess of depletion deductions over adjusted basis of property subject to depletion

+ Partner's contributions

− Since interest acquired, partner's share of partnership's
  - Debt decrease
  - Loss items
  - Nondeductible items not chargeable to a capital account
  - Special depletion deduction for oil and gas wells

− Partner's distributions and withdrawals.

The basis of a partner's interest can never be negative.

33. § 705(b).

Loss Limitations

Partnership losses flow through to the partners for use on their tax returns. However, the amount and nature of the losses that may be used by a partner for tax computational purposes may be limited. When limitations apply, all or a portion of the losses are held in suspension until a triggering condition occurs. At that later date, the losses can be used to determine the partner's tax liability.

Three different limitations may apply to partnership losses that are passed through to a partner. The first is the overall limitation contained in § 704(d). This limitation allows losses only to the extent the partner has adjusted basis for his or her partnership interest. Losses that are deductible under the overall limitation may then be subject to the at-risk limitation of § 465. Losses are only deductible under this provision if the partner has at-risk basis for the partnership interest. Any losses that survive this second limitation may be subject to a third limitation, the passive loss rules of § 469. Only losses that make it through these applicable limitations are deductible on the partner's tax return.

EXAMPLE 31

Meg is a partner in a partnership that does not invest in real estate. On January 1, 1993, Meg's adjusted basis for her partnership interest is $50,000, and her at-risk basis is $35,000. Her share of losses from the partnership for 1993 is $60,000, all of which is passive. She has one other passive income-producing investment that produced $25,000 of passive income during 1993.

Meg will be able to deduct $25,000 of partnership losses on her Form 1040 for 1993. Her deductible loss is calculated as follows:

Applicable Provision	Deductible Loss	Suspended Loss
Overall limitation	($50,000)	($10,000)
At-risk limitation	(35,000)	(15,000)
Passive loss limitation	(25,000)	(10,000)

Meg can deduct only $50,000 under the overall limitation. Of this $50,000, only $35,000 is deductible under the at-risk limitation. Under the passive loss limitation, passive losses can only be deducted against passive income. Thus, Meg can deduct only $25,000 on her return in 1993. ◆

Overall Limitation. A partner may only deduct losses flowing through from the partnership to the extent of the partner's adjusted basis in the partnership interest. A partner's basis in interest is determined at the end of the partnership's taxable year. It is adjusted for distributions and any partnership gains during the year, but it is determined before considering any losses for the year.

Losses that cannot be deducted because of this rule are suspended and carried forward (never back) for use against future increases in the partner's outside basis. Such increases might result from additional capital contributions, additional debts, or future income.

EXAMPLE 32

Carol and Dan do business as the CD Partnership, sharing profits and losses equally. All parties use the calendar year. At the start of the current year, the basis of Carol's partnership interest is $25,000. The partnership sustained an operating loss of $80,000 in the current year. For the current year, only $25,000 of Carol's $40,000 allocable share of the partnership loss (one-half of $80,000 loss) can be deducted under the overall limitation. As a result, the basis of Carol's partnership interest is zero as of January 1 of the following year, and she must carry forward the remaining $15,000 of partnership losses. ◆

EXAMPLE 33

Assume the same facts as in Example 32, and that the partnership earned a profit of $70,000 for the next calendar year. Carol reports net partnership income of $20,000 ($35,000 distributive share of income less the $15,000 carryforward loss). The basis of Carol's partnership interest becomes $20,000. ◆

In Example 32, Carol's entire $40,000 share of the current year partnership loss could have been deducted under the overall limitation in the current year if she had contributed an additional $15,000 or more in capital by December 31. Alternatively, if the partnership had incurred additional debt by the end of the current year, Carol's basis would have been increased to permit some or all of the loss to be deducted in that year. Thus, if partnership losses are projected for a given year, careful tax planning can ensure their deductibility under the overall limitation.

At-Risk Limitation. Under the at-risk rules, the losses from business and income-producing activities that individuals and closely held corporations can deduct are generally limited to amounts that are economically invested. Invested amounts include the adjusted basis of contributed property, cash contributions, and the earnings share that has not been withdrawn or used to absorb losses.[34] A closely held corporation exists when five or fewer individuals own more than 50 percent of the entity's stock under appropriate attribution and ownership rules.

Some or all of the partners are personally liable for partnership recourse debt. The debt is included in the adjusted basis of the partners who will have to pay this debt from their own resources if the partnership fails to pay the creditor. In general, these partners will also include the debt in their at-risk basis.

No partner, however, carries any financial risk on nonrecourse debt. Therefore, as a general rule, partners cannot include nonrecourse debt in their at-risk basis even though that debt is included in the adjusted basis of their partnership interest. There is an exception to this general rule, however, that applies in many cases. Real estate nonrecourse financing provided by a bank, retirement plan, or similar party, or by a Federal, state, or local government generally is deemed to be at risk.[35] Such debt is termed *qualified nonrecourse debt*. Consequently, although the general rule provides that nonrecourse debt is not at risk, the overriding exception may provide that it is deemed to be at risk.

When determining a partner's loss deduction, the overall limitation rule is invoked first (the deduction is limited to the partner's outside basis at the end of the partnership year). Then, the at-risk provisions are applied to see if the remaining loss is still deductible. Suspended losses are carried forward until a partner has a sufficient amount at risk in the activity to absorb them.[36]

EXAMPLE 34

Kelly invests $5,000 in the Kelly Green Limited Partnership as a general partner. Shortly thereafter, the partnership acquires the master recording of a well-known vocalist for $250,000 ($50,000 from the partnership and $200,000 secured from a local

34. § 465(a).
35. § 465(b)(6).
36. § 465(a)(2).

bank via a *recourse* mortgage). Kelly's share of the recourse debt is $10,000, and her basis in her partnership interest is $15,000 ($5,000 cash investment + $10,000 debt share). Since the debt is recourse, Kelly's at-risk amount is also $15,000. Kelly's share of partnership losses in the first year of operations is $11,000. She is entitled to deduct $11,000 of partnership losses because this amount is less than both her outside basis and her at-risk amount. ◆

Example 35

Assume the same facts as in Example 34, except that the bank loan is nonrecourse in nature (the partners have no direct liability under the terms of the loan in the case of a default). Kelly's basis in her partnership interest still is $15,000, but she can deduct only $5,000 of the flow-through loss. The amount that she has at risk in the investment does not include the nonrecourse debt. ◆

Passive Activity Rules. A partnership loss share also may be disallowed under the passive activity rules. Although these rules are not applicable solely to partnerships, they most assuredly affect how and when a partner's loss can be deducted. The rules require taxpayers to separate their activities into three groups:

- *Active.* Earned income, such as salary and wages; income or loss from a trade or business in which the taxpayer materially participates; and guaranteed payments from a partnership for services.
- *Portfolio.* Annuity income, interest, dividends, guaranteed payments from a partnership for interest on capital, royalties not derived in the ordinary course of a trade or business, and gains and losses from disposal of investment assets.
- *Passive.* Income from a trade or business in which the taxpayer does not materially participate on a regular, continuous, and substantial basis, or income from a rental activity.[37]

Material participation in an activity is determined annually. The burden is on the taxpayer to prove material participation. The IRS has provided a number of objective tests for determining material participation. These tests require the taxpayer to have substantial involvement in daily operations of the activity. Thus, a Maine vacation resort operator investing in a California grape farm or an electrical engineer employed in Virginia investing in an Iowa corn and hog farm may have difficulty proving material participation in the activities.

Rent income from real or personal property generally is passive income, regardless of the taxpayer's level of participation. Exceptions are made for rent income from activities where substantial services are provided (resorts) and from hotels, motels, and other transient lodging and for income from equipment rentals to various users for short periods.

Usually, passive activity losses can be offset only against passive activity income.[38] In determining the net passive activity loss for a year, generally losses and income from all passive activities are aggregated. The amount of suspended losses carried forward from a particular activity is determined by the ratio of the net loss from that activity to the aggregate net loss from all passive activities for the year. A special rule for rental real estate (discussed in the following section) allows a limited $25,000 offset against nonpassive income.[39]

---

37. §§ 469(c)(1) and (2).

38. § 469(a)(1).

39. § 469(i).

A taxpayer making a taxable disposition of an entire interest in a passive activity generally takes a full deduction for suspended losses in the year of disposal.[40] Suspended losses are deductible against income in the following order: income or gain from the passive activity, net income or gain from all passive activities, and other income. When a passive activity is transferred in a nontaxable exchange (e.g., a like-kind exchange or contribution to a partnership), suspended losses are deductible only to the extent of recognized gains. Remaining losses are deducted on disposal of the activity received in the exchange.

EXAMPLE 36

Debra has several investments in passive activities that generate aggregate losses of $10,000 in the current year. Debra wants to deduct all of these losses in the current year. To assure a loss deduction, she needs to invest in some passive activities that generate income. One of her long-time friends, an entrepreneur in the women's apparel business, is interested in opening a new apparel store in a nearby community. Debra is willing to finance a substantial part of the expansion but doesn't want to get involved with day-to-day operations. Debra also wants to limit any possible loss to her initial investment.

After substantial discussions, Debra and her friend decide to form a limited partnership, which will own the new store. Debra's friend will be the general partner, and Debra will be a limited partner. Debra invests $100,000, and her friend invests $50,000 and sweat equity (provides managerial skills and know-how). Each has a 50% interest in profits and losses. In the first year of operations, the store generates a profit of $30,000. Since Debra's share of the profit ($15,000) is passive activity income, it can be fully utilized against any passive activity losses. Thus, via her share of the apparel store profits, Debra assures a full deduction of her $10,000 of passive activity losses. ◆

Rental Real Estate Losses. Individuals can offset up to $25,000 of passive losses from rental real estate against active and portfolio income in any one year. The $25,000 maximum is reduced by 50 percent of the difference between the taxpayer's modified adjusted gross income (AGI) and $100,000. Thus, when the taxpayer's modified AGI reaches $150,000, the offset is eliminated.

The offset is available to those who actively (rather than materially) participate in rental real estate activities. Active participation is an easier test to meet. Unlike material participation, it does not require regular, continuous, and substantial involvement with the activity. However, the individual must own at least 10 percent of the fair market value of all interests in the rental property and either contribute to the activity in a significant and bona fide way regarding management decisions or actively participate in arranging for others to make such decisions.

EXAMPLE 37

Raoul invests $10,000 cash in the Sparrow Limited Partnership in the current year for a 10% limited interest in capital and profits. Shortly thereafter, the partnership purchases rental real estate subject to a nonconvertible qualified nonrecourse mortgage of $150,000 obtained from a commercial bank. Raoul has no other passive loss activities during the current year.

Raoul does not participate in any of Sparrow's activities. His share of losses from Sparrow's first year of operations is $27,000. His AGI before considering the loss is $60,000. Before considering the loss, Raoul's basis in the partnership interest is $25,000 [$10,000 cash + (10% × $150,000 debt)], and his loss deduction is limited to this amount under the overall limitation. The debt is included in Raoul's amount at risk because it is qualified nonrecourse financing. It seems that Raoul should be allowed to deduct the

40. § 469(g).

$25,000 loss share from portfolio or active income. However, the loss may not be offset against this income because Raoul is not an active participant. ◆

TRANSACTIONS BETWEEN PARTNERS AND PARTNERSHIPS

Many types of transactions may occur between a partnership and one of its partners. The partner may contribute property to the partnership, perform services for the partnership, or receive distributions from the partnership. The partner may borrow money from or lend money to the partnership. Property may be bought and sold between the partner and the partnership. Several of these transactions were discussed earlier in the chapter. The remaining types of partner-partnership transactions are the focus of this section.

Guaranteed Payments

If a partnership makes a payment to a partner in his or her capacity as a partner, the payment may be a draw against the partner's share of partnership income; a return of some or all of the partner's original capital contribution; or a guaranteed payment among other treatments. A *guaranteed payment* is a payment for services performed by the partner or for the use of the partner's capital. The payment may not be determined by reference to partnership income. Guaranteed payments are usually expressed as a fixed-dollar amount or as a percentage of capital that the partner has invested in the partnership.

EXAMPLE 38

David, Donald, and Dale formed the accrual basis DDD Partnership in 1993. According to the partnership agreement, David is to perform services for the partnership in exchange for $21,000 from the entity every year, payable in 12 monthly installments. Donald is to receive an amount that is equal to 18% of his capital account, as it is computed by the firm's accountant at the beginning of the year, payable in 12 monthly installments. Dale is the partnership's advertising specialist. He withdraws 3% of the partnership's net income every month for his personal use. David and Donald have received guaranteed payments from the partnership, but Dale has not. ◆

Guaranteed payments resemble the salary or interest payments of other businesses and receive similar treatment under partnership tax law.[41] Thus, in contrast to the provision that usually applies to withdrawals of assets by partners from their partnerships, guaranteed payments are deductible by the entity, and on the last day of the partnership's tax year, the recipients must report such income separately from their usual partnership allocations.

EXAMPLE 39

Continue with the situation that was introduced in Example 38. For calendar year 1993, David received the $21,000 that was provided by the partnership agreement, Donald's guaranteed payment for 1993 was $18,000, and Dale withdrew $20,000 under his personal expenditures clause. Before considering these amounts, the partnership's ordinary income for 1993 was $650,000.

41. § 707(c).

The partnership can deduct its payments to David and Donald, so the final amount of its 1993 ordinary income is $611,000 ($650,000 – $21,000 – $18,000). Thus, each of the equal partners is allocated $203,667 of ordinary partnership income for their 1993 individual income tax returns ($611,000 ÷ 3). In addition, David must report $21,000 of salary income, and Donald must include the $18,000 interest in his 1993 gross income. Dale's partnership draw is deemed to have come from his allocated $203,667 (or from the accumulated partnership income that was taxed to him in prior years) and is not taxed separately to him. ◆

EXAMPLE 40

Assume the same facts as in Example 39, except that Dale's withdrawals total $1,000, and ordinary partnership income (before considering the partners' distributions) was $30,000. The deductions for guaranteed payments to David and Donald reduce the final ordinary income of the partnership to a $9,000 loss ($30,000 – $21,000 – $18,000). Thus, David's individual income tax return includes his $21,000 salary and his $3,000 share of partnership loss. Donald's gross income includes the $18,000 interest and his allocable $3,000 partnership loss. Dale's return merely includes his $3,000 share of the partnership loss. Guaranteed payments, like any other deductible expenses of a partnership, can create an ordinary loss for the entity. In this manner, the partners can allocate a higher or lower proportion of the tax benefits among them. ◆

EXAMPLE 41

Assume the same facts as in Example 38, except that the partnership's tax year ends on March 31, 1994. The total amount of the guaranteed payments is taxable to the partners on that date. Thus, even though David receives 9 of his 12 payments for fiscal 1993 in calendar 1993, all of his guaranteed payments are recognized in 1994. Similarly, all of Donald's guaranteed payments are taxable to him in 1994 and not when it is received. The deduction for, and the gross income from, guaranteed payments are allowed on the same date that all of the other income and expense items relative to the partnership are allocated to the partners (on the last day of the entity's tax year). ◆

Other Transactions between Partners and Partnerships

Certain transactions between a partner and the partnership are treated as if the partner were an outsider, dealing with the partnership at arm's length.[42] Loan transactions, rental payments, and sales of property between the partner and the partnership are generally treated in this manner. In addition, payments for services are treated this way when the services are short-term technical services that the partner also provides for parties other than the partnership.

EXAMPLE 42

Emilio, a one-third partner in the CDE Partnership, owns a tract of land that the partnership wishes to purchase. The land has a fair market value of $30,000 and an adjusted basis to Emilio of $17,000. If Emilio sells the land to the partnership, he will recognize a $13,000 gain on the sale, and the partnership will take a $30,000 cost basis in the land. If the land had a fair market value of $10,000 on the sale date, Emilio would recognize a $7,000 loss. ◆

The timing of a payment by an accrual basis partnership to a cash basis service partner depends upon whether the payment is a guaranteed payment or a payment to a partner who is treated as an outsider. A guaranteed payment is includible in the partner's income when properly accrued by the partnership, even though the payment may not be made to the partner until the next taxable

42. § 707(a).

year. Conversely, the partner's method of accounting controls if the payment is treated as made to an outsider. This is because § 267(a)(2) provides that a deduction cannot be claimed for an amount owed to a related party until the recipient would be required to pay tax on the amount under the partner's method of accounting. Any partner is considered a related party under § 267(e). Thus, a partnership cannot claim a deduction until it actually makes a payment to the cash basis partner, but it would accrue a payment due to an accrual basis partner even if payment was not yet made.

EXAMPLE 43

Rachel, a cash basis taxpayer, is a partner in the accrual basis RTC Partnership. On December 31, 1993, the partnership accrues but does not pay $10,000 for deductible services that Rachel performed for the partnership during the year. Both Rachel and the partnership are calendar year taxpayers.

If the $10,000 accrual is a guaranteed payment, the partnership deducts the $10,000 in its calendar year ended December 31, 1993, and Rachel includes the $10,000 in her income for the 1993 calendar year. That Rachel is a cash basis taxpayer and does not actually receive the cash in 1993 is irrelevant.

Conversely, if the payment is classified as a payment to an outsider, the partnership cannot deduct the payment until Rachel actually receives the cash. If, for example, Rachel receives the cash on March 25, 1994, the partnership deducts the payment and Rachel recognizes the income on that date. ◆

Certain sales of property fall under special rules. No loss can be recognized on a sale of property between a person and a partnership when the person owns, directly or indirectly, more than 50 percent of partnership capital or profits.[43] The disallowed loss may not vanish entirely, however. If the transferee eventually sells the property at a gain, the disallowed loss reduces the gain that the transferee would otherwise recognize.

EXAMPLE 44

Barry sells land (adjusted basis to him, $30,000; fair market value, $45,000) to a partnership in which he controls a 60% capital interest. The partnership pays him $20,000 for the land. Barry cannot deduct his $10,000 realized loss. The sale apparently was not at arm's length, but the taxpayer's intentions are irrelevant. Barry and the partnership are related parties, and the loss is disallowed.

When the partnership sells the land to an outsider at a later date, it receives a sales price of $44,000. The partnership can offset the recognition of its realized gain on the subsequent sale ($44,000 sales proceeds – $20,000 adjusted basis = $24,000) by the amount of the prior disallowed loss ($30,000 – $20,000 = $10,000). Thus, it recognizes a $14,000 gain on its sale of the land. ◆

Using a similar rationale, any gain that is realized on a sale or exchange between a partner and a partnership in which the partner controls a capital or profit interest of 50 percent or more must be recognized as ordinary income, unless the asset is a capital asset to both the seller and the purchaser.[44]

EXAMPLE 45

Kristin purchases some land (adjusted basis, $30,000; fair market value, $45,000) for $45,000 from a partnership in which she controls a 90% profit interest. The land was a capital asset to the partnership. If Kristin holds the land for investment, the partnership

43. § 707(b).

44. § 707(b)(2).

recognizes a $15,000 capital gain. However, if Kristin is a land developer and the property is not a capital asset to her, the partnership must recognize $15,000 ordinary income from the same sale, even though the property was a capital asset to the entity. ◆

Partners as Employees

A partner generally does not qualify as an employee for tax purposes. Thus, a partner receiving guaranteed payments will not be regarded as an employee for purposes of withholding taxes. Moreover, since a partner is not an employee of his or her partnership, the entity cannot deduct its payments for the partner's fringe benefits. In fact, the partner's distributive share of ordinary partnership income is generally subject to the Federal self-employment tax.[45]

Concept Summary 22–3 reviews partner-partnership transactions.

DISTRIBUTIONS FROM THE PARTNERSHIP

The tax treatment of withdrawals from a partnership to a partner was introduced earlier. This section will expand that discussion by examining in greater detail the effect of nonliquidating distributions made during the normal operations of the partnership. Distributions to partners in complete liquidation of their ownership interests are not discussed in this text. See Chapter 11 of *West's Federal Taxation: Corporations, Partnerships, Estates, and Trusts* (1994 edition).

A *nonliquidating* distribution is any distribution from a continuing partnership to a continuing partner—that is, any distribution that is not a liquidating

CONCEPT SUMMARY 22–3
PARTNER-PARTNERSHIP TRANSACTIONS

1. Partners can transact business with their partnerships in a nonpartner capacity. These transactions include such things as the sale and exchange of property, rentals, etc.
2. A payment to a partner may be classified as a guaranteed payment if it is for services or use of the partner's capital and is not based on partnership income. A guaranteed payment may be deductible by the partnership and is included in the partner's income on the last day of the partnership's taxable year.
3. A payment to a partner may be treated as being to an outside (though related) party. Such a payment is deductible by the partnership at the time the partner must include the amount in income under his or her method of accounting.
4. Guaranteed payments and payments to a partner that are treated as being to an outside party are only deductible if the underlying reason for the payment constitutes an ordinary and necessary (rather than capitalizable) business expense.
5. Losses are disallowed between a partner or related party and a partnership when the partner or related party owns more than a 50% interest in the partnership's capital or profits. When there is income from a related-party sale, it is ordinary if the property is a capital asset to the transferor, but not to the transferee.

45. § 1402(a).

distribution and is not otherwise classified under the law (e.g., guaranteed payments, interest, rents paid to partners by the partnership). There are two types of nonliquidating distributions: draws or partial liquidations. A *draw* is a distribution of a partner's share of current or accumulated partnership profits that have been taxed to the partner in current or prior taxable years of the partnership. A *partial liquidation* is a distribution that reduces the partner's interest in partnership capital but does not liquidate the partner's entire interest in the partnership. The distinction between the two types of *nonliquidating* distributions is largely semantic, since the basic tax treatment typically does not differ.

EXAMPLE 46

Kay joins the calendar year KLM Partnership on January 1, 1993, by contributing $40,000 cash to the partnership in exchange for a one-third interest in partnership capital, profits, and losses. Her distributive share of partnership income for the year is $25,000. If the partnership were to distribute $65,000 ($25,000 share of partnership profits + $40,000 initial capital contribution) to Kay on December 31, 1993, the distribution would be a nonliquidating distribution as long as Kay continues to be a partner in the partnership. This is true even though Kay receives her share of profits plus her entire investment in the partnership. In this case, $25,000 would be considered a draw, and the remaining $40,000 would be a partial liquidation of Kay's interest. ◆

In general, neither the partner nor the partnership recognizes gain or loss when a nonliquidating distribution occurs.[46] The partner usually takes a carryover basis for the assets distributed. The distributee partner's outside basis is reduced (but not below zero) by the amount of cash and the adjusted basis of property distributed.[47]

Note the difference between the tax theory governing distributions from C corporations and partnerships. In a C corporation, a distribution from current or accumulated income (earnings and profits) is taxable as a dividend to the shareholder, and the corporation does not receive a deduction for the amount distributed. This results in corporate income being subject to double taxation. In a partnership, a distribution from current or accumulated profits is not taxable because Congress has decided that partnership income should be subject to only a single level of taxation. If a partner pays taxes on the share of income earned by the partnership, this income will not be taxed again when it is distributed to the partner.

This result makes sense under entity and aggregate concepts also. The entity concept is applicable to corporate dividends, so any amount paid as a dividend is a transfer between two parties and should be taxed accordingly. Under the aggregate theory, though, a partner receiving a distribution from partnership income is merely receiving a share of that income—whether the income is retained inside the partnership or outside in the hands of the partner should make no difference. The following examples illustrate that a distribution does not change a partner's economic position.

EXAMPLE 47

Jay is a one-fourth partner in the JP Partnership. His basis in his partnership interest is $40,000 on December 31, 1993. The fair market value of the interest is $70,000. The partnership distributes $25,000 cash to him on that date. The distribution is not taxable

46. § 731(a)(1).

47. § 732(a)(1).

to Jay or the partnership. The distribution reduces Jay's adjusted basis in the partnership to $15,000 ($40,000 – $25,000), and the fair market value of his partnership interest would, arguably, be reduced to $45,000 ($70,000 – $25,000). ◆

EXAMPLE 48

Assume the same facts as in Example 47, except that the partnership distributes both the $25,000 cash and land with an adjusted basis to the partnership of $13,000 and a fair market value of $30,000 on the date of distribution. The distribution is not taxable to Jay or the partnership. Jay reduces his basis in the partnership to $2,000 [$40,000 – ($25,000 + $13,000)] and takes a carryover basis of $13,000 in the land. The fair market value of Jay's remaining interest in the partnership would, arguably, be reduced to $15,000 [$70,000 – ($25,000 + $30,000)].

If Jay had sold his partnership interest for $70,000 rather than receiving the distribution, he would have realized and recognized gain of $30,000 ($70,000 selling price – $40,000 outside basis). Because he has not recognized any gain or loss on the distribution of cash and land, he should still have the $30,000 of deferred gain to recognize at some point in the future. This is exactly what will happen. If Jay were to sell the land and remaining partnership interest on January 1, 1994, the day after the distribution, he would realize and recognize gains of $17,000 ($30,000 – $13,000) on the land and $13,000 ($15,000 – $2,000) on the partnership interest. These gains total $30,000, which is the amount of the original deferred gain. ◆

Gain Recognition. A partner recognizes gain from a nonliquidating distribution to the extent that the cash received exceeds the outside basis of his or her interest in the partnership.[48]

EXAMPLE 49

Samantha is a one-third partner in the SF Partnership. Her basis in this ownership interest is $50,000 on December 31, 1993, after accounting for the calendar year entity's 1993 operations and for her 1993 capital contributions and withdrawals. On December 31, 1993, the partnership distributes $60,000 cash to Samantha. She must recognize a $10,000 gain from this distribution ($60,000 cash received – $50,000 basis in her partnership interest). Most likely, she will recognize a capital gain on this distribution. ◆

Whereas distributions *from* accumulated earnings are taxed differently to shareholders and partners (as a result of differing tax objectives), distributions *in excess* of accumulated profits are taxed similarly for corporate shareholders and partners in partnerships. The shareholder or partner is allowed to recover the cumulative capital invested in the entity tax-free. Any amount distributed to the shareholder or partner in excess of invested capital is taxed as if a sale of the stock or partnership interest had occurred. Allowing shareholders or partners to recover capital before recognizing gain is simply a matter of "legislative grace": Congress has decided that investors should be allowed to recover their entire investment before paying tax on a distribution in excess of that investment. This is because, in most cases, distributions are not guaranteed. Since the shareholder or partner may never receive any *future* distribution, it would not be fair to tax a *current* distribution that may represent a mere return of capital.

Recall from earlier in the chapter that the reduction of a partner's share of partnership debt is treated as a distribution of cash from the partnership to the partner. A reduction of a partner's share of partnership debt, then, reduces the partner's basis in the interest. Any reduction of a share of debt in excess of a partner's basis in the partnership interest is taxable as a gain.

48. § 731(a)(1).

EXAMPLE 50

Returning to the facts of Example 49, assume that Samantha's $50,000 basis in her partnership interest included a $60,000 share of partnership liabilities. If the partnership repays all of its liabilities, Samantha will be treated as receiving a $60,000 distribution from the partnership. Since this distribution exceeds the basis in her partnership interest, she must recognize a gain of $10,000. ◆

Property Distributions. In general, gains do not arise on property distributions (discussed more fully under Ordering Rules below). Exceptions to this general rule, however, do exist. A discussion of these exceptions is beyond the scope of this text.

EXAMPLE 51

Assume the same facts as in Example 49, except that instead of making a $60,000 cash distribution, the partnership distributes land it owns with a basis and a fair market value of $60,000. Samantha will not recognize any gain on this distribution because it is a distribution of property. However, Samantha should not be allowed to take a carryover basis of $60,000 in the land, when her basis in her partnership interest is only $50,000. Therefore, the Code provides that Samantha will take a substituted basis of $50,000 in the land. Her basis in her partnership interest is reduced by the basis she takes in the asset received, or $50,000. Therefore, Samantha has a basis of $50,000 in the land, a basis of $0 in her partnership interest, and recognizes no gain on this distribution. ◆

Ordering Rules. When the inside basis of the distributed assets exceeds the distributee partner's outside basis, the Code requires that the assets be deemed distributed in the following order:

- Cash is distributed first.
- Unrealized receivables and inventory are distributed second.
- All other assets are distributed last.

Since the partner will typically not recognize a gain from a *property* distribution, the Code provides that the bases of property received cannot exceed the partner's basis in the partnership interest immediately prior to the distribution. If the partnership's inside basis in an asset exceeds the partner's outside basis in the partnership interest, the partner takes a substituted basis in the asset distributed. That is, the partner's remaining basis in the partnership interest becomes the basis in the asset received from the partnership.

For each level of asset distribution, the relevant adjustments are made to the partner's basis in the interest and the partnership's basis in its assets. In other words, after a cash distribution, the partner's basis in the interest is recomputed before determining the effect of a distribution of unrealized receivables or inventory. The basis is again recomputed before determining the effect of a distribution of other assets. If the remaining outside basis is insufficient to cover the entire inside basis of the assets in either the second or third class, that remaining outside basis is allocated pro rata among the assets within that class in accordance with their relative inside bases.[49]

EXAMPLE 52

Assume the same facts as in Example 49, except that the partnership distributes cash of $12,000, cash basis receivables with an inside basis of zero and fair market value of $10,000,

49. § 732 and Reg. § 1.732–1(c)(1).

and two parcels of land to Samantha. These parcels have a basis to the partnership of $15,000 and $45,000, respectively. The fair market value of each parcel is $50,000.

Step 1. Determine the order in which these assets are distributed. According to the Code, the cash is treated as being distributed first, the unrealized receivables second, and the two parcels of land last.

Step 2. Determine if Samantha recognizes any gain as a result of the distribution. Since the $12,000 cash that Samantha received in the distribution does not exceed the basis for her partnership interest, she recognizes none of the $72,000 gain that she realized on the transfer. The realized gain consists of the $122,000 amount realized ($12,000 + 10,000 + $50,000 + $50,000) less Samantha's $50,000 basis in the partnership interest.

Step 3. Determine the basis Samantha takes in each distributed asset and the effect of the distribution on her outside basis. Samantha first assigns a $12,000 basis to the cash. After the cash distribution, the basis in her partnership interest is $38,000 ($50,000 – $12,000). Next, she assigns a zero carryover basis to the unrealized receivables that she receives from the partnership. Her remaining outside basis is still $38,000 [$50,000 – ($12,000 + $0)]. The land parcels are deemed distributed last. Samantha's remaining basis of $38,000 is less than the partnership's inside basis of $60,000 ($15,000 + $45,000) in the land parcels. Therefore, she must take a substituted basis of $38,000 in the land.

Samantha allocates the $38,000 outside basis to the land parcels proportionately based on their adjusted inside bases to the partnership (not according to their relative fair market values). Samantha takes a $9,500 basis in the first parcel of land, computed as follows:

$$\$38{,}000 \times \frac{\$15{,}000}{\$60{,}000} = \$9{,}500$$

The second parcel of land takes a $28,500 basis to Samantha, computed as follows:

$$\$38{,}000 \times \frac{\$45{,}000}{\$60{,}000} = \$28{,}500$$

◆

EXAMPLE 53

Assume the same facts as in Example 52. If Samantha sells both of the parcels early in 1994 at their fair market values, she will receive proceeds of $100,000 ($50,000 + $50,000) and will collect $10,000 for the cash basis receivables. She will recognize all of the $72,000 gain that she deferred upon receiving the property from the partnership [$100,000 amount realized – $38,000 adjusted basis for the two parcels ($9,500 + $28,500) + 10,000 received – $0 for the receivables]. ◆

Review the tax results of Example 52. Although Samantha need recognize none of the gain that she realizes from the distribution, she has a zero outside basis for her partnership interest. This zero basis will not be attractive to Samantha if she anticipates that the partnership will generate net losses in the near future. Since her tax basis in the entity is zero, she will be unable to deduct her share of the losses when they flow through to her on the last day of the partnership's tax year.

The low basis that Samantha has assigned to the parcels of land is of no tax detriment to her if she does not intend to sell the land in the near future. Since land does not generate cost recovery deductions, the substituted basis will be used only to determine Samantha's gain or loss upon her disposition of the asset in a taxable sale or exchange.

Concept Summary 22–4 summarizes the rules for nonliquidating distributions.

Choosing Partnership Taxation

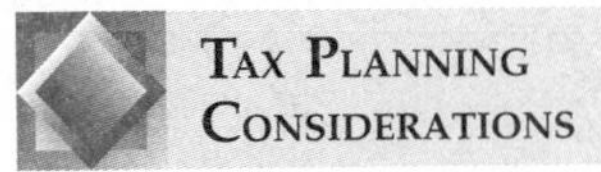
TAX PLANNING CONSIDERATIONS

Concept Summary 22–5 lists various factors that the owners of a business should consider in deciding whether to use a C corporation, S corporation, or partnership as a means of doing business.

Formation and Operation of a Partnership

Potential partners should be cautious in transferring assets to a partnership, so that they are not required to recognize any gain upon the creation of the entity. The exceptions to the nonrecognition provisions of § 721 are relatively straightforward and resemble the corresponding portions of § 351. However, any partner can make a tax-deferred contribution of additional assets to the entity after the inception of the partnership. This possibility is not available to less-than-controlling shareholders in a corporation.

The partners should anticipate the tax benefits and pitfalls that are presented in Subchapter K and should take appropriate actions to resolve any resulting problems. Typically, all that is needed is an appropriate provision in the partnership agreement (e.g., with respect to differing allocation percentages for gains and losses). Recall, however, that a special allocation of income, expense, or credit items in the partnership agreement must satisfy certain requirements before it will be respected by the IRS.

Transactions between Partners and Partnerships

Partners should be careful when engaging in transactions with the partnership to ensure that no negative tax results occur. A partner who owns a majority of the

CONCEPT SUMMARY 22–4
NONLIQUIDATING DISTRIBUTIONS (GENERAL RULES)

1. Generally, neither the distributee partner nor the partnership recognizes any gain or loss on a nonliquidating distribution. If cash (not property) distributed exceeds the distributee partner's outside basis, however, gain is recognized.
2. The distributee partner usually takes the same basis for the distributed property that it had to the partnership. However, where the inside basis of distributed property exceeds the partner's outside basis, the basis assigned to the distributed property cannot exceed that outside basis.
3. Gain recognized by the distributee partner on a nonliquidating distribution is generally capital in nature.

Calculations

1. Partner's outside basis. ________
2. Less: Cash distributed to partner, including reduction in share of liabilities. ________
3. Gain recognized by partner (excess of Line 2 over Line 1). ________
4. Partner's remaining outside basis (Line 1 – Line 2). If less than $0, enter $0. ________
5. Partner's basis in unrealized receivables and inventory distributed (enter lesser of Line 4 or the inside basis of the unrealized receivables and inventory). ________
6. Basis available to allocate to other property distributed (Line 4 – Line 5). ________
7. Inside basis of other property distributed. ________
8. Basis to partner of other property distributed (enter lesser of Line 6 or Line 7). ________
9. Partner's remaining outside basis (Line 6 – Line 8). ________

partnership generally should not sell property at a loss to the partnership, since the loss will be disallowed. Similarly, a majority partner typically would not want to sell a capital asset to the partnership at a gain, if the asset is to be used by the partnership as other than a capital asset. The gain on this transaction is taxed as ordinary income to the selling partner rather than as capital gain.

As an alternative to selling property to a partnership, the partner may want to lease it to the partnership. The partner will recognize rent income, and the partnership will have a rent expense. If the partner needs more cash immediately, the partner may wish to sell the property to an outside third party who will lease the property to the partnership for a fair rental.

The timing of payments by accrual basis partnerships to cash basis partners will vary depending on whether the payment is a guaranteed payment or is treated as a payment to an outsider. If the payment is a guaranteed payment, the timing will occur when the partnership properly accrues the payment. Conversely, if the payment is treated as a payment to an outsider, the actual date the payment is made will control the timing of the transaction.

CONCEPT SUMMARY 22–5
ADVANTAGES AND DISADVANTAGES OF THE PARTNERSHIP FORM

The partnership form may be attractive when one or more of the following factors is present:

- The entity is generating net taxable losses and/or valuable tax credits, which will be of use directly to the owners.
- The entity does not generate material amounts of tax preference and adjustment items, which would increase the alternative minimum tax liabilities of its owners.
- The entity is generating net passive income, which its owners can use to claim immediate deductions for net passive losses that they have generated from other sources.
- Other means by which to reduce the effects of the double taxation of business income (e.g., compensation to owners, interest, and rental payments) have been exhausted.
- Given the asset holdings and distribution practices of the entity, the possibility of liability under the accumulated earnings and personal holding company taxes is significant.
- Restrictions relative to S corporation status (e.g., the 35-shareholder maximum or the restriction to one class of outstanding stock) are not attractive, perhaps because of elaborate executive compensation arrangements or an anticipated public offering of stock.
- The owners wish to make special allocations of certain income or deduction items. Such allocations are not possible under the C or S corporation forms.
- The owners anticipate liquidation of the entity within a short period of time. Liquidation of a corporation would generate entity-level recognized gains relative to appreciated property distributed because of the liquidation.
- Adequate basis amounts in the partnership exist; these facilitate the deduction of flow-through losses and the assignment of an adequate basis to assets distributed in-kind to the partners.

The partnership form may be less attractive when one or more of the following factors is present:

- The entity is generating net taxable income, which will be taxed directly to the owners who do not necessarily receive any funds with which to pay the tax.
- The type of income that the entity is generating (e.g., business and portfolio income) is not as attractive to its owners as net passive income would be because the owners could use net passive income to offset the net passive losses that they have generated on their own.
- Congress enacts tax legislation raising the maximum marginal tax rate applicable to individuals above that applicable to C corporations.

Drafting the Partnership Agreement

Although a written partnership agreement is not required, many rules governing the tax consequences to partners and their partnership refer to such an agreement. Remember that a partner's distributive share of income, gain, loss, deduction, or credit is determined in accordance with the partnership agreement. Consequently, if taxpayers operating a business in partnership form want a measure of certainty as to the tax consequences of their activities, a carefully drafted partnership agreement is crucial. An agreement that sets forth the obligations, rights, and powers of the partners should prove invaluable in settling controversies among them and provide some degree of certainty as to the tax consequences of the partners' actions.

Overall Comparison: Forms of Doing Business

See Concept Summary 22–6 for a detailed comparison of the tax consequences of the following forms of doing business: sole proprietorship, partnership, S corporation, and corporation.

Concept Summary 22–6 Tax Attributes of Different Forms of Business (Assume Partners and Shareholders Are All Individuals)

	Sole Proprietorship	Partnership	S Corporation*	Regular Corporation**
Restrictions on type or number of owners	One owner. The owner must be an individual.	Must have at least 2 owners.	Only individuals, estates, and certain trusts can be owners. Maximum number of shareholders limited to 35.	None, except some states require a minimum of 2 shareholders.
Incidence of tax	Sole proprietorship's income and deductions are reported on Schedule C of the individual's Form 1040. A separate Schedule C is prepared for each business.	Entity not subject to tax. Partners in their separate capacity subject to tax on their distributive share of income. Partnership files Form 1065.	Except for certain capital gains, built-in gains, and violations of passive investment income tests when accumulated earnings and profits are present from Subchapter C tax years, entity not subject to Federal income tax. S corporation files Form 1120S. Shareholders are subject to tax on income attributable to their stock ownership. C corporations that claimed an investment tax credit and elect S status remain liable for any ITC recapture potential.	Income subject to double taxation. Entity subject to tax, and shareholder subject to tax on any corporate dividends received. Corporation files Form 1120.

	Sole Proprietorship	Partnership	S Corporation*	Regular Corporation**
Highest tax rate	31% at individual level.	31% at partner level.	31% at shareholder level.	39% at corporate level plus 31% on any corporate dividends at shareholder level.
Choice of tax year	Same tax year as owner.	Selection generally restricted to coincide with tax year of majority partners or principal partners, or to calendar year.	Restricted to a calendar year unless IRS approves a different year for business purposes or other exceptions apply.	Unrestricted selection allowed at time of filing first tax return.
Timing of taxation	Based on owner's tax year.	Partners report their share of income in their tax year with or within which the partnership's tax year ends. Partners in their separate capacity are subject to payment of estimated taxes.	Shareholders report their share of income in their tax year with or within which the corporation's tax year ends. Generally, the corporation uses a calendar year; but see "Choice of tax year" above. Shareholders may be subject to payment of estimated taxes. Corporation may be subject to payment of estimated taxes for any taxes imposed at the corporate level.	Corporation subject to tax at close of its tax year. May be subject to payment of estimated taxes. Dividends will be subject to tax at the shareholder level in the tax year received.
Basis for allocating income to owners	Not applicable (only one owner).	Profit and loss sharing agreement. Cash basis items of cash basis partnerships are allocated on a daily basis. Other partnership items are allocated after considering varying interests of partners.	Pro rata share based on stock ownership. Shareholder's pro rata share is determined on a daily basis according to the number of shares of stock held on each day of the corporation's tax year.	Not applicable.
Contribution of property to the entity	Not a taxable transaction.	Generally, not a taxable transaction.	Is a taxable transaction unless the § 351 requirements are satisfied.	Is a taxable transaction unless the § 351 requirements are satisfied.
Character of income taxed to owners	Retains source characteristics.	Conduit—retains source characteristics.	Conduit—retains source characteristics.	All source characteristics are lost when income is distributed to owners.
Basis for allocating a net operating loss to owners	Not applicable (only one owner).	Profit and loss sharing agreement. Cash basis items of cash basis partnerships are allocated on a daily basis. Other partnership items are allocated after considering varying interests of partners.	Prorated among shareholders on a daily basis.	Not applicable.

	Sole Proprietorship	Partnership	S Corporation*	Regular Corporation**
Limitation on losses deductible by owners	Investment plus liabilities.	Partner's investment plus share of liabilities.	Shareholder's investment plus loans made by shareholder to corporation.	Not applicable.
Subject to at-risk rules	Yes, at the owner level. Indefinite carryover of excess loss.	Yes, at the partner level. Indefinite carryover of excess loss.	Yes, at the shareholder level. Indefinite carryover of excess loss.	Yes, for closely held corporations. Indefinite carryover of excess loss.
Subject to passive activity loss rules	Yes, at the owner level. Indefinite carryover of excess loss.	Yes, at the partner level. Indefinite carryover of excess loss.	Yes, at the shareholder level. Indefinite carryover of excess loss.	Yes, for closely held corporations and personal service corporations. Indefinite carryover of excess loss.
Tax consequences of earnings retained by entity	Taxed to owner when earned and increases his or her basis in the sole proprietorship.	Taxed to partners when earned and increases their respective interests in the partnership.	Taxed to shareholders when earned and increases their respective basis in stock.	Taxed to corporation as earned and may be subject to penalty tax if accumulated unreasonably.
Nonliquidating distributions to owners	Not taxable.	Not taxable unless money received exceeds recipient partner's basis in partnership interest.	Generally not taxable unless the distribution exceeds the shareholder's AAA or stock basis. Existence of accumulated earnings and profits could cause some distributions to be dividends.	Taxable in year of receipt to extent of earnings and profits or if exceeds basis in stock.
Distribution of appreciated property	Not taxable.	No recognition at the partnership level.	Recognition at the corporate level to the extent of the appreciation. Conduit—amount of recognized gain is passed through to shareholders.	Taxable at the corporate level to the extent of the appreciation.
Splitting of income among family members	Not applicable (only one owner).	Difficult—IRS will not recognize a family member as a partner unless certain requirements are met.	Rather easy—gift of stock will transfer tax on a pro rata share of income to the donee. However, IRS can make adjustments to reflect adequate compensation for services.	Same as an S corporation, except that donees will be subject to tax only on earnings actually or constructively distributed to them. Other than unreasonable compensation, IRS generally cannot make adjustments to reflect adequate compensation for services and capital.
Organizational costs	Start-up expenditures are amortizable over 60 months.	Amortizable over 60 months.	Same as partnership.	Same as partnership.

	Sole Proprietorship	Partnership	S Corporation*	Regular Corporation**
Charitable contributions	Limitations apply at owner level.	Conduit—partners are subject to deduction limitations in their own capacity.	Conduit—shareholders are subject to deduction limitations in their own capacity.	Limited to 10% of taxable income before certain deductions.
Alternative minimum tax	Applies at owner level. AMT rate is 24%.	Applies at partner level rather than at the partnership level. AMT preferences and adjustments are passed through from the partnership to the partners.	Applies at the shareholder level rather than at the corporate level. AMT preferences and adjustments are passed through from the S corporation to the shareholders.	Applies at the corporate level. AMT rate is 20%.
ACE adjustment	Does not apply.	Does not apply.	Does not apply.	The adjustment is made in calculating AMTI. The amount of the adjustment is 75% of the excess of adjusted current earnings over unadjusted AMTI. If the unadjusted AMTI exceeds adjusted current earnings, the adjustment is negative.
Tax preference items	Apply at owner level in determining AMT.	Conduit—passed through to partners who must account for such items in their separate capacity.	Conduit—passed through to shareholders who must account for such items in their separate capacity.	Subject to AMT at corporate level.
Capital gains	Taxed at owner level using maximum rate of 28%.	Conduit—partners must account for their respective shares.	Conduit, with certain exceptions (a possible penalty tax), shareholders must account for their respective shares.	Taxed at corporate level using maximum rate of 34%. No other benefits.
Capital losses	Only $3,000 of capital losses can be offset each tax year against ordinary income. Indefinite carryover.	Conduit—partners must account for their respective shares.	Conduit—shareholders must account for their respective shares.	Carried back three years and carried forward five years. Deductible only to the extent of capital gains.
§ 1231 gains and losses	Taxable or deductible at owner level. Five-year lookback rule for § 1231 losses.	Conduit—partners must account for their respective shares.	Conduit—shareholders must account for their respective shares.	Taxable or deductible at corporate level only. Five-year lookback rule for § 1231 losses.
Foreign tax credits	Available at owner level.	Conduit—passed through to partners.	Generally conduit—passed through to shareholders.	Available at corporate level only.
§ 1244 treatment of loss on sale of interest	Not applicable.	Not applicable.	Available.	Available.

	Sole Proprietorship	Partnership	S Corporation*	Regular Corporation**
Basis treatment of entity liabilities	Includible in interest basis.	Includible in interest basis.	Not includible in stock basis.	Not includible in stock basis.
Built-in gains	Not applicable.	Not applicable.	Possible corporate tax.	Not applicable.
Special allocations to owners	Not applicable (only one owner).	Available if supported by substantial economic effect.	Not available.	Not applicable.
Availability of fringe benefits to owners	None.	None.	None unless a 2% or less shareholder.	Available within antidiscrimination rules.
Effect of liquidation/ redemption/ reorganization on basis of entity assets	Not applicable.	Usually carried over from entity to partner unless excessive cash is distributed.	Taxable step-up to fair market value.	Taxable step-up to fair market value.
Sale of ownership interest	Treated as the sale of individual assets. Classification of recognized gain or loss is dependent on the nature of the individual assets.	Treated as the sale of a partnership interest. Recognized gain or loss is classified as capital under § 741 subject to ordinary income treatment under § 751.	Treated as the sale of corporate stock. Recognized gain is classified as capital gain. Recognized loss is classified as capital loss subject to ordinary loss treatment under § 1244.	Treated as the sale of corporate stock. Recognized gain is classified as capital gain. Recognized loss is classified as capital loss subject to ordinary loss treatment under § 1244.

*Refer to Chapter 21 for additional details on S corporations.
**Refer to Chapters 16 through 20 for additional details on regular corporations.

Problem Materials

Discussion Questions

1. What is a partnership for Federal income tax purposes?
2. Distinguish between the entity concept and the aggregate or conduit concept of a partnership.
3. Compare the nonrecognition of gain or loss provision on contributions to a partnership with the similar provision with respect to corporate formation. What are the major differences and similarities?
4. If appreciated property is contributed to a partnership in exchange for a partnership interest, what basis does the partnership take in the property?
5. What effect does the contribution of property subject to a liability have on the basis of the contributing partner's interest? What is the effect on the basis of the other partners' interests?
6. What is the purpose of the three rules that implement the economic effect test?
7. Describe the three tests a partnership must use to determine its required taxable year, and list alternative years that may be available to the partnership.
8. Discuss the adjustments that must be made to a partner's basis in his or her partnership interest. When are such adjustments made?
9. To what extent can partners deduct their distributive shares of partnership losses? What happens to any unused losses?

10. Discuss the applicability of the at-risk rules to a partnership and its partners.
11. What are guaranteed payments?

PROBLEMS

12. Dan is an attorney who is financially quite successful. Mary is a real estate developer who has little cash for investment. The two decide to buy some real estate. Dan will contribute the money to buy the properties and have veto power over which properties to purchase. Mary will make all other decisions. Profits and losses from the operation will be shared equally.
    a. Is this a partnership for tax purposes? Why or why not?
    b. Would your answer change if Dan had no veto power and was to receive a guaranteed 10% annual return on his money?

13. James and Lynn form an equal partnership with a cash contribution of $50,000 from James and a property contribution (adjusted basis of $60,000 and a fair market value of $50,000) from Lynn.
    a. How much gain or loss, if any, does Lynn realize on the transfer? May Lynn recognize any gain or loss?
    b. What is James's basis in his partnership interest?
    c. What is Lynn's basis in her partnership interest?
    d. What basis does the partnership take in the property transferred by Lynn?
    e. Are there more effective ways to structure the formation?

14. Craig and Beth are equal members of the CB Partnership, formed on June 1 of the current year. Craig contributed land that he inherited from his father's estate three years ago. Craig's father purchased the land in 1946 for $6,000. The land was worth $50,000 when the father died. The fair market value of the land was $75,000 at the date it was contributed to the partnership.

    Beth has significant experience developing real estate. After the partnership is formed, she will prepare a plan for developing the property and secure zoning approvals for the partnership. She would normally bill a third party $25,000 for these efforts. Beth will also contribute $50,000 cash in exchange for her 50% interest in the partnership.
    a. How much gain or income will Craig recognize on his contribution of the land to the partnership? What is the character of any gain or income recognized?
    b. What basis will Craig take in his partnership interest?
    c. How much gain or income will Beth recognize on the formation of the partnership? What is the character of any gain or income recognized?
    d. What basis will Beth take in her partnership interest?
    e. Construct an opening balance sheet for the partnership reflecting the partnership's basis in assets and the fair market value of these assets.
    f. Outline any planning opportunities that may minimize current taxation to any of the parties.

15. Continue with the facts presented in Problem 14. At the end of the first year, the partnership distributes the $50,000 cash to Craig. No distribution is made to Beth.
    a. Under general tax rules, how would the payment to Craig be treated?
    b. How much income or gain would Craig recognize as a result of the payment?
    c. What basis would the partnership take in the land contributed to the partnership under general tax rules?
    d. What alternate treatment might the IRS try to impose?
    e. Under the alternate treatment, how much income or gain would Craig recognize?
    f. Under the alternate treatment, what basis would the partnership take in the land contributed by Craig?

16. The cash method Thrush Partnership, which reports on a calendar year basis, incurred the following organization and syndication costs in 1993:

Attorney fees for preparing partnership agreement	$2,100
Printing costs for preparing documents that were used to help sell the partnership interests	4,000
Accounting fees for tax advice of an organizational nature	2,400

The attorney fees and printing costs were incurred and paid in 1993. The accounting fees were incurred in December 1993 and paid in February 1994. If the partnership begins business in July 1993, how much of the organization costs can be amortized in 1993? In 1994?

17. Ron, Pat, and Matt form the RPM Partnership on January 1 of the current year. Ron is a 50% partner, and Pat and Matt are each 25% partners. Each partner and RPM use the cash method of accounting. For reporting purposes, Ron uses a calendar year, Pat uses an October 31 fiscal year, and Matt uses a June 30 fiscal year.

  a. What is RPM's required tax year under the least aggregate deferral method?
  b. Assuming that RPM cannot establish a natural business year that differs from your answer in (a), what tax year can RPM elect that provides the partners with the *greatest* aggregate additional deferral?

18. Lisa and Lori are equal members of the Redbird Partnership. They are real estate investors who formed the partnership two years ago with equal cash contributions. Redbird then purchased a piece of land.

On January 1 of the current year, to acquire a one-third interest in the entity, Lana contributed some land she had held for investment to the partnership. Lana purchased the land three years ago for $25,000; its fair market value at the contribution date was $20,000. No special allocation agreements were in effect before or after Lana was admitted to the partnership. The Redbird Partnership holds all land for investment.

Immediately before Lana's property contribution, the balance sheet of the Redbird Partnership was as follows:

	Basis	FMV		Basis	FMV
Land	$5,000	$40,000	Lisa, capital	$2,500	$20,000
			Lori, capital	2,500	20,000
	$5,000	$40,000		$5,000	$40,000

  a. At the contribution date, what is Lana's basis in her interest in the Redbird Partnership?
  b. When does the partnership's holding period begin for the contributed land?
  c. On June 30 of the current year, the partnership sold the land contributed by Lana for $20,000. How much is the recognized gain or loss, and how is it allocated among the partners?
  d. Prepare a balance sheet reflecting basis and fair market value for the partnership immediately after the land sale.

19. Assume the same facts as in Problem 18, with the following exceptions.

- Lana purchased the land three years ago for $25,000. Its fair market value was $20,000 when it was contributed to the partnership.
- Redbird sold the land contributed by Lana for $17,000.

  a. How much is the recognized gain or loss, and how is it allocated among the partners?
  b. Prepare a balance sheet reflecting basis and fair market value for the partnership immediately after the land sale, along with schedules that support the amount in each partner's capital account.

20. Earl and Zelda are equal partners in the accrual basis EZ Partnership. At the beginning of the current year, Earl's capital account has a balance of $10,000, and the

partnership has recourse debts of $30,000 payable to unrelated parties. All partnership recourse debt is shared equally between the partners. The following information about EZ's operations for the current year is obtained from the partnership's records.

Taxable income	$30,000
Tax-exempt interest income	2,000
§ 1231 gain	5,000
Long-term capital gain	430
Long-term capital loss	120
Short-term capital loss	600
IRS penalty	630
Charitable contribution to Girl Scouts	200
Cash distribution to Earl	14,000

Assume that year-end partnership debt payable to unrelated parties is $6,000.

a. What is Earl's basis in the partnership interest at the beginning of the year?
b. What is Earl's basis in the partnership interest at the end of the current year?

21. Lee, Bob, and Rick form the LBR Partnership on January 1 of the current year. In return for a 25% interest, Lee transfers property (basis of $15,000, fair market value of $17,500) subject to a nonrecourse liability of $10,000. The liability is assumed by the partnership. Bob transfers property (basis of $16,000, fair market value of $7,500) for a 25% interest, and Rick transfers cash of $15,000 for the remaining 50% interest.

a. How much gain must Lee recognize on the transfer?
b. What is Lee's basis in his interest in the partnership?
c. How much loss may Bob recognize on the transfer?
d. What is Bob's basis in his interest in the partnership?
e. What is Rick's basis in his interest in the partnership?
f. What basis does the LBR Partnership take in the property transferred by Lee?
g. What is the partnership's basis in the property transferred by Bob?

22. Assume the same facts as in Problem 21, except that the property contributed by Lee has a fair market value of $27,500 and is subject to a nonrecourse mortgage of $20,000.

a. What is Lee's basis in his partnership interest?
b. How much gain must Lee recognize on the transfer?
c. What is Bob's basis in his partnership interest?
d. What is Rick's basis in his partnership interest?
e. What basis does the LBR Partnership take in the property transferred by Lee?

23. Jen and Ken established the JK General Partnership on December 31 of the current year. The capital accounts are properly maintained, and each partner has to restore any deficit in their capital account. The partnership agreement provides that Jen will be allocated 90% of the partnership income, gains, losses, deductions, and credits until she has been allocated income and gains equal to her previous allocations of losses and deductions. Thereafter, all partnership items will be allocated equally. Each partner contributed $20,000 cash to the partnership in exchange for the partnership interest. The partnership used the $40,000 cash to help purchase a parcel of land for $100,000. The other $60,000 of financing for the land was obtained from a local bank. In addition to using the land as collateral, both partners are also personally liable on the note. How will the note be shared between the partners for purposes of computing the adjusted basis of each partnership interest?

24. The MGP General Partnership was created on January 1, 1993, by having Miguel, George, and Pat each contribute $10,000 cash to the partnership in exchange for a one-third interest in partnership income, gains, losses, deductions, and credits. On December 31, 1993, the partnership balance sheet reads as follows:

	Basis	FMV
Assets	$40,000	$55,000
Recourse debt	$12,000	$12,000
Miguel, capital	11,000	16,000
George, capital	11,000	16,000
Pat, capital	6,000	11,000
	$40,000	$55,000

Pat's capital account is less than Miguel's and George's capital accounts because Pat has withdrawn more cash than the other partners. How do the partners share the recourse debt as of December 31, 1993?

25. Chris is a 15% partner in the AC Partnership, which is a lessor of residential rental property. Her share of the partnership's losses for the current year is $60,000. Immediately before considering the deductibility of this loss, Chris's capital account (which, in this case, corresponds to her basis excluding liabilities) reflected a balance of $25,000. Her share of partnership recourse liabilities is $7,000, and her share of the nonrecourse liabilities is $11,000. The nonrecourse liability was obtained from an unrelated bank and is secured solely by the real estate. Chris is also a partner in the BC Partnership, which has generated $12,000 of income from long-term (more than 30 days) equipment rental activities. Chris performs substantial services for BC and spends several hundred hours a year working for the AC Partnership. Chris's modified adjusted gross income before considering partnership activities is $90,000. Based on this information, how much of the $60,000 loss can Chris deduct on her current calendar year return? Under what Code sections are nondeductible losses limited?

26. As of January 1 of last year, the outside basis and at-risk basis of Rashad's 25% interest in the RST Partnership were $24,000. Rashad and the partnership use the calendar year for tax purposes. The partnership incurred an operating loss of $100,000 last year and a profit of $8,000 for the current year. Rashad is a material participant in the partnership.

  a. How much loss, if any, may Rashad recognize for last year?
  b. How much net reportable income must Rashad recognize for the current year?
  c. What is Rashad's basis in the partnership interest as of January 1 of the current year?
  d. What is Rashad's basis in the partnership interest as of January 1 of the next year?
  e. What year-end tax planning would you suggest to ensure that Rashad can deduct his share of partnership losses?

27. Ned, an equal partner in the MN Partnership, is to receive a payment of $20,000 for services plus 50% of the partnership's profits or losses. After deducting the $20,000 payment to Ned, the partnership has a loss of $12,000.

  a. How much, if any, of the $12,000 partnership loss will be allocated to Ned?
  b. What is the net income from the partnership that Ned must report on his personal income tax return?

28. Sonya is a 50% owner of Philadelphia Cheese Treets, Inc., a C corporation that was formed February 1, 1993. She receives a $5,000 monthly salary from the corporation, and Cheese Treets generates $200,000 taxable income for its tax year ending January 31, 1994.

  a. How do these activities affect Sonya's 1993 AGI?
  b. Now assume that Cheese Treets is a partnership. Treat Sonya's salary as a guaranteed payment. How do these activities affect Sonya's 1993 AGI?

29. Four Lakes Partnership is owned by four sisters. Anne holds a 70% interest; each of the others own 10%. Anne sells investment property to the partnership for its fair market value of $54,000 (basis of $72,000).

a. How much loss, if any, may Anne recognize?
b. If the partnership later sells the property for $81,000, how much gain must it recognize?
c. If Anne's basis in the investment property were $20,000 instead of $72,000, how much, if any, capital gain would she recognize on the sale?

30. Comment on the following statements.

a. Since a partnership is not a taxable entity, it is not required to file any type of tax return.
b. Each partner can choose a different method of accounting and depreciation computation in determining the gross income from the entity.
c. Generally, a transfer of appreciated property to a partnership results in recognized gain to the contributing partner at the time of the transfer.
d. A partner can carry forward, for an unlimited period of time, any operating losses that exceed the basis in the entity, provided the partner retains an ownership interest in the partnership.
e. When a partner renders services to the entity in exchange for an unrestricted interest therein, that partner does not recognize any gross income.
f. Losses on sales between a partner and the partnership always are nondeductible.
g. A partnership may choose a year that results in the least aggregate deferral of tax to the partners, unless the IRS requires the use of a natural business year.
h. A partner's basis in a partnership interest includes that partner's share of partnership recourse and nonrecourse liabilities.
i. Built-in loss related to nondepreciable property contributed to a partnership must be allocated to the contributing partner to the extent the loss is eventually recognized by the partnership.
j. Property that was held as inventory by a contributing partner, but is a capital asset in the hands of the partnership, results in a capital gain if the partnership immediately sells the property.

31. For each of the following independent statements, indicate whether the tax attribute is applicable to regular corporations (C), partnerships (P), both business forms (B), or neither business form (N):

a. Restrictions are placed on the type and number of owners.
b. Business income is taxable to the owners rather than to the entity.
c. Distributions of earnings to the owners result in a tax deduction to the entity.
d. The characteristics of an entity's income flow through to the owners.
e. Capital gains are subject to tax at the entity level.
f. Organization costs can be amortized over a period of 60 months or more.

32. When Belinda's outside basis in the BCD Partnership is $16,000, the partnership distributes to her $8,000 cash and a parcel of land (fair market value of $20,000; inside basis to the partnership of $10,000). Belinda remains a partner in the partnership.

a. Determine the recognized gain or loss to the partnership as a result of this distribution.
b. Determine the recognized gain or loss to Belinda as a result of this distribution.
c. Determine Belinda's basis in the land and in the partnership after the distribution.

33. In each of the following independent cases, indicate:

- Whether the partner recognizes gain or loss.
- Whether the partnership recognizes gain or loss.
- The partner's adjusted basis for the property distributed.
- The partner's outside basis in the partnership after the distribution.

a. Lisa received $16,000 cash in partial liquidation of her interest in the partnership. Lisa's outside basis for her partnership interest immediately before the distribution was $15,000.

b. Susan received $6,000 cash and land with an inside basis to the partnership of $12,000 in partial liquidation of her interest. Susan's outside basis for her partnership interest immediately before the distribution was $20,000.
c. Assume the same facts as in (b), except that Susan's outside basis for her partnership interest immediately before the distribution was $15,000.
d. Jim received $8,000 cash and two tracts of land in partial liquidation of his partnership interest. The two tracts have adjusted bases to the partnership of $5,000 and $15,000, respectively. Each tract has a $20,000 fair market value. Jim's outside basis for his partnership interest immediately before the distribution was $20,000.

34. Sam is a 40% partner in the Oriole Partnership, which reports on a calendar year basis. On January 1 of the current year, his basis in his partnership interest is $15,000, including his $12,000 share of partnership liabilities. The partnership has no taxable income or loss for the current year, but repays all liabilities from cash on hand. In a nonliquidating distribution, the partnership distributes $4,000 cash. It also distributes inventory proportionately to all partners. Sam receives inventory with a basis of $4,000 and a fair market value of $6,000.

a. Determine the recognized gain or loss to the partnership as a result of current-year activities.
b. Determine the recognized gain or loss to Sam in the current year.
c. Determine Sam's basis in his partnership interest at the end of the current year.
d. Determine Sam's basis in inventory received.

35. In 1991, Gabriella contributed land with a basis of $16,000 and a fair market value of $25,000 to the Meadowlark Partnership in exchange for a 25% interest in capital and profits. In 1993, the partnership distributed this property to Juanita, also a 25% partner, in a nonliquidating distribution. The fair market value had increased to $30,000 at the time the property was distributed. Juanita's and Gabriella's bases in their partnership interests were each $30,000 at the time of the distribution.

a. How much gain or loss, if any, does Gabriella recognize on the distribution? What is Gabriella's basis in her partnership interest following the distribution?
b. What is Juanita's basis in the land she received in the distribution?
c. How much gain or loss, if any, does Juanita recognize on the distribution? What is Juanita's basis in her partnership interest following the distribution?
d. Would your answers to (a) and (b) change if Gabriella originally contributed the property to the partnership in 1984?

CHAPTER

EXEMPT ENTITIES

OBJECTIVES

Identify the different types of exempt organizations.

Differentiate between the tax consequences of public charities and private foundations.

Discuss the taxes imposed on the prohibited transactions of private foundations.

Explain the tax on unrelated business income and debt-financed income.

Explain the reporting requirements for exempt organizations.

Identify planning opportunities for exempt organizations.

OUTLINE

General Considerations

Ideally, any entity that generates profit would prefer not to be subject to the Federal income tax. All of the types of entities discussed thus far are subject to the Federal income tax at one (e.g., sole proprietorships, partnerships, and S corporations generally are only subject to single taxation) or more (e.g., C corporations are subject to double taxation) levels. However, organizations classified as exempt organizations may be able to escape Federal income taxation altogether.

Churches are among the types of organizations that are exempt from Federal income tax. Nevertheless, one must be careful not to conclude that everything labeled a church will qualify for exempt status.

During the 1970s and 1980s, a popular technique for attempting to avoid Federal income tax was the establishment of so-called mail-order churches. For example, in one typical scheme, a nurse obtained a certificate of ordination and a church charter from an organization that sold such documents.[1] The articles of incorporation stated that the church was organized exclusively for religious and charitable purposes, including a religious mission of healing the spirit, mind, emotions, and body. The nurse was the church's minister, director, and principal officer. Taking a vow of poverty, she transferred all her assets, including a house and car, to the church. The church assumed all of the nurse's liabilities, including the mortgage on her house and her credit card bills. The nurse continued to work at a hospital and deposited her salary in the church's bank account. The church provided her with a living allowance sufficient to maintain or improve her previous standard of living. She was also permitted to use the house and car for personal purposes.

The IRS declared that such organizations were shams and not bona fide churches. For a church to be tax-exempt under § 501(c)(3), none of its net earnings may be used to the benefit of any private shareholder or individual. In essence, the organization should serve a public rather than a private interest. Although the courts have consistently upheld the IRS position, numerous avoidance schemes such as this have been attempted.

As discussed in Chapter 1, the major objective of the Federal tax law is to raise revenue. If revenue raising were the only objective, however, the Code would not contain provisions that permit certain organizations to be either partially or completely exempt from Federal income tax. As Chapter 1 pointed out, social considerations may also affect the tax law. This objective bears directly on the decision by Congress to provide for exempt organization tax status. The House Report on the Revenue Act of 1938 provides as follows:[2]

> The exemption from taxation of money or property devoted to charitable and other purposes is based upon the theory that the Government is compensated for the loss of revenue by its relief from the financial burden which would otherwise have to be met by appropriations from public funds, and by the benefits resulting from the promotion of the general welfare.

In recognition of this social consideration objective, Subchapter F (Exempt Organizations) of the Code (§§ 501–528) provides the authority under which

1. Rev.Rul. 81–94, 1981–1 C.B. 330.
2. See 1939–1 (Part 2) C.B. 742 for a reprint of H.R. No. 1860, 75th Congress, 3rd Session.

certain organizations are exempt from Federal income tax. Exempt status is not open-ended in that two general limitations exist. First, the nature or scope of the organization may result in it being only partially exempt from tax.[3] Second, the organization may engage in activities that are subject to special taxation.[4]

TYPES OF EXEMPT ORGANIZATIONS

An organization qualifies for exempt status *only* if it fits into one of the categories provided in the Code. Examples of qualifying exempt organizations and the specific statutory authority for their exempt status are listed in Figure 23–1.[5]

REQUIREMENTS FOR EXEMPT STATUS

Exempt status frequently requires more than mere classification in one of the categories of exempt organizations. Many of the organizations that qualify for exempt status share the following characteristics:

- The organization serves some type of *common good.*[6]
- The organization is a *not for profit* entity.[7]
- *Net earnings* do not benefit the members of the organization.[8]
- The organization does not exert *political influence.*[9]

Serving the Common Good

The underlying rationale for all exempt organizations is that they serve some type of *common good.* However, depending on the type of the exempt organization, the term *common good* may be interpreted broadly or narrowly. If interpreted broadly, the group being served is the general public or some large subgroup thereof. If interpreted narrowly, the group is the specific group referred to in the statutory language. One of the factors in classifying an exempt organization as a private foundation is the size of the group it serves.

Not for Profit Entity

The organization may not be organized or operated for the purpose of making a profit. For some types of exempt organizations, the *for-profit prohibition* appears in the statutory language. For other types, the prohibition is implied.

---

3. See the subsequent discussion of Unrelated Business Taxable Income.
4. See the subsequent discussions of Prohibited Transactions and Taxes Imposed on Private Foundations.
5. Section 501(a) provides for exempt status for organizations described in §§ 401 and 501. The orientation of this chapter is toward organizations that conduct business activities. Therefore, the exempt organizations described in § 401 (qualified pension, profit sharing, and stock bonus trusts) are outside the scope of the chapter and are not discussed.
6. See, for example, §§ 501(c)(3) and (4).
7. See, for example, §§ 501(c)(3), (4), (6), (13), and (14).
8. See, for example, §§ 501(c)(3), (6), (7), (9), (10), (11), and (19).
9. See, for example, § 501(c)(3).

Net Earnings and Members of the Organization

What uses are appropriate for the net earnings of tax-exempt organizations? The logical answer would seem to be that the earnings should be used for the exempt purpose of the organization. However, where the organization exists for the good

FIGURE 23–1 **Types of Exempt Organizations**

Statutory Authority	Brief Description	Examples or Comments
§ 501(c)(1)	Corporations that are instrumentalities of the United States.	Commodity Credit Corporation, Federal Deposit Insurance Corporation, Federal Land Bank.
§ 501(c)(2)	Corporations holding title to property for and paying income to exempt organizations.	Corporation holding title to college fraternity house.
§ 501(c)(3)	Religious, charitable, educational, scientific, literary, etc., organizations.	Boy Scouts of America, Red Cross, Salvation Army, Episcopal Church, United Fund, University of Richmond.
§ 501(c)(4)	Civic leagues and employee unions.	Garden club, tenants' association promoting tenants' legal rights in entire community, League of Women Voters.
§ 501(c)(5)	Labor, agricultural, and horticultural organizations.	Teachers' association, organization formed to promote effective agricultural pest control, organization formed to test soil and to educate community members in soil treatment, garden club.
§ 501(c)(6)	Business leagues, chambers of commerce, real estate boards, etc.	Chambers of commerce, American Plywood Association, medical association peer review board, organization promoting acceptance of women in business and professions.
§ 501(c)(7)	Social clubs.	Country club, rodeo and riding club, press club, bowling club, college fraternities.
§ 501(c)(8)	Fraternal beneficiary societies.	Must operate under the lodge system *and* must provide for the payment of life, sickness, accident, or other benefits to members or their dependents.
§ 501(c)(9)	Voluntary employees' beneficiary associations.	Purpose is to provide for the payment of life, sickness, accident, or other benefits to members, their dependents, or their designated beneficiaries.
§ 501(c)(10)	Domestic fraternal societies.	Must operate under the lodge system; must not provide for the payment of life, sickness, accident, or other benefits; and must devote the net earnings exclusively to religious, charitable, scientific, literary, educational, and fraternal purposes.
§ 501(c)(11)	Local teachers' retirement fund associations.	Only permitted sources of income are amounts received from (1) public taxation, (2) assessments on teaching salaries of members, and (3) income from investments.
§ 501(c)(12)	Local benevolent life insurance associations, mutual or cooperative telephone companies, etc.	Local cooperative telephone company, local mutual water company, local mutual electric company.
§ 501(c)(13)	Cemetery companies.	Must be operated exclusively for the benefit of lot owners who hold the lots for burial purposes.
§ 501(c)(14)	Credit unions.	Excludes Federal credit unions that are exempt under § 501(c)(1).
§ 501(c)(15)	Mutual insurance companies.	Mutual fire insurance company, mutual automobile insurance company.
§ 501(c)(16)	Corporations organized by farmers' cooperatives for financing crop operations.	Related farmers' cooperative must be exempt from tax under § 521.
§ 501(c)(19)	Armed forces members' posts or organizations.	Veterans of Foreign Wars (VFW), Reserve Officers Association.
§ 501(c)(20)	Group legal service plans' organizations.	Group legal service plan provided by a corporation for its employees.
§ 501(d)	Religious and apostolic organizations.	Communal organization. Members must include pro rata share of the net income of the organization in their gross income as dividends.
§ 501(e)	Cooperative hospital service organizations.	Centralized purchasing organization for exempt hospitals.
§ 501(f)	Cooperative service organization of educational institutions.	Organization formed to manage universities' endowment funds.

of a specific group of members, such an open-ended interpretation could permit net earnings to benefit specific group members. Therefore, the Code specifically prohibits certain types of exempt organizations from using their earnings in this way.

> . . . no part of the net earnings . . . inures to the benefit of any private shareholder or individual . . .[10]

In other instances, a statutory prohibition is unnecessary because the definition of the exempt organization in the Code effectively prevents such use.

> . . . the net earnings of which are devoted exclusively to religious, charitable, scientific, literary, educational, and fraternal purposes . . .[11]

Political Influence

Religious, charitable, educational, etc., organizations are generally prohibited from attempting to influence legislation or participate in political campaigns. Participation in political campaigns includes participation both *on behalf of* a candidate and *in opposition to* a candidate.

Only in limited circumstances are such exempt organizations permitted to attempt to influence legislation. See the subsequent discussion under Prohibited Transactions.

Tax Consequences of Exempt Status: General

An organization that is appropriately classified as one of the types of exempt organizations is generally exempt from Federal income tax. Four exceptions to this general statement exist, however. An exempt organization that engages in a *prohibited transaction,* or is a so-called *feeder organization* is subject to tax. If the organization is classified as a *private foundation,* it may be partially subject to tax. Finally, an exempt organization is subject to tax on its *unrelated business taxable income* (which includes unrelated debt-financed income).

In addition to being exempt from Federal income tax, an exempt organization may be eligible for other benefits, including the following:

- The organization may be exempt from state income tax, state franchise tax, sales tax, or property tax.
- The organization may receive discounts on postage rates.
- Donors of property to the exempt organization may qualify for charitable contribution deductions on their Federal and state income tax returns.

Note, however, that *not* all exempt organizations are qualified charitable contribution recipients (e.g., the National Football League).

Prohibited Transactions

Engaging in a prohibited transaction can produce two potential results. First, part or all of the organization's income may be subject to Federal income tax. Even worse, the organization may forfeit its exempt status.

---

10. § 501(c)(6).

11. § 501(c)(10).

Failure to Continue to Qualify. Organizations initially qualify for exempt status only if they qualify as a type of exempt organization under § 501. The initial qualification requirements then effectively become maintenance requirements. Failure to continue to meet the qualifying requirements results in the loss of exempt status.

Election Not to Forfeit Exempt Status for Lobbying. Organizations exempt under § 501(c)(3) (religious, charitable, educational, etc., organizations) generally are prohibited from attempting to influence legislation (lobbying activities) or from participating in political campaigns.[12] Any violation can result in the forfeiture of exempt status.

Certain § 501(c)(3) exempt organizations are permitted to engage in lobbying activities on a limited basis.[13] Eligible for such treatment are most § 501(c)(3) exempt organizations (educational institutions, hospitals, and medical research organizations; organizations supporting government schools; organizations publicly supported by charitable contributions; certain organizations that are publicly supported by various sources including admissions, sales, gifts, grants, contributions, or membership fees; and certain organizations that support certain types of public charities). Churches, their integrated auxiliaries, and private foundations are not permitted to engage in lobbying activities, however.

The lobbying expenditures of electing § 501(c)(3) organizations are subject to a ceiling. Exceeding the ceiling can lead to the forfeiture of exempt status. Even when the ceiling is not exceeded, a tax may be imposed on some of the lobbying expenditures (discussed subsequently).

Two terms are key to the calculation of the ceiling amount: *lobbying expenditures* and *grass roots expenditures.* Lobbying expenditures are made for the purpose of influencing legislation through either of the following.

- Attempting to affect the opinions of the general public or any segment thereof.
- Communicating with any legislator or staff member or with any government official or staff member who may participate in the formulation of legislation.

Grass roots expenditures are made for the purpose of influencing legislation through attempting to affect the opinions of the general public or any segment thereof.

A statutory ceiling is imposed on both lobbying expenditures and grass roots expenditures.

- 150% × lobbying nontaxable amount = lobbying expenditures ceiling.
- 150% × grass roots nontaxable amount = grass roots expenditures ceiling.

A tax may be assessed on an electing exempt organization's *excess lobbying expenditures.*[14]

- 25% × excess lobbying expenditures = tax liability.

Excess lobbying expenditures are the greater of the following.[15]

- Excess of the lobbying expenditures for the taxable year over the lobbying nontaxable amount.
- Excess of the grass roots expenditures for the taxable year over the grass roots nontaxable amount.

---

12. § 501(c)(3).

13. § 501(h). An affirmative election to lobby must be made.

14. § 4911(a)(1).

15. § 4911(b).

Exempt Purpose Expenditures	Lobbying Nontaxable Amount Is
Not over $500,000	20% of exempt purpose expenditures*
Over $500,000 but not over $1,000,000	$100,000 + 15% of the excess of exempt purpose expenditures over $500,000
Over $1,000,000 but not over $1,500,000	$175,000 + 10% of the excess of exempt purpose expenditures over $1,000,000
Over $1,500,000	$225,000 + 5% of the excess of exempt purpose expenditures over $1,500,000

*Exempt purpose expenditures generally are the amounts paid or incurred for the taxable year to accomplish the following purposes: religious, charitable, scientific, literary, educational, fostering national or international amateur sports competition, or the prevention of cruelty to children or animals.

FIGURE 23–2
Calculation of Lobbying Nontaxable Amount

The *lobbying nontaxable amount* is the lesser of (1) $1,000,000 or (2) the amount determined in Figure 23–2.[16] The *grass roots nontaxable amount* is 25 percent of the lobbying nontaxable amount.[17]

EXAMPLE 1

Tan, Inc., a qualifying § 501(c)(3) organization, incurs lobbying expenditures of $500,000 for the taxable year and grass roots expenditures of $0. Exempt purpose expenditures for the taxable year are $5,000,000. Tan elects to be eligible to make lobbying expenditures on a limited basis.

Applying the data in Figure 23–2, the lobbying nontaxable amount is $400,000 [$225,000 + 5% ($5,000,000 – $1,500,000)]. The ceiling on lobbying expenditures is $600,000 (150% × $400,000). Therefore, the $500,000 of lobbying expenditures are within the permitted ceiling of $600,000. However, the election results in the imposition of tax on the excess lobbying expenditures of $100,000 ($500,000 lobbying expenditures – $400,000 lobbying nontaxable amount). The resulting tax liability is $25,000 ($100,000 × 25%). ◆

A § 501(c)(3) organization that makes disqualifying lobbying expenditures is subject to a 5 percent tax on the lobbying expenditures for the taxable year. A 5 percent tax may also be levied on the organization's management. The tax is imposed on management only if the managers knew that making the expenditures was likely to result in the organization no longer qualifying under § 501(c)(3) and if the managers' actions were willful and not due to reasonable cause. The tax does not apply to private foundations (see the subsequent discussion).[18]

Concept Summary 23–1 summarizes the rules on influencing legislation.

CONCEPT SUMMARY 23–1
EXEMPT ORGANIZATIONS AND INFLUENCING LEGISLATION

Factor	Tax Result
Entity subject to rule	§ 501(c)(3) organization.
Effect of influencing legislation	Subject to tax on lobbying expenditures under § 4912. Forfeit exempt status under § 501(c)(3). Not eligible for exempt status under § 501(c)(4).
Effect of electing to make limited lobbying expenditures	Subject to tax under § 4911.

16. § 4911(c)(2).
17. § 4911(c)(4).
18. § 4912.

Feeder Organizations

A *feeder organization* carries on a trade or business for the benefit of an exempt organization (remits its profits to the exempt organization). Such organizations are not exempt from Federal income tax. This provision is intended to prevent an entity whose primary purpose is to conduct a trade or business for profit from escaping taxation merely because all of its profits are payable to one or more exempt organizations.[19]

Some income and activities are *not* subject to the feeder organization rules:[20]

- Rent income that would be excluded from the definition of the term *rent* for purposes of the unrelated business income tax (discussed subsequently).
- A trade or business where substantially all the work is performed by volunteers.
- The trade or business of selling merchandise where substantially all the merchandise has been received as contributions or gifts.

Concept Summary 23–2 summarizes the consequences of exempt status.

PRIVATE FOUNDATIONS

Tax Consequences of Private Foundation Status

Certain exempt organizations are classified as private foundations. This classification produces two negative consequences. First, the classification may have an adverse impact on the contributions received by the donee exempt organization. Contributions may decline because the tax consequences for donors may not be as favorable as they would be if the exempt organization were not a private foundation.[21] Second, the classification may result in taxation at the exempt

CONCEPT SUMMARY 23–2
CONSEQUENCES OF EXEMPT STATUS

General	Exempt from Federal income tax.
	Exempt from most state and local income, franchise, sales, and property taxes.
	Qualify for reductions in postage rates.
	Gifts to the organization often can be deducted by donor.
Exceptions	May be subject to Federal income tax associated with the following. ■ Engaging in a prohibited transaction. ■ Being a feeder organization. ■ Being a private foundation. ■ Generating unrelated business taxable income.

19. § 502(a).
20. § 502(b).
21. § 170(e)(1)(B)(ii).

organization level. The reason for this less beneficial tax treatment is that private foundations define common good more narrowly and therefore are seen as not being supported by, and operated for the good of, the public.

Definition of a Private Foundation. The following § 501(c)(3) organizations are *not* private foundations.[22]

1. Churches; educational institutions; hospitals and medical research organizations; charitable organizations receiving a major portion of their support from the general public or the United States, a state, or a political subdivision thereof that is operated for the benefit of a college or university; and governmental units (favored activities category).
2. Organizations that are broadly supported by the general public (excluding disqualified persons), by governmental units, or by organizations described in (1) above.
3. Organizations organized and operated exclusively for the benefit of organizations described in (1) or (2) (a supporting organization).
4. Organizations organized and operated exclusively for testing for public safety.

To meet the broadly supported requirement in (2) above, both the following tests must be satisfied.

- External support test.
- Internal support test.

Under the *external support test,* more than one-third of the organization's support each taxable year *normally* must come from the three groups listed in (2) above, in the following forms.

- Gifts, grants, contributions, and membership fees.
- Gross receipts from admissions, sales of merchandise, performance of services, or the furnishing of facilities in an activity that is not an unrelated trade or business for purposes of the unrelated business income tax (discussed subsequently). However, such gross receipts from any person or governmental agency in excess of the greater of $5,000 or 1 percent of the organization's support for the taxable year are not counted.

The *internal support test* limits the amount of support *normally* received from the following sources to one-third of the organization's support for the taxable year.[23]

- Gross investment income (gross income from interest, dividends, rents, and royalties).
- Unrelated business taxable income (discussed subsequently) minus the related tax.

---

22. § 509(a).

23. Regulation § 1.509(a)–3(c) generally requires that the external and internal support tests be met in each of the four preceding tax years.

EXAMPLE 2

Lion, Inc., a § 501(c)(3) organization, received the following support during the taxable year.

Governmental unit A for services rendered	$30,000
Governmental unit B for services rendered	20,000
General public for services rendered	20,000
Gross investment income	15,000
Contributions from individual substantial contributors (disqualified persons)	15,000

For purposes of the *external support test,* the support from governmental unit A is counted only to the extent of $5,000 (greater of $5,000 or 1% of $100,000 support). Likewise, for governmental unit B, only $5,000 is counted as support. Thus, the total countable support is $30,000 ($20,000 from the general public + $5,000 + $5,000), and the result is 30% ($30,000/$100,000). The $15,000 received from disqualified persons is excluded from the numerator but is included in the denominator. Thus, Lion fails the test for the taxable year.

In calculating the *internal support test,* only the gross investment income of $15,000 is included in the numerator. Thus, the test is satisfied ($15,000/$100,000 = 15%) for the taxable year.

Since Lion did not satisfy both tests, it does not qualify as an organization that is broadly supported. ◆

The intent of the two tests is to exclude from private foundation status those § 501(c)(3) organizations that are responsive to the general public rather than to the private interests of a limited number of donors or other persons.

Examples of § 501(c)(3) organizations that are properly classified as private foundations receiving broad public support include the United Fund, the Boy Scouts, university alumni associations, symphony orchestras, and the PTA.

Taxes Imposed on Private Foundations

In general, a private foundation is exempt from Federal income tax. However, because a private foundation is usually not a broadly, publicly supported organization, it may be subject to the following taxes.[24]

- Tax based on investment income.
- Tax on self-dealing.
- Tax on failure to distribute income.
- Tax on excess business holdings.
- Tax on investments that jeopardize charitable purposes.
- Tax on taxable expenditures.

These taxes serve to restrict the permitted activities of private foundations. Two levels of tax may be imposed on the private foundation and the foundation manager: an initial tax and an additional tax. The initial taxes (first-level), with the exception of the tax based on investment income, are imposed because the private foundation engages in so-called *prohibited transactions.* The additional taxes (second-level) are imposed only if the prohibited transactions are not modified within a statutory time period.[25] See Concept Summary 23–3 for additional details. The tax on a failure to distribute income will be used to

24. §§ 4941–4945.

25. § 4961.

illustrate how expensive these taxes can be and the related importance of avoiding their imposition. For failure to distribute a sufficient portion of a private nonoperating foundation's income, both an initial tax (first-level) and an additional tax (second-level) may be imposed. The initial tax is imposed at a rate of 15 percent on the income for the taxable year that is not distributed during the current or the following taxable year. The initial tax is imposed on the undistributed income for each year until the IRS assesses the tax.

The additional tax is imposed at a rate of 100 percent on the amount of the inadequate distribution that is not distributed by the assessment date. The additional tax is effectively waived if the undistributed income is distributed within 90 days after the mailing of the deficiency notice for the additional tax. Extensions of this period may be obtained.

Undistributed income is the excess of the distributable amount (in effect, the amount that should have been distributed) over qualifying distributions made by the entity. The distributable amount is the excess of the minimum investment return over the sum of the (1) unrelated business income tax and (2) the excise tax based on net investment income.[26] The minimum investment return is 5

CONCEPT SUMMARY 23–3
TAXES IMPOSED ON PRIVATE FOUNDATIONS

Type of Tax	Code Section	Purpose	Private Foundation Initial Tax	Private Foundation Additional Tax	Foundation Manager Initial Tax	Foundation Manager Additional Tax
On investment income	§ 4940	Audit fee to defray IRS expenses.	2%*			
On self-dealing	§ 4941	Engaging in transactions with disqualified persons.	5%**	200%**	2.5%†	50%†
On failure to distribute income	§ 4942	Failing to distribute adequate amount of income for exempt purposes.	15%	100%		
On excess business holdings	§ 4943	Investments that enable the private foundation to control unrelated businesses.	5%	200%		
On jeopardizing investments	§ 4944	Speculative investments that put the private foundation's assets at risk.	5%	25%	5%††	5%†
On taxable expenditures	§ 4945	Expenditures that should not be made by private foundations.	10%	100%	2.5%††	50%†

*May be possible to reduce the tax rate to 1%. In addition, an exempt operating foundation [see §§ 4940(d)(2) and 4942(j)(3)] is not subject to the tax.

**Imposed on the disqualified person rather than the foundation.

†Subject to a statutory ceiling of $10,000.

††Subject to a statutory ceiling of $5,000.

26. § 4940.

percent of the excess of the fair market value of the foundation's assets over the unpaid debt associated with acquiring or improving these assets. Assets of the foundation that are employed directly in carrying on the foundation's exempt purpose are not used in making this calculation.

EXAMPLE 3

Gold, Inc., a private foundation, has undistributed income of $80,000 for its taxable year 1990. It distributes $15,000 of this amount during 1991 and an additional $45,000 during 1992. The IRS deficiency notice is mailed to Gold on August 5, 1993. The initial tax is $12,750 [($65,000 × 15%) + ($20,000 × 15%)].

At the date of the deficiency notice, no additional distributions have been made from the 1990 undistributed income. Therefore, since the remaining undistributed income of $20,000 has not been distributed by August 5, 1993, an additional tax of $20,000 ($20,000 × 100%) is imposed.

If Gold distributes the $20,000 of undistributed income for 1990 within 90 days of the deficiency notice, the additional tax is waived. Without this distribution, however, the foundation will owe $32,750 ($12,750 + $20,000) in taxes. ◆

UNRELATED BUSINESS INCOME TAX

As explained in the previous section, private foundations are subject to excise taxes for certain actions. One of these excise taxes penalizes the private foundation for using the foundation to gain control of unrelated businesses (tax on excess business holdings). However, *unrelated business* has different meanings for purposes of that excise tax and for unrelated business income tax.

The tax on unrelated business income treats the entity as if it were subject to the corporate income tax. Thus, the rates that are used are those applicable to a corporate taxpayer.[27] In general, *unrelated business income* is derived from activities not related to the exempt purpose of the exempt organization, and the tax is levied because the organization is engaging in substantial commercial activities.[28] Without such a tax, nonexempt organizations (regular taxable business entities) would be at a substantial disadvantage when trying to compete with the exempt organization. Thus, the unrelated business income tax is intended to neutralize the exempt entity's tax advantage.[29]

EXAMPLE 4

Historic, Inc., is an exempt private foundation. Its exempt activity is to maintain a restoration of eighteenth-century colonial life (houses, public buildings, taverns, businesses, and craft demonstrations) that is visited by over a million people each year. A fee is charged for admission to the "restored area." In addition to this "museum" activity, Historic operates two hotels and three restaurants that are available to the general public. The earnings from the hotel and restaurant business are used to defray the costs of operating the "museum" activity.

The "museum" activity is not subject to the Federal income tax, except to the extent of any tax liability for any of the aforementioned excise taxes that are levied on private foundations. However, even though the income from the hotel and restaurant business is used for exempt purposes, that income is unrelated business income and is subject to the tax on unrelated business income. ◆

27. § 511(a)(1).
28. § 512(a)(1).
29. Reg. § 1.513–1(b).

The tax on unrelated business income applies to all organizations that are exempt from Federal income tax under § 501(c), except Federal agencies. In addition, the tax applies to state colleges and universities.[30]

A materiality exception generally exempts an entity from being subject to the unrelated business income tax if such income is insignificant. See the later discussion of the $1,000 statutory deduction generally available to all exempt organizations.

Unrelated Trade or Business

An exempt organization may be subject to the tax on unrelated business income in the following circumstances.[31]

- The organization conducts a trade or business.
- The trade or business is not substantially related to the exempt purpose of the organization.
- The trade or business is regularly carried on by the organization.

The Code specifically excepts the following activities from classification as an unrelated trade or business. Thus, even if all of the above factors are present, the activity is not classified as an unrelated trade or business.[32]

- The individuals performing substantially all the work of the trade or business do so without compensation (e.g., an orphanage operates a retail store for sales to the general public, and all the work is done by volunteers).
- The trade or business consists of selling merchandise, and substantially all of the merchandise has been received as gifts or contributions (e.g., thrift shops).
- For § 501(c)(3) organizations and for state colleges or universities, the trade or business is conducted primarily for the convenience of the organization's members, students, patients, officers, or employees (e.g., a laundry operated by the college for laundering dormitory linens and students' clothing, a college bookstore).
- For most employee unions, the trade or business consists of selling to members, at their usual place of employment, work-related clothing and equipment and items normally sold through vending machines, snack bars, or food dispensing facilities.

Definition of Trade or Business. Trade or business, for this purpose, is broadly defined. It includes any activity conducted for the production of income through the sale of merchandise or the performance of services. An activity need not generate a profit to be treated as a trade or business. The activity may be part of a larger set of activities conducted by the organization, some of which may be related to the exempt purpose. Being included in a larger set does not cause the activity to lose its identity as an unrelated trade or business.[33]

EXAMPLE 5

Health, Inc., is an exempt hospital that operates a pharmacy. The pharmacy provides medicines and supplies to the patients in the hospital (i.e., it contributes to the conduct

30. § 511(a)(2) and Reg. § 1.511–2(a)(2).

31. § 513(a) and Reg. § 1.513–2(a).

32. § 513(a).

33. Reg. § 1.513–1(b).

of the hospital's exempt purpose). In addition, the pharmacy sells medicines and supplies to the general public. The activity of selling to the general public constitutes a trade or business for purposes of the unrelated business income tax. ◆

Not Substantially Related to the Exempt Purpose. Exempt organizations frequently conduct unrelated trades or businesses in order to provide income to help defray the costs of conducting the exempt purpose (like the hotel and restaurant business in Example 4). Providing financial support for the exempt purpose will not prevent an activity from being classified as an unrelated trade or business and thereby being subject to the tax on unrelated business income.

To be related to the accomplishment of the exempt purpose, the conduct of the business activities must be causally related and contribute importantly to the exempt purpose. Whether a causal relationship exists and the degree of its importance are determined by examining the facts and circumstances. One must consider the size and extent of the activities in relation to the nature and extent of the exempt function that the activities serve.[34]

EXAMPLE 6

Art, Inc., an exempt organization, operates a school for training children in the performing arts. As an essential part of that training, the children perform for the general public. The children are paid at the minimum wage for the performances, and Art derives gross income by charging admission to the performances.

The income from admissions is not income from an unrelated trade or business, because the performances by the children contribute importantly to the accomplishment of the exempt purpose of providing training in the performing arts. ◆

EXAMPLE 7

Assume the facts are the same as in Example 6, except that four performances are conducted each weekend of the year. Assume that this number of performances far exceeds that required for training the children. Thus, the part of the income derived from admissions for these excess performances is income from an unrelated trade or business. ◆

The trade or business may sell merchandise that has been produced as part of the accomplishment of the exempt purpose. The sale of such merchandise is normally treated as related to the exempt purpose. However, if the merchandise is not sold in substantially the same state it was in at the completion of the exempt purpose, the gross income subsequently derived from the sale of the merchandise is income from an unrelated trade or business.[35]

EXAMPLE 8

Help, Inc., an exempt organization, conducts programs for the rehabilitation of the handicapped. One of the programs includes training in radio and television repair. Help derives gross income by selling the repaired items. The income is substantially related to the accomplishment of the exempt purpose. ◆

An asset or facility used in the exempt purpose may also be used in a nonexempt purpose. Income derived from the use for a nonexempt purpose is income from an unrelated trade or business.[36]

34. Reg. § 1.513–1(d).

35. Reg. § 1.513–1(d)(4)(ii).

36. Regulation § 1.513–1(d)(4)(iii) addresses the allocation of expenses to exempt and nonexempt activities.

EXAMPLE 9

Civil, Inc., an exempt organization, operates a museum. As part of the exempt purpose of the museum, educational lectures are given in the museum's theater during the operating hours of the museum. In the evening, when the museum is closed, the theater is leased to an individual who operates a movie theater. The lease income received from the individual who operates the movie theater is income from an unrelated trade or business. ◆

Special Rule for Bingo Games. A special provision applies in determining whether income from bingo games is from an unrelated trade or business. Under this provision, a *qualified bingo game* is not an unrelated trade or business if both of the following requirements are satisfied.[37]

- The bingo game is legal under both state and local law.
- Commercial bingo games (conducted for a profit motive) ordinarily are not permitted in the jurisdiction.

EXAMPLE 10

Play, Inc., an exempt organization, conducts weekly bingo games. The laws of the state and municipality in which Play conducts the games expressly provide that exempt organizations may conduct bingo games, but do not permit profit-oriented entities to do so. Since both of the requirements for bingo games are satisfied, the bingo games conducted by Play are not an unrelated trade or business. ◆

EXAMPLE 11

Game, Inc., an exempt organization, conducts weekly bingo games in City X and City Y. State law expressly permits exempt organizations to conduct bingo games. State law also provides that profit-oriented entities may conduct bingo games in X, which is a resort community. Several businesses regularly conduct bingo games there.

The bingo games conducted by Game in Y are not an unrelated trade or business. However, the bingo games that Game conducts in X are an unrelated trade or business, because commercial bingo games are regularly permitted to be conducted there. ◆

Special Rule for Distribution of Low-Cost Articles. If an exempt organization distributes low-cost items as an incidental part of its solicitation for charitable contributions, the distributions may not be considered an unrelated trade or business. A low-cost article is one that costs $5 (to be indexed) or less. Examples are pens, stamps, stickers, stationery, and address labels. If more than one item is distributed to a person during the calendar year, the costs of the items are combined.[38]

Special Rule for Rental or Exchange of Membership Lists. If an exempt organization conducts a trade or business that consists of either exchanging with or renting to other exempt organizations the organization's donor or membership list (mailing lists), the activity is not an unrelated trade or business.[39]

Other Special Rules. Other special rules are used in determining whether each of the following activities is an unrelated trade or business.[40]

- Qualified public entertainment activities (e.g., a state fair).
- Qualified convention and trade show activities.

37. § 513(f).
38. § 513(h)(1)(A).
39. § 513(h)(1)(B).
40. §§ 513(d), (e), and (g).

- Certain services provided at cost or less by a hospital to other small hospitals.
- Certain pole rentals by telephone or electric companies.

Discussion of these special rules is beyond the scope of this text.

Unrelated Business Income

Even when an exempt organization conducts an unrelated trade or business, a tax is assessed only if the exempt organization regularly conducts the activity and the business produces unrelated business income.

Regularly Carried on by the Organization. An activity is classified as unrelated business income only if it is regularly carried on by the exempt organization. This provision assures that only activities that are actually competing with taxable organizations are subject to the unrelated business income tax. Accordingly, factors to be considered in assessing *regularly carried on* include the frequency of the activity, the continuity of the activity, and the manner in which the activity is pursued.[41]

EXAMPLE 12

Silver, Inc., an exempt organization, owns land that is located next to the state fairgrounds. During the 10 days of the state fair, Silver uses the land as a parking lot and charges individuals attending the state fair for parking there. The activity is not regularly carried on. ◆

EXAMPLE 13

Black, Inc., an exempt organization, has its offices in the downtown area. It owns a parking lot adjacent to its offices on which its employees park during the week. On Saturdays, it rents the spaces in the parking lot to individuals shopping or working in the downtown area. Black is conducting a business activity on a year-round basis, even though it is only for one day per week. Thus, an activity is regularly being carried on. ◆

Unrelated Business Income Defined. Unrelated business income is generally that derived from the unrelated trade or business. To convert it from a gross income measure to a net income measure, it must be reduced by the deductions directly connected with the conduct of the unrelated trade or business.[42]

Unrelated Business Taxable Income

General Tax Model. The model for unrelated business taxable income appears in Figure 23–3.

Positive adjustments[43]

1. The charitable contribution deduction is permitted without regard to whether the charitable contributions are associated with the unrelated trade or business. However, to the extent the charitable contributions

41. § 512(a)(1) and Reg. § 1.513–1(c).
42. § 512(a)(1).
43. §§ 512(a)(1) and (b) and Reg. § 1.512(b)–1.

deducted in calculating net unrelated business income (see Figure 23–3) exceed 10 percent of unrelated business taxable income (without regard to the charitable contribution deduction), the excess is treated as a positive adjustment.

EXAMPLE 14

Brown, Inc., an exempt organization, has unrelated business taxable income of $100,000 (excluding the charitable contribution deduction). Total charitable contributions (all associated with the unrelated trade or business) are $13,000. Assuming that the $13,000 is deducted in calculating net unrelated business income, the excess of $3,000 [$13,000 – 10% ($100,000)] is a positive adjustment in calculating unrelated business taxable income. ◆

2. Unrelated debt-financed income net of the unrelated debt-financed deductions (see the subsequent discussion of Unrelated Debt-Financed Income).
3. Certain interest, annuity, royalty, and rent income received by the exempt organization from an organization it controls (80 percent test). Note that this provision overrides the modifications for these types of income (point 3 under negative adjustments).

Negative adjustments

1. Income from dividends, interest, and annuities net of all deductions directly related to producing such income.
2. Royalty income, regardless of whether it is measured by production, gross income, or taxable income from the property, net of all deductions directly related to producing such income.
3. Rent income from real property and from certain personal property net of all deductions directly related to producing such income. Personal property rents are included in the negative adjustment only if the personal property is leased with the real property. In addition, the personal property rent income is ignored if it exceeds 10 percent of the total rent income under the lease. In both of the following cases, however, none of the rent income is treated as a negative adjustment.

   - More than 50 percent of the rent income under the lease is from personal property.
   - Rent income is calculated using the tenant's profits.

EXAMPLE 15

Beaver, Inc., an exempt organization, leases land and a building (realty) and computers (personalty) housed in the building. Under the lease, $46,000 of the rent is for the land and building, and $4,000 is for the computers. Expenses incurred for the land and building are $10,000. The net rent income from the land and building of $36,000 ($46,000 – $10,000) and the $4,000 from the computers are negative adjustments. ◆

FIGURE 23–3
Tax Formula for Unrelated Business Taxable Income

Gross unrelated business income
– Deductions
= Net unrelated business income
± Modifications
= Unrelated business taxable income

EXAMPLE 16

Assume the same facts as in Example 15, except that the rent income is $35,000 from the land and building and $15,000 from the computers. Since the rent income from the computers exceeds $5,000 (i.e., 10 percent of the total rent under the lease) and is not incidental, it is not a negative adjustment. ◆

EXAMPLE 17

Assume the same facts as in Example 15, except that the rent income is $20,000 from the land and building and $30,000 from the computers. Since over 50% of the rent income under the lease is from the computers, neither the rent income from the land and building nor that from the computers is a negative adjustment. ◆

4. Gains and losses from the sale, exchange, or other disposition of property *except for* inventory.

EXAMPLE 18

Beaver, the owner of the land, building, and computers in Example 15, sells these assets for $450,000. Their adjusted basis is $300,000. Beaver's recognized gain of $150,000 is a negative adjustment. ◆

5. Certain research income net of all deductions directly related to producing that income.
6. The charitable contribution deduction is permitted without regard to whether the charitable contributions are associated with the unrelated trade or business. Therefore, to the extent that the charitable contributions exceed those deducted in calculating net unrelated business income (see Figure 23–3), the excess is a negative adjustment in calculating unrelated business taxable income.

EXAMPLE 19

Canine, Inc., an exempt organization, has unrelated business taxable income of $100,000 (excluding the charitable contribution deduction). The total charitable contributions are $9,000, of which $7,000 (those associated with the unrelated trade or business) have been deducted in calculating net unrelated business income. Therefore, the remaining $2,000 of charitable contributions is deducted as a negative adjustment in calculating unrelated business taxable income. ◆

7. A specific deduction of $1,000 is permitted.

Unrelated Debt-Financed Income

In the formula for calculating the tax on unrelated business income (refer to Figure 23–3), unrelated debt-financed income is one of the positive adjustments. Examples of income from debt-financed property include the rental of real estate, rental of tangible personal property, and investments in corporate stock, including gains from the disposition of such property. Gains from property that is unrelated business income property are also included to the extent the gains are not otherwise treated as unrelated business income. Because of the importance of this item, it is discussed separately here.

Definition of Debt-Financed Income. *Debt-financed income* is the gross income generated from debt-financed property. *Debt-financed property* is all property of the exempt organization that is held to produce income and on which there is acquisition indebtedness, *except* for the following.[44]

44. § 514(b).

- Property where substantially all (at least 85 percent) of the use is for the achievement of the exempt purpose of the exempt organization.[45]
- Property whose gross income is otherwise treated as unrelated business income.
- Property whose gross income is from the following sources and is not otherwise treated as unrelated business income:

  1. Income from research performed for the United States, a Federal governmental agency, or a state or a political subdivision thereof.
  2. For a college, university, or hospital, income from research.
  3. For an organization that performs fundamental (as distinguished from applied) research for the benefit of the general public, income from research.

- Property used in a trade or business that is treated as not being an unrelated trade or business under one of the statutory exceptions (see page 23–13).

EXAMPLE 20

Deer, Inc., an exempt organization, owns a five-story office building on which there is acquisition indebtedness. Three of the floors are used for Deer's exempt purpose. The two other floors are leased to Purple Corporation. In this case, the *substantially all* test is not satisfied. Therefore, 40% of the office building is debt-financed property, and 60% is not. ◆

Certain land that is acquired by an exempt organization for later exempt use is excluded from debt-financed property if the following requirements are satisfied.[46]

- The principal purpose of acquiring the land is for (substantially all its) use in achieving the organization's exempt purpose.
- This use will begin within 10 years of the acquisition date.
- At the date when the land is acquired, it is located in the *neighborhood* of other property of the organization for which substantially all the use is for achieving the organization's exempt purpose.

Even if the third requirement is not satisfied (the property is not located in the neighborhood), the land still is excluded from debt-financed property if it is converted to use for achieving the organization's exempt purpose within the 10-year period. Qualification under this provision will result in a refund of taxes previously paid. If the exempt organization is a church, the 10-year period becomes a 15-year period, and the neighborhood requirement is waived.

Definition of Acquisition Indebtedness. Exempt organizations generally sustain acquisition indebtedness in association with the acquisition of property. More precisely, *acquisition indebtedness* consists of the unpaid amounts of the following for debt-financed property.[47]

---

45. Reg. § 1.514(b)–1(b)(1)(ii). If the 85% test is failed, the actual exempt-use percentage is excluded from debt-financed property.

46. § 514(b)(3).

47. § 514(c)(1). Educational organizations in certain limited circumstances can exclude debt incurred for real property acquisitions from classification as acquisition indebtedness.

- Debt incurred in acquiring or improving the property.
- Debt incurred before the property was acquired or improved, but which would not have been incurred without the acquisition or improvement.
- Debt incurred after the property was acquired or improved, but which would not have been incurred without the acquisition or improvement.

EXAMPLE 21

Red, Inc., an exempt organization, acquires land for $100,000. In order to finance the acquisition, Red mortgages the land with a bank and receives loan proceeds of $80,000. Red leases the land to Duck Corporation. The mortgage is acquisition indebtedness. ◆

EXAMPLE 22

Rose, Inc., an exempt organization, makes improvements to an office building that it rents to Bird Corporation. Excess working capital funds are used to finance the improvements. Rose is later required to mortgage its laboratory building, which it uses for its exempt purpose, to replenish working capital. The mortgage is acquisition indebtedness. ◆

Portion of Debt-Financed Income and Deductions Treated as Unrelated Business Taxable Income. Once the amount of the debt-financed income and deductions is determined, it is necessary to ascertain what portion of the debt-financed income and deductions is unrelated debt-financed income and deductions. Unrelated debt-financed income increases unrelated business taxable income, and unrelated debt-financed deductions decrease unrelated business taxable income.

The calculation is made for each debt-financed property. The gross income from the property is multiplied by the following percentage.[48]

$$\frac{\text{Average acquisition indebtedness for the property}}{\text{Average adjusted basis of the property}} = \begin{array}{c}\text{Debt/basis}\\ \text{percentage}\end{array}$$

This percentage cannot exceed 100. If debt-financed property is disposed of during the taxable year at a gain, average acquisition indebtedness in the formula is replaced with highest acquisition indebtedness. *Highest acquisition indebtedness* is the largest amount of acquisition indebtedness for the property during the 12-month period preceding the date of disposition.[49]

Deductions are allowed for expenses directly related to the debt-financed property and the income from it. However, depreciation deductions must apply the straight-line method. Once allowable deductions are determined, this amount is multiplied by the debt/basis percentage.[50]

EXAMPLE 23

White, Inc., an exempt organization, owns an office building that it leases to Squirrel Corporation for $120,000 per year. The average acquisition indebtedness is $300,000, and the average adjusted basis is $500,000. Since the office building is debt-financed property, the unrelated debt-financed income is:

$$\frac{\$300{,}000}{\$500{,}000} \times \$120{,}000 = \$72{,}000$$

◆

48. § 514(a)(1).
49. § 514(c)(7).
50. § 514(a)(3).

Average Acquisition Indebtedness. The *average acquisition indebtedness* for debt-financed property is the average amount of the outstanding debt for the taxable year (ignoring interest) during the portion of the year the property is held by the exempt organization. This amount is calculated by summing the outstanding debt on the first day of each calendar month the property is held by the exempt organization. Then this total is divided by the number of months the property is held by the organization. A partial month is treated as a full month.[51]

Example 24

On August 12, Yellow, Inc., an exempt organization, acquires an office building that is debt-financed property for $500,000. The initial mortgage on the property is $400,000. The principal amount of the debt on the first of each month is as follows.

Month	Principal Amount
August	$ 400,000
September	380,000
October	360,000
November	340,000
December	320,000
	$1,800,000

Average acquisition indebtedness is $360,000 ($1,800,000 ÷ 5 months). Note that even though August is only a partial month, it is treated as a full month. ◆

Average Adjusted Basis. The *average adjusted basis* of debt-financed property is calculated by summing the adjusted basis of the property on the first day during the taxable year the property is held by the exempt organization and the adjusted basis on the last day during the taxable year the property is held, and then dividing by two.[52]

Example 25

Assume the facts are the same as in Example 24. In addition, during the taxable year, depreciation of $5,900 is deducted. The average adjusted basis is $497,050 [($500,000 + $494,100) ÷ 2]. ◆

Concept Summary 23–4 summarizes the rules concerning the unrelated business income tax.

Reporting Requirements

Obtaining Exempt Organization Status

Not all exempt organizations are required to obtain IRS approval for their exempt status. Among those required by statute to do so are organizations exempt under §§ 501(c)(3), 501(c)(9), and 501(c)(20).[53] Even in these cases, exceptions are provided (e.g., churches).

51. § 514(c)(7) and Reg. § 1.514(a)–1(a)(3).

52. § 514(a)(1) and Reg. § 1.514(a)–1(a)(2).

53. §§ 505(c), 508(a), and 508(c).

Even when not required to obtain IRS approval, most exempt organizations do apply for exempt status. Typically, an organization does not want to assume that it qualifies for exempt status and describe itself in that way to the public, only to have the IRS rule later that it does not qualify.

If an organization is required to obtain IRS approval for its exempt status and does not do so, it does not qualify as an exempt organization.

Annual Filing Requirements

Most exempt organizations are required to file an annual information return.[54] The return is filed on Form 990 (Return of Organization Exempt from Income Tax). The following exempt organizations need not file Form 990.[55]

- Federal agencies.
- Churches.
- Organizations whose annual gross receipts do not exceed $25,000.
- Private foundations.

Private foundations are required to file Form 990–PF (Return of Private Foundation).

The due date for Form 990 or Form 990–PF is the fifteenth day of the fifth month after the end of the taxable year. These returns are filed with the appropriate IRS Service Center based on the location of the exempt organization's principal office. Requests for extensions on filing are made by filing Form 2758 (Applications for Extension of Time).

Concept Summary 23–4
Unrelated Business Income Tax

Purpose	To tax the entity on unrelated business income as if it were subject to the corporate income tax.
Applicable tax rates	Corporate tax rates.
Exempt organizations to which applicable	All organizations that are exempt under § 501(c) except corporations that are Federal agencies.
Entities subject to the tax	Organizations that regularly conduct a trade or business that is not substantially related to the exempt purpose of the organization.
Exceptions to the tax	**1.** All the work is performed by volunteers. **2.** Substantially all of the merchandise being sold has been received by gift. **3.** For § 501(c)(3) organizations, the business is conducted primarily for the benefit of the organization's members, students, patients, officers, or employees. **4.** For most employee unions, the trade or business consists of selling to members work-related clothing and equipment and items normally sold through vending machines, snack bars, or food dispensing facilities.
$1,000 provision	If the gross income from an unrelated trade or business is less than $1,000, it is not necessary to file a return associated with the unrelated business income tax.

54. § 6033(a)(1).

55. § 6033(a)(2).

EXAMPLE 26

Green, Inc., a § 501(c)(3) organization, has a fiscal year that ends June 30, 1993. The due date for the annual return is November 15, 1993. If Green were a calendar year entity, the due date for the 1993 annual return would be May 15, 1994. ◆

Exempt organizations that are subject to the unrelated business income tax may be required to file Form 990–T (Exempt Organization Business Income Tax Return). The return must be filed if the organization has gross income of at least $1,000 from an unrelated trade or business. The due date for the return is the fifteenth day of the fifth month after the end of the taxable year.

EXAMPLE 27

During the year, the First Church of Kentwood receives parishioner contributions of $450,000. Of this amount, $125,000 is designated as the church building fund. First Church is not required to file an annual return (Form 990) because churches are exempt from doing so. In addition, it is not required to file Form 990–T because it has no unrelated business income.

Colonial, Inc., is an exempt private foundation. Gross receipts for the year total $800,000, of which 60% is from admission fees paid by members of the general public who visit Colonial's museum of eighteenth-century life. The balance is endowment income. Because Colonial is a private foundation, it must file Form 990–PF.

Orange, Inc., is an exempt organization and is not a private foundation. Gross receipts for the year are $20,000. None of this amount is unrelated business income. Orange is not required to file Form 990 because its annual gross receipts do not exceed $25,000.

Restoration, Inc., is an exempt private foundation. Gross receipts for the year are $20,000. None of this amount is unrelated business income. Restoration must file Form 990–PF because private foundations are not eligible for the $25,000 filing exception.

During the year, the Second Church of Port Allen receives parishioner contributions of $300,000. In addition, the church has unrelated business income of $5,000. Second Church is not required to file Form 990 because churches are exempt from doing so. Form 990–T must be filed, however, because churches are not exempt from the unrelated business income tax and Second Church has exceeded the $1,000 floor. ◆

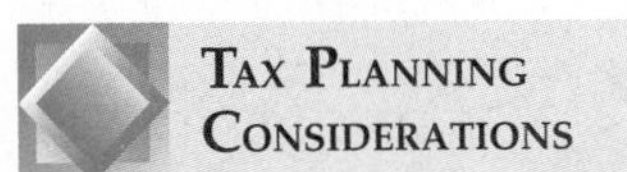

TAX PLANNING CONSIDERATIONS

General

Exempt organizations provide at least two potential tax benefits. First, the entity may be exempt from Federal income tax. Second, contributions to the entity may be deductible by the donor.

An organization that qualifies as an exempt organization may still be subject to certain types of Federal income tax, including the following.

- Tax on prohibited transactions.
- Tax on feeder organizations.
- Tax on private foundations.
- Tax on unrelated business income.

Therefore, classification as an exempt organization should not be interpreted to mean that the organization need not be concerned with any Federal income tax. Such a belief can result in the organization engaging in transactions that produce a substantial tax liability.

An organization is exempt from taxation only if it fits into one of the categories enumerated in the Code. Thus, particular attention must be given to the qualification requirements. These requirements must continue to be satisfied to avoid termination of exempt status.

Private Foundation Status

Exempt organizations that can qualify as public charities receive more beneficial tax treatment than those that qualify as private foundations. Thus, if possible, the organization should be structured to qualify as a public charity. The following can result when an exempt organization is classified as a private foundation.

- Taxes may be imposed on the private foundation.
  - Tax based on investment income.
  - Tax on self-dealing.
  - Tax on failure to distribute income.
  - Tax on excess business holdings.
  - Tax on investments that jeopardize charitable purposes.
  - Tax on taxable expenditures.
- Donors may receive less favorable tax deduction treatment under § 170 than they would if the exempt organization were not a private foundation.

EXAMPLE 28

David has IBM stock ($25,000 adjusted basis, $100,000 fair market value) that he is going to contribute to one of the following exempt organizations: Blue, Inc., a public charity, or Teal, Inc., a private nonoperating foundation. David has owned the stock for five years.

David asks the manager of each organization to describe the tax benefits of contributing to that organization. He tells them he is in the 31% tax bracket.

Based on the data provided by the managers, David decides to contribute the stock to Blue, Inc. He calculates the amount of the charitable contribution as follows.[56]

Donee	Contribution Deduction	Tax Rate	Contribution Borne by U.S. Government
Blue, Inc.	$100,000	31%	$31,000
Teal, Inc.	25,000 ($100,000 – $75,000)	31%	7,750

◆

CONCEPT SUMMARY 23–5
PRIVATE FOUNDATION STATUS

	Exempt Organization Is: A Private Foundation	Not a Private Foundation
Reason for classification	Does not serve the common good because it lacks an approved exempt purpose or does not receive broad public financial support.	Serves the common good
Eligible for exempt status?	Yes	Yes
Most beneficial charitable contribution deduction treatment available to donors?	Depends. No, if the private foundation is classified as a private *nonoperating* foundation.	Yes
Subject to excise taxes levied on prohibited transactions?	Yes	No
Subject to tax on unrelated business income?	Yes	Yes

56. See Chapter 10.

One method of avoiding private foundation status is to have a tax-exempt purpose that results in the organization not being classified as a private foundation (the *organization* approach). If this is not feasible, it may be possible to operate the organization so that it receives broad public support and thereby avoids private foundation status (the *operational* approach).

If the organization is a private foundation, care must be exercised to avoid the assessment of tax liability on prohibited transactions. This objective can best be achieved by establishing controls that prevent the private foundation from engaging in transactions that will trigger the imposition of the taxes. If an initial tax is assessed, corrective actions should be implemented to avoid the assessment of an additional tax. See Concept Summary 23–5 on the previous page.

Unrelated Business Income Tax

If the exempt organization conducts an unrelated trade or business, it may be subject to tax on the unrelated business income. Worse yet, the unrelated trade or business could result in the loss of exempt status if the IRS determines that the activity is the primary purpose of the organization. Thus, caution and planning should be used to eliminate the latter possibility and to minimize the former.

PROBLEM MATERIALS

DISCUSSION QUESTIONS

1. Are all churches exempt from Federal income tax?
2. Why are certain organizations either partially or completely exempt from Federal income tax?
3. What are the four general requirements for exempt status?
4. Under what circumstances may an exempt organization be subject to Federal income tax?
5. Religious organizations are generally prohibited from attempting to influence legislation or participating in political campaigns. Therefore, a church cannot participate in a political campaign on behalf of a candidate. Can a church participate in a political campaign *in opposition* to a political candidate?
6. Is a qualifying exempt organization ever subject to Federal income tax?
7. How can a § 501(c)(3) organization engage in lobbying without engaging in a prohibited transaction?
8. Aid, Inc., is a hospital that is exempt from Federal income tax under § 501(c)(3). Aid has made the required election to be permitted to engage in lobbying activities on a limited basis. It incurs lobbying expenditures, none of which are grass roots expenditures. Describe the tax to which Aid may be subject due to its lobbying activities.
9. What is a feeder organization, and why is it not exempt from Federal income tax?
10. What types of activities are not subject to the tax imposed on feeder organizations?
11. What is a private foundation, and what are the disadvantages of an exempt organization being classified as a private foundation?
12. Describe the internal support test for a private foundation.
13. What types of taxes may be levied on a private foundation? Why are the taxes levied?

14. A private foundation has net investment income of $50,000, yet its tax liability on net investment income is zero. Explain.
15. Describe the tax on excess business holdings including the purpose, rates, and on whom it is levied.
16. What is the purpose of the tax on unrelated business income?
17. What exempt organizations are subject to the tax on unrelated business income?
18. Can an exempt organization avoid the unrelated business income tax by using the profits generated from the unrelated trade or business to support the exempt purpose of the organization?
19. Under what circumstances can an exempt organization conduct bingo games and not have the income be treated as unrelated business income?
20. Under what circumstances can an exempt organization distribute low-cost articles and not have the activity be classified as an unrelated trade or business?
21. Passive income (e.g., interest, royalties, and annuities) generally is not unrelated business income. Under what circumstances do such items increase the amount of unrelated business taxable income?
22. What effect does unrelated debt-financed income have on unrelated business income?
23. Define each of the following with respect to unrelated debt-financed property:
    a. Debt-financed income.
    b. Debt-financed property.
    c. Acquisition indebtedness.
    d. Average acquisition indebtedness.
    e. Average adjusted basis.
24. Tom is the treasurer of the City Garden Club, a new garden club. A friend, who is the treasurer of the garden club in a neighboring community, tells Tom that it is not necessary for the garden club to file a request for exempt status with the IRS. Has Tom received correct advice?

PROBLEMS

25. Teach, Inc., a § 501(c)(3) educational institution, makes lobbying expenditures of $100,000. Teach incurs exempt purpose expenditures of $400,000 in carrying out its educational mission.
    a. Determine the tax consequences to Teach if it does not elect to be eligible to participate in lobbying activities on a limited basis.
    b. Determine the tax consequences to Teach if it does elect to be eligible to participate in lobbying activities on a limited basis.
26. Cardinal, Inc., a § 501(c)(3) organization, received support from the following sources.

Governmental unit A for services rendered	$ 4,000
General public for services rendered	60,000
Gross investment income	30,000
Contributions from disqualified persons	20,000
Contributions from other than disqualified persons	86,000

    a. Does Cardinal satisfy the test for receiving broad public support?
    b. Is Cardinal a private foundation?
27. Gray, Inc., a private foundation, has the following items of income and deductions.

Interest income	$10,000
Rent income	50,000
Dividend income	15,000
Royalty income	5,000

Unrelated business income	30,000
Rent expenses	12,000
Unrelated business expenses	7,000

Gray is not an exempt operating foundation and is not eligible for the 1% tax rate.

a. Calculate the net investment income.
b. Calculate the tax on net investment income.
c. What is the purpose of the tax on net investment income?

28. Eagle, Inc., is a private foundation that has been in existence for 10 years. During this period, it has been unable to satisfy the requirements for classification as a private operating foundation. At the end of 1992, it had undistributed income of $100,000. Of this amount, $40,000 was distributed in 1993, and $60,000 was distributed during the first quarter of 1994. The IRS deficiency notice was mailed on August 1, 1995.

a. Calculate the initial tax for 1992, 1993, and 1994.
b. Calculate the additional tax for 1995.

29. Fran is the foundation manager of Swan, Inc., a private foundation. James, a substantial contributor to Swan, engages in an act of self-dealing with the foundation. Fran is aware that the act is an act of self-dealing. The amount involved is $130,000.

a. Calculate the amount of the initial tax.
b. Calculate the amount of the additional tax if the act of self-dealing is not corrected within the correction period.

30. The board of directors of Pink, Inc., a private foundation, consists of Alice, Beth, and Carlos. They vote unanimously to provide a $100,000 grant to Doug, their business associate. The grant is to be used for travel and education and does not qualify as a permitted grant to individuals (i.e., it is a taxable expenditure under § 4945). Each director knows that Doug was selected for the grant because he is a friend of the organization and that the grant is a taxable expenditure.

a. Calculate the initial tax imposed on the private foundation.
b. Calculate the initial tax imposed on the foundation manager (i.e., board of directors).

31. A museum that is an exempt organization operates a gift shop. The annual operations budget of the museum is $2.5 million. Gift shop sales generate a profit of $750,000. Another $500,000 of endowment income is generated. Both the income from the gift shop and the endowment income are used to support the exempt purpose of the museum. The balance of $1.25 million required for annual operations is provided through admission fees.

a. Calculate the amount of unrelated business income.
b. Assume that the endowment income is reinvested rather than being used to support annual operations. Calculate the amount of unrelated business income.

32. Fish, Inc., an exempt organization, has unrelated business taxable income of $400,000 (excluding the deduction for charitable contributions). During the year, it makes charitable contributions of $45,000, of which $38,000 is associated with the unrelated trade or business.

a. Calculate unrelated business taxable income.
b. Assume that the charitable contributions are $39,000, of which $38,000 are associated with the unrelated trade or business. Calculate unrelated business taxable income.

33. Good, Inc., an exempt organization, leases a factory building, machinery, and equipment to Coal Corporation. Under the lease, the annual rent for the building is $150,000, and the rent for the machinery and equipment is $200,000. Depreciation on the building is $5,500, and depreciation on the machinery and equipment is $40,000.

a. Calculate the amount of unrelated business taxable income to Good.
b. Assume that the rent income from the machinery and equipment is only $20,000 and the related depreciation is $4,000. Calculate the amount of unrelated business taxable income to Good.

34. Grouse, Inc., an exempt organization, sells the following assets during the taxable year.

Asset	Gain (Loss)	Use
Building A	$ 40,000	In exempt purposes
Building B	(15,000)	Leased to Wall Corporation
Building C	30,000	In exempt purposes

Determine the effect of these transactions on unrelated business taxable income.

35. Dane, Inc., an exempt organization, leases a building to Dairy Corporation. The annual rent income is $150,000, and the annual depreciation expense is $30,000. Dane financed the initial acquisition of the building with a mortgage. Average acquisition indebtedness is $800,000. The adjusted basis of the building at the beginning of the taxable year is $900,000.

a. Calculate the unrelated debt-financed income and deductions.
b. Assume that, rather than leasing the building, Dane uses it in the performance of its exempt purpose. Calculate the unrelated debt-financed income and deductions.

36. Rodeo, Inc., is a social club that is exempt under § 501(c)(8). Its annual gross receipts are $250,000. Of this amount, $230,000 is from an unrelated trade or business. Rodeo's fiscal year ends on April 30.

a. Is Rodeo required to file an annual information return? If so, what form should be used?
b. Is Rodeo subject to the tax on unrelated business income? If so, what form should be used?
c. If tax returns must be filed, what are the due dates?

37. Historic Burg is an exempt organization that operates a museum depicting eighteenth-century life. Sally gives the museum an eighteenth-century chair that she has owned for 10 years. Her adjusted basis is $55,000, and the chair's appraised value is $100,000. Sally's adjusted gross income is $500,000.

a. Calculate Sally's charitable contribution deduction if Historic Burg is a private operating foundation.
b. Calculate Sally's charitable contribution deduction if Historic Burg is a private nonoperating foundation.

CHAPTER

TAXATION OF INTERNATIONAL TRANSACTIONS

OBJECTIVES

Describe the provisions of the foreign tax credit.

Explain the rules for sourcing income and allocating deductions.

Review U.S. taxation of nonresident aliens and foreign corporations.

Discuss U.S. taxation of foreign-source income of U.S. citizens and residents.

Summarize U.S. tax regarding controlled foreign corporations.

Discuss the tax treatment of foreign currency transactions.

OUTLINE

OVERVIEW OF INTERNATIONAL TAXATION

The U.S. government is not prohibited from taxing income earned outside the United States by U.S. persons, nor is it precluded from taxing income earned in the United States by non-U.S. persons. When the United States and another country both tax the income from an international transaction, double taxation may result. Knowledge of the laws and concepts applied by the United States in taxing international transactions, however, will aid taxpayers in arranging their transactions to minimize or eliminate double taxation.

This chapter covers U.S. Federal taxation of (1) transactions involving U.S. persons and foreign investment and (2) transactions involving foreign persons and U.S. investment. Tax planning suggestions are offered to aid taxpayers in minimizing the taxation of international transactions.

Significant Terminology

Some important terms related to U.S. international taxation include the following:

- *Effectively connected.* Income so designated is taxed differently than passive income that is not effectively connected with a U.S. trade or business.
- *Nonresident alien.* An individual must be both a nonresident and an alien to be classified as a non-U.S. person for Federal income tax purposes.
- *Controlled foreign corporation (CFC).* U.S. control of a foreign corporation can affect tax treatment under a number of tax law provisions. The CFC designation originated in Subpart F of the Internal Revenue Code.

THE FOREIGN TAX CREDIT

As previously noted, the United States retains the right to tax its citizens and residents on their worldwide taxable income. This approach can result in double taxation and presents a potential problem to U.S. persons who invest abroad.

EXAMPLE 1

Bob, a U.S. resident, has a business in Mexico from which he earns taxable income of $75,000 in 1993. He pays income tax of $20,000 on these earnings to the Mexican tax authorities. Bob must also include the $75,000 in gross income for U.S. tax purposes. Ignoring any foreign taxes he might pay, assume he would owe $21,000 in U.S. income taxes on this foreign-source income. This results in total taxes on the $75,000 of $41,000, or 55%. ◆

To reduce the possibility of double taxation, the U.S. Congress enacted the foreign tax credit (FTC) provisions. Under these provisions, a qualified taxpayer is allowed a tax credit for foreign income taxes paid. The credit is a dollar-for-dollar reduction of the U.S. income tax liability.

EXAMPLE 2

Bob in Example 1 takes an FTC of $20,000, reducing his U.S. tax liability on the foreign-source income to $1,000. Bob's total taxes on the $75,000 are $21,000. ◆

The Credit Provisions

The Direct Credit. Section 901 provides a direct FTC to U.S. taxpayers who pay or incur a foreign income tax. For purposes of the direct credit, only the taxpayer who bears the legal incidence of the foreign tax is eligible for the credit. Bob, in Example 1 above, would be eligible for the direct credit.

The Indirect Credit. If a U.S. corporation operates in a foreign country through a branch, the direct credit is available for foreign taxes paid. If, however, a U.S. corporation operates in a foreign country through a foreign subsidiary, the direct credit is not available for foreign taxes paid by the foreign corporation. Section 902 attempts to equate branch and subsidiary operations by making an indirect credit available to U.S. *corporate* taxpayers who receive actual or constructive dividends from foreign corporations that have paid a foreign tax on earnings. These foreign taxes are deemed paid by the corporate shareholders in the same proportion as the dividends actually or constructively received bear to the foreign corporation's post-1986 undistributed earnings and profits (E & P). A domestic corporation that chooses the FTC for deemed-paid foreign taxes must *gross up* dividend income by the amount of deemed-paid taxes.

EXAMPLE 3

Wren, Inc., a domestic corporation, owns 50% of Finch, Inc., a foreign corporation. Wren receives a dividend of $120,000 from Finch. Finch paid foreign taxes of $500,000 on post-1986 E & P. Finch's post-1986 E & P (after taxes) totals $1,200,000. Wren's deemed-paid foreign taxes for FTC purposes are $50,000:

Cash dividend from Finch	$120,000
Deemed-paid foreign taxes:	
$\$500{,}000 \times \dfrac{\$120{,}000}{\$1{,}200{,}000} =$	50,000
Gross income to Wren	$170,000

Wren must include the $50,000 in gross income due to the gross-up adjustment if the FTC is elected. ◆

Certain ownership requirements must be met before the indirect credit is available to a domestic corporation. The domestic corporation must own 10 percent or more of the voting stock of the foreign corporation. The credit is also available for deemed-paid foreign taxes of second- and third-tier foreign corporations if the 10 percent ownership requirement is met at the second- and third-tier level. Further, a 5 percent indirect ownership requirement must be met from tier to tier. The § 902 ownership requirements are summarized in Figure 24–1.

FTC Limitations. To prevent foreign taxes from being credited against U.S. taxes levied on U.S.-source taxable income, the FTC is subject to a limitation. Section 904 provides that the FTC for any taxable year shall not exceed the lesser of the actual foreign taxes paid or accrued, or the U.S. taxes (before the FTC) on foreign-source taxable income (the *general limitation*). The general limitation formula is as follows:

$$\begin{array}{c}\text{U.S. tax}\\ \text{before FTC}\end{array} \times \frac{\text{Foreign-source taxable income}^{1}}{\text{Worldwide taxable income}}$$

1. For FTC purposes, the taxable income of an individual, estate, or trust is computed without any deduction for personal exemptions. § 904(b)(1).

EXAMPLE 4

Terry, a U.S. resident, invests in foreign securities. Her worldwide taxable income for 1993 is $120,000, consisting of $100,000 in salary from a U.S. employer and $20,000 of income from foreign sources. Foreign taxes of $6,000 were withheld by foreign tax authorities. Assume that Terry's U.S. tax before the FTC is $33,600. Her FTC for 1993 is $5,600 [$33,600 × ($20,000/$120,000)]. Her net U.S. tax liability is $28,000 ($33,600 – $5,600). ◆

As Example 4 illustrates, the limitation can prevent some portion of foreign taxes paid in high tax jurisdictions from being credited. Taxpayers could overcome this problem by generating additional foreign-source income that is subject to no, or low, foreign taxation.

EXAMPLE 5

Compare Domestic Corporation's FTC situation when the corporation has only $500,000 of highly taxed foreign-source income with the situation where Domestic also has $100,000 of low-taxed foreign-source interest income.

	Only Highly Taxed Income	With Low-Taxed Interest
Foreign-source income	$500,000	$600,000
Foreign taxes	275,000	280,000
U.S.-source income	700,000	700,000
U.S. taxes (34%)	408,000	442,000
FTC limitation	170,000*	204,000**

*$408,000 × ($500,000/$1,200,000).
**$442,000 × ($600,000/$1,300,000).

FIGURE 24–1
Section 902 Ownership Requirements

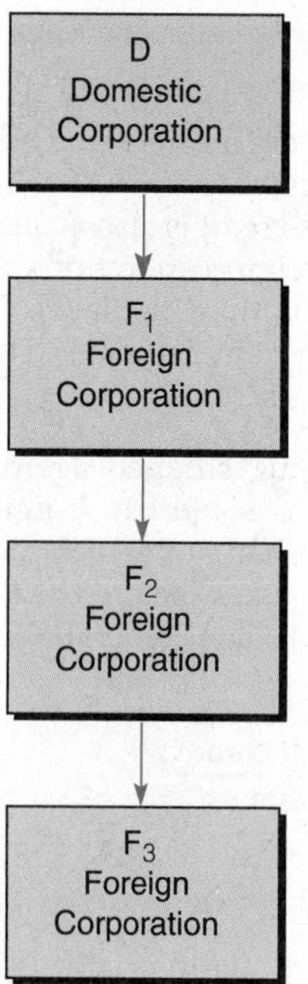
D
Domestic
Corporation
D must own directly at least 10% of the voting stock of F1 and must own indirectly at least 5% of the voting stock of F2 and F3 .
F1
Foreign
Corporation
F1 must own directly at least 10% of the voting stock of F2 .
F2
Foreign
Corporation
F2 must own directly at least 10% of the voting stock of F3 .
F3
Foreign
Corporation
There is no provision for a credit for deemed-paid foreign taxes from a foreign corporation below the third tier.

Domestic's foreign taxes increase by only $5,000, while its FTC limitation increases by $34,000. ◆

To prevent the *cross-crediting* of foreign taxes as in Example 5, Congress has enacted legislation providing for several separate limitation *baskets*. These provisions require that a separate limitation be calculated for certain categories of foreign-source taxable income and the foreign taxes attributable to that income. Section 904(d) provides separate limitation baskets for the following:

- Passive income.
- High withholding tax income.
- Financial services income.
- Shipping income.
- Dividends from each noncontrolled § 902 corporation.
- Dividends from a domestic international sales corporation (DISC) or former DISC to the extent they are treated as foreign-source income.
- Taxable income attributable to foreign trade income under § 923(b).
- Distributions from a foreign sales corporation (FSC) or former FSC out of E & P attributable to foreign trade income or qualified interest and carrying charges under § 263(c).

All other foreign-source income is included in a general (or overall) limitation basket. These separate limitations are diagrammed in Concept Summary 24–1.

A separate limitation under § 907 applies to foreign taxes paid on foreign oil and gas extraction income. This limitation is applied before consideration of the general limitation. Special provisions define the various income categories, particularly with regard to the possibility that an item of income could fall in more than one basket, such as passive income and high withholding tax interest.

In addition, in the case of controlled foreign corporations (CFCs), *look-through* rules are applied. These rules require the U.S. shareholder receiving, for example, dividend income to *look through* to the source (classification) of the income at the CFC level.

EXAMPLE 6

Delta, a domestic corporation, receives foreign-source dividend income from three noncontrolled § 902 foreign corporations, Ace, Box, and Cam. Delta's worldwide taxable income is $3,300,000, and its U.S. tax liability before the FTC is $1,122,000. The FTC is determined as follows:

Payer	Dividend	Foreign Taxes Paid and Deemed Paid	FTC Limitation	FTC
Ace	$ 50,000	$ 4,000	$17,000*	$ 4,000**
Box	100,000	40,000	34,000	34,000
Cam	150,000	7,500	51,000	7,500
	$300,000	$51,500		$45,500

*$1,122,000 × ($50,000/$3,300,000).
**Lesser of $4,000 or $17,000.

Without the separate basket limitation, Delta would have an FTC of $51,500 ($4,000 + $40,000 + $7,500). ◆

The limitations can result in unused (noncredited) foreign taxes for the tax year. Section 904 provides for a two-year carryback and five-year carryover of excess foreign taxes. The taxes can be credited in years when the formula limitation for that year exceeds the foreign taxes attributable to the same tax year. The carryback and carryover provision is available only within the separate baskets. In other words, excess foreign taxes in one basket cannot be carried over unless there is an excess limitation in the same basket for the carryover year.

The Alternative Minimum Tax FTC. For purposes of the alternative minimum tax, the FTC is limited to the lesser of the credit for regular tax purposes or 90 percent of the tentative minimum tax before the credit.[2] The 10 percent cutback is calculated on the tentative minimum tax without regard to the alternative tax NOL deduction. The general FTC limitation is calculated by using alternative minimum taxable income rather than taxable income in the denominator of the formula and the tentative minimum tax rather than the regular tax. The source of alternative minimum taxable income must be determined for the purpose of foreign-source taxable income.

Other Considerations. In order for a foreign levy to qualify for the FTC, it must be a tax, and its predominant character must be that of an income tax in the U.S. sense.[3] A levy is a tax if it is a compulsory payment, as contrasted with a payment for a specific economic benefit such as the right to extract oil. A tax's predominant character is that of an income tax in the U.S. sense if it reaches

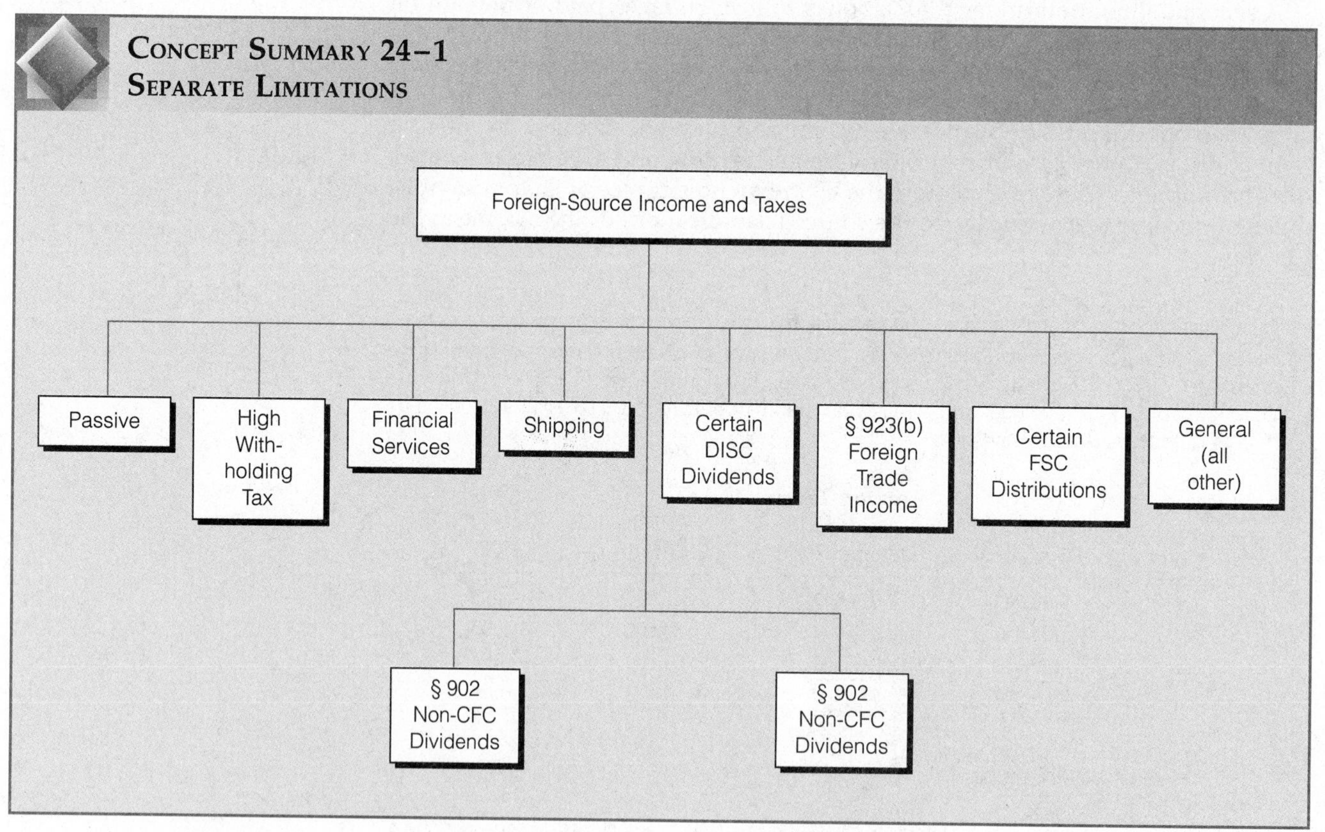

2. § 59. A "small corporation" exception is available.

3. Reg. § 1.901–2.

realized net gain and is not dependent on being credited against the income tax of another country (not a *soak-up* tax). A tax that is levied in lieu of an income tax is also creditable.[4]

EXAMPLE 7

Rigs, a domestic corporation, receives oil extraction income from operations in a foreign country. The tax laws of the foreign country levy a 50% tax on extraction income and a 30% tax on all other taxable income derived within the country. If Rigs pays $700,000 in taxes on its extraction income to the foreign country, only $420,000 [$700,000 × (30% ÷ 50%)] of that amount is creditable as an income tax. ◆

EXAMPLE 8

Hoops, a domestic corporation, generates $2 million of taxable income from operations in Larissa, a foreign country. Larissa's law levies a tax on income generated in Larissa by foreign residents only in cases in which the country of residence (such as the United States) allows a tax credit for foreign taxes paid. Hoops will not be allowed an FTC for taxes paid to Larissa because the foreign tax is a soak-up tax. ◆

Certain foreign taxes that generally would meet the definition of creditable may not be creditable due to § 901(j), which prohibits a credit for taxes paid to foreign governments that the United States does not recognize. Furthermore, where a person, or a member of a controlled group that includes such a person, participates in or cooperates with an unapproved international boycott during the taxable year, the FTC is reduced. Section 901 provides for the otherwise allowable FTC to be reduced by multiplying by the international boycott factor.[5]

For purposes of the FTC, foreign taxes are attributable to the year in which they are paid or accrued. Taxpayers using the cash method of accounting for tax purposes may elect to take the FTC in the year in which the foreign taxes accrue. The election is binding on the taxpayer for the year in which it is made and for all subsequent years. Taxes paid in a foreign currency are translated to U.S. dollars for FTC purposes at the exchange rate in effect when the taxes are actually paid.[6] Any adjustment of foreign taxes paid by a foreign corporation is translated at the rate in effect at the time of adjustment. Any refund or credit is translated at the rate in effect at the time the foreign taxes were originally paid.

The FTC is elective for any particular tax year. If the taxpayer does not choose to take the FTC, a deduction may be allowed for foreign taxes paid or incurred. However, a taxpayer cannot take a credit and a deduction for the same foreign income taxes.[7] A taxpayer can take a deduction in the same year as an FTC for foreign taxes that are not creditable (e.g., soak-up taxes).

Possessions Corporations

To encourage the economic development of U.S. possessions, Congress enacted a credit provision for income from operations in U.S. possessions. Domestic corporations may elect to receive a § 936 credit against U.S. taxes. The credit is equal to the portion of the U.S. tax attributable to the sum of possession-source taxable income and qualified investment income whether any tax is paid or due to the possession. This is referred to as a *tax-sparing* credit. No additional credit or deduction is allowed for income taxes actually paid to the possession. A number of pharmaceutical companies, including Eli Lilly Co., have used subsidiaries with operations in Puerto Rico to take advantage of this and local tax benefits.

4. § 903 and Reg. § 1.903–1.
5. §§ 908 and 999.
6. §§ 986(b) and 987.
7. § 275.

The credit is allowed against the U.S. tax attributable to foreign-source taxable income from the active conduct of a trade or business in a U.S. possession. It is also allowed on the sale or exchange of substantially all the assets used by the domestic corporation in that active trade or business and on qualified possession-source investment income. The credit is not allowed against certain taxes such as the accumulated earnings tax under § 531 and the personal holding company tax under § 541.

In order to elect the credit, the domestic corporation must meet certain conditions. Eighty percent or more of its gross income for the three-year period immediately preceding the taxable year for which the credit is taken must be derived from sources within a U.S. possession. In addition, 75 percent or more of its gross income for that period must have been derived from the active conduct of a trade or business within a U.S. possession. The credit is not available for income received in the United States unless it is possession-source income received from an unrelated person and is attributable to an active trade or business conducted in a possession.

Specific rules apply to intangible property income. The credit is not available for such income. Intangible property income is includible in taxable income by a domestic corporation as U.S.-source income. If a domestic corporation elects the credit, however, all of its shareholders who are U.S. persons must include their pro rata share of that income in their gross income as U.S.-source income. In this case, the domestic corporation is not taxed on such income.

EXAMPLE 9

A qualified possessions corporation has the following foreign-source income on which it pays the following foreign taxes:

Taxable Income	Source	Foreign Taxes
$400,000 active trade or business income	Possession	$40,000
50,000 qualified investment income	Possession	–0–
10,000 passive nonqualified income	Possession	–0–
40,000 investment income	Nonpossession	16,000

Assume that the corporation's worldwide taxable income is $500,000 and its U.S. tax before the FTC is $170,000. The § 936 possessions corporation credit is $153,000 (34% × $450,000), and the § 901 FTC is $13,600, the lesser of $16,000 or $13,600 [$170,000 × ($40,000/$500,000)]. ◆

SOURCING OF INCOME AND ALLOCATION OF DEDUCTIONS

The sourcing of income within or without the United States has a direct bearing on a number of tax provisions. The numerator of the FTC limitation formula is foreign-source taxable income. Generally, nonresident aliens and foreign corporations are subject to Federal taxation only on U.S.-source income. The foreign earned income exclusion is available only for foreign-source income.

Income Sourced within the United States

The determination of the source depends on the type of income realized. This makes the classification of income an important consideration (e.g., income from the sale of property versus income for the use of property). A detailed discussion of the characterization of income, however, is beyond the scope of this chapter. Section 861 contains source rules for most types of income. Other rules pertaining to the source of income are found in §§ 862–865.

Interest. Interest income received from the U.S. government, or the District of Columbia, and from noncorporate U.S. residents or domestic corporations is sourced within the United States. There are a few exceptions to this rule, most notably certain interest received from a resident alien individual or domestic corporation. This exception applies if an 80 percent foreign business requirement is met. Interest received on amounts deposited with a foreign branch of a U.S. corporation is also treated as foreign-source income if the branch is engaged in the commercial banking business.

EXAMPLE 10

John holds a bond issued by Delta, a domestic corporation. For the immediately preceding three tax years, 82% of Delta's gross income was active foreign business income. The interest income that John receives for the tax year from Delta is foreign-source income.[8] ◆

Dividends. Dividends received from domestic corporations (other than certain possessions corporations) are sourced within the United States. Generally, dividends paid by a foreign corporation are foreign-source income. However, an exception applies if 25 percent or more of a foreign corporation's gross income for the immediately preceding three tax years was effectively connected with the conduct of a U.S. trade or business. In this case, the dividends received in the taxable year are U.S.-source income to the extent of the proportion of gross income that was effectively connected with the conduct of a U.S. trade or business for the immediately preceding three-year period. Dividends from foreign sales corporations (FSCs) and domestic international sales corporations (DISCs) can be treated as U.S.-source income.

EXAMPLE 11

Ann receives dividend income from the following corporations for the tax year:

Amount	Corporation	Effectively Connected Income for Past 3 Years	Active Foreign Business Income for Past 3 Years	U.S.-Source Income
$500	Green, domestic	85%	15%	$500
600	Brown, domestic	13%	87%	600
300	Orange, foreign	80%	20%	240

The 80% active foreign business requirement would affect only interest income received from Green Corporation and Brown Corporation, not dividend income. Because Orange Corporation is a foreign corporation meeting the 25% test, 80% of the dividend from Orange is U.S.-source income. ◆

Personal Services Income. The source of income from personal services is determined by the location in which the services are performed (within or

8. § 861(c). Certain interest income, even though U.S.-source income, is not taxable if earned by nonresident aliens or foreign corporations.

without the United States). A limited *commercial traveler* exception is available. Personal services income must meet the following requirements to avoid U.S.-source treatment:

- The services must be performed by a nonresident alien who is in the United States for 90 days or less during the taxable year.
- The compensation for the services performed in the United States may not exceed $3,000 in total.
- The services must be performed on behalf of
  - a nonresident alien, foreign partnership, or foreign corporation that is not engaged in a U.S. trade or business, or
  - an office or place of business maintained in a foreign country or possession of the United States by an individual who is a citizen or resident of the United States, a domestic partnership, or a domestic corporation.

Example 12

Mark, a nonresident alien, is an engineer employed by a foreign oil company. He spent four weeks in the United States arranging the purchase of field equipment for his company. His salary for the four weeks was $3,500. Even though the oil company is not engaged in a U.S. trade or business, and Mark was in the United States for less than 90 days during the taxable year, the income is U.S.-source income because it exceeds $3,000. ◆

The issue of whether income is derived from the performance of personal services is important in determining the income's source. The courts have held that a corporation can perform personal services[9] and that, in the absence of capital as an income-producing factor, personal services income can arise even though there is no recipient of the services.[10] If payment is received for services performed partly within and partly without the United States, the income must be allocated for source purposes on some reasonable basis, such as days worked.[11]

Rents and Royalties. The source of income received for the use of tangible property is the country in which the property producing the income is located. The source of income received for the use of intangible property (e.g., patents, copyrights, secret processes, and formulas) is the country in which the property producing the income is used.

Sale or Exchange of Property. Income from the disposition of U.S. real property interests is U.S.-source income. The definition of a U.S. real property interest is discussed subsequently under the Foreign Investment in Real Property Tax Act (FIRPTA). Generally, the location of real property determines the source of any income derived from the property.

The source of income from the sale of personal property (property other than real property) depends on several factors, including whether the property was produced by the seller, the type of property sold (e.g., inventory or a capital asset), and the residence of the seller. The general rule under § 865 provides that

---

9. See *British Timken Limited,* 12 T.C. 880 (1949), and Rev.Rul. 60–55, 1960–1 C.B. 270.

10. See *Robida v. Comm.,* 72–1 USTC ¶9450, 29 AFTR2d 72–1223, 460 F.2d 1172 (CA–9, 1972). The taxpayer was employed in military PXs around the world. He had large slot machine winnings and claimed the foreign earned income exclusion. The IRS challenged the exclusion on the grounds that the winnings were not earned income because there was no recipient of Robida's services. The Court, however, found, that in the absence of capital, the winnings were earned income.

11. Reg. § 1.861–4(b).

the income, gain, or profit from the sale of personal property is sourced according to the residence of the seller. Income from the sale of purchased inventory, however, is sourced in the country in which the sale takes place.[12]

When the seller has produced the property, the income must be apportioned between the country of production and the country of sale. The regulations provide guidelines for allocating income between production and sales.[13] If the manufacturer or producer regularly sells to wholly independent distributors, this can establish an *independent* factory or production price that can be used to determine the split between production and sales income. However, if an independent price has not been established, taxable income from production and sales must be apportioned.

Losses from the sale of personal property are sourced according to the source of any income that may have been generated by the property prior to its disposition. This provision discourages the manipulation of the source of losses for tax purposes.

There are several exceptions to the general rule for the sourcing of income from the sale of personal property, such as the following:

1. Gain on the sale of depreciable personal property is sourced according to prior depreciation deductions to the extent of the deductions. Any excess gain is sourced as the sale of inventory.
2. Gain attributable to an office or fixed place of business maintained outside the United States by a U.S. resident is foreign-source income.
3. Gain on the sale of intangibles is sourced according to prior amortization deductions to the extent of the deductions. Contingent payments, however, are sourced as royalty income.

Transportation and Communication Income. Income from transportation beginning *and* ending in the United States is U.S.-source income. Fifty percent of the income from transportation beginning *or* ending in the United States is U.S.-source income, unless the U.S. point is only an intermediate stop. This rule does not apply to personal services income unless the transportation is between the United States and a possession.[14] Income from space and ocean activities conducted outside the jurisdiction of any country is sourced according to the residence of the person conducting the activity.

International communication income derived by a U.S. person is sourced 50 percent within the United States in cases where transmission is between the United States and a foreign country. International communication income derived by foreign persons is foreign-source income unless it is attributable to an office or other fixed place of business within the United States. In that case, it is U.S.-source income.

Income Sourced without the United States

The provisions for sourcing income without the United States are not as detailed and specific as those for determining U.S.-source income. Basically, § 862 provides that if interest, dividends, compensation for personal services, income from the use or sale of property, and other income is not U.S.-source income, then it is foreign-source income.

---

12. § 861(a)(6).The sale is deemed to take place where title passes. See Reg. § 1.861–7(c) regarding title passage. There has been considerable conflict in this area of tax law. See, for example, *Kates Holding Company, Inc.*, 79 T.C. 700 (1982) and *Miami Purchasing Service Corporation*, 76 T.C. 818 (1981).
13. Reg. § 1.863–3.
14. §§ 863(c) and (d).

Allocation and Apportionment of Deductions

The United States levies a tax on *taxable income.* Deductions and losses, therefore, must be allocated and apportioned between U.S.- and foreign-source gross income to determine U.S.- and foreign-source taxable income. A detailed discussion of Treasury Regulation § 1.861–8, which provides the basis for this allocation and apportionment, is beyond the scope of this chapter. Briefly, however, the Regulation calls for deductions directly related to an activity or property to be allocated to classes of income. This is followed by apportionment between the statutory and residual groupings on some reasonable basis. For FTC purposes, foreign-source income is the statutory grouping, and U.S.-source income is the residual grouping.

EXAMPLE 13

Ace, Inc., a domestic corporation has $2,000,000 of gross income and a $50,000 expense, all related to real estate activities. The expense is allocated and apportioned as follows:

	Gross Income			Apportionment	
	Foreign	**U.S.**	Allocation	**Foreign**	**U.S.**
Sales	$1,000,000	$500,000	$37,500*	$25,000	$12,500**
Rentals	400,000	100,000	12,500	10,000	2,500
			$50,000	$35,000	$15,000

*$50,000 × ($1,500,000/$2,000,000).
**$37,500 × ($500,000/$1,500,000).

If Ace could show that $45,000 of the expense was directly related to sales income, the $45,000 would be allocated to that class of gross income, with the remainder allocated ratably. ◆

Interest expenses are allocated and apportioned based on the theory that money is fungible. With limited exceptions, interest expense is attributable to all the activities and property of the taxpayer regardless of the specific purpose for incurring the debt on which interest is paid.[15] Generally, taxpayers must allocate and apportion interest expense on the basis of assets, using either the fair market value or the tax book value of assets.[16] Once the fair market value is used, the taxpayer must continue to use this method. Special rules apply in allocating and apportioning interest expense in an affiliated group of corporations.

EXAMPLE 14

Black, Inc., a domestic corporation, generates U.S.-source and foreign-source gross income for 1993. Black's assets (tax book value) are as follows:

Generating U.S.-source income	$18,000,000
Generating foreign-source income	5,000,000
	$23,000,000

15. Regulation § 1.861–10T(b) describes circumstances where interest expense can be directly allocated to specific debt. This exception to the fungibility concept is limited to cases in which specific property is purchased or improved with nonrecourse debt.

16. Reg. § 1.861–9T.

Black incurs interest expense of $800,000 for 1993. Using the asset method and the tax book value, interest expense is apportioned to foreign-source income as follows:

$$\frac{\$5,000,000 \text{ (foreign assets)}}{\$23,000,000 \text{ (total assets)}} \times \$800,000 = \$173,913$$

◆

Specific rules also apply to research and development expenditures, certain stewardship expenses, legal and accounting fees and expenses, income taxes, and losses.

A deduction not definitely related to any class of gross income is ratably allocated to all classes of gross income and apportioned between U.S.- and foreign-source income.

Section 482 Considerations

Taxpayers may be tempted to manipulate the source of income and the allocation of deductions arbitrarily to minimize taxation. This manipulation is more easily accomplished between or among related persons. The IRS uses § 482 to counter such actions. The provision gives the IRS the power to reallocate gross income, deductions, credits, or allowances between or among organizations, trades, or businesses owned or controlled directly or indirectly by the same interests. This can be done whenever the IRS determines that reallocation is necessary to prevent the evasion of taxes or to reflect income more clearly. Section 482 is a "one-edged" sword available only to the IRS. The taxpayer cannot invoke it to reallocate income and expenses.[17]

The reach of § 482 is quite broad. The IRS takes the position that a corporation and its sole shareholder who works full-time for the corporation can be treated as two separate trades or businesses for purposes of § 482.[18] Two unrelated shareholders who each owned 50 percent of a corporation were held to be acting in concert for their common good and, thus, together controlled the corporation.[19]

Section 482 is supplemented by legislative Regulations that provide rules for safe harbor charges in regard to loans, services, and the use of tangible property. The Regulations provide little specific guidance in the area of intangibles. Several court decisions in recent years have addressed this issue.[20]

The Regulations also provide three specific methods for determining an arm's length price on the sale of tangible property: the comparable uncontrolled price method, the resale price method, and the cost plus method. These methods are to be relied on in the order given.

After 1986, payments made by related parties for the sale or use of intangible property must be commensurate with the income attributable to the intangibles. Furthermore, the basis or inventory cost of imported property purchased from a related party cannot exceed the value declared for customs duty purposes.[21]

On October 19, 1988, the Treasury released its *Study of Intercompany Pricing* (the "White Paper"). It concluded that the market-based approach to intercompany pricing reflected in the current § 482 Regulations cannot be

---

17. Reg. § 1.482–1(b)(3).

18. Rev.Rul. 88–38, 1988–1 C.B. 246. But see *Foglesong v. Comm.*, 82–2 USTC ¶9650, 50 AFTR2d 82–6016, 691 F.2d 848 (CA–7, 1982), *rev'g*. 77 T.C. 1102 (1981).

19. See *B. Forman Company, Inc. v. Comm.*, 72–1 USTC ¶9182, 29 AFTR2d 72–405, 453 F.2d 1144 (CA–2, 1972).

20. See *Eli Lilly & Company and Subsidiaries v. Comm.*, 88–2 USTC ¶9502, 62 AFTR2d 88–5569, 856 F.2d 855 (CA–7, 1988), *aff'g*. in part, *rev'g*. in part, and *rem'g*. 84 T.C. 996 (1985); *Bausch & Lomb, Inc. & Consolidated Subsidiaries*, 933 F.2d. 1084 (CA–2, 1991), *aff'g*. 92 T.C. 525 (1989); and *G. D. Searle*, 88 T.C. 252 (1987).

21. § 1059A.

applied effectively due to the integration of the tangible property and the marketing and manufacturing intangibles in income generation. The Treasury concluded that the market-based approach should be supplemented by an alternative pricing approach that considers the return earned in the marketplace on a firm's factors of production. Accordingly, the Treasury has issued Proposed Regulations that reflect this approach.[22] As a further aid to reducing pricing disputes, the IRS has initiated an Advanced Pricing Agreement (APA) program whereby the taxpayer can propose a transfer pricing method for certain international transactions.[23] The taxpayer provides relevant data, which is then evaluated by the IRS. If accepted, the APA provides a safe harbor transfer pricing method for the taxpayer. Apple Computer, Inc., accomplished the first successful APA submission.

U.S. Taxation of Nonresident Aliens and Foreign Corporations

Generally, only the U.S.-source income of nonresident aliens (NRAs) and foreign corporations is subject to U.S. taxation. This reflects the reach of U.S. tax jurisdiction. The constraint, however, does not prevent the United States from also taxing the foreign-source income of NRAs and foreign corporations, when that income is effectively connected with the conduct of a U.S. trade or business.[24] The income of NRAs and foreign corporations subject to U.S. taxation can be divided into two classifications: *effectively connected* and *noneffectively connected* income. In some respects, foreign corporations enjoy preferential income tax treatment compared with NRA individuals. In addition, NRA individuals can be subject to the Federal estate and gift tax.

Nonresident Alien Individuals

An NRA individual is an individual who is not a citizen or resident of the United States. For example, Princess Diana is an NRA since she is not a citizen or resident of the United States. Citizenship is determined under the immigration and naturalization laws of the United States. Basically, the citizenship statutes are broken down into two categories, nationality at birth and nationality through naturalization.

Residency. For many years, the definition of residency for Federal income tax purposes was very subjective, requiring an evaluation of a person's intent and actions with regard to the length and nature of stay in the United States. In 1984, Congress enacted a more objective test of residency. A person is a resident of the United States for income tax purposes if he or she meets either the "green card" test or the substantial presence test. If either of these tests is met for the calendar year, the individual is deemed a U.S. resident for the year.[25]

An alien issued a green card is considered a U.S. resident on the first day he or she is physically present in the United States after issuance. The green card is Immigration Form I–551. Newly issued cards are now rose (off-pink), but the

22. Prop.Reg. §§ 1.482–1 and 1.482–2.
23. Rev.Proc. 91–22, 1991–1 C.B. 526.
24. §§ 871, 881, and 882.
25. § 7701(b). See also Reg. § 301.7701(b).

form is still referred to as the "green card." Status as a U.S. resident remains in effect until the green card has been revoked or the individual has abandoned lawful permanent resident status.

The substantial presence test is applied to an alien without a green card. It is a mathematical test involving physical presence in the United States. An individual who is physically present in the United States for at least 183 days during the calendar year is a U.S. resident for income tax purposes. This 183-day requirement can also be met over a three-year period that includes the two immediately preceding years and the current year. For this purpose, each day of the current calendar year is counted as a full day, each day of the first preceding year as one-third day, and each day of the second preceding year as one-sixth day.

EXAMPLE 15

Rudy, an alien, was present in the United States for 90 days in 1991, 180 days in 1992, and 110 days in 1993. For Federal income tax purposes, Rudy is a U.S. resident for 1993 since he was physically present for 185 days [(90 days × 1/6) + (180 days × 1/3) + (110 days × 1)] during the three-year period. ◆

The substantial presence test allows for several exceptions. Commuters from Mexico and Canada who are employed in the United States, but return home each day, are excepted. Also excepted are individuals who are prevented from leaving the United States due to a medical condition that arose while in the United States. Some individuals are exempt from the substantial presence test, including foreign government–related individuals (e.g., diplomats), qualified teachers, trainees and students, and certain professional athletes.

Residence, under the substantial presence test, begins the first day the individual is physically present in the United States and ends the last day of physical presence for the calendar year. This assumes the substantial presence test is not satisfied for the next calendar year. Nominal presence of 10 days or less can be ignored in determining whether the substantial presence test is met. A 31-day per-year exception and a 183-day current-year exception may apply to prevent residence under this test.[26]

The application of the income tax treaties that the United States has in force with other countries depends on the residence of the taxpayer. Most of the treaties have "tie breaker" provisions for situations in which a person may qualify as a resident of both treaty countries under each country's laws. Certain treaties override § 7701(b) for the purpose of income tax status (as resident or nonresident), but may not override residence under § 7701(b) for purposes of other tax provisions (e.g., the sourcing of income).

Nonresident Aliens Not Engaged in a U.S. Trade or Business. Section 871(a) subjects certain U.S.-source income that is not effectively connected with the conduct of a U.S. trade or business to a 30 percent tax. This income includes dividends, interest, rents, royalties, certain compensation, premiums, annuities, and other fixed, determinable, annual or periodic (FDAP) income. This tax generally is levied by a withholding mechanism that requires the payors of the income to withhold 30 percent of gross amounts.[27] This method eliminates the problems of assuring payment by nonresidents, determining allowable deductions, and, in many instances, the filing of tax returns by nonresidents. NRAs are allowed a deduction for casualty and theft losses related to property located

26. See § 7701(b)(3).

27. §§ 873 and 1441.

within the United States, a deduction for qualified charitable contributions, and one personal exemption. Residents of countries contiguous to the United States (i.e., Canada and Mexico) are allowed dependency exemptions as well. Interest received from certain portfolio debt investments, even though U.S.-source income, is exempt from taxation. Interest earned on deposits with banking institutions is also exempt as long as it is not effectively connected with the conduct of a U.S. trade or business.

Capital gains *not* effectively connected with the conduct of a U.S. trade or business are exempt from tax as long as the NRA individual was not present in the United States for 183 days or more during the taxable year. If an NRA has not established a taxable year, the calendar year will be treated as the taxable year. NRAs are not permitted to carry forward capital losses.[28]

Even though an NRA is not *actually* engaged in the conduct of a U.S. trade or business, any gains from the sale of U.S. real property interests are treated as effectively connected income. This is discussed in more detail subsequently. Furthermore, the taxpayer can elect to treat income from certain passive real estate activities (for example, a net lease arrangement) as effectively connected income. This allows the taxpayer to deduct any expenses incurred in earning the income attributable to the real estate in determining taxable income. Once made, the election is only revocable with IRS permission and generally cannot be reelected for five years.

Nonresident Aliens Engaged in a U.S. Trade or Business. As long as FDAP income and capital gains are not effectively connected income, the tax treatment of these income items is the same whether NRAs are engaged in a U.S. trade or business or not. Effectively connected income, however, is taxed at the same rates that apply to U.S. citizens and residents, and deductions for expenses attributable to that income are allowed.

Two important definitions determine the U.S. tax consequences to NRAs with U.S.-source income: *the conduct of a U.S. trade or business* and *effectively connected income.* Section 864 and the accompanying Regulations contain guidelines for making these determinations.

General criteria for determining if a U.S. trade or business exists include the location of production activities, management, distribution activities, and other business functions. Trading in commodities and securities ordinarily will not constitute a trade or business. Dealers, however, need to avoid maintaining a U.S. trading office and trading for their own account. Corporations (other than certain personal holding companies) that are not dealers can trade for their own account as long as their principal office is located outside the United States. There are no restrictions on individuals who are not dealers. An NRA individual who performs services in the United States for a foreign employer is not engaged in a U.S. trade or business.

A U.S. trade or business is a prerequisite to having effectively connected income. Section 864(c) provides a dual test for determining if income, such as FDAP income and capital gains, is effectively connected income. Income is effectively connected with a U.S. trade or business if it is derived from assets used in, or held for use in, the trade or business (asset-use test) or if the activities of the trade or business are a material factor in the production of the income (business-activities test).

28. § 871(a)(2).

Example 16

Ingrid, an NRA, operates a U.S. business. During the year, excess cash funds accumulate. Ingrid invests these funds on a short-term basis so that they remain available to meet her business needs. Any income earned from these investments is effectively connected income under the asset-use test. ◆

Estate and Gift Taxes. The value of property situated in the United States is included in a deceased NRA's gross estate for U.S. estate tax purposes.[29] Thus, the question of situs (location) of property owned by the decedent at the time of death is important.

Generally, the situs of real property is not subject to conflict. One probably would not question that a piece of land in Kansas is situated in the United States. Also, the situs of tangible personal property is easily determined (e.g., jewelry in a safe deposit box in a bank in New York City).

Specific rules are provided for certain intangible property. Stock owned and held by an NRA at the time of death is deemed situated in the United States only if it was issued by a domestic corporation.[30] Debt obligations of a U.S. person or the United States, a state or any political subdivision thereof, or the District of Columbia are deemed property situated within the United States. However, the proceeds of life insurance on the life of an NRA are not property situated within the United States. Furthermore, amounts on deposit in U.S. banks are not property situated within the United States if the interest income earned on the deposits is foreign-source income. A similar rule applies to portfolio debt obligations where the interest income earned on the debt is exempt from U.S. income taxation.

The tax rates applicable to the taxable estate of a deceased NRA are the same as those applicable to the taxable estate of a U.S. citizen or resident. Section 2102(c) allows a unified credit of only $13,000 against the estate tax imposed on an NRA's taxable estate. In fact, the credit is not *unified* since, for gift tax purposes, taxable gifts made by NRAs are subject to the same rates imposed on U.S. citizens and residents,[31] but a unified credit against the gift tax is not allowed to NRAs.[32] The gift tax is imposed only on an NRA's transfer of tangible property situated in the United States.[33]

The marital deduction is not available to NRAs. Nor is it available to U.S. persons (or their estates) on transfers to noncitizen spouses. However, a $100,000 annual gift tax exclusion is allowed on transfers to a noncitizen spouse. Under a limited exception for estate tax purposes, the marital deduction is available if the property passes to a qualified domestic trust or to a spouse who is a U.S. resident on the date of death of the decedent *and* becomes a U.S. citizen before the estate tax return is filed.

For purposes of the estate and gift tax, an individual is a *nonresident* if his or her domicile is not within the United States at the time of death or on the date the gift is transferred.[34] A person acquires a domicile in a place by living there with no definite present intention to change domicile at a later date. In other words, *action* and *intent* are required to establish domicile. Intent is more often subject to question than action. It is easy to determine whether an individual has actually lived and acquired permanent physical ties, such as a personal residence, in the United States. Some factors that the courts have considered in determining

29. The estate tax provisions of the Code applicable to NRAs are contained in §§ 2101–2108.
30. § 2104(a).
31. § 2502.
32. § 2505.
33. §§ 2501(a)(2) and 2511.
34. Reg. § 20.0–1.

intent are participation in local affairs, payment of taxes, voting status, location of personal property, and statements concerning residence. As a result of these provisions, a person can be classified as a U.S. resident for income tax purposes and an NRA for estate and gift tax purposes.

Foreign Corporations

Definition. The classification of an entity as a foreign corporation for U.S. tax purposes is an important consideration. Section 7701(a)(5) defines a foreign corporation as one that is not domestic. A domestic corporation is a corporation that is created or organized in the United States. Even though McDonald's is, in reality, a multinational corporation, it is considered a domestic corporation for U.S. tax purposes because it was organized in the United States.

The IRS looks at the corporate characteristics outlined in the Regulations under § 7701 to determine whether a foreign entity should be taxable as a corporation. See the discussion of these characteristics in Chapter 16. In determining the presence or absence of any of these characteristics, the IRS looks at the rights and duties of the foreign entity under the laws of the jurisdiction in which it resides. Classification of the foreign entity as a corporation, an association taxable as a corporation, a partnership, or some other form of entity can affect the U.S. tax consequences with regard to the entity and its owners. For example, stock in a foreign corporation is not included in the U.S. gross estate of an NRA individual even where all the assets of the corporation are located in the United States. Also, individuals expecting the pass-through of losses of a foreign partnership will be denied those losses if the foreign entity is deemed to be taxable as a corporation for U.S. tax purposes.

Income Not Effectively Connected with a U.S. Trade or Business. Under § 881, U.S.-source FDAP income of foreign corporations is taxed by the United States in the same manner as that of NRA individuals—at a flat 30 percent rate. Basically, foreign corporations qualify for the same exemptions from U.S. taxation for interest and dividend income as do NRA individuals. The U.S.-source capital gains of foreign corporations are exempt from the Federal income tax if they are not effectively connected with the conduct of a U.S. trade or business.

Effectively Connected Income. Section 882 subjects foreign corporations conducting a trade or business within the United States to Federal income taxation on effectively connected income. Additionally, any U.S.-source income other than noneffectively connected FDAP and capital gains is deemed effectively connected (e.g., casual sales of items by the home office). For such purposes, foreign corporations are subject to the same tax rates as domestic corporations.

Branch Profits Tax. In addition to the income tax imposed under § 882 on effectively connected income of a foreign corporation, a tax equal to 30 percent of the *dividend equivalent amount* for the taxable year is imposed on *any* foreign corporation.[35]

The objective of the branch profits tax is to afford equal tax treatment to income generated by a domestic corporation controlled by a foreign corporation and to income generated by other U.S. operations controlled by foreign corporations. If the foreign corporation operates through a U.S. subsidiary (a domestic corporation), the income of the subsidiary is taxable by the United States when

35. § 884.

derived and is also subject to a withholding tax when repatriated (returned as dividends to the foreign parent). Before the branch profits tax was enacted, a foreign corporation with a branch in the United States paid only the initial tax on its U.S. earnings; remittances were not taxed.

The dividend equivalent amount (DEA) is the foreign corporation's effectively connected earnings for the taxable year, adjusted for increases and decreases in the corporation's U.S. net equity (investment in the U.S. operations). The DEA is limited to current E & P and post-1986 accumulated E & P that are effectively connected, or treated as effectively connected, with the conduct of a U.S. trade or business. It does not include E & P that has been previously subject to the branch profits tax. E & P for this purpose does not include income otherwise exempt from U.S. taxation, certain FSC income, gain on sale of stock of a domestic corporation that is a U.S. real property holding corporation, and income that the taxpayer elects to treat as effectively connected under Subpart F. U.S. net equity is the sum of money and the aggregate adjusted basis of assets and liabilities directly connected to U.S. operations that generate effectively connected income. A decrease in net equity as the result of a deficit for the tax year is not subject to the branch profits tax.

Example 17

Robin, Inc., a foreign corporation, has a U.S. branch operation with the following tax results and other information for 1993:

E & P effectively connected with a U. S. trade or business	$2,000,000
U.S. corporate tax (at 34%)	680,000
Remittance to home office	1,000,000
Increase in U.S. net equity	320,000*

*$2,000,000 − $680,000 U.S. taxes − $1,000,000 remittance.

Robin's DEA and branch profits tax are computed as follows:

After-tax E & P effectively connected with a U.S. trade or business (1993)	$1,320,000
Less: Increase in U.S. net equity	(320,000)
DEA	$1,000,000
Branch profits tax rate	× 30%
Branch profits tax	$ 300,000

◆

The 30 percent rate of the branch profits tax may be reduced or eliminated by a treaty provision. A lower rate specified in a treaty applies where the treaty provides for a branch profits tax or withholding on dividends paid by a corporation resident in the treaty country. The rate reduction will not apply if the foreign corporation is not a qualified resident of the treaty country (for example, a foreign corporation owned by persons nonresident in the treaty country). The branch profits tax does not apply where prohibited by treaty under a nondiscrimination clause. If a foreign corporation is subject to the branch profits tax, no other tax is levied on the dividend actually paid by the corporation during the taxable year.

The Foreign Investment in Real Property Tax Act

Under prior law, NRAs and foreign corporations could avoid U.S. taxation on gains from the sale of U.S. real estate if the gains were treated as capital gains and were not effectively connected with the conduct of a U.S. trade or business.

Furthermore, the United States has a number of income tax treaties that allow for an annual election to treat real estate operations as a trade or business. Persons who were residents of the treaty countries could take advantage of the election for tax years prior to the year of sale and then revoke the election for the year in which the sale took place. In the mid-1970s, midwestern farmers put pressure on Congress to eliminate what they saw as a tax advantage that would allow nonresidents to bid up the price of farmland. This and other concerns regarding the foreign ownership of U.S. real estate led to enactment of the Foreign Investment in Real Property Tax Act (FIRPTA) of 1980.

Under FIRPTA, gains and losses realized by NRAs and foreign corporations from the sale or other disposition of U.S. real property interests are treated as effectively connected with the conduct of a U.S. trade or business even where those persons are not actually so engaged. NRA individuals must pay a tax equal to at least 21 percent of the lesser of their alternative minimum taxable income or net U.S. real property gain for the taxable year.

For these purposes, losses of individual taxpayers are taken into account only to the extent they are deductible under § 165(c) (business losses, losses on transactions entered into for profit, and losses from casualties and thefts).

U.S. Real Property Interest (USRPI). Any direct interest in real property situated in the United States and any interest in a domestic corporation (other than solely as a creditor) are U.S. real property interests (USRPIs). This definition applies unless the taxpayer can establish that a domestic corporation was not a U.S. real property holding corporation (USRPHC) during the shorter of the period after June 18, 1980, during which the taxpayer held an interest in the corporation, or the five-year period ending on the date on which the interest was disposed of (the base period). A domestic corporation is not a USRPHC if it holds no USRPIs on the date of disposition of its stock and if any USRPIs held by the corporation during the base period were disposed of in a transaction in which gain, if any, was fully recognized. This exception also applies if the USRPI disposed of by the corporation was stock of a second USRPHC that ceased to be a USRPHC by way of a taxable disposition of its USRPIs.

EXAMPLE 18

From January 1, 1988, through January 1, 1993, Francis (a foreign investor) holds shares in Door, Inc., a U.S. corporation. During this period, Door holds two parcels of U.S. real estate and stock of Sash, Inc., another U.S. corporation. Sash also owns U.S. real estate. The two parcels of real estate held directly by Door were disposed of on December 15, 1989, in a like-kind exchange in which Door acquired foreign realty. Sash disposed of its U.S. real estate in a taxable transaction on January 1, 1993. An interest in Door will be treated as a USRPI because Door did not recognize gain on the December 15, 1989, exchange of the USRPIs. If Door's ownership of U.S. real estate had been limited to its indirect ownership through Sash, as of January 2, 1993, an interest in Door would not constitute a USRPI. This is because Sash disposed of its USRPIs in a taxable transaction in which gain was fully recognized. ◆

A USRPHC is any corporation (whether foreign or domestic) where the fair market value of the corporation's USRPIs equals or exceeds 50 percent of the aggregate of fair market value of certain specific assets. These assets are the corporation's USRPIs, its interests in real property located outside the United States, plus any other of its assets that are used or held for use in a trade or business. Stock regularly traded on an established securities market is not treated as a USRPI where a person holds no more than 5 percent of the stock.

Withholding Provisions. Any purchaser or agent acquiring a USRPI from a foreign person must withhold 10 percent of the amount realized on the disposition.[36] The amount withheld must be submitted along with Form 8288 within at least 20 days after the transfer. The amount withheld need not exceed the transferor's maximum tax liability with regard to the transfer. A domestic partnership, trust, or estate with a foreign partner, foreign grantor treated as owner, or foreign beneficiary must withhold 34 percent (or 31 percent where allowed by the IRS) of the gain allocable to that person on a disposition of a USRPI. Foreign corporations are also subject to withholding provisions on certain distributions.

Failure to withhold can subject the purchaser or the purchaser's agent to interest on any unpaid amount. A civil penalty of 100 percent of the amount required to be withheld and a criminal penalty of up to $10,000 or five years in prison can be imposed for willful failure to withhold.[37]

Certain exemptions from withholding are provided. An agent for the purchaser or seller is liable for withholding only an amount equal to the compensation he or she received for handling the transaction.

Special Provisions

Taxpayers Married to Nonresident Aliens. A citizen or resident of the United States, who is married to an NRA at the close of the taxable year, may elect to file a joint return with the NRA spouse. Both spouses must consent to the election, and, once made, the election applies for the current year and all subsequent years unless revoked. With the election, the NRA is treated as a U.S. resident for income tax purposes, and his or her worldwide taxable income is subject to U.S. taxation.

Dual Resident Taxpayers. A taxpayer who is a dual resident (an NRA for a portion of the tax year and a U.S. resident for a portion of the tax year) can elect to file a joint return if he or she is a U.S. resident at the close of the taxable year and is married to a U.S. citizen or resident. Both spouses must consent to the election, which can be made only one time. The election also subjects the dual resident's worldwide taxable income for the entire tax year to U.S. taxation.

Community Income. Special rules set forth the tax treatment of community income in the case of a married couple where one or both persons are NRAs. Earned income, other than trade or business income and a partner's distributive share of partnership income, is treated as income of the spouse who rendered the personal services. Trade or business income is treated as income of the husband. However, if the wife exercises substantially all of the management and control of a trade or business, all the gross income and deductions attributable to the trade or business are treated as hers. A partner's distributive share of partnership income is treated as income of the partner. Other community income derived from separate property owned by one spouse is treated as that spouse's income. All other community income is treated as the applicable community property law provides.

Example 19

Howard, a U.S. citizen, is married to Wanda, an NRA. Howard and Wanda do not elect to file a joint return. Under the laws of their country of residence, dividends from stock owned jointly by married couples are considered the property of the husband. If Howard and Wanda receive dividends on stock they own jointly, Howard must include

36. § 1445.

37. §§ 6672 and 7202.

the entire dividend in gross income for U.S. tax purposes even where it is foreign-source income. ◆

Expatriation to Avoid Tax. An NRA individual who lost U.S. citizenship within 10 years immediately preceding the close of the current tax year is subject to U.S. taxation under § 877. An exception is made if the loss of citizenship did not have as one of its principal purposes the avoidance of the U.S. income, estate, or gift tax. Under § 877, only U.S.-source taxable income is subject to tax and only if the tax under § 877 is greater than the tax that the expatriate would otherwise owe with regard to U.S.-source taxable income. For this purpose, gain on the sale or exchange of property (other than stock or debt obligations) located in the United States is U.S.-source income. Gain on the sale or exchange of stock issued by a domestic corporation and debt obligations of U.S. persons or of the United States, a state or political subdivision thereof, or the District of Columbia also are deemed U.S.-source income under § 877. This source rule also applies to the sale or exchange of property that takes its basis in whole or in part by reference to the property described above.

Tax Treaties

Income Tax. Over 40 income tax treaties between the United States and other countries are in effect. These treaties generally provide *taxing rights* with regard to the taxable income of residents of one treaty country who have income sourced in the other treaty country. For the most part, neither country is prohibited from taxing the income of its residents. The treaties generally provide for primary taxing rights that require the other treaty partner to allow a credit for the taxes paid on income that is taxed under the primary taxing rights of one treaty partner and is also taxed by the other treaty partner.

EXAMPLE 20

Caterina, a resident of a foreign country with which the United States has an income tax treaty, earns income attributable to a permanent establishment (e.g., place of business) in the United States. Under the treaty, the United States has primary taxing rights with regard to this income. The other country can also require that the income be included in gross income and subject to its income tax, but must allow a credit for the taxes paid to the United States on the income. ◆

Primary taxing rights usually depend on the residence of the taxpayer or the presence of a permanent establishment in a treaty country, to which the income is attributable. Generally, a permanent establishment is a branch, office, factory, workshop, warehouse, or other fixed place of business.

The United States developed a Model Income Tax Treaty[38] as the starting point for negotiating income tax treaties with other countries. The most controversial of the articles in the model treaty is Article 16, Limitation on Benefits. This article is meant to prevent what is known as *treaty shopping.* Treaty shopping occurs when an entity resident in a treaty country takes advantage of the provisions of the treaty even though the majority of the owners of the entity are not residents of the treaty country. Article 16 disallows treaty benefits to an entity unless more than 75 percent of the beneficial interest in the entity is owned, directly or indirectly, by one or more individual residents of the same treaty country in which the entity is resident. The entity cannot be a conduit for meeting liabilities,

38. Treasury Department Model Income Tax Treaty (June 16, 1981).

such as interest or royalty payments, to persons who are not residents in either treaty country and who are not U.S. citizens. The United States' negotiating position with regard to Article 16 of the Model Income Tax Treaty has led to the termination of some treaties.

Several code provisions override the income tax treaties to some extent. Examples include § 884 (the branch profits tax) and § 897 (FIRPTA). The U.S. Treasury Department is currently considering the impact of the Tax Reform Act of 1986 on tax treaties that have been negotiated. Several international trade organizations have expressed concern that treaty override provisions inhibit treaty negotiations and international trade.

Estate and Gift Tax. The United States has estate tax treaties with fewer than 20 countries. Some of these treaties are combined estate and gift tax treaties. Like the income tax treaties, they provide primary taxing rights and a credit for taxes paid to the treaty country with the primary taxing rights. Primary taxing rights generally reside with the country where the property is located (older treaties) or the country of domicile of the donor or decedent (newer treaties). Primary taxing rights regarding real property and property of a permanent establishment for the most part reside with the country in which the property is situated.

U.S. Taxpayers Abroad

Citizens and residents of the United States are subject to Federal taxation on their worldwide taxable income. U.S. taxpayers who operate in a foreign country as a sole proprietor, or through a foreign branch or foreign partnership, must include foreign-source income in gross income for U.S. tax purposes. They are allowed a deduction for related expenses and losses.

Income tax treaties can reduce or eliminate the taxation of the income by the foreign country party to the treaty. Since, under the treaty, the United States reserves the right to tax its citizens and residents, relief from double taxation is achieved with the FTC. In addition to the FTC, several other tax provisions involve certain foreign-source income of U.S. citizens and residents.

The Foreign Earned Income Exclusion—§ 911

To help U.S. multinational entities be competitive in the world market, Congress enacted legislation granting an exclusion (from U.S. gross income) for a certain amount of qualified foreign earned income. This exclusion allows multinational entities to employ U.S. citizens and residents for foreign operations without having to pay them a wage or salary far in excess of that paid to nationals of the particular foreign country or countries. The United States taxes worldwide taxable income of its citizens and residents. Consequently, without the exclusion, the tax burden on a U.S. taxpayer working abroad could be much greater than that on a native of the foreign country. Currently, § 911 allows a foreign earned income exclusion for (1) a qualified housing cost amount and (2) foreign earned income not in excess of $70,000.

The exclusion is elective and is made by filing Form 2555 with the income tax return, or with an amended return, for the first taxable year for which the election is to be effective. An election once made remains in effect for that year and for all subsequent years unless revoked. If the election is revoked for any taxable year, the taxpayer may not make the election again (without consent of the IRS) until the sixth taxable year following the taxable year for which revocation was first effective.

Qualified Individuals. The exclusion is available to an individual whose tax home is in a foreign country and who is either (1) a U.S. citizen and bona fide resident of a foreign country or countries or (2) a citizen or resident of the United States who, during any 12 consecutive months, is physically present in a foreign country or countries for at least 330 full days. *Tax home* has the same meaning as under § 162(a)(2) relating to travel expenses while away from home. The issue of whether a stay abroad is temporary can be troublesome. If the stay abroad is deemed to be temporary, the taxpayer's tax home has not shifted to the foreign country. The IRS has held that an individual who worked in another city for 16 months was temporarily away from home.[39]

Only whole days count for the physical presence test. The taxpayer has some flexibility in choosing the 12-month period.

EXAMPLE 21

Carla, a U.S. citizen, arrived in Ireland from Boston at 3 P.M. on March 28, 1992. She remained in Ireland until 8 A.M. on March 1, 1993, when she departed for the United States. Among other possible 12-month periods, Carla was present in a foreign country an aggregate of 330 full days during each of the following 12-month periods: March 1, 1992, through February 28, 1993, and March 29, 1992, through March 28, 1993. ◆

Some factors considered in determining whether a bona fide foreign residence has been established are the taxpayer's intent, establishment of a home temporarily in a foreign country for an indefinite period, participation in community activities, and, in general, assimilation into the foreign environment.[40]

Section 911 is not available to a U.S. citizen or resident who resides and/or works in a foreign country in contravention of an executive order. These include countries with which the United States has broken diplomatic ties, such as Iran and Cuba. However, an individual who is required to leave a foreign country before meeting the bona fide residence or physical presence test may obtain a waiver on establishing that the requirements would have been met under normal conditions. Circumstances that trigger this exception include war, civil unrest, and similar adverse conditions that prevent the normal conduct of business.

If spouses both earn foreign earned income, each may be eligible for the foreign earned income exclusion. Each spouse is subject to a separate limitation, even when the couple files a joint return. Community property laws are ignored, and the income is treated as that of the spouse who actually performed the services.

The General Exclusion. The foreign earned income (general) exclusion is available for foreign earned income and is limited to the lesser of (1) $70,000 or (2) foreign earned income less the housing cost amount exclusion. The exclusion is available for the tax year in which income would be taken into account for tax purposes. The limitation, however, is determined for the tax year in which the

39. Rev.Rul. 83–82, 1983–1 C.B. 45.

40. *Sochurek v. Comm.*, 62–1 USTC ¶9293, 9 AFTR2d 883, 300 F.2d 34 (CA–7, 1962).

services were performed. Income received after the close of the taxable year following the taxable year in which the services were performed does not qualify for the exclusion.

EXAMPLE 22

Tom, a U.S. resident, is present in a foreign country for all of 1992. He earns $100,000 from the performance of personal services. On January 1, 1993, he returns to the United States and remains there. Of the $100,000 foreign earned income, Tom receives $60,000 in 1992 and $40,000 in 1993. Tom can take a foreign earned income exclusion of $60,000 for 1992 and $10,000 for 1993 ($70,000 statutory limit – $60,000 excluded for 1992). If Tom did not receive the $40,000 until 1994, no exclusion would be allowed for 1994 because he received the $40,000 after the close of the taxable year following the taxable year in which the services were performed. ◆

The statutory amount must be prorated on a daily basis where the taxpayer does not qualify for the exclusion for the full tax year. If Tom, in Example 22 qualified for only 11 months of the year, the statutory amount would be $64,055 [$70,000 × (334 days/365 days)].

Amounts paid by the United States, or any agency of the United States, to an employee do not qualify for the exclusion. Such persons usually are not subject to the income tax of the country where they work. Hence, relief from double taxation is not necessary since it does not exist.

The Housing Cost Amount. The housing cost amount is equal to the qualified housing expenses of an individual for the tax year less a base amount. The base amount is 16 percent of the salary of an employee of the United States for Step 1 Grade GS-14. The base amount is determined on a daily basis. For 1992, the base amount for a full year was $8,737. For a qualified individual employed overseas for 250 days of the year, the applicable base amount would be $5,984 [$8,737 × (250 days/365 days)].

Qualified housing expenses include reasonable expenses paid or incurred during the taxable year for housing for the individual (and spouse and dependents where appropriate) in a foreign country. Qualified housing expenses include housing costs provided by an employer, utilities, and insurance, but not interest and taxes deductible under § 163 or § 164. Under certain conditions, housing expenses for a second household will be allowed for a spouse and dependents.

If the taxpayer is an employee, all housing expenses are treated as provided by the employer. However, only housing expenses for which the employer actually incurs a cost are included in the taxpayer's gross income as foreign earned income. The housing cost amount exclusion is limited to foreign earned income.

EXAMPLE 23

Charles, a U.S. citizen, works as an engineer for a U.S. multinational company in Bahrain. He is a bona fide resident of Bahrain for the entire calendar and tax year and earns a salary of $80,000. In addition, his employer provides $16,000 in housing costs. If the base amount is $8,737 and Charles elects both exclusions, the housing cost amount exclusion is $7,263 ($16,000 – $8,737), and the foreign earned income exclusion is $70,000 (the lesser of $96,000 foreign earned income – $7,263 housing cost amount exclusion, or the $70,000 statutory limit). Charles's taxable income will include $18,737 of foreign earned income ($80,000 + $16,000 – $7,263 – $70,000). ◆

A self-employed individual is not eligible to exclude housing expenses, but can elect to deduct them. The § 911 Regulations provide guidelines for when an individual must allocate housing expenses between employer-provided amounts and expenses incurred as a self-employed person. The deduction for housing expenses is limited to the lesser of the housing cost amount or foreign earned income less the foreign earned income exclusion.

Foreign Corporations Controlled by U.S. Persons

To minimize current tax liability, taxpayers often attempt to defer the recognition of taxable income. One way of trying to defer income recognition is to shift the income-generating activity to a foreign entity that is not within the U.S. tax jurisdiction. A foreign corporation is the most suitable entity for such an endeavor since, unlike a partnership, it is not a conduit through which income is taxed directly to the owner.

Realizing that this tax planning device would hinder the collection of Federal tax revenues, Congress enacted §§ 951–964 in the Revenue Act of 1962. This and subsequent legislation have led to the present provisions for corporations controlled by U.S. persons.

Controlled Foreign Corporations

Subpart F, §§ 951–964 of the Code, provides that certain types of income generated by controlled foreign corporations (CFCs) are currently included in gross income by the U.S. shareholders. For Subpart F to apply, the foreign corporation must have been a CFC for an uninterrupted period of 30 days or more during the taxable year. When this is the case, U.S. shareholders must include in gross income their pro rata share of Subpart F income and increase in earnings that the CFC has invested in U.S. property for the tax year. This rule applies to U.S. shareholders who own stock in the corporation on the last day of the tax year in which the corporation is a CFC. The gross income inclusion must be made for the taxable year in which or with which the taxable year of the corporation ends.

Example 24

Gray, Inc., a calendar year corporation, is a CFC for all of 1993. Rex, a U.S. resident, owns 60% of Gray's one class of stock for the entire year. Subpart F income is $100,000, investment in U.S. property has not increased, and no distributions have been made during the year. Rex, a calendar year taxpayer, must include $60,000 in gross income as a constructive dividend for 1993. ◆

Example 25

Gray, Inc., is a CFC until July 1, 1994. Terry, a U.S. citizen, owns 30% of its one class of stock for the entire year. Subpart F income is $100,000. She must include $14,877 [$100,000 × 30% × (181 days/365 days)] in gross income as a constructive dividend for 1994. ◆

A CFC is any foreign corporation in which more than 50 percent of the total combined voting power of all classes of stock entitled to vote or the total value of the stock of the corporation is owned by U.S. shareholders on any day during the taxable year of the foreign corporation. For purposes of determining if a foreign corporation is a CFC, a *U.S. shareholder* is defined as a U.S. person who owns, or is considered to own, 10 percent or more of the total combined voting power of all classes of voting stock of the foreign corporation. Stock owned directly, indirectly, and constructively is counted.[41] The foreign subsidiaries of most multinational U.S. parent corporations are CFCs.

Indirect ownership involves stock held through a foreign entity, such as a foreign corporation, foreign partnership, or foreign trust. This stock is considered as actually owned proportionately by the shareholders, partners, or beneficiaries. The constructive ownership rules under § 318(a), with certain modifications, apply in determining if a U.S. person is a U.S. shareholder, in determining whether a foreign corporation is a CFC, and for certain related party provisions of Subpart F. The following are some of the modifications:

- Stock owned by a nonresident alien individual is not considered constructively owned by a U.S. citizen or resident alien individual.
- If a partnership, estate, trust, or corporation owns, directly or indirectly, more than 50 percent of the voting power of a corporation, it is deemed to own all of its stock.
- The threshold for corporate attribution is 10 percent rather than 50 percent.[42]

EXAMPLE 26

Shareholders of Foreign Corporation	Voting Power	Classification
Alan	30%	U.S. person
Bill	9%	U.S. person
Carla	41%	Foreign person
Dora	20%	U.S. person

Bill is Alan's son. Alan, Bill, and Dora are *U.S. shareholders.* Alan owns 39%, 30% directly and 9% constructively through Bill. Bill also owns 39%, 9% directly and 30% constructively through Alan. Dora owns 20% directly. The corporation is a CFC because U.S. shareholders own 59% of the voting power. If Bill were not related to Alan or to any other U.S. persons who were shareholders, Bill would not be a U.S. shareholder, and the corporation would not be a CFC. ◆

U.S. shareholders must include their pro rata share of the applicable income in their gross income only to the extent of their actual ownership. Stock held indirectly is considered actually owned for this purpose.

EXAMPLE 27

Bill, in Example 26 would recognize only 9% of the Subpart F income as a constructive dividend. Alan would recognize 30% and Dora would recognize 20%. If Bill were a foreign corporation, wholly owned by Alan, Alan would recognize 39% as a constructive dividend. If Carla owned only 40% of the stock and Ed, a U.S. person, owned 1% and was not related to any of the other shareholders, Ed would not be a *U.S. shareholder* and would not have to include any of the Subpart F income in gross income. ◆

Subpart F Income. Subpart F income consists of the following:

- Insurance income (§ 953).
- Foreign base company income (§ 954).

41. § 957.

42. § 958.

- International boycott factor income (§ 999).
- Illegal bribes.
- Income derived from a § 901(j) foreign country.

Insurance income is income attributable to any insurance or annuity contract in connection with property in, or liability arising out of activity in, or the lives or health of residents of a country other than the country under whose laws the CFC is created or organized. The income includes that from the reinsurance of such property, activity, or persons, and any arrangement with another corporation whereby the other corporation assumes these risks in exchange for the CFC's insurance of risks not described above.

If the foreign corporation is a *captive insurance company,* the U.S. shareholders must include any related-person insurance income in gross income as a constructive dividend if the U.S. shareholders own 25 percent or more of the voting power of the foreign corporation. For this purpose, any U.S. person owning *any* stock of the foreign corporation is deemed a *U.S. shareholder.* Related-person insurance income is that attributable to insurance or reinsurance where the primary insured is a U.S. shareholder or a person related to a U.S. shareholder. There are exceptions to this rule. A CFC can also elect to treat such income as effectively connected with a U.S. trade or business.

Foreign Base Company Income. There are five categories of foreign base company income (FBCI):

- Foreign personal holding company income.
- Foreign base company sales income.
- Foreign base company services income.
- Foreign base company shipping income.
- Foreign base company oil-related income.

Each of these income categories is defined in § 954. A *de minimis* rule provides that if the total amount of a foreign corporation's FBCI and gross insurance income for the taxable year is less than the lesser of 5 percent of gross income or $1 million, none of its gross income will be treated as FBCI for the tax year. The *de minimis* rule does not apply to other types of income under Subpart F, such as increases in investment in U.S. property. However, if a foreign corporation's FBCI and gross insurance income exceed 70 percent of total gross income, all the corporation's gross income for the tax year is treated as FBCI or insurance income.

FBCI and insurance income subject to high foreign taxes are not included under Subpart F if the taxpayer establishes that the income was subject to an effective rate, imposed by a foreign country, of more than 90 percent of the maximum corporate rate under § 11. For 1993, this rate must be greater than 30.6 percent (90% × 34%).

Foreign personal holding company (FPHC) income is gross income that consists of the following:

- Dividends, interest, royalties, rents, and annuities;
- Excess gains over losses from the sale or exchange of property (including an interest in a trust or partnership) that gives rise to FPHC income as described above or that does not give rise to any income;
- Excess gains over losses from transactions in any commodities (other than bona fide hedging transactions as part of an active business as a producer,

processor, merchant, or handler of commodities, or foreign currency gains or losses under § 988);
- Excess of foreign currency gains over foreign currency losses attributable to § 988 foreign currency transactions (other than any transaction directly related to the business needs of the CFC); and
- Any income equivalent to interest.

FPHC income does not include certain rents, royalties, dividends, and interest. These exceptions will not apply where the interest, rent, or royalty reduces the payor's Subpart F income.

Foreign base company (FBC) sales income is income derived from the purchase of personal property from or on behalf of a related person, or from the sale of personal property to or on behalf of a related person.

Example 28

A CFC owned 100% by Romus, a U.S. corporation, will generate FBC sales income in any one of the following situations:

- Purchase of widgets from anyone as commission agent for Romus Corporation.
- Purchase of widgets from Romus and sale to anyone.
- Purchase of widgets from anyone and sale to Romus Corporation.
- Sale of widgets to anyone as commission agent for Romus. ◆

An exception applies to property that is manufactured, produced, grown, or extracted in the country in which the CFC was organized or created and also to property sold for use, consumption, or disposition within that country. Certain income derived by a branch of the CFC in another country can be deemed FBC sales income. This would be the case if the effect of using the branch is the same as if the branch were a wholly owned subsidiary.

FBC services income is income derived from the performance of services for or on behalf of a related person and performed outside the country in which the CFC was created or organized. Income from services performed before and in connection with the sale of property by a CFC that has manufactured, produced, grown, or extracted such property is not FBC services income.

FBC shipping income includes several classifications of income, including dividends and interest received from a foreign corporation, to the extent that income is attributable to, or is derived from or in connection with, the shipping activity. Thus, income attributable to the use of any aircraft or vessel in foreign commerce, performance of services directly related to the use of that aircraft or vessel, or sale or exchange of any such aircraft or vessel is shipping income.

FBC oil-related income is income, other than extraction income, derived in a foreign country in connection with the sale of oil and gas products sold by the CFC or a related person for use or consumption within the country in which the oil or gas was extracted. Only corporations with production of at least 1,000 barrels per day are treated as deriving FBC oil-related income.

Distributions of Previously Taxed Income. Under § 959, distributions from a CFC are treated as being first from E & P attributable to increases in investment in U.S. property previously taxed as a constructive dividend, second from E & P attributable to previously taxed Subpart F income other than that described above, and last from other E & P. Thus, distributions of previously taxed income are not taxed as a dividend, but they reduce E & P.

EXAMPLE 29

Jet, Inc., a U.S. shareholder, owns 100% of a CFC from which Jet receives a $100,000 distribution. The CFC's E & P is composed of the following amounts:

- $50,000 attributable to previously taxed increases in investment in U.S. property,
- $30,000 attributable to previously taxed Subpart F income, and
- $40,000 attributable to other E & P.

Jet has a taxable dividend of only $20,000, all attributable to other E & P. The remaining $80,000 is previously taxed income. The CFC's E & P is reduced by $100,000. The remaining E & P is attributable to other E & P. ◆

A U.S. shareholder's basis in CFC stock is increased by constructive dividends included in income under Subpart F and decreased by subsequent distributions of previously taxed income. Under § 960, U.S. corporate shareholders who own at least 10 percent of the voting stock of a foreign corporation are allowed an indirect FTC for foreign taxes deemed paid on constructive dividends included in gross income under Subpart F. The indirect credit also is available for Subpart F income attributable to second- and third-tier foreign corporations as long as the 10 percent ownership requirement is met from tier to tier. Deemed-paid taxes for which an indirect FTC is allowed under § 960 are not creditable under § 902 when actual distributions of previously taxed income are made.

Foreign Sales Corporations

Prior to 1985, the Domestic International Sales Corporations (DISC) provisions (§§ 991–997) allowed for a deferral of the tax on a portion of the export income of a DISC until actual repatriation of the earnings. Over the years, Congress cut the amount of export income on which deferral was allowed. As the result of charges by the General Agreement on Trade and Tariffs (whose members include some of the United States' major trading partners) that the DISC provisions were a prohibited *export subsidy,* the DISC provisions were curtailed. As an alternative, the Foreign Sales Corporation (FSC) provisions (§§ 921–927) were enacted. The major short-term benefit of converting an export operation from a DISC to an FSC was that deferred DISC income that was forgiven would never be subject to U.S. taxation. The only remaining DISCs are interest charge ones—the price of deferral is an annual interest charge on the deferred taxes.[43] Only export sales up to $10 million qualify for deferral. Amounts in excess of $10 million are deemed distributed.

Most large multinational firms prefer CFCs to FSCs because they establish a more permanent active foreign presence, as in manufacturing. Mid-sized companies, such as Convex, often use FSCs, however, as do companies with very high profit margins (e.g., 50 to 60 percent).

FSCs are not allowed a tax deferral on export income. Instead, a certain percentage (about 15 or 16 percent, depending on taxpayer status) of export income is exempt from U.S. taxation (exempt foreign trade income). Pricing methods are provided for determining exempt foreign trade income.

To elect FSC status, a foreign corporation must meet a foreign presence requirement. An exception to this requirement is provided if the foreign corporation's export receipts do not exceed $5 million (the small FSC exception). The foreign presence requirement includes maintaining a foreign office, operating

43. § 995(f).

under foreign management, keeping a permanent set of books at the foreign office, conducting foreign economic processes (e.g., selling activities), and being a foreign corporation. Recall that a foreign corporation is one organized or created under the laws of a foreign country or any U.S. possession. In addition, the corporation must have no more than 25 shareholders at any time during the taxable year and have no preferred stock outstanding at any time during the taxable year.

Other Considerations

The Revenue Reconciliation Act of 1989 limits deductions of interest expense by certain foreign-controlled U.S. corporations. While primarily aimed at these foreign-controlled entities, this provision can also apply to U.S. parent corporations paying interest to their foreign subsidiaries. This rule is referred to as the *earnings stripping* provision since it will only apply if the payer's debt-to-equity ratio exceeds 1.5 to 1 and a high proportion of earnings is paid out as interest expense. Disallowed amounts can be carried over to future years.

The 1989 Act also requires that the tax years of CFCs and FPHCs conform to that of a more-than-50 percent U.S. owner. Additionally, a CFC is allowed to use a tax year ending such that no more than one month's deferral of income recognition is provided to the majority U.S. shareholder.

Foreign Currency Transactions

Changes in the relative value of a foreign currency and the U.S. dollar (the foreign exchange rate) affect the dollar value of foreign property held by the taxpayer, the dollar value of foreign debts, and the dollar amount of gain or loss on transactions denominated in a foreign currency.

Example 30

Dress, Inc., a domestic corporation, purchases merchandise for resale from Fiesta, Inc., a foreign corporation, for 50,000K. On the date of purchase, 1K (a foreign currency) is equal to $1 U.S. (1K:$1). At this time, the account payable is $50,000. On the date of payment by Dress (the foreign exchange date), the exchange rate is 1.25K:$1. In other words, the foreign currency has declined in value in relation to the U.S. dollar, and Dress will pay Fiesta 50,000K, which costs Dress $40,000. Dress must record the purchase of the merchandise at $50,000 and recognize a foreign currency gain of $10,000 ($50,000 – $40,000). ◆

Taxpayers may find it necessary to translate amounts denominated in foreign currency into U.S. dollars for any of the following purposes:

- Purchase of goods, services, and property.
- Sale of goods, services, and property.
- Collection of foreign receivables.
- Payment of foreign payables.
- FTC calculations.
- Recognizing income or loss from foreign branch activities.

The foreign currency exchange rates, however, have no effect on the transactions of a U.S. person who arranges all international transactions in U.S. dollars.

EXAMPLE 31

Sellers, Inc., a domestic corporation, purchases goods from Rose, Inc., a foreign corporation, and pays for these goods in U.S. dollars. Rose then exchanges the U.S. dollars for the currency of the country in which it operates. Sellers has no foreign exchange considerations with which to contend. If Sellers purchased goods from Rose and was required to pay Rose in a foreign currency, Sellers would have to exchange U.S. dollars for the foreign currency in order to make payment. If the exchange rate had changed from the date of purchase to the date of payment, Sellers would have a foreign currency gain or loss on the currency exchange. ◆

Tax Issues

The following are the major tax issues that must be considered in the taxation of foreign currency exchange:

- The character of the gain or loss (ordinary or capital).
- The date of recognition of any gain or loss.
- The source (U.S. or foreign) of the foreign currency gain or loss.

EXAMPLE 32

Batch, Inc., a domestic corporation, purchases computer parts for resale from Chips, a foreign corporation, for 125,000K. On the date of purchase, .75K (a foreign currency) is equal to $1 U.S. (.75K:$1). On the date of payment by Batch (the foreign exchange date), the exchange rate is .8K:$1. In other words, Batch paid 125,000K, which cost Batch $156,250 in U.S. dollars (125,000K/.8K). Batch, however, must record the purchase of the computer parts for inventory purposes at $166,667 (125,000K/.75K) and recognize a foreign currency gain of $10,417 ($166,667 – $156,250). ◆

Before 1987, there was little statutory authority dealing with the taxation of foreign currency transactions. The IRS rulings and the court decisions on the subject were not consistent. The Tax Reform Act of 1986 provided statutory rules for most business transactions involving foreign currency exchange. Many personal transactions involving foreign currency exchange are not covered by these provisions, however, and the law developed prior to TRA of 1986 still applies. For individuals, the post-1986 statutory provisions apply only to the extent that allocable expenses qualify as trade or business expenses under § 162 or expenses of producing income under § 212.[44]

The following concepts are important when dealing with the tax aspects of foreign exchange:

- Foreign currency is treated as property other than money.
- Gain or loss on the exchange of foreign currency is considered separately from the underlying transaction (e.g., the purchase or sale of goods).
- No gain or loss is recognized until a transaction is closed.

EXAMPLE 33

If, in Example 32 above, the foreign exchange rate on the date of purchase was .75K:$1, 1.2K:$1 on a date between the purchase and payment dates, and .75K:$1 on the payment date, Batch realizes no foreign currency gain or loss. The transaction was not closed at the time of the foreign exchange rate fluctuation. ◆

44. § 988(e).

Functional Currency

Prior to 1987, the Code contained no provisions for determining tax results when foreign operations could be recorded in a foreign currency. However, in 1981, the Financial Accounting Standards Board adopted FAS 52 on foreign currency translation. FAS 52 introduced the *functional currency* approach (the currency of the economic environment in which the foreign entity operates generally is to be used as the monetary unit to measure gains and losses). TRA of 1986 adopted this approach for the most part.

Under § 985, all income tax determinations are to be made in the taxpayer's functional currency. Generally, a taxpayer's functional currency will be the U.S. dollar. In certain circumstances, a qualified business unit (QBU) may be required to use a foreign currency as its functional currency. A QBU is a separate and clearly identified unit of a taxpayer's trade or business (e.g., a foreign branch). A corporation is a QBU. An individual is not a QBU; however, a trade or business conducted by an individual may be a QBU.

Section 988 Transactions

The disposition of a nonfunctional currency can result in a foreign currency gain or loss under § 988. Section 988 transactions include those in which gain or loss is determined with regard to the value of a nonfunctional currency, such as the following:

1. Acquisition of (or becoming obligor under) a debt instrument.
2. Accruing (or otherwise taking into account) any item of expense or gross income or receipts that is to be paid or received at a later date.
3. Entering into or acquiring any forward contract, futures contract, option or similar investment position unless the position is a regulated futures contract or nonequity option that would be marked-to-market under § 1256.[45]
4. Disposition of nonfunctional currency.

Section 988 generally treats exchange gain or loss falling within its provisions as ordinary income or loss. Certain exchange gain or loss will be apportioned in the same manner as interest income or expense. Capital gain or loss treatment may be elected with regard to forward contracts, futures contracts, and options that constitute capital assets in the hands of the taxpayer. These capital assets cannot be part of a straddle or marked-to-market under § 1256 and must meet certain identification requirements.

As under pre-1987 law, a closed or completed transaction is required. The residence of the taxpayer generally determines the source of a foreign exchange gain or loss. For this purpose, the residence of a QBU is the country in which its principal place of business is located.

Branch Operations

Where a QBU (a foreign branch, in this case) uses a foreign currency as its functional currency, the profit or loss must be computed in the foreign currency

45. Section 988(c)(1)(D)(ii) provides for an election to bring positions in regulated futures contracts and nonequity options that would be marked-to-market under § 1256 within the provisions of § 988. The election, once made, is binding for all future years. Special provisions apply with regard to qualified funds as defined under § 988(c)(1)(E)(iii).

each year and translated into U.S. dollars for tax purposes. Section 987 requires that the profit and loss method be used for this purpose. With this method, the entire amount of profit or loss, without taking remittances into account, must be translated using a weighted-average exchange rate for the taxable year. Exchange gain or loss is recognized on remittances from the QBU. This is done by comparing the U.S. dollar amount of the remittance at the exchange rate in effect on the date of remittance with the U.S. dollar value (at the appropriate weighted-average rate) of a pro rata portion of post-1986 accumulated earnings of the branch. This gain or loss is ordinary and is sourced according to the income to which the remittance is attributable.

EXAMPLE 34

Icon, a domestic corporation, began operation of a QBU (foreign branch) in 1991. The functional currency of the QBU is the K. The QBU's profits for 1991–1993 are as follows:

	Income (in Ks)	Exchange Rate	Income in U.S. Dollars
1991	200K	1K:$1	$200
1992	200K	1.25K:$1	160
1993	200K	1.6K:$1	125
	600K		$485

The income is taxed to Icon in the year earned regardless of whether any remittances take place. ◆

Distributions from Foreign Corporations

An actual distribution of E & P from a foreign corporation is included in income by the U.S. recipient at the exchange rate in effect on the *date of distribution*. Thus, no exchange gain or loss is recognized. Deemed dividend distributions under Subpart F must be translated at the weighted-average exchange rate for the CFC's tax year to which the deemed distribution is attributable. Exchange gain or loss can result when an actual distribution of this previously taxed income is made. The gain or loss is the difference in the exchange rates on the date the deemed distribution is included in income and the date of the actual distribution.

EXAMPLE 35

In 1993, the QBU (see Example 34) remits 300K to Icon when the exchange rate is 1.6K:$1. Icon has a foreign currency loss of $55, determined as follows:

		Difference
$62.50* from 1991 at 1K:$1 =	$100.00**	($37.50)
$62.50 from 1992 at 1.25K:$1 =	80.00	(17.50)
$62.50 from 1993 at 1.6K:$1 =	62.50	–0–
	$242.50	($55.00)

*[300K × (200K/600K)] at a rate of 1.6K:$1 = $62.50.
**[300K × (200K/600K)] at a rate of 1K:$1 = $100.

The loss is an ordinary loss for 1993. It is sourced by reference to the post-1986 accumulated earnings (1991–1993). The results would generally be the same if this was a distribution of previously taxed Subpart F income. ◆

For FTC purposes, foreign taxes are translated at the exchange rate in effect when the foreign taxes were paid. For purposes of the indirect FTC, any adjustment of foreign taxes paid by the foreign corporation is translated at the rate in effect at the time of adjustment. Any refund or credit is translated at the rate in effect at the time of original payment of the foreign taxes.

Example 36

Music, Inc., a foreign subsidiary of Keyboard, a U.S. corporation, has pre-tax income of 300K. Music pays 100K in foreign taxes. The exchange rate was .5K:$1 when the income was earned and the foreign taxes paid. None of the income is Subpart F income. If the 200K net earnings are distributed when the exchange rate is .4K:$1, the deemed-paid taxes are $200 [($500/$500) × $200]. The effective tax rate is 40%. ◆

Tax Planning Considerations

Tax legislation tends progressively to reduce the ability to plan transactions and operations in a manner that minimizes tax liability. However, taxpayers who are not limited by the constraints of a particular transaction or operation can use the following suggestions to plan for the maximum tax benefits.

The Foreign Tax Credit Limitation and Sourcing Provisions

The FTC limitation is partially based on the amount of foreign-source taxable income in the numerator of the limitation ratio. Consequently, the sourcing of income is extremely important. Income that is taxed by a foreign tax jurisdiction benefits from the FTC only to the extent that it is classified as foreign-source income under U.S. tax law. Thus, elements such as the place of title passage that affect the sourcing of income should be considered carefully before a transaction is undertaken.

A taxpayer who can control the timing of income and loss recognition will want to avoid recognizing losses in years in which the loss will be apportioned among the FTC limitation baskets. Otherwise, the foreign taxes for which a credit is allowed for the tax year will be reduced.

Example 37

Della, a U.S. citizen, has U.S.-source taxable income of $200,000, worldwide taxable income of $300,000, and a U.S. tax liability (before FTC) of $84,000. She receives foreign-source taxable income, pays foreign income taxes, and has an FTC as shown:

Basket	Amount	Foreign Taxes	FTC Limitation	FTC
Passive	$ 20,000	$ 800	$ 5,600	$ 800
General	50,000	20,500	14,000	14,000
Non-CFC § 902 corporation #1	15,000	3,000	4,200	3,000
Non-CFC § 902 corporation #2	15,000	4,500	4,200	4,200
	$100,000	$28,800		$22,000

If Della had a foreign-source loss of $10,000 that would fall in the shipping limitation basket, the FTC would be reduced by $1,820. The U.S. tax liability before the FTC would be $81,200; 50% of the loss would be apportioned to the general limitation basket reducing the FTC limitation for this basket to $12,600 [$81,200 × ($45,000/$290,000)]; and 15% would be apportioned to the non-CFC § 902 corporation #2 basket, reducing the FTC limitation for this basket to $3,780 [$81,200 × ($13,500/ $290,000)]. Della would avoid this result if she could defer recognition of the loss to a tax year in which it would not have a negative effect on the FTC. ◆

When negotiating the terms of the sale of an intangible, such as a patent, the taxpayer may be able to influence the source of the gain on the sale by controlling the amount of consideration that is contingent on the productivity or use of the intangible by the purchaser. Under § 865, contingent payments are sourced in the same manner as royalty income (where the intangible will be used). If the intangible will be used outside the United States, the greater the portion of the sales price that is contingent, the greater the foreign-source income. This will benefit the U.S. seller as long as any taxation of the contingent payments by the foreign tax authorities does not exceed the U.S. tax on those amounts.

The Foreign Corporation as a Tax Shelter

An NRA who is able to hold U.S. investments through a foreign corporation can accomplish much in the way of avoiding U.S. taxation. Any capital gains (other than dispositions of U.S. real property interests) are not subject to U.S. taxation. This assumes that they are not effectively connected with a U.S. trade or business and are not gains from commodity transactions entered into by a foreign corporation with its principal place of business in the United States. The NRA can dispose of the stock of a foreign corporation that holds U.S. real property and not be subject to taxation under § 897 (FIRPTA). Furthermore, the stock of a foreign corporation is not included in the U.S. gross estate of a deceased NRA even if all the assets of the foreign corporation are located in the United States.

Caution is advised where the foreign corporation may generate income effectively connected with the conduct of a U.S. trade or business. The income may be taxed at a higher rate than if the NRA individually generated the income. The trade-off between a higher U.S. tax on this income and protection from the U.S. estate tax and § 897 must be weighed.

Planning under Subpart F

The *de minimis* rule allows a CFC to avoid the classification of income as FBC income or insurance income and prevents the U.S. shareholder from having to include it in gross income as a constructive dividend. Thus, a CFC with total FBC income and insurance income in an amount close to the 5 percent or $1 million level should monitor income realization to assure that the *de minimis* rule applies for the tax year. At least as important is avoiding the classification of all the gross income of the CFC as FBC income or insurance income. This happens when the sum of the FBC income and gross insurance income for the taxable year exceeds 70 percent of total gross income.

Careful timing of increases in investment in U.S. property can reduce the potential for constructive dividend income to U.S. shareholders. The gross income of U.S. shareholders attributable to increases in investment in U.S. property is limited to the E & P of the CFC.[46] E & P that is attributable to amounts that have been included in gross income as Subpart F income either in the current year or a prior tax year is not taxed again when invested in U.S. property.

The Foreign Earned Income Exclusion

The tax benefit of the foreign earned income exclusion depends on the tax the income will incur in the country in which earned and the year in which received. If the foreign country levies little or no tax on the income, the U.S. taxpayer will be able to exclude the housing cost amount plus up to $70,000 of foreign earned

46. §§ 959(a)(1) and (2).

income and pay little or no tax on the income to the foreign tax jurisdiction. Since foreign earned income qualifies for the exclusion only if received in the year in which earned or the immediately succeeding tax year, the timely payment of such income is necessary.

In high tax jurisdictions, the taxpayer may benefit more from taking the FTC than from excluding the earnings from gross income. The taxpayer earning income in a high tax jurisdiction should compare the tax result of taking the exclusion with the tax result of forgoing either or both exclusions for the FTC. If U.S. taxes on the income are eliminated under all options and the taxpayer has excess foreign taxes to carry back or carry forward, then the FTC generally is more beneficial than the exclusion.

Taxpayers must also carefully monitor their trips to the United States when attempting to qualify for the exclusion under the physical presence test. Taxpayers who are attempting to establish a bona fide foreign residence must make sure that their ties to the foreign country predominate over their ties to the United States for the period for which bona fide foreign residence is desired.

Tax Treaties

The value of treaty benefits should never be overlooked by a taxpayer planning to perform services in a foreign country, enter into a transaction with a foreign person or in a foreign country, or conduct operations in a foreign country. Such persons should review the appropriate tax treaties carefully to apprise themselves of any benefits that may be available. International treaties not expressly labeled tax treaties also may contain provisions that are beneficial to U.S. or foreign persons entering into international transactions.[47]

Nonresident Aliens and U.S. Resident Status

An NRA who does not want worldwide income subject to U.S. taxation should not acquire a green card unless he or she has decided that U.S. resident status is worth the price of U.S. income taxation on a worldwide basis. Furthermore, an NRA who does not intend to become a U.S. resident for the tax year should avoid being physically present in the United States under any of the conditions that would lead to U.S. resident status for income tax purposes. Even if a person becomes a U.S. resident for income tax purposes, this does not necessarily mean that domicile has been changed to the United States. A resident alien can avoid the U.S. estate and gift tax in part at least by avoiding U.S. domicile. The showing of an intention to retain domicile in a foreign country suffices to retain foreign domicile for U.S. estate and gift tax purposes. Thus, to avoid U.S. domicile, the NRA or resident alien must maintain sufficient ties with a foreign country.

PROBLEM MATERIALS

DISCUSSION QUESTIONS

1. What income tax consequences need to be considered by a corporate shareholder which takes the indirect credit?
2. Explain the reasoning behind the foreign tax credit limitation.

---

47. *Arthur A. Amaral*, 90 T.C. 802 (1988).

3. What are some of the tax consequences affected by the sourcing of income as within or without the United States?
4. Why is the § 936 possessions corporation credit referred to as a "tax-sparing" credit?
5. Discuss the sourcing of losses rule and its effect.
6. What are the basic considerations in allocating interest expense between U.S.- and foreign-source income for deduction purposes?
7. What is the difference in the definition of "residency" for U.S. income tax purposes and for U.S. estate tax purposes?
8. What is the objective of the branch profits tax?
9. How are gains and losses on the sale of U.S. real property interests by NRAs treated under FIRPTA?
10. What requirements must be met and what tax consequences should be considered by a taxpayer and NRA spouse in making the election to file a joint return?
11. Describe "treaty shopping."
12. Why does the United States allow an exclusion for foreign earned income, but not for foreign unearned income such as dividends from foreign corporations?
13. How does the tax law prevent Subpart F income from being taxed more than once to the U.S. shareholders?
14. When would a U.S. corporation conducting international transactions *not* have to consider foreign exchange consequences?
15. Describe the effect of gain or loss on the exchange of foreign currency being considered separate from the underlying transaction (e.g., purchasing or selling goods).
16. When would the U.S. recipient of a constructive dividend (for example, under Subpart F) have a foreign exchange gain or loss?
17. Why can stock of a foreign corporation held by NRA individuals be considered a tax shelter for U.S. tax purposes?

PROBLEMS

18. For the tax year, George, a U.S. resident individual, has worldwide taxable income (without regard to personal exemptions) of $250,000, consisting of $200,000 U.S.-source income and $50,000 foreign-source dividend income. George's U.S. income tax liability before the FTC is $75,000, and the foreign tax paid on the dividend income is $12,500. What is George's FTC for the tax year?

19. Flim, a domestic calendar year corporation, has worldwide taxable income consisting of $400,000 U.S.-source income and a $100,000 foreign-source dividend received from Flam, a § 902 noncontrolled foreign corporation. Flam's post-1986 E & P after taxes is $2,000,000. Flam's foreign income taxes attributable to the E & P are $1,100,000.

    a. What is the amount of Flim's deemed-paid foreign taxes with regard to the dividend from Flam?
    b. What is Flim's FTC for the tax year?

20. How would the answers to Problem 19 change if the foreign tax authorities withheld $30,000 in taxes on the dividend from Flam, and the dividend Flim received amounted to only $70,000?
21. Given the following two separate ownership structures, may Delta, Inc., a domestic corporation, claim an FTC due to foreign taxes paid by Beta Corporation although Delta does not own any of Beta's stock? Alpha, Gamma, and Beta are foreign corporations.

    a. Delta owns 40% of Alpha Corporation, Alpha owns 40% of Gamma Corporation, and Gamma owns 50% of Beta Corporation.
    b. The same as (a) except that Gamma Corporation owns 30% of Beta rather than 50%.

22. World, Inc., a U.S. multinational corporation, has the following taxable income and pays the following taxes for 1993:

Category	Amount	Source	Foreign Taxes
Manufacturing	$150,000	Foreign	$ 60,000
	450,000	U.S.	–0–
Passive	50,000	Foreign	2,500
	120,000	U.S.	–0–
Dividends	60,000	Foreign*	15,000
	70,000	U.S.	–0–
Financial services	300,000	Foreign	120,000

*This is comprised of $30,000 from each of two § 902 noncontrolled foreign corporations. The foreign taxes attributable to the dividends were $12,000 and $3,000, respectively.

U.S. taxes before the FTC = $408,000.

a. What is World's FTC allowed for the tax year?
b. Are there any excess foreign taxes or excess limitations and, if so, how are they treated for FTC purposes?

23. Sarah, a U.S. resident, received the following dividend and interest income for 1993. What is the source (U.S. or foreign) of each income item?

a. Dividend income of $5,000 from Roberts, Inc., a domestic corporation, that has gross income of $1,700,000 from the active conduct of a foreign trade or business for the immediately preceding three-year period. Roberts's total gross income for the same period was $2,000,000.
b. Dividend of $10,000 from Fargo, Inc., a foreign corporation, that has gross income of $500,000 effectively connected with the conduct of a U.S. trade or business for the immediately preceding three-year period. Fargo's total gross income for the same period was $1,500,000.
c. Interest of $800 from Noel, an NRA individual, on a loan made by Sarah to Noel.
d. Interest of $15,000 on Hall Corporation bonds. Hall is a domestic corporation that derived $1,800,000 of its gross income for the immediately preceding three-year period from the active conduct of a foreign trade or business. Hall's total gross income for this same period was $2,100,000.
e. Interest of $2,000 from a savings account in a Chicago bank.

24. Amy, an NRA, is a resident of Costa Rica. She comes to the United States to perform with a musical group for five weeks in 1993. This is Amy's first and only visit to the United States during the year. She earns $5,000, which the group manager deposits directly into Amy's bank account in Costa Rica. Does Amy have U.S.-source income from this engagement?

25. Determine the source of income from the following sales:

a. Sale of inventory purchased by a U.S. resident in New York and sold to a Mexican company, title passing in Mexico.
b. Sale of inventory manufactured in Canada by a U.S. resident and sold to a German company, title passing in Germany.
c. Sale of equipment that had been used exclusively in a foreign trade or business by a domestic corporation to an unrelated foreign corporation, title passing in France.
d. Sale of Compaq stock by Richard, an NRA sale taking place on the New York Stock Exchange.

26. Jorge, a citizen and resident of Venezuela, comes to the United States for the first time on February 1, 1993, and remains until June 10 of the same year, at which time he returns to Venezuela. Jorge comes back to the United States on September 11, 1993, and remains until November 30, 1993, when he again returns to Venezuela. Jorge does not possess a green card. Is Jorge a U.S. resident for 1993 under the substantial

presence test? If so, is there any way that he can overcome the presumption of residence?

27. Anne, an NRA, has the following U.S.-source income for 1993. Determine Anne's U.S. tax liability assuming that she is single, has no § 165 losses and makes no charitable contributions.

Capital gain*	$15,000
Dividend from Bright Corporation**	10,000
Interest from U.S. bank account***	4,000
Net income from U.S. trade or business	50,000

*Not effectively connected to the U.S. business.
**Anne owns 30% of the stock of Bright, a U.S. corporation.
***The interest is not connected with the U.S. trade or business.

28. Stores, Inc., a foreign corporation, operates a trade or business in the United States. Stores's U.S.-source taxable income effectively connected with this trade or business is $400,000 for the current tax year. Stores's current E & P is $350,000. Stores's net U.S. equity at the beginning of the year was $1.5 million and at the end of the year was $1.6 million. Stores is resident in a country with which the United States does not have an income tax treaty. What is the effect of the branch profits tax on Stores for the current tax year?

29. Betty, a U.S. resident, is married to Henry, an NRA. Betty has taxable income of $80,000 for the tax year. Henry, who is retired, receives foreign-source investment income of $30,000 for the tax year. Can Betty and Henry file a joint return? If so, should they? Use 1993 tax rates to make the comparison.

30. Assume that Gary, a U.S. citizen, becomes a bona fide resident of a foreign country on March 28, 1992, and remains a resident until January 1, 1994. Gary is on the calendar year and cash tax basis in the United States. He earns a salary of $73,000 in 1993, but receives $60,000 of this amount in 1993 and $13,000 in 1994. Gary has no other foreign-source income in either year. How much of his salary is excludible under § 911 for 1993? How much for 1994? What would be the result if Gary received the $13,000 in 1995?

31. Calculate net taxable foreign-source earned income using the housing cost amount exclusion and the general exclusion for foreign-source earned income, given the following facts:

Total foreign-source earned income	$130,000*
Housing expenses paid by employer	35,000
Tax year	1993

*Includes the $35,000 of housing expenses.

For ease of calculation, use $9,000 as the base amount for purposes of the housing cost amount exclusion.

32. Referring back to Problem 31, calculate both exclusions under the assumption that the taxpayer was a qualified resident of the foreign country for only 11 months of the tax year.

33. Profit, Inc., a foreign corporation resident in Ireland, is owned 100% by Balance, Inc., a domestic corporation. Profit is a CFC. Determine Profit's Subpart F income (before expenses and cost of goods sold) for the tax year, given the following items of income:

   a. Insurance income of $150,000 from the insurance of risks of Loss, Inc., another foreign corporation owned by Balance and resident in Scotland.
   b. Income of $120,000 from the sale of merchandise to Balance. The merchandise was purchased from an unrelated manufacturer resident in Italy.
   c. Income of $240,000 from the sale of merchandise (purchased from Balance) to customers in France.

d. Commissions of $80,000 from the sale of merchandise on behalf of Balance to residents of Ireland for use within Ireland.
e. Income of $250,000 from the performance on a construction contract entered into by Balance. The services were performed by Profit's personnel in Italy.

34. Warren, a U.S. shareholder, owns 20% of the only class of stock of Tan, Inc., a CFC. Tan is a CFC until October 1 of the current tax year. Warren has held the stock since Tan was organized and continues to hold it for the entire year. Warren and Tan are both calendar year taxpayers. If Tan's Subpart F income for the tax year is $200,000, E & P is $250,000, and no distributions have been made for the tax year, what is the amount, if any, that Warren must include in gross income under Subpart F for the tax year?

35. On February 1 of the current year, a U.S. taxpayer executes a contract for the purchase of equipment for 200,000 francs when the rate is 20 francs = $1 U.S. Payment is made for the purchase on June 1 of the same year when the exchange rate is 10 francs = $1 U.S.

a. What is the basis of the equipment to the U.S. taxpayer?
b. Is there an exchange gain or loss on the purchase? If so, what amount?

36. Assume that Grove, Inc., a domestic corporation, organizes a foreign branch in 1991. The branch is a QBU and uses the K (a foreign currency) as its functional currency. The following income and taxes resulted in 1991–1993:

	Income	Foreign Taxes	Exchange Rate
1991	180K/$360	45K/$90	.5K:$1
1992	200K/$250	70K/$87.50	.8K:$1
1993	220K/$220	66K/$66	1K:$1

Assuming the maximum corporate rate of 34% applies for U.S. tax purposes, determine the net U.S. tax for each year, with respect to the branch income.

37. Referring to Problem 36, assume that in 1993, 400K is remitted to Grove's home office in the United States. Does this remittance trigger a foreign currency gain or loss? If so, what is its character (ordinary or capital)?

CHAPTER

TAX ADMINISTRATION AND PRACTICE

OBJECTIVES

Examine the various administrative pronouncements issued by the IRS and explain how they can be used in tax practice.

Summarize the administrative powers of the IRS including the examination of taxpayer records, the assessment and demand process, and collection procedures.

Review the audit process, including how returns are selected for audit and the various types of audits conducted by the IRS.

Explain and illustrate the taxpayer appeal process including various settlement options available.

Explain how interest on a deficiency or a refund is determined and when it is due.

Discuss the various penalties that can be imposed on acts of noncompliance by taxpayers.

Review the rules governing the statute of limitations on assessments and on refunds.

Summarize the statutory and nonstatutory prohibitions and guidelines for those engaged in tax practice.

OUTLINE

Few events arouse so much fear in the typical individual or corporation as the receipt of a letter from the Internal Revenue Service (IRS), notifying the taxpayer that prior years' tax returns are to be the subject of an audit. Almost immediately, calls are made to the tax adviser. Advice is sought as to what to reveal (or not reveal) in the course of the audit, how to delay or avoid the audit, and how friendly one should be with the auditor when he or she ultimately does arrive.

Indeed, many tax practitioners' reputations with their clients have been made or broken by the way they are observed to behave under the pressure of an audit situation. The strategy and tactics of audits—including such seemingly unimportant issues as whether the tax adviser brings donuts or other refreshments to the audit session, the color of his or her suit and tie, and the most effective negotiation techniques—are the subject of both cocktail party banter and scholarly review.

In actuality, the practitioner can render valuable services to the taxpayer in an audit context, thereby assuring that tax payments for the disputed years are neither under- nor overreported, as part of an ongoing tax practice. In this regard, the adviser must appreciate (1) the elements of the Treasury's tax administration process and opportunities for appeal within the structure of the IRS, (2) the extent of the negative sanctions that can be brought to bear against taxpayers whose returns are found to have been inaccurate, and (3) ethical and professional constraints on the advice given and actions taken by the tax adviser on behalf of the client, within the context of an adversarial relationship with the IRS.

TAX ADMINISTRATION

The Treasury has delegated the administration and enforcement of the tax laws to its subsidiary agency, the IRS. In this process, the Service is responsible for providing adequate information, in the form of publications and forms with instructions, to taxpayers so that they can comply with the laws in an appropriate manner. The IRS also has the responsibilities of identifying delinquent tax payments and carrying out assessment and collection procedures under the restrictions of due process and other constitutional guarantees.

In meeting these responsibilities, the Service conducts audits of selected tax returns. Fewer than 1 percent of all individual tax returns are subjected to audit in a given tax year. However, certain types of both taxpayers and income—including, for instance cash-oriented businesses, real estate transactions, and estate- and gift-taxable transfers—are subject to much higher probabilities of audit.

Recently, however, much of the IRS's effort has been devoted to developing statutory and administrative requirements relative to information reporting and document matching. For instance, when a taxpayer engages in a like-kind exchange or sells a personal residence, various parties to the transaction are required to report the nature and magnitude of the transaction to the IRS. Later the Treasury's computers determine whether the transaction has been reported properly by comparing the information reported by the third parties with the events included on the relevant taxpayers' returns for the year.

In addition, the IRS has been placing increasing pressure on the community of tax advisers. Severe penalties may be assessed on those who have prepared the appropriate return when the Service's interpretation of applicable law conflicts with that of the preparer.

IRS Procedure—Letter Rulings

Taxpayer dealings with the IRS commonly involve the issuance and receipt of informational publications, forms with instructions, and other direct correspondence. When a tax issue is controversial or a transaction involves considerable tax dollars, the taxpayer often wishes to obtain either assurance or direction from the IRS as to the treatment of the event. The letter ruling process is an effective means of dealing directly with the IRS while in the planning stages of a large or otherwise important transaction.

Rulings issued by the National Office provide a written statement of the position of the IRS concerning the tax consequences of a course of action contemplated by the taxpayer. Letter (individual) rulings do not have the force and effect of law, but they do provide guidance and support for taxpayers in similar transactions. The IRS will issue rulings only on uncompleted, actual (rather than hypothetical) transactions or on transactions completed before the filing of the tax return for the year in question.

The IRS will not issue a ruling in certain circumstances. It ordinarily will not rule in cases that essentially involve a question of fact.[1] For example, no ruling will be issued to determine whether compensation paid to employees is reasonable in amount and therefore allowable as a deduction.[2]

A letter ruling represents the current opinion of the IRS on the tax consequences of a transaction with a given set of facts. IRS rulings are not unchangeable. They are frequently declared obsolete or are superseded by new rulings in response to tax law changes. However, revocation or modification of a ruling is usually not applied retroactively to the taxpayer who received the ruling, if relied on in good faith and if the facts in the ruling request were in agreement with the completed transaction. The IRS may revoke any ruling if, upon subsequent audit, the agent finds a misstatement or omission of facts or substantial discrepancies between the facts in the ruling request and the actual situation. A ruling may be relied upon only by the taxpayer who requested and received it.

Letter rulings benefit both the IRS and the taxpayer. Not only do they help promote a uniform application of the tax laws, but they may also reduce the potential for litigation or disputes with revenue agents. In addition, they make the IRS aware of significant transactions being consummated by taxpayers. A fee is charged for processing a ruling request.

From the taxpayer's point of view, an advance ruling reduces the uncertainty of potential tax consequences resulting from a proposed course of action. Taxpayers frequently request a ruling before carrying out a tax-free corporate reorganization since severe tax consequences would result if the reorganization were subsequently deemed to be taxable. Liquidations, stock redemptions, and transfers to controlled corporations under § 351 are other sensitive areas where taxpayers may want some degree of assurance.

IRS Procedure—Additional Issuances

In addition to issuing unpublished letter rulings and published rulings and procedures, the IRS issues determination letters and technical advice memoranda.

The District Director will issue a determination letter for a completed transaction when the issue involved is covered by judicial or statutory authority,

1. Rev.Proc. 93–1, I.R.B. No. 1, 10.

2. Rev.Proc. 93–3, I.R.B. No. 1, 71.

Regulations, or rulings. Determination letters are issued for various death, gift, income, excise, and employment tax matters.

EXAMPLE 1

True Corporation recently opened a car clinic and has employed numerous mechanics. The corporation is not certain if the mechanics are to be treated as employees or as independent contractors for withholding and payroll tax purposes. True may request a determination letter from the appropriate District Director. ◆

EXAMPLE 2

Assume the same facts as in Example 1. True would like to establish a pension plan that qualifies for the tax advantages of §§ 401 through 404. To determine whether the plan qualifies, True should request and obtain a determination letter from the IRS. ◆

EXAMPLE 3

A group of physicians plans to form an association to construct and operate a hospital. The determination letter procedure is appropriate to ascertain the group's status—either subject to the Federal income tax or tax-exempt. ◆

A technical advice memorandum is issued by the National Office to the District Director and/or Regional Commissioner in response to a specific request by an agent, Appellate Conferee, or District Director. The taxpayer may ask that a request for a technical advice memorandum be made if an issue in dispute is not treated by the law or precedent and/or published rulings or Regulations. Technical advice memoranda are also appropriate when there is reason to believe that the IRS is not administering the tax law consistently. For example, a taxpayer may inquire why an agent proposes to disallow a certain expenditure when agents in other districts permit the deduction. Technical advice requests arise from the audit process, whereas ruling requests are issued before any IRS audit.

Administrative Powers of the IRS

Examination of Records. The Code authorizes the IRS to examine the taxpayer's books and records as part of the process of determining the correct amount of tax due. The IRS also has the authority to require the persons responsible to appear and to produce the necessary books and records.[3] Taxpayers are required to maintain certain record-keeping procedures and retain the records necessary to facilitate the audit. Therefore, the taxpayer and not the IRS has the burden of substantiating any item on the tax return that is under examination. The files, workpapers, and other memoranda of a tax practitioner may be subpoenaed, since communications between CPAs and their clients are not privileged.

Assessment and Demand. The Code permits the IRS to assess a deficiency and to demand payment for the tax.[4] However, no assessment or effort to collect the tax may be made until 90 days after a statutory notice of a deficiency (the *90-day letter*) is issued. The taxpayer therefore has 90 days to file a petition to the U.S. Tax Court, effectively preventing the deficiency from being assessed or collected pending the outcome of the case.[5]

3. § 7602.
4. § 6212.
5. § 6213.

This assessment procedure has certain exceptions.

- The IRS may issue a deficiency assessment without waiting 90 days if mathematical errors on the return incorrectly state the tax at less than the true liability.
- If the IRS believes the assessment or collection of a deficiency is in jeopardy, it may assess the deficiency and demand immediate payment.[6] The taxpayer can avoid (stay) the collection of the jeopardy assessment by filing a bond for the amount of the tax and interest. This action prevents the IRS from selling any property it has seized.

Following assessment of the tax, the IRS will issue a notice and demand for payment. The taxpayer is usually given 30 days after the notice and demand for payment to pay the tax.

IRS Collection Procedures. If the taxpayer neglects or refuses to pay the tax after receiving the demand for payment, a lien develops in favor of the IRS upon all property (whether it is realty or personalty, tangible or intangible) belonging to the taxpayer. This lien, commonly referred to as a statutory lien, is not valid until the IRS files Form 668 (Notice of Federal Tax Lien Under Internal Revenue Laws).

The levy power of the IRS is very broad. It allows the IRS to garnish (attach) wages and salary and to seize and sell all nonexempt property *by any means.* The IRS can also make successive seizures on any property owned by the taxpayer until the levy is satisfied.[7] In exceptional cases, the IRS will grant an extension for payment of a deficiency to prevent "undue hardship."[8]

If property is transferred and the tax is not paid, the subsequent owners of the property may be liable for the tax. For example, if an estate is insolvent and unable to pay the estate tax, the executor or the beneficiaries may be liable for the payment.[9]

The Audit Process

Selection of Returns for Audit. The IRS uses mathematical formulas to select tax returns that are most likely to contain errors and yield substantial amounts of additional tax revenues upon audit. The IRS does not openly disclose all of its audit selection techniques. However, the following observations can be made regarding the probability that a return will be selected for audit:

- Certain groups of taxpayers are subject to audit more frequently than others. These groups include individuals with gross income in excess of $50,000, self-employed individuals with substantial business income and deductions, and cash businesses where the potential for tax evasion is high.

EXAMPLE 4

Tracey owns and operates a liquor store. As nearly all of her sales are for cash, Tracey might be a prime candidate for an audit by the IRS. Cash transactions are easier to conceal than are those made on credit. ◆

6. § 6861.

7. The taxpayer can keep certain personal and business property and a minimal amount of his or her income as a subsistence allowance, even if a lien is outstanding. § 6334.

8. § 6161(b).

9. § 6901.

- If a taxpayer has been audited in a past year and the audit led to the assessment of a substantial deficiency, a return visit by the IRS often occurs.
- An audit might materialize if information returns (e.g., Form W–2, Form 1099) are not in substantial agreement with the income reported on a taxpayer's return. Obvious discrepancies do not necessitate formal audits (see below) but usually can be handled by correspondence with the taxpayer.
- If an individual's itemized deductions are in excess of norms established for various income levels, the probability of an audit increases. Certain deductions (e.g., casualty and theft losses, business use of the home, tax-sheltered investments) are sensitive areas since the IRS realizes that many taxpayers will determine the amount of the deduction incorrectly or may not be entitled to the deduction at all.
- The filing of a refund claim by the taxpayer may prompt an audit of the return.
- Certain returns are chosen on a random sample basis (known as the Taxpayer Compliance Measurement Program [TCMP]) to develop, update, and improve the mathematical formulas used in selecting returns. TCMP is a long-range project designed to measure and evaluate taxpayer compliance characteristics. TCMP audits are tedious and time-consuming because the taxpayer is generally asked to verify most or all items on the tax return.
- Information is often obtained from other sources (e.g., other government agencies, news items, informants). The IRS can pay rewards to persons who provide information that leads to the detection and punishment of those who violate the tax laws. The rewards are paid at the discretion of a District Director and will not exceed 10 percent of the taxes, fines, and penalties recovered as a result of the information.[10]

EXAMPLE 5

Phil reports to the police that burglars broke into his home while he was out of town and took a shoe box containing $25,000 in cash, among other things. A representative of the IRS reading the newspaper account of the burglary might wonder why Phil kept such a large amount of cash in a shoe box at home. ◆

EXAMPLE 6

After 15 years, Betty is discharged by her employer, Dr. Franklin. Shortly thereafter, the IRS receives a letter from Betty informing it that Franklin keeps two sets of books, one of which substantially understates the actual cash receipts. ◆

Many individual taxpayers mistakenly assume that if they do not hear from the IRS within a few weeks after filing their return or if they receive a refund check, no audit will be forthcoming. As a practical matter, most individual returns are examined about two years from the date of filing. If not, they generally remain unaudited. All large corporations, however, are subject to annual audits.

Verification and Audit Procedures. The tax return is initially checked for mathematical accuracy. A check is also made for deductions, exclusions, etc., that are clearly erroneous. An obvious error would be the failure to comply with the 7.5 percent limitation on the deduction for medical expenses. In such cases, the Service Center merely sends the taxpayer revised computations and a bill or

10. § 7623 and Reg. § 301.7623–1.

refund as appropriate. Taxpayers are usually able to settle such matters through direct correspondence with the IRS without the necessity of a formal audit.

Office audits are conducted by representatives of the District Director's Office, either in the office of the IRS or through correspondence. Individual returns with few or no items of business income are usually handled through an office audit. In most instances, the taxpayer is required merely to substantiate a deduction, credit, or item of income that appears on the return. The taxpayer will be asked to present documentation in the form of canceled checks, invoices, etc., for the items in question.

The *field audit* is commonly used for corporate returns and for returns of individuals engaged in business or professional activities. This type of audit generally involves a more complete examination of a taxpayer's transactions.

A field audit is conducted by IRS agents at the office or home of the taxpayer or at the office of the taxpayer's representative. The agent's work may be facilitated by a review of certain tax workpapers and discussions with the taxpayer's representative about items appearing on the tax return.

Prior to or at the initial interview, the IRS must provide the taxpayer with an explanation of the audit process that is the subject of the interview and describe the taxpayer's rights under that process. If the taxpayer clearly states at any time during the interview the desire to consult with an attorney, CPA, enrolled agent, or any other person permitted to represent the taxpayer before the IRS, then the IRS representative must suspend the interview.[11]

Any officer or employee of the IRS must, upon advance request, allow a taxpayer to make an audio recording of any in-person interview with the officer or employee concerning the determination and collection of any tax. The recording of IRS audit conferences may have significant legal implications. For example, if an IRS employee recklessly or intentionally disregards regulatory rules in the collection of Federal tax, the taxpayer can bring a civil action for damages in a U.S. District Court.[12]

Settlement with the Revenue Agent. Following an audit, the IRS agent may either accept the return as filed or recommend certain adjustments. The Revenue Agent's Report (RAR) is reviewed by the agent's group supervisor and the Review Staff within the IRS. In most instances, the agent's proposed adjustments are approved. However, the Review Staff or group supervisor may request additional information or raise new issues.

Agents must adhere strictly to IRS policy as reflected in published rulings, Regulations, and other releases. The agent cannot settle an unresolved issue based upon the probability of winning the case in court. Usually, issues involving factual questions can be settled at the agent level, and it may be advantageous for both the taxpayer and the IRS to reach agreement at the earliest point in the settlement process. For example, it may be to the taxpayer's advantage to reach agreement at the agent level and avoid any further opportunity for the IRS to raise new issues.

A deficiency (an amount in excess of tax shown on the return or tax previously assessed) may be proposed at the agent level. The taxpayer may wish to pursue to a higher level the disputed issues upon which this deficiency is based. The taxpayer's progress through the appeal process is discussed in subsequent sections of this chapter.

If agreement is reached upon the proposed deficiency, the taxpayer signs Form 870 (Waiver of Restrictions on Assessment and Collection of Deficiency in

11. § 7521(b).

12. § 7433.

Tax). One advantage to the taxpayer of signing Form 870 at this point is that interest stops accumulating on the deficiency 30 days after the form is filed.[13] When this form is signed, the taxpayer effectively waives the right to receive a statutory notice of deficiency (the 90-day letter) and to subsequently petition the Tax Court. In addition, it is no longer possible for the taxpayer to go to the Appeals Division. Signing Form 870 at the agent level generally closes the case. However, the IRS is not restricted by Form 870 and may assess additional deficiencies if deemed necessary.

The Taxpayer Appeal Process

If agreement cannot be reached at the agent level, the taxpayer receives a copy of the Revenue Agent's Report and a *30-day letter.* The taxpayer has 30 days to request an administrative appeal. If an appeal is not requested, a 90-day letter is issued. Figure 25–1 illustrates the taxpayer's alternatives when a disagreement with the IRS persists.

A taxpayer who wishes to appeal must make an appropriate request to the Appeals Division. The request must be accompanied by a written protest, except in the following cases:

- The proposed tax deficiency does not exceed $10,000 for any of the tax periods involved in the audit.
- The deficiency resulted from a correspondence or office audit (i.e., not as a result of a field audit).

The Appeals Division is authorized to settle all tax disputes based on the hazards of litigation. Since the Appeals Division has final settlement authority until a 90-day letter has been issued, the taxpayer may be able to negotiate a settlement. In addition, an overall favorable settlement may be reached by "trading" disputed issues. The Appeals Division occasionally may raise new issues if the grounds are substantial and of significant tax impact.

Both the Appeals Division and the taxpayer have the right to request technical advice memoranda from the National Office of the IRS. A technical advice memorandum that is favorable to the taxpayer is binding on the Appeals Division. Even if the technical advice memorandum is favorable to the IRS, however, the Appeals Division may nevertheless settle the case based on other considerations.

A taxpayer who files a petition with the U.S. Tax Court has the option of having the case heard before the informal Small Cases Division if the amount in dispute does not exceed $10,000.[14] If the Small Cases Division is used, neither party may appeal the case. The decisions of the Small Cases Division are not published or otherwise available as precedents for other cases.

The economic costs of a settlement offer from the Appeals Division should be weighed against the costs of litigation and the probability of winning the case. The taxpayer should also consider the impact of the settlement upon the tax liability for future periods, in addition to the years under audit.

If a settlement is reached with the Appeals Division, the taxpayer is required to sign Form 870AD. The IRS considers this settlement to be binding upon both parties unless fraud, malfeasance, concealment, or misrepresentation of material fact has occurred.

13. § 6601(c).

14. § 7463(a).

Offers in Compromise and Closing Agreements

The IRS can negotiate a compromise if there is doubt about the taxpayer's ability to pay the tax.[15] If the taxpayer is financially unable to pay the total amount of the tax, a Form 656 (Offer in Compromise) must be filed with the District Director or the IRS Service Center.

The IRS investigates the claim by evaluating the taxpayer's financial ability to pay the tax. In some instances, the compromise settlement will include an agreement for final settlement of the tax through payments of a specified percentage of the taxpayer's future earnings. The District Director must obtain approval from the IRS Regional Counsel if the amount involved exceeds $500. This settlement procedure usually entails lengthy periods of negotiation with the IRS and is used only in extreme cases.

Figure 25–1 **Income Tax Appeal Procedure**

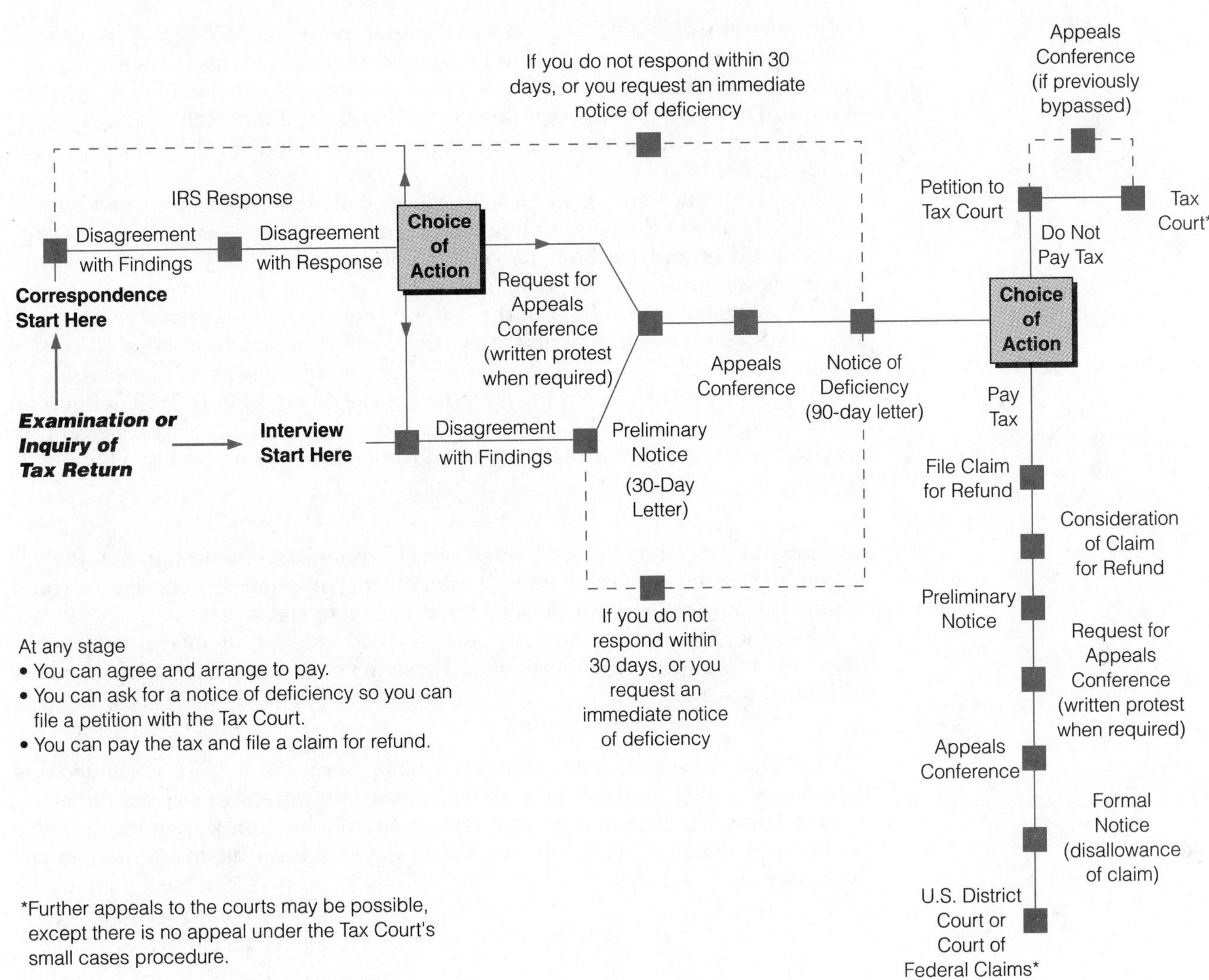

15. § 7122.

The IRS has statutory authority to enter into a written agreement allowing taxes to be paid on an installment basis if that arrangement will facilitate collection. The agreement may be modified or terminated because of (1) inadequate information, (2) subsequent change in financial condition, or (3) failure to pay any installment when due or to provide requested information.[16]

A closing agreement is binding on both the taxpayer and the IRS, except upon a subsequent showing of fraud, malfeasance, or misrepresentation of a material fact.[17] The closing agreement may be used when disputed issues carry over to future years. It may also be employed to dispose of a dispute involving a specific issue for a prior year or a proposed transaction involving future years. If, for example, the IRS is willing to make substantial concessions in the valuation of assets for death tax purposes, it may require a closing agreement from the recipient of the property to establish the income tax basis of the assets.

Interest

Determination of the Interest Rate. Several years ago, Congress recognized that the interest rates applicable to Federal tax underpayments (deficiencies) and overpayments (refunds) should be closer to the rates available in financial markets. The Code provides for rates to be determined quarterly.[18] For example, the rates that are determined during January are effective for the following April through June.

IRS interest rates are based on the Federal short-term rates published periodically by the IRS in Revenue Rulings. The Federal rates are based on the average market yield on outstanding marketable obligations of the United States with remaining maturity of three years or less.

Underpayments are subject to the Federal short-term rates plus three percentage points, and overpayments carry the Federal short-term rates plus two percentage points. Consequently, the rate for tax deficiencies is one percentage point higher than the rate for tax refunds. For the first quarter of 1993, interest on tax deficiencies was set at 7 percent, and interest on refunds was 6 percent. In previous years, interest rates have ranged from a low of 6 percent to a high of 20 percent.

Computation of the Amount of Interest. Interest is compounded daily.[19] Depending on the applicable interest rate, daily compounding conceivably could double the payable amount over a period of five to eight years.

Tables for determining the daily compounded amount are available from the IRS. The tables ease the burden of those who prepare late returns where additional taxes are due.[20]

IRS Deficiency Assessments. Interest usually accrues from the unextended due date of the return until 30 days after the taxpayer agrees to the deficiency by signing Form 870. If the taxpayer does not pay the amount shown on the IRS's "notice and demand" (tax bill) within 30 days, interest again accrues on the deficiency.

---

16. § 6159.
17. § 7121(b).
18. § 6621.
19. § 6622.
20. Rev.Proc. 83–7, 1983–1 C.B. 583.

Refund of Taxpayer's Overpayments. If the overpayment is refunded to the taxpayer within 45 days after the date the return is filed or is due, no interest is allowed. Interest is authorized, however, when the taxpayer files an amended return or makes a claim for refund of a prior year's tax (e.g., when net operating loss carrybacks result in refunds of a prior year's tax payments).

In the past, when interest rates were sometimes as high as 20 percent, many taxpayers found it advantageous to delay filing various tax returns that led to refunds. Thus, the IRS was placed in the unfortunate role of providing taxpayers with a high-yield savings account. Under current law, however, taxpayers applying for refunds receive interest as follows:

- When a return is filed after the due date, interest on any overpayment accrues from the date of filing. However, no interest is due if the IRS makes the refund within 45 days of the date of filing.

EXAMPLE 7

Naomi, a calendar year taxpayer, files her 1993 return on December 1, 1994. The return reflects an overwithholding of $2,500. On June 8, 1995, Naomi receives a refund of her 1993 overpayment. Interest on the refund began to accrue on December 1, 1994 (not April 15, 1994). ◆

EXAMPLE 8

Assume the same facts as in Example 7, except that the refund is paid to Naomi on January 5, 1995 (rather than June 8, 1995). No interest is payable by the IRS, since the refund was made within 45 days of the filing of the return. ◆

- In no event will interest accrue on an overpayment unless the return that is filed is in "processible form." Generally, this means that the return must contain enough information to enable the IRS to identify the taxpayer and to determine the tax (and overpayment) involved.

Taxpayer Penalties

To promote and enforce taxpayer compliance with the U.S. voluntary self-assessment system of taxation, Congress has enacted a comprehensive array of penalties.

Tax penalties may involve both criminal and civil offenses. Criminal tax penalties are imposed only after the usual criminal process, in which the taxpayer is entitled to the same constitutional guarantees as nontax criminal defendants. Normally, a criminal penalty provides for imprisonment. Civil tax penalties are collected in the same manner as other taxes and usually provide only for monetary fines. Criminal and civil penalties are not mutually exclusive; therefore, both types of sanctions may be imposed on a taxpayer.

The Code characterizes tax penalties as additions to tax; thus, they cannot subsequently be deducted by the taxpayer.

Ad valorem penalties are additions to tax that are based upon a percentage of the owed tax. *Assessable penalties,* on the other hand, typically include a flat dollar amount. Assessable penalties are not subject to review by the Tax Court, but *ad valorem* penalties are subject to the same deficiency procedures that apply to the underlying tax.

Failure to File and Failure to Pay. For a failure to file a tax return by the due date (including extensions), a penalty of 5 percent per month (up to a maximum of 25 percent) is imposed on the amount of tax shown as due on the return. If the failure to file is attributable to fraud, the penalty becomes 15 percent per month, to a maximum of 75 percent of the tax.[21]

For a failure to pay the tax due as shown on the return, a penalty of one-half percent per month (up to a maximum of 25 percent) is imposed on the amount of the tax. The penalty is doubled if the taxpayer fails to pay the tax after receiving a deficiency assessment.

In all of these cases, a fraction of a month counts as a full month. These penalties relate to the net amount of the tax due.

EXAMPLE 9

Conchita, a calendar year self-employed taxpayer, prepays $18,000 for income taxes during 1992. Her total tax liability for 1992 proves to be $20,000. Without obtaining an extension from the IRS, she files her Form 1040 in early August 1993 and encloses a check for the balance due of $2,000. The failure to file and the failure to pay penalties apply to the $2,000 (not the $20,000). ◆

During any month in which both the failure to file penalty and the failure to pay penalty apply, the failure to file penalty is reduced by the amount of the failure to pay penalty.

EXAMPLE 10

Jason files his tax return 10 days after the due date. Along with the return, he remits a check for $3,000, which is the balance of the tax owed. Disregarding any interest liabilities, Jason's total penalties are as follows:

Failure to pay penalty (½% × $3,000)		$ 15
Plus:		
Failure to file penalty (5% × $3,000)	$150	
Less: Failure to pay penalty for the same period	(15)	
Failure to file penalty		135
Total penalties		$150

The penalties for one full month are imposed even though Jason was delinquent by only 10 days. Unlike the method used to compute interest, any part of a month is treated as a whole month. ◆

Accuracy-Related Penalties. Major civil penalties relating to the accuracy of tax return data, including misstatements stemming from taxpayer negligence and improper valuation of income and deductions, are coordinated under the umbrella term *accuracy-related penalties.*[22] This consolidation of related penalties into a single levy eliminates the possibility that multiple penalties will be stacked together (i.e., when more than one type of penalty applies to a single understatement of tax).

The accuracy-related penalties each amount to 20 percent of the portion of the tax underpayment that is attributable to one or more of the following infractions: (1) negligence or disregard of rules and regulations; (2) substantial understatement of tax liability; (3) substantial valuation overstatement; and (4) substantial valuation understatement. The penalties apply only where the taxpayer fails to show either a reasonable cause for the underpayment or a good faith effort to comply with the tax law.

21. §§ 6651(a) and (f).

22. § 6662.

Negligence. For purposes of this accuracy-related penalty, *negligence* includes any failure to make a reasonable attempt to comply with the provisions of the tax law. The penalty also applies to any disregard (whether careless, reckless, or intentional) of rules and Regulations. The penalty can be avoided upon a showing of reasonable cause and that the taxpayer acted in good faith.

The negligence penalty is applicable to *all* taxes, but does not apply when fraud is involved.

A negligence penalty might be assessed when the taxpayer fails to report gross income, overstates deductions, or fails to keep adequate records. When the taxpayer takes a nonfrivolous position on the return that is contrary to a published pronouncement of the IRS, the penalty is waived if the taxpayer has disclosed the disputed position on Form 8275.

Substantial Understatements of Tax Liability. The understatement penalty is designed to strike at middle- and high-income taxpayers who play the so-called *audit lottery.* Some taxpayers take questionable and undisclosed positions on their tax returns in the hope that the return will not be selected for audit. Disclosing the positions would have called attention to the return and increased the probability of audit.

A *substantial understatement of a tax liability* transpires when the understatement exceeds the larger of 10 percent of the tax due or $5,000 ($10,000 for a C corporation). The understatement to which the penalty applies is the difference between the amount of tax required to be shown on the return and the amount of tax actually shown on the return.

The penalty can be avoided under any of the following circumstances:

- The taxpayer has *substantial authority* for the treatment.
- The relevant facts affecting the treatment are adequately disclosed in the return by attaching Form 8275.
- The taxpayer has reasonable cause and acts in good faith.

Penalty for Overvaluation. The objective of the overvaluation penalty is to deter taxpayers from inflating values (or basis), usually for charitable contributions of property, to reduce income taxes.[23]

- The penalty is 20 percent of the additional tax that would have been paid had the correct valuation (or basis) been used.
- The penalty applies only when the valuation (or basis) used is 200 percent or more of the correct valuation (or basis).
- The penalty applies only to the extent that the resulting income tax underpayment exceeds $5,000 ($10,000 for C corporations).

EXAMPLE 11

In 1985, Gretchen (a calendar year taxpayer) purchased a painting for $10,000. In early 1995 when the painting is worth $18,000 (as later determined by the IRS), Gretchen donates the painting to an art museum. Based on the appraisal of a cousin who is an amateur artist, she deducts $40,000 for the donation on a timely filed return for 1995. Since Gretchen was in a 31% tax bracket, overstating the deduction by $22,000 results in a tax underpayment of $6,820 for 1995.

Gretchen's penalty for overvaluation is $1,364 [20% × $6,820 (the underpayment that resulted from using $40,000 instead of $18,000)]. ◆

---

23. § 6662(b)(3).

The substantial valuation overstatement penalty can be avoided if the taxpayer can show reasonable cause and good faith. However, when the overvaluation involves *charitable deduction property*, the taxpayer must show *two additional* facts:

- The claimed value of the property is based on a qualified appraisal made by a qualified appraiser.
- The taxpayer made a good faith investigation of the value of the contributed property.

Based on these criteria, Gretchen of Example 11 would be unlikely to avoid the penalty. A cousin who is an amateur artist does not meet the definition of a qualified appraiser. Likewise, she apparently has not made a good faith investigation of the value of the contributed property.

Penalty for Undervaluation. When attempting to minimize the income tax, it is to the benefit of taxpayers to *overvalue* deductions. When attempting to minimize transfer taxes (i.e., estate and gift taxes), however, executors and donors may be inclined to *undervalue* the assets transferred. A lower valuation reduces estate and gift taxes. An accuracy-related penalty is imposed for substantial estate or gift tax valuation understatements.

The penalty is 20 percent of the additional transfer tax that would have been due had the correct valuation been used on Form 706 (estate and generation-skipping transfer tax return) or Form 709 (gift and generation-skipping transfer tax return). The penalty only applies if the value of the property claimed on the return is 50 percent or less than the amount determined to be correct. The penalty applies only to an additional transfer tax liability in excess of $5,000. The penalty is doubled if the reported valuation was 25 percent or less than the correct determination.

As with other accuracy-related penalties, reasonable cause and good faith on the part of the taxpayer is a defense.

Civil Fraud Penalty. A 75 percent civil penalty is imposed on any underpayment resulting from fraud by the taxpayer who has filed a return.[24] For this penalty, the burden of proof is *upon the IRS* to show by a preponderance of the evidence that the taxpayer had a specific intent to evade a tax.

Once the IRS has initially established that fraud has occurred, the taxpayer then bears the burden of proof to show by a preponderance of the evidence the portion of the underpayment that is not attributable to fraud.

Although the Code and the Regulations do not provide any assistance in ascertaining what constitutes civil fraud, it is clear that mere negligence on the part of the taxpayer (however great) will not suffice. Fraud has been found in cases of manipulation of the books,[25] substantial omissions from income,[26] and erroneous deductions.[27]

EXAMPLE 12

Frank underpaid his income tax for 1995 by $90,000. The IRS can prove that $60,000 of the underpayment was due to fraud. Frank responds by a preponderance of the evidence that $30,000 of the underpayment was not due to fraud. The civil fraud penalty is $45,000 (75% × $60,000). ◆

If the underpayment of tax is partly attributable to negligence and partly attributable to fraud, the fraud penalty is applied first.

24. § 6663.

25. *Dogget v. Comm.*, 60–1 USTC ¶9342, 5 AFTR2d 1034, 275 F.2d 823 (CA–4, 1960).

26. *Harvey Brodsky*, 21 TCM 578, T.C.Memo. 1962–105.

27. *Lash v. Comm.*, 57–2 USTC ¶9725, 51 AFTR 492, 245 F.2d 20 (CA–1, 1957).

Criminal Penalties In addition to civil fraud penalties, the Code provides numerous criminal sanctions that carry various monetary fines and/or imprisonment. The difference between civil and criminal fraud often is one of degree. A characteristic of criminal fraud is the presence of willfulness on the part of the taxpayer. Thus, § 7201, dealing with attempts to evade or defeat a tax, contains the following language:

> Any person who *willfully* attempts in any manner to evade or defeat any tax imposed by this title or the payment thereof shall, in addition to other penalties provided by law, be guilty of a felony and, upon conviction thereof, shall be fined not more than $100,000 ($500,000 in the case of a corporation), or imprisoned not more than five years, or both, together with the costs of prosecution. (Emphasis added.)

As to the burden of proof, the IRS must show that the taxpayer was guilty of willful evasion "beyond the shadow of any reasonable doubt." Recall that in the civil fraud area, the standard applied to measure culpability is "by a preponderance of the evidence."

Failure to Pay Estimated Taxes. A penalty is imposed for a failure to pay estimated income taxes. The penalty applies to individuals and corporations and is based on the rate of interest in effect for deficiency assessments.[28] The penalty also applies to trusts and certain estates that are required to make estimated tax payments.

The penalty is not imposed if the tax due for the year (less amounts withheld and credits) is less than $500. For employees, an equal amount of withholding is deemed paid on each due date.

The penalty *generally* can be avoided by individual taxpayers if the quarterly payments were based on one-fourth of the lesser of 90 percent (97 percent for corporations) of the current year's tax or 100 percent of the preceding 12-month year's tax (but only if a positive tax was due for corporate returns).

Quarterly payments are to be made on or before the fifteenth day of the fourth month (April 15 for a calendar year taxpayer), sixth month, and ninth month of the current year, and the first month of the following year. Corporations must make the last quarterly payment by the twelfth month of the same year. High-income individuals and large corporations (taxable income of $1 million or more in the last three years) can use the prior-year exception only on the first-quarter installment.

The penalty is levied on the amount of the underpayment for the period of the underpayment. Payments of estimated tax are credited against unpaid installments in the order in which the installments are required to be paid.

Example 13

Mrs. Prasad, who had no income tax withheld, made the following payments of estimated tax during 1995:

April 17, 1995	$1,400
June 15, 1995	2,300
September 15, 1995	1,500
January 15, 1996	1,800

28. §§ 6655 (corporations) and 6654 (other taxpayers).

Mrs. Prasad's actual tax for 1995 is $8,000. Her tax in 1994 was $10,000. Therefore, each installment should have been at least $1,800 [($8,000 × 90%) × 25%].

Of the payment on June 15, $400 is credited to the unpaid balance of the first quarterly installment due on April 17, thereby effectively stopping the underpayment penalty for the first quarterly period. Of the remaining $1,900 payment on June 15, $100 is credited to the September 15 payment, resulting in this third quarterly payment being $200 short. Then $200 of the January 15 payment is credited to the September 15 shortfall, ending the period of underpayment for that portion due. The January 15, 1996, installment is now underpaid by $200, and a penalty will apply from January 15, 1996, to April 15, 1996 (unless paid sooner). ◆

In computing the penalty, Form 2210 (Underpayment of Estimated Tax by Individuals) or Form 2220 (Underpayment of Estimated Tax by Corporations) is used.

False Information with Respect to Withholding. The Federal income tax system is based on a pay-as-you-go approach, an important element of which involves withholding from wages. One way employees might hope to avoid this withholding would be to falsify the information provided to the employer on Form W–4 (Employee Withholding Allowance Certificate). For example, by overstating the number of exemptions, income tax withholdings could be reduced or completely eliminated.

To encourage compliance, a civil penalty of $500 applies when a taxpayer claims withholding allowances based on false information. The criminal penalty for willfully failing to supply information or for willfully supplying false or fraudulent information in connection with wage withholding is an additional fine of up to $1,000 and/or up to one year of imprisonment.

Failure to Make Deposits of Taxes and Overstatements of Deposits. When the business is not doing well or cash-flow problems develop, employers have a great temptation to "borrow" from Uncle Sam. One way this can be done is to fail to pay over to the IRS the amounts that have been withheld from the wages of employees for FICA and income tax purposes. The IRS does not appreciate being denied the use of these funds and has a number of weapons at its disposal to discourage the practice, including the following:

- A penalty of up to 15 percent of any underdeposited amount not paid, unless the employer can show that the failure is due to reasonable cause and not to willful neglect.[29]
- Various criminal penalties.[30]
- A 100 percent penalty if the employer's actions are willful.[31] The penalty is based on the amount of the tax evaded, not collected, or not accounted for or paid over. Since the penalty is assessable against the "responsible person" of the business, more than one party may be vulnerable (e.g., the president *and* treasurer of a corporation). Although the IRS may assess the penalty against several persons, it cannot collect more than the 100 percent due.

In addition to these penalties, the actual tax due must be remitted. An employer remains liable for the amount that should have been paid even if the withholdings have not been taken out of the wages of its employees.[32]

---

29. § 6656.

30. See, for example, § 7202 (willful failure to collect or pay over a tax).

31. § 6672.

32. § 3403.

Statutes of Limitations

A statute of limitations defines the period of time during which one party may pursue against another party a cause of action or other suit allowed under the governing law. Failure to satisfy any requirement provides the other party with an absolute defense should the statute be invoked. Inequity would result if no limits were placed on such suits. Permitting an extended period of time to elapse between the initiation of a claim and its pursuit could place the defense at a serious disadvantage. Witnesses may have died or disappeared; records or other evidence may have been discarded or destroyed.

Assessment and the Statute of Limitations. In general, any tax that is imposed must be assessed within three years of the filing of the return (or, if later, the due date of the return).[33] Some exceptions to this three-year limitation exist:

- If no return is filed or a fraudulent return is filed, assessments can be made at any time. There is, in effect, no statute of limitations in these cases.
- If a taxpayer omits an amount of gross income in excess of 25 percent of the gross income stated on the return, the statute of limitations is increased to six years. The courts have interpreted this rule as including only items affecting income and not the omission of items affecting cost of goods sold.[34] In addition, gross income includes capital gains in the *gross* income amount (not reduced by capital losses).

EXAMPLE 14

During 1990, José had the following income transactions (all of which were duly reported on his timely-filed return):

Gross receipts		$ 480,000
Less: Cost of goods sold		(400,000)
Net business income		$ 80,000
Capital gains and losses—		
Capital gain	$ 36,000	
Capital loss	(12,000)	24,000
Total income		$ 104,000

José retains your services in 1995 as a tax consultant. It seems that he inadvertently omitted some income on his 1990 return and he wishes to know if he is "safe" under the statute of limitations. The six-year statute of limitations would apply, putting José in a vulnerable position, only if he omitted more than $129,000 on his 1990 return [($480,000 + $36,000) × 25%]. ◆

- The statute of limitations may be extended by mutual consent of the District Director and the taxpayer.[35] This extension covers a definite period and is made by signing Form 872 (Consent to Extend the Time to Assess Tax). The extension is frequently requested by the IRS when the lapse of the statutory period is imminent and the audit has not been completed. This practice is often applied to audits of corporate taxpayers and explains why many corporations have more than three "open years."

33. §§ 6501(a) and (b)(1).

34. *The Colony, Inc. v. Comm.*, 58–2 USTC ¶9593, 1 AFTR2d 1894, 78 S.Ct. 1033 (USSC, 1958).

35. § 6501(c)(4).

Special rules relating to assessment are applicable in the following situations:

- Taxpayers (corporations, estates, etc.) may request a prompt assessment of the tax.
- The period for assessment of the personal holding company tax is extended to six years after the return is filed only if certain filing requirements are met.
- If a partnership or trust files a tax return (a partnership or trust return) in good faith and a later determination renders it taxable as a corporation, the return is deemed to be the corporate return for purposes of the statute of limitations.
- The assessment period for capital loss, net operating loss, and investment credit carrybacks is generally related to the determination of tax in the year of the loss or unused credit rather than in the carryback years.

If the tax is assessed within the period of limitations, the IRS has 10 years from the date of assessment to collect the tax. However, if the IRS issues a statutory notice of deficiency to the taxpayer, who then files a Tax Court petition, the statute is suspended on both the deficiency assessment and the period of collection until 60 days after the decision of the Tax Court becomes final.

Refund Claims and the Statute of Limitations. To receive a tax refund, the taxpayer is required to file a valid refund claim. The official form for filing a claim is Form 1040X for individuals and Form 1120X for corporations. If the refund claim does not meet certain procedural requirements, including the following, it may be rejected with no consideration of its merit:

- A separate claim must be filed for each taxable period.
- The grounds for the claim must be stated in sufficient detail.
- The statement of facts must be sufficient to permit the IRS to evaluate the merits of the claim.

The refund claim must be filed within three years of the filing of the tax return or within two years following the payment of the tax if this period expires on a later date.[36]

EXAMPLE 15

On March 10, 1992, Louise filed her 1991 income tax return reflecting a tax of $10,500. On July 10, 1993, she filed an amended 1991 return showing an additional $3,000 of tax that was then paid. On May 18, 1995, she filed a claim for refund of $4,500.

Assuming Louise is correct in claiming a refund, how much tax can she recover? The answer is only $3,000. Because the claim was not filed within the three-year period, Louise is limited to the amount she actually paid during the last two years. ◆

Special rules are available for claims relating to bad debts and worthless securities. A seven-year period of limitations applies in lieu of the normal three-year rule.[37] The extended period is provided in recognition of the inherent difficulty of identifying the exact year in which a bad debt or security becomes worthless.

36. §§ 6511(a) and 6513(a).

37. § 6511(d)(1).

TAX PRACTICE

The Tax Practitioner

Definition. What is a tax practitioner? What service does the practitioner perform? To begin defining the term *tax practitioner,* one should consider whether the individual is qualified to practice before the IRS. Generally, practice before the IRS is limited to CPAs, attorneys, and persons who have been enrolled to practice before the IRS (called *enrolled agents [EAs]*). In most cases, EAs are admitted to practice only if they pass a special examination administered by the IRS. CPAs and attorneys are not required to take this examination and are automatically admitted to practice if they are in good standing with the appropriate licensing board regulating their profession.

Persons other than CPAs, attorneys, and EAs may be allowed to practice before the IRS in limited situations. Circular 230 (issued by the Treasury Department and entitled "Rules Governing the Practice of Attorneys and Agents Before the Internal Revenue Service") permits the following notable exceptions:

- A taxpayer may always represent him- or herself. A person also may represent a member of the immediate family if no compensation is received for such services.
- Regular full-time employees may represent their employers.
- Corporations may be represented by any of their bona fide officers.
- Partnerships may be represented by any of the partners.
- Trusts, receiverships, guardianships, or estates may be represented by their trustees, receivers, guardians, or administrators or executors.
- A taxpayer may be represented by whoever prepared the return for the year in question. However, such representation cannot proceed beyond the agent level.

EXAMPLE 16

Chang is currently undergoing audit by the IRS for tax years 1992 and 1993. He prepared the 1992 return but paid AddCo, a bookkeeping service, to prepare the 1993 return. AddCo may represent Chang in matters concerning only 1993. However, even for 1993, AddCo would be unable to represent Chang at an Appeals Division proceeding. Chang could represent himself, or he could retain a CPA, attorney, or EA to represent him in matters concerning both years under examination. ◆

Rules Governing Tax Practice. Circular 230 further prescribes the rules governing practice before the IRS. The following are imposed on CPAs, attorneys, and EAs:

- A requirement to make known to a client any error or omission the client may have made on any return or other document submitted to the IRS.
- A duty to submit records or information lawfully requested by the IRS.
- An obligation to exercise due diligence in preparing and filing tax returns accurately.
- A restriction against unreasonably delaying the prompt disposition of any matter before the IRS.

- A restriction against charging the client "an unconscionable fee" for representation before the IRS.
- A restriction against representing clients with conflicting interests.

Anyone can prepare a tax return or render tax advice, regardless of his or her educational background or level of competence. Likewise, nothing prevents the "unlicensed" tax practitioner from advertising his or her specialty, directly soliciting clients, or otherwise violating any of the standards of conduct controlling CPAs, attorneys, and EAs. Nevertheless, some restraints do govern all parties engaged in rendering tax advice or preparing tax returns for the general public:

- If the party holds him- or herself out to the general public as possessing tax expertise, he or she could be liable to the client if services are performed in a negligent manner. At a minimum, the practitioner would be liable for any interest and penalties the client incurs because of the practitioner's failure to exercise due care.
- If someone agrees to perform a service (e.g., prepare a tax return) and subsequently fails to do so, the aggrieved party may be in a position to obtain damages for breach of contract.
- The IRS requires any person who prepares tax returns for a fee to sign as preparer of the return.[38] Failure to comply with this requirement could result in penalty assessment against the preparer.
- The Code prescribes various penalties for the deliberate filing of false or fraudulent returns. These penalties apply to a tax practitioner who either was aware of the situation or actually perpetrated the false filing or the fraud.[39]
- Penalties are prescribed for tax practitioners who disclose to third parties information they have received from clients in connection with the preparation of tax returns or the rendering of tax advice.

EXAMPLE 17

Sarah operates a tax return preparation service. Her brother-in-law, Butch, has just taken a job as a life insurance salesman. To help Butch find contacts, Sarah furnishes him with a list of the names and addresses of all of her clients who report adjusted gross income of $10,000 or more. Sarah is subject to penalties. ◆

- All nonattorney tax practitioners should avoid becoming engaged in activities that constitute the unauthorized practice of law. If they engage in this practice, action could be instituted against them in the appropriate state court by the local or state bar association. What actions constitute the unauthorized practice of law are largely undefined, and the issue remains an open question.

Preparer Penalties. The Code also provides for the following penalties to discourage improper actions by tax practitioners:

1. A $250 penalty for understatements due to taking unrealistic positions.[40] Unless adequate disclosure is made, the penalty is imposed if two conditions are satisfied:

38. Reg. § 1.6065–1(b)(1). Rev.Rul. 84–3, 1984–1 C.B. 264, contains a series of examples illustrating when a person is deemed to be a preparer of the return.

39. § 7216.

40. § 6694(a).

- Any part of any understatement of tax liability on any return or claim for refund is due to a position that did not have a realistic possibility of being sustained on its merits.
- Any person who was an income tax return preparer for that return or claim knew (or should have known) of this position.

The penalty can be avoided by showing reasonable cause and by showing that the preparer acted in good faith.

2. A $1,000 penalty for willful and reckless conduct.[41] The penalty applies if any part of the understatement of a taxpayer's liability on a return or claim for refund is due to:

   - The preparer's willful attempt to understate the taxpayer's tax liability in any manner.
   - Any reckless or intentional disregard of IRS rules or Regulations by the preparer.

   Adequate disclosure can avoid the penalty. If both this penalty and the unrealistic position penalty (see item 1 above) apply to the same return, the total penalty cannot exceed $1,000.
3. A $1,000 ($10,000 for corporations) penalty per return or document is imposed against persons who aid in the preparation of returns or other documents that they know (or have reason to believe) would result in an understatement of the tax liability of another person. Clerical assistance in the preparation process does not incur the penalty.

   If this penalty applies, neither the unrealistic position penalty (item 1) nor the willful and reckless conduct penalty (item 2) is assessed.
4. A $50 penalty is assessed against the preparer for failure to sign a return or furnish the preparer's identifying number.[42]
5. A $50 penalty is assessed if the preparer fails to furnish a copy of the return or claim for refund to the taxpayer.
6. A $500 penalty may be assessed if a preparer endorses or otherwise negotiates a check for refund of tax issued to the taxpayer.

Ethical Considerations—"Statements on Responsibilities in Tax Practice"

Tax practitioners who are CPAs, attorneys, or EAs must abide by the codes or canons of professional ethics applicable to their respective professions. The various codes and canons have much in common with and parallel the standards of conduct set forth in Circular 230.

In the belief that CPAs engaged in tax practice require further guidance in the resolution of ethical problems, the Tax Committee of the AICPA began issuing periodic statements on selected topics. The first of these Statements on Responsibilities in Tax Practice was released in 1964. All were revised in August of 1988. The most important statements that have been issued to date are discussed below.[43]

Statements merely represent guides to action and are not part of the AICPA's Code of Professional Ethics. But because the statements are representative of standards followed by members of the profession, a violation might indicate a deviation from the standard of due care exercised by most CPAs. The standard of due care is usually at the heart of any suit charging negligence that is brought against a CPA.

---

41. § 6694(b).

42. § 6695.

43. For an additional discussion of tax ethics, see Raabe, Whittenburg, and Bost, *West's Federal Tax Research,* 3d ed. (St. Paul: West Publishing Co., 1993), Chapter 1.

Statement No. 1: Positions Contrary to IRS Interpretations. Under certain circumstances, a CPA may take a position that is contrary to that taken by the IRS. In order to do so, however, the CPA must have a good faith belief that the position, if challenged, has a realistic possibility of being sustained administratively or judicially on its merits.

The client should be fully advised of the risks involved and should know that certain penalties may result if the position taken by the CPA is not successful. The client should also be informed that disclosure on the return may avoid some or all of these penalties.

In no case should the CPA exploit the audit lottery; that is, to take a questionable position based on the probabilities that the client's return will not be chosen by the IRS for audit. Furthermore, the CPA should not "load" the return with questionable items in the hope that they might aid the client in a later settlement negotiation with the IRS.

Statement No. 2: Questions on Returns. A CPA should make a reasonable effort to obtain from the client, and provide to the IRS, appropriate answers to all questions on a tax return before signing as preparer. Reasonable grounds may exist for omitting an answer:

- The information is not readily available, and the answer is not significant in computing the tax.
- The meaning of the question as it applies to a particular situation is genuinely uncertain.
- The answer to the question is voluminous.

The fact that an answer to a question could prove disadvantageous to the client does not justify omitting the answer.

Statement No. 3: Procedural Aspects of Preparing Returns. In preparing a return, a CPA may in good faith rely without verification on information furnished by the client or by third parties. However, the CPA should make reasonable inquiries if the information appears to be incorrect, incomplete, or inconsistent. In this regard, the CPA should refer to the client's prior returns whenever appropriate.

EXAMPLE 18

A CPA normally can take a client's word for the validity of dependency exemptions. But suppose a recently divorced client wants to claim his three children (of whom he does not have custody) as dependents. A CPA must act in accordance with § 152(e)(2) in preparing the return. Claiming the dependency exemption will require evidence of a waiver by the custodial parent. Without this waiver, the CPA should not claim the dependency exemptions on the client's tax return. ◆

EXAMPLE 19

While preparing a client's income tax return for 1995, a CPA reviews her income tax return for 1994. In comparing the dividend income reported on the 1994 Schedule B with that received in 1995, the CPA notes a significant decrease. Further investigation reveals the variation is due to a stock sale in 1995 that, until now, was unknown to the CPA. Thus, the review of the 1994 return has unearthed a transaction that should be reported on the 1995 return. ◆

If the Code or the Regulations requires certain types of verification (as is the case with travel and entertainment expenditures), the CPA must advise the client of these rules. Further, inquiry must be made to ascertain whether the client has complied with the verification requirements.

Statement No. 4: Estimates. A CPA may prepare a tax return using estimates received from a taxpayer if it is impracticable to obtain exact data. The estimates must be reasonable under the facts and circumstances known to the CPA. When estimates are used, they should be presented in such a manner as to avoid implying that greater accuracy exists.

Statement No. 5: Recognition of Administrative Proceeding. As facts may vary from year to year, so may the position taken by a CPA. In these types of situations, the CPA is not bound by an administrative or judicial proceeding involving a prior year.

Example 20

Upon audit of Ramon Corporation's income tax return for 1994, the IRS disallowed $180,000 of the $400,000 salary paid to its president and sole shareholder on the grounds that it was unreasonable [§ 162(a)(1)]. A CPA has been engaged to prepare Ramon's income tax return for 1995. Again the corporation paid its president a salary of $400,000 and chose to deduct this amount. Because the CPA is not bound in 1995 by what the IRS deemed reasonable for 1994, the full $400,000 can be claimed as a salary deduction. ◆

Other problems that require a CPA's use of judgment include reclassification of corporate debt as equity (the thin capitalization possibility) and corporate accumulations beyond the reasonable needs of the business (the penalty tax under § 531).

Statement No. 6: Knowledge of Error. A CPA should promptly advise a client upon learning of an error on a previously filed return or upon learning of a client's failure to file a required return. The advice can be oral or written and should include a recommendation of the corrective measures, if any, to be taken. The error or other omission should not be disclosed to the IRS without the client's consent.

If the past error is material and is not corrected by the client, the CPA may be unable to prepare the current year's tax return. This situation might occur if the error has a carryover effect that prevents the CPA from determining the correct tax liability for the current year.

Example 21

In preparing a client's 1995 income tax return, a CPA discovers that final inventory for 1994 was materially understated. First, the CPA should advise the client to file an amended return for 1994 reflecting the correct amount in final inventory. Second, if the client refuses to make this adjustment, the CPA should consider whether the error will preclude preparation of a substantially correct return for 1995. Because this will probably be the case (the final inventory for 1994 becomes the beginning inventory for 1995), the CPA should withdraw from the engagement.

If the client corrects the error, the CPA may proceed with the preparation of the tax return for 1995. However, the CPA should ensure that the error is not repeated. ◆

Statement No. 8: Advice to Clients. In providing tax advice to a client, the CPA must use judgment to ensure that the advice reflects professional competence and appropriately serves the client's needs. No standard format or guidelines can be established to cover all situations and circumstances involving written or oral advice by the CPA.

The CPA may communicate with the client when subsequent developments affect previous advice on significant matters. However, the CPA cannot be expected to assume responsibility for initiating the communication, unless he or she is assisting a client in implementing procedures or plans associated with the advice. The CPA may undertake this obligation by specific agreement with the client.

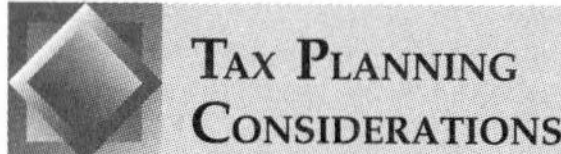

TAX PLANNING CONSIDERATIONS

Strategies in Seeking an Administrative Ruling

Determination Letters. In many instances, the request for an advance ruling or a determination letter from the IRS is a necessary or desirable planning strategy. The receipt of a favorable ruling or determination reduces the risk associated with a transaction when the tax results are in doubt. For example, the initiation or amendment of a qualified pension or profit sharing plan should be accompanied by a determination letter from the District Director. Otherwise, on subsequent IRS review, the plan may not qualify, and the tax deductibility of contributions to the plan will be disallowed. In some instances, the potential tax effects of a transaction are so numerous and of such consequence that proceeding without a ruling is unwise.

Letter Rulings. In some cases, it may not be necessary or desirable to request an advance ruling. For example, it is generally not desirable to request a ruling if the tax results are doubtful and the company is committed to complete the transaction in any event. If a ruling is requested and negotiations with the IRS indicate that an adverse determination will be forthcoming, it is usually possible to have the ruling request withdrawn. However, the National Office of the IRS may forward its findings, along with a copy of the ruling request, to the District Director. In determining the advisability of a ruling request, the taxpayer should consider the potential exposure of other items in the tax returns of all "open years."

A ruling request may delay the consummation of a transaction if the issues are novel or complex. Frequently, a ruling can be processed within six months, although in some instances a delay of a year or more may be encountered.

Technical Advice Memoranda. A taxpayer in the process of contesting a proposed deficiency with the Appeals Division should consider requesting a technical advice memorandum from the National Office of the IRS. If such advice is favorable to the taxpayer, it is binding on the Appeals Division. The request may be particularly appropriate when the practitioner feels that the agent or Appeals Division has been too literal in interpreting an IRS ruling.

Considerations in Handling an IRS Audit

As a general rule, a taxpayer should attempt to settle disputes at the earliest possible stage of the administrative appeal process. New issues may be raised by IRS personnel if the case goes beyond the agent level. It is usually possible to limit the scope of the examination by furnishing pertinent information requested by the agent. Extraneous information or thoughtless comments may result in the opening of new issues and should be avoided. Agents usually appreciate prompt and efficient responses to inquiries, since their performance may in part be judged by their ability to close or settle assigned cases.

To the extent possible, it is advisable to conduct the investigation of field audits in the practitioner's office, rather than the client's office. This procedure permits greater control over the audit investigation and facilitates the agent's review and prompt closure of the case.

Many practitioners feel that it is generally not advisable to have clients present at the scheduled conferences with the agent, since the client may give emotional or gratuitous comments that impair prompt settlement. If the client is not present, however, he or she should be advised of the status of negotiations. The client makes the final decision on any proposed settlement.

The tax practitioner's workpapers should include all research memoranda, and a list of resolved and unresolved issues should be continually updated during the course of the IRS audit. Occasionally, agents will request access to excessive amounts of accounting data in order to engage in a so-called "fishing expedition." Providing blanket access to workpapers should be avoided. Workpapers should be carefully reviewed to minimize opportunities for the agent to raise new issues not otherwise apparent. It is generally advisable to provide the agent with copies of specific workpapers upon request. An accountant's workpapers are not privileged and may be subpoenaed by the IRS.

In unusual situations, a Special Agent may appear to gather evidence in the investigation of possible criminal fraud. When this occurs, the taxpayer should be advised to seek legal counsel to determine the extent of his or her cooperation in providing information to the agent. It is frequently desirable for the tax adviser to consult personal legal counsel in such situations. If the taxpayer receives a Revenue Agent's Report (RAR), it generally indicates that the IRS has

CONCEPT SUMMARY 25–1
TAX ADMINISTRATION AND PRACTICE

1. The Internal Revenue Service (IRS) enforces the tax laws of the United States.
2. The IRS issues various pronouncements, communicating its position on certain tax issues. These pronouncements promote uniform enforcement of the tax law among taxpayers and among the internal divisions of the IRS. Taxpayers should seek such rulings and memoranda when the nature or magnitude of a pending transaction requires a high degree of certainty in the planning process.
3. IRS audits can take several forms. Taxpayers are selected for audit based on the probable return to the Treasury from the process. Offers in compromise and closing agreements can be a useful means of completing an audit without resorting to litigation.
4. Certain IRS personnel are empowered to consider the hazards of litigation in developing a settlement with the taxpayer during the audit process.
5. The IRS pays interest to taxpayers on overpaid taxes, starting essentially 45 days after the due date of the return, at two percentage points over the Federal short-term rate. Interest paid to the IRS on underpayments is computed at three points over this Federal rate, starting essentially on the due date of the return. Interest for both purposes is compounded daily.
6. The Treasury assesses penalties when the taxpayer fails to file a required tax return or pay a tax. Penalties also are assessed when an inaccurate return is filed due to negligence or other disregard of IRS rules. Tax preparers are subject to penalties for assisting a taxpayer in filing an inaccurate return, failing to follow IRS rules in an appropriate manner, or mishandling taxpayer data or funds.
7. Statutes of limitations place outer boundaries on the timing and amounts of proposed amendments to completed tax returns that can be made by the taxpayer or the IRS.
8. Tax practitioners must operate under constraints imposed on them by codes of ethics of pertinent professional societies and by Treasury Circular 230. These rules also define the parties who can represent others in an IRS proceeding.

decided not to initiate criminal prosecution proceedings. The IRS usually does not take any action upon a tax deficiency until the criminal matter has been resolved.

Penalties

Penalties are imposed upon a taxpayer's failure to file a return or pay a tax when due. These penalties can be avoided if the failure is due to reasonable cause and not to willful neglect. Reasonable cause, however, has not been liberally interpreted by the courts and should not be relied upon in the routine type of situation.[44] A safer way to avoid the failure to file penalty is to obtain an extension of time for filing the return from the IRS.

Since it is not deductible for income tax purposes, the penalty for failure to pay estimated taxes can become quite severe. Often trapped by the provision are employed taxpayers with outside income. Such persons may forget about their outside income and assume the amount withheld from wages and salaries will be adequate to cover their liability. Not only does April 15 provide a real shock (in terms of the additional tax owed) for these persons, but a penalty situation may have evolved. One possible way for an employee to mitigate this problem (presuming the employer is willing to cooperate) is described in the following example.

EXAMPLE 22

Patty, a calendar year taxpayer, is employed by Finn Corporation and earns (after withholding) a monthly salary of $4,000 payable at the end of each month. Patty also receives income from outside sources (interest, dividends, and consulting fees). After some quick calculations in early October 1995, Patty determines that she has underestimated her tax liability by $7,500 and will be subject to the penalty for the first two quarters of 1995 and part of the third quarter. Patty, therefore, completes a new Form W–4 in which she arbitrarily raises her income tax withholding by $2,500 a month. Finn accepts the Form W–4, and as a result, an extra $7,500 is paid to the IRS on Patty's account for the payroll period from October through December.

Patty avoids penalties for the underpayment for the first three quarters because withholding of taxes is allocated pro rata over the year involved. Thus, a portion of the additional $7,500 withheld in October–December is assigned to the January 1–April 15 period, the April 16–June 15 period, etc. Had Patty merely paid the IRS an additional $7,500 in October, this would not have affected the penalty for the earlier quarters. ◆

PROBLEM MATERIALS

DISCUSSION QUESTIONS

1. During the course of your research of a tax problem, you find that another company received a favorable unpublished (letter) ruling approximately two years ago, based on facts similar to your situation. What degree of reliance may you place upon this ruling?
2. Under what circumstances might the request for an advance ruling be considered a necessity? Are there situations in which a ruling should not be requested? If so, why?
3. In what situations might a taxpayer seek a determination letter?
4. What purpose does a request for a technical advice memorandum serve?

44. *Dustin v. Comm.*, 72–2 USTC ¶9610, 30 AFTR2d 72–5313, 467 F.2d 47 (CA–9, 1972), *aff'g*. 53 T.C. 491 (1969).

5. A taxpayer is fearful of filing a claim for refund for a prior year because she is convinced that the claim will cause the IRS to audit that year's return. Please comment.
6. In March 1993, Maria received a refund check from the IRS for the amount of overpayment she claimed when she filed her 1992 return in January. Does this mean that her 1992 return will not be audited? Explain.
7. Define and comment on each of the following:

    a. An RAR.
    b. Form 870.
    c. The 30-day letter.
    d. The 90-day letter.

8. Quon, a calendar year taxpayer, files her 1994 income tax return on February 9, 1995, on which she claims a $1,200 refund. If Quon receives her refund check on May 2, 1995, will it include any interest? Explain.
9. Indicate whether each of the following statements is true or false:

    a. The government never pays a taxpayer interest on an overpayment of tax.
    b. Penalties may be included as an itemized deduction on an individual's tax return, but net of the 2%-of-AGI floor.
    c. An extension of time for filing a return results in an automatic extension of the time in which the tax may be paid.
    d. The IRS can compromise on the amount of tax liability if there is doubt as to the taxpayer's ability to pay.
    e. The statute of limitations for assessing a tax never extends beyond three years from the filing of a return.
    f. A taxpayer's claim for a refund is not subject to a statute of limitations.

10. Define and illustrate the following terms or concepts:

    a. Fraud.
    b. Negligence.
    c. Reasonable cause.
    d. Civil penalty.
    e. Criminal penalty.

11. When can the taxpayer effect an "installment plan" for paying his or her delinquent taxes and associated interest and penalties?
12. Describe the following items:

    a. Closing agreement.
    b. Offer in compromise.

13. Lorraine, a vice president of Scott Corporation, prepared and filed the corporate Form 1120 for 1993. This return is being audited by the IRS in 1995.

    a. May Lorraine represent Scott during the audit?
    b. Can Lorraine's representation continue beyond the agent level (e.g., before the Appeals Division)?

PROBLEMS

14. Compute the failure to pay and failure to file penalties for John, who filed his 1993 income tax return on October 20, 1994, paying the $1,000 amount due. On April 1, 1994, John had received a four-month extension of time in which to file his return. He has no reasonable cause for failing to file his return by August 15 or for failing to pay the tax that was due on April 15, 1994. John's failure to comply with the tax laws was not fraudulent.
15. Kold Corporation estimates that its 1995 taxable income will be $900,000. Thus, it is subject to a flat 34% income tax rate and incurs a $306,000 liability. For each of the following independent cases, compute Kold's minimum quarterly estimated tax payments that will avoid an underpayment penalty.

a. For 1994, taxable income was ($100,000). Kold carried back all of this loss to prior years and exhausted the entire net operating loss in creating a zero 1994 liability.
b. For 1994, taxable income was $200,000, and tax liability was $68,000.
c. For 1993, taxable income was $2,000,000, and tax liability was $680,000. For 1994, taxable income was $200,000, and tax liability was $68,000.

16. Compute the overvaluation penalty for each of the following independent cases involving the taxpayer's reporting of the fair market value of charitable contribution property. In each case, assume a marginal income tax rate of 30%.

	Taxpayer	Corrected IRS Value	Reported Valuation
a.	Individual	$ 10,000	$ 20,000
b.	C corporation	10,000	30,000
c.	S corporation	10,000	30,000
d.	Individual	100,000	150,000
e.	Individual	100,000	300,000
f.	C corporation	100,000	500,000

17. Compute the undervaluation penalty for each of the following independent cases involving the executor's reporting of the value of a closely held business in the decedent's gross estate. In each case, assume a marginal estate tax rate of 50%.

	Reported Value	Corrected IRS Valuation
a.	$ 12,000	$ 15,000
b.	50,000	90,000
c.	50,000	150,000
d.	50,000	200,000

18. Discuss which penalties, if any, might be imposed on the tax adviser in each of the following independent circumstances. In this regard, assume that the tax adviser

a. suggested to the client various means by which to acquire excludible income.
b. suggested to the client various means by which to conceal cash receipts from gross income.
c. suggested to the client means by which to improve her cash flow by delaying for six months or more the deposit of the employees' share of Federal employment taxes.
d. kept in his own safe deposit box the cash of item (c).
e. failed, because of pressing time conflicts, to conduct the usual review of the client's tax return. The IRS later discovered that the return included fraudulent data.
f. failed, because of pressing time conflicts, to conduct the usual review of the client's tax return. The IRS later discovered a mathematical error in the computation of the personal exemption.

19. Olivia, a calendar year taxpayer, does not file her 1994 return until June 4, 1995. At this point, she pays the $3,000 balance due on her 1994 tax liability of $30,000. Olivia did not apply for and obtain any extension of time for filing the 1994 return. When questioned by the IRS on her delinquency, Olivia asserts: "If I was too busy to file my regular tax return, I was too busy to request an extension."

a. Is Olivia liable for any penalties for failure to file and for failure to pay?
b. If so, compute the penalty amounts.

20. Alec, a calendar year individual taxpayer, files his 1993 return on January 11, 1995. He did not obtain an extension for filing his return, and the return reflects additional income tax due of $3,800.

a. What are Alec's penalties for failure to file and to pay?
b. Would your answer change if Alec, before the due date of the return, had retained a CPA to prepare the return and it was the CPA's negligence that caused the delay?

21. Kim underpaid her taxes by $15,000. Of this amount $7,500 was due to negligence on her part. Determine the amount of any negligence penalty.

22. Dana underpaid his taxes by $250,000. A portion of the underpayment was attributable to negligence ($50,000) *and* another portion to civil fraud ($150,000). Compute the total penalties incurred.

23. Arnold made a charitable contribution of property that he valued at $20,000. He deducted this amount as an itemized deduction on his tax return. The IRS can prove that the real value of the property is $8,000. Arnold is in the 31% income tax bracket. Determine Arnold's overvaluation penalty.

24. Indicate which codes, canons, and other bodies of ethical statements apply to each of the following tax practitioners:

 a. CPAs who are members of the AICPA.
 b. CPAs who are not members of the AICPA.
 c. Attorneys.
 d. Enrolled agents.
 e. Tax preparers who are not CPAs, EAs, or attorneys.

25. What is the applicable statute of limitations in each of the following independent situations?

 a. No return was filed by the taxpayer.
 b. In 1990, the taxpayer incurred a bad debt loss that she failed to claim.
 c. On his 1990 return, a taxpayer inadvertently omitted a large amount of gross income.
 d. Same as (c), except that the omission was deliberate.
 e. For 1990, a taxpayer innocently overstated her deductions by a large amount.

26. During 1989, Suzanne (a calendar year taxpayer) had the following transactions, all of which were properly reported on a timely return:

Gross receipts		$960,000
Cost of goods sold		(800,000)
Gross profit		$160,000
Capital gain	$72,000	
Capital loss	(24,000)	48,000
Total income		$208,000

 a. Presuming the absence of fraud, how much of an omission from gross income is required before the six-year statute of limitations applies?
 b. Would it matter in your answer to (a) if cost of goods sold had been inadvertently overstated by $100,000?

27. On April 2, 1992, Mark filed his 1991 income tax return, which showed a tax due of $40,000. On June 1, 1994, he filed an amended return for 1991 that showed an additional tax of $12,000. Mark paid the additional amount. On May 18, 1995, Mark filed a claim for a refund of $18,000.

 a. If Mark's claim for a refund is correct in amount, how much tax will he recover?
 b. For what period will interest run in regard to Mark's claim for a refund?

28. Mimi had $40,000 withheld in 1991. Due to a sizable amount of itemized deductions, she figured that she had no further tax to pay for the year. For this reason, and because of personal problems, and without securing an extension, she did not file her 1991 return until July 1, 1992. Actually, the return showed a refund of $2,400, which Mimi ultimately received. On May 10, 1995, Mimi filed a $16,000 claim for refund of her 1991 taxes.

 a. How much, if any, of the $16,000 may Mimi recover?
 b. Would it have made any difference if Mimi had requested and secured from the IRS an extension of time for filing her 1991 tax return?

29. Rod's Federal income tax returns (Form 1040) for the past three years were prepared by the following persons:

Year	Preparer
1991	Rod
1992	Ann
1993	Cheryl

Ann is Rod's next-door neighbor and owns and operates a pharmacy. Cheryl is a licensed CPA and is engaged in private practice. In the event Rod is audited and all three returns are examined, who may represent him before the IRS at the agent level? Who may represent Rod before the Appeals Division?

30. Comment on the following statements relative to the "Statements on Responsibilities in Tax Practice":

   a. When a CPA has reasonable grounds for not answering an applicable question on a client's return, a brief explanation of the reason for the omission should not be provided, because it would flag the return for audit by the IRS.
   b. If a CPA discovers during an IRS audit that the client has a material error on the return under examination, he or she should immediately withdraw from the engagement.
   c. If the client tells you that she had contributions of $500 for unsubstantiated cash donations to her church, you should deduct an odd amount on her return (e.g., $499), because an even amount (i.e., $500) would indicate to the IRS that her deduction was based on an estimate.
   d. Basing an expense deduction on the client's estimates is not acceptable.
   e. If a CPA knows that the client has a material error on a prior year's return, he or she should not, without the client's consent, disclose the error to the IRS.
   f. If a CPA's client will not correct a material error on a prior year's return, the CPA should not prepare the current year's return for the client.

CHAPTER

THE FEDERAL GIFT AND ESTATE TAXES

OBJECTIVES

Illustrate the mechanics of the unified transfer tax.

Establish which persons are subject to this tax.

Review the formulas for the Federal gift and estate taxes.

Set forth the transfers that are subject to the Federal gift or estate tax.

Describe the exclusions and the deductions available in arriving at a taxable gift or a taxable estate.

Illustrate the computation of the Federal gift or estate tax by making use of all available credits.

Explain the objective of a program of lifetime giving.

Show how the gift and estate taxes can be reduced.

OUTLINE

TRANSFER TAXES—IN GENERAL

Until now, this text has dealt primarily with the various applications of the Federal income tax. Also important in the Federal tax structure are various excise taxes that cover transfers of property. Sometimes called transaction taxes, excise taxes are based on the value of the property transferred and not on the income derived from the property. Two such taxes—the Federal gift tax and the Federal estate tax—are the central focus of this chapter.

The importance of being familiar with rules governing transfer taxes can be shown with a simple illustration.

EXAMPLE 1

After 20 years of marriage to George, Helen decides to elope with Mark, a bachelor and long-time friend. Helen and Mark travel to a country in the Caribbean where Helen obtains a divorce, and she and Mark are married. Fifteen years later, Helen dies. Her will leaves all of her property (estimated value of $2,600,000) to Mark. Under the unlimited marital deduction (discussed later in the chapter), Helen's estate has no tax to pay. ◆

But the marital deduction applies only to transfers between husband and wife. Suppose the jurisdiction where Helen and Mark live does not recognize the validity of divorces granted by the Caribbean country involved? If this is the case, Helen and Mark are not married because Helen was never legally divorced from George. If Mark is not Helen's spouse, no marital deduction is available. Helen's estate must pay an estate tax of $780,800.

Nature of the Taxes

Before the enactment of the Tax Reform Act of 1976, Federal law imposed a tax on the gratuitous transfer of property in one of two ways. If the transfer was during the owner's life, it was subject to the Federal gift tax. If the property passed by virtue of the death of the owner, the Federal estate tax applied. Both taxes were governed by different rules including a separate set of tax rates. As Congress felt that lifetime transfers of wealth should be encouraged, the gift tax rates were lower than the estate tax rates.

The Tax Reform Act of 1976 significantly changed the approach taken by the Federal estate and gift taxes. Much of the distinction between life and death transfers was eliminated. Instead of subjecting these different types of transfers to two separate tax rate schedules, the Act substituted a unified transfer tax to cover all gratuitous transfers. Thus, gifts are subject to tax at the same rates as those applicable to transfers at death. In addition, current law eliminates the prior exemptions allowed under each tax and replaces them with a unified tax credit.

The Federal estate (or death) tax is designed to tax transfers at death. The tax differs, in several respects, from the typical inheritance tax imposed by many states and some local jurisdictions. First, the Federal *death tax* is imposed on the decedent's entire taxable estate. It is a tax on the right to pass property at death. *Inheritance taxes* are taxes on the right to receive property at death and are therefore levied on the heirs. Second, the relationship of the heirs to the decedent usually has a direct bearing on the inheritance tax. In general, the more closely related the parties, the larger the exemption and the lower the applicable rates.[1] Except for transfers to a surviving spouse that may result in a marital deduction, the relationship of the heirs to the decedent has no effect on the Federal estate tax.

The Federal gift tax, enacted several years after the enactment of the Federal estate tax, was designed to make the income and estate taxes more effective. Congress felt that individuals should not be able to give away property—thereby shifting the income tax consequences to others and avoiding estate taxes—without incurring some tax liability. The result is the Federal gift tax, which covers *inter vivos* (lifetime) transfers.

The Federal gift tax is imposed on the right of one person (the donor) to transfer property to another (the donee) for less than full and adequate consideration. The tax is payable by the donor.[2] If the donor fails to pay the tax when due, the donee may be held liable for the tax to the extent of the value of the property received.[3]

Persons Subject to the Taxes. To determine whether a transfer is subject to the Federal gift tax, first ascertain if the donor is a citizen or resident of the United States. If the donor is not a citizen or a resident, it is important to determine whether the property involved in the gift was situated within the United States.

The Federal gift tax is applied to all transfers by gift of property wherever located by individuals who, at the time of the gift, were citizens or residents of the United States. The term "United States" includes only the 50 states and the District of Columbia; it does not include U.S. possessions or territories.[4] For a U.S. citizen, the place of residence at the time of the gift is irrelevant.

For individuals who are neither citizens nor residents of the United States, the Federal gift tax is applied only to gifts of property situated within the United States.[5] A gift of intangible personal property (e.g., stocks and bonds) usually is not subject to the Federal gift tax when made by nonresident aliens.[6]

A gift by a corporation is considered a gift by the individual shareholders. A gift to a corporation is generally considered a gift to the individual shareholders. In certain cases, however, a gift to a charitable, public, political, or similar organization may be regarded as a gift to the organization as a single entity.[7]

The Federal estate tax is applied to the entire taxable estate of a decedent who, at the time of death, was a resident or citizen of the United States.[8] If the decedent was a U.S. citizen, the residence at death makes no difference.

If the decedent was neither a resident nor a citizen of the United States at the time of death, the Federal estate tax will be imposed on the value of any property located within the United States. In that case, the tax determination is controlled by a separate subchapter of the Internal Revenue Code.[9] In certain instances, these tax consequences outlined in the Code may have been modified by death tax conventions (treaties) between the United States and various foreign

---

1. For example, one state's inheritance tax provides an exemption of $50,000 for surviving spouses, with rates ranging from 5% to 10% on the taxable portion. This is to be contrasted with an exemption of only $1,000 for strangers (persons unrelated to the deceased), with rates ranging from 14% to 18% on the taxable portion. Other exemptions and rates fall between these extremes to cover beneficiaries variously related to the decedent.
2. § 2502(c).
3. § 6324(b).
4. § 7701(a)(9).
5. § 2511(a).
6. §§ 2501(a)(2) and (3). But see § 2511(b) and Reg. §§ 25.2511–3(b)(2), (3), and (4) for exceptions.
7. Reg. §§ 25.0–1(b) and 25.2511–1(h)(1). But note the exemption from the Federal gift tax for certain transfers to political organizations discussed later.
8. § 2001(a).
9. Subchapter B (§§ 2101 through 2108) covers the estate tax treatment of decedents who are neither residents nor citizens. Subchapter A (§§ 2001 through 2056A) covers the estate tax treatment of those who are either residents or citizens.

countries.[10] Further coverage of this area is beyond the scope of this text. The following discussion is limited to the tax treatment of decedents who were residents or citizens of the United States at the time of death.[11]

Formula for the Gift Tax. Like the income tax, which uses taxable income (and not gross income) as a tax base, the gift tax usually does not apply to the full amount of the gift. Deductions and the annual exclusion may be allowed to arrive at an amount called the *taxable gift*. However, unlike the income tax, which does consider taxable income from prior years, *prior taxable gifts* must be added to arrive at the tax base to which the unified transfer tax is applied. Otherwise, the donor could start over again each year with a new set of progressive rates.

EXAMPLE 2

Don makes taxable gifts of $500,000 in 1985 and $500,000 in 1993. Presuming no other taxable gifts and disregarding the effect of the unified tax credit, Don must pay a tax of $155,800 (see applicable tax rate schedule in Appendix A) on the 1985 transfer and a tax of $345,800 on the 1993 transfer (using a tax base of $1,000,000). If the 1985 taxable gift had not been included in the tax base for the 1993 gift, the tax would have been $155,800. The correct tax liability of $345,800 is more than twice $155,800! ◆

Because the gift tax is cumulative in effect, a credit is allowed for the gift taxes paid (or deemed paid) on prior taxable gifts included in the tax base. The deemed paid credit is explained later in the chapter.

EXAMPLE 3

Assume the same facts as in Example 2. Don will be allowed a credit of $155,800 against the gift tax of $345,800. Thus, his gift tax liability for 1993 becomes $190,000 ($345,800 − $155,800). ◆

The annual exclusion before 1982 was $3,000. The change to $10,000 was made to allow larger gifts to be exempt from the Federal gift tax. The increase improves taxpayer compliance and eases the audit function of the IRS. It also recognizes the inflationary trend in the economy.

The formula for the gift tax is summarized in Figure 26–1. [Note: Section (§) references are to the portion of the Internal Revenue Code involved.]

Formula for the Federal Estate Tax. The Federal unified transfer tax at death, commonly known as the Federal estate tax, is summarized in Figure 26–2. [Note: Section (§) references are to the portion of the Internal Revenue Code involved.]

The gross estate is determined by using the fair market value of the property on the date of the decedent's death (or on the alternate valuation date if applicable).

The reason post-1976 taxable gifts are added to the taxable estate to arrive at the tax base goes back to the scheme of the unified transfer tax. Starting in 1977, all transfers, whether lifetime or by death, are treated the same. Consequently,

---

10. At present, the United States has death tax conventions with the following countries: Australia, Austria, Denmark, Germany, Finland, France, Greece, Ireland, Italy, Japan, Netherlands, Norway, Republic of South Africa, Sweden, Switzerland, and the United Kingdom. The United States has gift tax conventions with Australia, Austria, France, Japan, and the United Kingdom.

11. Further information concerning Subchapter B (§§ 2101 through 2108) can be obtained from the relevant Code Sections (and the current Treasury Regulations thereunder). See also the Instructions to Form 706NA (U.S. Estate Tax Return of Nonresident Not a Citizen of the U.S.).

taxable gifts made after 1976 must be accounted for upon the death of the donor. Note that the double tax effect of including these gifts is eliminated by allowing a credit against the estate tax for the gift taxes previously paid or deemed paid.

Role of the Unified Tax Credit. Before the unified transfer tax, the gift tax allowed a $30,000 specific exemption for the lifetime of the donor. A comparable $60,000 exemption was allowed for estate tax purposes. The purpose of these exemptions was to allow donors and decedents to transfer modest amounts of wealth without being subject to the gift and estate taxes. Unfortunately, inflation took its toll, and more taxpayers became subject to these transfer taxes than Congress felt was appropriate. The congressional solution, therefore, was to rescind the exemptions and replace them with the unified tax credit.[12]

FIGURE 26–1
Gift Tax Formula

Determine whether the transfers are considered to be gifts by referring to §§ 2511 through 2519; list the fair market value of only the covered transfers		$xxx,xxx
Determine the deductions allowed by §§ 2522 (charitable) and 2523 (marital)	$xx,xxx	
Claim the annual exclusion ($10,000 per donee) under § 2503(b), if available	xx,xxx	(xx,xxx)
Taxable gifts [as defined by § 2503(a)] for the current period		$ xx,xxx
Add: Taxable gifts from prior years		xx,xxx
Total of current and past taxable gifts		$ xx,xxx
Compute the gift tax on the total of current and past taxable gifts by using the rates in Appendix A		$ x,xxx
Subtract: Gift tax paid or deemed paid on past taxable gifts and the unified tax credit		(xxx)
Gift tax due on transfers during the current period		$ xxx

FIGURE 26–2
Estate Tax Formula

Gross estate (§§ 2031–2046)		$xxx,xxx
Subtract:		
Expenses, indebtedness, and taxes (§ 2053)	$xx,xxx	
Losses (§ 2054)	xx,xxx	
Charitable bequests (§ 2055)	xx,xxx	
Marital deduction (§§ 2056 and 2056A)	xx,xxx	(x,xxx)
Taxable estate (§ 2051)		$ xx,xxx
Add: Post-1976 taxable gifts [§ 2001(b)]		x,xxx
Tax base		$xxx,xxx
Tentative tax on total transfers [§ 2001(c)]		$ xx,xxx
Subtract:		
Unified transfer tax on post-1976 taxable gifts (gift taxes paid or deemed paid)	$ x,xxx	
Other tax credits (including the unified tax credit) (§§ 2010–2016)	x,xxx	(x,xxx)
Estate tax due		$ x,xxx

12. §§ 2010 and 2505.

To curtail revenue loss, the credit was phased in as shown in Figure 26–3. The *exemption equivalent* is the amount of the transfer that will pass free of the gift or estate tax by virtue of the credit.

EXAMPLE 4

In 1993, Janet makes a taxable gift of $600,000. Presuming she has made no prior taxable gifts, Janet will not owe any gift tax. Under the applicable tax rate schedule (see Appendix A), the tax on $600,000 is $192,800, which is the exact amount of the credit allowed.[13] ◆

The Tax Reform Act of 1976 allowed donors one last chance to use the $30,000 specific exemption on lifetime gifts. If, however, the exemption was used on gifts made after September 8, 1976 (and before January 1, 1977), the unified tax credit must be reduced by 20 percent of the exemption utilized.[14] The credit must be readjusted whether the gift tax or the estate tax is involved. No adjustment is necessary for post-1976 gifts since the specific exemption was no longer available for such transfers.

EXAMPLE 5

Net of the annual exclusion, Myrtle, a widow, made gifts of $10,000 in June 1976 and $20,000 in December 1976. Assume Myrtle had never used any of her specific exemption and chose to use the full $30,000 to cover the 1976 gifts. Under these circumstances, the unified tax credit will be reduced by $4,000 (20% × $20,000). The use of the specific exemption on transfers made before September 9, 1976, has no effect on the credit. ◆

Key Property Concepts

When property is transferred either by gift or by death, the form of ownership can have a direct bearing on any transfer tax consequences. Understanding the different forms of ownership is necessary for working with Federal gift and estate taxes.

FIGURE 26–3
Unified Tax Credit Phase-In

Year of Death	Amount of Credit	Amount of Exemption Equivalent
1977	$ 30,000	$120,667
1978	34,000	134,000
1979	38,000	147,333
1980	42,500	161,563
1981	47,000	175,625
1982	62,800	225,000
1983	79,300	275,000
1984	96,300	325,000
1985	121,800	400,000
1986	155,800	500,000
1987 & thereafter	192,800	600,000

13. The rate schedules are contained in § 2001(c).

14. §§ 2010(c) and 2505(c).

Undivided Ownership. Assume Dan and Vicky own an undivided but equal interest in a tract of land. Such ownership can fall into any of four categories: joint tenancy, tenancy by the entirety, tenancy in common, or community property.

If Dan and Vicky hold ownership as joint tenants or tenants by the entirety, the right of survivorship exists. This means that the last tenant to survive receives full ownership of the property. Thus, if Dan predeceases Vicky, the land belongs entirely to Vicky. None of the land will pass to Dan's heirs or will be subject to administration by Dan's executor. A tenancy by the entirety is a joint tenancy between husband and wife.

If Dan and Vicky hold ownership as tenants in common or as community property, death does not defeat an owner's interest. Thus, if Dan predeceases Vicky, Dan's half interest in the land will pass to his estate or heirs.

Community property interests arise from the marital relationship. Normally, all property acquired after marriage, except by gift or inheritance, by husband and wife residing in a community property state becomes part of the community. The following states have the community property system in effect: Louisiana, Texas, New Mexico, Arizona, California, Washington, Idaho, Nevada, and Wisconsin. All other states follow the common law system of ascertaining a spouse's rights to property acquired after marriage.

Partial Interests. Interests in assets can be divided in terms of rights to income and rights to principal. Particularly when property is placed in trust, it is not uncommon to carve out various income interests that must be accounted for separately from the ultimate disposition of the property itself.

EXAMPLE 6

Under Bill's will, a ranch is to be placed in trust, life estate to Sam, Bill's son, with remainder to Sam's children (Bill's grandchildren). Under this arrangement, Sam is the life tenant and, as such, is entitled to the use of the ranch (including any income) during his life. Upon Sam's death, the trust terminates, and its principal passes to his children. Thus, Sam's children receive outright ownership of the ranch when Sam dies. ◆

THE FEDERAL GIFT TAX

General Considerations

Requirements for a Gift. For a gift to be complete under state law, the following elements must be present:

- A donor competent to make the gift.
- A donee capable of receiving and possessing the property.
- Donative intent on behalf of the donor.
- Actual or constructive delivery of the property to the donee or the donee's representative.
- Acceptance of the gift by the donee.

Whether transfers are gifts under state law is important in applying the Federal gift tax. But state law does not always control. For example, the tax law makes it clear that donative intent is not an essential factor in the application of the Federal gift tax.

Example 7

Barbara (age 24) consents to marry Harry (age 62) if he transfers $200,000 of his property to her. The arrangement is set forth in a prenuptial agreement, Harry makes the transfer, and he and Barbara are married. Harry lacked donative intent, and in most states no gift has been made by Harry to Barbara. Nevertheless, the transfer is subject to the Federal gift tax. ◆

The key to the result reached in Example 7 and to the status of other types of transfers is whether full and adequate consideration in money or money's worth was given for the property transferred. Although consideration is present in Example 7 (property for marriage) for purposes of state law, the consideration is not sufficient for the Federal gift tax. Under Regulation § 25.2512–8, "A consideration not reducible to a value in money or money's worth, as love and affection, promise of marriage, etc., is to be wholly disregarded, and the entire value of the property transferred constitutes the amount of the gift."

Incomplete Transfers. The Federal gift tax does not apply to transfers that are incomplete. Thus, if the transferor retains the right to reclaim the property or has not really parted with the possession of the property, a taxable event has not taken place.

Example 8

Lesly creates a trust with income payable to Mary for life, remainder to Paul. Under the terms of the trust instrument, Lesly can revoke the trust at any time and repossess the trust principal and income earned. No gift takes place on the creation of the trust; Lesly has not ceased to have dominion and control over the property. ◆

Example 9

Assume the same facts as in Example 8, except that one year after the transfer, Lesly relinquishes his right to terminate the trust. At this point, the transfer becomes complete, and the Federal gift tax applies. ◆

Business versus Personal Setting. In a business setting, full and adequate consideration is apt to exist. Regulation § 25.2512–8 provides that "a sale, exchange, or other transfer of property made in the ordinary course of business (a transaction that is bona fide, at arm's length, and free of any donative intent) will be considered as made for an adequate and full consideration in money or money's worth." If the parties are acting in a personal setting, a gift is usually the result. Do not conclude that the presence of *some* consideration may be enough to preclude Federal gift tax consequences. Again, the answer may rest on whether the transfer occurred in a business setting.

Example 10

Peter sells Bob some real estate for $40,000. Unknown to Peter, the property contains valuable mineral deposits and is really worth $100,000. Peter may have made a bad business deal, but he has not made a gift of $60,000 to Bob. ◆

Example 11

Assume the same facts as in Example 10, except that Peter and Bob are father and son. In addition, Peter is very much aware that the property is worth $100,000. Peter has made a gift of $60,000 to Bob. ◆

Certain Excluded Transfers. Transfers to political organizations are exempt from the application of the Federal gift tax.[15] This provision in the Code made

15. § 2501(a)(5).

unnecessary the previous practice whereby candidates for public office established multiple campaign committees to maximize the number of annual exclusions available to their contributors. As noted later, an annual exclusion of $10,000 (previously $3,000) for each donee passes free of the Federal gift tax.

The Federal gift tax does not apply to tuition payments made to an educational organization (e.g., a college) on another's behalf. Nor does it apply to amounts paid on another's behalf for medical care.[16] In this regard, the law is realistic since it is unlikely that most donors would recognize these items as being transfers subject to the gift tax.

Lifetime versus Death Transfers. Be careful to distinguish between lifetime (inter vivos) and death (testamentary) transfers.

EXAMPLE 12

Wilbur buys a U.S. savings bond, which he registers as follows: "Wilbur, payable to Alice upon Wilbur's death." No gift is made when Wilbur buys the bond; Alice has received only a mere expectancy (right to obtain ownership of the bond at Wilbur's death). Anytime before his death, Wilbur may redeem or otherwise dispose of the bond and cut off Alice's interest. On Wilbur's death, no gift is made because the bond passes to Alice by testamentary disposition. As noted later, the bond will be included in Wilbur's gross estate as property in which the decedent had an interest (§ 2033). ◆

Transfers Subject to the Gift Tax

Whether a transfer is subject to the Federal gift tax depends upon the application of §§ 2511 through 2519 and the Regulations thereunder.

Gift Loans. To understand the tax ramifications of gift loans, an illustration is helpful.

EXAMPLE 13

Before his daughter (Denise) leaves for college, Victor lends her $300,000. Denise signs a note that provides for repayment in five years. The loan contains no interest element, and neither Victor nor Denise expects any interest to be paid. Following Victor's advice, Denise invests the loan proceeds in income-producing securities. During her five years in college, she uses the income from the investments to pay for college costs and other living expenses. On the maturity date of the note, Denise repays the $300,000 she owes Victor. ◆

In a gift loan arrangement, the following consequences result:

- Victor has made a gift to Denise of the interest element. The amount of the gift is determined by the difference between the amount of interest charged (in this case, none) and the market rate (as determined by the yield on certain U.S. government securities).
- The interest element is included in Victor's gross income and is subject to the Federal income tax.
- Denise may be allowed an income tax deduction for the interest element, but may benefit from this result only if she is in a position to itemize her deductions *from* adjusted gross income.

The Code defines a gift loan as "any below-market loan where the forgoing of interest is in the nature of a gift."[17] Unless tax avoidance was one of the principal

---

16. § 2503(e).

17. § 7872(f)(3).

purposes of the loan, special limitations apply if the gift loan does not exceed $100,000. In such a case, the interest element may not exceed the borrower's net investment income.[18] Furthermore, if the net investment income does not exceed $1,000, it is treated as zero. Under a $1,000 *de minimis* rule, the interest element is to be disregarded.

Certain Property Settlements (§ 2516). Normally, the settlement of certain marital rights is not regarded as being for consideration and is subject to the Federal gift tax.[19] As a special exception to this general approach, Congress enacted § 2516. Under this provision, transfers of property interests made under the terms of a written agreement between spouses in settlement of their marital or property rights are deemed to be for adequate consideration. The transfers are exempt from the Federal gift tax if a final decree of divorce is obtained within the three-year period beginning on the date one year before the parties entered into the agreement. Likewise excluded are transfers to provide a reasonable allowance for the support of minor children (including legally adopted children) of a marriage. The agreement need not be approved by the divorce decree.

Disclaimers (§ 2518). A disclaimer is a refusal by a person to accept property that is designated to pass to him or her. The effect of the disclaimer is to pass the property to someone else.

EXAMPLE 14

Earl dies without a will and is survived by a son, Andy, and a grandson, Jay. At the time of his death, Earl owned real estate that, under the applicable state law, passes to the closest lineal descendant, Andy in this case. If, however, Andy disclaims his interest in the real estate, state law provides that the property passes to Jay. At the time of Earl's death, Andy has considerable property of his own, and Jay has none. ◆

Why might Andy want to consider disclaiming his inheritance and have the property pass directly from Earl to Jay? By doing so, an extra transfer tax may be avoided. If the disclaimer does not take place (Andy accepts the inheritance), and the property eventually passes to Jay (either by gift or by death), the later transfer will be subject to the application of either the gift tax or the estate tax.

For many years, whether a disclaimer would be effective in avoiding a Federal transfer tax depended on the application of state law. To illustrate by using the facts of Example 14, if state law determined that the real estate was deemed to have passed through Andy despite his disclaimer after Earl's death, the Federal gift tax would apply. In essence, Andy would be treated as if he had inherited the property from Earl and then given it to Jay. As state law was not always consistent in this regard and sometimes was not even known, the application or nonapplication of Federal transfer taxes could depend on where the parties lived. To remedy this situation and provide some measure of uniformity, §§ 2046 (relating to disclaimers for estate tax purposes) and 2518 were added to the Code.

In the case of the gift tax, when the requirements of § 2518 are met and Andy makes a timely lifetime disclaimer (refer to Example 14), the property is treated as if it goes directly from Earl to Jay. Since the property is not regarded as having passed through Andy (regardless of what state law holds), it is not subject to the Federal gift tax.

---

18. Net investment income has the same meaning given to the term by § 163(d). Generally, net investment income is investment income (e.g., interest, dividends) less related expenses.

19. See Reg. § 25.2512–8 and Example 7 in this chapter.

The tax law also permits the avoidance of the Federal gift tax in cases of a partial disclaimer of an undivided interest.

EXAMPLE 15

Assume the same facts as in Example 14, except that Andy wishes to retain half of the real estate for himself. If Andy makes a timely disclaimer of an undivided one-half interest in the property, the Federal gift tax will not apply to the portion passing to Jay. ◆

Other Transfers Subject to Gift Tax. Other transfers that may carry gift tax consequences (e.g., the exercise of a power of appointment, the creation of joint ownership) are discussed and illustrated in connection with the Federal estate tax.

Annual Exclusion

The first $10,000 of gifts made to any one person during any calendar year (except gifts of future interests in property) is excluded in determining the total amount of gifts for the year.[20] The annual exclusion applies to all gifts of a present interest made during the calendar year in the order in which they are made until the $10,000 exclusion per donee is exhausted. For a gift in trust, each beneficiary of the trust is treated as a separate person for purposes of the exclusion.

A *future interest* is defined as one that will come into being (as to use, possession, or enjoyment) at some future date. Examples of future interests include such rights as remainder interests that are commonly encountered when property is transferred to a trust. A *present interest* is an unrestricted right to the immediate use, possession, or enjoyment of property or of the income.

EXAMPLE 16

During the current year, Laura makes the following cash gifts: $8,000 to Rita and $12,000 to Maureen. Laura may claim an annual exclusion of $8,000 with respect to Rita and $10,000 with respect to Maureen. ◆

EXAMPLE 17

By a lifetime gift, Ron transfers property to a trust with a life estate (with income payable annually) to June and remainder upon June's death to Albert. Ron has made two gifts: one to June of a life estate and one to Albert of a remainder interest. The life estate is a present interest and qualifies for the annual exclusion. The remainder interest granted to Albert is a future interest and does not qualify for the exclusion. Note that Albert's interest does not come into being until some future date (on the death of June). ◆

Although Example 17 indicates that the gift of an income interest is a present interest, this is not always the case. If a possibility exists that the income beneficiary may not receive the immediate enjoyment of the property, the transfer is of a future interest.

EXAMPLE 18

Assume the same facts as in Example 17, except that the income from the trust need not be payable annually to June. It may, at the trustee's discretion, be accumulated and added to corpus. Since June's right to receive the income from the trust is conditioned on the trustee's discretion, it is not a present interest. No annual exclusion will be allowed. The mere possibility of diversion is enough. It would not matter if the trustee

---

20. § 2503(b).

never exercised the discretion to accumulate and did, in fact, distribute the trust income to June annually. ◆

Trust for Minors. Section 2503(c) offers an exception to the future interest rules just discussed. Under this provision, a transfer for the benefit of a person who has not attained the age of 21 years on the date of the gift may be considered a gift of a present interest. This is true even though the minor is not given the unrestricted right to the immediate use, possession, or enjoyment of the property. For the exception to apply, however, certain stringent conditions must be satisfied. One such condition is that all of the property and its income must be made available to the minor upon attaining age 21. Thus, the exception would allow a trustee to accumulate income on behalf of a minor beneficiary without converting the income interest to a future interest.

Deductions

In arriving at taxable gifts, a deduction is allowed for transfers to certain qualified charitable organizations. On transfers between spouses, a marital deduction may be available. Since both the charitable and marital deductions apply in determining the Federal estate tax, they are discussed later in the chapter.

Computing the Federal Gift Tax

The Unified Transfer Tax Rate Schedule. The top rates of the unified transfer tax rate schedule originally reached as high as 70 percent. For consistency with the maximum income tax rate applicable to individuals, which, until recently, was 50 percent, the top unified transfer tax rate was lowered to this amount. But the reduction was phased in, and the maximum of 50 percent was not reached until 1993 (see applicable tax rate schedule in Appendix A). For transfers (by gift or death) made from 1984 through 1992, the top rate was 55 percent. As noted later in the chapter, the benefits of the graduated rates are currently phased out for larger gifts. Keep in mind that the unified transfer tax rate schedule applies to all transfers (by gift or death) after 1976. Different rate schedules applied for pre-1977 gifts and pre-1977 death transfers.

The Deemed-Paid Adjustment. Review the formula for the gift tax (refer to Figure 26–1) and note that the tax base for a current gift includes *all* past taxable gifts. The effect of the inclusion is to force the current taxable gift into a higher bracket due to the progressive nature of the unified transfer tax rates (refer to Example 2). To mitigate such double taxation, the donor is allowed a credit for any gift tax previously paid or deemed paid (refer to Example 3).

Limiting the donor to a credit for the gift tax *actually paid* on pre-1977 taxable gifts would be unfair. Pre-1977 taxable gifts were subject to a lower set of rates than those in the unified transfer tax rate schedule. As a consequence, the donor is allowed a *deemed-paid* credit on pre-1977 taxable gifts. This is the amount that would have been due under the unified transfer tax rate schedule had it been applicable. *Post-1976* taxable gifts *also* are subject to the deemed-paid adjustment because the same rate schedule may not be involved in all gifts.

EXAMPLE 19

In early 1976, Lisa made taxable gifts of $500,000, upon which a Federal gift tax of $109,275 was paid. Assume Lisa makes further taxable gifts of $700,000 in 1993. The unified transfer tax on the 1993 gifts is determined as follows:

Taxable gifts made in 1993		$ 700,000
Add: Taxable gifts made in 1976		500,000
Total of current and past taxable gifts		$1,200,000
Unified transfer tax on total taxable gifts per Appendix A [$345,800 + (41% × $200,000)]		$ 427,800
Subtract:		
Deemed paid tax on pre-1977 taxable gifts per Appendix A	$155,800	
Unified tax credit for 1993	192,800	(348,600)
Gift tax due on the 1993 taxable gift		$ 79,200

Note that the gift tax actually paid on the 1976 transfer was $109,275. Nevertheless, Lisa is allowed a deemed-paid credit on the gift of $155,800, considerably different than the amount paid. ◆

The Election to Split Gifts by Married Persons. To understand the reason for the gift-splitting election of § 2513, consider the following situations:

EXAMPLE 20

Dick and Margaret are husband and wife and reside in Michigan, a common law state. Dick has been the only breadwinner in the family, and Margaret has no significant property of her own. Neither has made any prior taxable gifts or used the $30,000 specific exemption previously available for pre-1977 gifts. In 1993, Dick makes a gift to Leslie of $1,220,000. Presuming the election to split gifts did not exist, Dick's gift tax is as follows:

Amount of gift	$1,220,000
Subtract: Annual exclusion	(10,000)
Taxable gift	$1,210,000
Gift tax on $1,210,000 per Appendix A [$345,800 + (41% × $210,000)]	$ 431,900
Subtract: Unified tax credit for 1993	(192,800)
Gift tax due on the 1993 taxable gift	$ 239,100

◆

EXAMPLE 21

Assume the same facts as in Example 20, except that Dick and Margaret have always resided in California. Even though Dick is the sole breadwinner, income from personal services generally is community property. Consequently, the gift to Leslie probably involves community property. If this is the case, the gift tax is as follows:

	Dick	Margaret
Amount of the gift (50% × $1,220,000)	$ 610,000	$ 610,000
Subtract: Annual exclusion	(10,000)	(10,000)
Taxable gifts	$ 600,000	$ 600,000
Gift tax on $600,000 per Appendix A	$ 192,800	$ 192,800
Subtract: Unified tax credit for 1993	(192,800)	(192,800)
Gift tax due on the 1993 taxable gifts	$ -0-	$ -0-

◆

As the results of Examples 20 and 21 indicate, married donors residing in community property jurisdictions possessed a significant gift tax advantage over those residing in common law states. To rectify this inequity, the Revenue Act of 1948 incorporated the predecessor to § 2513 into the Code. Under this provision, a gift made by a person to someone other than his or her spouse may be considered, for Federal gift tax purposes, as having been made one-half by each spouse. Returning to Example 20, Dick and Margaret could treat the gift passing to Leslie as being made one-half by each of them, even though the property belonged to Dick. As a result, the parties are able to achieve the same tax consequence as in Example 21.

To split gifts, the spouses must be legally married to each other at the time of the gift. If they are divorced later in the calendar year, they may still split the gift if neither marries anyone else during that year. They both must indicate on their separate gift tax returns their consent to have all gifts made in that calendar year split between them. In addition, both must be citizens or residents of the United States on the date of the gift. A gift from one spouse to the other spouse cannot be split. Such a gift might, however, be eligible for the marital deduction.

The election to split gifts is not necessary when husband and wife transfer community property to a third party. It is needed if the gift consists of the separate property of one of the spouses. Generally, separate property is property acquired before marriage and property acquired after marriage by gift or inheritance. The election, then, is not limited to residents of common law states.

Procedural Matters

Having determined which transfers are subject to the Federal gift tax and the various deductions and exclusions available to the donor, the procedural aspects of the tax should be considered. The sections to follow discuss the return itself, the due dates for filing and paying the tax, and other related matters.

Concept Summary 26–1
Federal Gift Tax Provisions

1. The Federal gift tax applies to all gratuitous transfers of property made by U.S. citizens or residents. In this regard, it does not matter where the property is located.
2. In the eyes of the IRS, a gratuitous transfer is one not supported by full and adequate consideration. If the parties are acting in a business setting, such consideration usually exists. If purported sales are between family members, a gift element may be suspected.
3. If a lender loans money to another and intends some or all of the interest element to be a gift, the arrangement is categorized as a gift loan. To the extent that the interest provided for is less than the market rate, three tax consequences result. First, a gift has taken place between the lender and the borrower as to the interest element. Second, income may result to the lender. Third, an income tax deduction may be available to the borrower.
4. Property settlements can escape the gift tax if a divorce occurs within a prescribed period of time.
5. A disclaimer is a refusal by a person to accept property designated to pass to that person. The effect of a disclaimer is to pass the property to someone else. If certain conditions are satisfied, the issuance of a disclaimer will not be subject to the Federal gift tax.
6. Except for gifts of future interests, a donor is allowed an annual exclusion of $10,000. The future interest limitation does not apply to certain trusts created for minors.
7. The election to split a gift enables a married couple to be treated as two donors. The election doubles the annual exclusion and makes the unified tax credit available to the nonowner spouse.
8. The election to split gifts is not necessary if the property is jointly owned by the spouses. That is the case when the property is part of the couple's community.
9. In determining the tax base for computing the gift tax, all prior taxable gifts must be added to current taxable gifts. Thus, the gift tax is cumulative in nature.
10. Gifts are reported on Form 709 or Form 709–A. The return is due on April 15 following the year of the gift.

The Federal Gift Tax Return. For transfers by gift, a Form 709 (U.S. Gift Tax Return) must be filed whenever the gifts for any one calendar year exceed the annual exclusion or involve a gift of a future interest. A Form 709 need not be filed, however, for transfers between spouses that are offset by the unlimited marital deduction, regardless of the amount of the transfer.[21]

EXAMPLE 22

In 1993, Larry makes five gifts, each in the amount of $10,000, to his five children. If the gifts do not involve future interests, a Form 709 need not be filed to report the transfers. ◆

EXAMPLE 23

During 1993, Esther makes a gift of $20,000 cash of her separate property to her daughter. To double the amount of the annual exclusion allowed, Jerry (Esther's husband) is willing to split the gift. Since the § 2513 election can be made only on a gift tax return, a form must be filed even though no gift tax will be due as a result of the transfer. Useful for this purpose is Form 709–A (U.S. Short Form Gift Tax Return). This form is available to simplify the gift-splitting procedure. ◆

Presuming a gift tax return is due, it must be filed on or before the fifteenth day of April following the year of the gift.[22] As with other Federal taxes, when the due date falls on Saturday, Sunday, or a legal holiday, the date for filing the return is the next business day. Note that the filing requirements for Form 709 have no correlation to the accounting year used by a donor for Federal income tax purposes. Thus, a fiscal year taxpayer must follow the April 15 rule for any reportable gifts.

Extensions of Time and Payment of Tax. If sufficient reason is shown, the IRS is authorized to grant reasonable extensions of time for filing the return.[23] Unless the donor is abroad, no extension longer than six months may be granted. The application must be made before the due date of the return and must contain a full report of the causes for the delay. For a calendar year taxpayer, an extension of time for filing an income tax return also extends the time for filing Form 709. An extension of time to file the return does not extend the time for payment of the tax.

THE FEDERAL ESTATE TAX

The following discussion of the estate tax coincides with the formula that appeared earlier in the chapter. This formula can be summarized as follows (refer to page 26–5 for a more detailed presentation of the formula):

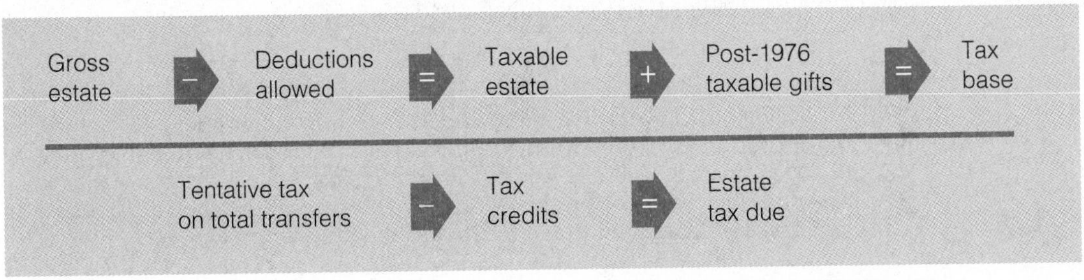

Gross estate − Deductions allowed = Taxable estate + Post-1976 taxable gifts = Tax base

Tentative tax on total transfers − Tax credits = Estate tax due

21. § 6019(a)(2).

22. § 6075(b).

23. § 6081.

The key components in the formula are the gross estate, the taxable estate, the tax base, and the credits allowed against the tentative tax.

Gross Estate

Simply stated, the gross estate comprises all property subject to the Federal estate tax. Thus, the gross estate depends on the provisions of the Internal Revenue Code as supplemented by IRS pronouncements and the judicial interpretations of Federal courts.

In contrast to the gross estate, the *probate estate* is controlled by state (rather than Federal) law. The probate estate consists of all of a decedent's property subject to administration by the executor or administrator of the estate. The administration is supervised by a local court of appropriate jurisdiction (usually called a probate court). An executor (or executrix) is the decedent's personal representative appointed under the decedent's will. When a decendent dies without a will or fails to name an executor in the will (or that person refuses to serve), the local probate court appoints an administrator (or administratrix).

The probate estate is frequently smaller than the gross estate. It contains only property owned by the decedent at the time of death and passing to heirs under a will or under the law of intestacy (the order of distribution for those dying without a will). As noted later, such items as the proceeds of many life insurance policies become part of the gross estate but are not included in the probate estate.

All states provide for an order of distribution in the event someone dies without a will. After the surviving spouse receives some or all of the estate, the preference is usually in the following order: down to lineal descendants (e.g., children, grandchildren), up to lineal ascendants (e.g., parents, grandparents), and out to collateral relations (e.g., brothers, sisters, aunts, and uncles).

Property Owned by the Decedent (§ 2033). Property owned by the decedent at the time of death is included in the gross estate. The nature of the property or the use to which it was put during the decedent-owner's lifetime has no significance as far as the estate tax is concerned. Thus, personal effects (such as clothing), stocks, bonds, furniture, jewelry, works of art, bank accounts, and interests in businesses conducted as sole proprietorships and partnerships are all included in the deceased's gross estate. No distinction is made between tangible or intangible, depreciable or nondepreciable, business or personal assets.

The application of § 2033 can be illustrated as follows:

EXAMPLE 24

Irma dies owning some City of Denver bonds. The fair market value of the bonds plus any interest accrued to the date of Irma's death is included in her gross estate. Although interest on municipal bonds is normally not taxable under the Federal income tax, it is property owned by Irma at the time of death. However, any interest accrued after death is not part of Irma's gross estate. ◆

EXAMPLE 25

Sharon dies on April 8, at a time when she owns stock in Robin Corporation and in Wren Corporation. On March 2, both corporations had authorized a cash dividend payable on May 1. For Robin, the dividend was payable to shareholders of record as of April 1. Wren's date of record is April 10. Sharon's gross estate includes the following: the stock in Robin Corporation, the stock in Wren Corporation, and the dividend on the Robin stock. It does not include the dividend on the Wren stock. ◆

EXAMPLE 26

Ray dies holding some promissory notes issued to him by his son. In his will, Ray forgives these notes, relieving the son of the obligation to make any payments. The fair market value of these notes will be included in Ray's gross estate. ◆

Dower and Curtesy Interests (§ 2034). In its common law (nonstatutory) form, dower generally gave a surviving widow a life estate in a portion of her husband's estate (usually the real estate he owned) with the remainder passing to their children. Most states have modified and codified these common law rules, and the resulting statutes often vary among jurisdictions. In some states, for example, by statute, a widow is entitled to outright ownership of a percentage of her deceased husband's real estate and personal property. Curtesy is a similar right held by the husband in his wife's property, taking effect in the event he survives her. Most states have abolished the common law curtesy concept and have, in some cases, substituted a modified statutory version.

Dower and curtesy rights are incomplete interests and may never materialize. Thus, if a wife predeceases her husband, her dower interest in her husband's property is lost.

EXAMPLE 27

Martin dies without a will, leaving an estate of $900,000. Under state law, Belinda (Martin's widow) is entitled to one-third of his property. The $300,000 Belinda receives will be included in Martin's gross estate. Depending on the nature of the interest Belinda receives in the $300,000, this amount could qualify Martin's estate for a marital deduction. (This possibility is discussed at greater length later in the chapter. For the time being, however, the focus is on what is or is not included as part of the decedent's gross estate.) ◆

Adjustments for Gifts Made within Three Years of Death (§ 2035). At one time, all taxable gifts made within three years of death were included in the donor's gross estate unless it could be shown that the gifts were not made in contemplation of death. The prior rule was designed to preclude tax avoidance since the gift tax and estate tax rates were separate and the former was lower than the latter. When the gift and estate tax rates were combined into the unified transfer tax, the reason for the rule for gifts in contemplation of death largely disappeared. The three-year rule has, however, been retained for the following items:

- Any gift tax paid on gifts made within three years of death. Called the *gross-up* procedure, this prevents the gift tax amount from escaping the estate tax.
- Any property interests transferred by gift within three years of death that would have been included in the gross estate by virtue of the application of § 2036 (transfers with a retained life estate), § 2037 (transfers taking effect at death), § 2038 (revocable transfers), and § 2042 (proceeds of life insurance). All except § 2037 transfers are discussed later in the chapter.

EXAMPLE 28

Before her death in 1993, Jennifer made the following taxable gifts:

Year of Gift	Nature of the Asset	Fair Market Value: Date of Gift	Fair Market Value: Date of Death	Gift Tax Paid
1987	Hawk Corporation stock	$100,000	$150,000	$ -0-
1991	Policy on Jennifer's life	40,000 (cash value)	200,000 (face value)	-0-
1992	Land	400,000	410,000	8,200

Jennifer's *gross estate* includes $208,200 ($200,000 life insurance proceeds + $8,200 gross-up for the gift tax on the 1992 taxable gift) as to these transfers. Referring to the formula for the estate tax (Figure 26–2), the other post-1976 taxable gifts are added to the *taxable estate* (at the fair market value on the date of the gift) in arriving at the tax base. Jennifer's estate is allowed a credit for the gift tax paid (or deemed paid) on the 1992 transfer. ◆

Transfers with a Retained Life Estate (§ 2036). Code §§ 2036 through 2038 were enacted on the premise that the estate tax can be avoided on lifetime transfers only if the decedent does not retain control over the property. The logic of this approach is somewhat difficult to dispute. One should not be able to escape the tax consequences of property transfers at death while remaining in a position during life to enjoy some or all of the fruits of ownership.

Under § 2036, the value of any property transferred by the deceased during lifetime for less than adequate consideration must be included if either of the following was retained:

- The possession or enjoyment of, or the right to the income from, the property.
- The right, either alone or in conjunction with any person, to designate the persons who shall possess or enjoy the property or the income.

"The possession or enjoyment of, or the right to the income from, the property," as it appears in § 2036(a)(1), is considered to have been retained by the decedent to the extent that such income, etc., is to be applied toward the discharge of a legal obligation of the decedent. The term "legal obligation" includes a legal obligation of the decedent to support a dependent during the decedent's lifetime.[24]

The practical application of § 2036 can be explained by turning to two illustrations.

EXAMPLE 29

Carl's will passes all of his property to a trust in which income goes to Alan for his life (Alan is given a life estate). Upon Alan's death, the principal goes to Melissa (Melissa is granted a remainder interest). On Alan's death, none of the trust property is included in his gross estate. Although Alan held a life estate, § 2036 is inapplicable because Alan was not the transferor (Carl was) of the property. Section 2033 (property owned by the decedent) causes any income distributions Alan was entitled to receive at the time of his death to be included in his gross estate. ◆

EXAMPLE 30

By deed, Nora transfers the remainder interest in her ranch to Marcia, retaining for herself the right to continue occupying the property until death. Upon Nora's death, the fair market value of the ranch will be included in her gross estate. Furthermore, Nora is subject to the gift tax. The amount of the gift is the fair market value of the ranch on the date of the gift less the portion applicable to Nora's retained life estate. ◆

Revocable Transfers (§ 2038). Another type of lifetime transfer that is drawn into a decedent's gross estate is covered by § 2038. The gross estate includes the value of property interests transferred by the decedent (except to the extent that the transfer was made for full consideration) if the enjoyment of the property transferred was subject, at the date of the decedent's death, to any power of the decedent to *alter, amend, revoke, or terminate* the transfer. This includes the power to change beneficiaries or to accelerate or increase any beneficiary's enjoyment of the property.

24. Reg. § 20.2036–1(b)(2).

The capacity in which the decedent could exercise the power is immaterial. If the decedent gave property in trust, making himself or herself the trustee with the power to revoke the trust, the property is included in his or her gross estate. If the decedent named another person as trustee with the power to revoke but reserved the power to later appoint himself or herself trustee, the property is also included in his or her gross estate. If, however, the power to alter, amend, revoke, or terminate was held at all times solely by a person other than the decedent and the decedent did not reserve a right to assume these powers, the property is not included in the decedent's gross estate.

The Code and the Regulations make it clear that one cannot avoid inclusion in the gross estate under § 2038 by relinquishing a power within three years of death.[25] Recall that § 2038 is one of several types of situations listed as exceptions to the usual rule excluding gifts made within three years of death from the gross estate.

In the event § 2038 applies, the amount includible in the gross estate is the portion of the property transferred that is subject, at the decedent's death, to the decedent's power to alter, amend, revoke, or terminate.

The classic § 2038 situation results from the use of a revocable trust.

EXAMPLE 31

Maria creates a trust, life estate to her children, remainder to her grandchildren. Under the terms of the trust, Maria reserves the right to revoke the trust and revest the trust principal and income in herself. As noted in Example 8, the creation of the trust does not result in a gift because the transfer is not complete. However, if Maria dies still retaining the power to revoke, the trust is included in her gross estate under § 2038. ◆

More subtle applications of § 2038 result from the use of a state Uniform Gifts to Minors Act. The Uniform Gifts to Minors Act permits the ownership of securities to be transferred to a minor with someone designated as custodian. The custodian has the right to sell the securities, collect any income, and otherwise act on behalf of the minor without court supervision. The custodianship arrangement is convenient and inexpensive. Under state law the custodianship terminates automatically when the minor reaches a specified age (usually age 21). If the custodian also has the power to terminate the arrangement, § 2038 could create estate tax problems.

EXAMPLE 32

Tom transfers securities to Sue under the state's Uniform Gifts to Minors Act naming himself as the custodian. Under the Act, the custodian has the authority to terminate the custodianship at any time and distribute the proceeds to the minor. Tom dies four years later before the custodianship is terminated. Although the transfer is effective for income tax purposes, it runs afoul of § 2038.[26] Under this Section, the fair market value of the securities on the date of Tom's death is included in his gross estate for Federal estate tax purposes. ◆

EXAMPLE 33

Assume the same facts as in Example 32, except that Tom dissolves the custodianship (thereby turning the securities over to Sue) within three years of death. The fair market value of the securities on the date of Tom's death is includible in his gross estate.[27] ◆

25. § 2038(a)(1) and Reg. § 20.2038–1(e)(1).
26. If the minor is under the age of 14, net unearned income may be taxed at the parents' income tax rate. Unearned income generally is passive income (e.g., dividends, interest) in excess of $1,200. §§ 1(i) and (j).
27. § 2035(d)(2).

EXAMPLE 34

Assume the same facts as in Example 32, except that Sue comes of age and the custodianship terminates before Tom's death. Nothing is included in Tom's gross estate upon his death. ◆

EXAMPLE 35

Gordon transfers securities to Patty under the state's Uniform Gifts to Minors Act naming Walter as the custodian. Nothing relating to these securities is included in Walter's gross estate upon his death during the term of the custodianship. Section 2038 is not applicable because Walter was not the transferor. Gordon's death during the custodianship causes no estate tax consequences; Gordon has retained no interest or control over the property transferred. ◆

In application, the provisions related to incomplete transfers (§§ 2036 and 2038) tend to overlap. It is not unusual to find that either or both Sections apply to a particular transfer.

Annuities (§ 2039). Annuities can be divided by their origin into commercial and noncommercial contracts. Noncommercial annuities are issued by private parties and, in some cases, charitable organizations that do not regularly issue annuities. The two varieties have much in common, but noncommercial annuities present special income tax problems and are not treated further in this discussion.

Regulation § 20.2039–1(b)(1) defines an annuity as representing "one or more payments extending over any period of time." According to the Regulation, the payments may be equal or unequal, conditional or unconditional, periodic or sporadic. Most commercial contracts fall into one of four general patterns:

1. *Straight-life annuity.* The insurance company promises to make periodic payments to Thomas (the annuitant) during his life. Upon Thomas's death, the company has no further obligation under the contract.
2. *Joint and survivor annuity.* The insurance company promises to make periodic payments to Thomas and Sally during their lives with the payments to continue, usually in a diminished amount, for the life of the survivor.
3. *Self and survivor annuity.* The company agrees to make periodic payments to Thomas during his life and, upon his death, to continue these payments for the life of a designated beneficiary. This and the preceding type of annuity are frequently used by married persons.
4. *Refund feature.* The company agrees to return to the annuitant's estate or other designated beneficiary a portion of the investment in the contract in the event of the annuitant's premature death.

In the case of a straight-life annuity, nothing is included in the gross estate of the annuitant at death. Section 2033 (property in which the decedent had an interest) does not apply because the annuitant's interest in the contract is terminated by death. Section 2036 (transfers with a retained life estate) does not cover the situation; a transfer made for full consideration is specifically excluded from § 2036 treatment. A commercial annuity is presumed to have been purchased for full consideration unless some evidence exists to indicate that the parties were not acting at arm's length.

EXAMPLE 36

Arnold purchases a straight-life annuity that will pay him $6,000 a month when he reaches age 65. Arnold dies at age 70. Except for the payments he received before his death, nothing relating to this annuity will affect Arnold's gross estate. ◆

In the case of a survivorship annuity (classifications 2 and 3), the estate tax consequences under § 2039(a) are usually triggered by the death of the first annuitant. The amount included in the gross estate is the cost from the same company of a comparable annuity covering the survivor at his or her attained age on the date of the deceased annuitant's death.

EXAMPLE 37

Assume the same facts as in Example 36, except that the annuity contract provides for Veronica to be paid $3,000 a month for life as a survivorship feature. Veronica is 62 years of age when Arnold dies. Under these circumstances, Arnold's gross estate includes the cost of a comparable contract that provides an annuity of $3,000 per month for the life of a female, age 62. ◆

Full inclusion of the survivorship element in the gross estate is subject to the important exception under § 2039(b). The amount includible is to be based on the proportion of the deceased annuitant's contribution to the total cost of the contract. This is expressed by the following formula:

$$\frac{\text{Decedent's contribution to purchase price}}{\text{Total purchase price of the annuity}}$$

Value of the annuity (or refund) at decedent's death

Amount includible in the deceased annuitant's gross estate

EXAMPLE 38

Assume the same facts as in Example 37, except that Arnold and Veronica are husband and wife and have always lived in a community property state. The premiums on the contract were paid with community funds. Since Veronica contributed half of the cost of the contract, only half of the amount determined under Example 37 is included in Arnold's gross estate. ◆

The result reached in Example 38 is not unique to community property jurisdictions. The outcome would have been the same in a noncommunity property state if Veronica had furnished half of the consideration from her own funds.

Joint Interests (§§ 2040 and 2511). Recall that joint tenancies and tenancies by the entirety are characterized by the right of survivorship. Thus, upon the death of a joint tenant, title to the property passes to the surviving tenant. None of the property is included in the *probate* estate of the deceased tenant. In the case of tenancies in common and community property, death does not defeat an ownership interest; rather, the deceased owner's interest is part of the probate estate.

The *Federal estate tax treatment* of tenancies in common or of community property follows the logical approach of taxing only the portion of the property included in the deceased owner's probate estate. Thus, if Homer, Wilma, and Thelma are tenants in common in a tract of land, each owning an equal interest, and Homer dies, only one-third of the value of the property is included in the gross estate. This one-third interest is also the same amount that will pass to Homer's heirs.

EXAMPLE 39

Homer, Wilma, and Thelma acquire a tract of land with ownership listed as tenants in common, each party furnishing $20,000 of the $60,000 purchase price. When the property is worth $90,000, Homer dies. If Homer's undivided interest in the property is 33⅓%, the gross estate *and* probate estate each include $30,000. ◆

Unless the parties have provided otherwise, each tenant is deemed to own an interest equal to the portion of the original consideration he or she furnished. The parties in Example 39 could have provided that Homer would receive an undivided half interest in the property although he contributed only one-third of the purchase price. In that case, Wilma and Thelma have made a gift to Homer when the tenancy was created, and Homer's gross estate and probate estate each include $45,000.

For certain joint tenancies, the tax consequences are different. All of the property is included in the deceased co-owner's gross estate unless it can be proven that the surviving co-owners contributed to the cost of the property.[28] If a contribution can be shown, the amount to be excluded is calculated by the following formula:

$$\frac{\text{Surviving co-owner's contribution}}{\text{Total cost of the property}} \times \text{Fair market value of the property}$$

In computing a survivor's contribution, any funds received as a gift *from the deceased co-owner* and applied to the cost of the property cannot be counted. However, income or gain from gift assets can be counted.

If the co-owners receive the property as a gift *from another,* each co-owner is deemed to have contributed to the cost of his or her own interest.

The preceding rules can be illustrated as follows:

EXAMPLE 40

Keith and Steve (father and son) acquire a tract of land with ownership listed as joint tenancy with right of survivorship. Keith furnished $40,000 and Steve $20,000 of the $60,000 purchase price. Of the $20,000 provided by Steve, $10,000 had previously been received as a gift from Keith. When the property is worth $90,000, Keith dies. Because only $10,000 of Steve's contribution can be counted (the other $10,000 was received as a gift from Keith), Steve has furnished only one-sixth ($10,000/$60,000) of the cost. Thus, Keith's gross estate must include five-sixths of $90,000, or $75,000. This presumes Steve can prove that he did in fact make the $10,000 contribution. In the absence of such proof, the full value of the property will be included in Keith's gross estate. Keith's death makes Steve the immediate owner of the property by virtue of the right of survivorship. None of the property is part of Keith's probate estate. ◆

EXAMPLE 41

Francis transfers property to Irene and Morden as a gift listing ownership as joint tenancy with the right of survivorship. Upon Irene's death, one-half of the value of the property is included in the gross estate. Since the property was received as a gift and the donees are equal owners, each is considered to have furnished half of the consideration. ◆

To simplify the joint ownership rules for *married persons,* § 2040(b) provides for an automatic inclusion rule upon the death of the first joint-owner spouse to die. Regardless of the amount contributed by each spouse, one-half of the value of the property is included in the gross estate of the spouse who dies first. The

28. § 2040(a).

special rule eliminates the need to trace the source of contributions and recognizes that any inclusion in the gross estate is neutralized by the marital deduction.

EXAMPLE 42

In 1986, Hank purchases real estate for $100,000 using his separate funds and listing title as "Hank and Louise, joint tenants with the right of survivorship." Hank predeceases Louise six years later when the property is worth $300,000. If Hank and Louise are husband and wife, Hank's gross estate includes $150,000 (½ of $300,000) as to the property. ◆

EXAMPLE 43

Assume the same facts as in Example 42, except that Louise (instead of Hank) dies first. Presuming the value at the date of death is $300,000, Louise's gross estate includes $150,000 as to the property. In this regard, it is of no consequence that Louise did not contribute to the cost of the real estate. ◆

In both Examples 42 and 43, inclusion in the gross estate of the first spouse to die will be neutralized by the unlimited marital deduction allowed for estate tax purposes (see the discussion of the marital deduction later in the chapter). Under the right of survivorship, the surviving joint tenant obtains full ownership of the property. The marital deduction generally is allowed for property passing from one spouse to another.

Whether or not a *gift* results when property is transferred into some form of joint ownership depends on the consideration furnished by each of the contributing parties for the ownership interest acquired.

EXAMPLE 44

Brenda and Sarah purchase real estate as tenants in common, each furnishing $40,000 of the $80,000 cost. If each is an equal owner in the property, no gift has occurred. ◆

EXAMPLE 45

Assume the same facts as in Example 44, except that of the $80,000 purchase price, Brenda furnishes $60,000 and Sarah furnishes only $20,000. If they are equal owners in the property, Brenda has made a gift to Sarah of $20,000. ◆

EXAMPLE 46

Martha purchases real estate for $240,000, the title to the property being listed as follows: "Martha, Sylvia, and Dan as joint tenants with the right of survivorship." If under state law the mother (Martha), the daughter (Sylvia), and the son (Dan) are deemed to be equal owners in the property, Martha will be treated as having made gifts of $80,000 to Sylvia and $80,000 to Dan. ◆

Several important *exceptions* exist to the general rule that the creation of a joint ownership with disproportionate interests resulting from unequal consideration triggers gift treatment. First, if the transfer involves a joint bank account, there is no gift at the time of the contribution.[29] If a gift occurs, it is when the noncontributing party withdraws the funds provided by the other joint tenant. Second, the same rule applies to the purchase of U.S. savings bonds. Again, any gift tax consequences are postponed until the noncontributing party appropriates some or all of the proceeds for his or her individual use.

---

29. Reg. § 25.2511–1(h)(4).

Life Insurance (§ 2042). Under § 2042, the gross estate includes the proceeds of life insurance on the decedent's life if (1) they are receivable by the estate, (2) they are receivable by another for the benefit of the estate, or (3) the decedent possessed an incident of ownership in the policy.

Life insurance on the life of another owned by a decedent at the time of death is included in the gross estate under § 2033 (property in which the decedent had an interest) and not under § 2042. The amount includible is the replacement value of the policy.[30] Under these circumstances, inclusion of the face amount of the policy is inappropriate as the policy has not yet matured.

EXAMPLE 47

At the time of his death, Luigi owned a life insurance policy on the life of Benito, face amount of $100,000 and replacement value of $25,000, with Sofia as the designated beneficiary. Since the policy had not matured at Luigi's death, § 2042 would be inapplicable. However, § 2033 (property in which the decedent had an interest) compels the inclusion of $25,000 (the replacement value) in Luigi's gross estate. If Luigi and Sofia owned the policy as community property, only $12,500 is included in Luigi's gross estate. ◆

The term "life insurance" includes whole life policies, term insurance, group life insurance, travel and accident insurance, endowment contracts (before being paid up), and death benefits paid by fraternal societies operating under the lodge system.[31]

As just noted, proceeds of insurance on the life of the decedent receivable by the executor or administrator or payable to the decedent's estate are included in the gross estate. The estate need not be specifically named as the beneficiary. Assume, for example, the proceeds of the policy are receivable by an individual beneficiary and are subject to an obligation, legally binding upon the beneficiary, to pay taxes, debts, and other charges enforceable against the estate. The proceeds are included in the decedent's gross estate to the extent of the beneficiary's obligation. If the proceeds of an insurance policy made payable to a decedent's estate are community assets and, under state law, one-half belongs to the surviving spouse, only one-half of the proceeds will be considered as receivable by or for the benefit of the decedent's estate.

Proceeds of insurance on the life of the decedent not receivable by or for the benefit of the estate are includible if the decedent at death possessed any of the incidents of ownership in the policy. In this connection, the term "incidents of ownership" means more than the ownership of the policy in a technical legal sense. Generally speaking, the term refers to the right of the insured or his or her estate to the economic benefits of the policy. Thus, it also includes the power to change beneficiaries, revoke an assignment, pledge the policy for a loan, or surrender or cancel the policy.[32]

EXAMPLE 48

At the time of death, Broderick was the insured under a policy (face amount of $100,000) owned by Gregory with Demi as the designated beneficiary. Broderick took out the policy five years ago and immediately transferred it as a gift to Gregory. Under the assignment, Broderick transferred all rights in the policy except the right to change beneficiaries. Broderick died without having exercised this right, and the policy

30. Reg. § 20.2031–8(a)(1).

31. Reg. § 20.2042–1(a)(1). As to travel and accident insurance, see *Comm. v. Estate of Noel*, 65–1 USTC ¶12,311, 15 AFTR2d 1397, 85 S.Ct. 1238 (USSC, 1965).

32. Reg. § 20.2042–1(c)(2).

proceeds are paid to Demi. Under § 2042(2), Broderick's retention of an incident of ownership in the policy (i.e., the right to change beneficiaries) causes $100,000 to be included in his gross estate. ◆

Assuming that the deceased-insured holds the incidents of ownership in a policy, how much will be included in the gross estate if the insurance policy is a community asset? Only one-half of the proceeds becomes part of the deceased spouse's gross estate.

In determining whether or not a policy is *community property* or what portion of it might be so classified, state law controls. The states appear to follow one of two general approaches. Under the inception of title approach, the classification depends on when the policy was originally purchased. If purchased before marriage, the policy is separate property regardless of how many premiums were paid after marriage with community funds. However, if the noninsured spouse is not the beneficiary of the policy, he or she may be entitled to reimbursement from the deceased-insured spouse's estate for half of the premiums paid with community funds. The inception of title approach is followed in at least three states: Louisiana, Texas, and New Mexico.

Some community property jurisdictions classify a policy using the tracing approach: The nature of the funds used to pay the premiums controls. Thus, a policy paid for 20 percent with separate funds and 80 percent with community funds will be 20 percent separate property and 80 percent community property. The point in time when the policy was purchased makes no difference. Conceivably, a policy purchased after marriage with the premiums paid exclusively with separate funds would be classified entirely as separate property. The tracing approach appears to be the rule in California and Washington.

Merely purchasing a life insurance contract and designating someone else as the beneficiary thereunder does not constitute a *gift*. As long as the purchaser still owns the policy, nothing has really passed to the beneficiary. Even on the death of the insured-owner, no gift takes place. The proceeds paid to the beneficiary constitute a testamentary and not a lifetime transfer. But consider the following possibility:

EXAMPLE 49

Kurt purchases an insurance policy on his own life and transfers the policy to Olga. Kurt retains no interest in the policy (such as the power to change beneficiaries). In these circumstances, Kurt has made a gift to Olga. Furthermore, if Kurt continues to pay the premiums on the transferred policy, each payment will constitute a separate gift. ◆

Under certain conditions, the death of the insured might represent a gift to the beneficiary of part or all of the proceeds. This occurs when the owner of the policy is not the insured.

EXAMPLE 50

Randolph owns an insurance policy on the life of Frank, with Tracy as the designated beneficiary. Up until the time of Frank's death, Randolph retained the right to change the beneficiary of the policy. The proceeds paid to Tracy by the insurance company by reason of Frank's death constitute a gift from Randolph to Tracy. ◆

Taxable Estate

After the gross estate has been determined, the next step is to determine the taxable estate. By virtue of § 2051, the taxable estate is the gross estate less the following: expenses, indebtedness, and taxes (§ 2053); losses (§ 2054); charitable transfers (§§ 2055 and 2522); and the marital deduction (§§ 2056 and 2056A). As previously noted, the charitable and marital deductions also have gift tax ramifications.

Expenses, Indebtedness, and Taxes (§ 2053). A deduction is allowed for funeral expenses; expenses incurred in administering property; claims against the estate; and unpaid mortgages and other charges against property, whose value is included in the gross estate (without reduction for the mortgage or other indebtedness).

Expenses incurred in administering community property are deductible only in proportion to the deceased spouse's interest in the community.[33]

Administration expenses include commissions of the executor or administrator, attorney's fees of the estate, accountant's fees, court costs, and certain selling expenses for disposition of estate property.

Claims against the estate include property taxes accrued before the decedent's death, unpaid income taxes on income received by the decedent before he or she died, and unpaid gift taxes on gifts made by the decedent before death.

Amounts that may be deducted as claims against the estate are only for enforceable personal obligations of the decedent at the time of death. Deductions for claims founded on promises or agreements are limited to the extent that the liabilities were contracted in good faith and for adequate and full consideration. However, a pledge or subscription in favor of a public, charitable, religious, or educational organization is deductible to the extent that it would have constituted an allowable deduction had it been a bequest.[34]

Deductible funeral expenses include the cost of interment, the burial plot or vault, a gravestone, perpetual care of the grave site, and the transportation expense of the person bringing the body to the place of burial. If the decedent had, before death, acquired cemetery lots for himself or herself and family, no deduction is allowed, but the lots are not included in the decedent's gross estate under § 2033 (property in which the decedent had an interest).

Losses (§ 2054). Section 2054 permits an estate tax deduction for losses from casualty or theft incurred during the period when the estate is being settled. As is true with casualty or theft losses for income tax purposes, any anticipated insurance recovery must be taken into account in arriving at the amount of the deductible loss. Unlike the income tax, however, the deduction is not limited by a floor ($100) or a percentage amount (the excess of 10 percent of adjusted gross income). If the casualty occurs to property after it has been distributed to an heir, the loss belongs to the heir and not to the estate. If the casualty occurs before the decedent's death, it should be claimed on the appropriate Form 1040. The fair market value of the property (if any) on the date of death plus any insurance recovery is included in the gross estate.

As is true of certain administration expenses, a casualty or theft loss of estate property can be claimed as an income tax deduction on the fiduciary return of the estate (Form 1041). But the double deduction prohibition of § 642(g) applies, and claiming the income tax deduction requires a waiver of the estate tax deduction.

---

33. *U.S. v. Stapf*, 63–2 USTC ¶12,192, 12 AFTR2d 6326, 84 S.Ct. 248 (USSC, 1963).

34. § 2053(c)(1)(A) and Reg. § 20.2053–5.

Transfers to Charity (§§ 2055 and 2522). A deduction is allowed for the value of property in the decedent's gross estate that is transferred by the decedent through testamentary disposition to (or for the use of) any of the following:

1. The United States or any of its political subdivisions.
2. Any corporation or association organized and operated exclusively for religious, charitable, scientific, literary, or educational purposes, as long as no benefit inures to any private individual and no substantial activity is undertaken to carry on propaganda or otherwise attempt to influence legislation or participate in any political campaign on behalf of any candidate for public office.
3. A trustee or trustees of a fraternal society, order, or association operating under the lodge system if the transferred property is to be used exclusively for religious, charitable, scientific, literary, or educational purposes, and no substantial activity is undertaken to carry on propaganda or otherwise attempt to influence legislation or participate in any political campaign on behalf of any candidate for public office.
4. Any veterans' organization incorporated by an Act of Congress (or any of its subdivisions) as long as no benefit inures to any private individual.

The organizations just described are identical to those that qualify for the Federal gift tax deduction under § 2522. With the following exceptions, they are also the same organizations that will qualify a donee for an income tax deduction under § 170:

- Certain nonprofit cemetery associations qualify for income tax but not death and gift tax purposes.
- Foreign charities may qualify under the estate and gift tax but not under the income tax.

No deduction is allowed unless the charitable bequest is specified by a provision in the decedent's will or the transfer was made before death and the property is subsequently included in the gross estate. Generally speaking, a deduction does not materialize when an individual dies intestate (without a will). The amount of the bequest to charity must be mandatory and cannot be left to someone else's discretion. It is, however, permissible to allow another person, such as the executor of the estate, to choose which charity will receive the specified donation. Likewise, a bequest may be expressed as an alternative and still be effective if the noncharitable beneficiary disclaims (refuses) the intervening interest before the due date for the filing of the estate tax return (nine months after the decedent's death plus any extensions of time granted for filing).

Marital Deduction (§§ 2056, 2056A, and 2523). The marital deduction originated with the Revenue Act of 1948 as part of the same legislation that permitted married persons to secure the income-splitting advantages of filing joint income tax returns. The purpose of these statutory changes was to eliminate the major tax variations that could develop between taxpayers residing in community property and common law states. The marital deduction was designed to provide equity in the estate and gift tax areas.

In a community property state, for example, no marital deduction generally was allowed since the surviving spouse already owned one-half of the community and that portion was not included in the deceased spouse's gross estate. In a common law state, however, most if not all of the assets often belonged to the breadwinner of the family. When that spouse died first, all of these assets were included in the gross estate. Recall that a dower or curtesy interest, (regarding a surviving spouse's right to some of the deceased spouse's property) does not reduce the gross estate. To equalize the situation, therefore, a marital deduction, usually equal to one-half of all separate assets, was allowed upon the death of the first spouse.

Ultimately, Congress decided to dispense with these historical justifications and recognize husband and wife as a single economic unit. Consistent with the approach taken under the income tax, spouses are considered as one for transfer tax purposes. By making the marital deduction unlimited in amount, neither the gift tax nor the estate tax is imposed on outright interspousal transfers of property. Unlike prior law, the unlimited marital deduction even includes one spouse's share of the community property transferred to the other spouse.

Under § 2056, the marital deduction is allowed only for property that is included in the deceased spouse's gross estate and that passes or has passed to the surviving spouse. In determining whether the parties are legally married, look to state law (see Example 1 earlier). Property that passes from the decedent to the surviving spouse includes any interest received as (1) the decedent's heir or donee; (2) the decedent's surviving tenant by the entirety or joint tenant; (3) the appointee under the decedent's exercise (or lapse or release) of a general power of appointment; or (4) the beneficiary of insurance on the life of the decedent.

EXAMPLE 51

At the time of his death in the current year, Matthew owned an insurance policy on his own life (face amount of $100,000) with Minerva (his wife) as the designated beneficiary. Matthew and Minerva also owned real estate (worth $250,000) as tenants by the entirety (Matthew had furnished all of the purchase price). As to these transfers, $225,000 ($100,000 + $125,000) is included in Matthew's gross estate, and this amount represents the property that passes to Minerva for purposes of the marital deduction.[35] ◆

Under certain conditions, disclaimers of property by the surviving spouse in favor of some other heir affect the amount that passes and reduce marital deduction. Thus, if Wife is entitled to $400,000 of Husband's property but disclaims $100,000 in favor of Son, the remainderperson under the will, the $100,000 passes from Husband to Son and not from Husband to Wife. Disclaimers by some other heir in favor of the surviving spouse may have the opposite effect. Suppose Wife, as remainder-person, will receive $300,000 under Husband's will, but the will also provides that Son is to receive a specific bequest of $100,000. If Son issues a timely disclaimer in favor of Wife, the amount passing from Husband to Wife for purposes of the marital deduction is increased from $300,000 to $400,000.

A similar problem arises when a property interest passing to the surviving spouse is subject to a mortgage or other encumbrance. In this case, only the net value of the interest after reduction by the amount of the mortgage or other encumbrance qualifies for the marital deduction. To allow otherwise would result in a double deduction since a decedent's liabilities are separately deductible under § 2053.

EXAMPLE 52

In his will, Oscar leaves real estate (fair market value of $200,000) to his wife. If the real estate is subject to a mortgage of $40,000 (upon which Oscar was personally liable), the

35. Inclusion in the gross estate falls under § 2042 (proceeds of life insurance) and § 2040 (joint interests). Although Matthew provided the full purchase price for the real estate, § 2040(b) requires inclusion of only half of the value of the property when one spouse predeceases the other.

marital deduction is limited to $160,000 ($200,000 – $40,000). The $40,000 mortgage is deductible under § 2053 as an obligation of the decedent (Oscar). ◆

However, if the executor is required under the terms of the decedent's will or under local law to discharge the mortgage out of other assets of the estate or to reimburse the surviving spouse, the payment or reimbursement is an additional interest passing to the surviving spouse.

EXAMPLE 53

Assume the same facts as in Example 52, except that Oscar's will directs that the real estate is to pass to his wife free of any liabilities. Accordingly, Oscar's executor pays off the mortgage by using other estate assets and distributes the real estate to Oscar's wife. The marital deduction now becomes $200,000. ◆

Federal estate taxes or other death taxes paid out of the surviving spouse's share of the gross estate are not included in the value of property passing to the surviving spouse. Therefore, it is usually preferable for the deceased spouse's will to provide that death taxes be paid out of the portion of the estate that does not qualify for the marital deduction.

Certain interests in property passing from the deceased spouse to the surviving spouse are referred to as *terminable interests.* Such an interest will terminate or fail after the passage of time, upon the happening of some contingency, or upon the failure of some event to occur. Examples are life estates, annuities, estates for terms of years, and patents. A terminable interest will not qualify for the marital deduction if another interest in the same property passed from the deceased spouse to some other person. By reason of the passing, that other person or his or her heirs may enjoy part of the property after the termination of the surviving spouse's interest.[36]

EXAMPLE 54

Vicky's will places her property in trust with a life estate to Brett, remainder to Andrew or his heirs. The interest passing from Vicky to Brett does not qualify for the marital deduction. Brett's interest will terminate on his death, and Andrew or his heirs will then possess or enjoy the property. ◆

EXAMPLE 55

Assume the same facts as in Example 54, except that Vicky created the trust during her life. No marital deduction is available for gift tax purposes for the same reason as in Example 54.[37] ◆

The justification for the terminable interest rule can be illustrated by examining the possible result of Examples 54 and 55 more closely. Without the rule, Vicky could have passed property to Brett at no cost because of the marital deduction. Yet, on Brett's death, none of the property would have been included in his gross estate. Section 2036 (transfers with a retained life estate) would not apply to Brett since he was not the original transferor of the property. The marital deduction should not be available in situations where the surviving spouse can enjoy the property and still pass it to another without tax consequences. The marital deduction merely postpones the transfer tax on the death of the first spouse and operates to shift any such tax to the surviving spouse.

---

36. §§ 2056(b)(1) and 2523(b)(1).

37. Both Examples 54 and 55 contain the potential for a qualified terminable interest property (QTIP) election discussed later in this section.

Consistent with the objective of the terminable interest rule, an alternative means for obtaining the marital deduction is available. Under this provision, the marital deduction is allowed for transfers of *qualified terminable interest property* (commonly referred to as QTIP). This is defined as property that passes from one spouse to another by gift or at death and for which the transferee-spouse has a qualifying income interest for life.

For a donee or a surviving spouse, a qualifying income interest for life exists under the following conditions:

- The person is entitled for life to all of the income from the property (or a specific portion of it), payable at annual or more frequent intervals.
- No person (including the spouse) has a power to appoint any part of the property to any person other than the surviving spouse during his or her life.[38]

If these conditions are met, an election can be made to claim a marital deduction as to the QTIP. For estate tax purposes, the executor of the estate makes the election on Form 706 (estate tax return). For gift tax purposes, the donor spouse makes the election on Form 709 (gift tax return). The election is irrevocable.

If the election is made, a transfer tax will be imposed upon the QTIP when the transferee-spouse disposes of it by gift or upon death. If the disposition occurs during life, the gift tax applies, measured by the fair market value of the property as of that time.[39] If no lifetime disposition takes place, the fair market value of the property on the date of death (or alternate valuation date if applicable) is included in the gross estate of the transferee-spouse.[40]

EXAMPLE 56

In 1993, Clyde dies and provides in his will that certain assets (fair market value of $400,000) are to be transferred to a trust under which Gertrude (Clyde's wife) is granted a life estate with the remainder passing to their children upon Gertrude's death. Presuming all of the preceding requirements are satisfied and Clyde's executor so elects, his estate will receive a marital deduction of $400,000. ◆

EXAMPLE 57

Assume the same facts as in Example 56, with the further stipulation that Gertrude dies in 1998 when the trust assets are worth $900,000. This amount is included in her gross estate. ◆

Because the estate tax will be imposed on assets not physically included in the probate estate, the law allows the liability for those assets to be shifted to the heirs. The amount shifted is determined by comparing the estate tax liability both with and without the inclusion of the QTIP. This right of recovery can be canceled by a provision in the deceased spouse's will.[41]

Computing the Federal Estate Tax

Once the taxable estate has been determined, post-1976 taxable gifts are added to arrive at the tax base. Note that pre-1977 taxable gifts do not enter into the computation of the tax base.

38. §§ 2523(f) and 2056(b)(7).
39. § 2519.
40. § 2044.
41. § 2207A(a).

EXAMPLE 58

Joyce dies in 1993, leaving a taxable estate of $800,000. During her life, Joyce made taxable gifts as follows: $50,000 in 1975 and $100,000 in 1982. For estate tax purposes, the Federal estate tax base becomes $900,000, determined as follows: $800,000 taxable estate + $100,000 taxable gift made in 1982. ◆

Next the tentative tax on the tax base is computed using the unified transfer tax rate schedule contained in § 2001(c). Using the facts in Example 58, the tax on $900,000 is $306,800 [$248,300 + (39% × $150,000)]—see Appendix A. (See the discussion below for the phase-out of the unified tax credit and the graduated tax rates for certain large estates.)

All available estate tax credits are subtracted from the tentative estate tax to arrive at the estate tax (if any) that is due.

Estate Tax Credits

Unified Tax Credit (§ 2010). Recall from previous discussion of this credit that the amount of the credit allowed depends upon the year of the transfer. Returning to Example 58, the credit allowed on the gift in 1982 was $62,800. Since the exemption equivalent of this amount is $225,000 (refer to Figure 26–3), no gift tax was due on the transfer. On Joyce's death in 1993, however, the unified tax credit is $192,800, which is less than the tentative tax of $306,800 (refer to the discussion following Example 58). Disregarding the effect of any other estate tax credits, Joyce's estate owes a tax of $114,000 ($306,800 tentative tax on a tax base of $900,000 – $192,800 unified tax credit for 1993).

An adjustment to the unified tax credit will be necessary if any portion of the specific exemption was utilized on gifts made after September 8, 1976, and before January 1, 1977. In this regard, refer to Example 5.

Under current law, the benefit of the unified tax credit and the graduated unified tax rates is phased out for taxable transfers exceeding a certain amount. The gift and estate tax liability for taxable transfers in excess of $10 million is increased by 5 percent of the excess until the benefit of the credit and graduated brackets is recaptured.

Credit for State Death Taxes (§ 2011). The Code allows a limited credit for the amount of any death tax actually paid to any state (or to the District of Columbia) attributable to any property included in the gross estate. Like the credit for foreign death taxes paid, this provision mitigates the harshness of subjecting the same property to multiple death taxes.

The credit allowed is limited to the lesser of the amount of tax actually paid or the amount provided for in a table contained in § 2011(b). (See Appendix A.) The table amount is based on the *adjusted taxable estate*, which for this purpose is the taxable estate less $60,000. No credit is allowed if the adjusted taxable estate is $40,000 or less.

EXAMPLE 59

Butch's taxable estate is $98,000, and the state of appropriate jurisdiction imposes a death tax of $1,500 on this amount. Since the adjusted taxable estate is $38,000 ($98,000 – $60,000), none of the $1,500 paid qualifies for the death tax credit. ◆

EXAMPLE 60

Butch's taxable estate is $200,000, and the state of appropriate jurisdiction imposes a death tax of $3,000 on this amount. Because the adjusted gross estate is $140,000 ($200,000 – $60,000), the table amount limits the death tax credit to $1,200. (See Appendix A.) ◆

As Examples 59 and 60 illustrate, the credit allowed by § 2011 may be less than the amount of state death taxes paid. The reverse is possible but usually is not the case. Most states make sure that the minimum tax payable to the jurisdiction is at least equal to the credit allowed by the table. Sometimes this result is accomplished by a soak-up or sponge tax superimposed on the regular inheritance tax. Thus, if the regular inheritance tax yielded $2,500, but the maximum credit allowed by the table is $3,200, a soak-up tax would impose an additional $700 in state death taxes. In other states, the state death tax liability depends entirely upon the amount allowed for Federal estate tax purposes under the table. In the previous illustration, the state death tax would be an automatic $3,200.

Credit for Gift Taxes (§ 2012). A credit is allowed against the estate tax for any Federal gift tax paid on a gift of property subsequently included in the donor-decedent's gross estate.

EXAMPLE 61

In 1965, Doreen transfers a remainder interest in a farm to her children, retaining a life estate for herself. As a result of the transfer, Doreen incurred and paid a Federal gift tax of $45,000. Doreen dies in 1993 when the property is worth $400,000. Under § 2036 (retention of a life estate), the farm is included in Doreen's gross estate. Thus, a double tax effect results. To mitigate this effect, § 2012 allows Doreen's estate a credit for some or all of the $45,000 previously paid in gift taxes. ◆

The adjustments needed to work out the amount of the credit can become somewhat complicated and are not discussed further.[42]

Only taxable gifts made after 1976 are added to the donor's taxable estate in arriving at the base for the application of the unified transfer tax at death. To the extent these gifts have exceeded the unified tax credit and have generated a tax, the tax paid (or deemed paid) is credited against the transfer tax due at death.

Credit for Tax on Prior Transfers (§ 2013). Suppose Floyd owns some property that he passes at death to Sarah. Shortly thereafter, Sarah dies and passes the property to Juan. Assuming both estates are subject to the Federal estate tax, the successive deaths result in a multiple effect. To mitigate the possible multiple taxation that might result, § 2013 provides relief in the form of a credit for a death tax on prior transfers. In the preceding hypothetical case, Sarah's estate may be able to claim as an estate tax credit some of the taxes paid by Floyd's estate.

The credit is limited to the lesser of the following:

1. The amount of the Federal estate tax attributable to the transferred property in the transferor's estate.
2. The amount of the Federal estate tax attributable to the transferred property in the decedent's estate.

To apply the limitations, certain adjustments must be made that are not covered in this text.[43] However, it is not necessary for the transferred property to be identified in the present decedent's estate or for it to be in existence at the time of the present decedent's death. It is sufficient that the transfer of property was subjected to the Federal estate tax in the estate of the transferor and that the transferor died within the prescribed period of time.

42. They are illustrated and explained in the instructions to Form 706 and in Reg. § 20.2012–1.

43. See the instructions to Form 706 and Reg. §§ 20.2013–2 and –3.

If the transferor dies within two years after or before the present decedent's death, the credit is allowed in full (subject to the preceding limitations). If the transferor died more than two years before the decedent, the credit is a certain percentage: 80 percent if the transferor died within the third or fourth year preceding the decedent's death, 60 percent if within the fifth or sixth year, 40 percent if within the seventh or eighth year, and 20 percent if within the ninth or tenth year.

EXAMPLE 62

Under Rosa's will, Imelda inherits property. One year later Imelda dies. Assume the estate tax attributable to the inclusion of the property in Rosa's gross estate was $15,000 and that attributable to the inclusion of the property in Imelda's gross estate is $12,000. Under these circumstances, Imelda's estate claims a credit against the estate tax of $12,000 (refer to limitation 2). ◆

EXAMPLE 63

Assume the same facts as in Example 62, except that Imelda dies three years after Rosa. The applicable credit is now 80% of $12,000, or $9,600. ◆

Credit for Foreign Death Taxes (§ 2014). A credit is allowed against the estate tax for any estate, inheritance, legacy, or succession tax actually paid to a foreign country. For purposes of this provision, the term "foreign country" means not only states in the international sense but also possessions or political subdivisions of foreign states and possessions of the United States.

Procedural Matters

A Federal estate tax return, if required, is due nine months after the date of the decedent's death.[44] The time limit applies to all estates regardless of the nationality or residence of the decedent. Frequently, an executor will request and obtain from the IRS an extension of time for filing Form 706 (estate tax return).

For the estate of a citizen or resident of the United States dying after 1976, Form 706 must be filed by the executor or administrator under the following conditions:[45]

Year of Death	Gross Estate in Excess of
1977	$120,000
1978	134,000
1979	147,000
1980	161,000
1981	175,000
1982	225,000
1983	275,000
1984	325,000
1985	400,000
1986	500,000
1987 & thereafter	600,000

The filing requirements parallel the exemption equivalent amounts of the unified tax credit available for each year (refer to Figure 26–3). The filing

44. § 6075(a).

45. § 6018(a).

requirements may be lower when the decedent has made taxable gifts after 1976 or has utilized any of the $30,000 specific gift tax exemption after September 8, 1976.

EXAMPLE 64

Carlos dies in 1993, leaving a gross estate of $595,000. If Carlos did not make any post-1976 taxable gifts or use the specific gift tax exemption after September 8, 1976, his estate need not file Form 706. ◆

EXAMPLE 65

Assume the same facts as in Example 64, except that Carlos made a taxable gift of $20,000 in 1980. Since the filing requirement now becomes $580,000 ($600,000 regular filing requirement for 1993 – $20,000 post-1976 taxable gift), Carlos's estate must file Form 706. ◆

Form 706 must be filed with the IRS Service Center serving the district in which the decedent lived at the time of death. The return must be accompanied by various documents related to the determination of tax liability.

THE GENERATION-SKIPPING TRANSFER TAX

In order to prevent partial avoidance of Federal gift and estate taxes on large transfers, the tax law imposes an additional generation-skipping transfer tax.

The Problem

Previously, it was possible to bypass a generation of transfer taxes by structuring the transaction carefully.

EXAMPLE 66

Under his will, Edward creates a trust, life estate to Stephen (Edward's son) and remainder to Ava (Edward's granddaughter) upon Stephen's death. Edward will be subject to the Federal estate tax, but no tax results on Stephen's death. Stephen held a life estate, but § 2036 does not apply. Stephen was not the grantor of the trust. Nor does § 2033 (property owned by the decedent) come into play because Stephen's interest disappeared upon his death. The ultimate result is that the property in trust skips a generation of transfer taxes. ◆

EXAMPLE 67

Amy gives assets to Eric (her grandson). Called a direct skip, the gift would circumvent any transfer taxes that would have resulted had the assets been channeled through Eric's parents. ◆

The Solution

The generation-skipping transfer tax (GSTT) is imposed when a younger generation is bypassed in favor of a later generation.[46] The GSTT applies to lifetime transfers by gift and to transfers by death. The tax rate imposed is the highest

46. The generation-skipping transfer tax provisions are contained in §§ 2601–2663.

rate under the gift and estate tax schedule—55 percent through 1992 and 50 percent thereafter. Consequently, the GSTT does not permit the use of the graduated rate structure.

The application of the GSTT depends upon the type of arrangement involved. In Example 66, the GSTT would be imposed upon the death of Stephen (the life tenant). The tax, however, is levied against the trust. In effect, it reduces the amount that is distributed to Ava (the remainderperson).

In Example 67, the GSTT is imposed upon Amy when the gift is made to Eric. In this situation, not only will Amy be subject to the GSTT, but the amount of the tax represents an additional gift to Eric.[47] Thus, if a gift is a direct skip (such as Example 67), the total transfer tax (the GSTT plus the gift tax) may exceed what the donee receives.

Though the GSTT may appear to yield a confiscatory result, every grantor is entitled to a $1 million exemption. The exemption can be applied to whichever transfers the grantor (or personal representative of the grantor) chooses. Any appreciation attributable to the exempted portion of the transfer is not subject to the GSTT.

EXAMPLE 68

Assume the same facts as in Example 66, except that the trust created by Edward contained assets valued at $1 million. Ten years later when Stephen dies, the trust is now worth $3 million. If the exemption of $1 million is used upon the creation of the trust, no GSTT results upon Stephen's death. ◆

The Federal Gift Tax

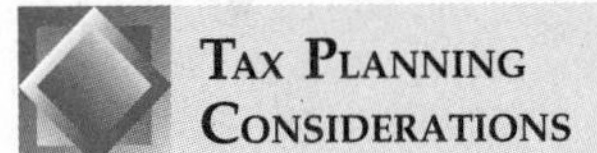

TAX PLANNING CONSIDERATIONS

For gifts that generate a tax, consideration must be given to the time value to the donor of the gift taxes paid. Since the donor loses the use of these funds, the expected interval between a gift (the imposition of the gift tax) and death (the imposition of the death tax) may make the gift less attractive from an economic standpoint. On the plus side, however, are the estate tax savings that result from any gift tax paid. Since these funds are no longer in the gross estate of the donor (except for certain gifts within three years of death), the estate tax thereon is avoided.

Gifts possess distinct advantages. First, and often most important, income from the property is generally shifted to the donee. If the donee is in a lower bracket than the donor, the family unit will save on income taxes. Second, the proper spacing of gifts can further cut down the Federal gift tax by maximizing the number of annual exclusions available. Third, all states impose some type of death tax, but only a minority impose a gift tax. Thus, a gift may completely avoid a state transfer tax.

In minimizing gift tax liability in lifetime giving, the optimum use of the annual exclusion can have significant results. Important in this regard are the following observations:

1. Because the annual exclusion is available every year, space the gifts over as many years as possible. To carry out this objective, start the program of lifetime giving as soon as is feasible. As an illustration, a donor could give as much as $100,000 to a donee if equally spaced over a 10-year period without using any of the unified tax credit and incurring any gift tax.

47. § 2515.

2. To the extent consistent with the wishes of the donor, maximize the number of donees. For example, a donor could give $500,000 to five donees over a 10-year period ($100,000 apiece) without using any of the unified tax credit and incurring any gift tax.
3. For the married donor, make use of the election to split gifts. As an example, a married couple can give $1 million to five donees over a 10-year period ($20,000 per donee each year) without using any of their unified tax credit and incurring any gift tax.
4. Watch out for gifts of future interests. As noted earlier in the chapter, the annual exclusion is available only for gifts of a present interest.

CONCEPT SUMMARY 26–2
FEDERAL ESTATE TAX PROVISIONS

1. Both the Federal gift and estate taxes are excise taxes on the transfer of wealth.
2. The starting point for applying the Federal estate tax is to determine which assets are subject to tax. Such assets constitute a decedent's gross estate. The gross estate must be distinguished from the probate estate. The latter classification includes assets subject to administration by the executor of the estate.
3. The gross estate generally will not include any gifts made by the decedent within three years of death. It does include any gift tax paid on these transfers.
4. Based on the premise that one should not continue to enjoy or control property and not have it subject to the estate tax, certain incomplete transfers are included in the gross estate.
5. Upon the death of a joint tenant, the full value of the property is included in the gross estate unless the survivor(s) made a contribution toward the cost of the property. Spouses are subject to a special rule that calls for automatic inclusion of half of the value of the property in the gross estate of the first tenant to die. As to joint tenancies (or tenancies by the entirety) between husband and wife, it makes no difference who furnished the original consideration. The creation of joint ownership is subject to the gift tax when a tenant receives a lesser interest in the property than is warranted by the consideration furnished.
6. If the decedent is the insured, life insurance proceeds are included in the gross estate if either of two conditions is satisfied. First, the proceeds are paid to the estate or for the benefit of the estate. Second, the decedent possessed incidents of ownership (e.g., the right to change beneficiaries) over the policy. A transfer of an unmatured life insurance policy is subject to the gift tax. A gift also occurs when a policy matures and the owner of the policy is not the insured or the beneficiary.
7. In moving from the gross estate to the taxable estate, certain deductions are allowed. Under § 2053, deductions are permitted for various administration expenses (e.g., executor's commissions, funeral costs), debts of the decedent, and certain unpaid taxes. Casualty and theft losses incurred during the administration of an estate can be deducted in arriving at the taxable estate.
8. Charitable transfers are deductible if the designated organization holds qualified status with the IRS at the time of the gift or upon death.
9. Transfers to a spouse qualify for the gift or estate tax marital deduction. Except as noted in (10), such transfers are subject to the terminable interest limitation.
10. The terminable interest limitation will not apply if the QTIP election is made. In the case of a lifetime transfer, the donor spouse makes the QTIP election. In the case of a testamentary transfer, the executor of the estate of the deceased spouse has the election responsibility.
11. The tax base for determining the estate tax is the taxable estate plus all post-1976 taxable gifts. All available credits are subtracted from the tax.
12. Of prime importance in the tax credit area is the unified tax credit. Except for large taxable transfers, the unified tax credit is $192,800 (exemption equivalent of $600,000).
13. Other Federal estate tax credits include credits for state death taxes, gift taxes, tax on prior transfers, and foreign death taxes.
14. If due, a Federal estate tax return (Form 706) must be filed within nine months of the date of the decedent's death. The IRS grants extensions for estates that encounter difficulty in complying with the deadline.

The Federal Estate Tax

Controlling the Amount of the Gross Estate. Presuming an estate tax problem is anticipated, the starting point for planning purposes is to reduce the size of the potential gross estate. Aside from initiating a program of lifetime giving, several other possibilities exist.

Incomplete Transfers. If property is to be excluded from a donee's gross estate by means of a lifetime transfer, the consequences of transfers deemed incomplete for estate tax purposes must be recognized. In general, transfers are considered incomplete if the transferor continues to exercise control over the property or to enjoy its use.

EXAMPLE 69

Ten years ago, Martha transferred title to her personal residence to Denise, her daughter. Until the time of her death in the current year, Martha continued to live in the residence. ◆

In Example 69, the residence will be included in Martha's gross estate if an express or implied agreement exists between the donor and the donee for continued occupancy of the property. This result is dictated by § 2036(a)(1): the transferor did not surrender the right to possession or enjoyment of the property.

If no express or implied agreement exists between the parties, may one be inferred by virtue of the fact that the transferor does not vacate the premises after the gift but continues to live there until his or her death? In this regard, the situation described in Example 69 could be precarious, to say the least.

An implied agreement will probably be found in Example 69 unless the parties can produce some strong proof to show otherwise. An affirmative answer to any of the following questions would be helpful, though not controlling, in excluding the residence from Martha's gross estate:

- Did Martha report the transfer on a gift tax return and, if appropriate, pay a Federal gift tax thereon?
- Did Martha pay a reasonable rental to Denise for her continued occupancy of the premises?
- Did Denise, as any owner might be expected to do, absorb the cost of maintaining the property?
- If the property was income producing (e.g., a farm or ranch), did Denise collect and report the income?

Life Insurance. If the insured wants to keep the proceeds of a life insurance policy out of his or her gross estate, no incidents of ownership can be retained. All too often, a policy is transferred, but the transferor has unsuspectingly retained some incident of ownership that may cause inclusion in the gross estate. The only way to prevent this from happening is to carefully examine the policy itself and ensure that all incidents of ownership have been released.

Recall that a gift of a life insurance policy made within three years of the death of the owner-insured will be ineffective in terms of keeping the maturity value of the policy out of the gross estate. In this regard, refer to Example 28. To avoid this trap concerning gifts of life insurance policies, the sooner transferred the better since death usually is an unpredictable event.

Proper Handling of Estate Tax Deductions. Estate taxes can be saved either by reducing the size of the gross estate or by increasing the total allowable deductions. Thus, the lower the taxable estate, the less the amount of estate tax generated. Planning in the deduction area generally involves the following considerations:

- Making proper use of the marital deduction.
- Working effectively with the charitable deduction.
- Properly handling other deductions and losses allowed under §§ 2053 and 2054.

Approaches to the Marital Deduction. When planning for the estate tax marital deduction, both tax and nontax factors have to be taken into account. In the tax area, planning is guided by two major goals: the *equalization* and *deferral* approaches.

- Attempt to equalize the estates of both spouses. Clearly, for example, the estate tax on $2,000,000 is more than double the estate tax on $1,000,000 [compare $780,800 with $691,600 ($345,800 × 2)].
- Try to postpone estate taxation as long as possible. On a $1,000,000 amount, for example, what is the time value of $345,800 in estate taxes deferred for a period of, say, 10 years?

Barring certain circumstances, the deferral approach generally is preferable. By maximizing the marital deduction on the death of the first spouse to die, not only are taxes saved, but the surviving spouse is enabled to trim his or her future estate by entering into a program of lifetime giving. By making optimum use of the annual exclusion, considerable amounts can be shifted without incurring *any* transfer tax.

Tax planning must remain flexible and be tailored to the individual circumstances of the parties involved. Before the equalization approach is cast aside, therefore, consider the following variables:

- Both spouses are of advanced age and/or in poor health, and neither is expected to survive the other for a prolonged period of time.
- The spouse who is expected to survive has considerable assets of his or her own. To illustrate, a spouse who passes a $250,000 estate to a survivor who already has assets of $1,000,000 is trading a 32 percent bracket for a later 43 percent bracket.
- Because of appreciation, property worth $250,000 when it passes to the surviving spouse today may be worth $1,000,000 five years later when the survivor dies.

The Marital Deduction—Sophistication of the Deferral Approach. When the saving of estate taxes for the family unit is the sole consideration, the equalization and deferral approaches can be combined with maximum effect.

Example 70

At the time of his death in 1993, Vito had never made any taxable gifts. Under Vito's will, his *disposable estate* of $1,100,000 passes to his wife, Zina.[48] ◆

48. For this purpose, the *disposable estate* includes the gross estate less all deductions (e.g., debts, administration and funeral expenses) except the marital deduction. The term is not in the Code but is useful in evaluating tax options.

EXAMPLE 71

Assume the same facts as in Example 70, except that Vito's will provides as follows: $600,000 to the children and the remainder ($500,000) to Zina. ◆

From a tax standpoint, which is the better plan? Although no estate tax results from either arrangement, Example 70 represents an overfunding in terms of the marital deduction. Why place an additional $600,000 in Zina's potential estate when it can pass free of tax to the children through the application of the $192,800 unified tax credit available for 1993? (The exemption equivalent of $192,800 is $600,000.) The exemption equivalent is known as the *bypass amount.* The arrangement in Example 71 is to be preferred, as it avoids unnecessary concentration of wealth in Zina's estate.

On occasion, the disclaimer procedure can be used to maximize the deferral approach.

EXAMPLE 72

At the time of his death in 1993, Pete had never made any taxable gifts. Under Pete's will, his disposable estate of $1,500,000 passes as follows: $700,000 to Jim (Pete's adult son) and the remainder ($800,000) to Clare (Pete's surviving spouse). Shortly after Pete's death, Jim issues a disclaimer as to $100,000 of his $700,000 bequest. This amount, therefore, passes to Clare as the remainderperson under Pete's will. ◆

Because the unified tax credit for 1993 is $192,800 (with an exemption equivalent of $600,000), Jim's disclaimer avoids an estate tax on $100,000. The end result is an increase of $100,000 in the marital deduction and the elimination of *any* estate tax upon Pete's death.

Effectively Working with the Charitable Deduction. As a general guide to obtain overall tax savings, lifetime charitable transfers are to be preferred over testamentary dispositions. For example, an individual who gave $10,000 to a qualified charity during his or her life would secure an income tax deduction, avoid any gift tax, and reduce the gross estate by the amount of the gift. By way of contrast, if the $10,000 had been willed to charity, no income tax deduction would be available, and the amount of the gift would be includible in the decedent's gross estate (though later deducted for estate tax purposes). In short, the lifetime transfer provides a double tax benefit (income tax deduction plus reduced estate taxes) at no gift tax cost. The testamentary transfer merely neutralizes the effect of the inclusion of the property in the gross estate (inclusion under § 2033 and then deduction under § 2055).

On occasion, a charitable bequest depends on the issuance of a disclaimer by a noncharitable heir. Such a situation frequently arises with special types of property or collections, which the decedent may feel a noncharitable heir should have a choice of receiving. If the charitable organization is the residuary legatee under a decedent's will, a disclaimer by a specific legatee passes the property to the holder of the residual interest and qualifies the estate for a charitable deduction under § 2055.

EXAMPLE 73

Megan specified in her will that her valuable art collection is to pass to her son or, if the son refuses, to a designated and qualified art museum. At the time the will was drawn, Megan knew that her son was not interested in owning the collection. If, after Megan's death, the son issues a timely disclaimer, the collection will pass to the designated museum, and Megan's estate is allowed a charitable deduction for its death tax value. ◆

EXAMPLE 74

Dick's will specifies that one-half of his disposable estate is to pass to his wife, and the remainder of his property to a designated and qualified charitable organization. If the wife issues a timely disclaimer after Dick's death, all of the property passes to the charity and qualifies for the § 2055 charitable deduction. ◆

Did the son in Example 73 act wisely if he issued the disclaimer in favor of the museum? Although the disclaimer will provide Megan's estate with a deduction for the value of the art collection, consider the income tax deduction alternative. If the son accepts the bequest, he can still dispose of the collection (and fulfill his mother's philanthropic objectives) through lifetime donation to the museum. At the same time, he obtains an income tax deduction under § 170. Whether this will save taxes for the family unit depends on a comparison of Megan's estate tax bracket with the estimated income tax bracket of the son. If the value of the collection runs afoul of the percentage limitations of § 170(b)(1), the donations can be spread over more than one year. If this is done, and to protect against the contingency of the son's dying before the entire collection is donated, the son can neutralize any potential death tax consequences by providing in his will for the undonated balance to pass to the museum.

The use of a disclaimer in Example 74 would be sheer folly. It would not reduce Dick's estate tax; it would merely substitute a charitable deduction for the marital deduction. Whether the wife issues a disclaimer or not, no estate taxes will be due. The wife should accept her bequest and, if she is so inclined, make lifetime gifts of it to a qualified charity. In so doing, she generates an income tax deduction for herself.

Proper Handling of Other Deductions and Losses under §§ 2053 and 2054. Many § 2053 and § 2054 deductions and losses may be claimed either as estate tax deductions or as income tax deductions of the estate on the fiduciary return (Form 1041), but a choice must be made.[49] The deduction for income tax purposes is not allowed unless the estate tax deduction is waived. It is possible for these deductions to be apportioned between the two returns.

PROBLEM MATERIALS

DISCUSSION QUESTIONS

1. Why can the unified transfer tax be categorized as an excise tax? In this regard, how does it differ from an income tax?
2. Upon whom is the Federal gift tax imposed? What happens if that party is unable to pay the tax?
3. What are the major differences between the Federal estate tax and the typical inheritance tax levied by many states?
4. Rudolph, a resident and citizen of Canada, owns real estate located in Rochester, New York.

   a. Would Rudolph be subject to the U.S. gift tax if he transferred this property as a gift to his Canadian son?
   b. Would Rudolph be subject to the U.S. estate tax if he died and left the property to his Canadian son?

49. § 642(g) and Reg. § 20.2053–1(d).

5. Hilda, a U.S. citizen, has established her residence in Costa Rica in order to avoid the U.S. estate tax. Comment on the value of Hilda's planning.
6. Explain what is meant by the statement that the Federal gift tax is cumulative in nature.
7. What effect, if any, do prior gifts made by a decedent have on the determination of the decedent's estate tax liability?
8. What is meant by the exemption equivalent of the unified tax credit?
9. Regulation § 25.2512–8 states: "A consideration not reducible to a value in money or money's worth, as love and affection, promise of marriage, etc., is to be wholly disregarded, and the entire value of the property transferred constitutes the amount of the gift."
   - **a.** What does this Regulation mean?
   - **b.** When might it apply?
10. Russell sells property to Karen for $50,000. If the property is really worth $100,000, has Russell made a gift to Karen? What additional facts would you want to know before answering this question?
11. In connection with gift loans, comment on the following points:
    - **a.** Since any interest element recognized by the lender as income can be deducted by the borrower, the income tax effect is neutralized for the family unit.
    - **b.** The borrower's net investment income for the year is less than $1,000.
    - **c.** The gift loan involved only $95,000.
    - **d.** The lender charged the borrower interest of 2%.
12. In the absence of § 2516, why would certain property settlements incident to a divorce be subject to the Federal gift tax?
13. In connection with § 2518 dealing with disclaimers, comment on the following:
    - **a.** The role of state law.
    - **b.** The avoidance of a Federal gift tax or the Federal estate tax.
    - **c.** The disclaimer of only a partial interest.
14. What is the justification for the annual exclusion? In what manner does it resemble the gift tax treatment of the following?
    - **a.** Tuition payments to an educational organization on behalf of another.
    - **b.** Medical care payments on behalf of another.
15. In connection with the gift-splitting provision of § 2513, comment on the following:
    - **a.** What it was designed to accomplish.
    - **b.** How the election is made.
    - **c.** Its utility in a community property jurisdiction.
16. In connection with the filing of a Federal gift tax return, comment on the following:
    - **a.** No Federal gift tax is due.
    - **b.** The § 2513 election to split gifts is to be used.
    - **c.** A gift of a future interest is involved.
    - **d.** The donor uses a fiscal year for Federal income tax purposes.
    - **e.** The donor obtained from the IRS an extension of time for filing his or her Federal income tax return.
17. Distinguish between the following:
    - **a.** The gross estate and the taxable estate.
    - **b.** The gross estate and the probate estate.
18. Explain the *gross-up* procedure on gift taxes paid on gifts made within three years of death. What purpose does it serve?
19. Using community property, Everette creates a trust with a life estate to Carolyn (Everette's wife), remainder to their children upon Carolyn's death.
    - **a.** Is there any estate tax effect upon Everette's death four years later?
    - **b.** Is there any estate tax effect upon Carolyn's death five years later?

20. At the time of Emile's death, he was a joint tenant with Colette in a parcel of real estate. With regard to the inclusion in Emile's gross estate under § 2040, comment on the following independent assumptions:

 a. Emile and Colette received the property as a gift from Douglas.
 b. Colette provided all of the purchase price of the property.
 c. Colette's contribution was received as a gift from Emile.
 d. Emile's contribution was derived from income generated by property he received as a gift from Colette.

21. Ramon owns a policy on the life of Winnie, with Latrica as the designated beneficiary. Upon Winnie's death, the insurance proceeds are paid to Latrica.

 a. Are any of the proceeds included in Winnie's gross estate?
 b. Does Winnie's death generate any tax consequences to Ramon?

22. In terms of the QTIP (qualified terminable interest property) election, comment on the following:

 a. Who makes the election.
 b. What the election accomplishes.
 c. The tax effect of the election upon the death of the surviving spouse.

23. Does the credit for state death taxes (§ 2011) eliminate the double taxation of an estate? Explain.

24. What is the purpose of the credit for tax on prior transfers (§ 2013)? Would the provision ever apply in the husband and wife–type of situation? Explain.

Problems

25. In each of the following independent situations, indicate whether or not the transfer by Phillip is, or could be, subject to the Federal gift tax:

 a. Phillip makes a contribution to an influential political figure.
 b. Phillip makes a contribution to Cardinal Corporation, of which he is not a shareholder.
 c. In consideration of his upcoming marriage to Teri, Phillip establishes a savings account in Teri's name.
 d. Same as (c). After their marriage, Phillip establishes a joint checking account in the names of "Phillip and Teri."
 e. Same as (d). One year after the checking account is established, Teri withdraws all of the funds.
 f. Phillip enters into an agreement with Teri where he will transfer property to her in full satisfaction of her marital rights. One month after the agreement, the transfer occurs. Later Phillip and Teri are divorced.
 g. Phillip purchases U.S. savings bonds, listing ownership as "Phillip and Teri." Several years later, and after Phillip's death, Teri redeems the bonds.

26. In each of the following independent situations, indicate whether or not the transfer by Jeff is, or could be, subject to the Federal gift tax:

 a. Jeff purchases real estate and lists title as "Jeff and Chris as joint tenants." Jeff and Chris are brothers.
 b. Same as (a), except that Jeff and Chris are husband and wife.
 c. Jeff creates a revocable trust with Chris as the designated beneficiary.
 d. Same as (c). One year after creating the trust, Jeff releases all power to revoke the trust.
 e. Jeff takes out an insurance policy on his life, designating Chris as the beneficiary.
 f. Same as (e). Two years later, Jeff dies and the policy proceeds are paid to Chris.

g. Jeff takes out an insurance policy on the life of Gretchen and designates Chris as the beneficiary. Shortly thereafter, Gretchen dies and the policy proceeds are paid to Chris.
h. Jeff pays for Chris's college tuition.

27. In 1975, Dale purchased real estate for $300,000, listing ownership as follows: "Dale and Paula, equal tenants in common." Dale predeceases Paula in 1993, when the property is worth $800,000. Before 1975, Dale had not made any taxable gifts or utilized the $30,000 specific exemption. Assume Dale and Paula are father and daughter.

    a. Determine Dale's gift tax consequences, if any, in 1975.
    b. How much, if any, of the property should be included in Dale's gross estate?

28. In 1984, Kim purchased real estate for $500,000, listing title to the property as follows: "Kim and Jacqueline, joint tenants with the right of survivorship." Jacqueline predeceases Kim in 1993, when the real estate is worth $900,000. Assume Kim and Jacqueline are sisters and that neither has made any other taxable gifts or utilized the $30,000 specific exemption.

    a. Determine Kim's gift tax consequences, if any, in 1984.
    b. How much, if any, of the property should be included in Jacqueline's gross estate?

29. Assume the same facts as in Problem 29, except that Kim and Jacqueline are husband and wife (rather than sisters).

    a. Determine Kim's gift tax consequences, if any, in 1984.
    b. How much, if any, of the property should be included in Jacqueline's gross estate? Will any such inclusion generate an estate tax liability? Explain.

30. In January 1993, Roger and Jean enter into a property settlement under which Roger agrees to pay $500,000 to Jean in return for the release of her marital rights. At the time the agreement is signed, Roger pays Jean $100,000 as a first installment. Although the parties intended to obtain a divorce, Roger dies in July 1993 before legal proceedings have been instituted. After Roger's death, the executor of his estate pays to Jean the $400,000 remaining balance due under the property settlement.

    a. What are the gift tax consequences of the $100,000 payment made upon the signing of the agreement? Why?
    b. What are the estate tax consequences of the $400,000 paid to Jean from estate assets after Roger's death? Why?

31. In 1993, Angela makes a gift to her daughter of securities worth $700,000. Angela has never made any prior taxable gifts or utilized her $30,000 specific exemption. Ed (Angela's husband), however, made a taxable gift of $500,000 in early 1976 upon which he paid a gift tax of $109,275. At the time of Ed's gift, he was not married to Angela.

    a. Determine Angela's gift tax liability on the 1993 transfer, assuming the parties chose not to make the election to split gifts under § 2513.
    b. What would be the liability if the election to split the gift were made?

32. Kirk dies on July 7, 1993, at a time when he owns stock in Hawk Corporation and Falcon Corporation. On June 3 of the same year, both corporations authorized cash dividends payable on August 4. For Hawk, the dividend was payable to shareholders of record as of July 2, and Falcon's date of record was July 9. After Kirk's death, the executor of the estate received dividends in the following amounts: $6,000 from Hawk Corporation and $8,000 from Falcon Corporation. Kirk also owned some City of Minneapolis tax-exempt bonds. As of July 7, the accrued interest on the bonds was $7,500. On December 1, the executor of the estate received $10,000 in interest ($2,500 accrued since Kirk's death) from the bonds. Concerning the dividends and interest, how much should be included in Kirk's gross estate?

33. Before his death in 1993, Willie (a widower) made the following transfers:

- A gift of real estate (basis of $90,000 and fair market value of $400,000) to Chester (Willie's son). The gift was made in 1991 and resulted in a Federal gift tax of $20,000, which Willie paid. On the date of Willie's death, the property is worth $450,000.
- A gift of an insurance policy on Willie's life to Rita (the designated beneficiary). The policy was worth $10,000 but had a maturity value of $70,000. The gift was made in 1991 and resulted in no Federal gift tax liability.
- A gift of stock (basis of $40,000 and fair market value of $80,000) to Timothy. The gift was made in 1981 and resulted in no Federal gift tax liability. On the date of Willie's death, the stock was worth $200,000.

How much should be included in Willie's gross estate as to these transfers?

34. In 1975, Judy created a revocable trust with securities worth $200,000. National Trust Company was designated as the trustee. Under the terms of the trust, Judy retained a life estate with remainder to her children. In 1991, Judy releases her right to revoke the trust. Judy dies in 1993 when the trust assets have a fair market value of $1 million.

a. What, if any, are Judy's gift tax consequences in 1975?
b. What, if any, is included in Judy's gross estate in 1993?
c. Would your answer to (b) change if Judy *also* released her life estate in 1991? Explain.

35. In each of the following independent situations, determine how much should be included in Burton's gross estate under § 2042 as to the various life insurance policies involved. Assume that none of the policies are community property.

a. At the time of his death, Burton owned a paid-up policy on the life of Suzanna, with Penny as the designated beneficiary. The policy had a replacement cost of $80,000 and a maturity value of $300,000.
b. Nancy owns a policy on the life of Burton ($300,000 maturity value) with Burton's estate as the designated beneficiary. Upon Burton's death, the insurance company pays $300,000 to his estate.
c. Four years before his death, Burton transferred a policy on his life ($300,000 maturity value) to Ann as a gift. Burton retained the power to change beneficiaries. At the time of the transfer, the designated beneficiary was Ann. Because Burton had never exercised his right to change beneficiaries, the insurance company pays Ann $300,000 upon his death.
d. Same as (c), except that Burton releases the power to change beneficiaries one year before his death.

36. Comment on how each of the following independent situations should be handled for estate tax purposes:

a. Before her death, Linda issued a note payable to her daughter in the amount of $100,000. Linda never received any consideration for the note. After Linda's death, the daughter files a claim against the estate and collects $100,000 on the note.
b. At the time of her death, Saleka (a widow) owned 10 cemetery lots (each worth $5,000), which she had purchased many years before for herself and her family.
c. At the time of his death, Stanley was delinquent in the payment of back Federal income taxes. Stanley's executor pays the taxes from assets of the estate.

37. At the time of his death in the current year, Jerome owned the following real estate:

Tract A	$1,000,000
Mortgage on tract A	(200,000)
Tract B	700,000
Mortgage on tract B	(100,000)

Under Jerome's will, both tracts of land pass to Janice (Jerome's surviving spouse). However, Jerome's will directs the executor to pay off the mortgage on tract B from the remainder interest passing to the children.

a. How much marital deduction will Jerome's estate be allowed?
b. What is the deduction for indebtedness under § 2053?

38. At the time of his death in the current year, Jacob holds the following assets:

Real estate (parcel A)	$1,600,000
Real estate (parcel B)	1,200,000
Life insurance	400,000

Parcel A is owned by Jacob and Roberta (Jacob's spouse) as tenants by the entirety. Roberta furnished all of the original purchase price of the property. Parcel B is held by Jacob and his two surviving sisters as equal tenants in common. Jacob and his sisters inherited the property from their mother. The $1,200,000 listed above represents the value of the *entire* property.

The insurance policy is owned by Jacob and is on his life. The maturity value of $400,000 is paid to Roberta as the designated beneficiary. Under Jacob's will, all uncommitted assets pass to Roberta.

a. As to these assets, how much is included in Jacob's gross estate?
b. How much marital deduction will be allowed to Jacob's estate?

39. Determine the credit for state death taxes in each of the following independent situations:

a. The adjusted taxable estate is $120,000. The amount of state death tax paid is $1,100.
b. The adjusted taxable estate is $440,000. The amount of state death tax paid is $9,000.
c. The adjusted taxable estate is $800,000. The state death tax is a soak-up tax that was paid.

40. Under Ira's will, Jill (Ira's sister) inherits property. Three years later, Jill dies. Determine Jill's credit for tax on prior transfers based on the following assumptions:

a. The estate tax attributable to the inclusion of the property in Ira's gross estate is $70,000, and the estate tax attributable to the inclusion of the property in Jill's gross estate is $50,000.
b. The estate tax attributable to the inclusion of the property in Ira's gross estate is $60,000, and the estate tax attributable to the inclusion of the property in Jill's gross estate is $80,000.

41. In each of the following independent situations, determine the decedent's final estate tax liability (net of any unified tax credit):

	Decedent			
	Seth	**Ted**	**Polly**	**Lori**
Year of death	1984	1985	1986	1993
Taxable estate	$600,000	$800,000	$700,000	$1,000,000
Pre-1977 taxable gift*	–0–	250,000	100,000	–0–
Post-1976 taxable gift	200,000	–0–	–0–	250,000
Gift tax actually paid on pre-1977 taxable gift	–0–	49,725	15,525	–0–
Gift tax actually paid on post-1976 taxable gift	38,000	–0–	–0–	70,800

*The $30,000 specific exemption was used in full for each of these gifts; Ted's gift occurred on October 1, 1976, and Polly's took place in June 1976.

42. In each of the following independent situations, determine the decedent's final estate tax liability (net of any unified tax credit):

	Decedent			
	Adam	Hazel	Floyd	Lupe
Year of death	1985	1986	1987	1993
Taxable estate	$800,000	$900,000	$1,100,000	$1,200,000
Pre-1977 taxable gift*	250,000	250,000	-0-	-0-
Post-1976 taxable gift	-0-	-0-	500,000	80,000
Gift tax actually paid on pre-1977 taxable gift	49,275	49,275	-0-	-0-
Gift tax actually paid on post-1976 taxable gift	-0-	-0-	155,800	18,200

*The $30,000 specific exemption was used in full for each of these gifts; Adam's gift occurred in December 1976, and Hazel's took place in December 1975.

CHAPTER

INCOME TAXATION OF TRUSTS AND ESTATES

OBJECTIVES

Develop working definitions with respect to trusts, estates, beneficiaries, and other parties.

Identify steps by which to determine the accounting and taxable income of a trust or estate, and the related taxable income of the beneficiaries.

Illustrate the uses and implications of distributable net income.

Examine effects of statutory restrictions on accounting periods and methods available to trusts and estates, and on the taxation of distributions from accumulation trusts.

Review various tax planning procedures that can be used to minimize the tax consequences of trusts and estates and their beneficiaries.

OUTLINE

AN OVERVIEW OF SUBCHAPTER J

Taxpayers create trusts for a variety of reasons. Some trusts are established primarily for tax purposes while others are designed to accomplish a specific financial goal or to provide for the orderly management of assets in case of emergency. Figure 27–1 lists some of the more common reasons for creating a trust.

Because a trust is a separate tax entity, its gross income and deductions must be measured and an annual tax return must be filed. Similarly, when an individual dies, a legal entity is created in the form of his or her estate. This chapter examines the rules related to the income taxation of trusts and estates.

The income taxation of trusts and estates is governed by Subchapter J of the Internal Revenue Code, §§ 641 through 692. Certain similarities are apparent between Subchapter J and the income taxation of individuals (e.g., the definitions of gross income and deductible expenditures), partnerships (e.g., the conduit principle), and S corporations (e.g., the conduit principle and the trust as a separate taxable entity). Trusts also involve several important new concepts, however, including the determination of distributable net income and the tier system of distributions to beneficiaries.

The primary concern of this chapter is the income taxation of estates and ordinary trusts. Grantor trusts and special trusts, such as alimony trusts, trusts to administer the requirements of a court in the context of a bankruptcy proceeding, and qualified retirement trusts, are beyond the scope of this text. Figure 27–2 illustrates the structure of a typical estate and trust.

What Is a Trust?

The Code does not contain a definition of a trust. However, the term usually refers to an arrangement created by a will or by an *inter vivos* (lifetime) declaration,

FIGURE 27–1
Motivations for Creating a Trust

Type of Trust	Financial and Other Goals
Life insurance trust	Holds life insurance policies on the insured, removes the proceeds of the policies from the gross estate (if an irrevocable trust), and safeguards against a young or inexperienced beneficiary receiving the proceeds.
"Living" (revocable) trust	Manages assets, reduces probate costs, provides privacy for asset disposition, protects against medical or other emergencies, and provides relief from the necessity of day-to-day management of the underlying assets.
Trust for minors	Provides funds for a college education, shifts income to lower-bracket taxpayers, and accumulates income without permanently parting with the underlying assets.
"Blind" trust	Holds and manages the assets of the grantor without his/her input or influence (e.g., while the grantor holds political office or some other sensitive position).
Retirement trust	A special tax-exempt trust that manages asset contributions under a qualified retirement plan.
Alimony trust	Manages the assets of an ex-spouse and assures they will be distributed in a timely fashion to specified beneficiaries.
Liquidation trust	Collects and distributes the last assets of a corporation that is undergoing a complete liquidation.

through which trustees take title to property for the purpose of protecting or conserving it for the beneficiaries.[1]

Typically, the creation of a trust involves at least three parties: (1) The *grantor* (sometimes referred to as the settler or donor) transfers selected assets to the trust entity. (2) The *trustee,* who may be either an individual or a corporation, is charged with the fiduciary duties associated with the trust. (3) The *beneficiary* is

Figure 27–2 **Structure of a Typical Trust and Estate**

TRUST

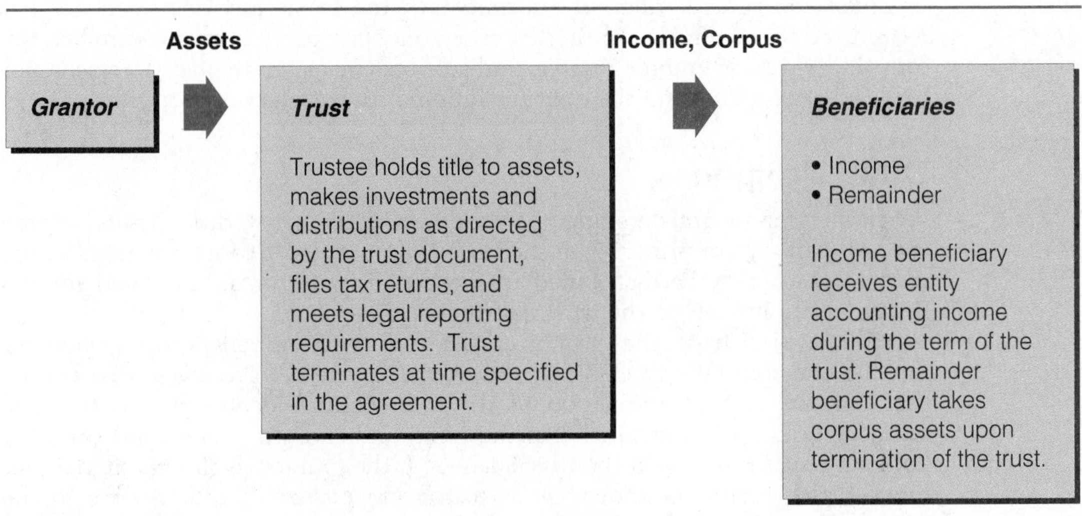

ESTATE

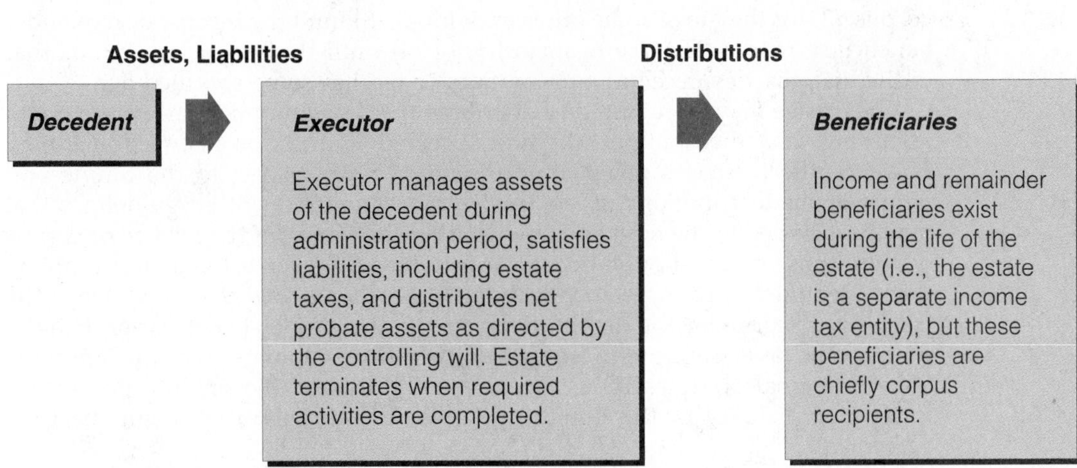

1. Reg. § 301.7701–4(a).

designated to receive income or property from the trust; the beneficiary's rights are defined by state law and by the trust document.

In some situations, fewer than three persons may be involved, as specified by the trust agreement. For instance, an elderly individual who can no longer manage his or her own property (e.g., because of ill health) may create a trust under which he or she is both the grantor and the beneficiary. In this case, a corporate trustee is charged with the management of the grantor's assets.

In another situation, the grantor might designate him- or herself as the trustee of the trust assets. For example, a parent who wants to transfer selected assets to a minor child could use a trust entity to ensure that the minor does not waste the property. By naming him- or herself as the trustee, the parent retains virtual control over the property that is transferred.

Under the general rules of Subchapter J, the trusts just described are not recognized for income tax purposes. When only one party is involved (when the same individual is grantor, trustee, and sole beneficiary of the trust), Subchapter J rules do not apply, and the entity is ignored for income tax purposes.

Other Definitions

When the grantor transfers title of selected assets to a trust, those assets become the *corpus* (body), or principal, of the trust. Trust corpus, in most situations, earns *income,* which may be distributed to the beneficiaries, or accumulated for the future by the trustee, as the trust instrument directs.

In the typical trust, the grantor creates two types of beneficiaries: one who receives the accounting income of the trust and one who receives trust corpus that remains at the termination of the trust entity. Beneficiaries in the first category hold an *income interest* in the trust, and those in the second category hold a *remainder interest* in the trust's assets. If the grantor retains the remainder interest, the interest is known as a *reversionary interest* (corpus reverts to the grantor when the trust entity terminates).

The trust document establishes the term of the trust. The term may be for a specific number of years (a *term certain*) or until the occurrence of a specified event. For instance, a trust might exist (1) for the life of the income beneficiary—in this case, the income beneficiary is known as a *life tenant* in trust corpus; (2) for the life of some other individual; (3) until the income or remainder beneficiary reaches the age of majority; or (4) until the beneficiary, or another individual, marries, receives a promotion, or reaches some specified age.

The trustee may be required to distribute the accounting income of the entity according to a distribution schedule specified in the agreement. Sometimes, however, the trustee is given more discretion with respect to the timing and nature of the distributions. If the trustee can determine, within guidelines that may be included in the trust document, either the timing of the income or corpus distributions or the specific beneficiaries who will receive them (from among those identified in the agreement), the trust is called a *sprinkling trust.* Here, the trustee can "sprinkle" the distributions among the various beneficiaries. Family-unit income taxes can be reduced by directing income to those who are subject to lower marginal tax rates. Thus, by giving the trustee a sprinkling power, the income tax liability of the family unit can be manipulated through the trust agreement.

For purposes of certain provisions of Subchapter J, a trust must be classified as either a *simple trust* or a *complex trust.* A simple trust (1) is required to distribute its entire accounting income to designated beneficiaries every year, (2) has no beneficiaries that are qualifying charitable organizations, and (3) makes no distributions of trust corpus during the year. A complex trust is any trust that is not a simple trust.[2] These criteria are applied to the trust every year. Thus, every trust will be classified as a complex trust in the year in which it terminates (because it will be distributing all of its corpus during that year).

What Is an Estate?

An estate is created upon the death of every individual. The estate is charged with collecting and conserving all of the individual's assets, satisfying all liabilities, and distributing the remaining assets to the heirs identified by state law or the will.

Typically, the creation of an estate involves at least three parties: the *decedent,* all of whose probate assets are transferred to the estate for disposition; the *executor* or *executrix,* who is appointed under the decedent's valid will (or the *administrator* or *administratrix,* if no valid will exists); and the *beneficiaries* of the estate, who are to receive assets or income from the entity, as the decedent indicated in the will. The executor or administrator holds the fiduciary responsibility to operate the estate as directed by the will, applicable state law, and the probate court.

Recall that the assets that make up the probate estate are not identical to those that constitute the gross estate for transfer tax purposes (refer to Chapter 26). Many of the gross estate assets are not a part of the *probate estate* and thus are not subject to disposition by the executor or administrator. For instance, property held by the decedent as a joint tenant passes to the survivor(s) by operation of the applicable state's property law rather than through the probate estate. Proceeds of insurance policies on the life of the decedent, over which the decedent held the incidents of ownership, are not under the control of the executor or administrator. The designated beneficiaries of the policy receive the proceeds outright under the insurance contract.

An estate is a separate taxable entity. Under certain circumstances, taxpayers may find it profitable to prolong an estate's existence. This situation is likely to arise when the heirs are already in a high income tax bracket. Therefore, they would prefer to have the income generated by the estate assets taxed at the estate's lower income tax rates. If an estate's existence is unduly prolonged, however, the estate is considered terminated for Federal income tax purposes after the expiration of a reasonable period for completing the duties of administration by the executor.[3]

NATURE OF TRUST AND ESTATE TAXATION

In general, the taxable income of a trust or an estate is taxed to the entity or to its beneficiaries to the extent that each has received the accounting income of the entity. Thus, Subchapter J creates a modified conduit principle relative to the income taxation of trusts, estates, and their beneficiaries: Whoever receives the accounting income of the entity, or some portion of it, is liable for the income tax that results.

2. Reg. § 1.651(a)–1.

3. Reg. § 1.641(b)–3(a).

EXAMPLE 1

Adam receives 80% of the accounting income of the Zero Trust. The trustee accumulated the other 20% of the income at her discretion under the trust agreement and added it to trust corpus. Adam is liable for income tax only on the amount of the distribution, and Zero is liable for the income tax on the accumulated portion of the income. ◆

The modified conduit principle of Subchapter J is subject to several exceptions. For instance, some trusts may be treated as associations and therefore will be subject to the corporate income tax.[4] In addition, part or all of the income of certain trusts is taxed to the grantor if too much control over the trust property or income is retained.[5]

Filing Requirements

The fiduciary is required to file a Form 1041 (U.S. Fiduciary Income Tax Return) in the following situations.[6]

- For an estate that has gross income for the year of $600 or more.
- For a trust that either has any taxable income or, if there is no taxable income, has gross income of $600 or more.

The fiduciary return (and any related tax liability) is due no later than the fifteenth day of the fourth month following the close of the entity's taxable year. The return should be filed with the Internal Revenue Service Center for the region in which the fiduciary resides or has his or her principal place of business.

Tax Accounting Periods, Methods, and Payments

An estate or trust may use many of the tax accounting methods available to individuals. The method of accounting used by the grantor of a trust or the decedent of an estate does not carry over to the entity.

An estate has the same options for choosing a tax year as any new taxpayer. Thus, the estate of a calendar year decedent dying on March 3 can select any fiscal year or report on a calendar year basis.[7] If the calendar year basis is selected, the estate's first taxable year will include the period from March 3 to December 31. If the first or last tax year of an estate is a short year (less than one calendar year), income for that year need not be annualized.

To eliminate the possibility of deferring the taxation of fiduciary-source income simply by using a fiscal tax year, trusts (other than tax-exempt trusts) use a calendar tax year.[8]

Trusts and certain estates are required to make estimated Federal income tax payments, using the same quarterly schedule that applies to individual taxpayers.[9] This requirement applies to estates only for tax years that end two or more years after the date of the decedent's death.

The two-year estimated tax exception for estates recognizes the liquidity problems that an executor often faces during the early months of administering

4. Refer to Chapter 16 for a discussion of associations taxed as corporations; see also *Morrissey v. Comm.*, 36–1 USTC ¶9020, 16 AFTR 1274, 56 S.Ct. 289 (USSC, 1936).

5. §§ 671–679.

6. § 6012(a).

7. § 441.

8. § 645.

9. § 6654(l).

the estate. The exception does not ensure, however, that an estate in existence less than 24 months will never be required to make an estimated tax payment.

EXAMPLE 2

Juanita died on March 15, 1994. Her executor elected a fiscal year ending on July 31 for the estate. Estimated tax payments will be required from the estate starting with the tax year that begins on August 1, 1995. ◆

Tax Rates and Personal Exemption

A compressed tax rate schedule applies to estates and trusts.[10] The 15 percent tax bracket is only $3,750 wide, so the ability to shift income in a tax-effective manner is restricted at present. Net long-term capital gains can be taxed at a nominal rate of no more than 28 percent. In addition to the regular income tax, an estate or trust may be subject to the alternative minimum tax.[11] Trusts may also be subject to a special tax imposed by § 644 on built-in gains from the sale or exchange of certain appreciated property.

Both trusts and estates are allowed a personal exemption in computing the fiduciary tax liability. All estates are allowed a personal exemption of $600. The exemption available to a trust depends upon the type of trust involved. A trust that is required to distribute all of its income currently is allowed an exemption of $300. All other trusts are allowed an exemption of only $100 per year.[12]

The classification of trusts as to the appropriate personal exemption is similar, but not identical, to the distinction between simple and complex trusts. The classification as a simple trust is more stringent.

EXAMPLE 3

Trust Alpha is required to distribute all of its current accounting income to Susan. Trust Beta is required to distribute all of its current accounting income, one-half to Tyrone and one-half to State University, a qualifying charitable organization. The trustee of Trust Gamma can, at her discretion, distribute the current accounting income or corpus of the trust to Dr. Chapman. None of the trusts makes any corpus distributions during the year. All of the accounting income of Trust Gamma is distributed to Dr. Chapman.

Trust Alpha is a simple trust; it will receive a $300 personal exemption. Trust Beta is a complex trust; it will receive a $300 personal exemption. Trust Gamma is a complex trust; it will receive a $100 personal exemption. ◆

Alternative Minimum Tax

The alternative minimum tax (AMT) may apply to a trust or estate in any tax year. Given the nature and magnitude of the tax preferences, adjustments, and exemptions that determine alternative minimum taxable income (AMTI), however, most trusts and estates are unlikely to incur the tax. Nevertheless, they could be vulnerable if they are actively engaged in a business that uses the accelerated cost recovery provisions. Similarly, an estate may be liable for the AMT if it receives a sizable portfolio of stock options shortly after the decedent's death under a deferred compensation plan. Charitable contributions of appreciated property may also cause an entity to incur AMT liability.

In general, derivation of AMTI for the entity follows the rules that apply to individual taxpayers. Thus, the corporate ACE adjustment does not apply to

10. § 1(e) (see Appendix A).

11. § 55.

12. § 642(b).

fiduciary entities, but AMTI may be created through the application of most of the other AMT preference and adjustment items discussed in Chapter 14.

The entity has a $20,000 annual exemption, similar to that available to a married individual who files a separate return. The exemption phases out at a rate of one-fourth of the amount by which AMTI exceeds $75,000.

A 24 percent alternative minimum tax rate is applied to AMTI. In addition, estimated tax payments for the entity must include any applicable AMT liability.

Taxable Income of Trusts and Estates

Generally, the taxable income of an estate or trust is computed in a manner similar to that used for an individual. Subchapter J does, however, include several important exceptions and provisions that make it necessary to use a systematic approach to calculating the taxable income of these entities. Figure 27–3 illustrates the computation method followed in this chapter.

Entity Accounting Income

The first step in determining the taxable income of a trust or estate is to compute the entity's accounting income for the period. Although this prerequisite is not apparent from a cursory reading of Subchapter J, a closer look at the Code reveals a number of references to the income of the entity. Wherever the term "income" is used in Subchapter J without some modifier (e.g., *gross* income or

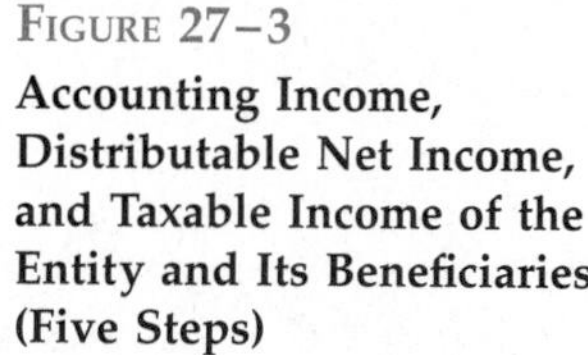

Figure 27–3
Accounting Income, Distributable Net Income, and Taxable Income of the Entity and Its Beneficiaries (Five Steps)

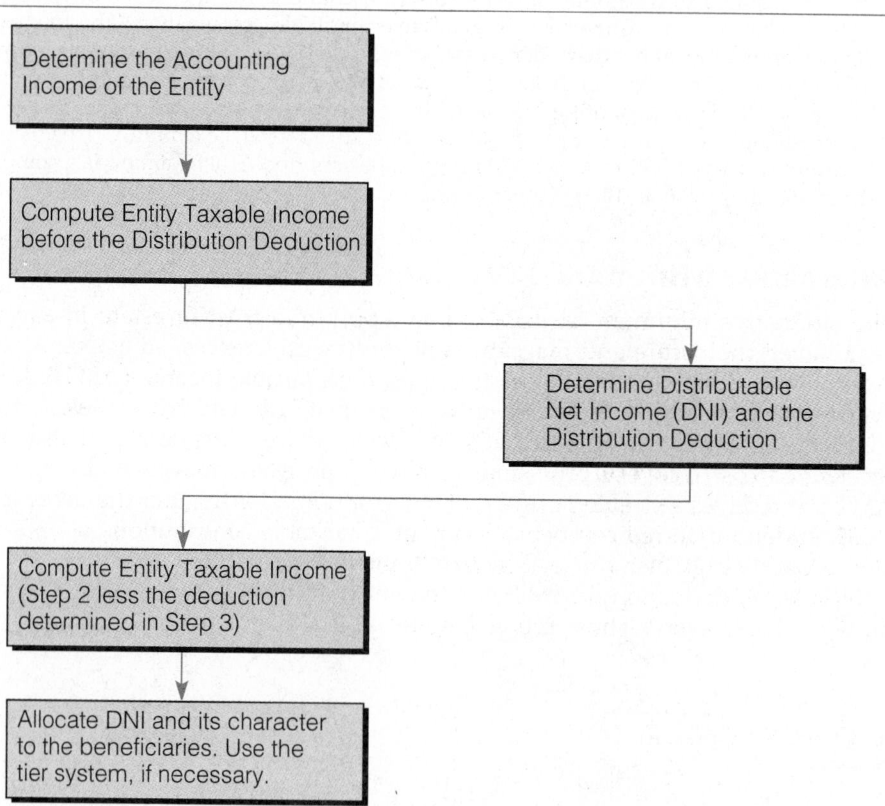
Determine the Accounting Income of the Entity
Compute Entity Taxable Income before the Distribution Deduction
Determine Distributable Net Income (DNI) and the Distribution Deduction
Compute Entity Taxable Income (Step 2 less the deduction determined in Step 3)
Allocate DNI and its character to the beneficiaries. Use the tier system, if necessary.

taxable income), the statute is referring to the accounting income of the trust or estate for the tax year.

A definition of entity accounting income is critical to understanding the Subchapter J computation of fiduciary taxable income. Under state law, entity accounting income is the amount that the income beneficiary of the simple trust or estate is eligible to receive from the entity. More importantly, the calculation of accounting income is virtually under the control of the grantor or decedent (through a properly drafted trust agreement or will). If the document has been drafted at arm's length, a court will enforce a fiduciary's good faith efforts to carry out the specified computation of accounting income.

By allocating specific items of income and expenditure either to the income beneficiaries or to corpus, the desires of the grantor or decedent are put into effect. Figure 27–4 shows typical assignments of revenue and expenditure items to fiduciary income or corpus.

Where the controlling document is silent as to whether an item should be assigned to income or corpus, state law prevails. These allocations are an important determinant of the benefits received from the entity by its beneficiaries and the timing of those benefits.

EXAMPLE 4

The Arnold Trust is a simple trust. Mrs. Bennett is its sole beneficiary. In the current year, the trust earns $20,000 in taxable interest and $15,000 in tax-exempt interest. In addition, the trust recognizes an $8,000 long-term capital gain. The trustee assesses a fee of $11,000 for the year. If the trust agreement allocates fees and capital gains to corpus, trust accounting income is $35,000, and Mrs. Bennett receives that amount. Thus, the income beneficiary receives no immediate benefit from the trust's capital gain, and she bears none of the financial burden of the fiduciary's fees.

Interest income	$35,000
Long-term capital gain—allocable to corpus	± –0–
Fiduciary's fees—allocable to corpus	± –0–
Trust accounting income	$35,000

◆

EXAMPLE 5

Assume the same facts as in Example 4, except that the trust agreement allocates the fiduciary's fees to income. The trust accounting income is $24,000, and Mrs. Bennett receives that amount.

Interest income	$35,000
Long-term capital gain—allocable to corpus	± –0–
Fiduciary's fees	–11,000
Trust accounting income	$24,000

◆

FIGURE 27–4
Common Allocations of Items to Income or Corpus

Allocable to Income	Allocable to Corpus
■ Ordinary and operating net income from trust assets.	■ Depreciation on business assets.
■ Interest, dividend, rent, and royalty income.	■ Casualty gain/loss on income-producing assets.
■ Stock dividends.	■ Insurance recoveries on income-producing assets.
■ One-half of fiduciary fees/commissions.	■ Capital gain/loss on investment assets.
	■ Stock splits.
	■ One-half of fiduciary fees/commissions.

EXAMPLE 6

Assume the same facts as in Example 4, except that the trust agreement allocates to income all capital gains and losses and one-half of the trustee's commissions. The trust accounting income is $37,500, and Mrs. Bennett receives that amount.

Interest income	$35,000
Long-term capital gain	+8,000
Fiduciary's fees—one-half allocable to corpus	−5,500
Trust accounting income	$37,500

◆

Gross Income

The gross income of an estate or trust is similar to that of an individual. In determining the gain or loss to be recognized by an estate or trust upon the sale or other taxable disposition of assets, the rules for basis determination are similar to those applicable to other taxpayers. Thus, the basis of property to an estate received from a decedent is stepped up or stepped down to gross estate value (refer to Chapter 12 for a more detailed discussion). Property received as a gift (the usual case in most trust arrangements) usually takes the donor's basis. Property purchased by the trust from a third party is assigned a basis equal to the purchase price.

Property Distributions. In general, the entity does not recognize gain or loss upon its distribution of property to a beneficiary under the provisions of the will or trust document. The beneficiary of the distribution assigns to the distributed property a basis equal to that of the estate or trust. Moreover, the distribution absorbs distributable net income (DNI) and qualifies for a distribution deduction (both of which are explained later in this chapter) to the extent of the lesser of the distributed asset's basis to the beneficiary or the asset's fair market value as of the distribution date.

EXAMPLE 7

The Howard Trust distributes a painting, basis of $40,000 and fair market value of $90,000, to beneficiary Kate. Kate's basis in the painting is $40,000. The distribution absorbs $40,000 of the trust's DNI, and Howard claims a $40,000 distribution deduction relative to the transaction. ◆

EXAMPLE 8

Assume the same facts as in Example 7, except that Howard's basis in the painting is $100,000. Kate's basis in the painting is also $100,000. The distribution absorbs $90,000 of the trust's DNI, and Howard claims a $90,000 distribution deduction. ◆

A trustee or executor can *elect* to recognize gain or loss with respect to all of its in-kind property distributions for the year.[13] If the election is made, the beneficiary's basis in the asset is equal to the asset's fair market value as of the distribution date. The distribution absorbs DNI and qualifies for a distribution deduction to the extent of the asset's fair market value. Note, however, that § 267 can restrict a trust's deduction for such losses.

13. § 643(e). The election applies to all distributions for the entity's tax year.

EXAMPLE 9

The Green Estate distributes an antique piano, basis to Green of $10,000 and fair market value of $15,000, to beneficiary Kyle. The executor elects that the estate recognize the related $5,000 gain on the distribution. Accordingly, Kyle's basis in the piano is $15,000 ($10,000 basis to Green + $5,000 gain recognized). Without the election, the estate would not recognize any gain, and Kyle's basis in the piano would be $10,000. ◆

EXAMPLE 10

Assume the same facts as in Example 9, except that Green's basis in the piano is $18,000. The executor elects that the estate recognize the related $3,000 loss on the distribution. Accordingly, Kyle's basis in the piano is $15,000 ($18,000 – $3,000). Without the election, the estate would not recognize any loss, and Kyle's basis in the piano would be $18,000. ◆

Income in Respect of a Decedent. The gross income of a trust or estate includes *income in respect of a decedent (IRD)*. For a cash basis decedent, IRD includes accrued salary, interest, rent, and other income items that were not constructively received before death. For both cash and accrual basis decedents, IRD includes, for instance, death benefits from qualified retirement plans and deferred compensation contracts.

The tax consequences of IRD are as follows.

- The fair market value of the right to IRD on the appropriate valuation date is included in the decedent's gross estate.[14] Thus, it is subject to the Federal estate tax.[15]
- The decedent's basis in the property carries over to the recipient (the estate or heirs). There is no step-up or step-down in the basis of IRD items.
- Gain or loss is recognized to the recipient of the income, measured by the difference between the amount realized and the adjusted basis of the IRD in the hands of the decedent. The character of the gain or loss depends upon the treatment that it would have received had it been realized by the decedent before death. Thus, if the decedent would have realized capital gain, the recipient must do likewise.[16]
- Expenses related to the IRD (such as interest, taxes, and depletion) that properly were not reported on the final income tax return of the decedent may be claimed by the recipient if the obligation is associated with the IRD. These items are known as *expenses in respect of a decedent*. They are deductible for both Federal estate and income tax purposes.
- If the IRD item would have created an AMT preference or adjustment for the decedent (e.g., with respect to the collection of certain tax-exempt interest by the entity), an identical AMT item is created for the recipient.

EXAMPLE 11

Amanda died on July 13 of the current year. On August 2, her estate received a check (before deductions) for $1,200 from Amanda's former employer; this was Amanda's compensation for the last pay period of her life. On November 23, Amanda's estate received a $45,000 distribution from her employer's qualified profit sharing plan, the full amount to which she was entitled under the plan. Both Amanda and the estate are calendar year, cash basis taxpayers.

---

14. § 2033. Refer to Chapter 26.

15. To mitigate the effect of double taxation (imposition of both the death tax and income tax), § 691(c) allows the recipient an income tax deduction for the estate tax attributable to the income.

16. § 691(a)(3) and Reg. § 1.691(a)–3.

The last salary payment and the profit sharing plan distribution constitute IRD to Amanda's estate. Amanda had earned these items during her lifetime, and the estate had an enforceable right to receive each of them after Amanda's death. Consequently, Amanda's gross estate includes $46,200 with respect to these two items. However, the income tax basis to the estate for these items is not stepped up (from zero to $1,200 and $45,000, respectively) upon distribution to the estate.

The estate must report gross income of $46,200 with respect to the IRD items. The gain recognized upon the receipt of the IRD is $46,200 [($1,200 + $45,000) amounts realized – $0 adjusted basis]. ◆

Including the IRD in both Amanda's gross estate and the gross income of the estate may seem harsh. Nonetheless, it is similar to the treatment that applies to all of a taxpayer's earned income. The amount is subject to income tax upon receipt, and to the extent that it is not consumed by the taxpayer before death, it is included in the gross estate.

Example 12

Assume the same facts as in Example 11, except that Amanda was an accrual basis taxpayer. IRD now includes only the $45,000 distribution from the qualified retirement plan. Amanda's last paycheck is included in the gross income of her own last return (January 1 through date of death). The $1,200 salary is already recognized properly under Amanda's usual method of tax accounting. It does not constitute IRD and is not gross income when received by the executor. ◆

Example 13

Assume the same facts as in Example 11. Amanda's last paycheck was reduced by $165 for state income taxes that were withheld by her employer. The $165 tax payment is an expense in respect of a decedent and is allowed as a deduction *both* on Amanda's estate tax return and on the estate's income tax return. ◆

Ordinary Deductions

As a general rule, the taxable income of an estate or trust is similar to that of an individual. Deductions are allowed for ordinary and necessary expenses paid or incurred in carrying on a trade or business; for the production or collection of income; for the management, conservation, or maintenance of property; and in connection with the determination, collection, or refund of any tax. Reasonable administration expenses, including fiduciary fees and litigation costs in connection with the duties of administration, also are deductible.

The trust or estate must apply the 2 percent-of-AGI floor to many of the § 212 expenses that it incurs. For this purpose, AGI appears to be the greater of (1) the pertinent-year AGI of the grantor of the trust or (2) the AGI of the trust or estate, computed as though the entity were an individual. The floor does not apply, however, to items like fiduciary fees or the personal exemption (i.e., items that would not be incurred by an individual).

Expenses attributable to the production or collection of tax-exempt income are not deductible.[17] The amount of the disallowed deduction is found by using a formula based upon the composition of the income elements of entity accounting income for the year of the deduction. The § 212 deduction is apportioned without regard to the accounting income allocation of such expenses to income or to corpus. The deductibility of the fees is determined strictly by the Code

17. § 265.

(under §§ 212 and 265), and the allocation of expenditures to income and to corpus is controlled by the trust agreement or will or by state law.

Under § 642(g), amounts deductible as administration expenses or losses for death tax purposes (under §§ 2053 and 2054) cannot be claimed by the estate for income tax purposes, unless the estate files a waiver of the death tax deduction. Although these expenses cannot be deducted twice, they may be allocated between Forms 706 and 1041 as the fiduciary sees fit; they need not be claimed in their entirety on either return. The prohibition against double deductions does not extend to expenses in respect of a decedent.

Trusts and estates are allowed cost recovery deductions. However, such deductions are assigned proportionately among the recipients of entity accounting income. An estate is allowed a deduction for depreciation, depletion, and amortization, to be apportioned among the estate and the heirs on the basis of the estate's accounting income allocable to each.[18]

EXAMPLE 14

Lisa and Martin are the equal income beneficiaries of the Needle Trust. Under the terms of the trust agreement, the trustee has complete discretion as to the timing of the distributions from Needle's current accounting income. The trust agreement allocates all depreciation expense to income. In the current year, the trustee distributes 40% of the current trust accounting income to Lisa and 40% to Martin; thus, 20% of the income is accumulated. The depreciation deduction allowable to Needle is $100,000. This deduction is allocated among the trust and its beneficiaries on the basis of the distribution of current accounting income: Lisa and Martin can each claim a $40,000 deduction, and the trust can deduct $20,000. ◆

EXAMPLE 15

Assume the same facts as in Example 14, except that the trust agreement allocates all depreciation expense to corpus. Lisa and Martin can each still claim a $40,000 depreciation deduction, and Needle retains its $20,000 deduction. The Code assigns the depreciation deduction proportionately to the recipients of current entity accounting income. Allocation of depreciation to income or to corpus is irrelevant in determining which party can properly claim the deduction. ◆

When a trust sells property received by transfer from the grantor, the amount of depreciation subject to recapture includes the depreciation claimed by the grantor before the transfer of the property to the trust. However, depreciation recapture potential disappears at death. Thus, when an entity receives depreciable property from a decedent, the recapture potential is reduced to zero.

EXAMPLE 16

Jaime transferred an asset to the Shoulder Trust via a lifetime gift. The asset's total depreciation recapture potential was $40,000. If the trust sells the asset at a gain, it will recognize ordinary income not to exceed $40,000. Had Jaime transferred the asset after his death to his estate through a bequest, the $40,000 recapture potential would have disappeared. ◆

Deductions for Losses

An estate or trust is allowed a deduction for casualty or theft losses not covered by insurance or other arrangement. Such losses may also be deductible by an

18. § 167(h) and §§ 611(b)(3) and (4).

estate for Federal death tax purposes under § 2054. As a result, an estate is not allowed an income tax deduction unless the death tax deduction is waived.

The net operating loss (NOL) deduction is available for estates and trusts. The carryback of an NOL may reduce the distributable net income of the trust or estate for the carryback year and therefore affect the amount taxed to the beneficiaries for that year.

Certain losses realized by an estate or trust may also be disallowed, as they are for all taxpayers. Thus, the wash sales provisions of § 1091 disallow losses on the sale or other disposition of stock or securities when the estate or trust acquires substantially identical stock or securities within the prescribed 30-day period. Likewise, § 267 disallows certain losses, expenses, and interest with respect to transactions between related taxpayers. Under § 267(b), the term "related taxpayers" includes, in addition to other relationships, the following:

- A grantor and a fiduciary of any trust.
- A fiduciary of a trust and a beneficiary of such trust.
- A fiduciary of a trust and a corporation, if more than 50 percent in value of the corporation's outstanding stock is owned by or for the trust or the grantor of the trust.

Except for the possibility of unused losses in the year of termination, the net capital losses of an estate or trust are used only on the fiduciary income tax return.[19] The tax treatment of these losses is the same as for individual taxpayers.

Charitable Contributions

An estate or complex trust is allowed a deduction for contributions to charitable organizations under the following conditions:

- The contribution must be made pursuant to the will or trust instrument.
- The recipient must be a qualified organization. For this purpose, qualified organizations include the same charities that qualify individual and corporate donors for the deduction, except that estates and trusts are permitted a deduction for contributions to certain foreign charitable organizations.
- Generally, the contribution must be paid in the tax year claimed, but a fiduciary can treat amounts paid in the year immediately following as a deduction for the preceding year.[20] Under this rule, estates and complex trusts receive more liberal treatment than individuals or corporations.

Unlike individuals and corporations, estates and complex trusts are not limited in the extent of their deductible charitable contributions for the year (e.g., to a percentage of taxable or adjusted gross income). Nonetheless, an entity's contribution may not fully qualify for a deduction. Specifically, the deduction is limited to amounts included in the gross income of the entity in the year of the contribution.

A contribution is deemed to have been made proportionately from each of the income elements of entity accounting income. Thus, in the event that the entity has tax-exempt income, the contribution is deductible only to the extent that the income elements of entity accounting income for the year of the deduction are included in the entity's gross income.

19. § 642(h).

20. § 642(c)(1) and Reg. § 1.642(c)–1(b).

This rule is similar to that used to limit the § 212 deduction for fiduciary fees and other expenses incurred to generate tax-exempt income. However, if the will or trust agreement requires that the contribution be made from a specific type of income or from the current income from a specified asset, the contribution will not have to be allocated to taxable and tax-exempt income.

EXAMPLE 17

The Capper Trust has 1994 gross rent income of $80,000, expenses attributable to the rents of $60,000, and tax-exempt interest from state bonds of $20,000. Under the trust agreement, the trustee is to pay 30% of the annual trust accounting income to the United Way, a qualifying organization. Accordingly, the trustee pays $12,000 (30% × $40,000) to the charity in 1995. The charitable contribution deduction allowed for 1994 is $9,600 [($80,000/$100,000) × $12,000]. ◆

EXAMPLE 18

Assume the same facts as Example 17, except that the trust instrument also requires that the contribution be paid from the net rent income. The agreement controls, and the allocation formula need not be applied. The entire $12,000 is allowed as a charitable deduction. ◆

Deduction for Distributions to Beneficiaries

The modified conduit approach of Subchapter J is embodied in the deduction allowed to trusts and estates for the distributions made to beneficiaries during the year. When the beneficiary receives a distribution from the trust, some portion of that distribution may be subject to income tax on his or her own return. At the same time, the distributing entity is to allowed a deduction for some or all of the distribution. Consequently, the modified conduit principle of Subchapter J is implemented. A good analogy is to the taxability of corporate profits distributed to employees as taxable wages. The corporation is allowed a deduction for the payment, but the employee receives gross income in the form of compensation.

A critical value that is used in computing the amount of the entity's distribution deduction is *distributable net income (DNI).* DNI serves several functions as it is defined in Subchapter J.

- DNI is the maximum amount of the distribution on which the beneficiaries can be taxed.[21]
- DNI is the maximum amount that can be used by the entity as a distribution deduction for the year.[22]
- The makeup of DNI carries over to the beneficiaries (the items of income and expenses retain their DNI character in the hands of the distributees).

Subchapter J defines DNI in a circular manner, however. The DNI value is necessary to determine the entity's distribution deduction and therefore its taxable income for the year. Nonetheless, the Code defines DNI as a modification of the entity's taxable income itself. Using the systematic approach to determining the taxable income of the entity and of its beneficiaries, as shown earlier in Figure 27–3, one first must compute *taxable income before the distribution deduction,* modify that amount to determine DNI and the distribution deduction, return to the calculation of *taxable income,* and apply the deduction that has resulted.

21. §§ 652(a) and 662(a).

22. §§ 651(b) and 661(c).

Taxable income before the distribution deduction includes all of the entity's items of gross income, deductions, gains, losses, and exemptions for the year. Therefore, to compute this amount, (1) determine the appropriate personal exemption for the year and (2) account for all of the other gross income and deductions of the entity.

The next step in Figure 27–3 is the determination of *distributable net income,* computed by making the following adjustments to the entity's *taxable income before the distribution deduction.*

- Add back the personal exemption.
- Add back *net* tax-exempt interest. To arrive at this amount, reduce the total tax-exempt interest by charitable contributions and by related expenses not deductible under § 265.
- Add back the entity's *net* capital losses.
- Subtract any net capital gains allocable to corpus. In other words, the only net capital gains included in DNI are those attributable to income beneficiaries or to charitable contributions.

Since taxable income before the distribution deduction is computed by deducting all of the expenses of the entity (whether they were allocated to income or to corpus), DNI is reduced by expenses that are allocated to corpus. The effect is to reduce the taxable income of the income beneficiaries. The actual distributions to the beneficiaries exceed DNI because the distributions are not reduced by expenses allocated to corpus. Aside from this shortcoming of Subchapter J, DNI offers a good approximation of the current-year economic income available for distribution to the entity's income beneficiaries.

DNI includes the net tax-exempt interest income of the entity, so that amount must be removed from DNI in computing the distribution deduction. Moreover, for estates and complex trusts, the amount actually distributed during the year may include discretionary distributions of income and distributions of corpus permissible under the will or trust instrument. Thus, the distribution deduction for estates and complex trusts is computed as the lesser of (1) the deductible portion of DNI or (2) the amount actually distributed to the beneficiaries during the year. For a simple trust, however, full distribution always is assumed, relative to both the entity and its beneficiaries, in a manner similar to the partnership and S corporation conduit entities.

EXAMPLE 19

The Zinc Trust is a simple trust. Because of severe liquidity problems, its 1992 accounting income is not distributed to its sole beneficiary, Mary, until early in 1993. Zinc is still allowed a full distribution deduction for, and Mary is still taxed upon, the entity's 1992 income in 1992. ◆

EXAMPLE 20

The Pork Trust is required to distribute its current accounting income annually to its sole income beneficiary, Barbara. Capital gains and losses and all other expenses are allocable to corpus. For the current year, the trust records the following items.

Dividend income	$25,000
Taxable interest income	15,000
Tax-exempt interest income	20,000
Net long-term capital gains	10,000
Fiduciary's fees	6,000

1. Trust accounting income is $60,000; this includes the tax-exempt interest income, but not the fees or the capital gains, pursuant to the trust document. Barbara receives $60,000 from the trust for the current year.
2. Taxable income before the distribution deduction is computed as follows.

Dividend income	$25,000
Interest income	15,000
Net long-term capital gains	10,000
Fiduciary's fees (40/60)	(4,000)
Personal exemption	(300)
Total	$45,700

The tax-exempt interest is excluded under § 103. Only a portion of the fees is deductible because some of the fees are traceable to the tax-exempt income. The trust receives a $300 personal exemption as it is required to distribute its annual trust accounting income.
3. DNI and the distribution deduction are computed in the following manner.

Taxable income before the distribution deduction (from above)		$ 45,700
Add back: Personal exemption		300
Subtract: Net long-term capital gains of the trust		(10,000)
Add back: Net tax-exempt income—		
Tax-exempt interest	$20,000	
Less: Disallowed fees	(2,000)	18,000
Distributable net income		$ 54,000
Distribution deduction ($54,000 DNI – $18,000 net tax-exempt income)		$ 36,000

4. Finally, return to the computation of the taxable income of the Pork Trust. Simply, it is as follows.

Taxable income before the distribution deduction	$ 45,700
Less: Distribution deduction	(36,000)
Taxable income, Pork Trust	$ 9,700

A simple test should be applied at this point to ensure that the proper figure for the trust's taxable income has been determined. On what is Pork to be taxed? All of the trust's gross income has been distributed to Barbara except the $10,000 net long-term capital gains. The $300 personal exemption reduces taxable income to $9,700. ◆

EXAMPLE 21

The Quick Trust is required to distribute all of its current accounting income equally to its two beneficiaries, Faith and the First Methodist Church, a qualifying charitable organization. Capital gains and losses and depreciation expenses are allocable to the income beneficiaries. Fiduciary fees are allocable to corpus. In the current year, Quick incurs fiduciary fees of $18,000 and the following.

1.	Rent income	$100,000
	Depreciation expense (rental property)	(15,000)
	Other expenses related to rent income	(30,000)
	Net long-term capital gains	20,000
	Accounting income, Quick Trust	$ 75,000

2.	Taxable rent income	$100,000
	Depreciation deduction	–0–
	Rent expense deductions	(30,000)
	Net long-term capital gains	20,000
	Fiduciary's fees	(18,000)
	Personal exemption	(300)
	Charitable contribution deduction	(37,500)
	Taxable income before the distribution deduction	$ 34,200

In the absence of tax-exempt income, a deduction is allowed for the full amount of the fiduciary's fees. Quick is a complex trust, but since it is required to distribute its full accounting income annually, a $300 exemption is allowed. The trust properly does not deduct any depreciation for the rental property. The depreciation deduction is available only to the recipients of the entity's accounting income for the period. Thus, the deduction will be split equally between Faith and the church. The deduction probably is of no direct value to the church as the church is not subject to the income tax. The trust's charitable contribution deduction is based upon the $37,500 that the charity actually received (one-half of trust accounting income).

3.	Taxable income before the distribution deduction	$34,200
	Add back: Personal exemption	300
	Distributable net income	$34,500
	Distribution deduction	$34,500

As there is no tax-exempt income, the only adjustment needed to compute DNI is to add back the trust's personal exemption. Subchapter J requires no adjustment for the charitable contribution. DNI is computed only from the perspective of Faith, who also received $37,500 from the trust.

4.	Taxable income before the distribution deduction	$34,200
	Less: Distribution deduction	(34,500)
	Taxable income, Quick Trust	$ (300)

Perform the simple test (referred to above) to ensure that the proper taxable income for the Quick Trust has been computed. All of the trust's gross income has been distributed to Faith and the church. As is the case with most trusts that distribute all of their annual income, the personal exemption is "wasted" by Quick. ◆

Tax Credits

An estate or trust may claim the foreign tax credit to the extent that it is not passed through to the beneficiaries. Similarly, other credits must be apportioned between the estate or trust and the beneficiaries on the basis of the entity accounting income allocable to each.

TAXATION OF BENEFICIARIES

The beneficiaries of an estate or trust receive taxable income from the entity under the modified conduit principle of Subchapter J. DNI determines the maximum amount that can be taxed to the beneficiaries for any tax year. The constitution of DNI also carries over to the beneficiaries (e.g., net long-term capital gains retain their character when they are distributed from the entity to the beneficiary).

The timing of any tax consequences to the beneficiary of a trust or estate presents a problem only when the parties involved use different tax years. A beneficiary must include in gross income an amount based upon the DNI of the trust for any taxable year or years of the trust or estate ending with or within his or her taxable year.[23]

EXAMPLE 22

An estate uses a fiscal year ending on March 31 for tax purposes. Its sole income beneficiary is a calendar year taxpayer. For the calendar year 1995, the beneficiary reports whatever income was assignable to her for the entity's fiscal year April 1, 1994 to March 31, 1995. If the estate is terminated by December 31, 1995, the beneficiary must also include any income assignable to her for the short year. This could result in a bunching of income in 1995. ◆

Distributions by Simple Trusts

The amount taxable to the beneficiaries of a simple trust is limited by the trust's DNI. However, since DNI includes net tax-exempt income, the amount included in the gross income of the beneficiaries could be less than DNI. When there is more than one income beneficiary, the elements of DNI must be apportioned ratably according to the amount required to be distributed currently to each.

EXAMPLE 23

A simple trust has ordinary income of $40,000, a long-term capital gain of $15,000 (allocable to corpus), and a trustee commission expense of $4,000 (payable from corpus). The two income beneficiaries, Allie and Bart, are entitled to the trust's annual accounting income, based on shares of 75% and 25%, respectively. Although Allie receives $30,000 as her share (75% × $40,000 trust accounting income), she will be allocated DNI of only $27,000 (75% × $36,000). Likewise, Bart is entitled to receive $10,000 (25% × $40,000), but he will be allocated DNI of only $9,000 (25% × $36,000). The $15,000 capital gain is taxed to the trust. ◆

Distributions by Estates and Complex Trusts

A problem arises with estates and complex trusts when more than one beneficiary receives a distribution from the entity and the controlling document does not require a distribution of the entire accounting income of the entity.

EXAMPLE 24

The trustee of the Wilson Trust has the discretion to distribute the income or corpus of the trust in any proportion between the two beneficiaries of the trust, Wong and Washington. Under the trust instrument, Wong must receive $15,000 from the trust every year. In the current year, the trust's accounting income is $50,000, and its DNI is $40,000. The trustee pays $35,000 to Wong and $25,000 to Washington for the current year. ◆

How is Wilson's DNI to be divided between Wong and Washington? Several arbitrary methods of allocating DNI between the beneficiaries could be devised. Subchapter J resolves the problem by creating a two-tier system to govern the

23. §§ 652(c) and 662(c).

taxation of beneficiaries in such situations.[24] The tier system determines which distributions will be included in the gross income of the beneficiaries in full, which will be included in part, and which will not be included at all.

Income that is required to be distributed currently, whether or not it is distributed, is categorized as a *first-tier distribution.* All other amounts properly paid, credited, or required to be distributed are considered to be *second-tier distributions.* The following formula is used to allocate DNI among the appropriate beneficiaries when only first-tier distributions are made and those amounts exceed DNI.

First-tier distributions to the beneficiary / First-tier distributions to all beneficiaries

Distributable net income

Beneficiary's share of distributable net income

When both first-tier and second-tier distributions are made and the first-tier distributions exceed DNI, the above formula is applied to the first-tier distributions. In this case, none of the second-tier distributions are taxed because all of the DNI has been allocated to the first-tier beneficiaries.

If both first-tier and second-tier distributions are made and the first-tier distributions do not exceed DNI, but the total of both first-tier and second-tier distributions does exceed DNI, the second-tier beneficiaries must recognize income as follows:

Second-tier distributions to the beneficiary / Second-tier distributions to all beneficiaries

Remaining distributable net income (after first-tier distributions)

Beneficiary's share of distributable net income

Example 25

The trustee of the Gray Trust is required to distribute $10,000 per year to both Harriet and Wally, the two beneficiaries of the entity. In addition, she is empowered to distribute other amounts of trust income or corpus at her sole discretion. In the current year, the trust has accounting income of $60,000 and DNI of $50,000. However, the trustee distributes only the required $10,000 each to Harriet and to Wally. The balance of the income is accumulated and added to trust corpus.

In this case, only first-tier distributions have been made, but the total amount of the distributions does not exceed DNI for the year. Although DNI is the maximum amount that is included by the beneficiaries for the year, they can include no more in gross income than is distributed by the entity. Thus, both Harriet and Wally are subject to tax on $10,000 as their proportionate shares of DNI. ◆

Example 26

Assume the same facts as in Example 25, except that DNI is $12,000. Harriet and Wally each receive $10,000, but they cannot be taxed in total on more than DNI. Each is taxed on $6,000 [$12,000 DNI × ($10,000/$20,000 of the first-tier distributions)]. ◆

24. §§ 662(a)(1) and (2).

EXAMPLE 27

Return to the facts in Example 24. Wong receives a first-tier distribution of $15,000. Second-tier distributions include $20,000 to Wong and $25,000 to Washington. Wilson Trust's DNI is $40,000. The DNI is allocated between Wong and Washington as follows.

1. First-tier distributions	
To Wong	$15,000 DNI
To Washington	–0–
Remaining DNI = $25,000 ($40,000 DNI – $15,000 distributed)	
2. Second-tier distributions	
To Wong (20/45 × $25,000)	$11,111 DNI
To Washington (25/45 × $25,000)	13,889 DNI

◆

Separate Share Rule. For the sole purpose of determining the amount of DNI for a complex trust with more than one beneficiary, the substantially separate and independent shares of different beneficiaries in the trust are treated as *separate trusts.* The need for this special rule can be illustrated as follows:

EXAMPLE 28

A trustee has the discretion to distribute or accumulate income on behalf of Greg and Hannah (in equal shares). The trustee also has the power to invade corpus for the benefit of either beneficiary to the extent of that beneficiary's one-half interest in the trust. For the current year, DNI is $10,000. Of this amount, $5,000 is distributed to Greg and $5,000 is accumulated on behalf of Hannah. In addition, the trustee pays $20,000 from corpus to Greg. Without the separate share rule, Greg is taxed on $10,000 (the full amount of the DNI). With the separate share rule, Greg is taxed on only $5,000 (his share of the DNI) and receives the $20,000 corpus distribution tax-free. The trust will be taxed on Hannah's $5,000 share of the DNI that is accumulated. ◆

The separate share rule is designed to prevent the inequity that results if the corpus payments are treated under the regular rules applicable to second-tier beneficiaries. In Example 28, the effect of the separate share rule is to produce a two-trust result: one trust for Greg and one for Hannah, each with DNI of $5,000.

Character of Income

Consistent with the modified conduit principle of Subchapter J, various classes of income (e.g., dividends, passive or portfolio gain and loss, AMT preferences and adjustments, and tax-exempt interest) retain the same character for the beneficiaries that they had when they were received by the entity. If there are multiple beneficiaries *and* if all of the DNI is distributed, a problem arises in allocating the various classes of income among the beneficiaries.

Distributions are treated as consisting of the same proportion as the items that enter into the computation of DNI. This allocation does not apply, however, if the governing instrument specifically allocates different classes of income to different beneficiaries or if local law requires such an allocation. Expressed as a formula, this generally means the following:

Beneficiary's total share of DNI distributed / Total DNI distributed

Total of DNI element deemed distributed (e.g., tax-exempt interest)

Beneficiary's share of the DNI element

If the entity distributes only a part of its DNI, the amount of a particular class of DNI that is deemed distributed must first be determined. This is done as follows:

Total distribution / Total distributable net income	×	Total of a particular class of distributable net income	=	Total of the DNI element deemed distributed (e.g., tax-exempt interest)

EXAMPLE 29

During the current year, a trust has DNI of $40,000, including the following: $10,000 of taxable interest, $10,000 of tax-exempt interest, and $20,000 of dividends. The trustee distributes, at her discretion, $8,000 to Mike and $12,000 to Nancy.

Beneficiary	Amount Received	Income Type	
Mike	$ 8,000	Taxable interest	
		[($8,000 distribution/$40,000 total DNI) × $10,000 taxable interest in DNI]	$2,000
		Tax-exempt interest	
		(8/40 × $10,000)	$2,000
		Passive income	
		(8/40 × $20,000)	$4,000
Nancy	$12,000	Taxable interest	
		[($12,000 distribution/$40,000 total DNI) × $10,000 taxable interest in DNI]	$3,000
		Tax-exempt interest	
		(12/40 × $10,000)	$3,000
		Passive income	
		(12/40 × $20,000)	$6,000 ◆

Special Allocations. Under certain circumstances, the parties may modify the character-of-income allocation method set forth above. A modification is permitted only to the extent that the allocation is required in the trust instrument and only to the extent that it has an economic effect independent of the income tax consequences of the allocation.

EXAMPLE 30

Return to the facts in Example 29. Assume that the beneficiaries are elderly individuals who have pooled their investment portfolios to avail themselves of the trustee's professional asset management skills. Suppose the trustee has the discretion to allocate different classes of income to different beneficiaries and that she designates all of Nancy's $12,000 distribution as being from the tax-exempt income. Such a designation *would not be recognized* for tax purposes, and the allocation method of Example 29 must be used.

Suppose, however, that the trust instrument stipulated that Nancy was to receive all of the income from tax-exempt securities because she alone contributed the exempt securities to trust corpus. Under this provision, the $10,000 of the nontaxable interest is paid to Nancy. This allocation *is recognized,* and $10,000 of Nancy's distribution is tax-exempt. ◆

Losses in the Termination Year

The ordinary net operating and capital losses of a trust or estate do not flow through to the entity's beneficiaries, as would such losses from a partnership or an S corporation. However, in the year in which an entity terminates its existence, the beneficiaries do receive a direct benefit from the loss carryovers of the trust or estate.

Net operating losses and net capital losses are subject to the same carryover rules that otherwise apply to an individual. Consequently, NOLs can be carried back 3 years and then carried forward 15 years while net capital losses can be carried forward only, and for an indefinite period of time. However, if the entity incurs an NOL in the last year of its existence, the excess of deductions over the entity's gross income is allowed to the beneficiaries (it will flow through to them directly). The net loss is available as a deduction *from* AGI in the beneficiary's tax year with or within which the entity's tax year ends. The amount allowed is in proportion to the relative amount of corpus assets that each beneficiary receives upon the termination of the entity, and it is subject to the 2 percent-of-AGI floor.

Any carryovers of the entity's other losses flow through to the beneficiaries in the year of termination in proportion to the relative amount of corpus assets that each beneficiary receives. The character of the loss carryforward is retained by the beneficiary, except that a carryover of a net capital loss to a corporate beneficiary is always treated as short term. Beneficiaries who are individuals use these carryforwards as deductions *for* AGI.

EXAMPLE 31

The Edgar Estate terminates on December 31, 1994. It had used a fiscal year ending July 31. For the termination year, the estate incurred a $15,000 NOL. In addition, the estate had an unused NOL carryforward of $23,000 from the year ending July 31, 1991, and an unused net long-term capital loss carryforward of $10,000 from the year ending July 31, 1993. Upon termination, Dawn receives $60,000 of corpus, and Blue Corporation receives the remaining $40,000. Dawn and Blue are calendar year taxpayers.

Dawn can claim an itemized deduction of $9,000 [($60,000/$100,000) × $15,000] for the entity's NOL in the year of termination. This deduction is subject to the 2% of AGI floor on miscellaneous itemized deductions. In addition, she can claim a $13,800 deduction *for* AGI in 1994 (60% × $23,000) for Edgar's other NOL carryforward, and she can use $6,000 of the estate's net long-term capital loss carryforward with her other 1994 capital transactions.

Blue Corporation receives ordinary business deductions in 1994 for Edgar's NOLs; $6,000 for the loss in the year of termination and $9,200 for the carryforward from fiscal year 1991. Moreover, Blue can use the $4,000 carryforward of Edgar's net capital losses to offset against its other 1994 capital transactions, although the loss must be treated as short term.

With respect to both Dawn and Blue, the losses flow through in addition to the other tax consequences of Edgar that they received on July 31, 1994 (at the close of the usual tax year of the entity), under Subchapter J. Moreover, if the beneficiaries do not use the NOL carryforward in calendar year 1994, the short year of termination will exhaust one of the years of the usual carryforward period (e.g., Dawn can use Edgar's NOL carryforward for 15 years). ◆

THE THROWBACK RULE

Generally, a trust's beneficiary is not taxed on any distributions in excess of the trust's DNI. Thus, trustees of complex trusts might be tempted to arrange distributions in a way that results in minimal income tax consequences to all of the parties involved. For instance, if the trust is subject to a lower income tax rate than are its beneficiaries, income could be accumulated at the trust level for several years before being distributed to the beneficiaries. Thus, the income that would be taxed to the beneficiaries in the year of distribution would be limited by the trust's DNI for that year. Further tax savings could be achieved by using multiple trusts. This device spreads the income during the accumulation period over more than one taxpaying entity and avoids the graduated tax rates.

To discourage the use of these tax minimization schemes, a *throwback rule* was added to the Code. Under the rule, a beneficiary's tax on a distribution of income accumulated by a trust in a prior year will approximate the increased tax that the beneficiary would have owed for that prior year if the income had been distributed in the year that it was earned by the trust. The tax as computed, however, is levied for the actual year of the distribution. The purpose of the throwback rule is to place the beneficiaries of complex trusts in the same nominal tax position they would have been in if they had received the distributions during the years in which the trust was accumulating the income.

A detailed description of the application of the throwback rule is beyond the scope of this text.

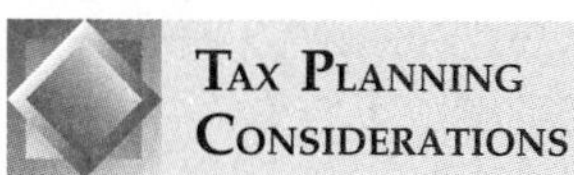

Tax Planning Considerations

Many of the tax planning possibilities for estates and trusts were discussed in Chapter 26. However, several specific tax planning possibilities are available to help minimize the income tax effects on estates and trusts and their beneficiaries.

Income Tax Planning for Estates

As a separate taxable entity, an estate can select its own tax year and accounting methods. The executor of an estate should consider selecting a fiscal year because this will determine when beneficiaries must include income distributions from the estate in their own tax returns. Beneficiaries must include the income for

Concept Summary 27–1
Income Taxation of Trusts and Estates

1. Estates and trusts are temporary entities, created to locate, maintain, and distribute assets and to satisfy liabilities according to the wishes of the decedent or grantor as expressed in the will or trust document.
2. Generally, the estate or trust acts as a conduit of the taxable income that it receives. To the extent that the income is distributed by the entity, it is taxed to the beneficiary. Taxable income retained by the entity is taxed to the entity itself.
3. The entity's accounting income must be determined first. Accounting conventions that are stated in the controlling document or, lacking such provisions, in state law allocate specific items of receipt and expenditure either to income or to corpus. Income beneficiaries typically receive payments from the entity that are equal to the accounting income.
4. The taxable income of the entity is computed using the scheme in Figure 27–3. The entity usually recognizes income in respect of a decedent. Deductions for fiduciary's fees and for charitable contributions may be reduced if the entity received any tax-exempt income during the year. Cost recovery deductions are assigned proportionately to the recipients of accounting income. Upon election, realized gain or loss on assets that properly are distributed in kind can be recognized by the entity.
5. A distribution deduction, computationally derived from distributable net income (DNI), is allowed to the entity. DNI is the maximum amount on which entity beneficiaries can be taxed. Moreover, the constitution of DNI is assigned to the recipients of the distributions.

their tax year with or within which the estate's tax year ends. Proper selection of the estate's tax year can result in a smoothing out of income and a reduction of the income taxes for all parties involved.

Caution should be taken in determining when the estate is to be terminated. If a fiscal year has been selected for the estate, a bunching of income to the beneficiaries can occur in the year in which the estate is closed. Prolonging the termination of an estate can be effective income tax planning, but the IRS carefully examines the purpose of keeping the estate open. Since the unused losses of an estate will pass through to the beneficiaries, the estate should be closed when the beneficiaries can enjoy the maximum tax benefit of the losses.

The timing and amounts of income distributions to the beneficiaries also present important tax planning opportunities. If the executor can make discretionary income distributions, he or she should evaluate the relative marginal income tax rates of the estate and its beneficiaries. By timing the distributions properly, the overall income tax liability can be minimized. Care should be taken, however, to time the distributions in light of the estate's DNI.

EXAMPLE 32

For several years before his death on March 7, Don had entered into annual deferred compensation agreements with his employer. These agreements collectively called for the payment of $200,000 six months after Don's retirement or death. To provide a maximum 12-month period within which to generate deductions to offset this large item of IRD, the executor or administrator of the estate should elect a fiscal year ending August 31. The election is made simply by filing the estate's first tax return for the short period of March 7 to August 31. ◆

EXAMPLE 33

Carol, the sole beneficiary of an estate, is a calendar year, cash basis taxpayer. If the estate elects a fiscal year ending January 31, all distributions during the period of February 1 to December 31, 1993, will be reported on Carol's tax return for calendar year 1994 (due April 15, 1995). Thus, any income taxes that result from a $50,000 distribution made by the estate on February 20, 1993, will be deferred until April 15, 1995. ◆

EXAMPLE 34

Assume the same facts as in Example 33. If the estate is closed on December 15, 1994, the DNI for both the fiscal year ending January 31, 1994, and the final tax year ending December 15, 1994, is included in Carol's tax return for the calendar year 1994. To avoid the effect of this bunching of income, the estate should not be closed until calendar year 1995. ◆

EXAMPLE 35

Assume the same facts as in Example 34, except that the estate has a substantial NOL for the period February 1 to December 15, 1994. If Carol is subject to a high income tax rate for calendar year 1994, the estate should be closed in that year so that the excess deductions are passed through to its beneficiary. However, if Carol anticipates being in a higher tax bracket in 1995, the termination of the estate should be postponed. ◆

In general, beneficiaries who are subject to high tax rates should be made beneficiaries of second-tier (but not IRD) distributions of the estate. Most likely, these individuals will have less need for an additional steady stream of (taxable) income while their income tax savings can be relatively large. Moreover, a special allocation of tax-favored types of income and expenses should be considered. For example, tax-exempt income can be directed more easily to beneficiaries in higher income tax brackets.

Income Tax Planning with Trusts

The great variety of trusts provides the grantor, trustee, and beneficiaries with excellent opportunities for tax planning. Many of the same tax planning opportunities available to the executor of an estate are available to the trustee. For instance, the distributions from a trust are taxable to the trust's beneficiaries to the extent of the trust's DNI. If income distributions are discretionary, the trustee can time the distributions to minimize the income tax consequences to all parties.

Remember that the throwback rule applies to complex trusts. Consequently, the benefit from the timing of distributions may be more limited than it is for estates. Indeed, improper timing could result in a greater nominal tax than if the distributions had been made annually.

Tax Year and Payment Planning. The TRA of 1986 reduced the benefits that arise from the traditional, tax-motivated use of trusts and estates by revising the rate schedules applicable to these entities. Specifically, accumulation within the entity of the otherwise taxable income of the trust or estate may no longer produce the same magnitude of tax benefits that were available under a more progressive tax rate schedule. The lower tax rates of the trust are exhausted more quickly. They are also very similar to those that apply to the potential beneficiaries and may be higher for a trust. As a result, the absolute and relative values of income shifting are reduced.

Distributions of In-Kind Property

The ability of the trustee or executor to elect to recognize the realized gain or loss relative to a distributed noncash asset allows the gain or loss to be allocated to the optimal taxpayer.

Example 36

The Yorba Linda Estate distributed some stock, basis of $40,000 and fair market value of $50,000, to beneficiary Larry. Yorba Linda is subject to a 15% income tax rate, and Larry is subject to a 31% tax rate. The executor of Yorba Linda should elect that the entity recognize the related $10,000 realized gain, thereby subjecting the gain to the estate's lower tax rate and reducing Larry's future capital gain income (by increasing his basis). ◆

Problem Materials

Discussion Questions

1. What is the importance of the accounting income of a trust or estate in determining its taxable income?
2. When must an income tax return be filed for an estate? A trust?
3. What is the general scheme of the income taxation of trusts and estates? How does the modified conduit principle relate to this general approach?
4. Under what circumstances can an estate or trust be taxed on a distribution of property to a beneficiary?
5. What is income in respect of a decedent? What are the tax consequences to a recipient of income in respect of a decedent?

6. How must an estate or trust treat its deductions for cost recovery? How does this treatment differ from the deductibility of administrative expenses or losses for estate tax purposes?
7. What happens to the NOL carryovers of an estate or trust if the entity is terminated before the deductions can be taken? How can this provision be used as a tax planning opportunity?
8. Discuss the income tax treatment of charitable contributions made by an estate or trust. How does this treatment differ from the requirements for charitable contribution deductions of individual taxpayers?
9. What is distributable net income? Why is this amount significant in the income taxation of estates and trusts and their beneficiaries?
10. Distinguish between first-tier and second-tier distributions from estates and complex trusts. Discuss the tax consequences to the beneficiaries receiving such distributions.
11. How must the various classes of income be allocated among multiple beneficiaries of an estate or trust?
12. What is the throwback rule? When is it applicable? Why was such a rule adopted?
13. Discuss the tax planning opportunities presented by the ability of an estate to select a noncalendar tax year.

PROBLEMS

14. The Prasad Trust operates a welding business. Its current-year MACRS (modified accelerated cost recovery system) deductions properly amounted to $35,000. Prasad's accounting income was $150,000, of which $80,000 was distributed to first-tier beneficiary Chuck, $60,000 was distributed to second-tier beneficiary Ruby, and $10,000 was accumulated by the trustee. Ruby also received a $15,000 corpus distribution. Prasad's DNI was $52,000. Discuss the treatment of Prasad's cost recovery deductions.
15. Brown incurred the following items in 1994.

Business income	$20,000
Tax-exempt interest income	5,000
Payment to charity from 1994 income, paid 3/1/95	3,000

Complete the following chart, indicating how the Code treats charitable contributions under the various assumptions.

Assumption	1994 Deduction for Contribution
Brown is a cash basis individual.	
Brown is an accrual basis corporation.	
Brown is a trust.	

16. In its first tax year, the Wittmann Estate generated $50,000 of taxable interest income and $25,000 of tax-exempt interest income. It paid fiduciary fees of $4,000. The estate is subject to a 37% marginal estate tax rate and a 31% marginal income tax rate.
   a. How should the executrix assign the deductions for the payment of the fees?
   b. How does the 2%-of-AGI floor apply to these fees assigned to the estate's income tax return?
17. Describe the nature and operations of each of the following trusts.
   a. A simple trust.
   b. A complex trust with a $300 personal exemption.
   c. A complex trust with a $100 personal exemption.

18. The Purple Trust incurred the following items this year.

Taxable interest income	$50,000
Tax-exempt interest income, not on private activity bonds	60,000
Tax-exempt interest income, on private activity bonds	40,000

Compute Purple's tentative minimum tax for the year. Purple does not have any credits available to reduce the AMT liability.

19. Complete the following chart, indicating the comparative attributes of the typical trust and estate by answering yes/no or explaining the differences between the entities where appropriate.

Attribute	Estate	Trust
Separate income tax entity	_____	_____
Controlling document	_____	_____
Termination date is determinable from controlling document	_____	_____
Legal owner of assets under fiduciary's control	_____	_____
Document identifies both income and remainder beneficiaries	_____	_____
Throwback rules apply	_____	_____
Separate share rules apply	_____	_____
Generally must use calendar tax year	_____	_____

20. The LMN Trust is a simple trust that correctly uses the calendar year for tax purposes. Its three income beneficiaries (Lynn, Mark, and Norelle) are entitled to the trust's annual accounting income in shares of one-third each. For the current calendar year, the trust has ordinary income of $60,000, a long-term capital gain of $18,000 (allocable to corpus), and a trustee commission expense of $6,000 (allocable to corpus).

   a. How much income is each beneficiary entitled to receive?
   b. What is the trust's DNI?
   c. What is the trust's taxable income?
   d. How much will be taxed to each of the beneficiaries?

21. Assume the same facts as in Problem 20, except that the trust instrument allocates the capital gain to income.

   a. How much income is each beneficiary entitled to receive?
   b. What is the trust's DNI?
   c. What is the trust's taxable income?
   d. How much will be taxed to each of the beneficiaries?

22. A trust is required to distribute $20,000 annually to its two income beneficiaries, Amber and Byron, in shares of 75% and 25%, respectively. If trust income is not sufficient to pay these amounts, the trustee is empowered to invade corpus to the extent necessary. During the current year, the trust has DNI of $12,000, and the trustee distributes $15,000 to Amber and $5,000 to Byron.

   a. How much of the $15,000 distributed to Amber must be included in her gross income?
   b. How much of the $5,000 distributed to Byron must be included in his gross income?
   c. Are these distributions considered to be first-tier or second-tier distributions?

23. Under the terms of the trust instrument, the trustee has discretion to distribute or accumulate income on behalf of Willie, Sylvia, and Drahman in equal shares. The trustee is also empowered to invade corpus for the benefit of any of the beneficiaries to the extent of their respective one-third interest in the trust. In the current year, the trust has DNI of $48,000. Of this amount, $16,000 is distributed to Willie and $10,000

is distributed to Sylvia. The remaining $6,000 of Sylvia's share of DNI and Drahman's entire $16,000 share are accumulated by the trust. Additionally, the trustee distributes $20,000 from corpus to Willie.

a. How much income is taxed to Willie?
b. To Sylvia?
c. To Drahman?
d. To the trust?

24. The trustee of the Miguel Trust is empowered to distribute accounting income and corpus to the trust's equal beneficiaries, Paula and George. In the current year, the trust incurs the following:

Taxable interest income	$40,000
Tax-exempt interest income	60,000
Long-term capital gains—allocable to corpus	35,000
Fiduciary's fees—allocable to corpus	12,000

The trustee distributed $25,000 to Paula and $28,000 to George.

a. What is Miguel's trust accounting income?
b. What is Miguel's DNI?
c. What is the amount of taxable income recognized by Paula from these activities? By George? By Miguel?

25. Determine the tax effects of the indicated losses for the Yellow Estate for both tax years. The estate holds a variety of investment assets, which it received from the decedent, Mrs. Yellow. The estate's sole income and remainder beneficiary is Yellow, Jr.

Tax Year	Loss Generated
1993 (first tax year)	Taxable income ($300) Capital loss ($15,000)
1994 (final tax year)	Taxable income ($1,000)

CHAPTER

WORKING WITH THE TAX LAW

OBJECTIVES

Become familiar with the statutory, administrative, and judicial sources of the tax law.

Develop the research skills to locate and work with appropriate tax law sources.

Determine the validity of the various tax law sources.

Apply research techniques and planning procedures.

Examine the influence of nontax factors.

Distinguish between tax evasion and tax avoidance.

Illustrate tax planning concepts through practical tax planning applications.

Learn about computer-assisted tax research.

OUTLINE

TAX SOURCES

Understanding taxation requires a mastery of the sources of the *rules of tax law.* These sources include not only legislative provisions in the form of the Internal Revenue Code, but also Congressional Committee Reports, Treasury Department Regulations, other Treasury Department pronouncements, and court decisions. Thus, the *primary sources* of tax information include pronouncements from all three branches of government: legislative, executive, and judicial.

In addition to being able to locate and interpret the sources of the tax law, a tax professional must understand the relative weight of authority within these sources. The tax law is of little significance, however, until it is applied to a set of facts and circumstances. This chapter, therefore, both introduces the statutory, administrative, and judicial sources of the tax law *and* explains how the law is applied to individual and business transactions. It also explains the application of research techniques and the effective use of planning procedures.

A large part of tax research focuses on determining the intent of Congress. While Congress often claims simplicity as one of its goals, a cursory examination of the tax law indicates that it has not been very successful. Commenting on his 48-page tax return, James Michener, the author, said, "it is unimaginable in that I graduated from one of America's better colleges, yet I am totally incapable of understanding tax returns."

Frequently, uncertainty in the tax law causes disputes between the Internal Revenue Service (IRS) and taxpayers. Due to these *gray areas* and the complexity of the tax law, a taxpayer may have more than one alternative for structuring a business transaction. In structuring business transactions and engaging in other tax planning activities, the tax adviser must be cognizant that the objective of tax planning is not necessarily to minimize the tax liability. Instead a taxpayer should maximize his or her after-tax return, which may include maximizing nontax as well as noneconomic benefits.

Statutory Sources of the Tax Law

Origin of the Internal Revenue Code. Before 1939, the statutory provisions relating to taxation were contained in the individual revenue acts enacted by Congress. The inconvenience and confusion that resulted from dealing with many separate acts led Congress to codify all of the Federal tax laws. Known as the Internal Revenue Code of 1939, the codification arranged all Federal tax provisions in a logical sequence and placed them in a separate part of the Federal statutes. A further rearrangement took place in 1954 and resulted in the Internal Revenue Code of 1954, which continued in effect until it was replaced by the Internal Revenue Code of 1986.

The following observations help clarify the codification procedure:

- Neither the 1939, the 1954, nor the 1986 Code changed all of the tax law existing on the date of enactment. Much of the 1939 Code, for example, was incorporated into the 1954 Code. The same can be said for the transition from the 1954 to the 1986 Code. This point is important in assessing judicial and administrative decisions interpreting provisions under prior codes. For example, a decision interpreting § 121 of the Internal Revenue Code of 1954 will have continuing validity since this provision carried over unchanged to the Internal Revenue Code of 1986.
- Statutory amendments to the tax law are integrated into the existing code. Thus, subsequent tax legislation, such as the Revenue Reconciliation Act of

1990, has become part of the Internal Revenue Code of 1986. In view of the frequency with which tax legislation was enacted during the 1980s, it appears that the tax law will continue to be amended frequently.

The Legislative Process. Federal tax legislation generally originates in the House of Representatives, where it is first considered by the House Ways and Means Committee. Tax bills originate in the Senate when they are attached as riders to other legislative proposals.[1] If acceptable to the Committee, the proposed bill is referred to the entire House of Representatives for approval or disapproval. Approved bills are sent to the Senate, where they are referred to the Senate Finance Committee for further consideration.

The next step involves referral from the Senate Finance Committee to the entire Senate. Assuming no disagreement between the House and Senate, passage by the Senate means referral to the President for approval or veto. If the bill is approved or if the President's veto is overridden, the bill becomes law and part of the Internal Revenue Code of 1986.

When the Senate version of the bill differs from that passed by the House, the Joint Conference Committee is called upon to resolve those differences. The Joint Conference Committee includes members of the House Ways and Means Committee and the Senate Finance Committee. The result of the Joint Conference Committee, usually a compromise of the two versions, is then voted on by both the House and the Senate. If both bodies accept the bill, it is referred to the President for approval or veto. The typical legislative process dealing with tax bills is summarized in Figure 28–1.

Referrals from the House Ways and Means Committee, the Senate Finance Committee, and the Joint Conference Committee are usually accompanied by Committee Reports. These Committee Reports often explain the provisions of the proposed legislation and are therefore a valuable source for ascertaining the *intent of Congress.* What Congress had in mind when it considered and enacted tax legislation is the key to interpreting the legislation. Since Regulations normally are not issued immediately after a statute is enacted, taxpayers and the courts look to legislative history materials to determine congressional intent.

The role of the Joint Conference Committee indicates the importance of compromise in the legislative process. The experience of the maximum income tax rates applicable to corporations in the TRA of 1986 (H.R. 3838) illustrates the practical effect of the committee process. See Figure 28–2.

Arrangement of the Code. In working with the Code, it helps to understand the format. Note the following partial table of contents:

Subtitle A. Income Taxes

Chapter 1. Normal Taxes and Surtaxes

Subchapter A. Determination of Tax Liability

Part I. Tax on Individuals

Sections 1–5

Part II. Tax on Corporations

Sections 11–12

* * *

1. The Tax Equity and Fiscal Responsibility Act of 1982 originated in the Senate, and its constitutionality was unsuccessfully challenged in the courts. The Senate version of the Deficit Reduction Act of 1984 was attached as an amendment to the Federal Boat Safety Act.

In referring to a provision of the Code, the key is usually the Section number. In citing Section 2(a) (dealing with the status of a surviving spouse), for example, it is unnecessary to include Subtitle A, Chapter 1, Subchapter A, Part I. Merely mentioning Section 2(a) will suffice, since the Section numbers run consecutively and do not begin again with each new Subtitle, Chapter, Subchapter, or Part. Not all Code Section numbers are used, however. Note that Part I ends with Section 5 and Part II starts with Section 11 (at present there are no Sections 6, 7, 8, 9, and 10). When the Code was drafted, the omission of Section numbers was intentional. This provides flexibility to incorporate later changes into the Code without disrupting its organization. When Congress does not leave enough space, subsequent Code Sections are given A, B, C, etc., designations. A good example is the treatment of Sections 280A through 280H.

Tax practitioners commonly refer to a specific area of income taxation by Subchapter designation. Some of the more common Subchapter designations include Subchapter C ("Corporate Distributions and Adjustments"), Subchapter K ("Partners and Partnerships"), and Subchapter S ("Tax Treatment of S Corporations and Their Shareholders"). Particularly in the last situation, it is much more convenient to describe the effect of the applicable Code provisions

FIGURE 28–1
Legislative Process for Tax Bills

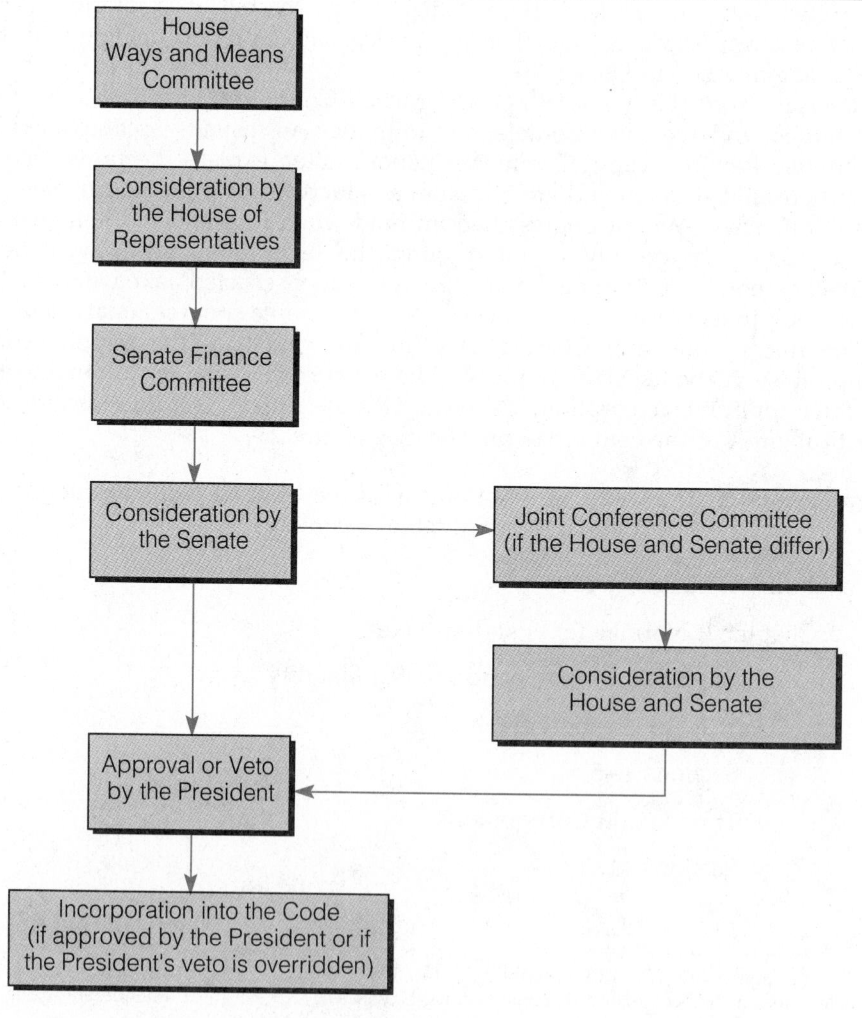

(Sections 1361–1379) as "S corporation status" than as the "Tax Treatment of S Corporations and Their Shareholders."

Citing the Code. Code Sections are often broken down into subparts.[2] Section 2(a)(1)(A) serves as an example.

§ 2 (a) (1) (A)
Abbreviation for "Section"
Section number
Subsection number[3]
Paragraph designation
Subparagraph designation

Broken down by content, Section 2(a)(1)(A) appears as follows:

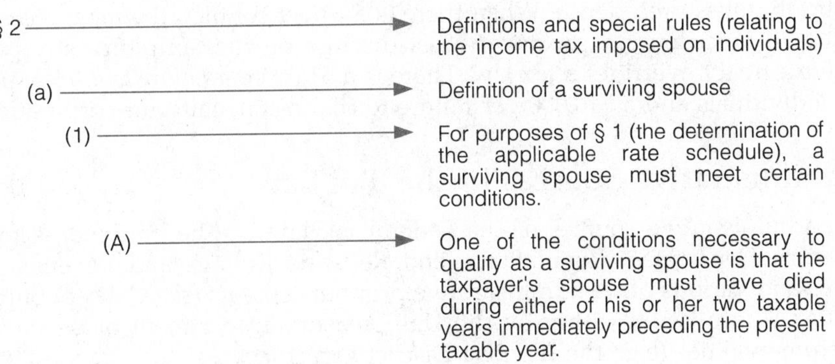
§ 2
Definitions and special rules (relating to the income tax imposed on individuals)
(a)
Definition of a surviving spouse
(1)
For purposes of § 1 (the determination of the applicable rate schedule), a surviving spouse must meet certain conditions.
(A)
One of the conditions necessary to qualify as a surviving spouse is that the taxpayer's spouse must have died during either of his or her two taxable years immediately preceding the present taxable year.

FIGURE 28–2
Role of Joint Conference Committee

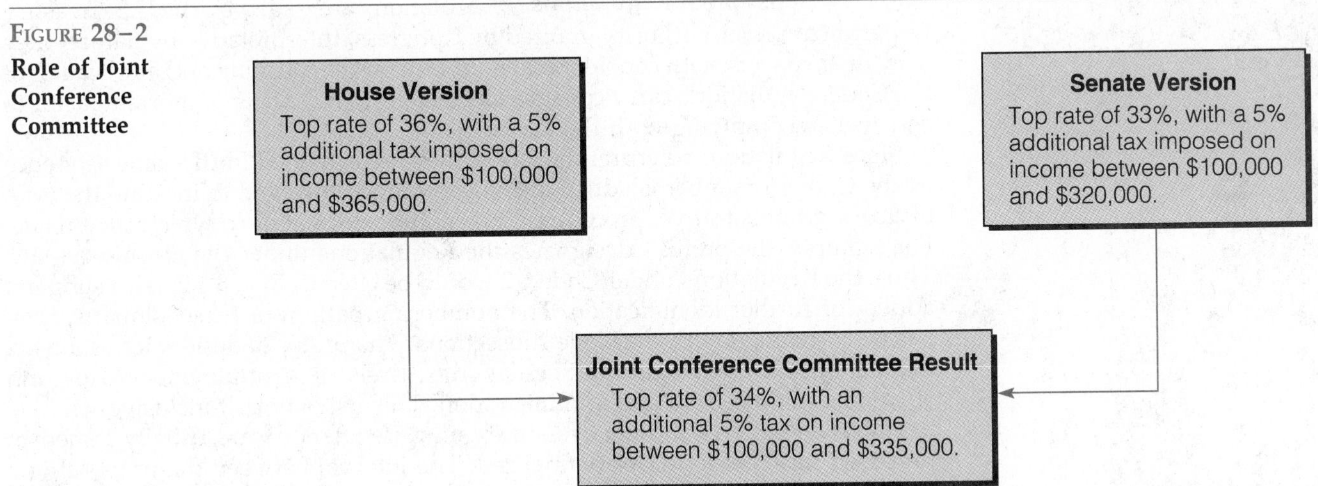
House Version
Top rate of 36%, with a 5% additional tax imposed on income between $100,000 and $365,000.
Senate Version
Top rate of 33%, with a 5% additional tax imposed on income between $100,000 and $320,000.
Joint Conference Committee Result
Top rate of 34%, with an additional 5% tax on income between $100,000 and $335,000.

2. Some Code Sections do not have subparts. See, for example, §§ 211 and 241.

3. Some Code Sections omit the subsection designation and use, instead, the paragraph designation as the first subpart. See, for example, §§ 212(1) and 1221(1).

Throughout the text, references to the Code Sections are in the form given above. The symbols "§" and "§§" are used in place of "Section" and "Sections." Unless otherwise stated, all Code references are to the Internal Revenue Code of 1986. The following table summarizes the format used in the text:

Complete Reference	Text Reference
Section 2(a)(1)(A) of the Internal Revenue Code of 1986	§ 2(a)(1)(A)
Sections 1 and 2 of the Internal Revenue Code of 1986	§§ 1 and 2
Section 2 of the Internal Revenue Code of 1954	§ 2 of the Internal Revenue Code of 1954
Section 12(d) of the Internal Revenue Code of 1939[4]	§ 12(d) of the Internal Revenue Code of 1939

Effect of Treaties. The United States signs certain tax treaties (sometimes called tax conventions) with foreign countries to render mutual assistance in tax enforcement and to avoid double taxation. Neither a tax law nor a tax treaty automatically takes precedence. When there is a direct conflict, the most recent item will take precedence. A taxpayer must disclose on the tax return any position where a treaty overrides a tax law. There is a $1,000 per *failure to disclose* penalty for individuals and a $10,000 per failure to disclose penalty for corporations.

Administrative Sources of the Tax Law

The administrative sources of the Federal tax law can be grouped as follows: Treasury Department Regulations, and Revenue Rulings and Revenue Procedures and various other administrative pronouncements (see Concept Summary 28–1). All are issued either by the U.S. Treasury Department or by one of its instrumentalities (e.g., the IRS or a District Director).

Treasury Department Regulations. Regulations are issued by the U.S. Treasury Department under authority granted by Congress. Interpretative by nature, they provide taxpayers with considerable guidance on the meaning and application of the Code. Regulations carry considerable weight. They are an important factor to consider in complying with the tax law.

Since Regulations interpret the Code, they are arranged in the same sequence as the Code. A number is added at the beginning, however, to indicate the type of tax or administrative, procedural, or definitional matter to which they relate. For example, the prefix 1 designates the Regulations under the income tax law. Thus, the Regulations under Code § 2 would be cited as Reg. § 1.2, with subparts added for further identification. The numbering pattern of these subparts often has no correlation with the Code subsections. The prefix 20 designates estate tax Regulations, 25 covers gift tax Regulations, 31 relates to employment taxes, and 301 refers to procedure and administration. This list is not all-inclusive.

New Regulations and changes in existing Regulations are usually issued in proposed form before they are finalized. The interval between the proposal of a Regulation and its finalization permits taxpayers and other interested parties to comment on the propriety of the proposal. Proposed Regulations under Code

4. § 12(d) of the Internal Revenue Code of 1939 is the predecessor to § 2 of the Internal Revenue Code of 1954 and the Internal Revenue Code of 1986.

§ 2, for example, are cited as Prop.Reg. § 1.2. The Tax Court indicates that proposed Regulations carry no more weight than a position advanced in a written brief prepared by a litigating party before the Tax Court. *Finalized* Regulations have the force and effect of law.

Sometimes the Treasury Department issues *temporary* Regulations relating to elections and other matters where speed is important. These Regulations are issued without the comment period required for proposed Regulations. Temporary Regulations have the same authoritative value as final Regulations and may be cited as precedents. Temporary Regulations now must also be issued as proposed Regulations and automatically expire within three years after the date of issuance.

Proposed, temporary and final Regulations are published in the *Federal Register* and are reproduced in major tax services. Final Regulations are issued as Treasury Decisions.

Regulations may also be classified as *legislative, interpretative,* or *procedural.* This classification scheme is discussed under Assessing the Validity of a Treasury Regulation later in the chapter.

Revenue Rulings and Revenue Procedures. *Revenue Rulings* are official pronouncements of the National Office of the IRS. Like Regulations, they are designed to provide interpretation of the tax law. However, they do not carry the same legal force and effect as Regulations and usually deal with more restricted problems. In addition, Regulations are approved by the Secretary of the Treasury, whereas Revenue Rulings are not. Both Revenue Rulings and Revenue Procedures serve an important function in that they provide guidance to IRS personnel and taxpayers in handling routine tax matters.

A Revenue Ruling often results from a specific taxpayer's request for a letter ruling. If the IRS believes that a taxpayer's request for a letter ruling deserves official publication due to its widespread impact, the holding will be converted

Concept Summary 28–1
Administrative Sources

Source	Location	Authority**
Regulations	*Federal Register**	Force and effect of law.
Proposed Regulations	*Federal Register** *Internal Revenue Bulletin* *Cumulative Bulletin*	Preview of final Regulations.
Temporary Regulations	*Federal Register** *Internal Revenue Bulletin* *Cumulative Bulletin*	May be cited as a precedent.
Revenue Rulings Revenue Procedures	*Internal Revenue Bulletin* *Cumulative Bulletin*	Do not have the force and effect of law.
General Counsel's Memoranda Actions on Decisions Technical Advice Memoranda	Tax Analysts' *Tax Notes;* RIA's *Internal Memoranda* of the IRS; CCH's *IRS Position Reporter*	May not be cited as a precedent.
Letter Ruling	Research Institute of America and Commerce Clearing House loose-leaf services	Applicable only to taxpayer addressed. No precedential force.

*Finalized, proposed, and temporary Regulations are published in soft-cover form by several publishers.
**Each of these sources may be substantial authority for purposes of the accuracy-related penalty in § 6662. A lower source has less weight than a higher source in this list. Notice 90–20, 1990–1 C.B. 328.

into a Revenue Ruling and issued for the information and guidance of taxpayers, tax practitioners, and IRS personnel. Names, identifying descriptions, and money amounts are changed to conceal the identity of the requesting taxpayer.

In addition to arising from taxpayer requests, Revenue Rulings may arise from Technical Advice to District Offices of the IRS, court decisions, suggestions from tax practitioner groups, and various tax publications.

Revenue Procedures are issued in the same manner as Revenue Rulings, but deal with the internal management practices and procedures of the IRS. Familiarity with these procedures increases taxpayer compliance and helps make the administration of the tax laws more efficient. The failure of a taxpayer to follow a Revenue Procedure can result in unnecessary delay or, in a discretionary situation, can cause the IRS to decline to act on behalf of the taxpayer.

Revenue Rulings and Revenue Procedures are published weekly by the U.S. Government in the *Internal Revenue Bulletin* (I.R.B.). Semiannually, the *Bulletins* for a six-month period are gathered together, reorganized by Code Section classification, and published in a bound volume called the *Cumulative Bulletin* (C.B.).[5]

The proper form for citing Rulings and Procedures depends on whether the item has been published in the *Cumulative Bulletin* or is available only in I.R.B. form. Consider, for example, the following transition:

Temporary Citation	Rev.Rul. 91–36, I.R.B. No. 26, 4. *Explanation:* Revenue Ruling Number 36, appearing on page 4 of the 26th weekly issue of the *Internal Revenue Bulletin* for 1991.
Permanent Citation	Rev.Rul. 91–36, 1991–2 C.B. 17. *Explanation:* Revenue Ruling Number 36, appearing on page 17 of Volume 2 of the *Cumulative Bulletin* for 1991.

Since the second volume of the 1991 *Cumulative Bulletin* was not published until August of 1992, the I.R.B. citation had to be used until that time. After the publication of the *Cumulative Bulletin,* the C.B. citation is proper. The basic portion of both citations (Rev.Rul. 91–36) indicates that this was the 36th Revenue Ruling issued by the IRS during 1991.

Revenue Procedures are cited in the same manner, except that "Rev.Proc." is substituted for "Rev.Rul." Procedures, like Rulings, are published in the *Internal Revenue Bulletin* (the temporary source) and later transferred to the *Cumulative Bulletin* (the permanent source).

Letter Rulings. Individual (letter) rulings are issued upon a taxpayer's request and describe how the IRS will treat a proposed transaction for tax purposes. They apply only to the taxpayer who asks for and obtains the ruling, but post-1984 letter rulings may be substantial authority for purposes of the accuracy-related penalty. This procedure may seem like the only real way to carry out effective tax planning. However, the IRS limits the issuance of individual rulings to restricted, preannounced areas of taxation. The main reason the IRS will not rule in certain areas is that they involve fact-oriented situations. Thus, it is not possible to obtain a ruling on many of the problems that are particularly troublesome to taxpayers.

Although letter rulings once were private and not available to the public, the law now requires the IRS to make such rulings available for public inspection

5. Usually, only two volumes of the *Cumulative Bulletin* are published each year. However, when Congress has enacted major tax legislation, other volumes may be published containing the Congressional Committee Reports supporting the Revenue Act. See, for example, the two extra volumes for 1984 dealing with the Deficit Reduction Act of 1984. The 1984–3 *Cumulative Bulletin,* Volume 1, contains the text of the law itself; 1984–3, Volume 2, contains the Committee Reports. This makes a total of four volumes of the *Cumulative Bulletin* for 1984: 1984–1; 1984–2; 1984–3, Volume 1; and 1984–3, Volume 2.

after identifying details are deleted. Published digests of private letter rulings can be found in RIA's *Private Letter Rulings*, BNA *Daily Tax Reports*, and Tax Analysts' *Tax Notes*. *IRS Letter Rulings Reports* (published by Commerce Clearing House) contain both digests and full texts of all letter rulings. *Letter Ruling Review* (published by Tax Analysts), a monthly publication, selects and discusses the more important of the over 300 letter rulings issued each month.

Letter rulings are issued multidigit file numbers, which indicate the year and week of issuance as well as the number of the ruling during that week. Consider, for example, Ltr.Rul. 9209004 dealing with investment interest expense:

92	09	004
Year 1992	9th week of issuance	Number of the ruling issued during the 9th week

Letter rulings may be either *mandatory* or *discretionary*. A taxpayer *must* obtain a favorable ruling for certain changes in accounting procedures (e.g., a change in accounting period under § 442 or a change in accounting method under § 446). Such rulings are mandatory rulings. Discretionary rulings are not required by law; taxpayers request them at their own discretion. Further, the IRS issues these rulings at its discretion. For example, a taxpayer might request a ruling as to the taxability of a corporate reorganization. In general, the IRS will rule on prospective transactions and on completed transactions where a return has not been filed for matters concerning income tax, gift tax, estate tax, generation-skipping transfer tax, and § 2032A ("Valuation of Certain Farm, Etc., Real Property").

Other Administrative Pronouncements. *Treasury Decisions* (TDs) are issued by the Treasury Department to promulgate new Regulations, amend or otherwise change existing Regulations, or announce the position of the Government on selected court decisions. Like Revenue Rulings and Revenue Procedures, TDs are published initially in the *Internal Revenue Bulletin* and subsequently transferred to the *Cumulative Bulletin.*

The IRS publishes other administrative communications in the *Internal Revenue Bulletin,* such as Announcements, Notices, LRs (proposed Regulations), and Prohibited Transaction Exemptions.

Like letter rulings, *determination letters* are issued at the request of taxpayers and provide guidance on the application of the tax law. They differ from letter rulings in that the issuing source is the District Director rather than the National Office of the IRS. Also, determination letters usually involve completed (as opposed to proposed) transactions. Determination letters are not published and are made known only to the party making the request.

Example 1

The shareholders of Red Corporation and Green Corporation want assurance that the consolidation of the corporations into Blue Corporation will be a nontaxable reorganization. The proper approach would be to ask the National Office of the IRS to issue a letter ruling concerning the income tax effect of the proposed transaction. ◆

Example 2

Chris operates a barber shop in which he employs eight barbers. To comply with the rules governing income tax and payroll tax withholdings, Chris wants to know whether the barbers working for him are employees or independent contractors. The proper procedure would be to request a determination letter on their status from the appropriate District Director. ◆

The National Office of the IRS releases *Technical Advice Memoranda* (TAMs) weekly. TAMs resemble letter rulings in that they give the IRS's determination of an issue. Letter rulings, however, are responses to requests by taxpayers, whereas TAMs are issued by the National Office of the IRS in response to questions raised by IRS field personnel during audits. TAMs deal with completed rather than proposed transactions and are often requested for questions relating to exempt organizations and employee plans. Although TAMs are not officially published and may not be cited or used as precedent, post-1984 TAMs may be substantial authority for purposes of the accuracy-related penalties.

The law now requires that several internal memoranda that constitute the working law of the IRS be released. These General Counsel Memoranda (GCMs) and Actions on Decisions (AODs) are not officially published, and the IRS indicates that they may not be cited as precedents by taxpayers. However, these working documents do explain the IRS's position on various issues.

Judicial Sources of the Tax Law

The Judicial Process in General. After a taxpayer has exhausted some or all of the remedies available within the IRS (no satisfactory settlement has been reached at the agent level or at the Appeals Division level), the dispute can be taken to the Federal courts. The dispute is first considered by a *court of original jurisdiction* (known as a trial court), with any appeal (either by the taxpayer or the IRS) taken to the appropriate appellate court. In most situations, the taxpayer has a choice of any of four trial courts: a Federal District Court, the U.S. Court of Federal Claims, the U.S. Tax Court, or the Small Claims Division of the U.S. Tax Court. The trial and *appellate court* system for Federal tax litigation is illustrated in Figure 28–3.

The broken line between the U.S. Tax Court and the Small Claims Division indicates that there is no appeal from the Small Claims Division. The jurisdiction of the Small Claims Division is limited to cases involving amounts of $10,000 or less.

American law, following English law, is frequently "made" by judicial decisions. Under the doctrine of *stare decisis,* each case (except in the Small Claims Division) has precedential value for future cases with the same controlling set of facts. Most Federal and state appellate court decisions and some decisions of trial

Figure 28–3
Federal Judicial Tax Process

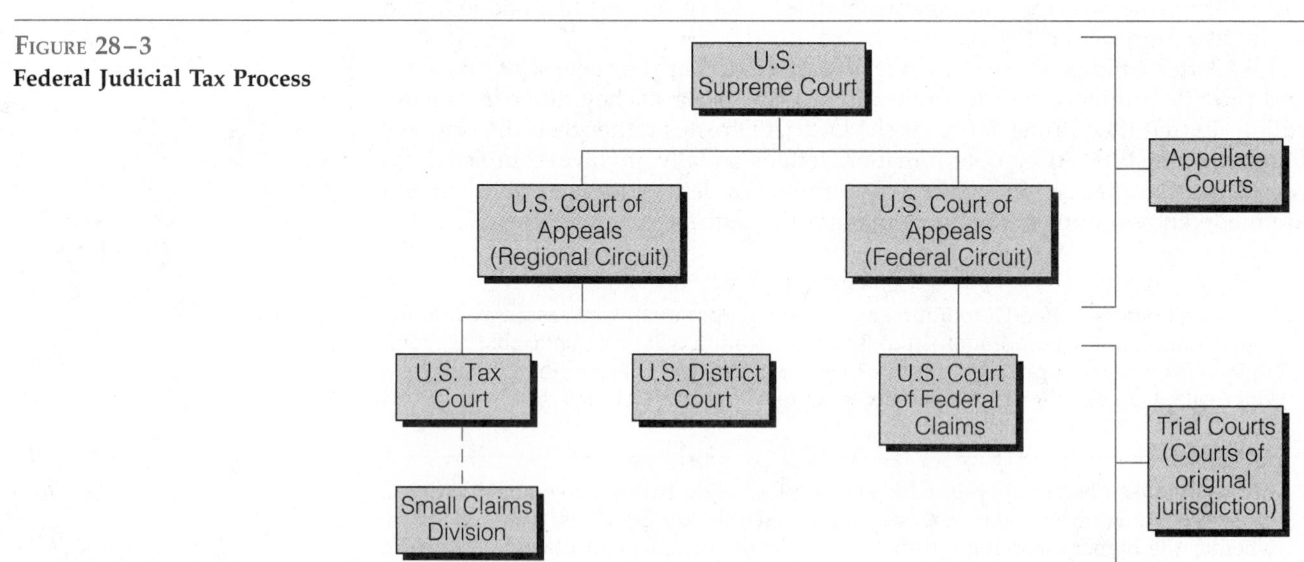

courts are published. Almost 3.5 million judicial opinions have been published in the United States, and over 30,000 cases are published each year. Published court decisions are organized by jurisdiction (Federal or state) and level of court (trial or appellate).

A decision of a particular court is called its *holding*. Sometimes a decision includes dicta or incidental opinions beyond the current facts. Such passing remarks, illustrations, or analogies are not essential to the current holding. Although the holding has precedential value under *stare decisis,* dicta are not binding on a future court.

Trial Courts. The differences between the various trial courts (courts of original jurisdiction) can be summarized as follows:

- *Number of courts.* There is only one U.S. Court of Federal Claims and only one Tax Court, but there are many Federal District Courts. The taxpayer does not select the District Court that will hear the dispute but must sue in the one that has jurisdiction.
- *Number of judges.* Each District Court has only 1 judge, the Court of Federal Claims has 16 judges, and the Tax Court has 19 regular judges. In the case of the Tax Court, however, the entire court will review a case (the case is sent to court conference) only when important or novel tax issues are involved. Most cases will be heard and decided by 1 of the 19 judges.
- *Location.* The Court of Federal Claims meets most often in Washington, D.C., while a District Court meets at a prescribed seat for the particular district. Each state has at least one District Court, and many of the populous states have more than one. Choosing the District Court usually minimizes the inconvenience and expense of traveling for the taxpayer and his or her counsel. The Tax Court is officially based in Washington, D.C., but the various judges travel to different parts of the country and hear cases at predetermined locations and dates. This procedure eases the distance problem for the taxpayer, but it can mean a delay before the case comes to trial and is decided.
- *Jurisdiction of the Court of Federal Claims.* The Court of Federal Claims has jurisdiction over any claim against the United States that is based upon the Constitution, any Act of Congress, or any regulation of an executive department. Thus, the Court of Federal Claims hears nontax litigation as well as tax cases. This forum appears to be more favorable for issues having an equitable or pro-business orientation (as opposed to purely technical issues) and those requiring extensive discovery.
- *Jurisdiction of the Tax Court and District Courts.* The Tax Court hears only tax cases and is the most popular forum. The District Courts hear nontax litigation as well as tax cases. Many Tax Court justices have been appointed from IRS or Treasury Department positions. For this reason, some people suggest that the Tax Court has more expertise in tax matters.
- *Jury trial.* The only court in which a taxpayer can obtain a jury trial is a District Court. Juries can decide only questions of fact and not questions of law. Therefore, taxpayers who choose the District Court route often do not request a jury trial. If a jury trial is not elected, the judge will decide all issues. Note that a District Court decision is controlling only in the district in which the court has jurisdiction.
- *Payment of deficiency.* Before the Court of Federal Claims or a District Court can have jurisdiction, the taxpayer must pay the tax deficiency assessed by the IRS and then sue for a refund. If the taxpayer wins (assuming no successful appeal by the Government), the tax paid plus appropriate

interest will be recovered. Jurisdiction in the Tax Court, however, is usually obtained without first paying the assessed tax deficiency. In the event the taxpayer loses in the Tax Court (and no appeal is taken or an appeal is unsuccessful), the deficiency must be paid with accrued interest. With the elimination of the deduction for personal (consumer) interest, the Tax Court route of delaying payment of the deficiency can become expensive. For example, to earn 7 percent after tax, a taxpayer with a 31 percent marginal tax rate will have to earn 10.14 percent. By paying the tax, a taxpayer limits underpayment interest and penalties on underpayment interest.

- *Appeals.* Appeals from a District Court or a Tax Court decision are to the appropriate U.S. Court of Appeals. Appeals from the Court of Federal Claims go to the Court of Appeals for the Federal Circuit.
- *Decision for taxpayer versus IRS.* The recent won and lost record of the IRS and taxpayers in the trial courts and the appellate courts is summarized in Figure 28–4. Although a taxpayer has little chance of a clear decision in the Tax Court, a split decision is more likely in that court.
- *Bankruptcy.* When a taxpayer files a bankruptcy petition, the IRS, like other creditors, is prevented from taking action against the taxpayer. Sometimes a bankruptcy court may settle a tax claim.

Appellate Courts. The losing party can appeal a trial court decision to a Circuit Court of Appeals. The 11 geographical circuits, the circuit for the District of Columbia, and the Federal Circuit are listed in Figure 28–5. The appropriate

FIGURE 28–4
Won and Lost Record of the IRS versus Taxpayers

	Decided in Favor of IRS	Decided in Favor of Taxpayer	Split Decision
Small Claims Division			
1990	46.0%	19.0%	35.0%
1989	46.4%	15.0%	38.6%
U.S. Tax Court			
1990	33.0%	3.0%	64.0%
1989	31.4%	3.6%	65.0%
1988	45.8%	5.0%	49.2%
District Courts			
1990	65.2%	23.2%	11.6%
1989	78.8%	17.7%	3.5%
1988	81.5%	15.1%	3.4%
Court of Federal Claims			
1990	73.5%	14.3%	12.2%
1989	89.1%	8.2%	2.7%
1988	93.4%	2.4%	4.2%
Courts of Appeals			
1990	75.9%	19.0%	5.1%
1989	88.5%	9.5%	2.0%
1988	75.8%	17.4%	6.8%
Supreme Court			
1990	75.0%	25.0%	0%
1989	66.7%	33.3%	0%
1988	66.7%	33.3%	0%

circuit for an appeal depends upon where the litigation originated. For example, an appeal from New York goes to the Second Circuit.

If the Government loses at the trial court level (District Court, Tax Court, or Court of Federal Claims), it need not (and frequently does not) appeal. The fact that an appeal is not made, however, does not indicate that the IRS agrees with the result and will not litigate similar issues in the future. The IRS may decide not to appeal for a number of reasons. First, the current litigation load may be heavy. As a consequence, the IRS may decide that available personnel should be assigned to other, more important cases. Second, the IRS may determine that this is not a good case to appeal. For example, the taxpayer may be in a sympathetic position, or the facts may be particularly strong in his or her favor. In that event, the IRS may wait to test the legal issues involved with a taxpayer who has a much weaker case. Third, if the appeal is from a District Court or the Tax Court, the Court of Appeals of jurisdiction could have some bearing on whether the IRS decides to pursue an appeal. Based on past experience and precedent, the IRS may conclude that the chance for success on a particular issue might be more promising in another Court of Appeals. If so, the IRS will wait for a similar case to arise in a different jurisdiction.

The Federal Circuit at the appellate level provides a taxpayer with an alternative forum to the Court of Appeals of his or her home circuit for the appeal. Appeals from both the Tax Court and the District Court go to a taxpayer's home circuit. Now, when a particular circuit has issued an adverse decision, the taxpayer may wish to select the Court of Federal Claims route since any appeal will be to the Federal Circuit.

District Courts, the Tax Court, and the Court of Federal Claims must abide by the precedents set by the Court of Appeals of jurisdiction. A particular Court of

Figure 28–5
Court of Appeals Jurisdictions

First

Maine
Massachusetts
New Hampshire
Rhode Island
Puerto Rico

Second

Connecticut
New York
Vermont

Third

Delaware
New Jersey
Pennsylvania
Virgin Islands

District of Columbia

Washington, D.C.

Fourth

Maryland
North Carolina
South Carolina
Virginia
West Virginia

Fifth

Canal Zone
Louisiana
Mississippi
Texas

Sixth

Kentucky
Michigan
Ohio
Tennessee

Seventh

Illinois
Indiana
Wisconsin

Eighth

Arkansas
Iowa
Minnesota
Missouri
Nebraska
North Dakota
South Dakota

Ninth

Alaska
Arizona
California
Hawaii
Idaho
Montana
Nevada
Oregon
Washington
Guam

Tenth

Colorado
Kansas
New Mexico
Oklahoma
Utah
Wyoming

Eleventh

Alabama
Florida
Georgia

Federal Circuit

All of the jurisdictions (where the case originates in the Court of Federal Claims)

Appeals need not follow the decisions of another Court of Appeals. All courts, however, must follow the decisions of the U.S. Supreme Court.

The Tax Court is a national court, meaning that it hears and decides cases from all parts of the country. For many years, the Tax Court followed a policy of deciding cases based on what it thought the result should be, even when its decision might be appealed to a Court of Appeals that had previously decided a similar case differently. A number of years ago this policy was changed in the *Golsen*[6] decision. Now the Tax Court will decide a case as it feels the law should be applied *only* if the Court of Appeals of appropriate jurisdiction has not yet passed on the issue or has previously decided a similar case in accord with the Tax Court's decision. If the Court of Appeals of appropriate jurisdiction has previously held otherwise, the Tax Court will conform even though it disagrees with the holding. This policy is known as the *Golsen* rule.

Example 3

Emily lives in Texas and sues in the Tax Court on Issue A. The Fifth Court of Appeals is the appellate court of appropriate jurisdiction. The Fifth Court of Appeals has already decided, in a case based on similar facts and involving a different taxpayer, that Issue A should be resolved against the Government. Although the Tax Court feels that the Fifth Court of Appeals is wrong, under its *Golsen* policy it will render judgment for Emily. Shortly thereafter, Rashad, a resident of New York, in a comparable case, sues in the Tax Court on Issue A. Assume that the Second Court of Appeals, the appellate court of appropriate jurisdiction, has never expressed itself on Issue A. Presuming the Tax Court has not reconsidered its position on Issue A, it will decide against Rashad. Thus, it is entirely possible for two taxpayers suing in the same court to end up with opposite results merely because they live in different parts of the country. ◆

Appeal to the U.S. Supreme Court is by *Writ of Certiorari.* If the Court accepts jurisdiction, it will grant the Writ (*Cert. Granted*). Most often, it will deny

Concept Summary 28–2
Federal Judicial System: Trial Courts

Issue	U.S. Tax Court	U.S. District Court	U.S. Court of Federal Claims
Number of judges per court	19*	1	16
Payment of deficiency before trial	No	Yes	Yes
Jury trial available	No	Yes	No
Types of disputes	Tax cases only	Most criminal and civil issues	Claims against the United States
Jurisdiction	Nationwide	Location of taxpayer	Nationwide
IRS acquiescence policy	Yes	No	No
Appeal route	U.S. Court of Appeals	U.S. Court of Appeals	U.S. Court of Appeals for the Federal Circuit

*There are also 14 special trial judges and 9 senior judges.

6. *Jack E. Golsen*, 54 T.C. 742 (1970).

jurisdiction (*Cert. Denied*). For whatever reason or reasons, the Supreme Court rarely hears tax cases. The Court usually grants certiorari to resolve a conflict among the Courts of Appeals (e.g., two or more appellate courts have assumed opposing positions on a particular issue) or where the tax issue is extremely important. The granting of a *Writ of Certiorari* indicates that at least four members of the Supreme Court believe that the issue is of sufficient importance to be heard by the full Court.

The *role* of appellate courts is limited to a review of the record of trial compiled by the trial courts. Thus, the appellate process usually involves a determination of whether the trial court applied the proper law in arriving at its decision. Usually, an appellate court will not dispute a lower court's fact-finding determination.

The result of an appeal can be any of a number of possibilities. The appellate court may approve (affirm) or disapprove (reverse) the lower court's finding, or it may send the case back for further consideration (remand). When many issues are involved, a mixed result is not unusual. Thus, the lower court may be affirmed (*aff'd.*) on Issue A and reversed (*rev'd.*) on Issue B, while Issue C is remanded (*rem'd.*) for additional fact finding.

When more than one judge is involved in the decision-making process, disagreements are not uncommon. In addition to the majority view, one or more judges may concur (agree with the result reached but not with some or all of the reasoning) or dissent (disagree with the result). In any one case, the majority view controls. But concurring and dissenting views can have influence on other courts or, at some subsequent date when the composition of the court has changed, even on the same court.

Knowledge of several terms is important in understanding court decisions. The term *plaintiff* refers to the party requesting action in a court, and the *defendant* is the party against whom the suit is brought. Sometimes a court uses the terms *petitioner* and *respondent.* In general, "petitioner" is a synonym for "plaintiff," and "defendant" is a synonym for "respondent." At the trial court level, a taxpayer is normally the plaintiff (or petitioner), and the Government is the defendant (or respondent). If the taxpayer wins and the Government appeals as the new petitioner (or appellee), the taxpayer becomes the new respondent.

Judicial Citations—General. Having briefly described the judicial process, it is appropriate to consider the more practical problem of the relationship of case law to tax research. As previously noted, court decisions are an important source of tax law. The ability to locate a case and to cite it is therefore a must in working with the tax law. Judicial citations usually follow a standard pattern: case name, volume number, reporter series, page or paragraph number, and court (where necessary). Specific citation formats for each court are presented in the following sections.

Judicial Citations—The U.S. Tax Court. A good starting point is the U.S. Tax Court (formerly the Board of Tax Appeals). The Court issues two types of decisions: Regular and Memorandum. The Chief Judge decides whether the opinion is issued as a Regular or Memorandum decision. The distinction between the two involves both substance and form. In terms of substance, *Memorandum* decisions deal with situations necessitating only the application of already established principles of law. *Regular* decisions involve novel issues not previously resolved by the Court. In actual practice, however, this distinction is not always preserved. Not infrequently, Memorandum decisions will be encountered that appear to warrant Regular status, and vice versa. At any rate, do not conclude that Memorandum decisions possess no value as precedents. Both represent the position of the Tax Court and, as such, can be relied upon.

The Regular and Memorandum decisions issued by the Tax Court also differ in form. Memorandum decisions are officially published in mimeograph form only. Regular decisions are published by the U.S. Government in a series called *Tax Court of the United States Reports.* Each volume of these *Reports* covers a six-month period (January 1 through June 30 and July 1 through December 31) and is given a succeeding volume number. But, as was true of the *Cumulative Bulletins,* there is usually a time lag between the date a decision is rendered and the date it appears in bound form. A temporary citation may be necessary to help the researcher locate a recent Regular decision. Consider, for example, the temporary and permanent citations for *Robert O. Fowler, Jr.,* a decision filed on April 22, 1992:

Temporary Citation	*Robert O. Fowler, Jr.,* 98 T.C. ____, No. 34 (1992). *Explanation:* Page number left blank because not yet known.
Permanent Citation	*Robert O. Fowler, Jr.,* 98 T.C. 503 (1992). *Explanation:* Page number now available.

Both citations tell us that the case will ultimately appear in Volume 98 of the *Tax Court of the United States Reports.* Until this volume is bound and made available to the general public, however, the page number must be left blank. Instead, the temporary citation identifies the case as being the 34th Regular decision issued by the Tax Court since Volume 97 ended. With this information, the decision can easily be located in either of the special Tax Court services published by Commerce Clearing House and Research Institute of America (formerly by Prentice-Hall). Once Volume 98 is released, the permanent citation can be substituted and the number of the case dropped.

Before 1943, the Tax Court was called the Board of Tax Appeals, and its decisions were published as the *United States Board of Tax Appeals Reports* (B.T.A.). These 47 volumes cover the period from 1924 to 1942. For example, the citation *Karl Pauli,* 11 B.T.A. 784 (1928) refers to the 11th volume of the *Board of Tax Appeals Reports,* page 784, issued in 1928.

One further distinction between Regular and Memorandum decisions of the Tax Court involves the IRS procedure of *acquiescence* (A or Acq.) or *nonacquiescence* (NA or Nonacq.). If the IRS loses in a Regular decision, it usually indicates whether it agrees or disagrees with the result reached by the Court. This acquiescence or nonacquiescence is published in the *Internal Revenue Bulletin* and the *Cumulative Bulletin.* This procedure is not followed for Memorandum decisions or for the decisions of other courts. The IRS can retroactively revoke an acquiescence. In addition, the IRS sometimes announces that it will or will not follow a decision of another Federal court on similar facts. Such an announcement is not considered to be an acquiescence or nonacquiescence.

Although Memorandum decisions are not published by the U.S. Government, they are published by Commerce Clearing House (CCH) and Research Institute of America (RIA [formerly by Prentice-Hall]). Consider, for example, the three different ways that *Jack D. Carr* can be cited:

Jack D. Carr, T.C.Memo. 1985–19
The 19th Memorandum decision issued by the Tax Court in 1985.

Jack D. Carr, 49 TCM 507
Page 507 of Vol. 49 of the CCH *Tax Court Memorandum Decisions.*

Jack D. Carr, RIA T.C.Mem.Dec. ¶85,019
Paragraph 85,019 of the RIA *T.C. Memorandum Decisions.*

Note that the third citation contains the same information as the first. Thus, ¶85,019 indicates the following information about the case: year 1985, 19th

T.C.Memo. decision.[7] Although the RIA citation does not include a specific volume number, the paragraph citation (85,019) indicates that the decision can be found in the 1985 volume of the RIA Memorandum Decision service.

Judicial Citations—The U.S. District Court, Court of Federal Claims, and Courts of Appeals. District Court, Court of Federal Claims, (formerly the Claims Court), Court of Appeals, and Supreme Court decisions dealing with Federal tax matters are reported in both the CCH *U.S. Tax Cases* (USTC) and the RIA *American Federal Tax Reports* (AFTR) series.

Federal District Court decisions, dealing with *both* tax and nontax issues, are also published by West Publishing Company in its *Federal Supplement Series.* A District Court case can be cited in three different forms as the following examples illustrate:

Simons-Eastern Co. v. U.S., 73–1 USTC ¶9279 (D.Ct.Ga., 1972).

Explanation: Reported in the first volume of the *U.S. Tax Cases* (USTC) published by Commerce Clearing House for calendar year 1973 (73–1) and located at paragraph 9279 (¶9279).

Simons-Eastern Co. v. U.S., 31 AFTR2d 73–640 (D.Ct.Ga., 1972).

Explanation: Reported in the 31st volume of the second series of the *American Federal Tax Reports* (AFTR2d) published by RIA and beginning on page 640. The "73" preceding the page number indicates the year the case was published but is a designation used only in recent decisions.

Simons-Eastern Co. v. U.S., 354 F.Supp. 1003 (D.Ct.Ga., 1972).

Explanation: Reported in the 354th volume of the *Federal Supplement Series* (F.Supp.) published by West Publishing Company and beginning on page 1003.

In all of the preceding citations, note that the name of the case is the same (Simons-Eastern Co. being the taxpayer), as are the references to the Federal District Court of Georgia (D.Ct.Ga.) and the year the decision was rendered (1972).[8]

Decisions of the Claims Court and the Courts of Appeals are published in the USTCs, AFTRs, and a West Publishing Company reporter called the *Federal Second Series* (F.2d). However, beginning in October 1982, decisions of the Claims Court are published in another West Publishing Company reporter entitled the *Claims Court Reporter.* The following examples illustrate the different forms:

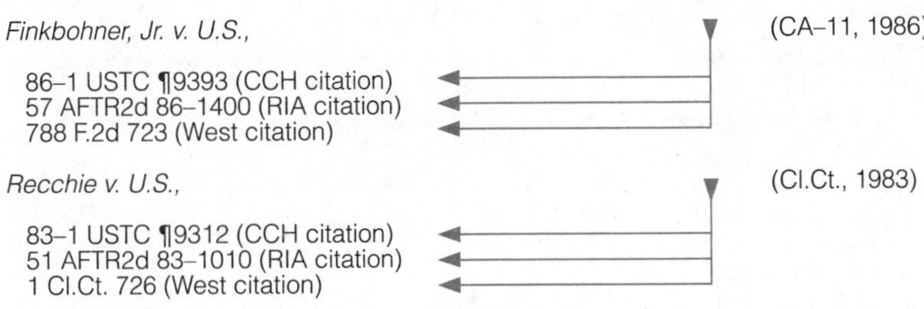

7. In this text, this Memorandum decision of the U.S. Tax Court would be cited as *Jack D. Carr*, 49 TCM 507, T.C.Memo. 1985–19.

8. In this text, the case would be cited in the following form: *Simons-Eastern Co. v. U.S.*, 73–1 USTC ¶9279, 31 AFTR2d 73–640, 354 F.Supp. 1003 (D.Ct.Ga., 1972). Prentice-Hall Information Services is now owned by Research Institute of America. Although new volumes will contain the RIA imprint, many of the older volumes will continue to have the P-H imprint.

Note that *Finkbohner, Jr.* is a decision rendered by the Eleventh Court of Appeals in 1986 (CA–11, 1986), while *Recchie* was issued by the Claims Court in 1983 (Cl.Ct., 1983).

Judicial Citations—The U.S. Supreme Court. Like all other Federal tax cases (except those rendered by the U.S. Tax Court), Supreme Court decisions are published by Commerce Clearing House in the USTCs and by RIA (formerly by Prentice-Hall) in the AFTRs. The U.S. Government Printing Office also publishes these decisions in the *United States Supreme Court Reports* (U.S.), as do West Publishing Company in its *Supreme Court Reporter* (S.Ct.) and the Lawyer's Co-operative Publishing Company in its *United States Reports, Lawyer's Edition* (L.Ed.). The following illustrates the different ways the same decision can be cited:

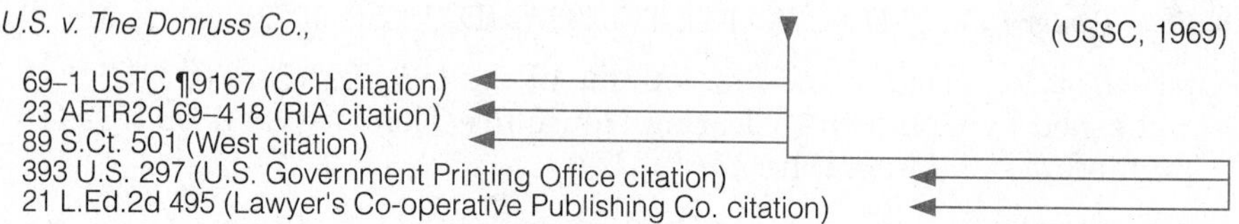

The parenthetical reference (USSC, 1969) identifies the decision as having been rendered by the U.S. Supreme Court in 1969. In this text, the citations of Supreme Court decisions are limited to the CCH (USTC), RIA (AFTR), and West (S.Ct.) versions. See Concept Summary 28–3.

CONCEPT SUMMARY 28–3
JUDICAL SOURCES

Court	Location	Authority
U.S. Supreme Court	S.Ct. Series (West) U.S. Series (U.S. Gov't.) L.Ed. (Lawyer's Co-op.) AFTR (RIA) USTC (CCH)	Highest authority
U.S. Courts of Appeal	Federal 2d (West) AFTR (RIA) USTC (CCH)	Next highest appellate court
Tax Court (Regular decisions)	U.S. Govt. Printing Office RIA/CCH separate services	Highest trial court*
Tax Court (Memorandum decisions)	RIA T.C.Memo (RIA) TCM (CCH)	Less authority than regular T.C. decision
U.S. Claims Court**	Claims Court Reporter (West) AFTR (RIA) USTC (CCH)	Similar authority as Tax Court
U.S. District Courts	F.Supp. Series (West) AFTR (RIA) USTC (CCH)	Lowest trial court
Small Claims Division of Tax Court	Not published	No precedent value

*Theoretically, the Tax Court, Claims Court, and District Courts are on the same level of authority. But some people believe that since the Tax Court hears and decides tax cases from all parts of the country (it is a national court), its decisions may be more authoritative than Claims Court or District Court decisions.
**Now the Court of Federal Claims (effective October 30, 1992).

WORKING WITH THE TAX LAW—TAX RESEARCH

Tax research is the method used to determine the best available solution to a situation that possesses tax consequences. In other words, it is the process of finding a competent and professional conclusion to a tax problem. The problem may originate from completed or proposed transactions. In the case of a completed transaction, the objective of the research is to determine the tax result of what has already taken place. For example, is the expenditure incurred by the taxpayer deductible or not deductible for tax purposes? When dealing with proposed transactions, the tax research process is concerned with the determination of possible tax consequences. To the extent that tax research leads to a choice of alternatives or otherwise influences the future actions of the taxpayer, it becomes the key to effective tax planning.

Tax research involves the following procedures:

- Identifying and refining the problem.
- Locating the appropriate tax law sources.
- Assessing the validity of the tax law sources.
- Arriving at the solution or at alternative solutions while giving due consideration to nontax factors.
- Effectively communicating the solution to the taxpayer or the taxpayer's representative.
- Following up on the solution (where appropriate) in light of new developments.

This process is depicted schematically in Concept Summary 28–4. The broken lines indicate steps of particular interest when tax research is directed toward proposed, rather than completed, transactions.

Identifying the Problem

Problem identification starts with a compilation of the relevant facts involved. In this regard, *all* of the facts that may have a bearing on the problem must be gathered, as any omission could modify the solution reached. To illustrate, consider what appears to be a very simple problem.

EXAMPLE 4

Early in December Fred and Megan review their financial and tax situation with their son, Sam, and daughter-in-law, Dana. Both Sam and Dana are age 21. Sam, a student at a nearby university, owns some publicly traded stock that he inherited from his grandmother. A current sale of the stock would result in approximately $7,000 of gross income. At this point, Fred and Megan provide about 55% of the support of Sam and Dana. Although neither is now employed, Sam has earned $960 and Dana has earned $900. The problem: Should the stock be sold, and would the sale prohibit Fred and Megan from claiming Sam and Dana as dependents? ◆

Refining the Problem

Initial reaction is that Fred and Megan in Example 4 could *not* claim Sam and Dana as dependents if the stock is sold, since Sam would then have earned more than the exemption amount under § 151(d). However, Sam is a full-time student, and § 151(c)(1)(B) allows a son or daughter who is a full-time student and is under age 24 to earn more than the exemption amount without penalizing the parents with the loss of the dependency exemption. Thus, Sam could sell the stock without penalizing his parents under the gross income test. However, the $7,000 income from the sale of the stock might lead to the failure of the greater than 50 percent support test, depending on how much Sam spends for his (or Dana's) support.

Assume, however, that further fact gathering reveals the following additional information:

- Sam does not really need to spend the proceeds from the sale of the stock.
- Sam receives a sizable portion of his own support from a scholarship.

With these new facts, additional research leads to § 152(d) and Regulation § 1.152–1(c), which indicate that a scholarship received by a student is not included for purposes of determining whether the parents furnished more than one-half of the child's support. Further, if Sam does not spend the proceeds from the sale of stock, the unexpended amount is not counted for purposes of the support test. Thus, it appears that the parents would not be denied the dependency exemptions for Sam and Dana.

Locating the Appropriate Tax Law Sources

Once the problem is clearly defined, what is the next step? This is a matter of individual judgment, but most tax research begins with the index volume of the tax service. If the problem is not complex, the researcher may bypass the tax service and turn directly to the Internal Revenue Code and the Treasury

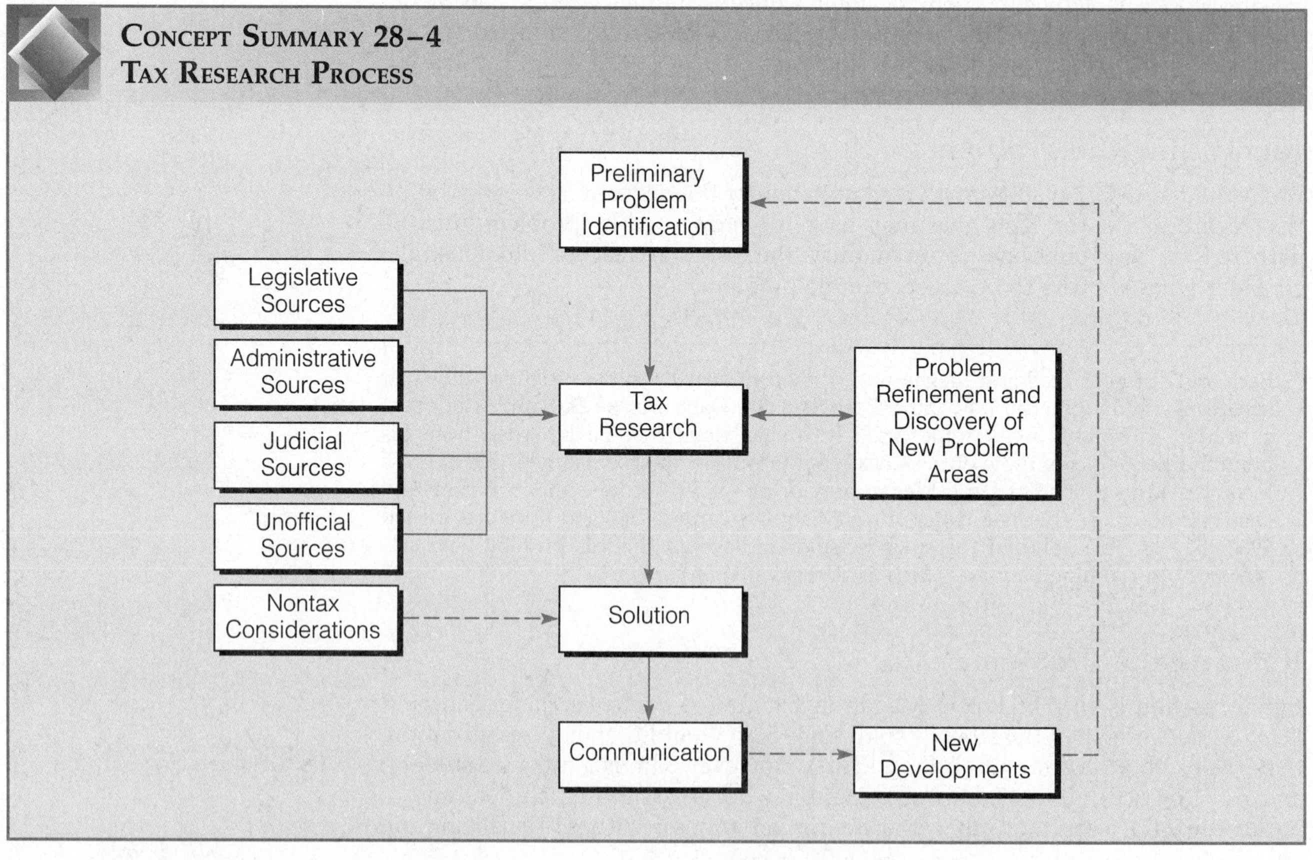

Regulations. For the beginner, the latter procedure saves time and will solve many of the more basic problems. If the researcher does not have a personal copy of the Code or Regulations, resorting to the appropriate volume(s) of a tax service is necessary.

The major tax services available are as follows:

Standard Federal Tax Reporter, Commerce Clearing House.

United States Tax Reporter, Research Institute of America (entitled *Federal Taxes* prior to July 1992).

Mertens Law of Federal Income Taxation, Callaghan and Co.

Federal Tax Coordinator 2d, Research Institute of America.

Tax Management Portfolios, Bureau of National Affairs.

Rabkin and Johnson, *Federal Income, Gift and Estate Taxation,* Matthew Bender, Inc.

Bender's Federal Tax Service, Matthew Bender, Inc.

Working with Tax Services. In this text, it is not feasible to explain the use of any particular tax service—this can be learned only by practice. However, several important observations about the use of tax services cannot be overemphasized. First, never forget to check for current developments. The main text of any service is revised too infrequently to permit reliance on that portion as the *latest* word on any subject. Where current developments can be found depends on which service is being used. The Commerce Clearing House service contains a special volume devoted to current matters. Both RIA's *U.S. Tax Reporter* and *Federal Tax Coordinator 2d* integrate the new developments into the body of the service throughout the year. Second, when dealing with a tax service synopsis of a Treasury Department pronouncement or a judicial decision, remember there is no substitute for the original source.

To illustrate, do not base a conclusion solely on a tax service's commentary on *Simons-Eastern Co. v. U.S.* If the case is vital to the research, look it up! It is possible that the facts of the case are distinguishable from those involved in the problem being researched. This is not to say that the case synopsis contained in the tax service is wrong—it might just be misleading or incomplete.

Tax Periodicals. The various tax periodicals are another source of information. The easiest way to locate a journal article on a particular tax problem is through Commerce Clearing House's *Federal Tax Articles.* This three-volume service includes a subject index, a Code Section number index, and an author's index. In addition, the RIA tax service has a topical "Index to Tax Articles" section that is organized using the RIA paragraph index system.

The following are some of the more useful tax periodicals:

The Journal of Taxation
Warren, Gorham and Lamont
210 South Street
Boston, MA 02111

Tax Law Review
Warren, Gorham and Lamont
210 South Street
Boston, MA 02111

Trusts and Estates
Communication Channels, Inc.
6255 Barfield Road
Atlanta, GA 30328

Estate Planning
Warren, Gorham and Lamont
210 South Street
Boston, MA 02111

Taxation for Accountants
Warren, Gorham and Lamont
210 South Street
Boston, MA 02111

The Tax Executive
1300 North 17th Street
Arlington, VA 22209

Oil and Gas Tax Quarterly
Matthew Bender & Co.
235 East 45th Street
New York, NY 10017

The International Tax Journal
Panel Publishers
14 Plaza Road
Greenvale, NY 11548

TAXES—The Tax Magazine
Commerce Clearing House, Inc.
4025 West Peterson Avenue
Chicago, IL 60646

National Tax Journal
21 East State Street
Columbus, OH 43215

The Tax Adviser
A.I.C.P.A.
1211 Avenue of the Americas
New York, NY 10036

The Practical Accountant
Warren, Gorham and Lamont
210 South Street
Boston, MA 02111

Journal of Corporate Taxation
Warren, Gorham and Lamont
210 South Street
Boston, MA 02111

Journal of Taxation for Individuals
Warren, Gorham and Lamont
210 South Street
Boston, MA 02111

The Tax Lawyer
American Bar Association
1800 M Street, N.W.
Washington, DC 20036

Journal of the American Taxation Association
American Accounting Association
5717 Bessie Drive
Sarasota, FL 34233

Tax Notes
6830 Fairfax Drive
Arlington, VA 22213

Assessing the Validity of the Tax Law Sources

Once a source has been located, the next step is to assess the source in light of the problem at hand. Proper assessment involves careful interpretation of the tax law and consideration of its relevance and validity.

Interpreting the Internal Revenue Code. The language of the Code can be extremely difficult to comprehend fully. For example, one subsection [§ 341(e)] relating to collapsible corporations contains *one* sentence of more than 450 words (twice as many as in the Gettysburg Address). Within this same subsection is another sentence of 300 words.

One author has noted 10 common pitfalls in interpreting the Code:[9]

1. Determine the limitations and exceptions to a provision. Do not permit the language of the Code Section to carry greater or lesser weight than was intended.
2. Just because a Section fails to mention an item does not necessarily mean that the item is excluded.
3. Read definitional clauses carefully.
4. Do not overlook small words such as "and" and "or." There is a world of difference between these two words.
5. Read the Code Section completely; do not jump to conclusions.
6. Watch out for cross-referenced and related provisions since many Sections of the Code are interrelated.
7. Congress is at times not careful when reconciling new Code provisions with existing Sections. Conflicts among Sections, therefore, do arise.

9. H. G. Wong, "Ten Common Pitfalls in Reading the Internal Revenue Code," *The Practical Accountant* (July–August 1972), pp. 30–33.

8. Be alert for hidden definitions; terms in a particular Code Section may be defined in the same Section *or in a separate Section.*
9. Some answers may not be found in the Code. Therefore, it may be necessary to consult the Regulations and/or judicial decisions.
10. Take careful note of measuring words such as "less than 50%," "more than 50%," and "at least 50%."

Assessing the Validity of a Treasury Regulation. Treasury Regulations are often said to have the force and effect of law. This is certainly true for most Regulations, but some judicial decisions have held a Regulation or a portion thereof invalid. Usually, this is done on the grounds that the Regulation is contrary to the intent of Congress. Most often the courts do not question the validity of Regulations because of the belief that "the first administrative interpretation of a provision as it appears in a new act often expresses the general understanding of the times or the actual understanding of those who played an important part when the statute was drafted."[10]

Keep in mind the following observations when assessing the validity of a Regulation:

- IRS agents must give the Code and the Regulations issued thereunder equal weight when dealing with taxpayers and their representatives.
- Proposed Regulations provide a preview of future final Regulations, but they are not binding on the IRS or taxpayers.
- In a challenge, the burden of proof is on the taxpayer to show that the Regulation is wrong. However, a court may invalidate a Regulation that varies from the language of the statute and has no support in the Committee Reports.
- If the taxpayer loses the challenge, the negligence penalty may be imposed. This accuracy-related penalty applies to any failure to make a reasonable attempt to comply with the tax law and to any disregard of rules and regulations.
- Final Regulations tend to be legislative, interpretative, or procedural. Procedural Regulations neither establish tax laws nor attempt to explain tax laws. Procedural Regulations are *housekeeping-type* instructions, indicating information that taxpayers should provide the IRS, as well as information about the internal management and conduct of the IRS itself.
- Some *interpretative* Regulations merely reprint or rephrase what Congress stated in the Committee Reports that were issued when the tax legislation was enacted. Such Regulations are *hard and solid* and almost impossible to overturn because they clearly reflect the intent of Congress.
- In some Code Sections, Congress has given to the *Secretary or his delegate* the authority to prescribe Regulations to carry out the details of administration or to otherwise complete the operating rules. Under such circumstances, it could almost be said that Congress is delegating its legislative powers to the Treasury Department. Regulations issued pursuant to this type of authority truly possess the force and effect of law and are often called *legislative* Regulations (e.g., consolidated return Regulations).

Assessing the Validity of Other Administrative Sources of the Tax Law. Revenue Rulings issued by the IRS carry less weight than Treasury Department Regulations. Revenue Rulings are important, however, in that they reflect the

---

10. *Augustus v. Comm.*, 41–1 USTC ¶9255, 26 AFTR 612, 118 F.2d 38 (CA–6, 1941).

position of the IRS on tax matters. In any dispute with the IRS on the interpretation of tax law, taxpayers should expect agents to follow the results reached in any applicable Revenue Rulings.

Revenue Rulings further tell the taxpayer the IRS's reaction to certain court decisions. Recall that the IRS follows a practice of either acquiescing (agreeing) or nonacquiescing (not agreeing) with the *Regular* decisions of the U.S. Tax Court. This does not mean that a particular decision of the Tax Court is of no value if the IRS has nonacquiesced in the result. It does, however, indicate that the IRS will continue to litigate the issue involved.

Assessing the Validity of Judicial Sources of the Tax Law. The judicial process as it relates to the formulation of tax law has been described. How much reliance can be placed on a particular decision depends upon the following variables:

- The level of the court. A decision rendered by a trial court (e.g., a Federal District Court) carries less weight than one issued by an appellate court (e.g., the Fifth Court of Appeals). Unless Congress changes the Code, decisions by the U.S. Supreme Court represent the last word on any tax issue.
- The legal residence of the taxpayer. If, for example, a taxpayer lives in Texas, a decision of the Fifth Court of Appeals means more than one rendered by the Second Court of Appeals. This is the case because any appeal from a District Court or the Tax Court would be to the Fifth Court of Appeals and not to the Second Court of Appeals.[11]
- A Tax Court Regular decision carries more weight than a Memorandum decision because the Tax Court does not consider Memorandum decisions to be binding precedents. Furthermore, a Tax Court *reviewed* decision carries even more weight. All of the Tax Court judges participate in a reviewed decision.
- A Circuit Court decision where certiorari has been requested and denied by the Supreme Court carries more weight than a Circuit Court decision that was not appealed. A Circuit Court decision heard *en banc* (all the judges participate) carries more weight than a normal Circuit Court case.
- Whether the decision represents the weight of authority on the issue. In other words, is it supported by the results reached by other courts?
- The outcome or status of the decision on appeal. For example, was the decision appealed and, if so, with what result?

In connection with the last two variables, a citator is helpful to tax research.[12] The use of a citator is not illustrated in this text.

Assessing the Validity of Other Sources. *Primary sources* of tax law include the Constitution, legislative history materials, statutes, treaties, Treasury Regulations, IRS pronouncements, and judicial decisions. In general, the IRS regards only primary sources as substantial authority. However, reference to *secondary materials* such as legal periodicals, treatises, legal opinions, General Counsel Memoranda, and written determinations may be useful. In general, secondary sources are not authority.

---

11. Before October 1, 1982, an appeal from the then-named U.S. Court of Claims (the other trial court) was directly to the U.S. Supreme Court.

12. The major citators are published by Commerce Clearing House, RIA, and Shepard's Citations, Inc.

Although the statement that the IRS regards only primary sources as substantial authority is generally true, there is one exception. In Notice 90–20,[13] the IRS expanded the list of substantial authority *for purposes of* the accuracy-related penalty in § 6662 to include:

> ... applicable provisions of the Internal Revenue Code and other statutory provisions; temporary and final regulations construing such statutes; court cases; administrative pronouncements (including revenue rulings and revenue procedures); tax treaties and regulations thereunder, and Treasury Department and other official explanations of such treaties; and congressional intent as reflected in committee reports, joint explanatory statements of managers included in conference committee reports, and floor statements made prior to enactment by one of the bill's managers.
>
> [T]he Service also will treat as authority General Explanations of tax legislation prepared by the Joint Committee on Taxation (the "Bluebook"), proposed regulations, information or press releases, notices, announcements and any other similar documents published by the Service in the Internal Revenue Bulletin. In addition, ... the Service will treat as authority private letter rulings, technical advice memoranda, actions on decisions, and general counsel memoranda after they have been released to the public and provided they are dated after December 31, 1984 (the date that is five years prior to the general effective date of the penalty provisions of the Act).

As under former § 6661, "authority" does not include conclusions reached in treatises, legal periodicals, and opinions rendered by tax professionals.

A letter ruling or determination letter is substantial authority only to the taxpayer to whom it is issued, except as noted above with respect to the accuracy-related penalty.

Upon the completion of major tax legislation, the staff of the Joint Committee on Taxation (in consultation with the staffs of the House Ways and Means and Senate Finance Committees) often will prepare a General Explanation of the Act, commonly known as the Bluebook because of the color of its cover. The IRS will not accept this detailed explanation as having legal effect. The Bluebook does, however, provide valuable guidance to tax advisers and taxpayers until Regulations are issued, and some letter rulings and General Counsel Memoranda of the IRS cite its explanations.

Arriving at the Solution or at Alternative Solutions

Example 4 raised the question of whether a taxpayer would be denied dependency exemptions for a son and a daughter-in-law if the son sold some stock near the end of the year. A refinement of the problem supplies the following additional information:

- Sam was a full-time student during four calendar months of the year.
- Sam and Dana anticipate filing a joint return.

Additional research leads to Regulation § 1.151–3(b), which indicates that to qualify as a student, Sam must be a full-time student during each of *five* calendar months of the year at an educational institution. Thus, proceeds from Sam's sale of the stock would cause his parents to lose at least one dependency exemption because Sam's gross income would exceed the exemption amount. The parents still might be able to claim Dana as an exemption if the support test is met.

---

13. 1990–1 C.B. 328; see also Reg. § 1.6661–3(b)(2).

Section 151(c)(2) indicates that a supporting taxpayer is not permitted a dependency exemption for a married dependent if the married individual files a joint return. Initial reaction is that a joint return by Sam and Dana would be disastrous to the parents. However, more research uncovers two Revenue Rulings that provide an exception if neither the dependent nor the dependent's spouse is required to file a return but does so solely to claim a refund of tax withheld. The IRS asserts that each spouse must have gross income of less than the exemption amount. Therefore, a sale of the stock by Sam combined with filing a joint return would cause the parents to lose a dependency exemption for both Sam and Dana. If the stock is not sold until January, both exemptions may still be available to the parents. However, under § 151(d)(2), a personal exemption is not available to a taxpayer who can be claimed as a dependent by another taxpayer (whether actually claimed or not). Thus, if the parents can claim Sam and Dana as dependents, Sam and Dana would lose their personal exemptions on their tax return.

Communicating Tax Research

Once the problem has been researched adequately, a memo setting forth the result may need to be prepared. The form such a memo takes could depend on a number of considerations. For example, does an employer or instructor recommend a particular procedure or format for tax research memos? Is the memo to be given directly to the client or will it first go to the preparer's employer? Whatever form it takes, a good research memo should contain the following elements:

- A clear statement of the issue.
- In more complex situations, a short review of the factual pattern that raises the issue.
- A review of the tax law sources (e.g., Code, Regulations, Revenue Rulings, judicial authority).
- Any assumptions made in arriving at the solution.
- The solution recommended and the logic or reasoning supporting it.
- The references consulted in the research process.

In short, a good tax memo should tell the reader what was researched, the results of that research, and the justification for the recommendation made.

Illustrations of the memorandum for the tax files and the client letter associated with Example 4 appear in Figures 28–6, 28–7, and 28–8.

Working with the Tax Law—Tax Planning

Tax research and tax planning are inseparable. The primary purpose of effective tax planning is to maximize the taxpayer's after-tax wealth. This does not mean that the course of action selected must produce the lowest possible tax under the circumstances. The minimization of tax liability must be considered in the context of the legitimate business goals of the taxpayer.

A secondary objective of effective tax planning is to reduce or defer the tax in the current tax year. Specifically, this objective aims to accomplish one or more results. Some possibilities are eradicating the tax entirely, eliminating the tax in the current year, deferring the receipt of income, proliferating taxpayers (i.e.,

Willis, Hoffman, Maloney, and Raabe, CPAs
50 Kellogg Boulevard
St. Paul, Minnesota 55164

FIGURE 28–6
Client Letter

September 2, 1993

Mr. and Ms. Fred Taxpayer
111 Boulevard
Williamsburg, Virginia 23185

Dear Mr. and Ms. Taxpayer:

This letter is in response to your request for us to review your family's financial and tax situation. Our conclusions are based upon the facts as outlined in your August 15th letter. Any change in the facts may affect our conclusions.

You provide over 50% of the support for your son, Sam, and his wife, Dana. The scholarship Sam receives is not included in determining support. If the stock is not sold, you will qualify for a dependency exemption for both Sam and Dana.

However, if the stock is sold, a gain of approximately $7,000 will result. This amount will result in the gross income requirement being violated (i.e., potential dependent's gross income must not exceed $2,350) for Sam. Therefore, you will not qualify to receive a dependency exemption for Sam. In addition, if Sam sells the stock and he and Dana file a joint return, you also will not qualify for a dependency exemption for Dana.

From a tax planning perspective, Sam should not sell the stock in 1993. This will enable you to claim dependency exemptions for both Sam and Dana. If the stock is sold, Sam and Dana should not file a joint return. This will still enable you to qualify for a dependency exemption for Dana.

Should you need more information or need to clarify our conclusions, do not hesitate to contact me.

Sincerely yours,

John J. Jones, CPA
Partner

FIGURE 28–7
Tax File Memorandum

August 19, 1993

TAX FILE MEMORANDUM

FROM: John J. Jones
SUBJECT: Fred and Megan Taxpayer
Engagement: Issues

Today I talked to Fred Taxpayer with respect to his August 15, 1993 letter requesting tax assistance. He wishes to know if his son, Sam, can sell stock worth $19,000 (basis of $12,000) without the parents losing the dependency exemptions for Sam and Sam's wife, Dana.

Fred Taxpayer is married to Megan, and Sam is a full-time student at a local university. Sam inherited the stock from his grandmother about five years ago. If he sells the stock, he will save the proceeds from the sale. Sam does not need to spend the proceeds if he sells the stock because he receives a $3,000 scholarship that he uses for his own support (i.e., to pay for tuition, books, and fees). Fred and Megan furnish approximately 55% of Sam and Dana's support.

ISSUE: If the stock is sold, would the sale prohibit Fred and Megan from claiming Sam and Dana as dependents? I told Fred that we would have an answer for him within two weeks.

forming partnerships and corporations or making lifetime gifts to family members), eluding double taxation, avoiding ordinary income, or creating, increasing, or accelerating deductions. However, this second objective should be approached with considerable reservation. Although the maxim "A bird in the hand is worth two in the bush" is generally valid, the rule frequently breaks down. For example, a tax election in one year may accomplish a current reduction in taxes, but it could saddle future years with a disadvantageous tax position.

Nontax Considerations

There is a danger that tax motivations may take on a significance that does not conform to the true values involved. In other words, tax considerations can operate to impair the exercise of sound business judgment. Thus, the tax planning process can lead to ends that are socially and economically objectionable. Unfortunately, a tendency exists for planning to go toward the opposing extremes of either not enough or too much emphasis on tax considerations. The happy medium is a balance that recognizes the significance of taxes, but not beyond the point at which planning detracts from the exercise of good business judgment.

FIGURE 28–8
Tax File Memorandum

August 27, 1993

TAX FILE MEMORANDUM

FROM: John J. Jones

SUBJECT: Fred and Megan Taxpayer
Engagement: Conclusions

Section 152(a) provides that in order for a taxpayer to take a dependency exemption, the taxpayer must provide over 50% of the support of the potential dependent. Fred and Megan provide about 55% of the support of their son, Sam, and their daughter-in-law, Dana. If Sam should sell the stock in 1993, he would not need to spend the proceeds for support purposes (i.e., would save the proceeds). Thus, the stock sale would not affect his qualifying for the support test. In calculating the percentage of support provided by Fred and Megan, a $3,000 scholarship received by Sam is not counted in determining the amount of support Sam provides for himself [see Reg. § 1.152–1(c)].

Section 151(c)(1) provides that in order to qualify for a dependency exemption, the potential dependent's gross income must be less than the exemption amount (i.e., $2,350 in 1993). Without the stock sale, the gross income of both Sam ($960) and Dana ($900) will be below the exemption amount in 1993. The $3,000 Sam receives as a scholarship is excluded from his gross income under § 117 because he uses the entire amount to pay for his tuition, books, and fees at a local university.

The key issue then is whether the stock, which will generate $7,000 gain for Sam, will cause the gross income test to be violated. The gain will increase Sam's gross income to $7,960 ($7,000 + $960). However, § 151(c)(1)(B) permits a child's gross income to exceed the exemption amount if the child is a student under the age of 24. Under Reg. § 1.151–3(b), to qualify as a student, the person must be a full-time student during each of five calendar months. A telephone call to Megan provided the information that Sam was a student for only four months in 1993. Thus, since Sam is not eligible for the student exception, the sale of the stock by Sam in 1993 would result in Fred and Megan losing the dependency exemption for Sam.

The stock sale would also result in the loss of the dependency exemption for Dana if Sam and Dana file a joint return for 1993 [see § 151(c)(2)].

From a tax planning perspective, Sam should not sell the stock until 1994. This will enable Fred and Megan to claim dependency exemptions on their 1993 return for Sam and Dana. Note, however, that neither Sam nor Dana will be permitted to take a personal exemption deduction on their 1993 tax return since they are claimed as dependents on someone else's return [see § 151 (d)(2)]. However, this will not produce any negative tax consequences since their tax liability will be zero if the stock is not sold in 1993.

The remark is often made that a good rule is to refrain from pursuing any course of action that would not be followed were it not for certain tax considerations. This statement is not entirely correct, but it does illustrate the desirability of preventing business logic from being "sacrificed at the altar of tax planning."

Tax Evasion and Tax Avoidance

A fine line exists between legal tax planning and illegal tax planning—tax avoidance versus tax evasion. Tax avoidance is merely tax minimization through legal techniques. In this sense, tax avoidance is the proper objective of all tax planning. Though eliminating or reducing taxes is also a goal of tax evasion, the term implies the use of subterfuge and fraud as a means to this end. Perhaps because common goals are involved, popular usage has blurred the distinction between the two concepts. Consequently, the association of tax avoidance with tax evasion has kept some taxpayers from properly taking advantage of planning possibilities. The now classic words of Judge Learned Hand in *Commissioner v. Newman* reflect the true values a taxpayer should have:

> Over and over again courts have said that there is nothing sinister in so arranging one's affairs as to keep taxes as low as possible. Everybody does so, rich or poor; and all do right, for nobody owes any public duty to pay more than the law demands: taxes are enforced extractions, not voluntary contributions. To demand more in the name of morals is mere cant.[14]

Follow-up Procedures

Because tax planning usually involves a proposed (as opposed to a completed) transaction, it is predicated upon the continuing validity of the advice based upon the tax research. A change in the tax law (either legislative, administrative, or judicial) could alter the original conclusion. Additional research may be necessary to test the solution in light of current developments (refer to the broken lines at the right in Concept Summary 28–4).

Tax Planning—A Practical Application

Returning to the facts of Example 4, what could be done to protect the dependency exemptions for the parents? If Sam and Dana were to refrain from filing a joint return, both could be claimed by the parents. This result assumes that the stock is not sold.

An obvious tax planning tool is the installment method. Could the securities be sold using the installment method under § 453 so that most of the gain is deferred into the next year? Under the installment method, certain gains may be postponed and recognized as the cash proceeds are received. The problem is that the installment method is not available for stock traded on an established securities market.

A little more research, however, indicates that Sam can sell the stock and postpone the recognition of gain until the following year by selling short an equal number of substantially identical shares and covering the short sale in the subsequent year with the shares originally held. Selling short means that Sam

---

14. *Comm. v. Newman*, 47–1 USTC ¶9175, 35 AFTR 857, 159 F.2d 848 (CA–2, 1947).

sells borrowed stock (substantially identical) and repays the lender with the stock held on the date of the short sale. This *short against the box* technique would allow Sam to protect his $7,000 profit and defer the closing of the sale until the following year. Further, if the original shares had been held for the required long-term holding period before the date of the short sale, Sam would be able to obtain long-term capital gain treatment. Thus, some research and planning would reap tax savings for this family. Note the critical role of obtaining the correct facts in attempting to resolve the proper strategy for the taxpayers.

Throughout this text, most chapters include observations on Tax Planning Considerations. Such observations are not all-inclusive but are intended to illustrate some of the ways in which the material covered can be effectively utilized to minimize taxes.

Computer-Assisted Tax Research

The computer is being used more frequently in the day-to-day practice of tax professionals, students, and educators. Many software vendors offer tax return software programs for individual, corporate, partnership, and fiduciary returns. The use of computers, however, is not limited to batch-processed tax returns. Computer timesharing for quantitative tax and problem-solving planning and calculations has added a new dimension to tax research.

The microcomputer has become the revolutionary tool of the present—much as the electronic calculator did in the 1970s. Electronic spreadsheets are replacing the 14-column worksheet. The electronic spreadsheet approach can be used anytime projections and calculations are needed. Examples include retirement planning, 1040 projections, real estate projections, partnership allocations, consolidated tax return problems, and compensation planning. Internally prepared tax-related programs are used by many public accounting firms. Microcomputer software is available for estate planning calculations.

LEXIS, a computerized legal data bank, has been available since 1973 as a complement to the conventional research approach. WESTLAW, a competitive system from West Publishing Company, has been operational since 1975. Commerce Clearing House's legal data base is called ACCESS, and Research Institute of America's is called TAXRIA. With these data banks, one has immediate access to the current tax law, Regulations, proposed Regulations, letter rulings, Revenue Rulings, judicial decisions, daily tax services, code commentaries, and much more. Note, however, that WESTLAW, LEXIS, ACCESS, and TAXRIA are document retrieval systems and cannot interpret the law.

Users have access to these computerized data banks through special terminals and long-distance telephone lines. A user selects key words, phrases, or numbers and types the search request on the terminal keyboard. A display screen shows the full text or portions of the various documents containing the words, phrases, or numbers in the search request. A printer can be used to obtain hard copy of any documents or portions of a document. For example, a researcher can obtain the decisions of a particular judge or court over a specified time period. It is also possible to access judicial opinions containing specific words or phrases of statutory language. These computer-assisted tax systems can be used as a citator by collecting all judicial decisions that have cited a particular decision or statute as well as all decisions that have a specific combination of two or more earlier decisions or statutes.

The latest development is the proliferation of Compact Disc–Read Only Memory (CD-ROM) products. By employing a key-word search technique, a person can browse through a tax service, IRS publications, and other tax information. Commerce Clearing House, Matthew Bender, Research Institute of America, and West Publishing Company offer CD-ROM products. For example,

West provides a complete Federal tax library on only ten CDs. Although CD-ROM does not offer the on-line updating provided by WESTLAW, LEXIS, ACCESS, and TAXRIA, the CDs can be replaced periodically.

Computer-assisted tax research is useful in searching for facts since human indexing centers on legal theories rather than fact patterns. Computer searching is also useful in finding new court decisions not yet in the printed indexes. Nevertheless, computer searching probably does not find as many relevant cases as manual searching does. Consequently, a combination of manual and computer searching is preferred.

PROBLEM MATERIALS

DISCUSSION QUESTIONS

1. Judicial decisions interpreting a provision of the Internal Revenue Code of 1939 or 1954 are no longer of any value in view of the enactment of the Internal Revenue Code of 1986. Assess the validity of this statement.
2. The Revenue Reconciliation Act of 1990 became part of the Internal Revenue Code of 1986. Explain this statement.
3. Trace the legislative route of a tax bill.
4. Why are Committee Reports of Congress important as a source of tax law?
5. Where may proposed Regulations first be found? How would a proposed Regulation under § 118 be cited?
6. Distinguish between legislative, interpretative, and procedural Regulations.
7. Distinguish between the following:
   - **a.** Treasury Regulations and Revenue Rulings.
   - **b.** Revenue Rulings and Revenue Procedures.
   - **c.** Revenue Rulings and letter rulings.
   - **d.** Letter rulings and determination letters.
8. Rank the following items from the highest authority to the lowest in the Federal tax law system:
   - **a.** Interpretative Regulation.
   - **b.** Legislative Regulation.
   - **c.** Letter ruling.
   - **d.** Revenue Procedure.
   - **e.** Internal Revenue Code.
   - **f.** Proposed Regulation.
9. Interpret each of the following citations:
   - **a.** Rev.Rul. 86–141, 1986–2 C.B. 151.
   - **b.** Rev.Proc. 74–33, 1974–2 C.B. 489.
   - **c.** Ltr.Rul. 8542034.
10. Discuss the two major types of letter rulings.
11. Summarize the trial and appellate court system for Federal tax litigation.
12. Which of the following statements would be considered advantages of the Small Claims Division of the Tax Court?
    - **a.** Appeal to the Court of Appeals for the Federal Circuit is possible.
    - **b.** A hearing of a deficiency of $11,200 is considered on a timely basis.
    - **c.** Taxpayer can handle the litigation without using a lawyer or certified public accountant.
    - **d.** Taxpayer can use Small Claims Division decisions for precedential value.

e. The actual hearing is held on an informal basis.
f. Travel time will probably be reduced.

13. List an advantage and a disadvantage of using the U.S. Tax Court as the trial court for Federal tax litigation.
14. List an advantage and a disadvantage of using a U.S. District Court as the trial court for Federal tax litigation.
15. List an advantage and a disadvantage of using the U.S. Court of Federal Claims as the trial court for Federal tax litigation.
16. A taxpayer lives in Michigan. In a controversy with the IRS, the taxpayer loses at the trial court level. Describe the appeal procedure for each of the following trial courts:

    a. Small Claims Division of the U.S. Tax Court.
    b. U.S. Tax Court.
    c. U.S. District Court.
    d. U.S. Court of Federal Claims.

17. Suppose the U.S. Government loses a tax case in the U.S. District Court of Idaho and does not appeal the result. What does the failure to appeal signify?
18. To what court are decisions of the following courts first appealed?

    a. Small Claims Court.
    b. Federal District Court.
    c. U.S. Court of Federal Claims.
    d. U.S. Tax Court.
    e. Federal Court of Appeals.

19. A taxpayer from a U.S. District Court in which of the following states could appeal a decision to the Ninth Court of Appeals?

    a. Arkansas.
    b. Arizona.
    c. Alabama.
    d. Maine.
    e. None of the above.

20. What is the Supreme Court's policy on hearing tax cases?
21. In assessing the validity of a prior court decision, discuss the significance of the following on the taxpayer's issue:

    a. The decision was rendered by the U.S. District Court of Wyoming. Taxpayer lives in Wyoming.
    b. The decision was rendered by the U.S. Court of Federal Claims. Taxpayer lives in Wyoming.
    c. The decision was rendered by the Second Court of Appeals. Taxpayer lives in California.
    d. The decision was rendered by the U.S. Supreme Court.
    e. The decision was rendered by the U.S. Tax Court. The IRS has acquiesced in the result.
    f. Same as (e), except that the IRS has nonacquiesced in the result.

22. What is the difference between a Regular and a Memorandum decision of the U.S. Tax Court?
23. Interpret each of the following citations:

    a. 54 T.C. 1514 (1970).
    b. 408 F.2d 117 (CA–2, 1969).
    c. 69–1 USTC ¶9319 (CA–2, 1969).
    d. 23 AFTR2d 69–1090 (CA–2, 1969).
    e. 293 F.Supp. 1129 (D.Ct., Miss., 1967).
    f. 67–1 USTC ¶9253 (D.Ct., Miss., 1967).
    g. 19 AFTR2d 647 (D.Ct., Miss., 1967).
    h. 56 S.Ct. 289 (USSC, 1935).

i. 36–1 USTC ¶9020 (USSC, 1935).
j. 16 AFTR 1274 (USSC, 1935).
k. 422 F.2d 1336 (Ct.Cls., 1970).

24. Explain the following abbreviations:

a. CA–2
b. Cls.Ct.
c. *aff'd.*
d. *rev'd.*
e. *rem'd.*
f. *Cert. denied*
g. *acq.*
h. B.T.A.
i. USTC
j. AFTR
k. F.2d
l. F.Supp.
m. USSC
n. S.Ct.
o. D.Ct.

25. Give the West Publishing Company citation for each of the following courts:

a. Small Claims Division of the Tax Court.
b. Federal District Court.
c. U.S. Supreme Court.
d. U.S. Claims Court.

26. Where can you locate a published decision of the U.S. Claims Court?

27. Which of the following items can probably be found in the *Cumulative Bulletin?*

a. Revenue Ruling.
b. Small Claims Division of the U.S. Tax Court decision.
c. Letter ruling.
d. Revenue Procedure.
e. Proposed Regulation.
f. District Court decision.
g. Senate Finance Committee Report.
h. Acquiescences to Tax Court decisions.
i. Tax Court Memorandum decision.

28. A friend majoring in sociology insists that tax advisers are immoral because they help people cheat the government. Defend tax planning by tax advisers.

PROBLEMS

29. Tom has just been audited by the IRS and, as a result, has been assessed a substantial deficiency (which he has not yet paid) in additional income taxes. In preparing his defense, Tom advances the following possibilities:

a. Although a resident of Kentucky, Tom plans to sue in a U.S. District Court in Oregon that appears to be more favorably inclined toward taxpayers.
b. If (a) is not possible, Tom plans to take his case to a Kentucky state court where an uncle is the presiding judge.
c. Since Tom has found a B.T.A. decision that seems to help his case, he plans to rely on it under alternative (a) or (b).
d. If he loses at the trial court level, Tom plans to appeal to either the U.S. Court of Federal Claims or the U.S. Second Court of Appeals. The reason for this choice is that he has relatives in both Washington, D.C., and New York. Staying with these relatives could save Tom lodging expense while his appeal is being heard by the court selected.
e. Even if he does not win at the trial court or appeals court level, Tom feels certain of success on an appeal to the U.S. Supreme Court.

Evaluate Tom's notions concerning the judicial process as it applies to Federal income tax controversies.

30. Using the legend provided, classify each of the following statements (more than one answer per statement may be appropriate):

Legend

D = Applies to the U.S. District Court
T = Applies to the U.S. Tax Court
C = Applies to the U.S. Court of Federal Claims
A = Applies to the U.S. Court of Appeals
U = Applies to the U.S. Supreme Court
N = Applies to none of the above

a. Decides only Federal tax matters.
b. Decisions are reported in the F.2d Series.
c. Decisions are reported in the USTCs.
d. Decisions are reported in the AFTRs.
e. Appeal is by *Writ of Certiorari.*
f. Court meets most often in Washington, D.C.
g. Offers the choice of a jury trial.
h. Is a trial court.
i. Is an appellate court.
j. Allows appeal to the Court of Appeals for the Federal Circuit and bypasses the taxpayer's particular Court of Appeals.
k. Has a Small Claims Division.
l. Is the only trial court where the taxpayer does not have to first pay the tax assessed by the IRS.

31. Using the legend provided, classify each of the following citations as to publisher:

Legend

RIA = Research Institute of America
CCH = Commerce Clearing House
W = West Publishing Company
U.S. = U.S. Government
O = Others

a. 83–2 USTC ¶9600.
b. 52 AFTR2d 83–5954.
c. 49 T.C. 645 (1968).
d. 39 TCM 32 (1979).
e. 393 U.S. 297.
f. RIA T.C.Memo ¶80,582.
g. 89 S.Ct. 501.
h. 2 Cl.Ct. 601.
i. 159 F.2d 848.
j. 592 F.Supp. 18.
k. Rev.Rul. 76–332, 1976–2 C.B. 81.
l. 21 L.Ed.2d 495.

32. Using the legend provided, classify each of the following statements:

Legend

A = Tax avoidance
E = Tax evasion
N = Neither

a. Terry writes a $250 check as a charitable contribution on December 28, 1993, but does not mail the check to the charitable organization until January 10. She takes a deduction in 1993.
b. Robert decided not to report interest income from a bank because it was only $11.75.
c. Jim pays property taxes on his home in December 1993 rather than waiting until February 1994.
d. Jane switches her investments from taxable corporate bonds to tax-exempt municipal bonds.
e. Ted encourages his mother to save most of her Social Security benefits so that he will be able to claim her as a dependent.

RESEARCH PROBLEMS

Chapter 2

RESEARCH PROBLEM 1 Jerry maintained a home in which he, his daughter (Fran), and his son-in-law (Ed) lived. Ed died in June 1990, and Fran continued to reside with Jerry for the rest of the year. Fran filed a joint return with Ed for 1990. Jerry filed his 1990 tax return as a head of household. The IRS claims that Jerry was not entitled to head-of-household status because Fran was considered married as of the end of 1990. Should Jerry accept the IRS position and file as a single taxpayer, or should he challenge them for the right to file as a head of household?

Research aids:
Hilliard v. U.S., 63–1 USTC ¶9126, 10 AFTR2d 6135, 310 F.2d 631 (CA–6, 1962).
§ 2(b).

RESEARCH PROBLEM 2 Emily's daughter, Sarah, graduated from high school on May 15, 1992. Emily and Sarah's father were divorced in 1990, and Emily was awarded custody of Sarah. Under the custody agreement, Sarah spent the last half of May and the entire months of June, July, and August with her father. Sarah returned to Emily's home on September 1, stayed there the first week of September, and then went away to college and lived on campus for the rest of the year. Can Emily file as head of household for 1992?

Chapter 3

RESEARCH PROBLEM 3 Sam purchased a newly issued convertible bond for $10,000 in 1990. The bond was issued by Hammer, Inc., and was convertible into 1,000 shares of the company's common stock. In 1993, Sam asked your opinion about the tax consequences of exercising his conversion rights. The value of the 1,000 shares of Hammer common stock is $13,000. Advise Sam whether he must recognize gain if he converts the bond into common stock.

RESEARCH PROBLEM 4 The Great Electric Company requires new customers to make a $100 deposit to secure future payments for electricity. After the customer has established a good payment record (usually within two years), the company refunds the deposit to the customer. If the services are terminated before refund, the deposit is usually applied against the final bill. The IRS agent insists that the company must include the deposits in gross income for the year the deposits are received. Can you find authority for excluding the deposits from income?

Chapter 4

RESEARCH PROBLEM 5 David is the minister at the First Baptist Church. As part of his compensation, David receives an $800 per month housing allowance. David is purchasing his residence, and he uses the $800 each month to make mortgage and property tax payments. The mortgage interest and property taxes are deducted (as itemized deductions) on David's tax return. The examining IRS agent thinks David would be enjoying a double benefit if the housing allowance is excluded and the itemized deductions are allowed. In addition, the agent contends that the housing allowance exclusion should apply only where the church provides the residence or the minister uses the funds to pay rent. Therefore, the agent maintains that David should include the $800 received each month in gross income. David has asked your assistance in this matter.

RESEARCH PROBLEM 6 Liz is a compulsive gambler. After losing $100,000 of her savings, she began to gamble on credit. That is, the casino would treat Liz's losses as an account receivable from Liz. Under state law, gambling debts are unenforceable. However, the casino has a very good collection rate. After Liz had accumulated an amount payable of $250,000, she refused to pay the casino. After threats on both sides, the casino finally accepted $50,000 in full payment of the debt. The IRS asserts that Liz has $200,000 income from discharge of indebtedness. What is the appropriate treatment of the $200,000?

Chapter 5

RESEARCH PROBLEM 7 Gray Chemical Company manufactured pesticides that were toxic. Over the course of several years, the toxic waste contaminated the air and water around the company's plant. Several employees suffered toxic poisoning, and the Environmental Protection Agency cited the company for violations. In court, the judge found Gray guilty and imposed fines of $15 million. The company voluntarily set up a charitable fund for the purpose of bettering the environment and funded it with $8 million. The company incurred legal expenses in setting up the foundation and defending itself in court. The court reduced the fine from $15 million to $7 million.

Gray Chemical Company deducted the $8 million paid to the foundation and the legal expenses incurred. The IRS disallowed both deductions on the grounds that the payment was, in fact, a fine and in violation of public policy.

Will Gray be able to deduct the $7 million fine? The $8 million payment to the foundation? The legal fees?

Research aids:
§§ 162(a) and (f).
Reg. § 1.162–21(b).

RESEARCH PROBLEM 8 Darlene is a graduate student working on her Ph.D. in microbiology. She attended the university under the G.I. bill, which pays for her tuition and books in full. The G.I. benefits are not taxable. She was appointed to a research team, and the university paid her a monthly stipend of $450 for the year. She was required to register and pay tuition for the semesters she was on the research team. Her tuition was still paid under the G.I. bill. Can she deduct the tuition as a business expense?

Research aids:
§ 265.
Rev.Rul. 83–3, 1983–1 C.B. 72.

Chapter 6

RESEARCH PROBLEM 9 Marcia owns six grocery stores and a warehouse that receives and stores goods and delivers the goods to different grocery stores as needed. How many separate activities does Marcia have? How are the income and expenses of the warehouse treated?

RESEARCH PROBLEM 10 George owns interests in three business activities, X, Y, and Z. George does not materially participate in any of the activities considered separately, but he does participate for 110 hours in Activity X, 160 hours in Activity Y, and 125 hours in Activity Z. George does not own interests in any other businesses. His net passive income (loss) for the taxable year from Activities X, Y, and Z is as follows:

	X	Y	Z
Gross income	$ 600	$ 700	$ 900
Deductions	(200)	(1,000)	(300)
Net income (loss)	$ 400	($ 300)	$ 600

How much of the gross income from the three activities is treated as income that is not from a passive activity?

Chapter 7

RESEARCH PROBLEM 11 While Ralph Jones was in the process of obtaining a divorce, his wife, without Ralph's knowledge, had the furniture removed from his apartment. Discuss whether Ralph is entitled to a tax deduction for the loss of the furniture.

Research aids:
Landis G. Brown, 30 TCM 257, T.C.Memo. 1971–60.
Goode v. Comm., 42 TCM 1209, T.C.Memo. 1981–548.

RESEARCH PROBLEM 12 George Johnson, a resident of St. Paul, Minnesota, parked his car on a lake while he was watching an iceboat race. During the race, the ice beneath his car unexpectedly gave way, and the car sank to the bottom of the lake. Discuss whether George can claim a casualty loss for the damage to the car.

Chapter 8

RESEARCH PROBLEM 13 Sandra operates several garbage dumps throughout the Chicago area. In 1993, she purchased a tract of land for $150,000. This land contained a pit that could accommodate 2,500,000 cubic yards of garbage. In 1993, the land was reasonably estimated to be worth $55,000 without the pit. The sellers indicated that they had charged a premium for the land because they knew Sandra needed land with a pit for dumping garbage in that area. At the end of 1993 and several times thereafter, Sandra had the property surveyed to determine the amount of space filled and the amount remaining. At the end of 1993, 2,300,000 cubic yards remained to be filled. Discuss whether Sandra can depreciate the value of the air space that is now being reduced by the dumping of the garbage.

RESEARCH PROBLEM 14 Gabriella is a professor of violin at the University of Minnesota. She is also a concert violinist. Gabriella purchased her violin for $80,000. Discuss whether Gabriella's violin is subject to cost recovery using MACRS with the violin being classified as five-year property.

Chapter 9

RESEARCH PROBLEM 15 Jesse maintains a home office that he uses exclusively for business. He is an employee of the Ace Company, which provides him with an office, and has a consulting business on the side.

He used his home office 80% of the time in his consulting business and 20% of the time in connection with his job with Ace. Can he deduct his home office expenses?

Research aid:
§ 280A(c)(1).

RESEARCH PROBLEM 16 Martha and Frank are wife and husband. Martha owns a small company that manufactures business machines. Many of the machine parts are made in Japan. On average, Martha spends three months in Japan on business each year. In 1993, Martha and Frank took a 63-day trip to Japan to discuss a new contract. Fifteen days were spent vacationing. Frank did not participate in the business meetings. Can Martha deduct any of Frank's expenses? Must she allocate expenses between business and personal days?

Research aid:
§ 274(c)(2)(B).

Chapter 10

Research Problem 17 Julio and his wife purchased a new residence. Because they were unable to obtain conventional mortgage financing, they borrowed the purchase price at City National Bank. Under the terms of the loan, they agreed to pay interest and make very modest repayments of the principal for three years. At the end of three years, the full amount of the loan would "balloon" and become due. During the three-year term of the loan, the couple made the interest payments and only some of the repayments of principal.

By the end of the three-year loan, Julio and his wife managed to obtain long-term (30-year) mortgage financing with State Savings and Loan. Thus, the outstanding amounts due City National were rolled over into a new mortgage with State Savings and Loan.

As a cost of securing the refinancing, the couple had to pay points. These were paid from their own funds and not from the mortgage proceeds. Julio and his wife concede that they did not possess the economic means to meet the balloon payment requirement under the City National loan agreement.

Determine the income tax treatment of the points paid to State Savings and Loan.

Research aid:
§ 461(g)(2).

Research Problem 18 Falcon Corporation is the owner and operator of a large daily metropolitan newspaper. For at least 80 years, Falcon has collected and maintained a "clippings library." The library is a collection of past news items from Falcon's and other newspapers. The 7,800,000 items are well preserved, cataloged, and cross-listed under various categories. Falcon estimates that it has spent in excess of $10 million compiling and organizing the library. However, since this amount was deducted as incurred, the income tax basis of the library is zero. The fair market value of the library is $3 million.

Falcon Corporation contributes the clippings library to the state historical society (a qualified organization) and claims a charitable contribution deduction of $3 million. Upon audit, the IRS disallows the entire amount of the deduction because the basis of the property is zero. Who is correct?

Research aids:
§§ 170(e)(1)(A) and 1221(3).

Chapter 11

Research Problem 19 Karen has been participating in a carpool arrangement from her home to her work with others in her office for a number of years. Carpooling has worked out well from her perspective because the physical and financial burdens of driving to and from work are reduced by being shared equally among several people. However, her family situation has changed recently, and she is now required to delay her departure for work until her 8-year-old child's school bus arrives each morning. Although she looked for help, she was unable to find anyone to care for her child during the early morning hours. Unfortunately, the others in the carpool were not willing to leave for work any later than previously. Therefore, the only recourse for Karen was to give up her carpool and begin driving to and from work by herself. Karen figures that the cost of individually driving to and from work for the year was $1,000, while the cost of the carpool arrangement was $200. Because the incremental $800 costs relate to and are necessary for the care of her dependent child, she feels that they should be considered qualifying expenditures for purposes of the credit for child and dependent care expenses. Karen asks your advice. How do you respond? Write a letter to Karen that contains your advice and prepare a memo for the tax files.

RESEARCH PROBLEM 20 Isabella, a lover of early-twentieth century American history and architecture, discovers a 1920s house in a downtown district of Atlanta during a recent visit. She decides not only to purchase and renovate this particular home, but also to move the structure to her hometown of Little Rock, Arkansas, so her community can enjoy its architectural features. Also, being aware of the availability of the tax credit for rehabilitation expenditures incurred on old structures, she wants to maximize her use of the provision once the renovation work begins in Arkansas. Comment on whether the renovation expenditures incurred will qualify for the tax credit for rehabilitation expenditures.

Chapter 12

RESEARCH PROBLEM 21 Wilma owns land that has an adjusted basis of $75,000 and a fair market value of $200,000. She has owned the land for five years. The land is subject to a mortgage of $100,000. Wilma, an alumna of State University, donates the land to State University. The university assumes Wilma's mortgage on the land. What are the tax consequences to Wilma?

Research aid:
Leo G. Ebben, 45 TCM 1283, T.C.Memo. 1983–200.

RESEARCH PROBLEM 22 You are the general manager of the San Diego Padres, Inc. In order for the Padres to become a serious contender for the pennant, you believe player changes are necessary. Discussions are in progress with the general manager of the Toronto Blue Jays. He has offered to trade Tony Fernandez (an all-star shortstop) and $5 million to the Padres in exchange for Joe Carter (an all-star outfielder) and Roberto Alomar (an all-star second baseman). You have countered by expressing an interest in receiving Fernandez and Fred McGriff (an all-star first baseman) rather than the cash. You believe that if you are going to give up the power provided by Carter, you need to get a power hitter in return (i.e., McGriff). In addition, you vaguely remember from your MBA days that a player trade with no cash involved provides better tax results. Before you finalize a trade, you need to know the tax consequences.

Chapter 13

RESEARCH PROBLEM 23 Airplay, Inc., recently purchased the assets, including the Federal Communications Commission (FCC) broadcast license, of WJBK, Inc. WJBK is a radio station in Tampa, Florida. Airplay paid $3 million for WJBK, of which $1 million is properly allocable to the broadcast license. The license is issued by the FCC, which must approve the transfer of the license from WJBK to Airplay. After reviewing Airplay's financial and other information, the FCC approved the transfer of the license. The license has six years to run before it must be renewed. Is the broadcast license a "franchise" and, if so, how is Airplay's deduction for the $1 million allocated to the broadcast license affected?

Research aids:
Jefferson-Pilot Corporation, et al. v. Comm., 98 T.C. No. 32 (1992).
§ 1253.

RESEARCH PROBLEM 24 Sidney owns a professional football franchise. He has received an offer of $80 million for the franchise, all the football equipment, the rights to concession receipts, the rights to a stadium lease, and the rights to all the player contracts he owns. Most of the players have been with the team for quite a long time and have contracts that were signed several years ago. The contracts have been substantially depreciated. Sidney is concerned about potential § 1245 recapture when the contracts are sold. He has heard about "previously unrecaptured depreciation with respect to initial contracts" and would like to know more about it. Find a definition for that phrase and write an explanation of it.

Research aid:
§ 1245(a)(4).

Chapter 14

RESEARCH PROBLEM 25 Tony is a full-time gambler whose only source of income is money that he wins from his gambling activities. The IRS contends that Tony's gambling losses should be treated as itemized deductions for purposes of computing the AMT. Tony argues that the gambling losses should be treated as trade or business expenses. Who is correct, Tony or the IRS?

RESEARCH PROBLEM 26 Carol owns two warehouses that were placed in service before 1987. Accelerated depreciation for 1990 on Warehouse A was $12,000, and straight-line depreciation would have been $8,000. On Warehouse B, accelerated depreciation was $6,000, and straight-line depreciation would have been $7,500. What was the amount of Carol's tax preference for excess depreciation in 1990?

Chapter 15

RESEARCH PROBLEM 27 RST Company discovered certain equipment used in its repair operations had been accounted for as inventory rather than as fixed assets. This incorrect treatment applied to all years in which the equipment had been used, and all of those years are open under the statute of limitations. RST filed amended returns for all years affected by the incorrect treatment to obtain a refund of overpayments of taxes for those years. The IRS refused to accept the amended returns. The IRS reasoned that RST was actually changing accounting methods, which can only be accomplished through a request for change in methods. In addition, the IRS concluded that an adjustment due to a voluntary change in accounting method must be taken into income for the year of the change. Is the IRS correct? Write a letter to RST Company that contains your advice and prepare a memo for the tax files.

RESEARCH PROBLEM 28 In November 1993, Anne agreed to purchase stock from Barry for $1 million. The transaction was to be closed on December 28, 1993. In early December 1993, Barry became concerned about the taxes due on the sale in 1993. He suggested that the transaction be deferred until January 1994, but Anne insisted that the stock be transferred on December 28, 1993. Anne and Barry agreed that the cash paid by Anne on December 28, 1993, would be held by the First Bank as Anne's escrow agent, and the funds would be dispersed to Barry on January 4, 1994. The IRS agent insists that the escrow amount was constructively received by Barry in 1993 and that Barry therefore cannot defer his gain until 1994 under the installment sales rules. Is the agent correct?

Research aid:
Reed v. Comm., 83–2 USTC ¶9728, 53 AFTR2d 84–335 (CA–1, 1983).

Chapter 16

RESEARCH PROBLEM 29 Joe and Tom are brothers and equal shareholders in Black Corporation, a calendar year taxpayer. In 1991, they incurred certain travel and entertainment expenditures, as employees, on behalf of Black Corporation. Because Black was in a precarious financial condition, Joe and Tom decided not to seek reimbursement for these expenditures. Instead, each brother deducted what he spent on his own individual return (Form 1040). Upon audit of the returns filed by Joe and Tom for 1991, the IRS disallowed these expenditures. Do you agree? Why or why not?

RESEARCH PROBLEM 30 Soon-Yi owns all the stock of White Corporation and 90% of the stock of Red Corporation. Red has had profitable years whereas White has suffered losses for several years. Red loaned White Corporation $90,000 in 1991 and did not charge White any interest on the loan. Upon audit of its 1991 return, the IRS determined that Red Corporation had interest income for 1991 in the amount of $9,900, causing Red to have a tax deficiency of $3,366 for 1991. Red is challenging the tax deficiency. It contends that White Corporation produced no taxable income from the use of the $90,000. Is the IRS correct in increasing the taxable income of Red Corporation?

Research aids:
Reg. §§ 1.482–2(a)(1) and 1.482–1(d)(4).

Chapter 17

RESEARCH PROBLEM 31 Chee and Hun, two doctors, form Brown, a professional association, to engage in the practice of medicine. Brown purchases X-ray equipment to be used in the business. Chee and Hun later form Black, an S corporation, to perform X-ray services for Brown, and transfer all the Black stock to their children. Brown transferred the X-ray equipment to Black, with Black executing a note payable to Brown for the equipment. Black then hires an X-ray technician to perform the X-ray services for Brown. The X-ray equipment and the X-ray technician's office are located in the building owned by Brown. Brown does all the billing for X-ray services and then remits a percentage of its collections to Black. Black then pays the technician for his services, pays rent to Brown for use of the building, and pays Brown on the note it executed for payment of the X-ray equipment. During the tax year, Black had a profit that the children of Chee and Hun reported on their individual income tax returns. Upon audit, the IRS assessed a deficiency against Brown, asserting that all income and expenses of Black must be attributed to Brown because Black was a sham corporation. The IRS also assessed a deficiency against Chee and Hun, stating that all distributions from Black to Chee's and Hun's children are constructive dividends to Chee and Hun from Brown Corporation. What are the results?

Research aids:
§§ 61 and 482.
Edwin D. Davis, 64 T.C. 1034 (1975).
Engineering Sales, Inc. v. U.S., 75–1 USTC ¶9347, 35 AFTR2d 75–1122, 510 F.d2 565 (CA–5, 1975).

RESEARCH PROBLEM 32 Robin Corporation, a qualified small business corporation under § 1244, was incorporated in 1986. Pat acquired 50 shares of Robin common stock in 1986. The stock had a tax basis to Pat of $50,000. In 1990, Robin Corporation redeemed Pat's 50 shares of common stock by issuing 10 shares of its preferred stock to her. In 1991, Robin experienced financial difficulties. It arranged for financing with a local bank, but the bank required adequate collateral. Pat agreed to transfer her shares in GM Corporation, a large publicly traded corporation, to Robin with the understanding that the GM shares would be used as collateral for the loan. Robin then issued 20 shares of its common stock to Pat. Pat had a tax basis of $40,000 in the GM stock. In 1992, Robin Corporation went bankrupt. Its shares, both preferred and common, were worthless. On her 1992 tax return (filed jointly with her husband), Pat claimed an ordinary loss of $90,000, her tax basis in her preferred and common stock in Robin Corporation. Upon audit of Pat's 1992 return, the IRS denied the $90,000 loss on the ground that neither the preferred stock nor the common stock qualified as § 1244 stock. According to the IRS, Pat has a capital loss of $90,000 and can deduct only $3,000 of that loss on her 1992 return. Pat contends that the 20 shares of common stock were issued to her in consideration of the cancellation of Robin Corporation's indebtedness to her. She argues that Robin owed her a debt when she contributed the GM stock to the corporation. The debt was then canceled when Robin issued its common stock to her.

Is Pat correct in contending that both her preferred stock and her common stock in Robin Corporation qualify as § 1244 stock? Explain.

Chapter 18

RESEARCH PROBLEM 33 Mark, the principal shareholder of Gray Corporation, diverted sums totaling $60,000 from the corporation during tax year 1992. Upon audit of Mark's return, the IRS contended these sums were taxable income to Mark under § 61 of the Code. Mark disagrees, stating that these amounts represent constructive dividends and are taxable only to the extent of Gray Corporation's E & P, which he argues had a deficit in 1991. The IRS contends that even if § 61 does not apply, the $60,000 would still be taxable income because Gray Corporation had income in 1992. Gray Corporation is on the cash basis. It had a deficit in its E & P account as of January 1, 1992. However, it had E & P of $65,000 in 1992. Its income tax liability for 1992 was $31,500. The IRS argues that $31,500 cannot be a charge against current E & P because the tax was not paid until 1993 and the corporation was on the cash basis. Consequently, the $60,000 would be taxable income to Mark in 1992, regardless of whether it is income under § 61 or under § 301. Mark comes to you for advice. What advice would you give him?

RESEARCH PROBLEM 34 Dave owns 40% of Brown Corporation; his father owns the remaining 60%. Dave also owns 70% of White Corporation, with the remaining 30% being owned by his wife. Dave terminates his entire interest in Brown Corporation through a stock redemption that he reports as a long-term capital gain pursuant to § 302(b)(3). Three years later, White Corporation enters into a contract with Brown Corporation whereby White is given exclusive management authority over Brown's operations. Upon audit, the IRS disallowed the long-term capital gain treatment on the stock redemption in Brown Corporation contending that Dave acquired an interest in Brown within 10 years from the date of the redemption because of White's management contract with Brown. What is the result?

Chapter 19

RESEARCH PROBLEM 35 Green Corporation was liquidated in 1992. In the year of liquidation, Green reported taxable gain of $8 million, based upon a value of its assets of $10 million and a basis of $2 million. After paying its tax liability of $2,720,000, Green distributed its remaining assets, valued at $7,280,000 ($10 million less the tax paid of $2,720,000), to its 10 shareholders. Shareholder Beth received $728,000 and reported a long-term capital gain in 1992 of $628,000 ($728,000 distribution – $100,000 stock basis). In 1993, the IRS audited Green Corporation and determined that the corporation had an additional gain of $1 million in the year of liquidation. The IRS assessed additional tax of $340,000 plus penalties and interest against Green Corporation and then against Beth, based on transferee liability. Beth comes to you for advice. She is not certain where the other shareholders are located.

a. If Beth is required to pay all of the tax liability, will she be entitled to deduct the amount paid as a loss?
b. What is the nature of the loss—capital or ordinary?
c. Would § 1341 apply?
d. How can a shareholder be protected from the problem facing Beth?

RESEARCH PROBLEM 36 Black Corporation, a supermarket development company, acquired 95% of all the stock in Brown Corporation in 1975 at a cost of $11 million. Brown Corporation owns and operates several grocery stores. In 1992, Black Corporation became concerned that it was not in its best interest to operate grocery stores through a subsidiary corporation. As a result, on December 1, 1992, Black sold all its stock in Brown Corporation to Gray Corporation for $500,000 cash and a promissory note in the amount of $6.5 million. Black then claimed a long-term capital loss of $4 million [$7 million (selling price of the Brown Corporation stock) – $11 million (cost of the stock)]. Black Corporation had a long-term capital gain of $5 million in 1989 and carried back the $4 million loss to offset this gain. As a result, Black Corporation claimed it was entitled to a substantial tax refund. Shortly after Black Corporation sold its Brown stock to Gray Corporation, Brown Corporation was merged into Gray Corporation and was liquidated. On January 15, 1993,

Black Corporation purchased 93% of the property formerly belonging to Brown Corporation from Gray Corporation in consideration of Gray canceling the note in the amount of $6.5 million.

The IRS audited Black Corporation's income tax returns in 1993. It disallowed the long-term capital loss of $4 million, contending that Black had, in effect, liquidated Brown Corporation. According to the IRS, because Black Corporation would have owned at least 80% of the stock of Brown before and during the deemed liquidation, § 332 applied to the transaction. Under § 332, gains and losses on the liquidation of an 80% owned subsidiary are not recognized. What is the result to Black Corporation?

Chapter 20

Research Problem 37 Tanya owns 100% of both Ash and Bond Corporations. Ash Corporation's accumulated earnings for 1989, 1990, 1991, and 1992 were reflected almost entirely in liquid assets, which were used to obtain bonding on the construction work of the sister corporation, Bond. Ash itself undertook no construction work as a general contractor and paid no dividends during the three-year period. Both corporations entered into an indemnity agreement under which both would be liable to the bonding company for any loss it suffered from the issuance of a bond to either of the corporations. Ash Corporation was merged into Bond in early January 1991. Assume that Ash Corporation would be subject to the accumulated earnings tax if the reasonable business needs of Bond Corporation are not considered. Would Ash Corporation be subject to the accumulated earnings tax in 1989, 1990, 1991, and 1992?

Research Problem 38 Geena Corporation derived most of its income from contracts involving the personal services of its sole shareholder, Bob. In October 1992, Bob discovered that his trusted accountant, Harry, had embezzled almost $300,000 from the corporation during the calendar years ending in 1989, 1990, and 1991. Harry wrote the checks, prepared the books, and completed the financial statements. He also neglected to file corporate tax returns for the same years. Geena Corporation claimed theft losses on its tax returns for 1989, 1990, and 1991. The IRS disallowed them since embezzlement losses are properly deducted in the year of discovery.

Happily, the theft losses were claimed in 1992 and carried back to 1989, 1990, and 1991, thereby eliminating most of the corporate tax liability. But the corporation was a PHC during the years 1989, 1990, and 1991. Bob discovered that the PHC did not have a loss carryback (just a one-year carryforward). The disallowed theft loss deduction resulted in undistributed PHC income. Bob also discovered that § 545 does not provide for a § 165(e) loss deduction in arriving at undistributed PHC income. Discuss Bob's dilemma.

Chapter 21

Research Problem 39 Felder Company, a calendar year corporation, is owned by a husband and wife who are having marital problems and living apart. On March 9, 1993, both shareholders held a shareholder meeting at their attorney's office and agreed to elect S corporation status. The lawyer prepared Form 2553 and gave it to the husband, Ron, on March 11.

When Ron could not locate his wife, Dorothy, by March 13, he mailed a letter asking for an extension of time for filing Form 2553. He was able to locate Dorothy on the evening of March 15. She signed Form 2553, and Ron mailed it at a nearby post office by 11:00 P.M. The envelope, however, was eventually postmarked on March 16. To protect his position, Ron hand delivered a copy of Form 2553 to the District Director on March 16. When is the S election effective?

Research Problem 40 Mel is a 40% owner of an S corporation, and at the end of 1993, he anticipates that his stock basis will not be large enough to absorb about $12,000 of his expected share of the corporation's NOL. Mel has not loaned any money to the corporation, but he has guaranteed about $14,000 of corporate debt owed to an unrelated party. Advise Mel as to how to obtain the loss flow-through.

Chapter 22

RESEARCH PROBLEM 41 Mark and John each contributed $10,000 cash to form a limited partnership. Mark is the general partner and John is the limited partner. The partnership used the $20,000 cash to make a down payment on a building. The rest of the building's $200,000 purchase price was financed with an interest-only nonrecourse loan of $180,000, which was obtained from an independent third-party bank. The partners share all partnership items equally except for the MACRS deductions and building maintenance, which are allocated 70% to John and 30% to Mark. The partnership definitely wishes to satisfy the "economic effect" requirements of Regulation §§ 1.704–1 and 1.704–2 and will reallocate MACRS, if necessary, to satisfy the requirements of the Regulations. Mark has an unlimited obligation to restore his capital account while John is subject to a qualified income offset provision. Assume all partnership items, except for MACRS, will net to zero throughout the first three years of the partnership operations. Also, assume that each year's MACRS deduction will be $10,000 (to simplify the calculations).

Evaluate the allocation of MACRS in each of the three years under Regulation §§ 1.704–1 and 1.704–2.

RESEARCH PROBLEM 42 Fred and Grady have formed the FG Partnership to operate a retail establishment selling antique household furnishings. Fred is the general partner, and Grady is the limited partner. Both partners contribute $15,000 to form the partnership. The partnership uses the $30,000 contributed by the partners and a recourse loan of $100,000 obtained from an unrelated third-party lender to acquire $130,000 of initial inventory.

The partners believe they will have extensive losses in the first year due to advertising and initial cash-flow requirements. Fred and Grady have agreed to share losses equally. To make sure the losses can be allocated to both partners, they have included a provision in the partnership agreement requiring each partner to restore any deficit balance in his partnership capital account upon liquidation of the partnership.

Fred was also willing to include a provision that requires him to make up any deficit balance within 90 days of liquidation of the partnership. As a limited partner, Grady argued that he should not be subject to such a time requirement. The partners compromised and included a provision that requires Grady to restore a deficit balance in his capital account within two years of liquidation of the partnership. No interest will be owed on the deferred restoration payment.

Determine whether FG will be able to allocate the $100,000 recourse debt equally to the two partners to ensure that they will be able to deduct their respective shares of partnership losses.

Chapter 23

RESEARCH PROBLEM 43 The ACAA, an athletic association that is exempt under § 501(c)(3), supervises the conduct of regional and national athletic events. The most prominent event and biggest revenue generator is the men's basketball tournament. The tournament includes 64 teams and is conducted at various sites throughout the country over a three-week period.

Through an agent, the ACAA publishes programs for the tournament and sells them to spectators. About 35% of the pages in the programs are advertisements sold by the agent to local and national companies. The ACAA has consistently treated the advertising revenue from the programs as exempt income under § 501(c)(3). An IRS agent has taken the position that the advertising revenue is income from an unrelated trade or business. Determine the appropriate treatment for the advertising revenue.

Research aid:
National Collegiate Athletic Association, 92 T.C. 456 (1989).

Chapter 24

RESEARCH PROBLEM 44 A U.S. bank (the lender) has a net loan agreement with several foreign borrowers. Under a net loan agreement, the borrower remits an agreed net amount to the lender, with the foreign borrower assuming the responsibility to withhold and pay over any foreign withholding tax due on the portion of any remittances that are interest income to the U.S. lender. The U.S. bank grossed up the interest income received (to include the foreign taxes) and took an FTC. Some borrowers sent letters with the payments to the U.S. bank stating that the tax was withheld and paid. Other borrowers sent letters stating that the tax was withheld. Does the U.S. bank have the necessary documentation to support taking the FTC?

Research aid:
Continental Illinois Corporation, 61 TCM 1916, T.C.Memo. 1991–66.

RESEARCH PROBLEM 45 Gustav, a citizen and resident of Norway, comes to the United States for the first time on June 1, 1992, and remains until December 15, 1992, when he returns to Norway. On April 1, 1993, Gustav returns to the United States with green card permanent resident status and remains until November 10, 1993, when he surrenders his green card and returns to Norway. Gustav does not qualify as a U.S. resident for 1994. For what period(s) does Gustav qualify as a U.S. resident for income tax purposes during 1992 and 1993?

Research aid:
Reg. § 301.7701(b)–4(e).

Chapter 25

RESEARCH PROBLEM 46 The Church of Freedom encourages its members to file "tax protester" returns with the IRS, objecting to both (a) the government's failure to use a gold standard in payment of tax liabilities and (b) its sizable expenditures for social welfare programs. The Tax Court routinely overturns these returns as frivolous, with delinquent taxes, penalties, and interest due, and the Church has engaged in a long-standing, sometimes ugly battle with the IRS over various constitutional rights to protest the Federal income tax. Meanwhile, Church members continue to file returns in this manner.

Alice overheard Church members talking about "roughing up" the IRS agents who were scheduled to conduct an audit of various members' returns. She went to the IRS and informed them of the danger that they might encounter.

At the IRS's direction, Alice then took a key clerical job at Church headquarters, where she had access to documents that would be useful to the Service. Over a period of a few months, Alice assisted the IRS in building a case of civil and criminal tax fraud against the Church and several of its members. She supplied the IRS with copies of Church mailing lists and computer disks, helped tape record key conversations among Church leaders, and searched the Church's trash and other documents.

All of these materials were given voluntarily to Alice in her capacity as an employee by Church leaders, who never suspected that she was working with the IRS. After delivering the various materials to the Service, Alice quit her job with the Church and severed all communications with the IRS.

After the parties were charged with fraud, the government's case was found to be insufficiently supported by the evidence, and no penalties were assessed. Afterward, Church leaders sued Alice in her role as IRS informant, charging that she had violated their First Amendment rights of free association and their Fourth Amendment rights against illegal search and seizure. Government employees are immune from such charges, but Alice was only an informant to the IRS and not its employee. Can the Church leaders collect damages from Alice for informing on them to the IRS?

RESEARCH PROBLEM 47 For many years, Butcher had attended meetings of tax protesters where the constitutionality of the Federal income tax and its means of collection were routinely challenged. Members of the protest groups were provided with materials to assist them in preparing returns that claimed little or no tax was due on such grounds as that only gold- or silver-backed currency need be submitted to pay the tax, or that a tax bill had originated in the Senate rather than the House of Representatives. Some of the groups maintained that individuals need not file returns at all, because the current Federal income tax law violated various provisions of the U.S. Constitution.

The Tax Court routinely overturned such means of avoiding the tax, holding that the protester returns were frivolously filed and charging the protesters with delinquent taxes, interest, and a variety of negligence and other accuracy-related penalties, especially where taxpayers failed to file altogether. The results of these cases were never discussed in the meetings that Butcher attended, though. Consequently, although he never joined any of the groups, Butcher felt comfortable with their arguments and never filed a Federal income tax return for himself or his profitable sole proprietorship carpentry business.

When the IRS discovered his failure to file and charged him with tax, interest, and penalties, Butcher went to the tax library and found that judicial precedent and administrative authority were against him. He asked the court for relief from the civil fraud penalties related to his failure to file and failure to pay tax, based on his good faith belief that the tax protester information he had received was an acceptable interpretation of the law. According to this argument, a taxpayer who believes in good faith that the Federal income tax is unconstitutional cannot be found to have willfully failed to file and pay. Should Butcher be required to pay civil fraud penalties?

Chapter 26

RESEARCH PROBLEM 48 On October 1, 1976, Homer made a gift of $66,000 to his son. In reporting the gift, Sonya (Homer's wife) made the election under § 2513. As a result, no gift tax was due. Sonya dies in 1993, and in completing Form 706, her executor claims a unified tax credit of $192,800.

a. Why was no gift tax due on the 1976 gift?
b. Did the executor of Sonya's estate act correctly in claiming a unified tax credit of $192,800 on Form 706? Why or why not?

RESEARCH PROBLEM 49 Hector dies on April 24, 1989, and under his will a major portion of the estate passes to a trust. The provisions of the trust grant a life estate to Ellen (Hector's surviving spouse), remainder to their adult children. The income is payable to Ellen quarter-annually or at more frequent intervals. Income accrued or held undistributed by the trust at the time of Ellen's death shall pass to the remainder interest.

On January 24, 1990, Hector's estate filed a Federal estate tax return and made the QTIP election. On July 3, 1990, Hector's estate filed an amended return based on the premise that the QTIP election was improper. As a result of the loss of the marital deduction, the amended return was accompanied by a payment of additional estate taxes.

On February 11, 1990, Ellen dies. All of her assets, including those in Hector's trust, pass to the children.

a. Why did Hector's estate file an amended return revoking the QTIP election?
b. Is the revocation of the election proper procedure?
c. Did Hector's estate ever qualify for the election?

Research aids:
§§ 2056(b)(7) and 2013.
Estate of Rose D. Howard, 91 T.C. 329 (1988), *rev'd* in 90–2 USTC ¶60,033, 66AFTR 2d 90–5994, 910 F.2d 633 (CA–9, 1990).

Chapter 27

RESEARCH PROBLEM 50 Thanks to a recent speech that you gave to the Kiwanis Club, Max has been convinced of the tax-saving opportunities available from the creation of trusts. He recognizes that a great deal of income can be shifted to the marginal income tax rates that apply to his three children, and he is willing to give up as much control over the trust corpus assets as is necessary to avoid a grantor trust classification.

Max is very enthusiastic about trusts—so much so that he instructs you to place $30,000 into each of 12 trusts for each of his children. These 36 trusts would be administered separately by you, as trustee, but they would differ only in the assets that are used to fund them and in the termination date specified in the trust instrument. Specifically, one of each child's 12 trusts is scheduled to terminate annually, beginning in 15 years. Can the proliferation of multiple trusts, given the same grantor, the same trustee, the same beneficiaries, but different corpus assets and termination dates, be accepted under prevailing tax law?

RESEARCH PROBLEM 51 Your client, Annie, has come to you for some advice regarding gifts of property. She has just learned that she must undergo major surgery, and she would like to make certain gifts before entering the hospital. On your earlier advice, she had established a plan of lifetime giving for four prior years. Consider each of the following assets that she is thinking of using as gifts to family and friends. In doing so, evaluate the income tax consequences of having the property pass through her estate to the designated legatee.

a. Annie plans to give a cottage to her son to fulfill a promise made many years ago. She has owned the cottage for the past 15 years and has a basis in it of $30,000 (fair market value of $20,000).

b. Annie has $100,000 of long-term capital losses that she has been carrying forward for the past few years. Now, she is considering making a gift of $200,000 in installment notes to her daughter. Her basis in the notes is $100,000, and the notes' current fair market value is $190,000.

c. Annie has promised to make a special cash bequest of $25,000 to her grandson in her will. However, she does not anticipate having that much cash immediately available after her death. Annie requests your advice concerning the income tax consequences to the estate if the cash bequest is settled with some other property.

APPENDIX

TAX RATE SCHEDULES AND TABLES

1992 Tax Rate Schedules

Single—Schedule X

If taxable income is: Over—	But not over—	The tax is:	of the amount over—
$0	$21,450	.........15%	**$0**
21,450	51,900	**$3,217.50 + 28%**	**21,450**
51,900	....	**11,743.50 + 31%**	**51,900**

Head of household—Schedule Z

If taxable income is: Over—	But not over—	The tax is:	of the amount over—
$0	$28,750	.........15%	**$0**
28,750	74,150	**$4,312.50 + 28%**	**28,750**
74,150	....	**17,024.50 + 31%**	**74,150**

Married filing jointly or Qualifying widow(er)—Schedule Y-1

If taxable income is: Over—	But not over—	The tax is:	of the amount over—
$0	$35,800	.........15%	**$0**
35,800	86,500	**$5,370.00 + 28%**	**35,800**
86,500	....	**19,566.00 + 31%**	**86,500**

Married filing separately—Schedule Y-2

If taxable income is: Over—	But not over—	The tax is:	of the amount over—
$0	$17,900	.........15%	**$0**
17,900	43,250	**$2,685.00 + 28%**	**17,900**
43,250	....	**9,783.00 + 31%**	**43,250**

1992 Tax Table

Use if your taxable income is less than $100,000. If $100,000 or more, use the Tax Rate Schedules.

Example. Mr. and Mrs. Brown are filing a joint return. Their taxable income on line 37 of Form 1040 is $25,300. First, they find the $25,300–25,350 income line. Next, they find the column for married filing jointly and read down the column. The amount shown where the income line and filing status column meet is $3,799. This is the tax amount they must enter on line 38 of their Form 1040.

Sample Table

At least	But less than	Single	Married filing jointly *	Married filing sepa-rately	Head of a house-hold
		Your tax is—			
25,200	25,250	4,275	3,784	4,736	3,784
25,250	25,300	4,289	3,791	4,750	3,791
25,300	25,350	4,303	(3,799)	4,764	3,799
25,350	25,400	4,317	3,806	4,778	3,806

If line 37 (taxable income) is—		And you are—			
At least	But less than	Single	Married filing jointly *	Married filing sepa-rately	Head of a house-hold
		Your tax is—			
0	5	0	0	0	0
5	15	2	2	2	2
15	25	3	3	3	3
25	50	6	6	6	6
50	75	9	9	9	9
75	100	13	13	13	13
100	125	17	17	17	17
125	150	21	21	21	21
150	175	24	24	24	24
175	200	28	28	28	28
200	225	32	32	32	32
225	250	36	36	36	36
250	275	39	39	39	39
275	300	43	43	43	43
300	325	47	47	47	47
325	350	51	51	51	51
350	375	54	54	54	54
375	400	58	58	58	58
400	425	62	62	62	62
425	450	66	66	66	66
450	475	69	69	69	69
475	500	73	73	73	73
500	525	77	77	77	77
525	550	81	81	81	81
550	575	84	84	84	84
575	600	88	88	88	88
600	625	92	92	92	92
625	650	96	96	96	96
650	675	99	99	99	99
675	700	103	103	103	103
700	725	107	107	107	107
725	750	111	111	111	111
750	775	114	114	114	114
775	800	118	118	118	118
800	825	122	122	122	122
825	850	126	126	126	126
850	875	129	129	129	129
875	900	133	133	133	133
900	925	137	137	137	137
925	950	141	141	141	141
950	975	144	144	144	144
975	1,000	148	148	148	148
1,000					
1,000	1,025	152	152	152	152
1,025	1,050	156	156	156	156
1,050	1,075	159	159	159	159
1,075	1,100	163	163	163	163
1,100	1,125	167	167	167	167
1,125	1,150	171	171	171	171
1,150	1,175	174	174	174	174
1,175	1,200	178	178	178	178
1,200	1,225	182	182	182	182
1,225	1,250	186	186	186	186
1,250	1,275	189	189	189	189
1,275	1,300	193	193	193	193

If line 37 (taxable income) is—		And you are—			
At least	But less than	Single	Married filing jointly *	Married filing sepa-rately	Head of a house-hold
		Your tax is—			
1,300	1,325	197	197	197	197
1,325	1,350	201	201	201	201
1,350	1,375	204	204	204	204
1,375	1,400	208	208	208	208
1,400	1,425	212	212	212	212
1,425	1,450	216	216	216	216
1,450	1,475	219	219	219	219
1,475	1,500	223	223	223	223
1,500	1,525	227	227	227	227
1,525	1,550	231	231	231	231
1,550	1,575	234	234	234	234
1,575	1,600	238	238	238	238
1,600	1,625	242	242	242	242
1,625	1,650	246	246	246	246
1,650	1,675	249	249	249	249
1,675	1,700	253	253	253	253
1,700	1,725	257	257	257	257
1,725	1,750	261	261	261	261
1,750	1,775	264	264	264	264
1,775	1,800	268	268	268	268
1,800	1,825	272	272	272	272
1,825	1,850	276	276	276	276
1,850	1,875	279	279	279	279
1,875	1,900	283	283	283	283
1,900	1,925	287	287	287	287
1,925	1,950	291	291	291	291
1,950	1,975	294	294	294	294
1,975	2,000	298	298	298	298
2,000					
2,000	2,025	302	302	302	302
2,025	2,050	306	306	306	306
2,050	2,075	309	309	309	309
2,075	2,100	313	313	313	313
2,100	2,125	317	317	317	317
2,125	2,150	321	321	321	321
2,150	2,175	324	324	324	324
2,175	2,200	328	328	328	328
2,200	2,225	332	332	332	332
2,225	2,250	336	336	336	336
2,250	2,275	339	339	339	339
2,275	2,300	343	343	343	343
2,300	2,325	347	347	347	347
2,325	2,350	351	351	351	351
2,350	2,375	354	354	354	354
2,375	2,400	358	358	358	358
2,400	2,425	362	362	362	362
2,425	2,450	366	366	366	366
2,450	2,475	369	369	369	369
2,475	2,500	373	373	373	373
2,500	2,525	377	377	377	377
2,525	2,550	381	381	381	381
2,550	2,575	384	384	384	384
2,575	2,600	388	388	388	388
2,600	2,625	392	392	392	392
2,625	2,650	396	396	396	396
2,650	2,675	399	399	399	399
2,675	2,700	403	403	403	403

If line 37 (taxable income) is—		And you are—			
At least	But less than	Single	Married filing jointly *	Married filing sepa-rately	Head of a house-hold
		Your tax is—			
2,700	2,725	407	407	407	407
2,725	2,750	411	411	411	411
2,750	2,775	414	414	414	414
2,775	2,800	418	418	418	418
2,800	2,825	422	422	422	422
2,825	2,850	426	426	426	426
2,850	2,875	429	429	429	429
2,875	2,900	433	433	433	433
2,900	2,925	437	437	437	437
2,925	2,950	441	441	441	441
2,950	2,975	444	444	444	444
2,975	3,000	448	448	448	448
3,000					
3,000	3,050	454	454	454	454
3,050	3,100	461	461	461	461
3,100	3,150	469	469	469	469
3,150	3,200	476	476	476	476
3,200	3,250	484	484	484	484
3,250	3,300	491	491	491	491
3,300	3,350	499	499	499	499
3,350	3,400	506	506	506	506
3,400	3,450	514	514	514	514
3,450	3,500	521	521	521	521
3,500	3,550	529	529	529	529
3,550	3,600	536	536	536	536
3,600	3,650	544	544	544	544
3,650	3,700	551	551	551	551
3,700	3,750	559	559	559	559
3,750	3,800	566	566	566	566
3,800	3,850	574	574	574	574
3,850	3,900	581	581	581	581
3,900	3,950	589	589	589	589
3,950	4,000	596	596	596	596
4,000					
4,000	4,050	604	604	604	604
4,050	4,100	611	611	611	611
4,100	4,150	619	619	619	619
4,150	4,200	626	626	626	626
4,200	4,250	634	634	634	634
4,250	4,300	641	641	641	641
4,300	4,350	649	649	649	649
4,350	4,400	656	656	656	656
4,400	4,450	664	664	664	664
4,450	4,500	671	671	671	671
4,500	4,550	679	679	679	679
4,550	4,600	686	686	686	686
4,600	4,650	694	694	694	694
4,650	4,700	701	701	701	701
4,700	4,750	709	709	709	709
4,750	4,800	716	716	716	716
4,800	4,850	724	724	724	724
4,850	4,900	731	731	731	731
4,900	4,950	739	739	739	739
4,950	5,000	746	746	746	746

Continued on next page

* This column must also be used by a qualifying widow(er).

1992 Tax Table—*Continued*

If line 37 (taxable income) is—		And you are—			
At least	But less than	Single	Married filing jointly *	Married filing sepa-rately	Head of a house-hold
		Your tax is—			
5,000					
5,000	**5,050**	754	754	754	754
5,050	**5,100**	761	761	761	761
5,100	**5,150**	769	769	769	769
5,150	**5,200**	776	776	776	776
5,200	**5,250**	784	784	784	784
5,250	**5,300**	791	791	791	791
5,300	**5,350**	799	799	799	799
5,350	**5,400**	806	806	806	806
5,400	**5,450**	814	814	814	814
5,450	**5,500**	821	821	821	821
5,500	**5,550**	829	829	829	829
5,550	**5,600**	836	836	836	836
5,600	**5,650**	844	844	844	844
5,650	**5,700**	851	851	851	851
5,700	**5,750**	859	859	859	859
5,750	**5,800**	866	866	866	866
5,800	**5,850**	874	874	874	874
5,850	**5,900**	881	881	881	881
5,900	**5,950**	889	889	889	889
5,950	**6,000**	896	896	896	896
6,000					
6,000	**6,050**	904	904	904	904
6,050	**6,100**	911	911	911	911
6,100	**6,150**	919	919	919	919
6,150	**6,200**	926	926	926	926
6,200	**6,250**	934	934	934	934
6,250	**6,300**	941	941	941	941
6,300	**6,350**	949	949	949	949
6,350	**6,400**	956	956	956	956
6,400	**6,450**	964	964	964	964
6,450	**6,500**	971	971	971	971
6,500	**6,550**	979	979	979	979
6,550	**6,600**	986	986	986	986
6,600	**6,650**	994	994	994	994
6,650	**6,700**	1,001	1,001	1,001	1,001
6,700	**6,750**	1,009	1,009	1,009	1,009
6,750	**6,800**	1,016	1,016	1,016	1,016
6,800	**6,850**	1,024	1,024	1,024	1,024
6,850	**6,900**	1,031	1,031	1,031	1,031
6,900	**6,950**	1,039	1,039	1,039	1,039
6,950	**7,000**	1,046	1,046	1,046	1,046
7,000					
7,000	**7,050**	1,054	1,054	1,054	1,054
7,050	**7,100**	1,061	1,061	1,061	1,061
7,100	**7,150**	1,069	1,069	1,069	1,069
7,150	**7,200**	1,076	1,076	1,076	1,076
7,200	**7,250**	1,084	1,084	1,084	1,084
7,250	**7,300**	1,091	1,091	1,091	1,091
7,300	**7,350**	1,099	1,099	1,099	1,099
7,350	**7,400**	1,106	1,106	1,106	1,106
7,400	**7,450**	1,114	1,114	1,114	1,114
7,450	**7,500**	1,121	1,121	1,121	1,121
7,500	**7,550**	1,129	1,129	1,129	1,129
7,550	**7,600**	1,136	1,136	1,136	1,136
7,600	**7,650**	1,144	1,144	1,144	1,144
7,650	**7,700**	1,151	1,151	1,151	1,151
7,700	**7,750**	1,159	1,159	1,159	1,159
7,750	**7,800**	1,166	1,166	1,166	1,166
7,800	**7,850**	1,174	1,174	1,174	1,174
7,850	**7,900**	1,181	1,181	1,181	1,181
7,900	**7,950**	1,189	1,189	1,189	1,189
7,950	**8,000**	1,196	1,196	1,196	1,196

If line 37 (taxable income) is—		And you are—			
At least	But less than	Single	Married filing jointly *	Married filing sepa-rately	Head of a house-hold
		Your tax is—			
8,000					
8,000	**8,050**	1,204	1,204	1,204	1,204
8,050	**8,100**	1,211	1,211	1,211	1,211
8,100	**8,150**	1,219	1,219	1,219	1,219
8,150	**8,200**	1,226	1,226	1,226	1,226
8,200	**8,250**	1,234	1,234	1,234	1,234
8,250	**8,300**	1,241	1,241	1,241	1,241
8,300	**8,350**	1,249	1,249	1,249	1,249
8,350	**8,400**	1,256	1,256	1,256	1,256
8,400	**8,450**	1,264	1,264	1,264	1,264
8,450	**8,500**	1,271	1,271	1,271	1,271
8,500	**8,550**	1,279	1,279	1,279	1,279
8,550	**8,600**	1,286	1,286	1,286	1,286
8,600	**8,650**	1,294	1,294	1,294	1,294
8,650	**8,700**	1,301	1,301	1,301	1,301
8,700	**8,750**	1,309	1,309	1,309	1,309
8,750	**8,800**	1,316	1,316	1,316	1,316
8,800	**8,850**	1,324	1,324	1,324	1,324
8,850	**8,900**	1,331	1,331	1,331	1,331
8,900	**8,950**	1,339	1,339	1,339	1,339
8,950	**9,000**	1,346	1,346	1,346	1,346
9,000					
9,000	**9,050**	1,354	1,354	1,354	1,354
9,050	**9,100**	1,361	1,361	1,361	1,361
9,100	**9,150**	1,369	1,369	1,369	1,369
9,150	**9,200**	1,376	1,376	1,376	1,376
9,200	**9,250**	1,384	1,384	1,384	1,384
9,250	**9,300**	1,391	1,391	1,391	1,391
9,300	**9,350**	1,399	1,399	1,399	1,399
9,350	**9,400**	1,406	1,406	1,406	1,406
9,400	**9,450**	1,414	1,414	1,414	1,414
9,450	**9,500**	1,421	1,421	1,421	1,421
9,500	**9,550**	1,429	1,429	1,429	1,429
9,550	**9,600**	1,436	1,436	1,436	1,436
9,600	**9,650**	1,444	1,444	1,444	1,444
9,650	**9,700**	1,451	1,451	1,451	1,451
9,700	**9,750**	1,459	1,459	1,459	1,459
9,750	**9,800**	1,466	1,466	1,466	1,466
9,800	**9,850**	1,474	1,474	1,474	1,474
9,850	**9,900**	1,481	1,481	1,481	1,481
9,900	**9,950**	1,489	1,489	1,489	1,489
9,950	**10,000**	1,496	1,496	1,496	1,496
10,000					
10,000	**10,050**	1,504	1,504	1,504	1,504
10,050	**10,100**	1,511	1,511	1,511	1,511
10,100	**10,150**	1,519	1,519	1,519	1,519
10,150	**10,200**	1,526	1,526	1,526	1,526
10,200	**10,250**	1,534	1,534	1,534	1,534
10,250	**10,300**	1,541	1,541	1,541	1,541
10,300	**10,350**	1,549	1,549	1,549	1,549
10,350	**10,400**	1,556	1,556	1,556	1,556
10,400	**10,450**	1,564	1,564	1,564	1,564
10,450	**10,500**	1,571	1,571	1,571	1,571
10,500	**10,550**	1,579	1,579	1,579	1,579
10,550	**10,600**	1,586	1,586	1,586	1,586
10,600	**10,650**	1,594	1,594	1,594	1,594
10,650	**10,700**	1,601	1,601	1,601	1,601
10,700	**10,750**	1,609	1,609	1,609	1,609
10,750	**10,800**	1,616	1,616	1,616	1,616
10,800	**10,850**	1,624	1,624	1,624	1,624
10,850	**10,900**	1,631	1,631	1,631	1,631
10,900	**10,950**	1,639	1,639	1,639	1,639
10,950	**11,000**	1,646	1,646	1,646	1,646

If line 37 (taxable income) is—		And you are—			
At least	But less than	Single	Married filing jointly *	Married filing sepa-rately	Head of a house-hold
		Your tax is—			
11,000					
11,000	**11,050**	1,654	1,654	1,654	1,654
11,050	**11,100**	1,661	1,661	1,661	1,661
11,100	**11,150**	1,669	1,669	1,669	1,669
11,150	**11,200**	1,676	1,676	1,676	1,676
11,200	**11,250**	1,684	1,684	1,684	1,684
11,250	**11,300**	1,691	1,691	1,691	1,691
11,300	**11,350**	1,699	1,699	1,699	1,699
11,350	**11,400**	1,706	1,706	1,706	1,706
11,400	**11,450**	1,714	1,714	1,714	1,714
11,450	**11,500**	1,721	1,721	1,721	1,721
11,500	**11,550**	1,729	1,729	1,729	1,729
11,550	**11,600**	1,736	1,736	1,736	1,736
11,600	**11,650**	1,744	1,744	1,744	1,744
11,650	**11,700**	1,751	1,751	1,751	1,751
11,700	**11,750**	1,759	1,759	1,759	1,759
11,750	**11,800**	1,766	1,766	1,766	1,766
11,800	**11,850**	1,774	1,774	1,774	1,774
11,850	**11,900**	1,781	1,781	1,781	1,781
11,900	**11,950**	1,789	1,789	1,789	1,789
11,950	**12,000**	1,796	1,796	1,796	1,796
12,000					
12,000	**12,050**	1,804	1,804	1,804	1,804
12,050	**12,100**	1,811	1,811	1,811	1,811
12,100	**12,150**	1,819	1,819	1,819	1,819
12,150	**12,200**	1,826	1,826	1,826	1,826
12,200	**12,250**	1,834	1,834	1,834	1,834
12,250	**12,300**	1,841	1,841	1,841	1,841
12,300	**12,350**	1,849	1,849	1,849	1,849
12,350	**12,400**	1,856	1,856	1,856	1,856
12,400	**12,450**	1,864	1,864	1,864	1,864
12,450	**12,500**	1,871	1,871	1,871	1,871
12,500	**12,550**	1,879	1,879	1,879	1,879
12,550	**12,600**	1,886	1,886	1,886	1,886
12,600	**12,650**	1,894	1,894	1,894	1,894
12,650	**12,700**	1,901	1,901	1,901	1,901
12,700	**12,750**	1,909	1,909	1,909	1,909
12,750	**12,800**	1,916	1,916	1,916	1,916
12,800	**12,850**	1,924	1,924	1,924	1,924
12,850	**12,900**	1,931	1,931	1,931	1,931
12,900	**12,950**	1,939	1,939	1,939	1,939
12,950	**13,000**	1,946	1,946	1,946	1,946
13,000					
13,000	**13,050**	1,954	1,954	1,954	1,954
13,050	**13,100**	1,961	1,961	1,961	1,961
13,100	**13,150**	1,969	1,969	1,969	1,969
13,150	**13,200**	1,976	1,976	1,976	1,976
13,200	**13,250**	1,984	1,984	1,984	1,984
13,250	**13,300**	1,991	1,991	1,991	1,991
13,300	**13,350**	1,999	1,999	1,999	1,999
13,350	**13,400**	2,006	2,006	2,006	2,006
13,400	**13,450**	2,014	2,014	2,014	2,014
13,450	**13,500**	2,021	2,021	2,021	2,021
13,500	**13,550**	2,029	2,029	2,029	2,029
13,550	**13,600**	2,036	2,036	2,036	2,036
13,600	**13,650**	2,044	2,044	2,044	2,044
13,650	**13,700**	2,051	2,051	2,051	2,051
13,700	**13,750**	2,059	2,059	2,059	2,059
13,750	**13,800**	2,066	2,066	2,066	2,066
13,800	**13,850**	2,074	2,074	2,074	2,074
13,850	**13,900**	2,081	2,081	2,081	2,081
13,900	**13,950**	2,089	2,089	2,089	2,089
13,950	**14,000**	2,096	2,096	2,096	2,096

* This column must also be used by a qualifying widow(er).

Continued on next page

1992 Tax Table—*Continued*

If line 37 (taxable income) is—		And you are—			
At least	But less than	Single	Married filing jointly *	Married filing sepa-rately	Head of a house-hold
		Your tax is—			
14,000					
14,000	14,050	2,104	2,104	2,104	2,104
14,050	14,100	2,111	2,111	2,111	2,111
14,100	14,150	2,119	2,119	2,119	2,119
14,150	14,200	2,126	2,126	2,126	2,126
14,200	14,250	2,134	2,134	2,134	2,134
14,250	14,300	2,141	2,141	2,141	2,141
14,300	14,350	2,149	2,149	2,149	2,149
14,350	14,400	2,156	2,156	2,156	2,156
14,400	14,450	2,164	2,164	2,164	2,164
14,450	14,500	2,171	2,171	2,171	2,171
14,500	14,550	2,179	2,179	2,179	2,179
14,550	14,600	2,186	2,186	2,186	2,186
14,600	14,650	2,194	2,194	2,194	2,194
14,650	14,700	2,201	2,201	2,201	2,201
14,700	14,750	2,209	2,209	2,209	2,209
14,750	14,800	2,216	2,216	2,216	2,216
14,800	14,850	2,224	2,224	2,224	2,224
14,850	14,900	2,231	2,231	2,231	2,231
14,900	14,950	2,239	2,239	2,239	2,239
14,950	15,000	2,246	2,246	2,246	2,246
15,000					
15,000	15,050	2,254	2,254	2,254	2,254
15,050	15,100	2,261	2,261	2,261	2,261
15,100	15,150	2,269	2,269	2,269	2,269
15,150	15,200	2,276	2,276	2,276	2,276
15,200	15,250	2,284	2,284	2,284	2,284
15,250	15,300	2,291	2,291	2,291	2,291
15,300	15,350	2,299	2,299	2,299	2,299
15,350	15,400	2,306	2,306	2,306	2,306
15,400	15,450	2,314	2,314	2,314	2,314
15,450	15,500	2,321	2,321	2,321	2,321
15,500	15,550	2,329	2,329	2,329	2,329
15,550	15,600	2,336	2,336	2,336	2,336
15,600	15,650	2,344	2,344	2,344	2,344
15,650	15,700	2,351	2,351	2,351	2,351
15,700	15,750	2,359	2,359	2,359	2,359
15,750	15,800	2,366	2,366	2,366	2,366
15,800	15,850	2,374	2,374	2,374	2,374
15,850	15,900	2,381	2,381	2,381	2,381
15,900	15,950	2,389	2,389	2,389	2,389
15,950	16,000	2,396	2,396	2,396	2,396
16,000					
16,000	16,050	2,404	2,404	2,404	2,404
16,050	16,100	2,411	2,411	2,411	2,411
16,100	16,150	2,419	2,419	2,419	2,419
16,150	16,200	2,426	2,426	2,426	2,426
16,200	16,250	2,434	2,434	2,434	2,434
16,250	16,300	2,441	2,441	2,441	2,441
16,300	16,350	2,449	2,449	2,449	2,449
16,350	16,400	2,456	2,456	2,456	2,456
16,400	16,450	2,464	2,464	2,464	2,464
16,450	16,500	2,471	2,471	2,471	2,471
16,500	16,550	2,479	2,479	2,479	2,479
16,550	16,600	2,486	2,486	2,486	2,486
16,600	16,650	2,494	2,494	2,494	2,494
16,650	16,700	2,501	2,501	2,501	2,501
16,700	16,750	2,509	2,509	2,509	2,509
16,750	16,800	2,516	2,516	2,516	2,516
16,800	16,850	2,524	2,524	2,524	2,524
16,850	16,900	2,531	2,531	2,531	2,531
16,900	16,950	2,539	2,539	2,539	2,539
16,950	17,000	2,546	2,546	2,546	2,546

If line 37 (taxable income) is—		And you are—			
At least	But less than	Single	Married filing jointly *	Married filing sepa-rately	Head of a house-hold
		Your tax is—			
17,000					
17,000	17,050	2,554	2,554	2,554	2,554
17,050	17,100	2,561	2,561	2,561	2,561
17,100	17,150	2,569	2,569	2,569	2,569
17,150	17,200	2,576	2,576	2,576	2,576
17,200	17,250	2,584	2,584	2,584	2,584
17,250	17,300	2,591	2,591	2,591	2,591
17,300	17,350	2,599	2,599	2,599	2,599
17,350	17,400	2,606	2,606	2,606	2,606
17,400	17,450	2,614	2,614	2,614	2,614
17,450	17,500	2,621	2,621	2,621	2,621
17,500	17,550	2,629	2,629	2,629	2,629
17,550	17,600	2,636	2,636	2,636	2,636
17,600	17,650	2,644	2,644	2,644	2,644
17,650	17,700	2,651	2,651	2,651	2,651
17,700	17,750	2,659	2,659	2,659	2,659
17,750	17,800	2,666	2,666	2,666	2,666
17,800	17,850	2,674	2,674	2,674	2,674
17,850	17,900	2,681	2,681	2,681	2,681
17,900	17,950	2,689	2,689	2,692	2,689
17,950	18,000	2,696	2,696	2,706	2,696
18,000					
18,000	18,050	2,704	2,704	2,720	2,704
18,050	18,100	2,711	2,711	2,734	2,711
18,100	18,150	2,719	2,719	2,748	2,719
18,150	18,200	2,726	2,726	2,762	2,726
18,200	18,250	2,734	2,734	2,776	2,734
18,250	18,300	2,741	2,741	2,790	2,741
18,300	18,350	2,749	2,749	2,804	2,749
18,350	18,400	2,756	2,756	2,818	2,756
18,400	18,450	2,764	2,764	2,832	2,764
18,450	18,500	2,771	2,771	2,846	2,771
18,500	18,550	2,779	2,779	2,860	2,779
18,550	18,600	2,786	2,786	2,874	2,786
18,600	18,650	2,794	2,794	2,888	2,794
18,650	18,700	2,801	2,801	2,902	2,801
18,700	18,750	2,809	2,809	2,916	2,809
18,750	18,800	2,816	2,816	2,930	2,816
18,800	18,850	2,824	2,824	2,944	2,824
18,850	18,900	2,831	2,831	2,958	2,831
18,900	18,950	2,839	2,839	2,972	2,839
18,950	19,000	2,846	2,846	2,986	2,846
19,000					
19,000	19,050	2,854	2,854	3,000	2,854
19,050	19,100	2,861	2,861	3,014	2,861
19,100	19,150	2,869	2,869	3,028	2,869
19,150	19,200	2,876	2,876	3,042	2,876
19,200	19,250	2,884	2,884	3,056	2,884
19,250	19,300	2,891	2,891	3,070	2,891
19,300	19,350	2,899	2,899	3,084	2,899
19,350	19,400	2,906	2,906	3,098	2,906
19,400	19,450	2,914	2,914	3,112	2,914
19,450	19,500	2,921	2,921	3,126	2,921
19,500	19,550	2,929	2,929	3,140	2,929
19,550	19,600	2,936	2,936	3,154	2,936
19,600	19,650	2,944	2,944	3,168	2,944
19,650	19,700	2,951	2,951	3,182	2,951
19,700	19,750	2,959	2,959	3,196	2,959
19,750	19,800	2,966	2,966	3,210	2,966
19,800	19,850	2,974	2,974	3,224	2,974
19,850	19,900	2,981	2,981	3,238	2,981
19,900	19,950	2,989	2,989	3,252	2,989
19,950	20,000	2,996	2,996	3,266	2,996

If line 37 (taxable income) is—		And you are—			
At least	But less than	Single	Married filing jointly *	Married filing sepa-rately	Head of a house-hold
		Your tax is—			
20,000					
20,000	20,050	3,004	3,004	3,280	3,004
20,050	20,100	3,011	3,011	3,294	3,011
20,100	20,150	3,019	3,019	3,308	3,019
20,150	20,200	3,026	3,026	3,322	3,026
20,200	20,250	3,034	3,034	3,336	3,034
20,250	20,300	3,041	3,041	3,350	3,041
20,300	20,350	3,049	3,049	3,364	3,049
20,350	20,400	3,056	3,056	3,378	3,056
20,400	20,450	3,064	3,064	3,392	3,064
20,450	20,500	3,071	3,071	3,406	3,071
20,500	20,550	3,079	3,079	3,420	3,079
20,550	20,600	3,086	3,086	3,434	3,086
20,600	20,650	3,094	3,094	3,448	3,094
20,650	20,700	3,101	3,101	3,462	3,101
20,700	20,750	3,109	3,109	3,476	3,109
20,750	20,800	3,116	3,116	3,490	3,116
20,800	20,850	3,124	3,124	3,504	3,124
20,850	20,900	3,131	3,131	3,518	3,131
20,900	20,950	3,139	3,139	3,532	3,139
20,950	21,000	3,146	3,146	3,546	3,146
21,000					
21,000	21,050	3,154	3,154	3,560	3,154
21,050	21,100	3,161	3,161	3,574	3,161
21,100	21,150	3,169	3,169	3,588	3,169
21,150	21,200	3,176	3,176	3,602	3,176
21,200	21,250	3,184	3,184	3,616	3,184
21,250	21,300	3,191	3,191	3,630	3,191
21,300	21,350	3,199	3,199	3,644	3,199
21,350	21,400	3,206	3,206	3,658	3,206
21,400	21,450	3,214	3,214	3,672	3,214
21,450	21,500	3,225	3,221	3,686	3,221
21,500	21,550	3,239	3,229	3,700	3,229
21,550	21,600	3,253	3,236	3,714	3,236
21,600	21,650	3,267	3,244	3,728	3,244
21,650	21,700	3,281	3,251	3,742	3,251
21,700	21,750	3,295	3,259	3,756	3,259
21,750	21,800	3,309	3,266	3,770	3,266
21,800	21,850	3,323	3,274	3,784	3,274
21,850	21,900	3,337	3,281	3,798	3,281
21,900	21,950	3,351	3,289	3,812	3,289
21,950	22,000	3,365	3,296	3,826	3,296
22,000					
22,000	22,050	3,379	3,304	3,840	3,304
22,050	22,100	3,393	3,311	3,854	3,311
22,100	22,150	3,407	3,319	3,868	3,319
22,150	22,200	3,421	3,326	3,882	3,326
22,200	22,250	3,435	3,334	3,896	3,334
22,250	22,300	3,449	3,341	3,910	3,341
22,300	22,350	3,463	3,349	3,924	3,349
22,350	22,400	3,477	3,356	3,938	3,356
22,400	22,450	3,491	3,364	3,952	3,364
22,450	22,500	3,505	3,371	3,966	3,371
22,500	22,550	3,519	3,379	3,980	3,379
22,550	22,600	3,533	3,386	3,994	3,386
22,600	22,650	3,547	3,394	4,008	3,394
22,650	22,700	3,561	3,401	4,022	3,401
22,700	22,750	3,575	3,409	4,036	3,409
22,750	22,800	3,589	3,416	4,050	3,416
22,800	22,850	3,603	3,424	4,064	3,424
22,850	22,900	3,617	3,431	4,078	3,431
22,900	22,950	3,631	3,439	4,092	3,439
22,950	23,000	3,645	3,446	4,106	3,446

* This column must also be used by a qualifying widow(er).

Continued on next page

1992 Tax Table—*Continued*

If line 37 (taxable income) is— At least	But less than	Single	Married filing jointly *	Married filing separately	Head of a household
		Your tax is—			
23,000					
23,000	23,050	3,659	3,454	4,120	3,454
23,050	23,100	3,673	3,461	4,134	3,461
23,100	23,150	3,687	3,469	4,148	3,469
23,150	23,200	3,701	3,476	4,162	3,476
23,200	23,250	3,715	3,484	4,176	3,484
23,250	23,300	3,729	3,491	4,190	3,491
23,300	23,350	3,743	3,499	4,204	3,499
23,350	23,400	3,757	3,506	4,218	3,506
23,400	23,450	3,771	3,514	4,232	3,514
23,450	23,500	3,785	3,521	4,246	3,521
23,500	23,550	3,799	3,529	4,260	3,529
23,550	23,600	3,813	3,536	4,274	3,536
23,600	23,650	3,827	3,544	4,288	3,544
23,650	23,700	3,841	3,551	4,302	3,551
23,700	23,750	3,855	3,559	4,316	3,559
23,750	23,800	3,869	3,566	4,330	3,566
23,800	23,850	3,883	3,574	4,344	3,574
23,850	23,900	3,897	3,581	4,358	3,581
23,900	23,950	3,911	3,589	4,372	3,589
23,950	24,000	3,925	3,596	4,386	3,596
24,000					
24,000	24,050	3,939	3,604	4,400	3,604
24,050	24,100	3,953	3,611	4,414	3,611
24,100	24,150	3,967	3,619	4,428	3,619
24,150	24,200	3,981	3,626	4,442	3,626
24,200	24,250	3,995	3,634	4,456	3,634
24,250	24,300	4,009	3,641	4,470	3,641
24,300	24,350	4,023	3,649	4,484	3,649
24,350	24,400	4,037	3,656	4,498	3,656
24,400	24,450	4,051	3,664	4,512	3,664
24,450	24,500	4,065	3,671	4,526	3,671
24,500	24,550	4,079	3,679	4,540	3,679
24,550	24,600	4,093	3,686	4,554	3,686
24,600	24,650	4,107	3,694	4,568	3,694
24,650	24,700	4,121	3,701	4,582	3,701
24,700	24,750	4,135	3,709	4,596	3,709
24,750	24,800	4,149	3,716	4,610	3,716
24,800	24,850	4,163	3,724	4,624	3,724
24,850	24,900	4,177	3,731	4,638	3,731
24,900	24,950	4,191	3,739	4,652	3,739
24,950	25,000	4,205	3,746	4,666	3,746
25,000					
25,000	25,050	4,219	3,754	4,680	3,754
25,050	25,100	4,233	3,761	4,694	3,761
25,100	25,150	4,247	3,769	4,708	3,769
25,150	25,200	4,261	3,776	4,722	3,776
25,200	25,250	4,275	3,784	4,736	3,784
25,250	25,300	4,289	3,791	4,750	3,791
25,300	25,350	4,303	3,799	4,764	3,799
25,350	25,400	4,317	3,806	4,778	3,806
25,400	25,450	4,331	3,814	4,792	3,814
25,450	25,500	4,345	3,821	4,806	3,821
25,500	25,550	4,359	3,829	4,820	3,829
25,550	25,600	4,373	3,836	4,834	3,836
25,600	25,650	4,387	3,844	4,848	3,844
25,650	25,700	4,401	3,851	4,862	3,851
25,700	25,750	4,415	3,859	4,876	3,859
25,750	25,800	4,429	3,866	4,890	3,866
25,800	25,850	4,443	3,874	4,904	3,874
25,850	25,900	4,457	3,881	4,918	3,881
25,900	25,950	4,471	3,889	4,932	3,889
25,950	26,000	4,485	3,896	4,946	3,896

If line 37 (taxable income) is— At least	But less than	Single	Married filing jointly *	Married filing separately	Head of a household
		Your tax is—			
26,000					
26,000	26,050	4,499	3,904	4,960	3,904
26,050	26,100	4,513	3,911	4,974	3,911
26,100	26,150	4,527	3,919	4,988	3,919
26,150	26,200	4,541	3,926	5,002	3,926
26,200	26,250	4,555	3,934	5,016	3,934
26,250	26,300	4,569	3,941	5,030	3,941
26,300	26,350	4,583	3,949	5,044	3,949
26,350	26,400	4,597	3,956	5,058	3,956
26,400	26,450	4,611	3,964	5,072	3,964
26,450	26,500	4,625	3,971	5,086	3,971
26,500	26,550	4,639	3,979	5,100	3,979
26,550	26,600	4,653	3,986	5,114	3,986
26,600	26,650	4,667	3,994	5,128	3,994
26,650	26,700	4,681	4,001	5,142	4,001
26,700	26,750	4,695	4,009	5,156	4,009
26,750	26,800	4,709	4,016	5,170	4,016
26,800	26,850	4,723	4,024	5,184	4,024
26,850	26,900	4,737	4,031	5,198	4,031
26,900	26,950	4,751	4,039	5,212	4,039
26,950	27,000	4,765	4,046	5,226	4,046
27,000					
27,000	27,050	4,779	4,054	5,240	4,054
27,050	27,100	4,793	4,061	5,254	4,061
27,100	27,150	4,807	4,069	5,268	4,069
27,150	27,200	4,821	4,076	5,282	4,076
27,200	27,250	4,835	4,084	5,296	4,084
27,250	27,300	4,849	4,091	5,310	4,091
27,300	27,350	4,863	4,099	5,324	4,099
27,350	27,400	4,877	4,106	5,338	4,106
27,400	27,450	4,891	4,114	5,352	4,114
27,450	27,500	4,905	4,121	5,366	4,121
27,500	27,550	4,919	4,129	5,380	4,129
27,550	27,600	4,933	4,136	5,394	4,136
27,600	27,650	4,947	4,144	5,408	4,144
27,650	27,700	4,961	4,151	5,422	4,151
27,700	27,750	4,975	4,159	5,436	4,159
27,750	27,800	4,989	4,166	5,450	4,166
27,800	27,850	5,003	4,174	5,464	4,174
27,850	27,900	5,017	4,181	5,478	4,181
27,900	27,950	5,031	4,189	5,492	4,189
27,950	28,000	5,045	4,196	5,506	4,196
28,000					
28,000	28,050	5,059	4,204	5,520	4,204
28,050	28,100	5,073	4,211	5,534	4,211
28,100	28,150	5,087	4,219	5,548	4,219
28,150	28,200	5,101	4,226	5,562	4,226
28,200	28,250	5,115	4,234	5,576	4,234
28,250	28,300	5,129	4,241	5,590	4,241
28,300	28,350	5,143	4,249	5,604	4,249
28,350	28,400	5,157	4,256	5,618	4,256
28,400	28,450	5,171	4,264	5,632	4,264
28,450	28,500	5,185	4,271	5,646	4,271
28,500	28,550	5,199	4,279	5,660	4,279
28,550	28,600	5,213	4,286	5,674	4,286
28,600	28,650	5,227	4,294	5,688	4,294
28,650	28,700	5,241	4,301	5,702	4,301
28,700	28,750	5,255	4,309	5,716	4,309
28,750	28,800	5,269	4,316	5,730	4,320
28,800	28,850	5,283	4,324	5,744	4,334
28,850	28,900	5,297	4,331	5,758	4,348
28,900	28,950	5,311	4,339	5,772	4,362
28,950	29,000	5,325	4,346	5,786	4,376

If line 37 (taxable income) is— At least	But less than	Single	Married filing jointly *	Married filing separately	Head of a household
		Your tax is—			
29,000					
29,000	29,050	5,339	4,354	5,800	4,390
29,050	29,100	5,353	4,361	5,814	4,404
29,100	29,150	5,367	4,369	5,828	4,418
29,150	29,200	5,381	4,376	5,842	4,432
29,200	29,250	5,395	4,384	5,856	4,446
29,250	29,300	5,409	4,391	5,870	4,460
29,300	29,350	5,423	4,399	5,884	4,474
29,350	29,400	5,437	4,406	5,898	4,488
29,400	29,450	5,451	4,414	5,912	4,502
29,450	29,500	5,465	4,421	5,926	4,516
29,500	29,550	5,479	4,429	5,940	4,530
29,550	29,600	5,493	4,436	5,954	4,544
29,600	29,650	5,507	4,444	5,968	4,558
29,650	29,700	5,521	4,451	5,982	4,572
29,700	29,750	5,535	4,459	5,996	4,586
29,750	29,800	5,549	4,466	6,010	4,600
29,800	29,850	5,563	4,474	6,024	4,614
29,850	29,900	5,577	4,481	6,038	4,628
29,900	29,950	5,591	4,489	6,052	4,642
29,950	30,000	5,605	4,496	6,066	4,656
30,000					
30,000	30,050	5,619	4,504	6,080	4,670
30,050	30,100	5,633	4,511	6,094	4,684
30,100	30,150	5,647	4,519	6,108	4,698
30,150	30,200	5,661	4,526	6,122	4,712
30,200	30,250	5,675	4,534	6,136	4,726
30,250	30,300	5,689	4,541	6,150	4,740
30,300	30,350	5,703	4,549	6,164	4,754
30,350	30,400	5,717	4,556	6,178	4,768
30,400	30,450	5,731	4,564	6,192	4,782
30,450	30,500	5,745	4,571	6,206	4,796
30,500	30,550	5,759	4,579	6,220	4,810
30,550	30,600	5,773	4,586	6,234	4,824
30,600	30,650	5,787	4,594	6,248	4,838
30,650	30,700	5,801	4,601	6,262	4,852
30,700	30,750	5,815	4,609	6,276	4,866
30,750	30,800	5,829	4,616	6,290	4,880
30,800	30,850	5,843	4,624	6,304	4,894
30,850	30,900	5,857	4,631	6,318	4,908
30,900	30,950	5,871	4,639	6,332	4,922
30,950	31,000	5,885	4,646	6,346	4,936
31,000					
31,000	31,050	5,899	4,654	6,360	4,950
31,050	31,100	5,913	4,661	6,374	4,964
31,100	31,150	5,927	4,669	6,388	4,978
31,150	31,200	5,941	4,676	6,402	4,992
31,200	31,250	5,955	4,684	6,416	5,006
31,250	31,300	5,969	4,691	6,430	5,020
31,300	31,350	5,983	4,699	6,444	5,034
31,350	31,400	5,997	4,706	6,458	5,048
31,400	31,450	6,011	4,714	6,472	5,062
31,450	31,500	6,025	4,721	6,486	5,076
31,500	31,550	6,039	4,729	6,500	5,090
31,550	31,600	6,053	4,736	6,514	5,104
31,600	31,650	6,067	4,744	6,528	5,118
31,650	31,700	6,081	4,751	6,542	5,132
31,700	31,750	6,095	4,759	6,556	5,146
31,750	31,800	6,109	4,766	6,570	5,160
31,800	31,850	6,123	4,774	6,584	5,174
31,850	31,900	6,137	4,781	6,598	5,188
31,900	31,950	6,151	4,789	6,612	5,202
31,950	32,000	6,165	4,796	6,626	5,216

* This column must also be used by a qualifying widow(er).

Continued on next page

1992 Tax Table—*Continued*

If line 37 (taxable income) is—		And you are—			
At least	But less than	Single	Married filing jointly *	Married filing separately	Head of a household
		Your tax is—			
32,000					
32,000	**32,050**	6,179	4,804	6,640	5,230
32,050	**32,100**	6,193	4,811	6,654	5,244
32,100	**32,150**	6,207	4,819	6,668	5,258
32,150	**32,200**	6,221	4,826	6,682	5,272
32,200	**32,250**	6,235	4,834	6,696	5,286
32,250	**32,300**	6,249	4,841	6,710	5,300
32,300	**32,350**	6,263	4,849	6,724	5,314
32,350	**32,400**	6,277	4,856	6,738	5,328
32,400	**32,450**	6,291	4,864	6,752	5,342
32,450	**32,500**	6,305	4,871	6,766	5,356
32,500	**32,550**	6,319	4,879	6,780	5,370
32,550	**32,600**	6,333	4,886	6,794	5,384
32,600	**32,650**	6,347	4,894	6,808	5,398
32,650	**32,700**	6,361	4,901	6,822	5,412
32,700	**32,750**	6,375	4,909	6,836	5,426
32,750	**32,800**	6,389	4,916	6,850	5,440
32,800	**32,850**	6,403	4,924	6,864	5,454
32,850	**32,900**	6,417	4,931	6,878	5,468
32,900	**32,950**	6,431	4,939	6,892	5,482
32,950	**33,000**	6,445	4,946	6,906	5,496
33,000					
33,000	**33,050**	6,459	4,954	6,920	5,510
33,050	**33,100**	6,473	4,961	6,934	5,524
33,100	**33,150**	6,487	4,969	6,948	5,538
33,150	**33,200**	6,501	4,976	6,962	5,552
33,200	**33,250**	6,515	4,984	6,976	5,566
33,250	**33,300**	6,529	4,991	6,990	5,580
33,300	**33,350**	6,543	4,999	7,004	5,594
33,350	**33,400**	6,557	5,006	7,018	5,608
33,400	**33,450**	6,571	5,014	7,032	5,622
33,450	**33,500**	6,585	5,021	7,046	5,636
33,500	**33,550**	6,599	5,029	7,060	5,650
33,550	**33,600**	6,613	5,036	7,074	5,664
33,600	**33,650**	6,627	5,044	7,088	5,678
33,650	**33,700**	6,641	5,051	7,102	5,692
33,700	**33,750**	6,655	5,059	7,116	5,706
33,750	**33,800**	6,669	5,066	7,130	5,720
33,800	**33,850**	6,683	5,074	7,144	5,734
33,850	**33,900**	6,697	5,081	7,158	5,748
33,900	**33,950**	6,711	5,089	7,172	5,762
33,950	**34,000**	6,725	5,096	7,186	5,776
34,000					
34,000	**34,050**	6,739	5,104	7,200	5,790
34,050	**34,100**	6,753	5,111	7,214	5,804
34,100	**34,150**	6,767	5,119	7,228	5,818
34,150	**34,200**	6,781	5,126	7,242	5,832
34,200	**34,250**	6,795	5,134	7,256	5,846
34,250	**34,300**	6,809	5,141	7,270	5,860
34,300	**34,350**	6,823	5,149	7,284	5,874
34,350	**34,400**	6,837	5,156	7,298	5,888
34,400	**34,450**	6,851	5,164	7,312	5,902
34,450	**34,500**	6,865	5,171	7,326	5,916
34,500	**34,550**	6,879	5,179	7,340	5,930
34,550	**34,600**	6,893	5,186	7,354	5,944
34,600	**34,650**	6,907	5,194	7,368	5,958
34,650	**34,700**	6,921	5,201	7,382	5,972
34,700	**34,750**	6,935	5,209	7,396	5,986
34,750	**34,800**	6,949	5,216	7,410	6,000
34,800	**34,850**	6,963	5,224	7,424	6,014
34,850	**34,900**	6,977	5,231	7,438	6,028
34,900	**34,950**	6,991	5,239	7,452	6,042
34,950	**35,000**	7,005	5,246	7,466	6,056

If line 37 (taxable income) is—		And you are—			
At least	But less than	Single	Married filing jointly *	Married filing separately	Head of a household
		Your tax is—			
35,000					
35,000	**35,050**	7,019	5,254	7,480	6,070
35,050	**35,100**	7,033	5,261	7,494	6,084
35,100	**35,150**	7,047	5,269	7,508	6,098
35,150	**35,200**	7,061	5,276	7,522	6,112
35,200	**35,250**	7,075	5,284	7,536	6,126
35,250	**35,300**	7,089	5,291	7,550	6,140
35,300	**35,350**	7,103	5,299	7,564	6,154
35,350	**35,400**	7,117	5,306	7,578	6,168
35,400	**35,450**	7,131	5,314	7,592	6,182
35,450	**35,500**	7,145	5,321	7,606	6,196
35,500	**35,550**	7,159	5,329	7,620	6,210
35,550	**35,600**	7,173	5,336	7,634	6,224
35,600	**35,650**	7,187	5,344	7,648	6,238
35,650	**35,700**	7,201	5,351	7,662	6,252
35,700	**35,750**	7,215	5,359	7,676	6,266
35,750	**35,800**	7,229	5,366	7,690	6,280
35,800	**35,850**	7,243	5,377	7,704	6,294
35,850	**35,900**	7,257	5,391	7,718	6,308
35,900	**35,950**	7,271	5,405	7,732	6,322
35,950	**36,000**	7,285	5,419	7,746	6,336
36,000					
36,000	**36,050**	7,299	5,433	7,760	6,350
36,050	**36,100**	7,313	5,447	7,774	6,364
36,100	**36,150**	7,327	5,461	7,788	6,378
36,150	**36,200**	7,341	5,475	7,802	6,392
36,200	**36,250**	7,355	5,489	7,816	6,406
36,250	**36,300**	7,369	5,503	7,830	6,420
36,300	**36,350**	7,383	5,517	7,844	6,434
36,350	**36,400**	7,397	5,531	7,858	6,448
36,400	**36,450**	7,411	5,545	7,872	6,462
36,450	**36,500**	7,425	5,559	7,886	6,476
36,500	**36,550**	7,439	5,573	7,900	6,490
36,550	**36,600**	7,453	5,587	7,914	6,504
36,600	**36,650**	7,467	5,601	7,928	6,518
36,650	**36,700**	7,481	5,615	7,942	6,532
36,700	**36,750**	7,495	5,629	7,956	6,546
36,750	**36,800**	7,509	5,643	7,970	6,560
36,800	**36,850**	7,523	5,657	7,984	6,574
36,850	**36,900**	7,537	5,671	7,998	6,588
36,900	**36,950**	7,551	5,685	8,012	6,602
36,950	**37,000**	7,565	5,699	8,026	6,616
37,000					
37,000	**37,050**	7,579	5,713	8,040	6,630
37,050	**37,100**	7,593	5,727	8,054	6,644
37,100	**37,150**	7,607	5,741	8,068	6,658
37,150	**37,200**	7,621	5,755	8,082	6,672
37,200	**37,250**	7,635	5,769	8,096	6,686
37,250	**37,300**	7,649	5,783	8,110	6,700
37,300	**37,350**	7,663	5,797	8,124	6,714
37,350	**37,400**	7,677	5,811	8,138	6,728
37,400	**37,450**	7,691	5,825	8,152	6,742
37,450	**37,500**	7,705	5,839	8,166	6,756
37,500	**37,550**	7,719	5,853	8,180	6,770
37,550	**37,600**	7,733	5,867	8,194	6,784
37,600	**37,650**	7,747	5,881	8,208	6,798
37,650	**37,700**	7,761	5,895	8,222	6,812
37,700	**37,750**	7,775	5,909	8,236	6,826
37,750	**37,800**	7,789	5,923	8,250	6,840
37,800	**37,850**	7,803	5,937	8,264	6,854
37,850	**37,900**	7,817	5,951	8,278	6,868
37,900	**37,950**	7,831	5,965	8,292	6,882
37,950	**38,000**	7,845	5,979	8,306	6,896

If line 37 (taxable income) is—		And you are—			
At least	But less than	Single	Married filing jointly *	Married filing separately	Head of a household
		Your tax is—			
38,000					
38,000	**38,050**	7,859	5,993	8,320	6,910
38,050	**38,100**	7,873	6,007	8,334	6,924
38,100	**38,150**	7,887	6,021	8,348	6,938
38,150	**38,200**	7,901	6,035	8,362	6,952
38,200	**38,250**	7,915	6,049	8,376	6,966
38,250	**38,300**	7,929	6,063	8,390	6,980
38,300	**38,350**	7,943	6,077	8,404	6,994
38,350	**38,400**	7,957	6,091	8,418	7,008
38,400	**38,450**	7,971	6,105	8,432	7,022
38,450	**38,500**	7,985	6,119	8,446	7,036
38,500	**38,550**	7,999	6,133	8,460	7,050
38,550	**38,600**	8,013	6,147	8,474	7,064
38,600	**38,650**	8,027	6,161	8,488	7,078
38,650	**38,700**	8,041	6,175	8,502	7,092
38,700	**38,750**	8,055	6,189	8,516	7,106
38,750	**38,800**	8,069	6,203	8,530	7,120
38,800	**38,850**	8,083	6,217	8,544	7,134
38,850	**38,900**	8,097	6,231	8,558	7,148
38,900	**38,950**	8,111	6,245	8,572	7,162
38,950	**39,000**	8,125	6,259	8,586	7,176
39,000					
39,000	**39,050**	8,139	6,273	8,600	7,190
39,050	**39,100**	8,153	6,287	8,614	7,204
39,100	**39,150**	8,167	6,301	8,628	7,218
39,150	**39,200**	8,181	6,315	8,642	7,232
39,200	**39,250**	8,195	6,329	8,656	7,246
39,250	**39,300**	8,209	6,343	8,670	7,260
39,300	**39,350**	8,223	6,357	8,684	7,274
39,350	**39,400**	8,237	6,371	8,698	7,288
39,400	**39,450**	8,251	6,385	8,712	7,302
39,450	**39,500**	8,265	6,399	8,726	7,316
39,500	**39,550**	8,279	6,413	8,740	7,330
39,550	**39,600**	8,293	6,427	8,754	7,344
39,600	**39,650**	8,307	6,441	8,768	7,358
39,650	**39,700**	8,321	6,455	8,782	7,372
39,700	**39,750**	8,335	6,469	8,796	7,386
39,750	**39,800**	8,349	6,483	8,810	7,400
39,800	**39,850**	8,363	6,497	8,824	7,414
39,850	**39,900**	8,377	6,511	8,838	7,428
39,900	**39,950**	8,391	6,525	8,852	7,442
39,950	**40,000**	8,405	6,539	8,866	7,456
40,000					
40,000	**40,050**	8,419	6,553	8,880	7,470
40,050	**40,100**	8,433	6,567	8,894	7,484
40,100	**40,150**	8,447	6,581	8,908	7,498
40,150	**40,200**	8,461	6,595	8,922	7,512
40,200	**40,250**	8,475	6,609	8,936	7,526
40,250	**40,300**	8,489	6,623	8,950	7,540
40,300	**40,350**	8,503	6,637	8,964	7,554
40,350	**40,400**	8,517	6,651	8,978	7,568
40,400	**40,450**	8,531	6,665	8,992	7,582
40,450	**40,500**	8,545	6,679	9,006	7,596
40,500	**40,550**	8,559	6,693	9,020	7,610
40,550	**40,600**	8,573	6,707	9,034	7,624
40,600	**40,650**	8,587	6,721	9,048	7,638
40,650	**40,700**	8,601	6,735	9,062	7,652
40,700	**40,750**	8,615	6,749	9,076	7,666
40,750	**40,800**	8,629	6,763	9,090	7,680
40,800	**40,850**	8,643	6,777	9,104	7,694
40,850	**40,900**	8,657	6,791	9,118	7,708
40,900	**40,950**	8,671	6,805	9,132	7,722
40,950	**41,000**	8,685	6,819	9,146	7,736

* This column must also be used by a qualifying widow(er).

Continued on next page

1992 Tax Table—*Continued*

If line 37 (taxable income) is—		And you are—			
At least	But less than	Single	Married filing jointly *	Married filing separately	Head of a household
		Your tax is—			
41,000					
41,000	**41,050**	8,699	6,833	9,160	7,750
41,050	**41,100**	8,713	6,847	9,174	7,764
41,100	**41,150**	8,727	6,861	9,188	7,778
41,150	**41,200**	8,741	6,875	9,202	7,792
41,200	**41,250**	8,755	6,889	9,216	7,806
41,250	**41,300**	8,769	6,903	9,230	7,820
41,300	**41,350**	8,783	6,917	9,244	7,834
41,350	**41,400**	8,797	6,931	9,258	7,848
41,400	**41,450**	8,811	6,945	9,272	7,862
41,450	**41,500**	8,825	6,959	9,286	7,876
41,500	**41,550**	8,839	6,973	9,300	7,890
41,550	**41,600**	8,853	6,987	9,314	7,904
41,600	**41,650**	8,867	7,001	9,328	7,918
41,650	**41,700**	8,881	7,015	9,342	7,932
41,700	**41,750**	8,895	7,029	9,356	7,946
41,750	**41,800**	8,909	7,043	9,370	7,960
41,800	**41,850**	8,923	7,057	9,384	7,974
41,850	**41,900**	8,937	7,071	9,398	7,988
41,900	**41,950**	8,951	7,085	9,412	8,002
41,950	**42,000**	8,965	7,099	9,426	8,016
42,000					
42,000	**42,050**	8,979	7,113	9,440	8,030
42,050	**42,100**	8,993	7,127	9,454	8,044
42,100	**42,150**	9,007	7,141	9,468	8,058
42,150	**42,200**	9,021	7,155	9,482	8,072
42,200	**42,250**	9,035	7,169	9,496	8,086
42,250	**42,300**	9,049	7,183	9,510	8,100
42,300	**42,350**	9,063	7,197	9,524	8,114
42,350	**42,400**	9,077	7,211	9,538	8,128
42,400	**42,450**	9,091	7,225	9,552	8,142
42,450	**42,500**	9,105	7,239	9,566	8,156
42,500	**42,550**	9,119	7,253	9,580	8,170
42,550	**42,600**	9,133	7,267	9,594	8,184
42,600	**42,650**	9,147	7,281	9,608	8,198
42,650	**42,700**	9,161	7,295	9,622	8,212
42,700	**42,750**	9,175	7,309	9,636	8,226
42,750	**42,800**	9,189	7,323	9,650	8,240
42,800	**42,850**	9,203	7,337	9,664	8,254
42,850	**42,900**	9,217	7,351	9,678	8,268
42,900	**42,950**	9,231	7,365	9,692	8,282
42,950	**43,000**	9,245	7,379	9,706	8,296
43,000					
43,000	**43,050**	9,259	7,393	9,720	8,310
43,050	**43,100**	9,273	7,407	9,734	8,324
43,100	**43,150**	9,287	7,421	9,748	8,338
43,150	**43,200**	9,301	7,435	9,762	8,352
43,200	**43,250**	9,315	7,449	9,776	8,366
43,250	**43,300**	9,329	7,463	9,791	8,380
43,300	**43,350**	9,343	7,477	9,806	8,394
43,350	**43,400**	9,357	7,491	9,822	8,408
43,400	**43,450**	9,371	7,505	9,837	8,422
43,450	**43,500**	9,385	7,519	9,853	8,436
43,500	**43,550**	9,399	7,533	9,868	8,450
43,550	**43,600**	9,413	7,547	9,884	8,464
43,600	**43,650**	9,427	7,561	9,899	8,478
43,650	**43,700**	9,441	7,575	9,915	8,492
43,700	**43,750**	9,455	7,589	9,930	8,506
43,750	**43,800**	9,469	7,603	9,946	8,520
43,800	**43,850**	9,483	7,617	9,961	8,534
43,850	**43,900**	9,497	7,631	9,977	8,548
43,900	**43,950**	9,511	7,645	9,992	8,562
43,950	**44,000**	9,525	7,659	10,008	8,576

If line 37 (taxable income) is—		And you are—			
At least	But less than	Single	Married filing jointly *	Married filing separately	Head of a household
		Your tax is—			
44,000					
44,000	**44,050**	9,539	7,673	10,023	8,590
44,050	**44,100**	9,553	7,687	10,039	8,604
44,100	**44,150**	9,567	7,701	10,054	8,618
44,150	**44,200**	9,581	7,715	10,070	8,632
44,200	**44,250**	9,595	7,729	10,085	8,646
44,250	**44,300**	9,609	7,743	10,101	8,660
44,300	**44,350**	9,623	7,757	10,116	8,674
44,350	**44,400**	9,637	7,771	10,132	8,688
44,400	**44,450**	9,651	7,785	10,147	8,702
44,450	**44,500**	9,665	7,799	10,163	8,716
44,500	**44,550**	9,679	7,813	10,178	8,730
44,550	**44,600**	9,693	7,827	10,194	8,744
44,600	**44,650**	9,707	7,841	10,209	8,758
44,650	**44,700**	9,721	7,855	10,225	8,772
44,700	**44,750**	9,735	7,869	10,240	8,786
44,750	**44,800**	9,749	7,883	10,256	8,800
44,800	**44,850**	9,763	7,897	10,271	8,814
44,850	**44,900**	9,777	7,911	10,287	8,828
44,900	**44,950**	9,791	7,925	10,302	8,842
44,950	**45,000**	9,805	7,939	10,318	8,856
45,000					
45,000	**45,050**	9,819	7,953	10,333	8,870
45,050	**45,100**	9,833	7,967	10,349	8,884
45,100	**45,150**	9,847	7,981	10,364	8,898
45,150	**45,200**	9,861	7,995	10,380	8,912
45,200	**45,250**	9,875	8,009	10,395	8,926
45,250	**45,300**	9,889	8,023	10,411	8,940
45,300	**45,350**	9,903	8,037	10,426	8,954
45,350	**45,400**	9,917	8,051	10,442	8,968
45,400	**45,450**	9,931	8,065	10,457	8,982
45,450	**45,500**	9,945	8,079	10,473	8,996
45,500	**45,550**	9,959	8,093	10,488	9,010
45,550	**45,600**	9,973	8,107	10,504	9,024
45,600	**45,650**	9,987	8,121	10,519	9,038
45,650	**45,700**	10,001	8,135	10,535	9,052
45,700	**45,750**	10,015	8,149	10,550	9,066
45,750	**45,800**	10,029	8,163	10,566	9,080
45,800	**45,850**	10,043	8,177	10,581	9,094
45,850	**45,900**	10,057	8,191	10,597	9,108
45,900	**45,950**	10,071	8,205	10,612	9,122
45,950	**46,000**	10,085	8,219	10,628	9,136
46,000					
46,000	**46,050**	10,099	8,233	10,643	9,150
46,050	**46,100**	10,113	8,247	10,659	9,164
46,100	**46,150**	10,127	8,261	10,674	9,178
46,150	**46,200**	10,141	8,275	10,690	9,192
46,200	**46,250**	10,155	8,289	10,705	9,206
46,250	**46,300**	10,169	8,303	10,721	9,220
46,300	**46,350**	10,183	8,317	10,736	9,234
46,350	**46,400**	10,197	8,331	10,752	9,248
46,400	**46,450**	10,211	8,345	10,767	9,262
46,450	**46,500**	10,225	8,359	10,783	9,276
46,500	**46,550**	10,239	8,373	10,798	9,290
46,550	**46,600**	10,253	8,387	10,814	9,304
46,600	**46,650**	10,267	8,401	10,829	9,318
46,650	**46,700**	10,281	8,415	10,845	9,332
46,700	**46,750**	10,295	8,429	10,860	9,346
46,750	**46,800**	10,309	8,443	10,876	9,360
46,800	**46,850**	10,323	8,457	10,891	9,374
46,850	**46,900**	10,337	8,471	10,907	9,388
46,900	**46,950**	10,351	8,485	10,922	9,402
46,950	**47,000**	10,365	8,499	10,938	9,416

If line 37 (taxable income) is—		And you are—			
At least	But less than	Single	Married filing jointly *	Married filing separately	Head of a household
		Your tax is—			
47,000					
47,000	**47,050**	10,379	8,513	10,953	9,430
47,050	**47,100**	10,393	8,527	10,969	9,444
47,100	**47,150**	10,407	8,541	10,984	9,458
47,150	**47,200**	10,421	8,555	11,000	9,472
47,200	**47,250**	10,435	8,569	11,015	9,486
47,250	**47,300**	10,449	8,583	11,031	9,500
47,300	**47,350**	10,463	8,597	11,046	9,514
47,350	**47,400**	10,477	8,611	11,062	9,528
47,400	**47,450**	10,491	8,625	11,077	9,542
47,450	**47,500**	10,505	8,639	11,093	9,556
47,500	**47,550**	10,519	8,653	11,108	9,570
47,550	**47,600**	10,533	8,667	11,124	9,584
47,600	**47,650**	10,547	8,681	11,139	9,598
47,650	**47,700**	10,561	8,695	11,155	9,612
47,700	**47,750**	10,575	8,709	11,170	9,626
47,750	**47,800**	10,589	8,723	11,186	9,640
47,800	**47,850**	10,603	8,737	11,201	9,654
47,850	**47,900**	10,617	8,751	11,217	9,668
47,900	**47,950**	10,631	8,765	11,232	9,682
47,950	**48,000**	10,645	8,779	11,248	9,696
48,000					
48,000	**48,050**	10,659	8,793	11,263	9,710
48,050	**48,100**	10,673	8,807	11,279	9,724
48,100	**48,150**	10,687	8,821	11,294	9,738
48,150	**48,200**	10,701	8,835	11,310	9,752
48,200	**48,250**	10,715	8,849	11,325	9,766
48,250	**48,300**	10,729	8,863	11,341	9,780
48,300	**48,350**	10,743	8,877	11,356	9,794
48,350	**48,400**	10,757	8,891	11,372	9,808
48,400	**48,450**	10,771	8,905	11,387	9,822
48,450	**48,500**	10,785	8,919	11,403	9,836
48,500	**48,550**	10,799	8,933	11,418	9,850
48,550	**48,600**	10,813	8,947	11,434	9,864
48,600	**48,650**	10,827	8,961	11,449	9,878
48,650	**48,700**	10,841	8,975	11,465	9,892
48,700	**48,750**	10,855	8,989	11,480	9,906
48,750	**48,800**	10,869	9,003	11,496	9,920
48,800	**48,850**	10,883	9,017	11,511	9,934
48,850	**48,900**	10,897	9,031	11,527	9,948
48,900	**48,950**	10,911	9,045	11,542	9,962
48,950	**49,000**	10,925	9,059	11,558	9,976
49,000					
49,000	**49,050**	10,939	9,073	11,573	9,990
49,050	**49,100**	10,953	9,087	11,589	10,004
49,100	**49,150**	10,967	9,101	11,604	10,018
49,150	**49,200**	10,981	9,115	11,620	10,032
49,200	**49,250**	10,995	9,129	11,635	10,046
49,250	**49,300**	11,009	9,143	11,651	10,060
49,300	**49,350**	11,023	9,157	11,666	10,074
49,350	**49,400**	11,037	9,171	11,682	10,088
49,400	**49,450**	11,051	9,185	11,697	10,102
49,450	**49,500**	11,065	9,199	11,713	10,116
49,500	**49,550**	11,079	9,213	11,728	10,130
49,550	**49,600**	11,093	9,227	11,744	10,144
49,600	**49,650**	11,107	9,241	11,759	10,158
49,650	**49,700**	11,121	9,255	11,775	10,172
49,700	**49,750**	11,135	9,269	11,790	10,186
49,750	**49,800**	11,149	9,283	11,806	10,200
49,800	**49,850**	11,163	9,297	11,821	10,214
49,850	**49,900**	11,177	9,311	11,837	10,228
49,900	**49,950**	11,191	9,325	11,852	10,242
49,950	**50,000**	11,205	9,339	11,868	10,256

* This column must also be used by a qualifying widow(er).

Continued on next page

1993 Tax Rate Schedules

Single—Schedule X

If taxable income is: Over—	But not over—	The tax is:	of the amount over—
$0	$22,100	.........15%	$0
22,100	53,500	$3,315.00 + 28%	22,100
53,500	....	12,107.00 + 31%	53,500

Head of household—Schedule Z

If taxable income is: Over—	But not over—	The tax is:	of the amount over—
$0	$29,600	.........15%	$0
29,600	76,400	$4,440.00 + 28%	29,600
76,400	....	17,544.00 + 31%	76,400

Married filing jointly or Qualifying widow(er)—Schedule Y-1

If taxable income is: Over—	But not over—	The tax is:	of the amount over—
$0	$36,900	.........15%	$0
36,900	89,150	$5,535.00 + 28%	36,900
89,150	....	20,165.00 + 31%	89,150

Married filing separately—Schedule Y-2

If taxable income is: Over—	But not over—	The tax is:	of the amount over—
$0	$18,450	.........15%	$0
18,450	44,575	$2,767.50 + 28%	18,450
44,575	....	10,082.50 + 31%	44,575

Income Tax Rates—Estates and Trusts

Tax Year 1993

If Taxable Income Is:	The Tax Is:
$3,750 or less	15% of the taxable income
Over $3,750 but not over $11,250	$562.50 plus 28% of the excess over $3,750
Over $11,250	$2,662.50 plus 31% of the excess over $11,250

Income Tax Rates—Corporations

Taxable Income	Tax Rate
$50,000 or less	15%
Over $50,000 but not over $75,000	25%
Over $75,000	34%
$100,000–$335,000	5%*

*Additional tax, "phases out" the lower marginal brackets.

UNIFIED TRANSFER TAX RATES

For Gifts Made and For Deaths after 1983 and before 1993

If the amount with respect to which the tentative tax to be computed is:	The tentative tax is:
Not over $10,000	18 percent of such amount.
Over $10,000 but not over $20,000	$1,800, plus 20 percent of the excess of such amount over $10,000.
Over $20,000 but not over $40,000	$3,800, plus 22 percent of the excess of such amount over $20,000.
Over $40,000 but not over $60,000	$8,200, plus 24 percent of the excess of such amount over $40,000.
Over $60,000 but not over $80,000	$13,000, plus 26 percent of the excess of such amount over $60,000.
Over $80,000 but not over $100,000	$18,200, plus 28 percent of the excess of such amount over $80,000.
Over $100,000 but not over $150,000	$23,800, plus 30 percent of the excess of such amount over $100,000.
Over $150,000 but not over $250,000	$38,800, plus 32 percent of the excess of such amount over $150,000.
Over $250,000 but not over $500,000	$70,800, plus 34 percent of the excess of such amount over $250,000.
Over $500,000 but not over $750,000	$155,800, plus 37 percent of the excess of such amount over $500,000.
Over $750,000 but not over $1,000,000	$248,300, plus 39 percent of the excess of such amount over $750,000.
Over $1,000,000 but not over $1,250,000	$345,800, plus 41 percent of the excess of such amount over $1,000,000.
Over $1,250,000 but not over $1,500,000	$448,300, plus 43 percent of the excess of such amount over $1,250,000.
Over $1,500,000 but not over $2,000,000	$555,800, plus 45 percent of the excess of such amount over $1,500,000.

Over $2,000,000 but not over $2,500,000........ $780,800, plus 49 percent of the excess of such amount over $2,000,000.

Over $2,500,000 but not over $3,000,000........ $1,025,800, plus 53 percent of the excess of such amount over $2,500,000.

Over $3,000,000*................................ $1,290,800, plus 57 percent of the excess of such amount over $3,000,000.

*For large taxable transfers (generally in excess of $10 million) there is a phase-out of the graduated rates and the unified tax credit.

Table for Computation of Maximum Credit for State Death Taxes

(A) Adjusted Taxable Estate* equal to or more than	(B) Adjusted Taxable Estate* less than	(C) Credit on amount in column (A)	(D) Rate of credit on excess over amount in column (A) (Percentage)
0	$ 40,000	0	None
$ 40,000	90,000	0	0.8
90,000	140,000	$ 400	1.6
140,000	240,000	1,200	2.4
240,000	440,000	3,600	3.2
440,000	640,000	10,000	4.0
640,000	840,000	18,000	4.8
840,000	1,040,000	27,600	5.6
1,040,000	1,540,000	38,800	6.4
1,540,000	2,040,000	70,800	7.2
2,040,000	2,540,000	106,800	8.0
2,540,000	3,040,000	146,800	8.8
3,040,000	3,540,000	190,800	9.6
3,540,000	4,040,000	238,800	10.4
4,040,000	5,040,000	290,800	11.2
5,040,000	6,040,000	402,800	12.0
6,040,000	7,040,000	522,800	12.8
7,040,000	8,040,000	650,800	13.6
8,040,000	9,040,000	786,800	14.4
9,040,000	10,040,000	930,800	15.2
10,040,000		1,082,800	16.0

* Adjusted Taxable Estate = Taxable Estate – $60,000

Appendix

Tax Forms

Form **1040EZ**

Department of the Treasury—Internal Revenue Service

Income Tax Return for Single Filers With No Dependents 1992

OMB No. 1545-0675

Name & address

Use the IRS label (see page 10). If you don't have one, please print.

LABEL HERE

Print your name (first, initial, last)

Home address (number and street). If you have a P.O. box, see page 10. Apt. no.

City, town or post office, state, and ZIP code. If you have a foreign address, see page 10.

Please print your numbers like this: 9 8 7 6 5 4 3 2 1 0

Your social security number

Please see instructions on the back. Also, see the Form 1040EZ booklet.

Presidential Election Campaign (See page 10.) Do you want $1 to go to this fund?

Note: *Checking "Yes" will not change your tax or reduce your refund.* ▶

Yes No

Dollars Cents

Report your income

Attach Copy B of Form(s) W-2 here. Attach tax payment on top of Form(s) W-2.

1 Total wages, salaries, and tips. This should be shown in box 10 of your W-2 form(s). Attach your W-2 form(s). 1

2 Taxable interest income of $400 or less. If the total is more than $400, you cannot use Form 1040EZ. 2

3 Add lines 1 and 2. This is your **adjusted gross income.** 3

4 Can your parents (or someone else) claim you on their return?

Note: *You must check Yes or No.*

☐ **Yes.** Do worksheet on back; enter amount from line E here.

☐ **No.** Enter 5,900.00. This is the total of your standard deduction and personal exemption. 4

5 Subtract line 4 from line 3. If line 4 is larger than line 3, enter 0. This is your **taxable income.** 5

Figure your tax

6 Enter your Federal income tax withheld from box 9 of your W-2 form(s). 6

7 **Tax.** Look at line 5 above. Use the amount on **line 5** to find your tax in the tax table on pages 22-24 of the booklet. Then, enter the tax from the table on this line. 7

Refund or amount you owe

8 If line 6 is larger than line 7, subtract line 7 from line 6. This is your **refund.** 8

9 If line 7 is larger than line 6, subtract line 6 from line 7. This is the **amount you owe.** Attach your payment for full amount payable to the "Internal Revenue Service." Write your name, address, social security number, daytime phone number, and "1992 Form 1040EZ" on it. 9

Sign your return

Keep a copy of this form for your records.

I have read this return. Under penalties of perjury, I declare that to the best of my knowledge and belief, the return is true, correct, and complete.

Your signature

X

Date

Your occupation

For IRS Use Only — Please do not write in boxes below.

For Privacy Act and Paperwork Reduction Act Notice, see page 4 in the booklet. Cat. No. 11329W Form 1040EZ (1992)

1992 Instructions for Form 1040EZ

Use this form if

- Your filing status is single.
- You were under 65* and not blind at the end of 1992.
- You do not claim any dependents.
- Your taxable income (line 5) is less than $50,000.
- You had **only** wages, salaries, tips, and taxable scholarship or fellowship grants, and your taxable interest income was $400 or less. **Caution:** *If you earned tips, including allocated tips, that are not included in box 13 and box 14 of your W-2, you may not be able to use Form 1040EZ. See page 12 in the booklet. Also, you cannot use this form if you had more than one employer and your total wages were over $55,500.*
- You did not receive any advance earned income credit payments.

* *If you turned 65 on January 1, 1993, you are considered to be age 65 at the end of 1992.*

If you are not sure about your filing status, see page 6 in the booklet. If you have questions about dependents, see Tele-Tax (topic no. 155) on page 20 in the booklet.

If you can't use this form, see Tele-Tax (topic no. 152) on page 20 in the booklet.

Filling in your return

Please print your numbers inside the boxes. Do not type your numbers. Do not use dollar signs.

Most people can fill in the form by following the instructions on the front. But you will have to use the booklet if you received a scholarship or fellowship grant or tax-exempt interest income, such as on municipal bonds. Also, use the booklet if you received a Form 1099-INT showing income tax withheld (backup withholding).

Remember, you must report your wages, salaries, and tips even if you don't get a W-2 form from your employer. You must also report all your taxable interest income, including interest from savings accounts at banks, savings and loans, credit unions, etc., even if you don't get a Form 1099-INT.

If you paid someone to prepare your return, that person must also sign it and show other information. See page 15 in the booklet.

Standard deduction worksheet for dependents who checked "Yes" on line 4

Fill in this worksheet to figure the amount to enter on line 4 if someone can claim you as a dependent, even if that person chooses not to claim you. To find out if someone can claim you as a dependent, see Tele-Tax (topic no. 155) on page 20 in the booklet.

A. Enter the amount from line 1 on the front.	**A.**	
B. Minimum amount.	**B.**	600.00
C. Look at lines A and B above. Enter the LARGER of the two amounts here.	**C.**	
D. Maximum amount.	**D.**	3,600.00
E. Look at lines C and D above. Enter the SMALLER of the two amounts here and on line 4 on the front.	**E.**	

If you checked "No" because no one can claim you as a dependent, enter 5,900.00 on line 4. This is the total of your standard deduction (3,600.00) and personal exemption (2,300.00).

Avoid common mistakes

This checklist is to help you make sure your form is filled in correctly.

1. Did you check your computations (additions, subtractions, etc.) especially when figuring your taxable income, Federal income tax withheld, and your refund or amount you owe?
2. Did you check the "Yes" box on line 4 if your parents (or someone else) can claim you as a dependent on their 1992 return, even if they choose not to claim you? If no one can claim you as a dependent, did you check the "No" box?
3. Did you enter an amount on line 4? If you checked the "Yes" box on line 4, did you fill in the worksheet above to figure the amount to enter? If you checked the "No" box, did you enter 5,900.00?
4. Did you use the amount from **line 5** to find your tax in the tax table? Did you enter the correct tax on line 7?
5. If you didn't get a label, did you enter your name, address (including ZIP code), and social security number in the spaces provided on Form 1040EZ?
6. If you got a label, does it show your correct name, address, and social security number? If not, did you enter the correct information?
7. Did you attach your W-2 form(s) to the left margin of your return? And did you sign and date Form 1040EZ and enter your occupation?

Mailing your return

Mail your return by **April 15, 1993**. Use the envelope that came with your booklet. If you don't have that envelope, see page 25 in the booklet for the address to use.

Form **1040A** Department of the Treasury—Internal Revenue Service

U.S. Individual Income Tax Return (T) 1992

IRS Use Only—Do not write or staple in this space.

OMB No. 1545-0085

Label (See page 14.)

Use the IRS label. Otherwise, please print or type.

LABEL HERE

Your first name and initial | Last name

If a joint return, spouse's first name and initial | Last name

Home address (number and street). If you have a P.O. box, see page 15. | Apt. no.

City, town or post office, state, and ZIP code. If you have a foreign address, see page 15.

Your social security number

Spouse's social security number

For Privacy Act and Paperwork Reduction Act Notice, see page 4.

Presidential Election Campaign Fund (See page 15.) | Yes | No

Do you want $1 to go to this fund?

If a joint return, does your spouse want $1 to go to this fund?

Note: *Checking "Yes" will not change your tax or reduce your refund.*

Check the box for your filing status

(See page 15.)

Check only one box.

1 ☐ Single

2 ☐ Married filing joint return (even if only one had income)

3 ☐ Married filing separate return. Enter spouse's social security number above and full name here. ▶

4 ☐ Head of household (with qualifying person). (See page 16.) If the qualifying person is a child but not your dependent, enter this child's name here. ▶

5 ☐ Qualifying widow(er) with dependent child (year spouse died ▶ 19 ____). (See page 17.)

Figure your exemptions

(See page 18.)

If more than seven dependents, see page 21.

6a ☐ **Yourself.** If your parent (or someone else) can claim you as a dependent on his or her tax return, **do not** check box 6a. But be sure to check the box on line 18b on page 2.

b ☐ **Spouse**

c **Dependents:**

(1) Name (first, initial, and last name)	(2) Check if under age 1	(3) If age 1 or older, dependent's social security number	(4) Dependent's relationship to you	(5) No. of months lived in your home in 1992

d If your child didn't live with you but is claimed as your dependent under a pre-1985 agreement, check here ▶ ☐

e Total number of exemptions claimed.

No. of boxes checked on 6a and 6b ____

No. of your children on 6c who:

• lived with you ____

• didn't live with you due to divorce or separation (see page 21) ____

No. of other dependents on 6c ____

Add numbers entered on lines above ☐

Figure your total income

Attach Copy B of your Forms W-2 and 1099-R here.

If you didn't get a W-2, see page 22.

Attach check or money order on top of any Forms W-2 or 1099-R.

7 Wages, salaries, tips, etc. This should be shown in box 10 of your W-2 form(s). Attach Form(s) W-2. — 7

8a **Taxable** interest income (see page 24). If over $400, also complete and attach Schedule 1, Part I. — 8a

b **Tax-exempt** interest. DO NOT include on line 8a. 8b

9 Dividends. If over $400, also complete and attach Schedule 1, Part II. — 9

10a Total IRA distributions. 10a — 10b Taxable amount (see page 25). — 10b

11a Total pensions and annuities. 11a — 11b Taxable amount (see page 25). — 11b

12 Unemployment compensation (see page 29). — 12

13a Social security benefits. 13a — 13b Taxable amount (see page 29). — 13b

14 Add lines 7 through 13b (far right column). This is your **total income.** ▶ 14

Figure your adjusted gross income

15a Your IRA deduction from applicable worksheet. 15a

b Spouse's IRA deduction from applicable worksheet. **Note:** *Rules for IRAs begin on page 31.* 15b

c Add lines 15a and 15b. These are your **total adjustments.** — 15c

16 Subtract line 15c from line 14. This is your **adjusted gross income.** If less than $22,370, see "Earned income credit" on page 39. ▶ 16

1992 Form 1040A page 2

Name(s) shown on page 1 | Your social security number

Figure your standard deduction, exemption amount, and taxable income

17 Enter the amount from line 16. 17

18a Check if: ☐ **You** were 65 or older ☐ Blind ☐ **Spouse** was 65 or older ☐ Blind } **Enter number of boxes checked** ▶ 18a ☐

b If your parent (or someone else) can claim you as a dependent, check here . . . . . . ▶ 18b ☐

c If you are married filing separately and your spouse files Form 1040 and itemizes deductions, see page 35 and check here ▶ 18c ☐

19 Enter the **standard deduction** shown below for your filing status. **But if you checked any box on line 18a or b,** go to page 35 to find your standard deduction. **If you checked box 18c,** enter -0-.

- Single—$3,600 • Head of household—$5,250
- Married filing jointly or Qualifying widow(er)—$6,000
- Married filing separately—$3,000 19

20 Subtract line 19 from line 17. (If line 19 is more than line 17, enter -0-.) 20

21 Multiply $2,300 by the total number of exemptions claimed on line 6e. 21

22 Subtract line 21 from line 20. (If line 21 is more than line 20, enter -0-.) This is your **taxable income.** ▶ 22

Figure your tax, credits, and payments

If you want the IRS to figure your tax, see the instructions for line 22 on page 36.

23 Find the tax on the amount on line 22. Check if from: ☐ Tax Table (pages 48–53) or ☐ Form 8615 (see page 37). 23

24a Credit for child and dependent care expenses. Complete and attach Schedule 2. 24a

b Credit for the elderly or the disabled. Complete and attach Schedule 3. 24b

c Add lines 24a and 24b. These are your **total credits.** 24c

25 Subtract line 24c from line 23. (If line 24c is more than line 23, enter -0-.) 25

26 Advance earned income credit payments from Form W-2. 26

27 Add lines 25 and 26. This is your **total tax.** ▶ 27

28a Total Federal income tax withheld. If any tax is from Form(s) 1099, check here. ▶ ☐ 28a

b 1992 estimated tax payments and amount applied from 1991 return. 28b

c **Earned income credit.** Complete and attach Schedule EIC. 28c

d Add lines 28a, 28b, and 28c. These are your **total payments.** ▶ 28d

Figure your refund or amount you owe

Attach check or money order on top of Form(s) W-2, etc., on page 1.

29 If line 28d is more than line 27, subtract line 27 from line 28d. This is the amount you **overpaid.** 29

30 Amount of line 29 you want **refunded to you.** 30

31 Amount of line 29 you want **applied to your 1993 estimated tax.** 31

32 If line 27 is more than line 28d, subtract line 28d from line 27. This is the **amount you owe.** Attach check or money order for full amount payable to the "Internal Revenue Service". Write your name, address, social security number, daytime phone number, and "1992 Form 1040A" on it. 32

33 Estimated tax penalty (see page 41). 33

Sign your return

Keep a copy of this return for your records.

Under penalties of perjury, I declare that I have examined this return and accompanying schedules and statements, and to the best of my knowledge and belief, they are true, correct, and complete. Declaration of preparer (other than the taxpayer) is based on all information of which the preparer has any knowledge.

▶ Your signature	Date	Your occupation
▶ Spouse's signature. If joint return, BOTH must sign.	Date	Spouse's occupation

Paid preparer's use only

Preparer's signature ▶	Date	Check if self-employed ☐	Preparer's social security no.
Firm's name (or yours if self-employed) and address ▶		E.I. No.	
		ZIP code	

Schedule 1 (Form 1040A)

Department of the Treasury—Internal Revenue Service

Interest and Dividend Income for Form 1040A Filers

1992

OMB No. 1545-0085

Name(s) shown on Form 1040A

Your social security number

Part I

Interest income

(See pages 24 and 54.)

Complete this part and attach Schedule 1 to Form 1040A if:

- You had over $400 in taxable interest, or
- You are claiming the exclusion of interest from series EE U.S. savings bonds issued after 1989.

If you received, as a nominee, interest that actually belongs to another person, see page 54.

Note: *If you received a Form 1099–INT, Form 1099–OID, or substitute statement, from a brokerage firm, enter the firm's name and the total interest shown on that form.*

			Amount
1	List name of payer—if any interest is from seller-financed mortgages, see page 54	1	
2	Add the amounts on line 1.	2	
3	Excludable interest on series EE U.S. savings bonds issued after 1989 from Form 8815, line 14. You MUST attach Form 8815 to Form 1040A.	3	
4	Subtract line 3 from line 2. Enter the result here and on Form 1040A, line 8a.	4	

Part II

Dividend income

(See pages 24 and 55.)

Complete this part and attach Schedule 1 to Form 1040A if you had over $400 in dividends.

If you received, as a nominee, dividends that actually belong to another person, see page 55.

Note: *If you received a Form 1099–DIV, or substitute statement, from a brokerage firm, enter the firm's name and the total dividends shown on that form.*

			Amount
5	List name of payer	5	
6	Add the amounts on line 5. Enter the total here and on Form 1040A, line 9.	6	

Form **1040** Department of the Treasury—Internal Revenue Service
U.S. Individual Income Tax Return (T) **1992**

IRS Use Only—Do not write or staple in this space.

For the year Jan. 1–Dec. 31, 1992, or other tax year beginning , 1992, ending , 19 OMB No. 1545-0074

Label
(See instructions on page 10.)
Use the IRS label. Otherwise, please print or type.

LABEL HERE

Your first name and initial | Last name | Your social security number

If a joint return, spouse's first name and initial | Last name | Spouse's social security number

Home address (number and street). If you have a P.O. box, see page 10. | Apt. no.

City, town or post office, state, and ZIP code. If you have a foreign address, see page 10.

For Privacy Act and Paperwork Reduction Act Notice, see page 4.

Presidential Election Campaign (See page 10.)
Do you want $1 to go to this fund? . . . . Yes No
If a joint return, does your spouse want $1 to go to this fund? . Yes No
Note: *Checking "Yes" will not change your tax or reduce your refund.*

Filing Status
(See page 10.)
Check only one box.

1 ☐ Single
2 ☐ Married filing joint return (even if only one had income)
3 ☐ Married filing separate return. Enter spouse's social security no. above and full name here. ▶
4 ☐ Head of household (with qualifying person). (See page 11.) If the qualifying person is a child but not your dependent, enter this child's name here. ▶
5 ☐ Qualifying widow(er) with dependent child (year spouse died ▶ 19). (See page 11.)

Exemptions
(See page 11.)

6a ☐ **Yourself.** If your parent (or someone else) can claim you as a dependent on his or her tax return, **do not** check box 6a. But be sure to check the box on line 33b on page 2 .
b ☐ **Spouse** . . . .

No. of boxes checked on 6a and 6b ____

c **Dependents:**

(1) Name (first, initial, and last name)	(2) Check if under age 1	(3) If age 1 or older, dependent's social security number	(4) Dependent's relationship to you	(5) No. of months lived in your home in 1992

If more than six dependents, see page 12.

No. of your children on 6c who:
• lived with you ____
• didn't live with you due to divorce or separation (see page 13) ____
No. of other dependents on 6c ____

d If your child didn't live with you but is claimed as your dependent under a pre-1985 agreement, check here ▶ ☐
e Total number of exemptions claimed . . . .

Add numbers entered on lines above ▶ ☐

Income

Attach Copy B of your Forms W-2, W-2G, and 1099-R here.

If you did not get a W-2, see page 9.

Attach check or money order on top of any Forms W-2, W-2G, or 1099-R.

7	Wages, salaries, tips, etc. Attach Form(s) W-2	7	
8a	**Taxable** interest income. Attach Schedule B if over $400	8a	
b	**Tax-exempt** interest income (see page 15). DON'T include on line 8a 8b		
9	Dividend income. Attach Schedule B if over $400	9	
10	Taxable refunds, credits, or offsets of state and local income taxes from worksheet on page 16	10	
11	Alimony received	11	
12	Business income or (loss). Attach Schedule C or C-EZ	12	
13	Capital gain or (loss). Attach Schedule D	13	
14	Capital gain distributions not reported on line 13 (see page 15) . . .	14	
15	Other gains or (losses). Attach Form 4797	15	
16a	Total IRA distributions . 16a b Taxable amount (see page 16)	16b	
17a	Total pensions and annuities 17a b Taxable amount (see page 16)	17b	
18	Rents, royalties, partnerships, estates, trusts, etc. Attach Schedule E . . .	18	
19	Farm income or (loss). Attach Schedule F	19	
20	Unemployment compensation (see page 17)	20	
21a	Social security benefits 21a b Taxable amount (see page 17)	21b	
22	Other income. List type and amount—see page 18	22	
23	Add the amounts in the far right column for lines 7 through 22. This is your **total income** . . ▶	23	

Adjustments to Income
(See page 18.)

24a	Your IRA deduction from applicable worksheet on page 19 or 20	24a	
b	Spouse's IRA deduction from applicable worksheet on page 19 or 20	24b	
25	One-half of self-employment tax (see page 20) . . .	25	
26	Self-employed health insurance deduction (see page 20)	26	
27	Keogh retirement plan and self-employed SEP deduction	27	
28	Penalty on early withdrawal of savings	28	
29	Alimony paid. Recipient's SSN ▶	29	
30	Add lines 24a through 29. These are your **total adjustments** . . . . ▶	30	

Adjusted Gross Income

31	Subtract line 30 from line 23. This is your **adjusted gross income.** *If this amount is less than $22,370 and a child lived with you, see page EIC-1 to find out if you can claim the "Earned Income Credit" on line 56* . . . . ▶	31	

Cat. No. 11320B

Form **1040** (1992)

Form 1040 (1992) Page 2

Tax Computation

(See page 22.)

32 Amount from line 31 (adjusted gross income) . . . 32

33a Check if: ☐ **You** were 65 or older, ☐ Blind; ☐ **Spouse** was 65 or older, ☐ Blind.
Add the number of boxes checked above and enter the total here . . . . ▶ 33a

b If your parent (or someone else) can claim you as a dependent, check here . ▶ 33b ☐

c If you are married filing separately and your spouse itemizes deductions or you are a dual-status alien, see page 22 and check here . . . ▶ 33c ☐

34 Enter the **larger** of your:
- **Itemized deductions** from Schedule A, line 26, **OR**
- **Standard deduction** shown below for your filing status. **But if you checked any box on line 33a or b,** go to page 22 to find your standard deduction. **If you checked box 33c,** your standard deduction is zero.
  - Single—$3,600
  - Head of household—$5,250
  - Married filing jointly or Qualifying widow(er)—$6,000
  - Married filing separately—$3,000

34

35 Subtract line 34 from line 32 . . . 35

36 If line 32 is $78,950 or less, multiply $2,300 by the total number of exemptions claimed on line 6e. If line 32 is over $78,950, see the worksheet on page 23 for the amount to enter . 36

If you want the IRS to figure your tax, see page 23.

37 **Taxable income.** Subtract line 36 from line 35. If line 36 is more than line 35, enter -0- . 37

38 Enter tax. Check if from **a** ☐ Tax Table, **b** ☐ Tax Rate Schedules, **c** ☐ Schedule D, or **d** ☐ Form 8615 (see page 23). Amount, if any, from Form(s) 8814 ▶ **e** ______ 38

39 Additional taxes (see page 23). Check if from **a** ☐ Form 4970 **b** ☐ Form 4972 . . 39

40 Add lines 38 and 39 . . . ▶ 40

Credits

(See page 23.)

41 Credit for child and dependent care expenses. Attach Form 2441 41

42 Credit for the elderly or the disabled. Attach Schedule R . . 42

43 Foreign tax credit. Attach Form 1116 . . . 43

44 Other credits (see page 24). Check if from **a** ☐ Form 3800 **b** ☐ Form 8396 **c** ☐ Form 8801 **d** ☐ Form (specify)______ 44

45 Add lines 41 through 44 . . . 45

46 Subtract line 45 from line 40. If line 45 is more than line 40, enter -0- . . . ▶ 46

Other Taxes

47 Self-employment tax. Attach Schedule SE. Also, see line 25. . . . 47

48 Alternative minimum tax. Attach Form 6251 . . . 48

49 Recapture taxes (see page 25). Check if from **a** ☐ Form 4255 **b** ☐ Form 8611 **c** ☐ Form 8828 . 49

50 Social security and Medicare tax on tip income not reported to employer. Attach Form 4137 . 50

51 Tax on qualified retirement plans, including IRAs. Attach Form 5329 . . . 51

52 Advance earned income credit payments from Form W-2 . . . 52

53 Add lines 46 through 52. This is your **total tax** . . . ▶ 53

Payments

Attach Forms W-2, W-2G, and 1099-R on the front.

54 Federal income tax withheld. If any is from Form(s) 1099, check ▶ ☐ 54

55 1992 estimated tax payments and amount applied from 1991 return . 55

56 **Earned income credit.** Attach Schedule EIC . . . 56

57 Amount paid with Form 4868 (extension request) . . . 57

58 Excess social security, Medicare, and RRTA tax withheld (see page 26) . 58

59 Other payments (see page 26). Check if from **a** ☐ Form 2439 **b** ☐ Form 4136 . . . 59

60 Add lines 54 through 59. These are your **total payments** . . . ▶ 60

Refund or Amount You Owe

Attach check or money order on top of Form(s) W-2, etc., on the front.

61 If line 60 is more than line 53, subtract line 53 from line 60. This is the amount you **OVERPAID**. . ▶ 61

62 Amount of line 61 you want **REFUNDED TO YOU**. . . ▶ 62

63 Amount of line 61 you want **APPLIED TO YOUR 1993 ESTIMATED TAX** ▶ 63

64 If line 53 is more than line 60, subtract line 60 from line 53. This is the **AMOUNT YOU OWE**. Attach check or money order for full amount payable to "Internal Revenue Service." Write your name, address, social security number, daytime phone number, and "1992 Form 1040" on it 64

65 Estimated tax penalty (see page 27). Also include on line 64 65

Sign Here

Keep a copy of this return for your records.

Under penalties of perjury, I declare that I have examined this return and accompanying schedules and statements, and to the best of my knowledge and belief, they are true, correct, and complete. Declaration of preparer (other than taxpayer) is based on all information of which preparer has any knowledge.

▶ Your signature	Date	Your occupation
▶ Spouse's signature. If a joint return, BOTH must sign.	Date	Spouse's occupation

Paid Preparer's Use Only

Preparer's signature ▶	Date	Check if self-employed ☐	Preparer's social security no.
Firm's name (or yours if self-employed) and address ▶		E.I. No.	
		ZIP code	

SCHEDULES A&B (Form 1040)
Department of the Treasury
Internal Revenue Service (T)

Schedule A—Itemized Deductions

(Schedule B is on back)

▶ **Attach to Form 1040.** ▶ **See Instructions for Schedules A and B (Form 1040).**

OMB No. 1545-0074
1992
Attachment Sequence No. **07**

Name(s) shown on Form 1040 | **Your social security number**

Medical and Dental Expenses		**Caution:** *Do not include expenses reimbursed or paid by others.*			
	1	Medical and dental expenses (see page A-1)	1		
	2	Enter amount from Form 1040, line 32 . 2			
	3	Multiply line 2 above by 7.5% (.075)	3		
	4	Subtract line 3 from line 1. If zero or less, enter -0- ▶		4	
Taxes You Paid (See page A-1.)	5	State and local income taxes	5		
	6	Real estate taxes (see page A-2)	6		
	7	Other taxes. List—include personal property taxes ▶	7		
	8	Add lines 5 through 7 ▶		8	
Interest You Paid (See page A-2.)	9a	Home mortgage interest and points reported to you on Form 1098	9a		
	b	Home mortgage interest not reported to you on Form 1098. If paid to an individual, show that person's name and address. ▶	9b		
Note: Personal interest is not deductible.	10	Points not reported to you on Form 1098. See page A-3 for special rules	10		
	11	Investment interest. If required, attach Form 4952. (See page A-3.)	11		
	12	Add lines 9a through 11 ▶		12	
Gifts to Charity (See page A-3.)		**Caution:** *If you made a charitable contribution and received a benefit in return, see page A-3.*			
	13	Contributions by cash or check	13		
	14	Other than by cash or check. If over $500, you **MUST** attach Form 8283	14		
	15	Carryover from prior year	15		
	16	Add lines 13 through 15 ▶		16	
Casualty and Theft Losses	17	Casualty or theft loss(es). Attach Form 4684. (See page A-4.) ▶		17	
Moving Expenses	18	Moving expenses. Attach Form 3903 or 3903F. (See page A-4.) ▶		18	
Job Expenses and Most Other Miscellaneous Deductions (See page A-5 for expenses to deduct here.)	19	Unreimbursed employee expenses—job travel, union dues, job education, etc. If required, you **MUST** attach Form 2106. (See page A-4.) ▶	19		
	20	Other expenses—investment, tax preparation, safe deposit box, etc. List type and amount ▶	20		
	21	Add lines 19 and 20	21		
	22	Enter amount from Form 1040, line 32 . 22			
	23	Multiply line 22 above by 2% (.02)	23		
	24	Subtract line 23 from line 21. If zero or less, enter -0- ▶		24	
Other Miscellaneous Deductions	25	Other—from list on page A-5. List type and amount ▶		25	
Total Itemized Deductions	26	Is the amount on Form 1040, line 32, more than $105,250 (more than $52,625 if married filing separately)? • **NO.** Your deduction is not limited. Add lines 4, 8, 12, 16, 17, 18, 24, and 25. • **YES.** Your deduction may be limited. See page A-5 for the amount to enter. ▶		26	
		Caution: *Be sure to enter on Form 1040, line 34, the* ***LARGER*** *of the amount on line 26 above or your standard deduction.*			

For Paperwork Reduction Act Notice, see Form 1040 instructions. Cat. No. 11330X **Schedule A (Form 1040) 1992**

Schedules A&B (Form 1040) 1992 — OMB No. 1545-0074 — Page 2

Name(s) shown on Form 1040. Do not enter name and social security number if shown on other side. | **Your social security number**

Schedule B—Interest and Dividend Income

Attachment Sequence No. 08

Part I Interest Income

(See pages 14 and B-1.)

If you had over $400 in taxable interest income OR are claiming the exclusion of interest from series EE U.S. savings bonds issued after 1989, you must complete this part. List ALL interest you received. If you had over $400 in taxable interest income, you must also complete Part III. If you received, as a nominee, interest that actually belongs to another person, or you received or paid accrued interest on securities transferred between interest payment dates, see page B-1.

Interest Income		Amount
1 List name of payer—if any interest income is from seller-financed mortgages, see page B-1 and list this interest first ▶	1	
2 Add the amounts on line 1	2	
3 Excludable interest on series EE U.S. savings bonds issued after 1989 from Form 8815, line 14. You MUST attach Form 8815 to Form 1040	3	
4 Subtract line 3 from line 2. Enter the result here and on Form 1040, line 8a. ▶	4	

Note: If you received a Form 1099-INT, Form 1099-OID, or substitute statement from a brokerage firm, list the firm's name as the payer and enter the total interest shown on that form.

Part II Dividend Income

(See pages 15 and B-1.)

If you had over $400 in gross dividends and/or other distributions on stock, you must complete this part and Part III. If you received, as a nominee, dividends that actually belong to another person, see page B-1.

Dividend Income		Amount
5 List name of payer—include on this line capital gain distributions, nontaxable distributions, etc. ▶	5	
6 Add the amounts on line 5	6	
7 Capital gain distributions. Enter here and on Schedule D* . . . 7		
8 Nontaxable distributions. (See the inst. for Form 1040, line 9.) 8		
9 Add lines 7 and 8	9	
10 Subtract line 9 from line 6. Enter the result here and on Form 1040, line 9 ▶	10	

**If you received capital gain distributions but do not need Schedule D to report any other gains or losses, see the instructions for Form 1040, lines 13 and 14.*

Note: If you received a Form 1099-DIV or substitute statement from a brokerage firm, list the firm's name as the payer and enter the total dividends shown on that form.

Part III Foreign Accounts and Foreign Trusts

(See page B-2.)

If you had over $400 of interest or dividends OR had a foreign account or were a grantor of, or a transferor to, a foreign trust, you must complete this part.	Yes	No
11a At any time during 1992, did you have an interest in or a signature or other authority over a financial account in a foreign country, such as a bank account, securities account, or other financial account? See page B-2 for exceptions and filing requirements for Form TD F 90-22.1		
b If "Yes," enter the name of the foreign country ▶		
12 Were you the grantor of, or transferor to, a foreign trust that existed during 1992, whether or not you have any beneficial interest in it? If "Yes," you may have to file Form 3520, 3520-A, or 926		

For Paperwork Reduction Act Notice, see Form 1040 instructions. — **Schedule B (Form 1040) 1992**

SCHEDULE C (Form 1040)

Department of the Treasury
Internal Revenue Service (T)

Profit or Loss From Business

(Sole Proprietorship)

▶ **Partnerships, joint ventures, etc., must file Form 1065.**

▶ **Attach to Form 1040 or Form 1041.** ▶ **See Instructions for Schedule C (Form 1040).**

OMB No. 1545-0074

1992

Attachment Sequence No. **09**

Name of proprietor | **Social security number (SSN)**

A Principal business or profession, including product or service (see page C-1) | **B** Enter principal business code (from page 2) ▶

C Business name | **D Employer ID number (Not SSN)**

E Business address (including suite or room no.) ▶ ....
City, town or post office, state, and ZIP code

F Accounting method: **(1)** ☐ Cash **(2)** ☐ Accrual **(3)** ☐ Other (specify) ▶ ....

G Method(s) used to value closing inventory: **(1)** ☐ Cost **(2)** ☐ Lower of cost or market **(3)** ☐ Other (attach explanation) **(4)** ☐ Does not apply (if checked, skip line H)

		Yes	No
H	Was there any change in determining quantities, costs, or valuations between opening and closing inventory? If "Yes," attach explanation		
I	Did you "materially participate" in the operation of this business during 1992? If "No," see page C-2 for limitations on losses		
J	Was this business in operation at the end of 1992?		
K	How many months was this business in operation during 1992? ▶		
L	If this is the first Schedule C filed for this business, check here ▶ ☐		

Part I Income

1	Gross receipts or sales. **Caution:** *If this income was reported to you on Form W-2 and the "Statutory employee" box on that form was checked, see page C-2 and check here* ▶ ☐	1	
2	Returns and allowances	2	
3	Subtract line 2 from line 1	3	
4	Cost of goods sold (from line 40 on page 2)	4	
5	**Gross profit.** Subtract line 4 from line 3	5	
6	Other income, including Federal and state gasoline or fuel tax credit or refund (see page C-2)	6	
7	**Gross income.** Add lines 5 and 6 ▶	7	

Part II Expenses (Caution: *Do not* enter expenses for business use of your home on lines 8–27. Instead, see line 30.)

8	Advertising	8		21	Repairs and maintenance	21	
9	Bad debts from sales or services (see page C-3)	9		22	Supplies (not included in Part III)	22	
10	Car and truck expenses (see page C-3—also attach **Form 4562**)	10		23	Taxes and licenses	23	
11	Commissions and fees	11		24	Travel, meals, and entertainment:		
12	Depletion	12		a	Travel	24a	
13	Depreciation and section 179 expense deduction (not included in Part III) (see page C-3)	13		b	Meals and entertainment		
14	Employee benefit programs (other than on line 19)	14		c	Enter 20% of line 24b subject to limitations (see page C-4)		
15	Insurance (other than health)	15		d	Subtract line 24c from line 24b	24d	
16	Interest:			25	Utilities	25	
a	Mortgage (paid to banks, etc.)	16a		26	Wages (less jobs credit)	26	
b	Other	16b		27a	Other expenses (**list type and amount**):		
17	Legal and professional services	17					
18	Office expense	18					
19	Pension and profit-sharing plans	19					
20	Rent or lease (see page C-4):						
a	Vehicles, machinery, and equipment	20a					
b	Other business property	20b		27b	Total other expenses	27b	

28	**Total expenses** before expenses for business use of home. Add lines 8 through 27b in columns ▶	28	
29	Tentative profit (loss). Subtract line 28 from line 7	29	
30	Expenses for business use of your home. Attach **Form 8829**	30	
31	**Net profit or (loss).** Subtract line 30 from line 29. If a profit, enter here and on Form 1040, line 12. Also, enter the net profit on Schedule SE, line 2 (statutory employees, see page C-5). If a loss, you MUST go on to line 32 (fiduciaries, see page C-5)	31	

32 If you have a loss, you MUST check the box that describes your investment in this activity (see page C-5)
If you checked 32a, enter the loss on Form 1040, line 12, and Schedule SE, line 2 (statutory employees, see page C-5). If you checked 32b, you MUST attach **Form 6198**.

32a ☐ All investment is at risk.
32b ☐ Some investment is not at risk.

For Paperwork Reduction Act Notice, see Form 1040 instructions. Cat. No. 11334P **Schedule C (Form 1040) 1992**

Schedule C (Form 1040) 1992 Page **2**

Part III Cost of Goods Sold (see page C-5)

33	Inventory at beginning of year. If different from last year's closing inventory, attach explanation	33	
34	Purchases less cost of items withdrawn for personal use	34	
35	Cost of labor. Do not include salary paid to yourself	35	
36	Materials and supplies	36	
37	Other costs	37	
38	Add lines 33 through 37	38	
39	Inventory at end of year	39	
40	**Cost of goods sold.** Subtract line 39 from line 38. Enter the result here and on page 1, line 4	40	

Part IV Principal Business or Professional Activity Codes

Locate the major category that best describes your activity. Within the major category, select the activity code that most closely identifies the business or profession that is the principal source of your sales or receipts. **Enter this 4-digit code on page 1, line B.** For example, real estate agent is under the major category of **"Real Estate,"** and the code is "5520." **Note:** *If your principal source of income is from farming activities, you should file* ***Schedule F*** *(Form 1040), Profit or Loss From Farming.*

Agricultural Services, Forestry, Fishing

Code

1990 Animal services, other than breeding
1933 Crop services
2113 Farm labor & management services
2246 Fishing, commercial
2238 Forestry, except logging
2212 Horticulture & landscaping
2469 Hunting & trapping
1974 Livestock breeding
0836 Logging
1958 Veterinary services, including pets

Construction

0018 Operative builders (for own account)

Building Trade Contractors, Including Repairs

0414 Carpentering & flooring
0455 Concrete work
0273 Electrical work
0299 Masonry, dry wall, stone, & tile
0257 Painting & paper hanging
0232 Plumbing, heating, & air conditioning
0430 Roofing, siding & sheet metal
0885 Other building trade contractors (excavation, glazing, etc.)

General Contractors

0075 Highway & street construction
0059 Nonresidential building
0034 Residential building
3889 Other heavy construction (pipe laying, bridge construction, etc.)

Finance, Insurance, & Related Services

6064 Brokers & dealers of securities
6080 Commodity contracts brokers & dealers; security & commodity exchanges
6148 Credit institutions & mortgage bankers
5702 Insurance agents or brokers
5744 Insurance services (appraisal, consulting, inspection, etc.)
6130 Investment advisors & services
5777 Other financial services

Manufacturing, Including Printing & Publishing

0679 Apparel & other textile products
1115 Electric & electronic equipment
1073 Fabricated metal products
0638 Food products & beverages
0810 Furniture & fixtures
0695 Leather footwear, handbags, etc.
0836 Lumber & other wood products
1099 Machinery & machine shops
0877 Paper & allied products
1057 Primary metal industries
0851 Printing & publishing
1032 Stone, clay, & glass products
0653 Textile mill products
1883 Other manufacturing industries

Mining & Mineral Extraction

1537 Coal mining
1511 Metal mining
1552 Oil & gas
1719 Quarrying & nonmetallic mining

Real Estate

5538 Operators & lessors of buildings, including residential
5553 Operators & lessors of other real property
5520 Real estate agents & brokers
5579 Real estate property managers
5710 Subdividers & developers, except cemeteries
6155 Title abstract offices

Services: Personal, Professional, & Business Services

Amusement & Recreational Services

9670 Bowling centers
9688 Motion picture & tape distribution & allied services
9597 Motion picture & video production
9639 Motion picture theaters
8557 Physical fitness facilities
9696 Professional sports & racing, including promoters & managers
9811 Theatrical performers, musicians, agents, producers & related services
9613 Video tape rental
9837 Other amusement & recreational services

Automotive Services

8813 Automotive rental or leasing, without driver
8953 Automotive repairs, general & specialized
8839 Parking, except valet
8896 Other automotive services (wash, towing, etc.)

Business & Personal Services

7658 Accounting & bookkeeping
7716 Advertising, except direct mail
7682 Architectural services
8318 Barber shop (or barber)
8110 Beauty shop (or beautician)
8714 Child day care
7872 Computer programming, processing, data preparation & related services
7922 Computer repair, maintenance, & leasing
7286 Consulting services
7799 Consumer credit reporting & collection services
8755 Counseling (except health practitioners)
7732 Employment agencies & personnel supply
7518 Engineering services
7773 Equipment rental & leasing (except computer or automotive)
8532 Funeral services & crematories
7633 Income tax preparation
7914 Investigative & protective services
7617 Legal services (or lawyer)
7856 Mailing, reproduction, commercial art, photography, & stenographic services
7245 Management services
8771 Ministers & chaplains
8334 Photographic studios
7260 Public relations
8733 Research services
7708 Surveying services
8730 Teaching or tutoring
7880 Other business services
6882 Other personal services

Hotels & Other Lodging Places

7237 Camps & camping parks
7096 Hotels, motels, & tourist homes
7211 Rooming & boarding houses

Laundry & Cleaning Services

7450 Carpet & upholstery cleaning
7419 Coin-operated laundries & dry cleaning
7435 Full-service laundry, dry cleaning, & garment service
7476 Janitorial & related services (building, house, & window cleaning)

Medical & Health Services

9274 Chiropractors
9233 Dentist's office or clinic
9217 Doctor's (M.D.) office or clinic
9456 Medical & dental laboratories
9472 Nursing & personal care facilities
9290 Optometrists
9258 Osteopathic physicians & surgeons
9241 Podiatrists
9415 Registered & practical nurses
9431 Offices & clinics of other health practitioners (dieticians, midwives, speech pathologists, etc.)
9886 Other health services

Miscellaneous Repair, Except Computers

9019 Audio equipment & TV repair
9035 Electrical & electronic equipment repair, except audio & TV
9050 Furniture repair & reupholstery
2881 Other equipment repair

Trade, Retail—Selling Goods to Individuals & Households

3038 Catalog or mail order
3012 Selling door to door, by telephone or party plan, or from mobile unit
3053 Vending machine selling

Selling From Showroom, Store, or Other Fixed Location

Apparel & Accessories

3921 Accessory & specialty stores & furriers for women
3939 Clothing, family
3772 Clothing, men's & boys'
3913 Clothing, women's
3756 Shoe stores
3954 Other apparel & accessory stores

Automotive & Service Stations

3558 Gasoline service stations
3319 New car dealers (franchised)
3533 Tires, accessories, & parts
3335 Used car dealers
3517 Other automotive dealers (motorcycles, recreational vehicles, etc.)

Building, Hardware, & Garden Supply

4416 Building materials dealers
4457 Hardware stores
4473 Nurseries & garden supply stores
4432 Paint, glass, & wallpaper stores

Food & Beverages

0612 Bakeries selling at retail
3086 Catering services
3095 Drinking places (bars, taverns, pubs, saloons, etc.)
3079 Eating places, meals & snacks
3210 Grocery stores (general line)
3251 Liquor stores
3236 Specialized food stores (meat, produce, candy, health food, etc.)

Furniture & General Merchandise

3988 Computer & software stores
3970 Furniture stores
4317 Home furnishings stores (china, floor coverings, drapes)
4119 Household appliance stores
4333 Music & record stores
3996 TV, audio & electronic stores
3715 Variety stores
3731 Other general merchandise stores

Miscellaneous Retail Stores

4812 Boat dealers
5017 Book stores, excluding newsstands
4853 Camera & photo supply stores
3277 Drug stores
5058 Fabric & needlework stores
4655 Florists
5090 Fuel dealers (except gasoline)
4630 Gift, novelty & souvenir shops
4838 Hobby, toy, & game shops
4671 Jewelry stores
4895 Luggage & leather goods stores
5074 Mobile home dealers
4879 Optical goods stores
4697 Sporting goods & bicycle shops
5033 Stationery stores
4614 Used merchandise & antique stores (except motor vehicle parts)
5884 Other retail stores

Trade, Wholesale—Selling Goods to Other Businesses, etc.

Durable Goods, Including Machinery Equipment, Wood, Metals, etc.

2634 Agent or broker for other firms—more than 50% of gross sales on commission
2618 Selling for your own account

Nondurable Goods, Including Food, Fiber, Chemicals, etc.

2675 Agent or broker for other firms—more than 50% of gross sales on commission
2659 Selling for your own account

Transportation, Communications, Public Utilities, & Related Services

6619 Air transportation
6312 Bus & limousine transportation
6676 Communication services
6395 Courier or package delivery
6361 Highway passenger transportation (except chartered service)
6536 Public warehousing
6114 Taxicabs
6510 Trash collection without own dump
6635 Travel agents & tour operators
6338 Trucking (except trash collection)
6692 Utilities (dumps, snow plowing, road cleaning, etc.)
6551 Water transportation
6650 Other transportation services

8888 Unable to classify

SCHEDULE D (Form 1040)

Department of the Treasury
Internal Revenue Service (T)

Capital Gains and Losses

(And Reconciliation of Forms 1099-B for Bartering Transactions)

▶ **Attach to Form 1040.** ▶ **See Instructions for Schedule D (Form 1040).**

▶ **For more space to list transactions for lines 1a and 9a, get Schedule D-1 (Form 1040).**

OMB No. 1545-0074

1992

Attachment Sequence No. **12A**

Name(s) shown on Form 1040 | **Your social security number**

Caution: *Add the following amounts reported to you for 1992 on Forms 1099-B and 1099-S (or on substitute statements):* ***(a)*** *proceeds from transactions involving stocks, bonds, and other securities, and* ***(b)*** *gross proceeds from real estate transactions not reported on another form or schedule. If this total does not equal the total of lines 1c and 9c, column (d), attach a statement explaining the difference.*

Part I Short-Term Capital Gains and Losses—Assets Held One Year or Less

(a) Description of property (Example, 100 shares 7% preferred of "XYZ" Co.)	(b) Date acquired (Mo., day, yr.)	(c) Date sold (Mo., day, yr.)	(d) Sales price (see page D-2)	(e) Cost or other basis (see page D-3)	(f) LOSS If (e) is more than (d), subtract (d) from (e)	(g) GAIN If (d) is more than (e), subtract (e) from (d)
1a Stocks, Bonds, Other Securities, and Real Estate. Include Form 1099-B and 1099-S Transactions. See page D-3.						
1b Amounts from Schedule D-1, line 1b. Attach Schedule D-1						
1c Total of All Sales Price Amounts. Add column (d) of lines 1a and 1b . . ▶		1c				
1d Other Transactions.						

		Line	(f)	(g)
2	Short-term gain from sale or exchange of your home from Form 2119, line 17 or 23 .	2		
3	Short-term gain from installment sales from Form 6252, line 26 or 37	3		
4	Short-term gain or (loss) from like-kind exchanges from Form 8824	4		
5	Net short-term gain or (loss) from partnerships, S corporations, and fiduciaries .	5		
6	Short-term capital loss carryover from 1991 Schedule D, line 36	6		
7	Add lines 1a, 1b, 1d, and 2 through 6, in columns (f) and (g).	7	( )	
8	**Net short-term capital gain or (loss).** Combine columns (f) and (g) of line 7		8	

Part II Long-Term Capital Gains and Losses—Assets Held More Than One Year

(a)	(b)	(c)	(d)	(e)	(f)	(g)
9a Stocks, Bonds, Other Securities, and Real Estate. Include Form 1099-B and 1099-S Transactions. See page D-3.						
9b Amounts from Schedule D-1, line 9b. Attach Schedule D-1						
9c Total of All Sales Price Amounts. Add column (d) of lines 9a and 9b . . ▶		9c				
9d Other Transactions.						

		Line	(f)	(g)
10	Long-term gain from sale or exchange of your home from Form 2119, line 17 or 23 .	10		
11	Long-term gain from installment sales from Form 6252, line 26 or 37	11		
12	Long-term gain or (loss) from like-kind exchanges from Form 8824.	12		
13	Net long-term gain or (loss) from partnerships, S corporations, and fiduciaries .	13		
14	Capital gain distributions	14		
15	Gain from Form 4797, line 8 or 10	15		
16	Long-term capital loss carryover from 1991 Schedule D, line 43	16		
17	Add lines 9a, 9b, 9d, and 10 through 16, in columns (f) and (g)	17	( )	
18	**Net long-term capital gain or (loss).** Combine columns (f) and (g) of line 17		18	

For Paperwork Reduction Act Notice, see Form 1040 instructions. Cat. No. 11338H **Schedule D (Form 1040) 1992**

Schedule D (Form 1040) 1992 Attachment Sequence No. **12A** Page **2**

Name(s) shown on Form 1040. Do not enter name and social security number if shown on other side. | **Your social security number**

Part III Summary of Parts I and II

19	Combine lines 8 and 18 and enter the net gain or (loss). If a gain, also enter the gain on Form 1040, line 13	19	
	Note: *If both lines 18 and 19 are gains, see Part IV below.*		
20	If line 19 is a (loss), enter here and as a (loss) on Form 1040, line 13, the **smaller** of:		
a	The (loss) on line 19; **or**		
b	($3,000) or, if married filing a separate return, ($1,500)	20	( )
	Note: *When figuring whether line 20a or 20b is* ***smaller,*** *treat both numbers as positive.*		
	Complete Part V if the loss on line 19 is more than the loss on line 20 OR if Form 1040, line 37, is zero.		

Part IV Tax Computation Using Maximum Capital Gains Rate

USE THIS PART TO FIGURE YOUR TAX ONLY IF BOTH LINES 18 AND 19 ARE GAINS, AND:

You checked filing status box:	AND	Form 1040, line 37, is over:	You checked filing status box:	AND	Form 1040, line 37, is over:
1		$51,900	3		$43,250
2 or 5		$86,500	4		$74,150

21	Enter the amount from Form 1040, line 37	21	
22	Enter the **smaller** of line 18 or line 19	22	
23	Subtract line 22 from line 21	23	
24	Enter: $21,450 if you checked filing status box 1; $35,800 if you checked filing status box 2 or 5; $17,900 if you checked filing status box 3; or $28,750 if you checked filing status box 4	24	
25	Enter the **greater** of line 23 or line 24	25	
26	Subtract line 25 from line 21	26	
27	Figure the tax on the amount on line 25. Use the Tax Table or Tax Rate Schedules, whichever applies	27	
28	Multiply line 26 by 28% (.28)	28	
29	Add lines 27 and 28. Enter here and on Form 1040, line 38, and check the box for Schedule D	29	

Part V Capital Loss Carryovers from 1992 to 1993

30	Enter the amount from Form 1040, line 35. If a loss, enclose the amount in parentheses					30	
31	Enter the loss from line 20 as a positive amount					31	
32	Combine lines 30 and 31. If zero or less, enter -0-					32	
33	Enter the **smaller** of line 31 or line 32					33	
	Note: *If both lines 8 and 20 are losses, go to line 34; otherwise, skip lines 34-38.*						
34	Enter the loss from line 8 as a positive amount					34	
35	Enter the gain, if any, from line 18			35			
36	Enter the amount from line 33			36			
37	Add lines 35 and 36					37	
38	**Short-term capital loss carryover to 1993.** Subtract line 37 from line 34. If zero or less, enter -0-					38	
	Note: *If both lines 18 and 20 are losses, go to line 39; otherwise, skip lines 39-45.*						
39	Enter the loss from line 18 as a positive amount					39	
40	Enter the gain, if any, from line 8			40			
41	Enter the amount from line 33	41					
42	Enter the amount, if any, from line 34	42					
43	Subtract line 42 from line 41. If zero or less, enter -0-			43			
44	Add lines 40 and 43					44	
45	**Long-term capital loss carryover to 1993.** Subtract line 44 from line 39. If zero or less, enter -0-					45	

Part VI Election Not To Use the Installment Method. Complete this part **only** if you elect out of the installment method and report a note or other obligation at less than full face value.

46	Check here if you elect out of the installment method	▶ ☐
47	Enter the face amount of the note or other obligation	▶
48	Enter the percentage of valuation of the note or other obligation	▶ %

Part VII Reconciliation of Forms 1099-B for Bartering Transactions. Complete this part **only** if you received one or more Forms 1099-B or substitute statements reporting **bartering income.**

			Amount of bartering income from Form 1099-B or substitute statement reported on form or schedule
49	Form 1040, line 22	49	
50	Schedule C, C-EZ, D, E, or F (specify) ▶	50	
51	Other form or schedule (identify). If nontaxable, indicate reason—attach additional sheets if necessary:	51	
52	**Total.** Add lines 49 through 51. This amount should be the same as the total bartering income on all Forms 1099-B and substitute statements received for bartering transactions	52	

SCHEDULE E (Form 1040)

Department of the Treasury
Internal Revenue Service (T)

Supplemental Income and Loss

(From rental real estate, royalties, partnerships, estates, trusts, REMICs, etc.)

▶ Attach to Form 1040 or Form 1041.
▶ See Instructions for Schedule E (Form 1040).

OMB No. 1545-0074

1992

Attachment Sequence No. **13**

Name(s) shown on return | **Your social security number**

Part I **Income or Loss From Rental Real Estate and Royalties** **Note:** *Report income and expenses from the rental of personal property on* ***Schedule C*** *or* ***C-EZ.*** *Report farm rental income or loss from* ***Form 4835*** *on page 2, line 39.*

1	Show the kind and location of each **rental real estate property:**	2 For each rental real estate property listed on line 1, did you or your family use it for personal purposes for more than the greater of 14 days or 10% of the total days rented at fair rental value during the tax year? (See page E-1.)		Yes	No
A			A		
B			B		
C			C		

		Properties A	Properties B	Properties C		Totals (Add columns A, B, and C.)
Income:						
3 Rents received	3				3	
4 Royalties received	4				4	
Expenses:						
5 Advertising	5					
6 Auto and travel (see page E-2)	6					
7 Cleaning and maintenance	7					
8 Commissions	8					
9 Insurance	9					
10 Legal and other professional fees	10					
11 Management fees	11					
12 Mortgage interest paid to banks, etc. (see page E-2)	12				12	
13 Other interest	13					
14 Repairs	14					
15 Supplies	15					
16 Taxes	16					
17 Utilities	17					
18 Other (list) ▶	18					
19 Add lines 5 through 18	19				19	
20 Depreciation expense or depletion (see page E-2)	20				20	
21 Total expenses. Add lines 19 and 20	21					
22 Income or (loss) from rental real estate or royalty properties. Subtract line 21 from line 3 (rents) or line 4 (royalties). If the result is a (loss), see page E-2 to find out if you must file **Form 6198**	22					
23 Deductible rental real estate loss. **Caution:** *Your rental real estate loss on line 22 may be limited. See page E-3 to find out if you must file* ***Form 8582***	23	( )	( )	( )		
24 **Income.** Add positive amounts shown on line 22. **Do not** include any losses					24	
25 **Losses.** Add royalty losses from line 22 and rental real estate losses from line 23. Enter the total losses here					25	( )
26 Total rental real estate and royalty income or (loss). Combine lines 24 and 25. Enter the result here. If Parts II, III, IV, and line 39 on page 2 do not apply to you, also enter this amount on Form 1040, line 18. Otherwise, include this amount in the total on line 40 on page 2					26	

For Paperwork Reduction Act Notice, see Form 1040 Instructions. Cat. No. 11344L **Schedule E (Form 1040) 1992**

Schedule E (Form 1040) 1992 Attachment Sequence No. 13 Page 2

Name(s) shown on return. Do not enter name and social security number if shown on other side. | Your social security number

Note: *If you report amounts from farming or fishing on Schedule E, you must enter your gross income from those activities on line 41 below.*

Part II Income or Loss From Partnerships and S Corporations

If you report a loss from an at-risk activity, you MUST check either column **(e)** or **(f)** of line 27 to describe your investment in the activity. See page E-3. If you check column **(f)**, you must attach **Form 6198**.

27	(a) Name	(b) Enter P for partnership; S for S corporation	(c) Check if foreign partnership	(d) Employer identification number	Investment At Risk? (e) All is at risk	(f) Some is not at risk
A						
B						
C						
D						
E						

	Passive Income and Loss		Nonpassive Income and Loss		
	(g) Passive loss allowed (attach Form 8582 if required)	(h) Passive income from Schedule K-1	(i) Nonpassive loss from Schedule K-1	(j) Section 179 expense deduction from Form 4562	(k) Nonpassive income from Schedule K-1
A					
B					
C					
D					
E					
28a Totals					
b Totals					

29	Add columns (h) and (k) of line 28a	29	
30	Add columns (g), (i), and (j) of line 28b	30	( )
31	Total partnership and S corporation income or (loss). Combine lines 29 and 30. Enter the result here and include in the total on line 40 below	31	

Part III Income or Loss From Estates and Trusts

32	(a) Name	(b) Employer identification number
A		
B		
C		

	Passive Income and Loss		Nonpassive Income and Loss	
	(c) Passive deduction or loss allowed (attach Form 8582 if required)	(d) Passive income from Schedule K-1	(e) Deduction or loss from Schedule K-1	(f) Other income from Schedule K-1
A				
B				
C				
33a Totals				
b Totals				

34	Add columns (d) and (f) of line 33a	34	
35	Add columns (c) and (e) of line 33b	35	( )
36	Total estate and trust income or (loss). Combine lines 34 and 35. Enter the result here and include in the total on line 40 below	36	

Part IV Income or Loss From Real Estate Mortgage Investment Conduits (REMICs)—Residual Holder

37	(a) Name	(b) Employer identification number	(c) Excess inclusion from Schedules Q, line 2c (see page E-4)	(d) Taxable income (net loss) from Schedules Q, line 1b	(e) Income from Schedules Q, line 3b

38	Combine columns (d) and (e) only. Enter the result here and include in the total on line 40 below	38	

Part V Summary

39	Net farm rental income or (loss) from **Form 4835**. Also, complete line 41 below	39	
40	TOTAL income or (loss). Combine lines 26, 31, 36, 38, and 39. Enter the result here and on Form 1040, line 18 ▶	40	
41	**Reconciliation of Farming and Fishing Income:** Enter your **gross** farming and fishing income reported in Parts II and III and on line 39 (see page E-4)	41	

Schedule R
(Form 1040)

Department of the Treasury
Internal Revenue Service (T)

Credit for the Elderly or the Disabled

▶ **Attach to Form 1040.** ▶ **See separate instructions for Schedule R.**

OMB No. 1545-0074
1992
Attachment
Sequence No. **16**

Name(s) shown on Form 1040

Your social security number

You may be able to use Schedule R to reduce your tax if by the end of 1992:

- You were age 65 or older, **OR** • You were under age 65, you retired on **permanent and total** disability, and you received taxable disability income.

But you must also meet other tests. See the separate instructions for Schedule R.
Note: *In most cases, the IRS can figure the credit for you. See page 23 of the Form 1040 instructions.*

Part I Check the Box for Your Filing Status and Age

If your filing status is:	And by the end of 1992:	Check only one box:
Single, Head of household, or Qualifying widow(er) with dependent child	1 You were 65 or older 1	☐
	2 You were under 65 and you retired on permanent and total disability . . . 2	☐
Married filing a joint return	3 Both spouses were 65 or older 3	☐
	4 Both spouses were under 65, but only one spouse retired on permanent and total disability 4	☐
	5 Both spouses were under 65, and both retired on permanent and total disability 5	☐
	6 One spouse was 65 or older, and the other spouse was under 65 and retired on permanent and total disability 6	☐
	7 One spouse was 65 or older, and the other spouse was under 65 and **NOT** retired on permanent and total disability 7	☐
Married filing a separate return	8 You were 65 or older and you did not live with your spouse at any time in 1992. 8	☐
	9 You were under 65, you retired on permanent and total disability, and you did not live with your spouse at any time in 1992 9	☐

If you checked box 1, 3, 7, or 8, skip Part II and complete Part III on the back. All others, complete Parts II and III.

Part II Statement of Permanent and Total Disability (Complete **only** if you checked box 2, 4, 5, 6, or 9 above.)

IF: 1 You filed a physician's statement for this disability for 1983 or an earlier year, or you filed a statement for tax years after 1983 and your physician signed line B on the statement, **AND**

2 Due to your continued disabled condition, you were unable to engage in any substantial gainful activity in 1992, check this box . . . . ▶ ☐

- If you checked this box, you do not have to file another statement for 1992.
- If you **did not** check this box, have your physician complete the following statement.

Physician's Statement (See instructions at bottom of page 2.)

I certify that ______________________________
Name of disabled person

was permanently and totally disabled on January 1, 1976, or January 1, 1977, **OR** was permanently and totally disabled on the date he or she retired. If retired after December 31, 1976, enter the date retired. ▶ __________

Physician: Sign your name on **either** line A or B below.

A The disability has lasted or can be expected to last continuously for at least a year . . . . ______________ Physician's signature Date

B There is no reasonable probability that the disabled condition will ever improve . . . . ______________ Physician's signature Date

Physician's name	Physician's address

For Paperwork Reduction Act Notice, see Form 1040 instructions. Cat. No. 11359K **Schedule R (Form 1040) 1992**

Part III Figure Your Credit

10 **If you checked (in Part I):** **Enter:**
Box 1, 2, 4, or 7 . . . . $5,000
Box 3, 5, or 6 . . . . $7,500
Box 8 or 9 . . . . $3,750 } **10**

Caution: *If you checked box 2, 4, 5, 6, or 9 in Part I, you* ***MUST*** *complete line 11 below. All others, skip line 11 and enter the amount from line 10 on line 12.*

11 **If you checked:**
- Box 6 in Part I, add $5,000 to the taxable disability income of the spouse who was under age 65. Enter the total here.
- Box 2, 4, or 9 in Part I, enter your taxable disability income here.
- Box 5 in Part I, add your taxable disability income to your spouse's taxable disability income. Enter the total here. } **11**

TIP: For more details on what to include on line 11, see the instructions.

12
- If you completed line 11 above, look at lines 10 and 11. Enter the **smaller** of the two amounts here.
- All others, enter the amount from line 10 here. } **12**

13 Enter the following pensions, annuities, or disability income that you (and your spouse if filing a joint return) received in 1992 (see instructions):

a Nontaxable part of social security benefits, and Nontaxable part of railroad retirement benefits treated as social security. } . . . **13a**

b Nontaxable veterans' pensions, and Any other pension, annuity, or disability benefit that is excluded from income under any other provision of law. } . . . **13b**

c Add lines 13a and 13b. (Even though these income items are not taxable, they **must** be included here to figure your credit.) If you did not receive any of the types of nontaxable income listed on line 13a or 13b, enter -0- on line 13c **13c**

14 Enter the amount from Form 1040, line 32 **14**

15 **If you checked (in Part I):** **Enter:**
Box 1 or 2 . . . . $7,500
Box 3, 4, 5, 6, or 7 . . . . . $10,000
Box 8 or 9 . . . . $5,000 } **15**

16 Subtract line 15 from line 14. If line 15 is more than line 14, enter -0- **16**

17 Divide line 16 above by 2 . . . . **17**

18 Add lines 13c and 17 . . . . **18**

19 Subtract line 18 from line 12. If line 18 is more than line 12, stop here; you **cannot** take the credit. Otherwise, go to line 21 . . . . **19**

20 Decimal amount used to figure the credit . . . . **20** × .15

21 Multiply line 19 above by the decimal amount (.15) on line 20. Enter the result here and on Form 1040, line 42. **Caution:** *If you file Schedule C, C-EZ, D, E, or F (Form 1040), your credit may be limited. See the instructions for line 21 for the amount of credit you can claim* **21**

Instructions for Physician's Statement

Taxpayer

If you retired after December 31, 1976, enter the date you retired in the space provided in Part II.

Physician

A person is permanently and totally disabled if **both** of the following apply:

1. He or she cannot engage in any substantial gainful activity because of a physical or mental condition, and

2. A physician determines that the disability has lasted or can be expected to last continuously for at least a year or can lead to death.

SCHEDULE SE (Form 1040)

Department of the Treasury Internal Revenue Service (T)

Self-Employment Tax

▶ See Instructions for Schedule SE (Form 1040).

▶ Attach to Form 1040.

OMB No. 1545-0074

1992

Attachment Sequence No. 17

Name of person with **self-employment** income (as shown on Form 1040)	Social security number of person with **self-employment** income ▶	

Who Must File Schedule SE

You must file Schedule SE if:

- Your wages (and tips) subject to social security AND Medicare tax (or railroad retirement tax) were less than $130,200; **AND**
- Your *net earnings from self-employment from other than church employee income* (line 4 of Short Schedule SE or line 4c of Long Schedule SE) were $400 or more;

  OR
- You had church employee income (as defined on page SE-1) of $108.28 or more.

Exception. If your only self-employment income was from earnings as a minister, member of a religious order, or Christian Science practitioner, AND you filed **Form 4361** and received IRS approval not to be taxed on those earnings, DO NOT file Schedule SE. Instead, write "Exempt–Form 4361" on Form 1040, line 47.

May I Use Short Schedule SE or MUST I Use Long Schedule SE?

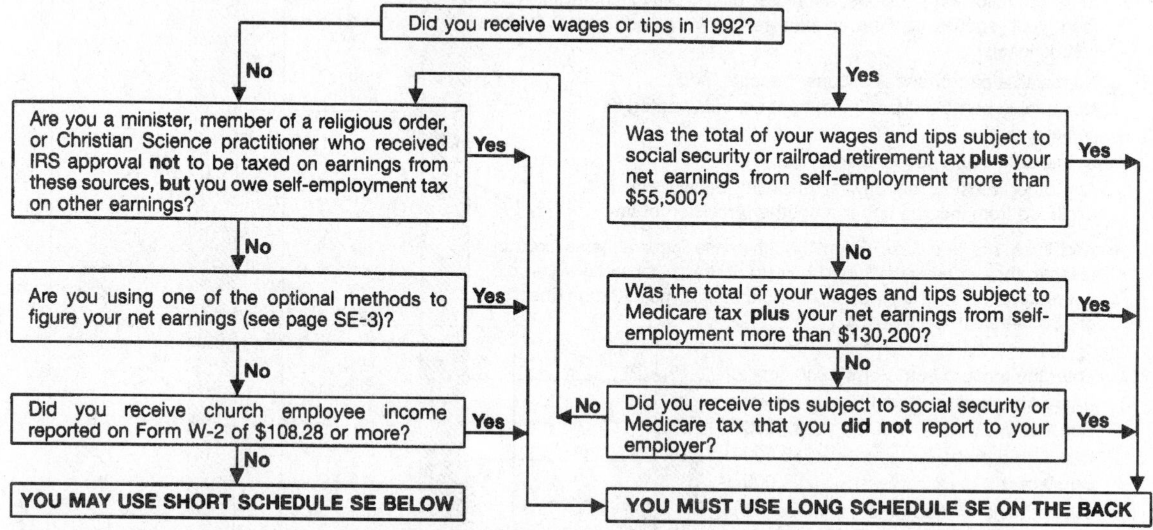

Did you receive wages or tips in 1992?
No
Yes
Are you a minister, member of a religious order, or Christian Science practitioner who received IRS approval **not** to be taxed on earnings from these sources, **but** you owe self-employment tax on other earnings?
Yes
No
Are you using one of the optional methods to figure your net earnings (see page SE-3)?
Yes
No
Did you receive church employee income reported on Form W-2 of $108.28 or more?
Yes
No
YOU MAY USE SHORT SCHEDULE SE BELOW
Was the total of your wages and tips subject to social security or railroad retirement tax **plus** your net earnings from self-employment more than $55,500?
Yes
No
Was the total of your wages and tips subject to Medicare tax **plus** your net earnings from self-employment more than $130,200?
Yes
No
Did you receive tips subject to social security or Medicare tax that you **did not** report to your employer?
No
Yes
YOU MUST USE LONG SCHEDULE SE ON THE BACK

Section A—Short Schedule SE. Caution: *Read above to see if you must use Long Schedule SE on the back (Section B).*

1	Net farm profit or (loss) from Schedule F, line 36, and farm partnerships, Schedule K-1 (Form 1065), line 15a	1	
2	Net profit or (loss) from Schedule C, line 31; Schedule C-EZ, line 3; and Schedule K-1 (Form 1065), line 15a (other than farming). See page SE-2 for other income to report	2	
3	Combine lines 1 and 2	3	
4	**Net earnings from self-employment.** Multiply line 3 by 92.35% (.9235). If less than $400, **do not** file this schedule; you do not owe self-employment tax . . . . . ▶	4	
5	**Self-employment tax.** If the amount on line 4 is: • $55,500 or less, multiply line 4 by 15.3% (.153) and enter the result. • More than $55,500 but less than $130,200, multiply the amount in excess of $55,500 by 2.9% (.029). Then, add $8,491.50 to the result and enter the total. • $130,200 or more, enter $10,657.80. Also, enter this amount on Form 1040, line 47 . . . . . **Note:** *Also, enter **one-half** of the amount from line 5 on **Form 1040, line 25**.*	5	

For Paperwork Reduction Act Notice, see Form 1040 instructions. Cat. No. 11358Z **Schedule SE (Form 1040) 1992**

Schedule SE (Form 1040) 1992 Attachment Sequence No. 17 Page 2

Name of person with **self-employment** income (as shown on Form 1040) | Social security number of person with **self-employment** income ▶

Section B—Long Schedule SE

A If you are a minister, member of a religious order, or Christian Science practitioner AND you filed **Form 4361,** but you had $400 or more of **other** net earnings from self-employment, check here and continue with Part I . . . . ▶ ☐

B If your only income subject to self-employment tax is church employee income and you are **not** a minister or a member of a religious order, skip lines 1 through 4b. Enter -0- on line 4c and go to line 5a.

Part I Self-Employment Tax

Line	Description	Sub-line	Sub-amount	Line	Amount	Cents
1	Net farm profit or (loss) from Schedule F, line 36, and farm partnerships, Schedule K-1 (Form 1065), line 15a. **Note:** *Skip this line if you use the farm optional method. See requirements in Part II below and on page SE-3*			1		
2	Net profit or (loss) from Schedule C, line 31; Schedule C-EZ, line 3; and Schedule K-1 (Form 1065), line 15a (other than farming). See page SE-2 for other income to report. **Note:** *Skip this line if you use the nonfarm optional method. See requirements in Part II below and on page SE-3*			2		
3	Combine lines 1 and 2			3		
4a	If line 3 is more than zero, multiply line 3 by 92.35% (.9235). Otherwise, enter amount from line 3			4a		
b	If you elected one or both of the optional methods, enter the total of lines 17 and 19 here			4b		
c	Combine lines 4a and 4b. If less than $400, **do not** file this schedule; you do not owe self-employment tax. **Exception.** If less than $400 and you had church employee income, enter -0- and continue ▶			4c		
5a	Enter your church employee income from Form W-2. **Caution:** *See page SE-1 for definition of church employee income*	5a				
b	Multiply line 5a by 92.35% (.9235). If less than $100, enter -0-			5b		
6	**Net earnings from self-employment.** Add lines 4c and 5b			6		
7	Maximum amount of combined wages and self-employment earnings subject to social security tax or the 6.2% portion of the 7.65% railroad retirement (tier 1) tax for 1992			7	55,500	00
8a	Total social security wages and tips (from Form(s) W-2) and railroad retirement (tier 1) compensation	8a				
b	Unreported tips subject to social security tax (from Form 4137, line 9)	8b				
c	Add lines 8a and 8b			8c		
9	Subtract line 8c from line 7. If zero or less, enter -0- here and on line 10 and go to line 12a ▶			9		
10	Multiply the **smaller** of line 6 or line 9 by 12.4% (.124)			10		
11	Maximum amount of combined wages and self-employment earnings subject to Medicare tax or the 1.45% portion of the 7.65% railroad retirement (tier 1) tax for 1992			11	130,200	00
12a	Total Medicare wages and tips (from Form(s) W-2) and railroad retirement (tier 1) compensation	12a				
b	Unreported tips subject to Medicare tax (from Form 4137, line 14)	12b				
c	Add lines 12a and 12b			12c		
13	Subtract line 12c from line 11. If zero or less, enter -0- here and on line 14 and go to line 15			13		
14	Multiply the **smaller** of line 6 or line 13 by 2.9% (.029)			14		
15	**Self-employment tax.** Add lines 10 and 14. Enter the result here and on Form 1040, line 47. **Note:** *Also, enter **one-half** of the amount from line 15 on **Form 1040, line 25.***			15		

Part II Optional Methods To Figure Net Earnings (See **Who Can File Schedule SE** on page SE-1 and **Optional Methods** on page SE-3.)

Farm Optional Method. You may use this method **only** if **(a)** Your gross farm income[1] was not more than $2,400 **or (b)** Your gross farm income[1] was more than $2,400 and your net farm profits[2] were less than $1,733.

Line	Description	Line	Amount	Cents
16	Maximum income for optional methods	16	1,600	00
17	Enter the **smaller** of: two-thirds (⅔) of gross farm income[1] **or** $1,600. Also, include this amount on line 4b above	17		

Nonfarm Optional Method. You may use this method **only** if **(a)** Your net nonfarm profits[3] were less than $1,733 and also less than 72.189% of your gross nonfarm income,[4] **and (b)** You had net earnings from self-employment of at least $400 in 2 of the prior 3 years. **Caution:** *You may use this method no more than five times.*

Line	Description	Line	Amount	Cents
18	Subtract line 17 from line 16	18		
19	Enter the **smaller** of: two-thirds (⅔) of gross nonfarm income[4] **or** the amount on line 18. Also, include this amount on line 4b above	19		

[1]From Schedule F, line 11, and Schedule K-1 (Form 1065), line 15b.
[2]From Schedule F, line 36, and Schedule K-1 (Form 1065), line 15a.
[3]From Schedule C, line 31; Schedule C-EZ, line 3; and Schedule K-1 (Form 1065), line 15a.
[4]From Schedule C, line 7; Schedule C-EZ, line 1; and Schedule K-1 (Form 1065), line 15c.

Form **1041** Department of the Treasury—Internal Revenue Service

U.S. Fiduciary Income Tax Return 1992

For the calendar year 1992 or fiscal year beginning , 1992, and ending , 19 OMB No. 1545-0092

A Type of Entity
- ☐ Decedent's estate
- ☐ Simple trust
- ☐ Complex trust
- ☐ Grantor type trust
- ☐ Bankruptcy estate
- ☐ Pooled income fund

B Number of Schedules K-1 attached (see instructions) ▶

Name of estate or trust (grantor type trust, see instructions)

Name and title of fiduciary

Number, street, and room or suite no. (If a P.O. box, see page 5 of instructions.)

City, state, and ZIP code

C Employer identification number

D Date entity created

E Nonexempt charitable and split-interest trusts, check applicable boxes (see instructions):
- ☐ Described in section 4947(a)(1)
- ☐ Not a private foundation
- ☐ Described in section 4947(a)(2)

F Check applicable boxes: ☐ Initial return ☐ Final return ☐ Amended return; Change in Fiduciary's ▶ ☐ Name ☐ Address

G Pooled mortgage account (see instructions) ☐ Bought ☐ Sold Date:

Income

1	Interest income	1	
2	Dividends	2	
3	Business income or (loss) (attach Schedule C or C-EZ (Form 1040))	3	
4	Capital gain or (loss) (attach Schedule D (Form 1041))	4	
5	Rents, royalties, partnerships, other estates and trusts, etc. (attach Schedule E (Form 1040))	5	
6	Farm income or (loss) (attach Schedule F (Form 1040))	6	
7	Ordinary gain or (loss) (attach Form 4797)	7	
8	Other income (state nature of income)	8	
9	**Total** income (combine lines 1 through 8) ▶	9	

Deductions

10	Interest. (Check if Form 4952 is attached ▶ ☐)	10	
11	Taxes	11	
12	Fiduciary fees	12	
13	Charitable deduction (from Schedule A, line 7)	13	
14	Attorney, accountant, and return preparer fees	14	
15a	Other deductions NOT subject to the 2% floor (attach schedule)	15a	
b	Allowable miscellaneous itemized deductions subject to the 2% floor	15b	
16	**Total** (add lines 10 through 15b)	16	
17	Adjusted total income or (loss) (subtract line 16 from line 9). Enter here and on Schedule B, line 1 ▶	17	
18	Income distribution deduction (from Schedule B, line 17) (see instructions) (attach Schedules K-1 (Form 1041))	18	
19	Estate tax deduction (including certain generation-skipping taxes) (attach computation)	19	
20	Exemption	20	
21	**Total** deductions (add lines 18 through 20) ▶	21	

Tax and Payments (Please attach check or money order here)

22	Taxable income of fiduciary (subtract line 21 from line 17)	22	
23	**Total** tax (from Schedule G, line 7)	23	
24	Payments: **a** 1992 estimated tax payments and amount applied from 1991 return	24a	
b	Estimated tax payments allocated to beneficiaries (from Form 1041-T)	24b	
c	Subtract line 24b from line 24a	24c	
d	Tax paid with extension of time to file: ☐ Form 2758 ☐ Form 8736 ☐ Form 8800	24d	
e	Federal income tax withheld	24e	
	Credits: **f** Form 2439 ; **g** Form 4136 ; **h** Other ; Total ▶	24i	
25	**Total** payments (add lines 24c through 24e, and 24i) ▶	25	
26	**Penalty** for underpayment of estimated tax (see instructions)	26	
27	If the total of lines 23 and 26 is larger than line 25, enter **TAX DUE**	27	
28	If line 25 is larger than the total of lines 23 and 26, enter **OVERPAYMENT**	28	
29	Amount of line 28 to be: **a Credited to 1993 estimated tax** ▶ ; **b Refunded** ▶	29	

Please Sign Here

Under penalties of perjury, I declare that I have examined this return, including accompanying schedules and statements, and to the best of my knowledge and belief, it is true, correct, and complete. Declaration of preparer (other than fiduciary) is based on all information of which preparer has any knowledge.

▶ Signature of fiduciary or officer representing fiduciary | Date | ▶ EIN of fiduciary (see instructions)

Paid Preparer's Use Only

Preparer's signature ▶ | Date | Check if self-employed ▶ ☐ | **Preparer's social security no.**

Firm's name (or yours if self-employed) and address ▶ | E.I. No. ▶ | ZIP code ▶

For Paperwork Reduction Act Notice, see page 1 of the separate instructions. Cat. No. 11370H Form **1041** (1992)

Form 1041 (1992) Page 2

Schedule A Charitable Deduction—Do not complete for a simple trust or a pooled income fund.

1	Amounts paid for charitable purposes from current year's gross income	1	
2	Amounts permanently set aside for charitable purposes from current year's gross income	2	
3	Add lines 1 and 2	3	
4	Tax-exempt income allocable to charitable contribution (see instructions)	4	
5	Subtract line 4 from line 3	5	
6	Amounts paid or set aside for charitable purposes other than from the current year's income	6	
7	**Total** (add lines 5 and 6). Enter here and on page 1, line 13	7	

Schedule B Income Distribution Deduction (see instructions)

1	Adjusted total income (from page 1, line 17) (see instructions)			1	
2	Adjusted tax-exempt interest			2	
3	Net gain shown on Schedule D (Form 1041), line 17, column (a). (see instructions)			3	
4	Enter amount from Schedule A, line 6			4	
5	Long-term capital gain included on Schedule A, line 3			5	
6	Short-term capital gain included on Schedule A, line 3			6	
7	If the amount on page 1, line 4, is a capital loss, enter here as a positive figure			7	
8	If the amount on page 1, line 4, is a capital gain, enter here as a negative figure			8	
9	Distributable net income (combine lines 1 through 8)			9	
10	Accounting income for the tax year as determined under the governing instrument	10			
11	Income required to be distributed currently			11	
12	Other amounts paid, credited, or otherwise required to be distributed			12	
13	Total distributions (add lines 11 and 12). (If greater than line 10, see instructions.)			13	
14	Enter the amount of tax-exempt income included on line 13			14	
15	Tentative income distribution deduction (subtract line 14 from line 13)			15	
16	Tentative income distribution deduction (subtract line 2 from line 9)			16	
17	Income distribution deduction. Enter the smaller of line 15 or line 16 here and on page 1, line 18			17	

Schedule G Tax Computation (see instructions)

1	Tax: a ☐ Tax rate schedule or ☐ Schedule D (Form 1041)	1a			
	b Other taxes	1b			
	c Total (add lines 1a and 1b) ▶			1c	
2a	Foreign tax credit (attach Form 1116)	2a			
b	Credit for fuel produced from a nonconventional source	2b			
c	General business credit. Check if from: ☐ Form 3800 or ☐ Form (specify) ▶	2c			
d	Credit for prior year minimum tax (attach Form 8801)	2d			
3	**Total** credits (add lines 2a through 2d) ▶			3	
4	Subtract line 3 from line 1c			4	
5	Recapture taxes. Check if from: ☐ Form 4255 ☐ Form 8611			5	
6	Alternative minimum tax (from Schedule H, line 39)			6	
7	**Total** tax (add lines 4 through 6). Enter here and on page 1, line 23 ▶			7	

Other Information (see instructions)

		Yes	No
1	Did the estate or trust receive tax-exempt income? (If "Yes," attach a computation of the allocation of expenses.) Enter the amount of tax-exempt interest income and exempt-interest dividends ▶ $		
2	Did the estate or trust have any passive activity losses? (If "Yes," get **Form 8582,** Passive Activity Loss Limitations, to figure the allowable loss.)		
3	Did the estate or trust receive all or any part of the earnings (salary, wages, and other compensation) of any individual by reason of a contract assignment or similar arrangement?		
4	At any time during the tax year, did the estate or trust have an interest in or a signature or other authority over a bank, securities, or other financial account in a foreign country? (See the instructions for exceptions and filing requirements for Form TD F 90-22.1.) If "Yes," enter the name of the foreign country ▶		
5	Was the estate or trust the grantor of, or transferor to, a foreign trust which existed during the current tax year, whether or not the estate or trust has any beneficial interest in it? (If "Yes," you may have to file Form 3520, 3520-A, or 926.)		
6	Check this box if this entity has filed or is required to file **Form 8264,** Application for Registration of a Tax Shelter ▶ ☐		
7	Check this box if this entity is a complex trust making the section 663(b) election ▶ ☐		
8	Check this box to make a section 643(e)(3) election (attach Schedule D (Form 1041)) ▶ ☐		
9	Check this box if the decedent's estate has been open for more than 2 years ▶ ☐		

SCHEDULE K-1 (Form 1041)

Department of the Treasury
Internal Revenue Service

Beneficiary's Share of Income, Deductions, Credits, Etc.

for the calendar year 1992, or fiscal year

beginning .... , 1992, ending .... , 19 ....

▶ Complete a separate Schedule K-1 for each beneficiary.

OMB No. 1545-0092

1992

Name of estate or trust

☐ Amended K-1
☐ Final K-1

Beneficiary's identifying number ▶	**Estate's or trust's employer identification number ▶**
Beneficiary's name, address, and ZIP code	Fiduciary's name, address, and ZIP code

	(a) Allocable share item	**(b)** Amount	**(c)** Calendar year 1992 Form 1040 filers enter the amounts in column (b) on:
1	Interest		Schedule B, Part I, line 1
2	Dividends		Schedule B, Part II, line 5
3a	Net short-term capital gain		Schedule D, line 5, column (g)
b	Net long-term capital gain		Schedule D, line 13, column (g)
4a	Business income and other non-passive income before directly apportioned deductions. (see instructions)		Schedule E, Part III
b	Depreciation		
c	Depletion		
d	Amortization		
5a	Rental, rental real estate, and other passive income before directly apportioned deductions. (see instructions)		
b	Depreciation		
c	Depletion		
d	Amortization		
6	Income for minimum tax purposes		
7	Income for regular tax purposes (add lines 1 through 3b, 4a, and 5a)		
8	Adjustment for minimum tax purposes (subtract line 7 from line 6) (see instructions)		Form 6251, line 5s
9	Estate tax deduction (including certain generation-skipping transfer taxes)		Schedule A, line 25
10	Foreign taxes (list on a separate sheet)		Form 1116 or Schedule A (Form 1040), line 7
11	Tax preference items (itemize):		
a	Accelerated depreciation		(Include on the applicable line of Form 6251)
b	Depletion		
c	Amortization		
d	Exclusion items		1993 Form 8801
12	Distributions in the final year of estate or trust:		
a	Excess deductions on termination (see instructions)		Schedule A, line 20
b	Short-term capital loss carryover		Schedule D, line 5, column (f)
c	Long-term capital loss carryover		Schedule D, line 13, column (f)
d	Net operating loss (NOL) carryover		Form 1040, line 22
e			(Include on the applicable line of appropriate tax form)
f			
13	Other (itemize):		
a	Trust payments of estimated taxes credited to you		Form 1040, line 55
b	Tax-exempt interest		Form 1040, line 8b
c			
d			
e			(Include on the applicable line of appropriate tax form)
f			
g			
h			

For Paperwork Reduction Act Notice, see page 1 of the Instructions for Form 1041. Cat. No. 11380D **Schedule K-1 (Form 1041) 1992**

Form **1065** Department of the Treasury Internal Revenue Service

U.S. Partnership Return of Income

For calendar year 1992, or tax year beginning .... , 1992, and ending .... , 19 .... .
▶ See separate instructions.

OMB No. 1545-0099

1992

A Principal business activity	Use the IRS label. Otherwise, please print or type. Name of partnership	D Employer identification number
B Principal product or service	Number, street, and room or suite no. (If a P.O. box, see page 9 of the instructions.)	E Date business started
C Business code number	City or town, state, and ZIP code	F Total assets (see Specific Instructions) $

G Check applicable boxes: (1) ☐ Initial return (2) ☐ Final return (3) ☐ Change in address (4) ☐ Amended return

H Check accounting method: (1) ☐ Cash (2) ☐ Accrual (3) ☐ Other (specify) ▶ ....

I Number of partners in this partnership . . . . ▶ ....

Caution: *Include **only** trade or business income and expenses on lines 1a through 22 below. See the instructions for more information.*

Income

1a Gross receipts or sales	1a		
b Less returns and allowances	1b	1c	
2 Cost of goods sold (Schedule A, line 8)		2	
3 Gross profit. Subtract line 2 from line 1c		3	
4 Ordinary income (loss) from other partnerships and fiduciaries *(attach schedule)*		4	
5 Net farm profit (loss) *(attach Schedule F (Form 1040))*		5	
6 Net gain (loss) from Form 4797, Part II, line 20		6	
7 Other income (loss) (see instructions) *(attach schedule)*		7	
8 **Total income (loss).** Combine lines 3 through 7		8	

Deductions (see instructions for limitations)

9a Salaries and wages (other than to partners)	9a		
b Less jobs credit	9b	9c	
10 Guaranteed payments to partners		10	
11 Repairs		11	
12 Bad debts		12	
13 Rent		13	
14 Taxes		14	
15 Interest		15	
16a Depreciation (see instructions)	16a		
b Less depreciation reported on Schedule A and elsewhere on return	16b	16c	
17 Depletion **(Do not deduct oil and gas depletion.)**		17	
18 Retirement plans, etc.		18	
19 Employee benefit programs		19	
20 Other deductions *(attach schedule)*		20	
21 **Total deductions.** Add the amounts shown in the far right column for lines 9c through 20		21	
22 **Ordinary income (loss)** from trade or business activities. Subtract line 21 from line 8		22	

Please Sign Here

Under penalties of perjury, I declare that I have examined this return, including accompanying schedules and statements, and to the best of my knowledge and belief, it is true, correct, and complete. Declaration of preparer (other than general partner) is based on all information of which preparer has any knowledge.

▶ Signature of general partner ▶ Date

Paid Preparer's Use Only

Preparer's signature ▶	Date	Check if self-employed ▶ ☐	Preparer's social security no.
Firm's name (or yours if self-employed) and address ▶		E.I. No. ▶	
		ZIP code ▶	

For Paperwork Reduction Act Notice, see page 1 of separate instructions. Cat. No. 11390Z Form **1065** (1992)

Form 1065 (1992) Page **2**

Schedule A **Cost of Goods Sold**

1	Inventory at beginning of year	1	
2	Purchases less cost of items withdrawn for personal use	2	
3	Cost of labor	3	
4	Additional section 263A costs (see instructions) *(attach schedule)*	4	
5	Other costs *(attach schedule)*	5	
6	**Total.** Add lines 1 through 5	6	
7	Inventory at end of year	7	
8	**Cost of goods sold.** Subtract line 7 from line 6. Enter here and on page 1, line 2	8	

9a Check all methods used for valuing closing inventory:
- **(i)** ☐ Cost
- **(ii)** ☐ Lower of cost or market as described in Regulations section 1.471-4
- **(iii)** ☐ Writedown of "subnormal" goods as described in Regulations section 1.471-2(c)
- **(iv)** ☐ Other (specify method used and attach explanation) ▶ ....

b Check this box if the LIFO inventory method was adopted this tax year for any goods *(if checked, attach Form 970)* ▶ ☐

c Do the rules of section 263A (for property produced or acquired for resale) apply to the partnership? ☐ **Yes** ☐ **No**

d Was there any change in determining quantities, cost, or valuations between opening and closing inventory? ☐ **Yes** ☐ **No**
If "Yes," attach explanation.

Schedule B **Other Information**

		Yes	No
1	Is this partnership a limited partnership?		
2	Are any partners in this partnership also partnerships?		
3	Is this partnership a partner in another partnership?		
4	Is this partnership subject to the consolidated audit procedures of sections 6221 through 6233? If "Yes," see **Designation of Tax Matters Partner** below		
5	Does this partnership meet **ALL THREE** of the following requirements?		
a	The partnership's total receipts for the tax year were less than $250,000;		
b	The partnership's total assets at the end of the tax year were less than $250,000; **AND**		
c	Schedules K-1 are filed with the return and furnished to the partners on or before the due date (including extensions) for the partnership return.		
	If "Yes," the partnership is not required to complete Schedules L, M-1, and M-2; Item F on page 1 of Form 1065; or Item J on Schedule K-1		
6	Does this partnership have any foreign partners?		
7	Is this partnership a publicly traded partnership as defined in section 469(k)(2)?		
8	Has this partnership filed, or is it required to file, **Form 8264,** Application for Registration of a Tax Shelter?		
9	At any time during calendar year 1992, did the partnership have an interest in or a signature or other authority over a financial account in a foreign country (such as a bank account, securities account, or other financial account)? (See the instructions for exceptions and filing requirements for form TD F 90-22.1.) If "Yes," enter the name of the foreign country. ▶		
10	Was the partnership the grantor of, or transferor to, a foreign trust that existed during the current tax year, whether or not the partnership or any partner has any beneficial interest in it? If "Yes," you may have to file Forms 3520, 3520-A, or 926		
11	Was there a distribution of property or a transfer (e.g., by sale or death) of a partnership interest during the tax year? If "Yes," you may elect to adjust the basis of the partnership's assets under section 754 by attaching the statement described under **Elections** on page 5 of the instructions		
12	Was this partnership in operation at the end of 1992?		
13	How many months in 1992 was this partnership actively operated? ▶		

Designation of Tax Matters Partner (See instructions.)

Enter below the general partner designated as the tax matters partner (TMP) for the tax year of this return:

Name of designated TMP ▶		Identifying number of TMP ▶	
Address of designated TMP ▶			

Form 1065 (1992) Page 3

Schedule K Partners' Shares of Income, Credits, Deductions, Etc.

	(a) Distributive share items		(b) Total amount
Income (Loss)	1 Ordinary income (loss) from trade or business activities (page 1, line 22)	1	
	2 Net income (loss) from rental real estate activities *(attach Form 8825)*	2	
	3a Gross income from other rental activities — 3a		
	b Expenses from other rental activities *(attach schedule)* — 3b		
	c Net income (loss) from other rental activities. Subtract line 3b from line 3a	3c	
	4 Portfolio income (loss) (see instructions): a Interest income	4a	
	b Dividend income	4b	
	c Royalty income	4c	
	d Net short-term capital gain (loss) *(attach Schedule D (Form 1065))*	4d	
	e Net long-term capital gain (loss) *(attach Schedule D (Form 1065))*	4e	
	f Other portfolio income (loss) *(attach schedule)*	4f	
	5 Guaranteed payments to partners	5	
	6 Net gain (loss) under section 1231 (other than due to casualty or theft) *(attach Form 4797)*	6	
	7 Other income (loss) *(attach schedule)*	7	
Deductions	8 Charitable contributions (see instructions) *(attach schedule)*	8	
	9 Section 179 expense deduction *(attach Form 4562)*	9	
	10 Deductions related to portfolio income (see instructions) (itemize)	10	
	11 Other deductions *(attach schedule)*	11	
Investment Interest	12a Interest expense on investment debts	12a	
	b (1) Investment income included on lines 4a through 4f above	12b(1)	
	(2) Investment expenses included on line 10 above	12b(2)	
Credits	13a Credit for income tax withheld	13a	
	b Low-income housing credit (see instructions):		
	(1) From partnerships to which section 42(j)(5) applies for property placed in service before 1990	13b(1)	
	(2) Other than on line 13b(1) for property placed in service before 1990	13b(2)	
	(3) From partnerships to which section 42(j)(5) applies for property placed in service after 1989	13b(3)	
	(4) Other than on line 13b(3) for property placed in service after 1989	13b(4)	
	c Qualified rehabilitation expenditures related to rental real estate activities *(attach Form 3468)*	13c	
	d Credits (other than credits shown on lines 13b and 13c) related to rental real estate activities (see instructions)	13d	
	e Credits related to other rental activities (see instructions)	13e	
	14 Other credits (see instructions)	14	
Self-Employment	15a Net earnings (loss) from self-employment	15a	
	b Gross farming or fishing income	15b	
	c Gross nonfarm income	15c	
Adjustments and Tax Preference Items	16a Depreciation adjustment on property placed in service after 1986	16a	
	b Adjusted gain or loss	16b	
	c Depletion (other than oil and gas)	16c	
	d (1) Gross income from oil, gas, and geothermal properties	16d(1)	
	(2) Deductions allocable to oil, gas, and geothermal properties	16d(2)	
	e Other adjustments and tax preference items *(attach schedule)*	16e	
Foreign Taxes	17a Type of income ▶ .... b Foreign country or U.S. possession ▶		
	c Total gross income from sources outside the United States *(attach schedule)*	17c	
	d Total applicable deductions and losses *(attach schedule)*	17d	
	e Total foreign taxes (check one): ▶ ☐ Paid ☐ Accrued	17e	
	f Reduction in taxes available for credit *(attach schedule)*	17f	
	g Other foreign tax information *(attach schedule)*	17g	
Other	18a Total expenditures to which a section 59(e) election may apply	18a	
	b Type of expenditures ▶		
	19 Tax-exempt interest income	19	
	20 Other tax-exempt income	20	
	21 Nondeductible expenses	21	
	22 Other items and amounts required to be reported separately to partners (see instructions) *(attach schedule)*		
Analysis	23a Income (loss). Combine lines 1 through 7 in column (b). From the result, subtract the sum of lines 8 through 12a, 17e, and 18a	23a	

b Analysis by type of partner:	(a) Corporate	(b) Individual i. Active	(b) Individual ii. Passive	(c) Partnership	(d) Exempt organization	(e) Nominee/Other
(1) General partners						
(2) Limited partners						

SCHEDULE K-1 (Form 1065)
Department of the Treasury
Internal Revenue Service

Partner's Share of Income, Credits, Deductions, Etc.

▶ See separate instructions.

For calendar year 1992 or tax year beginning , 1992, and ending , 19

OMB No. 1545-0099

1992

Partner's identifying number ▶

Partner's name, address, and ZIP code

Partnership's identifying number ▶

Partnership's name, address, and ZIP code

A Is this partner a general partner? . . . ☐ Yes ☐ No

B Partner's share of liabilities (see instructions):

Nonrecourse . . . . $ ....

Qualified nonrecourse financing . . $ ....

Other . . . . $ ....

C What type of entity is this partner? . ▶ ....

D Is this partner a ☐ domestic or a ☐ foreign partner?

E IRS Center where partnership filed return:

F Enter partner's percentage of:	(i) Before change or termination	(ii) End of year
Profit sharing	%	%
Loss sharing	%	%
Ownership of capital	%	%

G(1) Tax shelter registration number . ▶ ....

(2) Type of tax shelter ▶ ....

H Check here if this partnership is a publicly traded partnership as defined in section 469(k)(2) . . . . ☐

I Check applicable boxes: (1) ☐ Final K-1 (2) ☐ Amended K-1

J Analysis of partner's capital account:

(a) Capital account at beginning of year	(b) Capital contributed during year	(c) Partner's share of lines 3, 4, and 7, Form 1065, Schedule M-2	(d) Withdrawals and distributions	(e) Capital account at end of year (combine columns (a) through (d))
			( )	

		(a) Distributive share item		(b) Amount	(c) 1040 filers enter the amount in column (b) on:
Income (Loss)	1	Ordinary income (loss) from trade or business activities . . .	1		(See Partner's Instructions for Schedule K-1 (Form 1065).)
	2	Net income (loss) from rental real estate activities	2		
	3	Net income (loss) from other rental activities	3		
	4	Portfolio income (loss):			
	a	Interest	4a		Sch. B, Part I, line 1
	b	Dividends	4b		Sch. B, Part II, line 5
	c	Royalties	4c		Sch. E, Part I, line 4
	d	Net short-term capital gain (loss)	4d		Sch. D, line 5, col. (f) or (g)
	e	Net long-term capital gain (loss)	4e		Sch. D, line 13, col. (f) or (g)
	f	Other portfolio income (loss) *(attach schedule)*	4f		(Enter on applicable line of your return.)
	5	Guaranteed payments to partner	5		(See Partner's Instructions for Schedule K-1 (Form 1065).)
	6	Net gain (loss) under section 1231 (other than due to casualty or theft)	6		
	7	Other income (loss) *(attach schedule)*	7		(Enter on applicable line of your return.)
Deductions	8	Charitable contributions (see instructions) *(attach schedule)* . .	8		Sch. A, line 13 or 14
	9	Section 179 expense deduction	9		(See Partner's Instructions for Schedule K-1 (Form 1065).)
	10	Deductions related to portfolio income *(attach schedule)* . . .	10		
	11	Other deductions *(attach schedule)*	11		
Investment Interest	12a	Interest expense on investment debts	12a		Form 4952, line 1
	b	(1) Investment income included on lines 4a through 4f above .	b(1)		(See Partner's Instructions for Schedule K-1 (Form 1065).)
		(2) Investment expenses included on line 10 above	b(2)		
Credits	13a	Credit for income tax withheld	13a		(See Partner's Instructions for Schedule K-1 (Form 1065).)
	b	Low-income housing credit:			
		(1) From section 42(j)(5) partnerships for property placed in service before 1990	b(1)		Form 8586, line 5
		(2) Other than on line 13b(1) for property placed in service before 1990	b(2)		
		(3) From section 42(j)(5) partnerships for property placed in service after 1989	b(3)		
		(4) Other than on line 13b(3) for property placed in service after 1989	b(4)		
	c	Qualified rehabilitation expenditures related to rental real estate activities (see instructions)	13c		(See Partner's Instructions for Schedule K-1 (Form 1065).)
	d	Credits (other than credits shown on lines 13b and 13c) related to rental real estate activities (see instructions)	13d		
	e	Credits related to other rental activities (see instructions) . . .	13e		
	14	Other credits (see instructions)	14		

For Paperwork Reduction Act Notice, see Instructions for Form 1065. Cat. No. 11394R **Schedule K-1 (Form 1065) 1992**

Schedule K-1 (Form 1065) 1992 Page 2

	(a) Distributive share item		(b) Amount	(c) 1040 filers enter the amount in column (b) on:
Self-employment	15a Net earnings (loss) from self-employment	15a		Sch. SE, Section A or B
	b Gross farming or fishing income	15b		(See Partner's Instructions for Schedule K-1 (Form 1065).)
	c Gross nonfarm income	15c		
Adjustments and Tax Preference Items	16a Depreciation adjustment on property placed in service after 1986	16a		(See Partner's Instructions for Schedule K-1 (Form 1065) and Instructions for Form 6251.)
	b Adjusted gain or loss	16b		
	c Depletion (other than oil and gas)	16c		
	d (1) Gross income from oil, gas, and geothermal properties	d(1)		
	(2) Deductions allocable to oil, gas, and geothermal properties	d(2)		
	e Other adjustments and tax preference items *(attach schedule)*	16e		
Foreign Taxes	17a Type of income ▶			Form 1116, Check boxes
	b Name of foreign country or U.S. possession ▶			Form 1116, Part I
	c Total gross income from sources outside the United States *(attach schedule)*	17c		
	d Total applicable deductions and losses *(attach schedule)*	17d		
	e Total foreign taxes (check one): ▶ ☐ Paid ☐ Accrued	17e		Form 1116, Part II
	f Reduction in taxes available for credit *(attach schedule)*	17f		Form 1116, Part III
	g Other foreign tax information *(attach schedule)*	17g		See Instructions for Form 1116.
Other	18a Total expenditures to which a section 59(e) election may apply	18a		See Partner's Instructions for Schedule K-1 (Form 1065).
	b Type of expenditures ▶			
	19 Tax-exempt interest income	19		Form 1040, line 8b
	20 Other tax-exempt income	20		(See Partner's Instructions for Schedule K-1 (Form 1065).)
	21 Nondeductible expenses	21		
	22 Recapture of low-income housing credit:			
	a From section 42(j)(5) partnerships	22a		Form 8611, line 8
	b Other than on line 22a	22b		

Supplemental Information

23 Supplemental information required to be reported separately to each partner *(attach additional schedules if more space is needed):*

Form **1120-A**
Department of the Treasury
Internal Revenue Service

U.S. Corporation Short-Form Income Tax Return

See separate instructions to make sure the corporation qualifies to file Form 1120-A.
For calendar year 1992 or tax year beginning ...., 1992, ending............, 19....

OMB No. 1545-0890
1992

A Check this box if corp. is a personal service corp. (as defined in Temporary Regs. section 1.441-4T—see instructions) ▶ ☐

Use IRS label. Other-wise, please print or type.
Name
Number, street, and room or suite no. (If a P.O. box, see page 6 of instructions.)
City or town, state, and ZIP code

B Employer identification number
C Date incorporated
D Total assets (see Specific Instructions)
$

E Check applicable boxes: (1) ☐ Initial return (2) ☐ Change in address
F Check method of accounting: (1) ☐ Cash (2) ☐ Accrual (3) ☐ Other (specify) . . ▶

Income

1a	Gross receipts or sales ______ **b** Less returns and allowances ______ **c** Balance ▶	**1c**	
2	Cost of goods sold (see instructions)	**2**	
3	Gross profit. Subtract line 2 from line 1c	**3**	
4	Domestic corporation dividends subject to the 70% deduction	**4**	
5	Interest	**5**	
6	Gross rents	**6**	
7	Gross royalties	**7**	
8	Capital gain net income (attach Schedule D (Form 1120))	**8**	
9	Net gain or (loss) from Form 4797, Part II, line 20 (attach Form 4797)	**9**	
10	Other income (see instructions)	**10**	
11	**Total income.** Add lines 3 through 10 ▶	**11**	

Deductions (See instructions for limitations on deductions.)

12	Compensation of officers (see instructions)	**12**	
13a	Salaries and wages ______ **b** Less jobs credit ______ **c** Balance ▶	**13c**	
14	Repairs	**14**	
15	Bad debts	**15**	
16	Rents	**16**	
17	Taxes	**17**	
18	Interest	**18**	
19	Charitable contributions **(see instructions for 10% limitation)**	**19**	
20	Depreciation (attach Form 4562) . . . **20**		
21	Less depreciation claimed elsewhere on return . . . **21a**	**21b**	
22	Other deductions (attach schedule)	**22**	
23	**Total deductions.** Add lines 12 through 22 ▶	**23**	
24	Taxable income before net operating loss deduction and special deductions. Subtract line 23 from line 11	**24**	
25	**Less: a** Net operating loss deduction (see instructions) . . . **25a**		
	b Special deductions (see instructions) . . . **25b**	**25c**	

Tax and Payments

26	**Taxable income.** Subtract line 25c from line 24	**26**	
27	**Total tax** (from page 2, Part I, line 7)	**27**	
28	**Payments:**		
a	1991 overpayment credited to 1992 **28a**		
b	1992 estimated tax payments **28b**		
c	Less 1992 refund applied for on Form 4466 **28c** ( ) **Bal ▶ 28d**		
e	Tax deposited with Form 7004 . . . **28e**		
f	Credit from regulated investment companies (attach Form 2439) . . **28f**		
g	Credit for Federal tax on fuels (attach Form 4136). See instructions . **28g**		
h	**Total payments.** Add lines 28d through 28g	**28h**	
29	Estimated tax penalty (see instructions). Check if Form 2220 is attached ▶ ☐	**29**	
30	**Tax due.** If line 28h is smaller than the total of lines 27 and 29, enter amount owed	**30**	
31	**Overpayment.** If line 28h is larger than the total of lines 27 and 29, enter amount overpaid	**31**	
32	Enter amount of line 31 you want: **Credited to 1993 estimated tax ▶** ______ **Refunded ▶**	**32**	

Please Sign Here

Under penalties of perjury, I declare that I have examined this return, including accompanying schedules and statements, and to the best of my knowledge and belief, it is true, correct, and complete. Declaration of preparer (other than taxpayer) is based on all information of which preparer has any knowledge.

▶ Signature of officer | Date | ▶ Title

Paid Preparer's Use Only

Preparer's signature ▶ | Date | Check if self-employed ▶ ☐ | Preparer's social security number

Firm's name (or yours if self-employed) and address ▶ | E.I. No. ▶ | ZIP code ▶

For Paperwork Reduction Act Notice, see page 1 of the instructions. Cat. No. 11456E Form **1120-A** (1992)

Form 1120-A (1992) Page **2**

Part I Tax Computation (See instructions.)

1	Income tax. Check this box if the corporation is a qualified personal service corporation as defined in section 448(d)(2) (see instructions on page 14) ▶ ☐		1	
2a	General business credit. Check if from: ☐ Form 3800 ☐ Form 3468 ☐ Form 5884 ☐ Form 6478 ☐ Form 6765 ☐ Form 8586 ☐ Form 8830 ☐ Form 8826	2a		
b	Credit for prior year minimum tax (attach Form 8827)	2b		
3	**Total credits.** Add lines 2a and 2b		3	
4	Subtract line 3 from line 1		4	
5	Recapture taxes. Check if from: ☐ Form 4255 ☐ Form 8611		5	
6	Alternative minimum tax (attach Form 4626)		6	
7	**Total tax.** Add lines 4 through 6. Enter here and on line 27, page 1		7	

Part II Other Information (See instructions.)

1 Refer to the list in the instructions and state the principal:
- a Business activity code no. ▶
- b Business activity ▶
- c Product or service ▶

2 Did any individual, partnership, estate, or trust at the end of the tax year own, directly or indirectly, 50% or more of the corporation's voting stock? (For rules of attribution, see section 267(c).) ☐ Yes ☐ No

If "Yes," attach a schedule showing name and identifying number.

3 Enter the amount of tax-exempt interest received or accrued during the tax year ▶ $

4 Enter amount of cash distributions and the book value of property (other than cash) distributions made in this tax year ▶ $

5a If an amount is entered on line 2, page 1, see the worksheet on page 12 for amounts to enter below:
- (1) Purchases
- (2) Additional sec. 263A costs (see instructions—attach schedule)
- (3) Other costs (attach schedule)

b Do the rules of section 263A (for property produced or acquired for resale) apply to the corporation? ☐ Yes ☐ No

6 At any time during the 1992 calendar year, did the corporation have an interest in or a signature or other authority over a financial account in a foreign country (such as a bank account, securities account, or other financial account)? If "Yes," the corporation may have to file Form TD F 90-22.1 ☐ Yes ☐ No

If "Yes," enter the name of the foreign country ▶

Part III Balance Sheets

			(a) Beginning of tax year	(b) End of tax year
Assets	1	Cash		
	2a	Trade notes and accounts receivable		
	b	Less allowance for bad debts	( )	( )
	3	Inventories		
	4	U.S. government obligations		
	5	Tax-exempt securities (see instructions)		
	6	Other current assets (attach schedule)		
	7	Loans to stockholders		
	8	Mortgage and real estate loans		
	9a	Depreciable, depletable, and intangible assets		
	b	Less accumulated depreciation, depletion, and amortization	( )	( )
	10	Land (net of any amortization)		
	11	Other assets (attach schedule)		
	12	Total assets		
Liabilities and Stockholders' Equity	13	Accounts payable		
	14	Other current liabilities (attach schedule)		
	15	Loans from stockholders		
	16	Mortgages, notes, bonds payable		
	17	Other liabilities (attach schedule)		
	18	Capital stock (preferred and common stock)		
	19	Paid-in or capital surplus		
	20	Retained earnings		
	21	Less cost of treasury stock	( )	( )
	22	Total liabilities and stockholders' equity		

Part IV Reconciliation of Income (Loss) per Books With Income per Return *(You are not required to complete Part IV if the total assets on line 12, column (b) of Part III are less than $25,000.)*

1 Net income (loss) per books		6 Income recorded on books this year not included on this return (itemize)	
2 Federal income tax		7 Deductions on this return not charged against book income this year (itemize)	
3 Excess of capital losses over capital gains			
4 Income subject to tax not recorded on books this year (itemize)			
5 Expenses recorded on books this year not deducted on this return (itemize)		8 Income (line 24, page 1). Enter the sum of lines 1 through 5 less the sum of lines 6 and 7	

Form **1120**
Department of the Treasury
Internal Revenue Service

U.S. Corporation Income Tax Return

For calendar year 1992 or tax year beginning ...., 1992, ending ...., 19 ...
▶ **Instructions are separate. See page 1 for Paperwork Reduction Act Notice.**

OMB No. 1545-0123
1992

A Check if a:
(1) Consolidated return (attach Form 851) ☐
(2) Personal holding co. (attach Sch. PH) ☐
(3) Personal service corp. (as defined in Temporary Regs. sec. 1.441-4T—see instructions) ☐

Use IRS label. Other-wise, please print or type.
Name
Number, street, and room or suite no. (If a P.O. box, see page 6 of instructions.)
City or town, state, and ZIP code

B Employer identification number
C Date incorporated
D Total assets (see Specific Instructions)
$

E Check applicable boxes: (1) ☐ Initial return (2) ☐ Final return (3) ☐ Change in address

Income

1a	Gross receipts or sales ____ b Less returns and allowances ____ c Bal ▶	1c	
2	Cost of goods sold (Schedule A, line 8)	2	
3	Gross profit. Subtract line 2 from line 1c	3	
4	Dividends (Schedule C, line 19)	4	
5	Interest	5	
6	Gross rents	6	
7	Gross royalties	7	
8	Capital gain net income (attach Schedule D (Form 1120))	8	
9	Net gain or (loss) from Form 4797, Part II, line 20 (attach Form 4797)	9	
10	Other income (see instructions—attach schedule)	10	
11	**Total income.** Add lines 3 through 10 ▶	11	

Deductions (See instructions for limitations on deductions.)

12	Compensation of officers (Schedule E, line 4)	12	
13a	Salaries and wages ____ b Less jobs credit ____ c Balance ▶	13c	
14	Repairs	14	
15	Bad debts	15	
16	Rents	16	
17	Taxes	17	
18	Interest	18	
19	Charitable contributions **(see instructions for 10% limitation)**	19	
20	Depreciation (attach Form 4562) — 20		
21	Less depreciation claimed on Schedule A and elsewhere on return — 21a	21b	
22	Depletion	22	
23	Advertising	23	
24	Pension, profit-sharing, etc., plans	24	
25	Employee benefit programs	25	
26	Other deductions (attach schedule)	26	
27	**Total deductions.** Add lines 12 through 26 ▶	27	
28	Taxable income before net operating loss deduction and special deductions. Subtract line 27 from line 11	28	
29	**Less:** a Net operating loss deduction (see instructions) — 29a b Special deductions (Schedule C, line 20) — 29b	29c	

Tax and Payments

30	**Taxable income.** Subtract line 29c from line 28	30	
31	**Total tax** (Schedule J, line 10)	31	
32	**Payments:** a 1991 overpayment credited to 1992 — 32a		
b	1992 estimated tax payments — 32b		
c	Less 1992 refund applied for on Form 4466 — 32c ( ) d Bal ▶ 32d		
e	Tax deposited with Form 7004 — 32e		
f	Credit from regulated investment companies (attach Form 2439) — 32f		
g	Credit for Federal tax on fuels (attach Form 4136). See instructions — 32g	32h	
33	Estimated tax penalty (see instructions). Check if Form 2220 is attached ▶ ☐	33	
34	**Tax due.** If line 32h is smaller than the total of lines 31 and 33, enter amount owed	34	
35	**Overpayment.** If line 32h is larger than the total of lines 31 and 33, enter amount overpaid	35	
36	Enter amount of line 35 you want: **Credited to 1993 estimated tax** ▶ **Refunded** ▶	36	

Please Sign Here

Under penalties of perjury, I declare that I have examined this return, including accompanying schedules and statements, and to the best of my knowledge and belief, it is true, correct, and complete. Declaration of preparer (other than taxpayer) is based on all information of which preparer has any knowledge.

▶ Signature of officer | Date | ▶ Title

Paid Preparer's Use Only

Preparer's signature ▶ | Date | Check if self-employed ☐ | Preparer's social security number

Firm's name (or yours if self-employed) and address ▶ | E.I. No. ▶ | ZIP code ▶

Cat. No. 11450Q

Form 1120 (1992) Page 2

Schedule A Cost of Goods Sold (See instructions.)

1	Inventory at beginning of year	1	
2	Purchases	2	
3	Cost of labor	3	
4	Additional section 263A costs (attach schedule)	4	
5	Other costs (attach schedule)	5	
6	**Total.** Add lines 1 through 5	6	
7	Inventory at end of year	7	
8	**Cost of goods sold.** Subtract line 7 from line 6. Enter here and on page 1, line 2	8	

9a Check all methods used for valuing closing inventory:

(i) ☐ Cost (ii) ☐ Lower of cost or market as described in Regulations section 1.471-4

(iii) ☐ Writedown of "subnormal" goods as described in Regulations section 1.471-2(c)

(iv) ☐ Other (Specify method used and attach explanation.) ▶

b Check if the LIFO inventory method was adopted this tax year for any goods (if checked, attach Form 970) ▶ ☐

c If the LIFO inventory method was used for this tax year, enter percentage (or amounts) of closing inventory computed under LIFO 9c

d Do the rules of section 263A (for property produced or acquired for resale) apply to the corporation? ☐ Yes ☐ No

e Was there any change in determining quantities, cost, or valuations between opening and closing inventory? If "Yes," attach explanation ☐ Yes ☐ No

Schedule C Dividends and Special Deductions (See instructions.)

		(a) Dividends received	(b) %	(c) Special deductions: (a) × (b)
1	Dividends from less-than-20%-owned domestic corporations that are subject to the 70% deduction (other than debt-financed stock)		70	
2	Dividends from 20%-or-more-owned domestic corporations that are subject to the 80% deduction (other than debt-financed stock)		80	
3	Dividends on debt-financed stock of domestic and foreign corporations (section 246A)		see instructions	
4	Dividends on certain preferred stock of less-than-20%-owned public utilities		41.176	
5	Dividends on certain preferred stock of 20%-or-more-owned public utilities		47.059	
6	Dividends from less-than-20%-owned foreign corporations and certain FSCs that are subject to the 70% deduction		70	
7	Dividends from 20%-or-more-owned foreign corporations and certain FSCs that are subject to the 80% deduction		80	
8	Dividends from wholly owned foreign subsidiaries subject to the 100% deduction (section 245(b))		100	
9	**Total.** Add lines 1 through 8. See instructions for limitation			
10	Dividends from domestic corporations received by a small business investment company operating under the Small Business Investment Act of 1958		100	
11	Dividends from certain FSCs that are subject to the 100% deduction (section 245(c)(1))		100	
12	Dividends from affiliated group members subject to the 100% deduction (section 243(a)(3))		100	
13	Other dividends from foreign corporations not included on lines 3, 6, 7, 8, or 11			
14	Income from controlled foreign corporations under subpart F (attach Form(s) 5471)			
15	Foreign dividend gross-up (section 78)			
16	IC-DISC and former DISC dividends not included on lines 1, 2, or 3 (section 246(d))			
17	Other dividends			
18	Deduction for dividends paid on certain preferred stock of public utilities (see instructions)			
19	**Total dividends.** Add lines 1 through 17. Enter here and on line 4, page 1 ▶			
20	**Total deductions.** Add lines 9, 10, 11, 12, and 18. Enter here and on line 29b, page 1 ▶			

Schedule E Compensation of Officers (See instructions for line 12, page 1.)

Complete Schedule E only if total receipts (line 1a plus lines 4 through 10 on page 1, Form 1120) are $500,000 or more.

	(a) Name of officer	(b) Social security number	(c) Percent of time devoted to business	Percent of corporation stock owned: (d) Common	(e) Preferred	(f) Amount of compensation
1			%	%	%	
			%	%	%	
			%	%	%	
			%	%	%	
			%	%	%	

2	Total compensation of officers	
3	Compensation of officers claimed on Schedule A and elsewhere on return	
4	Subtract line 3 from line 2. Enter the result here and on line 12, page 1	

Form 1120 (1992) Page **3**

Schedule J Tax Computation (See instructions.)

1	Check if the corporation is a member of a controlled group (see sections 1561 and 1563) . . . . ▶ ☐		
2	If the box on line 1 is checked:		
a	Enter the corporation's share of the $50,000 and $25,000 taxable income bracket amounts (in that order): (i) $ (ii) $		
b	Enter the corporation's share of the additional 5% tax (not to exceed $11,750) ▶ $		
3	Income tax. Check this box if the corporation is a qualified personal service corporation as defined in section 448(d)(2) (see instructions on page 14) . . . . ▶ ☐	3	
4a	Foreign tax credit (attach Form 1118) . . .	4a	
b	Possessions tax credit (attach Form 5735) . . .	4b	
c	Orphan drug credit (attach Form 6765) . . .	4c	
d	Credit for fuel produced from a nonconventional source . . .	4d	
e	General business credit. Enter here and check which forms are attached: ☐ Form 3800 ☐ Form 3468 ☐ Form 5884 ☐ Form 6478 ☐ Form 6765 ☐ Form 8586 ☐ Form 8830 ☐ Form 8826 . . .	4e	
f	Credit for prior year minimum tax (attach Form 8827) . . .	4f	
5	**Total credits.** Add lines 4a through 4f . . .	5	
6	Subtract line 5 from line 3 . . .	6	
7	Personal holding company tax (attach Schedule PH (Form 1120)) . . .	7	
8	Recapture taxes. Check if from: ☐ Form 4255 ☐ Form 8611 . . .	8	
9a	Alternative minimum tax (attach Form 4626) . . .	9a	
b	Environmental tax (attach Form 4626) . . .	9b	
10	**Total tax.** Add lines 6 through 9b. Enter here and on line 31, page 1 . . .	10	

Schedule K Other Information (See instructions.)

		Yes	No
1	Check method of accounting: **a** ☐ Cash **b** ☐ Accrual **c** ☐ Other (specify) ▶		
2	Refer to the list in the instructions and state the principal: **a** Business activity code no. ▶ **b** Business activity ▶ **c** Product or service ▶		
3	Did the corporation at the end of the tax year own, directly or indirectly, 50% or more of the voting stock of a domestic corporation? (For rules of attribution, see section 267(c).) . . .		
	If "Yes," attach a schedule showing: (a) name and identifying number; (b) percentage owned; and (c) taxable income or (loss) before NOL and special deductions of such corporation for the tax year ending with or within your tax year.		
4	Did any individual, partnership, corporation, estate, or trust at the end of the tax year own, directly or indirectly, 50% or more of the corporation's voting stock? (For rules of attribution, see section 267(c).) If "Yes," complete a, b, and c below . . .		
a	Is the corporation a subsidiary in an affiliated group or a parent-subsidiary controlled group? . . .		
b	Enter the name and identifying number of the parent corporation or other entity with 50% or more ownership ▶		
c	Enter percentage owned ▶		
5	During this tax year, did the corporation pay dividends (other than stock dividends and distributions in exchange for stock) in excess of the corporation's current and accumulated earnings and profits? (See secs. 301 and 316.) . . .		
	If "Yes," file Form 5452. If this is a consolidated return, answer here for the parent corporation and on **Form 851,** Affiliations Schedule, for each subsidiary.		
6	Was the corporation a U.S. shareholder of any controlled foreign corporation? (See sections 951 and 957.) . . .		
	If "Yes," attach Form 5471 for each such corporation. Enter number of Forms 5471 attached ▶		
7	At any time during the 1992 calendar year, did the corporation have an interest in or a signature or other authority over a financial account in a foreign country (such as a bank account, securities account, or other financial account)? . . .		
	If "Yes," the corporation may have to file Form TD F 90-22.1. If "Yes," enter name of foreign country ▶		
8	Was the corporation the grantor of, or transferor to, a foreign trust that existed during the current tax year, whether or not the corporation has any beneficial interest in it? . . .		
	If "Yes," the corporation may have to file Forms 926, 3520, or 3520-A.		
9	Did one foreign person at any time during the tax year own, directly or indirectly, at least 25% of: **(a)** the total voting power of all classes of stock of the corporation entitled to vote, or **(b)** the total value of all classes of stock of the corporation? . . .		
	If "Yes," see page 17 of instructions and **a** Enter percentage owned ▶ **b** Enter owner's country ▶ **c** The corporation may have to file Form 5472. (See page 18 for penalties that may apply.) Enter number of Forms 5472 attached ▶		
10	Check this box if the corporation issued publicly offered debt instruments with original issue discount . ▶ ☐ If so, the corporation may have to file Form 8281.		
11	Enter the amount of tax-exempt interest received or accrued during the tax year ▶ $		
12	If there were 35 or fewer shareholders at the end of the tax year, enter the number ▶		
13	If the corporation has an NOL for the tax year and is electing under sec. 172(b)(3) to forego the carryback period, check here . . . ▶ ☐		

Form 1120 (1992) Page 4

Schedule L **Balance Sheets**

Assets	Beginning of tax year (a)	(b)	End of tax year (c)	(d)
1 Cash				
2a Trade notes and accounts receivable				
b Less allowance for bad debts	( )		( )	
3 Inventories				
4 U.S. government obligations				
5 Tax-exempt securities (see instructions)				
6 Other current assets (attach schedule)				
7 Loans to stockholders				
8 Mortgage and real estate loans				
9 Other investments (attach schedule)				
10a Buildings and other depreciable assets				
b Less accumulated depreciation	( )		( )	
11a Depletable assets				
b Less accumulated depletion	( )		( )	
12 Land (net of any amortization)				
13a Intangible assets (amortizable only)				
b Less accumulated amortization	( )		( )	
14 Other assets (attach schedule)				
15 Total assets				
Liabilities and Stockholders' Equity				
16 Accounts payable				
17 Mortgages, notes, bonds payable in less than 1 year				
18 Other current liabilities (attach schedule)				
19 Loans from stockholders				
20 Mortgages, notes, bonds payable in 1 year or more				
21 Other liabilities (attach schedule)				
22 Capital stock: a Preferred stock				
b Common stock				
23 Paid-in or capital surplus				
24 Retained earnings—Appropriated (attach schedule)				
25 Retained earnings—Unappropriated				
26 Less cost of treasury stock		( )		( )
27 Total liabilities and stockholders' equity				

Note: *You are not required to complete Schedules M-1 and M-2 below if the total assets on line 15, column (d) of Schedule L are less than $25,000.*

Schedule M-1 **Reconciliation of Income (Loss) per Books With Income per Return** (See instructions.)

1 Net income (loss) per books		7 Income recorded on books this year not included on this return (itemize):	
2 Federal income tax		Tax-exempt interest $	
3 Excess of capital losses over capital gains			
4 Income subject to tax not recorded on books this year (itemize):		8 Deductions on this return not charged against book income this year (itemize):	
5 Expenses recorded on books this year not deducted on this return (itemize):		a Depreciation . . . . $	
a Depreciation . . . . $		b Contributions carryover $	
b Contributions carryover $			
c Travel and entertainment $			
		9 Add lines 7 and 8	
6 Add lines 1 through 5		10 Income (line 28, page 1)—line 6 less line 9	

Schedule M-2 **Analysis of Unappropriated Retained Earnings per Books (Line 25, Schedule L)**

1 Balance at beginning of year		5 Distributions: a Cash	
2 Net income (loss) per books		b Stock	
3 Other increases (itemize):		c Property	
		6 Other decreases (itemize):	
		7 Add lines 5 and 6	
4 Add lines 1, 2, and 3		8 Balance at end of year (line 4 less line 7)	

Form **1120S** Department of the Treasury Internal Revenue Service

U.S. Income Tax Return for an S Corporation

For calendar year 1992, or tax year beginning ...., 1992, and ending ...., 19 ....
▶ See separate instructions.

OMB No. 1545-0130

1992

A Date of election as an S corporation	Use IRS label. Otherwise, please print or type.	Name	C Employer identification number
B Business code no. (see Specific Instructions)		Number, street, and room or suite no. (If a P.O. box, see page 8 of the instructions.)	D Date incorporated
		City or town, state, and ZIP code	E Total assets (see Specific Instructions) $

F Check applicable boxes: (1) ☐ Initial return (2) ☐ Final return (3) ☐ Change in address (4) ☐ Amended return

G Check this box if this S corporation is subject to the consolidated audit procedures of sections 6241 through 6245 (see instructions before checking this box) . ▶ ☐

H Enter number of shareholders in the corporation at end of the tax year . . . . ▶

Caution: *Include **only** trade or business income and expenses on lines 1a through 21. See the instructions for more information.*

Income	1a	Gross receipts or sales ______ **b** Less returns and allowances ______ **c** Bal ▶	1c	
	2	Cost of goods sold (Schedule A, line 8)	2	
	3	Gross profit. Subtract line 2 from line 1c	3	
	4	Net gain (loss) from Form 4797, Part II, line 20 *(attach Form 4797)*	4	
	5	Other income (loss) (see instructions) *(attach schedule)*	5	
	6	**Total income (loss).** Combine lines 3 through 5 ▶	6	
Deductions (See instructions for limitations.)	7	Compensation of officers	7	
	8a	Salaries and wages ______ **b** Less jobs credit ______ **c** Bal ▶	8c	
	9	Repairs	9	
	10	Bad debts	10	
	11	Rents	11	
	12	Taxes	12	
	13	Interest	13	
	14a	Depreciation (see instructions) — 14a		
	b	Depreciation claimed on Schedule A and elsewhere on return — 14b		
	c	Subtract line 14b from line 14a	14c	
	15	Depletion **(Do not deduct oil and gas depletion.)**	15	
	16	Advertising	16	
	17	Pension, profit-sharing, etc., plans	17	
	18	Employee benefit programs	18	
	19	Other deductions (see instructions) *(attach schedule)*	19	
	20	**Total deductions.** Add lines 7 through 19 ▶	20	
	21	Ordinary income (loss) from trade or business activities. Subtract line 20 from line 6	21	
Tax and Payments	22	**Tax:**		
	a	Excess net passive income tax *(attach schedule)* — 22a		
	b	Tax from Schedule D (Form 1120S) — 22b		
	c	Add lines 22a and 22b (see instructions for additional taxes)	22c	
	23	**Payments:**		
	a	1992 estimated tax payments — 23a		
	b	Tax deposited with Form 7004 — 23b		
	c	Credit for Federal tax paid on fuels *(attach Form 4136)* — 23c		
	d	Add lines 23a through 23c	23d	
	24	Estimated tax penalty (see instructions). Check if Form 2220 is attached. ▶☐	24	
	25	**Tax due.** If the total of lines 22c and 24 is larger than line 23d, enter amount owed. See instructions for depositary method of payment ▶	25	
	26	**Overpayment.** If line 23d is larger than the total of lines 22c and 24, enter amount overpaid ▶	26	
	27	Enter amount of line 26 you want: **Credited to 1993 estimated tax** ▶ ______ **Refunded** ▶	27	

Please Sign Here

Under penalties of perjury, I declare that I have examined this return, including accompanying schedules and statements, and to the best of my knowledge and belief, it is true, correct, and complete. Declaration of preparer (other than taxpayer) is based on all information of which preparer has any knowledge.

▶ Signature of officer — Date — ▶ Title

Paid Preparer's Use Only

Preparer's signature ▶	Date	Check if self-employed ▶ ☐	Preparer's social security number
Firm's name (or yours if self-employed) and address ▶		E.I. No. ▶	
		ZIP code ▶	

Form 1120S (1992) Page **2**

Schedule A **Cost of Goods Sold** (See instructions.)

1	Inventory at beginning of year	1	
2	Purchases	2	
3	Cost of labor	3	
4	Additional section 263A costs (see instructions) *(attach schedule)*	4	
5	Other costs *(attach schedule)*	5	
6	**Total.** Add lines 1 through 5	6	
7	Inventory at end of year	7	
8	**Cost of goods sold.** Subtract line 7 from line 6. Enter here and on page 1, line 2	8	

9a Check all methods used for valuing closing inventory:
- (i) ☐ Cost
- (ii) ☐ Lower of cost or market as described in Regulations section 1.471-4
- (iii) ☐ Writedown of "subnormal" goods as described in Regulations section 1.471-2(c)
- (iv) ☐ Other (specify method used and attach explanation) ▶ ....

b Check if the LIFO inventory method was adopted this tax year for any goods *(if checked, attach Form 970)* ▶ ☐

c If the LIFO inventory method was used for this tax year, enter percentage (or amounts) of closing inventory computed under LIFO . . . . **9c** |

d Do the rules of section 263A (for property produced or acquired for resale) apply to the corporation? ☐ Yes ☐ No

e Was there any change in determining quantities, cost, or valuations between opening and closing inventory? ☐ Yes ☐ No
If "Yes," attach explanation.

Schedule B **Other Information**

		Yes	No
1	Check method of accounting: **(a)** ☐ Cash **(b)** ☐ Accrual **(c)** ☐ Other (specify) ▶		
2	Refer to the list in the instructions and state the corporation's principal: **(a)** Business activity ▶ .... **(b)** Product or service ▶		
3	Did the corporation at the end of the tax year own, directly or indirectly, 50% or more of the voting stock of a domestic corporation? (For rules of attribution, see section 267(c).) If "Yes," attach a schedule showing: **(a)** name, address, and employer identification number and **(b)** percentage owned.		
4	Was the corporation a member of a controlled group subject to the provisions of section 1561?		
5	At any time during calendar year 1992, did the corporation have an interest in or a signature or other authority over a financial account in a foreign country (such as a bank account, securities account, or other financial account)? (See instructions for exceptions and filing requirements for form TD F 90-22.1.) If "Yes," enter the name of the foreign country ▶		
6	Was the corporation the grantor of, or transferor to, a foreign trust that existed during the current tax year, whether or not the corporation has any beneficial interest in it? If "Yes," the corporation may have to file Forms 3520, 3520-A, or 926		
7	Check this box if the corporation has filed or is required to file **Form 8264,** Application for Registration of a Tax Shelter ▶ ☐		
8	Check this box if the corporation issued publicly offered debt instruments with original issue discount ▶ ☐ If so, the corporation may have to file **Form 8281,** Information Return for Publicly Offered Original Issue Discount Instruments.		
9	If the corporation: **(a)** filed its election to be an S corporation after 1986, **(b)** was a C corporation before it elected to be an S corporation **or** the corporation acquired an asset with a basis determined by reference to its basis (or the basis of any other property) in the hands of a C corporation, and **(c)** has net unrealized built-in gain (defined in section 1374(d)(1)) in excess of the net recognized built-in gain from prior years, enter the net unrealized built-in gain reduced by net recognized built-in gain from prior years (see instructions) ▶ $		
10	Check this box if the corporation had subchapter C earnings and profits at the close of the tax year (see instructions) ▶ ☐		
11	Was this corporation in operation at the end of 1992?		
12	How many months in 1992 was this corporation in operation?		

Designation of Tax Matters Person (See instructions.)

Enter below the shareholder designated as the tax matters person (TMP) for the tax year of this return:

Name of designated TMP ▶

Identifying number of TMP ▶

Address of designated TMP ▶

Form 1120S (1992) Page **3**

Schedule K **Shareholders' Shares of Income, Credits, Deductions, etc.**

	(a) Pro rata share items		**(b)** Total amount
Income (Loss)	1 Ordinary income (loss) from trade or business activities (page 1, line 21)	1	
	2 Net income (loss) from rental real estate activities *(attach Form 8825)*	2	
	3a Gross income from other rental activities . . . 3a		
	b Expenses from other rental activities *(attach schedule)*. . 3b		
	c Net income (loss) from other rental activities. Subtract line 3b from line 3a	3c	
	4 Portfolio income (loss):		
	a Interest income	4a	
	b Dividend income	4b	
	c Royalty income	4c	
	d Net short-term capital gain (loss) *(attach Schedule D (Form 1120S))*	4d	
	e Net long-term capital gain (loss) *(attach Schedule D (Form 1120S))*	4e	
	f Other portfolio income (loss) *(attach schedule)*	4f	
	5 Net gain (loss) under section 1231 (other than due to casualty or theft) *(attach Form 4797)*	5	
	6 Other income (loss) *(attach schedule)*	6	
Deductions	7 Charitable contributions (see instructions) *(attach schedule)*	7	
	8 Section 179 expense deduction *(attach Form 4562)*.	8	
	9 Deductions related to portfolio income (loss) (see instructions) (itemize)	9	
	10 Other deductions *(attach schedule)*	10	
Investment Interest	11a Interest expense on investment debts	11a	
	b (1) Investment income included on lines 4a through 4f above	11b(1)	
	(2) Investment expenses included on line 9 above	11b(2)	
Credits	12a Credit for alcohol used as a fuel *(attach Form 6478)*	12a	
	b Low-income housing credit (see instructions):		
	(1) From partnerships to which section 42(j)(5) applies for property placed in service before 1990	12b(1)	
	(2) Other than on line 12b(1) for property placed in service before 1990.	12b(2)	
	(3) From partnerships to which section 42(j)(5) applies for property placed in service after 1989	12b(3)	
	(4) Other than on line 12b(3) for property placed in service after 1989	12b(4)	
	c Qualified rehabilitation expenditures related to rental real estate activities *(attach Form 3468)*	12c	
	d Credits (other than credits shown on lines 12b and 12c) related to rental real estate activities (see instructions).	12d	
	e Credits related to other rental activities (see instructions)	12e	
	13 Other credits (see instructions)	13	
Adjustments and Tax Preference Items	14a Depreciation adjustment on property placed in service after 1986	14a	
	b Adjusted gain or loss	14b	
	c Depletion (other than oil and gas)	14c	
	d (1) Gross income from oil, gas, or geothermal properties	14d(1)	
	(2) Deductions allocable to oil, gas, or geothermal properties	14d(2)	
	e Other adjustments and tax preference items *(attach schedule)*	14e	
Foreign Taxes	15a Type of income ▶		
	b Name of foreign country or U.S. possession ▶		
	c Total gross income from sources outside the United States *(attach schedule)*	15c	
	d Total applicable deductions and losses *(attach schedule)*	15d	
	e Total foreign taxes (check one): ▶ ☐ Paid ☐ Accrued	15e	
	f Reduction in taxes available for credit *(attach schedule)*	15f	
	g Other foreign tax information *(attach schedule)*	15g	
Other	16a Total expenditures to which a section 59(e) election may apply	16a	
	b Type of expenditures ▶		
	17 Tax-exempt interest income	17	
	18 Other tax-exempt income	18	
	19 Nondeductible expenses	19	
	20 Total property distributions (including cash) other than dividends reported on line 22 below	20	
	21 Other items and amounts required to be reported separately to shareholders (see instructions) *(attach schedule)*		
	22 Total dividend distributions paid from accumulated earnings and profits	22	
	23 **Income (loss).** (Required only if Schedule M-1 must be completed.) Combine lines 1 through 6 in column (b). From the result, subtract the sum of lines 7 through 11a, 15e, and 16a	23	

Form 1120S (1992) Page 4

Schedule L Balance Sheets

Assets	Beginning of tax year (a)	(b)	End of tax year (c)	(d)
1 Cash				
2a Trade notes and accounts receivable				
b Less allowance for bad debts				
3 Inventories				
4 U.S. Government obligations				
5 Tax-exempt securities				
6 Other current assets *(attach schedule)*				
7 Loans to shareholders				
8 Mortgage and real estate loans				
9 Other investments *(attach schedule)*				
10a Buildings and other depreciable assets				
b Less accumulated depreciation				
11a Depletable assets				
b Less accumulated depletion				
12 Land (net of any amortization)				
13a Intangible assets (amortizable only)				
b Less accumulated amortization				
14 Other assets *(attach schedule)*				
15 Total assets				
Liabilities and Shareholders' Equity				
16 Accounts payable				
17 Mortgages, notes, bonds payable in less than 1 year				
18 Other current liabilities *(attach schedule)*				
19 Loans from shareholders				
20 Mortgages, notes, bonds payable in 1 year or more				
21 Other liabilities *(attach schedule)*				
22 Capital stock				
23 Paid-in or capital surplus				
24 Retained earnings				
25 Less cost of treasury stock		( )		( )
26 Total liabilities and shareholders' equity				

Schedule M-1 Reconciliation of Income (Loss) per Books With Income (Loss) per Return (You are not required to complete this schedule if the total assets on line 15, column (d), of Schedule L are less than $25,000.)

1 Net income (loss) per books		5 Income recorded on books this year not included on Schedule K, lines 1 through 6 (itemize):	
2 Income included on Schedule K, lines 1 through 6, not recorded on books this year (itemize):		a Tax-exempt interest $	
3 Expenses recorded on books this year not included on Schedule K, lines 1 through 11a, 15e, and 16a (itemize):		6 Deductions included on Schedule K, lines 1 through 11a, 15e, and 16a, not charged against book income this year (itemize):	
a Depreciation $		a Depreciation $	
b Travel and entertainment $			
		7 Add lines 5 and 6	
4 Add lines 1 through 3		8 Income (loss) (Schedule K, line 23). Line 4 less line 7	

Schedule M-2 Analysis of Accumulated Adjustments Account, Other Adjustments Account, and Shareholders' Undistributed Taxable Income Previously Taxed (See instructions.)

	(a) Accumulated adjustments account	(b) Other adjustments account	(c) Shareholders' undistributed taxable income previously taxed
1 Balance at beginning of tax year			
2 Ordinary income from page 1, line 21			
3 Other additions			
4 Loss from page 1, line 21	( )		
5 Other reductions	( )	( )	
6 Combine lines 1 through 5			
7 Distributions other than dividend distributions			
8 Balance at end of tax year. Subtract line 7 from line 6			

SCHEDULE K-1 (Form 1120S)

Department of the Treasury
Internal Revenue Service

Shareholder's Share of Income, Credits, Deductions, etc.

▶ See separate instructions.

For calendar year 1992 or tax year beginning , 1992, and ending , 19

OMB No. 1545-0130

1992

Shareholder's identifying number ▶

Shareholder's name, address, and ZIP code

Corporation's identifying number ▶

Corporation's name, address, and ZIP code

A Shareholder's percentage of stock ownership for tax year (see Instructions for Schedule K-1) . . . . ▶ .... %

B Internal Revenue Service Center where corporation filed its return ▶ ....

C (1) Tax shelter registration number (see Instructions for Schedule K-1) . . . . ▶ ....

(2) Type of tax shelter ▶ ....

D Check applicable boxes: (1) ☐ Final K-1 (2) ☐ Amended K-1

		(a) Pro rata share items		(b) Amount	(c) Form 1040 filers enter the amount in column (b) on:
Income (Loss)	1	Ordinary income (loss) from trade or business activities	1		See Shareholder's Instructions for Schedule K-1 (Form 1120S).
	2	Net income (loss) from rental real estate activities	2		
	3	Net income (loss) from other rental activities	3		
	4	Portfolio income (loss):			
	a	Interest	4a		Sch. B, Part I, line 1
	b	Dividends	4b		Sch. B, Part II, line 5
	c	Royalties	4c		Sch. E, Part I, line 4
	d	Net short-term capital gain (loss)	4d		Sch. D, line 5, col. (f) or (g)
	e	Net long-term capital gain (loss)	4e		Sch. D, line 13, col. (f) or (g)
	f	Other portfolio income (loss) *(attach schedule)*	4f		(Enter on applicable line of your return.)
	5	Net gain (loss) under section 1231 (other than due to casualty or theft)	5		See Shareholder's Instructions for Schedule K-1 (Form 1120S).
	6	Other income (loss) *(attach schedule)*	6		(Enter on applicable line of your return.)
Deductions	7	Charitable contributions (see instructions) *(attach schedule)*	7		Sch. A, line 13 or 14
	8	Section 179 expense deduction	8		See Shareholder's Instructions for Schedule K-1 (Form 1120S).
	9	Deductions related to portfolio income (loss) *(attach schedule)*	9		
	10	Other deductions *(attach schedule)*	10		
Investment Interest	11a	Interest expense on investment debts	11a		Form 4952, line 1
	b	(1) Investment income included on lines 4a through 4f above	b(1)		See Shareholder's Instructions for Schedule K-1 (Form 1120S).
		(2) Investment expenses included on line 9 above	b(2)		
Credits	12a	Credit for alcohol used as fuel	12a		Form 6478, line 10
	b	Low-income housing credit:			
		(1) From section 42(j)(5) partnerships for property placed in service before 1990	b(1)		Form 8586, line 5
		(2) Other than on line 12b(1) for property placed in service before 1990	b(2)		
		(3) From section 42(j)(5) partnerships for property placed in service after 1989	b(3)		
		(4) Other than on line 12b(3) for property placed in service after 1989	b(4)		
	c	Qualified rehabilitation expenditures related to rental real estate activities (see instructions)	12c		See Shareholder's Instructions for Schedule K-1 (Form 1120S)
	d	Credits (other than credits shown on lines 12b and 12c) related to rental real estate activities (see instructions)	12d		
	e	Credits related to other rental activities (see instructions)	12e		
	13	Other credits (see instructions)	13		
Adjustments and Tax Preference Items	14a	Depreciation adjustment on property placed in service after 1986	14a		See Shareholder's Instructions for Schedule K-1 (Form 1120S) and Instructions for Form 6251
	b	Adjusted gain or loss	14b		
	c	Depletion (other than oil and gas)	14c		
	d	(1) Gross income from oil, gas, or geothermal properties	d(1)		
		(2) Deductions allocable to oil, gas, or geothermal properties	d(2)		
	e	Other adjustments and tax preference items *(attach schedule)*	14e		

For Paperwork Reduction Act Notice, see page 1 of Instructions for Form 1120S. Cat. No. 11520D **Schedule K-1 (Form 1120S) 1992**

Schedule K-1 (Form 1120S) (1992) Page 2

		(a) Pro rata share items		(b) Amount	(c) Form 1040 filers enter the amount in column (b) on:
Foreign Taxes	15a	Type of income ▶			Form 1116, Check boxes
	b	Name of foreign country or U.S. possession ▶			
	c	Total gross income from sources outside the United States *(attach schedule)*	15c		Form 1116, Part I
	d	Total applicable deductions and losses *(attach schedule)*	15d		Form 1116, Part I
	e	Total foreign taxes (check one): ▶ ☐ Paid ☐ Accrued	15e		Form 1116, Part II
	f	Reduction in taxes available for credit *(attach schedule)*	15f		Form 1116, Part III
	g	Other foreign tax information *(attach schedule)*	15g		See Instructions for Form 1116
Other	16a	Total expenditures to which a section 59(e) election may apply	16a		See Shareholder's Instructions for Schedule K-1 (Form 1120S).
	b	Type of expenditures ▶			
	17	Tax-exempt interest income	17		Form 1040, line 8b
	18	Other tax-exempt income	18		See Shareholder's Instructions for Schedule K-1 (Form 1120S).
	19	Nondeductible expenses	19		
	20	Property distributions (including cash) other than dividend distributions reported to you on Form 1099-DIV	20		
	21	Amount of loan repayments for "Loans From Shareholders"	21		
	22	Recapture of low-income housing credit:			
	a	From section 42(j)(5) partnerships	22a		Form 8611, line 8
	b	Other than on line 22a	22b		Form 8611, line 8

Supplemental Information

23 Supplemental information required to be reported separately to each shareholder *(attach additional schedules if more space is needed)*:

Form **2106**

Department of the Treasury
Internal Revenue Service (T)

Employee Business Expenses

▶ **See separate instructions.**

▶ **Attach to Form 1040.**

OMB No. 1545-0139

1992

Attachment Sequence No. **54**

Your name	**Social security number**	Occupation in which expenses were incurred

Part I **Employee Business Expenses and Reimbursements**

STEP 1 Enter Your Expenses		**Column A** Other Than Meals and Entertainment	**Column B** Meals and Entertainment
1 Vehicle expense from line 22 or line 29	1		
2 Parking fees, tolls, and local transportation, including train, bus, etc.	2		
3 Travel expense while away from home overnight, including lodging, airplane, car rental, etc. **Do not** include meals and entertainment	3		
4 Business expenses not included on lines 1 through 3. **Do not** include meals and entertainment	4		
5 Meals and entertainment expenses (see instructions)	5		
6 **Total expenses.** In Column A, add lines 1 through 4 and enter the result. In Column B, enter the amount from line 5	6		

Note: *If you were not reimbursed for any expenses in Step 1, skip line 7 and enter the amount from line 6 on line 8.*

STEP 2 Enter Amounts Your Employer Gave You for Expenses Listed in STEP 1

7 Enter amounts your employer gave you that were **not** reported to you in box 10 of Form W-2. Include any amount reported under code "L" in box 17 of your Form W-2 (see instructions) . . .	7		

STEP 3 Figure Expenses To Deduct on Schedule A (Form 1040)

8 Subtract line 7 from line 6	8		
Note: *If* ***both columns*** *of line 8 are zero,* ***stop here.*** *If Column A is less than zero, report the amount as income and enter -0- on line 10, Column A. See the instructions for how to report.*			
9 Enter 20% (.20) of line 8, Column B	9		
10 Subtract line 9 from line 8	10		

11 Add the amounts on line 10 of both columns and enter the total here. **Also, enter the total on Schedule A (Form 1040), line 19.** (Qualified performing artists and individuals with disabilities, see the instructions for special rules on where to enter the total.) . . . . ▶	11	

For Paperwork Reduction Act Notice, see instructions. Cat. No. 11700N Form **2106** (1992)

Form 2106 (1992) Page **2**

Part II **Vehicle Expenses** (See instructions to find out which sections to complete.)

Section A.—General Information

			(a) Vehicle 1	(b) Vehicle 2
12	Enter the date vehicle was placed in service	12	/ /	/ /
13	Total miles vehicle was driven during 1992	13	miles	miles
14	Business miles included on line 13	14	miles	miles
15	Percent of business use. Divide line 14 by line 13	15	%	%
16	Average daily round trip commuting distance	16	miles	miles
17	Commuting miles included on line 13	17	miles	miles
18	Other personal miles. Add lines 14 and 17 and subtract the total from line 13	18	miles	miles

19 Do you (or your spouse) have another vehicle available for personal purposes? ☐ Yes ☐ No

20 If your employer provided you with a vehicle, is personal use during off duty hours permitted? ☐ Yes ☐ No ☐ Not applicable

21a Do you have evidence to support your deduction? ☐ Yes ☐ No

21b If "Yes," is the evidence written? ☐ Yes ☐ No

Section B.—Standard Mileage Rate (Use this section only if you own the vehicle.)

22	Multiply line 14 by 28¢ (.28). Enter the result here and on line 1. (Rural mail carriers, see instructions.)	22	

Section C.—Actual Expenses

			(a) Vehicle 1		(b) Vehicle 2	
23	Gasoline, oil, repairs, vehicle insurance, etc.	23				
24a	Vehicle rentals	24a				
b	Inclusion amount (see instructions)	24b				
c	Subtract line 24b from line 24a	24c				
25	Value of employer-provided vehicle (applies only if 100% of annual lease value was included on Form W-2—see instructions)	25				
26	Add lines 23, 24c, and 25	26				
27	Multiply line 26 by the percentage on line 15	27				
28	Depreciation. Enter amount from line 38 below	28				
29	Add lines 27 and 28. Enter total here and on line 1	29				

Section D.—Depreciation of Vehicles (Use this section only if you own the vehicle.)

			(a) Vehicle 1		(b) Vehicle 2	
30	Enter cost or other basis (see instructions)	30				
31	Enter amount of section 179 deduction (see instructions)	31				
32	Multiply line 30 by line 15 (see instructions if you elected the section 179 deduction)	32				
33	Enter depreciation method and percentage (see instructions)	33				
34	Multiply line 32 by the percentage on line 33 (see instructions)	34				
35	Add lines 31 and 34	35				
36	Enter the limitation amount from the table in the line 36 instructions	36				
37	Multiply line 36 by the percentage on line 15	37				
38	Enter the **smaller** of line 35 or line 37. Also, enter this amount on line 28 above	38				

Form **2119**

Department of the Treasury
Internal Revenue Service

Sale of Your Home

▶ Attach to Form 1040 for year of sale.

▶ See separate instructions. ▶ Please print or type.

OMB No. 1545-0072

1992

Attachment Sequence No. **20**

Your first name and initial. If a joint return, also give spouse's name and initial.	Last name	Your social security number
Fill in Your Address Only If You Are Filing This Form by Itself and Not With Your Tax Return	Present address (no., street, and apt. no., rural route, or P.O. box no. if mail is not delivered to street address)	Spouse's social security number
	City, town or post office, state, and ZIP code	

Part I General Information

1 Date your former main home was sold (month, day, year) . . . ▶ **1** / /

2 Face amount of any mortgage, note (e.g., second trust), or other financial instrument on which you will get periodic payments of principal or interest from this sale (see instructions) . . . **2**

3 Have you bought or built a new main home? . . . ☐ Yes ☐ No

4 Is or was any part of either main home rented out or used for business? If "Yes," see instructions . . . ☐ Yes ☐ No

Part II Gain on Sale (Do not include amounts you deduct as moving expenses.)

5 Selling price of home. Do not include personal property items that you sold with your home . **5**

6 Expense of sale. Include sales commissions, advertising, legal, etc. . . . **6**

7 Amount realized. Subtract line 6 from line 5 . . . **7**

8 Basis of home sold (see instructions) . . . **8**

9 **Gain on sale.** Subtract line 8 from line 7 . . . **9**

- If line 9 is zero or less, **stop here** and attach this form to your return.
- If line 3 is "Yes," you **must** go to Part III or Part IV, whichever applies. Otherwise, go to line 10.

10 If you haven't replaced your home, do you plan to do so within the replacement period (see instructions)? ☐ Yes ☐ No

- If line 10 is "Yes," stop here, attach this form to your return, and see **Additional Filing Requirements** in the instructions.
- If line 10 is "No," you **must** go to Part III or Part IV, whichever applies.

Part III One-Time Exclusion of Gain for People Age 55 or Older (If you are not taking the exclusion, go to Part IV now.)

11 Who was age 55 or older on date of sale? . . . ☐ You ☐ Your spouse ☐ Both of you

12 Did the person who was age 55 or older own and use the property as his or her main home for a total of at least 3 years (except for short absences) of the 5-year period before the sale? If "No," go to Part IV now . . ☐ Yes ☐ No

13 **If line 12 is "Yes," do you elect to take the one-time exclusion?** If "No," go to Part IV now . . . ☐ Yes ☐ No

14 At time of sale, who owned the home? . . . ☐ You ☐ Your spouse ☐ Both of you

15 Social security number of spouse at time of sale if you had a different spouse from the one above at time of sale. If you were not married at time of sale, enter "None" . . . ▶ **15**

16 **Exclusion.** Enter the **smaller** of line 9 or $125,000 ($62,500, if married filing separate return). Then, go to line 17 . . . **16**

Part IV Adjusted Sales Price, Taxable Gain, and Adjusted Basis of New Home

17 Subtract line 16 from line 9 . . . **17**

- If line 17 is zero, stop here and attach this form to your return.
- If line 3 is "Yes," go to line 18 now.
- If you are reporting this sale on the installment method, stop here and see the line 2 instructions.
- All others, stop here and **enter the amount from line 17 on Schedule D, line 2 or line 10.**

18 Fixing-up expenses (see instructions for time limits) . . . **18**

19 Add lines 16 and 18 . . . **19**

20 **Adjusted sales price.** Subtract line 19 from line 7 . . . **20**

21a Date you moved into new home (month, day, year) ▶ / / **b** Cost of new home **21b**

22 Subtract line 21b from line 20. If the result is zero or less, enter -0- . . . **22**

23 **Taxable gain.** Enter the **smaller** of line 17 or line 22 . . . **23**

- If line 23 is zero, go to line 24 and attach this form to your return.
- If you are reporting this sale on the installment method, see the line 2 instructions and go to line 24.
- All others, **enter the amount from line 23 on Schedule D, line 2 or line 10,** and go to line 24.

24 Postponed gain. Subtract line 23 from line 17 . . . **24**

25 **Adjusted basis of new home.** Subtract line 24 from line 21b . . . **25**

Sign Here Only If You Are Filing This Form by Itself and Not With Your Tax Return

Under penalties of perjury, I declare that I have examined this form, including attachments, and to the best of my knowledge and belief, it is true, correct, and complete.

Your signature ▶ Date Spouse's signature ▶ Date

If a joint return, both must sign.

For Paperwork Reduction Act Notice, see separate instructions. Cat. No. 11710J Form **2119** (1992)

Instructions for Form 2119

Sale of Your Home

Paperwork Reduction Act Notice. We ask for the information on this form to carry out the Internal Revenue laws of the United States. You are required to give us the information. We need it to ensure that you are complying with these laws and to allow us to figure and collect the right amount of tax.

The time needed to complete and file this form will vary depending on individual circumstances. The estimated average time is: **Recordkeeping,** 46 min.; **Learning about the law or the form,** 13 min.; **Preparing the form,** 44 min.; and **Copying, assembling, and sending the form to the IRS,** 20 min.

If you have comments concerning the accuracy of these time estimates or suggestions for making this form more simple, we would be happy to hear from you. You can write to both the **Internal Revenue Service,** Washington, DC 20224, Attention: IRS Reports Clearance Officer, T:FP; and the **Office of Management and Budget,** Paperwork Reduction Project (1545-0072), Washington, DC 20503. **DO NOT** send this form to either of these offices. Instead, see **When and Where To File** on this page.

General Instructions

Purpose of Form

Use Form 2119 to report the sale of your main home. If you replaced your main home, use Form 2119 to postpone all or part of the gain. Form 2119 is also used by people who were age 55 or older on the date of sale to elect a one-time exclusion of the gain on the sale.

Caution: *If the home you sold was financed (in whole or in part) from a qualified mortgage credit certificate or the proceeds of a tax-exempt qualified mortgage bond, you may owe additional tax. Get* **Form 8828,** *Recapture of Federal Mortgage Subsidy, for details.*

Main Home. Your main home is the one you live in most of the time. It can be a house, houseboat, housetrailer, cooperative apartment, condominium, etc.

Date of Sale. See the instructions for line 1 on page 2.

More Than One Owner. If you owned the old home jointly with a person other than your spouse, you may postpone gain or elect the one-time exclusion only on your ownership interest in the home. For more details, see Pub. 523.

Additional Information

You may want to get **Pub. 523,** Selling Your Home, for more details.

Who Must File

You must file Form 1040 with Form 2119 for the year in which you sell your main home, even if the sale resulted in a loss, you are electing the one-time exclusion for people age 55 or older, or you are postponing all or part of the gain. There may be additional filing requirements as well. See **When and Where To File** on this page.

If part of your old home was rented out or used for business and in the year of sale you were entitled to deduct expenses related to the rental or business use, report that part of the sale on **Form 4797,** Sales of Business Property. See the instructions for line 4.

If you choose to report the gain from the sale of your home on the installment method, complete Form 2119 and **Form 6252,** Installment Sale Income.

If your home was damaged by fire, storm, or other casualty, see **Form 4684,** Casualties and Thefts, and its separate instructions, and **Pub. 547,** Nonbusiness Disasters, Casualties, and Thefts.

If your home was sold in connection with a divorce or separation, see Pub. 523. Also, get **Pub. 504,** Divorced or Separated Individuals.

If your home was condemned for public use, you can choose to postpone gain under the rules for a condemnation or you can choose to treat the transaction as a sale of your home. For details, see Pub. 523.

Which Parts To Complete

Parts I and II. You must complete Parts I and II.

Part III. Complete this part only if you qualify for the **One-Time Exclusion for People Age 55 or Older** (explained later), and you want to make the election for this sale.

Part IV. Complete line 17 even if you did not take the exclusion in Part III. Complete lines 18 through 25 only if line 17 is more than zero and you answered "Yes" on line 3.

When and Where To File

File Form 2119 with your tax return for the year of sale.

Additional Filing Requirements. If you have not replaced your home but plan to do so within the replacement period (defined on page 2), you will also have to complete a second Form 2119.

- You must file the second Form 2119 by itself if **all three** of the following apply:

1. You planned to replace your home within the replacement period.

2. You later replaced your home within the replacement period.

3. Your taxable gain (line 23 on the second Form 2119) is zero.

If your taxable gain is zero, no tax is due but you must still file the second form to show that you replaced your home within the replacement period. Enter your name and address, and sign and date the second form. If a joint return was filed for the year of sale, both you and your spouse must sign the second Form 2119. Send the form to the place where you would file your next tax return based on the address where you now live.

- You must file **Form 1040X,** Amended U.S. Individual Income Tax Return, for the year of sale with the second Form 2119 attached if **any** of the following applies:

1. You planned to replace your home when you filed your tax return, you later replaced your home within the replacement period, **and** you had a taxable gain on line 23 of the second Form 2119.

2. You planned to replace your home when you filed your tax return but **did not** do so within the replacement period.

3. You **did not** plan to replace your home when you filed your tax return and included the gain in income, but later you did replace your home within the replacement period.

Report the correct amount of gain from Form 2119 on Schedule D (Form 1040) and attach both forms to Form 1040X. Interest will be charged on any additional tax due. If you are due a refund, interest will be included with the refund.

One-Time Exclusion for People Age 55 or Older

Generally, you can elect to exclude from your income up to $125,000 ($62,500 if married filing a separate return) of the gain from one sale of any main home you choose. But for sales after July 26, 1978, the exclusion is available only once. To make the election for this sale, complete Part III and answer "Yes" on line 13. You can make the election if **all three** of the following apply:

1. You or your spouse were age 55 or older on the date of sale.

2. Neither you nor your spouse have ever excluded gain on the sale of a home after July 26, 1978.

3. The person who was age 55 or older owned and lived in the home for periods adding up to at least 3 years within the 5-year period ending on the date of sale.

For purposes of **3** above, if you were physically or mentally unable to care for yourself, count as time living in your main home any time during the 5-year period that you lived in a facility such as a nursing home. The facility must be licensed by a state (or political subdivision) to care for people in your condition. For this rule to apply, you must have owned and used your residence as your main home for a total of at least 1 year during the 5-year period. See Pub. 523 for more details.

The gain excluded is never taxed. But if the gain is more than the amount excluded, also complete Part IV to figure whether the excess gain is included in your income or postponed. If the gain is less than $125,000 ($62,500 if married filing a separate return), the difference **cannot** be excluded on a future sale of another main home. Generally, you can make or revoke the election within 3 years from the due date of your return (including extensions) for the year of sale. To make or revoke the election, file Form 1040X with Form 2119 attached. For more details, see Pub. 523.

Married Taxpayers. If you and your spouse owned the property jointly and file a joint return, only one of you must meet the age, ownership, and use tests to be able to make the election. If you did not own the property jointly, the spouse who owned the property must meet these tests.

If you were married at the time of sale, both you and your spouse must agree to exclude the gain. If you do not file a joint return with that spouse, your spouse must agree to exclude the gain by signing a statement saying, "I agree to the Part III election." The statement and signature may be made on a separate sheet or in the bottom margin of Form 2119.

If you sell a home while you are married and one spouse already made the election prior to the marriage, neither of you can exclude gain on the sale.

The election to exclude gain does not apply separately to you and your spouse. If you elect to exclude gain during marriage and later divorce, neither of you can make the election again.

Postponing Gain

If you buy or build another main home and move into it within the replacement period (defined below), you must postpone all or part of the gain in most cases. The amount of gain postponed is shown on line 24.

If one spouse dies after the old home is sold and before the new home is bought, the gain from the sale of the old home is postponed if the above requirements are met, the spouses were married on the date of death, and the surviving spouse uses the new home as his or her main home. This rule applies regardless of whether the title of the old home is in one spouse's name or is held jointly. For more details, see Pub. 523.

If you bought more than one main home during the replacement period, only the last one you bought qualifies as your new main home for postponing gain. If you sold more than one main home during the replacement period, any sale after the first one does not qualify for postponing gain. But these rules do not apply if you sold your home because of a job change that qualifies for a moving expense deduction. If this is the case, file a Form 2119 for each sale, for the year of the sale, and attach an explanation for each sale (except the first) to Form 2119. For more details on moving expenses, get **Pub. 521,** Moving Expenses.

Replacement Period. Generally, the replacement period starts 2 years before and ends 2 years after the date you sell your old main home. The replacement period may be longer if you are on active duty in the U.S. Armed Forces for more than 90 days or if you live and work outside the United States. For more details, see Pub. 523.

Applying Separate Gain to Basis of New Home. If you are married and the old home was owned by only one spouse but you and your spouse own the new home jointly, you and your spouse may elect to divide the gain and the adjusted basis. If you owned the old home jointly but you now own new homes separately, you may elect to divide the gain to be postponed. In either situation, you both must:

1. Use the old and new homes as your main homes, and

2. Sign a statement that says, "We agree to reduce the basis of the new home(s) by the gain from selling the old home." This statement can be made in the bottom margin of Form 2119 or on an attached sheet.

If you both do not meet these two requirements, you must report the gain in the regular way without allocation.

Line Instructions

You may not take double benefits. For example, you cannot use the moving expenses that are part of your moving expense deduction on **Form 3903,** Moving Expenses, to lower the amount of gain on the sale of your old home or to add to the cost of your new home.

Line 1. Enter the date of sale. If you received a **Form 1099-S,** Proceeds From Real Estate Transactions, the date should be shown in box 1. If you didn't receive a Form 1099-S, the date of sale is the earlier of **(a)** the date title transferred or **(b)** the date the economic burdens and benefits of ownership shifted to the buyer.

Line 2. If you report the gain from the sale of your home on Form 6252, using the installment method, first complete the lines on Form 2119 that apply to you. If you completed line 16 or line 24 of Form 2119, enter the total of those lines on line 15 of Form 6252. Otherwise, enter zero on line 15 of Form 6252. Do not enter the gain from Form 2119 on Schedule D (Form 1040).

Note: *If you received interest on a note (or other financial instrument), be sure to report that interest on Form 1040. For details, see the Form 1040 instructions for line 8a.*

Line 4. If any part of either home was rented out or used for business for which a deduction is allowed, answer "Yes" on line 4.

- If part of your old main home was rented out or used for business and in the year of sale you were entitled to deduct expenses for the part that was rented or used for business, treat the sale as two separate sales. Report the part of the sale that applies to the rental or business use on Form 4797. Report only the part of the sale that represents your main home on Form 2119. You must allocate the sales price, expenses of sale, and the basis of the property sold between Forms 2119 and 4797.

Note: *Only the part of the fixing-up expenses that applies to your main home may be included on line 18. These amounts are not allowed on Form 4797.*

Attach a statement showing the total selling price of the property and the method used to allocate the amounts between Forms 2119 and 4797. You cannot postpone or take the one-time exclusion on the part of the gain that is reported on Form 4797.

- If part of your new main home is rented out or used for business, enter on line 21b only the part of the total cost of the property that is allocable to your new main home. Attach a statement showing the total cost of the property and the allocation between the part that is your new main home and the part that is rented out or used for business.

Line 5. Enter the gross sales price of your old home. Generally, this includes the amount of money you received, plus all notes, mortgages, or other debts that are part of the sale, and the fair market value of any other property you received.

Line 6. Enter the total expenses you paid to sell your old home. These expenses include commissions, advertising, attorney and legal fees, appraisal fees, title insurance, transfer and stamp taxes, and recording fees. Loan charges, such as points charged to the seller, are also selling expenses. Do not include fixing-up expenses on this line. Instead, see the instructions for line 18.

Line 8. Include the cost of any capital improvements, and subtract any depreciation, casualty losses, or energy credits you reported on your tax return(s) that were related to your old home.

If you filed a Form 2119 when you originally bought your old home to postpone gain on a previous sale of a home, use the adjusted basis of the new home from the last line of that Form 2119 as the starting point to figure the basis of your old home. If you did not file a Form 2119 to postpone gain when you originally bought your old home, use the purchase price of the home including any expenses incurred to buy it as the starting point.

For more details or if you acquired your home other than by purchase, such as by gift, inheritance, trade, or you built your home, see Pub. 523 and **Pub. 551,** Basis of Assets.

Line 18. Enter the amount paid for work done on your old home to help sell it. The expenses must be—

- For work done during the 90-day period ending on the day you signed the contract to sell your home (not the day you signed the listing contract with the realtor), and
- Paid no later than 30 days after the date of sale.

Do not include amounts that are otherwise deductible or selling expenses included on line 6.

Also, do not include expenses for permanent improvements or replacements, which should be added to the basis of the property sold.

Line 21b. The cost of your new home includes one or more of the following:

- Cash payments,
- The amount of any mortgage or other debt on the new home,
- Commissions and other purchase expenses you paid that were not deducted as moving expenses, and
- Any capital expenses incurred within the replacement period (defined on this page).

If you built your new home, include the cost of the land and all construction costs incurred within the replacement period. Do not include the cost of land purchased before or after the replacement period or land acquired other than by purchase. Also, do not include the value of your own labor.

Note: *If line 23 of Form 2119 shows a taxable gain and you incur capital expenses after you file it but within the replacement period, you should refigure your taxable gain. If including the capital expenses in the cost of your new home reduces the gain you originally reported, file Form 1040X to correct your 1992 tax return.*

Line 25. Subtract line 24 from 21b. This is your adjusted basis in your new home. But if you built your new home and the land is not included in the amount entered on line 21b, your adjusted basis in your new home is the amount on line 25 plus the adjusted basis of the land.

Form **2441**

Department of the Treasury
Internal Revenue Service (T)

Child and Dependent Care Expenses

▶ Attach to Form 1040.

▶ See separate instructions.

OMB No. 1545-0068

1992

Attachment
Sequence No. **21**

Name(s) shown on Form 1040

Your social security number

Caution: • *If you have a child who was born in 1992 and the amount on Form 1040, line 32, is less than $22,370, see* ***A Change To Note*** *on page 1 of the instructions before completing this form.*

• *If you paid cash wages of $50 or more in a calendar quarter to an individual for services performed in your home, you must file an employment tax return. Get* ***Form 942*** *for details.*

Part I **Persons or Organizations Who Provided the Care—You must complete this part.** (See the instructions. If you need more space, use the bottom of page 2.)

1	**(a)** Care provider's name	**(b)** Address (number, street, apt. no., city, state, and ZIP code)	**(c)** Identifying number (SSN or EIN)	**(d)** Amount paid (see instructions)

2 Add the amounts in column (d) of line 1 2

Next: Did you receive employer-provided dependent care benefits?

• **YES.** Complete Part III on the back now.

• **NO.** Complete Part II below.

Part II **Credit for Child and Dependent Care Expenses**

3 Enter the number of qualifying persons cared for in 1992. See the instructions to find out who is a qualifying person. **Caution:** *To qualify, the person(s)* ***must*** *have shared the same home with you in 1992* . . . ▶

4 Enter the amount of **qualified** expenses you incurred and actually paid in 1992. See the instructions to find out which expenses qualify. **Caution:** *If you completed Part III on page 2,* **do not** *include on this line any excluded benefits shown on line 25* 4

5 Enter $2,400 ($4,800 if you paid for the care of two or more qualifying persons) 5

6 If you completed Part III on page 2, enter the **excluded benefits,** if any, from line 25. 6

7 Subtract line 6 from line 5. If the result is zero or less, skip lines 8 through 13; enter -0- on line 14, and go to line 15 7

8 Look at lines 4 and 7. Enter the **smaller** of the two amounts here 8

9 You **must** enter your **earned income**. See the instructions for the definition of earned income . . . 9

Note: *If you are not filing a joint return, go to "All other filers" on line 11 now.*

10 If you are filing a joint return, you **must** enter your spouse's earned income. If your spouse was a student or disabled, see the instructions for the amount to enter 10

11 • If you are filing a joint return, look at lines 8, 9, and 10. Enter the **smallest** of the three amounts here.

• All other filers, look at lines 8 and 9. Enter the **smaller** of the two amounts here. } 11

12 Enter the amount from Form 1040, line 32 12

13 Enter the decimal amount shown below that applies to the amount on line 12 . . . . . 13 ×

If line 12 is: Over—	**But not over—**	**Decimal amount is:**	**If line 12 is:** Over—	**But not over—**	**Decimal amount is:**
$0	10,000	.30	$20,000	22,000	.24
10,000	12,000	.29	22,000	24,000	.23
12,000	14,000	.28	24,000	26,000	.22
14,000	16,000	.27	26,000	28,000	.21
16,000	18,000	.26	28,000	No limit	.20
18,000	20,000	.25			

14 Multiply line 11 above by the decimal amount on line 13 14

15 Multiply any qualified expenses for 1991 that you paid in 1992 by the decimal amount that applies to the amount on your 1991 Form 1040, line 32, or Form 1040A, line 17. You must complete Part I and attach a statement. See the instructions 15

16 Add lines 14 and 15. See the instructions for the amount of credit you can claim 16

For Paperwork Reduction Act Notice, see separate instructions. Cat. No. 11862M Form **2441** (1992)

Form 2441 (1992) Page **2**

Part III **Employer-Provided Dependent Care Benefits**—Complete this part only if you received employer-provided dependent care benefits.

17 Enter the total amount of employer-provided dependent care benefits you received for 1992. This amount should be shown in box 22 of your W-2 form(s). **Do not** include amounts that were reported to you as wages in box 10 of Form(s) W-2		**17**	
18 Enter the amount forfeited, if any. **Caution:** *See the instructions*		**18**	
19 Subtract line 18 from line 17		**19**	
20 Enter the total amount of **qualified** expenses incurred in 1992 for the care of a qualifying person. See the instructions	**20**		
21 Look at lines 19 and 20. Enter the **smaller** of the two amounts here	**21**		
22 You **must** enter your **earned income**. See the instructions for lines 9 and 10 for the definition of earned income **Note:** *If you are not filing a joint return, go to "All other filers" on line 24 now.*	**22**		
23 If you are filing a joint return, you **must** enter your spouse's earned income. If your spouse was a student or disabled, see the instructions for lines 9 and 10 for the amount to enter	**23**		
24 • If you are filing a joint return, look at lines 22 and 23. Enter the **smaller** of the two amounts here. • All other filers, enter the amount from line 22 here.	**24**		
25 **Excluded benefits.** Enter here the **smallest** of the following: • The amount from line 21, or • The amount from line 24, or • $5,000 ($2,500 if married filing a separate return).		**25**	
26 **Taxable benefits.** Subtract line 25 from line 19. Enter the result, but not less than zero. Also, include this amount in the total on Form 1040, line 7. On the dotted line next to line 7, write "DCB"		**26**	

Next: If you are also claiming the child and dependent care credit, fill in Form 1040 through line 40. Then, complete Part II of this form.

Form **3903**

Department of the Treasury
Internal Revenue Service

Moving Expenses

▶ Attach to Form 1040.

▶ See separate instructions.

OMB No. 1545-0062

1992

Attachment
Sequence No. **62**

Name(s) shown on Form 1040 | **Your social security number**

1	Enter the number of miles from your **old home** to your **new workplace**	1	
2	Enter the number of miles from your **old home** to your **old workplace**	2	
3	Subtract line 2 from line 1. Enter the result but not less than zero ▶	3	

If line 3 is 35 or more miles, complete the rest of this form. If line 3 is less than 35 miles, you may not deduct your moving expenses. This rule does not apply to members of the armed forces.

Caution: *If you are a member of the armed forces, see the instructions before continuing.*

Part I Moving Expenses

Note: *Any payments your employer made for any part of your move (including the value of any services furnished in kind) should be included on your W-2 form. Report that amount on* ***Form 1040, line 7.*** *See* ***Reimbursements*** *in the instructions.*

Section A—Transportation of Household Goods							
4	Transportation and storage for household goods and personal effects					4	
Section B—Expenses of Moving From Old To New Home							
5	Travel and lodging **not** including meals			5			
6	Total meals	6					
7	Multiply line 6 by 80% (.80)			7			
8	Add lines 5 and 7					8	
Section C—Pre-move Househunting Expenses and Temporary Quarters (for any 30 days in a row after getting your job)							
9	Pre-move travel and lodging **not** including meals			9			
10	Temporary quarters expenses **not** including meals			10			
11	Total meal expenses for both pre-move househunting and temporary quarters	11					
12	Multiply line 11 by 80% (.80)			12			
13	Add lines 9, 10, and 12			13			
Section D—Qualified Real Estate Expenses							
14	Expenses of (check one): **a** ☐ selling or exchanging your old home, or **b** ☐ if renting, settling an unexpired lease.			14			
15	Expenses of (check one): **a** ☐ buying your new home, or **b** ☐ if renting, getting a new lease.			15			

Part II Dollar Limits and Moving Expense Deduction

16	Enter the **smaller** of: • The amount on line 13, or • $1,500 ($750 if married filing a separate return and at the end of 1992 you lived with your spouse who also started work in 1992).	16			
17	Add lines 14, 15, and 16	17			
18	Enter the **smaller** of: • The amount on line 17, or • $3,000 ($1,500 if married filing a separate return and at the end of 1992 you lived with your spouse who also started work in 1992).			18	
19	Add lines 4, 8, and 18. Enter the total here and on Schedule A, line 18. This is your **moving expense deduction** ▶			19	

For Paperwork Reduction Act Notice, see separate instructions. Cat. No. 12490K Form **3903** (1992)

Form **4562**

Department of the Treasury
Internal Revenue Service

Depreciation and Amortization
(Including Information on Listed Property)

▶ See separate instructions. ▶ Attach this form to your return.

OMB No. 1545-0172

1992

Attachment Sequence No. **67**

Name(s) shown on return

Identifying number

Business or activity to which this form relates

Part I **Election To Expense Certain Tangible Property (Section 179) (Note:** *If you have any "Listed Property," complete Part V before you complete Part I.)*

1	Maximum dollar limitation (see instructions)	1	$10,000
2	Total cost of section 179 property placed in service during the tax year (see instructions)	2	
3	Threshold cost of section 179 property before reduction in limitation	3	$200,000
4	Reduction in limitation. Subtract line 3 from line 2, but do not enter less than -0-	4	
5	Dollar limitation for tax year. Subtract line 4 from line 1, but do not enter less than -0-	5	

	(a) Description of property	(b) Cost	(c) Elected cost
6			
7	Listed property. Enter amount from line 26	7	

8	Total elected cost of section 179 property. Add amounts in column (c), lines 6 and 7	8	
9	Tentative deduction. Enter the smaller of line 5 or line 8	9	
10	Carryover of disallowed deduction from 1991 (see instructions)	10	
11	Taxable income limitation. Enter the smaller of taxable income or line 5 (see instructions)	11	
12	Section 179 expense deduction. Add lines 9 and 10, but do not enter more than line 11	12	
13	Carryover of disallowed deduction to 1993. Add lines 9 and 10, less line 12 ▶	13	

Note: *Do not use Part II or Part III below for automobiles, certain other vehicles, cellular telephones, computers, or property used for entertainment, recreation, or amusement (listed property). Instead, use Part V for listed property.*

Part II **MACRS Depreciation For Assets Placed in Service ONLY During Your 1992 Tax Year (Do Not Include Listed Property)**

(a) Classification of property	(b) Month and year placed in service	(c) Basis for depreciation (business/investment use only—see instructions)	(d) Recovery period	(e) Convention	(f) Method	(g) Depreciation deduction
14 General Depreciation System (GDS) (see instructions):						
a 3-year property						
b 5-year property						
c 7-year property						
d 10-year property						
e 15-year property						
f 20-year property						
g Residential rental property			27.5 yrs.	MM	S/L	
			27.5 yrs.	MM	S/L	
h Nonresidential real property			31.5 yrs.	MM	S/L	
			31.5 yrs.	MM	S/L	
15 Alternative Depreciation System (ADS) (see instructions):						
a Class life					S/L	
b 12-year			12 yrs.		S/L	
c 40-year			40 yrs.	MM	S/L	

Part III **Other Depreciation (Do Not Include Listed Property)**

16	GDS and ADS deductions for assets placed in service in tax years beginning before 1992 (see instructions)	16	
17	Property subject to section 168(f)(1) election (see instructions)	17	
18	ACRS and other depreciation (see instructions)	18	

Part IV **Summary**

19	Listed property. Enter amount from line 25	19	
20	**Total.** Add deductions on line 12, lines 14 and 15 in column (g), and lines 16 through 19. Enter here and on the appropriate lines of your return. (Partnerships and S corporations—see instructions)	20	
21	For assets shown above and placed in service during the current year, enter the portion of the basis attributable to section 263A costs (see instructions)	21	

For Paperwork Reduction Act Notice, see page 1 of the separate instructions. Cat. No. 12906N Form **4562** (1992)

Form 4562 (1992) Page 2

Part V **Listed Property—Automobiles, Certain Other Vehicles, Cellular Telephones, Computers, and Property Used for Entertainment, Recreation, or Amusement**

*For any vehicle for which you are using the standard mileage rate or deducting lease expense, complete **only** 22a, 22b, columns (a) through (c) of Section A, all of Section B, and Section C if applicable.*

Section A—Depreciation (Caution: *See instructions for limitations for automobiles.)*

22a Do you have evidence to support the business/investment use claimed? ☐ **Yes** ☐ **No** **22b** If "Yes," is the evidence written? ☐ **Yes** ☐ **No**

(a) Type of property (list vehicles first)	(b) Date placed in service	(c) Business/ investment use percentage	(d) Cost or other basis	(e) Basis for depreciation (business/investment use only)	(f) Recovery period	(g) Method/ Convention	(h) Depreciation deduction	(i) Elected section 179 cost
23 Property used more than 50% in a qualified business use (see instructions):								
		%						
		%						
		%						
24 Property used 50% or less in a qualified business use (see instructions):								
		%				S/L –		
		%				S/L –		
		%				S/L –		

25 Add amounts in column (h). Enter the total here and on line 19, page 1 . . . . **25**

26 Add amounts in column (i). Enter the total here and on line 7, page 1 . . . . **26**

Section B—Information Regarding Use of Vehicles—*If you deduct expenses for vehicles:*

- *Always complete this section for vehicles used by a sole proprietor, partner, or other "more than 5% owner," or related person.*
- *If you provided vehicles to your employees, first answer the questions in Section C to see if you meet an exception to completing this section for those vehicles.*

	(a) Vehicle 1		(b) Vehicle 2		(c) Vehicle 3		(d) Vehicle 4		(e) Vehicle 5		(f) Vehicle 6	
27 Total business/investment miles driven during the year (DO NOT include commuting miles)												
28 Total commuting miles driven during the year												
29 Total other personal (noncommuting) miles driven												
30 Total miles driven during the year. Add lines 27 through 29.												
	Yes	**No**	**Yes**	**No**	**Yes**	**No**	**Yes**	**No**	**Yes**	**No**	**Yes**	**No**
31 Was the vehicle available for personal use during off-duty hours?												
32 Was the vehicle used primarily by a more than 5% owner or related person?												
33 Is another vehicle available for personal use?												

Section C—Questions for Employers Who Provide Vehicles for Use by Their Employees

Answer these questions to determine if you meet an exception to completing Section B. **Note:** *Section B must always be completed for vehicles used by sole proprietors, partners, or other more than 5% owners or related persons.*

	Yes	**No**
34 Do you maintain a written policy statement that prohibits all personal use of vehicles, including commuting, by your employees?		
35 Do you maintain a written policy statement that prohibits personal use of vehicles, except commuting, by your employees? (See instructions for vehicles used by corporate officers, directors, or 1% or more owners.)		
36 Do you treat all use of vehicles by employees as personal use?		
37 Do you provide more than five vehicles to your employees and retain the information received from your employees concerning the use of the vehicles?		
38 Do you meet the requirements concerning qualified automobile demonstration use (see instructions)? . .		
Note: *If your answer to 34, 35, 36, 37, or 38 is "Yes," you need not complete Section B for the covered vehicles.*		

Part VI **Amortization**

(a) Description of costs	(b) Date amortization begins	(c) Amortizable amount	(d) Code section	(e) Amortization period or percentage	(f) Amortization for this year
39 Amortization of costs that begins during your 1992 tax year:					

40 Amortization of costs that began before 1992 . . . . **40**

41 Total. Enter here and on "Other Deductions" or "Other Expenses" line of your return . . . **41**

Form **4626**

Department of the Treasury
Internal Revenue Service

Alternative Minimum Tax—Corporations
(including environmental tax)

▶ See separate instructions.
▶ Attach to the corporation's tax return.

OMB No. 1545-0175

1992

Name | **Employer identification number**

1	Taxable income or (loss) before net operating loss deduction. (**Important:** See instructions if the corporation is subject to the environmental tax.)			1	
2	**Adjustments:**				
a	Depreciation of tangible property placed in service after 1986	2a			
b	Amortization of certified pollution control facilities placed in service after 1986	2b			
c	Amortization of mining exploration and development costs paid or incurred after 1986	2c			
d	Amortization of circulation expenditures paid or incurred after 1986 (personal holding companies only)	2d			
e	Basis adjustments in determining gain or loss from sale or exchange of property	2e			
f	Long-term contracts entered into after February 28, 1986	2f			
g	Installment sales of certain property	2g			
h	Merchant marine capital construction funds	2h			
i	Section 833(b) deduction (Blue Cross, Blue Shield, and similar type organizations only)	2i			
j	Tax shelter farm activities (personal service corporations only)	2j			
k	Passive activities (closely held corporations and personal service corporations only)	2k			
l	Certain loss limitations	2l			
m	Other adjustments	2m			
n	Combine lines 2a through 2m			2n	
3	**Tax preference items:**				
a	Depletion	3a			
b	Tax-exempt interest from private activity bonds issued after August 7, 1986	3b			
c	Appreciated property charitable deduction	3c			
d	Intangible drilling costs	3d			
e	Reserves for losses on bad debts of financial institutions	3e			
f	Accelerated depreciation of real property placed in service before 1987	3f			
g	Accelerated depreciation of leased personal property placed in service before 1987 (personal holding companies only)	3g			
h	Amortization of certified pollution control facilities placed in service before 1987	3h			
i	Add lines 3a through 3h			3i	
4	Pre-adjustment alternative minimum taxable income (AMTI). Combine lines 1, 2n, and 3i			4	
5	**Adjusted current earnings (ACE) adjustment:**				
a	Enter the corporation's ACE from line 10 of the worksheet on page 7 of the instructions	5a			
b	Subtract line 4 from line 5a. If line 4 exceeds line 5a, enter the difference as a negative number (see instructions for examples)	5b			
c	Multiply line 5b by 75% and enter the result as a positive number	5c			
d	Enter the excess, if any, of the corporation's total increases in AMTI from prior year ACE adjustments over its total reductions in AMTI from prior year ACE adjustments (see instructions). **Note:** *You **must** enter an amount on line 5d (even if line 5b is positive)*	5d			
e	ACE adjustment: • If you entered a positive number or zero on line 5b, enter the amount from line 5c on line 5e as a positive amount. • If you entered a negative number on line 5b, enter the smaller of line 5c or line 5d on line 5e as a negative amount.			5e	
6	Combine lines 4 and 5e. If zero or less, stop here (the corporation is not subject to the alternative minimum tax)			6	
7	Adjustment based on energy preferences. (Do not enter more than 40% of line 6.)			7	
8	Alternative tax net operating loss deduction. (Do not enter more than the excess, if any, of: **(a)** 90% of line 6, over **(b)** line 7.)			8	
9	**Alternative minimum taxable income.** Subtract the sum of lines 7 and 8 from line 6			9	

For Paperwork Reduction Act Notice, see separate instructions. Cat. No. 12955I Form **4626** (1992)

Form **4684**

Department of the Treasury
Internal Revenue Service

Casualties and Thefts

▶ See separate instructions.
▶ Attach to your tax return.
▶ Use a separate Form 4684 for each different casualty or theft.

OMB No. 1545-0177

1992

Attachment Sequence No. **26**

Name(s) shown on tax return	Identifying number

SECTION A.—Personal Use Property (Use this section to report casualties and thefts of property **not** used in a trade or business or for income-producing purposes.)

1 Description of properties (show kind, location, and date acquired for each):

Property **A** ....

Property **B** ....

Property **C** ....

Property **D** ....

		Properties (Use a separate column for each property lost or damaged from one casualty or theft.)			
		A	**B**	**C**	**D**
2 Cost or other basis of each property	2				
3 Insurance or other reimbursement (whether or not you submitted a claim). See instructions	3				
Note: *If line 2 is **more than** line 3, skip line 4.*					
4 Gain from casualty or theft. If line 3 is **more than** line 2, enter the difference here and skip lines 5 through 9 for that column. If line 3 includes an amount that you did not receive, see instructions .	4				
5 Fair market value **before** casualty or theft . . .	5				
6 Fair market value **after** casualty or theft	6				
7 Subtract line 6 from line 5	7				
8 Enter the **smaller** of line 2 or line 7	8				
9 Subtract line 3 from line 8. If zero or less, enter -0-	9				

10 Casualty or theft loss. Add the amounts on line 9. Enter the total	10	
11 Enter the amount from line 10 or $100, whichever is **smaller**	11	
12 Subtract line 11 from line 10	12	
Caution: *Use only one Form 4684 for lines 13 through 18.*		
13 Add the amounts on line 12 of all Forms 4684	13	
14 Combine the amounts from line 4 of all Forms 4684	14	
15 • If line 14 is **more than** line 13, enter the difference here and on Schedule D. Do not complete the rest of this section (see instructions). • If line 14 is **less than** line 13, enter -0- here and continue with the form. • If line 14 is **equal to** line 13, enter -0- here. Do not complete the rest of this section.	15	
16 If line 14 is **less than** line 13, enter the difference	16	
17 Enter 10% of your adjusted gross income (Form 1040, line 32). Estates and trusts, see instructions	17	
18 Subtract line 17 from line 16. If zero or less, enter -0-. Also enter result on Schedule A (Form 1040), line 17. Estates and trusts, enter on the "Other deductions" line of your tax return	18	

Form 4684 (1992) Attachment Sequence No. **26** Page **2**

Name(s) shown on tax return. Do not enter name and identifying number if shown on other side. | **Identifying number**

SECTION B.—Business and Income-Producing Property (Use this section to report casualties and thefts of property used in a trade or business or for income-producing purposes.)

Part I Casualty or Theft Gain or Loss (Use a separate Part I for each casualty or theft.)

19 Description of properties (show kind, location, and date acquired for each):

Property **A** ....

Property **B** ....

Property **C** ....

Property **D** ....

		Properties (Use a separate column for each property lost or damaged from one casualty or theft.)			
		A	B	C	D
20 Cost or adjusted basis of each property	20				
21 Insurance or other reimbursement (whether or not you submitted a claim). See the instructions for line 3	21				
Note: *If line 20 is **more than** line 21, skip line 22.*					
22 Gain from casualty or theft. If line 21 is **more than** line 20, enter the difference here and on line 29 or line 34, column (**c**), except as provided in the instructions for line 33. Also, skip lines 23 through 27 for that column. If line 21 includes an amount that you did not receive, see the instructions for line 4	22				
23 Fair market value **before** casualty or theft	23				
24 Fair market value **after** casualty or theft	24				
25 Subtract line 24 from line 23	25				
26 Enter the **smaller** of line 20 or line 25	26				
Note: *If the property was totally destroyed by casualty, or lost from theft, enter on line 26 the amount from line 20.*					
27 Subtract line 21 from line 26. If zero or less, enter -0-	27				

28 Casualty or theft loss. Add the amounts on line 27. Enter the total here and on line 29 **or** line 34 (see instructions). | 28 |

Part II Summary of Gains and Losses (from separate Parts I)

(**a**) Identify casualty or theft		(**b**) Losses from casualties or thefts: (*i*) Trade, business, rental or royalty property	(*ii*) Income-producing property	(**c**) Gains from casualties or thefts includible in income
Casualty or Theft of Property Held One Year or Less				
29		( )	( )	
		( )	( )	
30 Totals. Add the amounts on line 29	30	( )	( )	
31 Combine line 30, columns (b)(i) and (c). Enter the net gain or (loss) here and on Form 4797, line 15. If Form 4797 is not otherwise required, see instructions			31	
32 Enter the amount from line 30, column (b)(ii) here and on Schedule A (Form 1040), line 20. Partnerships, S corporations, estates and trusts, see instructions			32	
Casualty or Theft of Property Held More Than One Year				
33 Casualty or theft gains from Form 4797, line 34			33	
34		( )	( )	
		( )	( )	
35 Total losses. Add amounts on line 34, columns (b)(i) and (b)(ii)	35	( )	( )	
36 Total gains. Add lines 33 and 34, column (c)			36	
37 Add amounts on line 35, columns (b)(i) and (b)(ii)			37	
38 If the loss on line 37 is **more than** the gain on line 36:				
a Combine line 35, column (b)(i) and line 36, and enter the net gain or (loss) here. Partnerships and S corporations see the note below. All others enter this amount on Form 4797, line 15. If Form 4797 is not otherwise required, see instructions			38a	
b Enter the amount from line 35, column (b)(ii) here. Partnerships and S corporations see the note below. Individuals enter this amount on Schedule A (Form 1040), line 20. Estates and trusts, enter on the "Other deductions" line of your tax return			38b	
39 If the loss on line 37 is **equal to** or **less than** the gain on line 36, combine these lines and enter here. Partnerships, see the note below. All others, enter this amount on Form 4797, line 3			39	

Note: *Partnerships, enter the amount from line 38a, 38b, or line 39 on Form 1065, Schedule K, line 7. S corporations, enter the amount from line 38a or 38b on Form 1120S, Schedule K, line 6.*

Form **4797**

Department of the Treasury (T)
Internal Revenue Service

Sales of Business Property

(Also Involuntary Conversions and Recapture Amounts Under Sections 179 and 280F)

▶ **Attach to your tax return.** ▶ **See separate instructions.**

OMB No. 1545-0184

1992

Attachment Sequence No. **27**

Name(s) shown on return | **Identifying number**

1 Enter here the gross proceeds from the sale or exchange of real estate reported to you for 1992 on Form(s) 1099-S (or a substitute statement) that you will be including on line 2, 11, or 22 1

Part I **Sales or Exchanges of Property Used in a Trade or Business and Involuntary Conversions From Other Than Casualty or Theft—Property Held More Than 1 Year**

	(a) Description of property	(b) Date acquired (mo., day, yr.)	(c) Date sold (mo., day, yr.)	(d) Gross sales price	(e) Depreciation allowed or allowable since acquisition	(f) Cost or other basis, plus improvements and expense of sale	(g) LOSS ((f) minus the sum of (d) and (e))	(h) GAIN ((d) plus (e) minus (f))
2								

			(g)	(h)
3	Gain, if any, from Form 4684, line 39	3		
4	Section 1231 gain from installment sales from Form 6252, line 26 or 37	4		
5	Section 1231 gain or (loss) from like-kind exchanges from Form 8824	5		
6	Gain, if any, from line 34, from other than casualty or theft	6		
7	Add lines 2 through 6 in columns (g) and (h)	7	( )	

8 Combine columns (g) and (h) of line 7. Enter gain or (loss) here, and on the appropriate line as follows: 8

Partnerships—Enter the gain or (loss) on Form 1065, Schedule K, line 6. Skip lines 9, 10, 12, and 13 below.

S corporations—Report the gain or (loss) following the instructions for Form 1120S, Schedule K, lines 5 and 6. Skip lines 9, 10, 12, and 13 below, unless line 8 is a gain and the S corporation is subject to the capital gains tax.

All others—If line 8 is zero or a loss, enter the amount on line 12 below and skip lines 9 and 10. If line 8 is a gain and you did not have any prior year section 1231 losses, or they were recaptured in an earlier year, enter the gain as a long-term capital gain on Schedule D and skip lines 9, 10, and 13 below.

9 Nonrecaptured net section 1231 losses from prior years (see instructions) 9

10 Subtract line 9 from line 8. If zero or less, enter -0-. Also enter on the appropriate line as follows (see instructions): 10

S corporations—Enter this amount (if more than zero) on Schedule D (Form 1120S), line 13, and skip lines 12 and 13 below.

All others—If line 10 is zero, enter the amount from line 8 on line 13 below. If line 10 is more than zero, enter the amount from line 9 on line 13 below, and enter the amount from line 10 as a long-term capital gain on Schedule D.

Part II **Ordinary Gains and Losses**

11 Ordinary gains and losses not included on lines 12 through 18 (include property held 1 year or less):

(a)	(b)	(c)	(d)	(e)	(f)	(g)	(h)

			(g)	(h)
12	Loss, if any, from line 8	12		
13	Gain, if any, from line 8, or amount from line 9 if applicable	13		
14	Gain, if any, from line 33	14		
15	Net gain or (loss) from Form 4684, lines 31 and 38a	15		
16	Ordinary gain from installment sales from Form 6252, line 25 or 36	16		
17	Ordinary gain or (loss) from like-kind exchanges from Form 8824	17		
18	Recapture of section 179 expense deduction for partners and S corporation shareholders from property dispositions by partnerships and S corporations (see instructions)	18		
19	Add lines 11 through 18 in columns (g) and (h)	19	( )	

20 Combine columns (g) and (h) of line 19. Enter gain or (loss) here, and on the appropriate line as follows: 20

a For all except individual returns: Enter the gain or (loss) from line 20 on the return being filed.

b For individual returns:

(1) If the loss on line 12 includes a loss from Form 4684, line 35, column (b)(ii), enter that part of the loss here and on line 20 of Schedule A (Form 1040). Identify as from "Form 4797, line 20b(1)." See instructions . . . . 20b(1)

(2) Redetermine the gain or (loss) on line 20, excluding the loss, if any, on line 20b(1). Enter here and on Form 1040, line 15 . . 20b(2)

For Paperwork Reduction Act Notice, see page 1 of separate instructions. Cat. No. 13086I Form **4797** (1992)

Form 4797 (1992) Page 2

Part III Gain From Disposition of Property Under Sections 1245, 1250, 1252, 1254, and 1255

21 (a) Description of section 1245, 1250, 1252, 1254, or 1255 property:	(b) Date acquired (mo., day, yr.)	(c) Date sold (mo., day, yr.)
A		
B		
C		
D		

Relate lines 21A through 21D to these columns	▶	Property A	Property B	Property C	Property D
22 Gross sales price (**Note:** *See line 1 before completing.*)	22				
23 Cost or other basis plus expense of sale	23				
24 Depreciation (or depletion) allowed or allowable	24				
25 Adjusted basis. Subtract line 24 from line 23	25				
26 Total gain. Subtract line 25 from line 22	26				
27 **If section 1245 property:**					
a Depreciation allowed or allowable from line 24	27a				
b Enter the **smaller** of line 26 or 27a	27b				
28 **If section 1250 property:** If straight line depreciation was used, enter -0- on line 28g, except for a corporation subject to section 291.					
a Additional depreciation after 1975 (see instructions)	28a				
b Applicable percentage multiplied by the **smaller** of line 26 or line 28a (see instructions)	28b				
c Subtract line 28a from line 26. If line 26 is not more than line 28a, skip lines 28d and 28e	28c				
d Additional depreciation after 1969 and before 1976	28d				
e Applicable percentage multiplied by the **smaller** of line 28c or 28d (see instructions)	28e				
f Section 291 amount (corporations only)	28f				
g Add lines 28b, 28e, and 28f	28g				
29 **If section 1252 property:** Skip this section if you did not dispose of farmland or if this form is being completed for a partnership.					
a Soil, water, and land clearing expenses	29a				
b Line 29a multiplied by applicable percentage (see instructions)	29b				
c Enter the **smaller** of line 26 or 29b	29c				
30 **If section 1254 property:**					
a Intangible drilling and development costs, expenditures for development of mines and other natural deposits, and mining exploration costs (see instructions)	30a				
b Enter the **smaller** of line 26 or 30a	30b				
31 **If section 1255 property:**					
a Applicable percentage of payments excluded from income under section 126 (see instructions)	31a				
b Enter the **smaller** of line 26 or 31a	31b				

Summary of Part III Gains. Complete property columns A through D, through line 31b before going to line 32.

32 Total gains for all properties. Add columns A through D, line 26	32	
33 Add columns A through D, lines 27b, 28g, 29c, 30b, and 31b. Enter here and on line 14. See the instructions for Part IV if this is an installment sale	33	
34 Subtract line 33 from line 32. Enter the portion from casualty or theft on Form 4684, line 33. Enter the portion from other than casualty or theft on Form 4797, line 6	34	

Part IV Election Not to Use the Installment Method. Complete this part only if you elect out of the installment method and report a note or other obligation at less than full face value.

35 Check here if you elect out of the installment method ▶ ☐

36 Enter the face amount of the note or other obligation ▶ $

37 Enter the percentage of valuation of the note or other obligation ▶ %

Part V Recapture Amounts Under Sections 179 and 280F When Business Use Drops to 50% or Less

See instructions for Part V.

		(a) Section 179	(b) Section 280F
38 Section 179 expense deduction or depreciation allowable in prior years	38		
39 Recomputed depreciation (see instructions)	39		
40 Recapture amount. Subtract line 39 from line 38. See instructions for where to report	40		

Form **6251**

Department of the Treasury
Internal Revenue Service (T)

Alternative Minimum Tax—Individuals

► See separate instructions.

► Attach to Form 1040 or Form 1040NR.

OMB No. 1545-0227

1992

Attachment Sequence No. **32**

Name(s) shown on Form 1040 | Your social security number

Line	Description	Sub-line	Amount	Line	Amount
1	Enter the amount from Form 1040, line 35. If less than zero, enter as a negative amount			1	
2	Net operating loss deduction, if any, from Form 1040, line 22. Enter as a positive amount			2	
3	Overall itemized deductions limitation amount (see instructions)			3	( )
4	Combine lines 1, 2, and 3			4	
5	**Adjustments:** (See instructions before completing.)				
a	Standard deduction, if any, from Form 1040, line 34	5a			
b	Medical and dental expenses. Enter the smaller of the amount from Schedule A (Form 1040), line 4, or 2½% (.025) of Form 1040, line 32	5b			
c	Miscellaneous itemized deductions from Schedule A (Form 1040), line 24	5c			
d	Taxes from Schedule A (Form 1040), line 8	5d			
e	Refund of taxes	5e	( )		
f	Certain home mortgage interest	5f			
g	Investment interest expense	5g			
h	Depreciation of tangible property placed in service after 1986	5h			
i	Circulation and research and experimental expenditures paid or incurred after 1986	5i			
j	Mining exploration and development costs paid or incurred after 1986	5j			
k	Long-term contracts entered into after 2/28/86	5k			
l	Pollution control facilities placed in service after 1986	5l			
m	Installment sales of certain property	5m			
n	Adjusted gain or loss	5n			
o	Incentive stock options	5o			
p	Certain loss limitations	5p			
q	Tax shelter farm activities	5q			
r	Passive activities	5r			
s	Beneficiaries of estates and trusts	5s			
t	Combine lines 5a through 5s			5t	
6	**Tax preference items:** (See instructions before completing.)				
a	Appreciated property charitable deduction	6a			
b	Tax-exempt interest from private activity bonds issued after 8/7/86	6b			
c	Depletion	6c			
d	Accelerated depreciation of real property placed in service before 1987	6d			
e	Accelerated depreciation of leased personal property placed in service before 1987	6e			
f	Intangible drilling costs	6f			
g	Add lines 6a through 6f			6g	
7	Combine lines 4, 5t, and 6g			7	
8	Energy preference adjustment for certain taxpayers. Do not enter more than 40% of line 7. See instructions			8	
9	Subtract line 8 from line 7			9	
10	Alternative tax net operating loss deduction. See instructions for limitations			10	
11	**Alternative minimum taxable income.** Subtract line 10 from line 9. If married filing separately, see instructions			11	
12	Enter: $40,000 ($20,000 if married filing separately; $30,000 if single or head of household)			12	
13	Enter: $150,000 ($75,000 if married filing separately; $112,500 if single or head of household)			13	
14	Subtract line 13 from line 11. If zero or less, enter -0- here and on line 15 and go to line 16			14	
15	Multiply line 14 by 25% (.25)			15	
16	**Exemption.** Subtract line 15 from line 12. If zero or less, enter -0-. If completing this form for a child under age 14, see instructions for amount to enter			16	
17	Subtract line 16 from line 11. If zero or less, enter -0- here and on line 22 and skip lines 18 through 21			17	
18	Multiply line 17 by 24% (.24)			18	
19	Alternative minimum tax foreign tax credit. See instructions			19	
20	Tentative minimum tax. Subtract line 19 from line 18			20	
21	Enter your tax from Form 1040, line 38, minus any foreign tax credit on Form 1040, line 43. If an amount from Form 4970 is entered on line 39 of Form 1040, also include the amount from Form 4970 on this line			21	
22	**Alternative minimum tax.** Subtract line 21 from line 20. If zero or less, enter -0-. Enter this amount on Form 1040, line 48. If completing this form for a child under age 14, see instructions for amount to enter			22	

For Paperwork Reduction Act Notice, see separate instructions. Cat. No. 13600G Form **6251** (1992)

Form **8582**

Department of the Treasury
Internal Revenue Service

Passive Activity Loss Limitations

▶ See separate instructions.
▶ Attach to Form 1040 or Form 1041.

OMB No. 1545-1008

1992

Attachment Sequence No. 88

Name(s) shown on return | Identifying number

Part I **1992 Passive Activity Loss**

Caution: *See the instructions for Worksheets 1 and 2 on page 7 before completing Part I.*

Rental Real Estate Activities With Active Participation (For the definition of active participation see **Active Participation in a Rental Real Estate Activity** on page 3 of the instructions.)

1a Activities with net income (from Worksheet 1, column (a))	1a		
b Activities with net loss (from Worksheet 1, column (b))	1b	( )	
c Prior year unallowed losses (from Worksheet 1, column (c))	1c	( )	
d Combine lines 1a, 1b, and 1c		1d	

All Other Passive Activities

2a Activities with net income (from Worksheet 2, column (a))	2a		
b Activities with net loss (from Worksheet 2, column (b))	2b	( )	
c Prior year unallowed losses (from Worksheet 2, column (c))	2c	( )	
d Combine lines 2a, 2b, and 2c		2d	
3 Combine lines 1d and 2d. If the result is net income or zero, see the instructions for line 3. If this line and line 1d are losses, go to line 4. Otherwise, enter -0- on line 9 and go to line 10		3	

Part II **Special Allowance for Rental Real Estate With Active Participation**

Note: *Enter all numbers in Part II as positive amounts. (See instructions on page 7 for examples.)*

4 Enter the **smaller** of the loss on line 1d or the loss on line 3		4	
5 Enter $150,000. If married filing separately, see the instructions	5		
6 Enter modified adjusted gross income, but not less than zero (see instructions)	6		
Note: *If line 6 is equal to or greater than line 5, skip lines 7 and 8, enter -0- on line 9, and then go to line 10. Otherwise, go to line 7.*			
7 Subtract line 6 from line 5	7		
8 Multiply line 7 by 50% (.5). **Do not** enter more than $25,000. If married filing separately, see instructions		8	
9 Enter the **smaller** of line 4 or line 8		9	

Part III **Total Losses Allowed**

10 Add the income, if any, on lines 1a and 2a and enter the total	10	
11 **Total losses allowed from all passive activities for 1992.** Add lines 9 and 10. See the instructions to find out how to report the losses on your tax return	11	

For Paperwork Reduction Act Notice, see separate instructions. Cat. No. 63704F Form **8582** (1992)

Form **8615**

Department of the Treasury
Internal Revenue Service

Tax for Children Under Age 14 Who Have Investment Income of More Than $1,200

▶ See instructions below and on back.
▶ Attach ONLY to the child's Form 1040, Form 1040A, or Form 1040NR.

OMB No. 1545-0998
1992
Attachment Sequence No. **33**

General Instructions

Purpose of Form. For children under age 14, investment income (such as taxable interest and dividends) over $1,200 is taxed at the parent's rate if the parent's rate is higher than the child's rate. If the child's investment income is more than $1,200, use this form to figure the child's tax.

Investment Income. As used on this form, "investment income" includes all taxable income other than earned income as defined on page 2. It includes income such as taxable interest, dividends, capital gains, rents, royalties, etc. It also includes pension and annuity income and income (other than earned income) received as the beneficiary of a trust.

Who Must File. Generally, Form 8615 must be filed for any child who was under age 14 on January 1, 1993, and who had more than $1,200 of investment income. If neither parent was alive on December 31, 1992, do not use Form 8615. Instead, figure the child's tax in the normal manner.

Note: *The parent may be able to elect to report the child's interest and dividends on his or her return. If the parent makes this election, the child will not have to file a return or Form 8615. For more details, see the instructions for Form 1040 or Form 1040A, or get **Form 8814**, Parents' Election To Report Child's Interest and Dividends.*

Additional Information. For more details, get **Pub. 929,** Tax Rules for Children and Dependents.

Incomplete Information for Parent. If a child's parent or guardian cannot obtain the information needed to complete Form 8615 before the due date of the child's return, reasonable estimates of the parent's taxable income or filing status and the net investment income of the parent's other children may be made. The appropriate line(s) of Form 8615 must be marked "Estimated." For more details, see Pub. 929.

(Instructions continue on back.)

Child's name shown on return	Child's social security number
A Parent's name (first, initial, and last). **Caution:** *See instructions on back before completing.*	**B** Parent's social security number

C Parent's filing status (check one):
☐ Single ☐ Married filing jointly ☐ Married filing separately ☐ Head of household ☐ Qualifying widow(er)

Step 1 Figure child's net investment income

1	Enter child's investment income, such as taxable interest and dividend income. See instructions. If this amount is $1,200 or less, **stop here;** do not file this form	1	
2	If the child DID NOT itemize deductions on Schedule A (Form 1040 or Form 1040NR), enter $1,200. If the child ITEMIZED deductions, see instructions	2	
3	Subtract line 2 from line 1. If the result is zero or less, **stop here;** do not complete the rest of this form but ATTACH it to the child's return	3	
4	Enter child's **taxable** income from Form 1040, line 37; Form 1040A, line 22; or Form 1040NR, line 35	4	
5	Enter the **smaller** of line 3 or line 4 here ▶	5	

Step 2 Figure tentative tax based on the tax rate of the parent listed on line A

6	Enter parent's **taxable** income from Form 1040, line 37; Form 1040A, line 22; Form 1040EZ, line 5; or Form 1040NR, line 35. If the parent transferred property to a trust, see instructions	6	
7	Enter the total, if any, of the net investment income from Forms 8615, line 5, of ALL OTHER children of the parent. **Do not** include the amount from line 5 above	7	
8	Add lines 5, 6, and 7	8	
9	Tax on line 8 based on the **parent's** filing status. See instructions. If from Schedule D, enter amount from line 22 of that Schedule D here ▶	9	
10	Enter parent's tax from Form 1040, line 38; Form 1040A, line 23; Form 1040EZ, line 7; or Form 1040NR, line 36. If from Schedule D, enter amount from line 22 of that Schedule D here ▶	10	
11	Subtract line 10 from line 9. If line 7 is blank, enter on line 13 the amount from line 11; skip lines 12a and 12b	11	
12a	Add lines 5 and 7 — 12a		
b	Divide line 5 by line 12a. Enter the result as a decimal (rounded to two places)	12b	× .
13	Multiply line 11 by line 12b ▶	13	

Step 3 Figure child's tax

Note: *If lines 4 and 5 above are the same, go to line 16.*

14	Subtract line 5 from line 4 — 14		
15	Tax on line 14 based on the **child's** filing status. See instructions. If from Schedule D, enter amount from line 22 of that Schedule D here ▶	15	
16	Add lines 13 and 15	16	
17	Tax on line 4 based on the **child's** filing status. See instructions. If from Schedule D, check here ▶ ☐	17	
18	Enter the **larger** of line 16 or line 17 here and on Form 1040, line 38; Form 1040A, line 23; or Form 1040NR, line 36. Be sure to check the box for "Form 8615" even if line 17 is more than line 16 ▶	18	

For Paperwork Reduction Act Notice, see back of form. Cat. No. 64113U Form **8615** (1992)

Amended Return. If after the child's return is filed, the parent's taxable income is changed or the net investment income of any of the parent's other children is changed, the child's tax must be refigured using the adjusted amounts. If the child's tax is changed as a result of the adjustment(s), file **Form 1040X,** Amended U.S. Individual Income Tax Return, to correct the child's tax.

Alternative Minimum Tax. A child whose tax is figured on Form 8615 may owe the alternative minimum tax. For details, get **Form 6251,** Alternative Minimum Tax—Individuals, and its instructions.

Paperwork Reduction Act Notice. We ask for the information on this form to carry out the Internal Revenue laws of the United States. You are required to give us the information. We need it to ensure that you are complying with these laws and to allow us to figure and collect the right amount of tax.

The time needed to complete and file this form will vary depending on individual circumstances. The estimated average time is: **Recordkeeping,** 13 min.; **Learning about the law or the form,** 12 min.; **Preparing the form,** 44 min.; and **Copying, assembling, and sending the form to the IRS,** 17 min.

If you have comments concerning the accuracy of these time estimates or suggestions for making this form more simple, we would be happy to hear from you. You can write to both the IRS and the Office of Management and Budget at the addresses listed in the instructions of the tax return with which this form is filed.

Specific Instructions

(Section references are to the Internal Revenue Code.)

Lines A and B. If the child's parents were married to each other and filed a joint return, enter the name and social security number (SSN) of the parent who is listed first on the joint return. For example, if the father's name is listed first on the return and his SSN is entered in the block labeled "Your social security number," enter his name on line A and his SSN on line B.

If the parents were married but filed separate returns, enter the name and SSN of the parent who had the **higher** taxable income. If you do not know which parent had the higher taxable income, see Pub. 929.

If the parents were unmarried, treated as unmarried for Federal income tax purposes, or separated either by a divorce or separate maintenance decree, enter the name and SSN of the parent who had custody of the child for most of the year (the custodial parent).

Exception. If the custodial parent remarried and filed a joint return with his or her new spouse, enter the name and SSN of the person listed first on the joint return, even if that person is not the child's parent. If the custodial parent and his or her new spouse filed separate returns, enter the name and SSN of the person with the **higher** taxable income, even if that person is not the child's parent.

Note: *If the parents were unmarried but lived together during the year with the child, enter the name and SSN of the parent who had the **higher** taxable income.*

Line 1. If the child had no earned income (defined below), enter the child's adjusted gross income from Form 1040, line 32; Form 1040A, line 17; or Form 1040NR, line 31.

If the child had earned income, use the following worksheet to figure the amount to enter on line 1. But if the child files **Form 2555,** Foreign Earned Income, or **Form 2555-EZ,** Foreign Earned Income Exclusion, has a net loss from self-employment, or claims a net operating loss deduction, **do not** use the worksheet below. Instead, use the worksheet in Pub. 929 to figure the amount to enter on line 1.

Worksheet (keep a copy for your records)

1. Enter the amount from the child's Form 1040, line 23; Form 1040A, line 14; or Form 1040NR, line 23, whichever applies . . . ______
2. Enter the child's **earned income** (defined below) plus any deduction the child claims on Form 1040, line 28, or Form 1040NR, line 27, whichever applies ______
3. Subtract line 2 from line 1. Enter the result here and on Form 8615, line 1 . . ______

Earned income includes wages, tips, and other payments received for personal services performed. Generally, earned income is the total of the amounts reported on Form 1040, lines 7, 12, and 19; Form 1040A, line 7; or Form 1040NR, lines 8, 13, and 20.

Line 2. If the child itemized deductions, enter on line 2 the **greater** of:

- $600 plus the portion of the amount on Schedule A (Form 1040), line 26, or Schedule A (Form 1040NR), line 10, that is directly connected with the production of the investment income on Form 8615, line 1; **OR**
- $1,200.

Line 6. If the parent's taxable income is less than zero, enter zero on line 6. If the parent filed a joint return, enter the taxable income shown on that return even if the parent's spouse is not the child's parent. If the parent transferred property to a trust which sold or exchanged the property during the year at a gain, include any gain that was taxed to the trust under section 644 in the amount entered on line 6. Enter "Section 644" and the amount to the right of the line 6 entry. Also, see the instructions for line 10.

Line 7. If the individual identified as the parent on this Form 8615 is also identified as the parent on any other Form 8615, add the amounts, if any, from line 5 on each of the other Forms 8615 and enter the total on line 7.

Line 9. Figure the tax using the Tax Table, Tax Rate Schedules, or **Schedule D** (Form 1040), Capital Gains and Losses, whichever applies. If any net capital gain is included on lines 5, 6, and/or 7, the tax on the amount on line 8 may be less if Part IV of Schedule D can be used to figure the tax. See Pub. 929 for details on how to figure the net capital gain included on line 8 and how to complete Schedule D. Schedule D should be used to figure the tax if:

the parent's filing status is	**AND**	**the amount on Form 8615, line 8, is over:**
• Single		$51,900
• Married filing jointly or Qualifying widow(er)		$86,500
• Married filing separately		$43,250
• Head of household		$74,150

If Schedule D is used to figure the tax, enter on Form 8615, line 9, the amount from line 29 of that Schedule D. Also, enter the amount from line 22 of that Schedule D in the space next to line 9.

Line 10. If the parent filed a joint return, enter the tax shown on that return even if the parent's spouse is not the child's parent.

If line 6 includes any gain taxed to a trust under section 644, add the tax imposed under section 644(a)(2)(A) to the tax shown on the parent's return. Enter the total on line 10 instead of the tax from the parent's return. Also, enter "Section 644" to the right of the line 10 entry.

Line 15. Figure the tax using the Tax Table, Tax Rate Schedule X, or Schedule D, whichever applies. If line 14 is more than $51,900 and includes any net capital gain, the tax may be less if Schedule D is used to figure the tax. See Pub. 929 for details on how to figure the net capital gain included on line 14 and how to complete Part IV of Schedule D.

Line 17. Figure the tax as if these rules did not apply. For example, if the child files Schedule D and can use Part IV to figure his or her tax, complete Part IV on the child's actual Schedule D.

* U.S. GPO:1992-315-406

Form **8829** Department of the Treasury Internal Revenue Service (T)

Expenses for Business Use of Your Home

▶ File with Schedule C (Form 1040). Use a separate Form 8829 for each home you used for business during the year.

▶ See instructions on back.

OMB No. 1545-1266

1992

Attachment Sequence No. 66

Name(s) of proprietor(s) | Your social security number

Part I Part of Your Home Used for Business

1	Area used exclusively for business (see instructions). Include area that does not meet exclusive use test and either used for inventory storage or regularly used as part of a day-care facility	1	
2	Total area of home	2	
3	Divide line 1 by line 2. Enter the result as a percentage	3	%
	• **For day-care facilities not used exclusively for business, also complete lines 4–6.**		
	• **All others, skip lines 4–6 and enter the amount from line 3 on line 7.**		
4	Multiply days used for day care during year by hours used per day — 4: hr.		
5	Total hours available for use during the year (366 days × 24 hours). See instructions — 5: 8,784 hr.		
6	Divide line 4 by line 5. Enter the result as a decimal amount — 6: .		
7	Business percentage. For day-care facilities not used exclusively for business, multiply line 6 by line 3 (enter the result as a percentage). All others, enter the amount from line 3 ▶	7	%

Part II Figure Your Allowable Deduction

			(a) Direct expenses	(b) Indirect expenses		
8	Enter the amount from Schedule C, line 29, **plus** any net gain or (loss) derived from the business use of your home and shown on Schedule D or Form 4797. If more than one place of business, see instructions				8	
	See instructions for columns (a) and (b) before completing lines 9–20.					
9	Casualty losses. See instructions	9				
10	Deductible mortgage interest. See instructions	10				
11	Real estate taxes. See instructions	11				
12	Add lines 9, 10, and 11	12				
13	Multiply line 12, column (b) by line 7		13			
14	Add line 12, column (a) and line 13				14	
15	Subtract line 14 from line 8. If zero or less, enter -0-				15	
16	Excess mortgage interest. See instructions	16				
17	Insurance	17				
18	Repairs and maintenance	18				
19	Utilities	19				
20	Other expenses. See instructions	20				
21	Add lines 16 through 20	21				
22	Multiply line 21, column (b) by line 7		22			
23	Carryover of operating expenses from 1991 Form 8829, line 41		23			
24	Add line 21 in column (a), line 22, and line 23				24	
25	Allowable operating expenses. Enter the **smaller** of line 15 or line 24				25	
26	Limit on excess casualty losses and depreciation. Subtract line 25 from line 15				26	
27	Excess casualty losses. See instructions		27			
28	Depreciation of your home from Part III below		28			
29	Carryover of excess casualty losses and depreciation from 1991 Form 8829, line 42		29			
30	Add lines 27 through 29				30	
31	Allowable excess casualty losses and depreciation. Enter the **smaller** of line 26 or line 30				31	
32	Add lines 14, 25, and 31				32	
33	Casualty loss portion, if any, from lines 14 and 31. Carry amount to **Form 4684,** Section B				33	
34	Allowable expenses for business use of your home. Subtract line 33 from line 32. Enter here and on Schedule C, line 30. If your home was used for more than one business, see instructions ▶				34	

Part III Depreciation of Your Home

35	Enter the **smaller** of your home's adjusted basis or its fair market value. See instructions	35	
36	Value of land included on line 35	36	
37	Basis of building. Subtract line 36 from line 35	37	
38	Business basis of building. Multiply line 37 by line 7	38	
39	Depreciation percentage. See instructions	39	%
40	Depreciation allowable. Multiply line 38 by line 39. Enter here and on line 28 above. See instructions	40	

Part IV Carryover of Unallowed Expenses to 1993

41	Operating expenses. Subtract line 25 from line 24. If less than zero, enter -0-	41	
42	Excess casualty losses and depreciation. Subtract line 31 from line 30. If less than zero, enter -0-	42	

General Instructions

Paperwork Reduction Act Notice.—We ask for the information on this form to carry out the Internal Revenue laws of the United States. You are required to give us the information. We need it to ensure that you are complying with these laws and to allow us to figure and collect the right amount of tax.

The time needed to complete and file this form will vary depending on individual circumstances. The estimated average time is: **Recordkeeping,** 52 min.; **Learning about the law or the form,** 7 min.; **Preparing the form,** 1 hr., 13 min.; and **Copying, assembling, and sending the form to the IRS,** 20 min.

If you have comments concerning the accuracy of these time estimates or suggestions for making this form more simple, we would be happy to hear from you. You can write to both the IRS and the Office of Management and Budget at the addresses listed in the instructions for Form 1040.

Purpose of Form.—Use Form 8829 to figure the allowable expenses for business use of your home on **Schedule C** (Form 1040) and any carryover to 1993 of amounts not deductible in 1992. If all of the expenses for business use of your home are properly allocable to inventory costs, do not complete Form 8829. Expenses properly includible in inventory are figured in Part III of Schedule C and not on Form 8829.

You must meet specific requirements to deduct expenses for the business use of your home. Even if you meet these requirements, your deductible expenses are limited. For details, get **Pub. 587,** Business Use of Your Home.

Note: *If you file **Schedule F** (Form 1040) or you are an employee, **do not** use this form. Instead, use the worksheet in Pub. 587.*

Who May Deduct Expenses for Business Use of a Home.—Generally, you may deduct business expenses that apply to a part of your home **only** if that part is exclusively used on a regular basis:

- As your principal place of business for any of your trades or businesses; or
- As a place of business used by your patients, clients, or customers to meet or deal with you in the normal course of your trade or business; or
- In connection with your trade or business if it is a separate structure that is not attached to your home.

Exception for storage of inventory.—You may also deduct expenses that apply to space within your home if it is the **only** fixed location of your trade or business. The space must be used on a regular basis to store inventory from your trade or business of selling products at retail or wholesale.

Exception for day-care facilities.—If you use space in your home on a regular basis in your trade or business of providing day care, you may be able to deduct the business expenses even though you use the same space for nonbusiness purposes.

Specific Instructions

Lines 1 and 2.—To determine the area on lines 1 and 2, you may use square feet or any other reasonable method if it accurately figures your business percentage on line 7.

Do not include on line 1 the area of your home you used to figure any expenses allocable to inventory costs. The business percentage of these expenses should have been taken into account in Part III of Schedule C.

Line 4.—Enter the total number of hours the facility was used for day care during the year.

Example. Your home is used Monday through Friday for 12 hours per day for 250 days during the year. It is also used on 50 Saturdays for 8 hours per day. Enter 3,400 hours on line 4 (3,000 hours for weekdays plus 400 hours for Saturdays).

Line 5.—If you started or stopped using your home for day care in 1992, you must prorate the number of hours based on the number of days the home was available for day care. Cross out the preprinted entry on line 5. Multiply 24 hours by the number of days available and enter the result.

Line 8.—If all of the gross income from your trade or business is from the business use of your home, enter on line 8 the amount from Schedule C, line 29, **plus** any net gain or (loss) derived from the business use of your home and shown on Schedule D or Form 4797. If you file more than one Form 8829, include only the income earned and the deductions attributable to that income during the period you owned the home for which Part I was completed.

If part of the income is from a place of business other than your home, you must first determine the part of your gross income (Schedule C, line 7, and gains from Schedule D and Form 4797) from the business use of your home. In making this determination, consider the amount of time you spend at each location as well as other facts. After determining the part of your gross income from the business use of your home, subtract from that amount the **total expenses** shown on Schedule C, line 28, plus any losses from your business shown on Schedule D or Form 4797. Enter the result on line 8 of Form 8829.

Columns (a) and (b).—Enter as direct or indirect expenses only expenses for the business use of your home (i.e., expenses allowable only because your home is used for business). Other expenses not allocable to the business use of your home such as salaries, supplies, and business telephone expenses, are deductible elsewhere on Schedule C and should not be entered on Form 8829.

Direct expenses benefit only the business part of your home. They include painting or repairs made to the specific area or room used for business. Enter 100% of your direct expenses on the appropriate expense line in column (a).

Indirect expenses are for keeping up and running your entire home. They benefit both the business and personal parts of your home. Generally, enter 100% of your indirect expenses on the appropriate expense line in column (b).

Exception: If the business percentage of an indirect expense is different from the percentage on line 7, enter only the business part of the expense on the appropriate line in column (a), and leave that line in column (b) blank. For example, your electric bill is $800 for lighting, cooking, laundry, and television. If you reasonably estimate $300 of your electric bill is for lighting and you use 10% of your home for business, enter $30 on line 19 in column (a). **Do not** make an entry on line 19 in column (b) for any part of your electric bill.

Lines 9, 10, and 11.—Enter only the amounts that would be deductible whether or not you used your home for business (i.e., amounts allowable as itemized deductions on **Schedule A** (Form 1040)).

Treat **casualty losses** as personal expenses for this step. Figure the amount to enter on line 9 by completing Form 4684, Section A. When figuring line 17, enter 10% of your adjusted gross income excluding the gross income from business use of your home and the deductions attributable to that income. Include on line 9 of Form 8829 the amount from Form 4684, line 18. See line 27 to deduct part of the casualty losses not allowed because of the limits on Form 4684.

Do not file or use that Form 4684 to figure the amount of casualty losses to deduct on Schedule A. Instead, complete a separate Form 4684 to deduct the personal portion of your casualty losses.

On line 10, include only **mortgage interest** that would be deductible on Schedule A and that qualifies as a direct or indirect expense. **Do not** include interest on a mortgage loan that did not benefit your home (e.g., a home equity loan used to pay off credit card bills, to buy a car, or to pay tuition costs).

If you itemized your deductions, be sure to claim **only** the personal portion of your deductible mortgage interest and real estate taxes on Schedule A. For example, if your business percentage on line 7 is 30%, you can claim 70% of your deductible mortgage interest and real estate taxes on Schedule A.

Line 16.—If the amount of home mortgage interest you deduct on Schedule A is limited, enter the part of the excess mortgage interest that qualifies as a direct or indirect expense. Do not include mortgage interest on a loan that did not benefit your home (explained above).

Line 20.—If you rent rather than own your home, include the rent you paid on line 20, column (b).

Line 27.—Multiply your casualty losses in excess of the amount on line 9 by the business percentage of those losses and enter the result.

Line 34.—If your home was used in more than one business, allocate the amount shown on line 34 to each business using any method that is reasonable under the circumstances. For each business, enter on Schedule C, line 30, only the amount allocated to that business.

Lines 35 through 37.—Enter on line 35 the cost or other basis of your home, or if less, the fair market value of your home on the date you first used the home for business. **Do not** adjust this amount for depreciation claimed or changes in fair market value after the year you first used your home for business. Allocate this amount between land and building values on lines 36 and 37.

Show on an attached schedule the cost or other basis of additions and improvements placed in service after you began to use your home for business. Do not include any amounts on lines 35 through 38 for these expenditures. Instead, see the instructions for line 40.

Line 39.—If you first used your home for business in 1992, enter the percentage for the month you first used it for business.

Jan.	3.042%	**May**	1.984%	**Sept.**	0.926%
Feb.	2.778%	**June**	1.720%	**Oct.**	0.661%
March	2.513%	**July**	1.455%	**Nov.**	0.397%
April	2.249%	**Aug.**	1.190%	**Dec.**	0.132%

If you first used your home for business before 1992 and after 1986, enter 3.175%. If the business use began before 1987 or you stopped using your home for business before the end of the year, see **Pub. 534,** Depreciation, for the percentage to enter.

Line 40.—Include on line 40 depreciation on additions and improvements placed in service after you began using your home for business. See Pub. 534 to figure the amount of depreciation allowed on these expenditures. Attach a schedule showing how you figured depreciation on any additions or improvements. Write "See attached" below the entry space.

Complete and attach **Form 4562,** Depreciation and Amortization, if you first used your home for business in 1992 or you are depreciating additions or improvements placed in service in 1992. If you first used your home for business in 1992, enter on Form 4562, in column (c) of line 14h, the amount from line 38 of Form 8829. Then enter on Form 4562, in column (g) of line 14h, the amount from line 40 of Form 8829 (but **do not** include it on Schedule C, line 13).

APPENDIX

GLOSSARY OF TAX TERMS

The words and phrases in this glossary have been defined to reflect their conventional use in the field of taxation. The definitions may therefore be incomplete for other purposes.

A

Accelerated cost recovery system (ACRS). A method in which the cost of tangible property is recovered over a prescribed period of time. Enacted by the Economic Recovery Tax Act (ERTA) of 1981 and substantially modified by the Tax Reform Act (TRA) of 1986 (the modified system is referred to as MACRS), the approach disregards salvage value, imposes a period of cost recovery that depends upon the classification of the asset into one of various recovery periods, and prescribes the applicable percentage of cost that can be deducted each year. § 168.

Accelerated depreciation. Various methods of depreciation that yield larger deductions in the earlier years of the life of an asset than the straight-line method. Examples include the double declining-balance and the sum-of-the-years' digits methods of depreciation.

Accounting method. The method under which income and expenses are determined for tax purposes. Important accounting methods include the cash basis and the accrual basis. Special methods are available for the reporting of gain on installment sales, recognition of income on construction projects (the completed contract and percentage of completion methods), and the valuation of inventories (last-in, first-out and first-in, first-out). §§ 446–474. See also *accrual basis, cash basis, completed contract method, percentage of completion method.*

Accounting period. The period of time, usually a year, used by a taxpayer for the determination of tax liability. Unless a fiscal year is chosen, taxpayers must determine and pay their income tax liability by using the calendar year (January 1 through December 31) as the period of measurement. An example of a fiscal year is July 1 through June 30. A change in accounting period (e.g., from a calendar year to a fiscal year) generally requires the consent of the IRS. Some new taxpayers, such as a newly formed corporation, are free to select either an initial calendar or fiscal year without the consent of the IRS. §§ 441–444. See also *annual accounting period concept.*

Accrual basis. A method of accounting that reflects expenses incurred and income earned for any one tax year. In contrast to the cash basis of accounting, expenses do not have to be paid to be deductible, nor does income have to be received to be taxable. Unearned income (e.g., prepaid interest and rent) generally is taxed in the year of receipt regardless of the method of accounting used by the taxpayer. § 446(c)(2). See also *accounting method, cash basis,* and *unearned income.*

Accumulated adjustments account. An account that comprises an S corporation's post-1982 income, loss, and deductions for the tax year (including nontaxable income and nondeductible losses and expenses). After the year-end income and expense adjustments are made, the account is reduced by distributions made during the tax year.

Accumulated earnings credit. A reduction allowed in arriving at accumulated taxable income in determining the accumulated earnings tax. See also *accumulated earnings tax* and *accumulated taxable income.*

Accumulated earnings tax. A special tax imposed on corporations that accumulate (rather than distribute) their earnings beyond the reasonable needs of the business. The accumulated earnings tax and related interest are imposed on accumulated taxable income in addition to the corporate income tax. §§ 531–537.

Accumulated taxable income. The base upon which the accumulated earnings tax is imposed. Generally, it is the taxable income of the corporation as adjusted for certain items (e.g., the Federal income tax, excess charitable contributions, the dividends received deduction) less the dividends paid deduction and the accumulated earnings credit. § 535.

Accumulating trusts. See *discretionary trusts.*

Acquiescence. Agreement by the IRS on the results reached in most of the Regular decisions of the U.S. Tax Court; sometimes abbreviated *acq.* or *A.* See also *nonacquiescence.*

Acquisition. See *corporate acquisition.*

ACRS. See *accelerated cost recovery system.*

Ad valorem tax. A tax imposed on the value of property. The most common ad valorem tax is that imposed by states, counties, and cities on real estate. Ad valorem taxes can be imposed on personal property as well. See also *personalty.*

Adjusted basis. The cost or other basis of property reduced by depreciation allowed or allowable and increased by capital improvements. Other special adjustments are provided in § 1016 and the related Regulations. See also *basis.*

Adjusted current earnings (ACE) adjustment. An adjustment in computing corporate alternative minimum taxable income (AMTI), computed at 75 percent of the excess of adjusted current earnings and profits over AMTI. ACE computations reflect longer and slower cost recovery deductions and other restrictions on the timing of certain recognition events. Exempt interest, life insurance proceeds, and other receipts that are included in earnings and profits but not in taxable income also increase the ACE adjustment. See also *alternative minimum tax* and *earnings and profits.*

Adjusted gross estate. The gross estate of a decedent reduced by § 2053 expenses (e.g., administration, funeral) and § 2054 losses (e.g., casualty). The determination of the adjusted gross estate is necessary in testing for the extension of time for installment payment of estate taxes under § 6166. See also *gross estate.*

Adjusted gross income (AGI). A tax determination unique to individual taxpayers. Generally, it represents the gross income of an individual, less business expenses and less any appropriate capital gain or loss adjustment. See also *gross income.*

Adjusted ordinary gross income. A determination unique to the personal holding company tax imposed by § 541. In ascertaining whether a corporation is a personal holding company, personal holding company income divided by adjusted ordinary gross income must equal 60 percent or more. Adjusted ordinary gross income is the corporation's gross income less capital gains, § 1231 gains, and certain expenses. § 543(b)(2). See also *personal holding company income.*

Adjusted taxable estate. The taxable estate reduced by $60,000. The adjusted taxable estate is utilized in applying § 2011 for determining the limit on the credit for state death taxes paid that will be allowed against the Federal estate tax. See also *taxable estate.*

Administration. The supervision and winding up of an estate. The administration of an estate runs from the date of an individual's death until all assets have been distributed and liabilities paid.

Administrator. A person appointed by the court to administer (manage or take charge of) the assets and liabilities of a decedent (the deceased). The person may be a male (administrator) or a female (administratrix). See also *executor.*

AFTR. Published by Research Institute of America (formerly by Prentice-Hall), *American Federal Tax Reports* contain all of the Federal tax decisions issued by the U.S. District Courts, U.S. Court of Federal Claims, U.S. Courts of Appeals, and the U.S. Supreme Court.

AFTR2d. The second series of the *American Federal Tax Reports,* dealing with 1954 and 1986 Code case law.

Alimony. Alimony deductions result from the payment of a legal obligation arising from the termination of a marital relationship. Payments designated as alimony generally are included in the gross income of the recipient and are deductible *for* AGI by the payer.

Allocable share of income. Certain entities receive conduit treatment under the Federal income tax law. This means the earned income or loss is not taxed to the entity, but is allocated to the owners or beneficiaries, regardless of the magnitude or timing of corresponding distributions. The portion of the entity's income that is taxed to the owner or beneficiary is the allocable share of the entity's income or loss for the period. The allocations are determined by (1) the partnership agreement for partners, (2) a weighted-average stock ownership computation for shareholders of an S corporation, and (3) the controlling will or trust instrument for the beneficiaries of an estate or trust.

Allocation. The assignment of income for various tax purposes. The income and expense items of an estate or trust are allocated between income and corpus components. Specific items of income, expense, gain, loss, and credit can be allocated to specific partners or shareholders in an S corporation, if a substantial economic nontax purpose for the allocation is established. See also *apportionment* and *substantial economic effect.*

Alternate valuation date. Property passing from a person by death may be valued for death tax purposes as of the date of death or the alternate valuation date. The alternate valuation date is six months from the date of death or the date the property is disposed of by the estate, whichever comes first. To use the alternate valuation date, the executor or administrator of the estate must make an affirmative election. The election of the alternate valuation date is not available unless it decreases the amount of the gross estate *and* reduces the estate tax liability.

Alternative minimum tax (AMT). The AMT is a fixed percentage of alternative minimum taxable income (AMTI). AMTI generally starts with the taxpayer's adjusted gross income (for individuals) or taxable income (for other taxpayers). To this amount, the taxpayer (1) adds designated preference items (e.g., the appreciation on charitable contribution property), (2) makes other specified adjustments (e.g., to reflect a longer, straight-line cost recovery deduction), (3) subtracts certain AMT itemized deductions for individuals (e.g., interest incurred on housing but not taxes paid), and (4) subtracts an exemption amount (e.g., $40,000 on an individual joint return). The taxpayer must pay the greater of the resulting AMT (reduced by only the foreign tax credit) or the regular income tax (reduced by all allowable tax credits).

Amortization. The tax deduction for the cost or other basis of an intangible asset over the asset's estimated useful life. Examples of amortizable intangibles include patents, copyrights, and leasehold interests. The intangible goodwill cannot be amortized for income tax purposes because it possesses no estimated useful life. For tangible assets, see *depreciation.* For natural resources, see *depletion.* See also *estimated useful life* and *goodwill.*

Amount realized. The amount received by a taxpayer upon the sale or exchange of property. Amount realized is the sum of the cash and the fair market value of any property or services received by the taxpayer, plus any related debt assumed by the buyer. Determining the amount realized is the starting point for arriving at realized gain or loss. § 1001(b). See also *realized gain or loss* and *recognized gain or loss.*

Annual accounting period concept. In determining a taxpayer's income tax liability, only transactions taking place during a specified tax year are taken into consideration. For reporting and payment purposes, therefore, the tax life of taxpayers is divided into equal annual accounting periods. See also *accounting period* and *mitigation of the annual accounting period concept.*

Annual exclusion. In computing the taxable gifts for any one year, each donor may exclude the first $10,000 of a gift to each donee. Usually, the annual exclusion is not available for gifts of future interests. § 2503(b). See also *gift splitting* and *future interest.*

Annuitant. The party entitled to receive payments from an annuity contract. See also *annuity.*

Annuity. A fixed sum of money payable to a person at specified times for a specified period of time or for life. If the party making the payment (i.e., the obligor) is regularly engaged in this type of business (e.g., an insurance company), the arrangement is classified as a commercial annuity. A private annuity involves an obligor that is not regularly engaged in selling annuities (e.g., a charity or family member).

Anticipatory assignment of income. See *assignment of income.*

Appellate court. For Federal tax purposes, appellate courts include the Courts of Appeals and the Supreme Court. If the party losing in the trial (or lower) court is dissatisfied with the result, the dispute may be carried to the appropriate appellate court. See also *Court of Appeals* and *trial court.*

Arm's length. The standard under which unrelated parties would carry out a particular transaction. Suppose, for example, Cardinal Corporation sells property to its sole shareholder for $10,000. In determining whether $10,000 is an arm's length price, one would ascertain the amount for which the corporation could have sold the property to a disinterested third party.

Articles of incorporation. The legal document specifying a corporation's name, period of existence, purpose and powers, authorized number of shares, classes of stock, and other conditions for operation. The organizers of the corporation file the articles with the state of incorporation. If the articles are satisfactory and other conditions of the law are satisfied, the state will issue a charter recognizing the organization's status as a corporation.

Assessment. The process whereby the IRS imposes an additional tax liability. If, for example, the IRS audits a taxpayer's income tax return and finds gross income understated or deductions overstated, it will assess a deficiency in the amount of the tax that should have been paid in light of the adjustments made. See also *deficiency.*

Assignment of income. A procedure whereby a taxpayer attempts to avoid the recognition of income by assigning to another the property that generates the income. Such a procedure will not avoid the recognition of income by the taxpayer making the assignment if it can be said that the income was earned at the point of the transfer. In this case, usually referred to as an anticipatory assignment of income, the income will be taxed to the person who earns it.

Association. An organization treated as a corporation for Federal tax purposes even though it may not qualify as such under applicable state law. An entity designated as a trust or a partnership, for example, may be classified as an association if it clearly possesses corporate attributes. Corporate attributes include centralized management, continuity of life, free transferability of interests, and limited liability. § 7701(a)(3).

At-risk amount. A taxpayer has an amount at risk in a business or investment venture to the extent that personal assets have been subjected to the risks of the business. Typically, the taxpayer's at-risk amount includes (1) the amount of money or other property that the investor contributed to the venture for the investment, (2) the amount of any of the entity's liabilities for which the taxpayer personally is liable and that relate to the investment, and (3) an allocable share of nonrecourse debts incurred by the venture from third parties in arm's length transactions for real estate investments.

At-risk limitation. Generally, a taxpayer can deduct losses related to a trade or business, S corporation, partnership, or investment asset only to the extent of the at-risk amount.

Attribution. Under certain circumstances, the tax law applies attribution rules to assign to one taxpayer the ownership interest of another taxpayer. If, for example, the stock of Gold Corporation is held 60 percent by Marsha and 40 percent by Sidney, Marsha may be deemed to own 100 percent of Gold Corporation if Marsha and Sidney are mother and son. In that case, the stock owned by Sidney is attributed to Marsha. Stated differently, Marsha has a 60 percent direct and a 40 percent indirect interest in Gold Corporation. It can also be said that Marsha is the constructive owner of Sidney's interest.

Audit. Inspection and verification of a taxpayer's return or other transactions possessing tax consequences. See also *correspondence audit, field audit,* and *office audit.*

Automobile expenses. Automobile expenses are generally deductible only to the extent the automobile is used in business or for the production of income. Personal commuting expenses are not deductible. The taxpayer may deduct actual expenses (including depreciation and insurance), or the standard (automatic) mileage rate may be used (27.5 cents per mile for 1991, 28 cents per mile for 1992, and 28 cents per mile for 1993) during any one year. Automobile expenses incurred for medical purposes or in connection with job-related moving expenses are deductible to the extent of actual out-of-pocket expenses or at the rate of 9 cents per mile (12 cents for charitable activities).

B

Bailout. Various procedures whereby the owners of an entity can obtain the entity's profits with favorable tax consequences. With corporations, for example, the bailout of corporate profits without dividend consequences might be the desired objective. The alternative of distributing the profits to the shareholders as dividends generally is less attractive since dividend payments are not deductible. See also *preferred stock bailout.*

Bargain sale or purchase. A sale or purchase of property for less than fair market value. The difference between the sale or purchase price and the fair market value of the property may have tax consequences. If, for example, a corporation sells property worth $1,000 to one of its shareholders for $700, the $300 difference probably represents a constructive dividend to the shareholder. Suppose, instead, the shareholder sells the property (worth $1,000) to his or her corporation for $700. The $300 difference probably represents a contribution by the shareholder to the corporation's capital. Bargain sales and purchases among members of the same family may lead to gift tax consequences. See also *constructive dividends.*

Basis. The acquisition cost assigned to an asset for income tax purposes. For assets acquired by purchase, basis is cost (§ 1012). Special rules govern the basis of property received by virtue of another's death (§ 1014) or by gift (§ 1015), the basis of stock received on a transfer of property to a controlled corporation (§ 358), the basis of the property transferred to the corporation (§ 362), and the basis of property received upon the liquidation of a corporation (§ 334). See also *adjusted basis.*

Beneficiary. A party who will benefit from a transfer of property or other arrangement. Examples include the beneficiary of a trust, the beneficiary of a life insurance policy, and the beneficiary of an estate.

Bequest. A transfer of personal property by will. To bequeath is to leave such property by will. See also *devise* and *personal property.*

Blockage rule. A factor to be considered in valuing a large block of stock. Application of this rule generally justifies a discount in the fair market value since the disposition of a large amount of stock at any one time may depress the value of the shares in the market place.

Bona fide. In good faith, or real. In tax law, this term is often used in connection with a business purpose for carrying out a transaction. Thus, was there a bona fide business purpose for a shareholder's transfer of a liability to a controlled corporation? § 357(b)(1)(B). See also *business purpose.*

Book value. The net amount of an asset after reduction by a related reserve. The book value of machinery, for example, is the amount of the machinery less the reserve for depreciation.

Boot. Cash or property of a type not included in the definition of a nontaxable exchange. The receipt of boot will cause an otherwise nontaxable transfer to become taxable to the extent of the lesser of the fair market value of the boot or the realized gain on the transfer. For example, see transfers to controlled corporations under § 351(b) and like-kind exchanges under § 1031(b). See also *like-kind exchange* and *realized gain or loss.*

Bribes and illegal payments. Section 162 denies a deduction for bribes or kickbacks, fines and penalties paid to a government official or employee for violation of law, and two-thirds of the treble damage payments made to claimants for violation of the antitrust law. Denial of a deduction for bribes and illegal payments is based upon the judicially established principle that allowing such payments would be contrary to public policy.

Brother-sister corporations. More than one corporation owned by the same shareholders. If, for example, Chris and Pat each own one-half of the stock in Wren Corporation and Redbird Corporation, Wren and Redbird are brother-sister corporations.

B.T.A. The Board of Tax Appeals was a trial court that considered Federal tax matters. This Court is now the U.S. Tax Court.

Built-in gains tax. A penalty tax designed to discourage a shift of the incidence of taxation on unrealized gains from a C corporation to its shareholders, via an S election. Under this provision, any recognized gain during the first 10 years of S status generates a corporate-level tax on a base not to exceed the aggregate untaxed built-in gains brought into the S corporation upon its election from C corporation taxable years.

Burden of proof. The requirement in a lawsuit to show the weight of evidence and thereby gain a favorable decision. Except in cases of tax fraud, the burden of proof in a tax case generally is on the taxpayer. See also *fraud.*

Business bad debts. A tax deduction allowed for obligations obtained in connection with a trade or business that have become either partially or completely worthless. In contrast to nonbusiness bad debts, business bad debts are deductible as business expenses. § 166. See also *nonbusiness bad debts.*

Business purpose. A justifiable business reason for carrying out a transaction. It has long been established that mere tax avoidance is not an acceptable business purpose. The presence of a business purpose is crucial in the area of corporate reorganizations and certain liquidations. See also *bona fide.*

Buy-sell agreement. An arrangement, particularly appropriate in the case of a closely held corporation or a partnership, whereby the surviving owners (shareholders or partners) or the entity agrees to purchase the interest of a withdrawing owner. The buy-sell agreement provides for an orderly disposition of an interest in a business and may aid in setting the value of the interest for death tax purposes. See also *cross-purchase buy-sell agreement* and *entity buy-sell agreement.*

C

Calendar year. See *accounting period.*

Capital asset. Broadly speaking, all assets are capital except those specifically excluded by the Code. Major categories of noncapital assets include property held for resale in the normal course of business (inventory), trade accounts and notes receivable, and depreciable property and real estate used in a trade or business (§ 1231 assets). § 1221. See also *capital gain* and *capital loss.*

Capital contribution. Various means by which a shareholder makes additional funds available to the corporation (placed at the risk of the business) without the receipt of additional stock. The contributions are added to the basis of the shareholder's existing stock investment and do not generate income to the corporation. § 118.

Capital expenditure. An expenditure that should be added to the basis of the property improved. For income tax purposes, this generally precludes a full deduction for the expenditure in the year paid or incurred. Any cost recovery in the form of a tax deduction comes in the form of depreciation, depletion, or amortization. § 263.

Capital gain. The gain from the sale or exchange of a capital asset. See also *capital asset.*

Capital loss. The loss from the sale or exchange of a capital asset. See also *capital asset.*

Capital stock tax. A state-level tax, usually imposed on out-of-state corporations for the privilege of doing business in the state. The tax may be based on the entity's apportionable income or payroll, or on its apportioned net worth as of a specified date.

Cash basis. A method of accounting that reflects deductions as paid and income as received in any one tax year. However, deductions for prepaid expenses that benefit more than one tax year (e.g., prepaid rent and prepaid interest) usually must be spread over the period benefited rather than deducted in the year paid. § 446(c)(1). See also *constructive receipt of income.*

Cash surrender value. The amount of money that an insurance policy would yield if cashed in with the insurance company that issued the policy.

CCH. Commerce Clearing House (CCH) is the publisher of a tax service and of Federal tax decisions (USTC series).

C corporation. A regular corporation governed by Subchapter C of the Code. Distinguished from S corporations, which fall under Subchapter S of the Code.

Centralized management. A concentration of authority among certain persons who may make independent business decisions on behalf of the entity without the need for continuing approval by the owners of the entity. It is a characteristic of a corporation since day-to-day business operations are handled by appointed officers and not by the shareholders. Reg. § 301.7701–2(c). See also *association.*

Cert. den. By denying the Writ of Certiorari, the U.S. Supreme Court refuses to accept an appeal from a U.S. Court of Appeals. The denial of certiorari does not, however, mean that the U.S. Supreme Court agrees with the result reached by the lower court. See also *certiorari.*

Certiorari. Appeal from a U.S. Court of Appeals to the U.S. Supreme Court is by Writ of Certiorari. The Supreme Court need not accept the appeal and usually does not (*cert. den.*), unless a conflict exists among the lower courts that must be resolved or a constitutional issue is involved. See also *cert. den.*

Cf. Compare.

Charitable contributions. Contributions are deductible (subject to various restrictions and ceiling limitations) if made to qualified nonprofit charitable organizations. A cash basis taxpayer is entitled to a deduction solely in the year of payment. Accrual basis corporations may accrue contributions at year-end if payment is properly authorized before the end of the year and payment is made within two and one-half months after the end of the year. § 170.

Civil fraud. See *fraud.*

Claims Court. A trial court (court of original jurisdiction) that decides litigation involving Federal tax matters. Now known as the U.S. Court of Federal Claims, appeal from this court is to the Court of Appeals for the Federal Circuit.

Closely held corporation. A corporation where the stock ownership is not widely dispersed. Rather, a few shareholders are in control of corporate policy and are in a position to benefit personally from that policy.

Collapsing. To disregard a transaction or one of a series of steps leading to a result. See also *step-transaction approach, substance vs. form concept,* and *telescoping.*

Common law state. See *community property.*

Community property. Louisiana, Texas, New Mexico, Arizona, California, Washington, Idaho, Nevada, and Wisconsin have community property systems. The rest of the states are common law property jurisdictions. The difference between common law and community property systems centers around the property rights possessed by married persons. In a common law system, each spouse owns whatever he or she earns. Under a community property system, one-half of the earnings of each spouse is considered owned by the other spouse. Assume, for example, Jeff and Alice are husband and wife and their only income is the $50,000 annual salary Jeff receives. If they live in New York (a common law state), the $50,000 salary belongs to Jeff. If, however, they live in Texas (a community property state), the $50,000 salary is owned one-half each by Jeff and Alice. See also *separate property.*

Completed contract method. A method of reporting gain or loss on certain long-term contracts. Under this method of accounting, gross income and expenses are recognized in the tax year in which the contract is completed. Reg. § 1.451–3. See also *percentage of completion method.*

Complex trusts. Complex trusts are those that are not simple trusts. Such trusts may have charitable beneficiaries, accumulate income, and distribute corpus. §§ 661–663. See also *simple trusts.*

Component depreciation. The process of dividing an asset (e.g., a building) into separate components or parts for the purpose of calculating depreciation. The advantage of dividing an asset into components is to use shorter depreciation lives for selected components under § 167. Generally, the same cost recovery period must be used for all the components of an asset under § 168.

Concur. To agree with the result reached by another, but not necessarily with the reasoning or the logic used in reaching the result. For example, Judge Ricks agrees with Judges Stone and Talent (all being members of the same court) that the income is taxable but for a different reason. Judge Ricks would issue a concurring opinion to the majority opinion issued by Judges Stone and Talent.

Condemnation. The taking of property by a public authority. The taking is by legal action, and the owner of the property is compensated by the public authority.

Conduit concept. An approach assumed by the tax law in the treatment of certain entities and their owners. The approach permits specified tax characteristics to pass through the entity without losing their identity. Under the conduit concept, for example, long-term capital losses realized by a partnership are passed through as such to the individual partners. Varying forms of the conduit concept are applicable for partnerships, trusts, estates, and S corporations.

Consent dividends. For purposes of avoiding or reducing the penalty tax on the unreasonable accumulation of earnings or the personal holding company tax, a corporation may declare a consent dividend. In a consent dividend, no cash or property is distributed to the shareholders, although the corporation obtains a dividends paid deduction. The consent dividend is taxed to the shareholders and increases the basis in their stock investment. § 565.

Consolidated returns. A procedure whereby certain affiliated corporations may file a single return, combine the tax transactions of each corporation, and arrive at a single income tax liability for the group. The election to file a consolidated return is usually binding on future years. See §§ 1501–1505 and the related Regulations.

Consolidation. The combination of two or more corporations into a newly created corporation. Thus, White Corporation and Black Corporation combine to form Gray Corporation. A consolidation may qualify as a nontaxable reorganization if certain conditions are satisfied. §§ 354 and 368(a)(1)(A).

Constructive dividends. A taxable benefit derived by a shareholder from his or her corporation that is not actually called a dividend. Examples include unreasonable compensation, excessive rent payments, bargain purchases of corporate property, and shareholder use of corporate property. Constructive dividends generally are a problem limited to closely held corporations. See also *bargain sale or purchase, closely held corporation,* and *unreasonable compensation.*

Constructive ownership. See *attribution.*

Constructive receipt of income. If income is unqualifiedly available although not physically in the taxpayer's possession, it is subject to the income tax. An example is accrued interest on a savings account. Under the constructive receipt of income concept, the interest is taxed to a depositor in the year available, rather than the year actually withdrawn. The fact that the depositor uses the cash basis of accounting for tax purposes is irrelevant. See Reg. § 1.451–2. See also *cash basis.*

Continuity of life or existence. The death or other withdrawal of an owner of an entity does not terminate the existence of the entity. This is a characteristic of a corporation since the death or withdrawal of a shareholder does not affect the corporation's existence. Reg. § 301.7701–2(b). See also *association.*

Contributions to the capital of a corporation. See *capital contribution.*

Contributory qualified pension or profit sharing plan. A plan funded with both employer and employee contributions. Since the employee's contributions to the plan are subject to income tax, a later distribution of the contributions to the employee generally is tax-free. See also *qualified pension or profit sharing plan.*

Controlled foreign corporation. Any foreign corporation in which more than 50 percent of the total combined voting power of all classes of stock entitled to vote or the total value of the stock of the corporation is owned by "U.S. shareholders" on any day during the taxable year of the foreign corporation. For purposes of this definition, a U.S. shareholder is any U.S. person who owns, or is considered as owning, 10 percent or more of the total combined voting power of all classes of voting stock of the foreign corporation. Stock owned directly, indirectly, and constructively is used in this measure.

Controlled group. A controlled group of corporations is required to share the lower-level corporate tax rates and various other tax benefits among the members of the group. A controlled group may be either a brother-sister or a parent-subsidiary group.

Corporate acquisition. The takeover of one corporation by another if both parties retain their legal existence after the transaction. An acquisition can be effected via a stock purchase or through a tax-free exchange of stock. See also *corporate reorganization* and *merger.*

Corporate liquidation. Occurs when a corporation distributes its net assets to its shareholders and ceases to be a going-concern. Generally, a shareholder recognizes capital gain or loss upon the liquidation of the entity regardless of the corporation's balance in its earnings and profits account. However, the distributing corporation recognizes gain and loss on assets that it distributes to shareholders in kind.

Corporate reorganization. Occurs, among other instances, when one corporation acquires another in a merger or acquisition, a single corporation divides into two or more entities, a corporation makes a substantial change in its capital structure, or a corporation undertakes a change in its legal name or domicile. The exchange of stock and other securities in a corporate reorganization can be effected favorably for tax purposes if certain statutory requirements are followed strictly. The tax consequences include the nonrecognition of any gain that is realized by the shareholders except to the extent of boot received. See also *corporate acquisition* and *merger.*

Corpus. The body or principal of a trust. Suppose, for example, Grant transfers an apartment building into a trust, income payable to Ruth for life, remainder to Shawn upon Ruth's death. Corpus of the trust is the apartment building.

Correspondence audit. An audit conducted by the IRS by mail. Typically, the IRS writes to the taxpayer requesting the verification of a particular deduction or exemption. The completion of a special form or the remittance of copies of records or other support is all that is requested of the taxpayer. See also *audit, field audit,* and *office audit.*

Court of Appeals. Any of 13 Federal courts that consider tax matters appealed from the U.S. Tax Court, a U.S. District Court, or the U.S. Court of Federal Claims. Appeal from a U.S. Court of Appeals is to the U.S. Supreme Court by Writ of Certiorari. See also *appellate court* and *trial court.*

Court of Federal Claims. See *Claims Court.*

Credit for prior transfers. The death tax credit for prior transfers applies when property is taxed in the estates of different decedents within a 10-year period. The credit is determined using a decreasing statutory percentage, with the magnitude of the credit decreasing as the length of time between the multiple deaths increases.

Criminal fraud. See *fraud.*

Cross-purchase buy-sell agreement. Under this type of arrangement, the surviving owners of the business agree to buy out the withdrawing owner. Assume, for example, Ruth and Sam are equal shareholders in Eagle Corporation. Under a cross-purchase buy-sell agreement, Ruth and Sam would contract to purchase the other's interest should that person decide to withdraw from the business. See also *buy-sell agreement* and *entity buy-sell agreement.*

Current earnings and profits. A corporate distribution is deemed to be first from the entity's current earnings and profits and then from accumulated earnings and profits. Shareholders recognize dividend income to the extent of the earnings and profits of the corporation. A dividend results to the extent of current earnings and profits, even if there is a larger negative balance in accumulated earnings and profits.

Current use valuation. See *special use value.*

Curtesy. A husband's right under state law to all or part of his wife's property upon her death. See also *dower.*

D

Death benefit. A payment made by an employer to the beneficiary or beneficiaries of a deceased employee on account of the death of the employee. Under certain conditions, the first $5,000 of the payment is exempt from the income tax. § 101(b)(1).

Death tax. A tax imposed on property transferred by the death of the owner. See also *credit for prior transfers, estate tax,* and *inheritance tax.*

Decedent. An individual who has died.

Deduction. The Federal income tax is not imposed upon gross income. Rather, it is imposed upon taxable income. Congressionally identified deductions are subtracted from gross income to arrive at the tax base, taxable income.

Deductions in respect of a decedent. Deductions accrued to the point of death but not recognizable on the final income tax return of a decedent because of the method of accounting used. Such items are allowed as deductions on the estate tax return and on the income tax return of the estate (Form 1041) or the heir (Form 1040). An example of a deduction in respect of a decedent is interest expense accrued up to the date of death by a cash basis debtor.

Deferred compensation. Compensation that will be taxed when received and not when earned. An example is contributions by an employer to a qualified pension or profit sharing plan on behalf of an employee. The contributions will not be taxed to the employee until they are distributed (e.g., upon retirement). See also *qualified pension or profit sharing plan.*

Deficiency. Additional tax liability owed by a taxpayer and assessed by the IRS. See also *assessment* and *statutory notice of deficiency.*

Deficiency dividends. Once the IRS has established a corporation's liability for the personal holding company tax in a prior year, the tax may be reduced or avoided by the issuance of a deficiency dividend under § 547. The deficiency dividend procedure is not available in cases where the deficiency was due to fraud with intent to evade tax or to a willful failure to file the appropriate tax return [§ 547(g)]. Nor does the deficiency dividend procedure avoid the usual penalties and interest applicable for failure to file a return or pay a tax.

Deficit. A negative balance in the earnings and profits account.

Demand loan. A loan payable upon request by the creditor, rather than on a specific date.

Dependency deduction. See *personal and dependency exemptions.*

Depletion. The process by which the cost or other basis of a natural resource (e.g., an oil or gas interest) is recovered upon extraction and sale of the resource. The two ways to determine the depletion allowance are the cost and percentage (or statutory) methods. Under the cost method, each unit of production sold is assigned a portion of the cost or other basis of the interest. This is determined by dividing the cost or other basis by the total units expected to be recovered. Under the percentage (or statutory) method, the tax law provides a special percentage factor for different types of minerals and other natural resources. This percentage is multiplied by the gross income from the interest to arrive at the depletion allowance. §§ 613 and 613A.

Depreciation. The deduction for the cost or other basis of a tangible asset over the asset's estimated useful life. For intangible assets, see *amortization.* For natural resources, see *depletion.* See also *estimated useful life.*

Depreciation recapture. Upon the disposition of depreciable property used in a trade or business, gain or loss is measured by the difference between the consideration received (the amount realized) and the adjusted basis of the property. The gain recognized could be § 1231 gain and qualify for long-term capital gain treatment. The recapture provisions of the Code (e.g., §§ 219, 1245, and 1250) may operate to convert some or all of the § 1231 gain into ordinary income. The justification for depreciation recapture is that it prevents a taxpayer from converting a dollar of ordinary deduction (in the form of depreciation) into deferred tax-favored income (§ 1231 or long-term capital gain). The depreciation recapture rules do not apply when the property is disposed of at a loss or via a gift. See also *Section 1231 gains and losses.*

Determination letter. Upon the request of a taxpayer, an IRS District Director will comment on the tax status of a completed transaction. Determination letters are frequently used to clarify employee status, determine whether a retirement or profit sharing plan qualifies under the Code, and determine the tax-exempt status of certain nonprofit organizations.

Devise. A transfer of real estate by will. See also *bequest.*

Disabled access credit. A tax credit whose purpose is to encourage small businesses to make their businesses more accessible to disabled individuals. The credit is equal to 50 percent of the eligible expenditures that exceed $250 but do not exceed $10,250. Thus, the maximum amount for the credit is $5,000. The adjusted basis for depreciation is reduced by the amount of the credit. § 44. See also *general business credit.*

Disclaimer. The rejection, refusal, or renunciation of a claim, power, or property. Section 2518 sets forth the conditions required to avoid gift tax consequences as the result of a disclaimer.

Discretionary trusts. Trusts under which the trustee or another party has the right to accumulate (rather than distribute) the income for each year. Depending on the terms of the trust instrument, the income may be accumulated for future distributions to the income beneficiaries or added to corpus for the benefit of the remainderperson. See also *corpus* and *income beneficiary.*

Disproportionate. Not pro rata or ratable. Suppose, for example, Blue Corporation has two shareholders, Chris and Diane, each of whom owns 50 percent of its stock. If Blue Corporation distributes a cash dividend of $2,000 to Chris and only $1,000 to Diane, the distribution is disproportionate. The distribution would have been proportionate if Chris and Diane had received $1,500 each.

Disregard of corporate entity. To treat a corporation as if it did not exist for tax purposes. In that event, each shareholder accounts for an allocable share of all corporate transactions possessing tax consequences. See also *entity.*

Dissent. To disagree with the majority. If, for example, Judge Brown disagrees with the result reached by Judges Charles and Davis (all of whom are members of the same court), Judge Brown could issue a dissenting opinion.

Distributable net income (DNI). The measure that determines the nature and amount of the distributions from estates and trusts that the beneficiaries must include in income. DNI also limits the amount that estates and trusts can claim as a deduction for such distributions. § 643(a).

Distributions in kind. A transfer of property "as is." If, for example, a corporation distributes land to its shareholders, a distribution in kind has taken place. A sale of land followed by a distribution of the cash proceeds would not be a distribution in kind of the land.

District Court. A Federal District Court is a trial court for purposes of litigating Federal tax matters. It is the only trial court in which a jury trial can be obtained. See also *trial court.*

Dividend. A nondeductible distribution to the shareholders of a corporation. A dividend constitutes gross income to the recipient if it is from the current or accumulated earnings and profits of the corporation.

Dividends received deduction. A deduction allowed a shareholder that is a corporation for dividends received from a domestic corporation. The deduction usually is 70 percent of the dividends received, but it could be 80 or 100 percent depending upon the ownership percentage held by the recipient corporation. §§ 243–246.

Domestic corporation. A corporation created or organized in the United States or under the law of the United States or any state. § 7701(a)(4). Only dividends received from domestic corporations qualify for the dividends received deduction (§ 243). See also *foreign corporation.*

Domicile. A person's legal home.

Donee. The recipient of a gift.

Donor. The maker of a gift.

Dower. A wife's right to all or part of her deceased husband's property, unique to common law states as opposed to community property jurisdictions. See also *curtesy.*

E

Earned income. Income from personal services. Distinguished from passive, portfolio, and other unearned income (sometimes referred to as "active" income). See §§ 469, 911, and the related Regulations.

Earned income credit. A tax credit whose purpose is to provide assistance to certain low-income individuals who have a qualifying child. This refundable credit consists of three components: basic earned income credit, supplemental young child credit, and supplemental health insurance credit. See Chapter 11 for details.

Earnings and profits. Measures the economic capacity of a corporation to make a distribution to shareholders that is not a return of capital. Such a distribution will result in dividend income to the shareholders to the extent of the corporation's current and accumulated earnings and profits.

Employee stock ownership plan (ESOP). A type of qualified profit sharing plan that invests in securities of the employer. In a noncontributory ESOP, the employer usually contributes its shares to a trust and receives a deduction for the fair market value of the stock. Generally, the employee does not recognize income until the stock is sold after its distribution to him or her upon retirement or other separation from service. See also *qualified pension or profit sharing plan.*

En banc. The case was considered by the whole court. Typically, for example, only one of the judges of the U.S. Tax Court will hear and decide on a tax controversy. However, when the issues involved are unusually novel or of wide impact, the case will be heard and decided by the full Court sitting *en banc.*

Energy tax credit—business property. A 10 percent tax credit is available to businesses that invest in certain energy property. The purpose of the credit is to create incentives for conservation and to develop alternative energy sources. The credit is available on the acquisition of solar and geothermal property. §§ 46 and 48.

Entertainment expenses. These expenses are deductible only if they are directly related to or associated with a trade or business. Various restrictions and documentation requirements have been imposed upon the deductibility of entertainment expenses to prevent abuses by taxpayers. See, for example, the provision contained in § 274(n) that disallows 20 percent of entertainment expenses. § 274.

Entity. An organization or being that possesses separate existence for tax purposes. Examples are corporations, partnerships, estates, and trusts. See also *disregard of corporate entity.*

Entity accounting income. Entity accounting income is not identical to the taxable income of a trust or estate, nor is it determined in the same manner as the entity's financial accounting income would be. The trust document or will determines whether certain income, expenses, gains, or losses are allocated to the corpus of the entity or to the entity's income beneficiaries. Only the items that are allocated to the income beneficiaries are included in entity accounting income.

Entity buy-sell agreement. A buy-sell agreement whereby the entity is to purchase the withdrawing owner's interest. When the entity is a corporation, the agreement generally involves a stock redemption on the part of the withdrawing shareholder. See also *buy-sell agreement* and *cross-purchase buy-sell agreement.*

Escrow. Money or other property placed with a third party as security for an existing or proposed obligation. Ramon, for example, agrees to purchase Rashad's stock in Orange Corporation but needs time to raise the necessary funds. Rashad places the stock with Eve (the escrow agent), with instructions to deliver it to Ramon when the purchase price is paid.

Estate. An entity that locates, collects, distributes, and discharges the assets and liabilities of a decedent.

Estate tax. A tax imposed on the right to transfer property by death. Thus, an estate tax is levied on the decedent's estate and not on the heir receiving the property. See also *death tax* and *inheritance tax.*

Estimated useful life. The period over which an asset will be used by the taxpayer. Assets such as goodwill do not have an estimated useful life. The estimated useful life of an asset is essential to measuring the annual tax deduction for depreciation and amortization.

Estoppel. The process of being stopped from proving something (even if true) in court due to a prior inconsistent action. It is usually invoked as a matter of fairness to prevent one party (either the taxpayer or the IRS) from taking advantage of a prior error.

Excess lobbying expenditures. An excise tax is applied on otherwise tax-exempt organizations with respect to the excess of total lobbying expenditures over *grass roots lobbying expenditures* for the year.

Excise tax. A tax on the manufacture, sale, or use of goods; on the carrying on of an occupation or activity; or on the transfer of property. Thus, the Federal estate and gift taxes are, theoretically, excise taxes.

Executor. A person designated by a will to administer (manage or take charge of) the assets and liabilities of a decedent. The designated party may be a male (executor), female (executrix), or a trust company (executor). See also *administrator.*

Exemption. An amount by which the tax base is reduced for all qualifying taxpayers. Individuals can receive personal and dependency exemptions, and taxpayers apply an exemption in computing their alternative minimum taxable income. Often, the exemption amount is phased out as the tax base becomes sizable.

Exemption equivalent. The maximum value of assets that can be transferred to another party without incurring any Federal gift or death tax because of the application of the unified tax credit.

Exempt organization. An organization that is either partially or completely exempt from Federal income taxation. § 501.

F

Fair market value. The amount at which property would change hands between a willing buyer and a willing seller, neither being under any compulsion to buy or to sell, and both having reasonable knowledge of the relevant facts. Reg. § 20.2031–1(b).

Federal Register. The first place that the rules and regulations of U.S. administrative agencies (e.g., the U.S. Treasury Department) are published.

F.2d. An abbreviation for the Second Series of the *Federal Reporter,* the official series in which decisions of the U.S. Court of Federal Claims and of the U.S. Court of Appeals are published.

F.Supp. The abbreviation for the *Federal Supplement,* the official series in which the reported decisions of the Federal District Courts are published.

Feeder organization. An entity that carries on a trade or business for the benefit of an exempt organization. However, such a relationship does not result in the feeder organization itself being tax-exempt. § 502.

Fiduciary. A person who manages money or property for another and who must exercise a standard of care in the management activity imposed by law or contract. A trustee, for example, possesses a fiduciary responsibility to the beneficiaries of the trust to follow the terms of the trust and the requirements of applicable state law. A breach of fiduciary responsibility would make the trustee liable to the beneficiaries for any damage caused by the breach.

Field audit. An audit conducted by the IRS on the business premises of the taxpayer or in the office of the tax practitioner representing the taxpayer. See also *audit, correspondence audit,* and *office audit.*

FIRPTA. Under the Foreign Investment in Real Property Tax Act, gains or losses realized by nonresident aliens and non-U.S. corporations on the disposition of U.S. real estate create U.S.-source income and are subject to U.S. income tax.

First-in, first-out (FIFO). An accounting method for determining the cost of inventories. Under this method, the inventory on hand is deemed to be the sum of the cost of the most recently acquired units. See also *last-in, first-out (LIFO).*

Fiscal year. See *accounting period.*

Flat tax. In its pure form, a flat tax would eliminate all exclusions, deductions, and credits and impose a one-rate tax on gross income.

Foreign corporation. A corporation that is not created in the United States or organized under the laws of one of the states of the United States. § 7701(a)(5). See also *domestic corporation.*

Foreign currency transaction. An exchange that could generate a foreign currency gain or loss for a U.S. taxpayer. For instance, if a taxpayer contracts to purchase foreign goods, payable in a currency other than U.S. dollars, at a specified date in the future, any change in the exchange rate between the dollar and that currency will generate a foreign currency gain or loss upon completion of the contract. This gain or loss is treated as separate from the underlying transaction; it may create ordinary or capital gain or loss.

Foreign earned income exclusion. The Code allows exclusions for earned income generated outside the United States to alleviate any tax base and rate disparities among countries. In addition, the exclusion is allowed for housing expenditures incurred by the taxpayer's employer with respect to the non-U.S. assignment, and self-employed individuals can deduct foreign housing expenses incurred in a trade or business.

Foreign personal holding company (FPHC). A foreign corporation in which (1) 60 percent or more of the gross income for the taxable year is FPHC income and (2) more than 50 percent of the total combined voting power or the total value of the stock is owned, directly or indirectly, by five or fewer individuals who are U.S. persons (the U.S. group) at any time during the taxable year. The 60 percent of gross income test drops to 50 percent or more after the 60 percent requirement has been met for one tax year, until the foreign corporation does not meet the 50 percent test for three consecutive years or the stock ownership requirement is not met for an entire tax year.

Foreign sales corporation (FSC). An entity qualifying for a partial exemption of its gross export receipts from U.S. tax. Most FSCs must maintain a presence in a foreign country. In addition, an FSC cannot issue preferred stock, nor can it have more than 25 shareholders.

Foreign tax credit or deduction. A U.S. citizen or resident who incurs or pays income taxes to a foreign country on income subject to U.S. tax may be able to claim some of these taxes as a deduction or a credit against the U.S. income tax. §§ 27, 164, and 901–905.

Form 706. The U.S. Estate Tax Return. In certain cases, this form must be filed for a decedent who was a resident or citizen of the United States.

Form 709. The U.S. Gift Tax Return.

Form 709–A. The U.S. Short Form Gift Tax Return.

Form 870. The signing of Form 870 (Waiver of Restriction on Assessment and Collection of Deficiency in Tax and Acceptance of Overassessments) by a taxpayer permits the IRS to assess a proposed deficiency without issuing a statutory notice of deficiency (90-day letter). This means the taxpayer must pay the deficiency and cannot file a petition to the U.S. Tax Court. § 6213(d).

Form 872. The signing of this form by a taxpayer extends the period during which the IRS can make an assessment or collection of a tax. In other words, Form 872 extends the applicable statute of limitations. § 6501(c)(4).

Form 1041. The U.S. Fiduciary Income Tax Return, required to be filed by estates and trusts. See Appendix B for a specimen form.

Form 1065. The U.S. Partnership Return of Income. See Appendix B for a specimen form.

Form 1120. The U.S. Corporation Income Tax Return. See Appendix B for a specimen form.

Form 1120–A. The U.S. Short-Form Corporation Income Tax Return. See Appendix B for a specimen form.

Form 1120S. The U.S. Small Business Corporation Income Tax Return, required to be filed by S corporations. See Appendix B for a specimen form.

Fraud. Tax fraud falls into two categories: civil and criminal. Under civil fraud, the IRS may impose as a penalty an amount equal to as much as 75 percent of the underpayment [§ 6651(f)]. Fines and/or imprisonment are prescribed for conviction of various types of criminal tax fraud (§§ 7201–7207). Both civil and criminal fraud require a specific intent on the part of the taxpayer to evade the tax; mere negligence is not enough. Criminal fraud requires the additional element of willfulness (i.e., done deliberately and with evil purpose). In practice, it becomes difficult to distinguish between the degree of intent necessary to support criminal, rather than civil, fraud. In either situation, the IRS has the burden of proving fraud. See also *burden of proof.*

Free transferability of interests. The capability of the owner of an entity to transfer his or her ownership interest to another without the consent of the other owners. It is a characteristic of a corporation since a shareholder usually can freely transfer the stock to others without the approval of the existing shareholders. Reg. § 301.7701–2(e). See also *association.*

Fringe benefits. Compensation or other benefits received by an employee that are not in the form of cash. Some fringe benefits (e.g., accident and health plans, group term life insurance) may be excluded from the employee's gross income and thus are not subject to the Federal income tax.

Future interest. An interest that will come into being at some future point in time. It is distinguished from a present interest, which is already in existence. Assume, for example, that Dan transfers securities to a newly created trust. Under the terms of the trust instrument, income from the securities is to be paid each year to Wilma for her life, with the securities passing to Sam upon Wilma's death. Wilma has a present interest in the trust since she is currently entitled to receive the income from the securities. Sam has a future interest since he must wait for Wilma's death to benefit from the trust. The annual exclusion of $10,000 is not allowed for a gift of a future interest. § 2503(b). See also *annual exclusion* and *gift splitting.*

G

General business credit. The summation of various nonrefundable business credits, including the investment tax credit, jobs credit, research activities credit, and disabled access credit. The amount of general business credit that can be used to reduce the tax liability is limited to the taxpayer's net income tax reduced by the greater of (1) the tentative minimum tax or (2) 25 percent of the net regular tax liability that exceeds $25,000. Unused general business credits can be carried back 3 years and forward 15 years. § 38.

General partner. A partner who is fully liable in an individual capacity for the debts of the partnership to third parties. A general partner's liability is not limited to the investment in the partnership. See also *limited partner.*

General power of appointment. See *power of appointment.*

Gift. A transfer of property for less than adequate consideration. Gifts usually occur in a personal setting (such as between members of the same family). They are excluded from the income tax base but may be subject to a transfer tax.

Gift splitting. A special election for Federal gift tax purposes under which husband and wife can treat a gift by one of them to a third party as being made one-half by each. If, for example, George (the husband) makes a gift of $20,000 to Shirley, Barbara (the wife) may elect to treat $10,000 of the gift as coming from her. The major advantage of the election is that it enables the parties to take advantage of the nonowner spouse's (Barbara in this case) annual exclusion and unified credit. § 2513. See also *annual exclusion.*

Gift tax. A tax imposed on the transfer of property by gift. The tax is imposed upon the donor of a gift and is based on the fair market value of the property on the date of the gift.

Gifts within three years of death. Some taxable gifts automatically are included in the gross estate of the donor if death occurs within three years of the gift. § 2035.

Goodwill. The reputation and built-up business of a company. For accounting purposes, goodwill has no basis unless it is purchased. In the purchase of a business, goodwill generally is the difference between the purchase price and the fair market value of the assets acquired. The intangible asset goodwill cannot be amortized for tax purposes. Reg. § 1.167(a)–3. See also *amortization.*

Grantor. A transferor of property. The creator of a trust is usually referred to as the grantor of the trust.

Grantor trust. A trust under which the grantor retains control over the income or corpus (or both) to such an extent that he or she will be treated as the owner of the property and its income for income tax purposes. The result is to make the income from a grantor trust taxable to the grantor and not to the beneficiary who receives it. §§ 671–677. See also *reversionary interest.*

Grass roots lobbying expenditures. Exempt organizations are prohibited from engaging in political activities, but expenses incurred to influence the opinions of the general public relative to specific legislation are permitted by the law. See also *excess lobbying expenditures.*

Gross estate. The property owned or previously transferred by a decedent that is subject to the Federal estate tax. The gross estate can be distinguished from the probate estate, which is property actually subject to administration by the administrator or executor of an estate. §§ 2031–2046. See also *adjusted gross estate* and *taxable estate.*

Gross income. Income subject to the Federal income tax. Gross income does not include all economic income. That is, certain exclusions are allowed (e.g., interest on municipal bonds). For a manufacturing or merchandising business, gross income usually means gross profit (gross sales or gross receipts less cost of goods sold). § 61 and Reg. § 1.61–3(a). See also *adjusted gross income* and *taxable income.*

Gross up. To add back to the value of the property or income received the amount of the tax that has been paid. For gifts made within three years of death, any gift tax paid on the transfer is added to the gross estate. § 2035.

Group term life insurance. Life insurance coverage provided by an employer for a group of employees. Such insurance is renewable on a year-to-year basis, and typically no cash surrender value is built up. The premiums paid by the employer on the insurance are not taxed to the employees on coverage of up to $50,000 per person. § 79 and Reg. § 1.79–1(b).

Guaranteed payments. Payments made by a partnership to a partner for services rendered or for the use of capital to the extent that the payments are determined without regard to the income of the partnership. The payments are treated as though they were made to a nonpartner and thus are usually deductible by the entity.

Guardianship. A legal arrangement under which one person (a guardian) has the legal right and duty to care for another (the ward) and his or her property. A guardianship is established because the ward is unable to act legally on his or her own behalf (e.g., because of minority [he or she is not of age] or mental or physical incapacity).

H

Head of household. An unmarried individual who maintains a household for another and satisfies certain conditions set forth in § 2(b). This status enables the taxpayer to use a set of income tax rates that are lower than those applicable to other unmarried individuals but higher than those applicable to surviving spouses and married persons filing a joint return.

Heir. A person who inherits property from a decedent.

Hobby. An activity not engaged in for profit. The Code restricts the amount of losses that an individual can deduct for hobby activities so that these transactions cannot be used to offset income from other sources. § 183.

Holding period. The period of time during which property has been held for income tax purposes. The holding period is significant in determining whether gain or loss from the sale or exchange of a capital asset is long term or short term. § 1223.

Hot assets. Unrealized receivables and substantially appreciated inventory under § 751. When hot assets are present, the sale of a partnership interest or the disproportionate distribution of the assets can cause ordinary income to be recognized.

H.R. 10 plans. See *Keogh plans.*

I

Imputed interest. For certain long-term sales of property, the IRS can convert some of the gain from the sale into interest income if the contract does not provide for a minimum rate of interest to be paid by the purchaser. The application of this procedure has the effect of forcing the seller to recognize less long-term capital gain and more ordinary income (interest income). § 483 and the related Regulations.

Incident of ownership. An element of ownership or degree of control over a life insurance policy. The retention by an insured of an incident of ownership in a life insurance policy will cause the policy proceeds to be included in the insured's gross estate upon death. § 2042(2) and Reg. § 20.2042–1(c). See also *gross estate* and *insured.*

Includible gain. Section 644 imposes a built-in gains tax on trusts that sell or exchange property at a gain within two years after the date of its transfer in trust by the transferor. The provision applies only if the fair market value of the property at the time of the initial transfer exceeds the adjusted basis of the property immediately after the transfer. The tax imposed by § 644 is the amount of additional tax the transferor would pay (including any minimum tax) had the gain been included in the transferor's gross income for the tax year of the sale. However, the tax applies only to an amount known as *includible gain.* This is the lesser of the following: the gain recognized by the trust on the sale or exchange of any property, or the excess of the fair market value of the property at the time of the initial transfer in trust by the transferor over the adjusted basis of the property immediately after the transfer.

Income beneficiary. The party entitled to income from property. In a typical trust situation, Alan is to receive the income for life with corpus or principal passing to Gertrude upon Alan's death. In this case, Alan is the income beneficiary of the trust.

Income in respect of a decedent. Income earned by a decedent at the time of death but not reportable on the final income tax return because of the method of accounting that appropriately is utilized. Such income is included in the gross estate and will be taxed to the eventual recipient (either the estate or heirs). The recipient will, however, be allowed an income tax deduction for the estate tax attributable to the income. § 691.

Income shifting. Occurs when an individual transfers some of his or her gross income to a taxpayer who is subject to a lower tax rate, thereby reducing the total income tax liability of the group. Income shifting produces a successful assignment of income. It can be accomplished by transferring income-producing property to the lower-bracket taxpayer or to an effective trust for his or her benefit, or by transferring ownership interests in a family partnership or in a closely held corporation.

Incomplete transfer. A transfer made by a decedent during lifetime that, because of certain control or enjoyment retained by the transferor, is not considered complete for Federal estate tax purposes. Thus, some or all of the fair market value of the property transferred is included in the transferor's gross estate. §§ 2036–2038. See also *gross estate* and *revocable transfer.*

Individual retirement account (IRA). Individuals with earned income are permitted to set aside up to 100 percent of that income per year (not to exceed $2,000 or $2,250 for a spousal IRA) for a retirement account. The amount set aside can be deducted by the taxpayer and is subject to income tax only upon withdrawal. The Code limits the amount of this contribution that can be deducted *for* AGI depending upon (1) whether the taxpayer or spouse is an active participant in an employer-provided qualified retirement plan, and (2) the magnitude of the taxpayer's AGI before the IRA contribution is considered. § 219. See also *simplified employee pensions.*

Inheritance tax. A tax imposed on the right to receive property from a decedent. Thus, theoretically, an inheritance tax is imposed on the heir. The Federal estate tax is imposed on the estate. See also *death tax* and *estate tax.*

In kind. See *distributions in kind.*

Installment method. A method of accounting enabling certain taxpayers to spread the recognition of gain on the sale of property over the collection period. Under this procedure, the seller arrives at the gain to be recognized by computing the gross profit percentage from the sale (the gain divided by the contract price) and applying it to each payment received. § 453.

Insured. A person whose life is the subject of an insurance policy. Upon the death of the insured, the life insurance policy matures, and the proceeds become payable to the designated beneficiary. See also *life insurance.*

Intangible asset. Property that is a "right" rather than a physical object. Examples are patents, stocks and bonds, goodwill, trademarks, franchises, and copyrights. See also *amortization* and *tangible property.*

Inter vivos transfer. A transfer of property during the life of the owner. Distinguished from testamentary transfers, where the property passes at death.

Interest-free loans. Bona fide loans that carry no interest (or a below-market rate). If made in a nonbusiness setting, the imputed interest element is treated as a gift from the lender to the borrower. If made by a corporation to a shareholder, a constructive dividend could result. In either event, the lender may recognize interest income. § 7872.

Internal Revenue Code. The collected statutes that govern the taxation of income, property transfers, and other transactions in the United States and the enforcement of those provisions. Enacted by Congress, the Code is amended frequently, but it has not been reorganized since 1954. However, because of the extensive revisions to the statutes that occurred with the Tax Reform Act of 1986, Title 26 of the U.S. Code is now known as the Internal Revenue Code of 1986.

Interpolated terminal reserve. The measure used in valuing insurance policies for gift and estate tax purposes when the policies are not paid up at the time of their transfer. Reg. § 20.2031–8(a)(3), Ex. (3).

Intestate. No will exists at the time of death. In such cases, state law prescribes who will receive the decedent's property. The laws of intestate succession generally favor the surviving spouse, children, and grandchildren, and then parents and grandparents and brothers and sisters.

Investment income. Consisting of virtually the same elements as portfolio income, a measure by which to justify a deduction for interest on investment indebtedness. See also *investment indebtedness* and *portfolio income.*

Investment indebtedness. Debt incurred to carry or incur investments by the taxpayer in assets that will produce portfolio income. Limitations are placed upon interest deductions that are incurred in connection with the debt (generally to the corresponding amount of investment income).

Investment tax credit. A tax credit that usually was equal to 10 percent (unless a reduced credit was elected) of the qualified investment in tangible personalty used in a trade or business. If the tangible personalty had a recovery period of five years or more, the full cost of the property qualified for the credit. Only 60 percent qualified for property with a recovery period of three years. However, the regular investment tax credit was repealed by TRA of 1986 for property placed in service after December 31, 1985. § 46. See also *general business credit.*

Involuntary conversion. The loss or destruction of property through theft, casualty, or condemnation. Any gain realized on an involuntary conversion can, at the taxpayer's election, be deferred for Federal income tax purposes if the owner reinvests the proceeds within a prescribed period of time in property that is similar or related in service or use. § 1033.

IRA. See *individual retirement account.*

Itemized deductions. Personal and employee expenditures allowed by the Code as deductions from adjusted gross income. Examples include certain medical expenses, interest on home mortgages, and charitable contributions. Itemized deductions are reported on Schedule A of Form 1040. Certain miscellaneous itemized deductions are reduced by 2 percent of the taxpayer's adjusted gross income. In addition, a taxpayer whose adjusted gross income exceeds a certain level (indexed annually) must reduce the itemized deductions by 3 percent of the excess of adjusted gross income over that level. Medical, casualty and theft, and investment interest deductions are not subject to the 3 percent reduction. The 3 percent reduction may not reduce itemized deductions that are subject to the reduction to below 20 percent of their initial amount.

J

Jeopardy assessment. If the collection of a tax appears in question, the IRS may assess and collect the tax immediately without the usual formalities. The IRS can terminate a taxpayer's taxable year before the usual date if it feels that the collection of the tax may be in peril because the taxpayer plans to leave the country. §§ 6851 and 6861–6864.

Joint and several liability. Permits the IRS to collect a tax from one or all of several taxpayers. A husband and wife who file a joint income tax return usually are collectively or individually liable for the full amount of the tax liability. § 6013(d)(3).

Joint tenancy. The undivided ownership of property by two or more persons with the right of survivorship. Right of survivorship gives the surviving owner full ownership of the property. Suppose, for example, Bob and Tami are joint owners of a tract of land. Upon Bob's death, Tami becomes the sole owner of the property. For the estate tax consequences upon the death of a joint tenant, see § 2040. See also *tenancy by the entirety* and *tenancy in common.*

Joint venture. A one-time grouping of two or more persons in a business undertaking. Unlike a partnership, a joint venture does not entail a continuing relationship among the parties. A joint venture is treated like a partnership for Federal income tax purposes. § 7701(a)(2).

K

Keogh plans. Retirement plans available to self-employed taxpayers. They are also referred to as H.R. 10 plans. Under such plans, a taxpayer may deduct each year up to either 20 percent of net earnings from self-employment or $30,000, whichever is less.

Kiddie tax. See *tax on unearned income of a child under age 14.*

L

Lapse. The expiration of a right either by the death of the holder or upon the expiration of a period of time. Thus, a power of appointment lapses upon the death of the holder if he or she has not exercised the power during life or at death (through a will).

Last-in, first-out (LIFO). An accounting method for valuing inventories for tax purposes. Under this method, it is assumed that the inventory on hand is valued at the cost of the earliest acquired units. § 472. See also *first-in, first-out (FIFO).*

Leaseback. The transferor of property later leases it back. In a sale-leaseback situation, for example, Richard sells property to Sally and subsequently leases the property from Sally. Thus, Richard becomes the lessee and Sally the lessor.

Legacy. A transfer of cash or other property by will.

Legal age. The age at which a person may enter into binding contracts or commit other legal acts. In most states, a minor reaches legal age or majority (comes of age) at age 18.

Legal representative. A person who oversees the legal affairs of another; for example, the executor or administrator of an estate or a court-appointed guardian of a minor or incompetent person.

Legatee. The recipient of property under a will and transferred by the death of the owner.

Lessee. One who rents property from another. In the case of real estate, the lessee is also known as the tenant.

Lessor. One who rents property to another. In the case of real estate, the lessor is also known as the landlord.

LEXIS. An on-line database system with which the tax researcher can obtain access to the Internal Revenue Code, Regulations, administrative rulings, and court case opinions.

Life estate. A legal arrangement under which the beneficiary (the life tenant) is entitled to the income from property for his or her life. Upon the death of the life tenant, the property is transferred to the holder of the remainder interest. See also *income beneficiary* and *remainder interest.*

Life insurance. A contract between the holder of a policy and an insurance company (the carrier) under which the company agrees, in return for premium payments, to pay a specified sum (the face value or maturity value of the policy) to the designated beneficiary upon the death of the insured. See also *insured.*

Like-kind exchange. An exchange of property held for productive use in a trade or business or for investment (except inventory and stocks and bonds) for other investment or trade or business property. Unless non-like-kind property (boot) is received, the exchange is nontaxable. § 1031. See also *boot.*

Limited liability. The liability of an entity and its owners to third parties is limited to the investment in the entity. This is a characteristic of a corporation, as shareholders generally are not responsible for the debts of the corporation and, at most, may lose the amount paid in for the stock issued. Reg. § 301.7701–2(d). See also *association.*

Limited partner. A partner whose liability to third-party creditors of the partnership is limited to the amount he or she has invested in the partnership. See also *general partner* and *limited partnership.*

Limited partnership. A partnership in which some of the partners are limited partners. At least one of the partners in a limited partnership must be a general partner. See also *general partner* and *limited partner.*

Liquidating distribution. A distribution by a partnership or corporation that is in complete liquidation of the entity's trade or business activities. Typically, such distributions generate capital gain or loss to the investors without regard, for instance, to the earnings and profits of the corporation or to the partnership's basis in the distributed property. They can, however, lead to recognized gain or loss at the corporate level.

Liquidation. See *corporate liquidation.*

Lobbying expenditure. An expenditure made for the purpose of influencing legislation. Such payments can result in the loss of the exempt status of, and the imposition of Federal income tax on, an exempt organization.

Long-term capital gain or loss. Results from the sale or other taxable exchange of a capital asset that had been held by the seller for more than one year or from other transactions involving statutorily designated assets, including § 1231 property and patents.

Low-income housing credit. Beneficial treatment to owners of low-income housing is provided in the form of a tax credit. The calculated credit is claimed in the year the building is placed in service and in the following nine years. § 42. See also *general business credit.*

Lump-sum distribution. Payment of the entire amount due at one time rather than in installments. Such distributions often occur from qualified pension or profit sharing plans upon the retirement or death of a covered employee.

M

MACRS. See *accelerated cost recovery system (ACRS).*

Majority. See *legal age.*

Malpractice. Professional misconduct; an unreasonable lack of skill.

Marital deduction. A deduction allowed against the taxable estate or taxable gifts upon the transfer of property from one spouse to another.

Market value. See *fair market value.*

Merger. The absorption of one corporation by another with the corporation being absorbed losing its legal identity. Orange Corporation is merged into Blue Corporation, and the shareholders of Orange receive stock in Blue in exchange for their stock in Orange Corporation. After the merger, Orange Corporation ceases to exist as a separate legal entity. If a merger meets certain conditions, it is nontaxable to the parties involved. § 368(a)(1)(A). See also *corporate acquisition* and *corporate reorganization.*

Minimum tax. See *alternative minimum tax.*

Minority. See *legal age.*

Mitigate. To make less severe. See also *mitigation of the annual accounting period concept* and *mitigation of the statute of limitations.*

Mitigation of the annual accounting period concept. Various tax provisions that provide relief from the effect of the finality of the annual accounting period concept. For example, the net operating loss carryover provisions allow the taxpayer to apply the negative taxable income of one year against a corresponding positive amount in another tax accounting period. See also *annual accounting period concept.*

Mitigation of the statute of limitations. A series of tax provisions that prevents either the IRS or a taxpayer from obtaining a double benefit from the application of the statute of limitations. It would be unfair, for example, to permit a taxpayer to depreciate an asset previously expensed, but which should have been capitalized, if the statute of limitations prevents the IRS from adjusting the tax liability for the year the asset was purchased. §§ 1311–1314. See also *statute of limitations.*

Mortgagee. The party who holds the mortgage; the creditor.

Mortgagor. The party who mortgages the property; the debtor.

Most suitable use value. For gift and estate tax purposes, property that is transferred normally is valued in accordance with its most suitable or optimal use. Thus, if a farm is worth more as a potential shopping center, the value as a shopping center will control, even though the transferee (the donee or heir) continues to use the property as a farm. For an exception to this rule concerning the valuation of certain kinds of real estate transferred by death, see *special use value.*

Multitiered partnerships. See *tiered partnerships.*

N

Necessary. Appropriate and helpful in furthering the taxpayer's business or income-producing activity. §§ 162(a) and 212. See also *ordinary.*

Negligence. Failure to exercise the reasonable or ordinary degree of care of a prudent person in a situation that results in harm or damage to another. Code § 6651 imposes a penalty on taxpayers who exhibit negligence or intentional disregard of rules and Regulations with respect to the underpayment of certain taxes.

Net operating loss. To mitigate the effect of the annual accounting period concept, § 172 allows taxpayers to use an excess loss of one year as a deduction for certain past or future years. In this regard, a carryback period of 3 years and a carryforward period of 15 years currently are allowed. See also *mitigation of the annual accounting period concept.*

Net worth method. An approach used by the IRS to reconstruct the income of a taxpayer who fails to maintain adequate records. Under this method, the gross income for the year is estimated as the increase in net worth of the taxpayer (assets in excess of liabilities) with appropriate adjustment for nontaxable receipts and nondeductible expenditures. The net worth method often is used when tax fraud is suspected.

Ninety-day letter. See *statutory notice of deficiency.*

Nonacquiescence. Disagreement by the IRS on the result reached by the U.S. Tax Court in a Regular Decision. Sometimes abbreviated *non-acq.* or *NA.* See also *acquiescence.*

Nonbusiness bad debts. A bad debt loss that is not incurred in connection with a creditor's trade or business. The loss is classified as a short-term capital loss and will be allowed only in the year the debt becomes entirely worthless. In addition to family loans, many investor losses fall into the classification of nonbusiness bad debts. § 166(d). See also *business bad debts.*

Nonbusiness income. Income generated from investment assets or from the taxable disposition thereof.

Noncontributory qualified pension or profit sharing plan. A plan funded entirely by the employer with no contributions being made by the covered employees. See also *qualified pension or profit sharing plans.*

Nonliquidating distribution. A payment made by a partnership or corporation to the entity's owner is a nonliquidating distribution when the entity's legal existence does not cease thereafter. If the payer is a corporation, such a distribution can result in dividend income to the shareholders. If the payer is a partnership, the partner usually assigns a basis in the distributed property that is equal to the lesser of the partner's basis in the partnership interest or the basis of the distributed asset to the partnership. In this regard, the partner first assigns basis to any cash that he or she receives in the distribution. The partner's remaining basis, if any, is assigned to the noncash assets according to their relative bases to the partnership.

Nonrecourse debt. Debt secured by the property that it is used to purchase. The purchaser of the property is not personally liable for the debt upon default. Rather, the creditor's recourse is to repossess the related property. Nonrecourse debt generally does not increase the purchaser's at-risk amount.

Nonresident alien. An individual who is not a citizen or resident of the United States. Citizenship is determined under the immigration and naturalization laws of the United States. Residency is determined under § 7701(b) of the Internal Revenue Code.

Nonseparately stated income. The net income of an S corporation that is combined and allocated to the shareholders. Other items, such as capital gains and charitable contributions, that could be treated differently on the individual tax returns of the shareholders are not included in this amount but are allocated to the shareholders separately.

O

Obligee. The party to whom someone else is obligated under a contract. Thus, if Carol loans money to Dan, Carol is the obligee and Dan is the obligor under the loan.

Obligor. See *obligee.*

Office audit. An audit conducted by the IRS in the agent's office. See also *audit, correspondence audit,* and *field audit.*

On all fours. A judicial decision exactly in point with another as to result, facts, or both.

Optimal use value. Synonym for most suitable use value.

Ordinary. Common and accepted in the general industry or type of activity in which the taxpayer is engaged. It comprises one of the tests for the deductibility of expenses incurred or paid in connection with a trade or business; for the production or collection of income; for the management, conservation, or maintenance of property held for the production of income; or in connection with the determination, collection, or refund of any tax. §§ 162(a) and 212. See also *necessary.*

Ordinary and necessary. See *necessary* and *ordinary.*

Ordinary gross income. A concept peculiar to personal holding companies and defined in § 543(b)(1). See also *adjusted ordinary gross income.*

P

Partner. See *general partner* and *limited partner.*

Partnership. For income tax purposes, a partnership includes a syndicate, group, pool, or joint venture, as well as ordinary partnerships. In an ordinary partnership, two or more parties combine capital and/or services to carry on a business for profit as co-owners. § 7701(a)(2). See also *limited partnership* and *tiered partnerships.*

Passive foreign investment company (PFIC). A non-U.S. corporation that generates a substantial amount of personal holding company income. Upon receipt of an excess distribution from the entity or the sale of its shares, its U.S. shareholders are taxable on their pro rata shares of the tax that has been deferred with respect to the corporation's taxable income, plus an applicable interest charge.

Passive investment income. Passive investment income means gross receipts from royalties, certain rents, dividends, interest, annuities, and gains from the sale or exchange of stock and securities. With certain exceptions, if the passive investment income of an S corporation exceeds 25 percent of the corporation's gross receipts for three consecutive years, S status is lost.

Passive loss. Any loss from (1) activities in which the taxpayer does not materially participate and (2) rental activities. Net passive losses cannot be used to offset income from nonpassive sources. Rather, they are suspended until the taxpayer either generates net passive income (and a deduction of such losses is allowed) or disposes of the underlying property (at which time the loss deductions are allowed in full). Landlords who actively participate in the rental activities can deduct up to $25,000 of passive losses annually. However, this amount is phased out when the landlord's AGI exceeds $100,000. See also *portfolio income.*

Pecuniary bequest. A bequest of money to an heir by a decedent. See also *bequest.*

Percentage depletion. See *depletion.*

Percentage of completion method. A method of reporting gain or loss on certain long-term contracts. Under this method of accounting, the gross contract price is included in income as the contract is completed. Reg. § 1.451–3. See also *completed contract method.*

Personal and dependency exemptions. The tax law provides an exemption for each individual taxpayer and an additional exemption for the taxpayer's spouse if a joint return is filed. An individual may also claim a dependency exemption for each dependent, provided certain tests are met. The amount of the personal and dependency exemptions is $2,350 in 1993 ($2,300 in 1992). The exemption is subject to phase-out once adjusted gross income exceeds certain statutory threshold amounts.

Personal and household effects. Items owned by a decedent at the time of death. Examples include clothing, furniture, sporting goods, jewelry, stamp and coin collections, silverware, china, crystal, cooking utensils, books, cars, televisions, radios, stereo equipment, etc.

Personal holding company. A corporation that satisfies the requirements of § 542. Qualification as a personal holding company means a penalty tax will be imposed on the corporation's undistributed personal holding company income for the year.

Personal holding company income. Income as defined by § 543. It includes interest, dividends, certain rents and royalties, income from the use of corporate property by certain shareholders, income from certain personal service contracts, and distributions from estates and trusts. Such income is relevant in determining whether a corporation is a personal holding company and is therefore subject to the penalty tax on personal holding companies. See also *adjusted ordinary gross income.*

Personal property. Generally, all property other than real estate. It is sometimes referred to as personalty when real estate is termed realty. Personal property can also refer to property not used in a taxpayer's trade or business or held for the production or collection of income. When used in this sense, personal property can include both realty (e.g., a personal residence) and personalty (e.g., personal effects such as clothing and furniture). See also *bequest.*

Personalty. Personalty is all property that is not attached to real estate (realty) and is movable. Examples of personalty are machinery, automobiles, clothing, household furnishings, inventory, and personal effects. See also *ad valorem tax* and *realty.*

Portfolio income. Income from interest, dividends, rentals, royalties, capital gains, or other investment sources. Net passive losses cannot be used to offset net portfolio income. See also *passive loss* and *investment income.*

Power of appointment. A legal right granted to someone by will or other document that gives the holder the power to dispose of property or the income from property. When the holder may appoint the property to his or her own benefit, the power usually is called a general power of appointment. If the holder cannot benefit himself or herself but may only appoint to certain other persons, the power is a special power of appointment. For example, assume Gus places $500,000 worth of securities in trust granting Debbie the right to determine each year how the trustee is to divide the income between Ann and Bill. Under these circumstances, Debbie has a special power of appointment. If Debbie had the further right to appoint the income to herself, she probably possesses a general power of appointment. For the estate tax and gift tax effects of powers of appointment, see §§ 2041 and 2514. See also *testamentary power of appointment.*

Preferred stock bailout. A process where a shareholder used the issuance, sale, and later redemption of a preferred stock dividend to obtain long-term capital gains without any loss of voting control over the corporation. In effect, therefore, the shareholder was able to bail out corporate profits without suffering the consequences of dividend income treatment. This procedure led Congress to enact § 306, which, if applicable, converts the prior long-term capital gain on the sale of the stock to ordinary income. Under these circumstances, the amount of ordinary income is limited to the shareholder's portion of the corporation's earnings and profits existing when the preferred stock was issued as a stock dividend. See also *bailout.*

Present interest. See *future interest.*

Presumption. An inference in favor of a particular fact. If, for example, the IRS issues a notice of deficiency against a taxpayer, a presumption of correctness attaches to the assessment. Thus, the taxpayer has the burden of proof of showing that he or she does not owe the tax listed in the deficiency notice. See also *rebuttable presumption.*

Previously taxed income (PTI). Before the Subchapter S Revision Act of 1982, the undistributed taxable income of an S corporation was taxed to the shareholders as of the last day of the corporation's tax year and usually could be withdrawn by the shareholders without tax consequences at some later point in time. The role of PTI has been taken over by the accumulated adjustments account. See also *accumulated adjustments account.*

Principal. Property as opposed to income. The term is often used as a synonym for the corpus of a trust. If, for example, Gwen places real estate in trust with income payable to Abby for life and the remainder to Karen upon Abby's death, the real estate is the principal, or corpus, of the trust.

Private foundation. An exempt organization that is subject to additional statutory restrictions on its activities and on contributions made to it. Excise taxes may be levied on certain prohibited transactions, and the Code places more stringent restrictions on the deductibility of contributions to private foundations. § 509.

Pro rata. Proportionately. Assume, for example, a corporation has 10 shareholders, each of whom owns 10 percent of the stock. A pro rata dividend distribution of $1,000 would mean that each shareholder would receive $100.

Pro se. The taxpayer represents himself or herself before the court, without the benefit of counsel.

Probate. The legal process by which the estate of a decedent is administered. Generally, the probate process involves collecting a decedent's assets, liquidating liabilities, paying necessary taxes, and distributing property to heirs.

Probate court. The usual designation for the state or local court that supervises the administration (probate) of a decedent's estate.

Probate estate. The property of a decedent that is subject to administration by the executor or administrator of an estate. See also *administration.*

Property tax. An *ad valorem* tax, usually levied by a city or county government, on the value of real or personal property that the taxpayer owns on a specified date. Most states exclude intangible property and assets owned by exempt organizations from the tax base, and some exclude inventory, pollution control or manufacturing equipment, and other items to provide relocation or retention incentives for the taxpayer.

Prop.Reg. An abbreviation for Proposed Regulation. A Regulation may first be issued in proposed form to give interested parties the opportunity for comment. When and if a Proposed Regulation is finalized, it is known as a Regulation (abbreviated Reg.).

PTI. See *previously taxed income.*

Public policy limitation. A concept developed by the courts precluding an income tax deduction for certain expenses related to activities deemed to be contrary to the public welfare. In this connection, Congress has incorporated into the Code specific disallowance provisions covering such items as illegal bribes, kickbacks, and fines and penalties. §§ 162(c) and (f).

Q

Qualified pension or profit sharing plan. An employer-sponsored plan that meets the requirements of § 401. If these requirements are met, none of the employer's contributions to the plan will be taxed to the employee until distributed to him or her (§ 402). The employer will be allowed a deduction in the year the contributions are made (§ 404). See also *contributory qualified pension or profit sharing plan, deferred compensation,* and *noncontributory pension or profit sharing plan.*

Qualified terminable interest property (QTIP). Generally, the marital deduction (for gift and estate tax purposes) is not available if the interest transferred will terminate upon the death of the transferee spouse and pass to someone else. Thus, if Jim (the husband) places property in trust, life estate to Mary (the wife), and remainder to their children upon Mary's death, this is a terminable interest that will not provide Jim (or Jim's estate) with a marital deduction. If, however, the transfer in trust is treated as qualified terminable interest property (the QTIP election is made), the terminable interest restriction is waived and the marital deduction becomes available. In exchange for this deduction, the surviving spouse's gross estate must include the value of the QTIP election assets, even though he or she has no control over the ultimate disposition of the asset. Terminable interest property qualifies for this election if the donee (or heir) is the only beneficiary of the asset during his or her lifetime and receives income distributions relative to the property at least annually. For gifts, the donor spouse is the one who makes the QTIP election. For property transferred by death, the executor of the estate of the deceased spouse has the right to make the election. §§ 2056(b)(7) and 2523(f).

R

RAR. A Revenue agent's report, which reflects any adjustments made by the agent as a result of an audit of the taxpayer. The RAR is mailed to the taxpayer along with the 30-day letter, which outlines the appellate procedures available to the taxpayer.

Realized gain or loss. The difference between the amount realized upon the sale or other disposition of property and the adjusted basis of the property. § 1001. See also *adjusted basis, amount realized, basis,* and *recognized gain or loss.*

Realty. Real estate. See also *personalty.*

Reasonable needs of the business. The usual justification for avoiding the penalty tax on unreasonable accumulation of earnings. In determining the amount of taxable income subject to this tax (accumulated taxable income), § 535 allows a deduction for "such part of earnings and profits for the taxable year as are retained for the reasonable needs of the business." § 537.

Rebuttable presumption. A presumption that can be overturned upon the showing of sufficient proof. See also *presumption.*

Recapture. To recover the tax benefit of a deduction or a credit previously taken. See also *depreciation recapture.*

Recapture potential. A measure with respect to property that, if disposed of in a taxable transaction, would result in the recapture of depreciation (§§ 1245 or 1250), deferred LIFO gain, or deferred installment method gain.

Recognized gain or loss. The portion of realized gain or loss subject to income taxation. See also *realized gain or loss.*

Regulations. The U.S. Treasury Department Regulations (abbreviated Reg.) represent the position of the IRS as to how the Internal Revenue Code is to be interpreted. Their purpose is to provide taxpayers and IRS personnel with rules of general and specific application to the various provisions of the tax law. Regulations are published in the *Federal Register* and in all tax services.

Related parties. Various Code Sections define related parties and often include a variety of persons within this (usually detrimental) category. Generally, related parties are accorded different tax treatment from that applicable to other taxpayers who enter into similar transactions. For instance, realized losses that are generated between related parties are not recognized in the year of the loss. However, these deferred losses can be used to offset recognized gains that occur upon the subsequent sale of the asset to a nonrelated party. Other uses of a related-party definition include the conversion of gain upon the sale of a depreciable asset into all ordinary income (§ 1239) and the identification of constructive ownership of stock relative to corporate distributions, redemptions, liquidations, reorganizations, and compensation.

Remainder interest. The property that passes to a beneficiary after the expiration of an intervening income interest. If, for example, Gail places real estate in trust with income to Tom for life and remainder to Randy upon Tom's death, Randy has a remainder interest. See also *life estate* and *reversionary interest.*

Remand. To send back. An appellate court may remand a case to a lower court, usually for additional fact finding. In other words, the appellate court is not in a position to decide the appeal based on the facts determined by the lower court. Remanding is abbreviated *"rem'g."*

Reorganization. See *corporate reorganization.*

Research activities credit. A tax credit whose purpose is to encourage research and development. It consists of two components: the incremental research activities credit and the basic research credit. The incremental research activities credit is equal to 20 percent of the excess qualified research expenditures over the base amount. The basic research credit is equal to 20 percent of the excess of basic research payments over the base amount. § 41. See also *general business credit.*

Residential rental property. Buildings for which at least 80 percent of the gross rents are from dwelling units (e.g., an apartment building). This type of building is distinguished from nonresidential (commercial or industrial) buildings in applying the recapture of depreciation provisions. The term also is relevant in distinguishing between buildings that are eligible for a 27.5 year life versus a 31.5 year life for ACRS purposes. Generally, residential buildings receive preferential treatment.

Return of capital. When a taxpayer reacquires financial resources that he or she previously had invested in an entity or venture, the return of his or her capital investment itself does not increase gross income for the recovery year. A return of capital may result from an annuity or insurance contract, the sale or exchange of any asset, or a distribution from a partnership or corporation.

Revenue neutral. A change in the tax system that results in the same amount of revenue. Revenue neutral, however, does not mean that any one taxpayer will pay the same amount of tax as before. Thus, as a result of a tax law change, corporations could pay more taxes, but the excess revenue will be offset by lower taxes on individuals.

Revenue Procedure. A matter of procedural importance to both taxpayers and the IRS concerning the administration of the tax laws is issued as a Revenue Procedure (abbreviated Rev.Proc.). A Revenue Procedure is first published in an *Internal Revenue Bulletin* (I.R.B.) and later transferred to the appropriate *Cumulative Bulletin* (C.B.). Both the *Internal Revenue Bulletins* and the *Cumulative Bulletins* are published by the U.S. Government Printing Office.

Revenue Ruling. A Revenue Ruling (abbreviated Rev.Rul.) is issued by the National Office of the IRS to express an official interpretation of the tax law as applied to specific transactions. It is more limited in application than a Regulation. A Revenue Ruling is first published in an *Internal Revenue Bulletin* (I.R.B.) and later transferred to the appropriate *Cumulative Bulletin* (C.B.). Both the *Internal Revenue Bulletins* and the *Cumulative Bulletins* are published by the U.S. Government Printing Office.

Reversed (Rev'd.). An indication that a decision of one court has been reversed by a higher court in the same case.

Reversing (Rev'g.). An indication that the decision of a higher court is reversing the result reached by a lower court in the same case.

Reversionary interest. The property that reverts to the grantor after the expiration of an intervening income interest. Assume, for example, Phil places real estate in trust with income to Junior for 11 years, and upon the expiration of this term, the property returns to Phil. Under these circumstances, Phil holds a reversionary interest in the property. A reversionary interest is the same as a remainder interest, except that, in the latter case, the property passes to someone other than the original owner (e.g., the grantor of a trust) upon the expiration of the intervening interest. See also *grantor trust* and *remainder interest.*

Revocable transfer. A transfer of property where the transferor retains the right to recover the property. The creation of a revocable trust is an example of a revocable transfer. § 2038. See also *incomplete transfer.*

Rev.Proc. Abbreviation for an IRS Revenue Procedure. See *Revenue Procedure.*

Rev.Rul. Abbreviation for an IRS Revenue Ruling. See *Revenue Ruling.*

RIA. Research Institute of America is the publisher of two tax services and of Federal tax decisions (AFTR and AFTR2d series).

Right of survivorship. See *joint tenancy.*

S

Sales tax. A state- or local-level tax on the retail sale of specified property. Generally, the purchaser pays the tax, but the seller collects it, as an agent for the government. Various taxing jurisdictions allow exemptions for purchases of specific items, including certain food, services, and manufacturing equipment. If the purchaser and seller are in different states, a *use tax* usually applies.

Schedule PH. A tax form required to be filed by corporations that are personal holding companies. The form must be filed in addition to Form 1120 (U.S. Corporation Income Tax Return).

S corporation. The designation for a small business corporation. See also *Subchapter S.*

Section 306 stock. Preferred stock issued as a nontaxable stock dividend that, if sold or redeemed, would result in ordinary income recognition. § 306(c). See also *preferred stock bailout.*

Section 306 taint. The ordinary income that would result upon the sale or other taxable disposition of § 306 stock.

Section 1231 assets. Depreciable assets and real estate used in a trade or business and held for the appropriate holding period. Under certain circumstances, the classification also includes timber, coal, domestic iron ore, livestock (held for draft, breeding, dairy, or sporting purposes), and unharvested crops. § 1231(b). See also *Section 1231 gains and losses.*

Section 1231 gains and losses. If the combined gains and losses from the taxable dispositions of § 1231 assets plus the net gain from business involuntary conversions (of both § 1231 assets and long-term capital assets) is a gain, the gains and losses are treated as long-term capital gains and losses. In arriving at § 1231 gains, however, the depreciation recapture provisions (e.g., §§ 1245 and 1250) are first applied to produce ordinary income. If the net result of the combination is a loss, the gains and losses from § 1231 assets are treated as ordinary gains and losses. § 1231(a). See also *depreciation recapture* and *Section 1231 assets.*

Section 1244 stock. Stock issued under § 1244 by qualifying small business corporations. If § 1244 stock becomes worthless, the shareholders may claim an ordinary loss rather than the usual capital loss, within statutory limitations.

Section 1245 recapture. Upon a taxable disposition of § 1245 property, all depreciation claimed on the property is recaptured as ordinary income (but not to exceed recognized gain from the disposition).

Section 1250 recapture. Upon a taxable disposition of § 1250 property, some of the depreciation or cost recovery claimed on the property may be recaptured as ordinary income.

Separate property. In a community property jurisdiction, property that belongs entirely to one of the spouses is separate property. Generally, it is property acquired before marriage or acquired after marriage by gift or inheritance. See also *community property.*

Sham. A transaction without substance that will be disregarded for tax purposes.

Short-term capital gain or loss. Results from the sale or other taxable exchange of a capital asset that had been held by the seller for one year or less or from other transactions involving statutorily designated assets, including nonbusiness bad debts.

Simple trusts. Simple trusts are those that are not complex trusts. Such trusts may not have a charitable beneficiary, accumulate income, or distribute corpus. See also *complex trusts.*

Simplified employee pensions. An employer may make contributions to an employee's individual retirement account (IRA) in amounts not exceeding the lesser of 15 percent of compensation or $30,000 per individual. § 219(b)(2). See also *individual retirement account.*

Small business corporation. A corporation that satisfies the definition of § 1361(b), § 1244(c), or both. Satisfaction of § 1361(b) permits an S election, and satisfaction of § 1244 enables the shareholders of the corporation to claim an ordinary loss on the worthlessness of stock.

Small Claims Division of the U.S. Tax Court. Jurisdiction is limited to claims of $10,000 or less. There is no appeal from this court.

Special power of appointment. See *power of appointment.*

Special use value. An option that permits the executor of an estate to value, for death tax purposes, real estate used in a farming activity or in connection with a closely held business at its current use value rather than at its most suitable or optimal use value. Under this option, a farm is valued for farming purposes even though, for example, the property might have a higher potential value as a shopping center. For the executor of an estate to elect special use valuation, the conditions of § 2032A must be satisfied. See also *most suitable use value.*

Spin-off. A type of reorganization where, for example, Gold Corporation transfers some assets to Silver Corporation in exchange for enough Silver stock to represent control. Gold then distributes the Silver stock to its shareholders.

Split-off. A type of reorganization where, for example, Gold Corporation transfers some assets to Silver Corporation in exchange for enough Silver stock to represent control. Gold then distributes the Silver stock to its shareholders in exchange for some of their Gold stock.

Split-up. A type of reorganization where, for example, Gold Corporation transfers some assets to Silver Corporation and the remainder to Platinum Corporation. In return, Gold receives enough Silver and Platinum stock to represent control of each corporation. Gold then distributes the Silver and Platinum stock to its shareholders in return for all of their Gold stock. The result of the split-up is that Gold is liquidated, and its shareholders now have control of Silver and Platinum.

Sprinkling trust. When a trustee has the discretion to either distribute or accumulate the entity accounting income of the trust and to distribute it among the trust's income beneficiaries in varying magnitudes, a sprinkling trust exists. The trustee can "sprinkle" the income of the trust.

Standard deduction. The individual taxpayer can either itemize deductions or take the standard deduction. The amount of the standard deduction depends on the taxpayer's filing status (single, head of household, married filing jointly, surviving spouse, or married filing separately). For 1993, the amount of the standard deduction ranges from $3,100 (for married, filing separately) to $6,200 (for married, filing jointly). Additional standard deductions of either $700 (for married taxpayers) or $900 (for single taxpayers) are available if the taxpayer is either blind or age 65 or over. Limitations exist on the amount of the standard deduction of a taxpayer who is another taxpayer's dependent. The standard deduction amounts are adjusted annually for inflation. § 63(c).

Statute of limitations. Provisions of the law that specify the maximum period of time in which action may be taken on a past event. Code §§ 6501–6504 contain the limitation periods applicable to the IRS for additional assessments, and §§ 6511–6515 relate to refund claims by taxpayers.

Statutory depletion. See *depletion.*

Statutory notice of deficiency. Commonly referred to as the 90-day letter, this notice is sent to a taxpayer upon request, upon the expiration of the 30-day letter, or upon exhaustion by the taxpayer of his or her administrative remedies before the IRS. The notice gives the taxpayer 90 days in which to file a petition with the U.S. Tax Court. If a petition is not filed, the IRS will issue a demand for payment of the assessed deficiency. §§ 6211–6216. See also *deficiency* and *thirty-day letter.*

Step-down in basis. A reduction in the tax basis of property.

Step-transaction approach. Disregarding one or more transactions to arrive at the final result. Assume, for example, that the shareholders of Black Corporation liquidate the corporation and receive cash and operating assets. Immediately after the liquidation, the shareholders transfer the operating assets to newly formed Brown Corporation. Under these circumstances, the IRS may contend that the liquidation of Black should be disregarded (thereby depriving the shareholders of capital gain treatment). What may really have happened is a reorganization of Black with a distribution of boot (ordinary income) to Black's shareholders. If so, there will be a carryover of basis in the assets transferred from Black to Brown.

Step-up in basis. An increase in the tax basis of property. The classic step-up in basis occurs when a decedent dies owning appreciated property. Since the estate or heir acquires a basis in the property equal to the property's fair market value on the date of death (or alternate valuation date if available and elected), any appreciation is not subject to the income tax. Thus, a step-up in basis is the result, with no income tax consequences.

Stock attribution. See *attribution.*

Stock redemption. Occurs when a corporation buys back its own stock from a specified shareholder. Typically, the corporation recognizes any realized gain or loss on the noncash assets that it uses to effect a redemption, and the shareholder obtains a capital gain or loss upon receipt of the purchase price.

Subchapter S. Sections 1361–1379 of the Internal Revenue Code. An elective provision permitting certain small business corporations (§ 1361) and their shareholders (§ 1362) to elect to be treated for income tax purposes in accordance with the operating rules of §§ 1363–1379. Of major significance is the fact that S corporations usually avoid the corporate income tax and corporate losses can be claimed by the shareholders.

Substance vs. form concept. A standard used when one must ascertain the true reality of what has occurred. Suppose, for example, a father sells stock to his daughter for $1,000. If the stock is really worth $50,000 at the time of the transfer, the substance of the transaction is probably a gift to her of $49,000.

Substantial economic effect. Partnerships are allowed to allocate items of income, expense, gain, loss, and credit in any manner that is authorized in the partnership agreement, provided that the allocation has an economic effect aside from the corresponding tax results. The necessary substantial economic effect is present, for instance, if the post-contribution appreciation in the value of an asset that was contributed to the partnership by a partner was allocated to that partner for cost recovery purposes.

Surviving spouse. When a husband or wife predeceases the other spouse, the survivor is known as a surviving spouse. Under certain conditions, a surviving spouse may be entitled to use the income tax rates in § 1(a) (those applicable to married persons filing a joint return) for the two years after the year of death of his or her spouse.

Survivorship. See *joint tenancy.*

T

Tangible property. All property that has form or substance and is not intangible. See also *intangible asset.*

Tax benefit rule. A rule that limits the recognition of income from the recovery of an expense or loss properly deducted in a prior tax year to the amount of the deduction that generated a tax saving. Assume, for example, that last year Gary had medical expenses of $3,000 and adjusted gross income of $30,000. Because of the 7.5 percent limitation, Gary could deduct only $750 of these expenses [$3,000 – (7.5% × $30,000)]. If, in this year, Gary is reimbursed by his insurance company for $900 of these expenses, the tax benefit rule limits the amount of income from the reimbursement to $750 (the amount previously deducted with a tax saving).

Tax Court. The U.S. Tax Court is one of four trial courts of original jurisdiction that decide litigation involving Federal income, death, or gift taxes. It is the only trial court where the taxpayer must not first pay the deficiency assessed by the IRS. The Tax Court will not have jurisdiction over a case unless the statutory notice of deficiency (90-day letter) has been issued by the IRS and the taxpayer files the petition for hearing within the time prescribed.

Tax on unearned income of a child under age 14. Passive income, such as interest and dividends, that is recognized by such a child is taxed *to him or her* at the rates that would have applied had the income been incurred by the child's parents, generally to the extent that the income exceeds $1,200. The additional tax is assessed regardless of the source of the income or the income's underlying property. If the child's parents are divorced, the custodial parent's rates are used. The parents' rates reflect any applicable alternative minimum tax and the phase-outs of lower tax brackets and other deductions. § 1(g).

Tax preference items. Those items that may result in the imposition of the alternative minimum tax. §§ 55–58. See also *alternative minimum tax.*

TAXRIA. (Formerly called PHINet.) An on-line database system, with which the tax researcher can obtain access to the Internal Revenue Code, Regulations, administrative rulings, and court case opinions.

Tax year. See *accounting period.*

Taxable estate. Defined in § 2051, the taxable estate is the gross estate of a decedent reduced by the deductions allowed by §§ 2053–2057 (e.g., administration expenses, marital, charitable, and ESOP deductions). The taxable estate is subject to the unified transfer tax at death. See also *adjusted taxable estate* and *gross estate.*

Taxable gift. Defined in § 2503, a taxable gift is the amount of the gift that is subject to the unified transfer tax. Thus, a taxable gift has been adjusted by the annual exclusion and other appropriate deductions (e.g., marital and charitable).

Taxable income. The tax base with respect to the prevailing Federal income tax. Taxable income is defined by the Internal Revenue Code, Treasury Regulations, and pertinent court cases. Currently, taxable income includes gross income from all sources except those specifically excluded by statute. In addition, taxable income is reduced for certain allowable deductions. Deductions for business taxpayers must be related to a trade or business. Individuals can also deduct certain personal expenses in determining their taxable incomes. See also *gross income.*

Tax-free exchange. Transfers of property specifically exempted from income tax consequences by the tax law. Examples are a transfer of property to a controlled corporation under § 351(a) and a like-kind exchange under § 1031(a).

T.C. An abbreviation for the U.S. Tax Court used in citing a Regular Decision of the U.S. Tax Court.

T.C. Memo. An abbreviation used to refer to a Memorandum Decision of the U.S. Tax Court.

Telescoping. To look through one or more transactions to arrive at the final result. It is also referred to as the *step-transaction approach* or the *substance vs. form concept.*

Tenancy by the entirety. Essentially, a joint tenancy between husband and wife. See also *joint tenancy* and *tenancy in common.*

Tenancy in common. A form of ownership where each tenant (owner) holds an undivided interest in property. Unlike a joint tenancy or a tenancy by the entirety, the interest of a tenant in common does not terminate upon that individual's death (there is no right of survivorship). Assume, for example, Tim and Cindy acquire real estate as equal tenants in common, each having furnished one-half of the purchase price. Upon Tim's death, his one-half interest in the property passes to his estate or heirs, not to Cindy. For a comparison of results, see also *joint tenancy* and *tenancy by the entirety.*

Terminable interest. An interest in property that terminates upon the death of the holder or upon the occurrence of some other specified event. The transfer of a terminable interest by one spouse to the other may not qualify for the marital deduction. §§ 2056(b) and 2523(b). See also *marital deduction.*

Testamentary disposition. The passing of property to another upon the death of the owner.

Testamentary power of appointment. A power of appointment that can be exercised only through the will (upon the death) of the holder. See also *power of appointment.*

Thin capitalization. When debt owed by a corporation to the shareholders becomes too large in relation to the corporation's capital structure (i.e., stock and shareholder equity), the IRS may contend that the corporation is thinly capitalized. In effect, this means that some or all of the debt will be reclassified as equity. The immediate result is to disallow any interest deduction to the corporation on the reclassified debt. To the extent of the corporation's earnings and profits, interest payments and loan repayments on the reclassified debt are treated as dividends to the shareholders.

Thirty-day letter. A letter that accompanies a revenue agent's report issued as a result of an IRS audit of a taxpayer (or the rejection of a taxpayer's claim for refund). The letter outlines the taxpayer's appeal procedure before the IRS. If the taxpayer does not request any such procedures within the 30-day period, the IRS will issue a statutory notice of deficiency (the 90-day letter). See also *statutory notice of deficiency.*

Tiered partnerships. An ownership arrangement where one partnership (the parent or first tier) is a partner in one or more partnerships (the subsidiary/subsidiaries or second tier). Frequently, the first tier is a holding partnership, and the second tier is an operating partnership.

Trade or business. Any business or professional activity conducted by a taxpayer. The mere ownership of rental or other investment assets does not constitute a trade or business. Generally, a trade or business generates relatively little passive investment income.

Transfer tax. A tax imposed upon the transfer of property. See also *unified transfer tax.*

Transferee liability. Under certain conditions, if the IRS is unable to collect taxes owed by a transferor of property, it may pursue its claim against the transferee of the property. The transferee's liability for taxes is limited to the extent of the value of the assets transferred. For example, the IRS can force a donee to pay the gift tax when the tax cannot be paid by the donor making the transfer. §§ 6901–6905.

Treasury Regulations. See *Regulations.*

Trial court. The court of original jurisdiction; the first court to consider litigation. In Federal tax controversies, trial courts include U.S. District Courts, the U.S. Tax Court, the U.S. Court of Federal Claims, and the Small Claims Division of the U.S. Tax Court. See also *appellate court, Claims Court, District Court, Small Claims Division of the U.S. Tax Court,* and *Tax Court.*

Trust. A legal entity created by a grantor for the benefit of designated beneficiaries under the laws of the state and the valid trust instrument. The trustee holds a fiduciary responsibility to manage the trust's corpus assets and income for the economic benefit of all of the beneficiaries.

Trustee. An individual or corporation that takes the fiduciary responsibilities under a trust agreement.

U

Undistributed personal holding company income. The penalty tax on personal holding companies is imposed on the corporation's undistributed personal holding company income for the year. The adjustments necessary to convert taxable income to undistributed personal holding company income are set forth in § 545.

Unearned income. Income received but not yet earned. Normally, such income is taxed when received, even for accrual basis taxpayers.

Unified tax credit. A credit allowed against any unified transfer tax. §§ 2010 and 2505.

Unified transfer tax. A set of tax rates applicable to transfers by gift and death made after 1976. § 2001(c).

Uniform Gift to Minors Act. A means of transferring property (usually stocks and bonds) to a minor. The designated custodian of the property has the legal right to act on behalf of the minor without requiring a guardianship. Generally, the custodian possesses the right to change investments (e.g., sell one type of stock and buy another), apply the income from the custodial property to the minor's support, and even terminate the custodianship. In this regard, however, the custodian is acting in a fiduciary capacity on behalf of the minor. The custodian could not, for example, appropriate the property for his or her own use because it belongs to the minor. During the period of the custodianship, the income from the property is taxed to the minor. The custodianship terminates when the minor reaches legal age. See also *guardianship* and *legal age.*

Unrealized receivables. Amounts earned by a cash basis taxpayer but not yet received. Because of the method of accounting used by the taxpayer, these amounts have no income tax basis. When unrealized receivables are distributed to a partner, they generally convert a transaction from nontaxable to taxable or convert otherwise capital gain to ordinary income.

Unreasonable compensation. A deduction is allowed for "reasonable" salaries or other compensation for personal services actually rendered. To the extent compensation is "excessive" ("unreasonable"), no deduction is allowed. The problem of unreasonable compensation usually is limited to closely held corporations, where the motivation is to pay out profits in some form that is deductible to the corporation. Deductible compensation therefore becomes an attractive substitute for nondeductible dividends when the shareholders also are employed by the corporation.

Unrelated business income. Income recognized by an exempt organization that is generated from activities not related to the exempt purpose of the entity. For instance, the pharmacy located in a hospital often generates unrelated business income. § 511.

Unrelated business income tax. Levied on the unrelated business taxable income of an exempt organization.

Use tax. A sales tax that is collectible by the seller where the purchaser is domiciled in a different state.

U.S.-owned foreign corporation. A foreign corporation in which 50 percent or more of the total combined voting power or total value of the stock of the corporation is held directly or indirectly by U.S. persons. A U.S. corporation is treated as a U.S.-owned foreign corporation if the dividend or interest income it pays is classified as foreign source under § 861.

U.S. real property interest. Any direct interest in real property situated in the United States and any interest in a domestic corporation (other than solely as a creditor) unless the taxpayer can establish that a domestic corporation was not a U.S. real property holding corporation during the five-year period ending on the date of disposition of the interest (the base period).

USSC. An abbreviation for the U.S. Supreme Court.

U.S. Tax Court. See *Tax Court.*

USTC. Published by Commerce Clearing House, *U.S. Tax Cases* contain all of the Federal tax decisions issued by the U.S. District Courts, U.S. Court of Federal Claims, U.S. Courts of Appeals, and the U.S. Supreme Court.

V

Value. See *fair market value.*

Vested. Absolute and complete. If, for example, a person holds a vested interest in property, the interest cannot be taken away or otherwise defeated.

Voting trust. A trust that holds the voting rights to stock in a corporation. It is a useful device when a majority of the shareholders in a corporation cannot agree on corporate policy.

W

Wash sale. A loss from the sale of stock or securities that is disallowed because the taxpayer has, within 30 days before or after the sale, acquired stock or securities substantially identical to those sold. § 1091.

WESTLAW. An on-line database system, produced by West Publishing Company, which the tax researcher can obtain access to the Internal Revenue Code, Regulations, administrative rulings, and court case opinions.

Writ of Certiorari. See *certiorari.*

APPENDIX

TABLE OF CODE SECTIONS CITED

[See Title 26 U.S.C.A.]

Appendix

Comprehensive Tax Return Problems

Problem 1—Individual

1. Charles W. and Judy S. Clark are married and file a joint return for 1992. Both are 53 years of age. Charles is employed as a process engineer by Harding Chemical Corporation. Judy is a registered nurse who supervises the intensive care unit at St. Luke's Hospital. Their Social Security numbers are as follows: 308–42–4990 (Charles), 309–66–2780 (Judy). Both live at 4538 Mount Vernon Drive, San Diego, CA 92184.
2. The Clarks have two children, Mark (age 24) and Melina (age 22), who live with them (Social Security numbers: 312–90–8676 and 355–40–0339, respectively). Mark is a full-time law student at San Diego State University and earned $3,000 from a summer job. Melina is a full-time nursing student at the same university and earns $2,400 from part-time jobs. The Clarks furnish more than 50% of the support for both children.
3. Charles's widowed mother, Myrtle Clark (Social Security number 466–36–4590), lives with them. Myrtle suffers from Parkinson's disease and requires constant care. The Clarks hire a neighbor, Anne Hawkins, to help Myrtle while they are both at work. Anne's Social Security number is 449–86–9756; she lives at 4596 Mount Vernon Drive, San Diego, CA 92184. Expenses paid by the Clarks on behalf of Myrtle during the year are as follows:

Wages paid to Anne Hawkins	$3,750
Employer's portion of FICA	287
Surgical procedure (gallbladder operation), which includes physician and hospital charges and other medical expenses	3,200

   Anne has no formal medical training. Myrtle's only source of income is a modest Social Security benefit, which she does not spend.

4. On July 1, 1991, Myrtle gave Charles her personal residence and those furnishings she did not want to keep. No gift tax was due on the transfer. The property was converted to rental property on the same date. Information regarding the property is summarized below:

	Adjusted Basis to Myrtle	FMV on July 1, 1991
House	$40,000	$100,000
Land	5,000	10,000
Furnishings left in the house	10,000	12,000

On July 1, 1991, Charles listed the property (furnished) for rent, but a suitable tenant was not found until February 1, 1992. The house was then occupied under the following terms: renewable one-year lease at $550 rent per month (payable on the first of each month), damage deposit (refundable) of $400, and the last month's rent payable in advance. The tenant complied with all terms of the lease agreement.

The rental house is located at 3970 King Blvd., San Diego, CA 92184. It is a 20-year-old, single-story, frame house built on brick pilings.

Out-of-pocket expenses as to the property for the year are as follows:

Property taxes	$1,500
Special street paving assessment (7-1-92)	400
Minor repairs (e.g., screen door repair)	350
Casualty (e.g., fire, flood) insurance	500

Utilities and yard maintenance are the responsibility of the tenant. Depreciation is claimed under the MACRS method.

5. The Clarks have the following additional income:

Winnings from state lottery (losses were $1,200)		$ 1,000
Interest on CDs (Bank of America)		6,000
Interest on money market account (First Interstate Bank)		2,500
Dividends—		
Texaco, Inc.	$4,200	
Exxon, Inc.	3,100	
Chevron, Inc.	2,700	10,000
State Farm life insurance proceeds		100,000
Total		$119,500

The life insurance proceeds stemmed from a policy Judy's father had on his life with Judy as the designated beneficiary. The father died in June of 1992, and the proceeds were paid to Judy in the following month.

6. The Clarks had the following stock transactions:

Description of Property	Date Acquired	Date Sold	Sale Price	Cost or Other Basis
Ace Mining	1/18/90	6/3/92	$12,000	$20,000
S.W. Public Service	8/03/92	9/1/92	29,000	(see below)
S.D. Insurance Co.	6/03/91	(see below)	(see below)	14,000

The Clarks purchased Ace Mining as a speculative investment. However, when it significantly dropped in price on June 3, they became concerned and sold the stock. The same stock was repurchased on July 1, 1992, for $8,000 when the Clarks thought it had "bottomed out."

Judy inherited the S.W. Public Service stock from her father. The stock was acquired by the father on September 9, 1988, at a cost of $12,000. It had a fair market value of $28,000 on the date of the father's death.

Charles bought S.D. Insurance Co. stock on a tip from a friend who worked at the company. Although the stock was already depressed and the institution was rumored to be in financial difficulty, the friend thought that an eventual reorganization or liquidation would realize much more for the shareholders than the stock's listed price. In January of 1992, S.D. Insurance Co. was taken over by state regulators. In the same month, it was announced that assets were not even sufficient to cover deposits. In short, the shareholders would receive nothing, and their stock was worthless.

7. Although Charles is not involved in sales, he does, on occasion, do consulting for Harding Chemical Corporation. When one of Harding's customers has a problem with

a product, Charles may be sent out to investigate the matter. The employer estimates the expenses Charles will have for each trip and provides him with an allowance. Harding does not require its process engineers to account for the allowances. However, Charles maintains records and receipts for each trip.

A summary of these trips appears below:

Allowances provided by employer		$10,100
Expenses paid by Charles—		
Air fare	$3,200	
Lodging	1,100	
Meals	1,600	
Ground transportation	110	$ 6,010

8. Other expenditures for 1992 are as follows:

Medical (not including Myrtle)—		
Prescribed drugs	$ 320	
Doctor bills	6,200	
Medical insurance premiums	1,800	
Medical insurance reimbursements	(700)	$7,620
Taxes—		
State income taxes withheld from wages (Charles, $3,114; Judy, $2,914)	$6,028	
Property taxes on personal residence	3,200	9,228
Interest—		
Mortgage on personal residence	$4,800	
Consumer purchases	2,000	6,800
Charity—		
Church pledge	$2,400	
United Way	2,000	4,400
Other—		
Professional dues	$ 300	
Professional journals	400	
Safety shoes and glasses	150	
Nurse uniforms	320	
Laundry of nurse uniforms	240	1,410

The doctor bills ($6,200) included $5,000 for dental restorative work to correct Judy's overbite problem. Dental work is not covered by the Clarks' medical insurance.

9. Charles receives an annual salary of $52,000 from which his employer withheld $3,978 for Social Security and Medicare tax and $10,580 for Federal income tax.

   Judy receives an annual salary of $48,000 from which her employer withheld $3,672 for Social Security and Medicare tax and $7,200 for Federal income tax.

   On a timely basis, the Clarks have made four quarterly estimated Federal income tax payments of $800 each.

   The state income taxes listed above (item 8) do not include $300 the Clarks paid to California in 1992 for tax year 1991. The Clarks estimate that they will receive a $400 refund (in 1993) on the $6,500 withheld in 1992.

   The Clarks do not desire that $1 be directed to the Presidential Election Campaign Fund.

Requirements

You are to complete the Clark's Federal income tax return for 1992. Form 8582 is not required. If they have a refund due, they would like to receive the entire amount and not have it credited against tax for next year.

Problem 2—Individual

1. Paul J. and Judy L. Vance are married and file a joint return. Paul is 54 years of age, and Judy is 51. Paul is self-employed as a dentist, and Judy is a college professor. Paul's Social Security number is 333–45–6666, and Judy's is 566–77–8888. The Vances live at 621 Franklin Avenue, Cincinnati, OH 45211. They have a son, Vince (Social Security number 576–18–7928), age 23, who lives at home. Vince is a law student at the University of Cincinnati and worked part-time during the year, earning $1,500, which he spent for his own support. In addition, he received a $2,000 scholarship from the University of Cincinnati. Paul and Judy provided $2,000 toward Vince's support. They also provided over half the support of their daughter, Joan (Social Security number 575–92–4321), age 19, who is a full-time student at Edgecliff College. Joan worked part-time during the year, earning $1,200. She filed a joint return with her husband, Patrick, who earned $8,000 during the year.
2. Paul's mother, Vera (Social Security number 421–81–6945), age 87, lives with the Vances. Vera received $900 in Social Security benefits and $950 of interest during the year, all of which she used for her own support. Paul and his brother George each incurred out-of-pocket costs of $900 for Vera's support. In addition, Paul provided lodging for Vera during the entire year. Paul has determined that the fair rental value of the lodging is $1,200. George is willing to do whatever is necessary to enable Paul to claim Vera as a dependent.
3. Judy is a lecturer at Xavier University in Cincinnati, where she earned $40,000. The University withheld Federal income tax of $4,500, state income tax of $1,200, Cincinnati city income tax of $600, and $3,060 of Social Security and Medicare tax.
4. The Vances received $1,200 of interest from State Savings Bank on a joint account. They received interest of $1,000 on City of Cincinnati bonds they bought in January with the proceeds of a loan from Third National Bank of Cincinnati. They paid interest of $1,200 on the loan. Paul received a dividend of $540 on General Bicycle Corporation stock he owns. Judy received a dividend of $390 on Acme Clothing Corporation stock she owns. Paul and Judy received a dividend of $865 on jointly owned stock in Maple Company.
5. Paul practices under the name "Paul J. Vance, DDS." His business is located at 645 West Avenue, Cincinnati, OH 45211, and his employer identification number is 01–2222222. Paul's gross billings during the year were $170,000. Accounts receivable were $3,600 at the beginning of the year and $4,200 at the end of the year. The end-of-year balance does not include a $700 account from a customer who declared bankruptcy on November 9. The $700 was billed in July for work done during May and June. Paul uses the cash method of accounting for his business. Paul's business expenses are as follows:

Advertising	$ 1,200
Professional dues	490
Professional journals	360
Contributions to employee benefit plans	2,000
Malpractice insurance	3,200
Fine for overbilling State of Ohio for work performed on welfare patient	5,000
Insurance on office contents	720
Interest on money borrowed to refurbish office	900
Accounting services	1,800
Miscellaneous office expense	388
Office rent	6,000
Dental supplies	7,672
Utilities and telephone	3,360
Wages	30,000
Payroll taxes	2,400

In June, Paul decided to refurbish his office. This project was completed and the assets placed in service on July 1. Paul's expenditures included $8,000 for new office furniture, $6,000 for new dental equipment, and $2,000 for a new word processor. Paul elected to compute his cost recovery allowance using the MACRS percentage method.

6. Judy's mother, Sarah, died on July 2, 1977, leaving Judy her entire estate. Included in the estate was Sarah's residence (address 325 Oak Street, Cincinnati, OH 45211). Sarah's basis in the residence was $30,000. Fair market value of the residence on July 2, 1977, was $50,000. The property was distributed to Judy on September 9, 1977. The Vances have held the property as rental property and have managed it themselves. From March 1, 1978, until April 30 of 1992 the house was rented to the same tenant. The tenant was transferred to a branch office in California and moved out at the end of April. Since they did not want to bother finding a new tenant, Paul and Judy decided to sell the house, which they did on June 2. They received $140,000 for the house, less a six-percent commission charged by the broker. They had depreciated the house using the straight-line method of depreciation with an estimated useful life of 20 years and an estimated salvage value of zero. In computing depreciation, they had allocated a value of $5,000 to the lot on which the house is located. The Vances collected rent of $1,100 a month during the four months the house was occupied during the year. They incurred the following related expenses during this period:

Property insurance	$200
Property taxes (paid by buyer of the property but allocated to the Vances)	550
Maintenance	220

7. The Vances sold 1,000 shares of Capp Corporation stock they had received as a wedding present on June 25, 1963. The stock was worth $95 per share in January. By September 3, its value had dropped to $81 per share, and the Vances sold the stock on that date. They had been given the stock by Paul's father, who had paid $1 per share for it in 1953. Its value at the date of gift was $4.50 per share. No gift tax was paid on the gift.
8. During the year Paul purchased numerous state lottery tickets (cost of $400). One ticket won $10,000, which Paul received.
9. Judy is required by her employer to visit several high schools in the Cincinnati area to evaluate Xavier University students who are doing their practice teaching. However, she is not reimbursed for the expenses she incurs in doing this. During the year, she drove her personal automobile 6,800 miles in fulfilling this obligation. Total miles driven were 13,500 for the year.
10. Paul and Judy have given you a file containing the following receipts for expenditures during the year:

Medicines and drugs	$ 376
Doctor and hospital bills	1,148
Medical insurance premiums ($110/month)	1,320
Penalty for underpayment of last year's state income tax	362
Real estate taxes on personal residence	4,762
Interest on home mortgage (paid to Home State Savings & Loan)	8,250
Interest on credit cards (consumer purchases)	595
Cash contribution to St. Matthew's church	3,080
Payroll deductions for Judy's contributions to the United Way	150
Professional dues (Judy)	325
Professional subscriptions (Judy)	245
Fee for preparation of 1991 tax return	500

11. The Vances made timely estimated Federal income tax payments of $95,000 during the year. They made estimated state income tax payments of $1,400 and estimated city income tax payments of $700.

12. The Vances do not desire that $1 be directed to the Presidential Election Campaign Fund.

Requirements

You are to prepare Paul and Judy Vance's Federal income tax return for 1992.

SUBJECT INDEX

A

D

E

F

G

H

I

J

K

L

P

Q

R

S

T

U

V

W

Y

AMT Formula for Individuals

Regular taxable income

Plus or minus:	Adjustments
Plus:	Tax preferences
Equals:	Alternative minimum taxable income
Minus:	Exemption
Equals:	Alternative minimum tax base
Times:	24% rate
Equals:	Tentative minimum tax before foreign tax credit
Minus:	Alternative minimum tax foreign tax credit
Equals:	Tentative minimum tax
Minus:	Regular tax liability
Equals:	Alternative minimum tax (if amount is positive)

AMT Exemption Phase-out for Individuals

		Phase-out	
Status	**Exemption**	**Begins at**	**Ends at**
Married, filing jointly	$40,000	$150,000	$310,000
Single or Head of household	30,000	112,500	232,500
Married, filing separately	20,000	75,000	155,000

AMT Formula for Corporations

Regular taxable income before NOL deduction

Plus or minus:	Adjustments (except ACE adjustment)
Plus:	Tax preferences
Equals:	AMTI before ATNOL deduction and ACE adjustment
Plus or minus:	ACE adjustment
Equals:	Alternative minimum taxable income (AMTI) before ATNOL deduction
Minus:	ATNOL deduction (limited to 90% of AMTI before ATNOL deduction)
Equals:	Alternative minimum taxable income (AMTI)
Minus:	Exemption
Equals:	Alternative minimum tax base
Times:	20% rate
Equals:	AMT before AMT foreign tax credit
Minus:	AMT foreign tax credit (possibly limited to 90% of AMT before AMT foreign tax credit)
Equals:	Tentative minimum tax
Minus:	Regular tax liability before credits minus regular foreign tax credit
Equals:	Alternative minimum tax (AMT) if positive